My personal contribution in
the compilation of this dictionary
is dedicated to
my mother and her two close friends,
"Eileen" and "Cleo."

R. G. W.

Arabic Series: Number Six
General Editor: Richard S. Harrell
Institute of Languages and Linguistics
Georgetown University
Washington, D. C.

A DICTIONARY of IRAQI ARABIC

ENGLISH – ARABIC

edited by

Beverly E. Clarity   Karl Stowasser

Ronald G. Wolfe

Georgetown University Press
Washington, D. C.

The research reported herein was performed pursuant to a contract with the United States Office of Education, Department of Health, Education, and Welfare.

THE ARABIC SERIES
INSTITUTE OF LANGUAGES AND LINGUISTICS
GEORGETOWN UNIVERSITY

As an adjunct to its teaching and research program in the field of modern Arabic studies, Georgetown University's Institute of Languages and Linguistics inaugurated a publication series in Arabic studies in 1962. The present volume represents the sixth of the series. A list of currently available and forthcoming publications is to be found on the back cover of this book.

Inquiries as to prices, details of subscription, etc., should be sent to the Director of Publications, Institute of Languages and Linguistics, Georgetown University, Washington, D. C., 20007.

Copy Preparation by
WALTER CONWAY & ASSOCIATES, Inc.
Washington D. C., 20010

THE ARABIC RESEARCH PROGRAM
INSTITUTE OF LANGUAGES AND LINGUISTICS
GEORGETOWN UNIVERSITY

The Arabic Research Program was established in June of 1960 as a contract between Georgetown University and the United States Office of Education under the provisions of the Language Development Program of the National Defense Education Act.

The first two years of the research program, 1960-1962 (Contract number SAE-8706), were devoted to the production of six books, a reference grammar and a conversational English-Arabic dictionary in the cultivated spoken forms of Moroccan, Syrian, and Iraqi Arabic. The second two years of the research program, 1962-1964 (Contract number OE-2-14-029), call for the further production of Arabic-English dictionaries in each of the three varieties of Arabic mentioned above, as well as comprehensive basic courses in the Moroccan and Iraqi varieties.

The eleven books of this series, of which the present volume is one, are designed to serve as practical tools for the increasing number of Americans whose lives bring them into contact with the Arab world. The dictionaries, the reference grammars, and the basic courses are oriented toward the educated American who is a layman in linguistic matters. Although it is hoped that the scientific linguist and the specialist in Arabic dialectology will find these books both of interest and of use, matters of purely scientific and theoretical importance have not been directly treated as such, and specialized scientific terminology has been avoided as much as possible.

As is usual, the authors or editors of the individual books bear final scholarly responsibility for the contents, but there has been a large amount of informal cooperation in our work. Criticism, consultation, and discussion have gone on constantly among the senior professional members of the staff. The contribution of more junior research assistants, both Arab and American, is also not to be underestimated. Their painstaking assembling and ordering of raw data, often in manners requiring considerable creative intelligence, has been the necessary prerequisite for further progress.

Staff work has been especially important in the preparation of the dictionaries. Although the contributing staff members are named on the title page of the individual dictionaries, special mention must be made of Mr. Karl Stowasser's work. His lexicographical experience, acquired in his work on the English version of Professor Wehr's *Arabisches Wörterbuch für die Schriftsprache der Gegenwart*,*

---

*Hans Wehr, *A Dictionary of Modern Written Arabic,* ed. J Milton Cowan (Ithaca, N. Y.: Cornell University Press, 1961).

along with his thorough knowledge of Arabic, has been critically important for all our lexicographical work, covering the entire range from typography to substantive entries in the dictionaries.

In most cases the books prepared by the Arabic Research Program are the first of their kind in English, and in some cases the first in any language. The preparation of them has been a rewarding experience. It is hoped that the public use of them will be equally so. The undersigned, on behalf of the entire staff, would like to ask the same indulgence of the reader as Samuel Johnson requested in his first English dictionary: To remember that although much has been left out, much has been included.

Richard S. Harrell
Associate Professor of Linguistics
Georgetown University

Director,
Arabic Research Program

PREFACE

The compilation of this dictionary was begun in the summer of 1960 by Dr. Thomas B. Irving of the University of Minnesota, with the assistance of Munir Malayka of Baghdad, Iraq. Unfortunately, Dr. Irving was not able to see the dictionary through to its completion, and, for a variety of technical reasons, the mass of material which he had so conscientiously and diligently collected had largely to be abandoned.

The re-editing and completion of the work was undertaken by B. E. Clarity, formerly of the linguistics department of the Arabian-American Oil Company and now Professor at Beloit College, Beloit, Wisconsin. The work was then given a final revision by Ronald G. Wolfe under the editorial supervision of Karl Stowasser. The compilation of the dictionary was the work of many diligent hands and minds. Mr. Clarity's chief assistants, in addition to Ronald Wolfe, were Dan Woodhead, Munir Malayka, Husein Mustafa, and Faysal Al-Khalaf. Contributions were also made by Majid Damah, Basil Al-Bustani, Hasan Al-Hashimi, Jerome Hoffman, and Thomas Fox.

The long task of reading the proofs, both galley and page, was undertaken by Ronald Wolfe.

R. S. H.

Washington, D.C.
February, 1964

EDITORS' INTRODUCTION

This dictionary is based, in format, on the English-German section of the bilingual German and English *Dictionary of Everyday Usage**. The aim of this work has been to present, for the first time, a dictionary for English speakers containing the basic vocabulary of the Iraqi dialect. Technical terms have been largely avoided. The usage is primarily that of Muslim speakers from Baghdad, but some southern Iraqi usage is also included. The illustrative English sentences are based on everyday conversational usage with a deliberate avoidance of literary style. In a few cases somewhat awkward English constructions have been resorted to in order to give a clearer picture of Iraqi sentence structure.

The transcription system is identical to that of Wallace M. Erwin's *A Short Reference Grammar of Iraqi Arabic***, which should be consulted for further treatment of Iraqi phonology.

The consonants are as follows:

ʔ — glottal stop; not a distinctive feature of English, but similar to the variant for English t in button or bottle.

b — voiced bilabial stop; similar to English b as in bake.

p — voiceless bilabial stop; similar to English p as in pole.

t — voiceless dental stop; similar to English t as in take.

θ — voiceless interdental spirant; similar to English th as in thank.

j — voiced palatal affricate; similar to English j as in jail.

č — voiceless palatal affricate; similar to English ch as in cheese.

ح — voiceless pharyngeal spirant; no English equivalent, but same as Classical Arabic ح.

x — voiceless velar spirant; no English equivalent but similar to ch as in German Bach.

**German-English English-German Dictionary of Everyday Usage*, ed. by J. Alan Pfeffer (New York: Henry Holt and Company). Although the content of this dictionary is, in strictly legal terms, public domain since it was prepared as a part of the American war effort in World War II, we wish to express our thanks to the publishers for raising no copyright objections to our use of the material.

***A Short Reference Grammar of Iraqi Arabic*, by Wallace M. Erwin (Institute of Languages and Linguistics, Georgetown University, Arabic Series, 4). Washington, D. C., Georgetown University Press, 1964.

d — voiced dental stop; similar to English d as in desk.

δ — voiced interdental spirant; similar to English th as in than.

r — alveolar flap, generally voiced; unlike English r, but similar to the t or d flap of English Betty or body.

z — voiced dental spirant; similar to English z as in zeal.

s — voiceless dental spirant; similar to English s as in seen.

š — voiceless palatal spirant; similar to English sh as in sheep.

ṣ — voiceless dental spirant, emphatic; no equivalent in English.

δ̣ — voiceless interdental spirant, emphatic; no equivalent in English.

ṭ — voiceless dental stop, emphatic; no equivalent in English.

ε — voiced pharyngeal spirant; no equivalent in English, but same as Classical Arabic ع.

ġ — voiced velar spirant; no equivalent in English, but similar to some occurrences of French r.

f — voiceless labio-dental spirant; similar to English f as in fan.

q — voiceless post-velar stop; no equivalent in English.

k — voiceless velar stop; similar to English k as in kick.

g — voiced velar stop; similar to English g as in get.

l — voiced alveo-dental lateral; unlike most English l's, but similar to l as in million.

m — voiced bilabial nasal; similar to English m as in meat.

n — voiced dental nasal; similar to English n as in neat.

h — voiceless glottal spirant; similar to English h as in home.

The semivowels are as follows:

w — voiced high back rounded semivowel; similar to English w as in way.

y — voiced high front unrounded semivowel; similar to English y as in yell.

The short vowels are as follows:

a — short low central vowel; the quality of this vowel varies with its environment and is similar to the English a as in father, or a sound between the vowels of father and fought, or bet and bat.

i — short high front unrounded vowel; the quality of this vowel varies with its environment and is similar to the English i as in machine, bit, or the English e as in sister.

o — short mid back rounded vowel; similar to the first part of the diphthong in English boat.

u — short high back rounded vowel; the quality of this vowel varies with its environment, and is similar to the vowel of English boot, or to a sound between the vowels of bull and ball, or to the vowel sound of English book.

The long vowels are as follows:

aa — long low central vowel; this vowel, when not next to an emphatic, is between the vowels of English had and hod, but longer. Next to an emphatic, it ranges between the vowel of English hod and haul.

ee — long mid front unrounded vowel; this vowel is between the vowel sounds of English fez and phase, or else has diphthong quality, the first part being like the sound of eat, the second like the sound of let.

ii — long high front unrounded vowel; similar to the i of English as in machine.

oo — long mid back rounded vowel; this vowel, when not next to an emphatic, has the quality of the first element in the diphthong of English chose, or if next to an emphatic, it is similar to the vowel of English ball.

uu — long high back rounded vowel; if next to an emphatic, it is between the vowel of choose and the first element of the diphthong of chose in English, otherwise it is similar to the vowel of English choose.

A dot beneath a letter other than the three aforementioned emphatics (*ṣ*, *ẟ*, *ṭ*) indicates that the letter is also emphatic. As a general rule, the assimilation of a radical to a preceding or following consonant has not been shown. The notable expectation is that partial assimilation as to emphasis (velarization) is shown. For example *ṯṣiir* "you become" and *ṣṯubar* "he was patient".

English homonyms are treated in the same main entry. The Arabic equivalent of an English entry is usually followed by a contextual example which is designed to illustrate and define its semantic range or syntactic behavior, or both. Several Arabic equivalents separated by commas are interchangeable within these confines. An English entry which has no word-for-word equivalent in Arabic is followed by a colon and one or more contextual examples which demonstrate paraphrasitic possibilities. A double asterisk (**) preceding an English sentence or Arabic phrase signals idiomatic rendering.

An Arabic noun is regularly followed by its sound and/or broken plural, the former in abbreviation (*-a*, *-iyya*, or *-iin*, *-iyyiin* or *-aat*). The adjectives are given in masculine form with only broken plurals being indicated. An asterisk following an adjective ending in *-i* indicates that it follows this pattern: feminine *-iyya;* plural *-iyyiin*, *-iyyaat*.

An Arabic verb is quoted in the conventional third person singular (masculine) of the perfect. It is followed by parentheses containing the stem vowel of the imperfect and the verbal noun or nouns. If the verb has a passive voice it will be indicated by the proper prefix, *n–* or *t–*, following the closed parentheses. Following the passive form prefix appears the obligatory prepositional complement, if there is one; e.g. *ɛtiraf b–* "to admit", *ɛtimad ɛala* "to trust", whereas free prepositional complements are relegated to the illustrative sentences for demonstration.

A noun may occur in a verb entry either before or after the preposition. A tilde (˜) following a noun indicates that the noun is the object of the verb and takes the possessive pronominal suffix agreeing with the subject-doer of the verb: *daar (i) baal˜ ɛala* "to tend" becomes *daar baala̱ ɛaj–jihhaal* "He tended the children".

In a certain number of instances where the English verb is expressed in Arabic by a compound of verb plus noun, a hyphen (-) is placed after the noun to indicate annexion: *šaaf (u) manẓ̌ar–* "to view" becomes *šaaf manẓ̌ar il–ʒaadiθ* "He viewed the accident".

Elsewhere, the use of the hyphen in a compound of verb plus noun indicates that the noun is the subject of the Arabic verb and takes a pronominal suffix corresponding to the subject of the equivalent English sentence: *ġaabat (i) rooʒ–* "to faint" becomes *ġaabat rooʒa̱* "He fainted".

The abbreviations used are as follows:

coll. — collective
f. — feminine
m. — masculine
pl. — plural

The editors wish to express their appreciation to Georgetown University for providing an academic home during the compiling of this dictionary, and, above all, to the authors of the National Defense Education Act and its administrators in the Department of Health, Education, and Welfare, who made possible for us its undertaking.

B. E. C.
K. S.
R. G. W.

Washington, D. C.
February, 1964

A

a - 1. (no equivalent). Do you have a stamp and an envelope? *εindak ṭaabiε w-δaruf?* **2.** *fadd.* There is a man at the door. *ʔaku fadd rijjaal bil-baab.* **3.** *l-.* These eggs are fifty fils a dozen. *hal-beeδ id-darzan ib-xamsiin filis.*

to **abbreviate -** *xtiṣar (i xtiṣaar).* The British Broadcasting Corporation is abbreviated B.B.C. *maṣlaζat il-ʔiδaaεa l-bariiṭaaniyya muxtaṣara ʔila "bii bii sii".*

ability - *qaabliyya* pl. *-aat, qtidaar.* I don't doubt his ability. *ma-ašukk ib-qaabliita.*

able - *miqtidir, kafu* pl. *ʔakiffaaʔ.* I'm sure he's an able officer. *ʔaani mitʔakkid huwwa δaabuṭ kafu.*
  to be able - *gidar (a maqdira, qudra).* Will you be able to come? *raζ-tigdar tiji?*

aboard - *εala.* We went aboard the boat an hour before it sailed. *ṣεadna εal-markab saaεa gabuḷ-ma miša.*
  **all aboard! (ship) *kullkum ṣiεdu εal-markab.* (train) *kullkum rukbu bil-qiṭaar.*

to **abolish -** *liġa (i ʔilġaaʔ) n-.* When was slavery abolished in the United States? *šwakt inliġat il-εubuudiyya b-amriika?*

abortion - *taṭriiζ* pl. *-aat.* Abortion is against the law. *t-taṭriiζ δidd il-qaanuun.*
  to perform an abortion on - *ṭarraζ (i taṭriiζ) t-.* He was arrested for performing an abortion on a young girl. *twaqqaf li-ʔan ṭarraζ ibnayya ṣġayyra.*

about - 1. *ζawaali, taqriiban.* There were about thirty people present. *čaan ʔaku ζawaali tlaaθiin waaζid.* -- It's about the same. *taqriiban nafs iš-šii.* **2.** *εala wašak.* Lunch is about ready. *l-ġada εala wašak yiζδar.* -- He was about to leave when the phone rang. *čaan εala wašak yiṭlaε min dagg it-talafoon.* **3.** *εan, εala.* They were talking about the war. *čaanaw yiζčuun εann il-ζarub.* **4.** *b-.* My husband is very particular about his food. *rajli hwaaya diqdaaqi b-ʔakla.*
  **It's about time you got here. *ma-yaḷḷa εaad!* or *ween δalleet?*
  what ... about - *εala weeš.* What are you talking about? *ʔinta εala weeš da-tiζči?* or *ʔinta š-da-tiζči?*
  what about - *š-raʔyak, š-itguul.* What about this one? *š-raʔyak ib-haaδa?* or *šloonak bii?*
  to be about - 1. *εala weeš.* What's it all about? *εala weeš haaδa kulla?* or *š-ṣaar?* or *š-aku?* **2.** *εala.* It's about the money he owes me. *haay εal-ifluus il-ʔaṭlubh-iyyaa.* **3.** *čaan yriid.* I was about to send for you. *činit da-ariid adizz εaleek.* **4.** *εala wašak.* She was about to burst into tears. *čaanat εala wašak tibči.*

above - 1. *foog.* He is above average height. *ṭuula foog il-muεaddal.* **2.** *bis-saabiq.* As already mentioned above. *miθil-ma nδikar bis-saabiq.*
  above all - *wil-ʔahamm, la-siyyama, εala l-axaṣṣ, xuṣuuṣan.* Above all, remember to be on time. *wil-ʔahamm, iδδakkar laazim itkuun εal-wakit.* or *la-siyyama, la-titʔaxxar.*
  to be above - *(čaan) ʔaεla min, ʔarfaε min, foog.* She's above such petty things. *hiyya ʔarfaε min hal-ʔašyaaʔ iṭ-ṭafiifa.* -- He's above suspicion. *huwwa foog iš-šubhaat.*

abroad - *xaarij.* Are you going abroad this summer? *ʔinta msaafir lil-xaarij haṣ-ṣeef?* -- He lives abroad. *huwwa yεiiš bil-xaarij.* -- At home and abroad ... *bil-waṭan w-bil-xaarij ...*

abrupt - 1. *yaabis.* He has a very abrupt manner. *εinda ʔaxlaaqa hwaaya yaabsa.* **2.** *fujaaʔi*.* We noticed an abrupt change in his attitude. *laaζaδna taġayyur fujaaʔi b-mawqifa.*

abruptly - *b-jafaaf.* He treated me rather abruptly. *εaamalni b-jafaaf.*

absence - *ġiyaab.* No one noticed his absence. *maζζad laaζaδ ġiyaaba ʔaslan.*

absent - *ġaayib.* Three members were absent because of illness. *tlaθ ʔaεδaaʔ čaanaw ġaaybiin ib-sabab il-maraδ.*

absent-minded - *fikr- šaarid, daalġači.* He's very absent-minded. *haaδa kulliš fikra šaarid* or *huwwa kulliš daalġači.*

absolute - 1. *xaaliṣ, ṣirf, maζδ.* That's the absolute truth. *haaδa ṣ-ṣudug il-xaaliṣ.* -- That's an absolute fact. *haδiič l-ζaqiiqa l-maζδa.* **2.** *muṭlaq.* The dictator exercised absolute power. *d-diktatoor maaras sulṭa muṭlaqa.*

absolutely - *qaṭεan.* He's absolutely right. *l-ζaqq wiyyaa qaṭεan.*

to **absorb - 1.** *maṣṣ (u maṣṣ) n-.* The sponge absorbed the water quickly. *l-isfanja maṣṣat il-maay bil-εajal.* **2.** *hiδam (u haδum) n-.* You can't absorb all that material in a single lesson. *ma-tigdar tuhδum kull hal-maεluumaat ib-fadd daris.*

to be **absorbed -** *nhimak (i nhimaak).* He was so absorbed in his book, he didn't hear me come in. *čaan hal-gadd minhimik bil-iqraaya ma-ζass biyya min xaššeet.*

to **abuse - 1.** *ʔasaaʔ (i ʔisaaʔa) n- l-istiεmaal.* He's abusing his authority. *da-ysiiʔ istiεmaal ṣuluṭṭa.* **2.** *ʔasaaʔ (i ʔisaaʔa) n- l-muεaamala.* He abuses his wife. *huwwa ysiiʔ muεaamalat marta.*

academic - 1. *diraasi*.* The academic year. *s-sana d-diraasiyya.* **2.** *naδari*.* This is an academic matter. *haaδi qaδiyya naδariyya.*

academy - *majmaε* pl. *majaamiε.* Scientific academy. *majmaε εilmi.*

accelerator - *ʔaksaleeta.* The accelerator's broken. *l-ʔaksaleeta maksuura.*

accent - 1. *lakna, lahja.* He speaks with a German accent. *yiζči b-lakna ʔalmaaniyya.* **2.** *tašdiid* pl. *-aat.* Where is the accent in this word? *ween it-tašdiid ib-hal-kilma?*

to **accept -** *qibal (a qubuul) n-.* Are you going to accept that position? *raζ-tiqbal haδiič il-waδiifa?*

access - 1. *stiεmaal.* Access to the files is restricted to supervisors. *stiεmaal il-faaylaat maqṣuur εal-mulaaζiδiin.* **2.** *maxraj* pl. *maxaarij.* Iraq has access to the sea through the Shatt-al-Arab. *l-εiraaq εinda maxraj lil-baζar εan ṭariiq šaṭṭ il-εarab.*
  to have access to - 1. (things) *gidar (a) yistaεmil.* He has access to the files. *huwwa yigdar yistaεmil il-ʔiδbaaraat.* **2.** (persons) *gidar (a) yitwaṣṣal.* She has access to the minister of interior. *tigdar titwaṣṣal il-waziir id-daaxiliyya.*

accident - *ζaadiθa* pl. *ζawaadiθ, qadar* pl. *ʔaqdaar.* When did the accident happen? *šwakit ṣaarat il-ζaadiθa?*
  by accident - 1. *biṣ-ṣidfa.* I found it out by accident. *ktišafitha biṣ-ṣidfa.* **2.** *min keef-.* That didn't happen by accident. *haδiič ma-ṣaarat min keefha.*

accidentally - 1. *bila taεammud.* I dropped the plate accidentally. *waqqaεt il-maaεuun bila taεammud.* **2.** *ṣidfatan.* I accidentally learned the truth. *εiraft iṣ-ṣudug ṣidfatan.*

to **accommodate -** **We can accommodate three more people. *nigdar inhayyiʔ makaan l-itlaθ ašxaaṣ baεad* or *εidna makaan l-itlaaθa baεad.*

accommodating - *xaduum.* The manager was very accommodating. *l-mudiir čaan kulliš xaduum.*

accompaniment - *εazif.* Who's going to play the accompaniment? *minu raζ-yquum bil-εazif?*

to **accompany - 1.** *raafaq (i muraafaqa), ṣaaζab (i muṣaaζaba).* He accompanied her on the lute. *huwwa raafaqha εal-εuud.* -- I played the lute and Ali accompanied me on the flute. *ʔaani daggeet εuud* w-εali ṣaaζabni εan-naay. **2.** raaζ (u) wiyya. We'll accompany you to Damascus. nruuζ wiyyaak liš-šaam.

to **accomplish** – **1.** xallaṣ (i taxliiṣ) t–, kammal (i takmiil) t–. He accomplished what he set out to do. xallaṣ iš-šii l-bida bii or kammal il-raad ysawwii. **2.** ṭallaε (i taṭliiε) t–. For one day he accomplished quite a lot. ṭallaε ihwaaya šuġul ib-fadd yoom. **3.** ζaqqaq (i taζqiiq) t–. He's accomplished a good deal in his life. ζaqqaq ihwaaya ġaayaat ib-ζayaata. **4.** twaṣṣal (a tawaṣṣul). Did you accomplish anything in Washington? twaṣṣalit iš-šii b-waašintin?

accomplished – maahir. He's an accomplished musician. huwwa muusiiqi maahir.
**Mission accomplished. l-maṭluub ṣaar or l-ġaraḍ itζaqqaq.

accomplishment – **1.** ṣaniiεa pl. ṣanaayiε. His mother was proud of his accomplishments. ʔumma čaanat faxuura b-ṣanaayεa. **2.** εamal pl. ʔaεmaal. Really, that was no small accomplishment. ṣudug, čaan εamal muu šaqa.

accord – **1.** ttifaaq. They acted in complete accord with him. tṣarrifaw b-ittifaaq kaamil wiyyaa. **2.** keef–. He did it of his own accord. sawwaaha min keefa.

in **accordance with** – ζasab, b-muujib. In accordance with your request we are sending you three more copies. ζasab ṭalabak ʔiζna daazzii-lak itlaθ nusax baεad.

accordingly – **1.** εala hal-ʔasaas. I acted accordingly. tṣarrafit εala hal-ʔasaas. **2.** binaaʔan εalee. Accordingly, I wrote him a check for the full amount. binaaʔan εalee, kitabit-la čakk bil-mablaġ kulla.

according to – ζasab. Everything was carried out according to instructions. kullši tnaffaδ ζasab it-taεliimaat.

account – **1.** ζsaab pl. –aat. I have an account in this bank. εindi ζsaab ib-hal-ḅang. **2.** taqriir pl. taqaariir, waṣuf pl. ʔawṣaaf. His account of the accident isn't clear. taqriira εal-ζaadiθa muu waaḍiζ or waṣfa lil-ζaadiθa muu waaḍiζ.
on account of – εala ʔasaas, b-sabab. The game was postponed on account of rain. l-liεib itʔajjal ib-sabab il-muṭar.
on no account – b-ʔay ζaal, mahma ṣaar. On no account must you open this drawer. ʔinta ma-laazim itfukk hal-mijarr ib-ʔay ζaal or ma-laazim itfukk hal-mijarr mahma ṣaar.
to call to account – ζaasab (i muζaasaba) t–. I'll call him to account. raζ-aζaasba.
to give an account of – bayyan (i tabyiin) t–. You have to give me an account of every penny you spend. laazim itbayyin-li kull filis il-tuṣurfa ween yiruuζ.
**Give me an account of what happened. ζčii-li illi ṣaar or ʔooṣif-li illi ṣaar.
to take into account – ʔaxaδ ib-naḍar il-iεtibaar. You have to take all the facts into account. laazim taaxuδ kull il-ζaqaayiq ib-naḍar il-iεtibaar.
to account for – **1.** εallal (i taεliil) t–. How do you account for that? šloon itεallil haaδa? **2.** barrar (i tabriir). You'll have to account for your actions. laazim itbarrir aεmaalak.

to be **accountable for** – tζaasab (a taζaasub) εan. You alone will be accountable for the materials. ʔinta waζdak raζ-titζaasab εan hal-mawaadd.

accountant – muζaasib pl. –iin.

accurate – **1.** daqiiq. She's very accurate in her work. hiyya kulliš daqiiqa b-šuġulha. **2.** maḍbuuṭ. Is that watch accurate? has-saaεa maḍbuuṭa?

accurately – biḍ-ḍabuṭ, b-ṣuura maḍbuuṭa, b-diqqa. She figured it out accurately. ζisbatha biḍ-ḍabuṭ.

to **accuse** – tiham (i ttihaam) n–. You can't accuse me of being lazy. ma-tigdar tithimni bil-kasal. -- He was accused of theft. ntiham ib-booga.

accustomed – mitεawwid εala. She's not accustomed to that. hiyya ma-mitεawwda εala haaδa.
to get accustomed to – tεawwad (a taεawwud) εala. He can't get accustomed to the strict discipline. huwwa ma-yigdar yitεawwad εan-niḍaam id-daqiiq.

ace – ʔaas pl. –aat, billi pl. –iyyaat. He has all four aces. huwwa εinda l-ʔarbaε ʔaasaat.

to **ache** – wijaε (a wujaε). My ear aches. ʔiδni toojaεni.

to **achieve** – ζaqqaq (i taζqiiq) t–. He achieved his purpose. ζaqqaq maraama.

acid – **1.** ζaamuḍ pl. ζawaamiḍ. Bring me that bottle of acid. jiib-li δaak baṭl il-ζaamuḍ. **2.** laaδiε. He made a few acid remarks. εallaq šwayyat taεliiqaat laaδεa.

to **acknowledge** – εtiraf (i εtiraaf). We acknowledge receipt of your letter dated ... niεtirif b-istilaam maktuubak il-muʔarrax ...

acknowledged – muεtaraf. He is an acknowledged expert. huwwa xabiir muεtaraf bii.

acorn – balluuṭa pl. –aat coll. balluuṭ.

to **acquaint** – ʔaṭlaε (i ʔiṭlaaε) εala, εarraf (u taεriif) b–. First I want to acquaint you with the facts of the case. ʔawwalan ʔariid ʔaṭliεak εala ζaqaayiq il-qaḍiyya.
to acquaint oneself – tεarraf (a taεarruf), ṭṭilaε (i ṭṭilaaε). It'll take me a week to acquaint myself with all the problems. yinraad-li sbuuε ζatta ʔatεarraf εala kull il-mašaakil.
to get acquainted with – tεarraf (a taεarruf) εala. You two should get acquainted with each other. laazim ʔintu l-iθneen titεarrfuun εala baεaḍkum.

acquaintance – **1.** waaζid min il-maεaarif. He's an old acquaintance of mine. huwwa waaζid min maεaarfi l-εittag. **2.** maεrifa. I am pleased to make your acquaintance. ʔaani farζaan ib-maεriftak.

to **acquire** – **1.** ζaṣṣal (i ζuṣuul) t– εala. We acquired the house when our uncle died. ζaṣṣalna εal-beet min maat εammna. **2.** ktisab (i ktisaab). He's acquired considerable skill in tennis. ktisab ihwaaya mahaara bit-tanis.

to **acquit** – barra (i tabriya) t–. The judge acquitted him. l-ζaakim barraa.

across – b-ṣoob il-laax. The station is across the river. l-maζaṭṭa b-ṣoob il-laax imniš-šaṭṭ.
across the street – gḅaal. He lives across the street from us. huwwa yiskun igḅaalna.
to go across – εubar (u εubuur) n–. Let's go across the bridge. xal-niεbur ij-jisir.
**This bus goes right across town. hal-ṗaaṣ yijtaaz il-wlaaya εala ṭuul.

act – **1.** εamal pl. ʔaεmaal, fiεil pl. ʔafεaal. That wasn't a selfish act. haaδa ma-čaan εamal ʔanaani. **2.** faṣil pl. fuṣuul. I don't want to miss the first act. ma-ariid yfuutni l-faṣl il-ʔawwal.
**Don't put on an act! la-titṣannaε!
to act – **1.** tṣarraf (a taṣarruf). He's been acting like a child. čaan yitṣarraf miθl iz-zaεṭuuṭ. **2.** maθθal (i tamθiil) t–. She's going to act in that new play. raζ-itmaθθil ib-δiič it-tamθiiliyya j-jidiida.
to act on – ttixaδ (i ttixaaδ) ijraaʔ b–. They're going to act on our proposal tomorrow. raaζ yittaxδuun ijraaʔ b-iqtiraaζna baačir.

action – **1.** ζawaadiθ. The action of the novel takes place in Turkey. ζawaadiθ il-quṣṣa tijri b-turkiya. **2.** ʔijraaʔ pl. –aat. This situation requires firm action. hal-waḍiε yiṭṭallab ijraaʔ ζaazim. **3.** taṣarruf pl. –aat. His actions are hard to understand. taṣarrufaata ṣaεub tinfihim.
in action – bil-maεraka. He was killed in action. nkital bil-maεraka.
to bring action against – qaam (i ʔiqaama) n– daεwa εala. They will bring action against him. raζ-yqiimuun εalee daεwa.
to take action – ʔaxaδ (u ʔaxiδ) n– ʔijraaʔ. Has any action been taken on my case? nʔixaδ ʔay ijraaʔ ib-qaḍiiti?

active – **1.** εaamil. Are you an active member? ʔinta εuḍu εaamil? **2.** našiiṭ. He's still very active for his age. baεda kulliš našiiṭ bin-nisba l-εumra. **3.** faεεaal. He has always been very active in our club. huwwa čaan w-la-yzaal kulliš faεεaal ib-naadiina.

activity – **1.** našaaṭ. He had to give up all physical activity for a while. ḍṭarr yitruk kull našaaṭ jismi fadd mudda. **2.** ζaraka pl. –aat. There's not much activity around here on Sunday. ma-aku hwaaya ζaraka hnaa yoom il-aζζad. **3.** εamal pl. ʔaεmaal. She

engages in a lot of social activity. *tištirik b-ihwaaya ?aƐmaal ijtimaaƐiyya.*
feverish activity - *xabṣa* pl. *xabaṣaat.* What's all that feverish activity over there? *šinu hal-xabṣa hnaak?*

actor - *mumaθθil* pl. *-iin.*

actress - *mumaθθila* pl. *-aat.*

actual - 1. *ḥaqiiqi**, *fiƐli**. The actual reason was something entirely different. *s-sabab il-ḥaqiiqi čaan fadd šii yixtilif tamaaman.* 2. *?aṣli**. She works here, but her actual office is on the second floor. *hiyya tištuğuḷ ihnaa laakin muḥall šuğuḷha l-?aṣli biṭ-ṭaabiq iθ-θaani.*

actually - 1. *ḥaqiiqatan, fiƐlan, ṣudug.* Do you actually believe that story? *?inta ṣudug tiƐtiqid ib-haδiič l-ḥčaaya?* 2. *ṣaḥiiḥ.* Did he actually write this letter? *ṣaḥiiḥ kitab hal-maktuub?*

acute - 1. *ḥaadd.* He has acute dysentery. *Ɛinda dazantari ḥaadd.* -- This triangle has two acute angles. *hal-muθallaθ bii zaawiiteen ḥaadda.* 2. *šadiid.* If the pain becomes acute, call the doctor. *?iδa ṣaar il-?alam šadiid xaabur iṭ-ṭabiib.* 3. *qawi**. Dogs have an acute sense of smell. *l-ičlaab Ɛidha ḥaassat šamm qawiyya.*
ad - *?iƐlaan* pl. *-aat.* I'd like to put in an ad. *?ariid anšur iƐlaan.*
to **adapt** - 1. *tkayyaf (a takayyuf).* She adapts easily to new social situations. *hiyya titkayyaf ib-suhuula Ɛala l-ḥaala l-ijtimaaƐiyya j-jidiida.* 2. *tlaa?am (a talaa?um).* This method will adapt well to my purposes. *haṭ-ṭariiqa titlaa?am zeen wiyya ?ağraaδi.* 3. *kayyaf (i takyiif) t-.* He adapts himself easily. *huwwa ykayyif nafsa b-suhuula.*

to **add** - 1. *zaad (i zyaada).* You'll have to add some sugar. *yinraad-lak itziid išwayyat šakar.* 2. *δaaf (i ?iδaafa) n-.* I've nothing to add to that. *ma-Ɛindi sii ?aδiif il-haaδa.* 3. *jimaƐ (a jamiƐ) n-.* Add up these figures. *?ijmaƐ hal-arqaam.*
to add up to - *ṣaar (i).* How much will the bill add up to? *šgadd raḥ-iṭṣiir il-qaa?ima?*

addition - 1. *jamiƐ.* Is my addition correct? *jamƐi ṣaḥiiḥ?* 2. *mulḥaq* pl. *-aat.* They're building an addition on that building. *da-yibnuun mulḥaq il-haaδi l-binaaya.* 3. *ziyaada.* The addition of turpentine will thin the paint. *ziyaadt it-tarbantiin raḥ-itxaffif iṣ-ṣubuğ.*
in addition - *čmaal-, foog-.* In addition he asked for ten dollars. *čmaala ṭulab Ɛašir doolaaraat.*
in addition to - *bil-iδaafa Ɛala.* In addition to his fixed salary he gets commissions. *bil-iδaafa Ɛala maƐaaša yaaxuδ qoomisyoon.*

additional - 1. *?iδaafi**. He gave me an additional amount for incidentals. *nṭaani fadd mablağ iδaafi l-maṣaariif naθriyya.* 2. *?azyad.* An additional dollar gives you better quality. *fadd doolaar azyad yinṭiik nooƐ ?aḥsan.*

address - 1. *Ɛinwaan* pl. *Ɛanaawiin.* Send these books to this address. *dizz hal-kutub li-haaδa l-Ɛinwaan.* 2. *xiṭaab* pl. *-aat.* The President delivered an important address. *r-ra?iis ?alqa xiṭaab muhimm.*
to address - 1. *Ɛanwan (i) t-.* Address this letter to the manager. *Ɛanwin haaδa l-maktuub lil-mudiir.* 2. *xaaṭab (u muxaaṭaba).* How shall I address him? *šloon axaaṭba?* 3. *wajjah (i tawjiih) t-.* I would like to address a question to the speaker. *?aḥibb awajjih su?aal lil-mutakallim.*
adhesive tape - *šariiṭ lizzeeg.*

adjective - *ṣifa* pl. *-aat.*
to **adjoin** - 1. *ḥadd (i).* My garden adjoins his. *ḥadiiqti tḥidd ḥadiiqta.* 2. *jaawar (i mujaawara).* Their garage adjoins the house. *garaajhum yjaawir il-beet.*

to **adjourn** - *faδδ (u faδδ) n-.* He adjourned the meeting. *huwwa faδδ il-ijtimaaƐ.*

to **adjust** - 1. *δubaṭ (u δabuṭ) n-.* The mechanic adjusted the carburetor. *l-miikaaniiki δubaṭ il-kaabreeta.* 2. *ṣaḥḥaḥ (i taṣḥiiḥ) t-.* The manager will adjust your bill. *l-mudiir raḥ-yṣaḥḥiḥ qaa?imtak.* 3. *Ɛaddal (i taƐdiil) t-.* She adjusted her clothing. *Ɛaddilat ihduumha.* 4. *kayyaf (i takyiif) t-.* I can't adjust myself to the climate here. *ma-agdar akayyif nafsi l-haj-jaww.*

adjustable - *mitḥarrik.* Is this seat adjustable? *haaδa l-maqƐad mitḥarrik?*
to **administer** - 1. *daar (i ?idaara) n-.* Who's administering his estate? *minu da-ydiir tarikaata?* 2. *sawwa (i).* He showed us how he administers artificial respiration. *raawaana šloon ysawwi tanaffus iṣṭinaaƐi.*

administration - *?idaara* pl. *-aat.*

admiral - *?amiiraal* pl. *-aat, -iyya.*

admiration - *?iƐjaab.* He got the admiration of all his friends. *naal iƐjaab kull aṣdiqaa?a.*

to **admire** - *kaan muƐjab b-.* I admire her beauty. *?aani muƐjab ib-jamaalha.*
**I admire your patience. *yiƐjibni ṣabrak.*

admission - 1. *duxuul.* How much is the admission? *beeš id-duxuul?* 2. *qubuul.* I have an appointment with the Director of Admissions. *Ɛindi mawƐid wiyya mudiir il-qubuul.* 3. *Ɛtiraaf* pl. *-aat.* His admission proved my innocence. *Ɛtiraafa ?aθbat baraa?ti.*

admission charge - *?ujrat duxuul.* There's no admission charge. *ma-aku ?ujrat duxuul.*
to **admit** - 1. *daxxal (i tadxiil) t-, xaššaš (i taxšiiš) t-.* Give this card to the doorman and he'll admit you. *?inṭi hal-kart lil-bawwaab w-huwwa ydaxxlak.* 2. *qibal (a qubuul) n-.* We can't admit this type of student. *ma-nigdar niqbal hiiči tilmiiδ.* 3. *qarr (u ?iqraar) b-.* The accused finally admitted his guilt. *l-muttaham axiiran qarr ib-δanba.* 4. *Ɛtiraf (i Ɛtiraaf).* I admit I was wrong. *?aƐtirif činit ğalṭaan.*
to **adopt** - 1. *tbanna (a tabanni).* My friend has adopted a small boy. *ṣadiiqi tbanna walad iṣğayyir.* 2. *Ɛtinaq (i Ɛtinaaq).* They adopted Islam toward the end of the first century. *Ɛtinqaw il-?islaam ib-?awaaxir il-qarn il-?awwal.* 3. *ttixaδ (i ttixaaδ).* They adopted the measure unanimously. *ttixδaw il-qaraar bil-?ijmaaƐ.* 4. *ttibaƐ (i ttibaaƐ).* Better results could be obtained if we adopted this method. *nitwaṣṣal ?ila nataa?ij ?aḥsan ?iδa ttibaƐna haṭ-ṭariiqa.*

adult - *čibiir* pl. *kbaar.* There was milk for the children and coffee for the adults. *čaan aku ḥaliib liṣ-ṣiğaar w-gahwa lil-ikbaar.*

advance - 1. *taqaddum, taraqqi.* Great advances have been made in medicine during the last few years. *hwaaya taqaddum ṣaar biṭ-ṭibb bis-siniin il-?axiira.* 2. *sulfa* pl. *sulaf.* Can you give me an advance? *tigdar tinṭiini sulfa?*

in advance - *li-giddaam.* Let me know in advance if you're coming. *?ixbirni li-giddaam ?iδa raḥ-tiji.*

to advance - 1. *traqqa (a taraqqi).* He advanced rapidly in the company. *traqqa bil-Ɛajal biš-šarika.* 2. *raffaƐ (i tarfiiƐ) t-.* They just advanced him to assistant manager. *tawwhum raffiƐoo ?ila muƐaawin mudiir.* — He was advanced to chief clerk. *traffaƐ ?ila ra?iis kuttaab.* 3. *qaddam (i taqdiim) t-.* They advanced the date of the lecture. *qaddmaw taariix il-muḥaaδara.* 4. *tqaddam (a taqaddum).* Our army advanced twenty miles. *jeešna tqaddam Ɛišriin miil.* 5. *sallaf (i tasliif).* The bank advanced him one thousand dinars. *l-bang sallafa ?alif diinaar.*

advantage - *faa?ida* pl. *fawaa?id.* This method has advantages and disadvantages. *haṭ-ṭariiqa biiha fawaa?id w-Ɛiyuub.*
an advantage over - *?afδaliyya Ɛala.* Your technical education gives you an advantage over me. *θaqaaftak il-fanniyya tinṭiik ?afδaliyya Ɛalayya.*
to one's advantage - *l-maṣlaḥat ?aḥḥad.* This is to your advantage. *haaδa l-maṣlaḥtak.*
to take advantage of - 1. *ntihaz (i ntihaaz).* He takes advantage of every opportunity. *yintihiz kull furṣa.* 2. *stiğall (i stiğlaal).* Don't let people

take advantage of you. *la-txalli n-naas yistiġilluuk.*

advantageous – *mufiid, naafiƐ.*

adventure – *muxaaṭara* pl. *-aat, mujaazafa* pl. *-aat, muġaamara* pl. *-aat.*

adverb – *δaruf* pl. *δuruuf.*

to **advertise** – *Ɛilan (i ʔiƐlaan) n-.* The store advertised a sale. *l-maxzan Ɛilan tanziilaat.*

advertisement – *ʔiƐlaan* pl. *-aat.*

advertising – *diƐaaya, ʔiƐlaan.* Our company spends a lot on advertising. *šarikatna tuṣruf ihwaaya Ɛad-diƐaaya.*

advice – *naṣiiζa.* My advice is that you leave immediately. *naṣiiζti ʔan itruuζ ζaalan.*
to ask advice – *stašaar (i stišaara), ṭilab (u) naṣiiζa.* I asked his advice. *stišarta* or *ṭlabit naṣiiζta.*
to give advice – *niṣaζ (a) n-, ʔinṭa (i naṭi) naṣiiζa.* It is hard to give advice in this matter. *ṣaƐub waaζid yinṣaζ ib-hal-mawδuuƐ* or *ṣaƐub waaζid yinṭi naṣiiζa b-hal-mawδuuƐ.*

advisable – **1.** *l-ʔaƐqal.* I think it's advisable for you to stay home today. *ʔašuuf il-ʔaƐqal tibqa bil-beet il-yoom.* **2.** *mustaζsan.* Would that be an advisable step to take? *tiƐtiqid hal-xaṭwa mustaζsana?*

to **advise** – *niṣaζ (a) n-, šaar (i) n- Ɛala.* What do you advise me to do? *š-tinṣaζni ʔasawwi?*

adviser – **1.** Legal adviser. *mušaawir Ɛadli.* **2.** Political adviser. *mustašaar siyaasi.* **3.** Student adviser. *muršid.*

advisory – *stišaari*.*

aerial – *ʔeeryal* pl. *-aat.* The aerial on the radio isn't connected. *l-ʔeeryal maal ir-raadyo ma-mittiṣil.*

aerial warfare – *ζarub jawwiyya.*

affair – **1.** *ʔamur* pl. *ʔumuur.* I don't meddle in his affairs. *ma-atdaxxal ib-ʔumuura.* **2.** *šuġuḷ* pl. *ʔašġaal.* That's your affair. *haaδa šuġḷak ʔinta.* **3.** *šaʔin* pl. *šuʔuun.* He handled the affairs of the company badly. *daar šuʔuun iš-šarika b-ṣuura mxarubṭa.* **4.** *munaasaba* pl. *-aat.* Her party was a real nice affair. *ζaflatha čaanat munaasaba ḷaṭiifa jiddan.* **5.** *Ɛalaaqa* pl. *-aat.* The cook had an affair with the chauffeur. *ṭ-ṭabbaaxa ṣaar Ɛidha Ɛalaaqa (ġaraamiyya) wiyya s-saayiq.*

to **affect** – **1.** *ʔaθθar (i taʔθiir) Ɛala.* That damp climate affected his health. *haδaak iṭ-ṭaqis ir-raṭib ʔaθθar Ɛala ṣiζζta.* **2.** *tδ̣aahar (a taδ̣aahur).* He has affected an Egyptian accent. *yitδ̣aahar Ɛinda lakna miṣriyya.*
to be affected – *tʔaθθar (a taʔaθθur) b-.* His vision was affected by his illness. *naδ̣ara tʔaθθar ib-maraδ̣a.*

affected – **1.** *mitṣanniƐ.* She's terribly affected. *hiyya kulliš mitṣanniƐa.* **2.** *mitkallif.* Is his style in writing always that affected? *ʔisluuba bil-kitaaba daaʔiman hiiči mitkallif?*

to **afford** – *tmakkan (a tamakkun).* We can't afford to buy a car. *ma-nitmakkan ništiri sayyaara* or ***ma-ʔilna qaabliyyat sayyaara.*
**I can't afford that much. *haaδa ġaali Ɛalayya.*
**You can afford to laugh. *ζaqqak tiδζak* or *ʔiδζak, leeš laa.*

Afghanistan – *ʔafġaanistaan.*

to be **afraid** – *xiša (a xišya).* I'm afraid its going to rain. *ʔaxša raζ-tumṭur.*
to be afraid of – *xaaf (a xoof) n- min.* He's not afraid of anyone. *ma-yxaaf min ʔaζζad.*

Africa – *ʔafriiqya.*

African – *ʔafriiqi** pl. *-iyyiin.*

after – **1.** *baƐad.* Can you call me after supper? *tigdar itxaaburni baƐd il-Ɛaša?* **2.** *wara.* He arrived after me. *wiṣal waraaya.* **3.** *Ɛala.* Day after day, his health is improving. *yoom Ɛala yoom ṣiζζta da-titζassan.* — He named his son after his grandfather. *samma ʔibna Ɛala ʔisim jidda.* **4.** *Ɛala ʔaθar.* After the death of my father, I had to quit school. *Ɛala ʔaθar wafaat ʔabuuya δ̣ṭarreet abaṭṭil imnil-madrasa.*
after all – **1.** *mahma ykuun.* Why shouldn't I help him? After all, he's my friend. *luweeš ma-asaaƐda? mahma ykuun huwwa ṣadiiqi.* **2.** *taaliiha.* You are right, after all. *taaliiha l-ζaqq wiyyaak.*
after this – *minnaa w-ġaadi.* After this, please let us know in advance. *minnaa w-ġaadi ʔinṭiina xabar li-giddaam.*
to be after – *dawwar (u tadwiir) Ɛala.* The police have been after him for two weeks. *š-šurṭa da-tdawwur Ɛalee min muddat isbuuƐeen.*

afternoon – *Ɛaṣriyya* pl. *-aat.* I would like to see you one afternoon. *yiƐjibni ʔašuufak fadd Ɛaṣriyya.*
in the afternoon – *baƐd iδ-δuhur, wara δ-δuhur, l-Ɛaṣir.* I never drink coffee in the afternoon. *ʔaani ʔabad ma-ašrab gahwa wara δ-δuhur.*
this afternoon – *l-yoom il-Ɛaṣir.* Can you come this afternoon. *tigdar tiji il-yoom il-Ɛaṣir?*

afterwards – *baƐdeen.* We ate dinner and went to a movie afterwards. *tġaddeena w-baƐdeen riζna lis-siinama.*

again – **1.** *marra lux, marrt il-lux, marra θaanya.* I'll tell him again. *raζ-agul-la marra lux.* **2.** *min jiht il-lux.* Again, we should study the other proposal, too. *min jiht il-lux, hamm laazim nidrus il-iqtiraaζ iθ-θaani.* **3.** *baƐad.* He never made that mistake again. *huwwa ma-sawwa δiič il-ġalṭa baƐad.*
again and again – *marra wara marra, yaama w-yaama.* I warned him again and again. *ζaδδarta marra wara marra.*
over and over again – *marraat ihwaaya.* He tried over and over again. *huwwa ζaawal marraat ihwaaya.*
then again – *hammeen.* But then again, that's not always true. *laakin hammeen, haaδa muu daaʔiman ṣaζiiζ.*

against – **1.** *b-ṣaff.* Move this table over against the wall. *ζuṭṭ hal-meez ib-ṣaff il-ζaayiṭ.* **2.** *δidd.* We had to swim against the current. *δ̣ṭarreena nisbaζ δidd il-maay.* — He voted against me. *huwwa ṣawwaṭ δiddi.* **3.** *Ɛala.* He was leaning against the house. *čaan mintiči Ɛal-beet.*
as against – *muqaabil.* Fifty ships went through the canal as against thirty five last month. *xamsiin safiina marrat imnil-qanaal muqaabil xamsa w-θlaaθiin biš-šahr il-faat.*

age – **1.** *Ɛumur, sinn.* He's about my age. *huwwa taqriiban ib-Ɛumri* or *huwwa taqriiban ib-sinni.* **2.** *Ɛaṣir.* This is the atomic age. *haaδa Ɛaṣr iδ-δarra.*
in ages – *min zamaan.* We haven't seen them in ages. *ma-šifnaahum min zamaan.*
of age – *baaliġ sinn ir-rušud.* He'll come of age next year. *raζ-yibluġ sinn ir-rušud is-sana j-jaaya.*
old age – *kubur.* He died of old age. *maat imnil-kubur.*
to age – **1.** *šayyab (i).* He's aged a great deal lately. *šayyab ihwaaya bil-ʔayyaam il-ʔaxiira.* **2.** *Ɛattaq (i taƐtiiq) t-.* The brewery aged the beer ninety days. *maƐmal il-biira Ɛattaq il-biira tisƐiin yoom.* **3.** *tƐattaq (a).* They left the wine to age for a number of years. *xallaw iš-šaraab yitƐattaq čam sana.*

agency – **1.** *wakaala.* Our company has an agency in Beirut. *šarikatna Ɛidha wakaala b-beeruut.* **2.** *daaʔira* pl. *dawaaʔir.* Government agencies submit their budgets this month. *dawaaʔir il-ζukuuma yqaddimuun miizaaniyyaathum haš-šahar.*

agent – **1.** *wakiil* pl. *wukalaaʔ.* Your agent called on me yesterday. *wakiilak jaani l-baarζa.* **2.** *Ɛamiil* pl. *Ɛumalaaʔ.* He is said to be a communist agent. *l-šaayiƐ Ɛanna huwwa Ɛamiil šiyuuƐi.* **3.** *mumaθθil* pl. *-iin.* The insurance company sent its agent to the accident site. *šarikat it-taʔmiin dazzat wakiilha l-mukaan il-ζaadiθ.* **4.** *sirri* pl. *-iyyiin.* I think he's a police agent. *ʔaƐtiqid huwwa sirri mniš-šurṭa.* **5.** *Ɛaamil* pl. *Ɛawaamil.* This is a strong chemical agent. *haaδa Ɛaamil kiimyaawi faƐƐaal.*

to **aggravate** - **1.** *zahhag (i tzihhig, tazhiig) t-.* His bragging really aggravated me. *t-tabajjuʒ maala zahhagni hwaaya.* **2.** *ʔazzam (i taʔziim) t-.* The border incident aggravated the situation. *ʒaadiθ il-ʒuduud ʔazzam il-waḍiƐ.* **3.** *zayyad (i tazyiid) t-.* Scratching will aggravate the inflammation. *l-ʒakk raʒ-yzayyid il-iltihaab.*

aggravation - **1.** *ʔizƐaaj pl. -aat.* Her nagging is a source of constant aggravation. *ʔilʒaaʒha maṣdar izƐaaj mustamirr.* **2.** *taʔazzum, tadahwur.* Any aggravation of the situation may lead to war. *ʔay taʔazzum bil-ʒaala yimkin yʔaddi ʔila ʒarub.*

ago - *gabuḷ.* I was there two months ago. *čint ihnaak gabuḷ šahreen.*
a while ago - *gabuḷ mudda.* He left a while ago. *raaʒ gabuḷ mudda.*

agony - *tmurmur, Ɛaδaab.* I can't bear this agony. *ma-agdar atʒammal hat-tumurmur.*

to **agree** - **1.** *ttifaq (i ttifaaq).* Their opinions never agree. *ʔaraaʔhum ʔabad ma-tittifiq.* **2.** *waafaq (i muwaafaqa) Ɛala.* He agreed to buy the radio. *waafaq Ɛala ʔan yištiri r-raadyo.*
to agree on - *ttifaq (i ttifaaq) Ɛala.* We've agreed on everything. *ʔiʒna ttifaqna Ɛala kullši.*
to agree to - *waafaq (u muwaafaqa) Ɛala.* Do you agree to these terms? *twaafuq Ɛala haš-šuruuṭ?*
to agree with - **1.** *ttifaq (i ttifaaq) wiyya.* Do you agree with me? *tittifiq wiyyaaya?* **2.** *laaʔam (i mulaaʔama) t-, waalam (i muwaalama) t-.* This weather doesn't agree with me at all. *haj-jaww ma-ywaalimni ʔabadan.*

agreeable - **1.** *samiʒ.* She has an agreeable disposition. *Ɛidha fadd ṭabuƐ samiʒ.* **2.** *maqbuul.* These terms are not agreeable. *haš-šuruuṭ ma-maqbuula.*
to be agreeable - *waafaq (u muwaafaqa).* Is he agreeable to that? *huwwa ywaafuq Ɛala haaδa?*

agreement - **1.** *ttifaaqiyya pl. -aat.* The agreement has to be ratified by Parliament. *l-ittifaaqiyya laazim titṣaddaq min majlis il-umma.* **2.** *ttifaaq pl. -aat.* The contract was extended by mutual agreement. *l-muqaawala tmaddidat b-ittifaaq iṭ-ṭarafeen.*
to be in agreement - *ttifaq (i ttifaaq).* This is definitely not in agreement with the original terms of the contract. *haaδa qaṭƐiyyan ma-yittifiq wiyya šuruuṭ il-muqaawala l-ʔaṣliyya.* -- Are you in agreement with me? *ʔinta mittifiq wiyyaaya?*
to come to an agreement - *wuṣal (a wuṣuul) ʔila ttifaaq.* We came to an agreement on that point. *wuṣalna ʔila ttifaaq ʒawil haδiič in-nuqṭa.*

agricultural - *ziraaƐi*.*

agriculture - *ziraaƐa.* Inquire at the Department of Agriculture. *ʔisʔal ib-wizaart iz-ziraaƐa.* -- There isn't much agriculture in this region. *ma-aku hwaaya ziraaƐa b-hal-manṭiqa.*

ahead - **1.** *mitqaddim.* He's ahead of everybody in his studies. *huwwa mitqaddim Ɛala l-kull ib-diraasta.* -- I'm way ahead in my work. *ʔaani hwaaya mitqaddim ib-šuġli.* **2.** *gabuḷ.* Are you next? No, he's ahead of me. *hassa siraak? laa, huwwa gabḷi.* **3.** *saabiq, ġaaḷub.* My horse was ahead during the race. *ʒṣaani čaan ġaaḷub wakt is-sibaaq.* **4.** *giddaam, ʔamaam.* The soldiers marched ahead of the sailors in the parade. *j-jinuud mišaw giddaam il-baʒʒaara bil-istiƐraaḍ.*
straight ahead - *gubaḷ, Ɛadil.* Go straight ahead. *fuut gubaḷ.*
to get ahead - *tqaddam (a taqaddum).* He doesn't seem to get ahead. *ma-da-ybayyin Ɛalee yitqaddam.*
to go ahead - **1.** *miša (i) b-faal~.* Just go ahead, don't mind me. *ʔimši b-faalak. ma-Ɛleek minni.* **2.** *raaʒ (u) gabuḷ.* You go ahead, I'll follow you later. *ruuʒ gabḷi, ʔaani ʔaliʒgak baƐdeen.* **3.** *stimarr (i stimraar), daawam (u mudaawama).* Just go ahead with your work, don't let me stop you. *stimirr ib-šuġlak, la-txalliini ʔaƐaṭṭlak.*
**Go ahead and take it! *tfaḍḍaḷ ʔuxuδa.*
**Go ahead and tell him. *yaḷḷa, gul-la* or *ma-yxaalif, gul-la.*

aid - **1.** *ʔisƐaaf pl. -aat.* I gave him first aid. *sawweet-la ʔisƐaaf ʔawwali.* **2.** *musaaƐada.* That country received quite a bit of economic aid. *had-dawla stilmat kammiyya kbiira mnil-musaaƐadaat il-iqtiṣaadiyya.*
to aid - *saaƐad (i musaaƐada) t-, Ɛaawan (i muƐaawana) t-.* Can I aid you in any way? *ʔagdar asaaƐdak ib-ʔay ṭariiqa?*

aide - **1.** *muraafiq.* The British general and his aide went to Iraq. *l-janaraal il-bariiṭaani w-muraafqa raaʒaw lil-Ɛiraaq.* **2.** *muƐaawin pl. -iin, musaaƐid pl. -iin.* The minister consulted his top aides. *l-waziir istašaar ʔakbar muƐaawinii.*

ailing - *mariiḍ, wajƐaan.* She's always ailing. *hiyya Ɛala ṭuul mariiḍa.*

aim - **1.** *ġaaya pl. -aat, maqṣad pl. maqaaṣid, ġaraḍ pl. ʔaġraaḍ, hadaf pl. ʔahdaaf.* His aim is to become a good doctor. *ġaayta yṣiir ṭabiib zeen.* **2.** *niišaan pl. nyaašiin.* He took careful aim and fired. *ʔaxaδ niišaan zeen w-ḍirab.*
to aim - **1.** *neešan (i).* He aimed at a rabbit. *neešan Ɛala ʔarnab.* **2.** *nuwa (i niyya).* What do you aim to do this afternoon? *š-tinwi tsawwi hal-Ɛaṣriyya?* **3.** *wajjah (i tawjiih) t-.* He aimed an insult at me. *wajjah masabba ʔili.*
**You're aiming too high! *ʔinta da-tuḍrub bil-Ɛaali* or *j-janna ʔagrab* or *da-tuṭlub muṭar.*

air - **1.** *hawa.* The air in this room is bad. *l-hawa b-hal-ġurfa muu zeen.* **2.** *jaww.* The meeting was surrounded by an air of mystery. *l-ijtimaaƐ čaan muʒaaṭ ib-jaww ġaamuḍ.* **3.** *jawwi*.* Send us a letter by air mail. *dizz-inna maktuub bil-bariid ij-jawwi.*
**He's continually putting on airs. *huwwa daaʔiman yitḍaahar Ɛala ġeer ʒaqiiqta.*
to be on the air - *δaaƐ (i ʔiδaaƐa).* The president will be on the air this evening. *r-raʔiis raʒ-yδiiƐ hal-leela.*
to air - **1.** *hawwa (i tahwiya) t-.* Would you please air the room while I'm out? *ʔarjuuk hawwi l-ġurfa lamma ʔakuun barra.* **2.** *šarr (u šarr) n-.* I have to air the blanket this morning. *laazim ašurr il-baṭṭaaniyya haṣ-ṣubuʒ.*
**Don't air your personal problems in public. *la-tiṭliƐ in-naas Ɛala mašaaklak iš-šaxṣiyya.*

air base - *qaaƐida (pl. qawaaƐid) jawwiyya.*

aircraft carrier - *ʒaamilat ṭaaʔiraat.*

airfield - *maṭaar pl. -aat.* Let's meet at the airfield. *xalli nitlaaga bil-maṭaar.*

air force - *quwwa (pl. -aat) jawwiyya.*

air line - *xuṭuuṭ jawwiyya, šarikat ṭayaraan.*

air mail - *bariid jawwi.* Send the package by air mail. *dizz ir-ruzma bil-bariid ij-jawwi.*

airplane - *ṭiyyaara pl. -aat.* How long does it take by airplane? *šgadd yṭawwul biṭ-ṭiyyaara?*

airport - *maṭaar pl. -aat.*

air raid - *ġaara (pl. -aat) jawwiyya.*

air sick - **He gets air sick every time he flies. *tilizma ṣ-ṣufra kull-ma yṭiir.*

aisle - *mamša pl. mamaaši, mamarr pl. -aat.* He had to stand in the aisle. *ḍṭarr yoogaf bil-mamša.*

ajar - *mafkuuk šwayya.* The door was ajar. *l-baab čaanat mafkuuka šwayya.*

alarm - **1.** *jaraṣ ʔinδaar.* Who turned in the alarm? *minu dagg jaraṣ il-ʔinδaar?* **2.** *xoof.* She was full of alarm. *čaanat kullha xoof.* **3.** *munabbih pl. -aat.* Set the alarm for six. *ʔunṣub il-munabbih Ɛas-saaƐa sitta.*
to alarm - **1.** *xarraƐ (i taxriiƐ) t-, fazzaz (i tafziiz) t-.* Her screams alarmed the whole building. *Ɛyaatha xarraƐ kull il-binaaya.* **2.** *šawwaš (i tašwiiš) t-.* The news report alarmed

me. *n-našra l-ixbaariyya šawwišatni.*
to be alarmed - *xtiraε(i).* Don't be alarmed! *la-tixtiriε.*
alarm clock - *saaεa* (pl. *-aat*) *munabbiha.* I bought myself a new alarm clock yesterday. *štireet-li saaεa munabbiha jidiida l-baarȥa.*
album - *ʔalboom* pl. *-aat.* He gave me a photograph album. *nṭaani ʔalboom taṣaawiir.*
alcohol - *kuȥuul, spiirtu.* The medicine has alcohol in it. *d-dawa bii kuȥuul.* -- She started the fire with alcohol. *šiεalat in-naar bil-ispiirtu.*
Aleppo - *ȥalab.*
alert - **1.** *mityaqqið̣, mitnabbih.* He's an alert fellow. *huwwa fadd waaȥid mityaqqið̣.*
on alert - *taȥt il-ʔinðaar.* The defense minister put the army on alert. *waziir id-difaaε xalla j-jeeš taȥt il-ʔinðaar.*
to be on the alert - *twaqqaε (a tawaqquε), tȥað̣ð̣ar (a taȥað̣ð̣ur).* Be on the alert for a call from me. *twaqqaε nidaaʔ minni.*
to alert - *ȥað̣ð̣ar (i taȥð̣iir) t-.* They alerted us about the coming of a storm. *ȥað̣ð̣iroona b-majiiʔ εaaṣifa.*
Alexandria - *l-iskandariyya.*
Algeria - *l-jazaaʔir.*
Algerian - *jazaaʔiri*.*
Algiers - *madiinat il-jazaaʔir.*
alien - (m.) *muqiim ʔajnabi* pl. *muqiimiin ʔajaanib.* (f.) *muqiima ʔajnabiyya* pl. *muqiimaat ʔajnaabiyyaat.*
alike - **1.** *fadd šikil, fadd šii.* These tables are all alike. *hal-imyuuza kullha fadd šikil.* **2.** *suwa.* We treat all customers alike. *ʔiȥna nεaamil kull il-maεaamiil suwa.*
alive - **1.** *ȥayy, εadil, ṭayyib.* This fish is still alive. *has-simča li-hassa ȥayya.*
**The atmosphere was alive with tension. *j-jaww čaan mašȥuun bit-tawattur.*
**This marsh is alive with snakes. *hal-hoor kulla ȥayaaya.*
to be alive with - *εajj (i).* The pantry is alive with ants. *l-kilar yεijj bin-namil.*
to keep alive - **1.** *ð̣all (a) ṭayyib.* It's a wonder they kept alive. *l-muεjiza ð̣allaw ṭayybiin.* **2.** *buqa (a baqaaʔ) εaayiš.* How can you keep alive on this salary? *šloon tigdar tibqa εaayiš ib-hal-maεaaš?* **3.** *xalla (i) εaayiš.* The doctor kept him alive for two weeks. *ṭ-ṭabiib xallaa εaayiš isbuuεeen.*
all - **1.** *kull.* Did you all go? *kullkum riȥtu?* -- This will upset all my plans. *haaða raȥ-yxarbuṭ kull mašaariiεi.* -- The bread's all gone. *l-xubuz kulla xilaṣ.* **2.** *ṭuul.* I've been waiting all day. *ṣaar-li da-antið̣ir ṭuul in-nahaar.* **3.** *jamiiε.* He took a vote of all the officers. *ʔaxað aṣwaat jamiiε ið̣-ð̣abbaaṭ.*
**That's all. *haaða huwwa.*
**If that's all there is to it, I'll do it. *ʔiða b-has-suhuula, raȥ-asawwiiha* or *ʔiða hiiči sahla, raȥ-asawwiiha.*
**The captain's all for starting now. *l-qabṭaan yfað̣ð̣il nibdi hassa.*
**He isn't all there. *huwwa mašxuuṭ.*
all along - *εala ṭuul, daaʔiman.* We've suspected him all along. *ʔiȥna εala ṭuul činna nšukk bii.*
all hours - *ʔay wakit.* He comes home to lunch at all hours. *yiji lil-beet yitġadda ʔay wakit čaan.*
all in - *talfaan.* The kids are all in from playing. *j-jahhaal talfaaniin imnil-liεib.*
all in all - *šii εala šii.* All in all, the movie was good. *šii εala šii, l-filim čaan zeen.*
all of a sudden - *εala ġafḷa.* All of a sudden it got dark. *ṣaarat ð̣aḷma εala ġafḷa.*
all over - *kull makaan.* They came from all over. *ʔijaw min kull makaan.* -- He traveled all over the country. *saafar il-kull makaan bil-balad.* **2.** *kull.* He trembled all over from fright. *rijaf kulla mnil-xoof.* -- He has pimples all over his face *εinda danaabil ib-kull wijja.* **3.** *min jidiid.* You have to do it all over. *laazim itsawwiiha min jidiid.*
**He came back after the war was all over. *rijaε baεad-ma ntihat il-ȥarub.*
all right - **1.** *tamaam, maaši.* Is everything all right? *kullši maaši?* or *kullši tamaam?* -- I'd like to go, all right, but it's impossible. *tamaam ariid aruuȥ, bass haaða mustaȥiil.* -- He knows why, all right. *huwwa tamaam yuεruf luweeš* or *huwwa zeen yuεruf luweeš.* **2.** *ṭayyib, zeen.* All right, I'll do it. *ṭayyib, raȥ-asawwiiha* or *zeen, raȥ-asawwiiha.*
**Is that all right with you? *ma-εindak maaniε?*
all set - *ȥaað̣ir, mitȥað̣ð̣ir.* We were all set to leave. *činna mitȥað̣ð̣riin inruuȥ.*
all the better - *baεad aȥsan.* If that is so, all the better. *loo hiiči, baεad aȥsan.*
all the same - **1.** *fadd šii, nafs iš-šii.* That's all the same to me. *kullha fadd šii bin-nisba ʔili.* **2.** *walaw, maεa haaða, εala kull ȥaal.* All the same, you didn't have to do it. *walaw, ma-čaan laazim itsawwiiha.*
all the time - *εala ṭuul, daaʔiman, kull wakit.* She's complaining all the time. *hiyya kull wakit titšakka.*
all told - *šii εala šii.* All told, he's not a bad fellow. *šii εala šii, huwwa xooš walad.*
above all - *εala l-ʔaxaṣṣ, ʔahamm sii.* Above all, don't get discouraged. *εala l-ʔaxaṣṣ la-tiftar εaziimtak.*
at all - *ʔabad, ʔabadan, bil-marra, ʔaṣlan.* He has no patience at all. *maa εinda ṣabur ʔabadan.*
in all - *kull bil-kull.* How many are there in all? *šgadd ʔaku kull bil-kull?*
Allah - *ʔaḷḷa.*
alley - *darbuuna* pl. *daraabiin, εagid* pl. *εguud.*
alliance - *ȥilif* pl. *ʔaȥlaaf.* The two countries formed an alliance. *d-dawilteen šakklaw ȥilif.*
to **allow** - **1.** *simaȥ (a samaaȥ) n-.* He won't allow that. *ma-yismaȥ ib-haaða.* -- He doesn't allow himself a minute's rest. *ma-yismaȥ in-nafsa wala daqiiqa raaȥa.* **2.** *ȥisab (i ȥsaab) n-.* How much will you allow me for my old car? *beeš raȥ-tiȥsib sayyaarti l-εatiiga?* **3.** *xalla (i) t-.* How much should I allow for traveling expenses? *šgadd laazim axalli l-maṣaariif is-safar?* **4.** *raxxaṣ (a tarxiiṣ) t-.* They're not allowed to sell beer after midnight. *ma-mraxxaṣiin ybiiεuun biira baεad nuṣṣ il-leel.*
allowance - **1.** *xarjiyya* pl. *-aat.* Do you give your son an allowance? *tinṭi l-ʔibnak xarjiyya?* **2.** *muxaṣṣaṣaat.* In addition to the regular salary, there is a cost of living allowance. *bil-ʔið̣aafa ʔila r-raatib il-iεtiyaadi ʔaku muxaṣṣaṣaat ġalaaʔ il-maεiiša.*
to make allowance for - *ȥisab (i) ȥsaab l-.* You've got to make allowance for his inexperience. *laazim tiȥsib iȥsaab il-qillat xibirta.*
ally - *ȥaliif* pl. *ȥulafaaʔ.* They are our allies. *humma ȥulafaaʔna.*
to ally oneself - *tȥaalaf (a taȥaaluf).* They allied themselves with a neighboring country. *tȥaalfaw wiyya fadd dawla mujaawira.*
almond - *looza* pl. *-aat* coll. *looz.*
almost - **1.** *taqriiban.* I'm almost finished. *ʔaani taqriiban xallaṣit.* **2.** *εala wašak.* We were almost ready to surrender. *činna εala wašak insallim.* **3.** *ʔilla šwayya.* The glass almost broke when I dropped it. *l-iglaaṣ inkisar ʔilla šwayya min waggaεta.*
alms - *ṣadaqa* pl. *-aat.*
alone - **1.** *waȥid.* Do you live alone? *tiskun waȥdak?* **2.** *bass.* You alone can help me. *bass ʔinta tigdar itsaaεidni.*
all alone - *waȥiid.* He seems to be all alone in the world. *ybayyin waȥiid bid-dinya.*
to leave alone - *jaaz (u) n- min, εaaf (u).* Leave the radio alone! *juuz imnir-raadyo* or *εuuf ir-raadyo.*
along - **1.** *wiyya.* Do you want to come along with me? *triid tiji wiyyaaya?* -- How much baggage should I take along. *šgadd ġaraað̣ laazim aaxuð wiyyaaya.* **2.** *b-muȥaaðaat, wiyya.* We walked along the railroad tracks. *mšeena b-muȥaaðaat siččat il-qiṭaar.* **3.** *εala ṭuul, b-jaanib, b-ṣaff.* We have flowers planted along the walk. *εidna ʔawraad mazruuεa εala ṭuul il-mamša.* **4.** *b-ṣaff, wiyya.* He parked his car along the wall. *waggaf sayyaarta b-ṣaff il-ȥaayiṭ.* **5.** *ȥibla.* My wife is four months along. *marti ʔarbaεt išhur ȥibla.*
all along - **1.** *daaʔiman.* I said so all along. *činit daaʔiman aguul haaða.* **2.** *εala ṭuul.* We saw rabbits all along the road. *šifna ʔaraanib εala ṭuul iṭ-ṭariiq.*
alphabet - *ʔaliif baaʔ, ʔaliif bee.*
alphabetical - *ȥasab il-ʔaliif bee.*
already - **1.** *gabuḷ.* Haven't you been through this line already? *ʔinta ma-činit ib-has-sira gabuḷ?* **2.** *no equivalent.* They had already left when we arrived. *čaanaw raayȥiin lamma wṣalna.* I've eaten already. *ʔaani maakil.* -- It's already time to eat. *ṣaar wakt il-ʔakil.* -- So you'll already be there by the time I arrive? *laεad raȥ-itkuun ihnaak ib-wakt*

il-ʔooṣal?
also - *hamm, hammeen, ʔayð̣an.* We also discussed the test. *w-hammeen ibḥaθna l-imtiḥaan.*
altar - *miḥraab* pl. *maḥaariib* (mosque), *maðbaḥ* pl. *maðaabiḥ* (church or temple).
to **alter** - *baddal (i tabdiil) t- b-, ġayyar (i taġyiir) t- b-, εaddal (i taεdiil) t-, ṣallaḥ (i taṣliiḥ) t-.* The tailor is going to alter my suit. *l-xayyaaṭ raḥ-ybaddil ib-qaaṭi.*
alteration - *taεdiil* pl. *-aat, tabdiil* pl. *-aat, taġyiir* pl. *-aat, taṣliiḥ* pl. *-aat.* The alterations are free. *t-taεdiilaat ib-balaaš.* -- We'll have to make a few alterations in the text of the speech. *laazim insawwi šwayya taġyiiraat ib-naṣṣ il-xiṭaab.*
alternative - **1.** *xiyaar.* They left us no alternative. *ma-tirkoo-nna xiyaar.* **2.** *čaara.* You'll have to go. There's no alternative. *laazim itruuḥ. ma-aku čaara.* **3.** *ġeer.* I don't see any alternative solution. *ma-da-ašuuf ġeer ḥall.*
although - *walaw.* I'll be there, although I have very little time. *raḥ-akuun ihnaak, walaw wakti kulliš ð̣ayyiq.*
altitude - *rtifaaε* pl. *-aat, εilu.* The plane was flying at a very high altitude. *ṭ-ṭiyyaara čaanat ṭaayra εala rtifaaε εaali.*
altogether - **1.** *šii εala šii, kull bil-kull, bil-majmuuε.* Altogether there are thirty books. *kull bil-kull ʔaku θlaaθiin iktaab.* **2.** *b-ṣuura εaamma.* Altogether, this plan is good. *b-ṣuura εaamma hal-xuṭṭa zeena.* **3.** *bil-marra, fadd marra.* These prices are altogether too high. *hal-ʔasεaar εaalya bil-marra.* **4.** *tamaaman.* You're altogether right. *ʔinta ṣaḥiiḥ tamaaman.*
aluminum - *faafoon, ʔaliminyoom.*
always - *daaʔiman, εala ṭuul.* I'm always at home. *ʔaani daaʔiman bil-beet.* -- She's always been rich. *hiyya čaanat zangiina εala ṭuul* or ***ṭuul εumurha čaanat zangiina.*
amateur - *haawi* pl. *huwaat.* For an amateur he paints quite well. *ka-haawi yirsim kulliš zeen.*
to **amaze** - *εajjab (i taεjiib) t-.* He amazed us with his magic tricks. *εajjabna b-ʔalεaaba s-siḥriyya.*
to be amazed - *staġrab (i stiġraab).* I was amazed at his lack of concern. *staġrabit min εadam ihtimaama.*
amazing - *εajiib, mudhiš.*
ambassador - *safiir* pl. *sufaraaʔ.*
amber - *kahrab.*
ambergris - *εanbar.*
ambiguous - *ġaamið̣.*
ambiguity - *ġumuuð̣.*
ambition - *ṭumuuḥ.* He has no ambition. *ma-εinda ṭumuuḥ.*
ambitious - *ṭamuuḥ.*
ambulance - *sayyaarat ʔisεaaf.* This man is hurt! Call an ambulance! *har-rijjaal mitεawwir! xaabur εala sayyaarat ʔisεaaf!*
ambush - *kamiin* pl. *-aat.* They set up an ambush for him. *niṣboo-la kamiin.*
to be ambushed - *wigaε (a wuguuε) b-kamiin.* The patrol was ambushed outside the village. *d-dawriyya wigεat ib-kamiin xaarij il-qarya.*
**They ambushed the caravan. *hijmaw εal-qaafila εala ġafla.*
America - *ʔameerka, ʔamriika.*
American - *ʔameerki,* ʔamriiki,* ʔamriikaani** pl. *ʔamriikaan.*
Amman - *εammaan.*
ammunition - *εitaad, ðaxiira, muuna.*
amnesia - *daaʔ in-nisyaan, marað̣ in-nisyaan.*
amnesty - *εafu εaamm.*
among - **1.** *been.* You're among friends. *ʔinta been ʔaṣdiqaaʔ.* -- Look among the papers! *baawiε been il-waraq.* -- **2.** *beenaat, been.* We decided it among ourselves. *qarrarna beenaatna.* -- There were many nice people among them. *čaan ʔaku beenaathum xooš awaadim ihwaaya.* **3.** *min.* He's popular among most of the people. *huwwa maḥbuub min akθar in-naas.* **4.** *εala.* Pass the leaflets out among the crowd. *wazziε il-manaašiir εal-ḥaað̣riin.* **5.** *wiyya, been, b-nuṣṣ.* He lived four years among the Bedouins. *εaaš ʔarbaε isniin wiyya l-badu.*
among other things - *min jumlat il-ʔašyaaʔ, min ð̣imn il-ʔašyaaʔ.* Among other things he collects stamps. *min jumlat il-ʔašyaaʔ yjammiε ṭawaabiε.*
amount - **1.** *mablaġ* pl. *mabaaliġ.* Write a check for the full amount. *ʔiktib čakk bil-mablaġ kulla.* **2.** *kammiyya* pl. *-aat, miqdaar* pl. *miqaadiir.* We bought a large amount of coffee. *štireena kammiyya kabiira mnil-gahwa.* **3.** *majmuuε* pl. *majaamiiε.* Add up these numbers and tell me the amount. *ʔijmaε hal-ʔarqaam w-gul-li bil-majmuuε.*
to amount to - **1.** *sawwa (i), ṣaar (i).* How much does the bill amount to? *šgadd itsawwi l-qaaʔima?* **2.** *suwa (a).* He doesn't amount to much. *huwwa ma-yiswa šii.*
to **amputate** - *bitar (i batir) n-, gaṣṣ (u gaṣṣ) n-, giṭaε (a gaṭiε) n-.* The doctor amputated his leg. *ṭ-ṭabiib bitar rijla.*
amulet - *ḥiriz* pl. *ḥuruuz.*
to **amuse** - **1.** *wannas (i) t-.* That amuses me very much. *haaða ywannisni hwaaya.* **2.** *lahha (i) t-, salla (i tasliya) t-.* He amuses himself by reading. *ylahhi nafsa bil-iqraaya.* **3.** *ð̣aḥḥak (i tað̣ḥiik) t-.* The comedian amused the audience. *l-hazali ð̣aḥḥak il-ḥaað̣riin.*
amusement - *tasliya, lahu, winsa.* He paints for amusement only. *yirsim lit-tasliya faqaṭ.*
amusement tax - *ð̣ariibat malaahi.*
amusing - *mumtiε.* I read an amusing article in the paper today. *qreet maqaal mumtiε bij-jariida l-yoom.*
anarchist - *fawð̣awi* pl. *-iyyiin.*
anarchy - *fawð̣awiyya.*
analogous - *mšaabih, mmaaθil.*
analogy - *tamaaθul, tašaabuh.*
analysis - *taḥliil* pl. *-aat.* They made a chemical analysis during class. *sawwaw taḥliil kiimyaawi wakt id-daris.*
to **analyze** - *ḥallal (i taḥliil) t-.* First of all, analyze the problem. *ʔawwal šii, ḥallil il-muškila.*
anatomical - *tašriiḥi*.*
anatomy - **1.** *εilm it-tašriiḥ.* He studies anatomy at Cairo University. *yidrus εilm it-tašriiḥ ib-jaamiεat il-qaahira.* **2.** *tarkiib jismi.* We dissected the rabbit and studied its anatomy. *šarraḥna l-ʔarnab w-dirasna tarkiiba j-jismi.*
ancestor - *jidd* pl. *ʔajdaad, salaf* pl. *ʔaslaaf.*
anchor - *ʔangar* pl. *ʔanaagir.* The boat lost its anchor in the storm. *ð̣aaε ʔangar il-markab bil-εaaṣifa.*
**Our boat lay at anchor in the harbor. *markabna čaan raasi bil-miinaaʔ.*
to drop anchor - *ðabb (i ðabb) n- ʔangar.* The ship dropped anchor in the bay. *l-baaxira ðabbat ʔangar bil-xaliij.*
to weigh anchor - *šaal (i šeel) n- il-ʔangar, rufaε (a rafuε) n- il-ʔangar, jarr (u jarr) n- il-ʔangar.* We weighed anchor after the storm passed. *šilna l-ʔangar baεad-ma marrat il-εaaṣifa.*
to anchor - **1.** *risa (i rasu) n-.* They anchored the ship out in the bay. *risaw il-baaxira bil-xaliij.* **2.** *θabbat (i taθbiit) t-.* They anchored the telephone pole in cement. *θabbitaw εamuud it-talafoon bič-čibeentu.*
**He stood there as if he were anchored to the spot. *wugaf εabaalak imbasmar ib-mukaana.*
ancient - **1.** *qadiim* pl. *qudamaaʔ.* This is the palace of the ancient kings of Babylon. *haaða qaṣir miluuk baabil il-qudamaaʔ.* **2.** *qadiim, εatiig.* Why did you invest so much money in that ancient building? *leeš ḥaṭṭeet halgadd ifluus εala ðiič il-binaaya l-εatiiga?* -- I'm very much interested in ancient statues. *ʔaani kulliš muulaε bit-tamaaθiil il-qadiima.*
and - *w-.* They sell books and stationery. *ybiiεuun kutub w-qirṭaasiyya.*
and so forth (or **on**) - *w-ma ʔašbah, w-ʔila ʔaaxirihi.* I need paper, ink, and so forth. *ʔariid waraq, εibir, w-ma ʔašbah.*
anesthetic - *banj.*
angel - *malak, malaak* pl. *malaaʔika.*
anger - *ġað̣ab, zaεal.* In his anger, he said a lot of things he didn't mean. *b-ġað̣aba, gaal ihwaaya ʔašyaaʔ ma-yiqṣudha.*
to anger - **1.** *ziεal (a zaεal), ġið̣ab (a ġað̣ab).* He doesn't anger easily. *ma-yizεal bil-εajal.* **2.** *zaεεal (i tazεiil) t-, ʔaġð̣ab (i ʔiġð̣aab).* His remarks angered me. *ḥčaayaata zaεεalatni.*
angle - **1.** *zaawiya* pl. *zawaaya.* Measure each angle of the triangle. *qiis kull zaawiya min zawaaya l-muθallaθ.* **2.** *wijih* pl. *wujuuh, naaḥiya* pl. *nawaaḥi.* We considered the matter from all angles. *bḥaθna l-mawð̣uuε min kull il-wujuuh.* --
angry - *zaεlaan, ġað̣baan.* I haven't seen him angry very often. *ma-šifta zaεlaan ʔilla qaliil.*
to be angry - *ziεal (a zaεil), ġið̣ab (a ġað̣ab).* Please don't be angry with me! *ʔarjuuk la-tizεal*

minni. -- Are you angry at him? *ʔinta zaεlaan εalee?* or *ʔinta ġaḍbaan εalee?*

to make angry - *zaεεal (i tazεiil), ġaḍḍab (i taġḍiib).* That remark must have made him very angry. *hal-mulaaʒaḍa laazim ihwaaya zaεεlata.*

animal - *ʒaywaan* pl. *-aat.* Don't feed the animals. *la-tʔakkil il-ʒaywaanaat.*

Ankara - *ʔanqara.*

ankle - *mafṣal qadam.*

anniversary - *δikra sanawiyya.* The bank is celebrating the anniversary of its foundation. *l-bang da-yiʒtifil ib-δikraa s-sanawiyya l-taʔsiisa.*

to **announce** - **1.** *δaaε (i ʔiδaaεa).* They announced the results on the radio. *δaaεaw in-nataaʔij bir-raadyo.* **2.** *εilan (i ʔiεlaan).* They announced their engagement last night. *εilnaw xuṭbathum il-baarʒa bil-leel.*

announcement - **1.** *bayaan* pl. *-aat.* The government issued an announcement on their new policy. *l-ʒukuuma ʔaṣdirat bayaan εan siyaasatha j-jidiida.* **2.** *ʔiεlaan* pl. *-aat.* An announcement of their engagement was in the paper last night. *ʔiεlaan xuṭbathum čaan bij-jariida l-baarʒa bil-leel.*

announcer - *muδiiε* pl. *-iin.* The announcer has a pleasant voice. *l-muδiiε εinda ṣooṭ ʒilu.*

to **annoy** - *ziεaj (i ʔizεaaj) n-, ʔazεaj (i ʔizεaaj), ḍawwaj (i taḍwiij) t-.* He annoyed me all morning. *ʔazεajni ṭuul iṣ-ṣubuʒ.*

to get annoyed - *nziεaj (i ʔinziεaaj), ḍaaj (u ḍawajaan).* I got very annoyed at her. *nziεajit minha hwaaya.*

annoying - *muzεij.* That's very annoying. *haaδa kulliš muzεij.*

another - **1.** *laax* (f.) *lux* (pl.) *luxra, θaani* (f.) *θaanya.* Give me another cup of coffee please. *nṭiini finjaan gahwa laax rajaaʔan.* **2.** *ġeer, θaani.* Show me another pattern. *raawiini ġeer tufṣaal.* **3.** *baεad.* I don't want to hear another word about it. *ma-ard asmaε čilma baεad εanha.*

one another - **1.** *waaʒid εal-laax.* We depend on one another. *niεtimid waaʒid εal-laax.* **2.** *waaʒid wiyya l-laax.* Those two are always fighting with one another. *hal-iθneen yitεaarkuun waaʒid wiyya l-laax εala ṭuul.* **3.** *waaʒid bil-laax.* They don't trust one another. *ma-yθiquun waaʒid bil-laax.*

answer - **1.** *jawaab* pl. *ʔajwiba.* I'm waiting for an answer to my letter. *da-antiḍir jawaab il-maktuubi.* **2.** *ʒall* pl. *ʒluul.* How did you arrive at this answer? *šloon itwaṣṣalit il-hal-ʒall.*

to answer - *jaawab (i mujaawaba) t-, radd (i radd) n-.* He answered my question without any hesitation. *jaawab εala ʔasʔilti biduun taraddud.*

ant - *namla* pl. *-aat* coll. *namil.*

antelope - *ġazaal* pl. *ġizlaan.*

antenna - *ʔeeryal* pl. *-aat.*

anthem - *našiid* pl. *ʔanaašiid.* They played the national anthem before the game started. *εizfaw in-našiid il-waṭani gabuḷ-ma yibdaʔ il-liεib.*

antic - *tahriij* pl. *-aat.* His antics were very amusing. *tahriijaata čaanat ihwaaya tḍaʒʒik.*

to **anticipate** - *twaqqaε (a tawaqquε).* The attendance was larger than we had anticipated. *l-ʒaaḍriin čaanaw ʔazyad min-ma twaqqaεna.*

antidote - *duwa (ḍidd it-tasammum).* What is the antidote for arsenic poisoning? *šinu d-duwa ḍidd it-tasammum imniz-zarniix?*

Antioch - *ʔanṭaakya.*

antique - **1.** *εantiik.* He bought a very expensive antique watch. *štira saaεa εantiika kulliš ġaalya.* **2.** *qadiim.* We visited some antique ruins yesterday. *zirna baεaḍ il-ʔaaθaar il-qadiima l-baarʒa.*

anxiety - *qalaq.*

anxious - *qaliq.* We spent several anxious minutes waiting for their return. *qḍeena εiddat daqaayiq qalqa b-intiḍaar rujuuεhum.*

to be anxious - **1.** *mitʒammis, muštaaq.* I'm anxious to see the new book. *ʔaani mitʒammis ašuuf l-iktaab ij-jidiid.* **2.** *qaliq.* He's very anxious about his future. *huwwa qaliq εala mustaqbala.*

anxiously - *b-ištiyaaq.* They waited anxiously about an hour until the news came in. *ḍallaw yintaḍruun b-ištiyaaq ʒawaali saaεa ʔila ʔan wuṣlat l-axbaar.*

any - **1.** *ʔay.* Did you find any books there? *ligeet ʔay kutub ihnaak?* -- Any mechanic can fix that. *ʔay miikaaniiki yigdar yṣalliʒ haaδa.* **2.** *šii.* Don't eat any of it. *la-taakul šii minna.*

not .... any - *ma- .... kull, ma- .... ʔay.* There isn't any bread. *ma-aku kull xubuz.*

anybody - **1.** *ʔaʒʒad.* Was anybody at home? *čaan ʔaʒʒad bil-beet?* **2.** *ʔay waaʒid.* Anybody can do that. *ʔay waaʒid yigdar ysawwi haaδa.*

**If he's anybody at all in this town, I'd know him. *law čaan šaxṣiyya b-hal-balad, la-čaan εirafta.*

**We can't take just anybody. *ma-nigdar inεayyin yaahu č-čaan.*

anyhow - *εala ʔay ʒaal, εala kull ʒaal.* I would have gone anyhow. *ʔaani čaan riʒit, εala kull ʒaal.*

anyone - *ʔaʒʒad, ʔay waaʒid.* If anyone needs help, send him to me. *ʔiδa ʔaʒʒad yiʒtaaj musaaεada dizza εalayya.* -- Anyone can do that. *ʔay waaʒid yigdar ysawwi haaδa.*

anything - *ʔay šii, fadd šii, šii.* Is there anything for me here? *ʔaku ʔay šii ʔili hnaa?* -- Did he say anything? *gaal šii?* or *gaal fadd šii?*

**I wouldn't do that for anything. *ma-asawwi haaδa mahma čaan.*

**I was anything but pleased with his work. *ma-činit mirtaaʒ min εamala ʔabadan.*

anything but - *kullši bass.* You can do anything but that. *tigdar itsawwi kullši bass haaδa.*

anyway - *εala kull ʒaal.* She didn't want to come anyway. *ma-raadat tiji εala kull ʒaal.* -- I didn't go anyway. *ma-riʒit εala kull ʒaal.*

anywhere - **1.** *fadd mukaan, fadd maʒall.* Are you going anywhere today? *raayiʒ fadd mukaan il-yoom?* **2.** *ween-ma.* Anywhere you look there's dust. *ween-ma tbaawiε ʔaku εajaaj.*

not ... anywhere - *ma ... ʔay makaan, ma ... ʔay maʒall.* I couldn't find him anywhere. *ma-gidarit ʔalgaa b-ʔay mukaan.*

**That won't get you anywhere. *haaδi ma-raʒ-itwaṣṣlak il-fadd natiija.*

apart - **1.** *mfaṣṣix.* Is my watch still apart? *saaεati li-hassa mfaṣṣixa?* **2.** *miftiriq.* They were apart for two weeks. *čaanaw miftirqiin il-muddat isbuuεeen.* **3.** *minfaṣil.* They've been living apart since their quarrel. *čaanaw εaayšiin minfaṣliin min wakt iεraakhum.* **4.** *εala ʒida.* Let's consider each argument apart from the others. *xal-nunḍur ib-kull ʒijja εala ʒida εan il-ʒijaj il-uxra.*

**The two buses will leave five minutes apart. *l-paaṣeen yiṭlaεuun xamas daqaayiq waaʒid wara l-laax.*

apart from this - *ma-εada haay.* Apart from this, he's a good man. *ma-εada haay, huwwa xooš rijjaal.*

apartment - *šiqqa* pl. *šiqaq, ʔapartmaan* pl. *-aat.* We're looking for an apartment. *da-ndawwir εala šiqqa.*

apartment house - *εimaara (pl. -aat) lis-sukna.* They're building an apartment house on our street. *da-yibnuun εimaara lis-sukna b-šaariεna.*

ape - *šaadi* pl. *šwaadi, qird* pl. *qiruud.* We saw an ape at the zoo. *šifna fadd šaadi b-ʒadiiqt il-ʒaywaanaat.*

apiece - *kull waaʒid, kullman.* My brother and I earned six dollars apiece. *ʔaani w-axuuya ʒaṣṣalna kull waaʒid sitt doolaaraat.*

to **apologize** - *ṭilab (u ṭalab) il-εafu, εtiδar (i εtiδaar), tεaδδar (a taεaδδur).* I apologize. *ʔaṭlub il-εafu* or *ʔaani ʔaεtiδir.*

to apologize to - *tεaδδar (a) min, ʔila, εtiδar (i) min, ʔila.* Did you apologize to her? *εtiδarit ʔilha?*

apology - *εtiδaar* pl. *-aat, taεaδδur* pl. *-aat.*

apostrophe - *εalaamat (pl. -aat) ixtiṣaar, εalaamat (pl. -aat) iḍaafa.*

apostle - *rasuul* pl. *rusul, ʒawaari* pl. *-iyyiin.*

apostolic - *rasuuli*.* Could you direct me to the Apostolic Legation? *tigdar iddalliini εal-qaṣaada r-rasuuliyya.*

apparatus - *jihaaz* pl. *ʔajhiza.*

apparent - *mbayyin, ḍaahir, waaḍiʒ.* It's apparent that he didn't understand the question. *mbayyin ma-ftiham is-suʔaal.*

apparently - *εala-ma yiḍhar, ʒasab-ma yiḍhar.* He has apparently changed his mind. *εala-ma yiḍhar ġayyar fikra.*

appeal - **1.** *stiʔnaaf* pl. *-aat.* The appeal was denied. *l-istiʔnaaf irrufaḍ.* **2.** *ṭalab* pl. *-aat.* The United Nations got many appeals for help this year. *l-ʔumam il-muttaʒida stilmat εiddat ṭalabaat musaaεada has-sana.* **3.** *jaaδibiyya.* She's got a lot of sex appeal. *εidha jaaδibiyya jinsiyya hwaaya.*

to appeal - **1.** *εijab (i ʔiεjaab).* It doesn't appeal to me. *ma-tiεjibni.* **2.** *twassal (a tawassul).* He appealed to the president to pardon his son. *twassal imnir-raʔiis yiεfi εan*

ʔibna. 3. staʔnaf (i stiʔnaaf). The lawyer decided to appeal the case. l-muʒaami qarrar yistaʔnif id-daεwa. 4. stanjad (i stinjaad), stiġaaθ (i stiġaaθa). During the flood, the country appealed for help from the neighboring countries. b-wakt il-fayaðaan, il-balad istanjad musaaεada mnil-bilaad il-mujaawira.

to **appear** - 1. bayyan (i tbiyyin) t-. He appeared at the last moment. bayyan ib-ʔaaxir laʒð̣a. 2. ṭilaε (a ṭuluuε) n-. This paper appears every Thursday. haj-jariida tiṭlaε kull xamiis. 3. ð̣ihar (a ð̣uhuur) n-. A ship appeared on the horizon. fadd sifiina ð̣ihrat εal-ʔufuq.

appearance - 1. ð̣uhuur pl. ð̣awaahir. It's his first appearance on the stage. haaða ʔawwal ð̣uhuura εal-masraʒ. 2. mað̣har pl. mað̣aahir. You have to pay more attention to your appearance. laazim tihtamm ib-mað̣harak ʔazyad. -- Appearances are deceiving. l-mað̣aahir xaddaaεa.

appendicitis - ltihaab il-muṣraan l-aεwar, ltihaab iz-zaaʔida d-duudiyya.

appendix - 1. z-zaaʔida d-duudiyya, l-maṣraan l-aεwar. They took his appendix out when he was five years old. gaṣṣoo-la z-zaaʔida d-duudiyya min čaan εumra xams isniin. 2. mulʒaq pl. mulaaʒiq. Perhaps it's in the appendix. yimkin haaða bil-mulʒaq.

appetite - 1. šahiyya pl. -aat. Our boy has a good appetite. ʔibinna εinda šahiyya zeena. 2. raġba pl. -aat. He has a tremendous appetite for knowledge. εinda hwaaya raġba bil-εilim.

appetizer - mušahhi pl. -yaat.

appetizing - musahhi*.

to **applaude** - ṣaffag (u taṣfiig, tṣuffug) t-. We applauded heartily. ṣaffagna min kull galubna.

applause - taṣfiig, tṣuffug. They met him with applause. staqbiloo bit-taṣfiig.

apple - tiffaaʒa pl. -aat coll. tiffaaʒ.

appliance - jihaaz pl. ʔajhiza. We carry all kinds of electrical appliances. nitεaaṭa jamiiε il-ʔajhiza l-kahrabaaʔiyya. -- This place sells household appliances. hal-maʒall ybiiε ʔajhiza beetiyya.

application - 1. stimaara pl. -aat. Fill in this application and forward it to the university. ʔimli hal-istimaara w-dizzha lij-jaamiεa. 2. εariið̣a pl. εaraayið̣. He forwarded his application to the manager. qaddam εariið̣ta lil-mudiir. 3. taṭbiiq pl. -aat. The application of his theory wasn't practical. taṭbiiq nað̣ariita ma-čaan εamali. 4. ṭalab pl. -aat. His application was rejected. ṭalaba nrufað̣. 5. qaaṭ pl. qooṭ, ṭabaqa pl. -aat. You'll have to give it another application after this coat dries. laazim tuð̣rubha qaaṭ laax baεad-ma yeebis hal-qaaṭ.

to **apply** - 1. qaddam (i taqdiim) t-. I'd like to apply for the job. ʔaʒibb aqaddim εal-wað̣iifa. 2. ṭabbaq (i taṭbiiq) t-. You've applied this rule incorrectly. ṭabbaqit hal-qaaεida ġalaṭ. 3. ʒaṭṭ (u ʒaṭṭ) n-, staεmal (i stiεmaal). Apply a hot compress every two hours. ʒuṭṭ ð̣amaada ʒaarra kull saaεteen. -- I had to apply all my strength. ð̣ṭarreet aʒuṭṭ kull quuti. 4. ṭilab (u ṭalab) n-. My father applied for a loan. ʔabuuya ṭilab deen. 5. ʒaṭṭ (u ʒaṭṭ) n-, xalla (i txilli) t-. She applied another coat of polish to her fingernails. ʒaṭṭat qaaṭ ṣubuġ θaani εala ʔað̣aafirha. 6. šimal (i šumuul) n-, nṭubaq (u nṭibaaq) εala, sira (i saryaan). This order applies to everybody. hal-ʔamur yišmil il-kull.

to apply oneself - bið̣al (i bað̣il) n- jahid. He's smart but he doesn't apply himself. huwwa šaaṭir laakin ma-yibð̣il jahda.

to **appoint** - εayyan (i taεyiin) t-. The ministry appointed five new engineers. l-wuzaara εayyinat xamis muhandisiin jiddad.

appointment - 1. taεyiin pl. -aat. Congratulations on your appointment. t-tahaani εala taεyiinak. 2. mawεid pl. mawaaεiid. I had to cancel all appointments for tomorrow. ð̣ṭarreet algi kull il-mawaaεiid maal baačir. -- I have an appointment with him. εindi mawεid wiyyaa.

to make an appointment - twaaεad (a twaaεud). I made an appointment with Ali for five-o-clock. twaaεadit wiyya εali s-saaεa xamsa.

appraisal - taqdiir pl. -aat, taθmiin pl. -aat. A careful appraisal of the property showed that ... taqdiir il-muluk ib-ṣuura daqiiqa bayyan ʔan ...

to **appraise** - 1. ʒallal (i taʒliil) t-. We want you to appraise the situation and give us your opinion. nriidak itʒallil il-wað̣iε w-tinṭiina raʔyak. 2. qaddar (i taqdiir) t-, θamman (i taθmiin) t-. A broker's coming to appraise the house. fadd dallaal raʒ-yiji yqaddir il-beet.

to **appreciate** - 1. čaan (u) mimtann, mamnuun. I would appreciate it, if you could come. ʔakuun mamnuun ʔiða tigdar tiji. 2. qaddar (i taqdiir) t-. She doesn't appreciate what we've done for her. ma-da-tqaddir illi sawweena-lh-iyyaa. -- He doesn't appreciate good music. ma-yqaddir il-muusiiqa r-raaqya. 3. εiraf (u) n-. I quite appreciate that it can't be done overnight. ʔaεruf zeen haaða ma-yimkin yixlaṣ ib-fadd yoom.

appreciation - taqdiir pl. -aat. I don't expect any appreciation. ma-atwaqqaε ʔay taqdiir. -- She has no appreciation for art. ma-εidha taqdiir lil-fann.

appreciative - mamnuun. He doesn't seem very appreciative. ybayyin εalee muu mamnuun.

apprentice - ṣaaniε pl. ṣunnaaε (taʒt it-tadriib), εaamil pl. εummaal (taʒt it-tadriib).

approach - 1. madxal pl. madaaxil. They're repairing the approaches to the bridge. da-yṣallʒuun madaaxil ij-jisir. 2. ṭariiqa pl. ṭuruq. Am I using the right approach? da-astaεmil iṭ-ṭariiqa ṣ-ṣaʒiiʒa?

to approach - 1. tgarrab (a tagarrub). They approached the enemy's camp cautiously. tgarrbaw min muεaskar il-εaduww ib-ʒaðar. 2. faataʒ (i mufaataʒa) t-. I'm going to approach my boss about a raise. raʒ-afattiʒ ir-raʔiis maali bit-tarfiiε. 3. εaalaj (i muεaalaja) t-. How would you approach the problem? sloon itεaalij il-muškila?

appropriate - munaasib, mlaaʔim, laayig. This gift is very appropriate. haaði l-hadiyya kulliš munaasiba.

to appropriate - 1. stawla (i stiilaaʔ). My son has appropriated all my ties. ʔibni stawla εala kull ʔarbiṭṭi. 2. xaṣṣaṣ (i taxṣiiṣ) t-. The city has appropriated fifty thousand dinars to build a new library. l-baladiyya xaṣṣiṣat xamsiin ʔalif diinaar il-binaayat maktaba jdiida.

approval - muwaafaqa, muṣaadaqa. You'll have to get his approval on it. laazim taaxuð muwaafaqta εaleeha.

**This color will not meet her approval. ma-raʒ-itwaafiq εala hal-loon.

on approval - εala šarṭ il-muwaafaqa. They sent me the book on approval. dazzoo-li l-iktaab εala šarṭ il-muwaafaqa.

to **approve** - 1. waafaq (u muwaafaqa) t-. Do you approve of my suggestion? twaafuq εala qtiraaʒi? -- He doesn't approve of his son staying out late at night. ma-ywaafuq εala ʔibna yitʔaxxar bil-leel. 2. ṣaadaq (i muṣaadaqa) t-, waafaq (u muwaafaqa) t-. The president approved the housing project. r-raʔiis ṣaadaq εala mašruuε il-ʔiskaan. -- The National Assembly approved the new constitution. l-majlis il-waṭani ṣaadaq εala d-dustuur ij-jidiid.

approvingly - b-istiʒsaan. She nodded her head approvingly. hazzat raasha b-istiʒsaan.

approximate - taqriibi*. The approximate speed of the new planes is six-hundred miles an hour. s-surεa t-taqriibiyya liṭ-ṭiyyaaraat ij-jidiida sitt miit miil bis-saaεa.

approximately - ʒawaali, taqriiban. He left approximately a month ago. saafar gabuḷ šahar taqriiban.

apricot - mišimšaaya pl. -aat coll. mišmiš.

April - niisaan.

apron - ṣadriyya pl. -aat, ṣadaari.

apt - 1. munaasib, b-makaana. That was a very apt remark. haaði čaanat mulaaʒað̣a kulliš munaasiba. 2. muʒtamal. I'm apt to be out when you call. muʒtamal akuun barra lamma txaabur. 3. mnil-mitwaqqaε. When he's drunk, he's apt to do anything. lamma ykuun sakraan, imnil-mitwaqqaε ysawwi ʔay šii. 4. yjuuz. It's apt to be two o'clock before we get home. yjuuz itkuun is-saaεa θinteen gabuḷ-ma noosal il-beet.

**He is an apt pupil. yilguṭ bil-εajil.

Aqaba - l-εaqaba.

Arab - εarabi* pl. εarab.

arabesque - 1. zuxruf. He's very good at arabesque. huwwa kulliš zeen biz-zuxruf. 2. zuxrufi*. There's a beautiful arabesque engraving on the wall. ʔaku naqiš zuxrufi jamiil εal-ʒaayiṭ.

Arab League - j-jaamiεa l-εarabiyya.

Arabian Peninsula - j-jaziira l-εarabiyya.

Arabian Sea - l-baʒr il-εarabi.

Arabic - εarabi, l-luġa l-εarabiyya.

Arabist - *mustašriq* pl. *-iin*.
Aramaic - *l-luğa l-ʔaaraamiyya*.
arch - *ṭaag* pl. *ṭuug*. That bridge has a tremendous arch. *haδaak ij-jisir bii fadd ṭaag δaxim*.
fallen arches - *flaatfuut, ʔaqdaam musaṭṭaẓa*. He has fallen arches. *Ɛinda flaatfuut*.
to arch - *ẓina (i ẓinaaʔ) n-*. The cat arched it's back. *l-bazzuuna ẓinat δaharha*.
arched - *mṭawwag*. The church's ceiling is arched. *sagf il-kaniisa mṭawwag*.
architect - *muhandis miƐmaari* pl. *muhandisiin miƐmaariyyiin*.
architecture - *handasa miƐmaariyya*.
area - **1.** *manṭiqa* pl. *manaaṭiq*. The area around Baghdad is densely populated. *l-manṭiqa ẓawaali bağdaad kulliš mizdaẓma bis-sukkaan*. **2.** *masaaẓa* pl. *-aat*. The area of the city is four square miles. *masaaẓt il-madiina ʔarbaƐ ʔamyaal murabbaƐa*.
Argentina - *l-ʔarjantiin*.
to **argue** - *jaadal (i mujaadala, jadal) t-, naaqaš (i munaaqaša, niqaaš) t-, ẓaajaj (i muẓaajaja) t-*. Don't argue with me. *la-tjaadilni*. -- I won't argue that point. *ma-ʔajaadil Ɛala han-nuqṭa*. -- That's something that can't be argued. *haaδa fadd šii ma-yitjaadal bii*.
to argue (with someone) - *tjaadal (a tajaadul), tẓaajaj (a taẓaajuj), tnaaqaš (a tanaaquš)*. He'll argue with anyone about anything. *yitjaadil wiyya ʔay šaxiṣ Ɛala ʔay šii kaan*. -- They argue all the time. *yitjaadluun Ɛala ṭuul*.
argument - **1.** *ẓijja* pl. *ẓijaj*. They presented very convincing arguments. *qaddimaw ẓijaj kulliš muqniƐa*. **2.** *xilaaf* pl. *-aat, nizaaƐ*. It was just a small argument. *čaan fadd xilaaf baṣiiṭ*. **3.** *lağwa* pl. *-aat, lağaawi*. We had a violent argument. *ṣaarat beenaatna lağwa*.
to **arise** - **1.** *δihar (a δuhuur)*. The problem arose some time ago. *l-muškila δihrat gabul mudda*. **2.** *giƐad (u guƐuud) n-*. I arose at six this morning. *giƐadit iṣ-ṣubuẓ saaƐa sitta*. **3.** *gaam (u goom)*. He arose from his chair and left the room. *gaam imnil-kursi maala w-tirak il-ğurfa*. **4.** *sinaẓ (a sinuuẓ)*. As soon as the opportunity arises ... *ʔawwal-ma tisnaẓ il-furṣa ...*
arithmetic - *ẓisaab*.
arm - **1.** *δraaƐ* pl. *ʔaδruƐ*. He broke his arm. *kisar iδraaƐa*. **2.** *yadda* pl. *-aat*. The arms on this chair are too low. *yaddaat hal-iskamli kulliš naaṣya*. **3.** *slaaẓ* pl. *ʔasliẓa*. All arms have to be turned over to the police. *kull il-asliẓa laazim titsallam liš-šurṭa*.
underarm - *ʔubuṭ* pl. *ʔubaaṭ*.
under arms - *taẓt is-silaaẓ*. All ablebodied men were under arms. *kull ir-rijaal il-muqtadriin čaanaw taẓt is-silaaẓ*.
to be up in arms - *haaj (i hayajaan)*. Everybody was up in arms. *kull waaẓid čaan haayij*.
to arm - *sallaẓ (i tasliiẓ) t-*. The company armed its guards. *š-šarika salliẓat ẓurraasha*.
to be armed - *tsallaẓ (a tsilliẓ)*. The policeman is always armed with a revolver. *š-šurṭi daaʔiman yitsallaẓ ib-musaddas*. -- The gang is armed. *l-Ɛiṣaaba mitsallẓa*.
armchair - *kursi ʔabu yaddaat* pl. *karaasi ʔummahaat yaddaat*.
armistice - *hudna* pl. *-aat*.
armor - **1.** *diriƐ* pl. *druuƐ*. These shells can't penetrate the heavy armor of a battleship. *hal-qanaabil ma-tixtiriq dirƐ il-baarija l-ẓarbiyya*. **2.** *muṣaffaẓa* pl. *-aat*. Armor doesn't operate well in this mountainous terrain. *l-muṣaffaẓaat ma-tištuğul zeen ib-hal-manṭiqa j-jabaliyya*.
armored - *mṣaffaẓ*. Those tanks are heavily armored. *haaδi d-dabbaabaat imṣaffaẓa kulliš*.
army - *jeeš* pl. *jyuuš*. Did you serve in the army or the navy? *xidamit bij-jeeš loo bil-baẓriyya?*
around - **1.** *qariib*. He lives right around here. *yiskun qariib min ihnaa*. **2.** *ẓawaali*. I have around twenty dinars. *Ɛindi ẓawaali Ɛišriin diinaar*. **3.** *daayir*. He tied the rope around the barrel. *laff il-ẓabal daayir il-barmiil*. **4.** *b-*. There are some good movies around town this week. *ʔaku fadd ʔaflaam zeena bil-wlaaya hal-isbuuƐ*.
**Is there anybody around? *ʔaku ʔaẓẓad ihnaa?*
**The racetrack is a half mile around. *farrat is-saaẓa nuṣṣ miil*.
to **arouse** - **1.** *fazzaz (i tafziiz, tfizziz) t-*. A barking dog aroused me in the middle of the night. *fadd čalib yinbaẓ fazzazni b-nuṣṣ il-leel*. **2.** *ʔaθaar (i ʔiθaara) n-*. Her strange behavior aroused my suspicion. *taṣarrufha l-ğariib ʔaθaar šakki*. **3.** *waƐƐa (i twiƐƐi) t-*. What time shall I arouse you? *s-saaƐa beeš awaƐƐiik?*
arrack - *Ɛaraq*.
to **arrange** - **1.** *ṣaffaṭ (u taṣfiiṭ) t-, rattab (i tartiib) t-*. Who arranged the books? *minu ṣaffaṭ il-kutub?* **2.** *rattab (i tartiib) t-*. They arranged the room in two hours. *rattibaw il-ğurfa b-saaƐteen*. **3.** *dastar (i ddistir) t-, dabbar (i tadbiir) t-, rattab (i tartiib) t-*. I arranged with the guard to smuggle cigarettes to the prisoners. *dastaritha wiyya l-ẓaaris ẓatta yxaššiš jigaayir lil-masaajiin*.
arrangement - *tartiib* pl. *-aat, tadbiir* pl. *tadaabiir, ddistir*. How do you like this arrangement? *yƐijbak hat-tartiib?*
arrest - *ʔilqaaʔ qabuδ*. The arrest was made at his home. *ʔilqaaʔ il-qabuδ ṣaar ib-beeta*.
under arrest - *mawquuf, mwaqqaf*. He's been under arrest for two days. *čaan imwaqqaf yoomeen*.
to hold under arrest - *waqqaf (i tawqiif) t-*. They held him under arrest at the police station. *waqqufoo b-markaz iš-šurṭa*.
to arrest - *qubaδ (u qabuδ) n- Ɛala*. They arrested him and released him on bail. *qubδaw Ɛalee w-fakkoo b-kafaala*.
arrival - *wuṣuul*. His arrival caused a lot of enthusiasm. *wuṣuula sabbab ẓamaas ihwaaya*.
to **arrive** - **1.** *wuṣal (a wuṣuul)*. When did the train arrive? *šwakit wuṣal il-qiṭaar?* **2.** *twaṣṣal (a tawaṣṣul)*. Did they arrive at a decision? *twaṣṣalaw il-fadd qaraar?* **3.** *nwilad (i)*. The baby arrived at three this morning. *ṭ-ṭifil inwilad is-saaƐa tlaaθa ṣ-ṣubuẓ*.
arrow - **1.** *sahim* pl. *ʔashum*. The arrow points north. *s-sahim yʔaššir liš-šimaal*. **2.** *nišaaba* pl. *-aat* coll. *nišaab*. He killed the rabbit with an arrow. *qital il-ʔarnab ib-nišaaba*.
arsenic - *zarniix*.
art - *fann*. He knows a lot about art. *yuƐruf ihwaaya Ɛan il-fann*. -- There's an art to it. *yriid-ilha fadd fann*.
work of art - *qiṭƐa* (pl. *qiṭaƐ*) *fanniyya*. This building contains many works of art. *hal-binaaya tiẓwi qiṭaƐ fanniyya hwaaya*.
art gallery - *matẓaf* (pl. *mataaẓif*) *finuun*.
arthritis - *ltihaab il-mafaaṣil*.
article - **1.** *maqaal, maqaala* pl. *-aat*. There was a good article about it in the newspaper. *čaan ʔaku maqaal zeen Ɛanna bij-jariida*. **2.** *maadda* pl. *mawaadd*. Please read article three of the constitution. *rajaaʔan iqra l-maadda θ-θaalθa mnid-dastuur*. **3.** *šii* pl. *ʔašyaaʔ, maadda* pl. *mawaadd*. Many valuable articles were stolen. *hwaaya ʔašyaaʔ θamiina nbaagat*.
definite article - *ʔadaat it-taƐriif*.
artificial - *ṣṭinaaƐi**. Are those flowers artificial? *hal-warid iṣṭinaaƐi?* -- She has an artificial smile. *Ɛidha btisaama ṣṭinaaƐiyya*.
artillery - *madfaƐiyya*.
artist - *fannaan* pl. *-iin*. He is a famous artist. *huwwa fannaan mašhuur*.
as - **1.** *Ɛala-ma*. Leave it as it is. *xalliiha Ɛala-ma hiyya*. **2.** *miθil-ma*. Do as you please. *sawwi miθil-ma yƐijbak*. -- Everything stands as it was. *kullši baaqi miθil-ma čaan*. **3.** *Ɛala, ẓasab*. He's late, as usual. *huwwa mitʔaxxir, ẓasb il-Ɛaada*. **4.** *maadaam, li-ʔan*. As he is leaving tomorrow, we must hurry. *maadaam huwwa maaši baačir, laazim nistaƐjil*. **5.** *w-*. Did you see anyone as you came in? *šifit ʔaẓẓad w-inta daaxil*. **6.** *ka-, miθil*. I think of him as a brother. *ʔaƐtabra ka-ʔax*. -- He used his coat as a pillow. *staƐmal sitirta ka-mxadda*. **7.** *b-*. His house is as big as ours. *beeta b-kubur beetna*.
**I work as a clerk for them. *ʔaštuğul kaatib Ɛidhum*.
**I regard it as important. *ʔaƐtabra muhimm*.
as far as - **1.** *l-ẓadd*. The train goes as far as Nasriyya. *l-qiṭaar yruuẓ il-ẓadd in-naṣriyya*. **2.** *ẓasab-ma, Ɛala-ma*. As far as I can see, he's right. *ẓasab-ma ašuuf, huwwa ṣaẓiẓ*. **3.** *Ɛala madd*. The fields extend as far as you can see. *l-mazaariƐ timtadd Ɛala madd il-baṣar*.
as far as he's concerned - *bin-nisba ʔila, min naaẓiit~*. As far as he's concerned it's all right. *bin-nisba ʔila, zeena*.

as for – *ʔamma, min ṭaraf, bin-nisba l-, min naħiit-*. As for him, it's all right. *ʔamma huwwa, ma-εinda maaniε.*
as if – *εabaalak, ka-ʔan.* He acts as if he were the director himself. *da-yitṣarraf εabaalak il-mudiir nafsa.*
as soon as – *ʔawwal-ma, ħaal-ma.* Let me know as soon as you get here. *xabburni ʔawwal-ma tooṣal ihnaa.*
as yet – *l-ħadd al-ʔaan, li-hassa, lil-ʔaan, baεad.* Nothing has happened as yet. *ma-ṣaar šii l-ħadd al-ʔaan.*
asbestos – *ʔazbast, spasto.*
ascetic – *mitzahhid, mitnassik.*
asceticism – *tanassuk, tazahhud.*
to **be ashamed** – 1. *xijal (a xajal).* Don't be ashamed of this job. *la-tixjal min haš-šuġuḷ.* 2. *xtiħa (i xiħi).* He's not ashamed of anything. *ma-yixtiħi min ʔay šii.* 3. *staħa (i mistaħa).* He was ashamed to show his grades to his father. *staħa yraawi darajaata l-ʔabuu.*
ash can – *tanakat* (pl. *-aat*) *zibil.*
ashes – *rumaad.*
ashore – *lil-barr, lis-saaħil.* We weren't allowed to go ashore. *ma-čaan masmuuħ-inna ninzil lil-barr.*
ashtray – *ṭabla* pl. *-aat, nuffaaḍa* pl. *-aat.*
Asia Minor – *ʔaasya ṣ-ṣuġra.*
aside – *εala ṣafħa, εala jiha.* I have to put a little money aside for the trip. *laazim axalli šwayya fluus εala ṣafħa lis-safra.*
aside from – 1. *b-ġaḍḍ in-naḍar εan.* Aside from the paint, it's a good car. *b-ġaḍḍ in-naḍar εan iṣ-ṣubuġ hiyya xooš sayyaara.* 2. *ma-εada.* Aside from that, I have nothing else to add. *ma-εada haaða, ma-εindi šii ʔaḍiifa.*
to **ask** – 1. *siʔal (a suʔaal) n-.* I'll ask him right away. *raħ-ʔasʔala ħaalan.* — Ask at the ticket office in the railroad station. *ʔisʔal ib-šibbaač beeε it-taðaakir ib-maħaṭṭat il-qiṭaar.* 2. *ṭilab (u ṭalab) n-.* He asked for help. *ṭilab musaaεada.* 3. *ṭilab (u ṭalab) n-, raad (i reed) n-.* How much did he ask for washing the car? *šgadd ṭilab εala ġasl is-sayyaara?*
asleep – 1. *naayim.* I must have been asleep. *laazim činit naayim.* 2. *xadraan, mnammil.* My leg's asleep. *rijli xadraana.*
to fall asleep – *ġufa (i ġafu).* I fell asleep about three o'clock. *ġufeet ħawaali is-saaεa θlaaθa.*
aspect – 1. *naaħiya* pl. *nawaaħi.* We studied the problem from every aspect. *dirasna l-muškila min kull nawaaħiiha.* 2. *maḍhar* pl. *maḍaahir.* This is one of the aspects of Iraqi life. *haaða maḍhar min maḍaahir il-ħiyaat il-εiraaqiyya.*
asphalt – *giir, zifit, ʔasfalt.*
aspirin – *ʔaspiriina* pl. *-aat* coll. *ʔaspiriin.*
ass – *ħmaal* pl. *ħmaayiḷ, ħmaar* pl. *ħamiir.*
to **assassinate** – *ġtaal (a ġtiyaal).* His former friends assassinated him. *ʔaṣdiqaaʔa s-saabqiin iġtaaloo.*
assault – 1. *hujuum* pl. *-aat.* The assault on the island began at five o'clock. *l-hujuum εaj-jaziira btidat is-saaεa xamsa.* 2. *taεaddi.* He was charged with assault. *ntiham bit-taεaddi.*
to assault – 1. *tεadda (a taεaddi).* That man assaulted me. *tεadda εalayya ðaak ir-rijjaal.* 2. *hijam (i hujuum) n- εala, haajam (i muhaajama).* They assaulted the enemy position with everything they had. *hijmaw εala mawqiε il-εadu b-kull-ma εidhum.*
to **assemble** – 1. *tjammaε (a tajammuε), ltamm (a ltimaam).* The pupils assembled in the auditorium. *t-talaamiið itjammεaw bil-qaaεa.* 2. *jtimaε (i jtimaaε), tjammaε (a tajammuε).* The lawyers will assemble to discuss the case tomorrow morning. *l-muħaamiin raħ-yijtamεuun il-baħθ il-qaḍiyya bukra iṣ-ṣubuħ.* 3. *jimaε (a jamiε) n-.* You'll have to give me enough time to assemble the information. *laazim tinṭiini wakit kaafi ħatta ʔajmaε il-maεluumaat.* 4. *rakkab (u tarkiib) t-.* He assembles airplane engines. *yrakkub makaayin ṭayyaaraat.*
assembly – 1. *jamaaεa* pl. *-aat, ħašid* pl. *ħušuud, jamhuur* pl. *jamaahiir.* He spoke before a large assembly of lawyers. *xiṭab giddaam jamaaεa čbiira mnil-muħaamiin.* 2. *jamεiyya* pl. *-aat.* The General Assembly of the United Nations rejected the proposal. *j-jamεiyya l-εaamma lil-ʔumam il-muttaħida rufḍat il-iqtiraaħ.* 3. *qisim* pl. *ʔaqsaam, juzuʔ* pl. *ʔajzaaʔ.* We'll have to remove this entire assembly. *laazim inšiil hal-qisim kulla.*
assembly line – *xaṭṭ tarkiib, xaṭṭ tajmiiε.* I work on the assembly line in an automobile factory. *ʔaštuġul ib-xaṭṭ it-tarkiib maal maεmal is-sayyaaraat.*
to **assign** – 1. *εayyan (i taεyiin) t-, niṭa (i naṭi) n-.* The teacher assigned us a composition. *l-muεallim inṭaana ʔinšaaʔ.* 2. *xaṣṣaṣ (i taxṣiiṣ) t-, εayyan (i taεyiin) t-.* He assigned two men to guard the prisoner. *xaṣṣaṣ rajjaaleen il-ħiraasat il-masjuun.*
assignment – 1. *waḍiifa* pl. *waḍaayif, waajib* pl. *-aat.* Our teacher gave us a difficult assignment. *muεallimna nṭaana waajib ṣaεub.* 2. *šaġla* pl. *-aat, waḍiifa* pl. *waḍaayif, muhimma* pl. *mahaamm.* The boss gave me an interesting assignment. *l-mudiir inṭaani fadd šaġla laṭiifa.* 3. *tawziiε* pl. *-aat, taεyiin* pl. *-aat, taqsiim* pl. *-aat.* The assignment of jobs only took ten minutes. *tawziiε il-ašġaal ʔaxað εašir daqaaʔiq.*
to **assist** – *saaεad (i musaaεada), εaawan (i muεaawana).* Who assisted you? *minu εaawanak?*
assistance – *musaaεada* pl. *-aat, muεaawana* pl. *-aat.* He did it without any assistance. *sawwaaha b-layya musaaεada.*
assistant – *musaaεid* pl. *-iin, muεaawin* pl. *-iin.*
associate – *zamiil* pl. *zumalaaʔ, rafiiq* pl. *rufaqaaʔ* He's been my associate for many years. *ṣaar-la zamiili sniin ihwaaya.*
associate judge – *naaʔib ħaakim* pl. *nuwwaab ħukkaam.*
associate member – *εaḍu musaanid* pl. *ʔaεḍaaʔ musaanidiin.*
associate professor – *ʔustaað musaaεid* pl. *ʔasaatiða musaaεidiin.*
to associate – 1. *xaalaṭ (i muxaalaṭa), xtilaṭ (i xtilaaṭ) wiyya, εaašar (i εušra, muεaašara), tεaašar (a taεaašur).* He doesn't like to associate with them. *ma-yεijba yxaaliṭhum.* 2. *rabaṭ (u rabuṭ) εalaaqa.* I always associate big cars with rich people. *ʔaani daaʔiman ʔarbuṭ εalaaqa been is-sayyaaraat ič-čibiira wiz-zanaagiin.*
**He was associated with them for ten years. *čaanat ʔila εalaaqa wiyyaahum min εašr isniin.*
association – 1. *jamεiyya* pl. *-aat.* I don't think I'll join the association. *ma-aεtiqid raħ-aštirik bij-jamεiyya.* 2. *εalaaqa* pl. *-aat.* I wouldn't ever make that particular association. *ʔaani ʔabad ma-asawwi ðiič il-εalaaqa l-xaaṣṣa.*
assorted – *mšakkal, mnawwaε.* I want one kilo of assorted chocolates. *ʔariid keelu čukleet imšakkal.*
assortment – *taškiila* pl. *-aat.* They've got a large assortment of ties. *εidhum taškiila čbiira mnil-ʔarbiṭa.*
to **assume** – 1. *twaqqaε (a tawaqquε), qaddar (i taqdiir).* I assume that he'll be there too. *ʔatwaqqaε raħ-ykuun ihnaak ʔayðan.* — I assume the price will be less than twenty dinars. *ʔaqaddir is-siεir ykuun ʔaqall min εišreen diinaar.* 2. *tħammal (a taħammul).* I can't assume any responsibility for what happened. *ma-agdar atħammal ʔay-masʔuuliyya εan illi ṣaar.* 3. *tḍaahar (a taḍaahur).* Don't assume such an air of innocence! *l-titḍaahar ib-salaamt in-niyya.* 4. *furaḍ (u faraḍ) n-.* For example, let's assume birds can't fly. *maθalan, xalli nufruḍ iṭ-ṭiyuur ma-tigdar iṭṭiir.*
assurance – *taεahhud* pl. *-aat, taʔkiid* pl. *-aat.* He gave me his assurance that he'd pay. *nṭaani taεahhud raħ-yidfaε.*
to **assure** – *ʔakkad (i taʔkiid) t-, tεahhad (a taεahhud).* He assured us that he would be there. *ʔakkad-inna raħ-ykuun ihnaak.*
asthma – *tanag nifas, ḍiig nifas, rabu.*
at – 1. *b-.* I'll wait for you at the entrance. *raħ-antaḍrak bil-baab.* — I did it at his request. *sawweetha b-raġubta* or *sawweetha ħasab raġubta.* — The children are at school. *l-ʔaṭfaal bil-madrasa.* — It happened at night. *ṣaarat bil-leel.* — He came at three o'clock. *ʔija biθ-θilaaθa* or *jaa s-saaεa biθ-θilaaθa* or *jaa s-saaεa θlaaθa.* 2. *εind, εid.* We were at the tailor's. *činna εind il-xayyaaṭ.* — I met him at the dentist's. *qaabalta εid ṭabiib il-ʔasnaan.* 3. *min.* I was astonished at the size of the city. *ndihašit min kubr il-wlaaya.* 4. *ʔila.* We haven't arrived at a decision yet. *ma-twaṣṣalna ʔila fadd qaraar il-ħadd il-ʔaan.* 5. *εala.* He aimed at the target. *neešan εal-hadaf.* 6. *εala, min.* Don't get angry at me. *la-tiħεal εalayya* or *la-tiħεal minni.*

at all - *ʔabad, ʔabadan, ʔaṣlan, bil-marra.* I haven't got any money at all. *ma-Ɛindi fluus ʔabadan* or *ʔabad ma-Ɛindi ʔay ifluus.*

at all costs - *b-ʔay θaman.* We must get it at all costs. *laazim naaxδa b-ʔay θaman.*

at first - *bil-bidaaya, bil-ʔawwal, ʔawwalan.* At first we didn't like the town. *bil-bidaaya ma-ʒabbeena l-wlaaya.*

at last - *ʔaxiiran, bit-taali, taaliiha.* He came at last. *ʔaxiiran jaa.*

at least - 1. *Ɛal-ʔaqall.* There were at least a hundred people present. *čaanaw Ɛal-ʔaqall miit waaʒid ʒaaδriin.* 2. *ʔaqallan.* At least, mention my name to him. *ʔaqallan, ʔiδkur-la ʔismi.*

at most - *ʔakθar šii.* At most the bill will come to twenty dinars. *ʔakθar šii raʒ-itwaṣṣil il-qaaʔima il-Ɛišriin diinaar.*

at once - 1. *ʒaalan, hassa.* Do it at once. *sawwiiha ʒaalan.* 2. *b-fadd wakit, b-fadd marra.* I can't do everything at once. *ma-agdar asawwi kullši b-fadd marra.*

at that - *b-haš-šikil, Ɛind hal-ʒadd, Ɛala-ma huwwa.* Let's leave it at that. *xal-niturka b-haš-šikil.*

at times - *dooraat, ʔaʒyaanan, noobaat, marraat.* At times I'm doubtful. *dooraat ʔašukk.*

at will - *miθil-ma yriid, ʒasab-ma yriid, b-keef˜.* They come and go at will. *yirʒuun w-yijuun miθil-ma yirduun* or ***yisraʒuun w-yimraʒuun.*

atheism - *ʔilʒaad.*

atheist - *mulʒid* pl. *-iin.*

athlete - *riyaaδi* pl. *-iyyiin.*

athletic - *riyaaδi*.*

athletics - *riyaaδa.*

Atlantic - *l-muʒiiṭ il-ʔaṭlasi, ʔaṭlanṭiiki, ʔaṭlanṭi.*

atlas - *ʔaṭlas* pl. *ʔaṭaalis.* We're going to take the atlas with us on the trip. *raʒ-naaxuδ il-ʔaṭlas wiyyaana bis-safra.*

atmosphere - *jaww.* The atmosphere contains oxygen. *j-jaww yiʒtiwi Ɛala ʔaksiijiin.* — We work in a very nice atmosphere. *ništuğul ib-jaww kulliš zeen.*

atmospheric - *jawwi*.*

atom - *δarra* pl. *aat.* We live in the age of the atom. *nƐiiš ib-Ɛaṣr iδ-δarra.*

atomic - *δarri*.*

atrocity - *jariima* pl. *jaraaʔim.* The enemy committed many atrocities during the war. *l-Ɛadu rtikab jaraaʔim ihwaaya ʔaθnaaʔ il-ʒarub.*

to **attach** - 1. *šakkal (i taskiil) t-.* Please attach the envelope to the letter with a pin. *rajaaʔan šakkil iδ-δaruf bil-maktuub ib-dambuus.* 2. *rufaq (i ʔirfaaq) n-.* Don't forget to attach a picture with your application. *la-tinsa tirfiq ṣuura b-ƐariiδTak.* 3. *ʒijaz (i ʒajiz) n-.* We can attach his salary if he doesn't pay up. *nigdar niʒjiz raatba ʔiδa ma-yidfaƐ.* 4. *Ɛallaq (i taƐliiq) t-.* You attach too much importance to money. *tƐalliq ʔahammiyya hwaaya Ɛal-ifluus.*

to be attached to - *tƐallaq (a taƐalluq) b-.* I've become attached to this child. *ʔaani tƐallaqit ib-haṭ-ṭifil* or *ṣirit mitƐalliq ib-haṭ-ṭifil.*

attaché - *mulʒaq* pl. *-iin.*

attached - *miltiʒiq.* He's attached to the embassy. *huwwa miltiʒiq bis-safaara.*

attachments - 1. *mulʒaq* pl. *-aat.* I bought a vacuum cleaner with all its attachments. *štireet muknaasa kahrabaaʔiyya wiyya kull mulʒaqaatha.* 2. *muraffaq* pl. *-aat.* There are five attachments to the letter. *ʔaku xamas muraffaqaat wiyya l-maktuub.*

attack - *hajma* pl. *-aat* coll. *hujuum.* The attack was beaten back. *l-hajma nraddat.*

to attack - 1. *hijam (i hajuum) n-.* They attacked the castle in the middle of the night. *hijmaw Ɛal-qalƐa b-nuṣṣ il-leel.* 2. *haajam (i muhaajama) t-.* He attacked them in the newspaper. *haajmoohum bij-jariida.* 3. *tnaawal (i tanaawul).* Let's attack this problem from a slightly different angle. *xalli nitnaawil hal-muškila min jiha tixtilif išwayya.*

heart attack - *sakta* (pl. *-aat*) *qalbiyya.* He died from a heart attack. *maat bis-sakta l-qalbiyya.*

attempt - *muʒaawala* pl. *-aat.* At least make an attempt! *Ɛal-ʔaqall sawwi fadd muʒaawala.*

to attempt - *ʒaawal (i muʒaawala) t-.* Don't attempt to do too much at one time. *la-tʒaawil itsawwi ʔašyaaʔ ihwaaya b-fadd wakit.*

to **attend** - 1. *ʒiδar (a ʒuδuur) n-.* Did you attend the meeting? *ʒiδart il-ijtimaaƐ?* 2. *daawam (u mudaawama) t-.* I attended business school. *daawamit ib-madrasat tijaara.* 3. *raajaƐ (i muraajaƐa) t-, Ɛaalaj (muƐaalaja) t-.* What doctor attended you? *yaa ṭabiib raajaƐak?*

to attend to - *baašar (i mubaašara), Ɛaalaj (i Ɛilaaj, muƐaalaja) t-.* I still have some things to attend to. *baƐad Ɛindi baƐaδ il-ʔašyaaʔ laazim ʔabaaširha.*

attendance - *ʒuδuur.* Attendance is compulsory. *l-ʒuδuur ʔijbaari.*

attention - *ntibaah.* I tried to attract his attention. *ʒaawalit ʔajlib intibaaha.*

to call attention - *lifat (i lafit) n- in-naδar.* I've called attention to that repeatedly. *lifatit in-naδar iδ-δaak Ɛiddat marraat.*

to pay attention - *ntibah (i ntibaah), daar (i doora) baal˜.* Please pay attention! *ʔintibih min faδlak.*

attentively - *b-intibaah.* The children listened attentively. *j-jahhaal itṣanntaw b-intibaah.*

attitude - 1. *waδiƐ* pl. *ʔawδaaƐ.* I don't like his attitude in class. *ma-yiƐjibni waδƐa biṣ-ṣaff.* 2. *mawqif* pl. *mawaaqif, wajhat* (pl. *-aat*) *naδar.* I don't understand your attitude towards religion. *ma-da-aftihim mawqifak imnid-diin.*

attorney - *muʒaami* pl. *-iin.* Who's your attorney? *minu muʒaamiik?*

to **attract** - 1. *jaab (i jeeb) n-.* What's attracting the flies here? *š-da-yjiib iδ-δabbaan ihnaa?* 2. *jiδab (i jaδib) n-.* Magnets attract nails. *l-mağaaniṭ tijδib il-ibsaamiir.* 3. *jilab (i jalib) n-.* Be quiet! You're attracting attention. *ʔiskut, da-tijlib in-naδar.*

attraction - 1. *jaaδibiyya* pl. *-aat.* The attraction of the moon causes the tides. *jaaδibiyyat il-gumar ysabbib il-madd wij-jazir.* 2. *muğri* pl. *-iyyaat.* What's the big attraction around this town? *šinu l-muğri b-hal-wlaaya?*

attractive - 1. *jaδδaab.* She is very attractive. *hiyya kulliš jaδδaaba.* 2. *muğri.* He made me a very attractive offer. *Ɛiraδ Ɛalayya fadd Ɛariδ kulliš muğri.*

auction - *mazaad* pl. *-aat.*

audience - *l-ʒaaδriin.* The audience was enthusiastic. *l-ʒaaδriin čaanaw mitʒammsiin.*

August - *ʔaab.*

aunt - (paternal) *Ɛamma* pl. *-aat,* (maternal) *xaala* pl. *-aat.*

Austria - *n-namsa.*

Austrian - *namsaawi** pl. *-iyyiin.*

authentic - 1. *ʒaqiiqi*.* He wrote an authentic account of the war. *kitab waṣuf ʒaqiiqi lil-ʒarub.* 2. *ʔaṣli*, ʒaqiiqi*.* This is an authentic Babylonian vase. *haaδi mizhariyya baabiliyya ʔaṣliyya.*

author - 1. *muʔallif* pl. *-iin.* He always wanted to be an author. *daaʔiman čaan yriid yṣiir muʔallif.* 2. *ṣaaʒib* pl. *ʔaṣʒaab.* The prime minister is the author of the plan. *raʔiis il-wuzaraaʔ ṣaaʒib hal-xiṭṭa.*

authorities - *ṣulṭaat, maraajiƐ.* The local authorities condemned the building. *ṣ-ṣulṭaat il-maʒalliyya ʔumrat ib-hadm il-binaaya.*

authority - 1. *ṣalaaʒiyya* pl. *-aat, taxwiil* pl. *-aat.* He has no authority to sign the check. *ma-Ɛinda ṣalaaʒiyya ywaqqiƐ iṣ-ṣakk.* -- Do you have the authority to sign this contract for him? *Ɛindak taxwiil itwaqqiƐ Ɛanna hal-Ɛaqid?* 2. *ṣulṭa* pl. *-aat.* The police have no authority over diplomats. *š-šurṭa ma-Ɛidha ṣulṭa Ɛad-diblumaasiyyiin.* 3. *ʒujja* pl. *ʒujaj.* He's an authority on the Koran. *huwwa ʒujja bil-qurʔaan.*

to **authorize** - *xawwal (i taxwiil) t-.* Who authorized you to spend that money? *minu xawwalak tuṣruf hal-ifluus?*

authorized - *mxawwal* pl. *-iin.* He's authorized to sign the receipts. *huwwa mxawwal ywaqqiƐ il-wuṣuulaat.*

automatic - 1. *musaddas* pl. *-aat, warwar* pl. *waraawir.* Officers carry automatics. *δ-δubbaaṭ šaayliin musaddasaat.* 2. *ʔootoomaatiiki*.* Is this an automatic pump? *hal-maδaxxa ʔootoomaatiikiyya?*

automatically - *b-ṣuura tilqaaʔiyya, b-ṣuura ʔootoomaatiikiyya, b-layya šuƐuur.* He picked up the phone automatically. *šaal it-talafoon ib-ṣuura tilqaaʔiyya.*

automobile - *sayyaara* pl. *-aat.*

autopsy - *tašriiʒ* pl. *-aat.*

autumn - *xariif.* I hope to stay through the autumn. *ʔatʔammal ʔabqa n-nihaayat il-xariif.*

available - 1. *mawjuud.* They used all available

cars. *staᶓmilaw kull is-sayaaraat il-mawjuuda.* -- Is this pen available in red? *hal-qalam il-ṗaandaan mawjuud ᶓala ʔaẓmar?* **2.** *jawwa l-ʔiid.* I have two houses available. *ᶓindi beeteen jawwa l-ʔiid.* **3.** *faariġ.* When will the director be available? *šwakit il-mudiir ykuun faariġ?* **4.** *maysuur, mityassir.* Vegetables are available in the market. *l-muxaḍḍraat mityassira bis-suug.*

avenue - *šaariᶓ* pl. *šawaariᶓ.*

average - **1.** *muᶓaddal* pl. *-aat.* He has a good average in school. *ᶓinda xooš muᶓaddal bil-madrasa.* **2.** *mustawa ᶓtiyaadi.* He's of average intelligence. *mustawa ḍakaaʔa ᶓtiyaadi.*

on the average - *b-muᶓaddal.* I go to the movies on the average of once a week. *ʔaruuẓ lis-siinama b-muᶓaddal marra bil-isbuuᶓ.*

to average - *ṭallaᶓ (i taṭliiᶓ) muᶓaddal.* He averages sixty dollars a week. *ytalliᶓ muᶓaddal sittiin doolaar bil-isbuuᶓ.*

to **avoid** - *tẓaaša (a tẓaaši), tjannab (i tajannub).* Why is he avoiding me? *luweeš da-yitẓaašaani?*

to **await** - *ntiḍar (i ntiḍaar), traqqab (a taraqqub), twaqqaᶓ (a tawaqquᶓ).* They were ordered to await the signal. *jaahum ʔamur yintaḍruun il-ʔišaara.*

awake - *ṣaaẓi, gaaᶓid.* Are you awake? *ʔinta ṣaaẓi?*

to awake - *ṣaẓa (i ṣaẓu), giᶓad (u gaᶓid), faaq (i feeq).* I awoke at seven o'clock. *gᶓadit is-saaᶓa sabᶓa.*

to **awaken** - *qaᶓᶓad (i tqiᶓᶓid) t-, ṣaẓẓa (i tṣaẓẓi) t-, fayyaq (i tfiyyiq) t-.* A noise awakened me. *fadd ẓiss ṣaẓẓaani.*

aware - **1.** *ᶓaarif, daari, ᶓinda xabar.* I'm aware of the difficulties involved in the subject. *ʔaani ᶓaarif biṣ-ṣuᶓuubaat id-daaxla bil-mawḍuuᶓ.* -- He's not aware of his brother's death yet. *li-hassa ma-ᶓinda xabar ib-mootat axuu.* **2.** *ẓaass.* He was aware of movements behind him. *čaan ẓaass ib-ẓarakaat waraa.*

away - *ġaayib.* Have you been away? *činit ġaayib?*

to be away - *ġaab (i ġiyaab).* He was away from school for a week. *ġaab ᶓan il-madrasa l-muddat isbuuᶓ.*

**The station is far away from our house. *l-maẓaṭṭa kulliš ibᶓiida min beetna.*

**Park the car away from the house. *waggif is-sayyaara bᶓiid ᶓann il-beet.*

awful - **1.** *faḍiiᶓ.* It was an awful accident. *čaan ẓaadiθ faḍiiᶓ.* **2.** *qabiiẓ.* That coat is awful. *has-sitra qabiiẓa.* **3.** *wakiẓ.* The kids have been awful today. *j-jahhaal čaanaw wakẓiin il-yoom.*

**It's been an awful day. *čaan yoom ʔaswad.*

awfully - *kulliš, hwaaya.* I'm awfully tired. *ʔaani kulliš taᶓbaan.*

awhile - *fatra, šwayya.* He was here awhile this afternoon. *čaan ihnaa fadd fatra il-yoom il-ᶓasir.* -- I want to think about it awhile. *ʔariid afakkir biiha šwayya.*

awkward - **1.** *mxarbaṭ.* Why is he so awkward in everything he does? *luweeš huwwa hiiči mxarbaṭ ib-kullši l-ysawwii?* **2.** *muẓrij.* It was an awkward situation. *čaanat fadd waḍᶓiyya muẓrija.*

awning - *šamsiyya* pl. *-aat, šamaasi.*

axe - *faas* pl. *fuus, faasa* pl. *-aat.*

axis - *miẓwar* pl. *maẓaawir.* The world turns on its axis once a day. *l-ʔarḍ itduur ẓawil miẓwarha marra bil-yoom.*

axle - *ʔaksil* pl. *-aat.* The axle is broken. *l-ʔaksil maksuur.*

B

baby - **1.** *ṭifil* pl. *ʔaṭfaal.* The baby is crying. *ṭ-ṭifil da-yibči.* They treat me like a baby. *yᶓaamluuni miθil ṭifil.* **2.** *jaahil* pl. *jihhaal.* My sons are still babies. *wildi baᶓadhum jihhaal.*

to baby - *dallal (i tadliil).* You baby your children more than necessary. *ʔinta tdallil jihhaalak akθar imnil-laazim.*

to baby oneself - *daara (i mudaaraa) nafis~.* He babies himself very much. *huwwa ydaari nafsa kulliš ihwaaya.*

baby carriage - *ᶓarabaana maal jaahil* pl. *ᶓarabaayin maal jihhaal.*

bachelor - *ʔaᶓzab* pl. *ᶓuzzaab.* My older brother is still a bachelor. *ʔaxuuya č-čibiir baᶓda ʔaᶓzab.*

back - **1.** *ḍahar* pl. *ḍhuur.* He was lying on his back. *čaan minjiṭil ᶓala ḍahra.* -- This chair has a high back. *hal-iskamli ḍahra ᶓaali.* -- My back aches. *ḍahri yoojaᶓni.* **2.** *warraani*.* The back rooms are dark. *l-gubab il-warraaniyya ḍalma.*

**They did it behind my back. *sawwaaha bala ẓissi.*

**He walked back and forth in the room. *ḍall yruuẓ w-yiji bil-gubba.*

in back - *li-wara.* I prefer to sit in back. *ʔafaḍḍil agᶓud li-wara.*

in back of - *wara.* There's a garden in back of the house. *ʔaku ẓadiiqa wara l-beet.* — I wonder who is in back of this plan? *ᶓajaba minu wara hal-mašruuᶓ?*

in the back of - *b-ʔaaxir.* You'll find it in the back of the book. *raẓ-tilgaaha b-ʔaaxir il-iktaab.*

**I have had it in the back of my mind to tell you for a long time. *haay ṣaar-ilha mudda ib-fikri ʔariid ʔagul-lak-iyyaaha.*

to be back - *rijaᶓ (a rujuuᶓ).* He isn't back yet. *li-hassa baᶓad ma-rijaᶓ.*

to come back - *rijaᶓ (a rujuuᶓ).* When is he coming back? *šwakit raẓ-yirjaᶓ?*

to go back - *rijaᶓ (a rujuuᶓ).* When are you going back to Basra? *šwakit raẓ-tirjaᶓ lil-baṣra?*

to go back over - *raajaᶓ (i muraajaᶓa).* He went back over his work in order to find his mistakes. *raajaᶓ šuġla ẓatta yilgi ġaliṭṭa.*

to step back - **1.** *rijaᶓ (a rujuuᶓ) li-wara.* Step back a bit. *ʔirjaᶓ šwayya li-wara.* **2.** *twaxxar (a tawaxxur).* Please step back out of the way. *baḷḷa twaxxar ᶓan iṭ-ṭariiq.*

to back - *ʔayyad (i taʔyiid) t-.* All parties are backing him. *kull il-aẓzaab itʔayyda.*

to back down - *traajaᶓ (a taraajuᶓ).* He finally backed down and admitted his error. *ʔaxiiran itraajaᶓ w-iᶓtiraf ib-ġaliṭṭa.*

to back up - *rijaᶓ (a) li-wara.* **1.** I still can't back up. *ʔaani baᶓadni ma-agdar arjaᶓ li-wara.* **2.** *saanad (i musaanada).* He backs me up in all my decisions. *ysaanidni ib-kull qaraaraati.* **3.** *rajjaᶓ (i tarjiiᶓ, trajjaᶓ) li-wara.* Back up your car a little. *rajjiᶓ sayyaartak li-wara šwayya.*

backbone - **1.** *ᶓamuud faqari* pl. *ʔaᶓmida faqariyya.* They performed an operation on her backbone. *sawwaw ᶓamaliyya bil-ᶓamuud il-faqari maalha.* **2.** *jurʔa.* If only he had a little backbone he'd tell her to shut up. *loo čaan ᶓinda šwayyat jurʔa čaan gall-ilha "yeezi ᶓaad".*

background - **1.** *gaaᶓiyya* pl. *-aat.* The cloth has a black background with white dots. *l-igmaaš gaaᶓiita sooda w-imnaggaṭ b-abyaḍ.* **2.** *xibra.* We want someone with a wide background for this job. *nriid waaẓid ᶓinda xibra waasᶓa l-hal-waḍiifa.*

in the background - *biṣ-ṣufuuf il-xalfiyya.* His father remained in the background throughout the elections. *ʔabuu ḍall ib-ṣufuuf il-xalfiyya xilaal il-intixaabaat* or *ʔabuu ma-bayyan nafsa xilaal il-intixaabaat.*

back talk - *jasaara, tajaasur.* I won't listen to any back talk. *ma-raẓ-asmaᶓ ib-ʔay tajaasur.*

backward - **1.** *mitʔaxxir.* The people there are very backward. *n-naas ihnaak ihwaaya mitʔaxxiriin.* **2.** *baliid.* Her son is a bit backward. *ʔibinha šwayya baliid.*

backward(s) - **1.** *li-wara.* He fell backwards. *wugaᶓ li-wara.* **2.** *bil-magluub.* You've got that sweater on backwards. *ʔinta laabis hal-ibluuz bil-magluub.*

**He knows the lesson backwards and forwards. *yuᶓruf id-daris čilma ᶓala čilma.*

bad - **1.** *baṭṭaal, muu zeen, sayyiʔ.* He has a bad reputation. *ᶓinda sumᶓa muu zeena.* **2.** *qawi.* I have a bad cold today. *ᶓindi fadd našla qawiyya l-yoom.* **3.** *baʔs b-.* That is not a bad idea. *haaḍi fikra la-baʔs biiha.* **4.** *ma- ... zeen.* He has bad eyes. *ᶓyuuna ma-tšuuf zeen* or *naḍara ḍaᶓiif.* I feel bad today. *ʔaani muu zeen hal-yoom* or *ma-ali xulug il-yoom.* **5.** *šeen.* We have to take the good with the bad. *laazim nirḍa biz-zeen w-iš-šeen.*

**His business is going from bad to worse. *šuğla da-yitdahwar.*

too bad - **1.** *mu?sif.* That's too bad! *haaδa šii mu?sif.* **2.** *maɛa l-asaf.* Too bad that you couldn't come. *maɛa l-?asaf ?inta ma-gdarit tiji.*

to feel bad - *t?aθθar (a ta?aθθur).* Now he feels very bad about what happened. *huwwa hassa kulliš mit?aθθir imn illi jira.*

bag - **1.** *čiis* pl. *čyaas.* Put these apples in a bag. *zutt hat-tiffaaz ib-čiis.* **2.** *janṭa* pl. *jinaṭ.* She took some change out of her bag. *ṭallɛat išwayya xurda min janṭatha.* -- Where can I check my bag? *ween agdar a?ammin janṭati?* **3.** *guuniyya* pl. *gwaani, čiis* pl. *čyaas.* Have them put the bags of rice in the truck. *xalliihum yzuṭṭuun igwaani it-timman bil-loori.*

**He has the money and I'm left holding the bag. *huwwa yiδrub bid-dijaaj w-aani ?atlagga l-ɛajaaj* or *n-naas taakul bit-tamur w-aani n-nuwaaya zişşati.*

**They moved in on us, bag and baggage. *?ijaw kullhum fadd nooba w-giɛdaw ɛala gluubna.*

baggage - *ğaraaδ.* I want to send my baggage on ahead. *?ariid adizz ğaraaδi li-giddaam.*

bail - *kafaala.* The court fixed his bail at two thousand dinars. *l-mazkama qarrirat ?an itkuun kafaalta b-?alfeen diinaar.*

to put up bail - *kifal (a kafaala) n-.* Who is going to put up bail for him? *minu raz-yikfala?*

to bail out - **1.** *ğiraf (u ğaruf) n-.* We used our helmets to bail the water out of the boat. *staɛmalna xuwaδna zatta nuğruf il-maay imnil-balam.* **2.** *ṭufar (u ṭafur).* I had to bail out of my plane at an elevation of five thousand feet. *?aani njabarit ?aṭfur min ṭiyyaarti min ɛilu xamist aalaaf gadam.*

bait - *ṭuɛum.* He put bait on the hook so he could catch himself a fish. *xalla ṭuɛum biš-šuşş zatta yşiid-la simča.*

to **bake** - **1.** *xubaz (u xabuz) n-.* My mother baked bread yesterday. *?ummi xubzat il-baarza.* **2.** *sawwa (i) bil-firin.* She baked the baklava in the oven. *sawwat il-baqlaawa bil-firin.*

baker - *xabbaaz* pl. *-iin, xabaabiiz, čurukči* pl. *-iyya.* This baker has good bread. *hal-xabbaaz ɛinda xooš xubuz.*

bakery - *maxbaz* pl. *maxaabiz, firin* pl. *?afraan.* The bakery is around the corner. *l-maxbaz ib-looft iš-šaariɛ.*

baking powder - *beekin pawdar.*

baking soda - *sooda maal keek, beekin sooda, soodat xubuz.*

balance - **1.** *miizaan* pl. *myaaziin.* The jeweler put the bracelets on the balance and weighed them. *ş-şaayiğ zaṭṭ il-iswaaraat bil-miizaan w-wuzanhum.* **2.** *muwaazana.* I lost my balance. *xtallat muwaazanti.* **3.** *baaqi.* Pay one-third down and the balance in monthly installments. *?inṭi θilθ il-qiima li-giddaam wil-baaqi b-?aqsaaṭ šahriyya.*

**His life hung in the balance. *tɛallag been il-zayaat wil-moot.*

to balance - **1.** *waazan (i muwaazana) t-.* Can you balance a stick on your forehead? *tigdar itwaazin ɛuuda ɛala guşşṭak?* -- Our bookkeeper balances his books at the end of each month. *muzaasibna ywaazin dafaatra b-nihaayat kull šahar.* **2.** *ṭaabag (u muṭaabaga).* Does the account balance? *l-izsaab da-yṭaabug?*

balcony - **1.** *balkoon* pl. *-aat.* I have an apartment with a balcony. *ɛindi šiqqa biiha balkoon.* **2.** *galari* pl. *-yaat.* We had seats in the first balcony. *čaan ɛidna maqaaɛid ib-?awwal galari.*

bald - *?aşlaɛ* pl. *şalɛiin.* He was bald at thirty. *čaan ?aşlaɛ biθ-θilaaθiin.*

bald spot - *şalɛa* pl. *-aat.* He has a small bald spot. *ɛinda şalɛa şgayyra.*

ball - **1.** *ṭooba, kura.* They played ball all afternoon. *liɛbaw ṭooba l-ɛaşir kulla.* **2.** *kabbuuba* pl. *-aat, kubbaaba* pl. *-aat.* I'd like a ball of white wool. *?ariid kabbuubat şuuf abyaδ.* **3.** *ṭooba* pl. *-aat, ṭuwab; kura* pl. *-aat.* He butted the ball with his head. *nigar iṭ-ṭooba b-raasa.*

balled up - **1.** *mxarbaṭ.* I found everything all balled up. *ligeet kullši mxarbaṭ.* **2.** *mirtibik.* He was all balled up. *čaan kulliš mirtibik.*

balloon - *baaloon* pl. *-aat, nuffaaxa* pl. *-aat.*

ballot - *waragat* (pl. *?awraag*) *intixaab.* Have all the ballots been counted? *kull awraag il-intixaab inɛaddat?*

secret ballot - *ntixaab sirri.*

ballroom - *qaaɛa* (pl. *-aat*) *maal rigiş.*

Baltic Sea - *bazr il-balṭiiq.*

bamboo - *xayzaraan.*

to **ban** - *minaɛ (a maniɛ) n-.* The government has banned the sale of narcotics. *l-zukuuma minɛat beeɛ il-muxaddiraat.*

banana - *mooza* pl. *-aat* coll. *mooz.*

band - **1.** *jooq* pl. *?ajwaaq.* The band played dance music all evening. *j-jooq dagg muusiiqat rigiş ṭuul il-leel.* **2.** *šariiṭ* pl. *šaraayiṭ.* The Christians tie a black band on their arm in mourning. *l-masiiziyyiin yšidduun šariiṭ ?aswad ɛala ?iidhum lil-zuzin.* **3.** *ɛişaaba* pl. *-aat.* The police caught the leader of the bank of smugglers. *š-šurṭa lizmat ra?iis ɛişaabat il-muharribiin.* **4.** *mawja* pl. *-aat.* You can get that station on the 25 meter band. *tigdar itzaşşil hal-mazaṭṭa ɛala mawja xamsa w-ɛišriin.*

bandage - *laffaaf* pl. *-aat.* Don't undo the bandage. *la-tfukk il-laffaaf.*

to bandage - *laff (i) ib-laffaaf.* You'd better bandage the cut at once. *?azsan-lak itliff ij-jariz ib-laffaaf hassa.*

bandit - *zaraami* pl. *-iyya, sallaab* pl. *-a.*

bang - *ṭagga* pl. *-aat.* The loud bang startled her. *ṭ-ṭagga l-ɛaalya jafflatha.*

to bang - *δirab (u δarub).* He banged his shoe on the table. *δirab qundarta ɛal-meez.*

to **banish** - **1.** *?abɛad (i ?ibɛaad).* They banished the troublemakers from the capital for two years. *?abɛidaw il-mušaağibiin imnil-ɛaaşima l-muddat santeen.* **2.** *nifa (i nafi) n-.* They banished the party leaders from the country. *nifaw zuɛamaa? il-zizib imnil-bilaad.*

banister - *mzajjar* pl. *-aat.* Hold on to the banister. *?ilzam l-imzajjar.*

bank - **1.** *bang* pl. *bunuug.* I keep my money in the bank. *?aani ?aδumm ifluusi bil-bang.* **2.** *šaaṭi* pl. *šwaaṭi.* He swam to the nearby bank. *sibaz liš-šaaṭi l-giriib.*

to bank on - **1.** *ɛtimad (i ɛtimaad) ɛala.* You can bank on that. *tigdar tiɛtimid ɛala δaak.*

banker - *şarraaf* pl. *şraariif.*

bank note - *nooṭ* pl. *nwaaṭ.*

bankrupt - **1.** *miflis, minkisir.* He is bankrupt. *huwwa miflis.* **2.** *kasir.* The company went bankrupt. *š-šarika ṭilɛat kasir.*

to go bankrupt - *filas (a ?iflaas), nkisar (i nkisaar).* He went bankrupt. *filas.*

bankruptcy - *?iflaas, kasir.* The firm had to announce its bankruptcy. *š-šarika njubrat tiɛlin iflaasha.*

banner - *beeraq* pl. *byaariq, ɛalam* pl. *ɛlaam.*

banquet - *ɛaziima* pl. *ɛazaayim, zafla* pl. *-aat.*

to **baptize** - *ɛammad (i taɛmiid) t-.* He baptized him in the Jordan River. *ɛammada b-nahr il-?ardun.*

bar - **1.** *qaalab* pl. *qwaalib.* Here's a bar of soap. *haak haaδa qaalab şaabuun.* **2.** *šiiš* pl. *šyaaš.* We are going to need more iron bars to finish this foundation. *raz-niztaaj baɛad šiiš zatta nşalliz hal-?asaas.* **3.** *baar* pl. *-aat.* Let's meet in the bar in an hour. *xal-nitlaaga bil-baar baɛad saaɛa.* -- Let's have a drink at the bar. *xal-nišrab-inna fadd šii bil-baar.* **4.** *mayxaana* pl. *-aat.* There was a fight in this cheap bar last night. *şaarat ɛarka b-haay il-mayxaana l-baarza bil-leel.* **5.** *faaşla* pl. *-aat.* He played a few bars of the tune. *dagg ɛam faaşla mnin-nağma.* **6.** *naqaabat il-muzaamiin.* When were you admitted to the bar? *šwakit inqibalit b-naqaabat il-muzaamiin?* **7.** *jazra* pl. *-dat.* Let's swim out to the bar. *xal-nisbaz lij-jazra.*

to bar - **1.** *sadd (i sadd) n-.* He forgot to bar the stable door. *nisa ysidd baab iṭ-ṭoola.* **2.** *minaɛ (a maniɛ) n-.* They posted soldiers at the entrances to bar people from entering. *zaṭṭaw junuud bil-madaaxil zatta yimnaɛuun in-naas imnid-dixuul.*

barbed wire - *silk šaa?ik* pl. *?aslaak šaa?ika.*

barber - *mzayyin* pl. *mzaayna, zallaaq* pl. *-iin.* Is there a good barber in town? *?aku mzayyin zeen bil-wlaaya?*

barber shop - *şaaloon* (pl. *-aat*) *zilaaqa, dukkaan* (pl. *dakaakiin*) *imzayyin.*

bare - **1.** *mşallax* pl. *mşaaliix, ɛaryaan* pl. *-iin.* Little kids are always swimming bare. *l-wulid iş-şiğaar daa?iman yisbazuun mşaaliix.* **2.** *mkaššaf.* Don't go out in the sun with your head bare. *la-tiṭlaɛ barra biš-šamis imkaššaf ir-raas.* **3.** *xaali.* I looked in the cupboard and found the shelves were bare. *baawaɛit bid-diilaab w-ligeet* *ir-rufuuf čaanat xaalya.* -- These are the bare facts. *haaδi hiyya l-ʒaqaayiq xaalya min kull rituuš.*

to bare - 1. *kaššaf (i tkiššif) t-.* The nurse told me to bare my right arm. *l-mumarriδa gaalat-li ʔakaššif iδraaƐi l-yamiin.* **2.** *tfarraƐ (a tafarruƐ).* The men bared their heads when the flag passed. *r-riyaajiil itfarrƐaw min marr il-Ɛalam.*

barefoot - *ʒaafi* pl. *ʒiffaay.* Children, don't play barefoot. *ǧǧaar, la-tilƐabuun ʒiffaay.*

barely - 1. *duub, yaaduub.* He's barely ten. *huwwa duub Ɛašr isniin.* -- I barely had time to finish the book. *l-wakt il-čaan Ɛindi yaaduub kaffa ʔaxallis l-iktaab.* **2.** *bil-kaad.* He barely managed it. *bil-kaad dabbarha.*

bargain - 1. *šarwa* pl. *-aat.* This book was a good bargain. *hal-iktaab čaan xooš šarwa.* **2.** *ṣafqa* pl. *-aat.* That's just part of the bargain. *δaak fadd qisim imniṣ-ṣafqa.* **3.** *ttifaaq* pl. *-aat.* According to our bargain you were to pay half. *ʒasb ittifaaqna čaan laazim tidfaƐ in-nuṣṣ.*

**All right, it's a bargain! *zeen, ṣaar!* or *zeen, mwaafiq!*

to bargain - 1. *tƐaamal (a Ɛimla).* She bargains for hours with the shopkeepers. *titƐaamal saaƐaat wiyya d-dukkančiyya.* **2.** *faawaδ (i mufaawaδa).* The workmen are bargaining with their employer for a raise. *l-Ɛummaal da-yfaawδuun mustaxdimhum ʒawil ziyaada bil-ʔujuur.*

**He got more than he bargained for. *ʒaṣṣal ʔakθar min-ma twaqqaƐ.*

bark - 1. *gišra* pl. *gšuur.* The eucalyptus trees have a thin bark. *ʔašjaar il-yuukaaliptus ʔilha gišra xafiifa.* **2.** *nabʒa* pl. *-aat.* The dog's bark is worse than his bite. *nabʒat ič-čalib ʔangas min Ɛaδδta.*

to bark - *nibaʒ (a nbaaʒ), Ɛawwa (i tƐuwwi).* The dog barked loudly. *č-čalib Ɛawwa b-ṣooṭ Ɛaali.*

barley - *šƐiir.*

barometer - *baroomatir* pl. *-aat.*

barrack(s) - *θakana* pl. *-aat, muƐaskar* pl. *-aat.* Our barracks were built of concrete. *θakanatna mabniyya b-simant.*

barrel - 1. *barmiil* pl. *baraamiil.* We used up a whole barrel of oil. *staƐmalna barmiil kaamil imnid-dihan.* **2.** *sabaṭaana* pl. *-aat.* Show the boy how to clean the barrel of his gun. *raawi l-walad išloon ynaδδuf sabaṭaanat bundiqiita.*

barren - 1. *qaaʒil.* Except for a strip along the river, all the land is barren. *b-istiθnaaʔ wuṣla muʒaaδiya lin-nahar, kull il-ʔaraaδi qaaʒla.* **2.** *Ɛaaqir.* He divorced his wife because she is barren. *ṭallag marta li-ʔanha Ɛaaqir.*

barricade - *maaniƐ* pl. *mawaaniƐ.* The rebels set up barricades in the streets. *θ-θuwwaar niṣbaw mawaaniƐ biš-šawaariƐ.*

to barricade - *sadd (i sadd) n-, gitaƐ (a gaṭiƐ) n-.* They barricaded all the roads into the area. *saddaw kull iṭ-ṭuruq l-itfuut lil-manṭiqa.*

base - 1. *qaaƐida* pl. *qawaaƐid.* The base of the statue was still standing. *qaaƐidat it-timθaal čaanat baƐadha baaqya.* -- The planes returned to their base. *ṭ-ṭiyyaaraat rijƐat il-qaaƐidatha.* **2.** *ʔasaas* pl. *-aat.* The water pipe passes under the base. *buuri l-maay yfuut jawwa l-ʔasaas.*

**Paint the bathroom walls with an oil-base paint. *ʔuṣbuǧ ʒiiṭaan il-ʒammaam ib-dihin.*

to base - 1. *bina (i binaaʔ) n-.* On what do you base your figures? *Ɛala-weeš ibneet iʒsaabak?* **2.** *sawwa (i taswiya) markaz.* The company decided to base its operations in Basra. *š-šarika qarrirat itsawwi markazha bil-baṣra.*

basement - *sirdaab* pl. *saraadiib.*

bashful - *xajuul.* She is very bashful. *hiyya fadd wiʒda kulliš xajuula.*

to be bashful - 1. *xijal (a xajal), stiʒa (i stiʒaaʔ).* She is bashful with people. *tistiʒi mnin-naas.* -- Don't be bashful, ask him. *la-tixjal, ʔisʔala.*

basic - *raʔiisi*, ʔasaasi*, jawhari*.* He earns enough money for his basic needs. *yʒaṣṣil ifluus itkaffi ʒaajaata r-raʔiisiyya.* -- The argument came up because of a basic difference of opinion. *n-niqaaš ṣaar ib-sabab xilaaf raʔiisi bir-raʔi.*

basically - *jawhariyyan.* There is nothing basically wrong with your idea. *fikirtak ma-biiha Ɛeeb jawhariyyan.*

basil - *riiʒaan* pl. *riyaaʒiin.*

basin - 1. *njaana* pl. *-aat.* Please bring me a basin of warm water. *ʔarjuuk jiib-li njaana maay daafi.* **2.** *ʒooδ* pl. *ʔaʒwaaδ, waadi* pl. *wudyaan.* The basin of the Tigris and Euphrates is the most fertile in Iraq. *ʒooδ nahr dijla wil-furaat ʔaxṣab ʔarδ bil-Ɛiraaq.*

basis - *ʔasaas* pl. *ʔusus.* We can't continue on this basis. *ma-nigdar nistimirr Ɛala hal-ʔasaas.*

basket - *salla* pl. *-aat, slaal.* Put the clothes in the basket. *ʒuṭṭ l-ihduum bis-salla.*

basketball - *kurat is-salla, baaskitbool.*

to **baste - 1.** *kawwak (u tkuwwuk, takwiik) t-.* It's better to baste the hem first. *ʔawwal loo tkawwuk iṭ-ṭawya ʔaʒsan.* **2.** *saaqa (i musaaqaa).* Baste the chicken with the oil from time to time while it's cooking. *saaqi d-dijaaja bid-dihin min ʒiin il-ʔaxar lamma tinṭubux.*

bat - 1. *xaffaaš* (pl. *xafaafiiš*) *il-leel, xaššaaf il-leel.* I'm afraid of bats. *ʔaani ʔaxaaf min xafaafiiš il-leel.*

to bat - *δirab (u), ṭaffar (u).* He batted the ball over the fence. *δirab iṭ-ṭooba l-xaarij is-siyaaj.*

**He really went to bat for me. *ṣudug wugaf-li.*

**He told his story without batting an eye. *ʒiča ʒčaayta bala-ma tiṭruf-la Ɛeen.*

batch - 1. *xabṭa* pl. *-aat.* This batch of cement won't be enough. *hal-xabṭa mnič-čimantu ma-raʒ-itkaffi.* **2.** *jooga* pl. *-aat.* The second batch of pilgrims will arrive tomorrow. *j-jooga θ-θaanya mnil-ʒijjaaj raʒ-tooṣal baačir.* **3.** *tannuur* pl. *-aat, tanaaniir.* How many batches of bread do you bake a day? *čam tannuur xubuz tuxbuz bil-yoom?* **4.** *baṭin* pl. *bṭuun.* This is the biggest batch of kittens our cat has ever had. *haay ʔakbar baṭin jaabata bazzuunatna.*

bath - *ʒammaam* pl. *-aat.* I'd like to take a hot bath. *da-ariid aaxuδ ʒammaam ʒaarr.* Have you a room with bath? *Ɛindak ǧurfa biiha ʒammaam?*

to **bathe - 1.** *ǧisal (i ǧasil) n-.* Bathe the baby in lukewarm water. *ʔiǧsil iṭ-ṭifil ib-maay daafi.* -- We usually bathe at the public bathhouse. *ʔiʒna Ɛaadatan niǧsil bil-ʒammaam il-Ɛumuumi.* **2.** *sibaʒ (a sibiʒ) n-.* We went bathing in the river almost every day. *sibaʒna biš-šaṭṭ taqriiban kull yoom.*

bathhouse - 1. *ʒammaam Ɛaamm* pl. *-aat Ɛaamma.* There are many public bathhouses in the city. *ʔaku hwaaya ʒammaamaat Ɛaamma bil-wlaaya.* **2.** *manzaƐ* pl. *manaaziƐ.* There is a bathhouse at the beach where we can change our clothes. *ʔaku manzaƐ bil-masbaʒ nigdar ninzaƐ ihduumna bii.*

bathing suit - *maayo* pl. *-waat* (for women), *čiswa* pl. *čisaw* (for men).

bathrobe - *roob* pl. *-aat, burnuṣ* pl. *baraaniṣ.*

bathroom - *ʒammaam* pl. *-aat.* I'm looking for the toilet not the bathroom. *da-adawwur Ɛal-mirʒaaδ muu l-ʒammaam.*

bath towel - *manšafa* pl. *manaašif.*

bathtub - *baanyo* pl. *-waat.*

batter - *Ɛajiina* pl. *-aat.* Is the batter for the cake mixed? *l-Ɛajiina maal il-keek maxbuuṭa?*

to batter in - *kassar (i taksiir) t-.* The firemen battered in the door and saved the man. *rijaal il-ʔiṭfaaʔ kassraw il-baab w-xallṣaw ir-rijjaal.*

battered-up - *mhaššam.* He bought a battered-up old car. *štira sayyaara Ɛatiiga mhaššama.*

battery - *paatri* pl. *-iyyaat.* My car has to have a new battery. *sayyaarti yinraad-ilha paatri jdiid.*

battle - *maƐraka* pl. *maƐaarik.*

battlefield - *saaʒat il-maƐraka, miidaan* pl. *mayaadiin.*

battle ship - *baarija* pl. *bawaarij.*

to **bawl -** *ṣirax (u ṣraax), Ɛayyaṭ (i Ɛyaaṭ).* The child has been bawling for an hour. *ṭ-ṭifil ṣaar-la saaƐa da-yuṣrux.*

to bawl out - *razzal (i tarziil, trizzil) t-.* Why did he bawl you out? *luweeš razzalak?*

bay - *xaliij* pl. *xiljaan.* There's a steamship anchored out in the bay. *ʔaku baaxira raasiya bil-xaliij.*

bayonet - *sungi* pl. *sanaagi, ʒarba* pl. *-aat, ʒraab.*

to **be - 1.** *čaan (ykuun koon).* Are you planning to be there? *b-niitak itkuun ihnaak?* -- When will you be at home? *šwakit raʒ-itkuun bil-beet?* -- Where have you been? *ween činit?* -- I was planning to go with you. *činit naawi ʔaruuʒ wiyyaak.* -- I wasn't at home when you phoned me. *ma-činit bil-beet min xaabaritni.* -- He had climbed that hill when he was a child. *čaan mitsalliq hat-tall min čaan jaahil.* -- When I got to the office, he was about to leave. *lamma wuṣalt id-daaʔira, čaan da-yiṭlaƐ.* -- His children were playing with ours. *jihhaala čaanaw da-yilƐabuun wiyya jihhaalna.* **2.** *ṣaar (i ṣayra).*

Be good while I'm away, children. *yaa jhaal, ṣiiru εiqqaal ib-ġiyaabi.* — Don't be rude! *la-tṣiir xašin!* — He wants to be an engineer. *yriid yṣiir muhandis.* — How much is it going to be? *šgadd raȥ-yṣiir?* — Would it be all right if we used this room? *yṣiir nistaεmil hal-ġurfa?* — How much will that be? *šgadd ṣaar?* — If that were true, we'd all be rich. *loo haaδa ṣudug, čaan kullna ṣirna zanaagiin.* — He has been climbing that hill everyday for years. *ṣaar-la sniin yitsallaq δaak it-tall kull yoom.* — He had already been there a month when he resigned. *čaan ṣaar-la šahar ihnaak min qarrar yistiqiil.* **3.** (no equivalent). How much is this? *haaδa beeš?* -- The man is a merchant. *r-rijjaal huwwa taajir* or *r-rijjaal fadd waaȥid taajir.* -- His name is Salih. *ʔisma ṣaaliȥ.* -- They are all company employees. *kullhum mustaxdamiin biš-šarika.* -- He is ill. *huwwa mariiδ̣.* He seems to be ill. *ybayyin (huwwa) mariiδ̣.* -- The children are playing in the street. *j-jihaal da-yilεabuun bid-darub.* If I were you, I'd forget the whole thing. *loo ʔaani b-makaanak, ʔansa kullši.*

there is, are - *ʔaku.* There are five men at the door. *ʔaku xams iryaajiil bil-baab.*

there isn't, aren't - *ma-aku.* There isn't anyone at home. *ma-aku ʔaȥȥad bil-beet.*

there was, were - *čaan ʔaku.* There were many people ahead of me. *čaan aku hwaaya naas gabḷi.*

there wasn't, weren't - *ma-čaan aku.* There wasn't anyone at the door. *ma-čaan aku ʔaȥȥad bil-baab.*

beach - *balaaj* pl. *-aat.* We built a fire on the beach. *šεalna naar εal-balaaj.*

bead - **1.** *xirza* pl. *xiraz.* How many beads are there on this string? *čam xirza ʔaku b-hal-xeet?* **2.** *ȥabba* pl. *-aat.* Beads of sweat covered his forehead. *ȥabbaat il-εarag ġaṭṭat guṣṣta.*

beads - *glaada* pl. *-aat, glaayid.* She lost her beads on the way home from the party. *δ̣ayyεat iglaadatha b-ṭariiqha lil-beet imnil-ȥafla.*

prayer beads - *sibȥa* pl. *sibaȥ.* I never saw him without his prayer beads in his hand. *ʔabad ma-šifta min ġeer sibȥa b-ʔiida.*

beam - **1.** *jisir* pl. *jsuura.* The roof was supported by strong beams. *s-saguf čaan masnuud b-ijsuura qawiyya.* **2.** *šeelmaana* pl. *-aat* coll. *šeelmaan.* The warehouse has a framework of steel beams. *l-maxzan haykala min šeelmaan.* **3.** *šuεaaε* pl. *ʔašiεεa.* Throw a beam of light on it. *wajjih šuεaaε δ̣uwa εalee.*

to beam - **1.** *ʔašraq (u ʔišraaq).* Her face beams every time he talks to her. *yišruq wijihha kull-ma yiȥči wiyyaaha.* **2.** *šaεε (i ʔisεaaε).* The face of the pious man beams with light. *wučč ir-rijjaal iṣ-ṣaaliȥ yšiεε nuur.* **3.** *wajjah (i tawjiih).* This program is being beamed to the Middle East. *hal-manhaj imwajjah ʔila š-šarq il-ʔawṣaṭ.*

beans - *faaṣuuliyya.*

broad beans - *baagillaaya* pl. *-aat* coll. *baagilla.*

bear - *dibb* pl. *dibaba.* Are there any bears in this forest? *ʔaku dibaba b-hal-ġaaba?*

to bear - **1.** *tȥammal (a taȥammul).* I can't bear the suspense any longer. *ma-agdar atȥammal hal-ġumuuδ̣ baεad.* He has to bear all the responsibility himself. *huwwa waȥda laazim yitȥammal kull il-masʔuuliyya.* **2.** *šaal (i šeel) n-.* This date tree didn't bear last year. *han-naxla ma-šaalat is-sana l-faatat.* **3.** *wilad (i wilaad) n-.* She bore her first child when she was eighteen. *wildat ʔawwal ṭifilha min čaan εumurha θmanṭaεaš.*

to bear down - **1.** *daas (u doos) n-.* Don't bear down so hard on the pencil, it might break. *la-tduus εal-qalam zeel, tara yinkisir.* **2.** *twajjah (i).* The car bore down upon us at a terrible speed. *s-sayyaara twajjhat εaleena b-surεa haaʔla.* **3.** *δ̣igaṭ (u δ̣agiṭ) n-.* The boss is beginning to bear down on us more everyday. *l-mudiir gaam yuδ̣ġuṭ εaleena ʔakθar yoom εala yoom.*

to bear fruit - *ʔaθmar (i ʔiθmaar).* The apricot trees did not bear much fruit this year. *ʔašjaar il-mišmiš ma-ʔaθmirat has-sana.* After many years, his efforts finally bore fruit. *baεad ihwaaya sniin, juhuuda ʔaxiiran ʔaθmirat.*

bearable - *mumkin iȥtimaala.* It is bearable for a while, but not continually. *haaδa mumkin iȥtimaala fatra bass muu εala ṭuul.*

to be bearable - *nṭaaq (a ntaaqa), nȥimal (i nȥimaal).* The heat is still bearable. *l-ȥarr baεda yinȥimil.*

beard - *liȥya* pl. *liȥa.* He has a long beard. *huwwa mṭawwil-la liȥya.* -- I'm letting my beard grow. *da-arabbi liȥiiti.*

bearing - *beerin* pl. *-aat.* This motor needs new bearings. *hal-makiina yinraad-ilha beerinaat jidiida.*

to get one's bearing - *εayyan (i taεyiin) t-mawqiε~.* First let's get our bearings. *xalli ʔawwil inεayyin mawqiεna.*

to have bearing on - *ʔila εalaaqa b-.* What bearing does that have on what we're doing? *haaδaak š-ila εalaaqa biš-šii d-da-nsawwii.*

beast - **1.** *daabba* pl. *dawaabb.* The horse, the donkey and the mule are beasts of burden. *l-iȥṣaan wuz-zumaaḷ wil-baġaḷ dawaabb.* **2.** *ȥaywaan* pl. *-aat, ȥwaawiin.* He paced up and down in the room like a caged beast. *raaȥ w-jaa bil-ġurfa miθl il-ȥaywaan il-maȥṣuur.*

beat - **1.** *nabuδ̣.* His heartbeat has become stronger. *nabuδ̣ gaḷba ṣaar ʔaqwa.* **2.** *dagga* pl. *-aat, δ̣arba* pl. *-aat.* Count the heartbeats. *ʔiȥsib daggaat il-gaḷub.*

to beat - **1.** *δ̣irab (u δ̣arub) n-, buṣaṭ (u baṣiṭ) n-.* If you keep on throwing stones at my car, I'll beat you up. *ʔiδa tδ̣all itδibb iȥjaar εala sayyaarti, tara ʔabuṣṭak.* **2.** *dagg (u dagg) n-.* If you want to beat your drum, go outside. *ʔiδa triid itdugg ṭablak, ʔiṭlaε barra.* -- Her heart was beating wildly from fear. *gaḷubha čaan da-ydugg ȥeel imnil-xoof.* **3.** *ṭirag (u ṭarig) n-.* Beat two eggs. *ʔuṭrug beeδ̣teen.* **4.** *ġiḷab (u ġuḷub) n-.* We beat them in today's game. *ʔiȥna ġḷabnaahum bil-liεib il-yoom.* **5.** *sibaq (i sabiq) n-.* He beats me to work every day. *yisbiqni liš-šuġuḷ kull yoom.*

to beat down - *gaṣṣ (u gaṣṣ) n-.* I was able to beat down the price 10 Dinars. *gdarit ʔaguṣṣ εašr idnaaniir mnis-siεir.*

to beat in - *xubaṭ (u xabuṭ) n-, mizaj (i mazij) n-.* Beat the eggs into the mixture. *ʔuxubṭi l-beeδ̣ ib-hal-xaliiṭ.*

to beat off - *ṭarrad (i ṭarid) t-.* I beat off the dogs with a club. *ṭarradit l-ičlaab ib-tuuθiyya.*

to beat up - *buṣaṭ (u baṣiṭ) n-, δ̣irab (u δ̣arub) n-, kital (i katil) n-.* They beat him up. *buṣṭoo.*
**Beat it! *walli!*

beautician - *ʔaxiṣṣaaʔi* (pl. *-iyyiin*) *bit-tajmiil.*

beautiful - **1.** *ȥilu, jamiil, badiiε.* What a beautiful day! *šloon nahaar ȥilu!* The bride is a beautiful girl. *l-εaruus ibnayya ȥilwa.* **2.** *badaaεa, mumtaaz.* He did a beautiful job on that. *sawwa šaġla badaaεa b-haaδa.*

beautifully - *kulliš zeen.* Your daughter sews beautifully. *bintak itxayyiṭ kulliš zeen.*

to **beautify** - *jammal (i tajmiil) t-.* The plans for beautifying the city are almost finished. *l-xiṭaṭ il-tajmiil il-madiina εala wašak tithayyaʔ.*

beauty - **1.** *jamaal.* They stood there a long time enjoying the beauty of the sunset. *wugfaw ihnaak mudda ṭuwiila yitmattaεuun ib-jamaal il-ġuruub.* **2.** *badaaεa, falla.* She's a real beauty! *hiyya badaaεa* or *hiyya ṣudug falla.* -- The fish we caught were beauties. *s-simač iṣ-ṣidna čaan falla.*

beauty parlor - *ṣaaloon* (pl. *-aat*) *tajmiil.*

became - see become.

because - *li-ʔan, b-sabab.* He didn't come because he was sick. *ma-jaa li-ʔan čaan mariiδ̣.* I didn't buy it because the price wasn't agreeable to me. *ma-štireeta li-ʔan is-siεir ma-waafaqni.*

because of - **1.** *li-ʔan, b-sabab.* Ali, I'm going to be late because of you. *ya εali, ʔaani raȥ-atʔaxxar ib-sababak.* **2.** *εala muud, l-xaaṭir.* I did it because of her. *sawweeta εala muudha.* -- I don't want you to do it just because of me. *ma-ariidak itsawwiiha bass il-xaaṭiri.*

to **become** - *ṣaar (i), ʔaṣbaȥ (a).* What became of them? *š-ṣaar minhum?* or *ween ʔaṣbiȥaw?* What has become of my purse? *jizdaani ween ṣaar?* It has become a matter of ''pull''. *l-qaδ̣iyya ʔaṣbaȥat waaṣṭa.*

to be **becoming** - *laag (u) l-.* That color is very becoming to you. *hal-loon ihwaaya yluug-lič.*

bed - **1.** *fraaš* pl. *furiš.* I want a room with two beds. *ʔariid ġurfa biiha fraašeen.* -- My bed hasn't been made. *fraaši ma-msawwa.* **2.** *sariir* pl. *sraayir.* The government is building a new hospital with 80 beds. *l-ȥukuuma da-tibni mustašfa jidiid bii θmaaniin sariir.* **3.** *čarpaaya* pl. *-aat.* Where was this bed (stead) made? *hač-čarpaaya ween maεmuula?* **4.** *jiwwa* pl. *jiwaw.* I want you to weed the rose beds today. *ʔariidak tišlaε il-ȥašiiš min jiwaw il-warid il-yoom.* **5.** *gaaεiyya* pl. *-aat.* Put the

box in the middle of the truck bed. *ζuṭṭ iṣ-ṣanduug ib-nuṣṣ gaaƐiit il-loori.*
**He must have gotten up on the wrong side of the bed today. *huwwa ma-adri b-wijj man imṣabbuζ hal-yoom.*
to go to bed – *naam (a, noom).* I went to bed late. *nimit mitʔaxxir.*
to put to bed – *nawwam (u tanwiim) t-, nayyam (i tanwiim) t-.* Tell the nurse to put the children to bed early. *guul lil-murabbiya tnayyim ij-jihhaal min wakit.*
to stay in bed – *buqa (a) bil-ifraaš, ð̣all (a) bil-ifraaš.* He still has to stay in bed. *baƐda laazim yibqa bil-ifraaš.*
bed bug – *baggat l-ifraaš.*
bed clothes – *čaraačif.*
bedding – *l-furiš wič-čaraačif.* Air the bedding today. *hawwi l-furiš wič-čaraačif hal-yoom.*
Bedouin – *badwi** pl. *-iyyiin* coll. *badu.*
bed pan – *qiƐƐaada* pl. *-aat.*
bed rock – *ṭ-ṭabaqa ṣ-ṣaxriyya.*
bed room – *ġurfat* (pl. *ġuraf*) *noom, gubbat* (pl. *gubab, gbaab*) *noom.*
bedspread – *čarčaf* pl. *čaraačif, ġiṭa maal ifraaš.*
bedstead – *sariir* pl. *sraayir* (wooden), *čarpaaya* pl. *-aat* (metal).
bee – *naζla* pl. *naζal, zanbuur* pl. *zanaabiir.*
beech tree – *zaan.*
beef – *laζam hooš.* Do you like beef? *tζibb laζm il-hooš?*
beehive – *kuurat* (pl. *kuwar*) *naζal, kuurat* (pl. *kuwar*) *zanaabiir.*
been – see be.
beer – *biira.* I'd like a glass of beer, please. *ʔariid fadd iglaaṣ biira, rajaaʔan.*
beet – *šwandara* pl. *-aat* coll. *šwandar.*
beetle – *xunfusaana* pl. *-aat* coll. *xunfusaan.* The beetles have eaten all the leaves. *l-xunfusaan ʔaklaw kull waraq iš-šajar.*
before – *gabuḷ.* I'll be there before two o'clock. *raζ-akuun ihnaak gabḷ is-saaƐa θneen.* -- The telegram should be there before evening. *l-barqiyya laazim toosal ihnaak gabḷ il-miġrub.* -- Call me up before you come. *xaaburni gabuḷ-ma tiji.*
**Business before pleasure. *š-šuġul gabḷ il-liƐib.*
before long – 1. *baƐd išwayya.* Before long he'll be able to help you. *raζ-yigdar yƐaawnak baƐd išwayya.* 2. *ð̣all išwayya.* Before long the money we've been saving will come to a hundred dinars. *ð̣all išwayya l-fluus il-da-nlimmha tṣiir miit diinaar.*
never ... before – *ma- ... gabuḷ ʔabad, b-Ɛumr~ ma-.* I've never been there before. *ʔaani ma-raayiζ l-ihnaak gabuḷ ʔabad* or -- *b-Ɛumri ma-riζit l-ihnaak.*
the day before – 1. *gabḷ ib-yoom.* It had rained the day before. *muṭrat gabḷ ib-yoom.* 2. *l-yoom is-saabiq l-.* I didn't get my passport until the day before I left. *ma-ζaṣṣalit paaṣpoorti lil-yoom is-saabiq is-safari.*
the day before yesterday – *ʔawwal il-baarζa.* He was here the day before yesterday. *čaan ihnaa ʔawwal il-baarζa.*
beforehand – *li-giddaam.* I knew it beforehand. *ʔaani Ɛrafitha li-giddaam.*
to **beg** – 1. *jadda (i jidya).* He spends most of his day begging in the market. *yigð̣i muƐð̣am yooma yjaddi bis-suug.* 2. *twassal (a twissil, tawassul) b-.* The children begged their father for some money. *l-ʔaṭfaal itwasslaw b-abuuhum Ɛala čam filis.* -- They begged us to help them. *twasslaw biina nsaaƐidhum.*
beggar – 1. *mgaddi* pl. *mgaadi, mjaddi* pl. *mjaadi.* There's a beggar at the door. *ʔaku mjaddi bil-baab.*
**Beggars can't be choosers. *laazim nirð̣a bil-maqsuum* or *l-buṭar muu zeen.*
to **begin** – 1. *bida (i badwa, bidaaya) n-.* When did you begin working in your present job? *šwakit bideet tištuġul ib-waðiiftak ij-jidiida?* 2. *ballaš (i tabliiš) t-.* The oil company has begun drilling. *šarikt in-nafuṭ ballšat bil-ζafur.* -- As soon as they met on the street, they began to curse one another. *min itlaagaw biš-šaariƐ ballšaw yšattmuun waaζid Ɛal-laax.* 3. *gaam (u qiyaam).* All at once, the donkey began to bray. *fujʔatan, l-iζmaal gaam yjooƐir.*
to begin with – *ʔawwalan, gabuḷ kullši.* To begin with, we haven't got enough money. *ʔawwalan, ma-Ɛidna fluus kaafya.*
beginner – *mubtadiʔ* pl. *-iin.* He's still a beginner. *baƐda mubtadiʔ.*
beginning – *bidaaya.* The box office remains open until 10 minutes after the beginning of the film. *maζall il-biṭaaqaat yibqa maftuuζ Ɛašir daqaayiq baƐad bidaayt il-filim.*
to **begrudge** – *ζisad (i ζasad).* Why should he begrudge me my job? *leeš yiζsidni Ɛala waðiifti?* -- I don't begrudge him his success, he deserves it. *ma-aζisda Ɛala najaaζa, huwwa yistaζiqqa.*
on **behalf of** – *bin-niyaaba Ɛan.* I want to thank you on behalf of our organization. *ʔaζibb ʔaškurak bin-niyaaba Ɛan muʔassasatna.*
to **behave** – 1. *tṣarraf (a taṣarruf).* He doesn't know how to behave. *ma-yuƐruf šloon yitṣarraf.* 2. *tʔaddab (a taʔaddub), ζassan (i taζsiin) t- siluuk~.* Behave yourself! *tʔaddab, ζassin siluukak!* or *ṣiir xooš walad!*
behind – *wara.* There's a garage behind the house. *ʔaku garaaj wara l-beet.* -- The attack came from behind. *ʔija l-hujuum min wara.*
to be behind – 1. *tʔaxxar (a tʔuxxur).* My watch is always ten minutes behind. *saaƐati daaʔiman mitʔaxxra Ɛašir daqaayiq.* 2. *ʔayyad (i taʔyiid) t-.* All the people are behind the president of the republic. *kull in-naas yʔayyiduun raʔiis ij-jamhuuriyya.* 3. *wara.* Who's behind this project? *minu wara hal-mašruuƐ?*
to fall behind – *tʔaxxar (a tʔuxxur).* He has fallen behind in his work. *huwwa mitʔaxxir ib-šuġla.*
to leave behind – 1. *tirak (u tarik) n-.* We had to leave our trunk behind. *ð̣ṭarreena nitruk ṣanduugna.* 2. *xalla (i).* We left the dog behind to watch the house. *xalleena č-čalib ydiir baala Ɛal-beet.*
belch – *taryuuƐa* pl. *-aat.*
to belch – *ttaryaƐ (a ttiryiƐ).* He ate radishes and began belching a lot. *ʔakal fijil w-gaam yittaryaƐ ihwaaya.*
Belgian – *baljiiki** pl. *-iyyiin.*
Belgium – *baljiika.*
belief – 1. *ʔiimaan.* My belief in him was seriously shaken. *ʔiimaani bii ð̣iƐaf kulliš ihwaaya.* 2. *Ɛtiqaad.* Belief in superstitions is wide-spread among illiterates. *l-iƐtiqaad bil-xaraafaat šaayiƐ been il-ʔummiyyiin.*
to **believe** – 1. *ṣaddag (i taṣdiig) t-.* Don't believe anything he says. *la-tṣaddig ʔay šii l-yguula.* 2. *Ɛtiqad (i Ɛtiqaad).* I don't believe he did it. *ʔaani ma-aƐtiqid huwwa sawwaaha.*
to believe in – *ʔaaman (i) b-.* Do you believe in his sincerity? *inta tʔaamin b-ixlaaṣa?*
bell – *jaraṣ* pl. *jraaṣ.* The bell doesn't work. *j-jaraṣ ma-yištuġul.*
belligerent – 1. *mušaakis* pl. *-iin.* He is always belligerent and rude to the people that work with him. *huwwa daaʔiman mušaakis w-xašin wiyya n-naas il-yištaġluun wiyyaa.* 2. *mitζaarub* pl. *-iin.* They have arranged a truce between the two belligerent nations. *dabbiraw hudna been id-dawilteen il-mitζaarubteen.* 3. *mitxaaṣum* pl. *-iin.* The leaders of both the belligerent parties have been arrested. *zuƐamaaʔ il-fariiqeen il-mitxaaṣmeen twaqqfaw.*
bellows – 1. *minfaax* pl. *manaafiix.* Where can I buy a pair of bellows? *ween ʔagdar ʔaštiri minfaax?* 2. *jraab.* The bellows on my camera is ripped. Can you fix it? *l-ijraab maal kaameerti mašguug, tigdar itṣallζa?*
belly – 1. *baṭin* pl. *bṭuun.* This strap goes around the horse's belly. *has-seer yiltaff Ɛala baṭn il-iζṣaan.* -- The plane made a forced landing and slid two hundred meters on its belly. *ṭ-ṭiyyaara nizlat nizuul ið̣ṭiraari w-ziζfat Ɛala baṭinha miiteen matir.* 2. *kariš* pl. *kruuš.* He has a very big belly. *Ɛinda kariš čibiir.*
to **belong to** – 1. *Ɛaad (u) l-.* This building belongs to the oil company. *hal-ibnaaya tƐuud iš-šarikt in-nafuṭ.* 2. *xaṣṣ (u).* These files belong to the Personnel Section. *hal-faaylaat itxuṣṣ šuƐbat ið-ðaatiyya.* 3. *maal.* Who does this car belong to? *has-sayyaara maal man?* 4. *(čaan) Ɛuð̣u b-.* He also belongs to the club. *huwwa hamm Ɛuð̣u bin-naadi.*
below – 1. *jawwa.* The temperature here seldom gets below zero. *darajt il-ζaraara hnaa naadir tinzil jawwa ṣ-ṣifir.* 2. *taζat.* The Dead Sea is below sea-level. *l-baζr il-mayyit taζat mustawa l-baζar.*
belt – 1. *ζzaam* pl. *ζizim.* Do you wear a belt? *tilbas iζzaam?* 2. *gaayiš* pl. *-aat.* My pump needs a new belt. *makiinti yird-ilha gaayiš jidiid.*
**He's got a few under his belt. *širab-la čam*

peek.

**That's hitting below the belt. *haaδi naδaala.*

bench - *maṣṭaba* pl. *-aat, maṣaaṭib.* The benches were just painted. *l-maṣṭabaat tawwha maṣbuuġa.*

bend - *looḟa* pl. *-aat, lawya* pl. *-aat.* We can cross the river at the bend. *nigdar nuɛbur iš-šaṭṭ bil-looḟa.*

to bend - 1. *ɛuwaj (u ɛawij) n-, luwa (i lawi) n-.* He bent the wire. *ɛuwaj is-siim.* **2.** *maal (i mayl, mayalaan).* The tree bends when the wind blows. *š-šajara tmiil min yhibb il-hawa.* **3.** *ẓina (i ẓani) n-.* Bend your head forward. *ʔiẓni raasak li-giddaam.*

**We must bend every effort. *laazim nibδil kull majhuud.*

to bend down - *naṣṣa (i tanṣiya) t-.* I can't bend down. *ʔaani ma-agdar anaṣṣi.*

beneath - 1. *jawwa.* He was buried beneath the tree. *huwwa ndifan jawwa š-šajara.* -- I put it beneath all the other papers. *xalleetha jawwa kull il-ʔawraaq il-luxra.* **2.** *ʔanzal min.* That's beneath his level. *haδiič ʔanzal min mustawaa.*

benefactor - *naṣiir* pl. *nuṣaraaʔ, ɛaḍiid* pl. *ɛuḍadaaʔ.* He was both a friend and a benefactor to me. *čaan-li ṣadiiq w-ɛaḍiid.*

beneficial - *mufiid* pl. *-iin, naafiɛ* pl. *-iin.* The new treatment has proved very beneficial to my back. *l-ɛilaaj ij-jidiid ʔaθbat kawna jiddan mufiid iδ-δahri.*

beneficiary - *mustafiid* pl. *-iin.* He made me the beneficiary of his life insurance policy. *sawwaani l-mustafiid min ɛagd il-taʔmiin ɛala ẓayaata.*

benefit - *faaʔida* pl. *fawaaʔid.* I don't expect to get any benefit out of it. *ma-atwaqqaɛ ʔaẓaṣṣil ʔay faaʔida minha.*

to benefit - *faad (i faaʔida) n-.* The trip did not benefit us much. *s-safra ma-faadatna hwaaya.*

bent - 1. *minẓini.* He is bent with age. *huwwa minẓini mnil-kubur.* **2.** *ʔaɛwaj.* The nail is bent. *l-bismaar ʔaɛwaj.* **3.** *maayil.* The tree is bent from the force of the wind. *š-šajara maayla min quwwat il-hawa.* **4.** *mitqawwis, mqawwas.* His leg is bent this way because he had rickets when he was young. *rijla mqawwsa hiiči li-ʔan ṣaar bii maraḍ il-kisaaẓ min čaan jaahil.*

bent out of shape - *mitɛawwij, maɛwuuj, mɛawwaj.* The pan is all bent out of shape. *j-jidir kulla mitɛawwij.*

berry - no generic equivalent. see specific kinds.

berth - *manaam* pl. *-aat, fraaš* pl. *furiš.* I couldn't get a berth in the late train. *ma-gdarit ʔaẓaṣṣil ɛala manaam bil-qiṭaar il-ʔaxiir.*

**Whenever I see her I try to give her a wide berth. *kull-ma ʔašuufha ʔaẓaawil atjannabha.*

beside - 1. *yamm.* Please put this trunk beside the other one. *ʔarjuuk ẓuṭṭ haṣ-ṣanduuq yamm iṣ-ṣanduuq il-laax.* -- Who's that standing beside your father? *minu δaak il-waaguf yamm ʔabuuk?*

**That's beside the point. *haaδi waẓẓad.*

to be beside oneself - *txabbaḷ (a txubbuḷ, xbaal).* He was beside himself when I heard the news. *txabbaḷ ixbaal min simaɛ il-xabar.* He was beside himself with rage. *čaan mitxabbuḷ imnil-ġaḍab.* -- She was beside herself with grief. *čaanat mitxabbḷa mnil-ẓizin.*

besides - 1. *bil-ʔiḍaafa ʔila.* Besides his being a large landowner, he has a soap factory. *bil-ʔiḍaafa ʔila kawna muzaariɛ ɛinda maɛmal ṣaabuun.* **2.** *ɛalaawa ɛala.* He's a good worker, and besides, everybody likes him. *huwwa šaaġuul w-ɛalaawa ɛala δaak kull waaẓid yẓibba.* **3.** *čmaala.* And besides, he is not related to me. *w-ičmaala, huwwa muu garaaybi.* **4.** *foog.* Besides his wages, he gets tips. *foog ʔujuura yẓaṣṣil baxšiiš.*

best - 1. *ʔaẓsan.* We don't want anything but the best. *ʔiẓna ma-nriid ġeer il-ʔaẓsan.* -- I work best in the morning. *ṣ-ṣubuẓ ʔaẓsan wakit ʔagdar ʔaštaġuḷ bii.* -- I think this is the best way. *ʔaɛtiqid haaδi ʔaẓsan ṭariiqa.* **2.** *ʔaɛazz.* He's my best friend. *huwwa ʔaɛazz ʔaṣdiqaaʔi.* **3.** *ʔazyad šii.* I like your hair best this way. *šaɛrič yiɛjibni hiiči ʔazyad šii.*

**Perhaps it's all for the best. *belki biiha l-xeer.*

at best - *mahma ykuun, š-ma ykuun.* At best, potatoes are a very poor substitute for rice. *mahma tkuun, il-ṗuteeta muu xooš bidal lit-timman.*

to get the best of - 1. *qašmar (u qašmara) t-.* We have to be careful that he doesn't get the best of us. *laazim indiir baanna ẓatta la-yqašmurna.* **2.** *ġiḷab (u ġuḷub).* I think we got the best of this bargain. *ʔaɛtiqid ġiḷabna b-haṣ-ṣafqa.*

**This cold will get the best of me. *hal-našla ma-raẓ-itxalli biyya ẓeel.*

to make the best of - *riḍa (a raḍi) b-.* We don't like our new apartment, but we'll have to make the best of it. *ma-tiɛjibna šiqqatna j-jidiida laakin laazim nirḍa biiha.*

bet - *rahan* pl. *ruhuun.* When are you going to pay me the bet? *šwakit raẓ-tidfaɛ-li r-rahan?*

**That's your best bet. *haδaak ʔaẓsan šii ʔilak.*

to bet - 1. *traahan (a taraahun) ɛala.* Want to bet? *titraahan?* **2.** *raahan (i muraahana).* I'll bet you haven't seen anything like this before. *ʔaraahnak ʔinta ma-šaayif šii miθil haaδa gabuḷ.*

to bet on - *liɛab (a liɛib) n- ɛala, traahan (a) ɛala.* I bet five dinars on the black horse. *ʔaani ʔalɛab xams idnaaniir ɛal-iẓṣaan il-aswad.*

to betray - 1. *xaan (u xiyaana) n-.* He betrayed his best friend. *xaan ʔaẓsan ʔaṣdiqaaʔa.* **2.** *xayyab (i taxyiib).* She betrayed my confidence. *hiyya xayybat θiqti.*

better - 1. *ʔaẓsan.* Don't you have a better room? *ma-ɛindak ġurfa ʔaẓsan?* -- They got better after they had practiced a little. *ṣaaraw ʔaẓsan baɛad-ma tmarrnaw šwayya.* -- Do you feel better? *tiššur ʔaẓsan?* -- We'd better go before it rains. *ʔaẓsan-inna nruuẓ gabuḷ-ma tumṭur.* -- You'd better go. *ʔaẓsan-lak loo truuẓ.*

to be better off - 1. *ʔaẓsan l-.* We'll be better off if we move to another house. *ʔaẓsan-inna ʔiδa nitẓawwal il-ġeer beet.* **2.** *(čaan) ʔaẓsan.* We used to be better off before the war. *ẓaalatna čaanat ʔaẓsan gabḷ il-ẓarub.* -- We'd have been better off without his help. *čaan ʔaẓsan-inna bila musaaɛada minna.*

to get the better of - *ġilab (u ġulub) n-.* He tried to get the better of you. *raad yġuḷbak.*

between - 1. *been.* We'll meet between six and seven. *raẓ-nitlaaga been is-sitta wis-sabɛa.* **2.** *beenaat, been.* This is just between you and me. *haaδi beeni w-beenak.* -- Just between us it's his own fault. *l-ẓači beenaatna, tara ṣuuča.*

**Honest people are few and far between. *l-xooš awaadim qaliiliin w-naadir yiltiguun.*

beverage - 1. (alcoholic) *mašruub* pl. *-aat.* **2.** (non-alcoholic) *muraṭṭibaat.*

to **beware of** - *tqayyad (a taqayyud) min.* Beware of him! *tqayyad minna!* **2.** *daar (i deer) baal min.* Beware of pickpockets! *diir baalak min ḍarraabiin ij-jiyuub.*

to **bewilder** - *tẓayyar (a taẓayyur).* I was completely bewildered. *tẓayyarit tamaaman.*

beyond - 1. *ġaadi.* The house is beyond the river. *l-beet ġaadi mniš - šaṭṭ.* **2.** *wara.* The house is right beyond the hospital. *l-beet wara l-mustašfa tamaaman.* **3.** *ʔakθar min, foog.* We are living beyond our means. *da-nuṣruf ʔakθar min ṭaaqatna.* -- Our neighbors are living beyond their means. *jiiraanna da-yɛiišuun foog mustawaahum.*

**He is beyond help. *ma-tṣiir-la čaara.*

to go beyond - *faaq (u).* That goes beyond my authority. *haaδa yfuuq ṣuluṭṭi.*

biased - *mitẓayyiz, muġriδ.* He is very biased. *huwwa kulliš mitẓayyiz.*

Bible - *l-kitaab il-muqaddas.*

bicarbonate of soda - *kaarboonaat.*

bicycle - *ṗaaysikil* pl. *-aat, darraaja* pl. *-aat.* My bicycle needs fixing. *l-ṗaaysikil maali yirraad-la taṣliiẓ.*

bid - *ɛaṭaaʔ* pl. *-aat.* All the bids for the new building must be in by the fifteenth of the month. *kull il-ɛaṭaaʔaat lil-binaaya j-jidiida laazim itkuun ihnaa gabḷ ixmuṣṭaɛaš biš-šahar.*

to bid - *zaayad (i muzaayada).* He bid ten dinars for the rug. *zaayad ɛašr idnaaniir ɛas-sijjaada.*

big - *čbiir* pl. *kbaar.* The live in a big house. *ysuknuun ib-beet ičbiir.* -- Her father is a big lawyer. *ʔabuuha muẓaami čbiir.* -- He talks big. *yiẓči kbaar.*

**He's a big shot now. *ṣaar šaxṣiyya hassa.*

bill - 1. *qaaʔima* pl. *qawaaʔim.* We have to pay this bill today. *laazim nidfaɛ hal-qaaʔima l-yoom.* **2.** *nooṭ* pl. *nwaaṭ.* Give me some small bills, please. *ʔarjuuk inṭiini nwaaṭ iṣġayyra.* **3.** *laaʔiẓa* pl. *lawaaʔiẓ.* The bill was passed. *l-laaʔiẓa tṣaddqat.* **4.** *mungaar* pl. *manaagiir.* Storks have long bills. *l-lagaalig ɛidha manaagiir iṭwiila.* **5.** *ʔiɛlaan* pl. *-aat.* Posting bills is forbidden here. *lasq il-ʔiɛlaanaat mamnuuɛ ihnaa.*

to fill the bill - *wufa (i wafaa?) bil-maraam.* I don't think that these will fill the bill. *ma-aðunn haðoola yoofuun bil-maraam.*

to foot the bill - *difaƐ (a dafiƐ) l-iḥsaab.* Who's going to foot the bill for all this? *minu raḥ-yidfaƐ kull haaða l-iḥsaab?*

to bill - *dazz (i) qaa?ima.* Bill me for the account. *dizz-li qaa?ima bil-iḥsaab.*

billboard - *looḥat* (pl. *-aat*) *iƐlaan.*

billfold - *jizdaan* pl. *jizaadiin.*

billiards - *bilyaard.* Let's play a game of billiards. *xal-nilƐab fadd geem bilyaard.*

billion - *bilyoon* pl. *balaayiin.* That runs into billions. *haaða yooṣal ?ila balaayiin.*

to **bind** - **1.** *jallad (i tajliid) t-.* Can you bind these magazines for me? *tigdar itjallid-li hal-majallaat?* **2.** *ḥiṣar (i ḥaṣir).* This coat binds a little under the arms. Can you let it out? *has-sitra tiḥṣirni šwayya jawwa l-?ubuṭ. tigdar itkabburha?* **3.** *lizam (i).* Your signature binds you to fulfill the contract on time. *tawqiiƐak ylizmak ib-?injaaz il-Ɛaqid Ɛal-wakit.* **4.** *šadd (i sadd), rubaṭ (u rabuṭ).* The police bound the thief's hands with his handkerchief. *š-šurṭa šaddaw ?iideen il-ḥaraami b-čaffiita.* -- Put glue on both surfaces and bind them together tightly with wire. *ḥuṭṭ ġira Ɛaṣ-ṣafiḥteen w-šiddhum suwa b-teel ḥeel.*

to bind up - *ðammad (i taðmiid).* Bind up his wounds and give him two aspirins with some water. *ðammid ijruuḥa w-inṭii ?aspiriinteen wiyya šwayya maay.*

binder - **1.** *mujallid* pl. *-iin.* The newspapers are at the binder's. *j-jaraayid Ɛind il-mujallid.* **2.** *maḥfaða* pl. *maḥaafið.* You'd better buy a binder for those loose papers. *?aḥsan loo tištiri maḥfaða l-hal-?awraaq il-mafluula.*

bindery - *maḥall* (pl. *-aat*) *tajliid il-kutub.*

binding - *tajliid* pl. *-aat.* The binding is damaged. *t-tajliid talfaan.*

to be binding - *(čaan) mulzim.* This contract is binding on both parties. *hal-Ɛaqid mulzim Ɛaṭ-ṭarafeen.*

binoculars - *doorbiin* pl. *-aat, naaðuur* pl. *nawaaðiir.*

bird - *ṭeer* pl. *ṭyuur.* What kind of bird is this? *šinu nooƐ hat-ṭeer?*

**A bird in the hand is worth two in the bush. *Ɛaṣfuur bil-?iid ?aḥsan min Ɛašra Ɛaš-šajara.* --

**He killed two birds with one stone. *ðirab Ɛaṣfuureen b-ḥjaara.*

birth - **1.** *miilaad* pl. *mawaaliid, wilaada* pl. *-aat.* They announced the birth of their son. *Ɛilnaw miilaad ?ibinhum.* **2.** *wilaada, jeebuuba.* This time it was an easy birth. *hal-marra l-wilaada čaanat sahla.*

by birth - *bil-wilaada.* Are you an American by birth? *?inta ?amriiki bil-wilaada?*

date of birth - *taariix il-wilaada.* You forgot to put down your date of birth? *niseet itḥuṭṭ taariix wilaadtak.*

place of birth - *maḥall il-wilaada.* My place of birth is Bagdad. *maḥall wilaadti baġdaad.*

birth control - *taḥdiid in-nasil.*

birthday - *Ɛiid miilaad.* We are celebrating our son's birthday today. *da-niḥtifil ib-Ɛiid miilaad ?ibinna l-yoom.*

birthday party - *ḥaflat Ɛiid il-miilaad.* My wife is giving a birthday party tomorrow for our daughter. Can you come? *marti da-tsawwi ḥaflat Ɛiid miilaad il-binitna baačir, tigdar tiji?*

birth rate - *nisbat il-wilaada.* The government is concerned about the rapid rise in the birth rate. *l-ḥukuuma maqluuqa mniz-ziyaada č-čibiira b-nisbat il-wilaada.*

bishop - **1.** *maṭraan* pl. *maṭaarna.* His uncle is a bishop. *Ɛamma maṭraan.* **2.** *fiil* pl. *fyaal.* You've already lost one bishop and the game has just begun. *nkital Ɛindak fiil wil-liƐib tawwa bida.*

bit - **1.** *lijaam* pl. *-aat.* The horse's mouth has been injured by the bit. *ḥalg il-iḥṣaan majruuḥ imnil-lijaam.* **2.** *šwayya.* The tea is a bit strong. *č-čaay šwayya ṭoox.* -- I'm sorry but you'll have to wait a bit longer. *mit?assif laakin laazim tintiðir baƐad išwayya.* **3.** *nitfa* pl. *nitaf.* There's a bit of lint on your coat. *?aku nitfat guṭin Ɛala sitirtak.*

**That's going a bit too far. *θaxxanitha.*

**That doesn't make a bit of difference. *ma-yhimm ?abadan.*

bit by bit - *šwayya šwayya.* We learned the story bit by bit. *Ɛirafna l-iḥčaaya šwayya šwayya.*

not a bit - *wala šwayya, ?abadan, wala wuṣla.* There's not a bit left. *maa baaqi wala šwayya.* -- There isn't a bit of bread in the house. *ma-aku wala wuṣlat xubuz bil-beet.* --

bite - **1.** *Ɛaðða* pl. *-aat.* The bite itches. *l-Ɛaðða tḥukk.* -- He took a bite out of the apple. *?axað-la fadd Ɛaðða mnit-tiffaaḥa.* **2.** *wuṣla* pl. *wuṣal.* We haven't a bite left. *ma-buqa Ɛidna wala wuṣla.* **3.** *lugma* pl. *lugam.* Won't you have a bite with us? *ma-taakul-lak fadd lugma wiyyaana?*

to bite - **1.** *Ɛaðð (a Ɛaðð) n-.* Will the dog bite? *č-čalib yƐaðð?* **2.** *nigar (u nagir).* The fish are biting well today. *s-simač da-yungur zeen hal-yoom.*

**I tried twice but he didn't bite. *niṣabit-la fuxx marrteen laakin ma-wugaƐ* or *ðabbeet-la ṭuƐum marrteen laakin ma-nṣaad.*

biting - *gaṣṣ (u gaṣṣ).* It's a biting wind. *haaða fadd hawa yguṣṣ.*

bitter - **1.** That tastes bitter. *ðaak ṭaƐma murr.* -- He has had some bitter experiences. *marr ib-tajaarub murra.* **2.** *qaasi, šadiid.* It was bitter cold. *čaan il-barid qaasi.* **3.** *laduud* pl. *?aliddaa?.* They are bitter enemies. *humma ?aƐdaa? ?aliddaa?.*

**They fought to the bitter end. *ḥaarbaw lil-moot.*

bitterly - *b-ḥurga, b-?alam, b-maraara.* He complained to me bitterly. *tšakkaa-li b-ḥurga.*

black - **1.** (m) *?aswad* (f) *sooda* pl. *suud.* His hair is black. *šaƐra ?aswad.* **2.** *zunji** pl. *zunuuj.* He has become a leader of the black people. *ṣaayir zaƐiim iz-zunuuj.*

to turn black - *swadd (a).* The sky turned black before the storm. *d-dinya swaddat gabḷ il-Ɛaaṣifa.*

black bird - *zarzuur* pl. *zaraaziir.*

blackboard - *ṣabbuura* pl. *-aat, lawḥa* pl. *-aat.* Write it on the blackboard. *kitba Ɛaṣ-ṣabbuura.*

to **blacken** - *sawwad (i taswiid) t-.* The smoke from the fire blackened the ceiling. *d-duxxaan imnin-naar sawwad is-saguf.*

black market - *s-suuq is-sawdaa?.*

blackness - *sawaad.*

blackout - *taƐtiim* pl. *-aat.* The army is going to carry out a trial blackout tomorrow. *j-jeeš raḥ-yquum ib-tamriin taƐtiim baačir.*

to black out - *Ɛattam (i taƐtiim) t-.* The government has decided to blackout the city for ten minutes. *l-ḥukuuma qarrirat itƐattim il-madiina l-muddat Ɛašir daqaayiq.*

Black sea - *l-baḥr il-?aswad.*

blacksmith - *ḥaddaad* pl. *-iin.*

bladder - *maθaana* pl. *-aat.*

blade - *muus* pl. *mwaas, mwaasa; raas ḥaadd* pl. *ruus ḥaadda.* I need a knife with two blades. *?aḥtaaj siččiina ?umm raaseen.* -- These blades don't fit my razor. *hal-imwaas ma-yirhamuun Ɛala makiinat iz-ziyaan maalti.*

blame - **1.** *mas?uuliyya* pl. *-aat.* He took the blame for their mistake. *?axað mas?uuliyyat ġalṭathum Ɛala nafsa.* **2.** *loom.* Don't put the blame on me! *la-tðibb il-loom Ɛalayya.*

to blame - *laam (u loom) n-, bila (i balwa) n-.* Don't blame me. *la-tibliini ?ili.* -- Under these circumstances I could hardly blame her. *b-hal-ḥaala kulliš ṣaƐub ?agdar ?aluumha.* -- This child can't be blamed for anything. *haaða ṭifil ma-yinlaam Ɛala šii.*

to be to blame for - *čaan muṣwič b-.* Who's to blame for the collision? *minu l-muṣwič bil-iṣṭidaam?*

blank - **1.** *stimaara* pl. *-aat.* Would you help me to fill out this blank form? *tigdar itsaaƐidni b-taris hal-istimaara?* **2.** *faraaġ* pl. *-aat.* Fill in all blanks. *ḥašši kull il-faraaġaat.* **3.** (m) *?abyaḍ* (f) *beeða* pl. *biið.* The envelope contained only a blank sheet of paper. *ð-ðaruf ma-bii ġeer warqa beeða.* **4.** *xaali.* Did you notice her blank expression? *laaḥaðit išloon wujihha xaali min kull taƐbiir?*

**My mind is a complete blank. *fikri waaguf tamaaman.*

blanket - **1.** *baṭṭaaniyya* pl. *-aat.* Take another blanket and you won't be cold any more. *?uxuð baṭṭaaniyya lux w-baƐad ma-tubrad.* **2.** *šaamil.* He made a blanket statement which satisfied no one. *ṣarraḥ taṣriiḥ šaamil ma-raððа ?aḥḥad.*

to blanket - *ġaṭṭa (i tġiṭṭi, taġṭiya).* A thick fog blanketed the airfield. *ðubaab kaθiif ġaṭṭa l-maṭaar.*

blast - *nfijaar* pl. *-aat.* You can hear the blast for miles. *tigdar tismaƐ l-infijaar min biƐid ?amyaal.*

full blast - *leel-nahaar, b-kull ṭaaqa.* The plant is going full blast. *l-maƐmal da-yištuġul* *leel-nahaar.*

to blast - 1. *fajjar (i tfijjir, tafjiir) t-.* They're blasting a tunnel. *da-yfajjruun nafag.* **2.** *nisaf (i nasif) n-.* The guerrillas blasted the bridge last night. *l-fidaaʔiyyin nisfaw ij-jisir il-baarḥa bil-leel.*

blaze - 1. *ḥariiq* pl. *ḥaraayiq.* The blaze destroyed a whole block. *l-ḥariiq dammar kull il-manṭiqa lli-been iš-šaarʕeen.* **2.** *naar* pl. *niiraan.* Come and warm your hands over the blaze. *taʕaal w-daffi ʔiideek ʕan-naar.*

to blaze (up) - *ltihab (i ltihaab).* Don't put kerosene in the brazier or the fire will blaze up. *la-tḥuṭṭ nafuṭ bil-manqal tara n-naar tiltihib.*

blazing - *laafiḥ.* We had to stand for half an hour in the blazing sun. *ḍṭarreena noogaf ḥawaali nuṣṣ saaʕa jawwa š-šams il-laafḥa.*

to **bleach - 1.** *kišaf (i kašif).* The wash is bleaching in the sun. *l-ihduum da-tikšif biš-šamis.*

to **bleed -** *nizaf (i nazif).* My nose is bleeding. *xašmi da-yinzif.*

to bleed to death - *maat (u moot) mnin-naziif.* He nearly bled to death. *maat imnin-naziif ʔilla šwayya.*

blend - *xabṭa* pl. *-aat, xaliiṭ, maziij.* I make the blend I smoke myself. *ʔaani ʔasawwi l-xabṭa l-adaxxinha b-iidi.*

to **bless -** *baarak (i mubaaraka) t-.* May God bless you! *baarak aḷḷaa fiik!*

blessing - *baraka* pl. *-aat, raḥma* pl. *-aat.* It was really a blessing that she came. *jayyatha čaanat fadd raḥma min ʔaḷḷa.* -- Go with my blessing! *ruuḥ bil-baraka.*

blew - see blow.

blind - 1. *qiim* pl. *-aat.* Shall I pull up the blinds? *ʔaṣaʕʕid il-qiimaat?* **2.** (m) *ʔaʕmi* (f) *ʕamya* pl. *ʕimyaan, baṣiir* pl. *-iin.* This building is a home for the blind. *hal-binaaya hiyya daar lil-ʕimyaan.* -- We helped the blind man across the street. *ʕaawanna r-rijjaal il-ʔaʕmi ḥatta yuʕbur iš-šaariʕ.* **3.** *ġaafil.* I'm not blind to her faults. *ʔaani muu ġaafil ʕan ġalṭaatha.*

blind (in one eye) - (m) *ʔaʕwar* (f) *ʕoora* pl. *ʕuur.* He's been blind in one eye from birth. *čaan ʔaʕwar imnil-wilaada.*

to go blind - *ʕima (a ʕama).* I hope he's not going to go blind. *ʔatʔammal huwwa ma-yiʕma.*

to blind - *ʕima (i ʕami) n-.* The sun is blinding me. *š-šamis da-tiʕmiini.*

blind alley - *darbuuna* (pl. *daraabiin*) *ma-tiṭlaʕ.* I drove into a blind alley and had to back all the way out. *xaššeet ib-darbuuna ma-tiṭlaʕ w-iḍṭarreet ʔarjaʕ baak.*

to **blink - 1.** *rimaš (i ramiš).* He blinked his eyes when I turned the light on. *rimaš ʕeena min šiʕalt iḍ-ḍuwa.* **2.** *šiʕal w-ṭaffa (i-i).* Blink your lights to attract his attention. *ʔišʕil w-ṭaffi l-laayt maalak ḥatta tijlib intibaaha.*

blister - *buṭbaaṭa* pl. *-aat, buṭaabiiṭ.* He has a blister on his foot. *ʕinda buṭbaaṭa b-rijla.*

blizzard - *ʕaaṣifa* (pl. *ʕawaaṣif*) *θaljiyya.* This is the worst blizzard we've had in ten years. *haaði ʔarḍal ʕaaṣifa θaljiyya marrat ʕaleena b-xilaal ʕašr isniin.*

bloc - *kutla* pl. *kutal.* There are a number of political blocs in Parliament. *ʔaku ʕiddat kutal siyaasiyya bil-barlamaan.*

block - 1. *qiṭʕa* pl. *qiṭaʕ.* What do you plan to do with these blocks of wood? *š-raḥ-itsawwi b-hal-qiṭaʕ xišab?* **2.** *mukaʕʕab* pl. *-aat.* Jamil, put your blocks away. *jamiil, ḍumm il-mukaʕʕabaat maaltak.* **3.** *šaariʕ* pl. *šawaariʕ.* Walk three blocks and then turn right. *ʔimši tlaθ šawaariʕ w-baʕdeen duur lil-yimna.*

**The fire destroyed the whole block. *l-ḥariiq dammar kull il-ibnaayaat been haš-šawaariʕ il-ʔarbaʕa.*

to block - 1. *sadd (i sadd) n-, qiṭaʕ (a qaṭiʕ) n-.* The road is blocked. *ṭ-ṭariiq masduud.* **2.** *ḥaṭṭ (u) n- b-qaalab.* I'd like to have my old hat blocked. *ʔariid šafiqti l-ʕatiiga tinḥaṭṭ ib-qaalab.*

blond - (m) *ʔašgar* (f) *šagra* pl. *šugur.* She has blond hair. *ʕidha šaʕar ʔašgar.*

blonde - *šagra* pl. *-aat.* Who's that good-looking blonde over there? *minu haðiič iš-šagra l-ḥilwa hnaak?*

blood - *damm* pl. *dmuum, dimaaʔ.* The doctor took a sample of my blood. *d-diktoor ʔaxað numuuðaj min dammi.* -- She fainted at the sight of all the blood on the floor. *xirbat min šaafat l-idmuum bil-gaaʕ.*

**Blood is thicker than water. *ʔaani w-ʔaxuuya ʕala bin ʕammi w-ʔaani w-bin ʕammi ʕala l-ġariib.*

in cold blood - *bala raḥma.* They were murdered in cold blood. *nqitlaw bala raḥma.*

**He shot them in cold blood. *rimaahum bir-riṣaaṣ wala ʕinda bil-qeed.*

blood poisoning - *tasammum id-damm.*

blood pressure - *ḍaġiṭ damm.* He has high blood pressure. *ʕinda ḍaġiṭ damm ʕaali.*

blood shed - *ʔiraaqat id-dimaaʔ.* We must avoid bloodshed at all costs. *laazim nitjaada ʔiraaqat id-dimaaʔ ib-ʔay θaman.*

blood shot - *miḥmarr.* His eyes are bloodshot from loss of sleep. *ʕyuuna miḥmarra min qillat in-noom.*

blood stain - *lakkat* (pl. *-aat*) *damm.* The bloodstains on my shirt will not come out. *lakkaat id-damm ʕala θoobi ma-tiṭlaʕ.*

blood type - *nooʕ* (pl. *ʔanwaaʕ*) *damm.*

bloody - 1. *mdamma.* His handkerchief was all bloody. *čaffiita čaanat kullha mdammaaya.* **2.** *damawi*.* Did you hear the rumors about the bloody battle between the tribes. *smaʕt il-ʔišaaʕaat ʕan il-maʕraka d-damawiyya been il-ʕašaayir.*

bloom - 1. *warda* pl. *-aat* coll. *warid.* She picked the choicest blooms in the garden for us. *guṭṭat-ilna ʔaḥsan warid il-bil-bistaan.* **2.** *šarix* He died in the bloom of his youth. *maat ib-šarix šabaaba.*

in bloom - *mwarrad.* The apricot trees are now in bloom. *ʔašjaar il-mišmiš hassa mwarrda.*

to bloom - *warrad (i tawriid).* My roses didn't bloom well last year. *l-warid maali ma-warrad zeen is-sana l-faatat.*

blossom - 1. *warda* pl. *-aat* coll. *warid.* The blossoms are falling off the pomegranate bushes. *l-warid da-yoogaʕ min šajart ir-rummaan.* **2.** *(citrus) qiddaaḥ.* The scent from the orange blossoms filled the whole garden. *riiḥt il-qiddaaḥ tirsat il-ḥadiiqa.*

to blossom - *warrad (i tawriid).* The carnations will start to blossom next week. *l-iqrinfil raḥ-yibdi ywarrid isbuuʕ ij-jaay.*

blot - *lakka* pl. *-aat.* The page is full of blots. *ṣ-ṣafḥa kullha lakkaat.*

to blot - *naššaf (i tanšiif) t-.* Blot the signature before you fold the letter. *naššif il-ʔimḍaaʔ gabul-ma tiṭwi l-maktuub.*

to blot out - *sadd (i sadd).* The trees blot out the view. *l-ʔašjaar itsidd il-manðar.*

to blot up - *naššaf (i tanšiif).* Blot up the ink with a blotter. *naššif il-ḥibir bin-niššeef.*

blotch - *ṭugʕa* pl. *ṭugaʕ.* What caused these red blotches on your face? *š-sabbab haṭ-ṭugaʕ il-ḥamra b-wiččak?*

blotter - *niššeefa* pl. *-aat* coll. *niššeef, niššaafa* pl. *-aat* coll. *niššaaf.* Quick, give me a blotter! *nṭiini niššeef bil-ʕajal!*

blotting paper - *waraqa* (pl. *-aat*) *niššaaf* coll. *waraq niššaaf.* I'd like three sheets of blotting paper. *ʔariid itlaθ waraqaat niššaaf.*

blow - *ḍarba* pl. *-aat.* That was a hard blow. *ðiič čaanat fadd ḍarba qawiyya.* -- That blow struck home. *ðiič iḍ-ḍarba jatti b-makaanha* or ***had-dagga ḍirbat bid-damaar.*

to blow - 1. *habb (i habb).* The wind is blowing from the North. *l-hawa da-yhibb imniš-šimaal.* **2.** *gabb (u gabb).* Last night a severe sandstorm blew in on Baghdad. *l-baarḥa gabbat ʕajja qawiyya ʕala baġdaad.* **3.** *dagg (u dagg).* When do they blow taps? *šwakit ydugguun buuq in-noom?* **4.** *dagg (u dagg), ṭawwaṭ (u ṭṭuwwuṭ) t-.* Blow the horn three times. *dugg il-hoorin itlaθ daggaat.* **5.** *ṣoofar (i mṣoofra) t-.* The umpire blew his whistle three times. *l-ḥakam ṣoofar ib-ṣaafirta tlaθ marraat.* **6.** *nufax (u nafux).* Blow on the coffee, if you want to cool it. *ʔunfux ʕal-gahwa ʔiða triid itbarridha.*

to blow away - 1. *ṭaar (i).* The paper blew away. *l-warga ṭaarat.* **2.** *ṭayyar (i ṭṭiyyir).* The wind blew the papers away. *l-hawa ṭayyar il-waraq.*

to blow one's nose - *muxaṭ (u maxiṭ).* I have to blow my nose. *laazim ʔamxuṭ.*

to blow out - 1. *ṭaffa (i taṭfiya).* Take a deep breath and blow out the candle. *ʔuxuð nafas ṭuwiil w-ṭaffi š-šamʕa.* **2.** *ṭagg (u ṭagg).* The old tire blew out. *t-taayar il-ʕatiig ṭagg.* **3.** *fakk (u) bil-hawa.* Blow out the clogged tube. *fukk il-buuri*

l-masduud b-waasiṭṭ il-hawa. **4.** ʒirag (i ʒarig). Be careful you don't blow out the fuse. *diir baalak la-taʒrig l-ifyuuz.*
to blow over - 1. *hida (a hiduuʔ).* The storm will blow over soon. *l-εaaṣifa raʒ-tihda baεad išwayya.* **2.** *burad (a).* Her anger will soon blow over. *ġaðabha raʒ-yibrad baεad išwayya.*
to blow up - 1. *nfijar (i nfijaar).* The powder plant blew up. *maεmal il-baaruud infijar.* **2.** *nisaf (i nasif).* The enemy blew up all the bridges. *l-εadu nisaf kull ij-jisuur.* **3.** *nufax (u nafux).* Blow up the balloons for the children. *ʔinfux in-nuffaaxaat lij-jihhaal.*
blowout - *pančar* pl. *panaačir.* We had a blowout on the way home. *b-ṭariiqna lil-beet ṣaar εidna pančar.*
blue - 1. (m) *ʔazrag* (f) *zarga* pl. *zurug.* She has beautiful blue eyes. *εidha εyuun zurug ʒilwa.* **2.** *maqhuur.* She looks blue this morning. *ybayyin εaleeha maqhuura hwaaya l-yoom.*
**He arrived out of the blue. *nizal εaleena mnis-sima.*
to get the blues - *nqubað (u nqibaað).* I get the blues when it rains. *ʔanqubuð min timṭur* or *nafsi tinqubuð min timṭur.*
to turn blue - *zragg (a).* Your face has turned blue with cold. *wiččak izragg imnil-barid.*
blueing - *čuwiit.*
blueness - *zaraag.*
blue print - *xariiṭa* pl. *xaraayiṭ, taṣmiim* pl. *taṣaamiim.* Show him how to read the blueprint. *raawii šloon yiqra l-xariiṭa.*
bluff - 1. *juruf εaali* pl. *jruuf εaalya.* He's building his house on a bluff overlooking the river. *da-yibni beeta εala juruf εaali yṭill εaš-šaṭṭ.* **2.** *qašmara, balfa* pl. *-aat.* That's only a bluff. *haaði muu ʔakθar min fadd balfa.*
to bluff - 1. *qašmar (u qašmara) t-.* He's only bluffing. *haaða da-yqašmur.* **2.** *bilaf (i balif) n-.* When he took another card, I knew he was bluffing. *min ʔaxað warqat il-lux εirafit da-yiblif.*
**If I were you, I'd have called his bluff. *loo čint ib-makaanak, čaan xalleeta yikšif liεibta.*
blunder - *ġalṭa* pl. *-aat.* I made an awful blunder. *ʔaani sawweet fadd ġalṭa faðiiεa.*
blunt - (m) *ʔaεmi* (f) *εamya.* This knife is too blunt. *has-siččiina kulliš εamya.*
**Said is awfully blunt. *saεiid yṭugg il-iʒčaaya ib-wučč il-waaʒid.*
bluntly - **He told me the truth very bluntly. *ṭagg il-ʒaqiiqa b-wučči.*
to **blush -** *ʒmarr (a ʒmiraar).* She blushes easily. *hiyya tiʒmarr bil-εajal.*
board - 1. *looʒa* pl. *-aat, lwaaʒ* coll. *looʒ.* We need some large boards. *niʒtaaj čam looʒa čbiira.* -- Write it on the board. *kitba εal-looʒa.* **2.** *ʔakil.* My board costs me more than my room. *ʔakli ykallifni ʔazyad min ʔiijaari.*
on board (ship) - *bil-markab.* There was a famous actress on board ship with us. *čaan ʔaku mumaθθila mašhuura bil-markab wiyyaana.*
on board (train) - *bil-qiṭaar.* Is everybody on board the train? *l-kull rikbaw bil-qiṭaar?*
room and board - *ġurfa maεa ʔakil.* How much do you pay for room and board? *šgadd tidfaε εann il-ġurfa maεa l-ʔakil?*
to board - 1. *ʔakal (u) b-ifluus.* I would like to arrange to board with an Iraqi family. *ʔariid ʔasawwi tartiib wiyya εaaʔila εiraaqiyya ʒatta ʔaakul εidhum b-ifluus.* **2.** *rikab (u rukub) n-.* We boarded the train in Washington. *rikabna l-qiṭaar ib-waašinṭin.*
boarder - **Do you take in boarders? *εidkum tartiib in-naas yaakluun ib-beetkum b-ifluus?*
board of health - *daaʔirt iṣ-ṣiʒʒa.*
to **boast - 1.** *tbajjaʒ (a tabajjuʒ).* Stop boasting! *ma-yeezi titbajjaʒ!* **2.** *tbaaha (a tabaahi).* He is always boasting about how much influence his family has. *εala ṭuul yitbaaha b-nufuuð εaaʔilta.*
boat - 1. *balam* pl. *blaam.* We went fishing in his boat. *riʒna nṣiid simač bil-balam maala.* **2.** *markab* pl. *maraakub, baaxira* pl. *bawaaxir.* This boat goes to Australia. *hal-markab yruuʒ il-ʔusturaalya.*
**We're all in the same boat. *kullna fil-hawa sawa.*
bobby pin - *firkeeta* pl. *-aat, maaša* (pl. *-aat*) *maal šaεir.*
body - 1. *jisim* pl. *ʔajsaam, jasad* pl. *ʔajsaad.* He has a rash on his body. *εinda šira b-jisma.* -- There are solid, liquid, and gaseous bodies. *ʔaku ʔajsaam ṣalba, w-saaʔla w-ġaaziyya.* **2.** *lašša* pl. *-aat, jiθθa* pl. *jiθaθ.* The body of the dog is still lying in the middle of the road. *laššt ič-čalib baεadha maðbuuba b-nuṣṣ iš-šaariε.* -- The body was cremated. *j-jiθθa nʒirgat.*
**They barely manage to keep body and soul together. *ma-εidhum εaša leela.*
in a body - *b-jooga, b-jamaaεa.* They left the hall in a body. *ṭilεaw imnil-qaaεa b-joogathum.*
bodyguard - *ʒaaris* pl. *ʒurraas.*
to **bog down - 1.** *ṭumaṣ (u ṭamuṣ) n-.* The car bogged down in the mud. *s-sayyaara ṭumṣat biṭ-ṭiin.* **2.** *ṭammas (u ṭṭummus) t-.* This illness bogged me down financially. *hal-marað ṭammasni bid-deen.*
boil - 1. *dimbila* pl. *dnaabil.* He has a boil on his neck. *εinda dimbila b-rugubta.* **2.** (Baghdad boil). *ʔuxut* pl. *xawaat.* That round scar on his face is a Baghdad boil. *han-nadba l-imdawwra b-wučča ʔuxut.*
to boil - 1. *faar (u fawaraan), ġila (i ġalayaan) n-.* The water is boiling. *l-maay da-yfuur.* **2.** *fawwar (u tafwiir, tfuwwur) t-.* Boil the water before you give it to the baby. *fawwr il-maay gabul-ma tintii lij-jaahil.* -- Boil the vegetables in salted water. *fawwr il-xuðrawaat ib-maay w-miliʒ.* **3.** *silag (i salig) n-.* Please boil the eggs two minutes. *baḷḷa ʔislig il-beeð daqiiqteen.*
to boil with rage - *gila mnil-ġaðab.* He was boiling with rage. *čaan da-yigli mnil-ġaðab* or ***čaan ṣaayir naar.*
boiler - *booylar* pl. *-aat, qazaan* pl. *-aat.* The boiler exploded. *ṭagg il-booylar.*
bold - *jasir* pl. *-iin, jariʔ* pl. *-iin.* That was a bold statement. *haaða taṣriiʒ jariʔ.*
bolt - 1. *burgi* pl. *baraaġi.* This nut doesn't fit the bolt. *has-sammuuna ma-tirham εal-burġi.* **2.** *ṭool* pl. *twaal.* There are only ten yards of material left in this bolt. *buqat bass εašir yardaat iqmaaš ib-haṭ-ṭool.* **3.** *lisaan* pl. *-aat, lisin; ṣiqqaaṭa* pl. *-aat.* Did you push the bolt shut? *saddeet il-lisaan.* **4.** *ṣaaεiqa* pl. *ṣawaaεiq.* The news came like a bolt from the blue. *ðiič il-ʔaxbaar nizlat miθl iṣ-ṣaaεiqa.*
to bolt - 1. *ʒaṭṭ (u) ṣiqqaaṭa b-.* You forgot to bolt the garage door. *ʔinta niseet itʒuṭṭ iṣ-ṣiqqaaṭa b-baab il-garaaj.* **2.** *šadd (i šadd), rakkab (i).* Bolt the plate onto the work bench. *šidd ir-raaṣṭa εat-tizgaa.* **3.** *jimaʒ (a jmuuʒ).* Suddenly the horse shied and bolted. *εala ġafḷa jifal l-iʒṣaan w-jimaʒ.*
bomb - *qumbula* pl. *qanaabil, bamba* pl. *-aat.* The whole district has been destroyed by bombs. *l-manṭiqa kullha čaanat imdammra bil-qanaabil.*
to bomb - *qiṣaf (u qaṣuf) n-.* The planes bombed the factory again during the night. *ṭ-ṭiyyaaraat quṣfat il-maεmal marra lux bil-leel.*
bomber - *qaaṣifa* pl. *-aat.* The Air Force is using a new type of long-range bomber. *l-quwwa j-jawwiyya da-tistaεmil nooε jidiid imnil-qaaṣifaat biεiidt il-madad.*
bond - 1. *sanad* pl. *-aat.* He invested all his money in stocks and bonds. *kull ifluusa šaġġalha bil-ʔashum wis-sanadaat.* **2.** *raabiṭa* pl. *rawaabuṭ.* There's a firm bond between the two friends. *ʔaku fadd raabiṭa qawiyya been iṣ-ṣadiiqeen.*
bone - *εaðma* pl. *-aat, εaðum* pl. *εðaam.* Give the dog a bone. *nṭii lič-čalib fadd εaðma.* -- He's nothing but skin and bones. *huwwa bass jild w-εaðum.* -- This fish has an awful lot of bones. *has-simča malyaana εðaam.*
**He made no bones about his intentions. *huwwa ma-ʒaawal ysawwi šii jawwa l-εabaa.*
**I feel chilled to the bone. *da-aʒiss jimdat iεðaami.*
bonfire - *naar* pl. *niiraan.*
bonnet - *klaaw* pl. *-aat.*
bonus - *εlaawa* pl. *-aat, minʒa* pl. *minaʒ.* The employees here get a bonus at the end of each year. *l-mustaxdamiin ihnaa yaaxðuun iεlaawa b-nihaayat kull sana.*
book - *ktaab* pl. *kutub.* Did you like the book? *εijabak l-iktaab?*
bookbindery - *maʒall* (pl. *-aat*) *tajliid il-kutub.*
bookcase - *diilaab* pl. *dwaaliib, maktaba* pl. *-aat.* Close the bookcase. *sidd id-diilaab maal il-kutub* or *sidd baab il-maktaba.*
book end - *sannaada* (pl. *-aat*) *maal kutub.*
bookkeeper - *muʒaasib* pl. *-iin.*
bookkeeping - *muʒaasaba, masik dafaatir.*

booklet – *kurraasa* pl. *-aat.*
bookstore – *maktaba* pl. *-aat.* Were you in this bookstore? *ʔinta xaašš ib-hal-maktaba?*
boom – **1.** *dawya* pl. *-aat.* You can hear the boom of the cannon. *tigdar tismaε dawyat il-madfaε.* **2.** *wakt in-niεma, wakt il-xeer.* He made all his money in the boom during the war. *ʒaṣṣal kull ifluusa b-wakt in-niεma ʔaθnaaʔ il-ʒarub.* -- How do you explain this sudden boom? *šloon itfassir hal-xeer iṣ-ṣaar εala ġafla?*
to boom – **1.** *laεlaε (i laεlaεa), duwa (i dawi).* He has a booming voice. *εinda ṣoot ylaεliε.* **2.** *raaj (u rawaaj), zdihar (i zdihaar).* Our business is booming now. *šuġulna hassa raayij.*
to **boost** – *ṣaεεad (i taṣεiid) t-.* The drought has boosted the prices of wheat. *qillat il-muṭar ṣaεεidat ʔasεaar il-ʒunṭa.*
boot – **1.** *juzma* pl. *juzam.* When I go fishing I wear high boots. *lamma aruuʒ iṣ-ṣeed is-simač ʔalbas juzma.* **2.** *puṣṭaal* pl. *paṣaaṭiil.* Soldiers wear black boots. *j-jinuud yilbasuun paṣaaṭiil suud.*
to boot – *cmaala, εlaawa.* He paid me for my work and gave me five dinars to boot. *difaε-li ʒaqqi w-inṭaani xams idnaaniir ičmaala.*
to boot – *čallaq (i tačliiq) t-.* They booted him out of the coffee house. *čalliqoo mnil-gahwa.*
bootblack – *ṣabbaaġ (pl. ṣabaabiiġ) qanaadir.*
booth – **1.** *maʒall* pl. *-aat.* There were many display booths at the fair. *čaan aku hwaaya maʒallaat εariδ̣ bil-maεraδ̣.* **2.** *maqṣuura* pl. *-aat.* I'm calling from a phone booth. *da-axaabur min maqṣuurat talafoon.*
border – **1.** *ʒiduud* (pl.). When do we reach the border? *šwakit nooṣal lil-ʒiduud?* **2.** *ʒaašya* pl. *ʒawaaši.* The border of this rug is getting worn. *ʒaašyat haz-zuuliyya saayfa.*
to be bordered by – *nʒadd (a), (čaan) maʒduud b-.* Holland is bordered on the south by Belgium. *hoolanda maʒduuda mnij-jinuub ib-baljiika.*
to border on – *kaad (a) yooṣal l-.* That borders on the ridiculous. *haaδa ykaad yooṣal il-darajt is-saxaafa.*
border line – **1.** *ʒiduud.* The border line of my property is marked by a row of trees. *ʒiduud mulki mεayyan ib-qaṭar ʔašjaar.* **2.** *bayna bayn.* That is a border line case. *hal-qaδ̣iyya bayna bayn.*
to **bore** – **1.** *ziraf (u zuruf) n-.* We'll have to bore a hole through the wall. *ʔiʒna laazim nizruf zuruf bil-ʒaayiṭ.* **2.** *δ̣awwaj (i tδ̣uwwuj, taδ̣wiij) t-.* His speech bored me. *l-ʒadiiθ maala δ̣awwajni.*
to be **bored** – *mall (i malal) n-, δ̣aaj (u δ̣ooj, δ̣awajaan).* I'm bored of always seeing the same faces. *malleet min šoofat nafs il-wujuuh.*
boredom – *δ̣uwaaja.* I almost died of boredom. *mitit imniδ̣-δ̣uwaaja ʔilla šwayya.*
boric acid – *ʒaamiδ̣ il-booriik.*
to be **born** – *nwilad (i), jaa (i jayya) lid-dinya, mawluud.* Where were you born? *ʔinta ween inwiladit?* -- She was born blind. *jatti lid-dinya εamya.* -- My grandfather was born in Basra. *ʔabu jiddi nwilad bil-baṣra.*
to **borrow** – *tdaayan (a), ṭilab (u ṭalab).* She borrowed the book from him. *ṭulbat minna l-iktaab.*
bosom – *ṣadir* pl. *ṣduur.*
**They are bosom pals. *δoola ʔaṣdiqaaʔ ṭoox.*
boss – **1.** *raʔiis* pl. *ruʔasaaʔ.* Do you know my boss? *tuεruf ir-raʔiis maali?* **2.** *l-kull bil-kull.* Talk to his wife, she's the boss. *ʔiʒči wiyya marta hiyya l-kull bil-kull.*
**Who wouldn't want to be his own boss? *minu ma-yriid yṣiir malik nafsa?*
to boss (around) – *tʔammar (a taʔammur).* Who gave him the right to boss me around? *minu nṭaa sulṭa yitʔammar εalayya?*
to **botch up** – *xarbaṭ (u xarbaṭa) t-.* Your workman botched the job up and you'll have to repair it. *ṣaanεak xarbaṭ iš-šaġla w-inta laazim itṣalliʒha.*
both – *θ-θineen.* Both brothers are in the navy. *l-ʔuxwa θ-θineen bil-baʒriyya.* -- We both visited him. *ʔiʒna θneenna zirnaa.* -- I like to do both equally well. *yiεjibni ʔasawwi θ-θineen ib-duun tafδ̣iil.*
bother – **1.** *kuluufa* pl. *-aat.* It's no bother at all. I'm always at your service. *ma-aku ʔay kuluufa, ʔaani daaʔiman bil-xidma.* **2.** *dooxat raas.* Getting ready for the holiday is a big bother. *l-istiεdaad lil-εiid dooxat raas čibiira.* -- His constant questions are getting to be a bother. *ʔasʔilta l-mitkarrira ṣaarat dooxat raas.* **3.** *maġaθθa.* This job is all bother and strain with no profit in it. *haš-šaġla ma-biiha ġeer il-maġaθθa w-šilεaan il-galub w-maa min waraaha faaʔida.* **4.** *ʔizεaaj.* Pardon the bother, but I have to see you. *ʔarju l-maεδira εan ʔizεaajak, laakin laazim ʔašuufak.*
to bother – **1.** *ziεaj (i ʔizεaaj) n-.* Please don't bother me! *ʔarjuuk la-tizεijni.* -- Does my cigarette smoke bother you? *d-duxxaan maal jigaarti da-yziεjak?* -- Does the cough bother you much? *l-gaʒʒa da-tziεjak ihwaaya?* **2.** *dawwax (u tduwwux, tadwiix) t- raas.* I really hate to bother you. *ʔaani bil-ʒaqiiqa ma-ard adawwux raasak.* -- I can't bother with that. *ma-agdar adawwux raasi b-δiič.* **3.** *ġaθθ (u ġaθθ) n-.* What's bothering you? *šinu l-ġaaθθak?* or *ʔinta min eeš maġθuuθ?* or *š-da-yġuθθak?* **4.** *ʔannab (i taʔniib), εaδδab (i taεδiib).* His conscience bothered him. *δ̣amiira ʔannaba.*
to bother oneself – *tkallaf (a takalluf).* Please don't bother yourself on my account. *ʔarjuuk la-titkallaf εala muudi.*
bottle – *buṭil* pl. *bṭuula, šiiša* pl. *šiyaš.* Shall I get a few bottles of beer? *tirduun ʔajiib čam buṭil biira?* -- I'd like a bottle of ink. *ʔariid šiišat ʒibir.*
bottle neck – **1.** *εaqaba* pl. *-aat.* The only bottle neck on Rashid Street is the Mirjan mosque. *l-εaqaba l-waʒiida b-saariε ir-rašiid hiyya jaamiε mirjaan.* **2.** *εarqala* pl. *εaraaqiil.* The main bottle neck in the Post Office is the sorting section *l-εarqala r-raʔiisiyya b-daaʔirt il-bariid, šuεbat it-tafriiq.*
bottom – **1.** *čaεab* pl. *čεuub.* He found it at the bottom of the trunk. *ligaa b-čaεb iṣ-ṣanduug.* -- Bottoms up! – *čaεb ʔabyaδ̣!* **2.** *ʔasaas* pl. *ʔusus.* We have to get to the bottom of this affair. *ʔiʒna laazim nuεruf ʔasaas hal-qaδ̣iyya.* **3.** *ʔaεmaaq.* I thank you from the bottom of my heart. *ʔaškurak min ʔaεmaaq galbi.* **4.** *jawwaani*.* Your shirts are in the bottom drawer. *θyaabak bil-imjarr il-jawwaani.*
from top to bottom – **1.** *min foog li-jawwa.* They searched the house from top to bottom. *dawwraw il-beet min foog li-jawwa.* **2.** *mnir-raas lič-čaεab.* The policeman searched me from top to bottom. *š-šurṭi fattašni mnir-raas lič-čaεab.*
to reach rock bottom – *wuṣal (a) il-ʔasfal darak.* We've reached rock bottom! Things can't get worse. *wṣalna l-ʔasfal darak! l-ʒaala ma-mumkin itṣiir ʔatεas.*
to touch bottom – *gayyaš (i geeš).* Can you touch bottom here? *tigdar itgayyiš ihnaa.* -- The boat has touched bottom. *l-balam gayyaš.*
to **bounce** – **1.** *gumaz (u gamuz).* This ball doesn't bounce. *haṭ-ṭooba ma-tugmuz.* **2.** *gammaz (u tagmiiz, tgummuz) t-.* He bounced the ball. *huwwa gammaz iṭ-ṭooba.*
to get (or be) bounced – *nṭirad (i).* He was bounced yesterday. *nṭirad il-baarʒa.*
bound – **1.** *mčattaf.* We found the man bound with a sheet. *liqeena r-rijjaal imčattaf ib-čarčaf.* **2.** *mjallad.* I bought a book bound in red leather. *štireet iktaab imjallad ib-jilid ʔaʒmar.* **3.** *mirtibiṭ.* I am bound by contract to finish this building in two months. *ʔaani mirtibiṭ ib-εaqid ʔaxalliṣ hal-ibnaaya b-šahreen.*
to be bound (for) – *twajjah (i) ʔila.* That boat is bound for America. *hal-markab mitwajjih ʔila ʔamriika.*
**She's bound to be late. *tara raʒ-titʔaxxar min kull budd.*
**It was bound to happen sooner or later. *haaδa ʔawwal w-taali ma-čaan minna mafarr.*
boundary – *ʒadd* pl. *ʒiduud.* There is no boundary separating his property and mine. *ma-aku ʒadd faaṣil been mulka w-mulki.*
to be **bounded by** – *(čaan) maʒduud b-.* Germany is bounded on the south by Switzerland. *ʔalmaanya maʒduuda mnij-jinuub b-iswiisra.*
boundless – *ma-la ʒadd.* He has boundless self-confidence. *θiqta b-nafsa ma-lha ʒadd.*
bounds – *ʒadd* pl. *ʒiduud.* His greed knows no bounds. *ṭamaεa ma-la ʒadd.*
out of bounds – **1.** *foog ʒadd.* The price he is asking is way out of bounds. *s-siεr il-da-yṭulba foog kull ʒadd.* **2.** *ʔaawt.* The ball went out of bounds. *ṭ-ṭooba ṭilεat aawt.*
within the bounds – *δ̣imin ʒiduud.* I don't care what you do so long as you stay within the bounds of decency. *ma-adiir baal iš-ma-tsawwi ṭuul-ma*

tibqa δimin ẓiduud in-nazaaha.
bouquet – *šadda* pl. *-aat, baaga* pl. *-aat.* Where did you get that beautiful bouquet of roses? *mneel-lak haš-šaddat il-warid il-ẓilwa?*
bow – **1.** *ṣadir* pl. *ṣduur.* I like to stand at the bow of the ship. *yiεjibni ʔoogaf ib-ṣadr il-markab.* **2.** *ẓanya* pl. *-aat.* He greeted me with a polite bow of the head. *ẓayyaani b-ẓanyat raas muʔaddaba.*
to bow – **1.** *nẓina (i).* He bowed and left the stage. *nẓina w-tirak il-masraẓ.* **2.** *ẓina (i ẓani) n-.* He bowed his head in shame. *ẓina raasa mnil-xajal.* **3.** *xiδaε (a xuδuuε).* He bowed to his father's wishes. *xiδaε il-raġbat abuu.*
bow – **1.** *qaws* pl. *ʔaqwaas, gooz* pl. *gwaaza.* Boys like to play with bows and arrows. *l-wilid yẓibbuun yliεbuun bil-gooz win-niššaab.* **2.** *qurdeela* pl. *-aat.* She had a pretty bow in her hair. *čaanat laabsa qurdeela ẓilwa b-šaεarha.* **3.** *qaws* pl. *ʔaqwaas.* The violinist is tightening the strings of his bow. *l-kamanjaati da-yδubb ixyuuṭ il-qaws maala.* **4.** *εawaaj* pl. *-aat.* This pole has a bow in it. Find me a straight one. *hal-εamuud bii εawaaj. ʔilqii-li waaẓid εadil.* **5.** *yadda* pl. *-aat.* Can you adjust the bows of my glasses? *tiqdar itεaddil-li yaddaat manδarti?*
bowl – *minčaasa* pl. *-aat, manaačiis, ṭaasa* pl. *-aat.* Put these apples into a bowl. *ẓuṭṭ hat-tiffaaẓaat ib-fadd minčaasa.*
to bowl over – *ṣiεaq (a) n-.* I was bowled over when I heard the news. *nṣiεaqit min simiεt il-xabar.*
bowlegged – (m) *ʔaεwaj* (f) *εooja* pl. *εuuj; mqawwas.* He's bowlegged. *rijla εooja* or *rijla mqawwsa.*
bow tie – *warda* pl. *-aat.* Teach me how to tie a bow tie. *εallimni šloon ašidd warda.*
box – **1.** *ṣanduug* pl. *ṣnaadiig, quuṭiyya* pl. *qwaaṭi.* Shall I put the shoes in a box? *ʔaẓuṭṭ il-qundira b-quuṭiyya?* -- I have another box of cigars. *εindi quuṭiyya lux ičruud.* -- Would you drop this letter in the box for me? *tigdar itδibb-li hal-maktuub ib-ṣanduug il-bariid?* **2.** *looj* pl. *-aat, lwaaj, maqṣuura* pl. *-aat.* All boxes are sold out for the play. *kull il-loojaat maal ir-ruwaaya mabyuuεa.*
to box – *laakam (i mulaakama), tlaakam (a talaakum).* Would you like to box? *tẓibb titlaakam?*
boxer – **1.** *mulaakim* pl. *-iin.* He has become a famous boxer. *ṣaar mulaakim šahiir.* **2.** *čalib* (pl. *člaab*) *booksar.* My brother brought back a boxer from England. *ʔaxuuya jaab wiyyaa čalib booksar min ʔingiltara.*
box office – *maẓall* (pl. *-aat*) *biṭaaqaat.* The box office is open from ten to four. *maẓall il-biṭaaqaat maftuuẓ imnil-εašra lil-ʔarbaεa.*
boy – **1.** *walad* pl. *wulid.* This boy is Ali's son. *hal-walad ibin εali.* **2.** *ṣaaniε* pl. *ṣinnaaε.* I'll have the boy deliver them. *raẓ-axalli ṣ-ṣaaniε yjiib-ilkum-iyyaahum.*
**Boy, what a night! *yaa yaaba šloon leela!*
boycott – *muqaaṭaεa* pl. *-aat.* The boycott was lifted. *nšaalat il-muqaaṭaεa.*
to boycott – *qaaṭaε (i muqaaṭaεa) t-.* We should boycott foreign products. *laazim inqaaṭiε il-maṣnuuεaat il-ʔajnabiyya.*
boy scout – *kaššaaf* pl. *kaššaafa.* They have asked the Boy Scouts to take part in the parade. *ṭilbaw imnil-kaššaafa yištarkuun bil-istiεraaδ.*
boy's school – *madrasa* (pl. *madaaris*) *maal wulid.* That's a boy's school. *haδiič madrasa maal wulid.*
brace – **1.** *mašadd* pl. *-aat.* He's still wearing a brace on his left leg. *huwwa baεda laabis mašadd εala rijla l-yisra.* **2.** *masnad* pl. *masaanid.* This chair needs four braces to hold it firm. *ʔhal-kursi yinraad-la ʔarbaε masaanid itlizma.* **3.** *mizraf* pl. *mazaaruf, bariina* pl. *baraayin.* Get a brace and bit and drill the holes in this board where I have marked. *jiib mizraf w-sawwi zruuf ib-hal-looẓa bil-makaanaat il-ʔaššaritha.*
to brace – *qawwa (i taqwiya).* Brace the corners with wooden cross-pieces. *qawwi z-zuwaaya b-xišbaat εurδaaniyya.*
to brace oneself – **1.** *tẓaδδar (a taẓaδδur).* Brace yourself, here they come. *tẓaδδar, tara ʔijaw.* **2.** *δabb (i δabb) n- nafs˜.* They both braced themselves against the door and didn't let anyone in. *θneenhum δabbaw nafishum wara l-baab w-ma-xallaw ʔaẓẓad yxušš.*
to brace oneself up – *našnaš (i) t-.* I need a shot to brace me up. *ʔariid-li fadd peek ẓatta ʔanašniš.*
**Brace up! *šidd ẓeelak!* or *tšajjaε!*
to be **braced** – *nsinad (i).* The wall will need to be braced in two places. *l-ẓaayiṭ yinraad-la yinsinid ib-mukaaneen.*
bracelet – *swaar* pl. *-aat.* I've lost my bracelet. *δayyaεt iswaari.*
bracket – **1.** *εikis* pl. *εkuus.* One of the brackets for the shelf has come loose. *waaẓid min iεkuus ir-rafj mašluuε.* **2.** *qaws* pl. *ʔaqwaas.* Put the foreign words in brackets. *ẓuṭṭ il-kalimaat il-ʔajnabiyya been qawseen.* **3.** *fiʔa* pl. *-aat.* My last raise put me in a higher income-tax bracket. *tarfiiεi l-ʔaxiir ẓaṭṭni b-fiʔa maal δariibt id-daxal ʔaεla.*
to **brag** – **1.** *tbajjaẓ (a tabajjuẓ).* Does he always brag that way? *huwwa daaʔiman yitbajjaẓ haš-šikil?* **2.** *tbaaha (a tabaahi).* Don't brag so much about your ancestors. *la-titbaaha hal-gadd ib-ʔajdaadak.*
braid – **1.** *gṣiiba* pl. *giṣaayib, δufiira* pl. *δufaayir.* I admire her thick braids. *ʔaani muεjab ib-giṣaayibha l-mitiina.* **2.** *šariiṭ* pl. *šaraayiṭ.* The doorman was wearing a uniform ornamented with gold braid. *l-bawwaab čaan laabis badla mzarkaša b-šaraayiṭ δahab.*
to braid – *δufar (u δafur) n-.* Her mother braids her hair for her. *ʔummha tuδfur-ilha šaεarha.*
brain – *muxx* pl. *mxaax, damaaġ* pl. *ʔadmiġa.* The bullet penetrated his brain. *r-riṣaaṣa xaššat ib-damaaġa.* -- He hasn't a brain in his head. *ma-εinda muxx* or *haaδa muxx sizz.*
to rack one's brain – *šaġġal (i tašġiil) fikr˜, dawwax (u tadwiix) raas˜.* There's no use racking your brains over it. *ma-ẓaaja tšaġġil fikrak ihwaaya biiha.*
to brain – *kisar (i kasir) n- raas.* If you do that again I'll brain you. *ʔaksir raasak ʔiδa tsawwiiha marra lux.*
brake – *breek* pl. *-aat.* The brake doesn't work. *l-ibreek ma-yištuġul.*
to put on the brakes – *lizam (a) breek.* I tried to put on the brakes, but I didn't make it. *ʔaani ẓaawalit ʔalzam ibreek laakin ma-laẓẓagit.*
branch – **1.** *ġuṣin* pl. *ġṣuun, ʔaġṣaan.* The wind broke off several branches. *l-hawa kisar čam ġuṣin.* **2.** *fariε* pl. *fruuε.* Our firm has a branch in Mosul. *šarikatna εidha fariε bil- mooṣil.* -- The bank has two branches in town. *l-bang εinda farεeen bil-wlaaya.*
to branch – *tfarraε (a tafarruε).* The road branches off here. *ṭ-ṭariiq yitfarraε ihnaa.*
brand – **1.** *maarka* pl. *-aat.* What brand of cigarettes do you smoke? *ʔay maarkat jigaayir ʔinta tdaxxin?* **2.** *nooε* pl. *ʔanwaaε, ṣinif* pl. *ʔaṣnaaf.* We carry all the best brands of tea. *εidna kull il-ʔaṣnaaf iz-zeena mnič-čaay.* **3.** *damġa* pl. *-aat, ṭamġa* pl. *-aat, waṣum* pl. *wṣaam.* We recognized our cattle from the brand mark. *εirafna baqarna mniṭ-ṭamġa.*
to brand – **1.** *wuṣam (i waṣum) n-.* He was branded as a traitor. *nwuṣam bij-jaasuusiyya.* **2.** *dumaġ (u damuġ) n-, tumaġ (u tumuġ) n-.* Have they finished branding the new horses yet? *xallṣaw ydamġuun l-iẓṣuuna j-jidiida loo baεad?*
brand-new – *bil-kaaġad.* It's still brand-new. *baεda bil-kaaġad.*
brandy – *braandi.*
brass – **1.** *prinj* (for castings). The mortar is cast from brass. *l-haawan maṣbuub min iprinj.* **2.** *ṣifir.* Some of our kitchen pans are of sheet brass. *qisim min ij-jiduur ib-muṭbaxna min ṣifir.* **3.** *δ-δubbaaṭ.* All the high brass were present. *kaaffat kibaar iδ-δubbaaṭ čaanaw ẓaaδriin.*
brassiere – *zixma* pl. *zixam.*
brat – *malεuun* pl. *malaaεiin.* He's a nasty brat. *haaδa fadd malεuun zafir.*
brave – *šujaaε* pl. *šujεaan.* The brave die but one death. *š-šujεaan ymuutuun moota wiẓda.*
bravery – *šajaaεa.*
brawl – *εarka* pl. *-aat.* Those two taxi-drivers started the brawl. *has-suwwaaq it-taaksi l-iθneen bidaw il-εarka.*
to brawl – *tεaarak (a εraak).* Those people were always brawling and disturbing the whole neighborhood. *haδoola čaanaw daaʔiman yitεaarkuun w-yizεijuun kull il-imẓalla.* -- That man and his wife are always brawling with each other. *har-rijjaal w-marta daaʔiman yitεaarkuun waaẓid wiyya l-laax.*
bread – **1.** *xubza* pl. *-aat* coll. *xubuz.* Our baker makes the best bread in town. *xabbaazna ysawwi ʔaẓsan xubuz bil-wlaaya.* **2.** (Flat rounds of bread) *gurṣa* pl. *guraṣ.* Give me six loaves of Arab flat bread. *nṭiini sitt guraṣ.* **3.** (Small raised loaves)

ṣammuuna pl. *-aat* coll. *ṣammuun.* May I have another half bread roll, please. *ʔarjuuk inṭiini nuṣṣ ṣammuuna ƐwaaƷa.* -- Divide the bread into four pieces. *qassim iṣ-ṣammuuna ʔila ʔarbaƐ wuṣal.* -- You had better buy three extra bread rolls for dinner tonight. *laazim tištiri tlaθ ṣammuunaat lil-Ɛaša hal-leela.*

breadth - *Ɛuruð, ttisaaƐ.*

break - **1.** *kasir* pl. *ksuur.* They are trying to find the break in the water main. *da-yẓaawluun yilguun il-kasir bil-ʔabbi.* **2.** *nqiṭaaƐ* pl. *-aat.* A break in relations between the two countries can no longer be avoided. *nqiṭaaƐ il-Ɛalaaqaat been il-baladeen la-budd minna.* **3.** *faṭir* pl. *fṭuur.* Germs enter the body through a break in the skin. *l-mikroobaat itxušš ib-jismak min faṭir bij-jilid.* **4.** *raaẓa* pl. *-aat.* Take a short break before you start the next job. *ʔuxuð-lak fadd raaẓa qṣayyra gabuḷ-ma tbaašir ib-waðiiftak ij-jidiida.* -- Whenever they want a break, give it to them. *kull-ma yriiduun raaẓa ʔinṭiihum-iyyaa.* **5.** *furṣa* pl. *furaṣ.* We have an hour break for lunch. *Ɛidna furṣa saaƐa wiẓda lil-ġada.* **6.** *ẓaðð.* He's had a lot of bad breaks in his life. *ṣaadafa hwaaya suuʔ ẓaðð ib-ẓayaata.*

**That's a tough break! *šloon ẓaðð naẓis!*

to give someone a break - **1.** *niṭa (i) furṣa.* Give me a break. *nṭiini furṣa.* **2.** *tsaahal (a) wiyya.* I'll give you a break this time but don't do it again. *hal-marra raẓ-atsaahal wiyyaak, laakin la-tsawwiiha baƐad.*

to break - **1.** *kisar (i kasir) n-.* I broke my leg. *ksarit rijli.* -- My watch is broken. *saaƐti maksuura.* -- The boys broke the window pane. *l-wilid kisraw j-jaama maal iš-šibbaač.* -- He won't break his word. *huwwa ma-yiksir čilimta.* **2.** *fuṣax (u faṣix) n-.* She broke her engagement. *hiyya fuṣxat xuṭbatha.* **3.** *niṭa (i).* We'll have to break the news to him gently. *laazim ninṭii l-xabar b-luṭuf.* **4.** *giṭaƐ (a gaṭiƐ) n-.* He broke the string on the package. *giṭaƐ xeeṭ ir-ruzma.* -- He broke a string on his violin. *giṭaƐ watar ib-kamanjta.* -- The wires are broken. *l-waayaraat magṭuuƐa.* **5.** *ngiṭaƐ (i ngiṭaaƐ).* The string broke. *l-xeeṭ ingiṭaƐ.* **6.** *xaalaf (i muxaalafa).* He has broken the law. *huwwa xaalaf il-qaanuun.* **7.** *jawwaz (i tajwiiz).* I'll break him of that habit. *raẓ-ajawwza min hal-Ɛaada.*

to break down - **1.** *xirab (a xaraab).* The machine broke down this morning. *l-makiina xurbat hal-yoom iṣ-ṣubuẓ.* **2.** *twaqqaf (a tawaqquf), tƐaṭṭal (a taƐaṭṭul).* The internal organization of the country broke down near the end of the war. *t-tanðiimaat id-daaxiliyya lil-mamlaka twaqqfat qurub nihaayt il-ẓarub.* **3.** *fiqad (u fuqdaan) ṣayṭara Ɛala Ɛawaaṭif~.* He broke down when he heard the news. *fiqad iṣ-ṣayṭara Ɛala Ɛawaaṭfa min simaƐ il-xabar.*

to break in - **1.** *darrab (u tadriib).* I'll have to break in another beginner. *ʔaani raẓ-aðṭarr adarrub waaẓid laax jidiid Ɛaš-šuġuḷ.* **2.** *nizal (i nuzuul) Ɛala, siṭa (i saṭu) n- Ɛala.* Last night thieves broke in our neighbor's house. *ẓaraamiyya nizlaw Ɛala beet ij-jiiraan il-baarẓa bil-leel.* **3.** *kisar (i kasir).* They lost the key and had to break in the door. *ðayyƐaw il-miftaaẓ w-iðṭarraw ykisruun il-baab.*

to break off - **1.** *giṭaƐ (a gaṭiƐ) n-.* They have broken off relations with our country. *giṭƐaw Ɛalaaqaathum wiyya dawlatna.* **2.** *nkisar (i nkisaar).* Then, the branch broke off. *t-taali, nkisar il-ġuṣin.*

to break oneself - *jaaz (u jooz).* I broke myself of that habit long ago. *jizit min hal-Ɛaada min zimaan.*

to break out - **1.** *nhizam (i haziima).* He broke out of prison. *nhizam imnis-sijin.* **2.** *ðihar (a ðuhuur).* The plague has broken out in the south. *marið iṭ-ṭaaƐuun ðihar bij-jinuub.* **3.** *nišab (i nušuub), bida (i btidaaʔ).* The fire broke out towards midnight. *nišab il-ẓariiq gabuḷ nuṣṣ il-leel b-išwayya.* **4.** (with measles) *ẓaṣṣab (u taẓṣiib).* My oldest boy broke out with measles this morning. *ʔibni č-čibiir ẓaṣṣab hal-yoom iṣ-ṣubuẓ.* **5.** (with small pox) *jaddar (i tajdiir).* If you have broken out with small pox when you were young, you won't do so again. *ʔiða jaddarit min činit jaahil, ma-raẓ-itjaddir baƐad.*

to break up - **1.** *farraq (i tafriiq, tfirriq), faðð (u faðð) n-.* The police broke up the demonstration. *š-šurṭa farriqaw il-muðaahara.* -- The party broke up early. *l-ẓafla faððat min wakit.* -- The police came and broke up the fight. *š-šurṭa ʔijaw w-faððaw il-Ɛarka.* **2.** *tfarraq (a).* We broke up about midnight. *tfarraqna ẓawaali nuṣṣ il-leel.* **3.** *nkisar (i nkisaar).* The cold spell is about to break up. *mawjat il-barid raẓ-tinkisir.*

**Break it up! *bass Ɛaad!* or *yeezi Ɛaad!* or *fuððuuha!*

breakdown - **1.** *Ɛaṭal, Ɛawaara, xalaal.* The breakdown happened about five miles outside of town. *l-Ɛaṭal ṣaar ẓawaali xams amyaal xaarij il-balad.* **2.** *ngiṭaaƐ* pl. *-aat, fašal.* We must avoid a breakdown in the negotiations at all costs. *laazim nitẓaaša fašal il-mufaawaðaat ib-ʔay θaman.*

nervous breakdown - *nhiyaar Ɛaṣabi.* She had a nervous breakdown. *ṣaar Ɛidha inhiyaar Ɛaṣabi.*

breakfast - *riyuug, fṭuur.* I always have an egg for breakfast. *ʔaani daaʔiman ʔaakul-li fadd beeða lir-riyuug.*

to give (someone his) breakfast - *rayyag (i).* His mother gave him his breakfast. *ʔumma rayyigata.*

to have breakfast - *trayyag (a), fuṭar (u fuṭuur).* Have you had your breakfast yet? *trayyagit loo baƐad?*

breast - *nahid* pl. *nhuud, dees* pl. *dyuus, ṣadir* pl. *ṣduur.*

breath - *nafas* pl. *ʔanfaas.* Hold your breath. *ʔigṭaƐ nafasak.*

to be out of breath - *nihag (a).* I'm completely out of breath. *da-anhag imnit-taƐab.*

to catch one's breath - *jarr (u) nafas, ʔaxað (u) nafas.* I have to catch my breath first. *xalli šwayya ʔajurr nafasi ʔawwal.*

to **breathe** - *tnaffas (a tanaffus).* He's breathing regularly. *da-yitnaffas b-intiðaam.*

**Don't breathe a word of this to anyone. *la-tṭalliƐ haay min ẓalqak.*

**He is breathing his last. *da-yƐaalij* or or *da-yilfuð ʔanfaasa.*

**I'll breathe again when I'm done with this job. *min ʔaxalliṣ haš-šaġla yinzaaẓ kaabuus Ɛan ṣadri.*

to **breed** - **1.** *waalad (i muwaalada).* My uncle breeds horses. *Ɛammi ywaalid il-xeel.* **2.** *twaalad (a tawaalud).* Rabbits breed faster than many animals. *l-ʔaraanib titwaalad ʔasraƐ min ihwaaya mnil-ẓaywaanaat.*

breeze - *nasmat* (pl. *-aat*) *hawa, hawa ṭayyib.* At night we got a cool breeze from the lake. *bil-leel habbat Ɛaleena nasma barda mnil-buẓeera.* -- There's not a breeze stirring. *ma-aku wa-laa nasmat hawa titẓarrak* or *l-hawa waaguf tamaaman.*

to **brew** - *xammar (u taxmiir, txummur) t-.* We brew our own beer. *ʔiẓna nxammur biiratna b-iidna.*

brewery - *maƐmal* (pl. *maƐaamil*) *biira.* Bavaria is known for its good breweries. *baavaarya mašhuura b-maƐaamil biiratha.*

bribe - *rašwa* pl. *-aat, rašaawi.* He was caught accepting a bribe. *nlizam da-yaaxuð rašwa.*

to bribe - *riša (i rašwa) n-.* You can't bribe him. *ma-tigdar tiršii.*

brick - *ṭaabuuga* pl. *-aat* coll. *ṭaabuug.* Their house is built of yellow brick. *beethum mabni b-ṭaabuug.*

mud brick - *libna* pl. *-aat* coll. *libin.* The farmer and his sons are making mud bricks. *l-fallaaẓ w-wilda da-ysawwuun libin.*

bricklayer - *banna* pl. *bnaani.* He's a bricklayer. *huwwa banna.*

bride - *Ɛaruus* pl. *Ɛaraayis.*

bridegroom - *Ɛaruus* pl. *Ɛirsaan.*

bridge - **1.** *jisir* pl. *jsuur.* There's a bridge across the river a mile from here. *Ɛala biƐid miil minnaa ʔaku jisir Ɛan-nahar.* -- The dentist is making a new bridge for me. *ṭabiib il-ʔasnaan da-ysawwii-li jisir jidiid.* **2.** *maẓall qiyaada, ġurfat* (pl. *ġuraf*) *qiyaada.* Can you see the captain on the bridge? *da-tšuuf ir-rubbaan waaguf ib-ġurfat il-qiyaada?* **3.** *brij.* Do you play bridge? *ʔinta tilƐab brij?*

**He burned his bridges behind him. *ma-xallaa-la xaṭṭ rajƐa.*

to bridge - *bina (i) jisir.* There is some talk of bridging the river at a point near our village. *ʔaku ẓači raẓ-yibnuun jisir Ɛaš-šaṭṭ yamm qaryatna.*

bridle - *risan* pl. *risin.*

brief - **1.** *qṣayyir, qaṣiir.* He paid me a brief visit before he left. *zaarni zyaara qṣiira gabuḷ-ma saafar.* **2.** *muxtaṣar.* His speech was brief and helpful. *xiṭaaba čaan muxtaṣar w-mufiid.*

in brief - *b-ixtiṣaar, muxtaṣar mufiid.* In brief, our plan is this. *muxtaṣar mufiid, haaða manhajna.*

to brief - *nawwar (u tanwiir), zawwad (i tazwiid) t-.* Our leader briefed us on every detail of the operation. *qaa?idna nawwarna ƹan kull tafaaṣiil il-ƹamaliyya.* -- Tuesday you will be briefed with the final information. *yoom iθ-θalaaθaa? raẓ-titzawwduun bil-maƹluumaat in-nihaa?iyya.*

to be brief - *xtiṣar (i xtiṣaar).* Please be brief. *xtiṣir, min faðlak.*

brief case - *junṭa* (pl. *-aat*) *maal kutub.*

briefing - *tawziid bil-maƹluumaat.* The briefing session lasted more than an hour. *jalsat it-tazwiid bil-maƹluumaat istamarrat ?akθar min saaƹa.*

bright - **1.** *wahhaaj.* I like a bright fire. *tiƹjibni n-naar il-wahhaaja.* **2.** *zaahi.* She likes to wear bright colors. *yiƹjibha tilbas ?alwaan zaahya.* **3.** *ðaki.* He's a bright boy. *huwwa walad ðaki.* **4.** *ẓaṣiif.* That was a bright idea. *haay čaanat fikra ẓaṣiifa.*

**She's always bright and cheerful. *ƹala ṭuul ƹaṣaafiirha ṭayra w-bašuuša.*

bright and early - *ġubša.* We're going to start out bright and early. *raẓ-niṭlaƹ min ġubša* or *raẓ-inġabbuš.*

brilliant - **1.** *ṣaarix.* You can tell his paintings by the brilliant colors. *tigdar tuƹruf irsuuma mnil-?alwaan ṣ-ṣaarxa lli yistaƹmilha.* **2.** *baariƹ.* He's a brilliant speaker. *huwwa fadd xaṭiib baariƹ.* **3.** *ðaki.* He's the most brilliant man I know. *huwwa ?aðka waaẓid ?aƹurfa.*

brim - **1.** *raas* pl. *ruus.* The glass is filled to the brim. *l-iglaaṣ matruus lir-raas.* **2.** *ẓaašya* pl. *ẓawaaši.* The brim of your hat will protect your face and neck from the sun. *ẓaašyat šafiqtak raẓ-tuẓfuð wiččak w-rugubtak imniš-šamis.*

to **bring** - *jaab (i jeeb) n-.* Bring me a glass of water. *jiib-li fadd iglaaṣ maay.* -- Won't you please bring me the other folder? *ma-tjiib-li l-malaffa l-lux, min faðlak?* -- He brought the children a present. *jaab fadd hadiyya lil-?aṭfaal.*

to bring about - *?antaj (i ?intaaj), sabbab (i tasbiib).* The depression brought about a change in living standards. *l-kasaad ?antaj tabaddul ib-mustawa l-ẓayaat.*

to bring along - *jaab (i) wiyya.* Bring your children along. *jiib il-jihhaal wiyyaak.*

to bring back - *rajjaƹ (i trijjiƹ, tarjiiƹ) t-.* Please bring the book back. *?arjuuk rajjiƹ l-iktaab.*

to bring down - *nazzal (i tnizzil, tanziil) t-.* I also brought down the big box. *hamm nazzalit iṣ-ṣanduug ič-čibiir.*

to bring in - **1.** *jaab (i).* The dance brought in a hundred dollars. *ẓaflat ir-rigiṣ jaabat miit doolaar.* **2.** *daxxal (i tadxiil), xaššaš (i taxšiiš).* Bring the boxes in the house. *xaššiš iṣ-ṣanaadiig bil-beet.*

to bring out - **1.** *ṭallaƹ (i taṭliiƹ).* Bring out the chairs and put them on the terrace. *ṭalliƹ il-karaasi w-ẓuṭṭhum biṭ-ṭarma.* -- They're bringing out a new edition of my book. *raẓ-yṭallƹuun ṭabƹa jdiida min iktaabi.* **2.** *ƹirað (i ƹarið) n-.* He brought out his point convincingly. *huwwa ƹirað ra?ya b-ṭariiqa muqniƹa.*

to bring to - *ṣaẓẓa (i taṣẓiya).* Cold water will bring him to. *l-maay l-baarid yṣaẓẓii.*

to bring to bear - *staƹmal (i stiƹmaal).* He brought all his influence to bear. *staƹmal kull nufuuða.*

to bring up - **1.** *rabba (i tarbiya).* Her aunt brought her up. *ƹammatha rabbatha.* **2.** *ṣaƹƹad (i taṣƹiid).* Bring up my coat when you come. *ṣaƹƹid sitirti min tiṣƹad.* **3.** *θaar (i ?iθaara).* I'll bring it up at the next meeting. *raẓ-aθiirha bij-jalsa j-jaaya.*

brisk - **There is a brisk wind blowing today. *l-hawa da-yilƹab il-yoom.*

briskly - *b-našaaṭ.* He walks very briskly for such an old man. *yimši kulliš ib-našaaṭ il-waaẓid šaayib miθla.*

bristle - *šaƹra* pl. *-aat* coll. *šaƹar.* The bristles of this brush are beginning to fall out. *šaƹar hal-firča bida yoogaƹ.*

British - *bariiṭaani** pl. *-iyyiin.*

brittle - *hašš.*

broad - *ƹariið.* He has broad shoulders. *čtaafa ƹariiða.*

**It happened in broad daylight. *ṣaarat ib-raabiƹt in-nahaar.*

**That's as broad as it's long. *kullha yak ẓasaab* or *mneem-ma tijiiha siwa.*

broadcast - *?iðaaƹa* pl. *-aat.* Did you listen to the broadcast? *smaƹt il-?iðaaƹa?*

to broadcast - **1.** *ðaaƹ (i ?iðaaƹa) n-.* They will broadcast directly from London. *raẓ-yðiiƹuun min landan ra?san.* -- If you tell her, she'll broadcast it all over the neighborhood. *?iða tgul-lha tara tðiiƹ-ilk-iyyaa b-kull il-maẓalla.* **2.** *nišar (u našir) n-.* I wouldn't broadcast it if I were you. *ma-anšurha, loo b-makaanak.*

broadcloth - *čoox* pl. *čwaax.* I bought a good piece of broadcloth today. *štireet qiṭƹa čoox zeena l-yoom.*

broad-minded - *ṣadra raẓib.* She's a very broad-minded person. *ṣadirha raẓib ihwaaya.*

brochure - *kurraasa* pl. *-aat.* There is a very interesting brochure on that subject. *?aku kurraasa mumtiƹa ƹan hal-mawðuuƹ.*

to **broil** - *šuwa (i šawi) n-.* Broil the chicken on a skewer. *?išwi d-dijaaja b-šiiš.*

broke - *miflis* pl. *mafaaliis.* I was broke at that time and couldn't afford to buy it. *činit miflis ðaak il-wakit w-ma-gdarit aštirii.*

to go broke - **1.** *filas (i ?iflaas), ?aflas (i).* Ali went broke again. *ƹali hamm ?aflas.* **2.** *nkisar (i).* The merchant is about to go broke. *it-taajir ƹala wašak yinkisir.*

broker - *dallaal* pl. *-iin.* If you want to sell your house quickly, get a broker. *?iða triid itbiiƹ beetak ib-saaƹ, šuuf-lak dallaal.*

customs broker - *mṭalliƹči* pl. *-iyya.* Can you find me a customs broker to take on this job? *tigdar tilgii-li mṭalliƹči yaaxuð haay ƹala ƹaatqa?*

bronchitis - *ltihaab il-qaṣabaat.* Your boy has a bad case of bronchitis. *?ibnak ƹinda ltihaab qaṣabaat šadiid.*

bronze - *brunz.*

brooch - *brooš* pl. *-aat.* I'd like to buy a nice brooch for my wife. *?ariid ?aštiri brooš ẓilu l-marti.*

brood - *fruux, fraariij.* The hen and her brood come when you call her. *d-dijaaja w-fruuxha yijuun min itṣiiẓha.*

to brood - **1.** *nġamm (a ġamm), nhamm (a hamm).* Don't brood about it; try and forget it. *la-tinġamm ƹala muud haaða, ẓaawil tinsaa.* **2.** *(čaan) maġmuum, (čaan) mahmuum.* What are you brooding about? *leeš maġmuum?* or *?inta leeš mahmuum?*

brooder - *makiinat* (pl. *makaayin*) *tafriix.* If I can find a small brooder I'm going to hatch my own chickens. *?iða ?algi makiinat tafriix iṣġayyra raẓ-afaggis dijaaji b-nafsi.*

brook - *majra* pl. *majaari, saagya* pl. *swaagi.* The brook dries up in the summer. *yjiff il-majra biṣ-ṣeef* or *s-saagya teebas biṣ-ṣeef.*

broom - **1.** *makinsa, muknaasa* pl. *makaanis.* Get the broom and sweep the floor. *jiib il-muknaasa w-iknus il-gaaƹ.*

broth - *maay laẓam.* Drink a little of this chicken broth; it will do you good. *?išrab išwayya min hal-mayy dijaaj, ynifƹak.*

brothel - *karxaana* pl. *-aat, kallačiyya* pl. *-aat.* The club turned out to be nothing but a brothel. *n-naadi ṭilaƹ bil-ẓaqiiqa karxaana.*

brother - *?ax* pl. *?uxwaan, ?uxwa.* Have you a brother? *ƹindak ?ax?* -- I bought it from Hasso Bros. *štireeta min ẓassu xwaan.*

brotherhood - *?uxuwwa.* His speech was all about brotherhood and pan-Arabism. *xiṭaaba kulla čaan ƹann il-?uxuwwa wil-ƹuruuba.*

brother-in-law - **1.** *nisiib* pl. *nisbaan, rajil uxut* pl. *riyaajiil xawaat.* **2.** (wife's sister's husband). *ƹadiil* pl. *ƹidlaan.*

brow - *guṣṣa* pl. *guṣaṣ.* He wiped the sweat off his brow. *misaẓ il-ƹarag min guṣṣta.*

brown - **1.** *bunni*, qahwaa?i*, ?asmar* pl. *sumur.* Her hair and eyes are brown. *loon šaƹarha w-iƹyuunha bunni.*

to brown - **1.** *ẓmarr (i).* Leave the meat in the oven until it browns. *xalli l-laẓam bil-firin ?ila ?an yiẓmarr.* **2.** *ẓimas (i ẓamis).* First brown the onions in a little fat. *?awwal ?iẓmis il-buṣal b-išwayya dihin.*

to **browse** - *tfarraj (a tafarruj).* I love to browse for books in a good book store. *yiƹjibni ?atfarraj ƹal-kutub ib-maktaba zeena.*

brucellosis - *l-ẓumma l-maalṭiyya.*

bruise - *raðða* pl. *-aat.* He had a bruise on his left foot. *čaan ƹinda raðða b-rijila l-yisra.*

to bruise - *raðð (u raðð) n-.* The boy bruised his

knee. *l-walad raδδ rukubta.*

brunette - *samra* pl. *sumur.*

brunt - *šidda.* The infantry bore the brunt of the attack. *šiddat il-hujuum wugaE Eal-mušaat.*

brush - *firča* pl. *firač, pirča* pl. *pirač.* You can use this brush for your shoes. *tigdar tistaEmil hal-firča l-qanaadrak.* -- Who left the brush in the paint? *minu tirak il-firča biṣ-ṣubuġ?*

to brush - *farrač (i tfirrič) t-, parrač (i tpirrič) t-.* I brush my hair every evening. *ʔaani ʔafarrič šaEri kull leela.* -- I have to brush my teeth. *laazim ʔafarrič isnuuni.*

to brush aside - *tjaahal (a tajaahul).* He brushed my protests aside. *tjaahal iʒtijaajaati.*

to brush up on - *raajaE (i muraajaEa).* I'm brushing up on German. *da-araajiE il-luġa l-ʔalmaaniyya.*

brush off - *dafEa.* She gave me the brush off. *nṭatni dafEa* or *ligat-li ʒijja.*

to brush off - *farrač (i tafriič) t-.* Brush off your overcoat. *farrič miEṭafak* or *farrič qappuuṭak.*

brutal - *waʒši*, faδδ* pl. *ʔafδaaδ, šaris* pl. *-iin.*

brute - *waʒiš* pl. *wuʒuuš, šaris* pl. *-iin.* He's a brute. *huwwa šaris.*

brute strength - *quwwat δiraaE.* We raised the car by brute strength. *ṭallaEna s-sayyaara b-quwwat iδraaEaatna.*

bubble - *buqbaaqa* pl. *-aat, buqaabiiq; fuqaaEa* pl. *-aat.* You can see the bubbles rise to the surface of the water. *tigdar itšuuf il-buqbaaqaat da-tiṭlaE foog il-maay.*

to bubble - *baqbaq (u baqbaqa).* The water is beginning to bubble. *l-maay bida ybaqbuq.*

to **buck** - *qaawam (u muqaawama).* We had to buck the current all the way. *δṭarreena nqaawum it-tayyaar ṭuul il-masaafa.*

bucket - *ṣaṭla* pl. *-aat, ṣṭuul.*

buckle - *bziim* pl. *-aat.* I lost the buckle of my leather belt. *δayyaEit l-ibziim maal iʒzaami.*

to buckle - **1.** *šadd (i šadd) n-.* I can't buckle the strap. *ma-ʔagdar ʔašidd is-seer.* -- I can't buckle my belt. *ma-agdar ašidd iʒzaami.* **2.** *ṭallaE (i) baṭin.* The wall buckled. *l-ʒaayiṭ ṭallaE baṭin.* **3.** *tEawwaj (a tEuwwuj).* The linoleum buckled from the heat. *l-imšammaE itEawwaj imnil-ʒarr.* **4.** *nEuwaj (i).* The beams buckled from the weight of roof. *š-šeelmaan inEuwaj min θugl is-saguf.*

**It's about time we buckled down to work. *ṣaar il-wakit ʒatta nšidd ʒeelna liš-šuġul* or *ṣaar il-wakit ʒatta nδibb nafisna Eaš-šuġul.*

bud - **1.** (flower) *jumbuda* pl. *janaabid* coll. *jumbud.* The cold killed all the buds. *l-barid kital kull ij-jumbud.* **2.** (new growth) *burEum* pl. *baraaEum.* In spring, buds appear on the trees, *bir-rabiiE il-baraaEum tiṭlaE bil-ʔašjaar.*

**The uprising was nipped in the bud. *l-Eiṣyaan inqiδa Ealee w-huwwa bil-mahad.*

to bud out - *ṭagṭag (i ṭagṭaga).* The new cuttings are budding out. *l-iqlaam ij-jidiida da-ṭṭagṭig.*

budding - *naaši?* pl. *-iin.* He's a budding author. *huwwa fadd muʔallif naaši?.*

to **budge** - *ʒaʒʒaʒ (i ʒaʒʒaʒa).* I couldn't budge it. *ma-gdarit ʔaʒaʒʒiʒha.*

budget - *miizaaniyya* pl. *-aat.* Our budget doesn't allow that. *miizaaniyyatna ma-titʒammal haδaak.* -- This is not in this year's budget. *haaδa ma-daaxil ib-miizaaniyyat has-sana.*

to budget - *waazan (i muwaazana) t-.* You'll have to budget your expenses with your salary. *ʔinta laazim itwaazin maṣrafak wiyya raaṭbak.*

to **buff** - *ṣiqal (u ṣaqil).* They buff the trays to give them a high polish. *yṣiqluun iṣ-ṣuwaani ʒatta tṣiir biiha lamEa.*

buffalo - (water buffalo) *jaamuus* pl. *jawaamiis.*

buffet - *buufya* pl. *-aat, buufee* pl. *-yaat.* The dishes are in the buffet. *l-imwaaEiin bil-buufya.*

bug - **1.** *ʒašara* pl. *-aat.* This spray is good for all kinds of bugs. *had-duwa mufiid δidd kull il-ʒašaraat.* **2.** *bagga* pl. *-aat* coll. *bagg.* The leaves were covered with bugs. *l-ʔawraaq čaanat imġaṭṭaaya bil-bagg.* **3.** *gaariṣ, bagg.* I couldn't sleep because of bed bugs. *ma-gdart anaam ib-sabab il-gaariṣ.* **4.** *barġaša* pl. *-aat* coll. *barġaš.* At night on the river the flying bugs give you a lot of trouble. *bil-leel yamm iš-šaṭṭ il-barġaš yδawwj il-waaʒid.*

bugle - *buuq* pl. *ʔabwaaq.*

to **build** - *bina (i binaaʔ) n-, Eammar (u taEmiir) t-.* Our neighbor is building a new house. *jaarna da-yibni beet jidiid.* -- The company is going to build houses for its employees. *š-šarika raʒ-itEammur ibyuut il-Eummaalha.*

to build in - *bina (i) bil-ʒaayiṭ.* I'm going to build in bookcases here. *raʒ-abni hnaa maktaba bil-ʒaayiṭ.*

to build on - *δaaf (i ʔiδaafa) n-.* We're going to build on a new wing to the hospital. *raʒ-inδiif janaaʒ jidiid lil-mustašfa.*

to build up - *namma (i tanmiya) t-, kabbar (u takbiir) t-.* He built up the business. *nammaa liš-šuġuļ* or *kabbar il-maṣlaʒa.*

building - *binaaya* pl. *-aat, Eimaara* pl. *-aat.* Both offices are in one building. *d-daaʔirteen ib-fadd binaaya.* -- They're going to build a ten story building on this piece of ground. *raʒ-yibnuun Eimaara biiha Eašir ṭawaabiq Eala hal-qiṭEat il-ʔarδ.*

bulb - **1.** *gloob* pl. *-aat.* This bulb is burnt out. *hal-igloob maʒruug.* **2.** *buṣla* pl. *-aat, ʔabṣaal,* coll. *buṣaļ.* I have some Dutch bulbs in my garden. *Eindi ʔabṣaal hoolandiyya b-ʒadiiqti.*

bulge - *ntifaax* pl. *-aat.* What's that bulge in your pocket? *šinu hal-intifaax ib-jeebak?*

to bulge - **1.** *ṭallaE (i) baṭin.* The wall is bulging dangerously. *l-ʒaayiṭ imṭalliE baṭin ib-ṣuura muxṭira.* **2.** *ntufax (u ntifaax).* Their stomachs were bulging with so much food. *baṭinhum intufxat imnil-ʔukil.*

bulging - *manfuux, waarum.* His briefcase was bulging with papers. *januṭṭa čaanat manfuuxa bil-ʔawraaq.*

bulk - **1.** *muEδam.* The bulk of my salary goes for rent and food. *muEδam maEaaši yruuʒ lil-ʔajar wil-ʔakil.* **2.** *bil-wazin, falla.* Buying bulk tea is cheaper than packaged tea. *širaaʔ ič-čaay bil-wazin ʔarxaṣ min čaay l-iqwaaṭi.*

in bulk - *bij-jumla.* We buy dates in the bulk and package them ourselves. *ništiri tamur bij-jumla w-inEallba b-nafisna.*

bulky - *čibiir* pl. *kbaar.* The sofa is too bulky to go through the door. *l-qanafa kulliš čibiira ma-tfuut imnil-baab.*

bull - *θoor* pl. *θiiraan.*

to **bulldoze (level)** - **1.** *siʒag (a saʒig).* First of all, we have to bulldoze all this rock and gravel level. *ʔawwalan laazim nisʒag haṣ-ṣaxar wil-ʒaṣu kulla.* **2.** *waxxar (i) bil-buldoozar.* Bulldoze them out of the way. *waxxirhum imniṭ-ṭariiq bil-buldoozar.*

bulldozer - *buldoozar* pl. *-aat.* The contractor is in the market for a new bulldozer. *l-qunṭarči da-yriid yištiri buldoozar jidiid.*

bullet - *riṣaaṣa* pl. *-aat* coll. *riṣaaṣ.* The bullet lodged in his shoulder. *r-riṣaaṣa staqarrat ib-čitfa.*

bully - *ʔašqiyaaʔ* pl. *-iyya.* He is the bully of the school. *huwwa ʔašqiyaaʔ il-madrasa.*

to bully - *baaE (i beeE) šaqaawa.* They are complaining about him bullying the smaller children. *da-yitšakkuun minna li-ʔan da-ybiiE šaqaawa Eaj-jihaal.*

bum - *mhatlaf* pl. *-iin, Eaaṭil* pl. *-iin.*

bump - **1.** *Einjurra* pl. *-aat, Eanaajiir.* Where did you get that bump on your head? *mneen jattak δiič il-Einjurra b-raasak?* **2.** *Eukra* pl. *Eukar, ṭaṣṣa* pl. *-aat.* The car went over a bump. *s-sayyaara ṭaṣṣat ib-Eukra.*

to bump (into) - **1.** *Eiθar (a Euθuur) n-.* He bumped into a chair in the dark. *Eiθar b-iskamli biδ-δalma.* **2.** *ṣaadaf (i muṣaadafa) t-.* Guess who I bumped into yesterday. *ʔiʒzir il-man ṣaadafit il-baarʒa.*

bumper - *daEEaamiyya* pl. *-aat.* He bent the bumper when he ran into me. *Euwaj id-daEEaamiyya lamma diEamni.*

bumpy - *(bii) ṭaṣṣaat.* We drove for about an hour over a bumpy road. *siqna ʒawaali saaEa b-darub kulla ṭaṣṣaat.*

bunch - *baaga* pl. *-aat, šadda* pl. *-aat, δabba* pl. *-aat.* Let me have a bunch of radishes, please. *balla nṭiini fadd baaga fijil.*

bundle - **1.** *rabṭa* pl. *-aat, buqča* pl. *buqač.* Is that bundle too heavy for you? *hal-buqča θagiila Ealeek?* **2.** *δabba* pl. *-aat.* I want two bundles of iron rods. *ʔariid δabbteen šiiš.* **3.** *šadda* pl. *-aat, laffa* pl. *-aat.* I gave him a bundle of newspapers. *nṭeeta šaddat jaraayid.*

to **bungle** - *laaṣ (u looṣ).* It was a delicate job and he bungled it. *čaanat fadd šaġla daqiiqa w-huwwa laaṣha.*

to **bunk (with)** - *baat (a).* If you don't have a place to sleep, you can bunk with us. *ʔiδa ma-Eindak makaan itnaam bii, tigdar itbaat Eidna.*

burden - **1.** *θugul.* I don't want to be a burden to you. *ma-ariid ʔaṣiir θugul ɛaleek.* **2.** *mašaqqa* pl. *-aat, taɛab.* Most of the burden of bringing up the children fell on the mother. *ʔakθar mašaqqat tarbiyat il-ʔaṭfaal wuqɛat ib-raas il-ʔumm.* **The burden of proof lies with the complaintant. *l-bayyina ɛal-muddaɛi* or *l-muddaɛi laazim yiθbit.*

to burden - *kallaf (i takliif) t-, ẓammal (i taẓmiil) t-.* I don't want to burden you with my troubles. *ʔaani ma-ariid ʔakallifak ib-masaakli.* -- She is burdened with a lot of responsibilities. *mẓammla masʔuuliyyaat ihwaaya.*

bureau - **1.** *diilaab* pl. *dawaaliib, kuntoor* pl. *kanaatiir.* The bottom drawer of the bureau is stuck. *l-imjarr ij-jawwaani maal diilaab l-ihduum ɛaaṣi.* **2.** *daaʔira* pl. *dawaaʔir.* Bureau of Vital Statistics. *daaʔirat il-ʔiẓṣaaʔ.*

burglar - *ẓaraami* pl. *-iyya, liṣṣ* pl. *liṣuuṣ.*

burglary - *booqa* pl. *-aat, sariqa* pl. *-aat, saṭu, ẓaadiθat saṭu.* When was the burglary committed? *šwakit ṣaarat il-booqa?*

burial - *dafin, dafna* pl. *-aat.*

burn - *ẓarig* pl. *ẓruug, čawya* pl. *-aat.* This is a serious burn. *haaδa ẓarig xaṭiir.*

to burn - **1.** *ẓirag (i ẓarig) n-.* Have the boy burn the papers. *xalli l-farraaš yiẓrig il-ʔawraaq.* **2.** *ẓtirag (i ẓtiraag), štiɛal (i štiɛaal).* This wood burns well. *hal-ẓaṭab yiẓtirig zeen.* **3.** *čuwa (i čawi) n-.* Don't touch the iron; it will burn your fingers. *la-ṭṭuxx il-uuti; tara yičwi ʔaṣaabɛak.* **4.** *čawwa (i tčuwwi) t.* The sand is so hot it burns the feet. *r-ramul hal-gadd ẓaarr yčawwi r-rijil.*

**I'm burning with curiosity. *ʔaani mayyit imnil-fuδuul.*

**He's burnt his bridges behind him. *giṭaɛ kull ʔamal lir-rajɛa* or *ma-xallaa-la xaṭṭ rajɛa.*

**He has money to burn. *ɛinda fluus miθil iz-zibil.*

**The building has burned down to the ground. *l-ibnaaya dammarha n-naar* or *n-naar sawwat l-ibnaaya qaaɛ ṣafṣaf.*

to get burned - *nčuwa (i).* I got burned on the iron. *nčuweet bil-ʔuuti.*

to burn oneself - *nčuwa (i).* I burned myself once already and I don't want to do it again. *nčuweet marra w-ma-ariid ančuwi marra lux.*

to burn out - *ẓtirag (i ẓtiraag).* This bulb burned out. *hal-igluub iẓtirag.*

to burn up - *ẓtirag (i ẓtiraag).* His books burned up in the fire. *kutba ẓtirgat bil-ẓariiq.*

to be burnt up - *tgarδam (a tgurδum).* He's burnt up because he can't come along. *da-yitgarδam li-ʔan ma-yigdar yiji wiyyaana.*

burning hot - *miθl in-naar.* The soup is burning hot. *š-šoorba miθl in-naar.*

burr - *šooka* pl. *-aat* coll. *šook.* The sheep's wool was filled with burrs. *l-ġanam ṣuufhum čaan malyaan šook.*

to **burst** - *nfijar (i nfijaar), ṭagg (u ṭagg) n-, nkisar (i nkisaar).* The water pipe burst. *buuri l-maay infijar.* -- She's bursting with curiosity. *raẓ-iṭṭugg imnil-fuδuul.* -- Last year the dam burst. *s-sana l-faatat inkisar is-sadd.*

to burst into - **1.** *čifat (i čafit) n- l-.* He burst into the room. *čifat lil-gubba.* **2.** *ṭagg (u ṭagg) n-.* She burst into tears. *ṭaggat idmuuɛha.* -- **3.** *gaam(u).* He burst into loud laughter. *gaam yqahqih.* -- She burst into crying. *gaamat tibči.*

to burst out - *ṭagg (u ṭagg) min.* The rice is bursting out through the seams of the bag. *t-timman ṭagg imnil-guuniyya.*

to **bury** - **1.** *difan (i dafin) n-.* We buried her yesterday. *difannaaha l-baarẓa.* **2.** *ṭumar (u ṭumur) n-.* He buried my application under the rest of the papers on purpose. *ṭumar ɛariiδti jawwa baaqi l-ʔawraaq ɛamdan.*

bus - *paaṣ* pl. *-aat.* Would you rather go by bus? *tfaδδil itruuẓ bil-paaṣ?* -- There's a bus every ten minutes. *yfuut paaṣ kull ɛašir daqaayiq.*

bush - **1.** *daġla* pl. *-aat* coll. *daġla.* He hid behind a bush. *xital wara d-daġla.* **2.** *zariɛ.* He is hiding in the bushes. *huwwa xaatil wara z-zariɛ.*

to beat around the bush - *laff (i) w-daar (u).* Don't keep on beating around the bush. *la-tδill itliff w-itduur.*

bushel - (no equivalent).

business - **1.** *tijaara* pl- *-aat.* They're selling their business. *da-ysaffuun tijaarathum.* **2.** *šuġuḷ.* Business is flourishing. *š-šuġuḷ maaši* or *s-suug zeen.* That's none of your business. *haaδa muu šuġlak* or **haaδa ma-yxuṣṣak* or **ʔinta maa lak daxal.* -- What business is he in? *šinu šuġḷa?* or *š-yištiġuḷ?* -- You have no business around here. *ʔinta maa ʔilak šuġuḷ ihnaa.* -- Mind your own business. *la-titdaaxal* or *ɛaleek ib-šuġlak.* **3.** *šaġla, masʔala, qaδiyya.* Let's settle this business right away. *xal-infuδδ haš-šaġla ẓaalan.* **4.** *šaʔin* pl. *šiʔuun.* Don't meddle in other people's business. *la-titdaaxal ib-šiʔuun ġeerak.*

**What business is it of yours. *ʔinta yaahu maaltak?*

**Business comes before pleasure. *j-jadd qabl il-liɛib.*

on business - *b-šuġuḷ* I have to see him on business. *laazim ʔašuufa b-šuġuḷ.*

to go into business for oneself - *štiġal (u) ɛala ẓsaab~.* They have gone into business for themselves. *gaamaw yištaġluun ɛala ẓsaabhum.* -- Going into business for oneself requires a lot of capital. *š-šuġuḷ ɛala ẓsaab il-waaẓid yinraad-la hwaaya raasmaal.*

businessman - *rajul* (pl. *rijaal*) *ʔaɛmaal.* He's a successful businessman. *huwwa fadd rajuḷ ʔaɛmaal naajiẓ.*

bust - **1.** *timθaal niṣfi* pl. *tamaaθiil niṣfiyya.* The sculptor is doing a bust of Ahmad. *n-naẓẓaat da-ysawwi timθaal niṣfi l-ʔaẓmad.* **2.** *ṣadir* pl. *ṣduur.* The blouse is a little too tight across the bust. *hal-ibluuz išwayya δayyig min yamm iṣ-ṣadir.*

busy - **1.** *mašġuuḷ* pl. *-iin.* I'm even too busy to read the paper. *ma-agdar ʔaqra j-jariida halgadd-ma mašġuuḷ.* -- We're very busy at the office. *bid-daaʔira ʔiẓna hwaaya mašġuuḷiin* or **ma-nigdar inẓukk raasna bid-daaʔira mniš-šuġuḷ.* -- The line's busy. *l-xaṭṭ mašġuuḷ.* **2.** *bii ẓaraka.* They live on a busy street. *ysiknuun ib-šaariɛ bii ẓaraka w-šuġuḷ.*

but - **1.** *bass, laakin.* We can go with you, but we'll have to come back early. *nigdar inruuẓ wiyyaak bass laazim nirjaɛ min wakit.* -- But you'll admit she's pretty. *bass ʔinta tiɛtirif hiyya ẓilwa.* -- But you know that I can't go. *laakin ʔinta tidri ʔaani ma-agdar ʔaruuẓ.* -- I didn't mean you but your friend. *ʔaani ma-ɛneetak inta laakin ɛineet ṣadiiqak.* **2.** *ġeer.* Nobody was there but me. *ma-čaan aku ʔaẓẓad ihnaak ġeeri.* **3.** *ʔilla.* All but one escaped. *l-kull xilṣaw ʔilla waaẓid.* -- Nothing but lies! *ma-aku ʔilla č-čiδib!* -- Now nothing but an operation can save him. *hassa ma-txaḷḷṣa ʔilla ɛamaliyya.*

**I was anything but pleased with it. *ʔaani wala raaδi bii ʔabadan.*

but then - *laakin ɛaad.* The suit is expensive, but then it fits well. *l-qaaṭ ġaali, laakin ɛaad tugɛud ɛalayya zeen.*

butcher - *gaṣṣaab* pl. *-iin, giṣaaṣiib.* I always buy the meat at the same butcher's. *ʔaani daaʔiman aštiri l-laẓam min nafs il-gaṣṣaab.*

butcher shop - *dukkaan gaṣṣaab* pl. *dukaakiin gaṣaaṣiib.*

butt - **1.** *miqbaδ* pl. *maqaabiδ.* Take the gun by the butt. *ʔilzam il-bunduqiyya mnil-miqbaδ.* **2.** *guṭuf* pl. *gṭuuf.* The ash tray is full of butts. *n-nuffaaδa matruusa gṭuuf.* **3.** *maδẓaka.* Doesn't he realize that he's the butt of their jokes? *haaδa ma-da-yẓiss huwwa ṣaayir maδẓaka maalhum?*

to butt - *niṭaẓ (a naṭiẓ) n-.* The goat kept butting his head against the fence. *ṣ-ṣaxla δallat tinṭaẓ bil-imẓajjar.*

to butt in - **1.** *tdaxxal (a tadaxxul).* This is none of your business, so don't butt in! *haaδa muu šuġḷak, fa-la titdaxxal.* **2.** *nabb (i nabb) n- ɛala.* Every time we talk, her little brother butts in with a question. *kull-ma nizči ynibb ʔaxuuha l-iṣġayyir ɛaleena b-fadd suʔaal.*

to butt together - **1.** *raawas (i muraawasa) t-.* Butt the two boards together. *raawis il-looẓteen.* **2.** *ṭubag (u ṭabug) n- suwa.* Butt the desks together this way. *ʔuṭbug il-meezaat suwa hiiči.*

butter - *zibid.* Let me have a pound of butter, please. *ntiini paawan zibid min faδlak.*

to butter - *ẓaṭṭ (u) zibid.* Shall I butter your bread? *triid aẓuṭṭ-lak zibid ɛal-xubuz?*

butterfly - *faraaša* pl. *-aat* coll. *faraaš.*

button - **1.** *dugma* pl. *digam.* She sewed the button on for me. *xayyṭat-li d-dugma.* **2.** *zirr* pl. *zraar.* You have to press the button. *laazim itduus iz-zirr.*

to button (up) - *daggam (u tduggum) t-.* Button up your overcoat. *daggum qappuuṭak.*

buttonhole - *beet dugma* pl. *byuut dugam, zuruf dugma* pl. *zruuf dugam.* This buttonhole needs fixing. *beet id-dugma haaδa yirraad-la taṣliiz.*
buy - *šarwa* pl. *-aat.* That's a good buy. *haaδi šarwa tiswa.*
to buy - *štira (i šira) n-.* What did you buy at Ali's shop? *š-ištireet min dukkaan Ɛali?*
to buy a ticket - *gaṣṣ (u) biṭaaqa, giṭaƐ (a) biṭaaqa, štira (i) biṭaaqa.* Buy me a ticket too. *ˀili hamm guṣṣ-li biṭaaqa.* -- Did you buy the theater tickets? *giṭaƐit il-biṭaaqaat lir-ruwaaya?*
to buy into - *štira (i) ˀashum b-.* I'm thinking of buying into that company. *da-ˀafakkir aštiri ˀashum ib-haš-šarika.*
to buy up - *lamm (i lamm) n-.* That monopolist bought up all the sugar in the market. *hal-muẓtakir lamm kull iš-šakar il-bis-suug.*
buzz - **1.** *ṭaniin.* The buzz of the mosquito kept me awake. *ṭaniin il-bagga ma-xallaani ˀanaam.* **2.** *wašwaša.* A buzz of voices filled the courtroom. *ṣaarat fadd wašwaša b-qaaƐat il-maẓkama.*
to buzz - *ṭanṭan (i ṭanṭana).* The bee buzzes. *n-naẓla tṭanṭin.*
buzzer - *jaraṣ* pl. *jraaṣ.* Push the buzzer. *dugg ij-jaraṣ.*
by - **1.** *qariib min.* The house stands close by the river. *l-beet mabni qariib min iš-šaṭṭ.* **2.** *yamm, b-jaanib.* He went by me without saying a word. *faat min yammi bala-ma yguul wala čilma.* **3.** *b-.* The club has been closed by order of the police. *nsadd in-naadi b-ˀamur imniš-šurṭa.* -- That horse won by a length. *δaak l-iẓṣaan ġilab b-ṭuul waaẓid.* -- We came by car. *jeena b-sayyaara.* — He'll be back by five o'clock. *raẓ-yirjaƐ bil-xamsa* or *raẓ-yirjaƐ saaƐa xamsa.* -- The table is four feet by six. *l-meez kubra ˀarbaƐa fuutaat ib-sitta.* **4.** *b-, Ɛala.* She can't work by artificial light. *ma-tigdar tištuġuḷ b-δuwa ṣṭinaaƐi.* **5.** *b-waasṭa, b-.* I'll send it to you by mail. *raẓ-adizz-lak-iyyaaha b-waasṭat il-bariid.*
**This book was written by a Frenchman. *haaδa l-iktaab il-waaẓid fransi.*
**Little by little he fought his way through the crowd. *šwayya šwayya šagg-la ṭariiq min been in-naas.*
**I got the story out of him word by word. *čilma čilma ṭallaƐit l-iẓčaaya min ẓalga.*
**That's done by machine. *haaδa šuġuḷ makiina.*
by and by - **1.** *bit-tadriij.* You'll get used to it by and by. *raẓ-titƐallam Ɛaleeha bit-tadriij.* **2.** *baƐd išwayya.* He told me he'd let me know by and by. *gal-li yinṭiini xabar baƐd išwayya.*
by and large - *Ɛal-Ɛumuum.* By and large, the results were satisfactory. *Ɛal-Ɛumuum, in-nataayij čaanat zeena.*
by far - *b-ihwaaya.* This is by far the best hotel in town. *haaδa ˀaẓsan ˀuuteel bil-wlaaya b-ihwaaya.*
by name - *bil-ˀisim.* I just know him by name. *ˀaani ˀaƐurfa bass bil-ˀisim.*
by oneself - *waẓẓad-, b-nafis-.* He did that by himself. *huwwa sawwaaha waẓẓda* or *sawwaaha b-nafsa.*
by sight - *biš-šikil.* I know him only by sight. *ˀaani ˀaƐurfa biš-šikil.*
by that - **1.** *min haaδa.* What do you understand by that? *š-tifhim min haaδa?* **2.** *b-haaδa.* What do you mean by that? *š-tiƐni b-haaδa?*
by the hour - *bis-saaƐa.* Do you know of a place where they rent boats by the hour? *tuƐruf makaan yˀajjiruun bii blaam bis-saaƐa?*
by the way - *bil-munaasaba.* By the way, I met a friend of yours yesterday. *bil-munaasaba, ṣaadafit waaẓid min ˀaṣdiqaaˀak il-baarẓa.*
by way of - *Ɛala ṭariiq.* Are you going to Europe by way of Beirut? *ˀinta raayiẓ il-ˀooruppa Ɛala ṭariiq beeruut?*
day by day - *yoom wara yoom, yoom Ɛala yoom.* Day by day his condition improves. *yoom wara yoom ẓaalta da-titẓassan.*
one by one - *waaẓid wara waaẓid, waaẓid wara l-laax, waaẓid waaẓid.* One by one they left the room. *waaẓid wara l-laax ṭilƐaw imnil-ġurfa.*
bylaw - *niδaam* pl. *ˀanδima.* The bylaws of the society are available from the secretary. *niδaam ij-jamƐiyya yitẓaṣṣal imnis-sikirteer.*

C

cab - *taksi* pl. *-iyyaat, sayyaarat* (pl. *-aat*) *ˀujra.*
cabbage - *lahaana.* Cabbage is hard to digest. *l-lahaana ṣaƐub tinhuδum.*
cabin - **1.** *kapra* pl. *-aat.* We have a cabin in the mountains. *Ɛidna kapra bij-jibal.* **2.** *qamaara* pl. *-aat, kabiina* pl. *-aat.* Would you please tell me which deck my cabin is on? *qul-li, min faδlak, ib-ˀay daraja l-qamaara maalti?*
cabinet - **1.** *diilaab* pl. *dwaaliib.* We keep our good dishes in a small cabinet. *nδumm immaaƐiinna z-zeena b-diilaab iṣġayyir.* **2.** *wazaara.* The cabinet met with the President of the Republic yesterday. *l-baarẓa jtimaƐ il-wazaara wiyya raˀiis ij-jamhuuriyya.*
cabinet maker - *ṣaaniƐ* (pl. *ṣunnaaƐ*) *moobiilyaat.*
cable - **1.** *silk* pl. *ˀaslaak.* The cables support the bridge. *l-ˀaslaak laazimta lij-jisir.* Can the cable be laid within ten days? *mumkin tinnuṣub il-ˀaslaak ib-xilaal Ɛaširt iyyaam?* **2.** *barqiyya* pl. *-aat.* I want to send a cable to New York. *ˀariid adizz barqiyya li-nyu yoork.*
to cable - *ˀabraq (i ˀibraaq).* Cable immediately when you arrive. *ˀibruq barqiyya ˀawwal-ma tooṣal.*
cadet - *tilmiiδ ẓarbi* pl. *talaamiiδ ẓarbiyyiin.*
cafe - *gahwa* pl. *gahaawi, maqha* pl. *maqaahi.*
cage - *qafaṣ* pl. *qfaaṣ.* The room is just like a cage. *l-ġurfa Ɛabaalak qafaṣ.*
cake - **1.** *keeka* pl. *-aat* coll. *keek.* I'd like cake with my coffee. *ˀariid keek wiyya gahuuti.* **2.** *qaalab* pl. *qwaalib.* Can you bring me a cake of soap and a towel? *tigdar itjiib-li fadd qaalab ṣaabuun w-xaawli?*
calamity - *nakba* pl. *-aat, kaariθa* pl. *kawaariθ, faajiƐa* pl. *fawaajiƐ.*
calcium - *kaalisyoom.*
to **calculate** - **1.** *ẓisab (i ẓisaab) n-.* It was difficult to calculate the costs. *čaan ṣaƐub il-waaẓid yiẓsib il-kulfa.* **2.** *qaddar (i taqdiir) t-.* Let's call in an expert to calculate the extent of the damage. *xalli njiib xabiir ẓatta yqaddir mada δ-δarar.*
calculated - *maẓsuub.* This is a calculated risk. *haaδi mujaazafa maẓsuub-ilha ẓsaab.*
calculating - *nafƐi*, maṣlaẓi*.* She's a shrewd calculating woman. *haay fadd mara daahya nafƐiyya.*
calculating machine - *ˀaalat* (pl. *-aat*) *ẓaasiba.*
calendar - **1.** *taqwiim* pl. *taqaawiim, ruznaama* pl. *-aat.* I've noted it on my calendar. *ˀaani ˀaššaritha bit-taqwiim maali.* **2.** *manhaj* pl. *manaahij, birnaamij* pl. *baraamij.* What events are on the calendar this month? *šaku faƐaaliyyaat bil-manhaj haš-šahar?*
calf - **1.** *Ɛijil* pl. *Ɛjuul.* Cows and calves were grazing in the field. *l-ihwaayiš wil-iƐjuul čaanaw da-yirƐuun bil-marƐa.* -- That bag is made of genuine calf. *haj-janṭa msawwaaya min jilid Ɛijil ˀaṣli.* **2.** *karša* pl. *-aat.* The bullet struck him in the calf of his leg. *r-riṣaaṣa ṣaabata b-karšat rijla.*
caliph - *xaliifa* pl. *xulafaaˀ.*
caliphate - *xilaafa* pl. *-aat.*
call - **1.** *nidaaˀ* pl. *-aat, muxaabara* pl. *-aat.* Were there any calls for me? *čaan ˀaku ˀili nidaaˀaat?* -- How much was the call? *šgadd kallaf in-nidaaˀ?* **2.** *daƐwa.* He was the first to answer the call to arms. *čaan ˀawwal man labba d-daƐwa lij-jihaad.*
**I thought I heard a call for help. *ˀaƐtiqid simaƐit waaẓid yistanjid.*
to call - **1.** *ṣaaẓ (i syaaẓ) n-, naada (i nidaaˀ).* I called him but he didn't hear me. *ṣiẓit Ɛalee laakin ma-simaƐni.* -- Shall I call you a cab? *ˀaṣiiẓ-lak taksi?* **2.** *xaabar (u muxaabara) t-.* You can call me any time at my office. *tigdar itxaaburni lid-daaˀira šwakit-ma triid.* **3.** *dazz (i dazz) n- Ɛala.* Call a doctor! *dizz Ɛala ṭabiib!* **4.** *samma (i tasmiya) t-.* What do you call this in Arabic? *š-itsammi haaδa bil-Ɛarabi?* -- Let's call him Ali. *xalli nsammii Ɛali.*
to call attention to - *jilab (i jalb) n- intibaah*

l-, nabbah (i tanbiih) t- εala. I called his attention to it. *jilabt intibaaha ʔilha* or *nabbahta εalee.*

to call down - *zaff (i zaff) n-.* My boss called me down for being late. *raʔissi zaffni li-ʔan ʔatʔaxxar.*

to call for - **1.** *marr (u muruur) n- εala, jaa (i majiiʔ) εala.* Will you call for me at the hotel? *tigdar itmurr εalayya bil-ʔuuteel?* **2.** *raaζ (u rooζ) εala.* I have to call for my laundry. *laazim ʔaruuζ εala hduumi εind il-makwi.* **3.** *stadεa (i stidεaaʔ), haaδi tistadεi ζtifaal.* **4.** *nraad (a) l-.* That calls for a drink. *haaδa yinraad-la ṗeek.* **5.** *ṭilab (u ṭalab) n-.* The president called for a vote on the matter. *r-raʔiis ṭilab it-taṣwiit εal-mawδuuε.* **6.** *qarrar (i taqriir) t-.* The director has called for a rehearsal for four o'clock. *l-muxrij qarrar ysawwi tamriin saaεa ʔarbaεa.* **7.** *εayyan (i taεyiin) t-.* He called the conference for Monday, the fourth. *εayyan wakt il-muʔtamar yoom iθ-θineen ʔarbaεa biš-šahar.*

to call in - *lamm (i lamm) n-.* All old notes are being called in. *kull il-ʔawraaq in-naqdiyya l-εatiiga da-tinlamm.*

**Call him in. *ʔuṭluba* or *dizz εalee* or *ṣiiζa.*

**We had to call in a specialist. *δṭarreena nistišiir ixtiṣaaṣi* or *čaan laazim nuṭlub raʔi xtiṣaaṣi.*

to call off - *ʔalğa (i ʔilğaaʔ) n-.* Today's broadcast was called off for technical reasons. *ʔiδaaεat il-yoom inliğat il-ʔasbaab fanniyya.*

to call on - **1.** *zaar (u zyaara) n-, jaa (i majiiʔ).* We'll call on you next Sunday. *raζ-inzuurak yoom il-ʔaζζad ij-jaay* or *raζ-nijiik yoom il-ʔaζζad ij-jaay.* -- Our agent will call on you tomorrow. *wakiilna raζ-yijiik baačir.* **2.** *stanjad (i stinjaad).* You can call on me for help in case of necessity. *tigdar tistanjid biyya εind iδ-δuruura.*

to call out - **1.** *ṭilab (u ṭalab) n-.* They had to call out the firemen to put out the fire. *δṭarraw yṭulbuun il-ʔiṭfaaʔiyya ζatta yṭaffuun in-naar.* **2.** *naada (i nidaaʔ) t-.* The demonstrators began to call out his name with enthusiasm. *l-mutaδaahriin qaamaw ynaaduun ʔisma b-ζamaas.* **3.** *εilan (i ʔiεlaan) n-.* The conductor calls out all the stops. *j-jaabi yiεlin ʔisim kull il-maζaṭṭaat.* **4.** *ṣaaζ (i ṣiyaaζ) n-.* They stopped in front of the door and called out my name. *wugfaw giddaam il-baab w-ṣaaζaw ʔismi.*

to call together - *lamm (i lamm) n- siwa, jimaε (a jamiε) n-.* He called all of us together in his office. *lammna kullna siwa b-ğurufta.*

to call (up) - **1.** *xaabar (u muxaabara).* I'll call you up tomorrow. *ʔaani raζ-axaabrak baačir.* **2.** *diεa (i daεwa) n-.* I heard they are calling up year group 1944 for duty. *simaεit raζ-yidεuun mawaaliid ʔalf w-tisiε miyya w-ʔarbaεa w-ʔarbaεiin il-xidmat il-εalam.*

caller - **1.** *zaaʔir* pl. *zuwwaar, xuṭṭaar* pl. *xṭaaṭiir.* I'm expecting a gentleman caller this afternoon. *da-antiδir fadd rijjaal xuṭṭaar il-yoom il-εaṣir.* **2.** *muraajiε* pl. *-iin.* Did I have any callers while I was out of the office? *ʔijooni muraajiεiin lil-maktab min činit ṭaaliε?*

calling card - *kaart šaxṣi* pl.*-aat šaxṣiyya, biṭaaqa* pl. *-aat.*

callus - *bismaar* pl. *bsaamiir.* I got calluses on my hand from digging. *ṭilaε-li bismaar ib-ʔiidi mnil-ζafur.*

calm - **1.** *saakin, haadiʔ.* The sea is calm again. *l-baζar saakin marra lux.* **2.** *haadiʔ.* He remained calm and in control of the situation. *biqa haadiʔ w-imṣayṭir εal-waδiε.*

to keep calm - *ζtifaδ (u ζtifaaδ) b-huduuʔ~.* Keep calm, everybody. *ζtafδu b-huduuʔkum kullkum.*

to calm - *hadda (i tahdiʔa) t-, barrad (i tabriid) t-.* We tried to calm the frighten animals. *ζaawalna nhaddi l-ζaywaanaat ij-jaafla.*

to calm down - **1.** *haffat (i tahfiit) t-.* Try to calm him down. *ζaawul ithaffta.* **2.** *hifat (i hafit), hidaʔ (a huduuʔ) n-.* It took her some time to calm down. *nraad-ilha mudda ζatta tihfit.* -- The wind has calmed down. *l-hawa hifat* or *l-hawa wugaf* or *hidaʔ il-hawa.*

to calm oneself - *ṭawwal (i taṭwiil) baal~, sakkan (i taskiin) ruuζ~, barrad (i) nafis~, hadda (i) nafis~, hidaʔ (a huduuʔ).* Calm yourself! *ṭawwul baalak!* or *ʔihdaʔ!*

calmly - *b-huduuʔ, b-buruud.* She took the news calmly. *ʔaxδat il-xabar ib-huduuʔ.*

camel - *jimal* pl. *jimaal, biεiir* pl. *biεraan.*

camel dung - *baεra* pl. *-aat* coll. *baεar, baεruura* pl. *-aat* coll. *baεruur.*

camel litter - *hawdaj* pl. *hawaadij.*

camera - *kaamira* pl. *-aat, makiinat* (pl. *makaayin*) *rasim.*

camouflage - *tamwiih.*

to **camouflage** - *mawwah (i tamwiih) t-.*

camp - **1.** *muεaskar* pl. *-aat.* At what camp did you get your training? *b-yaa muεaskar itdarrabit?* **2.** *muxayyam* pl. *-aat.* The boy scout camp is going to be in the north. *l-kaššaafa raζ-ykuun muxayyamhum biš-šimaal.*

to camp - **1.** *xayyam (i taxyiim).* We camped in the woods. *xayyamna bil-ğaabaat.* **2.** *εaskar (i tεiskir).* The division camped a mile outside the city. *l-firqa εaskirat εala buεud miil imnil-wlaaya.*

campaign - *ζamla* pl. *-aat.* He took part in the African campaign. *štirak bil-ζamla l-ʔafriiqiyya.* His election campaign lasted three months. *l-ζamla l-intixaabiyya maalta ṭawwilat iθlatt išhur.*

to campaign - *qaam (u) b-ζamla.* He campaigned to get himself elected to the presidency. *qaam ib-ζamla l-ğarδ intixaaba lir-riyaasa.*

camphor - *kaafuur.*

can - *quuṭiyya* pl. *qwaaṭi, εilba* pl. *εilab.* Give me a can of green peas. *nṭiini quuṭiyya bazaalya xaδra.*

can - **1.** *gidar (a maqdira) n-, tmakkan (a tamakkun), ʔamkan (i ʔimkaan), staṭaaε (i stiṭaaεa).* Can you speak English? *tigdar tiζči ngiliizi?* or *b-ʔimkaanak tiζči ngiliizi?* -- Could I look at it, please. *ʔagdar ʔašuufha min faδlak?* -- She could be wrong. *yimkin ğalṭaana.* -- Can't that be simplified? *ma-yimkin tabṣiiṭ haaδa?* -- Can't you delay this a few hours. *ma-mumkin itεaṭṭil haaδa čam saaεa.* -- He did everything he could. *sawwa kull-ma čaan b-imkaana.* -- He could have come. *čaan ib-ʔimkaana yiji.* -- If you can bring me the book tomorrow, I'll appreciate it. *ʔiδa titmakkan itjiib-li l-iktaab baačir iṣ-ṣubζ ʔakuun mamnuun.* **2.** *yjuuz.* He could have said that. *yjuuz gaala l-haaδa.*

**I can't say yet whether I'll run for election or not. *l-hassa ma-aεruf baεad ʔiδa raζ-atqaddam lil-intixaab loo laa.*

to can - *εallab (i taεliib) t-.* This factory is set up to process and can all kinds of vegetables. *hal-maεmal munšaʔ il-tahyiʔat w-taεliib anwaaε il-muxaδδaraat.*

canal - **1.** *qanaal* pl. *-aat, qanaat* pl. *ʔaqniya, qanawaat.* We came by way of the Suez Canal. *jeena εala ṭariiq qanaal is-suweez.* **2.** *saagya* pl. *swaagi, saajya* pl. *swaaji, turεa* pl. *turaε.* We'll have to dig a canal here to drain the land. *laazim nuζfur saajya hnaa l-bazl il-ʔaruδ.*

canary - *kanaari* pl. *-iyya.*

to **cancel** - **1.** *ʔalğa (i ʔilğaaʔ) n-, baṭṭal (i tabṭiil, tbuṭṭil) t-.* They have cancelled the order. *ʔalğaw l-ʔamur.* -- I'd like to cancel my newspaper subscription. *ʔaζibb alği štiraaki bij-jariida.* -- I had to cancel my doctor's appointment. *δṭarreet alği mawεidi wiyya ṭ-ṭabiib.* -- The meeting was canceled. *l-ijtimaaε inliğa.* **2.** *ṣaqqaṭ (i taṣqiiṭ) t-.* He cancelled the rest of my debt. *ṣaqqaṭ il-baaqi min deena εalayya.* -- These postage stamps are canceled. *haṭ-ṭawaabiε il-bariidiyya mṣaqqaṭa.*

cancer - *saraṭaan.* They discovered too late that he had cancer. *ligaw εinda saraṭaan baεad-ma faat il-wakit.*

candid - *ṣariiζ.*

candidacy - *taršiiζ.*

candidate - *muraššaζ* pl. *-iin.* Our party isn't putting up a candidate. *ζizibna ma-raζ-yraššiζ muraššaζ.* -- We have three candidates for the position. *εidna tlaθ muraššaζiin lil-waδiifa.*

candle - *šamεa* pl. *šmuuε.* We had to light a candle. *δṭarreena nišεil šamεa.*

candlestick - *šamiεdaan* pl. *-aat.*

candy - *šakraaya* pl. *-aat* coll. *šakaraat.*

chocolate candy - *čukleetaaya* pl. *-aat* coll. *čukleet.*

to candy - *šakkar (i taskiir) t-.* He brought us a box of candied fruits. *jaab-inna quuṭiyya fawaakih imšakkira.*

cane - **1.** *guṣba* pl. *-aat* coll. *guṣab.* The marsh dwellers build their houses of cane. *sukkaan il-ahwaar yibnuun ibyuuthum min guṣab.* **2.** *εuučiyya*

pl̄. -aat, Ɛawaači. Ever since I broke my leg I have
been walking with a cane. min wakit-ma nkisrat rijli
gimit amši Ɛal-Ɛuučiyya. 3. baaṣṭoon pl. -aat.
He only carries the cane for show. huwwa šaayil
il-baaṣṭoon lil-kašxa bass. 4. Ɛaṣa pl. Ɛiṣi.
The blind man feels his way with the cane. l-ʔaƐmi
yitʓassas ṭariiqa bil-Ɛaṣa.

canned goods – muƐallabaat. Canned goods can be kept
a long time. muƐallabaat il-ʔaṭƐima tinʓufuð mudda
ṭawiila.

cannibal – ʔaakil (pl. ʔakilat) laʓam il-bašar.

cannon – madfaƐ pl. madaafiƐ, ṭoob pl. ṭwaab.

can opener – fattaaʓa pl. -aat.

cantaloupe – baṭṭiixa pl. -aat coll. baṭṭiix.

canteen – 1. maṭṭaara pl. -aat. Did you fill your
canteen? trast il-maṭṭaara maaltak? 2. kaantiin
pl. -aat. The soldiers are waiting for the canteen
to open. j-junuud yintaðruun il-kaantiin yfattiʓ.

canvas – 1. čunfaaṣ, junfaaṣ. My gym shoes are made
of canvas. qundart il-riyaaða maalti msawwaaya min
čunfaaṣ. 2. kittaan pl. -aat. This picture is
painted on canvas. haṣ-ṣuura marsuuma Ɛala kittaan.

to canvass – 1. marr (u muruur) n- Ɛala. They asked
me to canvass the whole group to get their opinions.
ṭilbaw minni ʔamurr Ɛala kull ij-jamaaƐa w-astaṭliƐ
ʔaraaʔhum. 2. jass (i jass) nabuð. Before we
change anything, let's canvass the group. gabuḷ-ma
nǧayyir šii, xalli njiss nabð ij-jamaaƐa.

cap – 1. Ɛaraqčiin pl. -aat, klaaw pl. -aat. He's
wearing a small cap under his head cloth. laabis
Ɛaraqčiin jawwa ǧuṭurta. 2. raas pl. ruus. I've
lost the cap to my fountain pen. ðayyaƐit ir-raas
maal qalam il-ʓibir maali. 3. ǧuṭa pl. ǧuṭaayaat,
qabaǧ pl. -aat. Put the cap back on the bottle.
rajjiƐ qabaǧ il-buṭil ib-makaana. 4. talbiisa pl.
-aat. The cap is cutting my gums. t-talbiisa
da-tijraʓ laθθti. 5. kaaṗ pl. -aat. The jockey's
cap fell off during the race. wugaƐ il-kaaṗ maal
il-jaaki ʔaθnaaʔ is-sibaaq.

   to cap – 1. labbas (i talbiis) t-. This tooth
needs capping. has-sinn yinraad-la talbiis.
2. qabbaǧ (i tqubbuǧ, taqbiiǧ) t-. They cap the
bottles with metal caps. yqabbuǧuun l-ibṭuula
b-qabaǧaat maƐdan.

capability – maqdira.

capable – miqtidir, qaadir. She's a very capable
person. hiyya fadd waʓda kulliš miqtadra. — He's
capable of anything. huwwa qaadir Ɛala kullši or
**yiṭlaƐ min ʔiida kullši.

capacity – 1. siƐa pl. -aat. The tank has a capacity
of one hundred gallons. siƐat it-taanki miit gaḷin.
2. sifa pl. -aat. I am here in my capacity as
guardian. ʔaani hnaa b-ṣifati waṣi. 3. ṭaaqa pl.
-aat. It is already working up to full capacity.
min hassa da-tištuǧul kull ṭaaqatha.
   **The tank is full to capacity. t-taanki malyaan
lir-raas or t-taanki matruus il-ʔamaana.

cape – raas pl. ruus. The Cape of Good Hope. raas
ir-rijaaʔ is-ṣaaliʓ.

capital – 1. Ɛaaṣima pl. Ɛawaaṣim. Have you ever
been in the capital? b-Ɛumrak raayiʓ lil-Ɛaaṣima?
2. raasmaal. How much capital do you need to start
your business? šgadd tiʓtaaj raasmaal ʓatta tibdi
šuǧḷak? 3. maal pl. ʔamwaal. His capital is
invested abroad. ʔamwaala mustaθmara bil-xaarij.
4. ʓaruf čibiir pl. ʓuruuf čibiira. When you write
English, begin every sentence with a capital. min
tiktib bil-ingiliizi ʔibdi kull jumla b-ʓaruf iččbiir.
5. ṣarmaaya pl. -aat. Ahmed is going to provide me
with a capital of ID 1,000 to open a shop. ʔaʓmad
raʓ-yinṭiini ṣarmaaya ʔalif diinaar afattiʓ biiha
dukkaan.

capitalist – raʔismaali pl. -iyyiin.

capitalism – raʔismaaliyya.

capitalistic – raʔismaali*.

to capitalize – staǧall (i stiǧlaal). We are planning
to capitalize on the situation. b-niyyatna nistiǧill
il-waðiƐ.

capital offense – jinaaya pl. -aat.

capital punishment – Ɛuquubat il-ʔiƐdaam.

capon – diič maxṣi pl. dyuuč maxṣiyya.

capricious – hawaaʔi*, sweeƐati*.
   **She is capricious. saaƐaatha muu suwa.

capsule – ʓillaaja pl. -aat coll. ʓillaaj, gullaaja pl.
-aat coll. gullaaj, kabsuula pl. -aat coll. kabsuul.

captain – qabṭaan pl. -iyya, raʔiis pl. ruʔasaaʔ. The
captain was the last to leave the sinking ship.
l-qabṭaan čaan ʔaaxir man tirak is-sifiina l-ǧargaana.
— The captain was taken prisoner with his entire

company. r-raʔiis itʔassar, huwwa wil-fawj maala
kulla. — Who's the captain of the team? minu
raʔiis il-fariiq?

to captivate – ʔisar (yiʔsar ʔasir) n-. She captivated
us all with her charm and good looks. ʔisratna
kullna b-fitnatha w-jamaalha.

captive – 1. ʔasiir pl. ʔasra. The captives are
arriving from the front in large numbers. l-ʔasra
da-yooṣluun imnij-jabha b-ʔaƐdaad čibiira. — The
captive tiger hasn't eaten for two days. n-nimr
il-ʔasiir ṣaar-la yoomeen ma-ʔakal. 2. rahiina
pl. rahaayin. He was held captive by the band until
his family paid the ransom. buqa rahiina Ɛind
il-Ɛiṣaaba ʔila ʔan Ɛaaʔilta difƐaw il-xaawa.
3. masʓuur pl. -iin. He held his audience captive
with his tales of adventure. tirak is-saamƐiin
masʓuuriin ib-qiṣaṣ muǧaamaraata.

captivity – ʔasir.

to capture – 1. ʔassar (i tʔissir, taʔsiir) t-. They
captured a general and his entire staff. ʔassraw
janaraaḷ w-kull ʔarkaan ʓarba. 2. stawla
(i stiilaa?). Our armies have captured two cities.
jeešna stawla Ɛala madinteen. 3. ʔaxað (u ʔaxið)
n-. We captured the town without a shot being fired.
ʔaxaðna l-madiina bila ʔiṭlaaq naar.

car – 1. sayyaara pl. -aat. Would you like to ride in
my car? yƐijbak tirkab ib-sayyaarti? 2. faargoon
pl. -aat, faraagiin. Two cars went off the track.
faargooneen ṭilƐat imnis-sičča.

carafe – saraaʓi, saraaʓiyya pl. -aat. Get the carafe
of water out of the refrigerator. jiib saraaʓi
l-maay imniθ-θillaaja.

carat – qiiraaṭ pl. -aat, qaraariiṭ; ʓabba pl. -aat.
These earrings are made of eighteen carat gold.
hat-taraači ðahabha θmunṭaƐaš qiiraaṭ.

caravan – karwaan pl. karaawiin, qaafila pl. qawaafil.

caravansary – xaan pl. -aat.

carbon – kaarboon.

carbon paper – waraq (pl. ʔawraaq) karboon. I need
some new carbon paper. ʔaʓtaaj šwayya waraq
kaarboon ijdiid.

carburetor – kaabreeta pl. -aat.

card – 1. waraqa pl. ʔawraaq coll. waraq. They played
cards all evening. liƐbaw waraq ṭuul il-leel.
2. biṭaaqa pl. -aat. They have a fine selection of
greeting cards in that shop. Ɛidhum majmuuƐa
badiiƐa min biṭaaqaat tahaani b-ðaak il-maxʓan. —
He sent me a card from Beirut. ʔarsal-li biṭaaqa
min beeruut. 3. kaart pl. -aat. He left me his
card with his telephone number. tirak-li kaarta
maƐa raqam talafoona.
   **He's quite a card! huwwa fadd nimra xaaṣṣa!
   to card – 1. mišaṭ (i mašiṭ) n. The women spent
the whole day carding the wool. n-nisaaʔ giðaw kull
in-nahaar ymišṭuun iṣ-ṣuuf. 2. nidaf (i nadif) n-.
The cotton in this mattress needs carding. l-guṭin
maal haaða l-ifraaš yinraad-la nadif.

cardboard – mqawwaaya pl. -aat coll. mqawwa. Put a
piece of cardboard in between. ʓuṭṭ fadd imqawwaaya
bin-nuṣṣ. — Put them in a cardboard box. ʓuṭṭhum
ib-ṣanduug imqawwa.

cardomom – heel. Don't put too much cardomom in the
tea. la-tʓuṭṭ heel ihwaaya bič-čaay.

care – 1. mdaaraa. Regular care of the teeth is
important. mdaaraat l-isnuun b-intiðaam muhimm
jiddan. 2. Ɛinaaya. He's under the doctor's care.
huwwa taʓat Ɛinaayat iṭ-ṭabiib. 3. ʔamaana. May
I leave these documents in your care. ʔagdar axalli
hal-mustanadaat ib-ʔamaantak?
   in care of – b-waaṣṭaṭ, Ɛala Ɛinwaan. Send me the
letter care of Ahmed Husayn. dizz-li l-maktuub
Ɛala Ɛinwaan aʓmad iʓseen.
   to take care – 1. htamm (a htimaam). I took care
to mention everything. htammeet ʔaðkur kullši.
2. tʓaaša (a taʓaaši). I took care not to mention
anything. tʓaašeet aðkur ʔay sii.
   to take care of – 1. daar (i deer) n- baal~. The
maids work is to take care of the children.
l-xaadma šuǧulha deer baalha Ɛaj-jihhaal. — Take
care of my money for me. diir baalak Ɛala fluusi.
2. sawwa (i taswiya) t-, xallaṣ (i taxliiṣ) t-.
I still have a few things to take care of. ʔaani
baƐad Ɛindi baƐð il-ʔašyaaʔ laaʓim asawwiiha.
3. Ɛtina (i Ɛtinaaʔ) b-, ʓaafað (i muʓaafaða) t-.
He takes care of his clothes. yiƐtini b-ihduuma.
   **That takes care of that. xilsaṭ wis-salaam or
hal-muškila nʓallat or haaða ntiha ʔamra or šii
ysidd šii.
   **Good-by; take care of yourself. fiimaanilla,

ʔaḷḷa wyaak! or *fiimaanillaa, ʔamaant aḷḷa εala nafsak!*

to care - 1. *maal (i meel) l-.* I don't care much for movies. *ma-amiil ihwaaya lis-siinama.* **2.** *daar (i deer) n- baal.* Who cares? *minu ydiir baal?*

**What do I care? *w-aani š-aεlayya?*

**I don't care what he thinks. *ma-yhimmni huwwa š-yiftikir.*

**For all I care, you can go wherever you like. *wala yhimmni, tigdar itruuζ ween-ma yεijbak.*

**I don't care to go to the movies tonight. *ma-yiεjibni ʔaruuζ lis-siinama hal-leela.*

to care for - 1. *εtina (i εtinaaʔ) b-, tiεab (a taεab, taεbaan) εala.* This garden is well cared for. *hal-ζadiiqa miεtiniin biiha hwaaya* or *hal-ζadiiqa taεbaaniin εaleeha hwaaya.* **2.** *daar (i deer) n- baal˜, daara (i mudaaraa).* My sister is caring for the children today. *ʔuxti da-tdiir baalha εal-ʔaṭfaal hal-yoom.* **3.** *ζabb (i ζubb).* Do you care for her? *tζibbha?*

**Would you care for gravy on the meat? *yεijbak marag εala l-laζam?*

to be cared for - *čaan matεuub εala, ndaar (a) baal εala.* The children are well cared for. *l-ʔaṭfaal ihwaaya matεuub εaleehum.*

career - 1. *mihna* pl. *mihan.* Her career is more important for her than her marriage. *mihnatha ʔahamm-ilha mniz-zawaaj.* -- He made medicine his career. *ttixaδ iṭ-ṭibb mihna ʔila.* **2.** *siira* pl. *siyar.* I have been following his career with great interest. *da-atεaqqab siirta b-ihtimaam šadiid.* **3.** *maslak* pl. *masaalik.* He spent his life in this career. *qiḍa εumra b-hal-maslak.* **4.** *maslaki*.* He is a career diplomat. *huwwa dabloomaasi maslaki.*

carefree - *εadam mubaalaat.* He leads a carefree life. *yεiiš εiišat εadam mubaalaat.*

careful - 1. *daqiiq.* He's a very careful person. *huwwa šaxiṣ kulliš daqiiq.* **2.** *ζaδir, mitζaδδir.* He is very careful about how he invests his money. *huwwa kulliš ζaδir b-istiθmaar ifluusa.*

to be careful - 1. *daar (i deer) n- baal˜.* Be careful not to break this vase. *diir baalak la-truuζ tiksir hal-mazhariyya.* **2.** *čaan ζariiṣ.* I was careful not to mention anything. *kunit ζariiṣ la-ajiib δikir fadd šii.*

carefully - 1. *b-εinaaya.* They lifted the stretcher carefully. *šaalaw is-sadya b-εinaaya.* **2.** *b-diqqa.* Check the figures carefully. *ʔifζaṣ il-ʔarqaam ib-diqqa.* **3.** *b-ζaδar.* He drives carefully. *ysuug is-sayyaara b-ζaδar.*

careless - *muhmil.* She's become careless lately. *ṣaayra muhmil bil-ʔayyaam il-ʔaxiira.*

**He's careless with his money. *ma-ydiir baala εala fluusa.*

cargo - *ζumuula* pl. *-aat, šaζna* pl. *-aat.*

carnation - *qranfila* pl. *-aat* coll. *qranfil.*

carpenter - *najjaar* pl. *-iin, najaajiir.*

carpet - *zuuliyya* pl. *zwaali, sijjaada* pl. *sijjaad.* This is a nice carpet. *haz-zuuliyya ζilwa* or *haaδi xoos sijjaada.*

to have someone on the carpet - *razzal (i razaala) t-, wabbax (i tawbiix) t-.* The boss had him on the carpet again this morning. *l-mudiir razzala l-yoom iṣ-ṣubuζ marra lux.*

to carpet - *furaš (u fariš) n- b-sijjaad, ġaṭṭa (i taġṭiya) t- b-sijjaad.* All the stairs were carpeted. *kull id-darjaat čaanat mafruuša b-sijjaad.*

carrot - *jizra* pl. *-aat* coll. *jizar.*

to **carry - 1.** *šaal (i šeel) n-.* He'll carry your bags for you. *huwwa raζ-yšiil-lak ij-junaṭ.* **2.** *ζimal (i ζamil) n-.* This truck carries five tons. *hal-loori yiζmil xamis aṭnaan.* **3.** *baaε (i beeε) n-.* Do you carry men's shirts? *tbiiε iθyaab maal iryaajiil?* **4.** *niqal (u naqil) n-.* Mosquitoes carry malaria. *l-bagg yinqul il-malaarya.* **5.** *faaz (u fooz) n-.* He carried the election with an overwhelming majority, *faaz bil-intixaabaat ib-ʔakθariyya saaζiqa.* **6.** *niṭa (i naṭi) bid-deen.* The grocer agreed to carry us until I get another job. *l-baggaal waafag yinṭiina bid-deen ζatta algi šuġul.* 7. *qibal (a qubuul) n-.* The motion was carried. *l-iqtiraaζ inqibal.*

**This crime carries the death penalty. *haaδi l-jariima εaleeha εuquubt il-ʔiεdaam.*

**The captain carries himself well. *r-raʔiis šamurta ζilwa.*

**Isn't that carrying things a little too far? *muu θixnat εaad?*

to carry away - 1. *jiraf (u jaruf) n-.* The flood carried the house away. *l-fayaḍaan jiraf il-beet.* **2.** *ṭirab (u ṭarab) n-.* The music carried me away. *l-moosiiqa ṭirbatni.* **3.** *hazz (i hazz) n- εawaaṭif, siζar (a saζir) n-.* The crowd was carried away by the eloquence of the speaker. *j-jamhuur inhazzat εawaaṭfa b-faṣaaζat il-xaṭiib.* **4.** *ʔaxaδ (u ʔaxiδ) n-.* He was carried away by the idea. *nʔixaδ bil-fikra.*

to carry on - *waaṣal (i muwaaṣala) t-.* His son carries on his business. *ʔibna da-ywaaṣil tijaarta.*

to carry out - 1. *naffaδ (i tanfiiδ) t-.* We'll try to carry out your plan. *raζ-inζaawil innaffiδ il-xiṭṭa maaltak.* **2.** *ṭallaε (i taṭliiε, ṭṭilliε) t-.* Carry out the garbage. *ṭalliε iz-zibil barra.*

to carry weight - *(čaan) ʔila wazin, (čaan) ʔila ʔahammiyya.* His opinion carries great weight. *raʔya ʔila wazin čibiir.*

cart - *εarabaana* pl. *εarabaayin.* The cart was so loaded that he could hardly push it. *l-εarabaana čaanat mašζuuna ʔila daraja ʔan čaan bil-kaad yidfaεha.*

to cart - *ζimal (i ζamil) n-.* The sand has to be carted away. *r-ramul laazim yinζimil minnaa.*

cartridge - 1. *fišga* pl. *fišag, ṭalqa* pl. *-aat.* Three shots remained in the revolver. *buqat bil-musaddas itlaθ ṭalqaat.* **2.** *ʔigna* pl. *-aat.* I want to change the cartridge on my recordplayer. *ʔariid abaddil il-ʔigna maal foonooġraafi.*

to **carve - 1.** *niqaš (u naqiš) n-.* This is the man who carved the teak doors of the mosque. *haaδa r-rajil ʔilli niqaš ʔabwaab iṣ-ṣaaj maal il-masjid.* **2.** *niζat (a naζit) n-.* The Assyrians used to carve winged bulls from stone. *l-ʔaašuuriyyiin iεtaadaw yinζatuun θiiraan imjannaζa mniṣ-ṣaxar.* **3.** *gaṣgaṣ (i tigiṣgiṣ) t-.* Will you carve the turkey? *tζibb itgaṣgiṣ il-εališiiš?* **4.** *ζufar (u ζafur) n-.* He carved his name on the trunk of the tree. *ζufar ʔisma εala jiδε iš-šajara.*

case - 1. *ṣanduug* pl. *ṣnaadiig.* Leave the bottles in the case. *xalli l-ibṭuula biṣ-ṣanduug.* **2.** *beet* pl. *byuut, quuṭiyya* pl. *qwaaṭi.* I need a new case for my glasses. *ʔaζtaaj beet jidiid lil-manaaḍir maalti.* **3.** *ʔiṣaaba* pl. *-aat.* There were five new cases of malaria. *čaan aku xamis ʔiṣaabaat jidiida bil-malaarya.* **4.** *qaḍiyya* pl. *qḍaaya, ζaadiθ* pl. *ζwaadiθ.* I read about the case in the newspaper. *qreet εan il-qaḍiyya bij-jariida.* -- He presented his case well. *εiraḍ qaḍiita εariḍ zeen.* **5.** *daεwa* pl. *-aat, daεaawi.* He's lost his case. *huwwa xiṣar daεuuta.* **6.** *ζaala* pl. *-aat.* That being the case... *ṭaal-ma l-ζaala hiiči...*

**The doctor is out on a case. *ṭ-ṭabiib raaζ yšuuf mariiḍ.*

in any case - *εala kull ζaal, mahma kaan.* I'll call in any case. *ʔaani ʔaxaabur εala kull ζaal.*

in case - *ʔiδa.* Wait for me in case I'm late. *stanḍirni ʔiδa tʔaxxarit.*

in case of - *b-ζaalat.* In case of fire, use the emergency exit. *staεmil baab iṭ-ṭawaari b-ζaalat il-ζariiq.*

cash - 1. *naqid.* I have no cash with me. *ma-εindi naqid wiyyaaya* or *ma-šaayil ifluus.* **2.** *naqdi*, naqdan.* I'll pay cash. *raζ-adfaε naqdi.* -- We sell only for cash. *ʔiζna ma-nbiiε ġeer naqdi* or *nbiiε bass bin-naqdi.*

to cash - *ṣarraf (u taṣriif) t-.* Can you cash a check for me? *tigdar itṣarruf-li čakk?*

cashier - *ṣarraaf* pl. *-iin, ṣraariif, ʔamiin* (pl. *ʔumanaaʔ*) *ṣanduuq.*

cashmere - *kašmiir.* I bought my sister a cashmere sweater. *štireet il-ʔuxti bluuz kašmiir.*

casket - *taabuut* pl. *twaabiit.* Six of his best friends carried his casket. *sitta min ʔaζsan ʔaṣdiqaaʔa šaalaw taabuuta.*

cast - 1. *majmuuεa* pl. *-aat, hayʔa* pl. *-aat.* The new play has an excellent cast of actors. *t-tamθiiliyya j-jidiida biiha xooš majmuuεat mumaθθiliin.* **2.** *qaalab* pl. *qwaalib.* How long will you have to wear the cast? *šgadd laazim tilbas il-qaalab?*

to cast - 1. *ṣabb (u ṣabb) n-.* The statue will be cast in bronze. *t-timθaal raζ-yinṣabb min ibrunz.* **2.** *niṭa (i naṭi).* I cast my vote for the majority party nominee. *nṭeet ṣooti l-muraššaζ ζizb il-ʔakθariyya.*

**The die is cast. *quḍiya l-ʔamr.*

to cast anchor - *risa (i rasu) n-, δabb (i δabb) n- ʔangar.* We cast anchor at dawn. *δabbeena ʔangar wiyya l-fajir.* -- The ship cast anchor. *l-baaxira* *risat.*

castle - *qalɛa* pl. *qilaaɛ.* Have you seen the old castle? *šift il-qalɛa l-qadiima?* -- I'm taking the pawn with the castle. *raẓ-aktul ij-jundi bil-qalɛa.*

castor oil - *dihn il-xirwiɛ.*

casual - *ɛaabir, ṭaari?, ṣaṭẓi*, ɛaraḍi*.* It was nothing more than a casual remark. *ma-čaanat ?azyad min mulaaẓaḍa ɛaabira.* -- He's only a casual acquaintance. *?aɛurfa bass maɛrifa ṣaṭẓiyya.*

to be casual about - *ma-htamm (a) b-, ma-?axaḍ (u) iɛtibaar l-.* I wish I could be as casual about it as he is. *yaa reet agdar aṣiir miθla w-ma-aaxuḍ lil-mawḍuuɛ ihwaaya ɛtibaar.*

casually - **1.** *ɛaraḍan, ṣidfatan.* He said it to me quite casually. *gaal-li-yyaaha ɛaraḍan.* **2.** *ṣaṭẓiyyan, b-ṣuura ṣaṭẓiyya.* I only know him casually. *?aɛurfa b-ṣuura ṣaṭẓiyya.*

casualties - *?iṣaabaat, xasaa?ir.* Our casualties in Africa were small. *xasaa?irna b-?afriiqya čaanat qaliila.*

cat - **1.** *bazzuun* pl. *bzaaziin, hirr* pl. *hruura.* Our cat had kittens yesterday. *bazzuunatna jaabat ifruux il-baarẓa.* **2.** *qiṭṭ* pl. *qiṭaṭ.* When the cat's away, the mice will play. *ġaab il-qiṭṭ, ?ilɛab yaa faar.*

catalogue - *kataloog* pl. *-aat.* The sample clothes patterns in this catalogue are better. *namaaḍij tafṣiil il-malaabis ib-hal-kataloog ?aẓsan.* -- Why don't you arrange your (card) catalogue alphabetically? *leeš ma-trattbuun il-kataloog ẓasab il-ẓuruuf il-?abjadiyya?*

catastrophe - *kaariθa* pl. *kawaariθ, nakba* pl. *-aat.*

catch - **1.** *zuqfaala* pl. *-aat, quful* pl. *qfaala.* The catch on the camera is broken. *z-zuqfaala maal il-kaameera maksuura.* **2.** *ṣeeda* pl. *-aat.* Ten fish is a good catch. *ɛašir simčaat xooš ṣeeda.* -- That girl is a good catch. *hal-ibnayya xooš ṣeeda.* **3.** *ẓiila* pl. *ẓiyal, liɛba* pl. *laɛab.* There must be a catch to it. *laazim biiha liɛba.*

to catch - **1.** *ṣaad (i ṣeed) n-.* We caught a lot of fish. *ṣidna simič ihwaaya.* **2.** *ligaf (u laguf) n-.* Here, catch it! *yaḷḷa, ?ilgufha!* **3.** *laẓẓag (i talẓiig) t- b-.* I have to catch a train at five o'clock. *laazim alaẓẓig ib-qiṭaar is-saaɛa xamsa.* **4.** *lizam (a lazim) n-.* I caught him at it. *?aani lzamta biiha.* -- They caught him red-handed. *lizmoo mitlabbis bij-jariima.* -- They caught him before he could get over the border. *lizmoo gabuḷ-ma yigdar yuɛbur il-ẓiduud.* **5.** *qibaḍ (u qabuḍ) n- ɛala, kumaš (u kamuš) n-.* The police caught the thief. *š-šurṭa qibḍaw ɛala l-ẓaraami.* **6.** *?axaḍ (u ?axiḍ) n-.* The lock doesn't catch well. *l-qifil ma-da-yaaxuḍ zeen.* **7.** *simaɛ (a samiɛ) n-.* I didn't catch his name. *ma-smaɛit ?isma zeen.* **8.** *šakkal (i taškiil) t-.* My coat caught on a nail. *sitirti šakklat ib-fadd bismaar.* **9.** *ẓiṣar (i ẓaṣir) n-.* I've caught my finger in the door. *?iṣibɛi nẓiṣar bil-baab.*

to catch cold - *nnišal (i), ?axaḍ (u ?axiḍ) barid.* You'll catch cold. *?inta raẓ-tinnišil.*

to catch fire - **1.** *štiɛal (i stiɛaal), ẓtirag (i ẓirag).* The wood is so dry that it will catch fire quickly. *l-xišab halgadd-ma yaabis yištiɛil ib-saaɛ.* **2.** *ɛtilag (i).* The wood didn't catch fire. *l-ẓaṭab ma-ɛtilag.*

to catch hold - *lizam (a lazim) n-.* Catch hold of the other end. *?ilzam min ṣafẓat il-lux.*

to catch on - **1.** *diraj (u darij).* That song caught on very quickly. *hal-?uġniya dirjat bil-ɛajal.* **2.** *ligaf (u laguf) n-, ftiham (i ftihaam).* He catches on quickly. *yilgufha bil-ɛajal.* -- She immediately caught on to the idea. *hiyya bil-ɛajal iftihmatha lil-fikra.*

to catch the eye - *lifat (i lafit) n- naḍar, jilab (i jalib) n- naḍar.* The neckties in the window caught my eye. *l-?arbiṭa biš-šibbaač liftat naḍari.*

to catch the measles - *ẓaṣṣab (u tẓiṣṣib) t-, ?axaḍ (u ?axiḍ) n- il-ẓaṣba, nṣaab (a) bil-ẓaṣba.* I caught the measles from him. *?axaḍit il-ẓaṣba minna.*

to catch up - **1.** *laẓẓag (i tliẓẓig).* Try to catch up in your work. *ẓaawil itlaẓẓig ib-šuġļak.* -- Go ahead, I'll catch up with you. *ruuẓ, ɛuud ?aani alaẓẓig biik.* **2.** *ɛawwaḍ (i taɛwiiḍ) t-.* I have to catch up on my sleep. *laazim aɛawwiḍ ɛan noomi.*

catching - *muɛdi.* Measles are catching. *l-ẓaṣba muɛdiya.*

caterpillar - *duudat* (pl. *-aat* coll. *duud) qazz.*

cathedral - *kaatidraa?iyya* pl. *-aat.*

cattle - *mawaaši, hawaayiš, baqar.* They raise fine cattle in this part of the country. *yrabbuun xooš mawaaši b-hal-qisim imnil-balad.*

to get **caught** - **1.** *wugaf (a waguf, wuguuf).* A fish bone got caught in his throat. *ɛaḍmat simač wugfat ib-lahaata.* **2.** *nlizam (i lazim).* I got caught in a shower on the way home. *nlizamit ib-maṭra b-ṭariiqi lil-beet.* -- Don't get caught! *la-txalli nafsak tillizim* or *la-txalli nafsak tinkumuš.*

cauliflower - *qarnaabiiṭ.*

cause - *sabab* pl. *?asbaab, ġaaya* pl. *-aat.* What is the cause of the delay? *šinu sabab it-ta?xiir?* -- He died for a good cause. *huwwa maat ib-sabiil ġaaya šariifa.*

to cause - *sabbab (i tasbiib) t-.* What caused the accident? *š-sabbab il-ẓaadiθ?* -- He causes her a lot of grief. *huwwa ysabbib-ilha hwaaya qahar.*

caution - *ẓaḍar, taẓḍiir, ẓtiyaaṭ, ẓtiraas.* Caution in this work is just as important as speed. *l-ẓaḍar ib-haaḍa š-šuġuḷ muhimm miθil ?ahammiyyat is-surɛa.*

cautious - *mitẓaḍḍir, miẓtiris, mintibih.* He's very cautious. *huwwa kulliš mitẓaḍḍir.*

cave - *kahaf* pl. *khuuf, maġaara* pl. *-aat, maġaayir.* We hid in a cave. *?iẓna xtalna b-fadd kahaf.*

to cave in - *ṭubag (u ṭabug).* I'm afraid the house is going to cave in. *da-axaaf il-beet raẓ-yiṭbug.*

cavity - *ẓafur* pl. *ẓfuur.* I have a cavity in this tooth. *ɛindi ẓafur ib-has-sinn.*

to **cease** - **1.** *kaff (u kaff) n-.* The company has decided to cease publication of its monthly magazine. *š-šarika qarrirat itkuff ɛan našir majallatha š-šahriyya.*

cease-fire - *waqf iṭlaaq in-naar.* A cease-fire is expected before midnight. *waqf iṭlaaq in-naar muntaḍar gabuḷ nuṣṣ il-leel.*

cedar - *?arza* pl. *-aat* coll. *?ariz.*

ceiling - **1.** *saguf* pl. *sguuf.* The ceiling is painted white. *s-saguf maṣbuuġ ib-?abyaḍ.* **2.** *ẓadd ?aqṣa.* We shouldn't exceed the ceiling the government has set. *laazim ma-nitjaawaz il-ẓadd il-?aqṣa ?illi ɛayynata l-ẓukuuma.*

to **celebrate** - *ẓtifal (i ẓtifaal).* We're celebrating his birthday tomorrow. *raẓ-niẓtifil ib-ɛiid miilaada baačir.*

celebration - *ẓtifaal* pl. *-aat.* The celebration took place yesterday. *l-iẓtifaal ṣaar il-baarẓa.*

cell - **1.** *zinzaana* pl. *-aat.* Take the prisoner to his cell. *waddi l-maẓbuus il-zinzaanta.* **2.** *xaliyya* pl. *xalaaya, ẓjayra* pl. *-aat.* We were able to observe the structure of the cells under the microscope. *tmakkanna nšuuf tarkiib il-xalaaya taẓt il-mijhar.* **3.** *xaliyya* pl. *xalaaya.* The cell is the basic unit in the organization of the party. *l-xaliyya hiyya l-wuẓda l-?asaasiyya l-munaḍḍamat il-ẓizib.*

cellar - *sirdaab* pl. *saraadiib.*

cement - *simint, čbintu, čmintu.* Put more sand than cement in the mixture next time. *ẓuṭṭ ramuḷ ?azyad imnis-simant bil-xabṭa marra lux.*

to cement - *ṣabb (u ṣabb) n- b-ičbintu, bina (i binaa?) n- b-ičbintu.* Are you going to cement the basement floor or leave it dirt? *raẓ-itṣubb qaaɛ is-sirdaab bil-čibintu loo txalliiha traab?* -- Are you going to cement it? *raẓ-tibniih ib-čibintu?*

cemetery - *maqbara* pl. *maqaabur.*

censor - *raqiib* pl. *ruqabaa?.*

to censor - *raaqab (i muraaqaba, riqaaba) t-.* During the state of emergency the government will censor all letters leaving the country. *b-ẓaalat iṭ-ṭawaari? il-ẓukuuma raẓ-itraaqib kull il-makaatiib il-mursala xaarij il-bilaad.*

censorship - *muraaqaba, riqaaba.* The censorship has been lifted. *nrufiɛat ir-riqaaba.*

census - *?iẓṣaa?.*

cent - **1.** *sant* pl. *-aat.* There are a hundred cents in a dollar. *d-doolaar bii miit sant.* **2.** *filis* pl. *fluus.* I haven't a cent in change. *ma-ɛindi wala filis xurda.* -- He doesn't have a cent. *ma-ɛinda filis* or *huwwa miflis.* -- I wouldn't give a cent for it. *ma-aštiriiha b-filis.*

**I'm almost down to my last cent. *?aani taqriiban iflasit.*

**Do you have to put in your two cents worth? *šinu hal-laġwa l-faarġa?* or *yaɛni laazim itḍibbha l-had-durra?*

center - **1.** *nuṣṣ* pl. *nṣaaṣ, wasaṭ* pl. *?awsaaṭ.* The table is standing in the center of the room. *l-meez manṣuub ib-nuṣṣ il-ġurfa.* -- He lives in the center of the town. *yiskun ib-nuṣṣ il-wlaaya.* **2.** *markaz* pl. *maraakiz.* She's the center of attention. *hiyya markaz ihtimaam il-kull.*

to center - *rakkaz (i tarkiiz, trikkiz) t-.* Center the slide under the lens. *rakkiz is-slaayd taɀt il-ƹadasa.* -- All his thoughts were centered on her. *kull afkaara čaanat mitrakkza ƹaleeha.*

centigrade - *miʔawi*.* The temperature today is 20° centigrade. *l-ɀaraara l-yoom ƹišriin miʔawiyya.*

centimeter - *saantiimatir* pl. *-aat.*

centrally - *waṣaṭi*, markazi*, bil-waṣaṭ.* The hotel is centrally located. *l-ʔuuteel ṣaayir ib-maɀall waṣaṭi.*

century - *qirin* pl. *quruun.*

ceremony - *ɀtifaal* pl. *-aat.* The ceremony will take place in the Embassy. *l-iɀtifaal raɀ-yijri bis-safaara.*

certain - **1.** *muɀaqqaq, muʔakkad.* He's certain to pass the exam. *najaaɀa bil-imtiɀaan fadd šii muʔakkad.* **2.** *mitʔakkid.* I am certain that I signed the papers myself. *ʔaani mitʔakkid waqqaƹt il-ʔawraaq ib-nafsi.* **3.** *muƹayyan.* I mean certain people I'd rather not name. *ʔaƹni ʔašxaaṣ muƹayyaniin ma-ariid ajiib ʔasmaaʔhum.* **4.** *baƹaḍ.* There are certain things I want to discuss with you. *ʔaku baƹḍ ašyaaʔ ʔariid ʔabɀaθha wiyyaak.* **5.** *ʔakiid, muqarrar.* The date is certain but the time hasn't been set yet. *l-mawƹid ʔakiid laakin is-saaƹa ma-tƹayynat baƹad.*

certainly - **1.** *bit-taʔkiid.* She's certainly right. *hiyya bit-taʔkiid ṣaɀiiɀa.* **2.** *maƹluum, ṭabƹan, yaqiin.* Why, certainly! *maƹluum!* -- He's certainly coming. *yaqiin raɀ-yiji.*

certificate - *šahaada* pl. *-aat, taqriir* pl. *-aat.* He needs a doctor's certificate. *yiɀtaaj šahaada ṭibbiyya.* -- Submit a copy of your birth certificate with the other papers. *qaddim nusxa min šahaadat wilaadtak wiyya baqiit il-ʔawraaq.* -- Do you have a Certificate of Good Conduct? *ƹindak šahaadat ɀusn is-siluuk?*

certified - **1.** *qaanuuni*.* He is a certified public accountant. *huwwa muɀaaṣib qaanuuni.* **2.** *muṣaddaq.* This is a certified copy. *haay nusxa muṣaddaqa.*

to **certify** - **1.** *šihad (a šahaada) n-.* He says he will certify that they were all present at the time. *yguul raɀ-yišhad bi-ʔan kullhum čaanaw ɀaaḍriin ḍaak il-wakit.* **2.** *ṣaddaq (i taṣdiiq) t- ƹala.* A notary public has to certify the signature. *kaatib ƹadil laazim yṣaddiq ƹat-tawqiiƹ.*

chain - **1.** *maƹḍad* pl. *maƹaaḍid.* She wears a golden chain. *tilbas maƹḍad ḍahab.* **2.** *zanjiil* pl. *zanaajiil.* Do you have a chain I can use to tow the car? *ƹindak zanjiil agdar astaƹmila l-saɀb is-sayyaara?* **3.** *silsila* pl. *salaasil.* This firm operates a chain of food stores. *haš-šarika tdiir silsilat maxaazin il-beeƹ il-maʔkuulaat.*

to chain - *zanjal (i zanjala) t-, rubaṭ (u rabuṭ) n- b-zanjiil.* They chained the prisoners together. *zanjilaw il-masaajiin waaɀid bil-laax.*

chair - **1.** *kursi* pl. *karaasi, skamli* pl. *-iyaat.* Please sit down in this chair. *ʔarjuuk ʔugƹud ƹala hal-kursi.* **2.** *qulṭuġ* pl. *-aat.* Sit in the upholstered chair. *ʔugƹud ƹal-qulṭuġ* or *ʔugƹud ƹal-kursi l-baṭṭiixa.*

chalk - *ṭabaašiir.* How many sticks of chalk are in the box? *čam qaalab ṭabaašiir ʔaku bil-quuṭiyya.*
**Chalk that up to experience. *qayyidha xibra lil-mustaqbal.*

challenge - *taɀaddi* pl. *-iyaat.* Our team accepted their challenge. *fariiqna qibal taɀaddiihum.*

to challenge - *tɀadda (a taɀaddi).* I challenge the winner. *ʔaani ʔatɀadda l-ġaalub.*

chambermaid - *xaadma* pl. *-aat.*

chamber of commerce - *ġurfat* (pl. *ġuraf*) *tijaara.*

chamber pot - *qaƹƹaada* pl. *-aat.*

champagne - *šampaanya* pl. *-aat.*

champion - *baṭal* pl. *ʔabṭaal.*

championship - *buṭuula.* They're wrestling for the championship. *da-yitṣaarƹuun ƹala l-buṭuula.*

chance - **1.** *furṣa* pl. *furaṣ.* Give me a chance. *nṭiini fadd furṣa.* -- I had a chance to go to the ruins of Babel. *ṣaar ƹindi fadd furṣa ʔaruuɀ il-xaraaʔib baabil.* **2.** *ʔamal* pl. *ʔaamaal.* Is there any chance of catching the train. *ʔaku ʔamal inlaɀɀig bil-qiṭaar?* -- Not a chance. *ma-biiha ʔamal.* **3.** *yaanaṣiib.* Won't you buy a chance? *triid tištiri yaanaṣiib?*

by chance - *ṣidfatan, biṣ-ṣidfa.* I met him by chance. *laageeta biṣ-ṣidfa.*

to take a chance - *xaaṭar (i muxaaṭara) t-, jaazaf (i mujaazafa).* Let's take a chance on it. *xalli nxaaṭir biiha.*

to chance - *xaaṭar (i muxaaṭara) t-, jaazaf (i mujaazafa).* I'll chance it. *raɀ-axaaṭir bii* or *raɀ-ajarrub ɀaḍḍi.*

chandelier - *θurayya* pl. *-aat.*

change - **1.** *taġyiir* pl. *-aat, tabdiil* pl. *-aat.* Have there been any changes in my absence? *ʔay taġyiiraat ṣaarat ʔaθnaaʔ ġiyaabi?* -- You need a change of air. *yinraad-lak šwayya taġyiir hawa.* -- I'm for a change in the present administration. *ʔaani min muʔayyidiin taġyiir in-niḍaam il-ɀaali.* **2.** *xurda* pl. *-awaat.* Have you any change ? *ƹindak xurda?*

for a change - *lit-tabdiil, lit-taġyiir.* For a change I'd like to go to the movies tonight. *lit-tabdiil yiƹjibni ʔaruuɀ lis-siinama hal-leela.*

to change - **1.** *ṣarraf (u taṣriif) t-.* Can you change a dinar for me? *tigdar itṣarruf-li diinaar?* **2.** *ġayyar (i taġyiir) t-.* We may have to change our plans. *ʔaku ɀtimaal niḍṭarr inġayyir manhajna.* **3.** *tġayyar (a taġayyur).* The weather is going to change. *ṭ-ṭaqis raɀ-yitġayyar.* -- You won't believe when you see him how much he has changed. *ma-tṣaddig min itšuufa šgadd mitġayyir.* Nothing has changed. *ma-tġayyar šii.* **4.** *baddal (i tabdiil, tbiddil) t-.* Can you wait until I change my clothes? *tigdar tintiḍir ʔila ʔan ʔabaddil ihduumi?* -- I haven't changed my mind. *ma-baddalit fikri.* -- You'll have to change your tone if you want to talk to me. *ʔiḍa triid tiɀči wiyyaaya laazim itbaddil lahijtak.* -- We have to change trains at the next station. *laazim inbaddil il-qiṭaar bil-maɀaṭṭa j-jaaya* or *laazim inġayyir il-qiṭaar bil-maɀaṭṭa j-jaaya.* **5.** *tbaddal (a tabaddul).* The management of this hotel has changed hands a number of times. *ʔidaarat hal-ʔuteel itbaddlat čam marra.* **6.** *ɀawwal (i taɀwiil, taɀawwul) t- ʔila.* Our plan is to change this hotel into a hospital. *xiṭṭatna ʔan inɀawwil hal-ʔuteel ʔila mustašfa.* **7.** *tɀawwal (i taɀwiil, taɀawwul).* This store has changed hands often. *had-dukkaan itɀawwal min ʔiid il-ʔiid.* **8.** *ngilab (i ngilaab).* She has changed from an ugly girl into a real beauty. *ngulbat min bašƹa ʔila ʔaaya bij-jamaal.*

changeable - **1.** *mitġayyir.* The weather is very changeable at this time of year. *l-hawa mitġayyir ihwaaya haaḍa l-wakit imnis-sana.* **2.** *mitqallib.* She has a changeable disposition. *ƹidha ṭabuƹ mitqallib.*

channel - **1.** *majra* pl. *majaari, qanaat* pl. *qanawaat.* The two lakes are joined by a narrow channel. *l-buɀayraat iθ-θinteen mittaṣla b-majra ḍayyig.* -- The application will have to go through proper channels. *l-ƹariiḍa laazim taaxuḍ majraaha l-ʔuṣuuli.* **2.** *qanaal* pl. *-aat.* We crossed the English Channel in the storm. *ƹubarna l-qanaal il-ingiliizi ʔaθnaaʔ il-ƹaaṣifa.* **3.** *maɀaṭṭa* pl. *-aat.* How many channels can you get on your television set? *čam maɀaṭṭa tigdar itɀaṣṣil ib-talafizyoonak?*

to channel - *wajjah (i tawjiih) t-.* I'm trying to help him channel his efforts into useful activities. *da-aɀaawil ʔasaaƹda ywajjih jihuuda ʔila ʔaƹmaal mufiida.*

to **chant** - **1.** *waḍḍan (i tawḍiin) t-, ʔaḍḍan (i taʔḍiin) t-.* We hear the muezzin chanting from the minaret every morning. *nismaƹ il-muwaḍḍin ywaḍḍin imnil-manaara kull yoom iṣ-ṣubuɀ.* **2.** *jawwad (i tajwiid) t-.* We are learning to chant the Koran in religion class. *da-nitƹallam tajwiid il-qurʔaan ib-dars id-diin.* **3.** *rattal (i tartiil) t-.* He chants the passages from the Koran at the Friday service. *yrattil ʔaayaat il-qurʔaan ib-ṣalaat ij-jumƹa.*

chaos - *fawḍa, hoosa.*

chaotic - *fawḍawi*.*

to **chap** - **1.** *maššag (i tmiššig) t.* The wind chapped my face today. *l-hawa maššag wičči l-yoom.* **2.** *faṭṭar (i tafṭiir) t-.* My lips are chapped. *šfaafi mfaṭṭira.*

chapter - **1.** *faṣil* pl. *fṣuul.* Did you read the last chapter of this book? *qreet il-faṣl il-ʔaxiir min hal-iktaab?* **2.** *juzuʔ* pl. *ʔajzaaʔ.* That's a closed chapter in my life. *haaḍa juzuʔ mintihi min ɀayaati.* **3.** *ṣuura* pl. *ṣuwar.* The Koran is divided into 114 chapters. *l-qurʔaan imqassam ʔila miyya w-ʔarbaṭaƹaš ṣuura.*

character - **1.** *xuluq* pl. *ʔaxlaaq.* I've misjudged his character. *ʔaxṭaaʔit ib-ɀukmi ƹala ʔaxlaaqa.* -- Your son has character. *ʔibnak ƹinda xuluq.* **2.** *šaxṣiyya* pl. *-aat.* How many characters are there in the play? *čam šaxṣiyya ʔaku bir-ruwaaya?* **3.** *ṣuura* pl. *-aat.* This man is a familiar character here. *har-rijjaal ṣuura maʔluufa hnaa.* **4.** *ʔintiika* pl. *-aat, ɛantiika* pl. *-aat.* He's quite a character. *haaða ṣudug ɛantiika.* **5.** *ramiz* pl. *rumuuz.* He is trying to decipher the cuneiform characters on the stone. *da-yḥaawil ḥall ir-rumuuz il-mismaariyya ɛala ṣ-ṣaxar.*

characteristic – 1. *ṣifa* pl. *-aat.* He has many good characteristics. *ɛinda hwaaya ṣifaat zeena.* **2.** *miiza* pl. *-aat, mazaaya.* That's characteristic of our times. *haaði miizat haz-zamaan.* **3.** *xaaṣṣiyya* pl. *xawaaṣṣ.* One of the characteristics of salt is its solubility. *ʔiḥda xawaaṣṣ il-miliḥ qaabliita lið-ðawabaan.*

charcoal – *faḥma* pl. *-aat* coll. *faḥam.*

charge – 1. *kulfa* pl. *kulaf, ʔujra* pl. *ʔujuur.* What is the charge for shortening trousers? *šgadd kulfat tagṣiir il-panṭiruun?* **2.** *tuhma* pl. *tuham.* What are the charges against this man? *šinu t-tuham ð̣idd har-rijjaal?* **3.** *quwwa* pl. *-aat.* The charge of dynamite is sufficient to destroy the whole building. *quwwat id-dinaameet kaafya l-hadim il-binaaya kullha.*

free of charge – *balaaš, majjaanan, biduun rusuum.* We'll mail it to you free of charge. *raḥ-indizz-lak-iyyaaha bil-bariid majjaanan.*

in charge – *masʔuul.* Who's in charge of this section? *minu masʔuul ɛan haš-šuɛba?*

to take charge – *twalla (a tawalli) r-riʔaasa, traʔʔas (a taraʔʔus).* He's taking charge of the new branch. *raḥ-yitwalla riʔaasat iš-šuɛba j-jidiida.*

to charge – 1. *saam (u soom) n-.* This merchant charges twice what the others do. *hat-taajir ysuum ð̣iɛf il-baaqiin.* **2.** *kallaf (i takliif) t-, ʔaxað (u ʔaxið) min, ɛala.* How much are you going to charge me for the stitching? *šgadd raḥ-itkallifni ɛala l-xiyaaṭa?* **3.** *šiḥan (a šaḥin) n-.* We can charge your battery for you for a dirham. *nigdar nišḥan-lak il-baaṭri b-dirham.* **4.** *hijam (i hujuum) n- ɛala.* The mounted police charged the crowd of demonstrators. *š-šurṭa l-xayyaala hijmaw ɛal-mutaḍaahiriin.* **5.** *ḥisab (i ḥsaab) n- ɛala, qayyad (i taqyiid) t- b-iḥsaab.* You have charged me for something I never got. *ḥisabit ɛalayya siɛir šii maa maaxða.* -- **I'd like to charge it, please. *ḥuṭṭa ɛala l-iḥsaab, rajaaʔan.* **6.** *ttiham (i ttihaam), tiham (i tahim) n-.* They charged him with theft. *ttihmoo bis-sariqa.*

charitable – 1. *xeeri**. She is a member of several charitable organizations. *hiyya ɛuḍwa b-jamɛiyyaat xeeriyya mutaɛaddida.* **2.** *muḥsin* pl. *-iin.* He is a charitable man; loves to do good. *huwwa muḥsin, muḥibb il-ɛamal il-xeer.*

charity – 1. *xeer, l-barr wil-ʔiḥsaan.* He gives all his money to charity. *yinṭi fluusa kullha lil-xeer.* **2.** *ṣadaqa* pl. *-aat, ʔiḥsaan.* She's too proud to accept charity. *haay tistankif tiqbal ṣadaqa.*
**Charity begins at home. *l-ʔaqrabuun ʔawla bil-maɛruuf.*

charm – 1. *siḥir, fitna.* She has a lot of charm. *ɛidha fadd siḥir qawi.* **2.** *ḥiriz* pl. *ḥuruuz, dillaaɛa* pl. *-aat.* He always carries a charm against the evil eye. *yšiil ḥiriz daaʔiman ð̣idd il-ɛeen.*

to charm – *siḥar (a siḥir) n-, fitan (i fatin) n-.* She charmed us with her wit and pleasant personality. *siḥratna b-ð̣araafatha w-šaxṣiyyatha l-laṭiifa.*

charming – *saaḥir, fattaan.* His sister is a very charming person. *ʔuxta kulliš fattaan.*

charter – *miiθaaq* pl. *mawaaθiiq.* He took part in drawing up the United Nations' charter. *ʔištirak ib-waḍiɛ miiθaaq il-ʔumum il-muttaḥida.*

to charter – *staʔjar (i stiʔjaar).* Our group is going to charter a bus for the trip. *jamaaɛatna raḥ-tistaʔjir paaṣ lis-safra.*

chase – 1. *muṭaarada* pl. *-aat.* A wild chase began. *fadd muṭaarada ɛaniifa bidat.* **2.** *taɛqiib, qtifaaʔ.* The chase led them thru the market and down to the shore. *t-taɛqiib qaadhum lis-suuq w-lis-saaḥil.*

to chase – 1. *liḥaq (a laḥiq) n-.* Before he was married he used to chase the girls all the time. *gabul-ma yitzawwaj čaan yilḥag il-banaat ɛala ṭuul.* **2.** *looḥag (i tlooḥig).* Their dog is always chasing our cat. *čalibhum ɛala ṭuul ylooḥig bazzuunatna.*

to chase around – *daar (u door), ftarr (a ftiraar).* My son chases around with a pretty wild crowd. *ʔibni da-yduur wiyya fadd jamaaɛa wikkaḥ.*

to chase away – *kašš (i kašš) n-.* Chase the birds away from the tomato vines. *kišš iṭ-ṭiyuur min xuð̣rat iṭ-ṭamaaṭa.*

to chase down – *tɛaqqab (a taɛaqqub).* I spent three days chasing down that reference. *qið̣eet itlaθt iyyaam atɛaqqab hal-marjaɛ.*

to chase out – *ṭarrad (i taṭriid) t-.* I chased him out of the house. *ṭarradta mnil-beet.*

chassis – *šaaṣi* pl. *-yaat.*

chaste – *ɛafiif, ṭaahir.*

chastity – *ɛiffa, ṭuhur.*

chat – *ḥači.* We had a nice chat. *jira beenna ḥači laṭiif.*

to chat – *soolaf (i tsoolif) t-.* We spent a very pleasant hour chatting with each other. *gið̣eena saaɛa laṭiifa nsoolif.*

chatter – *θarθara, lağwa.* Stop that foolish chatter. *baṭṭil haθ-θarθara.*

to chatter – 1. *θarθar (i θarθara), liğa (i lağwa).* They chatter incessantly. *yilğuun ɛala ṭuul.* **2.** *ṣṭakk (a), ṭagṭag (i).* My teeth are chattering. *snuuni da-tiṣṭakk* or *snuuni da-ṭṭagṭig.*

chatterbox – *θarθaar* pl. *-iin.*

chauffeur – *saayiq* pl. *suwwaaq, dreewil* pl. *-iyya.*

cheap – 1. *rixiiṣ* pl. *rxaaṣ.* Fruit is cheap this year. *l-fawaakih rixiiṣa has-sana.* -- He offered it to me cheap. *ɛiraḍha ɛalayya b-siɛir rixiiṣ* or *nṭaani-yyaaha rixiiṣ.* **2.** *ma-yiswa.* That's cheap stuff. *haaða šii ma-yiswa.* **3.** *waaṭi.* Her manners are cheap. *ʔaxlaaqha waaṭya.* **4.** *mubtaðal.* She looks cheap in those clothes. *tbayyin ɛabaalak mubtaðala b-hal-ihduum.* **5.** *danii*.* He played a cheap trick on me. *sawwa biyya ḥiila daniiʔa.* **6.** *waḍiiɛ.* She is a cheap, vulgar woman. *haay fadd waḥda waḍiiɛa.* **7.** *duuni**. These goods are cheap quality. *hal-baḍaayiɛ duuniyya.* -- He ruined his feet from wearing cheap shoes. *ɛidam rijla min libs il-qanaadir id-duuniyya.*
**His openhandedness made me feel cheap. *karama xajjilatni.*

cheat – *ğaššaaš* pl. *-iin.* They all know he's a cheat. *kullhum yɛurfuun huwwa fadd waaḥid ğaššaaš.*

to cheat – 1. *ğašš (u ğišš) n-.* Be careful you don't get cheated. *diir baalak la-tinğašš.* -- He always cheats at cards. *daaʔiman yğušš ib-liɛib il-ʔawraaq.* **2.** *sawwa (i taswiya) qoopya.* He's always cheating at exams. *daaʔiman ysawwi qoopya bil-imtiḥaanaat.* **3.** *xaan (u xiyaana).* His wife is cheating on him. *zoojta da-txuuna.* **4.** *zaağal (i zuğul) wiyya.* I know he's cheating me but I can't prove it. *da-aɛruf da-yzaağil wiyyaaya laakin ma-agdar aθibta.* **5.** *qašmar (i qašmara) t-, laflaf (i laflafa).* He cheated him out of all his money. *qašmara w-axað kull ifluusa* or *laflaf kull ifluusa.*

check – 1. *čakk* pl. *-aat, ṣakk* pl. *ṣukuuk.* I'll send you a check tomorrow. *ɛuud adizz-lak čakk baačir.* **2.** *waṣil* pl. *wṣuulaat.* Give your baggage check to the porter. *ʔinṭi l-waṣil maal ğaraaḍak lil-ḥammaal.* Here's your hat check, sir. *sayyid, tfað̣ð̣al waṣl iš-šafqa maaltak.* **3.** *ʔišaara* pl. *-aat, ɛalaama* pl. *-aat.* Put a check before the name of each one as he reports in. *ḥuṭṭ ʔišaara giddaam ʔisim kull waaḥid min yiji.* **4.** *ḥsaab* pl. *-aat.* Waiter, the check please. *booy, l-iḥsaab min faḍlak.*

in check – *makšuuš.* Your king is in check. *l-malik maalak makšuuš.*

to keep in check – *ð̣ubaṭ (u ð̣abuṭ) n-.* I'm no longer able to keep him in check. *ma-agdar að̣ubṭa baɛad.*

to check – 1. *ʔamman (i taʔmiin) t-, waddaɛ (i tawdiiɛ) t-.* Check your hat and coat here. *ʔammin šafuqtak w-qappuuṭak ihnaa.* **2.** *ʔamman (i taʔmiin) t-.* Can I check this suitcase at the station? *ʔagdar aʔammin haj-junṭa bil-maḥaṭṭa?* **3.** *ʔaššar (i taʔšiir) t-.* Check the items you want. *ʔaššir il-ʔašyaaʔ li-triidha.* **4.** *čayyak (i tačyiik) t-, fuḥaṣ (a faḥiṣ) n-.* Please check the oil. *ʔarjuuk ifḥaṣ id-dihin.* **5.** *fattaš (i taftiiš) t-.* They will check your passports at the border. *raḥ-yfattišuun paaṣpoortaatkum bil-ḥiduud.* **6.** *daqqaq (i tadqiiq) t-.* Will you please check the bill once more? *ʔarjuuk ma-tdaqqiq l-iḥsaab marra lux?* **7.** *raaqab (i muraaqaba) t-.* We have been asked to check on the water table levels at all seasons of the year. *nṭilab min ɛidna nraaqib mustawa l-ṃaay ib-kull fuṣuul is-sana.* -- We are required to check on each man's daily output. *maṭluub minna nraaqib išgadd* *kull waazid yṭalliɛ bil-yoom.* **8.** *raajaɛ (i muraajaɛa) t-.* Check with me again before you go. *raajiɛni marrt il-lux gabuḷ-ma truuz.* **9.** *kašš (i kašš) n-.* You gave me a chance to check your king. *nṭeetni furṣa ʔakušš il-malik maalak.*

to check in - 1. *sajjal (i tasjiil) t-.* They checked in at the hotel at 2 P.M. *sajjlaw bil-ʔuteel saaɛa biθ-θinteen.* **2.** *ziδar (a zuδuur).* What time do we have to check in? *šwakit laazim nizδar?*

to check off - *ʔaššar (i taʔšiir) t-.* Check them off as you go. *ʔašširhum w-inta maaši.*

to check out - *ġaadar (i muġaadara), tirak (u tarik).* What time did he check out of the hotel? *šwakit ġaadar il-ʔuteel?*

to check over - *fuzaṣ (a faziṣ) n-.* Check over the list and see if we can use any of the items. *ʔifzaṣ il-qaaʔima w-šuuf ʔiδa niztaaj šii min hal-mawaadd.*

to check through - *dazz (i dazz) n- l-, waṣṣal (i tawṣiil) t-.* I want this baggage checked through Mosul. *ʔariid hal-ġaraaδ tindazz lil-muuṣil.*

to check up - 1. *daqqaq (i tadqiiq) t-.* We had better check up on the accuracy of his accounts. *l-ʔazsan indaqqiq ṣizzat zisaabaata.* **2.** *zaqqaq (i tazqiiq) t-, staɛlam (i stiɛlaam).* Did you check up on him? *zaqqaqit ɛanna?* or *sawweet tazqiiq ɛanna* or *staɛlamit ɛanna.* **3.** *tzaqqaq (a tazaqquq).* We have to check up on his statements. *laazim nitzaqqaq min kalaama.*

to check with - *ttifaq (i ttifaaq) wiyya, ṭaabaq (i muṭaabaqa) t-.* That checks with what he told me. *haaδa yittifiq wiyya lli gal-li-yyaa.*

check book - *daftar* (pl. *dafaatir*) *čakkaat.*

check point - *nuqṭat* (pl. *nuqaṭ*) *taftiiš, markaz* (pl. *maraakiz*) *taftiiš.*

check room - *ġurfat* (pl. *ġuraf*) *taɛliiq il-ihduum.*

check-up - *faziṣ, kašif.* You should see your doctor for a general check-up once a year. *laazim itruuz liṭ-ṭabiib zatta ysawwii-lak faziṣ ɛaamm marra bis-sana.*

cheek - *xadd* pl. *xuduud.* My cheek is all swollen. *xaddi kulla mwarrum.*

cheer - *hitaaf* pl. *-aat.* We heard the cheers from quite a distance. *smaɛna l-hitaaf min masaafa bɛiida.* -- Three cheers for our team. *θlaθ hitaafaat il-fariiqna.*

**They gave him a cheer. *hitfoo-la.*

to cheer - 1. *hitaf (i hitaaf) n-.* The crowd cheered. *j-jamaahiir hitfat.* -- The crowd cheered the speaker. *l-mujtamɛiin hitfaw lil-xaṭiib.*

to cheer up - 1. *farraz (i tafriiz) t-, sarr (i).* The news cheered her up. *l-ʔaxbaar farrizatha.* **2.** *tšajjaɛ (a tašajjuɛ).* Cheer up, he'll be back soon. *tšajjaɛ, huwwa raz-yirjaɛ qariiban.*

cheerful - *farzaan, fariz, mitwannis.* He's very cheerful today. *huwwa kulliš farzaan il-yoom.* -- Isn't this a cheerful room. *baḷḷa muu hal-gubba kulliš farza?.*

cheese - *jibin* pl. *ʔajbaan.* What kind of cheese do you have? *yaa nooɛ jibin ɛindak?*

chef - *baaštabbaax* pl. *-iin.*

chemical - *kiimyaawi*.* He's working in a chemical laboratory. *huwwa yištuġuḷ ib-fadd muxtabar kiimyaawi.*

chemist - *kiimyaaʔi* pl. *-yyiin, kiimyaawi* pl. *-yyiin.*

cherry - *karaza* pl. *-aat,* coll. *karaz.* These are good cherries. *haaδa xooš karaz.*

chess - *šiṭranj.* Do you know how to play chess? *tuɛruf tilɛab šiṭranj?*

chess set - *šiṭranj* pl. *-aat.* All the chess sets are in use. *kull iš-šiṭranjaat da-tilɛab.*

chest - 1. *ṣadir* pl. *ṣduur.* He has a broad chest. *ɛinda ṣadir ɛariiδ.* -- That's a load off my chest. *haaδa čaan fadd zimil w-inzaaz ɛan ṣadri.* **2.** *ṣanduug* pl. *ṣanaadiig.* Put the tools in the chest. *zuṭṭ il-ʔadawaat biṣ-ṣanduug.* **3.** *diilaab* pl. *dwaaliib.* She bought a beautiful chest of drawers. *štirat diilaab ʔabu mjarraat zilu.*

chestnut - 1. *kistaanaaya* pl. *-aat* coll. *kistaana.* Let's buy some roasted chestnuts. *xal-ništiri šwayya kistaana mzammṣa.* **2.** *kastanaaʔi*.* Her hair is chestnut. *šaɛarha kastanaaʔi.*

chestnut tree - *šajarat il-kistaana.*

to **chew -** *ɛilač (i ɛalič) n-, ɛilas (i ɛalis) n-, muδaġ (u maδiġ) n-.* Chew your food well. *ʔiɛlis ʔaklak zeen.*

chewing gum - *ɛilič.* How many sticks of chewing gum are there in the package? *čam qiṭɛat ɛilič ʔaku bil-paakeet?*

chic - *šiik, ʔaniiq.*

chicken - *dijaaja* pl. *-aat* coll. *dijaaj.* We're having chicken for dinner. *ɛašaana dijaaj.*

chicken pox - *jidri maay.*

chick peas - *zummuṣ, lablabi.*

chief - 1. *raʔiis* pl. *ruʔasaaʔ.* Who's the chief of the division? *minu raʔiis il-qisim?* **2.** *mudiir* pl. *mudaraaʔ.* Where's the office of the Chief of Police? *ween daaʔirat mudiir iš-šurṭa?* **3.** *baaš.* He has worked in our office as chief clerk for five years. *ṣaar-la xams isniin yištuġuḷ baaš kaatib ib-daaʔiratna.* **4.** *ʔawwal.* He is chief legal advisor to the company. *huwwa l-mušaawir il-qaanuuni l-ʔawwal liš-šarika.* **5.** *raʔiisi*.* These are the chief reasons why we should accept the plan. *haay il-ʔasbaab ir-raʔiisiyya lli tijɛalna niqbal il-xiṭṭa.* -- What are the chief exports of Iraq? *šinu ṣaadiraat il-ɛiraaq ir-raʔiisiyya?*

child - *jaahil* pl. *jihaal, juhhaal, ṭifil* pl. *ʔaṭfaal, ṣġayyir* pl. *ṣġaar.* They took the child along on a trip. *ʔaxδaw ij-jaahil wiyyaahum ib-safra.* -- Next year we have budgeted more money for child welfare. *s-sana j-jaaya xaṣṣaṣna fluus ʔazyad il-riɛaayt il-ʔaṭfaal.* -- I've been used to it ever since I was a child. *haaδi mitɛallim ɛaleeha min ʔaani ṣġayyir.*

childhood - *ṭufuula, ṣuġur, juhul.* I spent part of my childhood in the country. *gδeet qisim min ṭufuulti bir-riif.* -- In his childhood he didn't have much contact with other children. *b-juhla ma-ṣaar ɛinda hwaaya ttiṣaal ib-baqiit il-ʔaṭfaal.*

childish - 1. *zaɛṭuuṭ* pl. *zaɛaaṭiiṭ.* He is very childish in his demands. *huwwa kulliš zaɛṭuuṭ ib-ṭalabaata.* **2.** *mazɛaṭa* pl. *-aat.* This is childish. *haay mazɛaṭa.* -- The whole thing was childish. *l-masʔala čaanat mazɛaṭa.* **3.** *ṣibyaani*.* What you did was childish. *ɛamalak čaan ṣibyaani.*

to act childish - *tzaɛṭaṭ (a tziɛṭiṭ), ṣaar zaɛṭuuṭ.* Don't act so childish; you're old enough to know better. *la-tṣiir zaɛṭuuṭ hal-gadd; ʔinta čibiir w-tiftihim.*

chill - 1. *barid.* I've got a chill. *ʔaani maaxiδ barid.* **2.** *qašɛariira.* Suddenly I felt a chill. *ɛala ġafḷa šiɛarit ib-qašɛariira.*

to chill - *barrad (i tabriid) t-.* Chill them before you serve them. *barridha gabuḷ-ma tqaddimha.*

**I'm chilled to the bone. *l-barid yabbas ɛaδaami.*

chilly - 1. *baarid.* It's chilly outside. *baarda barra.* -- They received us in a chilly manner. *staqbiloona stiqbaal baarid.* **2.** *bardaan.* I'm chilly. *ʔaani bardaan.*

chimney - 1. *madxana* pl. *madaaxin.* They are repairing the chimney. *da-yṣallzooha lil-madxana.* **2.** *šiiša* pl. *šiyaš.* Where's the chimney for the lamp? *ween iš-šiiša maal il-faanuus?*

chimpanzee - *šimbaanzi* pl. *-yaat.*

chin - *zinič* pl. *znuuč, δiqin* pl. *δiquun.* He has a protruding chin. *ɛinda zinič baariz.*

**Chin up! *tšajjaɛ* or *šidd zeelak.*

China - *ṣ-ṣiin.* He lived in China for a long time. *ɛaaš biṣ-ṣiin mudda ṭwiila.*

china - *faxfuuri, farfuuri.* We got this set of china as a wedding present. *haṭ-ṭaxm il-faxfuuri jaana hadiyyat zawaaj.*

Chinese - *ṣiini** pl. *-iyyiin.* The owner of this store is a Chinese. *ṣaazib hal-mazall ṣiini.* I got a Chinese vase. *zaṣṣalit ɛala mazhariyya ṣiiniyya.*

chip - 1. *θilma* pl. *θilam.* There is a chip out of the plate. *ʔaku θilma ṭaayra mnil-maaɛuun.* **2.** *šugfa* pl. *šugaf.* Fill in the spaces between the stones with chips. *ʔitris il-faraaġat been iṭ-ṭaabuug ib-šugaf.* **3.** *fiiša* pl. *-aat, fiyaš.* When the game finished, I had three white chips left. *min xilaṣ il-liɛib čaan baɛad ɛindi tlaθ fiyaš beeδa.* **4.** *njaara, šugfa* pl. *šugaf.* The carpenter left the floor littered with chips. *n-najjaar ɛaaf il-gaaɛ matruusa njaara.* -- Where did this chip of wood come from? *haš-šugfat il-xišab imneen jatti?*

**He always has a chip on his shoulder. *haaδa ydawwur zirša.*

to chip - 1. *θilam (i θalim) n-, gaššaṭ (i tagšiiṭ) t-.* Be careful you don't chip the dishes when you wash them. *diir baalak la-tiθlim il-imwaaɛiin min tigsilha.* -- The rim of this glass is chipped; bring me another. *zaašyat hal-iglaaṣ maθluuma; jiib-li ġeera.* -- The edge of the table is chipped. *zaašiit il-meez magšuuṭa.* **2.** *nijar (u najir) n-.* This man can chip the bricks in any shape you want. *har-rajjaal yigdar yinjur iṭ-ṭaabuug ib-ʔay sikil* *triida.* **3.** *tgaššaṭ (a tgiššiṭ).* The paint is beginning to chip. *ṣ-ṣubuġ bida yitgaššaṭ.*

to **chirp** – *zaqzaq (i zaqzaqa).* A little bird was chirping at the window and woke me up. *ṭeer iṣġayyir čaan yzaqziq biš-šibbaač w-gaƐƐadni.*

chisel – *minqaar* pl. *manaaqiir.*

to chisel – *ʒufar (u ʒafur) n–.* Have them chisel the name on the stone in both languages. *xalliihum yʒafruun il-ʔism bil-ʒajar bil-luġteen.*

chocolate – *čukleet.* Is this chocolate bitter or sweet? *hač-čukleet murr loo ʒilu?* -- I want to buy a box of chocolate. *ʔariid aštiri fadd quuṭiyya čukleet.*

choice – **1.** *xtiyaar* pl. *-aat, xiyaar* pl. *-aat.* I had no other choice. *ma-čaan Ɛindi ġeer ixtiyaar.* -- If I had a choice, I'd do it. *loo b-iidi xiyaar, sawweeta.* **2.** *taškiila.* They have a wide choice of colors to choose from. *Ɛidhum taškiila čibiira mnil-ʔalwaan tixtaar minha.* **3.** *mumtaaz.* These are choice cuts of meat. *haaδi wuṣal mumtaaza mnil-laʒam.* **4.** *muxtaar, mistanga.* He has a choice but small collection of books. *Ɛinda majmuuƐa muxtaara wa-loo ṣġayyra mnil-kutub.*

choir – *kooras* pl. *-aat.* He sings in a choir in the church. *yġanni b-kooras bil-kaniisa.*

choke – *čook.* The choke doesn't work. *č-čook ma-da-yuštuġul.*

to choke – **1.** *xinag (i xanig) n–.* I could choke you. *min widdi ʔaxungak.* -- The collar is choking me. *l-yaaxa xaangatni.* **2.** *xtinag (i xtinaag).* I nearly choked on a fishbone. *xtinagit ib-Ɛaδm is-simča ʔilla šwayya.*

to choke back – *minaƐ (a maniƐ) n–, ʒišar (i ʒašir) n–, δubaṭ (u δabuṭ) n–.* She choked back her tears. *minƐat dumuuƐha.*

to choke up – *sadd (u sadd) n–.* The stovepipe is choked up. *buuri d-duxxaan masduud.*

cholera – *hayδa, kuleera.*

to **choose** – *ntixab (i ntixaab), stanga (i), xtaar (a xtiyaar).* The editors chose the book of the month for their readers. *l-muʒarririin ixtaaraw kitaab iš-šahar il-qurraaʔhum.* -- Choose the oranges you want. *ʔistangi l-purtiqaalaat li-triidha.* -- They chose him as candidate for the party. *ntixboo muraššaʒ Ɛann il-ʒizib.*

choosy – *diqdaaqi*.* There's no need to be so choosy. *ma-aku ʒaaja tṣiir hal-gadd diqdaaqi.*

to **chop** – *faššag (i tafšiig, tfiššig) t–, kassar (i taksiir) t–.* Did you chop some wood? *faššagit šwayyat ʒatab?*

to chop down – *gaṣṣ (u gaṣṣ) n–.* They chopped the dead tree down. *gaṣṣooha liš-šajara l-mayyta.*

to chop off – *gaṣṣ (u gaṣṣ) n–, giṭaƐ (a gaṭiƐ) n–.* Be careful you don't chop your finger off. *diir baalak la-tguṣṣ iṣibƐak.*

to chop up – **1.** *θarram (i tθurrum) t–, θiram (u θarum) n–.* Chop the meat up fine. *θarrim il-laʒam naaƐim.* -- This dish calls for chopped meat. *haṭ-ṭabxa yinraad-ilha laʒam maθruum.* **2.** *gaṣgaṣ (i tgiṣgiṣ) t–.* Have the butcher chop up the meat for you. *xalli l-gaṣṣaab ygaṣgiṣ-lak il-laʒam.*

chops – **1.** *qulbaaṣṭi.* I'd like the lamb chops with vegetables and rice. *yiƐjibni l-gulbaaṣṭi wiyya xuδra w-timman.* **2.** *čaap.* Can you cut me some lamb chops? *tigdar itguṣṣ-li šwayyat čaap?* **3.** *buuz.* The dog licked his chops. *č-čalib liʒas buuza.*

to lick one's chops – *maṭṭag (i tamṭiig) t–.* The food he makes makes you lick your chops. *l-ʔakl il-ysawwii yxalli l-waaʒid ymaṭṭig.*

Christ – *l-masiiʒ.*

Christian – *masiiʒi** pl. *-iyyiin, naṣraani** pl. *naṣaara.* He's a member of the Young Men's Christian Association. *huwwa ƐuΦu b-jamƐiyyat iš-šubbaan il-masiiʒiyyiin.*

Christianity – *l-masiiʒiyya.*

Christmas – *Ɛiid il-miilaad, krismis.* Christmas comes on a Wednesday this year. *Ɛiid il-miilaad has-sana raʒ-yoogaƐ yoom ʔarbaƐa.*

chromium – *kroom.*

chronic – *muzmin.* He has a chronic disease. *Ɛinda maraδ muzmin.*

to **chuckle** – *δiʒak (a δaʒik) waʒd˜, sanṭaawi.* He chuckles whenever he thinks of it. *yiδʒak waʒda kull-ma tiji b-baala.*

church – **1.** *kaniisa* pl. *kanaayis.* Is there a Catholic church here? *ʔaku kaniisa kaaθoolikiyya hnaa?* **2.** *ṭaaʔifa* pl. *ṭawaaʔif.* What church do you belong to? *min ʔay ṭaaʔifa ʔinta?* or *šinu diinak?*

cider – *Ɛaṣiir tiffaaʒ.*

cigar – *siigaar* pl. *-aat, čarid* pl. *čruud.*

cigarette – *jigaara* pl. *jigaayir.* Have a cigarette. *tfaδδal fadd jigaara.*

cigarette case – *quuṭiyyat (*pl. *qwaaṭi) jigaayir.* I've lost my cigarette case. *ʔaani δayyaƐit quuṭiit ij-jigaayir maalti.*

cigarette lighter – *qiddaaʒa* pl. *-aat.*

cinch – **1.** *seer* pl. *syuur.* The saddle is loose; tighten the cinch. *s-sarij raaxi; δubb is-seer.* **2.** *muʔakkada.* That's a cinch. *haay muʔakkada.*

cinder – *faʒma (*pl. *-aat) maʒruuga,* coll. *faʒam maʒruug.* What are they doing with this big pile of cinders? *š-ysawwuun ib-hal-koom ič-čibiir imnil-faʒam il-maʒruug?* -- I've got a cinder in my eye. *xaššat faʒma ṣġayyra b-Ɛeeni.*

cinnamon – *daarsiin.*

circle – **1.** *daaʔira* pl. *dawaaʔir.* Draw the circle with a compass. *ʔirsim id-daaʔira b-purgaal.* **2.** *ʒalaqa* pl. *-aat.* He has a wide circle of friends. *Ɛinda fadd ʒalaqa čbiira mnil-ʔaṣdiqaaʔ.* **3.** *waṣaṭ* pl. *ʔawṣaaṭ.* They are well-known in diplomatic circles. *δoola maƐruufiin zeen bil-ʔawṣaaṭ id-dibloomaasiyya.*

to circle – **1.** *ftarr (a farr), ʒaam (u ʒoom) n .* The airplane is circling over the town. *ṭ-ṭayyaara da-tiftarr foog il-wlaaya.* **2.** *daar (u dawaraan) n–, ftarr (a farr).* The moon circles around the earth. *l-gumar yduur ʒawl il-ʔarδ.*

circular – **1.** *daaʔiri*.* Apply the polish with a circular movement. *ʔuδrub il-pooliš ib-ʒarakaat daaʔiriyya.* **2.** *mdawwar.* A circular staircase leads to the top of the minaret. *fadd daraj imdawwar yquud il-qummat il-manaara.* **3.** *manšuur* pl. *manaašiir.* We need some boys to distribute circulars. *niʒtaaj čam walad il-tawziiƐ il-manaašiir.*

to **circulate** – *daar (u dawaraan) n–.* Cold water circulates through these pipes constantly. *l-maay il-baarid yduur ib-hal-buuriyyaat Ɛala ṭuul.* -- There's a strange rumor circulating. *ʔaku fadd ʔišaaƐa ġariiba daayra.*

circulation – **1.** *dawaraan.* His blood circulation is not too good. *dawaraan damma muu kulliš zeen.* **2.** *tawziiƐ, ntišaar.* Our paper has a circulation of a hundred and fifty thousand. *tawziiƐ ij-jariida maalatna ywaṣṣil ila miyya w-xamsiin ʔalf.* **3.** *tadaawul.* The government has put new bills into circulation. *l-ʒukuuma nazlat nwaaṭ jidiida bit-tadaawul.*

circumference – *muʒiiṭ* pl. *-aat.* How do you get the circumference of the circle? *šloon iṭṭalliƐ muʒiiṭ id-daaʔira?*

circumstances – **1.** *δaruf* pl. *δuruuf.* Under these circumstances I can't blame her. *ʒaʒat haδ-δuruuf ma-agdar aluumha.* **2.** *ʔaʒwaal, ʔumuur.* He's in very good circumstances. *ʔaʒwaala zeena* or *ʔumuura maašya.*

circus – *sarkiis* pl. *-aat.*

citation – *stišhaad* pl. *-aat.* His speech is full of citations from the Koran. *xiṭaaba ʒaafil b-istišhaadaat imnil-qurʔaan.*

to **cite** – *stašhad (i stišhaad) b–.* Cite the passage exactly as the author wrote it. *ʔistašhid bil-maqṭaƐ tamaaman miθil-ma kitaba l-muʔallif.*

citizen – *muwaaṭin* pl. *iin.* Fellow citizens, choose your candidate carefully. *ʔayyuha l-muwaaṭiniin, ʔintaxbu muraššaʒkum ib-diqqa.*

**I am an Iraqi citizen. *ʔaani Ɛiraaqi.*

citizenship – *jinsiyya* pl. *-aat.* I have Iraqi citizenship. *Ɛindi jinsiyya Ɛiraaqiyya.*

city – **1.** *madiina* pl. *mudun, wlaaya* pl. *-aat.* How far is the nearest city from here? *šgadd tibƐid ʔaqrab madiina minnaa?* **2.** *baladi*.* She is in the City Hospital. *hiyya bil-mustašfa l-baladi.*

city dweller – *saakin (*pl. *sukkaan) mudin, ʒaδari* pl. *ʒaδar.* He is a city dweller and doesn't know much about agriculture. *huwwa min sukkaan il-mudin w-ma-yuƐruf ihwaaya Ɛann iz-ziraaƐa.* -- The bedouins and the city dwellers do not get on well together. *l-badu wil-ʒaδar ma-yitraahmuun.*

city hall – *saraay* pl. *-aat.*

city life – *ʒayaat il-madiina.* She is not accustomed to city life. *ma-mitƐawwda Ɛala ʒayaat il-madiina.*

civil – **1.** *naazik, muʔaddab.* At least he was civil to us. *hamm-zeen čaan naazik wiyyaana.* **2.** *madani*.* This is the concern of the civil authorities. *haaδi min ixtiṣaaṣ is-sulṭaat il-madaniyya.* **3.** *ʔahli*.* The difficulty almost led to civil war. *l-muškila* taqriiban ʔaddat ila ζaruub ʔahliyya.

civil code - l-qaanuun il-madani.

civilian - madani* pl. -iyyiin. There were civilians and soldiers in the crowd. čaan ʔaku madaniyyiin w-εaskariyyiin been ij-jamhuur. -- Was he wearing civilian clothes? čaan laabis ihduum madaniyya? or čaan laabis suwiil? -- He used to work as a teacher in civilian life. čaan yištuġul muεallim ʔaθnaaʔ ζayaata l-madaniyya.

civilization - madaniyya pl. -aat, ζaδ̣aara pl. -aat. The Babylonians had an advanced civilization. l-baabiliyyiin čaan εidhum ζaδ̣aara mitqaddma.

to **civilize** - maddan (i tamdiin) t-, ζaδ̣δ̣ar (i taζδ̣iir) t-. They were unable to civilize them. They remain savages. ma-gidraw ymaddinuuhum. buqaw mitwaζζišiin.

civilized - mitmaddin, mitζaδ̣δ̣ir.

civil service - xidma madaniyya.

claim - 1. ddiεaaʔ pl. -aat. You must submit your claim within ten days. laazim itqaddim iddiεaaʔak xilaal εaširt iyyaam. -- I don't believe his claim that he won the lottery. ma-aṣaddig iddiεaaʔa ʔinnahu rubaζ il-yaanaṣiib. 2. ζaqq pl. ζuquuq. I have no claim to that. maa εindi ζaqq biiha.

to claim - 1. ṭaalab (i muṭaalaba) t- b-. I claim my share. ʔaani ʔaṭaalib ib-ζuṣṣti. -- Where do I claim my baggage? ween aṭaalib b-ijnaaṭi? 2. ddaεa (i ddiεaaʔ). She claims to know the man. hiyya tiddiεi taεurfa lir-rijjaal.

to **clap** - ṣaffag (u taṣfiig, ṭṣuffug). He clapped to summon the waiter. ṣaffag ζatta yṣiiζ il-booy.

to **clarify** - waδ̣δ̣aζ (i tawδ̣iiζ) t-, fassar (i tafsiir) t-. We have asked you to come in and clarify a few points for us. ṭilabnaak tiji ζatta twaδ̣δ̣iζ-ilna čam nuqṭa.

clash - 1. štibaak pl. -aat. He was wounded in a clash on the border. njiraζ b-ištibaak εal-ζiduud. 2. taṣaadum pl. -aat, muṣaadama pl. -aat. The real source of the trouble is a clash of personalities. s-sabab il-ζaqiiqi lil-muškila huwwa t-taṣaadum biš-šaxṣiyyaat.

to clash - 1. ṭṣaadam (a taṣaadum). Government troops clashed briefly with rebel forces yesterday. quwwaat il-ζukuuma ṭṣaadmat il-baarζa l-mudda qaṣiira wiyya quwwaat iθ-θuwwaar. 2. ṭδ̣aarab (a taδ̣aarub). The interests of the two parties clashed over the question of government subsidies. maṣaaliζ il-ζizbeen itδ̣aarbat ζawl il-musaaεadaat il-ζukuumiyya. -- These two colors clash with each other unpleasantly. hal-looneen yitδ̣aarbuun waaζid wiyya l-laax ib-ṣuura maa ζilwa.

clasp - 1. qabδ̣a pl. -aat. He has a firm handclasp. εinda qabδ̣at ʔiid qawwiyya. 2. ṭubbaaga pl. -aat. Can you fix the clasp on my purse? tigdar itṣalliζ iṭ-ṭubbaaga maal junuṭṭi. 3. čillaab pl. člaaliib, šakkaala pl. -aat. Hook the clasp on my necklace please. šakkil ič-čillaab maal iglaadti rajaaʔan.

to clasp - lizam (a lazim) n-. They walked down the street clasping hands. tmaššaw biš-šaariε laazmiin waaζid ʔiid il-laax.

class - 1. ṣinif pl. ṣunuuf, ʔaṣnaaf. Arrange the items according to their classes. rattib il-mawaadd ζasab ʔaṣnaafha. 2. daris pl. druus. You're going to be late for class. raζ-titʔaxxar εala d-daris. -- There are no classes on Friday. ma-aku druus yoom ij-jumεa. 3. ṣaff pl. ṣfuuf. Our class is going on a field trip tomorrow. ṣaffna raζ-yitlaε safra baačir. 4. ṭabaqa pl. -aat. He is popular with all classes of society. maζbuub min kull iṭ-ṭabaqaat il-ijtimaaεiyya. -- This word is not used by the educated classes. hal-kalima ma-mustaεmala min qibal iṭ-ṭabaqaat il-muθaqqafa. 5. wajba pl. -aat, dafεa pl. -aat. We are all alumni of the class of 1934. kullna min xirriijiin wajbat ʔalf w-tisiεmiyya w-ʔarbaε w-itlaaθiin. 6. daraja pl. -aat. You'll find the first class coaches ahead just behind the engine. tilgi εarabaat id-daraja l-ʔuula li-giddaam mubaašaratan wara l-makiina. 7. ṭiraaz pl. ʔaṭriza. He is a first class politician. huwwa siyaasi mniṭ-ṭiraaz il-ʔawwal.

classical - 1. klaasiiki*. He prefers classical music to jazz. yfaδ̣δ̣il il-moosiiqa l-iklaasiikiyya εala j-jaaz. 2. faṣiiζ. He is making good progress in his study of classical Arabic. da-yitqaddam zeen ib-diraasta lil-luġa l-εarabiyya l-faṣiiζa. 3. taqliidi*. This is a classical example of Eastern architecture. haaδa fadd maθal taqliidi lil-handasa š-šarqiyya.

classification - taṣniif.

classified - 1. mubawwab. I found the car advertised in the classified ad section of the newspaper. ligeet is-sayyaara maεluun εanha b-ṣafζat il-iεlaanaat il-mubawwaba mnij-jariida. 2. sirri*. These papers are all classified. hal-ʔawraaq kullha sirriyya.

to **classify** - ṣannaf (i taṣniif) t-, bawwab (i tabwiib) t-. The remaining items are hard to classify. l-mawaadd il-baaqya yiṣεab taṣniifha.

classroom - ṣaff pl. ṣfuuf. The teacher is still in the classroom. l-muεallim baεda biṣ-ṣaff.

clatter - 1. ṭagṭaga. The clatter of dishes in the kitchen disturbs the guests. ṭagṭagat l-imwaaεiin bil-maṭbax tiζεij il-xuṭṭaar. 2. ṭargaεa. We heard the clatter of the wagon wheels as he went through the alley. simaεna ṭargaεat ičruux il-εarabaana min marr bil-εagid. 3. ṭarbaga. We awakened to the clatter of horses' hooves on the pavement. giεadna εala ζiss ṭarbagat ζawaafir il-xeel biš-šaariε.

to clatter - ṭargaε (i ṭargaεa). She clattered down the stairs in her clogs. nizlat id-daraj w-qubqaabha yṭargiε.

clause - band pl. bnuud, šarṭ pl. šruuṭ. I won't sign the contract if it has that clause in it. ma-amδ̣i l-εaqid ʔida bii hal-band.

claw - 1. maxlab pl. maxaalib. The hawk had a mouse in his claws. ṣ-ṣigar laazim ijreedi b-maxaalba. 2. δ̣ifir pl. ʔaδ̣aafir. The cat has sharp claws. l-bazzuuna εidha ʔaδ̣aafir ζaadda.

clay - ṭiin pl. ʔaṭyaan. Is this clay good for pottery? haṭ-ṭiin zeen lil-ikwaaza? -- The floor is made of clay pounded hard. l-gaaεiyya msawwaaya min ṭiin madčuuč.

clean - 1. naδ̣iif pl. nδ̣aaf. This plate is not clean. hal-maaεuun muu naδ̣iif. 2. baṣiiṭ. I like the clean lines of that building. yiεjibni t-taṣmiim il-baṣiiṭ maal δiič il-ibnaaya.

**Wipe the pane clean. naδ̣δ̣uf ij-jaama zeen.

to clean - 1. naδ̣δ̣af (u tanδ̣iif) t-. Has the maid cleaned the room yet? l-xaadma naδ̣δ̣fat il-ġurfa loo baεad? -- Please clean the chicken for me. ʔarjuuk naδ̣δ̣uf-li d-dijaaja. -- Where can I have my clothes cleaned? ween agdar awaddi hduumi lit-tanδ̣iif? -- We still have to clean the windows. baεad laazim innaδ̣δ̣uf iš-šibaabiič. 2. εazzal (i taεziil) t-. We gave the house a thorough cleaning today. εazzalna l-beet taεziila zeena l-yoom.

**He cleaned house in the poker game last night. l-baarζa bil-leel šaal kull il-gaaε bil-pookar.

to clean out - 1. farraġ (i tafriiġ) t-. This drawer has to be cleaned out. hal-imjarr laazim yitfarraġ. 2. ʔaxaδ il-ʔaku wil-maaku min. They cleaned me out all right. ʔaxδaw minni l-ʔaku wil-maaku or **δ̣irboo-li jyuubi ʔuuti.

to clean up - 1. ġassal (i taġsiil) t-. I'd like to clean up before dinner. ʔariid aġassil gabḷ il-εaša. 2. naδ̣δ̣af (u tanδ̣iif) t-. When are you going to clean up this mess on your desk? šwakit raζ-itnaδ̣δ̣uf hal-xarbaṭa min εala meezak?

cleaner - 1. munaδ̣δ̣if pl. -aat. This cleaner will remove all the spots. hal-munaδ̣δ̣if raζ-yrawwiζ kull il-lakkaat. 2. mukawwi, makwi. Do you know a good cleaners in this area? tuεruf fadd makwi zeen ib-hal-manṭiqa?

cleaning - tanδ̣iif, taεziil. The house needs a good cleaning. l-beet yinraad-la tanδ̣iif zeen.

cleaning plant - maζall (pl. -aat) kawi. They have their own cleaning plant. εidhum maζall kawi xaaṣṣ biihum.

cleaning woman - ṣaanεa pl. -aat. Where can I find a good cleaning woman? ween ʔagdar ʔalgi fadd ṣaanεa?

cleanser - munaδ̣δ̣if pl. -aat. This cleanser cleans pans well. hal-munaδ̣δ̣if ynaδ̣δ̣if il-ijduur tanδ̣iif zeen.

clear - 1. ṣaafi. The water is deep and clear. l-maay ġamiij w-ṣaafi. -- Try to keep a clear head. ζaawil itxalli fikrak ṣaafi. 2. waaδ̣iζ. His voice was very clear over the radio. ṣoota čaan kulliš waaδ̣iζ bir-raadyo. 3. ṣaζu, mṣaζζi. We have had clear weather all week. čaan ij-jaww εidna ṣaζu ṭuul il-ʔisbuuε. 4. δ̣aahir. It is clear from the letter that he isn't satisfied. δ̣aahir min maktuuba ʔinna muu raaδ̣i. 5. maftuuζ, masluuk. Is the road clear up ahead? ṭ-ṭariiq giddaam maftuuζ? 6. mirtaaζ. My conscious is clear. δ̣amiira mirtaaζ. 7. bari pl. ʔabriyaaʔ. We're going to release you; you're in the clear. raζ-inhiddak, ʔinta bari.

to clear - 1. ṣiζa (a ṣaζu). The sky is beginning to clear. s-sima bidat tiṣζa. 2. naδ̣δ̣af (u tanδ̣iif) *t-*. We've finished eating; you may clear the table now. *xallaṣna l-ʔakal hassa tigdar itnaððuf il-meez.* 3. *fakk (u fakk) n-*. These drops will clear your head and sinuses. *hal-qaṭra tfukk raasak w-ijyuubak il-ʔanfiyya.* 4. *ɛubar (u ɛubuur) n- foog, faat (u foot) n- foog.* The plane just barely cleared the tree tops as it took off. *ṭ-ṭiyyaara bil-kaad ɛubrat foog ruus il-ʔašjaar min ṭaarat.* 5. *barra (i tabriya) t-*. The court cleared him of the charges against him. *l-maζkama barrata mnit-tuham iδ-δidda.* 6. *xallaṣ (i taxliiṣ) t-*. Look and see if I'm going to clear that car. *baawiɛ-li w-šuuf ʔiδa ʔaxalliṣ min has-sayyaara.* 7. *ʔaxla (i ʔixlaaʔ).* Clear the court room. *ʔixlu qaaɛt il-maζkama.* 8. *ṭilaɛ (a ṭuluuɛ).* Your residence permit will take a week or two to clear. *ʔiqaamtak raζ-taaxuδ isbuuɛ loo sbuuɛeen ζatta tiṭlaɛ.* 9. *marr (u marr) n-*. It took us an hour to clear customs. *ʔaxδatna saaɛa ζatta nmurr bil-kumrug.*

to clear away - *šaal (i šeel) n-*. Tell her to clear away the dishes. *gul-lha xalli tšiili l-imwaaɛiin.*

to clear off - *šaal (i šeel) n- min.* Clear this stuff off your table. *šiil hal-ʔašyaaʔ min ɛala meezak.*

to clear one's throat - *tnaζnaζ (a naζnaζa).* He cleared his throat before he entered the room. *tnaζnaζ gabuḷ-ma yxušš lil-gubba.*

to clear out - 1. *farraġ (i tafriiġ) t-*. I'll clear out this closet so you can hang your clothes in it. *raζ-afarriġ hal-diilaab ζatta tigdar itɛallig ihduumak biiha.* 2. *šilaɛ (a šaliɛ).* He cleared out in the middle of the night. *šilaɛ ib-nuṣṣ il-leel* or ***šammaɛ il-xeeṭ ib-nuṣṣ il-leel.*

to clear up - 1. *ṣaζζa (i), ṣifa (a ṣafaaʔ).* The weather has cleared up and the rain has stopped. *ṣaζζat id-dinya wil-muṭar baṭṭal.* 2. *ṣifa (a ṣafaaʔ).* The dust storm is over; the weather has cleared up. *raaζat il-ɛajja; ṣifa j-jaww.* 3. *waδδaζ (i tawδiiζ) t-, fassar (i tafsiir) t-*. Several points remain to be cleared up. *ɛiddat nuqaṭ baɛad yinraad-ilha tawδiiζ.*

clearance - 1. *majaal* pl. *-aat.* I don't think there is enough clearance here for the truck to turn around. *ma-aɛtiqid ʔaku majaal kaafi lil-loori ydeewur ihnaa.* 2. *muwaafaqa* pl. *-aat, muṣaadaqa* pl. *-aat.* Foreigners have to get clearance from the proper authorities to work in Iraq. *l-ʔajaanib laazim yaaxδuun muwaafaqat iṣ-ṣulṭaat il-muxtaṣṣa lil-ɛamal bil-ɛiraaq.*

clearly - *b-wuδuuζ, b-ṣuura waaδζa.* Please speak more clearly. *ʔarjuuk itkallim ib-wuδuuζ ʔakθar.*

clergy - *ʔikliirus.*

clerical - *kitaabi**. I am looking for a clerical job. *da-adawwir-li fadd šaġla kitaabiyya.*

clerk - *kaatib* pl. *kuttaab.* He's a clerk in a big office. *huwwa kaatib ib-daaʔira čbiira.*

clever - 1. *δaki, faṭin.* He's a clever fellow. *huwwa fadd waaζid δaki.* 2. *maahir, ζaaδiq.* He's a very clever tailor. *huwwa fadd xayyaaṭ kulliš maahir.* 3. *labiq.* He's a clever speaker. *huwwa fadd xaṭiib labiq.* 4. *šaaṭir, ζaaδiq, faahim.* He's a clever business man. *huwwa fadd rajul ʔaɛmaal šaaṭir.*

click - *ṭagga* pl. *-aat.* I heard the click of the lock. *smaɛit ṭaggat il-keeluun.*

to click - 1. *ṭagg (u ṭagg) n-*. He clicked his heels and saluted me. *ṭagg-li salaam.* 2. *ṭagṭag (i ṭagṭaga).* I heard her heels clicking as she came toward me down the hall. *smaɛit čaɛab qundaratha ṭṭagṭig min jatt mittajha ɛalayya bil-mamarr.* 3. *nijaζ (a najaaζ).* The show clicked from the first night on. *t-tamθiiliyya nijζat min ʔawwal leela.*

**Everything clicked beautifully. *kullši miša miθl is-saaɛa.*

client - *maɛmiil* pl. *mɛaamiil, muraajiɛ* pl. *-iin.*

cliff - *juruf* pl. *jruuf.*

climate - 1. *manaax.* The climate here is not suitable for planting coconut. *hnaa l-manaax ma-ylaaʔim zariɛ jooz il-hind.* 2. *jaww* pl. *ʔajwaaʔ.* The political climate is favorable for his return to power. *j-jaww is-siyaasi ysaaɛid ɛala rijuuɛa lil-ζukum.*

climax - 1. *δarwa* pl. *-aat.* The climax of the excitement came when the president appeared on the balcony. *δarwat il-ζamaas ṣaar lamma r-raʔiis δihar bil-baalqoon.* 2. *ʔawj.* Islamic art reached a climax in the era of Haroun Al-Rashid. *l-fann il-ʔislaami wuṣal ʔila ʔawja b-ɛahad haaruun ir-rašiid.*

climb - *ṣaɛda, tasalluq.* You'll find the climb difficult. *raζ-itšuuf iṣ-ṣaɛda ṣaɛba.*

to climb - 1. *ṣiɛad (a ṣiɛuud) n-*. She can't climb the stairs anymore due to old age. *ma-tigdar tiṣɛad id-darab baɛad imnil-kubur.* -- They climb the date palms about five times a year. *yiṣɛaduun ɛala n-naxal ζawaali xamis marraat bis-sana.* 2. *tšalbah (a tšilbih, šalbaha).* The children enjoy climbing on the fence. *j-jihaal yζibbuun it-tišilbih ɛal-imζajjar.* 3. *ɛalla (i), rtifaɛ (i rtifaaɛ).* The jet planes climb rapidly after take-off. *ṭ-ṭiyyaarat ij-jatt itɛalli b-surɛa baɛad-ma ṭṭiir.*

to climb down - *nizal (i nizuul) n-*. The cat is afraid to climb down the tree. *l-bazzuuna txaaf tinzil imniš-šajara.*

to climb up - *ṣiɛad (a ṣiɛuud).* I climbed up on the rock first and then helped the rest of them up. *ṣiɛadit foog iṣ-ṣaxra ʔawwal w-saaɛadit il-baaqiin ɛaṣ-ṣaɛda.*

to **cling** - 1. *čallab (i tačliib).* The child is clinging to its mother. *j-jaahil imčallib ib-ʔumma.* 2. *lizag (a lazig) n-*. My shirt was clinging to my back with sweat. *θoobi čaan laazig ɛala δahri mnil-ɛarag.*

clinic - *ɛiyaada* pl. *-aat.* You can get a blood analysis at the clinic. *tigdar itsawwi taζliil damm bil-ɛiyaada.* -- This hospital has an out-patient clinic. *hal-mustašfa biiha ɛiyaada xaarijiyya.*

clip - 1. *danbuus* pl. *danaabiis.* She put a golden clip on her dress. *šakklat danbuus δahab ɛala nafnuufha.* 2. *klips* pl. *-aat, šikkaala* pl. *-aat.* Please give me a box of paper clips. *ʔarjuuk inṭiini paakeet iklips.* 3. *mišiṭ* pl. *mšuuṭ, mšaaṭ.* Can you show me how to put the clip in the rifle? *tigdar itraawiini šloon aζuṭṭ il-mišiṭ bil-bunduqiyya?*

to clip - 1. *gaṣṣ (u gaṣṣ) n-*. Don't clip my hair too short. *la-tguṣṣ šaɛri kulliš igṣayyir.* -- I clipped this article out of the magazine. *gaṣṣeet hal-maqaala mnil-majalla.* 2. *garṭaf (u garṭafa) t-*. The gardener clipped the hedges. *l-bistanči garṭaf is-siyaaj.* 3. *šakkal (i taškiil) t-*. Clip these papers together. *šakkil hal-awraaq suwa.*

clipping - *quṣaaṣa* pl. *-aat.* He showed me some clippings from the local newspapers. *raawaani čam quṣaaṣa mnij-jaraayid il-maζalliyya.*

cloak - 1. *ɛaba* pl. *-ɛibi.* The sheikh's cloak is made of pure camel wool. *l-ɛaba maal is-seex min wubar xaaliṣ.* 2. *ɛabaaya* pl. *-aat.* Only her face was visible in the cloak. *bass wuččha čaan imbayyin imnil-ɛabaaya.*

to cloak - *sitar (u satir) n-*. He is using his social position to cloak his membership in the secret organization. *da-yistiġill markaza l-ijtimaaɛi ζatta yistur ɛuδwiita bij-jamɛiyya s-sirriyya.*

clock - *saaɛa* pl. *-aat.* We set our clock by the radio. *nuδbuṭ saaɛatna ɛar-raadyo.*

to clock - *lizam (a lazim) wakit, waqqat (i tawqiit) t-*. Will you clock me for the hundred-meter run? *tilzam-li wakit ir-rikδ il-miit matir?* -- Clock the workers and see how much work they put out a day. *waqqit hal-ɛummaal w-šuuf išgadd yṭalliɛuun šuġuḷ bil-yoom.*

to **clog** - 1. *sadd (i sadd) n-*. The pipes are clogged. *l-ibwaari masduuda.* 2. *sadsad (i tsidsid) t-*. The holes in the strainer are clogged up. *ɛuyuun l-maṣfi msadsida.*

clogs - *qubqaab* pl. *qabaaqiib.* She wears clogs instead of sandals. *tilbas qubqaab badal in-naɛaal.*

close - 1. *ζamiim* pl. *-iin.* We are close friends. *ʔiζna ʔaṣdiqaaʔ ζamiimiin.* 2. *giriib, qariib.* The hotel is close to the station. *l-ʔuteel qariib imnil-maζaṭṭa.* -- This is close to what I had in mind. *haaδa giriib imniš-šii l-čaan ib-baali.* -- He is one of my closest friends. *huwwa min ʔaqrab ʔaṣdiqaaʔi.* -- The car drove up very close. *s-sayyaara wugfat kulliš qariib.* 3. *yamm.* We sat close together. *giɛadna waaζid yamm il-laax.* 4. *qurub, gurub.* We use to live close to each other. *činna niskun qurub baɛaδna.* 5. *maζṣuur, waxim.* The air is very close in this room. *l-hawa kulliš maζṣuur ib-hal-qubba.* 6. *zeen.* Pay close attention. *diir baalak zeen.* 7. *δaʔiil.* He won the election by a close margin of the vote. *ribaζ il-intixaab ib-fariq δaʔiil bil-aṣwaat.* 8. *daqiiq.* This problem needs close study. *hal-muškila tiζtaaj diraasa daqiiqa.* 9. *naaɛim.* The barber gave me a close shave this morning. *l-imzayyin zayyan-li wučči naaɛim il-yoom iṣ-ṣubuζ.*

**He had a close call. *xilaṣ b-iɛjuuba.*

close by - *b-qurub.* Is there a restaurant close by? *ʔaku maṭɛam ib-hal-qurub?*
close - *nihaaya, ʔaaxir.* I'll see you at the close of the meeting. *ʔašuufak ib-nihaayt il-ijtimaaɛ.*
to close - **1.** *sadd (i sadd) n-.* Please close the door. *min faḍlak, sidd il-baab.* -- The museum is closed Sundays. *l-matḥaf yinsadd ʔayyaam il-ʔaḥḥad.* **2.** *ġilag (u ġalig) n-, sadd (i sadd) n-.* The road is closed. *ṭ-ṭariiq maġluug.* **3.** *ɛazzal (i taɛziil) t-.* They close at six. *yɛazzluun bis-sitta.* **4.** *xitam (i xitaam) n-.* They closed the program with the national anthem. *xitmaw il-manhaj bin-našiid il-waṭani.* **5.** *ġammaḍ (u tġummuḍ) t-.* Close your eyes and go to sleep! *gammuḍ ɛuyuunak w-naam!*
to close one's eyes - *tɛaama (a taɛaami).* Don't close your eyes to the facts. *la-titɛaama ɛann il-ḥaqaayiq.*
closely - *b-diqqa.* Look at it closely. *baawuɛha b-diqqa.*
closet - *diilaab* pl. *dwaaliib, xazaana* pl. *xazaayin.* Her closet is full of new clothes. *diilaabha matruus ihduum jidiida.*
close up - **1.** *ṣuura* (pl. *ṣuwar) muqarraba.* Have you seen the close-ups we took of the baby. *šift iṣ-ṣuwar l-muqarraba l-ʔaxaḍnaaha lij-jaahil.* **2.** *min giriib, ɛan qurub.* From close up it looks different. *min giriib itbayyin ġeer šikil.*
cloth - **1.** *qmaaš* pl. *-aat, ʔaqmiša.* In the cloth market you find cloth for dresses, shirts, and pajamas. *b-suug l-iqmaašaat tilgi qmaaš maal nafaaniif, w-iθyaab, w-beejaamaat.* -- The book has a cloth binding. *ġilaaf l-iktaab min iqmaaš.* **2.** *xirga* pl. *xirag.* Use a clean cloth for the dusting. *ʔistaɛmil xirga nḍiifa lit-tanḍiif.*
**He made the story up out of whole cloth. *xilaq l-iḥčaaya min baṭna* or ***xilaq l-iḥčaaya min jawwa l-gaaɛ.*
to **clothe** - *kisa (i ʔiksaaʔ) n-.* The Red Crescent feeds and clothes the poor from its funds. *l-hilaal il-ʔaḥmar yiṭɛum w-yiksi l-fuqaraaʔ min mawaarda.*
clothes - *hduum, malaabis.* I want these clothes cleaned and pressed. *ʔariid hal-ihduum titnaḍḍaf w-tinḍurub ʔuuti.*
clothes hanger - *tiɛlaaga* pl. *-aat.*
clothes hook - *ɛillaaga* pl. *-aat.* We need a few more clothes hooks to hang up the clothes. *niḥtaaj baɛad fadd čam ɛillaaga l-taɛliig l-ihduum.*
clothesline - *ḥabil* (pl. *ḥbaal) šarr il-ihduum.*
clothespin - *qirraaṣa* pl. *-aat.* What has become of the clothespins? *š-ṣaar imnil-qirraaṣaat?*
clothes rack - *šimmaaɛa* pl. *-aat.* There's a clothes rack in the hall. *ʔaku šimmaaɛa bil-mamarr.*
clothing - *malaabis, hduum.*
cloud - *ġeema* pl. *ġyuum* coll. *ġeem.* The sun has disappeared behind the clouds. *š-šamis ixtifat wara l-ġeem.*
**He always has his head in the clouds. *haaḍa daalġači* or *haaḍa dallaaġ.*
to cloud up - *ġayyam (i taġyiim).* Just after we started the sky clouded up. *baɛad-ma bdeena b-šwayya ġayymat id-dinya.*
cloudy - *mġayyim.*
clover - *barsiim.*
club - **1.** *doonki* pl. *-iyyaat.* The policeman had to use his club. *š-šurṭi njubar yistaɛmil doonkiyya.* **2.** *migwaar* pl. *migaawiir, klung* pl. *-aat.* They fought with clubs and sickles. *tɛaarkaw bil-migaawiir wil-manaajil.* **3.** *naadi* pl. *nwaadi.* Are you a member of the club? *ʔinta ɛuḍu bin-naadi?* **4.** *sinak.* I played the ace of clubs. *ḍabbeet il-billi s-sinak.*
to club - *ḍirab (u ḍarub) n- bil-migwaar.* The man was clubbed. *r-rijjaal inḍirab bil-migwaar.*
clue - **1.** *ʔišaara* pl. *-aat.* Can you give me a clue? *tigdar tinṭiini fadd ʔišaara?* **2.** *daliil* pl. *ʔadilla.* The police found no clues. *š-šurṭa ma-ligaw ʔay daliil.*
clumsy - **1.** *mxarbaṭ.* That's a clumsy sentence. *haaḍi jumla mxarbuṭa.* **2.** *θgiil.* He's as clumsy as a bear. *huwwa θgiil miθil id-dibb.*
clutch - **1.** *klač* pl. *-aat.* Push in the clutch. *duus ɛal-iklač.* **2.** *qabḍa.* He fell into the clutches of some gangsters. *wugaɛ ib-qabḍat čam ʔašqiyaaʔ.*
**He had him in his clutches. *xallaa jawwa ɛbaaṭa.*
to clutch - **1.** *ɛiṣar (i ɛaṣir) n-, čallab (i tačliib) t- b-.* The child clutched my hand. *ṭ-ṭifil ɛiṣar iidi.* **2.** *madd (i madd) n- ʔiid~.* He clutched at the rope but he wasn't able to get ahold of it. *madd iida ɛal-ḥabil laakin ma-gidar ykumša.*
coach - **1.** *ɛarabaana* pl. *ɛarabaayin, fargoon* pl. *-aat.* The train consists of the engine and four coaches. *l-qiṭaar yitʔallif min makiina w-ʔarbaɛ fargoonaat.* **2.** *mudarrib* pl. *-iin.* He's the best coach in this school. *huwwa ʔaḥsan mudarrib ib-hal-madrasa.*
to coach - **1.** *darrab (i tadriib) t-.* He coaches the soccer team. *ydarrib firqat kuurat il-qadam.* **2.** *ɛallam (i taɛliim) t-.* Students in the back of the room began coaching him when he was asked a question. *ṭ-ṭullaab ib-ʔaxiir il-ġurfa bidaw yɛallmuu lamma nsiʔal suʔaal.*
coal - *faḥma* pl. *-aat* coll. *faḥam.* We have to order coal. *laazim nuṭlub faḥam.*
coal bin - *maxzan* (pl. *maxaazin) faḥam.*
coarse - *xašin.* This material is very coarse. *hal-uqmaaš kulliš xašin.* -- He's a very coarse person. *huwwa fadd waaḥid kulliš xašin.*
coast - *saaḥil* pl. *sawaaḥil.* We approached the coast at night. *tqarrabna mnis-saaḥil bil-leel.*
to coast - *tdahdar (a tdihdir).* We coasted for three hundred meters. *tdahdarna tlaθ miit matir.*
coast guard - *xafar is-sawaaḥil.*
coat - **1.** *qappuuṭ* pl. *-aat, miɛṭaf* pl. *maɛaaṭif.* You can't go out without a coat in this weather. *ma-tigdar titlaɛ iblayya qappuuṭ ib-haj-jaww.* **2.** *sitra* pl. *sitar.* The pants are fine but the coat's too tight. *l-panṭaruun maḍbuuṭ laakin is-sitra kulliš ḍayyga.* **3.** *qaaṭ* pl. *quuṭ.* This house needs another coat of paint. *hal-beet yinraad-la qaaṭ subuġ θaani.*
coated - *mġaṭṭa.* The car was coated with mud. *s-sayyaara čaanat imġaṭṭaaya biṭ-ṭiin.*
coat hanger - *tiɛlaaga* pl. *-aat.*
cobweb - *ɛišš ɛankabuut, beet ɛankabuut, xyuuṭ ɛankabuut.*
cockroach - *ṣurṣur* pl. *ṣaraaṣir, ṣarṣuur* pl. *ṣaraaṣiir, bint* (pl. *banaat) murdaan.*
cocktail - *kookteel* pl. *-aat.*
cocoa - *kakaaw.*
coconut - *joozat* (pl. *-aat) hind,* coll. *jooz hind.*
code - **1.** *rumuuz, ʔišaaraat.* They sent the telegram in Morse code. *dazzaw il-barqiyya b-rumuuz moors.* **2.** *šafra.* They tried to decipher the code. *ḥaawlaw yfassiruun iš-šafra.*
code of ethics - *qawaaɛid ʔadabiyya.*
code of Hammurabi - *šariiɛat ḥamuraabi.*
code of morals - *qawaaɛid ʔaxlaaqiyya.*
coffee - *gahwa.* The coffee is freshly roasted. *l-gahwa stawha tḥammṣat.*
coffee pot - *dalla* (pl. *-aat, dlaal) maal gahwa.*
coffin - *taabuut* pl. *twaabiit.*
cog - *sinn* pl. *snuun.* One of the cogs is broken off this gear. *waaḥid imn-isnuun had-dišli maksuur.*
cognac - *koonyaak.*
coil - *laffa* pl. *-aat.* You'll have to buy a coil of wire. *laazim tištiri laffat waayar.*
ignition coil - *kooyil* pl. *-aat.*
to coil - *ltaff (a ltifaaf).* The snake coiled around the man's arm. *l-ḥayya ltaffat ḥawl iḍraaɛ ir-rajjaal.*
to coil up - *laff (i laff) n-.* He coiled up the wire. *laff is-siim.*
coin - *ɛumla* pl. *-aat.* He collects old gold coins. *yjammiɛ ɛumla ḏahabiyya qadiima.*
to coin - **1.** *ḍurab (a ḍarub) n-.* This money was coined in Belgium. *hal-ɛumla nḍurbat ib-baljiika.* **2.** *xilaq (i xaliq) n-.* Scientists are coining new words every day. *l-ɛulamaaʔ da-yxilquun kalimaat ijdiida kull yoom.*
coincidence - *ṣudfa* pl. *ṣudaf.* What a strange coincidence! *šloon ṣudfa ġariiba!*
coke - *faḥam il-kuuk.* We use coke for heating. *nistaɛmil faḥam il-kuuk lit-tadfiʔa.*
cold - **1.** *barid.* I can't stand this cold. *ma-agdar atḥammal hal-barid.* **2.** *bardaan.* I'm cold. *ʔaani bardaan.* **3.** *barid, našla, zukaam.* He has a bad cold. *ɛinda našla qawiyya.* **4.** *baarid.* It was a cold night. *čaanat leela baarda.*
**The blow knocked him cold. *ḍ-ḍarba ʔafqidat šuɛuura.*
to **collaborate** - **1.** *tɛaawan (a taɛaawun).* She collaborated with the enemy. *tɛaawnat wiyya l-ɛadu.* **2.** *štirak (i štiraak), tɛaawan (a taɛaawun).* Two teams of scientists collaborated in the experiment. *firiqteen imnil-ɛulamaaʔ ištirkat ib-ɛamal it-tajruba.*
to **collapse** - **1.** *nhaar (a nhiyaar), nhidam (i nhidaam), tdahwar (a tadahwur).* The bridge suddenly collapsed. *j-jisir inhaar ɛala ġafla.* **2.** *wugaɛ (a wguuɛ),*

xirab (a). He collapsed in the middle of the street. *wugaɛ ib-nuṣṣ ij-jaadda.*

collar – *yaaxa* pl. *-aat.* Do you want your collars starched or not? *triid yaaxaatak imnaššaaya loo laa?*

collar bone – *ɛaḍm* (pl. *ɛḍaam*) *ṭurquwa.*

to **collect** – **1.** *jimaɛ (a jamiɛ) n-, jammaɛ (i tajmiiɛ) t-, lamm (i lamm) n-.* I collect stamps. *ʔajammiɛ ṭawaabiɛ.* -- Give me a chance to collect my thoughts. *nṭiini majaal ʔajmaɛ fikri.* **2.** *ltamm (a ltimaam).* People collected in the square. *n-naas iltammaw bis-saaẓa.*

collected – **1.** *ḍaabuṭ il-aɛṣaab.* In spite of the danger, he remained calm and collected. *b-raġm il-xaṭar, buqa haadiʔ w-ḍaabuṭ aɛṣaaba.* **2.** *majmuuɛ.* I bought the collected works of Taha Hussein. *štireet il-muʔallafaat il-majmuuɛa li-ṭaaha ẓseen.*

collection – *majmuuɛa, majaamiiɛ.* The library has a famous collection of books on America. *l-maktaba biiha majmuuɛa mašhuura mnil-kutub ɛan ʔamriika.*

**What time is the last mail collection? *šwakit ʔaaxir marra yinlamm il-bariid?*

**They took up a collection for the beggar. *jimɛaw ifluus lil-faqiir.*

college – *kulliyya* pl. *-aat.*

to **collide** – *ṣṭidam (i ṣṭidaam), tṣaadam (a taṣaadum).* The cars collided at the intersection. *s-sayyaaraat itṣaadmat ib-mafraq iṭ-ṭariiq.*

collision – *taṣaadum* pl. *-aat, ṣṭidaam* pl. *-aat.*

colloquial – *ɛammi*, jilfi*.* How do I say this in the colloquial language? *šloon aguul haay bil-luġa l-ɛammiyya?*

cologne – *riiẓa, qaloonya.*

colon – **1.** *nuquṭṭeen.* Use a comma instead of a colon. *ʔistaɛmil faariẓa badal nuquṭṭeen.* **2.** *kooloon* pl. *-aat.* Your colon is in an inflammed condition. *l-kooloon maalak miltihib.*

colonel – *ɛaqiid* pl. *ɛuqadaaʔ.*

to **colonize** – *staɛmar (i stiɛmaar).* They colonized the island. *staɛmiraw ij-jaziira.*

colony – *mustaɛmara* pl. *-aat.* We were a colony until two years ago. *činna mustaɛmara ʔila gabuḷ santeen.* -- There's a colony of ants in our back yard. *ʔaku mustaɛmarat namil ib-ẓadiiqatna.* **2.** *jaaliya.* The majority of the American colony lives in this district. *ʔakθariyyat il-jaaliya l-ʔamiirkiyya tiskun ib-hal-manṭiqa.*

color – *loon* pl. *ʔalwaan.* I don't like any of these colors. *ma-aẓibb ʔay loon min hal-ʔalwaan.* -- The team wore its school colors. *l-fariiq libas loon madrasta.*

to color – *lawwan (i talwiin) t-.* She colored some pictures. *lawwinat čam ṣuura.*

colored – **1.** *mulawwan* pl. *-iin.* Several colored families live near here. *ɛiddat ɛawaaʔil imnil-mulawwiniin itɛiiš qariib min ihnaa.* -- Do you have any colored handkerchiefs? *ɛindak ʔay icfaafi mlawwna?* **2.** *maṣbuuġ.* His ideas are colored by Communism. *ʔaaraaʔa maṣbuuġa biš-šuyuuɛiyya.*

color-blindness – *ɛama l-ʔalwaan.*

colt – *muhur* pl. *muhuur.*

column – **1.** *ɛamuud* pl. *ʔaɛmida, ɛawaamiid.* You can recognize the house by its white columns. *tigdar tuɛruf il-beet imnil-ɛawaamiid il-biiḍ il-bii.* -- Write your name in the right-hand column. *ʔiktib ismak bil-ɛamuud illi ɛal-yimna.* **2.** *ṭaabuur* pl. *ṭwaabiir, ratil* pl. *ʔartaal.* Four columns of soldiers marched down the road. *ʔarbaɛ artaal imnij-jinuud mišat bis-saariɛ.* -- I believe she's a member of the fifth column. *ʔaɛtiqid hiyya mnir-ratl il-xaamis.*

comb – **1.** *mišiṭ* pl. *mšaaṭ.* Where can I buy a comb? *mneen agdar aštiri mišiṭ?* **2.** *xaliyya* pl. *xalaaya.* The comb is full of honey. *l-xaliyya malyaana ɛasal.*

to comb – *maššaṭ (i tamšiiṭ, tmiššiṭ) t-.* Did your mother comb your hair? *ʔummak maššiṭat saɛrak?* -- The police combed the whole city. *š-šurṭa maššṭooha lil-wlaaya kullha.*

combination – *jamiɛ.* How do you like the combination of red and gray? *šloon yɛijbak ij-jamiɛ been il-ʔaẓmar wir-rumaadi?*

**We are the only ones who know the combination to the safe. *ʔiẓna l-waẓiidiin illi nuɛruf tartiib rumuuz fatẓ il-qaaṣa.*

to come – **1.** *jaa (i majiiʔ).* When does he come to town? *šwakit yiji lil-wlaaya?* -- Joking comes natural to him. *t-tankiit yijii b-ṣuura ṭabiiɛiyya.* -- This cloth comes only in two colors. *hal-iqmaaš ma-yiji ġeer ib-looneen.* **2.** *ṣaadaf (i muṣaadafa), tṣaadaf (a taṣaaduf).* My birthday comes on a Monday this year. *ɛiid miilaadi yṣaadif has-sana yoom il-iθneen.* **3.** *taɛaal.* Come here a minute, Nizar. *taɛaal fadd daqiiqa, nazaar.* -- Hey boys, come over here! *yaa ʔawlaad, taɛaalu!*

**I don't know whether I'm coming or going. *ma-da-aɛruf iš-da-asawwi.*

**Come now, I'm not that foolish. *bass ɛaad, ʔaani mu l-had-daraja ġabi.*

to come about – *jira (i majra), ṣaar (i ṣeer).* How did all this come about? *šloon jira haaḍa kulla?*

to come across – **1.** *ɛubar (u ɛabur) n-.* He had to come across the bridge to visit us. *ḍṭarr yuɛbur ij-jisir ẓatta yzuurna.* **2.** *liga (i lagi) n-.* I accidentally came across my friend's name in this book. *lgeet ʔisim ṣadiiqi b-hal-iktaab biṣ-ṣidfa.*

**He's the wisest man I've ever come across. *huwwa ʔaɛqal šaxiṣ šifta.*

to come after (or for) – *jaa (i majiiʔ) ɛala.* I've come after my passport. *jeet ɛala paaspoorti.*

to come along – *miša (i maši).* How's your work coming along? *šloon da-yimsi šuġlak?*

to come apart – *tfaṣṣax (a tafaṣṣux), tfallaš (a tfilliš).* This chair is coming apart. *hal-kursi da-yitfaṣṣax.*

to come around – *ɛaawad (i muɛaawada).* The beggar comes around to us every Friday. *l-imjaddi yɛaawidna kull yoom jimɛa.*

to come back – **1.** *rijaɛ (a rujuuɛ).* They're coming back tomorrow. *yirjaɛuun baačir.*

to come by – **1.** *marr (u muruur) min.* He's coming by here this afternoon. *raẓ-ymurr minnaa l-yoom il-ɛaṣir.* **2.** *dabbar (u tadbiir) t-.* How did he come by all that money? *šloon dabbar kull hal-ifluus?*

to come down – **1.** *nizal (i nuzuul).* Can you come down a moment? *tigdar tinzil fadd laẓḍa?* **2.** *xaffaḍ (u taxfiiḍ, txuffuḍ) t-, nazzal (i tanziil, tnizzil) t-.* We can't come down a bit on this price. *ma-nigdar inxaffuḍ has-siɛir wala filis.* **3.** *nṣaab (a ʔiṣaaba).* He came down with a bad cold. *nṣaab ib-fadd našla qawiyya.*

to come in – **1.** *dixal (u duxuul), xašš (u xašš).* Please come in. *ʔarjuuk idxul* or *rajaaʔan xušš.* **2.** *wuṣal (a wuṣuul).* What time does the train come in? *šwakit yooṣal il-qiṭaar?* **3.** *jaa (i majiiʔ).* Requests for help are coming in daily. *ṭalabaat il-musaaɛada da-tiji yoomiyyan.*

to come in handy – *faad (i faaʔida), nifaɛ (a nafiɛ).* It'll come in very handy to you later. *raẓ-itfiidak baɛdeen.*

to come off – **1.** *nšilaɛ (i).* One leg of the table has come off. *wiẓda min rijleen il-meez inšilɛat.* **2.** *ngiṭaɛ (i ngiṭaaɛ).* The button has come off. *d-dugma ngiṭɛat.* **3.** *gaam (u goom), nẓakk (a).* The color comes off these gloves. *ṣ-ṣubuġ da-yguum min hač-čifuuf.* **4.** *ṭilaɛ (ṭuluuɛ).* The play came off real well. *t-tamθiiliyya ṭilɛat zeena.*

to come out – **1.** *ṭilaɛ (a ṭuluuɛ).* Are you going to come out to the farm with us? *raẓ-tiṭlaɛ wiyyaana lil-mazraɛa?* -- The ink spot won't come out of this shirt. *buqɛat il-ẓibir ma-tiṭlaɛ min haθ-θoob.* -- Who came out on top in the fight? *minu ṭilaɛ ġaaḷub bil-mulaakama?* or *minu ġiḷab bil-mulaakama?* or *minu faaz bil-mulaakama?* **2.** *ḍihar (a ḍuhuur), ʔija (i majiiʔ), ṭilaɛ (a ṭuluuɛ).* Their product came out on the market a month ago. *mantuujhum ḍihar bis-suug gabuḷ šahar.* **3.** *bayyan (i tbiyyin) t-.* The truth finally came out. *l-ẓaqiiqa bayyinat bit-taali.* **4.** *ḍihar (a ḍuhuur), bayyan (i tbiyyin).* The president came out in favor of high taxes. *r-raʔiis ḍihar yfaḍḍil iḍ-ḍaraaʔib il-ɛaalya.*

to come over – **1.** *ʔija (i majiiʔ).* Some friends are coming over to see us this evening. *baɛḍ il-ʔaṣdiqaaʔ raẓ-yjuun ɛidna hal-leela.* **2.** *ṣiɛad (a ṣuɛuud), faaḍ (i feeḍ).* The water's starting to come over the curb. *l-mayy bida yiṣɛad ɛala ẓaaffat ir-raṣiif.* **3.** *ɛubar (u ɛabur) n-.* They came over the bridge on their way to town. *ɛubraw ij-jisir ib-ṭariiqhum lil-madiina.*

**I don't know what's come over him. *ma-adri š-bii.*

to come through – **1.** *marr (u muruur) n- b-.* Did you come through the woods on your way here? *marreet bil-ġaaba b-ṭariiqak l-ihnaa.* -- He came through the operation safely. *marr bil-ɛamaliyya b-salaama.* **2.** *xaaḍ (u xooḍ) n- b-, marr (u muruur) n- b-.* He had to come through mud to get here. *ḍṭarr yxuuḍ*

ib-ṭiin ħatta yooṣal l-ihnaa.
to come to – 1. *waṣṣal (i twiṣṣil).* The bill comes to two dollars. *l-qaaʔima twaṣṣil doolaareen.* **2.** *ṣiħa (i ṣaħu).* After a few minutes she came to. *ṣiħat baεad fadd čam daqiiqa.* **3.** *ṣaar (i ṣeer).* Who knows what all this will come to? *minu yidri š-raħ-yṣiir?* **4.** *ʔija, jaa (i majiiʔ) b–.* Her name doesn't come to me right now. *ʔisimha ma-yiji b-baali hassa.*
to come true – *tħaqqaq (a taħaqquq).* Her dream came true. *tħaqqaq ħilimha.*
to come up – 1. *ṭilaε (a ṭuluuε).* The diver came up after three minutes under water. *l-ġawwaaṣ ṭilaε li-foog baεad-ma čaan iθlaθ daqaayiq taħt il-mayy.* -- The wheat is beginning to come up. *l-ħunṭa bida tiṭlaε.* **2.** *ð̣ihar (a ð̣uhuur).* This problem comes up every day. *hal-muškila tið̣har kull yoom.* **3.** *ṣaar (i ṣeer).* A thunderstorm is coming up. *raħ-iṣṣiir εaaṣifa.* **4.** *ṣiεad (a ṣuεuud, ṣaεid).* Can you come up for a minute? *tigdar tiṣεad il-fadd daqiiqa?* **5.** *jaab (i jeeb) n–.* If you can come up with a better idea, go right ahead. *ʔiða tigdar itjiib fikra ʔaħsan, itfað̣ð̣al.*
to come upon – 1. *twaṣṣal (a tawaṣṣul) l–.* I came upon the solution by accident. *twaṣṣalit lil-ħall biṣ-ṣidfa.* **2.** *ʔija, jaa (i majiiʔ) εala.* We came upon a man lying in the street. *jeena εala rijjaal waagiε biš-šaariε.*
to come up to – *ṭaabaq (i muṭaabaqa), nṭubaq (u nṭibaaq) εala.* The new bridge didn't come up to government specifications. *j-jisir ij-jidiid ma-ṭaabaq muwaaṣafaat il-ħukuuma.*
comedy – *ruwaaya* (pl. *-aat*) *hazaliyya.* Did you like the comedy? *εijbatak ir-ruwaaya l-hazaliyya?*
comet – *muðannab* pl. *-aat.*
comfort – *wasiilat* (pl. *wasaaʔil*) *raaħa.* This hotel has all the comforts you can ask for. *hal-funduq bii jamiiε wasaaʔil ir-raaħa lli tuṭlubha.*
to comfort – *εazza (i taεziya).* We went to comfort her after her son died. *riħna nεazziiha baεad-ma maat ibinha.*
comfortable – 1. *muriiħ.* This chair is very comfortable. *hal-kursi kulliš muriiħ.* **2.** *mirtaaħ.* I don't feel very comfortable. *ʔaani ma-mirtaaħ.*
to make oneself comfortable – *stiraaħ (i stiraaħa).* Sit down and make yourself comfortable. *ʔugεud w-istiriiħ* or *ʔugεud w-xuð raaħtak.*
comical – *hazali*, fukaahi*, muð̣ħik.* The movie was very comical. *l-filim čaan kulliš hazali.*
comma – *faariza* pl. *fawaariz.*
command – 1. *ʔamur* pl. *ʔawaamir.* Why wasn't my command carried out? *leeš ma-tnaffað ʔamri?* **2.** *ṣayṭara.* He has an excellent command of English. *εinda ṣayṭara taamma εal-luġa l-ingiliiziyya.*
in command – *ʔaamir.* Who's in command of these soldiers? *minu ʔaamir hal-jinuud?*
to command – 1. *ʔumar (u ʔamur).* He commanded the soldiers to return. *ʔumar ij-junuud bir-rujuuε.* **2.** *jilab (i jalib) n–.* He commands respect everywhere he goes. *yijlib iħtiraam ween-ma yruuħ.* **3.** *qaad (u qiyaada) n–.* My father commands the Fifth Army. *ʔabuuya yquud ij-jeeš il-xaamis.*
to command a view – *ṭall (u ʔiṭlaal), ʔašraf (i ʔišraaf).* Our house commands a view of the entire lake. *beetna yṭull εal-buħeera kullha.*
commander – *qaaʔid* pl. *quwwaad.* He's been appointed commander of the Fourteenth Army. *huwwa tεayyan qaaʔid lij-jeeš ir-raabiε εašar.*
to **commend – 1.** *midaħ (a madiħ) n–, ħimad (i ħamid) n–.* He commended the soldiers for their bravery in the battle. *midaħ ij-junuud il-basaalathum bil-maεraka.* **2.** *sallam (i tasliim) t–.* He commended his soul to God. *sallam rooħa l-ʔaḷḷa.*
comment – *taεliiq* pl. *-aat, mulaaħað̣a* pl. *-aat.* Did he have any comments on the subject? *čaanat εinda taεliiqaat εal-mawð̣uuε?*
to comment – *εallaq (i taεliiq) t–.* The editor commented on the president's visit. *l-muħarrir εallaq εala ziyaarat ir-raʔiis.*
commercial – *tijaari*.* He's well known in commercial circles. *huwwa zeen maεruuf bil-ʔawsaaṭ it-tijaariyya.*
to **commit – 1.** *rtikab (i rtikaab).* Who committed the crime? *minu rtikab ij-jariima?* **2.** *daxxal (i tadxiil).* They committed her to a mental hospital. *daxxlooha b-mustašfa l-ʔamraað̣ il-εaqliyya.*
to commit one's self – *tεahhad (a taεahhud), ltizam (i ltizaam).* The president refused to commit himself. *r-raʔiis rufað̣ yitεahhad.*
to commit suicide – *ntiħar (i ntiħaar).* He committed suicide last week. *ntiħar bil-ʔisbuuε il-maað̣i.*
committee – *lujna* pl. *lijaan.*
common – 1. *šaayiε.* Some French words are in common use in the Lebanese dialect. *baεað̣ ič-čilam il-fransiyya šaayεat il-istiεmaal bil-lahja l-lubnaaniyya.* **2.** *muštarak.* We have common goals. *εidna ġaayaat muštaraka.* **3.** *εaammi* pl. *εawaamm.* The common people don't care about politics. *l-εawaamm ma-yihtammuun bis-siyaasa.*
common knowledge – *l-maεruuf εan.* It is common knowledge that he lies. *l-maεruuf εanna huwwa yičðib.*
common market – *suuq muštarak.*
commotion – *haraj w-maraj.* There was a terrific commotion in the street. *čaan ʔaku haraj w-maraj biš-šaariε.*
to **communicate – 1.** *ttiṣal (i ttiṣaal).* We communicate with them daily by radio. *nittiṣil biihum yoomiyyan bir-raadyo.* **2.** *tfaaham (a tafaahum).* They have difficulty communicating because of a language problem. *b-ṣuεuuba yitfaahmuun ib-sabab muškilt il-luġa.*
communication – 1. *muwaaṣalaat.* He works in the communication branch. *da-yištuġul ib-qism il-muwaaṣalaat.* **2.** *muraasala* pl. *-aat.* We received their communication a week ago. *stilamna muraasalathum gabuḷ isbuuε.*
Communism – *šiyuuεiyya.*
Communist – *šiyuuεi** pl. *-iyyiin.*
community – *wlaaya* pl. *-aat.* He lives in a small community about four miles from Baghdad. *yεiiš b-wlaaya ṣġayyra ħawaali ʔarbaε imyaal min baġdaad.*
compact – 1. *quuṭiyyat* (pl. *-aat*) *poodra.* She bought a new compact. *štireet quuṭiyyat poodra jdiida.* **2.** *maħšuuk, marṣuuṣ.* That's a very compact package. *har-ruzma maħšuuka ħašik.*
company – 1. *fawj* pl. *ʔafwaaj.* I served in his company. *xidamit bil-fawj maala.* **2.** *šarika* pl. *-aat.* What company do you represent? *ʔay šarika tmaθθilha?* **3.** *xiṭṭaar, ð̣uyuuf.* We are expecting company this evening. *nitwaqqaε xiṭṭaar hal-leela.* **4.** *jamaaεa, ʔaṣdiqaaʔ, rifjaan.* A man is known by the company he keeps. *r-rajul maεruuf imnij-jamaaεa lli yimši wiyyaahum.* **5.** *rafiiq* pl. *rufaqaaʔ, rifiij* pl. *rifjaan.* I find him very good company. *šifta kulliš xooš rafiiq.*
**Keep me company for a while. *ʔubqa wiyyaaya fadd išwaaya.*
comparatively – *nisbiyyan.* The test was comparatively easy. *l-ixtibaar čaan nisbiyyan saahil.*
to **compare** – *qaaran (i muqaarana) t- been.* We compared the two methods. *qaarenna been iṭ-ṭariiqteen.*
comparison – *muqaarana* pl. *-aat.* Can you make another comparison between the two? *tigdar itsawwi muqaarana ʔuxra been il-iθneen?*
**There is no comparison between the two. *ween haaða min ðaak?* or *haaða ween w-ðaak ween?*
compartment – 1. *maqṣuura* pl. *-aat.* All compartments in this car are crowded with people. *kull il-maqṣuuraat ib-hal-εaraba mizdaħma bin-naas.* **2.** *xaana* pl. *-aat, beet* pl. *-byuut.* The drawer has compartments for knives, forks, and spoons. *j-jaraar bii xaanaat lis-sičaačiin wič-čaṭalaat wil-xawaašiig.*
compass – 1. *booṣla* pl. *-aat.* Without the compass we would have been lost. *loo maa l-booṣla čaan ðiεna.* **2.** *purgaaḷ* pl. *paraagiiḷ.* I can draw a circle without a compass. *ʔagdar ʔarsim daaʔira blayya purgaaḷ.*
to **compel** – *jubar (u jabur) n–, ð̣ṭarr (a ð̣ṭiraar).* The accident compelled us to leave a day early. *l-ħaadiθ jubarna nitruk yoom gabuḷ.*
compensation – *taεwiið̣* pl. *-aat.* I demand full compensation. *ʔaṭaalub ib-taεwiið̣ kaamil.*
to **compete – 1.** *tnaafas (a tanaafus), tsaabaq (a tasaabuq).* The two teams are competing for the silver cup. *l-firiqteen yitnaafsuun εal-kaʔs il-fuð̣ð̣i.* **2.** *naafas (i munaafasa), zaaħam (i muzaaħama).* I won't ever be able to compete with him in the exams. *ma-raħ-agdar ʔanaafsa bil-imtiħaanaat.*
competent – *muqtidir, kafu.*
competition – *munaafasa, muzaaħama.* Competition is necessary in business. *l-munaafasa ð̣aruuriyya bil-ħayaat it-tijaariyya.*
competitor – *munaafis* pl. *-iin, muzaaħim* pl. *-iin.* Our competitor's product is no good. *ʔintaaj munaafisna muu zeen.*
to **compile** – *jammaε (i tjimmiε) t–.* He's compiling

material for his new book. *da-yjammi£ mawaadd l-iktaaba j-jidiid.*
to **complain** - *štika (i tšikki), tšakka (a tšikki).* She complains of severe pains. *da-tištiki min wuja£ šadiid.* 2. *tðammar (a taðammur), štika (i tšikki), tšakka (a tšikki).* He complains about his work. *da-yitðammar min suġla.*
complaint - 1. *šakwa* pl. *šakaawi, šakaaya* pl. *-aat.* Do you have any complaints? *£indak ʔay šakwa?* 2. *da£wa* pl. *da£aawi.* I filed a complaint with the police after the assault took place. *sajjalit da£wa £ind iš-šurṭa ba£ad-ma ṣaar il-i£tidaaʔ.*
complete - *kaamil.* This volume makes my collection complete. *haj-juzuʔ ysawwi majmuu£ati kaamla.* 2. *tamaam, bil-marra.* He's a complete fool. *huwwa ʔaẓmaq tamaam.*
to complete - *kammal (i tkimmil) t-, xaḷḷaṣ (i txiḷḷiṣ) t-, tammam (i ttimmim) t-, ʔanha (i ʔinhaaʔ) n-.* We'll complete the arrangements for the trip tomorrow. *raẓ-inkammil it-tartiibaat lis-safra bukra.*
completely - 1. *tamaaman.* He convinced me completely. *ʔaqna£ni tamaaman.* 2. *bil-marra.* You're completely wrong. *ʔinta ġalṭaan bil-marra.*
complexion - *bušra* pl. *-aat.* He has a very dark complexion. *l-bušra maalta kulliš samra.*
to **complicate** - *£aqqad (i ta£qiid).* Don't complicate matters any more than they are. *la-t£aqqid il-ʔumuur ʔakθar mim-ma hiyya.*
complicated - *m£aqqad.*
compliment - 1. *madiẓ, θanaaʔ* pl. *-aat.* Thanks for the compliment. *ʔaškurak £ala l-madiẓ.* 2. *taẓiyya* pl. *-aat.* Please accept this gift with the compliments of the company. *rajaaʔan itqabbal hal-hadiyya ma£a taẓiyyat iš-šarika.*
to compliment - *midaẓ (a madiẓ) n-, ʔaθna (i θanaaʔ) n- £ala.* He complimented me on my cooking. *midaẓni £ala ṭabxi* or *ʔaθna £alayya b-ṭabxi.*
to **comply** - 1. *labba (i talbiya) t-.* We regret that we cannot comply with your request. *ʔaasfiin ma-nigdar inlabbi ṭalabak.* 2. *tjaawab (a tajaawub), ṭaa£ (i ʔiṭaa£a).* He refused to comply with the rules of the university. *rufaḍ yṭii£ qawaaniin ij-jaami£a* or *rufaḍ yitjaawab wiyya qawaaniin ij-jaami£a.*
to **compose** - 1. *ʔallaf (i taʔliif) t-.* He composed a piece of music for the occasion. *ʔallaf qiṭ£a muusiiqiyya lil-munaasaba.* -- This sentence is composed of a subject and a predicate. *haj-jumla titʔallaf min mubtadaʔ w-xabar.* 2. *ḍubaṭ (u ḍabuṭ), hadda? (i thiddiʔ, tahdiʔa).* Just try to compose yourself a bit. *ẓaawil tiḍbuṭ nafsak išwayya.*
composed - 1. *ḍaabuṭ in-nafis, haadiʔ, mṣaytir £ala n-nafis.* He remained composed during the whole trial. *buqa ḍaabuṭ nafsa ṭuul il-muẓaakama.* 2. *mitkawwin.* This fabric is composed of rayon and silk. *hal-iqmaaš mitkawwin min riiyoon w-ẓariir.*
composition - 1. *taʔliif* pl. *taʔaaliif.* The orchestra is going to play his compositions tonight. *l-firqa l-muusiiqiyya raẓ-ti£zif taʔaaliifa hal-leela.* 2. *murakkabaat, mukawwinaat.* The composition of this rock isn't known. *murakkabaat haṣ-ṣaxra muu ma£ruufa.* 3. *ʔinšaaʔ* pl. *-aat.* Have you done your English composition? *sawweet ʔinšaaʔak il-ingiliizi?*
compress - *ḍamaada* pl. *-aat, kammaada* pl. *-aat.* A cold compress will relieve the pain. *ḍamaada barda raẓ-itxaffuf il-wuja£.*
to compress - *ḍiġaṭ (u ḍaġiṭ) n-.* It is difficult to compress water. *mniṣ-ṣa£ub tuḍġuṭ il-mayy.*
compromise - *taraaḍi.* The problem cannot be solved but by compromise. *l-masʔala ma-tinẓall ʔilla bit-taraaḍi.*
to compromise - 1. *traaḍa (i taraaḍi), tsaahal (a tasaahul), saawa (i musaawaa).* They don't want to compromise. *ma-yirduun yitraaḍuun.* 2. *£arraḍ (i ta£riiḍ) t- lil-xaṭar.* You have compromised the security of our country. *£arraḍit salaamat baladna lil-xaṭar.*
comrade - *rafiiq* pl. *rufaqaaʔ, rifaaq; zamiil* pl. *zumalaaʔ.*
to **conceal** - *ḍamm (u ḍamm) n-, ʔaxfa (i ʔixfaaʔ) n-.* He concealed himself behind a tree. *ḍamm nafsa wara fadd šijara.* -- He attempted to conceal the truth from the judge. *ẓaawal yixfi l-ẓaqiiqa £an il-ẓaakim.*
conceited - *mitkabbur, maġruur, šaayif in-nafis.* Those girls are all very conceited. *hal-banaat kullhin mitkabburaat.*
conceivable - *mumkin ʔidraak.* A few years ago a trip to the moon wasn't even conceivable. *gabuḷ čam sana is-safar lil-gumar ma-čaan mumkin ʔidraaka.*
to **conceive** - *tṣawwar (a taṣawwur).* I can't conceive of her doing such a thing. *ma-yimkin ʔatṣawwarha tsawwi hiiči šii.*
concentrate - *murakkaz.* Mix one can of orange juice concentrate with three cans of water. *ʔixluṭ quuṭiyyat £aṣiir purṭaqaal murakkaz wiyya tlaθ qawaaṭi mayy.*
to concentrate - 1. *ẓaššad (i taẓšiid, tẓiššid) t-.* The commanders concentrated the armies at the base of the hill. *l-quwwaad ẓaššdaw ij-juyuuš jawwa j-jibal.* 2. *rakkaz (i tarkiiz) t-.* We're going to concentrate on pronunciation today. *raẓ-inrakkiz £at-talaffuḍ il-yoom.* -- The textile industry is concentrated in the North. *ṣinaa£at in-nasiij mitrakkza biš-šimaal.*
concern - 1. *šarika* pl. *-aat.* How long have you been with this concern? *šgadd ṣaar-lak ib-haš-šarika?* 2. *da£wa* pl. *da£aawi, šuġuḷ* pl. *ʔašġaal.* She said it was no concern of mine. *gaalat ma-ʔili da£wa biiha.* 3. *qalaq.* There's no reason for concern. *ma-aku daa£i lil-qalaq.*
to concern - *xaṣṣ (u), hamm (i hamm).* This bulletin concerns everyone in this office. *hal-manšuur yhimm kull waaẓid ib-had-daaʔira.*
to be concerned - *htamm (i htimaam), qilaq (a qaliq).* She gets very concerned over the smallest thing. *da-tihtamm ihwaaya £ala ʔaqall šii.* -- The police are concerned with this increase in crime. *š-šurṭa mihtamma b-izdiyaad ij-jaraaʔim haaḍi.*
as far as one's concerned - *bin-nisba ʔila, min naaẓiya~, min yamm.* As far as I'm concerned you can do as you like. *bin-nisba ʔili tigdar itsawwi š-ma-triid.*
concerning - *b-xuṣuuṣ.* Nothing was said concerning the vacation. *ma-ngaal šii b-xuṣuuṣ il-£uṭla.*
to **conclude** - 1. *ʔanha (i ʔinhaaʔ), xitam (i xatim) n-, faḍḍ (u faḍḍ) n-.* They concluded the meeting yesterday afternoon. *ʔanhaw l-ijtimaa£ il-baarẓa l-£aṣir.* 2. *£iqad (i £aqid) n-, ʔabram (i ʔibraam) n-.* The two countries concluded the trade agreement two days ago. *l-baladeen £iqdaw l-ittifaaqiyya t-tijaariyya gabuḷ yoomeen.* 3. *stantaj (i stintaaj).* What do you conclude from his remark? *š-tistantij min mulaaẓaḍta?*
conclusion - 1. *natiija* pl. *nataaʔij, stintaaj* pl. *-aat.* What conclusions did you draw from the debate? *šinu n-nataaʔij illi stalxaṣitha mnil-munaaqaša?* 2. *xitaam.* In conclusion, I should like to state that .... *w-bil-xitaam, ʔaẓibb ʔan ʔabayyin ʔinna ....*
concrete - 1. *kankiriit, kankari.* The bridge is built of concrete. *j-jisir mabni b-kankari.* 2. *maḍbuuṭ, qawi.* Give me a concrete example. *nṭiini fadd maθal maḍbuuṭ.*
to **condemn** - 1. *ẓikam (u ẓukum) n-.* The judge condemned him to death. *l-ẓaakim ẓikama bil-ʔi£daam.* 2. *ðamm (i ðamm) n-.* They condemned him for his actions. *ðammoo l-ʔa£maala.* 3. *ʔumar (u ʔamur) n- b-hadim.* The municipality condemned the old building. *l-baladiyya ʔumrat ib-hadm il-binaaya l-qadiima.*
condition - 1. *ẓaala* pl. *aat, ʔaẓwaal.* The house was in good condition. *l-beet čaan ib-ẓaala zeena.* 2. *šariṭ* pl. *šuruuṭ.* I'll accept the offer on one condition. *raẓ-aqbal il-£ariḍ ib-šarṭ waaẓid.*
conduct - *siluuk, siira* pl. *siyar.* Your conduct is disgraceful. *siluukak šaaʔin.*
to conduct - 1. *qaad (u qiyaada) n-.* Who's conducting the orchestra tonight? *minu da-yquud il-firqa l-muusiiqiyya hal-leela?* 2. *dawwar (i tadwiir), farrar (i tafriir, tfirrir), dalla (i ddilli).* The guide conducted us around the ruins. *d-daliil dawwarna been il-ʔaaθaar.* 3. *waṣṣal (i tawṣiil) t-.* Metal conducts heat better than wood. *l-ma£dan ywaṣṣil il-ẓaraara ʔaẓsan imnil-xišab.* 4. *daar (i ʔidaara) n-.* He conducts his work very well. *da-ydiir ʔašġaala kulliš zeen.*
to conduct oneself - *silak (u siluuk), tṣarraf (a taṣarruf).* She conducts herself like a lady. *tisluk siluuk is-sayyida.*
conductor - 1. *mufattiš* pl. *-iin, tiiti* pl. *-iyyaat.* Did the conductor punch your ticket? *l-mufattiš giraḍ it-tikit maalak?* 2. *muuṣila* pl. *-aat.* Silver is a good conductor of electricity. *l-fuḍḍa muuṣila zeena lil-kahrabaaʔiyya.* 3. *qaaʔid* pl. *quwwaad.* Who is the conductor of the orchestra? *minu qaaʔid*

il-firqa l-muusiiqiyya?

cone – *maxruuṭ* pl. *maxaariiṭ*. The vase was made in the shape of a cone. *l-mizhariyya čaanat maʕmuula b-šikil maxruuṭ.*

conference – **1.** *jtimaaʕ* pl. *-aat*. He had a conference with the doctor. *čaan ʕinda jtimaaʕ wiyya ṭ-ṭabiib.* **2.** *muʔtamar* pl. *-aat*. He wrote an article on the disarmament conference. *kitab maqaal ʕan muʔtamar nazʕ is-silaaḥ.* **3.** *mudaawala* pl. *-aat*. After a short conference with my wife, I agreed to buy the car. *baʕad mudaawala qaṣiira wiyya zawijti waafaqit aštiri s-sayyaara.*

to **confess** – *ʕtiraf (i ʕtiraaf), qaar (u qaar) n-.* The defendant confessed. *l-muttaham iʕtiraf.*

confession – *ʕtiraaf* pl. *-aat*, *ʔiqraar* pl. *-aat*. The criminal made a full confession. *l-mujrim iʕtiraf iʕtiraaf kaamil.*

confidence – *θiqa*. I have confidence in him. *ʕindi θiqa bii.*

confident – *waaθiq, mitʔakkid, mitqayyin*. I'm confident that everything will turn out all right. *ʔaani waaθiq kullši raḥ-yṣiir ḥasb il-ʔuṣuul.*

confidential – *sirri**. This letter is confidential. *hal-maktuub sirri.*

confidentially – *ḥaači beenaat-, b-ṣuura sirriyya.* Confidentially, I don't like that proposal. *ḥaači beenaatna ma-yiʕjibni hal-iqtiraaḥ.*

to **confirm** – **1.** *ʔayyad (i taʔyiid, tʔiyyid) t-, ʔakkad (i taʔkiid, tʔikkid) t-.* The president confirmed the news report. *r-raʔiis ʔayyad našrat il-ʔaxbaar.* -- You'll have to confirm the reservation tomorrow. *laazim itʔakkid il-ḥajiz iṣ-ṣubuḥ.* **2.** *θabbat (i taθbiit, tθibbit).* That confirms my faith in him. *haaδa yθabbit ʔiimaani bii.*

conflict – **1.** *nizaaʕ* pl. *-aat*, *taṣaadum* pl. *-aat*, *ʕraak*. Four men were killed in the border conflict. *ʔarbaʕ riyaajiil inkitlaw ib-nizaaʕ il-ḥuduud.* **2.** *ṣiraaʕ, nizaaʕ* pl. *aat*. It's the eternal conflict between good and evil. *huwwa ṣ-ṣiraaʕ il-ʔabadi been il-xeer wiš-šarr.* **3.** *tanaaquḍ* pl. *-aat, taʕaaruḍ* pl. *-aat*. Because of the conflict between the two reports another committee went to investigate the matter. *b-sabab it-tanaaquḍ been it-taqriireen lujna lux raaḥat titḥarra ʕan il-qaḍiyya.*

to conflict – **1.** *tʕaaraḍ (a taʕaaruḍ).* Will this appointment conflict with your schedule? *hal-mawʕid raḥ-yitʕaaraḍ wiyya manhajak?* **2.** *tʕaaraḍ (a taʕaaruḍ), tnaaqaḍ (a tanaaquḍ).* His philosophy conflicts with the basic tenets of Islam. *falsafta titʕaaraḍ wiyya mabaadiʔ il-ʔislaam il-ʔasaasiyya.*

to **confuse** – **1.** *xarbaṭ (u txurbuṭ) t-, ʔarbak (i ʔirbaak) n-, ḥayyar (i tḥiyyir) t-.* The map confused me. *l-xariiṭa xarbuṭatni.* -- The problem confused me. *l-muškila ḥayyiratni.* **2.** *štibah (i štibaah) b-.* He must have confused me with someone else. *laazim ištibah biyya b-šaxiṣ ʔaaxar.*

confusion – **1.** *rtibaak*. That will cause a lot of confusion. *haaδi raḥ-itsabbib irtibaak ihwaaya.* **2.** *xabṣa* pl. *-aat, hoosa* pl. *-aat, harja* pl. *-aat.* He escaped in the confusion. *nhijam bil-xabṣa.*

to **congratulate** – *hanna (i thinni, tahniya) t-, baarak (i mubaaraka) t-.* We congratulated him on his success. *hanneenaa b-najaaḥa.*

congratulations – *tahaani, mabruuk, ʕal-baaraka.* Congratulations on your appointment! *tahaaniina ʕala taʕyiinak!*

congress – *majlis* pl. *majaalis*.

to **connect** – **1.** *waṣṣal (i twiṣṣil, tawṣiil) t-.* A short hallway connects our offices. *mamarr qaṣiir ywaṣṣil dawaaʔirna baʕaḍha b-baʕaḍ.* -- Have they connected the telephone for you yet? *waṣṣloo-lak it-talafoon loo baʕad?* **2.** *rubaṭ (u rabuṭ) n-, waṣṣal (i twiṣṣil, tawṣiil) t-.* Connect these wires to the battery. *ʔurbuṭ hal-waayaraat bil-paatri.* **3.** *rubaṭ (u rabuṭ) n-.* The police have connected the crime to two men who were seen in the area. *s-surṭa rubṭat ij-jariima b-rijjaaleen inšaafaw bil-manṭiqa.*

connection – **1.** *ttiṣaal* pl. *-aat*. I can't hear you very well. There must be a bad connection. *ma-agdar asimʕak zeen. laazim ʔaku ttiṣaal muu zeen.* **2.** *ʕalaaqa* pl. *-aat*. He has very good connections with the government. *ʕinda kulliš xooš ʕalaaqaat wiyya l-ḥukuuma.* **3.** *munaasaba* pl. *-aat, ʕalaaqa* pl. *-aat*. In what connection did he mention it? *b-ʔay munaasaba δikarha?* **4.** *ṣila* pl. *-aat, ʕalaaqa* pl. *-aat*. There's no connect between the two. *ma-aku ṣila been l-iθneen.*

to **conquer** – **1.** *fitaḥ (a fatiḥ) n-.* He wanted to conquer the whole world. *raad yiftaḥ il-ʕaalam kulla.* **2.** *qihar (a qahir) n-.* Scientists have conquered polio. *l-ʕulamaaʔ qihraw maraḍ šalal il-ʔaṭfaal.*

conquest – *fatiḥ* pl. *fituuḥaat*.

conscience – *ḍamiir* pl. *ḍamaaʔir, wujdaan* pl. *-aat*. I have a clear conscience. *ḍamiiri mirtaaḥ.*

conscientious – *mujidd*. He's a conscientious student. *huwwa ṭaalib mujidd.*

conscious – *ḥaasis, waaʕi, ṣaaḥi.* You can talk to him now. He's conscious. *tigdar itḥaačii hassa. huwwa ḥaasis.*

consent – *riḍa, muwaafaqa, qubuul.* This was done without my consent. *haaδi ṣaarat biduun riḍaaya.*

to consent – *waafaq (i muwaafaqa), qibal (a qubuul), riḍa (a riḍa).* He consented to stay. *waafaq yibqa.*

consequence – *ʕaaqiba* pl. *ʕawaaqib, natiija* pl. *nataaʔij*. I'm afraid of the consequences. *ʔaani xaayif imnil-ʕawaaqib.*

consequently – *wa-ʕaleehi, binaaʔan ʕala δaalik, bin-natiija.*

conservative – **1.** *muḥaafiḍ*. He's a very conservative politician. *huwwa siyaasi muḥaafiḍ kulliš.* **2.** *miqtiṣid*. You'll have to be more conservative with your allowance. *laazim itkuun miqtiṣid akθar ib-muxaṣṣaṣaatak.*

to **consider** – **1.** *ʕtubar (u ʕtibaar), ḥisab (i ḥsaab) n-.* I consider him an able chemist. *ʔaʕtabra kiimyaawi qadiir.* **2.** *niḍar (u naḍar) n- b-.* We're still considering your request. *li-hassa da-nunḍur ib-ṭalabak.*

considerable – *ḍaxim, muḥtaram.* Building this house cost me a considerable sum of money. *binaaʔ hal-beet kallafni mablaġ ḍaxim* or ***binaaʔ hal-beet kallafni mablaġ laa baʔis bii.*

considerate – *muqaddir, munṣif.* My boss is very considerate. *raʔiisi fadd waaḥid muqaddir.*

consideration – **1.** *naḍar*. We have three plans under consideration. *ʕidna tlaθ mašaariiʕ taḥt in-naḍar.* **2.** *ʕtibaar*. He hasn't any consideration for anybody. *ma-ʕinda ʕtibaar il-kull ʔaḥḥad.*

consignment – *wadiiʕa, ʔamaana.* He took the goods on consignment. *ʔaxaδ il-biḍaaʕa bil-ʔamaana.*

to **consist of** – *štimal (i štimaal) ʕala, trakkab (a tarakkub) min, ḥuwa (i ḥawi) ʕala.* The meal consisted of fish, vegetables, and coffee. *l-wajba štimlat ʕala simač w-xuḍrawaat w-gahwa.*

consistent – *muttifiq, mulaaʔim.* His ideas are consistent with those of his party. *ʔafkaara muttafqa maʕa ʔafkaar ḥizba.*

to **consolidate** – *waḥḥad (i tawḥiid, twiḥḥid) t-.* The two presidents consolidated the two oil companies. *r-raʔiiseen waḥḥidaw šarikteen in-nafuṭ.*

conspiracy – *muʔaamara, taʔaamur.*

constant – **1.** *mistimirr, daaʔimi**. This constant noise is making me nervous. *haṣ-ṣoot il-mistimirr da-ysawwiini ʕaṣabi.* **2.** *mitkarrir, mistimirr, daaʔimi**. These constant trips to the doctor are costing me money. *haz-ziyaaraat il-mitkarrira liṭ-ṭabiib da-yitkallafni fluus.* **3.** *θaabit*. Wheat prices have remained constant for two months. *ʔasʕaar il-ḥunṭa buqat θaabta šahreen.* **4.** *nisba* (pl. *nisab*) *θaabita*. If you know the constant you can solve the problem. *loo tuʕruf in-nisba θ-θaabita tigdar itḥill il-masʔala.*

constantly – *b-istimraar, ʕala ṭuul, daaʔiman.* The The telephone rang constantly. *t-talifoon dagg b-istimraar.*

constellation – *majmuuʕat* (pl. *-aat*) *nujuum.*

constitution – **1.** *dastuur* pl. *dasaatiir*. Our freedom is guaranteed by the constitution. *ḥurriyyatna maḍmuuna bid-dastuur.* **2.** *bunya* pl. *-aat*. He has a very strong constitution. *ʕinda bunya kulliš qawiyya.*

to **construct** – *bina (i binaaʔ) n-.* We're going to construct a new hotel here. *raḥ-nibni fadd funduq jidiid ihnaa.*

construction – *binaaʔ*. The construction of this dam will take five years. *binaaʔ has-sadd raḥ-yṭawwil xams isniin.* -- My father works for a construction company. *ʔabuuya da-yištuġul ʔila šarikat il-binaaʔ.*

consul – *qunṣul* pl. *qanaaṣil*.

consulate – *qunṣuliyya*. Were you at the American consulate? *činit bil-qunṣuliyya l-ʔamriikiyya?*

to **consult** – *stišaar (i stišaara).* You should have consulted us. *čaan laazim tistišiirna.*

to **consume** – *stahlak (i stihlaak), ṣiraf (u ṣaruf) n-.* My car consumes a lot of gas. *sayyaarti tistahlik ihwaaya banziin.*

consumption – **1.** *stihlaak*. Consumption has gone up fifty per cent. *l-istihlaak zaad xamsiin bil-miyya.* **2.** *sill.* He has consumption. *Ɛinda sill.*

contact - 1. *ttiṣaal* pl. *-aat.* He's never had any contact with foreigners. *ʔabad ma-čaan Ɛinda ʔay ittiṣaal wiyya l-ʔajaanib.* **2.** *Ɛalaaqa* pl. *-aat.* I've made several new contacts. *sawweet Ɛiddat Ɛalaaqaat jidiida.*

to come into contact with - *mass (i mass) n-.* By accident, his hand came into contact with a bare electric wire. *biṣ-ṣudfa ʔiida massat silik kahrabaaʔi Ɛaari.*

to contact - *ttiṣal (i ttiṣaal) b-.* I'll contact you as soon as I arrive. *raz-attiṣil biik ʔawwal-ma ʔooṣal.*

contagious - *muƐdi.*

to **contain - 1.** *zuwa (i zawi), ztiwa (i ztiwaaʔ) Ɛala.* That trunk contains clothing. *haṣ-ṣanduug yizwi hduum* or ***haṣ-ṣanduug bii hduum.* **2.** *lizam (a lazim), ḍubaṭ (u ḍabuṭ).* Don't get excited! Try to contain yourself. *la-tinxubuṣ. zaawil tilzam nafsak.*

contempt - *stixfaaf, zdiraaʔ.*

content - 1. *muqdaar* pl. *maqaadiir.* The alcoholic content is very low. *muqdaar il-kuhuul kulliš qaliil.* **2.** *qaaniƐ, raaḍi.* He was content with what we offered him. *čaan qaaniƐ b-illi Ɛraḍnaa Ɛalee.*

contents - *muztawayaat.* Dissolve the contents of this package in one glass of water. *ḍawwub muztawayaat hal-paakeet ib-fadd iglaaṣ ṃaay.*

table of contents - *fihras* pl. *fahaaris.*

contest - *sibaaq* pl. *-aat, musaabaqa* pl. *-aat, munaafasa* pl. *-aat.* Who won the contest? *minu faaz bil-musaabaqa?*

to contest - *ṭaƐan (a ṭaƐan) n-.* They're contesting the validity of the will. *da-yṭiƐnuun ib-ṣizzat il-waṣiyya.*

continent - *qaarra* pl. *-aat.*

continual - *mistimirr, mitwaaṣil.* This continual arguing is annoying me. *haj-jidaal il-mistimirr da-yizƐijni.*

continually - *daaʔiman, b-istimraar, Ɛala ṭuul.* The line is continuaaly busy. *l-xaṭṭ mašġuul daaʔiman.*

to **continue - 1.** *stamarr (i stimraar) b-, daawam (i dawaam, mudaawama), waaṣal (i muwaaṣala).* Let's continue with our work. *xaali nistimirr ib-šuġulna.* **2.** *waaṣal (i muwaaṣala).* We'll continue our discussion tomorrow. *raz-inwaaṣil munaaqašatna baačir.* **3.** *ḍall (u ḍall), stamarr (i stimraar).* His condition continued to be the same. *zaalta ḍallat Ɛala-ma hiyya.*

continuously - *b-istimraar, daaʔiman, Ɛala ṭuul.* The phone has been ringing continuously. *t-talifoon da-ydugg b-istimraar.*

contract - *muqaawala* pl. *-aat, qunṭaraat, Ɛaqid* pl. *Ɛuquud.* I refuse to sign that contract. *ʔarfuḍ awaqqiƐ hal-Ɛaqid.*

to contract - 1. *tqallaṣ (a taqalluṣ).* Which metal contracts the most? Iron or copper? *ʔay maƐdan yitqallaṣ ʔakθar? l-zadiid loo n-nuzaas?* **2.** *tqaawal (a taqaawul), sawwa (i tsiwwi) qanṭaraat.* They've contracted to build the building in five months. *tqaawlaw yibnuun il-Ɛimaara b-xamist išhur.* **3.** *ʔaxaḍ (u ʔaxiḍ) n-.* I contracted pneumonia. *ʔaxaḍit nimoonya.*

contractor - *qunṭarči* pl. *-iyya, muqaawil* pl. *-iin.*

to **contradict** - *Ɛaaraḍ (i muƐaaraḍa), naaqaḍ (i munaaqaḍa).* Don't contradict me! *la-tƐaariḍni.*

contradictory - *mitnaaqiḍ, mitxaalif.* We heard the most contradictory reports on it. *smaƐna Ɛanha taqaariir kulliš mitnaaqḍa.*

contrary - 1. *Ɛnaadi*.* She's very contrary. *hiyya kulliš iƐnaadiyya.* **2.** *b-Ɛakis, b-xilaaf, ḍidd.* Contrary to what we expected he passed the exam. *b-Ɛakis-ma twaqqaƐna nijaz bil-imtizaan.* **3.** *muxaalif, muƐaakis.* That's contrary to our agreement. *haaḍa muxaalif l-ittifaaqna.*

on the contrary - *bil-Ɛakis.* On the contrary, nothing could be worse. *bil-Ɛakis, ma-aku ʔatƐas minna.*

contrast - *xtilaaf* pl. *-aat, tabaayun.* There's a big contrast between the two brothers. *ʔaku xtilaaf čibiir been il-ʔuxwa l-iθneen.*

to contrast - *bayyan (i tbiyyin) t- xtilaaf.* He contrasted the programs of the two parties. *bayyan il-ixtilaaf been manaahij il-zizbeen.*

to **contribute - 1.** *tbarraƐ (a tabarruƐ) b-.* I contributed five dinars to the Red Cross. *tbarraƐit ib-xams idnaaniir liṣ-ṣaliib il-ʔazmar.* **2.** *saaƐad (i musaaƐada).* The interference of the police just contributed to the confusion. *tadaxxul iš-šurṭa bass saaƐad Ɛal-irtibaak.* **3.** *qaddam (i tqiddim, taqdiim) t-.* He's continually contributing articles to the daily newspaper. *daaʔiman da-yqaddim maqaalaat lij-jariida l-yoomiyya.*

contribution - *tabarruƐ* pl. *-aat, musaaƐada* pl. *-aat.* We received your contribution yesterday. *stilamna tabarruƐak il-baarza.*

control - 1. *sayṭara, ḍabuṭ.* He lost control of the car. *fuqad is-sayṭara Ɛala s-sayyaara.* **2.** *muraaqaba.* The control tower is at the north end of the runway. *murj il-muraaqaba ṣaayir biṭ-ṭaraf iš-šimaali mnil-madraj.* **3.** *sulṭa, sayṭara.* The police have no control over diplomats. *š-šurṭa ma-Ɛidha sulṭa Ɛad-dibloomaasiyyiin.* **4.** *qiyaada.* Let me take over control for a while. *xalliini ʔastilim il-qiyaada šwayya.* -- The co-pilot took over the controls. *muƐaawin iṭ-ṭayyaar istilam ʔaalaat il-qiyaada.*

to control - *ḍubaṭ (u ḍabuṭ) n-, sayṭar (i tsayṭar) t-.* The teacher couldn't control the class. *l-muƐallim ma-gidar yuḍbuṭ iṣ-ṣaff.*

convenience - *wasiilat* (pl. *wasaaʔil*) *raaza.* Our apartment has every modern convenience. *šiqqatna biiha kull wasaaʔil ir-raaza l-zadiiθa.*

**Call me at your earliest convenience. *xaaburni b-ʔawwal wakit ynaasbak.*

convenient - *munaasib, mulaaʔim, murii ̣z.* Will five o'clock be convenient for you? *s-saaƐa xamsa raz-itkuun munaasiba lak?*

conveniently - *b-ṣuura mulaaʔima, b-ṣuura munaasiba.* The telephone is conveniently located so everybody can reach it. *t-talifoon maẓṭuuṭ ib-ṣuura mulaaʔima zatta kull waazid yigdar yooṣal-la.*

convent - *deer* (pl. *ʔadyira*) *lir-raahibaat.*

convention - 1. *muʔtamar* pl. *-aat.* Were you at the convention last year? *činit bil-muʔtamar is-sana l-faatat?* **2.** *Ɛurf, Ɛaada.* Everything he does is according to convention. *kullši ysawwii zasb il-Ɛurf.*

conventional - *mutƐaaraf Ɛalee, muƐtaad Ɛalee.* I prefer the conventional methods. *ʔafaḍḍil iṭ-ṭuruq il-mutƐaaraf Ɛaleeha.*

conversation - *mukaalama* pl. *-aat, zači, zadiiθ* pl. *ʔazaadiiθ.* Our telephone conversation lasted an hour. *mukaalamatna t-talifooniyya ṭawwilat saaƐa.*

convert - 1. *mitnaṣṣir* pl. *-iin.* His wife became a Christian convert. *zawijta ṣaarat mitnaṣṣira.* -- **2.** *mistaslim* pl. *-iin.* There are many converts to Islam living here. *ʔaku mistasilmiin ihwaaya yƐiišuun ihnaa.* **3.** *mithawwid* pl. *-iin.* This man is a convert to Judaism. *har-rijjaal mithawwid.*

to convert - 1. *baddal (i tbiddil, tabdiil) t-, zawwal (i tazwiil, tziwwil) t-.* Where can I convert these dollars into dinars? *ween ʔagdar abaddil had-doolaaraat ila danaaniir?* **2.** *zawwal (i tazwiil, tziwwil) t-, gilab (u galub) n-.* This experiment converts starch into sugar. *hat-tajruba tzawwil in-niša ʔila šakar.* -- He converted his house into a restaurant. *zawwal beeta ʔila matƐam.* **3.** *gilab (u galub) n-.* You cannot convert this atheist to any religion. *ma-tigdar tuglub hal-mulzid il-ʔay diin.*

convict - *mudaan* pl. *-iin, mazkuum Ɛalee* (pl. *-hum*). Three convicts escaped. *tlaθ mazkuum Ɛaleehum hirbaw.*

to convict - *ʔadaan (i ʔidaana).* The judge convicted him of murder. *l-zaakim ʔadaana b-jariimat il-qatil.*

to **convince** - *qannaƐ (i tqinniƐ, taqniiƐ) t-, ʔaqnaƐ (i ʔiqnaaƐ).* You can't convince me. *ma-tigdar itqanniƐni.*

cook - *ṭabbaax* pl. *-iin.* She a very good cook. *hiyya ṭabbaaxa kulliš zeena.*

**Too many cooks spoil the broth. *s-safiina, ʔiḍa kiθraw imlaaliizha, tiġrag.*

to cook - *ṭubax (u ṭabux) n-.* We don't have time to cook tonight. *ma-Ɛidna wakit niṭbux hal-leela.*

cookie - *kleečaaya* pl. *-aat* coll. *kleeča.* I brought you some cookies. *jibit-lak šwayya kleeča.*

cool - 1. *baarid.* The weather is cool here, especially at night. *d-dinya baarda hnaa, xuṣuuṣan bil-leel.* -- Bring me some cool water. *jiib-li šwayya ṃayy baarid.* **2.** *haadiʔ, baarid.* I tried to keep cool after the accident. *zaawalit abqa haadiʔ baƐd il-zaadiθ.*

to cool - 1. *burad (a buruud).* Don't let the soup cool too long. *la-txalli š-šoorba tubrad ihwaaya.* **2.** *hidaʔ (a huduuʔ), burad (a buruud).* Leave him alone. He'll cool off after a while. *xallii wazda. raz-yihdaʔ baƐd išwayya.* **3.** *barrad* (*i tbirrid, tabriid) t-*. The air conditioner cools the entire house. *l-mukayyifa tbarrid il-beet kulla.* **4.** *hadda*ʔ *(i tahdiʔa, thiddiʔ) t-, barrad (i tabriid, tbirrid) t-*. Try to cool him down a bit. *ζaawil ithaddiʔa šwayya.*

coop - *beet* pl. *byuut*. Clean out the chicken coop. *nað̣ð̣uf beet id-dijaaj.*

to coop up - *ζibas (i ζabis) n-, ζiṣar (i ζaṣir) n-*. I cooped the children up in the house this morning for being naughty. *ζbasit ij-jihhaal iṣ-ṣubuζ bil-beet li-ʔan čaanaw yʔaððuun.*

to **co-operate** - *tεaawan (a taεaawun)*. I wish they would co-operate with us more. *ʔatmanna yitεaawnuun wiyyaana ʔakθar.*

co-operation - *taεaawun*. Can we count on your co-operation? *nigdar niεtimid εala taεaawnak?*

copper - *ṣifir, nζaas.*

Copt - *qabṭi* pl. *ʔaqbaaṭ.*

copy - **1.** *nusxa* pl. *nusax, ṣuura* pl. *ṣuwar*. I made a copy of the letter. *sawweet nusxa mnil-maktuub.* **2.** *nusxa* pl. *nusax*. Do you have a copy of this morning's paper? *εindak nusxa mnij-jariida ṣ-ṣabaaζiyya maalt il-yoom.*

to copy - **1.** *niqal (u naqil) n-*. Copy these two sentences off the blackboard. *ʔiniqlu haj-jumalteen imniṣ-ṣabbuura.* **2.** *sawwa (i taswiya, tsiwwi) qoopya*. The teacher gave him a zero in the examination because he copied. *l-muεallim niṭaa ṣifir bil-imtiζaan li-ʔanna sawwa qoopya.* **3.** *qallad (i tqillid, taqliid) t-*. He copies his father in everything. *yqallid ʔabuu b-kullši.*

coral - *marjaan*. I'd like to buy a coral necklace. *ʔariid aštiri ġlaada marjaan.*

cord - **1.** *xeeṭ* pl. *xyuuṭ*. My son doesn't have enough cord to fly his kite. *ʔibni ma-εinda xeeṭ kaafi yṭayyir iṭ-ṭiyyaara bii.* **2.** *waayar* pl. *-aat*. We'll have to get a new cord for the iron. *laazim injiib waayar jidiid lil-ʔuuti.*

cordial - *ζaarr, qalbi**. The host gave us a cordial welcome. *l-imεazzib istaqbalna stiqbaal ζaarr.*

cork - *tabbaduur* pl. *-aat, filliina* pl. *-aat*. The cork fell into the bottle. *t-tabbaduur wugaε bil-buṭil.*

to cork - *sadd (i sadd) n- bit-tabbaduur*. Don't forget to cork the bottle. *la-tinsa tsadd il-buṭil bit-tabbaduur.*

corkscrew - *burġi* pl. *baraaġi.*

corn - **1.** *ʔiðra*. He doesn't grow much corn. *ma-yizraε ʔiðra hwaaya.* **2.** *bismaar* pl. *bisaamiir*. Doctor, this corn on my foot is bothering me. *daktoor, hal-bismaar li-b-rijli da-yoojaεni.*

corn bread - *xubuz ʔiðra.*

corner - **1.** *rukun* pl. *ʔarkaan*. The man stood by the corner of the building. *r-rajul wugaf yamm rukn il-ibnaaya.* **2.** *zwiyya* pl. *-aat*. Put the books in the corner. *ζuṭṭ il-kutub biz-zuwiyya.*

to corner - *ζiṣar (i ζaṣir) n-*. I cornered him this morning and demanded my money. *ζiṣarta ṣ-ṣubuζ w-itlabit ifluusi.*

corn flour - *ṭζiin ʔiðra.*

corporal - *naayib εariif* pl. *nuwwaab εurafaaʔ.*

corpse - *jiθθa* pl. *jiθaθ.*

corral - *ziriiba* pl. *zaraayib.*

correct - *ṣaζiiζ, tamaam, mað̣buuṭ*. Is this the correct address? *haaða l-εinwaan iṣ-ṣaζiiζ.*

to correct - **1.** *ṣaζζaζ (i taṣζiiζ, tṣiζζiζ) t-, ṣallaζ (i taṣliiζ, tṣilliζ) t-*. Please correct the mistakes in my French. *ʔarjuuk ṣaζζiζ ʔaġlaaṭi bil-ifransi.* **2.** *ð̣ubaṭ (u ð̣abuṭ) n-, εaddal (i taεdiil, tεiddil) t-, ṣaζζaζ (i) t-, ṣallaζ (i)* These glasses will correct your vision. *hal-manaað̣ir raζ-tuð̣buṭ nað̣arak.*

correction - *taṣζiiζ* pl. *-aat, taṣliiζ* pl. *-aat, taεdiil* pl. *-aat, ð̣abuṭ*. Please make the necessary corrections. *ʔarjuuk sawwi it-taṣζiiζaat il-laazma.*

to **correspond** - **1.** *ṭaabaq (u muṭaabaqa) t-*. The translation does not correspond with the original. *t-tarjuma ma-ṭṭaabuq il-ʔaṣil.* **2.** *traasal (a taraasul), tkaatab (a takaatub)*. We've been corresponding for six years. *ṣaar-inna sitta sniin nitraasal.*

correspondence - *muraasala* pl. *-aat, mukaataba* pl. *-aat*. My job is answering the correspondence. *šuġli ʔajiib εal-muraasalaat.*

correspondent - *muraasil* pl. *-iin*. He's a correspondent for the Times. *huwwa muraasil jariidat it-taaymz.*

corridor - *mamša* pl. *mamaaši, dihliiz* pl. *dahaaliiz, mamarr* pl. *-aat, mjaaz* pl. *-aat.*

corrugated - *mεarraj.*

cosmetic - *masζuuq* pl. *masaaζiiq*. She uses a lot of cosmetics. *da-tistaεmil masaaζiiq ihwaaya.*

cost - **1.** *takliif* pl. *takaaliif, kulfa* pl. *-aat*. He was forced to sell everything at less than cost. *njubar ybiiε kullši b-ʔaqall imnit-takliif.* -- The cost of living is rising. *kulfat il-maεiiša da-tirtifiε.* **2.** *qiima* pl. *qiyam, siεir* pl. *ʔasεaar, θaman* pl. *ʔaθmaan, takliif* pl. *takaaliif, kulfa* pl. *kulaf*. The cost of this item on the market is twenty dinars. *qiimat haš-šii bis-suug εišriin diinaar.*

at any cost - *b-ʔay θaman, mahma ykuun iθ-θaman.* He wants it at any cost. *yriidha b-ʔay θaman.*

to cost - *kallaf (i takliif)*. How much do these shoes cost? *hal-qundara šgadd itkallif?* -- The battle cost the enemy the loss of many lives. *l-maεraka kallifat il-εadu xasaaʔir ihwaaya bil-ʔarwaaζ.*

costly - *ġaali*. She uses very costly perfume. *da-tistaεmil riiζa ġaalya hwaaya.*

costume - *zayy* pl. *ʔazyaaʔ, libis*. The dancer wore a beautiful costume. *r-raaqiṣa libsat zayy ζilu.*

cot - *čarpaaya (*pl. *-aat) safariyya, siriir safari* pl. *saraayir safariyya.*

cottage cheese - *liban imnaššaf*. Give me a half kilo of cottage cheese. *nṭiini nuṣṣ kiilu liban imnaššaf.*

cotton - *guṭin*. Bring me a piece of cotton. *jiib-li fadd wuṣlat guṭin.* -- I'd like to buy a pair of cotton socks. *ʔariid aštiri fadd zooj ijwaariib guṭin.*

couch - *qanafa* pl. *-aat.*

cough - *gaζζa* pl. *-aat*. Do you have something that's good for a cough? *εindak šii zeen lil-gaζζa?*

to cough - *gaζζ (u gaζζ)*. The baby coughed all night. *ṭ-ṭifil gaζζ ṭuul il-leel.*

could - see under can.

council - *majlis* pl. *majaalis.*

councilman - *εuð̣u (*pl. *ʔaεð̣aaʔ) majlis.*

counsel - **1.** *naṣiiζa* pl. *naṣaayiζ, mašuura* pl. *-aat, stišaara* pl. *-aat*. Let me give you some good counsel. *xalli ʔanṭiik fadd naṣiiζa zeena.* **2.** *muζaami* pl. *-iin*. The counsel for the defense arrived late. *muζaami d-difaaε wuṣal mitʔaxxir.*

count - **1.** *tiεdaad* pl. *-aat, εadd, ζsaab* pl. *-aat*. The count has not been taken yet. *t-tiεdaad ma-ṣaar baεad.* **2.** *koont* pl. *-aat*. She married a count. *tzawwjat koont.*

to count - *ζisab (i ζsaab) n-, εadd (i tiεdaad, εadd) n-*. Please count your change. *ʔarjuuk iζsib il-xurda maaltak.*

to count on - *εtimad (i εtimaad) εala, wiθaq (i θiqa) n- b-*. You can not count on him at all. *ma-tigdar tiεtimid εalee bil-marra.*

counter - **1.** *kaawntir* pl. *-aat*. Your package is on the counter. *r-ruzma maaltak εal-kaawntir.* **2.** *ð̣idd*. This is counter to our beliefs. *haaða ð̣idd muεtaqadaatna.*

counterfeit - **1.** *mzayyaf, qalib*. This money is counterfeit. *hal-ifluus imzayyifa.* **2.** *mzawwar*. This signature is counterfeit. *hat-tawqiiε imzawwar.*

to counterfeit - *zayyaf (i tazyiif, tziyyif) t-, zawwar (i tazwiir, tziwwir) t-*. He counterfeited one thousand dinars. *zayyaf ʔalif diinaar.*

countess - *koonteesa* pl. *-aat.*

country - **1.** *balad* pl. *buldaan, blaad, quṭur* pl. *ʔaqṭaar, dawla* pl. *duwal*. I've seen many countries. *šifit buldaan ihwaaya.* **2.** *riif* pl. *ʔaryaaf*. We spent our vacation in the country. *ġð̣eena εuṭlatna bir-riif.* **3.** *manṭiqa* pl. *manaaṭiq*. The country around Baghdad is agricultural. *l-manṭiqa ζawaali baġdaad ziraaεiyya.*

couple: A young couple sat in front of us in the movie. *fadd šaabb w-šaabba giεdaw giddaamna bis-siinama.* -- I'm living with an elderly couple. *ʔaani saakin wiyya fadd šaayib w-εajuuz.*

a couple of - *fadd* and foll. noun in dual. I bought a couple of ties. *štireet fadd rabuṭṭeen.* -- Hand me a couple of nails. *naawušni fadd bismaareen.* -- He was here a couple of days ago. *čaan ihnaa gabuḷ fadd yoomeen.*

to couple - *šakkal (i taškiil, tšikkil)*. They coupled the coach to the train. *šakkilaw il-fargoon bil-qiṭaar.*

coupling - *ṣammuuna* pl. *-aat*. They connected the two pipes with a rubber coupling. *rubṭaw il-buuriyyeen ib-ṣammuuna laastiik.*

coupon - *koopoon* pl. *-aat.*

courage - *šajaaεa, jurʔa*. Don't lose your courage. *la-tufqud šajaaεtak.*

course - **1.** *ttijaah* pl. *-aat, tariiq* pl. *turuq.* The plane is holding a straight course. *t-tiyyaara laazma ttijaah ɛadil.* **2.** *ttijaah* pl. *-aat, majra* pl. *majaari.* The river changed its course. *n-nahar ġayyar ittijaaha.* **3.** *daris* pl. *druus.* How many courses did you take? *čam daris axaδit?* **4.** *tariiqa* pl. *turuq, xutta* pl. *xutat, sabiil* pl. *subul.* Tell me the course of action you're going to follow. *gul-li tariiqt il-ɛamal il-raz-titbaɛha.* **5.** *saaza* pl. *-aat.* It takes almost a half hour to walk around the course. *ttawwil zawaali nuss saaɛa maši zawl is-saaza.* **6.** *dafɛa* pl. *-aat.* They served the meal in three courses. *qaddimaw l-ʔakil ɛala tlaθ dafɛaat.*

in due course - *b-wakitha.* We will notify you in due course. *raz-inxabbrak ib-wakitha.*

in the course - *b-xilaal, ʔaθnaaʔ.* He got two promotions in the course of one year. *zassal ɛala tarfiiɛeen ib-xilaal sana wizda.*

of course - *tabɛan, bit-tabuɛ.* Of course I know what you mean! *tabɛan, ʔaɛruf iš-tuqsud.*

court - **1.** *mazkama* pl. *mazaakim.* I'll see you in court tomorrow. *raz-ašuufak bil-mazkama baačir.* **2.** *saaza* pl. *-aat.* The tennis court is still wet. *saazt it-tinis baɛadha ratba.* **3.** *zooš* pl. *zawaaš, saaza* pl. *-aat.* The maid is washing the clothes in the court. *l xaddaama da-tiġsil l ihduum bil-zooš.* **4.** *zaašiya.* The king attended the game with his court. *l-malik ziδar is-sibaaq wiyya zaašiita.*

to court - *tqarrab (a taqarrub) ila, tzabbab (a tazabbub) ila.* He tried to court her several times. *zaawal yitqarrab ilha ɛiddat marraat.*

courteous - *mujaamil.* Try to be courteous while they're here. *zaawil itkuun mujaamil lamma ykuunuun ihnaa.*

courtesy - *mujaamala.* You should learn some courtesy. *laazim titɛallam šwayya mujaamala.*

courtroom - *qaaɛat* (pl. *-aat*) *mazkama.*

cousin: father's brother's son, *ʔibin* (pl. *wulid*) *ɛamm;* father's brother's daughter, *bint* (pl. *banaat*) *ɛamm;* father's sister's son, *ʔibin* (pl. *wulid*) *ɛamma;* father's sister's daughter, *bint* (pl. *banaat*) *ɛamma;* mother's brother's son, *ʔibin* (pl. *wulid*) *xaal;* mother's brother's daughter, *bint* (pl. *banaat*) *xaal;* mother's sister's son, *ʔibin* (pl. *wulid*) *xaala;* mother's sister's daughter, *bint* (pl. *banaat*) *xaala.*

cover - **1.** *ġata* pl. *ġataayaat, čarčaf* pl. *čaraačif.* The cover to this chair is dirty. *ġata hal-kursi wasix.* **2.** *qabaġ* pl. *-aat, ġata* pl. *ġataayaat.* Where is the cover for this box? *ween qabaġ hal-quutiyya?* **3.** *ġlaaf* pl. *-aat.* Who tore the cover off this book? *minu šaggag iġlaaf hal-iktaab?* **4.** *malјaʔ* pl. *malaajiʔ.* Deer don't have good cover in this area. *l-ġizlaan ma-ɛidha maljaʔ zeen ib-hal-mantiqa.* **5.** *lzaaf* pl. *lizif, lizfaan; ġata* pl. *ġataayaat.* Fatma, take the covers off the bed. *faatma, šiili l-lizif imnil-ifraaš.*

to cover - **1.** *ġatta (i taġtiya, tġitti) t-.* We covered the ground with a blanket. *ġatteena l-gaaɛ ib-battaaniyya.* **2.** *gatta (i), kaffa (i tkiffi) t-.* Will fifty dollars cover your expenses? *xamsiin doolaar itġatti masaariifak?* **3.** *ġatta (i), δamδam (u tδumδum), tamtam (u ttumtum).* She's always covering for her friend. *hiyya daaʔiman itġatti l-sadiiqatha.* **4.** *šimal (i šumuul) n-.* I believe that covers everything. *ʔaɛtiqid haaδa yišmil kullši.* **5.** *qitaɛ (a qatiɛ) n-.* We covered the distance in four hours. *qtaɛna l-masaafa b-ʔarbaɛ saaɛaat.* **6.** *sallat (i tasliit, tsillit) t- ɛala.* He covered us with a revolver. *sallat ɛaleena l-musaddas.*

**Is your house covered by insurance? *beetak imʔamman ɛalee?* or *beetak imsoogar?*

cow - *baqara* pl. *-aat* coll. *baqar, haayša* pl. *hwaayiš* coll. *hooš.* The cows were milked this morning. *l-ihwaayiš inzilbaw has-subuz.*

coward - *jabaan* pl. *jubanaaʔ, xawwaaf* pl. *-iin.* Don't be such a coward! *la-tsiir haš-šikil jabaan.*

cozy - *mčaknam.* I like this room because it's cozy. *ʔazabb hal-ġurfa li-ʔanha mčaknima.*

crab - **1.** *ʔabu j-jinneeb.* We saw four crabs at the seashore. *šifna ʔarbaɛ ʔabu j-jinneeb ɛala saazil il-bazar.* **2.** *niqnaaqi* pl. *-iyyiin.* He's an old crab. *huwwa fadd waazid niqnaaqi.*

crab lice - *gamul šiɛra.*

to crab - *naqnaq (i tniqniq).* Stop crabbing. *bass ɛaad itnaqniq.*

crack - **1.** *fatir* pl. *ftuur, faliɛ* pl. *fluuɛ, šagg* pl. *šguug.* The crack in the dam is getting larger. *l-fatir il-bis-sadd da-yikbar.* **2.** *tagga* pl. *-aat.* I think I heard the crack of a rifle. *ʔaδunn ismaɛit tagga maal bunduqiyya.* **3.** *tahakkum* pl. *-aat.* That crack was very appropriate. *hat-tahakkum čaan kulliš ib-mazalla.* **4.** *maahir.* He's a crack shot. *huwwa raami maahir.*

**We got up at the crack of dawn. *gɛadna wiyya tarrat il-fajir.*

to crack - **1.** *futar (u fatir) n-.* I've cracked the crystal of my watch. *ftarit ij-jaama maal saaɛti.* **2.** *kassar (i taksiir, tkissir) t-.* Who's going to crack the nuts? *minu raz-ykassir ij-jooz?* **3.** *zall (i zall) n-.* The police finally cracked the code. *š-šurta ʔaxiiran zallat rumuuz iš-šafra.* **4.** *tagg (u tagg) n-.* He cracked the whip several times. *tagg il-qamči ɛiddat marraat.* -- Crack another bottle of wine for the guests. *tugg butil šaraab θaani liδ-δuyuuf.* **5.** *tagtag (i ttigtig) t-.* He's always cracking his knuckles. *huwwa daaʔiman ytagtig isaabiiɛa.*

**He didn't crack a smile. *wala btisam.*

to crack jokes - *nakkat (i tankiit, tnikkit).* He's always cracking jokes. *huwwa daaʔiman ynakkit.*

to crack open - *filaɛ (a faliɛ) n-.* He dropped the watermelon and cracked it open. *waggaɛ ir-raggiyya w-filaɛha.*

to crack up - **1.** *txabbal (a txubbul, xbaul).* He cracked up under the strain. *txabbal imnil-ʔijhaad.* **2.** *zattam (i taztiim) t-.* He cracked up his car three weeks ago. *zattam sayyaarta gabul itlaθ asaabiiɛ.*

cradle - *mahad* pl. *mhaad, kaaruuk* pl. *kwaariik.*

craft - *mihna* pl. *mihan, šaġla* pl. *-aat, sanɛa* pl. *-aat.* Rugmaking is a difficult craft. *ɛamal iz-zuwaali mihna saɛba.*

to cram - **1.** *zišak (i zašik) n-, zišar (i zašir) n-, zišar (u zašir) n-.* He crammed everything into one trunk. *zišak kullši b-sanduug waazid.* **2.** *zašša (i tazšiya, tzišši) t- δihin~.* I started cramming the night before the exam. *bdeet azašši δihni bil-leela l-gabl il-imtizaan.*

cramp - *ʔabu š-širgeel, ʔabu š-širgeet, tašannuj* pl. *-aat.* I have a cramp in my leg. *ɛindi ʔabu š-širgeel ib-rijli.*

crane - **1.** *ġarnuuq* pl. *ġaraaniiq.* We saw a flock of cranes in the marsh. *šifna majmuuɛa mnil-ġaraaniiq bil-hoor.* **2.** *sling* pl. *-aat.* They're using a crane to destroy the house. *da-yistaɛmiluun isling il-tafliiš il-beet.*

crank - **1.** *hindir* pl. *-aat.* We have to use the crank to start the car. *laazim nistaɛmil il-hindir zatta nšaġġil is-sayyaara.* **2.** *yadda* pl. *-aat.* The window crank is rusty and won't turn. *yaddat iš-šibbaač imzanjira w-ma-tinfarr.*

cranky - *niqnaaqi** pl. *-iyyiin.* Why are you so cranky this morning? *ʔinta leeš hiiči niqnaaqi has-subuz?*

crash - **1.** *stidaam* pl. *-aat, tasaadum* pl. *-aat, sadma* pl. *-aat.* Was anyone hurt in the crash? *ʔazzad itʔaδδa bil-istidaam?* **2.** *soot* pl. *ʔaswaat, ziss* pl. *zsuus.* We heard a crash when the tree fell. *smaɛna ziss lamma š-šijra wugɛat.*

to crash - *stidam (i stidaam) b-, sidam (i sadim) n-.* The car crashed into the wall. *s-sayyaara stidmat bil-zaayit.*

crate - *qufas* pl. *qfaas.* I bought a crate of oranges. *štireet qufas purtaqaal.*

to crawl - **1.** *zizaf (a zazif).* The dog crawled under the table. *č-čalib zizaf jawwa l-meez.* **2.** *ziba (i zabi), zizaf (a zazif).* Her child is beginning to crawl. *tifilha bida yizbi.* **3.** *diba (i dabi).* An ant was crawling on my hand. *fadd namla čaanat tidbi ɛala ʔiidi.*

crazy - **1.** *majnuun* pl. *majaaniin, mxabbal* pl. *mxaabiil.* They put him in the hospital because he was crazy. *daxxloo l-mustašfa li-ʔan čaan majnuun.* **2.** *mitxabbul* pl. *-iin, majnuun* pl. *majaaniin.* He's crazy about that girl. *huwwa mitxabbul ɛala δiič il-ibnayya.* **3.** *saxiif.* That's a crazy idea. It'll never work. *haay fikra saxiifa. ma-tsiir ʔabadan.*

to creak - *jazjaz (i juzjuz, jazjaza).* The wooden stairs are creaking. *d-daraaj il-xišab da-yjazjiz.*

cream - **1.** *kriim.* You'll have to buy the cream canned. *laazim tištiri l-ikriim imɛallab.* **2.** *dihin* pl. *duhuunaat, kriim.* This cream is good for the complexion. *had-dihin zeen lil-bašara.* **3.** *zaliibi**. The color of the walls is cream. *loon il-zayaatiin zaliibi.*

**These students are the cream of the crop. *hat-tullaab humma l-ɛiina.*

Devonshire cream (clotted) - *ġeemar.*
crease - *kasra* pl. *-aat.* The rain took the crease out of my pants. *l-muṭar rawwaz kasrat il-panṭuruun maali.*
to **create** - **1.** *xilaq (i xaliq) n-, kawwan (i takwiin, tkiwwin) t-.* God created the world. *ʔaḷḷa xilaq il-ɛaalam.* **2.** *ʔazdaθ (i ʔizdaaθ) n-, xilaq (i xaliq) n-, ʔawjad (i ʔiijaad) n-.* We have to create a position for him. *laazim nizdiθ-la waḍiifa.*
creature - *maxluuq* pl. *-aat, kaaʔin* pl. *-aat.* He wrote a story about the creatures in the forest. *kitab quṣṣa ɛan maxluuqaat il-ġaaba.*
credentials - *waθaaʔiq, ʔawraaq il-iɛtimaad, mustanadaat.*
credible - **1.** *ṣaadiq.* He's a credible witness. *huwwa šaahid ṣaadiq.* **2.** *mṣaddag.* His story wasn't credible. *zčaayta ma-čaanat imṣaddiga.*
credit - **1.** *deen* pl. *dyuun, zsaab* pl. *-aat.* We can buy the furniture on credit. *nigdar ništiri l-ʔaθaaθ bid-deen.* **2.** *mafxara* pl. *mafaaxir, faxar, faḍil* pl. *ʔafḍaal.* The credit for his success goes to his teacher. *b-najaaza yɛuud il-faxar il-muɛallim maala.* -- He's a credit to his profession. *huwwa fadd mafxara l-mihinta.* **3.** *ɛtimaad* pl. *-aat.* They don't have enough credit to import this many cars. *ma-ɛidhum iɛtimaad kaafi l-istiiraad halgadd sayyaaraat.*
to credit - **1.** *ʔaḍaaf (i ʔiḍaafa) n-, zisab (i zsaab) n-.* We're going to credit this amount to your account. *raz-inḍiif hal-mablaġ ɛala zsaabak.* **2.** *niṭa (i naṭi) n- faḍil.* They credited him with saving her life. *niṭoo l-faḍil b-inqaaδ zayaatha.*
creditor - *daaʔin* pl. *dayyaana.*
to **creep** - **1.** *zizaf (a zazif).* My son is always creeping around the house. *ʔibni daaʔiman yizzaf bil-beet.* **2.** *kazbar (u tkizbur) t.* That movie made my skin creep. *δaak il-film xalla jildi ykazbur.*
crescent - *hlaal* pl. *ʔahilla.* The star and crescent is a symbol of Islam. *n-najma wil-hilaal ramz il-ʔislaam.*
the Fertile Crescent - *l-hilaal il-xaṣiib.*
the Red Crescent - *l-hilaal il-ʔazmar.*
crew - **1.** *jamaaɛa* pl. *-aat, firqa* pl. *firaq.* The entire crew drowned when the ship sank. *jamaaɛt il-bazzaara kullhum ġirgaw lamma l-markab ġirag.* **2.** *mallaaziin.* The plane's crew consists of five persons. *mallaaziin it-taaʔira ɛadadhum xamsa.* **3.** *jooga* pl. *-aat.* The foreman divided his workmen into three crews with a special job for each. *l-ʔuṣṭa qassam il-ɛammaala ʔila tlaθ joogaat; kull jooga ʔilha šuġuḷ xaaṣṣ.*
crib - **1.** *maɛlaf* pl. *maɛaalif.* Did you put hay in the crib? *zaṭṭeet it-tibin bil-maɛlaf?* **2.** *kaaruuk* pl. *kwaariik, mahad* pl. *mhaad.* Don't take him out of the crib. *la-tšiila mnil-kaaruuk.*
cricket - *ṣurṣur* pl. *ṣaraaṣiir.*
crime - *jariima* pl. *jaraaʔim.* He committed several crimes. *rtikab ɛiddat jaraaʔim.*
criminal - **1.** *mujrim* pl. *-iin.* He's a well-known criminal. *huwwa fadd mujrim mašhuur.* **2.** *jinaaʔi*.* He's studying criminal law. *huwwa da-yidrus il-qaanuun ij-jinaaʔi.*
cripple - *muqɛad* pl. *-iin, mgarram* pl. *-iin, ṣigaṭ* pl. *ṣigaṭ.* It is hard for cripples to get a job. *l-muqɛadiin ṣaɛub ɛaleehum yzaṣṣluun ɛala šuġuḷ.*
to cripple - *garram (u tgurrum) t-, ṣaggaṭ (i taṣgiiṭ) t-.* He was crippled in an automobile accident. *tṣaggaṭ ib-zaadiθ sayyaara.*
crippled - *muqɛad* pl. *-iin, mgarram* pl. *-iin, ṣigaṭ* pl. *ṣigaṭ.* They're going to open a school for crippled children. *raz-yiftazuun madrasa lil-ʔaṭfaal il-muqɛadiin.*
crisis - **1.** *ʔazma* pl. *-aat.* The country is facing an economic crisis in the near future. *l-balad da-yjaabih ʔazma qtiṣaadiyya bil-mustaqbal il-qariib.* **2.** *šidda* pl. *šadaaʔid.* The patient passed the crisis safely. *l-mariiḍ marr biš-šidda b-salaama.*
crisp - **1.** *mgassib* pl. *-iin, mjassib* pl. *-iin.* The bread is fresh and crisp. *l-xubuz taaza w-imgassib.* **2.** *hašš.* This cucumber is crisp, not wilted. *hal-ixyaara hašša, muu δaabla.*
**The air is a bit crisp tonight. *l-hawa bii garṣat barid il-leela.*
critic - *naaqid* pl. *nuqqaad.* Did you read the movie critic's article before you saw the film? *qreet maqaal in-naaqid is-sinamaaʔi gabuḷ-ma šift il-filim?*
critical - **1.** *muntaqid.* He is sharply critical of social conventions. *huwwa muntaqid laaδiɛ lil-ʔawḍaaɛ il-ijtimaaɛiyya.* **2.** *xaṭiir, xaṭir.* His condition is critical. *zaalta xaṭra.*
criticism - *ntiqaad* pl. *-aat, naqid.* He can't stand criticism. *huwwa ma-yitzammal intiqaad.* -- She has nothing to offer but criticism. *maa ɛidha ġeer il-intiqaad.*
to **criticize** - *ntiqad (i ntiqaad), ɛayyab (i tɛiyyib) t-.* They severely criticized him. *ntiqdoo ntiqaad murr.* -- She criticizes the way I dress. *hiyya tɛayyib ɛala libsi.*
to **crochet** - *zaak (u ziyaaka) n-.* His mother crocheted a pair of slipper tops for him. *ʔumma zaakat-la zooj iklaaš.*
crock - *bastuuga* pl. *basaatiig.* When you go to the market buy a crock of pickles. *lamma truuz lis-suug štiri bastuugat ṭurši.*
crockery - *faxxaar.* This is made of crockery. *haaδa maɛmuul imnil-faxxaar.*
crocodile - *timsaaz* pl. *tamaasiiz.*
crocus - *zaɛufraan.*
crook - **1.** *ɛoočiyya* pl. *-aat, ɛaṣaaya* pl. *-aat.* The shepherd struck the lamb with his crook. *r-raaɛi ḍurab iṭ-ṭili bil-ɛoočiyya.* **2.** *mqurbaaz* pl. *-iyya, -iin; muztaal* pl. *-iin, ġaššaaš* pl. *-iin.* He's a crook. *huwwa mqurbaaz.*
crooked - **1.** *ʔaɛwaj, maɛwuuj, mɛawwaj.* This pin is crooked. *had-danbuus maɛwuuj.* **2.** *mqurbaaz* pl. *-iyya, -iin; muztaal* pl. *-iin, ġaššaaš* pl. *-iin.* All the merchants in this street are crooked. *kull it-tijjaar ib-has-suug imqurbaaziyya.*
crop - **1.** *zaaṣil* pl. *zaaṣil, mazṣuul* pl. *mazaaṣiil.* The farmers expect a good crop this year. *l-fallaaziin yitwaqqɛuun zaaṣil zeen has-sana.* **2.** *zooṣla* pl. *zawaaṣil.* The chickens are so full their crops are almost touching the ground. *d-dijaaj šabɛaan ʔila daraja zawaaṣla qariiban itdugg il-gaaɛ.*
to crop up - *ḍihar (a ḍuhuur).* Many new problems are sure to crop up. *mašaakil jidiida hwaaya mnil-muʔakkad tiḍhar.*
cross - **1.** *ṣaliib* pl. *ṣulbaan.* Do you see the church with the big cross on the steeple? *tšuuf il-kaniisa lli ɛala burujha ṣaliib čibiir?* -- The central office of the International Red Cross is in Geneva. *d-daaʔira l-markaziyya l-jamɛiyyat iṣ-ṣaliib il-ʔazmar il-ɛaalamiyya maqarrha b-janeef.* **2.** *mḍarrab.* The mule is a cross between a horse and a donkey. *l-baġal imḍarrab been il-izṣaan wil-izmaar.*
to cross - *ɛubar (u ɛubuur) n-.* Cross at the intersection of the street. *ʔuɛbur min raas iš-šaariɛ.* -- When do we cross the border? *šwakit nuɛbur il-zuduud?* **2.** *tqaaṭaɛ (a taqaaṭuɛ) wiyya.* Rashid St. crosses Amin St. at Amin Sq. *šaariɛ ir-rašiid yitqaaṭaɛ wiyya šaariɛ il-ʔamiin ib-saazt il-ʔamiin.*
**Cross your heart! *twajjah ɛal-qibla w-izlif!*
to cross out - *šiṭab (u šaṭub) n-, čazz (i čazz) n-.* Cross out the items you don't want. *ʔisṭub il-mawaadd illi ma-triidha.*
to **crossbreed** - *ḍarrab (i taḍriib) t-.* On this farm they crossbreed varieties of sheep with each other. *b-hal-mazraɛa yḍarrbuun ʔanwaaɛ il-ʔaġnaam maɛa baɛaḍha.*
cross-eyed - m. *ʔazwal* pl. *zool, zooliin,* f. *zoola* pl. *-aat.* She's cross-eyed. *hiyya zoola.*
crossing - **1.** *mafraq* pl. *mafaariq.* There's no traffic light at this crossing. *ma-aku ḍuwa maal muruur ib-hal-mafraq.* **2.** *ɛubuur.* How far are we from the crossing point. *šgadd nibɛid ɛan nugṭat il-ɛubuur?* **3.** *ɛibra* pl. *-aat.* On the ferry they charge ten fils for each crossing. *bil-ɛabbaara yaaxδuun ɛašr ifluus ɛan kull ɛibra.*
cross section - *maqṭaɛ* pl. *maqaaṭiɛ.*
crosswise - *bil-ɛuruḍ.* Cut this cucumber crosswise. *guṣṣ hal-ixyaara bil-ɛuruḍ.*
crossword puzzle - *l-kalimaat il-mutaqaaṭiɛa.*
to **crouch** - *naṣṣa (i tniṣṣi) nafs~.* He crouched down behind the table so I couldn't see him. *huwwa naṣṣa nafsa wara l-meez zatta ma-ašuufa.*
crow - *ġraab* pl. *ġirbaan, zaaġ* pl. *-aat.* The black and white crows are bigger than the black crows. *l-ġirbaan ʔakbar imniz-zaaġ.*
to crow - *ɛooɛa (i tɛooɛi), ṣaaz (i ṣyaaz).* I woke up when the rooster crowed. *gɛadt imnin-noom lamma d-diič ɛooɛa.*
crowbar - *hiim* pl. *hyaama.*
crowd - **1.** *zdizaam* pl. *-aat, jamhuur* pl. *jamaahiir.* Have you seen the crowd in front of the theater? *šift il-izdizaam ib-baab is-siinama?* -- There was a

small crowd standing at the bus stop. *čaan aku jamhuur iṣġayyir mawjuud ib-mawqif il-paaṣ.* 2. *jamaaƐa* pl. *-aat.* He goes around with a bad crowd. *yruuz wiyya jamaaƐa muu zeena.*
to crowd - 1. *zdizam (i zdizaam), ndizas (i ndizaas).* We all crowded into the bus. *kullatna zdizamna bil-paaṣ.* 2. *zišak (a zašik) n-, zišar (u zašir) n-.* I don't think you can crowd another thing in there. *ma-aƐtiqid tigdar tizšik šii laax ihnaak.*

crowded - *muzdazim.* The bus was crowded, as usual. *l-paaṣ čaan muzdazim kal-Ɛaada.*
crowded to capacity - *mqappuṭ.* The hall was crowded to capacity. *l-qaaƐa čaanat imqappṭa.*

crown - *taaj* pl. *tiijaan, tuuj.* He wore a gold crown. *libas taaj ðahabi.*
to crown - *tawwaj (i tatwiij) t-.* They crowned him king in 1925. *tawwijoo malik sanat alf w-tisiƐmiyya w-xamsa w-Ɛišriin.*

crown prince - *waliyy* (pl. *ʔawliyaaʔ*) *Ɛahid.*

to **crucify** - *ṣilab (u ṣalub) n-.* The Romans used to crucify their prisoners. *r-ruumaaniyyiin čaanaw yṣilbuun masaajiinhum.*

crude - 1. *xašin, faðð.* He's a rather crude person. *huwwa fadd waazid xašin.* 2. *xaam.* These barrels contain crude oil. *hal-baraamiil biiha nafuṭ xaam.*

cruel - *qaasi* pl. *-iin, qusaat.* Why are you this cruel? *ʔinta luweeš hiiči qaasi?*

cruelty - *qasaawa.*

cruiser - *ṭarraad* pl. *-aat.* My brother is assigned to a cruiser. *ʔaxuuya mƐayyan ib-ṭarraad.*

crumb - *ftaata* pl. *-aat* coll. *ftaat.* He left bread crumbs on the table. *tirak iftaat xubuz Ɛal-meez.*
to crumb - *fattat (i taftiit, tfittit) t-.* Crumb the bread and mix it with the meat. *fattit il-xubuz w-xubṭa wiyya l-lazam.*

to **crush - 1.** *fuƐaṣ (u faƐuṣ) n-.* You're crushing my hat. *ʔinta da-tufƐuṣ šafuqti.* 2. *sizag (a sazig) n-.* The army remained loyal and crushed the insurrection. *j-jeeš buqa muxliṣ w-sizag it-tamarrud.* -- He crushed out the cigarette with his foot. *sizag ij-jigaara b-rijla.* 3. *jiraš (u jariš) n-.* When are you going to crush the wheat? *šwakit raz-tijruš il-zunṭa?* 4. *kassar (i taksiir, tkissir) t-.* This machine crushes the rocks. *hal-makiina tkassir iṣ-ṣuxuur.* 5. *ṣidam (i ṣadim) n-.* The news crushed him. *ṣidama l-xabar.*

crust - *gišra* pl. *-aat.* I can't eat the crust. *ma-agdar aakul il-gišra.* -- The thickness of the earth's crust is several miles. *gišrat il-ʔaruð simukha Ɛiddat ʔamyaal.*

crutch - *Ɛikkaaza* pl. *-aat.* He has to walk on crutches. *laazim yimši Ɛala Ɛikkaazaat.*

cry - 1. *ṣeeza* pl. *-aat, Ɛeeṭa* pl. *-aat, ṣarxa* pl. *-aat.* We heard a loud cry and went to investigate. *smaƐna ṣeeza Ɛaalya w-rizna nitzarra.* 2. *bačya* pl. *-aat.* She'll feel better after a good cry. *raz-tirtaaz baƐad fadd bačya zeena.*
to cry - 1. *biča (i biča, bači).* The baby was crying for its mother. *ṭ-ṭifil čaan yibči Ɛala ʔumma.* 2. *ṣaaz (i ṣyaaz).* I heard an animal crying in the forest. *smaƐit zaywaan yṣiiz bil-ġaaba.*
to cry out - *ṣirax (a ṣraax), Ɛaaṭ (i Ɛyaaṭ), ṣaaz (i ṣyaaz).* He cried out from the pain. *ṣirax imnil-ʔalam.*
to cry to oneself - *naaz (u nooz).* We saw her at her son's grave crying to herself. *šifnaaha Ɛala gabur ʔibinha tnuuz.*

crystal - 1. *balluura* pl. *-aat* coll. *balluur.* We studied salt crystals under the microscope. *drasna balluuraat il-miliz tazt il-mikriskoop.* -- I broke the last piece of crystal that I had. *ksarit ʔaaxir qiṭƐa mnil-balluur illi Ɛindi.* -- They bought a crystal chandelier for the reception room. *štiraw iθrayya balluur il-ġurfat il-istiqbaal.* 2. *jaama* pl. *-aat.* I need a new crystal for my watch. *ʔaztaaj jaama jdiida s-saaƐti.*

cube - *mukaƐƐab* pl. *-aat.* Draw a cube on the blackboard. *ʔirsim mukaƐƐab Ɛaṣ-ṣabbuura.*

cucumber - *xyaara* pl. *-aat* coll. *xyaar.*

to **cuddle - 1.** *ziðan (u zaðin) n-.* The mother cuddled her children. *l-ʔumm ziðnat jahhaalha.* 2. *tlaflaf (a tliflif).* The children cuddled up in their blankets. *l-ʔaṭfaal itlafilfaw ib-baṭṭaaniyyaathum.*

cue - 1. *ʔišaara* pl. *-aat.* I'll give you the cue to start talking. *raz-anṭiik ʔišaart il-ibtidaaʔ bil-kalaam.* 2. *Ɛaṣa* pl. *Ɛiṣi, kyuu* pl. *-aat.* He hit his friend on the head with a billiard cue. *ðurab ṣadiiqa Ɛala raasa b-Ɛaṣa bilyaard.*

cuff - *ṭawya* pl. *-aat, kaffa* pl. *-aat, θanya* pl. *-aat.* I tore my pants cuff. *šaggeet ṭawyat il-panṭaroon maali.*
on the cuff - *bid-deen.* Can you put it on the cuff until tomorrow? *tigdar tizsibha bid-deen il-baačir?*

cuff link - *dugmat* (pl. *digam*) *irdaan.* I lost one of my cuff links. *ðayyaƐit wizda min digam irdaani.*

culprit - *muðnib* pl. *-iin.* They found the culprit. *ligaw il-muðnib.*

cultural - *θaqaafi*.* He is Iraq's cultural attache. *huwwa mulzaq iθ-θaqaafi maal il-Ɛiraaq.*

culture - 1. *zaðaara* pl. *-aat.* He's a specialist in ancient Greek culture. *huwwa muxtaṣṣ ib-zaðaarat il-yunaan il-qadiim.* 2. *θaqaafa.* He is a man of high culture. *huwwa ṣaazib θaqaafa Ɛaalya.* 3. *zariƐ* pl. *zruuƐ.* He is studying microbe culture. *da-yidrus zariƐ il-mikroobaat.*

cultured - *mhaððab, mθaqqaf.* She's a cultured woman. *hiyya fadd wizda mhaððba.*

culvert - *burbux* pl. *baraabix.*

cuneiform - *mismaari*.*

cunning - *muraawiġ, zayyaal, šeeṭaan, makkaar.* The fox is a very cunning animal. *θ-θaƐlab fadd zaywaan muraawiġ ihwaaya.*

cup - 1. *finjaan* pl. *fnaajiin.* He drank three cups of coffee. *širab iθlaθ ifnaajiin gahwa.* 2. *kuub* pl. *kwaaba.* I asked our neighbors for a cup of sugar. *ṭlabit min jiiraanna kuub šakar.* 3. *kaʔis* pl. *kuʔuus.* Who won the cup? *minu zaṣṣal Ɛal-kaʔis?*

cupboard - *diilaab* (pl. *dwaaliib*) *imwaaƐiin.*

curb - 1. *raṣiif* pl. *-aat.* I stood on the curb watching the parade. *wgafit Ɛar-raṣiif atfarraj Ɛal-istiƐraað.* 2. *taqyiid* pl. *-aat.* The government put a curb on emigration. *l-zukuuma xallat taqyiid Ɛal-hijra.*
to curb - 1. *qayyad (i taqyiid, tqiyyid) t-.* The government has begun curbing foreign imports. *l-zukuuma btidat itqayyid il-istiiraadaat il-xaarijiyya.* 2. *ðubaṭ (u ðabuṭ) n-.* You have to try to curb your temper. *laazim itzaawil tuðbuṭ ʔaƐṣaabak.*

cure - *duwa* pl. *ʔadwiya, Ɛilaaj* pl. *-aat.* There is no cure for cancer. *ma-aku duwa liṣ-ṣaraṭaan.*
to cure - 1. *ṭayyab (i ṭṭiyyib) t-, šaafa (i šifaaʔ) t-.* The doctors cured his deafness. *d-dakaatra ṭayyibaw it-ṭaraš maala.* 2. *xammar (u taxmiir, txummur) t-.* They cure the tobacco in these warehouses. *yxammruun it-titin ib-hal-maxaazin.*

curfew - *maniƐ tajawwul.*

curiosity - 1. *zubb istiṭlaaƐ.* She aroused my curiosity. *ʔaθaarat zubb istiṭlaaƐi.* 2. *ġariib* pl. *ġaraayib.* He brought with him some curiosities from India. *jaab wiyyaa ġaraayib imnil-hind.*

curious - 1. *muzibb lil-istiṭlaaƐ.* Don't be so curious. *la-tṣiir hal-gadd muzibb lil-istiṭlaaƐ.* 2. *ġariib.* This is a very curious situation. *haaði fadd waðƐiyya ġariiba kulliš.*

curl - *tajƐiid* pl. *-aat, kaƐkuula* pl. *-aat.* Her hair is all curls. *šaƐarha kulla tajƐiidaat.*
to curl - *jaƐƐad (i tajƐiid) t-, kaƐkal (i tkiƐkil) t-.* Fatma, who curled your hair? *faaṭma, minu jaƐƐad šaƐarič?*
to curl up - *lamlam (i tlimlim) nafs~, tlamlam (a tlimlim).* The dog curled up and went to sleep. *č-čalib itlamlam w-naam.*

currency - *naqid* pl. *nuquud, Ɛumla* pl. *-aat.* Their currency is made in this country. *nuquudhum maƐmuula b-hal-balad.*

current - 1. *tayyaar* pl. *-aat.* The current is very swift here. *t-tayyaar kulliš sariiƐ ihnaa.* -- The electric current has been turned off. *nqiṭaƐ it-tayyaar il-kahrabaaʔi.* 2. *jaari, zaali*.* The bill for the current month is attached. *l-qaaʔima maal iš-šahr ij-jaari murfaqa.* 3. *daarij.* Wearing of the fez was current in Baghdad before the First World War. *libs il-fiina čaan daarij ib-baġdaad gabuḷ il-zarb il-Ɛaalamiyya l-ʔuula.*

curse - *šattuuma* pl. *-aat, štaayim; laƐna* pl. *-aat, naƐla* pl. *-aat, šatma* pl. *-aat, masabba* pl. *-aat.* I don't want to hear another curse out of you. *ma-ard asmaƐ šattuuma lux minnak.*
to curse - *šattam (i tšittim) t-, sabb (i sabb) n-, šitam (i šatim) n-.* He cursed him for his slow driving. *šattam Ɛalee s-siyaaqta l-baṭiiʔa.*

curtain - *parda* pl. *-aat, sitaar* pl. *sitaaʔir.*

curtain rod - *šiiš* (pl. *šyaaš*) *parda.*

curve - *munƐaṭaf* pl. *-aat, loofa* pl. *-aat.* This road

has a lot of curves. *haṭ-ṭariiq bii loofaat ihwaaya.*
to curve - *daar (u dawaraan), laaf (u loof), nƐiṭaf (u nƐiṭaaf).* The road curves to the right. *ṭ-ṭariiq yduur lil-yamiin.*
cushion - *kušin* pl. *-aat, mxadda* pl. *mxaadiid, mindar* pl. *manaadir, maqƐad* pl. *maqaaƐid.*
cuspidor - *mibṣaqa* pl. *mabaaṣiq.*
custody - *tawqiif, ẓajiz.* They took him into custody. *ˀaxδoo lit-tawqiif.*
custom - **1.** *Ɛaada* pl. *-aat.* This is an old Iraqi custom. *haaδi Ɛaada Ɛiraaqiyya qadiima.* **2.** *tunṣaa.* His cars are all custom-made. *kull sayyaaraata maƐmuula tuuṣaa.*
customary - *ẓasb il-Ɛaada, ẓasb il-Ɛuruf, Ɛtiyaadi*.*
customer - *maƐmiil* pl. *maƐaamiil, zabuun* pl. *zabaayin.* He's my best customer. *huwwa ˀaẓsan maƐmiil Ɛindi.*
customs - **1.** *gumrug* pl. *gamaarig.* Do we have to pay customs on this? *laazim nidfaƐ gumrug Ɛala haay?* **2.** *gumrugi*.* We had to go through a customs inspection when we arrived. *lamma wṣalna čaan laazim inmurr ib-taftiiš gumrugi.*
cut - **1.** *jariẓ* pl. *jruuẓ.* The cut is nearly healed. *j-jariẓ indimal taqriiban.* **2.** *taxfiiḍ* pl. *-aat, tanziil* pl. *-aat, taqliil* pl. *-aat, tangiiṣ* pl. *-aat.* He had to take a cut in his salary. *ḍṭarr yiqbal taxfiiḍ ib-raatba.* **3.** *tifṣaal* pl. *-aat, tafṣiil* pl. *-aat.* I don't like the cut of this coat. *ma-yiƐjibni tifṣaal has-sitra.* **4.** *ẓuṣṣa* pl. *ẓuṣaṣ.* You'll get your cut after everything is sold. *raẓ-taaxuδ ẓuṣṣtak baƐad-ma kullši yinbaaƐ.* **5.** *ġiyaab* pl. *-aat, ngiṭaaƐ* pl. *-aat.* He gave me a cut for being a quarter of an hour late for class. *sajjal Ɛalayya ġiyaab li-ˀann itˀaxxarit rubuƐ saaƐa Ɛan id-daris.* **6.** *wuṣla* pl. *wuṣal, qiṭƐa* pl. *qiṭaƐ.* Give me a good cut of beef. *nṭiini wuṣlat laẓam hooš zeena.*
cut rate - *siƐir muxaffaḍ.* He bought it cut-rate. *štiraaha b-siƐir muxaffaḍ.*
to cut - **1.** *gaṣṣ (u gaṣṣ) n-, jiraẓ (a jariẓ) n-.* I cut my finger. *jraẓit iṣibƐi.* -- That remark cut him a great deal. *hal-mulaaẓaḍa jirẓata kθiir.* **2.** *gaṣṣ (u gaṣṣ) n-.* Will you cut the watermelon please? *baḷḷa ma-tguṣṣ ir-raggiyya rajaaˀan?* -- Would you cut the cards please? *baḷḷa ma-tguṣṣ il-waraq rajaaˀan?* **3.** *xaffaḍ (u taxfiiḍ, txuffuḍ) t-, nazzal (i tanziil, tnizzil) t-, qallal (i taqliil, tqillil) t-, naggaṣ (i tangiiṣ, tniggiṣ) t-.* They've cut the prices on winter clothes. *xaffiḍaw il-ˀasƐaar lil-malaabis iš-šitwiyya.* **4.** *ġaab (i ġiyaab), ngiṭaƐ (ngiṭaaƐ).* He cut class three days in a row. *ġaab Ɛan iṣ-ṣaff itlatt iyyaam mitwaalya.* **5.** *xaffaf (i taxfiif, txiffif) t-.* Cut the paint with a gallon of turpentine. *xaffif iṣ-ṣubug ib-gaḷin tarpantiin.* **6.** *ṭallaƐ (i ṭṭilliƐ) t-.* Our son is beginning to cut his teeth. *ˀibinna btida yṭalliƐ isnuun.*
to cut across - *gaṣṣ (u gaṣṣ) n-, Ɛubar (u Ɛabur) n-.* We cut across the orange grove on our way home. *gaṣṣeena bistaan il-purtaqaal ib-jayyatna lil-beet.*
to cut back - *xaffaḍ (i), nazzal (i), naggaṣ (i), qallal (i).* They've cut back production fifty percent. *xaffiḍaw il-ˀintaaj xamsiin bil-miyya.*
to cut in - *tdaxxal (a tadaxxul).* He's always cutting in when we're having a discussion. *huwwa daaˀiman yitdaxxal lamma tkuun Ɛidna munaaqaša.*
to cut off - **1.** *qiṭaƐ (a qaṭiƐ) n-.* They cut off his allowance. *qiṭƐaw muxaṣṣaṣaata.* -- The police cut off the roads leading to town. *š-šurṭa qiṭƐat iṭ-ṭuruq il-muˀaddiya lil-wlaaya.* -- The company cut off the electricity. *š-šarika qiṭƐat il-kahrabaaˀ.* **2.** *bitar (i batir) n-, gaṣṣ (u gaṣṣ) n-.* He cut off the dog's tail. *bitar δeel ič-čalib.*
to cut out - **1.** *baṭṭal (i tabṭiil) min.* Cut out that running around the house. *baṭṭilu min har-rakuḍ bil-beet.* **2.** *gaṣṣ (u).* The censor cut two sentences out of the letter. *r-raqiib gaṣṣ jumulteen imnil-maktuub.* **3.** *yeezi Ɛaad, bass Ɛaad.* Cut it out! Stop making that noise. *yeezi Ɛaad! baṭṭilu min hal-laġwa.*
**He's not cut out to be a teacher. *huwwa muu maal muƐallim* or *huwwa muu wijih muƐallim.*
to cut up - *gaṣgaṣ (i tgiṣgiṣ) t-, gaṭṭaƐ (i tgiṭṭiƐ) t-.* Cut up the carrots in small pieces. *gaṣgiṣ il-jizar wusal iṣġaar.*
cute - *laṭiif, ẓabbuub.* She's a very cute girl. *hiyya fadd ibnayya hwaaya ẓabbuuba.* -- He told a cute story. *ẓiča quṣṣa laṭiifa.*
cycle - *dawra* pl. *-aat.* This machine completes it's cycle in five minutes. *hal-makiina tkammil dawratha b-xamas daqaayiq.*
cylinder - **1.** *silindar* pl. *-aat.* This engine has six cylinders. *hal-makiina biiha sitt silindaraat.* **2.** *ṣṭuwaana* pl. *-aat.* The volume of a cylinder is equal to multiplying the area of the base times its height. *ẓajm il-iṣṭuwaana ysaawi ḍarb masaaẓat il-qaaƐida bil-irtifaaƐ.*
cymbal - *ṭaas* pl. *ṭuus.*
Cypriot - *qubruṣi** pl. *-iyyiin.*
Cyprus - *qubruṣ.*
czar - *qayṣar* pl. *qayaaṣira.*

D

dad - *yaaba, yaab, baaba.* Dad, can I use the car? *yaab, ˀagdar astaƐmil is-sayyaara?*
daddy - *baaba.* Is your daddy home? *baaba bil-beet?*
daffodil - *narjisa* pl. *-aat* coll. *narjis.*
dagger - *xanjar* pl. *xanaajir.*
daily - **1.** *bil-yoom, kull yoom.* The mail is delivered twice daily. *l-bariid yitwazzaƐ marrteen bil-yoom.* **2.** *yoomi*.* The daily rate is three dollars. *l-ˀujra l-yoomiyya tlaθ doolaaraat.*
dairy - **1.** *maƐmal* (pl. *maƐaamil) ˀalbaan.* I bought the butter at the dairy. *štireet iz-zibda min maƐmal il-ˀalbaan.* **2.** *ˀalbaan.* My uncle has a dairy farm. *Ɛammi Ɛinda mazraƐat ˀalbaan.*
dam - *sadd* pl. *suduud.* The dam is broken. *s-sadd maksuur.*
damage - *ḍarar* pl. *ˀaḍraar, talaf* pl. *-iyyaat.* How much damage took place? *šgadd ṣaar ḍarar?*
to damage - *tilaf (i talif).* The storm damaged the roof. *l-Ɛaaṣifa tilfat iṣ-ṣaṭiẓ.*
damages - *taƐwiiḍaat.* He had to pay damages. *ḍṭaar yidfaƐ taƐwiiḍaat.*
Damascene - *dimišqi** pl. *-iyyiin, šaami** pl. *-iyyiin, šwaam.*
Damascus - *dimašq, š-šaam.*
damn - *malƐuun.* Throw that damn cat out! *ṭalliƐ hal-bazzuuna l-malƐuuna barra!*
**I don't give a damn what he says. *ẓčaayta w-qundarti.*
to damn - **1.** *liƐan (a laƐin) n-.* Damn him! *ˀaḷḷa yilƐana!* **2.** *liƐan (a laƐin) n- maδhab, niƐal (a naƐil) n- maδhab, šiƐal (a šaƐil) n- diin.* She damned me up and down for running over her cat. *niƐlat maδhabi li-ˀan disit bazzuunatha b-sayyaarti.* -- I'll be damned if I'll do it! *ˀanniƐil ˀiδa asawwiiha!*
damned - *malƐuun, manƐuul.*
damp - *raṭib, naadi.* Everything gets damp in the cellar. *kullši yṣiir raṭib bis-sirdaab.*
dampness - *ruṭuuba, nida.*
dance - **1.** *rigṣa* pl. *-aat.* May I have the next dance? *tismaẓii-li bir-rigṣa j-jaaya?* **2.** *ẓaflat* (pl. *-aat) rigiṣ.* Are you going to the dance? *raẓ-itruuẓ il-ẓaflat ir-rigiṣ?*
to dance - *rigaṣ (u rigaṣ).* They danced until midnight. *rigṣaw ˀila nuṣṣ il-leel.*
dancer - *raaqiṣa* pl. *-aat.* They have a good dancer at the Select Night Club. *Ɛidhum raaqiṣa zeena b-malha salakt.*
**He's a good dancer. *yirguṣ zeen.*
danger - *xaṭar.* The doctor says she is out of danger now. *t-tabiib gaal il-xaṭar zaal Ɛanha hassa.* -- Caution! Danger! *ntibih lil-xaṭar!*
in danger of - *muƐarraḍ.* He's in danger of losing his job. *huwwa muƐarraḍ il-fuqdaan waḍiifta.*
dangerous - *muxṭir.* Is swimming here dangerous? *s-sibiẓ ihnaa muxṭir?*
to **dare** - *jiraˀ (a jurˀa), jisar (u jisaara).* I didn't dare leave the baby alone. *ma-jraˀit atruk iṭ-ṭifil waẓda.* -- How dare you open my mail? *šloon tijsur tiftaẓ bariidi?*

dark - 1. *ðalma.* The road is hard to find in the dark. *ṭ-ṭariiq ṣaεub yinligi biδ-ðalma.* **2.** *ðalaam.* Don't keep me in the dark this way. *la-titrukni b-ðalaam hiici.* **3.** *ṭoox.* I want a darker color. *ˀariid loon ˀaṭwax.* **4.** *ˀasmar* pl. *sumur.* She is quite dark. *hiyya samra kulliš.*

to get dark - *ðlamm (a ðalaam).* In summer it gets dark late. *biṣ-ṣeef tiðlamm faayit wakit.*

darling - 1. *mdallal* pl. *-iin.* He's his mother's pampered darling. *huwwa mdallal maal ˀumma.* **2.** *ζabiib.* What's the matter, darling? *š-biik, ζabiibi?*

**What a darling child! *šloon jaahil yinζaṭṭ bil-gaḷub!*

to **darn -** *xayyaṭ (i xyaaṭa).* Did you darn my socks? *xayyaṭṭii-li jwaariibi?*

**I'll be darned if it isn't Jalil! *ˀaguṣṣ ˀiidi ˀiδa haaδa muu jaliil.*

dash - 1. *xaṭṭ* pl. *xuṭuuṭ, šuxuṭ* pl. *šxuuṭ.* Put a dash after the first word. *ζuṭṭ xaṭṭ baεd il-kalima il-ˀuula.* **2.** *ζabba* pl. *-aat.* All it needs is a dash of salt. *ma-yinraad-la ġeer ζabbat miliζ.* **3.** *rikið.* Who won the hundred meter dash? *minu ġilab ib-rikð il-miit matir.*

to dash - 1. *rašš (u rašš), δabb (i δabb).* He came to when I dashed some water in his face. *raddat ruuζa lamma raššeet šwayya maay εala wujja.* **2.** *ṭufar (u ṭafur).* He grabbed his hat and made a dash for the door. *ligaf šafuqta w-ṭufar ṭafur bil-baab.*

to dash off - *εallag (i taεliig).* He dashed off before I could answer. *εallag, gabuḷ-ma ˀajaawba.*

dashboard - *dašbuul* pl. *-aat.*

date - 1. *tamra* pl. *-aat* coll. *tamur.* How much is a kilo of dates? *beeš kiilu t-tamur.* **2.** *taariix* pl. *tawaariix.* What's the date today? *šinu taariix il-yoom?* or ***l-yoom išgadd biš-šahar?* **3.** *mawεid* pl. *mawaaεiid.* I have a date for lunch today. *εindi mawεid lil-ġada hal-yoom.* **4.** *yoom* pl. *ˀayyaam.* You set the date. *ˀinta εayyin il-yoom.*

to date - *li-hassa, ˀila l-ˀaan.* We haven't heard from him to date. *ma-smaεna minna li-hassa.*

to date - *ˀarrax (i taˀriix) t-.* The letter is dated June 6. *l-maktuub imˀarrax ib-sitta ζazayraan.*

to date from - *rijaε (a rujuuε) it-taariix ˀila.* The oldest house in town dates from the 17th century. *ˀaεtag beet bil-madiina yirjaε taariixa ˀila l-qarn is-saabiε εašar.*

date palm - *naxla* pl. *-aat* coll. *naxal.*

daughter - *bitt, bint* pl. *banaat.*

daughter-in-law - *čanna* pl. *-aat, čnaayin.*

dawn - *fajir.* We had to get up at dawn. *ðṭarreena nigεud imnil-fajir.*

to dawn - 1. *ṣabbaζ (i taṣbiiζ).* The day dawned, clear and sunny. *ṣabbaζ in-nahaar ṣaaζi w-mišmis.* **2.** *wuðaζ (a wuðuuζ) l-, ˀadrak (i ˀidraak).* It finally dawned on me what he meant. *ˀaxiiran wuðaζ-li qaṣda* or *ˀaxiiran ˀadrakit iš-εina.*

day - 1. *yoom* pl. *ˀayyaam.* I haven't seen him since that day. *ma-šifta min δaak il-yoom.* -- I'll drop by your house some day. *raζ-amurr il-beetkum fadd yoom imnil-ˀayyaam.* -- One of these days you'll be sorry. *raζ-tindam fadd yoom.* **2.** *nahaar* pl. *-aat.* He's been sleeping all day. *ṣaar-la naayim ṭuul in-nahaar.*

**Let's call it a day! *paaydoos!*

a day - *bil-yoom.* Take three pills a day. *ˀiblaε itlaθ ζabbaat bil-yoom.*

by the day - 1. *yoom baεad yoom, yoom εala yoom.* It gets more difficult by the day. *da-yṣiir ˀaṣεab yoom εala yoom.* **2.** *εala ˀasaas il-ˀayyaam, kull yoom ib-yooma.* You can rent this room by the day. *tiġdar itˀajjir hal-ġurfa εala ˀasaas il-ˀayyaam.*

day after day - *yoom wara yoom.* Day after day he tells us the same old story. *yoom wara yoom yεiid w-yiṣqul ib-nafs il-quṣṣa.*

day by day - *yoom εala yoom, yoom baεad yoom, yoom wara yoom.* Day by day his condition is improving. *yoom εala yoom ζaalta da-titζassan.*

day off - *εuṭla* pl. *εuṭal.* Tuesday is my day off. *εuṭilti yoom iθ-θilaaθaa.*

every day - *kull yoom.* He works every day except Friday. *yištugul kull yoom ma-εada yoom ij-jumεa.*

daybreak - *fajir.* We're leaving at daybreak. *raζ-insaafir il-fajir.*

to **daze -** *dawwax (u), siṭar(u saṭir) n-.* The explosion dazed him. *l-infijaar dawwaxa.*

dazed - *daayix, masṭuur.* He seemed completely dazed. *čaan imbayyin εalee daayix tamaaman.*

dead - 1. *mayyit* pl. *mawta, ˀamwaat.* They buried their dead. *difnaw mawtaahum.* -- The meeting was pretty dead. *j-jalsa čaanat mayyta* or *j-jalsa ma-čaan biiha ζayaat.* **2.** *tamaaman.* I'm dead tired. *ˀaani taεbaan tamaaman.* -- I'm dead certain I put it there. *ˀaani mitˀakkid tamaaman xalleetha hnaak.*

**The fire is dead. *n-naar xumdat.*

dead-end - *ma-bii ṭalεa, ma-yiṭlaε.* This is a dead-end street. *haaδa šaariε ma-yiṭlaε.*

deadly - *qaatil, qattaal, mumiit.* This poison is deadly. *has-samm qaatil.*

deaf - m. *ˀaṭraš* pl. *ṭaršiin,* f. *ṭarša* pl. *-aat, -iin.* He's completely deaf. *huwwa ˀaṭraš tamaaman.*

to **deafen -** *ṭarraš (i taṭriiš).* That noise is deafening. *haṣ-ṣoot yṭarriš.*

deal - 1. *ṣafqa* pl. *-aat.* He made a lot of money on that deal. *sawwa xooš ifluus ib-haṣ-ṣafqa.* **2.** *ζuṣṣa* pl. *ζuṣaṣ.* All I want is a fair deal. *kull-ma ˀariida huwwa ζuṣṣa εaadla.* **3.** *tawziiε* pl. *-aat.* Whose deal is it now? *door man hassa bit-tawziiε?* or *minu ywazziε waraq?* **4.** *dagga.* That's a good deal! *haay xooš dagga!*

**They gave him a raw deal. *εaamloo muu xooš* or *ġumṭaw ζaqqa.*

a good deal - *ihwaaya.* There's a good deal to be done yet. *ˀaku baεad ihwaaya yirraad-la msaawaa.*

to deal - *wazzaε (i tawziiε) t-, qassam (i taqsiim) t-, farrag (i tafriig) t-.* Who dealt the cards? *minu wazzaε il-waraq?*

to deal with - 1. *tεaamal (a taεaamul) maεa, wiyya.* He dealt fairly with me. *tεaamal wiyyaaya b-εadil.* -- He deals directly with the company. *yitεaamal maεa š-šarika raˀsan.* **2.** *tεallaq (a taεalluq) b-.* The book deals with labor problems. *l-iktaab yitεallaq ib-mašaakil il-εummaal.*

**This problem has been dealt with. *hal-muškila nbiζθat w-xilṣat.*

dealer - 1. *taajir* pl. *tijjaar.* He's a dealer in Persian rugs. *huwwa taajir bis-sijjaad il-εajmi.* **2.** *bayyaaε* pl. *-iin.* There's a used car dealer near our house. *ˀaku bayyaaε sayyaaraat mustaεmila yamm beetna.*

dear - 1. *εaziiz.* His sister is very dear to him. *ˀuxta kulliš εaziiza εalee.* **2.** *ġaali.* Everything in the market is very dear these days. *kullši bis-suug kulliš ġaali hal-ˀayyaam.*

oh dear - *ˀaax yaaba.* Oh dear, we'll be late again. *ˀaax yaaba! raζ-inkuun mitˀaxxriin marra lux!*

dearly - *ġaali.* He had to pay dearly for his mistake. *ðṭarr yidfaε ġaali εala galiṭṭa.*

death - 1. *moot* pl. *ˀamwaat, wafaat, wafiyya* pl. *-aat.* His death was announced in the newspapers. *moota nεilan bij-jaraayid.* **2.** *ˀiεdaam.* This crime carries the death penalty. *hal-jariima tiṭðamman εuquubat il-ˀiεdaam.*

**You'll catch your death of cold. *raζ-yṣiibak barid ymawwtak.*

**He'll be the death of me yet. *raζ-yimawwitni waḷḷa.*

**Don't work yourself to death. *la-tihlik nafsak imniš-šuġuḷ.*

**He's in the throes of death. *gaεad ynaaziε.*

debate - *munaaqaša* pl. *-aat.* The debate lasted for hours. *l-munaaqaša daamat εiddat saaεaat.*

to debate - *naaqaš (i munaaqaša).* The students debated the subject among themselves. *ṭ-ṭullaab naaqšaw il-mawðuuε beenaathum.* — The question was debated for a long time. *s-suˀaal ṭawwlat manaaqašta mudda ṭwiila.*

to debate with oneself - *daanaš (i mudaanaša) in-nafis.* I debated with myself whether or not to go. *daanašit nafsi ˀaruuζ loo laa.*

debt - *deen* pl. *dyuun.* This payment settles your debt. *had-dafεa tinhi deenak.*

in debt - 1. *madyuun.* Is he still in debt? *huwwa baεda madyuun.* **2.** *bid-deen.* He's up to his ears in debt. *huwwa ṭaamus bid-deen.*

debtor - *madyuun* pl. *-iin.*

decade - *εaqid* pl. *εuquud.*

decay - *nζilaal.* Some means must be found to prevent any further decay in our economic system. *fadd wasiila laazim tinligi l-maniε ˀayy inζilaal ˀaaxar ib-niðaamna l-iqtiṣaadi.*

to decay - 1. *xaas (i xees, xayasaan).* The vegetables decayed rapidly in the heat. *l-xuðrawaat xaasat bil-εajal min ζaraart ij-jaww.* **2.** *sawwas (i taswiis) t-.* The tooth decayed. *s-sinn sawwas.*

decayed - 1. *xaayis.* Throw all the decayed vegetables

into the garbage can. *δibb kull il-xuδ̣rawaat il-xaaysa b-tanakt iz-zibil.* 2. *mitsawwis, msawwis.* The tooth is decayed and I'll have to pull it. *s-sinn imsawwis w-laazim ʔašlaεa.* 3. *mitfassix.* The body was so decayed that it could not be identified. *j-juθθa halgadd-ma mitfassxa maa mumkin it-taεarruf εala hawiyyat ṣaaʒibha.*

deceit - *ġišš, muxaatala, xidaaε, qašmara.*

deceitful - *muxaadiε.* She is a lying, deceitful woman. *haay fadd mara čaδδaaba w-muxaadiεa.*

to **deceive** - 1. *ġašš (i ġašš) n-, xidaε (a xidaaε) n-, qašmar (u qašmara).* Appearances are deceiving. *l-maδ̣aahir tixdaε.* -- He deceived us. *ġaššna.* 2. *xaan (u xiyaana), xidaε (a xidaaε) n-.* His wife is deceiving him. *zawijta da-txuuna.*

December - *kaanuun il-ʔawwal.*

decency - *ʔadab, liyaaqa.* He didn't even have the decency to thank me. *ma-kaan εinda ʒatta ʔadab kaafi yiškurni.*

decent - 1. *muʒtaram, muʔaddab.* He's a decent fellow. *huwwa fadd waaʒid muʒtaram.* -- He lives a decent life. *yεiiš εiiša muʒtarama.* 2. *šariif.* He did the decent thing and married her. *sawwa šii šariif w-itzawwajha.* 3. *zeen.* I make a decent living from this job. *haš-šaġla twaffir-li εiiša zeena.*

to **decide** - *qarrar (i taqriir) t-.* I decided to stay. *qarrarit ʔabqa.* -- What did you decide on? *š-qarrarit?*

decided - *θaabit, ʒatman.* His height gave him a decided advantage in the flight. *ṭuula nṭaa ʔafδ̣aliyya ʒatman bil-εarka.*

decidedly - *ʒatman, ʔakiid.* He is decidedly worried about the examination. *ʒatman huwwa qaliq imnil-imtiʒaan.*

decision - 1. *qaraar pl. -aat.* At last he has come to a decision. *w-ʔaxiiran wuṣal ʔila qaraar.* 2. *ʒukum pl. ʔaʒkaam.* The judge hasn't come to his decision yet. *l-ʒaakim ma-wuṣal ʔila ʒukma baεad.*

deck - 1. *saṭiʒ (pl. suṭuuʒ) baaxira.* Is he in his cabin or on the deck? *huwwa b-maqṣuurta loo εala saṭʒ il-baaxira.* 2. *dasta pl. -aat, šadda pl. -aat.* Let's take a new deck of cards. *xan-naaxuδ dastat waraq jidiida.*

to deck out - *zayyan (i tazyiin) t-, zarwaq (u zarwaqa) t-.* The city was all decked out with lights. *l-madiina čaanat mzayyna bil-ʔaδ̣wiya.*

declaration - 1. *taṣriiʒa pl. -aat.* He presented his customs declaration to the customs inspector. *qaddam taṣriiʒta l-gumrugiyya l-mufattiš il-gumrug.* 2. *ʔiεlaan pl. -aat, ʔišhaar pl. -aat.* He broadcasted the declaration of war over the radio. *δaaε ʔiεlaan il-ʒarub bir-raadyo.*

to **declare** - 1. *ʔaεlan (i ʔiεlaan).* They declared war on us. *ʔaεlinaw εaleena ʒarub.* 2. *qaddam (i taqdiim) taṣriiʒa b-.* Do I have to declare the tobacco at the customs? *laazim aqaddim taṣriiʒa bit-tibig bil-gumrug?*

decline - 1. *tanaaguṣ.* The decline in new cases of cancer continued this month. *t-tanaaguṣ bil-iṣaabaat ij-jidiida biṣ-ṣaraṭaan istamarr haš-šahar.* 2. *tadahwur.* The empire's decline continued for several years. *tadahuur il-imparaaṭooriyya stamarr εiddat isniin.*

to decline - 1. *nʒaṭṭ (a nʒiṭaaṭ).* His health has declined over the past year. *ṣiʒʒta nʒaṭṭat xilaal is-sana il-maaδ̣iya.* 2. *tnaagaṣ (a tanaaguṣ).* Club membership has declined recently. *ʔuδ̣wiyyat in-naadi tnaagṣat muʔaxxaran.* 3. *rifaδ̣ (u rafuδ̣) n-.* They had to decline his invitation. *δ̣ṭarraw yrufδ̣uun daεuuta.*

to **decorate** - 1. *ṣannaε (i taṣniiε) t-.* The baker decorated the cake for our party. *baayiε il-keek ṣannaε il-keeka l-ʒaflatna.* 2. *zayyan (i tazyiin) t-.* They decorated the school for graduation. *zayyinaw il-madrasa l-ʒaflat it-taxarruj.* 3. *zaxraf (u zaxrafa) t-.* The walls of the mosque are decorated. *ʒiiṭaan ij-jaamiε mzaxrafa.*

decoration - 1. *ziina pl. -aat.* The government is putting up decorations in the street for Republic Day. *l-ʒukuuma da-tʒuṭṭ ziina biš-šawaariε il-εiid ij-jamhuuriyya.* 2. *wisaam pl. ʔawsima.* What did they give him the decoration for? *εala weeš inṭoo l-wisaam?*

decrease - *nxifaaδ̣ pl. -aat, nuqṣaan.* Statistics show a decrease in the death rate in the last few years. *l-ʔiʒṣaaʔiyyaat itbayyin inxifaaδ̣ ib-εadad il-wafiyyaat bis-siniin il-ʔaxiira.*

decree - *marsuum pl. maraasiim.* The decree goes into effect tomorrow. *l-marsuum yitnaffaδ min baačir.*

to decree - *ṣaddar (i taṣdiir) marsuum b-.* The government decreed a holiday. *l-ʒukuuma ṣaddirat marsuum ib-ʔiʒdaaθ εuṭla.*

to **deduct** - *xiṣam (u xaṣum), staqṭaε (i stiqṭaaε).* Deduct ten per cent. *ʔixṣum εašra bil-miyya.*

deed - 1. *ʒijja pl. ʒijaj.* The deed to the house is at the lawyer's. *ʒijjat il-beet εind il-muʒaami.* 2. *εamal pl. ʔaεmaal.* There are good deeds and bad deeds. *ʔaku ʔaεmaal il-xeer w-ʔaεmaal iš-šarr.*

to deed - *sajjal (i tasjiil) b-isim, kitab (i kitaaba) b-isim.* My father has deeded the house to me. *ʔabuuya kitab il-beet b-ismi.*

deep - *εamiiq, ġamiij.* This subject is too deep for me. *hal-mawδ̣uuε kulliš εamiiq bin-nisba ʔili.* **The lake is ten feet deep. *l-buʒayra ġumijha εašir ʔaqdaam.*

deeply - *kulliš, hwaaya.* He was deeply affected by their story. *čaan kulliš mitʔaθθir ib-quṣṣathum.*

defeat - *hazima, nkisaar.* The enemy suffered a crushing defeat. *l-εadu qaasaw haziima saaʒiqa.*

to **defeat** - 1. *ġilab (u ġulub) n-.* He defeated three candidates and got a seat in parliament. *ġilab itlaθ muraššaʒiin w-ʒaṣṣal in-niyaaba.* 2. *rifaδ̣ (u rafuδ̣) n-.* The motion was defeated. *l-iqtiraaʒ inrifaδ̣.*

defect - *εeeb pl. εuyuub.* There's a natural defect in this cloth. *ʔaku εeeb ʔaṣli b-hal-iqmaaš.*

defective - *bii εeeb, bii xalal.* The radio is defective; either exchange it or give me my money back. *r-raadyo bii εeeb; ʔamma tbaddla loo tinṭiini fluusi.*

to **defend** - *daafaε (i difaaε) εan.* They decided not to defend the town. *qarriraw ʔan ma-ydaafεuun εan il-madiina.* -- There's no need to defend yourself. *ma-aku ʒaaja tdaafiε εan nafsak* or ***ma-aku majaal tiεtiδir.*

defense - *difaaε.* The defense was weak. *d-difaaε čaan δ̣aεiif.* -- He works for the Ministry of Defense. *yištuġul ib-wizaart id-difaaε.*

to **define** - 1. *ʒaddad (i taʒdiid) t- maεna, εarraf (u taεriif) t- maεna.* Can you define the word "democracy"? *tiġdar itʒaddid maεna kalimat "dimooqraaṭiyya"?* 2. *εayyan (i taεyiin) t-.* The boundaries were defined by the treaty. *l-ʒuduud itεayyinat bil-muεaahada.*

definite - *muʒaddad, muεayyan.* Do you have any definite plan? *εindak ʔay xuṭṭa muεayyna?*

definitely - *bit-taʔkiid, ʔakiid.* I'm definitely coming. *ʔaani jaay bit-taʔkiid.*

to **defy** - *tʒadda (a taʒaddi).* The opposition defied the government to find a solution to the problem. *l-muεaaraδ̣a tʒaddat il-ʒukuuma ʔan yilguun ʒall lil-muškila.*

degree - 1. *daraja pl. -aat.* Last night the temperature dropped ten degrees. *l-baarʒa bil-leel inxufδ̣at darajat il-ʒaraara εašir darajaat.* 2. *šahaada pl. -aat.* I got my degree last year. *ʔaxaδit šahaadti bis-sana l-faatat.*

delay - *taʔxiir.* What's causing the delay? *šinu lli msabbib it-taʔxiir?*

to delay - 1. *ʔaxxar (i taʔxiir) t-, εaṭṭal (i taεṭiil) t-, εawwag (i taεwiig) t-.* I was delayed on the way. *ʔaani tεawwagit biṭ-ṭariiq.* 2. *ʔajjal (i taʔjiil) t-, ʔaxxar (i taʔxiir) t-.* We're going to delay the trip for a week. *raʒ-inʔajjil is-safra l-muddat isbuuε.*

delegate - *manduub pl. -iin.* The delegates will arrive tomorrow. *l-manduubiin raʒ-yooṣluun baačir.*

delegation - *wafid pl. wufuud, baεθa pl. -aat.* The delegation arrived yesterday. *l-wafid wuṣal il-baarʒa.*

deliberate - *mutaεammad, maqṣuud.* That was a deliberate insult. *haay čaanat ʔihaana maqṣuuda.*

deliberately - *εan qaṣid, εan εamid, qaṣṭani*.* I don't think he did it deliberately. *ma-aεtiqid sawwaaha εan qaṣid.*

delicate - 1. *δ̣aεiif, naazik.* Her health is very delicate. *ṣiʒʒatha kulliš δ̣aεiifa.* 2. *muʒrij.* That's a delicate question. *haaδa suʔaal muʒrij.* 3. *daqiiq.* Repairing watches is a delicate job. *taṣliiʒ is-saaεaat šaġla daqiiqa.* 4. *ʒassaas.* That's a delicate instrument. *haay ʔaala ʒassaasa.*

delicious - *laδiiδ.* This is delicious candy. *haaδi ʒalawiyyaat laδiiδa.*

delighted - *masruur, farʒaan, mkayyif.* I was delighted to see him. *činit farʒaan ib-šoofta.*

delightful - *laṭiif, badiiε, raaʔiε.* It was a delight-

ful evening. *čaanat is-sahra laṭiifa.*
to **deliver** - **1.** *sallam (i tasliim) t-, waṣṣal (i tawṣiil) t-.* We'll deliver it to you tomorrow. *raz-insallmak-iyyaaha baačir.* -- Please deliver these packages to my house. *ʔarjuuk waṣṣil har-rizam il-beeti.* **2.** *wazzaɛ (i tawziiɛ) t-.* How often is the mail delivered here? *čam marra yitwazzaɛ il-bariid ihnaa?* **3.** *wallad (i tawliid) t-.* The doctor only charged 5 dinars to deliver the baby. *ṭ-ṭabiib ʔaxað xams idnaaniir bass il-tawliid iṭ-ṭifil.*
delivery - **1.** *tasliim* pl. *-aat.* I'll pay you on delivery. *ʔadfaɛ-lak ɛind it-tasliim.* **2.** *tawziiɛ.* There's no mail delivery today. *ma-aku tawziiɛ bariid il-yoom.*
demand - *ṭalab* pl. *-aat.* There's a big demand for fresh fruit. *ʔaku hwaaya ṭalab ɛala l-fawaakih it-taaza.* -- The library can't supply the demand for books. *l-maktaba ma-tigdar toofi ṭ-ṭalab ɛal-kutub.* -- Their demands never cease. *ṭalabaathum ma-tixlaṣ.*
**This job makes heavy demands on my time. *haay iš-šaġla maaxða waqti kulla.*
in demand - *maṭluub, ɛalee ṭalab.* This model is very much in demand and is sold out. *haaða l-muudeel ɛalee ṭalab ihwaaya w-nifað.*
to demand - *ṭilab (u ṭalub), ṭaalab (u muṭaalaba).* He's demanding more money. *da-yiṭlub ifluus ʔakθar.*
democracy - *dimuuqraaṭiyya.*
democratic - *dimuuqraaṭi*.*
to **demolish** - *haddam (i tahdiim) t-.* The workers demolished the building. *l-ɛummaal haddimaw il-binaaya.*
demon - *jinni* pl. *jinuun* coll. *jinn.*
to **demonstrate** - **1.** *raawa (i truwwi), bayyan (i tabyiin).* Now I'm going to demonstrate to you how the machine works. *hassa raz-araawiikum išloon tištuġul il-makiina.* **2.** *tðaahar (a taðaahur).* There is a group of students demonstrating in front of the embassy. *ʔaku jamaaɛa mniṭ-ṭullaab da-yitðaahruun giddaam is-safaara.*
demonstration - *muðaahara* pl. *-aat.* There was a demonstration in the street yesterday. *čaan aku muðaahara biš-šaariɛ il-baarẓa.*
den - **1.** *maġaara* pl. *-aat.* There's a fox den over there. *ʔaku maġaara maal θaɛlab ihnaak.* **2.** *ɛariin* pl. *ɛurun.* We found a lion's den, but the lion wasn't there. *ligeena ɛariin ʔasad, laakin il-ʔasad ma-čaan ihnaak.*
denial - *ʔinkaar.* Nobody believed his denial of the charge. *mazzad ṣaddag inkaara lit-tuhma.*
dense - **1.** *kaθiif.* We drove through a dense fog. *siqna b-ðabaab kaθiif.* **2.** *baliid* pl. *-iin, buladaaʔ; ġabi* pl. *ʔaġbiyaaʔ.* Most of the time he's very dense. *b-ʔakθar il-zaalaat huwwa hwaaya baliid.*
dent - *ṭaɛja* pl. *-aat, daɛma* pl. *-aat.* There's a new dent in the fender of my car. *ʔaku ṭaɛja jdiida bil-čaamulluġ maal sayyaarti.*
to dent - *ṭiɛaj (a ṭaɛij) n-, diɛam (a daɛim).* The bumper was badly dented. *d-daɛɛaamiyya čaanat maṭɛuuja ṭaɛja qawwiyya.*
dentist - *ṭabiib* (pl. *ʔaṭibbaaʔ*) *ʔasnaan.* Is there a good dentist around here? *ʔaku ṭabiib ʔasnaan zeen ihnaa?*
to **deny** - **1.** *nikar (u ʔinkaar).* He denies having been a member of that party. *yinkur kawna ɛuðu b-hal-zizib.* **2.** *rifað (u rafuð) n-.* I couldn't deny him such a small favor. *ma-gdarit arfuð-la maɛruuf ṣġayyir miθil haaða.*
to **depart from** - **1.** *xiraj (u xuruuj) ɛala.* You're not allowed to depart from standard procedure. *maa masmuuz-lak tuxruj ɛala niðaam il-muttabaɛ.* **2.** *ġaadar (i muġaadara), tirak (u tarik).* The train departed from the station at six o'clock. *l-qiṭaar tirak il-mazaṭṭa s-saaɛa sitta.*
department - **1.** *qisim* pl. *ʔaqsaam.* Which department does he work in. *b-ʔay qisim yištuġuḷ?* **2.** *wizaara* pl. *-aat.* This is a matter for the Department of State. *haay masʔala itxuṣṣ wizaarat il-xaarijiyya.*
departure - *safar.* The departure is scheduled for three o'clock. *s-safar itqarrar is-saaɛa tlaaθa.*
to **depend** - **1.** *ɛtimad (i ɛtimaad).* Can I depend on him? *ʔagdar aɛtimid ɛalee?* **2.** *twaqqaf (a tawaqquf).* That depends on the circumstances. *haaði titwaqqaf ɛað-ðuruuf.*
dependent - *mittikil, miɛtimid.* I'm financially dependent on him. *maaliyyan ʔaani mittikil ɛalee.*
**How many dependents do you have? *čam waazid itɛiil?*
to **deport** - *ʔabɛad (i ʔibɛaad) n-, saffar (i tasfiir).* They deported him. *ʔabɛidoo.*
to **depose** - *xilaɛ (a xaliɛ) n-, ɛizal (i ɛazil) n-ɛan.* They want to depose the king. *yirduun yxilɛuun il-malik.*
deposit - **1.** *taʔmiin* pl. *-aat, ɛarabuun* pl. *-aat.* We'll lay it aside for you, if you leave a deposit. *niẓtufuð-lak biiha ʔiða tẓuṭṭ ɛarabuun.* -- I had to pay five fils deposit for the bottle. *ðṭarreet adfaɛ xams ifluus taʔmiinaat ɛal-buṭil.*
2. *rawaasib.* They've just discovered a rich deposit of iron in the north. *hassa ktišfaw rawaasib ġaniyya maal l-zadiid biš-šimaal.*
to deposit - *waddaɛ (i tawdiiɛ), ʔawdaɛ (i ʔiidaaɛ).* I'm going to deposit some money in the bank. *raz-awaddiɛ išwayya fluus bil-bang.*
to **depress** - *qubað (u qabuð) nafis, zizan (i zuzin).* His letters always depress me. *makaatiiba tuqbuð nafsi daaʔiman.*
depressed - *kaʔiib, zaziin.* He's been very depressed lately. *huwwa kulliš kaʔiib bil-ʔayyaam il-ʔaxiira.*
depressing - *muqbið lin-nafis.*
depression - **1.** *kasaad.* We lost all our money in the depression. *xsarna kull ifluusna bil-kasaad.*
2. *hamm, ġamm, zuzin.* No one can bring him out of his depression. *mazzad yigdar yfarrij ɛan hamma.*
to **deprive** - *zíram (u zirmaan) n-.* I wouldn't want to deprive you of your cigarettes. *ma-ariid azarmak min jigaayrak.* -- They were deprived of all their rights. *nzirmaw min kull zuquuqhum.*
depth - *ɛumuq* pl. *ʔaɛmaaq, ġumij* pl. *ġmuuj.* The depth of the lake has never been measured. *ɛumuq hal-buzayra ʔabadan ma-yinqaas.*
deputy - *naaʔib* pl. *nuwwaab.* He's the deputy from our district. *huwwa n-naaʔib min manṭiqatna.*
chamber of deputies - *majlis* (pl. *majaalis*) *nuwwaab.*
to **derail** - *ʔaxraj (i ʔixraaj) ɛan il-xaṭṭ.* The saboteurs derailed the train. *l-muxarribiin ʔaxrijaw il-qiṭaar ɛan il-xaṭṭ.*
derrick - **1.** *burij* pl. *bruuj, ʔabraaj.* They left the derrick up after they struck oil. *tirkaw il-burij ib-mazalla baɛad-ma xiraj in-nafuṭ.* **2.** *slink* pl. *-aat.* They set up a derrick on the dock to unload boat cargo. *nuṣbaw islink ɛar-raṣiif zatta yfarriġuun zumuulat is-sifiina.*
dervish - *daarwiiš* pl. *daraawiiš.*
to **descend** - **1.** *nizal (i nuzuul), hubaṭ (u hubuuṭ), nzidar (i nzidaar).* I'd never have thought she'd descend so low. *ʔabadan ma-tṣawwaritha tinzil il-hal-mustawa.* -- He's descended from a prominent family. *huwwa minzidir min ɛaaʔila ɛariiqa.*
2. *nizal (i).* His relatives descended on him. *garaayba nizlaw ɛalee.*
descendent - *ðurriyya* pl. *-aat, saliil* pl. *sulaala.* This is a picture of Abu Khalil with all his descendents. *haay ṣuurat ʔabu xaliil wiyya kull ðurriita.*
to **describe** - *wuṣaf (u waṣuf).* He described it accurately. *wṣafha b-ðabuṭ.*
description - *waṣuf* pl. *ʔawṣaaf.* Can you give me a detailed description? *tigdar tinṭiini waṣuf tafṣiili?*
desert - *ṣazraaʔ* pl. *ṣazaari.* They crossed the desert in twenty days. *qiṭɛaw iṣ-ṣazraaʔ ib-ɛisriin yoom.*
to desert - **1.** *tirak (u tarik).* Don't desert me now! *la-titrukni hassa!* **2.** *hijar (u hajir, hijraan), ɛaaf (u ɛoof).* He deserted his wife and children. *hijar zawijta w-ʔawlaada.* **3.** *hirab (u harab, huruub), farr (u farr, firaar).* The soldiers deserted in droves. *j-junuud hirbaw ib-ʔaɛdaad.*
deserted - *mahjuur.* After a long march they came to a deserted village. *baɛad mašya ṭwiila wuṣlaw ʔila qarya mahjuura.*
to **deserve** - *stazaqq (i stizqaaq), staahal (i).* Such a good worker deserves higher pay. *miθla waazid šaaġuul yistaziqq raatib ʔaɛla.*
design - **1.** *taṣmiim* pl. *taṣaamiim, taxṭiiṭ* pl. *-aat.* He is working on the design for a new house. *da-yištuġuḷ ib-taṣmiim beet jidiid.* **2.** *naqiš* pl. *nuquuš, rasim* pl. *rusuum.* The tablecloth has a simple design. *n-naqiš illi ɛala ġaṭa l-meez basiiṭ.*
to design - *ṣammam (i taṣmiim), faṣṣal (i tafṣiil).* She designs her own clothes. *hiyya tṣammim ihduumha b-iideeha.*
desirable - **1.** *marġuub bii.* A change would be very desirable now. *t-taġyiir fadd šii kulliš marġuub bii hassa.* **2.** *marġuub.* This is a very desirable neighborhood for a hotel. *haay manṭiqa marġuuba*

il-binaa? findiq biiha.
desire - *raģba* pl. *-aat.* My desires are easily satisfied. *raģbaati mumkin titzaqqaq ib-suhuula.*
desk - *meez* pl. *-aat, myuuza, minðada* pl. *manaaðid.* This desk is too small for me. *hal-meez kulliš işġayyir Ɛalayya.*
information desk - *maktab* (pl. *makaatib*) *istiƐlaamaat.* Ask at the information desk over there. *?is?al ib-maktab l-istiƐlaamaat.*
desolate - *muuziš.* This must be a desolate place in winter. *haaða laazim ykuun makaan muuziš biš-šita.*
despair - *ya?is, qunuuṭ.* She was about to commit suicide in her despair. *raadat tintizir min ya?isha.*
desperate - *yaa?is, m?ayyis, may?uus min, mistaktil, bila ?amal.* She's in a desperate situation. *zaalatha yaa?sa.* -- The situation's desperate. *l-waðiƐ may?uus minna.*
to **despise** - *ztiqar (i ztiqaar).* I despise that man. *?aani ?aztiqir haaða r-rajjaal.*
dessert - *zalaa, zalawiyyaat.* You forgot to bring the dessert. *niseet itjiib il-zalawiyyaat.*
destination - *zadd.* My destination is Baghdad. *?aani zaddi l-bağdaad.*
destiny - *maşiir* pl. *maşaa?ir.*
to **destroy** - **1.** *tilaf (i talif) n-.* All my papers were destroyed in the fire. *kull ?awraaqi ntilfat bil-zariiq.* **2.** *dammar (u tadmiir) t-, xarrab (u taxriib) t-.* The earthquake destroyed a third of the town. *z-zilzaal dammar θilθ il-madiina.*
destroyer - *mudammira* pl. *-aat.*
destruction - *taxriib, damaar.* The fire caused a lot of destruction. *n-naar sabbibat ihwaaya damaar.*
detail - *tafşiil* pl. *-aat, tafaaşiil.* Today's paper gives more details. *jariidat il-yoom biiha tafaaşiil ?akθar.*
in detail - *bit-tafşiil.* He described the incident in detail. *wuşaf il-zaadiθ bit-tafşiil.*
detailed - *mfaşşal.* He gave me a detailed report. *qaddam-li taqriir imfaşşal.*
to **detain** - *zijaz (i zajiz) n-.* The police detained him for questioning. *š-šurṭa zijzata lit-tazqiiq.* **2.** *?axxar (i ta?xiir) t-.* Authorities detained the plane a half hour to look for a bomb. *ş-şulṭaat ?axxirat iṭ-ṭiyyaara nuşş saaƐa lil-baziθ Ɛan il-qumbula.*
determination - *taşmiim, Ɛazim.* He showed definite determination. *huwwa bayyan Ɛazim ?akiid.*
determined - *muşammim, muşirr.* She's determined to have her way. *hiyya mşammima Ɛala ?an itsawwi lli triida* or *hiyya muşirra Ɛala ra?iiha.*
to **detour** - *laaf (u loof), ltaaf (a ltifaaf), ltaff (a ltifaaf).* Rashid St. is closed at the Defence building and we had to detour by way of Waziria St. *šaariƐ ir-rašiid masduud yamm id-difaaƐ w-iðṭarreena nluuf Ɛala šaariƐ il-waziiriyya.*
deuce - *θneen, ?abu-θneen.* He held three deuces and two kings. *čaan Ɛinda tlaθ iθneenaat w-šaaybeen.*
to **develop** - **1.** *ġisal (i ġasil) n-.* Could you develop this film for me? *mumkin tiġsil-li hal-filim?* **2.** *ṭṭawwar (a taṭawwur).* The situation's developed a lot in the last week. *l-mawgif ihwaaya ṭṭawwar bil-isbuuƐ il-?axiir.* **3.** *Ɛammar (i taƐmiir) t-, zassan (i tazsiin) t-.* The government is developing this area. *l-zukuuma da-tƐammir hal-manṭiqa.*
development - **1.** *taṭawwur* pl. *-aat.* Do you know anything about the latest developments? *tuƐruf ?ay šii Ɛan ?aaxir it-taṭawwuraat?* **2.** *?iƐmaar.* The development plan requires more money. *xiṭṭat il-?iƐmaar tiztaaj ?ila fluus ?akθar.*
device - **1.** *tadbiir* pl. *tadaabiir, xiṭṭa* pl. *xiṭaṭ.* That's an ingenious device for getting his approval. *haaði fadd tadbiir baariƐ l-istizşaal muwaafaqta.* **2.** *jihaaz* pl. *?ajhiza.* He invented a device to peel potatoes. *xtiraƐ jihaaz il-tagšiir il-puteeta.*
devil - *šeeṭaan* pl. *šayaaṭiin, ?ibliis* pl. *?abaaliis, ?abaalisa.*
to **devote** - **1.** *karras (i tkirris, takriis), xaşşaş (i txişşiş, taxşiiş).* He devoted all his spare time to study. *karras kull wakit faraaġa lid-diraasa.* **2.** *wihab (i wahib) n-.* He devoted his life to science. *wihab zayaata lil-Ɛilim.*
to be devoted - *barr (u birr).* He's very devoted to his mother. *huwwa kulliš baarr ib-?umma.*
dew - *nida.*
diabetes - *marað is-sukkar.*
diagonal - *munzarif, qiraaj.* Now draw a diagonal line. *hassa ?irsim xaṭṭ munzarif.*
diagonally - *qiraaj.* You have to park diagonally here. *laazim itşuff is-sayyaara qiraaj ihnaa.*
dial - *quruş* pl. *?aqraaş.* The dial on the telephone is broken. *qurş it-talifoon maksuur.* -- The dial on my watch is dirty. *qurş saaƐti waşix.*
to dial - *farr (u farr) n- numra, daar (u deer) n- numra.* She dialed the wrong number. *farrat in-nimra l-ġalaṭ.*
dialect - *lahja* pl. *-aat.* Many dialects are spoken here. *hwaaya lahjaat tinziči hnaa.*
diameter - *quṭur daa?ira* pl. *?aqṭaar dawaa?ir.*
diamond - **1.** *?almaasa* pl. *-aat* coll. *?almaas.* This ring has four diamonds. *hal-mihbas bii ?arbaƐ ?almaasaat.* **2.** *maƐiin* pl. *-aat.* The new traffic signs are diamond-shaped. *?išaaraat il-muruur ij-jidiida Ɛala šikil il-maƐiin.* **3.** *dinaari*.* I've got a diamond flush. *Ɛindi flooš dinaari* or *Ɛindi flooš baqlaawa.*
diarrhea - *?ishaal.*
dice - see under **die**.
to **dictate** - **1.** *?amla (i ?imlaa?), malla (i ?imlaa?).* He's dictating a letter. *huwwa da-yimli maktuub.* -- He's dictating a letter to his secretary. *da-ymalli kitaab Ɛas-sikirtaara maalta.* **2.** *t?ammar (a ta?ammur).* I can't stand anyone dictating to me! *?aani ma-aqbal waazid yit?ammar Ɛalayya.*
dictation - *?imlaa?.* I gave my class a dictation today. *nṭeet şaffi ?imlaa? il-yoom.*
dictator - *diktaatoor* pl. *-iyyiin.*
dictatorial - *diktaatoori*.*
dictatorship - *diktaatooriyya.*
die - **1.** *qaalab* pl. *qawaalib.* The die for that part is broken. *qaalab hal-?aala maksuur.* **2.** *zaar* pl. *-aat.* They play chuck-a-luck with three dice. *yilƐabuun lagaw b-iθlaθ zaaraat.*
**The die is cast. *quðiya l-?amr.*
to die - **1.** *maat (u moot), twaffa (a tawiffi, wafaat).* He died today at two o'clock. *twaffa l-yoom saaƐa θinteen.* **2.** *ðibal (a ðabil).* The tree is dying. *š-šajara da-tiðbal.* **3.** *nṭufa (i nṭufaa?), ṭaffa (i ṭṭiffi) t-.* The motor died. *l-makiina nṭufat.*
**I'm dying to find out what he said. *mazruug bass ?ariid aƐruf huwwa š-gaal.*
to die away - *tlaaša (a talaaši).* The noise of the train died away in the distance. *tlaaša şoot il-qiṭaar lamman ibtiƐad.*
to die down - *xumad (i xamud), nṭufa (i).* We let the fire die down. *trakna n-naar tixmid* or *trakna n-naar tinṭufi wazidha.* -- The excitement will die down in a few days. *hal-hiyaaj raz-yixmid ib-kam yoom.*
to die laughing - *ṭagg (u ṭagg) imnið-ðizik, maat (u moot) imnið-ðizik.* I just about died laughing when I heard that. *ṭaggeet imnið-ðizik min ismaƐitha.*
to die off - *ðmazall (i ðmizlaal).* The older generation is dying off. *j-jiil il-qadiim gaƐad yiðmazill.*
diet - **1.** *rajiim.* I have to go on a diet. *laazim asawwi rajiim.* **2.** *?akil.* For weeks our diet consisted of nothing but fish. *xilaal Ɛiddat asaabiiƐ ?akilna ma-čaan ġeer simač.*
to diet - *sawwa (i taswiya) rajiim.* I've been dieting for a month, but I still haven't lost any weight. *?aani msawwi rajiim şaar-li šahar w-ma-fqadit šii min wazni.*
to **differ** - **1.** *xtilaf (i xtilaaf).* They differ in every respect. *yixtalfuun ib-kullši.* -- I beg to differ with you. *?aani ?axtilif wiyyaak* or *?aani ma-awaafqak.* **2.** *tðaarab (a taðaarub).* Opinions differ on this topic. *l-?aaraa? mitðaarba b-hal-mawðuuƐ.*
difference - **1.** *xtilaaf* pl. *-aat, fariq* pl. *furuuq.* Can you show me the difference? *tigdar itbayyin-li l-fariq?* — It makes no difference when you come. *ma-aku fariq išwakit-ma tiji.* **2.** *xilaaf* pl. *-aat.* They ironed out their differences. *şaffaw xilaafaathum.*
to make a difference - *firaq (u fariq).* Does it make any difference to you if I write in pencil? *tifruq-lak ?iða ?aktib ib-qalam rişaaş?*
different - **1.** *muxtalif.* The brothers are very different. *l-?uxwa kulliš mixtalfiin.* **2.** *mitðaarub, mitbaayin.* The two ideas are different. *l-fikirteen mitbaayna.* **3.** *ġeer, ?aaxar.* That's a different matter. *haaða ġeer mawðuuƐ* or *haay mas?ala tixtilif.*
differently - *ġeer šikil, b-šikil ?aaxar, b-šikil muxtalif.* I think differently about it. *?aani ?anður-ilha ġeer šikil.*

difficult - **1.** *ṣaεub.* It's difficult to understand what he means. *ṣaεub tifham iš-yaεni.* -- That's a difficult assignment. *haaδi muhimma ṣaεba.* **2.** *mitṣaεεub.* He's difficult (to deal with). *huwwa mitṣaεεub.*

difficulty - *ṣuεuub* pl. *-aat, ṣiεaab.* He overcame the difficulties. *tġallab εala ṣ-ṣuεuubaat.*

to **dig** - *ḥufar (u ḥafur) n-.* Dig the hole a little deeper. *ʔiḥfur il-ḥufra šwayya ʔaġmaj.*

to dig up - *nibaš (i nabiš) n-.* The dog dug up a bone he had buried in the ground. *č-čalib nibaš εaδum čaan daafna bil-gaaε.*

**Dig up the rose bush. *ʔiḥfur daayir εirg il-warid w-ṭallεa.*

to **digest** - *hiḍam (u haḍum) n-.* Nuts are hard for us to digest. *č-čarazaat ṣaεub εaleena nihḍumha.*

digestion - *haḍum.*

dignified - *waquur.* His father was a dignified old gentlemen. *ʔabuu čaan fadd šeex waquur.*

dim - *miεtim, xaafit, ḍaεiif.* I couldn't see anything in the dim light. *ma-gdarit ašuuf šii biḍ-ḍuwa l-miεtim.*

to dim - *xaffaḍ (i taxfiiḍ) t-.* Dim your lights! *xaffiḍ ḍawaak!*

dimple - *raṣεa* pl. *-aat.* She has a nice dimple. *εidha raṣεa ḥilwa.*

dinar - *diinaar* pl. *danaaniir.*

to **dine** - *tεašša (a taεašši).* They're dining with us tonight. *da-yitεaššuun wyaana hal-leela.* -- We dine out occasionally. *ʔiḥna ʔaḥyaanan nitεašša barra.*

dining room - *ġurfat* (pl. *ġuraf*) *ʔakil, ġurfat* (pl. *ġuraf*) *ṭaεaam.* Bring another chair into the dining room. *jiib kursi laax il-ġurfat il-ʔakil.*

dinner - **1.** *εaša* pl. *-aayaat.* Dinner is ready. *l-εaša jaahiz.* **2.** *εaziima* pl. *εazaayim.* We're giving a dinner in his honor. *raḥ-insawwi εaziima εala šarafa.*

to have dinner - *tεašša (a taεašši).* We have dinner at six o'clock every day. *nitεašša s-saaεa sitta yoomiyya.*

dip - **1.** *ḥadra* pl. *-aat, nazla* pl. *-aat.* There's a dip in the road ahead of us. *ʔaku ḥadra biṭ-ṭariiq giddaamna.* **2.** *ġaṭṭa* pl. *-aat, ṭamsa* pl. *-aat.* There's nothing like a dip in the river to refresh you on a hot day. *ma-aku miθil il-ġaṭṭa biš-šaṭṭ tiniεšak ib-yoom ḥaarr.*

to dip - *ṭammas (u ṭṭummus, taṭmiis).* I dipped my finger into the water. *ṭammasit ʔiṣbaεi bil-maay.*

direct - **1.** *mubaašir.* There is no direct route. *ma-aku ṭariiq mubaašir* or ***ma-aku ṭariiq yiṭlaε raʔsan.* **2.** *tamaaman.* It's the direct opposite of what we expected. *hiyya εakis-ma twaqqaεna tamaaman.*

to direct - **1.** *ʔumar (u ʔamur).* He directed us to follow the old regulations. *ʔumarna ʔan nitbaε it-taεliimaat il-qadiima.* **2.** *wajjah (i tawjiih).* A policeman is directing the traffic. *šurṭi da-ywajjih il-muruur.* **3.** *dalla (i tdilli).* Can you direct me to the post office? *tigdar itdalliini εala markaz il-bariid.* **4.** *xarraj (i taxriij), ʔaxraj (i ʔixraaj).* Who is directing the play? *minu da-yxarrij it-tamθiiliyya?*

direct current - *tayyaar mubaašir, diisi.*

direction - **1.** *jiha* pl. *-aat, ttijaah* pl. *-aat.* Which direction did he go? *l-ʔay jiha raaḥ?* **2.** *ʔiršaad* pl. *-aat.* His directions are clear. *ʔiršaadaata waaḍḥa.* **3.** *ʔidaara, ʔišraaf.* They have made great progress under his direction. *xiṭaw xaṭwaat waasεa taḥat ʔišraafa* or *ḥaqqiqaw taqaddum kabiir taḥat ʔidaarta.* **4.** *taεliim* pl. *-aat.* The government issued directions concerning the election. *l-ḥukuuma ʔaṣdirat taεliimaat titεallaq bil-intixaabaat.*

directly - *mubaašaratan, raʔsan.* Let's go directly to the hotel. *xalli nruuḥ lil-ʔuteel raʔsan.* -- Our house is directly opposite the store. *beetna muqaabil il-maxzan mubaašaratan.*

dirham - *dirhim* pl. *daraahim.*

dirt - **1.** *traab* pl. *ʔatriba.* How many trucks of dirt do we need to fill this in? *čam loori traab niḥtaaj il-dafin haay?* **2.** *zimiij.* The dirt in the flower pots should be replaced this year. *z-zimiij b-isnaadiin il-warid laazim yitbaddal has-sana.* **3.** *wuṣax.* There is some dirt on your shirt. *ʔaku šwayya wuṣax ib-θoobak.*

dirt-cheap - *ʔaxu l-balaaš, ʔuxt il-balaaš.* I bought the car dirt-cheap. *štireet is-sayyaara ʔuxt il-balaaš.*

dirty - **1.** *waṣix.* The floor is dirty. *l-gaaε waṣxa.* **2.** *baδiiʔ.* Most of his stories are pretty dirty. *muεḍam quṣaṣa baδiiʔa.* **3.** *daniiʔ, ḥaqiir.* He played a dirty trick on us. *sawwa biina nukta daniiʔa.*

**He gave us a dirty look. *niḍarna b-izdiraaʔ* or *baawaεna b-iḥtiqaar.*

**That is a dirty lie. *haay čiδba qadra.*

to dirty - *waṣṣax (i tawṣiix, twiṣṣix).* Don't dirty the carpet with your muddy shoes. *la-twaṣṣix iz-zuuliyya b-qundartak l-imṭayyna.*

disability - *εajiz.* He can't play soccer because of a disability. *ma-yigdar yilεab kurat il-qadam ib-sabab il-εajiz.*

to **disable** - *sawwa (i) εajiz.* The auto accident disabled him. *ḥaadiθ is-sayyaara sawwaa εajiz.*

to be disabled - *nṣaab (a) ib-εajiz.* The soldier was permanently disabled. *j-jundi nṣaab ib-εajiz daaʔim.*

disadvantage - *maḍaar.* You'll have to weigh the advantages and disadvantages before you decide. *laazim itwaazin been il-maḍaar wil-manaafiε gabuḷ-ma tqarrir.*

to **disagree** - **1.** *xtilaf (i xtilaaf).* I disagree with you. *ʔaani ʔaxtilif wiyyaak.* **2.** *xaalaf (i muxaalafa).* I disagree with the method. *ʔaani ʔaxaalif iṭ-ṭariiqa* or *ʔaani ma-aʔayyid haṭ-ṭariiqa.* **3.** *ma-waalam (i muwaalama).* Melons disagree with me. *l-baṭṭiix ma-ywaalimni* or ***ʔaani muu ṣuḥba wiyya l-baṭṭiix.*

to **disappear** - *xtifa (i xtifaaʔ).* He disappeared in the crowd. *xtifa bil-xabṣa.* **2.** *tlaaša (a talaaši).* The river disappears in the desert. *n-nahar yitlaaša biṣ-ṣaḥraaʔ.*

to **disappoint** - *xaab (i xayabaan) ʔamal.* I was very much disappointed. *xaab ʔamali hwaaya.*

disappointment - *xeebat* (pl. *-aat*) *ʔamal.* It was a great disappointment. *čaanat xeebat ʔamal čibiira.*

to **disapprove** - *stankar (i stinkaar).* He disapproves of our plans. *yistankir xuṭaṭna.*

to **disarm** - *jarrad (i tajriid) t- mnis-silaaḥ.* They disarmed the prisoners immediately. *jarridaw il-ʔasra mnis-silaaḥ bil-ḥaal.*

disarmament - *nazε is-silaaḥ.*

disaster - *nakba* pl. *-aat, kaariθa* pl. *kawaariθ, muṣiiba* pl. *maṣaayib.* The airplane crash was a great disaster. *suquuṭ iṭ-ṭiyyaara čaan kaariθa čibiira.*

disastrous - *murwiε, muriiε.* The collision was disastrous. *t-taṣaadum čaan kulliš murwiε.*

discharge - *tasriiḥ* pl. *-aat.* Your discharge is in November. *tasriiḥak ib-tišriin iθ-θaani.*

to discharge - **1.** *fuṣal (u faṣul) n-, ṭirad (u ṭarid) n-.* The company discharged him for his carelessness. *š-šarika fuṣlata il-ʔihmaala.* **2.** *sarraḥ (i tasriiḥ) t-.* You're going to be discharged when the war ends. *raḥ-titsarraḥuun lamma tintihi l-ḥarub.* **3.** *xallaṣ (i taxliiṣ), ʔanha (i ʔinhaaʔ), ʔadda (i tʔiddi).* He discharges his responsibilities promptly. *yxalliṣ waajibaata b-surεa.* **4.** *farraġ (i tafriiġ) t-, nazzal (i tanziil) t-.* The ship discharged its cargo on the dock. *s-safiina farrġat šuḥnatha εar-raṣiif.* **5.** *ḍiεaf (a ḍuεuf).* Turn off the lights, don't discharge the battery. *ṭuffi l-uḍwiya, la-tiḍεif il-baatri.* **6.** *ṭilaε (a ṭuluuε).* The hospital discharged him after 10 days. *l-mustašfa ṭilεata baεad εaširt iyyaam.*

discipline - *ḍabuṭ, ṭaaεa, niḍaam.* The teacher can't maintain discipline in class. *l-ʔustaaδ ma-yigdar yḥaafuḍ εaḍ-ḍabuṭ ib-ṣaffa.*

to discipline - *jaaza (i mujaazaa).* The lieutenant disciplined his troops for disobediance. *l-mulaazim jaaza j-jinuud il-εadam ṭaaεathum.*

to **disclose** - *kišaf (i kašif) εan, ʔaḍhar (i ʔiḍhaar).* The investigation disclosed new facts. *t-taḥqiiq kišaf εan ḥaqaayiq jidiida.*

to **disconnect** - *fiṣal (i faṣil) n-.* If we disconnect these two wires the lights will go out. *ʔiδa fiṣalna hal-waayreen tinṭufi l-ʔuḍwiya.*

discontented - *ma-raaḍi.* He's discontented in his present job. *huwwa ma-raaḍi b-šuġla l-ḥaaliyya.*

to **discontinue** - *baṭṭal (i), waggaf (i), qiṭaε (a qaṭiε) n-.* We're going to discontinue mail service in this area. *raḥ-inbaṭṭil xidmat il-bariid ib-hal-manṭiqa.*

discount - *xaṣum.* Can you get a discount on these books? *tigdar itḥaṣṣil xaṣum εala hal-kutub?*

to **discourage** - *θabbaṭ (i taθbiiṭ) t- εaziima.* He did his best to discourage me from going. *ḥaawal kullši ḥatta yθabbuṭ εaziimti w-ma-aruuḥ.* -- He gets discouraged easily. *yitθabbaṭ εaziimta b-suhuula.*

discouraging - *muθabbiṭ lil-ɛazim, ġeer mušajjiɛ.* The results are discouraging. *n-nataa?ij muθabbiṭa lil-ɛazim.*
to **discover** - *ktišaf (i ktišaaf).* Columbus discovered America. *kaloombis iktišaf ?amriika.*
discovery - *ktišaaf* pl. *-aat.* He made an important discovery in science. *zaqqaq iktišaaf muhimm bil-ɛilim.*
to **discuss** - *naaqaš (i munaaqaša), bizaθ (a baziθ).* They discussed the subject from all sides. *naaqišaw il-mawḍuuɛ min kull in-nawaazi.* -- Discuss the matter with him. *?ibzaθ il-mawḍuuɛ wiyyaa.*
discussion - *munaaqaša* pl. *-aat, baziθ.*
disease - *maraḍ* pl. *?amraaḍ.* This disease is contagious. *haaḍa l-maraḍ muɛdi.*
to **disfigure** - *šawwah (i tašwiih) t-.* The injury disfigured his face. *j-jariz šawwah wujja.*
disgrace - *ɛaar, xizi, faḍiiza* pl. *faḍaayiz.* He brought disgrace on his family. *jaab il-xizi l-ɛaa?ilta.*
to disgrace - *fuḍaz (a faḍiiza) n-.* She disgraced her family. *fuḍzat ɛaa?ilatha.*
to **disguise** - *nakkar (i tankiir, tnikkir) t-.* He disguised himself to avoid capture. *tnakkar zatta yitjannab il-qabuḍ ɛalee.*
disguised - *mitnakkir.* Haroun al-Rashid had the habit of walking in the streets of Baghdad disguised as a merchant. *haaruun ir-rašiid čaanat ɛaadta yimši b-šawaariɛ baġdaad mitnakkir ka-taajir.*
disgust - *šmi?zaaz, taqazzuz.* He turned away in disgust. *daar wujja b-išmi?zaaz.*
to disgust - *qazzaz (i taqziiz) t- nafis.* His conduct disgusts me. *taṣarrufaata tqazziz nafsi.*
to be disgusted - *šmi?azz (i šmi?zaaz), tqazzaz (a taqazzuz).* I was disgusted by his conduct. *šmi?azzeet min taṣarrufaata.*
**I'm disgusted with everything. *?aani baz?aan min kullši* or *ṭaafra ruuzi min kullši.*
dish - 1. *maaɛuun* pl. *mwaaɛiin, ṣazan* pl. *ṣzuun.* He dropped the dish. *waggaɛ il-maaɛuun.* -- I'd like a dish of ice cream. *?ariid maaɛuun doondirma.* 2. *loon* (pl. *?alwaan) ?akil.* I have a recipe for a new dish. *ɛindi waṣfa l-loon jidiid imnil-?akil.*
dishonest - *ġeer šariif, ġaššaaš, muu šariif.*
to **disinfect** - *ɛaqqam (i taɛqiim) t-, ṭahhar (i taṭhiir) t-.* Did you disinfect the wound? *ɛaqqamta lij-jariz?*
disinfectant - *muṭahhir, muɛaqqim.* I need a disinfectant. *?aztaaj muṭahhir.*
to **disinherit** - *ziram (a zirmaan) imnil-?iriθ.* His father threatened to disinherit him. *?abuu haddada b-zirmaana mnil-?iriθ.*
to **disintegrate** - *tzallal (a tazallul).* The empire disintegrated. *l-imbiraaṭooriyya tzallilat.*
dislike - *nufuur, karaaha, ɛadam mazabba.* I couldn't conceal my dislike for him. *ma-gdarit aktim nufuuri minna.*
to dislike - *ma-zabb (i zabb), nufar (u nafur) min.* I dislike that fellow. *ma-azibb haaḍa r-rajjaal.*
to **dislocate** - *xilaɛ (a xaliɛ) n-.* He dislocated his shoulder. *xilaɛ čitfa.*
disloyal - *ġeer muxliṣ, xaayin.*
dismal - *ka?iib.* It's a dismal day today. *hal-yoom ka?iib* or **hal-yoom yuqbuḍ iṣ-ṣadir.*
to **dismiss** - 1. *ṭirad (i ṭarid).* She was dismissed after two weeks. *nṭiradat wara sbuuɛeen.* 2. *rufaḍ (u rafuḍ) n-.* The court dismissed the complaint. *l-mazkama rufḍat iš-šakwa.* 3. *ṣiraf (u ṣaruf) n-.* He dismissed the soldiers after an hour's drill. *ṣiraf ij-jinuud baɛad tadriib saaɛa.*
dispensary - *mustawṣif* pl. *-aat.*
display - *waajiha* pl. *-aat.* Have you seen the beautiful displays in the shops on Rashid St.? *šifit waajihaat il-maxaazin il-zilwa b-šaariɛ ir-rašiid?*
on display - *maɛruuḍ.* The statute is on display at the museum. *t-timθaal maɛruuḍ bil-matzaf.*
to display - 1. *raawa (i muraawaat), bayyan (i tabyiin), ?aḍhar (i ?iḍhaar).* He displayed great courage. *bayyan šajaaɛa faa?iqa.* -- There's no need to display your ignorance. *ma-aku zaaja tiḍhir jahlak.* 2. *ɛiraḍ (u ɛariḍ) n-.* You can't display your fruit on the side walks of a main street. *ma-tigdar tuɛruḍ fawaakhak ɛar-raṣiif ib-šaariɛ ɛaamm.* 3. *xalla (i txilli, taxliya), rifaɛ (a rafiɛ).* All the houses displayed flags. *kull il-ibyuut xallat iɛlaam.*
disposal - *?amur.* I'm at your disposal. *?aani tazat ?amrak.* 2. *taṣriif.* There's no garbage disposal plant in this village. *ma-aku mazall taṣriif il-miyaah il-qaḍra b-hal-qarya.*
**They agreed to put a car at my disposal. *waafqaw yxalluun sayyaara jawwa ?iidi.*
to **dispose** - *txallaṣ (a taxalluṣ).* They will leave as soon as they dispose of their furniture. *raz-yturkuun ?awwal-ma yitxallṣuun min ?aθaaθhum.*
disposition - *ṭabuɛ.* He has a poor disposition. *ṭabɛa muu zeen.*
to **disregard** - 1. *himal (i ?ihmaal) n-.* If I were in your place, I'd disregard the letter. *loo b-makaanak, ahimla lil-maktuub.* 2. *tġaaḍa (a tġaaḍi) ɛan.* We can't disregard his objections. *ma-nigdar nitġaaḍa ɛan iɛtiraaḍaata.*
to **disrupt** - *giṭaɛ (a gaṭiɛ) n-.* Communications were disrupted by the storm. *l-muwaaṣilaat ingiṭɛat imnil-ɛaaṣifa.*
dissatisfied - *muu raaḍi.* You look dissatisfied. *ybayyin ɛaleek muu raaḍi.*
to **dissipate** - 1. *baddad (i tabdiid) t-.* He dissipated his entire fortune. *baddad kull θaruuta.* 2. *nqišaɛ (i nqišaaɛ).* We'd better wait until the fog dissipates a bit. *?azsan nintiḍir ?ila ?an yinqišiɛ iḍ-ḍabaab išwayya.*
**He leads a dissipated life. *huwwa mušrif bil-malaḍḍaat.*
to **dissolve** - 1. *ḍaab (u ḍawabaan), tzallal (a tazallul).* Salt dissolves in water. *l-miliz yḍuub bil-ṃaay.* 2. *ḍawwab (i taḍwiib).* Dissolve the tablet in a glass of water. *ḍawwib il-quruṣ b-iglaaṣ ṃaay.*
distance - 1. *masaafa* pl. *-aat, buɛad* pl. *?abɛaad.* The distance between Baghdad and Najaf is about 180 kilometers. *l-masaafa been baġdaad win-najaf zawaali miyya w-θmaaniin kiiloomatir.* 2. *masaafa, biɛiid.* You can see the tower from a distance. *tigdar itšuuf il-burij min biɛiid.*
to keep one's distance - *lizam (a lazim) zadd~, ḍibat (u ḍabut) zadd~.* He knows how to keep his distance. *yuɛruf ween yilzam zadda.*
distant - *min biɛiid.* She's a distant relative of mine. *hiyya garaaybi min ibɛiid.*
distinct - *waaḍiz, mbayyin, ḍaahir.* There's a distinct difference between the two. *?aku xtilaaf waaḍiz been il-?iθneen.*
distinctly - *b-wuḍuuz.* I told him distinctly not to come. *?aani fahhamta b-kull wuḍuuz ?an ma-yiji.*
to **distinguish** - 1. *farzan (i tfirzin), mayyaz (i tamyiiz) t-.* I couldn't distinguish the features of his face in the dark. *ma-gdarit afarzin malaamiz wujja biḍ-ḍalma.* -- I could hardly distinguish one from the other. *b-ṣuɛuuba gdarit amayyiz ɛan baɛaḍhum.* 2. *mayyaz (i tamyiiz), farraq (i tafriiq).* Can you distinguish between the two? *tigdar itfarriq been il-iθneen?* 3. *?abraz (i ?ibraaz).* He distinguished himself by his courage. *?abraz nafsa b-šajaaɛta.* -- He's a distinguished soldier and statesman. *huwwa jundi w-rajul dawla baariz.*
distress - 1. *šidda, ḍiiq.* The Red Crescent did everything possible to relieve the distress. *jamɛiyyat il-hilaal il-?azmar sawwat kull-ma mumkin lit-taxfiif imniš-šidda.* — The ship was in distress. *l-baaxira čaanat ib-ḍiiq.* 2. *ġamm.* He caused his mother much distress. *sabbab il-?umma hwaaya ġamm.*
to **distribute** - *wazzaɛ (i tawziiɛ) t-, qassam (i taqsiim) t-.* The profits were evenly distributed. *l-?arbaaz itqassimat bit-tasaawi.*
district - 1. *manṭiqa* pl. *manaaṭiq, naaziya* pl. *nawaazi.* This is a very poor district. *haaḍi manṭiqa kulliš faqiira.* 2. *qisim* pl. *?aqsaam, manṭiqa* pl. *manaaṭiq.* The city is divided into ten districts. *l-madiina mqassma ?ila ɛašir ?aqsaam.*
to **distrust** - *ma-wiθaq (i) b-.* I distrust him. *?aani ma-aθiq bii.*
to **disturb** - 1. *?azɛaj (i ?izɛaaj), šawwaš (i tašwiiš).* Don't disturb the others! *la-tizɛij il-?aaxariin.* 2. *qilaq (i qaliq).* The news disturbed me. *l-?axbaar qilqatni.* 3. *xarbaṭ (u txurbuṭ).* Someone has disturbed my papers. *waazid xarbaṭ ?awraaqi.*
ditch - *saaqya* pl. *swaaqi.* The car got stuck in the ditch. *s-sayyaara ṭumsat bis-saaqya.*
to **dive** - 1. *ḍabb (i ḍabb) zarig.* Do you know how to dive? *tuɛruf išloon itḍibb zarig?* 2. *ġaaṣ (u ġooṣ).* They dive for pearls in Kuwait. *yġuuṣuun min ?ajil il-lu?lu? bil-kuweet.*
diver - *ġawwaaṣ* pl. *-iin.* They hired a diver to inspect the wreck of the ship. *sta?jiraw ġawwaaṣ*

il-faζiṣ ζiṭaam is-safiina.
**He's a good diver. *huwwa yδibb zarig zeen.*

to **divide** – **1.** *qisam (i qasim) n–, qassam (i taqsiim) t–.* Divide the total by four. *ʔiqsim il-majmuuε εala ʔarbaεa.* -- The book is divided into two parts. *l-iktaab minqisim ʔila qismeen.* -- Divide the group into two teams. *qassim ij-jamaaεa ʔila fariiqeen.* **2.** *tfarraε (a tafarruε), tfarraq (a tafarruq).* The road divides at the end of the village. *ṭ-ṭariiq yitfarraε ib-ṭaraf il-qarya.* **3.** *qaasam (i muqaasama).* I divide the profits between me and my partner. *ʔaani ʔaqaasim il-ʔarbaaζ beeni w-been šariiki.*

division – **1.** *qisim* pl. *ʔaqsaam.* He works in another division. *yištuġuḷ ib-qisim laax.* **2.** *firqa* pl. *firaq.* Ten divisions were destroyed. *εašir firaq itdammrat.* **3.** *qisma, taqsiim.* When are you going to learn division? *šwakit raζ-titεallam l-qisma?*

divorce – *ṭalaag.* She's suing for divorce. *gaayma b-daεwat ṭalaag.*
to divorce – *ṭallag (i taṭliig, ṭṭillig) t–.* It's been several years since he divorced his wife. *ṣaar-la εiddat sanawaat min ṭallag marta.*

divorced – *mṭallag.* She's divorced. *hiyya mṭallga.*
**He's divorced. *huwwa čaan mitzawwaj w-ṭallag.*

dizzy – *daayix.* I feel dizzy. *ʔaani daayix* or ***ʔašεur ib-dooxa.*

to **do** – **1.** *sawwa (i taswiya), εamal (i εamal).* Let him do it by himself. *xalli ysawwiiha b-nafsa.* -- What are we going to do now? *š-raζ-insawwi hassa?* -- Do it the way I do. *sawwiiha biṭ-ṭariiqa lli ʔasawwii.* -- I don't do things like that. *ʔaani ma-asawwi hiiči ʔašyaaʔ.* **2.** *qaam (u qiyaam) b–, sawwa (i).* He can't do this work because he has a hernia. *ma-yigdar yquum ib-haš-šuġul li-ʔan εinda fatiq.* -- Can I do anything for you? *ʔagdar aquum-lak ib-ʔay xidma?* **3.** *kaffa (i kifaaya).* This meat will have to do for four people. *hal-laζam laazim ykaffi l-ʔarbaε ʔašxaaṣ.* -- That will do for now. *haaδa ykaffi hassa.* **4.** *ṣilaζ (a ṣalaaζ), nifaε (a nafiε), faad (i faaʔida).* This screwdriver won't do. *had-darnafiis ma-yiṣlaζ.* **5.** *giðạ (i gaðị).* He did five years in jail. *giðạ xams isniin bis-sijin.* **6.** *xaṣṣ (u).* That has nothing to do with the matter. *haaδa ma-yxuṣṣ il-mawðụuε* or ***haaδa maa ʔila εalaaqa bil-mawðụuε.* **7.** *ṭallaε (i taṭliiε).* This car won't do more than forty miles per hour. *has-sayyaara ma-ṭṭaliiε ġeer ʔarbaεiin miil bis-saaεa.* **8.** *rattab (i tartiib).* It takes her an hour to do her hair. *yinraad-ilha saaεa ζatta trattib šaεarha.* **9.** *miša (i maši).* Your son is doing well in school this year. *ʔibnak maaši zeen bil-madrasa has-sana.* -- My tomato plants are doing well. *ṭ-ṭamaaṭa maalti maašya zeen.*
**He wears his hat just the way I do. *yilbas šafuqta tamaaman biš-šikil miθil-ma ʔalbasha ʔaani.*
to do away with – *txallaṣ (a taxalluṣ) min.* They want to do away with most of the redtape. *da-yriiduun yitxallṣuun min ʔakθar il-ruutiiniyyaat.*
to do good – **1.** *ʔaζsan (i ʔiζsaan), εamal (i εamal) xeer.* Our neighbor was well-known for his piety and doing good. *jaarna čaan mašhuur bit-taqwa wil-ʔiζsaan.* **2.** *faad (i faaʔida).* Complaining won't do you much good. *š-šakwa ma-raζ-itfiidak ihwaaya.* -- If you take a vacation, it will do you lots of good. *loo taaxuδ εuṭla, tfiidak ihwaaya.*
to do harm – **1.** *ðạrr (ʔiðṛaar).* Rerouting the traffic to the new street has done much harm to my business. *taġyiir il-muruur liš-šaariε ij-jidiid ðạrr šuġḷi hwaaya.* **2.** *ʔaδδa (i ʔiiδaaʔ).* His interference in our work has done us more harm than good. *tadaxxula b-šuġuḷna ʔaδδaana ʔakθar min-ma faadna.*
to do in – *kital (u katil) n–.* They did him in. *kitloo.* -- Working in this heat has done me in. *š-šuġuḷ ib-hal-ζarr kitalni.*
to do one's best – *biδal (i baδil) jahid~.* I'll do my best to finish it on time. *raζ-abδil jahdi ζatta ʔaxaḷḷuṣha εal-wakit.*
to do out of – *sawwa (i) b–.* He did me out of all my money. *sawwaaha biyya w-ʔaxaδ kull ifluusi.*
to do without – *staġna (i stiġnaaʔ) εan.* Can you do without this pencil for a while? *tiġdar tistaġni εan hal-qalam il-fadd fatra?*

dock – *raṣiif* (pl. *ʔarṣifat*) *miinaaʔ.* I nearly fell off the dock. *wugaεit min raṣiif il-miinaaʔ ʔilla šwayya.*
to dock – **1.** *waččа (i tuwičči, toočiya).* Where do most of the tugboats dock? *ween itwačči ʔakθar il-maaṭooraat ib-baġdaad?* **2.** *risa (i rasu) n–.* The ship will dock at Basra at seven o'clock. *l-baaxira raζ-tirsi bil-baṣra saaεa sabεa.* **3.** *staqṭaε (i stiqṭaaε) min.* I was late 15 minutes, but they docked me an hour's wages. *ʔaani činit mitʔaxxir bass rubuε saaεa laakin istaqṭiεaw minni ʔujrat saaεa.*

doctor – *ṭabiib* pl. *ʔaṭibbaaʔ, daktoor* pl. *dakaatra.* Please send for a doctor. *dizz εala ṭabiib, min faðḷak.*
to doctor – *ṭabbab (i taṭbiib), daawa (i mudaawaat).* We doctored him ourselves. *ṭabbabnaa b-nafisna.*

doctorate – *diktoora* pl. *–aat.* He has a doctorate. *εinda diktoora.*

document – *waθiiqa* pl. *waθaayiq, mustanad* pl. *–aat.* Do you have all the documents? *εindak kull il-waθaayiq?*

dodge – *ζiila* pl. *ζiyal, liεba* pl. *–aat.* What dodge has he thought of now? *ʔay ζiila fakkar biiha hassa?*
to dodge – **1.** *zaaġ (u zooġ), tjannab (a tajannub, tjinnib).* If I hadn't dodged, he would have hit me. *loo ma-azuuġ minna, čaan ðịrabni.* **2.** *tmaḷḷaṣ (a tamaḷḷuṣ, tmiḷḷiṣ).* He tried to dodge the question. *ζaawal yitmaḷḷaṣ imnis-suʔaal.*

dog – *čalib* pl. *člaab, kalib* pl. *kilaab.* Take that dog out of here! *waxxir hač-čalib minnaa!*
**He's going to the dogs. *da-ydammur nafsa b-iida.*

dog-eared – *maθni.* The pages are all dog-eared. *ṣ-ṣafζaat kullha maθniyya.*

dogma – *εaqiida* pl. *εaqaaʔid.*

dogmatic – *mitεaṣṣub ib-ʔafkaar~.* Our Arabic teacher is very dogmatic. *mudarris il-εarabi maalna mutεaṣṣub ib-ʔafkaara kulliš.*

doll – *laεεaaba* pl. *–aat.* She likes to play with dolls. *yiεjibha tilεab bil-laεεaabaat.*

dollar – *doolaar* pl. *–aat, duulaar* pl. *–aat.*

domestic – **1.** *beeti**. She is studying to be a Domestic Science teacher. *da-tidrus ζatta tkuun mudarrisa lil-funuun il-beetiyya.* **2.** *maζalli**, *waṭani**. These are all domestic products. *haaδi kullha muntajaat waṭaniyya.* **3.** *beet.* It is hard to find domestic help these days. *yiṣεab tilgi xaddaamiin beet hal-ʔayyaam.*

domesticated – *ʔahli**, *daajin.* The chicken is a domesticated animal. *d-dijaaj imnil-ζaywaanaat il-ʔahliyya.*

to **donate** – *tbarraε (a tabarruε) b–.* I donated two dinars to the Red Crescent. *tbarraεit ib-diinaareen lil-hilaal il-ʔaζmar.*

donation – *tabarruε* pl. *–aat.* Donations are welcome. *baab it-tabarruεaat maftuuζ.*

done – **1.** *msawwa, mxallaṣ, xalṣaan.* All my lessons are done. *waðạayfi kullha msawwaaya.* **2.** *laaζiq, mistiwi.* In ten minutes the meat will be done. *b-xilaal εašir daqaayiq il-laζam raζ-ykuun laaζig.*
done in – *halkaan, manhuuk.* I'm done in from working in this weather. *ʔaani halkaan imniš-šuġuḷ ib-haj-jaww.*
to be done for – *ntiha (i ntihaaʔ) ʔamur.* If the boss finds this out I'm done for. *ʔiδa ζass biiha ir-raʔiis, ʔintiha ʔamri.* -- These tires are done for. *hat-taayiraat mintihi ʔamurha.*

donkey – *zmaaḷ* pl. *zmaayil, ζmaar* pl. *ζamiir.*

door – *baab* pl. *ʔabwaab, biibaan.* Please open the door. *ʔarjuuk fukk il-baab.*

doorbell – *jaraṣ* (pl. *ʔajraṣ*) *baab.*

doorknob – *yaddat* (pl. *–aat*) *baab, qabðạt* (pl. *–aat*) *baab.*

doorman – *bawwaab* pl. *–iin.*

doorway – *madxal* pl. *madaaxil.* Please don't stand in the doorway! *rijaaʔan la-toogaf bil-madxal.*

dope – *muxaddir* pl. *–aat.* He uses dope. *yistaεmil muxaddiraat.*

dormitory – *radha* pl. *–aat.*

dose – *jarεa* pl. *–aat.* That's too big a dose for a child. *haj-jarεa kulliš čibiira liṭ-ṭifil.* -- Take it in small doses. *ʔuxuδha b-jarεaat iṣġayyra.*

dossier – *ʔiðḅaara* pl. *–aat, malaffa* pl. *–aat, faayil* pl. *–aat.* Let me see Ali's dossier. *xalliini ʔašuuf ʔiðḅaarat εali.*

dot – *nuqṭa* pl. *nuqaṭ.* Wear your dress with the blue dots. *libsi l-badla ʔumm in-nuqaṭ iz-zarga.* -- Add three dots. *ζuṭṭ itlaθ nuqaṭ.*
on the dot – **1.** *bið-ðạbuṭ.* I'll see you at three on the dot. *raζ-ašuufak saaεa tlaaθa bið-ðạbuṭ.* **2.** *εal-mawεid, εal-wakit, bil-wakit.* He came right on the dot. *ʔija εal-wakit.*

double - *dabil, ð̣uεuf.* We got paid double today. *stilamna ð̣uεuf raatib il-yoom.* -- Bring me a double portion of ice cream. *jiib-li dabil doondirma.* -- It's double the size of mine. *haaði ð̣uεf il-ħajim maali.*
**He could be your double. *huwwa ṣuura ṭabq il-ʔaṣil minnak.*
to double - *ð̣aaεaf (u muð̣aaεafa).* He doubled his capital in two years. *ð̣aaεaf raasmaala b-santeen.*
double-breasted - *ʔabu siraween.* He wore a double-breasted suit. *libas qaaṭ ʔabu siraween.*
doubles - *zawji, θneen-iθneen.* Let's play doubles. *xal-nilεab zawji.*
doubt - *šakk* pl. *šukuuk.* Do you have any doubts? *εindak ʔay šakk?* -- Without a doubt he's the best man for the job. *biduun šakk huwwa ʔaħsan waaħid liš-šaġla.*
in doubt - *maškuuk b-.* The result is still in doubt. *n-natiija baεadha maškuuk biiha.*
to doubt - *šakk (u šakk).* I doubt that the story is true. *ʔašukk ʔan ykuun il-quṣṣa ṣaħiiħa.* -- I don't doubt it in the least. *ʔaani ʔabadan ma-ašukk biiha.*
doubtful - **1.** *maškuuk b-.* It is doubtful if he'll get well. *maškuuk bii ʔan yṭiib.* **2.** *šaakik b-.* I'm still doubtful about it. *ʔaani baεadni šaakik biiha* or ***baεad εindi šakk biiha.*
dough - *εajiin.* He put the dough in the oven. *xalla l-εajiin bil-firin.*
down - **1.** *riiš naεim.* This pillow is filled with down. *hal-imxadda mħaššaaya riiš naεim.* **2.** *zaġab.* The chick is covered with down. *farx id-dijaaja mġaṭṭa biz-zaġab.* **3.** *jawwa.* Did you look down there? *baawaεit jawwa hnaak?*
**Down with imperialism! *yasquṭ il-istiεmaar!*
to down - *waggaε (i tawgiiε) t-.* I downed the duck with one shot. *waggaεt il-baṭṭa b-fadd ṭalqa.*
downgrade - *nħidaar.* The road has a steep downgrade. *ṭ-ṭariiq bii nħidaar šadiid.*
downhearted - *maqhuur, ħaziin.* He looks downhearted. *ybayyin εalee maqhuur.*
downhill - *minħidir.* From here on the road is downhill all the way. *minnaa w-hiiči ṭ-ṭariiq minħidir εala ṭuul.*
down payment - *muqaddam, εarabuun* pl. *-aat.* How much of a down payment can you make? *šgadd tigdar tidfaε muqaddam?*
downpour - *zaxx.* We were caught in the downpour. *liħmatna z-zaxx.*
downstairs - *jawwa.* I'll be waiting downstairs. *raħ-antið̣ir jawwa.*
**He tripped and fell downstairs. *εiθar w-wugaε imnid-daraj.*
downtown - **Let's go downtown. *xal-ninzil lil-wlaaya* or *xal-inruuħ lis-suug.* **He's downtown right now. *huwwa bis-suug hassa.*
dowry - *ħagg.* How much dowry did he pay her? *šgadd difaε-ilha ħagg?*
to **doze** - *ʔaxað (u) ġaffa, ġafwa, ġafya.* I've just been dozing. *bass činit maaxið ġaffa.*
to doze off - *ġifa (i ġafi).* He dozed off after supper. *ġifa wara l-εaša.*
dozen - *darzan* pl. *daraazin.* Please give me a dozen eggs. *balla nṭiini darzan beeð̣.*
draft - **1.** *tayyaar* (pl. *-aat*) *hawa.* I can't stand the draft in this room. *ma-agdar atħammal tayyaar il-hawa b-hal-ġurfa.* -- The fire went out because there wasn't enough draft. *xumdat in-naar li-ʔan ma-čaan aku tayyaar hawa kaafi.* **2.** *miftaaħ* (pl. *mafaatiiħ*) *hawa.* Did you open the draft on the heater? *fakkeet miftaaħ il-hawa biṣ-ṣooba?* **3.** *miswadda* pl. *-aat.* The first draft is ready. *l-miswadda l-ʔuula ħaað̣ra.* **4.** *tajniid.* You have to report to the draft officer. *laazim itraajiε ð̣aabuṭ it-tajniid.*
to draft - *ʔaxað (u ʔaxið) lij-jundiyya, jannad (i tajniid).* They drafted him last month. *ʔaxðoo lij-jundiyya biš-šahr il-faat.*
to **drag** - **1.** *siħal (a saħil) n-.* I had to drag the trunk into the house myself. *ð̣tarreet ʔasħal iṣ-ṣanduug lil-beet ib-nafsi.* -- Your coat is dragging on the floor. *qappuuṭak da-yisħal bil-gaaε.* **2.** *marr (u marr) ib-buṭuʔ.* Time drags when you don't have anything to do. *l-wakit ymurr ib-buṭuʔ lumman maa εindak šii tsawwii.* **3.** *jarr (u jarr).* He could hardly drag himself to work. *bil-moot yaḷḷa yjurr nafsa liš-šuġuḷ.*
to drag on - *maṭmaṭ (u maṭmaṭa).* The meeting dragged on for three hours. *l-ijtimaaε maṭmaṭ itlaθ saaεaat.*
dragon - *tinniin* pl. *tanaaniin.*
drain - *balluuεa* pl. *balaaliiε.* The drain is stopped up again. *l-balluuεa nsaddat marra lux.*
to drain - *farraġ (i tafriiġ) t-.* They drained the swimming pool only yesterday. *bass il-baarħa farrġaw maay il-masbaħ.*
to drain off - *ṭṣarraf (a taṣarruf).* The water doesn't drain off quickly. *l-mayy ma-da-yiṭṣarraf ib-surεa.*
drastic - *ṣaarim, šadiid.* The government took drastic measures. *l-ħukuuma ttixðat ʔijraaʔaat ṣaarima.*
to **draw** - **1.** *risam (i rasim) n-.* He likes to draw pictures of animals. *yħibb yirsim ṣuwar ħaywanaat.* **2.** *siħab (a saħib) n-.* He drew the winning number in the lottery. *siħab ir-raqam ir-raabiħ bil-yaanaṣiib.* **3.** *jiðab (i jaðib) n-.* The concert is sure to draw a big crowd. *ʔakiid il-ħafla l-mawsiiqiyya raħ-tijðib jamhuur kabiir.* **4.** *ṭabb (u ṭabb).* The train is just drawing into the station. *l-qiṭaar hassa da-yṭubb lil-maħaṭṭa.* **5.** *jarr (u jarr) n-, ħišar (u ħašir) n-.* I was drawn into this argument against my will. *nħišarit il-hal-mujaadala ð̣idd raġubti.*
to draw conclusions - *stantaj (i stintaaj), staxliṣ (i stixlaaṣ).* Draw whatever conclusions you want to. *stantij iš-ma triid.*
to draw in - **1.** *jarr (u jarr) n-.* Draw in your breath. *jurr in-nafis.* **2.** *qallaṣ (i tqulluṣ, taqliiṣ).* Draw in your stomach. *qalliṣ baṭnak.*
to draw out - **1.** *siħab (a saħib) n-.* I'll have to draw out fifty dinars from the bank. *laazim asħab xamsiin diinaar imnil-bang.* **2.** *stadraj (i stidraaj).* See if you can draw him out. *jarrub tistadrij.*
to draw up - *wuð̣aε (a wað̣iε) n-.* Who drew up the plan for your house. *minu wuð̣aε xuṭṭat beetak?* -- I'm going to draw up the report. *ʔaani raħ-oođ̣aε it-taqriir.*
drawer - *mjarr* pl. *-aat, dirij* pl. *druuj.* You'll find it in the top drawer. *tilgii bil-imjarr il-foogaani.*
drawn - *manhuuk.* His face looks drawn. *ybayyin εala wijja manhuuk.*
dread - *xoof, xišya.* I have a dread of doctors. *εindi xoof imnil-ʔaṭibbaaʔ.*
to dread - *xaaf (a xoof), xiša (a xaši).* I dread the dark. *ʔaxaaf imnið̣-ð̣ilma.*
dreadful - *fað̣iiε, muriiε.* She wears dreadful clothes. *tilbas ihduum fað̣iiεa.* -- That was a dreadful accident. *haaði čaanat ħaadiθa muriiεa.*
dream - *ħilim* pl. *ʔaħlaam.* I had a strange dream last night. *šifit ħilim ġariib leelt il-baarħa.*
to dream - *ħilam (a ħalim).* Last night I dreamed that I was home. *ħilamit ʔaani činit ib-beeti l-baarħa bil-leel.*
**I wouldn't dream of doing it. *ma-aṭṣawwar aguum biiha ħatta b-manaami.*
dreary - *kaʔiib.* It was an awfully dreary day. *čaan fadd nahaar kulliš kaʔiib.*
dredge - *ħaffaara* pl. *-aat.* The dredge is being repaired right now. *l-ħaffaara da-tiṭṣallaħ hassa.*
to dredge - *kira (i kari) n-.* After the flood they had to dredge the river. *baεad il-fayað̣aan ið̣ṭarraw yikruun in-nahar.*
dress - *nafnuuf* pl. *nafaaniif.* She wants to buy a new dress. *triid tištiri nafnuuf jidiid.*
to dress - **1.** *libas (a libis) n-.* I'll dress quickly. *raħ-albas bil-εajal.* -- He's always well-dressed. *daaʔiman laabis zeen* or *daaʔiman yilbas zeen.* **2.** *labbas (i talbiis).* Mother is dressing the baby. *ʔummi da-tlabbis iṭ-ṭifil.* **3.** *ð̣ammad (i tað̣miid).* Did you dress the wound? *ð̣ammadt ij-jariħ?*
to dress up - *kišax (a kašix).* Look at him, all dressed up. *šuufa šloon kaašix.*
dresser - **1.** *diilaab, duulaab* pl. *dwaaliib.* The handkerchiefs are in the dresser. *č-čifaafi bid-diilaab.* **2.** *muð̣ammid* pl. *-iin.* The doctor looked at my injuries and told the dresser to treat them. *ṭ-ṭabiib kišaf εaj-juruuħ maalti w-xalla l-muð̣ammid yεaalijha.*
dressing - *ð̣ammaad* pl. *-aat, šdaad* pl. *-aat, lfaaf* pl. *-aat.* The nurse changes his dressings every morning. *l-mumarriða tbaddil ð̣ammaadaata kull yoom iṣ-ṣubuħ.*
dressing gown - *burnuṣ* pl. *baraaniṣ, roob* pl. *-aat.*
dressing table - *meez* (pl. *-aat*) *itwaaleet.*
dressmaker - *xayyaaṭa* pl. *-aat.*
dried - *yaabis.* Buy me a kilo of dried beans.

štirii-li keelu faaṣuuliyya yaabsa.

to **drift** - *sayyas (i tasyiis).* They cut the motor and let the boat drift. *waggifaw il-muzarrik w-xallaw il-maaṭoor ysayyis.*

drill - **1.** *mizraf* pl. *mazaarif.* The mechanic needs another drill. *l-miikaaniiki yiztaaj mizraf laax.* -- I just bought a new set of drills. *hassa štireet ṭaxum jidiid mazaarif.* **2.** *tamriin* pl. *tamaariin.* There are two drills on this rule on the fifth page. *ˀaku tamaariin iθneen εala hal-qaaεida biṣ-ṣafza l-xaamsa.* **3.** *tadriib* pl. *-aat.* I was late for drill today and they gave me extra duty. *tˀaxxarit εan it-tadriib il-yoom w-inṭooni waajib iḍaafi.*

to drill - **1.** *ziraf (u zaruf) n-, sawwa (i taswiya) zuruf.* Drill a hole in the beam. *sawwi zuruf biš-šeelmaana.* **2.** *zufar (u zafur) n-.* The dentist had to drill the tooth. *ṭabiib il-ˀasnaan iḍṭarr yizfur is-sinn.* **3.** *zaffaḍ (i tazfiiḍ).* The teacher drilled us in the multiplication table. *l-muεallim zaffaḍna jadwil iḍ-ḍarub.* **4.** *marran (i tamriin) t-, darrab (i tadriib) t-.* The soldiers drill every day. *j-jinuud yitmarranuun kull yoom.*

drink - **1.** *mašruub* pl. *-aat.* Lemonade is a refreshing summer drink. *l-leemuunaat mašruub ṣeefi munεiš.* -- What kind of drinks have you got? *yaa nooε imnil-mašruubaat εindak?* **2.** *jurεa* pl. *-aat, juraε, gumuε* pl. *gmuuε.* He's choking, give him a drink of water. *da-yixtinig, ˀinṭii jurεat maay.* **3.** *šwayya.* May I have a drink of water. *tismaz-li b-išwayyat mayy.*

to drink - *širab (a šurub) n-.* Drink plenty of water! *ˀišrab ihwaaya mayy!* -- Let's drink to your return. *xal-nišrab εala šaraf rujuuεak.*

to **drip** - **1.** *nigaṭ (u naguṭ).* Let it drip dry. *xallii yinguṭ lamma yinšif.* **2.** *naggaṭ (i tnigguṭ).* The faucet is dripping. *l-zanafiyya da-tnaggiṭ.*

drive - *zamla* pl. *-aat.* We raised five thousand dollars in the last drive. *jimaεna xamist aalaaf diinaar bil-zamla l-ˀaxiira.*

**We took a drive. *ṭlaεna bis-sayyaara.*

to drive - **1.** *saaq (u siyaaqa) n-.* Can you drive a truck? *tigdar itsuuq loori?* **2.** *saag (u siyaaga) n-.* Drive the sheep to the pasture. *suug il-ġanam lil-marεa.* **3.** *difaε (a dafiε) n-.* Hunger drove him to stealing. *j-juuε difaεa lil-boog.* **4.** *zaθθ (i zaθθ).* The foreman drives his workers continually. *raˀiis il-εummaal yziθθ εummaala εal-εamal b-istimraar.* **5.** *dagg (u dagg) n-.* Drive the nail into the wall. *dugg il-bismaar bil-zaayiṭ.*

**What are you driving at? *š-tuqṣud?* or *š-tiεni?*

to drive away - *ṭirad (u ṭarid) n-, biεad (u baεid) n-.* Drive the dog away. *ˀibεad ič-čalib.*

to drive crazy - *xabbaḷ (u txubbuḷ) t-.* You'll drive me crazy. *raz-itxabbuḷni.*

to drive off - *zaad (i zeed) n- εan.* The boat was driven off its course by the wind. *l-markab inzaad εan ittijaaha b-sabab ir-riyaaz.*

driver - **1.** *saayiq* pl. *suwwaaq.* He's a good driver. *huwwa xooš saayiq.* **2.** *εarabanči* pl. *-iyya.* The driver lost control of his horses. *l-εarabanči fuqad is-sayṭara εala xyuula.*

driving license - *ˀijaazat (pl. -aat) siyaaqa.* Let me see your driving license. *xalli ˀašuuf ˀijaazat siyaaqtak.*

to **drizzle** - *naθθ (i naθθ), naff (i naff).* It's been drizzling all day. *ṣaar-ilha tniθθ in-nahaar kulla.*

to **droop** - *ðuwa (i ðawi), ðibal (a ðabil).* The flowers are beginning to droop. *l-warid bida yiðbal.* -- The flower is drooping. *l-warid ðaawi.*

drooping - *mhaddil, raaxi.* He has drooping shoulders. *čtaafa mhaddila.*

drop - *qaṭra* pl. *-aat, nuqṭa* pl. *-aat.* Put three drops in a glass of water. *zuṭṭ itlaθ qaṭraat b-iglaaṣ mayy.*

to drop - *wugaε (a wuguuε).* The box dropped out of the window. *ṣ-ṣanduug wugεat imniš-šibbaač.* -- Some of them dropped from exhaustion. *baεaḍhum wugεaw imnit-taεab.* **2.** *waggaε (i tawgiiε) t-.* You dropped something. *waggaεit šii.* **3.** *nizal (i nuzuul), nxufaḍ (u nxifaaḍ).* The temperature dropped very rapidly. *darajat il-zaraara nizlat ib-surεa.* **4.** *tirak (u tarik) n-, himal (i ˀihmaal) n-.* Let's drop the subject. *xal-nitruk il-mawḍuuε.* **5.** *nazzal (i tanziil) t-.* Please drop me at the corner. *rajaaˀan nazzilni bil-loofa.* **6.** *ṭirad (u ṭarid) n-, ṭilaε (a ṭuluuε) n-.* I'll be dropped from the club. *raz-anṭarid imnin-naadi.* **7.** *ðabb (i ðabb) n-.* Please drop this card in the mail box. *rajaaˀan ðibb hal-kaart ib-ṣanduug il-bariid.*

to drop a hint - *lammaz (i talmiiz).* She dropped a hint to me that she wanted to go. *lammzat-li hiyya triid itruuz.*

to drop in - *marr (u marr).* Drop in sometime. *murr fadd yoom.*

drought - *jafaaf.* The drought hurt the crop very much. *j-jafaaf ihwaaya ˀaððа l-zaaṣil.*

drove - **1.** *qaṭiiε* pl. *qiṭεaan.* We waited for the drove of sheep to pass. *ntiḍarna zatta ymurr qaṭiiε il-ġanam.* **2.** *jamaaεa* pl. *-aat.* People came in droves. *n-naas ˀijaw ib-jamaaεaat.*

to **drown** - **1.** *ġirag (a ġarig).* He drowned in the river. *ġirag biš-šaṭṭ.* **2.** *ġarrag (i taġriig).* She had to drown the kittens. *ḍṭarrat itġarrig l-ibzaaziin l-iṣġaar.*

to drown out - *ṭiġa (i ṭaġi, ṭuġiyaan) εala.* The noise drowned out his remarks. *l-hoosa ṭiġat εala ṣoota.*

drowsy - *naεsaan.* I feel drowsy. *da-aziss naεsaan.*

drug - **1.** *duwa* pl. *ˀadwiya.* This drug is sold only on prescription. *had-duwa ma-yinbaaε ˀilla b-waṣfa.* **2.** *muxaddir* pl. *-aat.* He became addicted to drugs. *ṣaar mudmin εal-muxaddiraat.*

drugstore - *ṣaydaliyya* pl. *-aat.* Where is the nearest drugstore? *ween ˀaqrab ṣaydaliyya?*

drum - **1.** *ṭabul* pl. *ṭubuul, dumbug* pl. *danaabug.* Can you here sound of the drums? *tigdar tismaε ziss iṭ-ṭubuul?* **2.** *barmiil* pl. *baraamiil, piip* pl. *pyaap.* They unloaded six drums of kerosene. *farrġaw sitt baraamiil nafuṭ.*

to drum - *dagg (u dagg).* Please stop drumming on the table. *baṭṭa bass εaad itdugg εal-meez.*

drunk - *sakraan* pl. *sakaara.* Was that drunk annoying you? *čaan da-yziεjič has-sakraan?* -- He's dead drunk; if you pull on him, he won't feel a thing. *sakraan ṭiina; ˀiða tjurra ma-yziss.*

to get drunk - *sikar (a sukur).* He got drunk at her birthday party. *sikar ib-zaflat εiid miilaadha.*

dry - **1.** *naašif, yaabis, jaaff.* Is the wash dry yet? *l-ġasiil naašif loo baεad?* -- My throat is dry. *zarduumi yaabis.* or *riigi naašif.* -- The well is dry. *l-biir naašfa.* **2.** *jaaff.* It has been a dry summer. *čaan ṣeef jaaff.* -- The lecture was so dry, I walked out. *ˀaani ṭlaεit min wakit li-ˀan il-muzaaḍara čaanat kullis jaaffa.* **3.** *yaabis.* Let's gather some dry wood. *xalli nijmaε išwayya zaṭab yaabis.*

to dry - **1.** *yibas (a yibaas), nišaf (a našif), jaff (i jafaaf).* The paint dries in five hours. *ṣ-ṣubuġ yinšaf ib-xamis saaεaat.* **2.** *naššaf (i tanšiif).* Who's going to dry the dishes? *minu raz-ynaššif l-imwaaεiin?* -- Dry yourself well. *naššif nafsak zeen.*

to dry up - *jaff (i jafaaf), yibas (a yibaas), nišaf (a našif).* Every summer this stream dries up. *kull ṣeef hal-majra yinšaf.*

dry cleaner - *mukawwi* pl. *-iin.* I sent your gray suit to the dry cleaner. *dazzeet qaaṭak ir-rumaadi lil-mukawwi.*

dual - *muθanna, θunaaˀi*.*

duck - *baṭṭa* pl. *-aat* coll. *baṭṭ.* We're having roast duck for dinner. *εašaana lazam baṭṭ mišwi.*

to duck - **1.** *naṣṣa (i tnuṣṣi, tanṣiya), zina (i zani) n-, giṭaf (i gaṭif).* He ducked his head. *naṣṣa raasa.* **2.** *ġiṭaṣ (u ġaṭiṣ), ġaṭṭ (u ġaṭṭ).* The duck ducked under the water. *l-baṭṭa ġiṭṣat bil-mayy.* **3.** *ġaṭṭaṣ (i tġiṭṭiṣ, taġṭiiṣ), ġaṭṭaṭ (i tġiṭṭiṭ).* He ducked his brother's head under the water. *ġaṭṭaṭ raas ˀaxuu bil-mayy.*

due - *zaqq* pl. *zuquuq.* That's his due. *haaða zaqqa.*

**He's due to arrive at ten. *muntaḍar wuṣuula saaεa εašra.*

due to - *b-sabab, b-natiija.* Due to an oversight, she wasn't invitated. *ma-nεizmat ib-sabab sahu.* -- That was due to a mistake. *ṣaar ib-natiijat ġalṭa.*

to be due - *stazaqq (i stizqaaq).* The rent is due next Monday. *l-ˀiijaar mistiziqq iθ-θineen ij-jaay.*

duel - *ṣiraaε, mubaaraza.*

dues - *badalaat.* I pay membership dues every month. *ˀaani ˀadfaε badalaat il-ištiraak kull šahar.*

dull - **1.** *ˀaεmi, εimyaan* pl. *εimi.* This knife is dull. *has-siččiina εamya.* **2.** *baliid* pl. *buladaaˀ.* He's terribly dull. *huwwa kulliš baliid.* **3.** *θaqiil.* I feel a dull pain in my side. *ˀašεur ib-wajaε θaqiil ib-ṣafuzti.* **4.** *šaazib.* She likes dull colors. *tiεjibha l-ˀalwaan iš-šaazba.*

dumb - **1.** *ˀaxras* pl. *xarsiin.* He's deaf and dumb. *huwwa ˀaṭraš w-ˀaxras.* **2.** *ġabi, baliid, dimaaġsizz.*

He's too dumb to notice. *hal-ġabi ma-ylaaziδ.*

to strike dumb - *δihal (i δahil) n-, lijam (i lajim) n-.* We were struck dumb when we heard the news. *nδihalna lamman simaεna l-xabar.*

dumbfounded - *maδhuul.* I was dumfounded when I heard it. *ṣirit maδhuul lumman simaεit biiha.*

dump - *mazbala* pl. *mazaabil.* Where's the dump? *ween il-mazbala?*

**Their house is an awful dump. *beethum kulliš imxarbaṭ.*

down in the dumps - *maqbuuδ in-nafis.* I've been down in the dumps all day. *činit maqbuuδ in-nafis ṭuul in-nahaar* or ***nafsi čaanat maqbuuδa ṭuul in-nahaar.*

to dump - *δabb (i δabb) n-.* Don't dump the sand in front of the door. *la-tδibb ir-ramul giddaam il-baab.* -- Don't dump the coffee grounds in the sink. *la-tδibb it-tilif maal il-gahwa b-zalg il-maġsal.*

dumpy - *mdazdaz.* She has a dumpy figure. *εidha jisim imdazdaz.*

dune - *kaθiib* pl. *kuθbaan.* The sand dunes extend for miles. *kuθbaan ir-ramul timtadd il-biεid ʔamyaal.*

dung - *dimin.* Do you use chemical fertilizer or dung in your garden? *tistaεmil samaad kiimyaawi loo dimin ib-zadiiqtak?*

duplicate - *nusxa* pl. *nusax.* You need a duplicate of your birth certificate. *tiztaaj nusxa š-šihaadat miilaadak.*

to duplicate - *stansax (i stinsaax).* I'll have the secretary duplicate them for you. *raz-axalli s-sikirteera tistansixhum ʔilak.*

duplication - *zdiwaaj* pl. *-aat.* We must avoid duplication in the work. *laazim nitzaaša l-izdiwaaj biš-šuġul.*

to be **durable** - *daawam (u dawaam).* These tires are cheap but they are not durable. *hat-taayaraat irxiiṣa laakin ma-tdaawum.*

during - *ʔaθnaaʔ, xilaal.* I met him during the war. *εirafta xilaal il-zarub.*

dust - *ġubaar, traab, εajaaj.* There's a heavy layer of dust on the table. *ʔaku ṭabaqa θixiina mnil-ġubaar εal-meez.*

to dust - **1.** *naffaδ (u tanfiiδ) imnil-εajaaj.* Please dust my desk. *ʔarjuuk naffuδ meezi mnil-εajaaj.* **2.** *rašš (u rašš).* They dusted a chemical substance on the cotton fields by plane. *raššaw mawaadd kiimyaawiyya εala zuquul il-guṭin imnit-ṭayyaara.*

dust storm - *εajaaj* pl. *-aat.*

Dutch - *hoolandi** pl. *-iyyiin.*

duty - **1.** *waajib* pl. *-aat.* It was his duty to support his parents. *ʔaṣbaz min waajba ʔan yεiil ʔumma w-abuu.* -- Answering the phone is one of my duties. *l-ʔijaaba εat-talifoon min waajibaati.* -- I'm on duty all night. *ʔaani bil-waajib ṭuul il-leel* or *ʔaani xafaara ṭuul il-leel.* **2.** *gumrug, rsuum gumrugiyya.* I paid 300 dinars duty on it. *difaεit itlaθ miit diinaar gumrug εalee.*

dwarf - *gurri* pl. *-iyya.*

to **dwell** - **1.** *εaaš (i εeeš) n-.* The Bedouins dwell in the desert most of the year. *l-badu yεiišuun bil-barr miεδam is-sana.* **2.** *stimarr (i stimraar).* There's no point in dwelling on this subject any longer. *ma-aku daaεi nistimirr bil-mawδuuε ʔakθar.*

dye - *ṣubuġ* pl. *ʔaṣbaaġ.* Please get me a package of blue dye. *ʔarjuuk jiib-li paakeet ṣubuġ ʔazrag.*

to dye - *ṣubaġ (u ṣubuġ).* I dyed my blue dress with black dye. *ṣbaġit nafnuufi l-ʔazrag ib-ṣubuġ ʔaswad.*

dynamic - *našiṭ, zarik.* He's a dynamic businessman. *huwwa rajul ʔaεmaal našiṭ.*

dysentery - *dizantari.*

E

each - **1.** *kull.* Each one of us received a pack of cigarettes. *kull waazid min εidna ʔaxaδ paakeet jigaayir.* -- He comes here each week. *yiji hnaa kull isbuuε.* -- Give one to each child. *ʔinṭi wazda l-kull jaahil.* **2.** *waazid.* These apples are ten fils each. *hat-tiffaaz wizda b-εašr ifluus.*

each and every one - *jamiiε.* You can count on each and every one of us. *tigdar tiεtimid εala jamiiεna.*

each other - **1.** *waazid il-laax, baεaδhum baεaδ.* They see each other every day. *yšuufuun waazid il-laax kull yoom.* -- They have nothing to do with each other. *ma-lhum lizuum waazid bil-laax.* **2.** (sometimes expressed in sixth form of verb). They've been writing to each other for a year. *čaanaw yitraasluun il-muddat sana.* -- They're not not talking to each other. *ma-yitzaačuun.*

eager - *muštaaq, mitšawwiq.* I am eager to meet your friend. *ʔaani muštaaq atεarraf ib-ṣadiiqak.*

eagle - *nisir* pl. *nisuur.*

ear - **1.** *ʔiδin* pl. *ʔaδaan, ʔiiδaan* pl. *-aat.* She's deaf in her right ear. *ʔiδinha l-yimna ṭarša.* -- I have no ear for music. *ma-εindi ʔiδin mawsiiqiyya.* **2.** *εarnuuṣ* pl. *εaraaniiṣ.* Make popcorn out of these ears of corn. *sawwi šaamiyya min εaraaniiṣ il-ʔiδra haaδi.* **3.** *sunbula* pl. *sanaabil.* This ear of wheat has fifty grains on it. *has-sunbult il-zunṭa biiha xamsiin zabba.*

**He's up to his ears in debt. *ṭaamus bid-deen ʔila raasa.*

earlier - *gabuḷ.* Come earlier than usual. *taεaal gabḷ il-muεtaad.*

earliest - **1.** *ʔawwal* pl. *ʔawaaʔil.* The earliest immigrants came from Europe. *ʔawaaʔil il-muhaajiriin ʔijaw min ʔooruppa.* **2.** *ʔaqdam.* He is one of the earliest advocates of this idea. *huwwa min ʔaqdam duεaat hal-fikra.*

early - **1.** *min wakit, εala wakit.* Please wake me up early. *ʔarjuuk gaεεidni min wakit.* **2.** *εaajil, sariiε.* We expect an early reply. *nitwaqqaε jawaab εaajil.* **3.** *mubakkir.* She got married at an early age. *tzawwjat ib-εumur mubakkir.*

**He will arrive early next month. *raz-yooṣal ib-ʔawaaʔil iš-šahr ij-jaay.*

to **earmark** - *xaṣṣaṣ (i taxṣiiṣ) t-.* We earmarked two million dinars for the new bridge. *xaṣṣaṣna milyooneen diinaar lij-jisir ij-jidiid.*

to **earn** - **1.** *zaṣṣal (i tazṣiil) t-, ṭallaε (i taṭliiε) t-.* How much do you earn a week? *šgadd itzaṣṣil bil-isbuuε?* -- She earns her living as a dressmaker. *ṭṭalliε εiišatha mnil-ixyaaṭa.* **2.** *ktisab (i ktisaab).* He earned his reputation the hard way. *ktisab šuhurta b-šaqq il-ʔanfus.* **3.** *kisab (i kasib) n-.* His conduct earned him universal respect. *taṣarrufaata kisbat-la ztiraam ij-jamiiε.*

earnings - *mazṣuul* pl. *mazaaṣiil, maksab* pl. *makaasib.*

earrings - *tirčiyya* pl. *taraači.* She bought a new pair of earrings. *štirat zooj taraači jidiida.*

earth - **1.** *dinya, εaalam, ʔarδ.* Nothing on earth can save him. *ma-aku šii bid-dinya yxallṣa.* **2.** *ʔarδ.* The earth is a sphere. *l-ʔarδ kurawiyya.* **3.** *traab.* This ditch has to be filled with earth. *han-nugra laazim tindifin b-itraab.*

**There is nothing like it on the face of the earth. *haaδa ma-aku minna εala wajh il-baṣiiṭa.*

**He is very down to earth. *haaδa kulliš waaqiεi.*

earthquake - *zilzaal* pl. *zalaazil.* The earthquake destroyed twenty houses. *z-zilzaal dammar εišriin beet.*

ease - *suhuula, baṣaaṭa.* Did you notice the ease with which he does things? *laazaδit išloon ysawwi l-ʔašyaaʔ ib-suhuula?*

at ease - *mirtaaz.* I never feel quite at ease when I'm with her. *ʔabadan ma-ʔašεur mirtaaz min ʔakuun wiyyaaha.*

**At ease! *stariiz!*

to ease - **1.** *xaffaf (u taxfiif) t-.* This medicine will ease the pain. *had-duwa yxaffuf il-wujaε.* **2.** *hawwan (i tahwiin) t-.* Nothing will ease my grief. *ma-aku šii yhawwin qahri.*

**We have to ease the box through the narrow door. *laazim infawwit iṣ-ṣanduug εala keefna mnil-baab iδ-δayyig.*

to ease up - *xaff (u xiffa), qall (i qilla).* The pressure is beginning to ease up. *δ-δagiṭ bida yxuff.*

easily - *b-suhuula, b-baṣaaṭa.* He did it easily. *sawwaaha b-suhuula.* -- This can easily be believed. *haay titṣaddag ib-suhuula.*

east - **1.** *šarq.* The arrow points east. *s-sahim yʔaššir liš-šarq.* **2.** *šarji.* It's an east wind.

l-hawa šarji.
the Far East – *š-šarq il-ʔaqṣa.*
the Middle East – *š-šarq il-ʔawṣaṭ.*
the Near East – *š-šarq il-ʔadna.*
Easter – *εiid il-qiyaama, εiid il-fuṣiζ.* Easter comes early this year. *εiid il-qiyaama yiji min wakit has-sana.*
eastern – *šarqi**. I know the eastern part very well. *ʔaεruf il-qism iš-šarqi kulliš zeen.*
easy – **1.** *sahil, baṣiiṭ.* That was an easy question. *δaak čaan suʔaal sahil.*
**Take it easy, don't get mad. *εala keefak, la-tizεal* or *yawaaš, la tizεal.*
easy-going – *mitsaahil.* He's an easy-going fellow. *huwwa fadd waaζid mitsaahil.*
to **eat** – **1.** *ʔakal (u ʔakil) n-.* I haven't eaten a thing in two days. *ṣaar-li yoomeen ma-akalit šii.* — He walked in just as we sat down to eat. *ṭabb min giεadna naakul.* **2.** *ziraf (u zaruf).* The acid ate three holes in my pants. *l-ζaamuδ ziraf itlaθ izruuf bil-panṭaroon maali.*
to eat out – **1.** *ʔakal (u), ziraf (u).* Rust ate out the bottom of the pan. *z-zinjaar ʔakal čaεb ij-jidir.* **2.** *ʔakal (u) barra.* Why don't we eat out tonight? *leeš ma-naakul barra hal-leela?*
echo – *ṣada* pl. *ʔaṣdaaʔ.* If you listen you can hear the echo. *ʔiδa titṣannaṭ tigdar tismaε iṣ-ṣada.*
to echo – **1.** *niṭa (i) ṣada.* The sound of the shot echoed through the hills. *ṣoot iṭ-ṭalqa niṭa ṣada been il-itlaal.* **2.** *raddad (i tardiid).* Stop echoing every word he says. *bass εaad itraddid kull čilma yguulha.*
eclipse – **1.** *xusuuf* pl. *-aat.* There will be a partial lunar eclipse tomorrow night. *raζ-yṣiir xusuuf juzʔi baačir bil-leel.* **2.** *kusuuf* pl. *-aat.* We watched the solar eclipse from the top of the building. *šifna l-kusuuf min saṭζ il-ibnaaya.*
to eclipse – *ṭiğa (a ṭuğyaan) εala.* She eclipsed everybody else at the party. *ṭiğat εala kull il-baaqyaat bil-ζafla.*
to be eclipsed – **1.** *xisaf (i xusuuf).* The moon will be eclipsed tonight. *l-gumar raζ-yixsif hal-leela.* **2.** *kisaf (i kusuuf).* Don't forget that the sun will be eclipsed this afternoon. *la-tinsa š-šamis raζ-tiksif hal-εaṣriyya.*
economic – *qtiṣaadi**. Their economic situation is improving. *ζaalathum il-iqtiṣaadiyya da-titζassan.*
economical – **1.** *muqtaṣid, mudabbir.* She's a very economical woman. *haay fadd mara kulliš muqtaṣida.* **2.** *qtiṣaadi**. This car is very economical. *has-sayyaara kulliš iqtiṣaadiyya.*
economics – *qtiṣaad.* He's studying economics. *da-yidrus iqtiṣaad.*
to **economize** – *qtiṣad (i qtiṣaad).* She economizes in household expenditures. *hiyya tiqtiṣid ib-maṣaariif il-beet.*
edge – **1.** *ṭaraf* pl. *ʔaṭraaf.* He lives at the edge of town. *yiskun ib-ṭaraf il-wlaaya.* **2.** *ζaašya* pl. *ζawaaši.* Don't put the glass real close to the edge. *la-tζuṭṭ l-iglaaṣ kulliš giriib lil-ζaašya.* **3.** *ζadd* pl. *ζduud.* The knife's edge is dull. *ζadd is-siččiina ʔaεmi.* **4.** *ʔafḍaliyya.* He has the edge on me. *ʔila l-ʔafḍaliyya εalayya.*
on edge – *miζtadd.* She's on edge today. *hiyya miζtadda l-yoom.*
edible – *ṣaaliζ lil-ʔakil.* Is this edible? *haaδa ṣaaliζ lil-ʔakil?*
to **edit** – *ζarrar (i taζriir) t-.* He has been editing this magazine for several years. *ṣaar-la εiddat isniin yζarrir hal-majalla.*
edition – *ṭabεa* pl. *-aat, εadad,* pl. *ʔaεdaad.* Have you seen the new edition of his book? *šift iṭ-ṭabεa j-jidiida min iktaaba?*
editor – *muζarrir* pl. *-iin.* My brother has just become editor of our local newspaper. *ʔaxuuya stawwa ṣaar muζarrir jariidatna l-maζalliyya.*
editorial – *maqaal iftitaaζi* pl. *maqaalaat iftitaaζiyya.* Did you read the editorial? *qireet il-maqaal il-iftitaaζi?*
editor-in-chief – *raʔiis* (pl. *ruʔasaaʔ*) *taζriir.* You have to see the editor-in-chief about this. *laazim itraajiε raʔiis it-taζriir ζawil haaδa.*
to **educate** – **1.** *εallam (i taεliim) t-.* We have to educate our children to tolerance. *laazim inεallim ʔaṭfaalna εat-tasaamuζ.* **2.** *θaqqaf (i taθqiif) t-, εallam (i).* We need many more teachers to educate the masses. *niζtaaj ihwaaya baεad muεallimiin il-taθqiif ʔabnaaʔ iš-šaεab.*
educated – *mθaqqaf* pl. *-iin, mitεallim* pl. *-iin.* He's an educated person. *haaδa šaxiṣ imθaqqaf.*
education – **1.** *θaqaafa, taεliim.* Her parents neglected her education. *ʔahalha himlaw θaqaafatha.* **2.** *diraasa, taεliim, taζṣiil, θaqaafa.* I completed my education in England. *kammalit diraasti b-ingiltara.* **3.** *tarbiya.* He has an M.A. in education. *εinda maajisteer bit-tarbiya.*
ministry of education – *wizaarat il-maεaarif.*
educational – *diraasi**. The new law provides many educational opportunities. *l-qaanuun ij-jidiid yhayyiʔ furaṣ diraasiyya hwaaya.*
effect – **1.** *taʔθiir* pl. *-aat.* His appeal produced the desired effect. *stiğaaθta ʔantijat it-taʔθiir il-marğuub.* **2.** *mafεuul.* The effect of this medicine is not what I would like it to be. *mafεuul had-duwa muu miθil-ma ʔariida.* **3.** *taḍaahur.* He does it for effect. *ysawwiiha l-ğaraḍ it-taḍaahur.* **4.** *musabbab* pl. *-aat.* This is a cause, not an effect. *haaδa sabab, muu musabbab.*
to go into effect – *sira (i sarayaan) mafεuul.* This law will go into effect next month. *hal-qaanuun raζ-yisri mafεuula š-šahr ij-jaay.*
to have an effect – *ʔaθθar (i taʔθiir).* Scolding has no effect on him. *t-tarziil ma-yʔaθθir bii.*
to take effect – *sira (i) mafεuul.* This injection is beginning to take effect. *l-ʔubra bida yisri mafεuulha.*
to effect – *sawwa (i taswiya) t-, ʔajra (i ʔijraaʔ), ζaqqaq (i taζqiiq) t-.* He effected the change without difficulty. *sawwa t-tağyiir bila ṣuεuuba.*
effective – **1.** *muʔaθθir.* They produced a very effective new weapon. *ʔantijaw silaaζ jidiid kulliš muʔaθθir.* **2.** *faεεaal.* The committee was very effective in handling the dispute. *l-lujna čaanat kulliš faεεaala b-muεaalajat in-nizaaε.* **3.** *mafεuul.* These pills have proved to be very effective. *hal-ζubuub θibat mafεuulha qawi.* **4.** *εtibaaran min.* Effective Monday, we'll go on summer time. *εtibaaran min yoom iθ-θineen raζ-nistaεmil it-tawqiit iṣ-ṣeefi.*
efficiency – *kafaaʔa, qtidaar.* We all admire his efficiency. *kullna nqaddir kafaaʔta.*
efficient – *kafuʔ* pl. *ʔakiffaaʔ, muqtadir* pl. *-iin.* He's very efficient. *haaδa kulliš kafuʔ.*
effort – **1.** *juhud* pl. *juhuud, majhuud* pl. *-aat.* All his efforts were in vain. *kull juhuuda raaζat εabaθ.* **2.** *masεa* pl. *masaaεi.* I wouldn't have got the job without your efforts. *ma-čaan ζaṣṣalt il-waḍiifa blayya masaaεiik.* **3.** *taεab* pl. *ʔatεaab.* That isn't worth the effort. *haaδa ma-yiswa t-taεab.*
**We spared no effort to make the program a success. *biδalna l-ğaali wir-rixiiṣ ζatta nijεal l-mašruuε naajiζ.*
to make an effort – *siεa (a saεi), jtihad (i jtihaad), biδal (i baδil) masεa.* I will make a real effort to get you the job. *raζ-asεa min ṣudug ζatta aζaṣṣil-lak il-waḍiifa.*
egg – *beeḍa* pl. *-aat* coll. *beeḍ.* How much is a dozen eggs? *beeš darzan il-beeḍ?*
**Don't put all your eggs in one basket. *la-tikšif kull ʔawraaqak* or *daaʔiman xallii-lak xaṭṭ rajεa.*
eggplant – *beetinjaana* pl. *-aat* coll. *beetinjaan.*
Egypt – *miṣir.*
Egyptian – *miṣri** pl. *-iyyiin.*
eight – **1.** *θmaanya.* It's eight o'clock. *s-saaεa θmaanya.* **2.** *θman.* He has eight children. *εinda θman ʔaṭfaal.*
eighteen – *θmunṭaεaš.*
eighteenth – *θ-θmunṭaεaš.* That's the eighteenth time he hasn't come to work this month. *haay il-marra θ-θumunṭaεaš ma-ʔija liš-šuğul haš-šahar.*
eighth – **1.** *θumun.* He could only get an eighth of a pound of butter. *gidar yaaxuδ θumun paawan zibid bass.* **2.** *θaamin.* That is his eighth book. *haaδa ktaaba θ-θaamin.*
eightieth – *θ-θimaaniin.* They celebrated his eightieth birthday. *ζtiflaw εiid miilaada θ-θimaaniin.*
eighty – *θmaaniin.*
either – **1.** *fadd waaζid min θineen.* Does either of these roads lead to Baghdad? *ʔaku fadd ṭariiq min haθ-θineen yruuζ il-bağdaad.* **2.** *ʔay waaζid imniθ-θineen.* Either (one) is correct. *ʔay waaζid imniθ-θineen ṣaζiiζ.* **3.** *-een.* There are trees on either side of the road. *ʔaku ʔašjaar εala jihteen iš-šaariε.* **4.** *ʔamma, loo.* I leave either tonight or tomorrow morning. *ʔasaafir ʔamma l-yoom ʔaw baačir iṣ-ṣubuζ* or *ʔasaafir loo l-yoom loo baačir iṣ-ṣubuζ.* **5.** *hamm.* He doesn't know it either. *huwwa hamm ma-yuεrufha.*

elaborate - *mufaṣṣal.* He gave us an elaborate description of it. *nṭaana waṣuf mufaṣṣal ɛanha.*
  to elaborate - *faṣṣal (i tfiṣṣil, tafṣiil), waḍḍaʒ (i twiḍḍiʒ, tawḍiiʒ) ˀakθar.* Can you elaborate upon your decision? *tigdar itwaḍḍiʒ taqriirak ˀakθar?*
elastic - **1.** *laastiig.* Do you need any elastic for the blouse? *tiʒtaajiin ˀay laastiig lil-ibluuz?* **2.** *marin.* This metal is very elastic. *hal-maɛdan kulliš marin.*
elbow - *ɛikis* pl. *ɛukuus.* I banged my elbow. *ḍirabit ɛiksi.*
  to elbow - **1.** *šagg (u šagg) b-ɛikis˜.* She elbowed her way through the crowd. *šaggat ṭariiqha b-ɛikisha bil-xabṣa.* **2.** *naġġ (u naġġ) b-ɛikis˜.* He shut up after she elbowed him in his ribs. *sikat baɛad-ma naġġata b-ɛikisha b-iḍluuɛa.*
to **elect** - *ntixab (i ntixaab).* Whom did they elect president? *ˀilman intixbaw raˀiis?*
election - *ntixaab* pl. *-aat.*
electric - *kahrabaaˀi*.* Where can I plug in my electric razor? *ˀaku plaak ˀašakkil bii makiinat iz-ziyaan il-kahrabaaˀiyya maalti?*
electric bulb - *gloob* pl. *-aat.*
electrician - *ˀabu* (pl. *ˀahil) kahrabaaˀ.*
electricity - *kahrabaaˀ.* The electricity's been cut off! *l-kahrabaaˀ ingiṭaɛ!*
electron - *ˀalakitroon* pl. *-aat.*
electronic - *ˀalakitrooni*.*
elegant - *ˀaniiq.*
element - **1.** *ɛunṣur* pl. *ɛanaaṣir.* What are the elements of water? *šinu hiyya ɛanaaṣir il-maay?* -- This group constitutes the important element of the population. *haj-jamaaɛa tkawwan il-ɛunṣur il-muhimm bil-majmuuɛ.* **2.** *muʒiiṭ* pl. *-aat.* He's out of his element. *huwwa muu b-muʒiiṭa l-mulaaˀim.*
elementary - **1.** *ˀasaasi*.* Practice is elementary to learning any language. *t-tamriin šii ˀasaasi l-taɛallum ˀay luġa.* **2.** *ˀawwali*, btidaaˀi*.* I studied in an elementary school in Baghdad. *drasit ib-madrasa btidaaˀiyya b-baġdaad.*
elephant - *fiil* pl. *fyaal, fyaala.*
elevation - *rtifaaɛ.* The elevation of this village is six hundred meters above sea level. *rtifaaɛ hal-qarya ɛan mustawa l-baʒar sitt miit matir.*
elevator - **1.** *maṣɛad* pl. *maṣaaɛid.* Let's take the elevator. *xalli naaxuḍ il-maṣɛad.* **2.** *maxzan* pl. *maxaazin.* How much wheat does this elevator hold? *šgadd hal-maxzan yilzam imnil-ʒunṭa?*
eleven - *daɛaš, hdaɛaš.* I had to fill out eleven forms. *čaan laazim amli hdaɛaš istimaara.*
eleventh - *d-daɛaš, l-ihdaɛaš.* Take the tenth book and give me the eleventh. *ˀuxuḍ il-iktaab il-ɛaašir w-inṭiini il-ihdaɛaš.*
to **eliminate** - **1.** *zaal (i ˀizaala), miʒa (i maʒu, maʒi).* The robbers eliminated all traces of the crime. *l-ʒaraamiyya zaalaw kull ˀaaθaar ij-jariima.* **2.** *ṣaqqaṭ (u tṣuqquṭ taṣqiiṭ) t-.* They eliminated him in the third race. *ṣaqqṭoo b-θaaliθ musaabaqa.* **3.** *ʒiḍaf (i ʒaḍif) n-.* His name was eliminated from the candidate list. *ˀisma nʒiḍaf min qaaˀimat il-muraššaʒiin.* **4.** *ˀalġa (i ˀilġaaˀ) n-.* They finally eliminated taxes. *bil-ˀaxiir alġaw iḍ-ḍaraayib.*
eloquence - *balaaġa.*
else - **1.** *baɛad, ˀaaxar.* What else can we do? *š-nigdar insawwi baɛad?* -- Do you want something else? *triid šii ˀaaxar?* **2.** *laax, baaqi.* I'll take everything else. *raʒ-aaxuḍ kullši laax.*
  or else - *tara.* Hurry, or else we'll be late. *bil-ɛajil, tara raʒ-nitˀaxxar.*
elsewhere - *maʒall ˀaaxar, ġeer mukaan.* If you don't like it here, we can go elsewhere. *ˀiḍa ma-yɛijbak hal-maʒall nigdar inruuʒ il-maʒall ˀaaxar.*
embargo - *maniɛ.* The government issued an embargo on all goods to that island. *l-ʒukuuma ṣaddirat maniɛ ɛala jamiiɛ il-baḍaayiɛ itruuʒ il-haj-jaziira.*
to **embarrass** - *xajjal (i txijjil, taxjiil) t-, faššal (i tafšiil) t-.* That child is always embarrassing me in front of people. *haṭ-ṭifil daaˀiman yxajjilni giddaam in-naas.*
embarrassed - *xajlaan, fašlaan.* I was terribly embarrassed. *činit xajlaan il-daraja muzɛija.*
embarrassing - *mxajjil, mfaššil.* It was an embarrassing situation. *čaanat fadd waḍɛiyya mxajjila.*
embassy - *safaara* pl. *-aat.* Where is the American Embassy? *ween is-safaara l-ˀamriikiyya?*
to **embezzle** - *xtilas (i xtilaas).* How much has he embezzled? *šgadd ixtilas?*
to **embrace** - **1.** *ʒiḍan (i ʒaḍin).* He embraced his mother tenderly. *ʒiḍan ˀumma b-ʒanaan.* **2.** *ḍamm (u ḍamm) n-.* Islam embraces people from many various nationalities. *l-ˀislaam yḍumm naas min muxtalif iš-šuɛuub.*
emerald - *zmurrada* pl. *-aat* coll. *zmurrad.*
to **emerge** - **1.** *ṭilaɛ (a ṭuluuɛ), xiraj (u xuruuj).* He emerged from the meeting smiling. *ṭilaɛ imnil-ijtimaaɛ w-wujha yibtisim.* **2.** *biraz (i buruuz).* He emerged as one of the leaders of the party. *biraz ka-ˀaʒʒad zuɛamaaˀ il-ʒizib.* **3.** *nišaˀ (i našiˀ), ḍahar (a ḍuhuur).* These facts emerged from the study of the problem. *hal-ʒaqaayiq nišˀat min diraasat il-muškila.* **4.** *bizaġ (a bizuuġ).* The sun emerged from behind the hills. *bizġat iš-šamis min wara j-jibaal.*
emergency - **1.** *ṭaariˀa* pl. *ṭawaariˀ.* A state of emergency was declared. *ʒaalat iṭ-ṭawaariˀ inɛilnat.* **2.** *ḍṭiraari*, mustaɛjal.* This is an emergency case. *haaḍi ʒaala ḍṭiraariyya.* **3.** *ḍaruura.* In case of emergency call the doctor. *ɛind iḍ-ḍaruura xaabur iṭ-ṭabiib.*
emergency brake - *handibreek* pl. *-aat.*
emergency exit - *baab* (pl. *bwaab*) *ṭawaariˀ.*
emigrant - *muhaajir* pl. *-iin.* Lebanese emigrants have settled all over the world. *l-muhaajiriin il-lubnaaniyyiin istawṭinaw ib-kull makaan bil-ɛaalam.*
to **emigrate** - *haajar (i muhaajara).* In recent years many people have emigrated from Europe. *bis-siniin il-ˀaxiira hwaaya naas haajraw min ˀawruppa.*
eminent - *baariz.*
emir - *ˀamiir* pl. *ˀumaraaˀ.*
emotion - *ɛaaṭifa* pl. *ɛawaaṭif, šuɛuur.* He couldn't hide his emotion. *ma-gidar yixfi ɛaaṭifta.*
emperor - *ˀimbiraaṭoor* pl. *-iin.*
emphasis - *ˀahammiyya, taˀkiid.*
to **emphasize** - *ˀakkad (i taˀkiid) t-.* He emphasized the need for more teachers. *ˀakkad il-ʒaaja ˀila muɛallimiin ˀakθar.*
emphatically - *b-šidda, b-taˀkiid.* I'll have to deny that emphatically. *raʒ-aḍṭarr ˀanfi haḍaak ib-šidda.*
empire - *ˀimbiraaṭooriyya* pl. *-aat.*
to **employ** - *staxdam (i stixdaam), šaġġal (i tšiġġil, tašġiil) t-.* This factory employs a thousand workers. *hal-maɛmal yistaxdim ˀalif ɛaamil.*
  **Where are you employed? *ˀinta ween tištuġul?*
employee - *mustaxdam* pl. *-iin, muwaḍḍaf* pl. *-iin.*
employer - *mustaxdim* pl. *-iin.*
employment - **1.** *šuġuḷ.* What kind of employment did you finally get? *taaliiha šinu nooɛ iš-šuġuḷ illi ʒaṣṣalta?* **2.** *stixdaam.* The employment of children is forbidden by law. *stixdaam iṣ-ṣiġaar mamnuuɛ qaanuunan.*
empty - *faariġ, xaali.* Do you have an empty box? *ɛindak fadd ṣanduug faariġ?* -- He made empty threats. *haddad tahdiidaat faarġa.*
  to empty - **1.** *farraġ (i tfurriġ, tafriiġ) t-, ˀaxla (i ˀixlaaˀ) n-.* Please empty this tank. *rajaaˀan farriġ hat-tanki.* **2.** *xila (i ˀixlaaˀ).* The hall emptied in five minutes. *l-qaaɛa xilat ib-xamis daqaayiq.* **3.** *ṣabb (u ṣabb).* This river empties into the ocean. *han-nahar yṣubb bil-muʒiiṭ.*
to **enable** - *makkan (i tmikkin) t-, ˀahhal (i tˀihhil) t-.* This experience will enable you to get a good position. *hat-tajruba la-budd itmakkinak imnil-ʒuṣuul ɛala waḍiifa zeena.*
to **enact** - *sann (i sann) n-.* This law was enacted in 1920. *hal-qaanuun insann ib-sanat ˀalf w-tisiɛmiyya w-ɛišriin.*
to **enclose** - *rifaq (i ˀirfaaq) n-.* I've enclosed herewith the newspaper clippings you wanted. *rfaqit ṭayyan quṣaaṣaat ij-jaraayid ir-riditha.* -- The sum due you is enclosed herewith. *l-mablaġ il-maṭluub bii ˀilak murfaq ṭayyan.*
to **encourage** - *šajjaɛ (i tašjiiɛ) t-.* He encouraged me to stick it out. *huwwa šajjaɛni ɛal-ˀiṣraar ɛaleeha.*
encouragement - *tašjiiɛ.*
to **encroach** - *ɛtida (i ɛtidaaˀ), tjaawaz (a tajaawuz).* That would be encroaching upon his rights. *ḍaak ykuun iɛtidaaˀ ɛala ʒuquuqa.*
encyclopedia - *daaˀirat* (pl. *dawaaˀir*) *maɛaarif, ˀinsikloopiidya* pl. *-aat, mawsuuɛa* pl. *-aat.*
end - **1.** *ˀaaxir* pl. *ˀawaaxir, nihaaya* pl. *-aat.* I'll pay you the balance at the end of the month. *raʒ-adfaɛ-lak il-baaqi b-ˀaaxir iš-šahar.* **2.** *nihaaya* pl. *-aat.* Tie the two ends together. *ˀurbuṭ in-nihaayteen suwa.* -- That is the end of the program. *haaḍi nihaayat il-barnaamij.* **3.** *ġaaya*

pl. *-aat.* He believes that the end justifies the means. *yiεtiqid ʔinna l-ġaaya tbarrir il-waaṣṭa.* **4.** *zadd.* Can't you put an end to these squabbles? *ma-tigdar itzuṭṭ zadd il-han-nizaaε?*
**He scolded a bit and that was the end of it. *rabrab išwayya w-intiha l-mawḍuuε.*
**Except for a few loose ends, everything is done. *kullši kimal ma-εada baεḍ il-ʔašyaaʔ il-basiiṭa.*
to end - 1. *ʔanha (i ʔinhaaʔ) n-, xallaṣ (i txilliṣ) t-.* He ended his speech with a quotation from the Koran. *ʔanha muzaaḍarta b-ʔaaya qurʔaaniyya.* **2.** *xilaṣ (a xalaaṣ), ntiha (i ntihaaʔ).* Won't this back-biting ever end? *hal-qaal w-qiil ma-raz-yixlaṣ ʔabad?*
endeavor - *masεa* pl. *masaaεi.* He did not succeed in his endeavor. *ma-nijaz ib-masεaa.*
to **endorse - 1.** *jayyar (i tajyiir) t-, ḍahhar (i taḍhiir) t-.* Endorse the check, please. *jayyir ič-čakk rajaaʔan.* **2.** *ʔayyad (i taʔyiid) t-.* He endorsed my program. *ʔayyad barnaamiji.*
to **endure** - *tzammal (a tazammul).* She endured the grief quietly. *tzammlat il-faajiεa b-kull huduuʔ.*
enema - *zuqna* pl. *zuqan.*
enemy - *εadu* pl. *ʔaεdaaʔ.*
energy - 1. *zayawiyya, našaaṭ.* He's full of energy. *haaḏa malyaan zayawiyya* or *kulla zayawiyya.* **2.** *ṭaaqa.* I read a book on atomic energy. *qreet iktaab εan iṭ-ṭaaqa ḏ-ḏarriyya.*
to **enforce** - *ṭabbaq (u taṭbiiq) t-, naffaḏ (i tanfiiḏ) t-.* This law has never been strictly enforced. *hal-qaanuun ʔabadan ma-ṭṭabbaq biḍ-ḍabuṭ.*
to **engage - 1.** *staxdam (i stixdaam).* We've just engaged a new maid. *hastawwna staxdamna xaadma jdiida.* **2.** *tεaaqad (a taεaaqud) wiyya.* We engaged him for two concerts. *tεaaqadna wiyyaa b-zafilteen mawsiiqiyya.* **3.** *tdaxxal (a tadaxxul).* I don't engage in politics. *ʔaani ma-atdaxxal bis-siyaasa.* **4.** *ṣaadam (i muṣaadama).* They engaged the enemy on the hill. *ṣaadmaw il-ʔaεdaaʔ εat-tall.*
engaged - 1. *maxṭuub.* How long have they been engaged? *šgadd ṣaar-ilhum maxṭuubiin?* **2.** *mašġuul.* I'm presently engaged in research. *ʔaani hassa mašġuul ib-baziθ.*
engagement - 1. *mawεid* pl. *mawaaεid.* I have an engagement this evening. *εindi mawεid hal-masa.* **2.** *xuṭba* pl. *-aat, xuṭab.* They announced her engagement. *ʔaεlinaw xuṭbatha.*
engine - *makiina* pl. *makaayin.* You left the engine running. *ʔinta xalleet il-makiina tištuġul.* — This train has two engines. *hal-qiṭaar bii makiinteen.* — The factory is equipped with electric machines. *l-maεmal imjahhaz bil-makaayin il-kahrabaaʔiyya.*
engineer - 1. *muhandis* pl. *-iin.* I've asked the engineer to draw a new set of plans. *ṭlabit imnil-muhandis ʔan yirsim majmuuεa jdiida mnil-muxaṭṭaṭaat.* **2.** *saayiq* (pl. *suwwaaq*) *qiṭaar.* The engineer stopped the train. *saayiq il-qiṭaar waggaf il-qiṭaar.* **3.** *makiinači* pl. *-iin, -iyya.* The engineer says there's something wrong with the boiler. *l-makiinači gaal ʔaku fadd εaṭub bil-marjal.*
to engineer - *naḍḍam (u tanḍiim, tnuḍḍum) t-.* Who engineered this plan? *minu naḍḍam hal-xuṭṭa?*
engineering - *handasa.*
English - 1. *ʔingiliizi.* He speaks English very well. *yizči ʔingiliizi kulliš zeen.* **2.** *ʔingiliizi*.* That's an old English custom. *haaḏi εaada ʔingiliiziyya qadiima.* — **3.** *ʔingiliizi* pl. *ʔingiliiz.* The English fight well. *l-ʔingliiz yzaarbuun zeen.*
to **engrave - 1.** *zufar (u zafur) n-.* My name is engraved on my watch. *ʔismi mazfuur εala saaεti.* **2.** *niqaš (u naquš) n-.* What is this design engraved on the sword? *šinu han-naqaš manquuš εala s-seef?*
to **enjoy - 1.** *tmattaε (a tamattuε) b-.* He's enjoying his life. *huwwa mitmattiε ib-zayaata.* -- He's enjoying excellent health. *yitmattaε ib-ṣizza mumtaaza.*
to enjoy oneself - *twannas (a tawannus).* Did you enjoy yourself at the dance? *twannasit bir-rigiṣ?*
enjoyment - *tamattuε, laḏḏa.*
to **enlarge - 1.** *kabbar (u tkubbur) t-.* Do you enlarge pictures? *ʔinta tkabbur ṣuwar?* **2.** *wassaε (i tawsiiε, twissiε) t-, kabbar (u tkubbur) t-.* We're going to have to enlarge this room. *laazim inwassiε hal-ġurfa.*
enlargement - *ṣuura* (pl. *ṣuwar*) *mukabbara.* How many enlargements do you want? *čam ṣuura mukabbara triid?*
to **enlist** - *ṭṭawwaε (taṭawwuε).* He enlisted in the navy two days ago. *ṭṭawwaε ib-silk il-bazriyya gabuḷ yoomeen.*
enormous - *ḍaxim, haaʔil, jasiim, εaḍiim.* That's an enormous project. *haaḏa fadd mašruuε ḍaxim.* — He spent enormous amounts of money on this building. *difaε mabaaliġ εaḍiima b-hal-binaaya.*
enormously - *b-daraja εaḍiima, b-ḍaxaama, b-ṣuura kabiira.* The need for raw materials has grown enormously. *l-zaaja lil-mawaadd il-ʔawwaliyya zdaadat ib-daraja εaḍiima.*
enough - *kifaaya, kaafi.* Have you had enough to eat? *ʔakalit kifaaya?* -- Do you have enough money? *εindak ifluus kaafya?*
**Would you be kind enough to open the window? *tismaz tiftaz iš-šabbaač?*
to be enough - *kaffa (i tkiffi).* Will that be enough? *haaḏa ykaffi?*
to have enough - *šibaε (a šibiε), tkaffa (a tkiffi).* I've had enough of that talk. *šbaεit min hal-zači.*
to **enroll - 1.** *sajjal (i tasjiil) t-.* I'm going to enroll my son in first grade. *ʔaani raz-asajjil ibni biṣ-ṣaff il-ʔawwal.* **2.** *tsajjal (a tasajjul).* He's going to enroll in night school. *raz-yitsajjal ib-madrasa masaaʔiyya.*
enslavement - *stiεbaad.*
to **enter - 1.** *xašš (u xašš), dixal (u duxuul), ṭabb (u ṭabb).* Everyone rose when the guest of honor entered. *kull waazid gaam min xašš ḍeef iš-šaraf.* **2.** *daxxal (i tdixxil) t-.* Enter these names in the list. *daxxil hal-ʔasmaaʔ bil-qaaʔima.*
enterprise - *mašruuε* pl. *mašaariiε.* The enterprise was successful. *l-mašruuε nijaz.*
enterprising - *muntij.* He's the most enterprising one in the company. *huwwa ʔakθar waazid muntij biš-šarika.*
to **entertain** - *wannas (i twunnis) t-.* He entertained the guests with his amusing stories. *wannas il-xiṭṭaar ib-quṣaṣa j-jaḏḏaaba.*
**They entertain a great deal. *humma ysawwuun ihwaaya εazaayim.*
entertainment - 1. *tasliya.* Who's going to provide the program of entertainment? *minu raz-yqaddim manhaj it-tasliya?* **2.** *lahu.* What do you do for entertainment around here? *šaku wasaaʔil lahu b-hal-manṭiqa?*
enthusiasm - *zamaas.* He didn't show any enthusiasm. *ma-raawa ʔay zamaas.*
enthusiastic - *mitzammis.* I'm quite enthusiastic about it. *ʔaani kulliš mitzammis il-haay.*
entire - *kull, kaamil, jamiiε.* The entire amount has to be paid in cash. *kull il-mablaġ laazim yindifiε naqdan.* —
**The entire evening was wasted. *ḍaaεat εalayya l-leela b-kaamilha.*
entirely - 1. *tamaaman.* You're entirely right. *ʔinta muziqq tamaaman.* **2.** *kulliyyan, bil-kulliyya.* These two things are entirely different. *haš-šiyyeen mixtalfiin kulliyyan.*
entrance - *madxal* pl. *madaaxil, baab* pl. *bwaab.*
entry - 1. *tanziil* pl. *-aat.* The last entry in the account was five dinars. *ʔaaxir tanziil bil-izsaab čaan xams idnaaniir.* **2.** *duxuul.* Entry into this room is not allowed. *d-duxuul il-hal-ġurfa mamnuuε.*
envelope - *ḍaruf* pl. *ḍruuf.* I need an envelope for the letter. *ʔaztaaj ḍaruf lil-maktuub.*
environment - *biiʔa* pl. *-aat, muziiṭ* pl. *-aat.* He was raised in a poor environment. *trabba b-biiʔa muu zeena.*
envoy - *manduub* pl. *-iin, mumaθθil dawli* pl. *mumaθθiliin dawliyyiin.*
envy - 1. *ġiira, zasad.* He was green with envy. *da-ymuut min ġiirta.* **2.** *mazsuud.* You'll be the envy of all your friends. *raz-itkuun mazsuud min kull ʔaṣdiqaaʔak.*
to envy - *zisad (i zasad) n-, ġaar (a ġiira) n- min.* I envy you! *ʔaani ʔazisdak!*
epidemic - *wabaaʔ* pl. *ʔawbiʔa.* An epidemic has broken out among the cattle. *fadd wabaaʔ intišar been il-maašiya.*
epilepsy - *ṣaraε.*
epoch - *door* pl. *ʔadwaar.*
epsom salts - *milz ifringi.*
equal - *mitsaawi.* Cut this bread into three equal parts. *guṣṣ haṣ-ṣammuuna ʔila tlaθ ʔaqsaam mitsaawiya.* **2.** *kafuʔ* pl. *ʔakfaaʔ.* I don't think I'm equal to that job. *ma-aεtiqid ʔaani kafuʔ il-hal-εamal.*
to equal - 1. *εaadal (i muεaadala), tεaadal*

(a taɛaadul) wiyya. It will be hard to equal him. mniṣ-ṣuɛuuba titɛaadal wiyyaa. 2. saawa (i musaawaa). Five plus five equals ten. xamsa zaaʔidan xamsa ysaawi ɛašara.
equality – musaawaat. I'm a believer in equality among men. ʔaani muʔmin bil-musaawaat been in-naas.
equally – 1. bit-tasaawi. The two books are equally important. l-iktaabeen muhimma bit-tasaawi. 2. b-gadd. I liked his first play equally well. zabbeet tamθiiliita l-ʔuula b-gadd haay.
equation – muɛaadala pl. -aat.
equator – xaṭṭ (pl. xṭuuṭ) istiwaaʔ.
equilibrium – tawaazun, muwaazana.
to **equip** – jahhaz (i tajhiiz) t-, hayyaʔ (i tahyiʔa) t-. Our planes are equipped with the latest instruments. ṭayyaaraatna mujahhaza b-ʔazdaθ il-wasaaʔil.
equipment – 1. ʔadawaat. They make welding equipment. ysawwuun ʔadawaat il-liziim. 2. lawaazim, ġaraaḍ. He put the hunting equipment in the trunk of the car. xalla lawaazim iṣ-ṣeed ib-ṣanduug is-sayyaara.
equivalent – muɛaadil, musaawi, mukaafiʔ.
era – ɛaṣir pl. ɛuṣuur.
to **erase** – misaz (a masiz) n-, miza (i mazi) n-. He erased the signature. misaz il-ʔimḍaaʔ. -- Will you please erase the board? ʔarjuuk ʔimsaz is-sabbuura?
eraser – 1. missaaza pl. -aat, mazzaaya pl. -aat. I bought two pencils and an eraser. štireet qalameen w-missaaza. 2. missaaza pl. -aat. We need some chalk and an eraser. niztaaj išwayya tabaašiir w-fadd missaaza.
to **erect** – bina (i binaaʔ) n-. Who erected this building? minu bina hal-ibnaaya?
erosion – taʔaakul.
to **err** – ġilaṭ (a ġalaaṭ).
errand – šaġla pl. -aat. I have a few errands I want to do. ɛindi čam šaġla ʔariid asawwiiha.
erroneous – maġluuṭ. The information he gave us was erroneous. l-maɛluumaat lli nṭaana-yyaaha čaanat maġluuṭa.
error – ġalṭa pl. -aat, ʔaġlaaṭ. I made four errors on the exam. ġlaṭit ʔarbaɛ ġalṭaat bil-imtizaan.
escape – 1. huruub, haziima pl. hazaayim. The prisoners' escape was cleverly planned. huruub il-imsaajiin čaan imdabbar ib-mahaara. 2. taxalluṣ. We had a narrow escape. txalluṣna čaan ib-ʔiɛjuuba.
to escape – 1. hirab (a huruub), nhizam (i nhizaam). Two prisoners have escaped from the penitentiary. masjuuneen inhizmaw imnis-sijin. 2. raaz (u rawaaz) min baal. Her face is familiar but her name escapes me. wujihha muu ġariib laakin ʔisimha raaz min baali. 3. xilaṣ (a xalaaṣ) min, faat (u foot). Nothing escapes her. ma-aku fadd šii yixlaṣ minha or ma-yfuutha šii. 4. txallaṣ (a taxalluṣ) min, xallaṣ (i txilliṣ) min. That's the third time he's escaped punishment. haay il-marra θ-θaalθa xallaṣ biiha mnil-ɛiqaab.
especially – la-siyyama, b-ṣuura xaaṣṣa, xuṣuuṣan. She's been trying especially hard lately. da-tzaawil jahidha la-siyyama bil-mudda l-ʔaxiira. -- She's especially interested in sports. hiyya mihtamma bir-riyaaḍa b-ṣuura xaaṣṣa.
espionage – tajassus, jaasuusiyya.
essay – maqaala pl. -aat, ʔinšaaʔ pl. -aat.
essence – 1. jawhar pl. jawaahir. What was the essence of his lecture? šinu čaan jawhar zadiiθa? 2. ɛaṭir pl. ɛuṭuur, riiza pl. riiz. This contains essence of roses. haay tiztiwi ɛaṭir il-warid.
essential – ʔasaasi*, ḍaruuri*, jawhari*. Fresh vegetables are essential to good health. l-xuḍrawaat iṭ-ṭariyya šii ʔasaasi liṣ-ṣizza z-zeena.
essentials – ʔusus. You can learn the essentials in an hour. tigdar titɛallam il-ʔusus ib-saaɛa wizda.
to **establish** – 1. ʔassas (i taʔsiis) t-, ʔanšaʔ (i ʔinšaaʔ) n-. This firm was established in 1905. haš-šarika tʔassisat ib-sana ʔalf w-tisiɛmiyya w-xamsa. 2. θibat (i θabaat) n-. This is an established rule. haay qaaɛida θaabta. 3. qarrar (i taqriir) t-. Contrary to regulations established in the law. xilaafan lit-taɛliimaat il-muqarrara bil-qaanuun. 4. ḍirab (u ḍarub). He established a new record. ḍirab raqam qiyaasi jidiid.
establishment – muʔassasa pl. -aat, munšiʔa pl. -aat.
estate – muluk pl. ʔamlaak. His entire estate went to his eldest son. kull mulka raaz il-ʔibna č-čibiir.
real estate – ɛiqaar pl. -aat.
esteem – ztiraam.
estimate – 1. taqdiir pl. -aat. My estimate was absolutely accurate. taqdiiri čaan maḍbuuṭ tamaaman. 2. siɛir taqdiiri pl. ʔasɛaar taqdiiriyya. The painter made us an estimate. ṣ-ṣabbaaġ inṭaana fadd siɛir taqdiiri.
to estimate – qaddar (i taqdiir) t-, xamman (i taxmiin) t-. The flood damage was estimated at a million dinars. ḍarar il-fayaḍaan itqaddar ib-milyoon diinaar.
et cetera – ʔila ʔaaxirihi.
eternal – ʔazali*, ʔabadi*, xaalid. The Imam spoke on eternal life. l-ʔimaam ziča ɛan il-zayaat il-ʔabadiyya.
ether – ʔaθiir.
Ethiopia – l-zabaša.
Ethiopian – 1. zabaši pl. -iyyiin, ʔazbaaš. Four Ethiopians visited our town today. ʔarbaɛ ʔazbaaš zaaraw madiinatna l-yoom. 2. zabaši*. I'd like to learn the Ethiopian language. yiɛjibni ʔatɛallam il-luġa l-zabašiyya.
etiquette – ʔuṣuul, ʔadaab.
Euphrates – l-furaat.
Europe – ʔooruppa.
European – ʔooruppi* pl. -iyyiin.
to **evacuate** – ʔaxla (i ʔixlaaʔ) n-. We have to evacuate the town or else we'll be killed. laazim nixli l-madiina w-ʔilla ninkitil.
evacuation – ʔixlaaʔ.
to **evade** – tharrab (a taharrub), tmallaṣ (a tamalluṣ). She evaded the question. tharrbat imnis-suʔaal.
to **evaluate** – ɛaadal (i muɛaadala). The college evaluated my diploma and accepted me. l-kulliyya ɛaadlat šihaadti w-qiblatni.
to **evaporate** – tbaxxar (a tabaxxur), ṭaar (i ṭeeraan). The alcohol has all evaporated. l-kuzuul kulla tbaxxar.
even – 1. zawji*. Two, four, and six are even numbers. θneen w-arbaɛa w-sitta ʔarqaam zawjiyya. 2. haadiʔ. He has an even disposition. ɛinda ṭabuɛ haadiʔ. 3. ɛadil. I have an even dozen left. buqa ɛindi darzan ɛadil. 4. zatta. Even a layman can understand that. zatta š-šaxṣ il-mu-muxtaṣṣ yigdar yiftihimha l-haay. -- Not even he knows the truth. zatta huwwa ma-yuɛruf il-zaqiiqa. -- That's even better. haaḍi zatta baɛad ʔazsan.
even now – zatta baɛad hassa. Even now I can't convince him. zatta baɛad hassa ma-agdar aqinɛa.
even so – maɛa haaḍa. Even so I can't agree with you. maɛa haaḍa ʔaani ma-attifiq wiyyaak.
even though – walaw. Even though he succeeds in everything, he's not satisfied. walaw yinjaz ib-kullši huwwa ma-raaḍi.
not even – zatta ma-. I couldn't even see him. ʔaani zatta ma-gdart ašuufa.
to be even – twaafa (a tawaafi), tpaawak (a tapaawuk). He took his money from me and we were even. ʔaxaḍ ifluusa minni w-twaafeena.
to get even – tpaawak (a tapaawuk), ʔaxaḍ (u) zeel~. Just you wait! I'll get even with you! ʔuṣbur-li šwayya! ʔatpaawuk wiyyaak! or ʔusbur-li šwayya! raz-aaxuḍ zeeli minnak!
to even up – ɛaadal (i muɛaadala). Your team is stronger than ours. Let's even them up before we play. firqatkum ʔaqwa min firqatna. xalli nɛaadilhum gabul-ma nilɛab.
evening – masaaʔ, masa pl. ʔumsiyaat, leela pl. lyaali. The evenings here are cool. l-ʔumsiyaat ihna baarda. -- Good evening! masaaʔ il-xeer! -- We take a walk every evening. nitmašša kull leela.
evenly – bit-tasaawi, bit-taɛaadul. The paint isn't spread evenly. ṣ-ṣubuġ ma-mitwazziɛ bit-tasaawi. -- Divide the apples evenly among you. qismu t-tiffaaz beenaatkum bit-tasaawi.
event – 1. zadaθ pl. ʔazdaaθ, zaadiθa pl. zawaadiθ. It was the most important event of the year. čaanat ʔahamm zadaθ bis-sana. 2. zaal pl. ʔazwaal. I'll be there in any event. raz-akuun ihnaak ɛala ʔay zaal. 3. zaala pl. -aat. In the event of an accident, call the police. b-zaalat wuquuɛ zaadiθa, ʔixbir iš-šurṭa.
eventually – ʔaxiiran, bil-ʔaxiir.
ever – ʔabad, ʔabadan (with negative). Haven't you ever been in the United States? ʔinta ʔabad ma-raayiz lil-wilaayaat il-muttazida? -- Don't ever do this again. la-tsawwi haaḍa marra θaaniya ʔabadan.
**Who ever heard of such a thing! minu saamiɛ ib-hiiči šii!
ever since – min, min wakit. Ever since the

accident I've had pains in my leg. *min wakt il-zaadiθ buqa Eindi ?alam ib-rijli.* --

hardly ever - *naadiran, mnin-naadir.* I hardly ever have a headache. *naadiran yoojaEni raasi.*

every - *kull.* He comes here every week. *huwwa yiji hnaa kull isbuuE.* -- Give every child one. *?inṭi wizda l-kull ṭifil.* -- It rains every time we want to go out. *kull marra nriid niṭlaE tumṭur id-dinya.*

every now and then - *been kull mudda w-mudda.* He takes a drink every now and then. *yaaxuδ-la fadd peek been kull mudda w-mudda.*

every other - *been- w-, kull -een.* They have meat every other day. *yaakluun lazam been yoom w-yoom* or *yaakluun lazam kull yoomeen.*

everybody - *kull waazid, kull in-naas.* Everybody has to do his duty. *kull waazid laazim yquum ib-waajba.* -- I told it to everybody. *gilitha l-kull in-naas.*

everybody else - *kull il-?aaxariin, kull il-baaqiin.* I have no objection if everybody else is agreed. *?aani ma-Eindi maaniE ?iδa kull il-?aaxariin imwaafqiin.*

everything - *kullši.* He's mixed up everything. *xarbaṭ kullši.*

everywhere - *b-kull makaan.* I've looked everywhere for that book. *dawwarit Eala δaak il-iktaab ib-kull makaan.*

to **evict** - *ṭallaE (i taṭliiE) t-.* The landlord evicted them from the house. *ṣaazb il-muluk ṭallaEhum imnil-beet.*

evidence - *bayyna* pl. *-aat, burhaan* pl. *baraahiin, zijja* pl. *zijaj, daliil* pl. *?adilla.* He was convicted on the basis of false evidence. *nzikam istinaadan Eala bayynaat kaaδiba.*

evident - *ẓaahir, waaẓiz.* It was evident that she was sick. *čaan waaẓiz hiyya mariiẓa.*

evil - **1.** *šarr* pl. *šuruur, ?ašraar.* He chose the lesser of the two evils. *xtaar ?ahwan iš-šarreen.* **2.** *sayyi?.* He has evil intention. *Einda qaṣid sayyi?.*

evolution - *taṭawwur, rtiqaa?.*

ewe - *naEja* pl. *-aat.*

exact - *ṭabq il-?aṣil, tamaam.* Is this an exact copy? *haaδi nusxa ṭabq il-?aṣil?*

**Write down the exact amount. *?iktib il-mablaġ biẓ-ẓabuṭ.*

exactly - *tamaaman, biẓ-ẓabuṭ, maẓbuuṭ.* That is exactly the same. *haaδi miθilha biẓ-ẓabuṭ.* -- That wasn't exactly nice of you. *haδiič čaanat muu zilwa tamaaman minnak.*

to **exaggerate** - *baalaġ (i mubaalaġa) t-, hawwal (i tahwiil) t-, ẓaxxam (u taẓxiim) t-, ġaala (i muġaalaat) t-.* You're exaggerating as usual. *?inta da-tbaaliġ zasb il-?uṣuul.*

exaggeration - *tahwiil, mubaalaġa, muġaalaat, taẓxiim.* There's no need for exaggeration. *ma-aku zaaja l-hat-tahwiil.*

exam - *mtizaan* pl. *-aat.*

examination - **1.** *mtizaan* pl. *-aat.* The examination was easy. *l-imtizaan čaan sahil.* **2.** *fazis* pl. *fuzuuṣ.* What did the examination show? *š-ṭilaE bil-faziṣ?* **3.** *stijwaab* pl. *-aat.* The examination of the witnesses lasted two hours. *stijwaab iš-šuhuud ṭawwal saaEteen.*

to **examine** - **1.** *fuzaṣ (a faziṣ) n-.* The doctor examined me thoroughly. *ṭ-ṭabiib fuzaṣni faziṣ daqiiq.* **2.** *stajwab (i stijwaab).* The witnesses haven't been examined yet. *li-hassa baEad ma-stajwibaw iš-šuhuud.* **3.** *daqqaq (i tadqiiq).* I'm here to examine the books. *?aani hnaa da-adaqqiq id-dafaatir.* **4.** *mtizan (i mtizaan), xtibar (i xtibaar).* He examined me in geography first. *mtizanni bij-juġraafiya bil-?awwal.*

example - **1.** *maθal* pl. *?amθaal.* Give me an example. *nṭiini maθal.* **2.** *qudwa* pl. *-aat, miθaal* pl. *?amθaal.* You should take him as an example in studying. *laazim tittaxδa qudwa bid-diraasa.* **3.** *Eibra* pl. *Eibar, miθaal* pl. *?amθaal.* The government punished him so he'd be an example to others. *l-zukuuma Eaaqbata zatta ykuun Eibra l-ġeera.*

for example - *maθalan, Eala sabiil il-miθaal, bil-maθal.* Let's take Russia, for example ... *xalli naaxuδ ruusya maθalan ...*

excavation - **1.** *zafur.* When will the excavation for the new houses begin? *šwakit raz-yibdi zafr il-?asaasaat lil-ibyuut ij-jidiida?* **2.** *zafriyya* pl. *-aat, tanqiib* pl. *-aat.* Excavations in Iraq uncovered many relics of the past. *l-zafriyyaat bil-Eiraaq kišfat Ean muxallafaat ?aθariyya kaθiira Ean il-maaẓi.*

to **exceed** - **1.** *zaad (i ziyaada) Eala, Ean.* The country's imports exceed the exports. *l-waaridaat bil-balad da-tziid Ean iṣ-ṣaadiraat.* **2.** *tjaawaz (a tajaawuz).* They caught him exceeding the speed limit. *lizmoo mitjaawaz il-zadd il-?aqṣa lis-surEa.* **3.** *faaq (u fooq), zaad (i ziyaada) Eala.* The enemy's strength exceeded ours. *quwwat il-Eadu faaqat quwwatna.*

exceedingly - *kulliš.* She's exceedingly beautiful. *hiyya zilwa kulliš.*

to **excel** - **1.** *faaq (u fawq) n-, tfawwaq (a tafawwuq) Eala.* He excelled them all. *faaqhum kullhum.* **2.** *biraE (a baraaEa) b-, biraz (i buruuz) b-.* He excelled in sports. *biraE bir-riyaaẓa.*

excellency - *maEaali.* I'd like to present my brother to your excellency. *?azibb aqaddim il-maEaaliikum ?axuuya.*

excellent - *mumtaaz, baariE, falla.* He's an excellent tennis player. *huwwa laaEib tanis mumtaaz.*

except - *ma-Eada, ?illa, ġeer, b-istiθnaa?.* Everyone believed it except him. *l-kull iEtiqdaw biiha ma-Eadaa.* -- I like the book except for one chapter. *?azibb il-iktaab b-istiθnaa? faṣil waazid.*

exception - *stiθnaa?* pl. *-aat.* We make no exceptions. *ma-Eidna stiθnaa?aat* or *ma-nistaθni ?azzad.*

excerpt - *maqṭaE* pl. *maqaaṭiE.* He read me an excerpt from the new book. *qiraa-li maqṭaE imnil-iktaab il-ijdiid.*

excess - *zaayid.* Pour off the excess fat. *diir id-dihin iz-zaayid.*

to excess - *b-?ifraaṭ.* I drink sometimes, but not to excess. *?aani ?azyaanan ašrab, laakin muu b-?ifraaṭ.*

excessive - *faadiz, baaziẓ.* Their charges are excessive. *?ujuurhum faadza.* -- They've been making excessive profits. *čaanaw da-yzaqqiquun ?arbaaz faadiza.*

exchange - **1.** *tabaadul.* We've arranged for an exchange of prisoners. *tdabbarna mas?alat tabaadul il-?asra.* **2.** *baddaala* pl. *-aat.* The rebels have captured the telephone exchange. *θ-θuwwaar stawlaw Eala baddaalat it-talafoon.*

rate of exchange - *siEir il-Eumla.* What's the rate of exchange today? *šinu siEir il-Eumla l-yoom?*

stock exchange - *boorṣa.* Where's the stock exchange? *ween il-boorṣa?*

to exchange - **1.** *baddal (i tabdiil) t-.* I want to exchange this book for another one. *?ariid abaddil hal-iktaab wiyya waazid laax.* **2.** *tbaadal (a tabaadul).* The ministers met to exchange views. *l-wuzaraa? ijtimEaw yitbaadal wujhaat in-naẓar.*

to **excite** - **1.** *hayyaj (i tahyiij) t-.* The way she walks excites me. *ṭariiqat mašiiha thayyijni.* **2.** *zammas (i zamaas) t-.* His speech excited the people. *xiṭaaba zammas in-naas.*

to get excited - **1.** *zimaq (a zamaaqa), ṣaar (i) Eaṣabi, haaj (i hayajaan).* Don't get excited, I'll do it later on. *la-tizmaq, raz-asawwiiha baEdeen.* **2.** *thayyaj (a tahayyuj).* Don't get excited dear, we've got all night. *la-tithayyaj Eaziizi, l-leel kulla ?ilna.* **3.** *ẓṭirab (i ẓṭiraab).* He got excited when he saw the enemy. *ẓṭirab min šaaf il-Eadu.* **4.** *tzammas (a tazammus).* The crowd got excited and stormed the embassy. *j-jamaahiir itzammisat w-haajimat is-safaara.* -- I'm so excited about the elections. *?aani kulliš mitzammis bil-intixaabaat.*

exclamation mark - *Ealaamat taEajjub.*

to **exclude** - *staθna (i stiθnaa?).* Our club rules exclude women. *qawaaEid naadiina tistaθni in-niswaan.*

exclusive - **1.** *ma-Eada.* Your bill comes to 50 dinars exclusive of tax. *qaa?imtak itsawwi xamsiin diinaar ma-Eada ẓariiba.* **2.** *muṭlaq.* We have exclusive rights to this invention. *Eidna zaqq muṭlaq ib-hal-ixtiraaE.* **3.** *xaaṣṣ.* This is quite an exclusive club. *haaδa naadi kulliš xaaṣṣ.*

excuse - **1.** *Euδur* pl. *?aEδaar.* That's no excuse! *haaδa muu Euδur!* **2.** *mubarrir* pl. *-aat.* There's no excuse for this. *ma-aku mubarrir il-haay.*

to excuse - *simaz (a samiz) l-.* Excuse my broken Arabic. *?ismaz-li b-luġat il-Earabiyya l-imkassira.* **2.** *Eifa (i Eafi, ?iEfaa?) n-.* They excused him from military service. *Eifoo mnil-xidma l-Easkariyya.*

to **execute** - **1.** *Eidam (i ?iEdaam) n-.* The government executed the murderer at daybreak. *l-zukuuma Eidmat il-qaatil il-fajir.* **2.** *naffaδ (i tanfiiδ) t-.* They executed his orders promptly. *naffiδaw ?awaamra zaalan.*

execution - **1.** *?iEdaam* pl. *-aat.* When will his execution take place? *šwakit raz-yijri l-?iEdaam* *bii?* 2. *tanfiiδ.* When do you expect to put the plan into execution? *šwakit tit?ammal itzuṭṭ il-xiṭṭa mawδiɛ it-tanfiiδ?*

executive - *?idaari*, tanfiiδi*.* The executive branch has been given wide powers. *ṣ-ṣulṭa l-?idaariyya nniṭat ṣulṭaat waasɛa.*

to **exempt** - **1.** *ɛifa (i ɛafi) n-.* I've been exempted from the exam. *nɛifeet imnil-imtizaan.* **2.** *staθna (i stiθnaa?), ɛifa (i).* The government exempted army officers from paying the new tax. *l-zukuuma staθnat ḍubbaat ij-jeeš min dafɛ iδ-δaraayib ij-jidiida.*

exercise - **1.** *tamriin* pl. *tamaariin.* The tenth exercise is difficult. *t-tamriin il-ɛaašir ṣaɛub.* **2.** *riyaaḍa.* Walking is good exercise. *l-maši xooš riyaaḍa.*

to exercise - **1.** *rayyaḍ (i taryiiḍ) t-.* I exercise the horse every day. *?arayyiḍ il-izṣaan kull yoom.* **2.** *trayyaḍ (a tarayyuḍ).* You have to exercise every morning. *laazim titrayyaḍ kull yoom iṣ-ṣubuz.* **3.** *maaras (i mumaarasa) t-.* He exercised his authority to end the strike. *maaras ṣulṭaata il-?inhaa? il-?iḍraab.*

to **exert** - **1.** *jihad (i ?ijhaad, jahid).* He never exerts himself. *ma-yijhid nafsa ?abadan.* **2.** *firaḍ (u fariḍ) n-.* That group exerts considerable influence on the party's decisions. *haj-jimaaɛa tufruḍ ta?θiir kabiir ɛala qaraaraat il-zizib.*

to **exhaust** - **1.** *stanfaδ (i stinfaaδ).* I've exhausted all possibilities. *stanfaδit kull il-iztimaalaat.* **2.** *xallaṣ (i taxliiṣ) t-.* We've almost exhausted our ammunition. *ɛala wašak inxalliṣ ɛiṭaadna.* **3.** *stanzaf (i stinzaaf).* The oil reserves in this area are exhausted. *ztiyaaṭ in-nafuṭ ib-hal-manṭiqa mustanzaf.* **4.** *nihak (i ?inhaak) n-.* Traveling eight hours by train is exhausting. *safrat iθman saaɛaat bil-qiṭaar tinhik.*

exhaustion - *?iɛyaa?.* The runner dropped from exhaustion. *r-raakuuḍ wugaɛ imnil-?iɛyaa?.*

exhaust pipe - *gzooz* pl. *-aat.* The exhaust pipe is broken. *l-igzooz maksuur.*

exhibit - *maɛraḍ* pl. *maɛaariḍ.* Did you see the science exhibit? *šift il-maɛraḍ il-ɛilmi?*

to exhibit - **1.** *raawa (i muraawa?a).* His wife loves to exhibit her jewelry. *marta yiɛjibha traawi mujawharaatha.* **2.** *?aḍhar (i ?iḍhaar).* He exhibited great courage in the battle. *?aḍhar šajaaɛa faa?iqa bil-maɛraka.* **3.** *ɛiraḍ (u ɛariḍ) n-.* The Russians exhibited their new farm machinery at the fair. *r-ruus ɛirḍaw ?aalaathum iz-ziraaɛiyya ij-jidiida bil-maɛraḍ.*

exhibition - *maɛraḍ* pl. *maɛaariḍ.*

exile - *manfa* pl. *manaafi.* He is in exile. *huwwa bil-manfa.* **2.** *manfi* pl. *-iyyiin.* I met several exiles in Beirut. *ltigeet wiyya ɛiddat manfiyyiin ib-beeruut.*

to **exist** - **1.** *wujad (a wijuud) n-.* As far as I'm concerned, Israel doesn't exist. *bin-nisba ?ili, ?israa?iil ġeer mawjuuda.* **2.** *ɛaaš (i ɛeeš).* How does he manage to exist on that amount of money? *šloon yigdar yɛiiš ɛala hal-mablaġ?*

existence - **1.** *ɛiiša* pl. *-aat.* He's leading a miserable existence. *da-yɛiiš ɛiisa taɛsa.* **2.** *wujuud.* He's not even aware of my existence. *wala yidri b-wujuudi.* **3.** *baqaa?.* The professor explained the theory of the struggle for existence. *l-?ustaaδ širaz naḍariyyat iṣ-ṣiraaɛ min ?ajl il-baqaa?.*

in existence - **1.** *mawjuud.* This business has been in existence for fifty years. *haš-šaġla ṣaar-ilha mawjuuda xamsiin sana.* **2.** *bil-wujuud.* There is no such thing in existence. *ma-aku hiiči šii bil-wujuud.*

exit - *baab* (pl. *biibaan*) *ṭalɛa, maxraj* pl. *maxaarij.* I can't find the exit! *ma-agdar ?algi baab iṭ-ṭalɛa.*

to **expand** - *wassaɛ (i tawsiiɛ) t-.* They're planning to expand the communications network. *gaɛad yooδaɛuun xiṭṭa it-tawsiiɛ šabakat il-muwaaṣalaat.*

expansion - *tawassuɛ.* Expansion of trade is beneficial to the country. *tawassuɛ it-tijaara mufiid lil-balad.*

to **expect** - **1.** *twaqqaɛ (a tawaqquɛ), t?ammal (a ta?ammul).* I expect him at three o'clock. *?atwaqqaɛa saaɛa tlaaθa.* -- Does he expect a tip? *haaδa yit?ammal baxšiiš?* **2.** *ntiḍar (i ntiḍaar), t?ammal (a), twaqqaɛ (a).* You can't expect that of him. *ma-mumkin tintiḍir haaδi minna.*

expectation - *tawaqquɛ.* Contrary to my expectations, the experiment succeeded. *ḍidd tawaqquɛi, t-tajruba nijzat.*

expedition - *biɛθa* pl. *-aat.* He's a member of the archaeological expedition. *huwwa ɛuḍu bil-biɛθa l-?aθariyya.*

to **expel** - *ṭirad (u ṭarid) n-.* The boy was expelled from school. *l-walad inṭirad imnil-madrasa.*

expenditure - *maṣruuf* pl. *-aat, maṣaariif.* Government expenditures will decrease this year. *maṣruufaat il-zukuuma raz-itqill has-sana.*

expense - *maṣraf* pl. *maṣaariif, nafaqa* pl. *-aat.* I can't afford the expense. *ma-atzammal hal-maṣraf.*

at the expense of - *ɛala zsaab, ɛala nafaqa.* He made the trip at the expense of the company. *gaam bis-safra ɛala zsaab iš-šarika.*

expensive - **1.** *ġaali.* This house is very expensive. *hal-beet kulliš ġaali.* **2.** *θamiin, ġaali.* He was wearing a very expensive watch. *čaan laabis saaɛa θamiina jiddan.*

experience - **1.** *xibra.* Do you have any experience in these matters? *ɛindak ?ay xibra b-hal-?umuur?* **2.** *tajruba* pl. *tajaarub.* I had a strange experience last night. *marrat ɛalayya tajruba ġariiba l-baarza bil-leel.*

to experience - *marr (u marr) b-.* I never experienced anything like it before. *ma-marreet ib-šii miθil haaδa gabuḷ.*

experienced - **1.** *mujarrib.* He's an experienced mechanic. *huwwa mujarrib miikaaniiki.* **2.** *muzannak, mujarrib.* He's an experienced politician. *haaδa siyaasi muzannak.*

experiment - *tajruba* pl. *tajaarub.* The experiment was successful. *t-tajruba čaanat naajza.*

to experiment - **1.** *sawwa (i) tajruba.* The scientist is experimenting with rabbits. *l-ɛaalim da-ysawwi tajaarub ɛal-?araanib.* **2.** *jarrab (u tajriib) t-.* The artist experimented with a new technique. *l-fannaan jarrab ṭariiqa jdiida.*

experimental - *tajrubi*.* This medicine is still in the experimental stage. *had-duwa baɛda biṭ-ṭawr it-tajrubi.*

expert - **1.** *xabiir* pl. *xubaraa?.* The experts declared the document a forgery. *l-xubaraa? ṣarrizaw ?inna l-waθiiqa muzawwara.* **2.** *maahir, xabiir.* He's an expert salesman. *haaδa bayyaaɛ maahir.*

to **expire** - *xilṣat (tixlaṣ) muddat-, ntiha (i) mafɛuul-.* His visa expired last week. *l-viiza maalta xilṣat muddatha l-isbuuɛ il-faat* or *l-viiza maalta ntiha mafɛuulha l-isbuuɛ il-faat.*

to **explain** - *fassar (i tafsiir) t-, širaz (a šariz) n-.* I explained it to him. *fassart-ilh-iyyaa.*

explanation - *tafsiir, šariz.* His explanation wasn't very clear. *tafsiira ma-čaan kulliš waaḍiz.*

explicit - *waaḍiz, jali*.* We gave her explicit instructions. *nṭeenaaha taɛliimaat waaḍza.*

to **explode** - **1.** *nfijar (i nfijaar).* A shell exploded near our house. *fadd qumbula nfijrat yamm beetna.* **2.** *fajjar (i tafjiir) t-.* The government exploded an atomic bomb. *l-zukuuma fajjirat qumbula δarriyya.*

exploit - **1.** *ma?θara* pl. *ma?aaθir, mafxara* pl. *mafaaxir.* He never stops talking about his exploits. *ma-yiɛjaz imnil-zači ɛan-ma?aaθra.* **2.** *šeeṭana.* He doesn't talk about his exploits with women. *ma-yjiib ṭaari šeeṭanta wiyya n-niswaan.*

to exploit - *staġall (i stiġlaal).* He exploits his workers. *yistiġill ɛummaala.* -- You've just begun to exploit the country's resources. *tawwkum bideetu tistiġilluun mawaarid id-dawla.*

to **explore** - **1.** *ktišaf (i ktišaaf).* Sections of the Rub al Khali haven't been explored yet. *baɛḍ ajzaa? ir-rubɛ il-xaali baɛadha ma-muktašafa.* **2.** *bizaθ (a baziθ) n-.* We explored all the possibilities of understanding. *bizaθna jamiiɛ iztimaalaat it-tafaahum.*

explorer - *muktašif* pl. *-iin, raa?id* pl. *ruwwaad.*

explosion - *nfijaar* pl. *-aat.* The explosion was heard for miles. *l-infijaar čaan yinsimiɛ ɛala buɛd amyaal.*

export - *taṣdiir.* The government has stopped the export of wheat. *l-zukuuma waggfat tasdiir il-zunṭa.*

exports - *ṣaadiraat.* This year our exports exceeded our imports. *has-sana ṣaadiraatna zaadat ɛala stiiraadaatna.*

to export - *ṣaddar (i taṣdiir) t-.* Germany exports lenses. *?almaanya tṣaddir ɛadasaat.*

exporter - *muṣaddir* pl. *-iin.*

to **expose** - **1.** *ɛiraḍ (i ɛariḍ) n-, ɛarraḍ (i taɛriiḍ) t-.* How long did you expose the shot? *šgadd ɛiraḍt iṣ-ṣuura liḍ-ḍuwa?* -- He's constantly exposed to danger. *huwwa muɛarraḍ lil-xaṭar daa?iman.* **2.** *fuḍaz (a faḍiz) n-, šinaɛ (a šaniɛ) n-.* He was exposed as a spy. *nfuḍaz ka-jaasuus.* **3.** *kišaf (i kašif) n-, ṭallaɛ (i taṭliiɛ).* She exposed her navel before

the crowd. *kišfat ṣurratha giddaam ij-jamaahiir.*
exposure - *taʕarruḍ.* He died from exposure to the sun. *maat imnit-taʕarruḍ liš-šamis.*
express - **1.** *ʔiksiþras.* I went to Basra by the express. *riɀit lil-baṣra bil-ʔiksiþras.* **2.** *ṣariiɀ.* It was his express wish. *haaði čaanat raġubta ṣ-ṣariiɀa.* **3.** *muʕayyan.* The tool was bought for this express purpose. *hal-ʔaala nširat il-hal-ġaraḍ il-muʕayyan.*
to express - **1.** *ʕabbar (u taʕbiir) t- ʕan, ʔabda (i ʔibdaaʔ).* He expressed his opinion freely. *ʕabbar ʕan raʔya b-ɀurriyya.* **2.** *ʔaʕrab (i ʔiʕraab) ʕan.* Did he express any wish? *ma-ʔaʕrab ʕan ʔay raġba?* **3.** *bayyan (i tabyiin) t-.* He expressed his concern about the situation. *bayyan qalaqa ɀawl il-ɀaala.*
expression - **1.** *taʕbiir* pl. *-aat.* There's no better expression for it. *ma-ʔilha ʔaɀsan min hat-taʕbiir.* **2.** *malaamiɀ, taʕbiir.* I can tell by the expression on your face that you don't like it. *ʔagdar aʕruf min malaamiɀ wujjak ʔanna ma-yʕijbak.*
expressive - *muʕabbir.* She has very expressive eyes. *ʕidha ʕyuun kulliš muʕabbira.*
expressly - *ṣaraaɀatan.* The law expressly says ... *l-qaanuun ynuṣṣ ṣaraaɀatan ʕala ...*
expulsion - *ṭarid.* We threatened him with expulsion from the party. *haddadnaa biṭ-ṭarid imnil-ɀizib.*
exquisite - *raaʔiʕ.* She has exquisite features. *ʕidha malaamiɀ raaʔiʕa.*
extemporaneous - *rtijaali*, murtajal.* The minister gave an extemporaneous speech. *l-waziir ʔalqa xiṭaab irtijaali.*
to **extend** - **1.** *mtadd (a mtidaad).* The dunes extend for miles. *r-rawaabi timtadd il-buʕud ʔamyaal.* **2.** *madd (i madd) n-.* He extended a helping hand to me. *madd-li yadd il-musaaʕada.* **3.** *maddad (i tamdiid) t-.* I'd like to extend this visa. *ʔaɀibb amaddid hal-viiza.* **4.** *qaddam (i taqdiim) t-.* We'd like to extend our sincere congratulations. *nwidd ʔan inqaddim tahaaniina l-qalbiyya.*
extended - *ṭuwiil.* He remained in the hospital for an extended period. *buqa bil-mustašfa mudda ṭuwiila.*
extension - **1.** *tamdiid* pl. *-aat.* He gave me another week's extension. *nṭaani tamdiid l-muddat isbuuʕ laax.* -- The extension of the new road to Mosul will be finished next year. *tamdiid iṭ-ṭariiq ij-jidiid lil-mooṣil raɀ-yikmal is-sana j-jaaya.* **2.** *fariʕ* pl. *furuuʕ.* We need two more extensions for our telephone. *niɀtaaj farʕeen baʕad lit-talafoon maalna.*
extension cord - *waayir sayyaar* pl. *waayraat sayyaara.*
extensive - *waasiʕ.* He was given extensive powers. *nniṭa ṣulṭaat waasʕa.*
extent - **1.** *daraja, ɀadd.* To a certain extent, he's responsible for the disaster. *ʔila daraja muʕayyana, huwwa masʔuul ʕan il-kaariθa.* **2.** The extent of his influence is still not known. *mada nufuuða baʕad ma-maʕruuf.*
**He resembles his father to some extent. *yišbah ʔabuu baʕḍ iš-šabah.*
exterior - **1.** *xaariji*, barraani*.* This is an exterior view of the house. *haaða manḍar xaariji lil-beeṭ.*
to **exterminate** - *qiḍa (i qaḍaaʔ) n- ʕala, staʔṣal (i stiʔṣaal).* We hired a man to exterminate the termites. *šaġġalna rijjaal ɀatta yiqḍi ʕal-ʔarḍa.*
external - *xaariji*.* This medicine is for external use only. *had-duwa lil-istiʕmaal il-xaariji faqaṭ.*
extinct - *munqariḍ.* The dinosaur is an extinct animal. *d-daynaṣoor ɀaywaan munqariḍ.*
to **extinguish** - *ṭaffa (i taṭfiya) t-.* The fire department extinguished the fire. *daaʔirt il-ʔiṭfaaʔ ṭaffat il-ɀariiq.*
extra - **1.** *zaayid, ʔiḍaafi*.* Do you have a few extra pencils? *ʕindak čam qalam zaayid?* **2.** *jiddan.* These are extra large eggs. *hal-beeḍ ikbaar jiddan.*
extract - *xulaaṣa* pl. *-aat.* Give me a bottle of lemon extract. *nṭiini šiiša min xulaaṣt il-leemuun.*
to extract - **1.** *šilaʕ (a šaliʕ) n-.* The dentist extracted two of my teeth. *ṭabiib il-ʔasnaan šilaʕ iθneen min isnuuni.* **2.** *staxlaṣ (i stixlaaṣ).* He has a factory for extracting aluminum from its ore. *ʕinda maʕmal l-istixlaaṣ il-ʔalaminyoom min maaddta l-xaam.*
extradition - *tasliim il-mujrimiin.* We have extradition agreements with many countries. *ʕidna muʕaahadaat tasliim il-mujrimiin wiyya hwaaya duwal.*
extraordinary - **1.** *ġeer iʕtiyaadi*.* Only an extraordinary person could do that. *bass fadd šaxiṣ ġeer iʕtiyaadi yigdar ysawwi haaða.* -- The president is given extraordinary powers in time of war. *r-raʔiis yinniṭi ṣulṭaat ġeer iʕtiyaadiyya b-wakt il-ɀarub.* **2.** *foog il-ʕaada.* The cabinet will have an extraordinary session tomorrow. *l-wuzaara raɀ-tiʕqud ijtimaaʕ foog il-ʕaada baačir.* **3.** *xaariq.* That's something really extraordinary. *haaða fadd šii ṣudug xaariq.*
extravagant - *muṣrif* pl. *-iin, mubaððir* pl. *-iin.* She's very extravagant. *haay kulliš muṣrifa.*
extreme - **1.** *šadiid.* We had to resort to extreme measures. *ḍṭarreena niljaʔ ʔila ʔijraaʔaat šadiida.* **2.** *miṭṭarrif.* He is an extreme nationalist. *haaða waṭani miṭṭarrif.*
extremely - *lil-ġaaya, jiddan, hwaaya, kulliš.* This news is extremely sad. *hal-xabar muɀzin lil-ġaaya.* -- I am extremely surprised. *ʔaani mindihiš jiddan.*
eye - **1.** *ʕeen* pl. *ʕyuun.* On a clear day you can see the town from here with the naked eye. *b-yoom ṣaɀu tigdar itšuuf il-madiina minnaa bil-ʕeen il-mujarrada.* -- I've had my eye on that for a long time. *ṣaar-li mudda ṭuwiila ɀaaṭṭ ʕeeni ʕala haaða.* -- Keep your eye on the children while I'm out. *ɀuṭṭ ʕeenak ʕaj-jihhaal min aṭlaʕ.* **2.** *xurum* pl. *xruum.* The eye of this needle is very small. *xurum hal-ʔubra kulliš iṣġayyir.* **3.** *naḍar.* I've been trying to catch your eye for a half hour. *ṣaar-li nuṣṣ saaʕa da-aɀaawil ʔalfit naḍarak.* -- All are equal in the eyes of the law. *l-kull mitsaawiin ib-naḍar il-qaanuun.*

**He's lowered himself in her eyes. *wugaʕ min ʕeenha.*
to eye - *baawaʕ (i mbaawaʕa) ʕala.* He eyed the chocolate longingly. *baawaʕ ʕač-čukleet ib-šahya.*
eyebrow - *ɀaajib* pl. *ɀwaajib.* He has thick eyebrows. *ʕinda ɀwaajib θixiina.*
eyedrops - *qaṭra* pl. *-aat.* Use these eyedrops three times a day. *staʕmil hal-qaṭra θlaθ marraat bil-yoom.*
eyeglasses - *manḍara, manaaḍir* pl. *manaaḍir, ʕweenaat.* Do you wear eyeglasses? *tilbas manaaḍir?*
eyelash - *ramiš* pl. *rmuuš, hadab* pl. *ʔahdaab.* You have pretty black eyelashes. *ʕindič irmuuš sooda ɀilwa.*
eyelid - *jifin* pl. *jfuun.* She's wearing eyeshadow on her eyelids. *hiyya xaalla kuɀul ʕala jfuunha.*
eyesight - *baṣar, naḍar.* You have weak eyesight. *baṣarak ḍaʕiif.*

F

fabric - *qmaaš.* My wife bought some fabric to make a new jacket. *marti štirat iqmaaš ɀatta txayyiṭ sitra.*
face - **1.** *wujih* pl. *wjuuh.* If I'd been in your place, I'd have told him to his face. *loo b-makaanak, čaan gitt-la b-wujha.* -- She slammed the door in my face. *saddat il-baab ib-wujhi.* **2.** *ḍaahir.* On the face of it, it looks like a good proposition. *ɀasb iḍ-ḍaahir, ybayyin xooš iqtiraaɀ.*
at face value - *b-maḍaahir xaarijiyya.* She takes everything at face value. *taaxuð kullši b-maḍaahirha l-xaarijiyya.*
to face - **1.** *waajah (i muwaajaha) t-.* Let's face the facts. *xalli nwaajih il-ɀaqaayiq.* -- I can't face him. *ma-agdar awaajha.* -- Face the wall. *waajih il-ɀaayiṭ.* **2.** *ttijah (i ttijaah), waajah (i).* Our windows face south. *šbaabiična tittijih lij-jinuub.*
**The building is faced with red brick. *waajhat il-ibnaaya mabniyya b-ṭaabuug ʔaɀmar.*
facing - *gbaal, mwaajih, muqaabil.* He lives in the house facing the theater. *yiskun bil-beet li-gbaal is-siinama.*
fact - *ɀaqiiqa* pl. *ɀaqaayiq, waaqiʕ* pl. *waqaayiʕ.* That's a well-known fact. *haðiič ɀaqiiqa kulliš*

maεruufa. --
**He has a matter-of-fact way about him. *huwwa rajul waaqεi.*

factor - *εaamil* pl. *εawaamil.* That's an important factor. *haaδa fadd εaamil muhimm.*

factory - *maεmal* pl. *maεaamil, maṣnaε* pl. *maṣaaniε.* He's working in a factory. *huwwa da-yištuġul ib-maεmal.*

factual - *waaqεi**. His reports are always factual. *taqaariira daaʔiman waaqεiyya.*

to **fade** - **1.** *kišaf (i kašif).* My socks faded in the wash. *jwaariibi kišfat bil-ġasil.* -- The wallpaper is all faded. *kull ʔawraaq il-ƶyaaṭiin loonha kišaf.* **2.** *δibal (i δubuul).* These roses faded very quickly. *hal-warid δibal kulliš bil-εajal.* **3.** *tlaaša (a talaaši).* The music faded in the distance. *l-mawsiiqa tlaašat min biεiid.*

to **fail** - **1.** *fišal (a fašal).* His experiment failed. *tajrubta fišlat.* -- All our efforts failed. *kull muƶaawalaatna fišlat.* **2.** *ṣiqaṭ (u ṣuquuṭ) b-, risab (i rusuub) b-.* Five students failed in geometry. *xamis talaamiiδ ṣiqṭaw bil-handasa.* **3.** *xaan (u xiyaana) n-.* If my eyes don't fail me, that's him. *haaδa huwwa ʔiδa ma-txuunni εeeni.* **4.** *δ̣iεaf (a δ̣uεuf).* His eyesight is failing. *naδ̣ara da-yiδ̣εaf.*
**I won't fail you. *ma-axayyib δ̣annak.*
don't fail ... - *la-ykuun ma-...* Don't fail to see that picture. *la-ykuun ma-tšuuf hal-filim.*
without fail - *min kull budd, ƶatman.* I'll be there without fail. *ʔaani raƶ-akuun ihnaak min kull budd.*

failure - **1.** *fašal.* The failure of the experiment was due to carelessness. *fašal it-tajruba čaan sababa l-ʔihmaal.* **2.** *faašil.* As a businessman he was a complete failure. *ka-rajul ʔaεmaal kaan faašil tamaaman.* **3.** *sakta.* He died of heart failure. *maat ib-sakta qalbiyya.*

faint - **1.** *δ̣aεiif, xaafit.* I heard a faint noise. *smaεit ƶiss xaafit.* -- There's only a faint hope left. *ma-buqa ġeer ʔamal kulliš δ̣aεiif.* **2.** *daayix.* I feel faint. *ʔaƶiss daayix.*
**I haven't the faintest idea. *ma-εindi ʔaqall fikra.*
to faint - *ġaabat (tġiib) rooƶ-, ġima (i ʔiġmaaʔ) εala.* She fainted with fright. *ġaabat rooƶha mnil-xoof* or *ġima εaleeha mnil-xoof.*

fair - **1.** *maεraδ̣* pl. *maεaariδ̣.* Are you going to the Damasaus International Fair? *ʔinta raayiƶ il-maεraδ̣ dimašq id-dawli?* **2.** *muεtadil, munaasib.* That's a fair price. *haaδa siεir muεtadil.* **3.** *ṣaaƶi.* Tomorrow the weather will be fair and cool. *baačir ij-jaww raƶ-ykuun ṣaaƶi w-šwayya barid.* **4.** *ʔašgar* pl. *šugur.* She has blue eyes and fair hair. *εidha εyuun zurug w-šaεar ʔašgar.* **5.** *mitwaṣṣiṭ.* The work is only fair. *š-šuġuḷ mitwaṣṣiṭ.*
**That wouldn't be fair! *haδaak ma-ykuun ʔinṣaaf!*

fairy tale - *qiṣṣa* (pl. *quṣuṣ*) *xaraafiyya.*

faith - **1.** *diin* pl. *ʔadyaan.* I don't know what his faith is. *ma-aεruf diina šinu.* **2.** *θiqa.* I lost faith in him. *ʔaani fqadit θiqti bii.*

faithful - *muxliṣ.* He's faithful to his wife. *huwwa muxliṣ il-zawijta.* -- She's very faithful in her work. *hiyya kulliš muxliṣa b-šuġuḷha.*

fake - *muqallad, mzayyaf, kaaδib.* This picture is a fake. *haṣ-ṣuura muqallada.* -- He's not a real doctor, he's a fake. *huwwa muu ṭabiib ƶaqiiqi, huwwa mzayyaf.*
to fake - **1.** *zayyaf (i tziyyif, tazyiif) t-, qallad (i taqliid, tqillid) t-.* The documents are faked. *l-waθaayiq muzayyfa.* **2.** *tδ̣aahar (a taδ̣aahur) b-.* He faked poverty. *tδ̣aahar bil-fuqur.*

fall - **1.** *wagεa* pl. *-aat.* He hasn't recovered from his fall yet. *baεad li-hassa ma-ṣiƶa min wagiεta.* **2.** *suquuṭ.* What do you know about the fall of the Roman Empire? *š-tuεruf εan suquuṭ id-dawla r-roomaaniyya?* **3.** *xariif.* I'll be back next fall. *ʔaani raƶ-arjaε il-xariif ij-jaay.*
to fall - **1.** *wugaε (a wuguuε).* He fell from the ladder. *huwwa wugaε imnid-daraj.* **2.** *siqaṭ (u suquuṭ).* How did the Roman Empire fall? *šloon siqṭat id-dawla r-roomaaniyya?*
to fall apart - **1.** *tkassar (a tkissir, taksiir), tfaṣṣax (a tfuṣṣux, tafṣiix).* The chair is already falling apart. *l-kursi min hassa da-yitkassar.* **2.** *wugaε (a wuguuε), tfallaš (a tafalluš).* That old house is falling apart. *haδaak il-beet il-εatiig da-yoogaε.*
to fall asleep - *ġufa (i ġafu).* I fell asleep. *ʔaani ġufeet.*
to fall back on - *ltija (i ltijaaʔ) l-, lijaʔ (a ʔiljaaʔ) n- ʔila.* We can always fall back on what we've saved. *ʔiƶna daaʔiman nigdar niltiji l-illi waffarnaa.*
to fall behind - *tʔaxxar (a taʔaxxur).* We fell behind in the rent. *ʔiƶna tʔaxxarna εan dafε il-ʔajaar.*
to fall for - *nxidaε (i nxidaaε) b-.* I fell for his story. *nxidaεit b-iƶčaayta.*
to fall off - **1.** *wugaε (a wuguuε).* The lid fell off. *l-qabaġ wugaε.* **2.** *nizal (i nuzuul).* Receipts have been falling off lately. *l-waarid da-yinzil hal-ʔayyaam il-ʔaxiira.*
to fall through - *fišal (a fašal).* The plans for the trip fell through. *manaahij is-safra fišlat.*

fallen arches - *flaatfuut.*

false - **1.** *ġalaṭ, xaṭaʔ, kaaδib.* Is this true or false? *haaδa ṣaƶiiƶ loo ġalaṭ?* **2.** *εaari*, mustaεaar.* Many people have false teeth. *hwaaya naas εidhum isnuun εaariyya.*

familiar - **1.** *miṭṭiliε.* I'm not familiar with that. *ʔaani ma-miṭṭiliε εala haay.* **2.** *maʔluuf.* Soldiers are a familiar sight these days. *tšuuf jinuud fadd šii maʔluuf hal-ʔayyaam.* **3.** *maεruuf.* It's good to see a familiar person. *zeen waaƶid yšuuf fadd šaxiṣ maεruuf.*

family - **1.** *εaaʔila* pl. *εawaaʔil, ʔahal* pl. *ʔahaali, ʔusra* pl. *ʔusar.* Did you notify his family? *ʔaxbarit εaaʔilta?* **2.** *faṣiila* pl. *faṣaaʔil.* Is this animal of the cat family? *hal-ƶaywaan min faṣiilat il-qiṭṭ?*

famine - *majaaεa* pl. *-aat, qaƶaṭ.* Many people died during the famine. *hwaaya naas maataw ʔaθnaaʔ il-majaaεa.*

famous - *mašhuur, maεruuf.* His book made him famous. *kitaaba sawwaa mašhuur.*
to become famous - *štihar (i štihaar).* The restaurant became famous in a short time. *l-maṭεam ištihar b-mudda qaṣiira.*
to make famous - *šihar (i šuhra).* Her records made her famous. *ṣṭiwaanaatha šihratha.*

fan - **1.** *panka* pl. *-aat, mirwaƶa* pl. *maraawiƶ.* Turn on the fan. *šaġġil il-panka.* **2.** *mhaffa* pl. *mahaafiif.* Hand each one of the guests a fan. *ʔinṭi mhaffa l-kull waaƶid imnil-xuṭṭaar.*

fancy - **1.** *hawa* pl. *ʔahwaaʔ, meel* pl. *myuul, walaε.* It's just a passing fancy with her. *haaδa fadd hawa wakti jaa b-raasha.* **2.** *faxim, ʔaniiq.* She doesn't like fancy clothes. *ma-tiεjibha l-malaabis il-faxma.*
**Don't you look fancy! *ʔamma kaašix tamaaman!*

fantastic - *xayaali*, taṣawwuri**.

far - **1.** *biεiid* pl. *biεaad.* People came from far and near. *n-naas ʔijaw min giriib w-min biεiid.* -- That's not far wrong. *haaδa muu biεiid εan il-ƶaqiiqa.* -- I'm far from satisfied with your work. *ʔaani biεiid εan ir-riδ̣a εan šuġuḷak.* **2.** *li-bεiid.* Don't go far. *la-truuƶ li-bεiid.*
**This joke has gone far enough. *hal-mahzala tεaddat ƶuduudha.*
as far as - **1.** *l-ƶadd.* We walked together as far as the R.R. station. *mišeena suwa l-ƶadd maƶaṭṭat il-qiṭaar.* -- As far as it goes, your idea is good. *l-ƶadd, fikirtak zeena.* **2.** *ƶasab-ma.* As far as I can see, his papers are o.k. *ƶasab-ma ašuuf, ʔawraaqa zeena.*
by far - *b-ihwaaya.* This is the best book by far I have read this year. *hal-iktaab b-ihwaaya ʔaƶsan iktaab qareeta has-sana.*
so far - *li-hassa, l-hal-ƶadd.* So far, you've been pretty lucky. *li-hassa, ʔinta činit kulliš maƶδ̣uuδ̣.*

farce - *mahzala* pl. *mahaazil.* The elections were a farce. *l-intixaabaat čaanat mahaazil.*

fare - *ʔujra* pl. *ʔujar.* How much is the fare? *šgadd il-ʔujra?*

Far East - *š-šarq il-ʔaqṣa.*

farewell - *tawdiiε, wadaaε.* They gave him a farewell party. *sawwoo-la ƶaflat tawdiiε.*

farm - *mazraεa* pl. *mazaariε.* The village is surrounded by farms. *l-qarya muƶaaṭa bil-mazaariε.*
to farm - *ziraε (a ziraaεa) n-.* My sons and I can farm the land by ourselves. *ʔaani w-wuldi nigdar nizraε hal-gaaε waƶƶadna.*

farmer - *zarraaε* pl. *zurraaε, muzaariε* pl. *-iin.* Most of the farmers have already harvested their crops. *ʔakθar iz-zurraaε ƶiṣdaw il-ƶaaṣil maalhum.*

farming - *ziraaεa.* There isn't much farming in this region. *ma-aku ziraaεa hwaaya b-hal-manṭiqa.*

farther – *ʔabεad.* You'll have to walk a little farther. *laazim timši šwayya ʔabεad.*

to **fascinate** – *fitan (i fatin) n–, siζar (a saζir) n–, jiðab (i jaðib) n–.* The entire audience was fascinated by his story. *kull il-ζaaðriin insiζraw b-iζcaayta.*

fascinating – *jaððaab, fattaan, musζir.* This is a fascinating book. *haaða ktaab jaððaab.*

fashion – 1. *mooda* pl. *-aat.* Is that the latest fashion? *haaða ʔaaxir mooda?* 2. *ṭariiqa* pl. *ṭuruq, ṭaraaz* pl. *-aat, šikil* pl. *ʔaškaal, namaṭ* pl. *ʔanmaaṭ.* I want you to do it in this fashion. *ʔaζibbak itsawwiiha εala haṭ-ṭariiqa.* 3. *ʔisluub* pl. *ʔasaaliib.* He tries to write after the fashion of Manfaluti. *yζaawil yqallid ʔisluub il-manfaluuṭi.*

fashionable – *daarij, mooda.* It is fashionable now for Iraqi women to wear western clothing. *daarij ib-hal-wakit il-imrayya l-εiraaqiyya tilbas malaabis ġarbiyya.*

fast – 1. *ṣiyaam, ṣoom.* Ramadan is the month of the fast. *ramaðaan šahr iṣ-ṣiyaam.* 2. *bil-εajal, b-surεa, sariiε.* Don't talk so fast. *la-tiζči hal-gadd bil-εajal.* 3. *faasiq.* He travels in fast company. *huwwa yimši wiyya jamaaεa faasqiin.* 4. *θaabit.* Are those colors fast? *hal-ʔalwaan θaabta?* -- In this case you can't make hard and fast rules. *b-hal-ζaala ma-tigdar itζuṭṭ qawaaεid θaabta.* 5. *saabiq, raakið.* My watch is ten minutes fast. *saaεti saabqa εašir daqaayiq.* 6. *mustaġriq.* I was fast asleep. *ʔaani činit mustaġriq ib-noomi.*

to fast – *ṣaam (u ṣoom).* I'm fasting. *ʔaani ṣaayim.*

to **fasten** – *šadd (i šadd) n–, rubaṭ (u rubuṭ) n–.* Where can I fasten the string? *ween ʔagdar ašidd il-xeeṭ?*

fat – 1. *šaζam.* This meat has very much fat on it. *hal-laζam bii kulliš ihwaaya šaζam.* 2. *dihiin.* The meat is too fat. *l-laζam kulliš dihiin.* 3. *simiin* pl. *smaan.* He's gotten fat. *huwwa ṣaayir simiin.*

fatal – *qattaal, mumiit.* The blow was fatal. *ð̣-ð̣arba čaanat qattaala.*

fate – *qaðaaʔ w-qadar, qisma, baxat.*

father – *ʔabu, ʔab* pl. *ʔaabaaʔ, ʔabbahaat; waalid.* He has no father. *ma-εinda ʔab.* -- The father was killed, but the mother is still alive. *l-ʔabb inkital laakin il-ʔumm baεadha ṭayyba.* -- How's your father? *šloon ʔabuuk?*

father-in-law – *ʔabu z-zawj, ʔabu z-zawja.* His father-in-law is a merchant. *ʔabu zawijta taajir.*

faucet – *ζanafiyya* pl. *-aat; mzambila, mzammila* pl. *-aat.* The faucet is dripping. *l-ζanafiyya da-tnaggiṭ.*

fault – 1. *εeeb* pl. *εyuub.* We all have our faults. *kullna εidna εyuub.* 2. *ġalṭa* pl. *-aat, ʔaġlaaṭ; xaṭaʔ* pl. *-aat.* It's not his fault. *hiyya muu ġaliṭṭa.*

to find fault – *ntiqad (i ntiqaad).* You're always finding fault. *ʔinta εala ṭuul tintiqid* or ***ʔinta εala ṭuul da-ttalliε min galbak ζači.*

faulty – 1. *xaṭaʔ, muxṭiʔ, maġluuṭ.* That's faulty thinking. *haaða tafkiir xaṭaʔ.* 2. *b- εeeb.* This machine is faulty. *hal-makiina biiha εeeb.*

favor – 1. *jamiil* pl. *-aat, ʔiζsaan* pl. *-aat, faðil* pl. *ʔafðaal, maεruuf, minniyya* pl. *-aat.* I want you to do me a favor. *ʔariidak itsawwii-li fadd jamiil.* 2. *jaanib, maṣlaζa.* She spoke in my favor. *ζičat min jaanbi.*

in favor of – *b-jaanib.* I'm in favor of immediate action. *ʔaani b-jaanib fikrat il-ibtidaaʔ ζaalan.*

to favor – *faððal (i tafðiil) t–.* He favors the youngest child. *huwwa yfaððil il-ʔibn il-ʔaṣġar.*

favorable – 1. *mulaaʔim, mnaasib.* He bought the house on very favorable terms. *štira l-beet ib-šuruuṭ kulliš mulaaʔima.* 2. *mwaati.* I'm only waiting for a favorable opportunity. *ʔaani bass da-antiðir il-furṣa l-imwaatiya.*

favorite – *mufaððal, maζbuub.* This is my favorite book. *haaða ktaabi l-mufaððal.* -- This book is a great favorite with children. *hal-iktaab ihwaaya maζbuub imnil-ʔaṭfaal.*

fear – *xoof* pl. *maxaawuf.* He doesn't know the meaning of fear. *ma-yuεruf maεna l-xoof.* -- Your fears are unfounded. *maxaawfak ma-ʔilha ʔasaas.*

for fear of – *xoofan min ʔan.* He took a taxi for fear of missing the train. *ʔaxað taaksi xoofan min ʔan yfuuta l-qiṭaar.*

to fear – *xaaf (a xoof) n– min.* He doesn't fear death. *ma-yxaaf imnil-moot.*

fearful – 1. *xaayif.* Mother is so fearful about my health. *ʔummi kulliš xaayfa εala ṣiζζti.* 2. *muxiif, yxawwuf.* That's a fearful wound you have. *haaða jariζ yxawwuf εindak.*

feat – *εamal εaðiim* pl. *ʔaεmaal εaðiima.* That was quite a feat. *ðaak čaan fadd εamal εaðiim.*

feather – *riiša* pl. *-aat* coll. *riiš.* The feathers are coming out of the pillow. *r-riiš da-yiṭlaε imnil-imxadda.* -- This hat is light as a feather. *haš-šafqa xafiifa miθl ir-riiša.*

feature – *naaζiya* pl. *nawaaζi.* This plan has many good features. *hal-mašruuε bii εiddat nawaaζi zeena.* **When does the main feature begin? *šwakit yibdi il-ʔasaaṣi?*

features – *taqaaṭiiε.* Her facial features are beautiful. *taqaaṭiiε wijihha ζilwa.*

February – *šbaaṭ.*

fee – *ʔujra* pl. *ʔujuur.* The doctor's fee was thirty dinars. *ʔujuur iṭ-ṭabiib čaanat itlaaθiin diinaar.*

feeble – *ðaεiif* pl. *ðuεafaaʔ, εaajiz* pl. *-iin, εajaza.* My grandmother is very feeble. *jiddti kulliš ðaεiifa.*

feed – 1. *luguṭ.* Did you tell them to bring the feed for the chickens? *gilt-ilhum yjiibuun il-luguṭ lid-dijaaj?* 2. *εalaf.* Did you tell them to bring the feed for the cows? *gilt-ilhum yjiibuun il-εalaf lil-hawaayiš?*

to feed – *ṭaεεam (u tṭuεεum) t–, wakkal (i twikkil).* She's feeding the chickens. *hiyya da-tṭaεεum id-dijaaj.*

to be fed up with – *ðaaj (u ðooj) min, bizaε (a bazaε) min.* I'm fed up with this whole business. *ʔaani ðijit min haš-šaġla kullha.*

to **feel** – 1. *jass (i jass) n–.* The doctor felt my pulse. *ṭ-ṭabiib jass nabði.* 2. *šiεar (u šuεuur), ζass (i ζass).* He doesn't feel well. *huwwa ma-da-yišεur zeen.* -- He feels very strongly against women drinking. *kulliš yišεur ðidd širb in-niswaan lil-mašruubaat.* -- All of a sudden I felt a sharp pain in my back. *εala ġafla šiεarit ib-ʔalam ζaadd ib-ðahri.* 3. *kamkaš (i tkumkiš), tζassas (a tζissis).* He felt his way to the window. *huwwa kamkaš ṭariiqa liš-šibbaač.*

to feel about – *šiεar (u šuεuur) b–.* How do you feel about this matter? *ʔinta š-tišεur ib-hal-qaðiyya?* or ***š-raʔyak ib-hal-mawðuuε?*

to feel for – *tʔaθθar (a taʔaθθur) εala, nkisar (i nkisaar) galub- εala.* I really feel for you. *ʔaani ṣudug atʔaθθar εala ζaalak.*

to feel out – *tζassas (a taζassus) ζaalat-.* I'll feel him out and let you know. *ʔaani raζ-atζassas ζaalta w-agul-lak.*

feeling – 1. *ʔiζsaas.* I have no feeling in my right arm. *ʔiidi l-yimna ma-biiha kull ʔiζsaas.* 2. *šuεuur.* I really didn't mean to hurt your feelings. *ma-čaan qaṣdi ʔajraζ šuεuurak ʔabadan.*

fellow – *ʔinsaan* pl. *naas, šaxiṣ* pl. *ʔašxaaṣ.* He's a nice fellow. *huwwa fadd ʔinsaan ṭayyib.* -- How many fellows were there? *čam šaxiṣ čaan ʔaku hnaak?* **Poor fellow! *miskiin!*

felt – *čoox.*

female – *niθya* pl. *niθaaya.* Is this cat a male or a female? *hal-bazzuuna faζal loo niθya?*

feminine – *muʔannaθ.* This word is feminine in Arabic. *hal-kalima muʔannaθa bil-εarabi.*

fence – *siyaaj* pl. *-aat, ζaajiz* pl. *ζawaajiz.* There's a hole in the fence. *ʔaku zuruf bis-siyaaj.*

to fence – *tbaaraz (a tabaaruz), liεab (a liεib) saas.* Do you know how to fence? *tuεruf išloon titbaaraz?*

to fence in – *sayyaj (i tsiyyij) t–.* We fenced in the orchard. *sayyajna l-bistaan.*

to **ferment** – *txammar (a taxmiir).* The wine is fermenting. *š-šaraab da-yitxammar.*

fertile – *xaṣib.* The soil here is very fertile. *t-turba hnaa kulliš xaṣba.* -- He has a very fertile imagination. *εinda xayaal xaṣib.*

to **fertilize** – 1. *sammad (i tasmiid) t–.* We fertilize the garden twice a year. *nsammid il-ζadiiqa marrteen bis-sana.* 2. *laqqaζ (i talqiiζ) t–.* The female fish lays the eggs somewhere, and the male comes along and fertilizes them. *s-simča n-niθya txalli l-beeð ib-mukaan wil-faζal yiji ylaqqiζa.*

fertilizer – 1. *smaad.* I'd advise you to use a chemical fertilizer. *ʔanṣiζak tistaεmil ismaad kiimyaawi.* 2. *dimin, smaad.* Your shoes are covered with fertilizer. *qundartak kullha mġaṭṭaaya b-dimin.*

to **fester** – *tqayyaζ (a tqiyyiζ).* Is the wound still festering? *j-jariζ baεda mitqayyiζ?*

festival - *ʒtifaal* pl. *-aat, mahrajaan* pl. *-aat.* The festival was cancelled at the last minute. *il-iʒtifaal inliġa b-ʔaaxir laʒδa.*
festive - *mufriʒ, mubhij.*
festivity - *ʒtifaal* pl. *-aat.*
to **fetch** - *jaab (i jeeba) n-.* Fetch me the newspaper. *jiib-li j-jariida.*
fever - **1.** *ṣxuuna, ʒumma.* Do you have any fever? *ʕindak iṣxuuna?* **2.** *ʒaraara.* They were all in a fever of excitement. *kullhum čaanaw ib-ʒaraarat il-hayajaan.*
feverish - *mṣaxxin, maʒmuum.* He's feverish. *jisma mṣaxxin.*
**Why all the feverish activity over there? *luweeš kull hal-iδṭiraabaat ihnaak?*
feverishly - *b-ʒaraara, b-našaaṭ, b-jidd.* They're working feverishly on the new project. *da-yištaġluun ib-ʒaraara bil-mašruuʕ ij-jidiid.*
few - **1.** *šwayya, qaliil.* Few people come to see us in the summer. *šwayya naas yjuun yzuuruuna biṣ-ṣeef.* -- Good people are few and far between. *l-xooš awaadim qaliiliin w-ṣaʕub yiltiguun.* **2.** *čam.* May I ask a few questions? *mumkin ʔasʔal fadd čam suʔaal?* or *mumkin ʔasʔal šwayyat ʔasʔila?* -- We go to see him every few days. *ʔiʒna nruuʒ inšuufa kull čam yoom.*
quite a few - *ʕadad la-baʔis bii.* Quite a few people were present. *ʕadad la-baʔis bii mnin-naas čaanaw ʒaaδriin.*
fiance - *xaṭiib* pl. *xuṭbaan.* Give my regards to your fiance. *sallimii-li ʕala xaṭiibič.*
fiancee - *xaṭiiba* pl. *-aat.* My fiancee writes me every day. *xaṭiibti tiktib-li kull yoom.*
fickle - *hawaaʔi*, mitqallib.* She's a very fickle person. *hiyya fadd waʒda kulliš hawaaʔiyya.*
fiddle - *kamanja* pl. *-aat.* Quit scratching on that fiddle. *bass ʕaad itwaṣwuṣ ib-hal-kamanja.*
**He's not satisfied playing second fiddle to anyone. *huwwa ma-yirδa yquum ib-ʕamal θaanawi.*
to fiddle - *liʕab (a liʕib).* Don't keep on fiddling with the radio! *la-tδill tilʕab bir-raadyo!*
to fiddle away - *daʕfas (i tdiʕfis).* He fiddled away the whole day doing absolutely nothing. *δall ydaʕfis ṭuul il-yoom w-kullši ma-sawwa.*
field - **1.** *ʒaqil* pl. *ʒuquul.* We walked across the fields. *mišeena bil-ʒuquul.* **2.** *saaʒa* pl. *-aat.* The teams are coming onto the field. *l-firaq raʒ-tinzil lis-saaʒa.* **3.** *xtiṣaaṣ.* He's the best man in his field. *huwwa ʔaʒsan waaʒid b-ixtiṣaaṣa.*
fierce - **1.** *ʒaadd.* He have me a fierce look. *niδarni fadd naδra ʒaadda.* **2.** *šaris.* The lion is a fierce animal. *l-ʔasad ʒaywaan šaris.* **3.** *šadiid.* The heat's fierce today. *l-ʒaraara šadiida hal-yoom.*
fiery - *naari*.* He made a fiery speech. *ʔalqa xiṭaab naari.*
fifteen - *xumuṣṭaʕaš.*
fifteenth - *l-xumuṣṭaʕaš.* This is my fifteenth car. *haay sayyaarti l-xumuṣṭaʕaš.*
fifth - **1.** *xumus.* I got only a fifth of the money. *ʔaxaδit bass xums il-ifluus.* **2.** *xaamis.* This is my fifth car. *haay sayyaarti l-xaamsa.*
fifties - *xamsiinaat.* He's in his fifties. *huwwa bil-xamsiinaat.*
fiftieth - *l-xumuṣṭaʕaš.* This is my fifteenth car. day. *l-ʕiid intiha bil-yoom il-xamsiin.*
fifty - *xamsiin.* I gave him fifty dinars. *nṭeeta xamsiin diinaar.*
fifty-fifty - *xamsiin bil-miyya, nuṣṣ w-nuṣṣ.* I'll go fifty-fifty with you on the expenses. *raʒ-ašaarkak xamsiin bil-miyya mnil-maṣruufaat.*
fight - **1.** *mukaafaʒa* pl. *-aat, kifaaʒ* pl. *-aat.* He played an important part in the fight against tuberculosis. *huwwa liʕab door muhimm ib-mukaafaʒt is-sill.* **2.** *maʕraka* pl. *maʕaarik.* It was a fight to the finish. *čaanat fadd maʕraka lil-moot* or ***stamaataw bil-qitaal.* **3.** *ʕarka* pl. *-aat, maʕraka* pl. *maʕaarik, mbaaṣaṭ.* When the police arrived the fight was already over. *min wuṣlaw iš-šurṭa l-ʕarka caanat xalṣaana.* **4.** *mulaakama* pl. *-aat.* Were you at the fight last night? *činit bil-mulaakama l-baarʒa bil-leel?* **5.** *muqaawama.* He hasn't any fight left in him. *baʕad ma-buqa ʕinda ʔay muqaawama.*
**He had a flight with his wife. *tʕaarak wiyya marta.*
to fight - **1.** *ʒaarab (i muʒaaraba).* They fought bravely in World War II. *ʒaarbaw ib-šajaaʕa bil-ʒarb il-ʕaalamiyya θ-θaanya.* **2.** *qaawam (u muqaawama) t-.* You've got to fight that habit. *ʔinta laazim itqaawum hal-ʕaada.* -- I'm going to fight this suit to the end. *raʒ-aqaawum had-daʕwa lil-ʔaaxir.* **3.** *tʕaarak (a ʕarka).* Have you two been fighting again? *hamm itʕaarakta marra lux?*
**Let them fight it out by themselves. *xalliihum yinjaazuun biiha b-nafishum.*
figure - **1.** *raqam* pl. *ʔarqaam.* Add up these figures. *ʔijmaʕ hal-ʔarqaam.* **2.** *kasim* pl. *ʔaksaam, jisim* pl. *ʔajsaam.* She has a nice figure. *ʕidha kasim ʒilu.* **3.** *šikil* pl. *ʔaškaal.* Figure seven in the book shows you the parts of the locomotive engine. *š-šikil raqam sabʕa bil-iktaab yraawiik ʔajzaaʔ makiint il-qiṭaar.* **4.** *šaxṣiyya* pl. *-aat.* He's a mighty important figure in this town. *huwwa fadd šaxṣiyya kulliš muhimma b-hal-madiina.*
**Are you good at figures? *ʔinta zeen bil-ʔiʒsaab?*
to figure - *qaddar (i taqdiir) t-.* I figure it's about five-thirty. *ʔaqaddir is-saaʕa bil-xamsa w-nuṣṣ.*
**The way I figure, it will cost about twenty dinars. *b-iʒsaabi hiyya tkallif ʒawaali ʕišriin diinaar.*
to figure on - *ʒisab (i ʒsaab) n- iʒsaab.* We didn't figure on having company. *ma-ʒsabna ʒsaab yijiina xiṭṭaar.*
to figure out - **1.** *ʒall (i ʒall) n-.* Can you figure out this problem? *tigdar itʒill hal-muškila?* **2.** *ʒisab (i ʒsaab) n-.* Figure out how much it will cost. *ʔiʒsib išgadd raʒ-itkallif.* **3.** *fiham (a fahim) n-, ftiham (i fahim).* Can you figure out what he means? *tigdar tifham iš-yuqṣud?* **4.** *ʒizar (i ʒazir) n-.* I can't figure you out. *ma-agdar aʒizrak.*
to figure up - **1.** *ʒisab (i ʒsaab) n-.* Figure up how much I owe you. *ʔiʒsib išgadd ʔaani madyuun ʔilak.* -- Did you figure up the first column? *ʒsabt il-ʕamuud il-ʔawwal?* **2.** *waṣṣal (i tawṣiil).* The bill figures up to a hundred dollars. *l-qaaʔima twaṣṣil ʔila miit doolaar.*
file - **1.** *mubrad* pl. *mabaarid.* You need a finer file than that. *tiʒtaaj mubrad ʔanʕam min haaδa.* **2.** *malaffa* pl. *-aat, ʔiδbaara* pl. *-aat, faayil* pl. *-aat.* File the report in the Iraqi Oil Company file. *ʔiʒfuδ it-taqriir ib-malaffat šarikat in-nafṭ il-ʕiraaqiyya.* **3.** *miʒfaδa* pl. *maʒaafiδ, duulaab* pl. *dwaaliib.* Isn't her address in the file? *ma-mawjuud ʕinwaanha bil-miʒfaδa?* **4.** *sira* pl. *siraayaat, siraawaat; xaṭṭ* pl. *xṭuuṭ.* Line up in single file! *ṣṭaffu bis-sira waaʒid!*
on file - *maʒfuuδ.* Do we have his application on file? *ʕariiδta maʒfuuδa ʕidna?*
to file - **1.** *burad (u burid) n-.* I have to file this down first. *laazim ʔabrud haaδa ʔawwal.* **2.** *ʒufaδ (u ʒafuδ) n-.* The letters have not yet been filed. *l-makaatiib baʕad li-hassa ma-nʒufδat.* **3.** *qaddam (i taqdiim) t-.* I filed my application today. *qaddamit ṭalabi hal-yoom.*
filing cabinet - *duulaab* pl. *dwaaliib.*
fill - **I've had my fill of it. *wuṣlat il-xašmi.*
to fill - **1.** *tiras (u taris) n-, mila (i mali) n-.* Fill this bottle with water. *ʔitrus hal-buṭil maay.* -- The hall was filled to capacity. *l-qaaʕa čaanat matruusa tamaaman.* **2.** *šiġal (i ʔišġaal), mila (i).* The position has been filled. *l-waδiifa nšiġlat.* **3.** *ʔaxaδ (u ʔaxiδ) n-, tiras (u taris) n-.* The sofa just about fills half the room. *l-qanafa taqriiban taaxuδ nuṣṣ il-ġurfa.* **4.** *ʒašša (i taʒšiya) t-.* This tooth will have to be filled. *has-sinn laazim yitʒašša.* **5.** *jahhaz (i tajhiiz) t-.* The order hasn't been filled yet. *ṭ-ṭalabiyya baʕadha ma-tjahhzat.* **6.** *difan (i dafin) n-.* We filled the ditch in an hour. *difanna n-nugra b-saaʕa.*
to fill in - **1.** *difan (i dafin) n-.* The ditch has been filled in. *ndifnat in-nugra.* **2.** *mila (i mali) n-, tiras (u taris) n-.* Fill in all the blanks. *ʔimli kull il-faraaġaat.*
**Fill your name in here. *ʔiktib ʔismak ihnaa.*
**I'm just filling in here temporarily. *ʔaani bass da-aquum bil-ʕamal ib-ṣuura muwaqqata.*
to fill up - **1.** *tiras (u taris) n-, mila (i mali) n-.* He filled up the glasses. *tiras il-iglaaṣaat.* -- Fill 'er up! *ʔitrisha!* **2.** *ntiras (i), nmila (i).* The theater was slowly filling up. *s-siinama čaanat da-tintiris išwayya šwayya.*
filling - **1.** *ʒašwa.* I've lost a filling from my tooth. *wugʕat il-ʒašwa maal sinni.* **2.** *ʒašu.* The cookie filling is walnuts and sugar. *l-ʒašu maal il-ikleeča jooz w-šakar.*
film - **1.** *ṭabaqa* pl. *-aat.* A thin film of oil formed on the water. *ṭabaqa xafiifa mnid-dihin tkawwnat ʕal-*

ṃaay. 2. *filim* pl. *ʔaflaam.* I don't like funny films. *ma-aḥibb il-ʔaflaam il-hazaliyya.* -- I have to get another roll of film. *laazim ʔaštiri filim laax.*

to film - *ṣawwar (i taṣwiir) t-, ʔaxaδ (u ʔaxiδ) n- rasim.* They filmed the entire ceremony. *ṣawwraw kull il-iḥtifaal.*

filter - 1. *maṣfi* pl. *maṣaafi.* The water comes from the river and goes through the filter. *l-ṃayy yiji mnin-nahar w-yidxul bil-maṣfi.* 2. *ʔumm guṭna, mzabban.* I bought a pack of filter cigarettes. *štireet ṗaakeet jigaayir ʔumm guṭna.*

to filter - *ṣaffa (i taṣfiya) t-.* The water will have to be filtered. *l-ṃaay laazim yitṣaffa.*

final - 1. *nihaaʔi*.* How did you make out on your final exam? *šloon sawweet bil-imtiḥaan in-nihaaʔi?* 2. *qaṭεi*, nihaaʔi*.* Is this your final decision? *haaδa qaraarak in-nihaaʔi?* 3. *ʔaxiir, xitaami*.* This is the final lecture. *haaδi l-muḥaaδ̣ara l-ʔaxiira.* 4. *mtiḥaan nihaaʔi* pl. *mtiḥaanaat nihaaʔiyya.* I passed the final. *nijaḥit bil-imtiḥaan in-nihaaʔi.* 5. *sibaaq nihaaʔi* pl. *sibaaqaat nihaaʔiyya, liεib nihaaʔi* pl. *ʔalεaab nihaaʔiyya.* The finals are being played tomorrow. *s-sibaaqaat in-nihaaʔiyya raḥ-itṣiir baačir.*

finally - 1. *ʔaxiiran, bil-ʔaxiir.* He finally yielded. *ʔaxiiran ʔaδεan.* 2. *taali-ma-taali, taaliiha.* So they finally got married. *laεad taali-ma-taali tzawwjaw.*

financial - *maali*.* Our financial situation is improving. *waδ̣iεna l-maali da-yitḥassan.*

find - *ligya* pl. *-aat.* This book is a real find. *hal-iktaab ṣudug ligya.*

to find - 1. *liga (i lagi) n-.* I found this pencil in the street. *ligeet hal-qalam biš-šaariε.* -- I can never find my way around here. *ʔaani mustaḥiil ʔalgi darbi hnaa.* 2. *wujad (i wujuud) n-.* I found him at home. *wujadta bil-beet.*

to find out - 1. *šaaf (u šoof).* Let's go out and find out what is going on. *xal-niṭlaε barra w-inšuuf šaku.* 2. *ktišaf (i ktišaaf), εiraf (u maεrifa).* I found out he doesn't speak English. *ktišafit ʔanna ma-yiḥči ngiliizi.*

fine - 1. *ġaraama* pl. *-aat.* He had to pay a fine. *δ̣tarr yidfaε ġaraama.* 2. *naaεim.* Strain it through a fine piece of cloth. *ṣaffii b-wuṣlat iqmaaš naaεma.* 3. *xooš, zeen.* That's a fine car you've got. *xooš sayyaara εindak* or *sayyaartak zeena.* 4. *εaal, zeen, ṭayyib.* That's fine! *εaal.* 5. *daqiiq.* That's too fine a distinction. *haaδa tafriiq kulliš daqiiq.* 6. *luṭuf.* That was mighty fine of him. *haaδa čaan luṭuf kabiir minna.* 7. *rifiiε.* I'd like a fountain pen with a fine point. *ʔariid ṗaandaan sillaayta rifiiεa.* 8. *zeen.* Thanks, I'm feeling fine. *šukran, ʔaani zeen.*

to fine - *ġarram (i taġriim) t-, jazza (i jazaaʔ) t-.* The judge fined him half a dinar. *l-ḥaakim ġarrama nuṣṣ diinaar.*

finger - *ʔiṣbiε* pl. *ʔaṣaabiε.* I cut my little finger. *jiraḥit ʔiṣibεi l-iṣġayyir.*

**He let the opportunity slip through his fingers. *δ̣ayyaε il-furṣa min ʔiida.*

**Keep your fingers crossed. *twakkal εal-aḷḷa.*

forefinger - *sabbaaba* pl. *-aat.*

little finger - *xunṣur* pl. *xanaaṣir.*

middle finger - *ʔiṣbiε* (pl. *ʔaṣaabiε*) *wuṣṭa.*

ring finger - *bunṣur* pl. *banaaṣir.*

finger print - *ṭabεat ʔiṣbiε* pl. *ṭabεaat ʔaṣaabiε.* Have you taken his fingerprints? *ʔaxaδit ṭabεaat ʔaṣaabεa?*

finish - 1. *nihaaya* pl. *-aat, ʔaxiir.* I read the book from start to finish. *qireet l-iktaab imnil-bidaaya lin-nihaaya.* -- It was a fight to the finish. *čaanat maεraka lil-ʔaxiir.* 2. *ṣubuġ.* You're rubbing off the finish of the car. *da-tjalliġ ṣubġ is-sayyaara.*

to finish - *xallaṣ (i taxliiṣ), kammal (i takmiil).* Have you finished washing the car? *xaḷḷaṣit ġasl is-sayyaara?* -- I couldn't even finish my coffee. *ḥatta ma-gdarit akammil gahuuti.*

**If he does it once more, he'll be finished. *ʔiδa sawwaaha marra lux yintihi ʔamra.*

fire - 1. *naar* pl. *niiraan.* Has the fire gone out? *n-naar inṭufat?* -- We were under fire all day. *činna taḥt in-naar ṭuul il-yoom.* 2. *ḥariiq* pl. *ḥaraayiq, ḥariijiyya* pl. *-aat.* The fire damaged the building. *l-ḥariiq dammar il-binaaya.*

to be on fire - *ḥtirag (i ḥtiraag), štiεal (i štiεaal).* The house is on fire. *l-beet da-yiḥtirig.*

to catch fire - *ʔaxaδ (u ʔaxiδ) naar.* The hay caught fire. *t-tibin ʔaxaδ naar.*

to set on fire - *ḥirag (i ḥarig) n-.* He set the car on fire. *ḥirag is-sayyaara.*

to fire - 1. *rima (i rami), ʔaṭlaq (i ʔiṭlaaq) naar.* He fired two shots. *rima ramiiteen* or *ʔaṭlaq naar marrteen.* 2. *δ̣urab (u δ̣arub).* He fired the gun twice. *δ̣urab il-bunduqiyya marrteen.* 3. *ṭallaε (i taṭliiε) t-, ṭirad (u ṭarid) n-, lazzam (i talziim) t- baab, fuṣal (i faṣil) n-.* I fired my driver when he wrecked the car. *ṭallaεt is-saayiq maali min diεam is-sayyaara* or *lazzamt is-saayiq il-baab min diεam is-sayyaara.* -- We are going to fire five workers. *raḥ-nuṭrud xamis εummaal.*

fire department - *daaʔirt ʔiṭfaaʔ, ʔiṭfaaʔiyya.* Call the fire department. *xaabur daaʔirt il-ʔiṭfaaʔ.*

fire extinguisher - *ʔaalat* (pl. *-aat*) *ʔiṭfaaʔ il-ḥariiq.*

fireman - *ʔiṭfaaʔči* pl. *-iyya.*

fireplace - *šoomiina* pl. *-aat.*

fireproof - *δ̣idd in-naar.* The walls are fireproof. *l-ḥiiṭaan δ̣idd in-naar.*

firm - 1. *šarika* pl. *-aat.* What firm do you represent? *ʔay šarika ʔinta tmaθθil?* 2. *raasix, waṭiid, θaabit.* I have a firm belief in God. *εindi ʔiimaan raasix ib-ʔaḷḷa.* 3. *ṣalib, qawi*.* The ground is firm here. *l-gaaε ṣalba hnaa.* 4. *qaaṭiε.* We have a firm agreement with your company to supply our paper needs. *εidna ttifaaq qaaṭiε wiyya šarikatkum il-tajhiizna b-kull ḥaajaatna mnil-waraq.*

firmly - *b-ṣuura jaazima.* I'm firmly convinced that she is innocent. *ʔaani miqtiniε ib-ṣuura jaazima ʔanha bariiʔa.*

first - 1. (m) *ʔawwal* (f) *ʔuula.* It's the first house on the left. *huwwa ʔawwal beet εal-yisra.* -- She's the first woman to become a minister. *hiyya ʔawwal mara ṣaarat waziira* or *hiyya l-mara l-ʔuula lli ṣaarat waziira.* -- I get paid on the first of the month. *ʔaaxuδ raatib ib-ʔawwal iš-šahar.* 2. *gabuḷ, ʔawwal.* The doctor will see the women first. *d-diktoor raḥ-yšuuf in-nisaaʔ gabuḷ.* 3. *ʔawwalan.* First let me ask you a question. *ʔawwalan xalli ʔasʔalak suʔaal.* 4. *ʔawwali*.* They gave him first aid. *sawwoo-la ʔisεaaf ʔawwali.*

at first - *bil-ʔawwal.* I didn't believe it at first. *ma-ṣaddagitha bil-ʔawwal.*

first of all - *gabuḷ kullši, ʔawwalan.* First of all, you misunderstood me. *gabuḷ kullši, ʔinta ma-ftihamitni.*

first-class - 1. *daraja ʔuula.* I always travel first-class. *ʔaani daaʔiman asaafir bid-daraja l-ʔuula.* 2. *faaxir, mumtaaz.* It's a first-class job. *haay šaġḷa faaxra.*

fish - *simča* pl. *-aat* coll. *simač.* Do you like fish? *tḥibb is-simač?*

to fish - 1. *ṣaad (i ṣeed) simač.* Do you want to go fishing? *triid itruuḥ itṣiid simač?* 2. *dawwar (u tduwwur), xamm (u xamm).* He fished in his pocket for ten fils. *dawwar ib-jeeba εala εašr ifluus.*

fishbone - *εaδ̣um* (pl. *εδ̣aam*) *simač.* A fishbone caught in his throat. *εaδ̣um simač wugaf ib-zarduuma.*

fisherman - *sammaač* pl. *-iin, ṣayyaad* (pl. *-iin*) *simač.*

fish glue - *ġira.*

fist - *qabδ̣at* (pl. *-aat*) *ʔiid.* He shook his fist at me. *hazz qabδ̣at ʔiida b-wučči.*

fit - *nooba.* Every time I mention it, he has a fit of anger. *kull-ma ʔaδkurha tṣiiba noobat ġaδ̣ab.*

**This suit isn't a good fit. *hal-qaaṭ ma-gaaεid zeen.*

to be fit - 1. *laag (u liyaaga).* Is he fit for this kind of work? *huwwa laayig il-han-nooε šuġuḷ?* 2. *ṣilaḥ (a ṣalaaḥ).* This meat isn't fit to eat. *hal-laḥam muu ṣaaliḥ lil-ʔakil.*

to fit - 1. *riham (a rahum).* These shoes don't fit me. *hal-ḥiδaaʔ ma-yirham εalayya.* 2. *rahham (u tarhiim) t-.* Can you fit these rings to the pistons? *tigdar itrahhum har-ringaat εal-pasaatin?*

to fit together - *tṭaabaq (a muṭaabaqa).* These parts don't fit together. *hal-qiṭaε ma-tiṭṭaabaq.*

fitting - 1. *ṗraawa* pl. *-aat.* When will the suit be ready for a fitting? *šwakit ykuun il-qaaṭ ḥaaδ̣ir lil-iṗraawa.* 2. *mnaasib.* Let's wait for a more fitting time. *xal-nintiδ̣ir ʔila wakit imnaasib ʔakθar.*

five - 1. *xamis.* I bought it for five dinars. *štireeta b-xams idnaaniir.* -- There are five starlings on the tree. *ʔaku xams izraaziir εaš-šijra.* 2. *xamist.* His salary is five thousand dinars a year. *raatba xamist aalaaf diinaar bis-sana.* -- I spent five days on my uncle's farm. *gδ̣eet xamist* iyyaam ib-mazraɛat ɛammi. **3.** xamsa. Take five of them and leave the rest. ʔuxuð xamsa minha w-xalli l-baaqi. -- Take the five from here and add it to this number. ʔuxuð il-xamsa minnaa w-ðiifha ɛala har-raqum.

fix - warṭa pl. -aat. He's in a terrible fix. waaqiɛ ib-warṭa čibiira.

to fix - **1.** zaddad (i tazdiid) t-. The price was fixed at ten dinars. s-siɛir itzaddad ib-ɛašr idnaaniir. **2.** ɛaddal (i taɛdiil) t-. Fix your tie. ɛaddil booyinbaaġak. **3.** ṣallaz (i taṣliiz) t-. Can you fix the typewriter for me? tigdar itṣalliz-li ʔaalat iṭ-ṭaabiɛa. **4.** sawwa (i taswiya) t-, hayyaʔ (i tahyiʔa) t-. I have to fix supper now. laazim ʔasawwi l-ɛaša hassa.

flag - ɛalam pl. ʔaɛlaam. The colors of the American flag are red, white, and blue. ʔalwaan il-ɛalam il-ʔamiirki ʔazmar, w-abyaḍ, w-azraq.

flake - nidfa pl. nidaf. The snow is falling in big flakes. θ-θalij da-yinzil ib-nidaf ikbaar.

flames - šuɛla, lahab. The whole house was in flames. l-beet kulla čaan ṣaayir šuɛla.

flare - nuur kaššaaf pl. ʔanwaar kassaafa. They fired flares so it would be known where they were. ʔaṭliqaw ʔanwaar kaššaafa zatta yinɛarfuun ween.

to flare up - **1.** ðṭiram (i ðṭiraam). The fire flared up when I poured some gasoline on it. n-naar iðṭirmat min čabbeet ɛaleeha šwayya baanziin. **2.** θaar (u θawra). He flares up at the slightest provocation. haaða yθuur min ʔaqall zirša.

flash - **1.** lamaɛaan. Did you see the flash of lightning? šifit lamaɛaan il-bariq? **2.** lazða. It was all over in a flash. kullši xilaṣ ib-lazða or kullši xilaṣ miθil il-barq.

to flash - **1.** limaɛ (a lamaɛaan). His eyes flashed with anger. ɛyuuna limɛat imnil-ġaḍab. **2.** xiṭar (u xuṭraan). Many thoughts flashed through my mind. hwaaya ʔafkaar xiṭrat ɛala baali. **3.** šiɛal (i šaɛil) n-. He flashed the light in my face. šiɛal iḍ-ḍuwa b-wučči. **4.** xiṭaf (u xaṭuf). The bird flashed by the window. ṭ-ṭeer xiṭaf min yamm iš-šibbaač.

flashlight - toorič pl. -aat. Can you lend me your flashlight? tigdar itɛiirni t-toorič maalak?

flat - **1.** šaqqa pl. šiqaq. I just moved into a new flat. stawwni tzawwalit ʔila šaqqa jidiida. **2.** pančar pl. panaačir. On the way back we had a flat. b-ṭariiq rajɛatna ṣaar ɛidna pančar. **3.** minbaṣiṭ, mabṣuuṭ, mustawi. The country around Baghdad is flat. l-ʔaraaḍi zawil baġdaad minbaṣṭa. **4.** faahi, bila ṭaɛam. The soup is flat. š-šoorba faahya. **5.** baat, qaaṭiɛ. His answer was a flat ''no''. jawaaba čaan nafi baat. **6.** mfalṭaz. He has a flat nose. ɛinda xašim imfalṭaz.

flat feet - flaatfuut. He has flat feet. ɛinda flaatfuut.

flat iron - ʔuuti pl. -iyyaat.

to **flatten** - **1.** waggaɛ (i twiggiɛ). He flattened him with one punch. waggaɛa b-boox waazid. **2.** ṭabbag (u ṭṭubbug) t-. Flatten the cardboard boxes and stack them on the shelf. ṭabbug iṣ-ṣinaadiig il-imqawwa w-ṣaffuṭha ɛar-raazuuna.

**He stepped on my hat and flattened it. daas ɛala šafuqti w-sawwaaha wiyya l-gaaɛ.

to **flatter** - tmallaq (a tamalluq) l-. He tried to flatter me. zaawal yitmallaq-li.

to flatter oneself - tbaaha (a tabaahi). He flatters himself that he's a good judge of character. yitbaaha b-kawna yigdar yizzir ʔaṭbaaɛ in-naas.

flattery - malaq, tamalluq. Flattery won't get you anywhere. l-malaq ma-yfiidak.

flavor - ṭaɛam. The coffee has lost all its flavor. l-gahwa ma-buqa biiha ṭaɛam.

flight - **1.** qaaṭ pl. quuṭ, ṭaabiq pl. ṭawaabiq. How many more flights do we have to climb? čam qaaṭ baɛad laazim niṣɛad? **2.** ṭayaraan. The flight to Rome took an hour. ṭ-ṭayaraan ila rooma ṭawwal saaɛa.

**There are four flights a day to Mecca. ʔaku ʔarbaɛ ṭayyaaraat yṭiir yoomiyya ʔila makka.

to **fling** - šumar (u šamur) n-, ðabb (i ðabb) n-. He flung his jacket on a chair and rushed to the telephone. šumar sitirta ɛala skamli w-rikaḍ ɛat-talafoon.

to **flirt** - **1.** ġaazal (i muġaazala) t-. She flirts with every man she meets. haay itġaazil ʔay rijjaal itlaagii or titġaazal wiyya ʔay rijjaal itlaagii.

**I've been flirting with this idea for a long time. hal-fikra ṣaar-ilha mudda tdaaɛib ɛaqli.

float - **1.** ɛawwaama pl. -aat. Let's swim to the float. xal-nisbaz lil-ɛawwaama. **2.** ṭawwaafa pl. -aat. When the float starts bobbing around, you know there's a fish on the hook. min gaamat titzarrak iṭ-ṭawwaafa ɛrafit aku simča biš-šuṣṣ.

to float - **1.** ṭaaf (u ṭoof), ɛaam (u ɛoom). What is that floating on the water? šinu ðaak iṭ-ṭaayif ɛal-mayy? **2.** sayyas (i tasyiis). They floated a raft loaded with watermelons down to Baghdad. sayysaw kalak imzammal raggi ʔila baġdaad. -- The logs were floated down the river. jðuuɛ il-ʔašjaar itsayysat biš-šaṭṭ.

flock - **1.** qaṭiiɛ pl. qiṭɛaan. They followed him like a flock of sheep. tibɛoo miθil qaṭiiɛ ġanam. **2.** sirib pl. ʔasraab. We saw a flock of birds flying south. šifna sirib iṭyuur ṭaayir lij-jinuub.

to flock - tgaaṭar (a tagaaṭur). The children flocked into the circus. l-ʔaṭfaal itgaaṭraw ɛas-sarkis.

**People came flocking to hear him. n-naas ʔijaw joogaat joogaat zatta yismaɛuu.

flood - fayaḍaan pl. -aat. Many perished in the flood. hwaaya maataw bil-fayaḍaan.

to flood - **1.** faaḍ (i fayaḍaan). The river floods every year. š-šaṭṭ yfiiḍ kull sana. **2.** ġirag (a ġarag). The whole street was flooded. š-šaariɛ kulla ġirag. **3.** ġarrag (i taġriig). The rain water flooded the basement. mayy il-muṭar ġarrag is-sirdaab. -- They flooded the market with Egyptian cigarettes. ġarrigaw is-suug ib-jigaayir miṣriyya.

floor - **1.** gaaɛ pl. giiɛaan. My glasses fell on the floor. manaaḍri wugɛat bil-gaaɛ. **2.** ṭaabiq pl. ṭawaabiq. I live on the second floor. ʔaskun biṭ-ṭaabiq iθ-θaani. **3.** zaqq il-kalaam. May I have the floor, Mr. Chairman? yaa zaḍrat ir-raʔiis, ʔagdar ʔaaxuð zaqq il-kalaam?

flop - faašil pl. -iin. He's a flop as a singer. haaða faašil ka-muġaani.

to flop - **1.** ðabb (i ðabb) nafis~. She flopped into a chair. ðabbat nafisha ɛala kursi. **2.** fišal (a fašil). The play flopped. r-ruwaaya fišlat. **3.** lubaṭ (u labuṭ). The fish flopped around on the bottom of the boat. s-simča lubṭat ib-gaaɛiit il-balam.

flour - ṭiziin. I want a sack of flour. ʔariid čiis ṭiziin.

to **flourish** - zdihar (i zdihaar). A highly developed civilization flourished here 2,000 years ago. fadd zaḍaara mitqaddma jiddan izdihrat ihnaa gabuḷ ʔalfeen sana.

flourishing - muzdahir. We had a flourishing trade with Syria. čaanat ɛidna tijaara muzdahra wiyya suurya.

flow - wuruud. The flow of food supplies was cut. ngiṭaɛ wuruud il-mawaadd il-ġiðaaʔiyya.

to flow - **1.** jira (i jarayaan). The Tigris flows from north to south. nahar dijla yijri mniš-šimaal lij-jinuub. **2.** ṣabb (u ṣabb). The Shatt al-Arab flows into the Persian Gulf. šaṭṭ il-ɛarab yṣubb bil-xaliij il-faarisi.

flower - warda pl. -aat coll. warid. He took some flowers to a sick friend. wadda šwayya warid il-fadd ṣadiiq mariiḍ.

flu - ʔanfluwanza. Our whole family had the flu. kull ɛaaʔilatna ṣaar biihum ʔanfluwanza.

to **fluctuate** - **1.** tqallab (a taqallub). Prices fluctuate. l-ʔasɛaar titqallab. **2.** tðabðab (a taðabðub, ðabðaba). The gas gauge began to fluctuate. geej il-baanziin bida yitðabðab.

fluently - b-ṭalaaga. He speaks Persian fluently. yizči faarsi b-ṭalaaga.

fluid - **1.** saaʔil pl. sawaaʔil. You should drink more water to replace your body fluids. laazim tišrab mayy ʔazyad zatta tɛawwuḍ sawaaʔil jismak. **2.** maayiɛ. I watched them pour the fluid metal into the mold. raaqabithum ydiiruun il-maɛdam il-maayiɛ bil-qaalab.

flush - **1.** flašš pl. -aat. He always beats me with a flush. ɛala ṭuul da-yiġlubni bil-iflašš. **2.** wiyya. The shelf is built flush with the wall. r-raazuuna mabniya wiyya l-zaayit.

to flush - **1.** zmarr (a zmiraar). His face flushed with anger. wičča zmarr imnil-ġaḍab. **2.** šayyaš (i tašyiiš) t-. We'll have to flush your radiator. laazim inšayyiš ir-raadeeta maalak.

**Don't forget to flush the toilet. la-tinsa tjurr is-siifoon.

fly - ðibbaana pl. -aat coll. ðibbaan. The flies around here are terrible. ð-ðibbaan ihnaa muzɛij.

to fly – **1.** *ṭaar (i ṭayaraan).* The birds are flying south. *ṭ-ṭuyuur da-yṭiiruun lij-jinuub.* — We're flying to Paris tomorrow. *raz-inṭiir il-paariis baačir.* **3.** *ṭayyar (i taṭyiir) t-.* Can you fly a plane? *tigdar iṭṭayyir ṭiyyaara?* **4.** *ʔaxaδ (u) ib-ṭiyyaara, wadda (i) ib-ṭiyyaara.* The child was flown to a hospital. *ṭ-ṭifil innixaδ lil-mustašfa b-ṭiyyaara.* **5.** *rufaƐ (a rafuƐ) n-.* The ship was flying the Indian flag. *l-baaxira čaanat raafƐa l-Ɛalam il-hindi.*

flyer – *ṭayyaar* pl. *-iin.* He's a famous flyer. *haaδa fadd ṭayyaar mašhuur.*

foam – **1.** *waġaf.* There's more foam than beer. *ʔaku waġaf akθar min il-biira.* **2.** *zabad.* The water below the falls was covered with foam. *l-maay jawwa š-šallaal čaan imġaṭṭa biz-zabad.*

to foam – *zabbad (i tzibbid).* He was foaming at the mouth. *zalga čaan yzabbid.*

to **focus** – **1.** *ẓibaṭ (u ẓabuṭ) n-.* Focus the camera at 50 feet. *ʔiẓbuṭ il-kaamira Ɛala xamsiin qadam.* **2.** *rakkaz (i tarkiiz).* Try to focus your eyes on this dot. *zaawil itrakkiz iƐyuunak Ɛala han-nuqṭa.*

fog – *ẓubaab.* A dense fog shut out the view. *ẓubaab kaθiif sadd il-manẓar.*

fold – **1.** *θanya* pl. *-aat.* The curtains are faded at the folds. *l-pardaat kuušfa mniθ-θanyaat.* **2.** *ṭayya* pl. *-aat.* He hid the knife in the folds of his clothes. *ẓamm is-siččiina b-ṭayyaat ihduuma.*

to fold – *ṭawwa (i taṭwiya) t-, ṭabbag (u taṭbiig) t-, ṭiwa (i ṭawi) n-.* Help me fold the blanket. *saaƐidni ʔaṭawwi l-baṭṭaaniyya.*

to fold one's arms – *tčattaf (a tačattuf).* He folded his arms. *tčattaf.*

to fold up – *fišal (a fašil).* His business folded up last year. *šaġilta fišlat is-sana l-faatat.*

folder – *malaffa* pl. *-aat.* The copies are in the blue folder. *n-nusax bil-malaffa z-zarga.*

folks – **1.** *waaldeen.* How are your folks? *šloon waaldeek?* **2.** *rabuƐ, jamaaƐa.* Let's go, folks! *xalli nruuz, yaa rabuƐ!*

to **follow** – **1.** *lizag (a lazig) n-, tibaƐ (a tabiƐ).* You lead the way and we'll follow you. *ʔinta tqaddam w-izna nilzagak.* **2.** *tƐaqqab (a taƐaqqub).* Somebody's following us. *fadd waazid da-yitƐaqqabna.* **3.** *tibaƐ (a) n-.* Follow these instructions exactly. *ʔitbaƐ hat-taƐliimaat ib-diqqa.* — He's following in his father's footsteps and becoming a doctor. *da-yitbaƐ xaṭawaat ʔabuu w-da-yṣiir ṭabiib.* **4.** *Ɛiqab (i Ɛaqib) n-, tibaƐ (a tabiƐ) n-.* Rain followed the hot weather. *j-jaww il-zaarr Ɛiqaba muṭar.* **5.** *ttabbaƐ (a tatabbuƐ).* Have you been following the news lately? *ʔinta mittabbiƐ il-ʔaxbaar hal-ʔayyaam?* — I couldn't follow his explanation. *ma-gdarit attabbaƐ it-tafsiir maala* or *ma-gdarit afham tafsiira.*

**From this fact it follows that... *yubna Ɛala hal-zaqiiqa ʔanna ...*

as follows – *ka-ma yali.* The letter reads as follows ... *l-maktuub yiqra ka-ma yali ...*

follower – *taabiƐ* pl. *ʔatbaaƐ, naṣiir* pl. *ʔanṣaar.* He's one of the party's most faithful followers. *haaδa waazid min ʔaxlaṣ ʔatbaaƐ il-zizib.*

following – **1.** *taali.* The following day it rained. *muṭrat bil-yoom it-taali.* — I need the following items. *ʔaztaaj il-ʔašyaaʔ it-taaliya.* **2.** *baƐad.* Following the party we went to his house. *baƐad il-zafla rizna l-beeta.*

**He has a very large following. *Ɛinda ʔatbaaƐ ihwaaya.*

fond – **1.** *muulaƐ.* We're fond of music. *ʔizna muulaƐiin bil-mawsiiqa* or ***Ɛidna walaƐ bil-mawsiiqa.*— She's fond of children. *hiyya muulaƐa bil-ʔaṭfaal* or ***hiyya tzibb il-ʔaṭfaal.* **2.** *mitƐalliq.* Our boy is very fond of you. *ʔibinna hwaaya mitƐalliq biik.*

to become fond of – *tƐallaq (a taƐalluq) b-.* The children became very fond of their teacher. *j-jihhaal itƐallqaw kulliš ib-muƐallimathum.*

food – **1.** *ʔakil.* The food is excellent in this restaurant. *l-ʔakil mumtaaz ib-hal-maṭƐam.* **2.** *maʔuuna.* Food got scarcer day after day. *l-maʔuuna qallat yoom wara yoom.*

**This will give you food for thought. *haaδa yinṭiik maadda lit-tafkiir.*

foodstuff – *mawaadd ġiδaaʔiyya.* We've got to increase our production of foodstuff. *laazim inzayyid intaajna mnil-mawaadd il-ġiδaaʔiyya.*

fool – *ġabi* pl. *ʔaġbiyaaʔ, ʔazmaq* pl. *zumuq.* He's a fool if he believes that story. *huwwa ġabi ʔiδa yṣaddig hal-izčaaya.*

**He's nobody's fool. *mazzad yigdar yiẓzak Ɛalee* or *haaδa ma-yitqašmar.*

to fool – **1.** *tšaaqa (a tašaaqi).* I was only fooling. *činit bass da-atšaaqa.* **2.** *qašmar (u qašmara).* You can't fool me. *ma-tigdar itqašmurni.* **3.** *liƐab (a laƐib) n-, naġbaš (u naġbaša) t-.* Don't fool with the radio while I'm gone. *la-tilƐab bir-raadyo min ʔaani ṭaaliƐ.*

to fool around – *taxxam (i tatxiim) t-.* I just fooled around all afternoon. *taxxamit il-Ɛaṣriyya kullha.*

foolish – *saxiif.* Don't be foolish! *la-tṣiir saxiif.*

foot – **1.** *rijil* pl. *-een.* The shoe is tight on my foot. *l-qundara ẓayyga Ɛala rijli.* **2.** *qadam* pl. *ʔaqdaam, fuut* pl. *-aat.* He's over six feet tall. *ṭuula foog sitt aqdaam.* **3.** *čaƐab.* They camped at the foot of the mountain. *xayymaw ib-čaƐb ij-jibal.*

**It'll take a month to get back on our feet after the fire. *yinraad-ilna šahar zatta nistaƐdil baƐd il-zariiq.*

**They'll keep on until you put your foot down. *raz-yẓalluun ysawwuuha ʔila ʔan itraawiihum Ɛeen zamra.*

**I really put my foot in it that time! *jilaṭitha xooš jalṭa han-nooba!*

on foot – *bir-rijil, maši.* We had to cover the rest of the distance on foot. *ẓṭarreena nigṭaƐ baaqi l-masaafa bir-rijil.*

on one's feet – *waaguf Ɛala zeel~.* He's on his feet all day long. *haaδa waaguf Ɛala zeela ṭuul in-nahaar.*

footprint – *ʔaθar qadam* pl. *ʔaaθaar ʔaqdaam.* We followed the footprints. *tbaƐna ʔaaθaar il-ʔaqdaam.*

for – **1.** *ka-.* For an American, he speaks Arabic well. *ka-waazid ʔamriikaani, yizči Ɛarabi zeen.* — What do you use for firewood? *š-tistaƐmil ka-zaṭab lin-naar?* **2.** *l-.* He married her for her money. *tzawwajha l-fluusha.* Aspirin is good for headaches. *l-ʔaspiriin zeen il-wujaƐ ir-raas.* — They continued talking about it for several days. *ẓallaw yizčuun biiha l-Ɛiddat ʔayyaam.* — Take this fifty fils for some breakfast. *ʔuxuδ hal-xamsiin filis ir-ruyuugak.* **3.** *b-.* You can buy this table for a dinar. *tigdar tištiri hal-meez ib-diinaar.* — An eye for an eye, and a tooth for a tooth. *l-Ɛeen bil-Ɛeen, wis-sinn bis-sinn.* **4.** *ʔila.* I've got some letters for you. *ʔaku ʔilak čam maktuub Ɛindi.* **5.** *Ɛan, Ɛala.* Did anyone ask for me? *ʔazzad siʔal Ɛanni?* **6.** *l-, min.* I haven't heard from him for a long time. *ma-smaƐit minna l-mudda ṭuwiila.* — They laughed at him for his stupidness. *ẓizkaw Ɛalee min saxaafta.*

**I've been wearing this coat for three years. *ṣaar-li tlaθ isniin da-albas hal-qappuuṭ.*

for heaven's sake – *l-xaaṭir ʔaḷḷa, yaa mƐawwad.* For heaven's sake, stop! *l-xaaṭir ʔaḷḷa, bass Ɛaad!*

what ... for – **1.** *l-ʔay šii.* What's that good for? *l-ʔay šii haaδa yinfaƐ?* **2.** *leeš, luweeš.* What did you do that for? *leeš sawweet haaδa?*

force – **1.** *quwwa* pl. *-aat.* We had to use force. *ẓṭarreena nistaƐmil il-quwwa.* — How large is the Baghdad police force? *šgadd quwwat iš-šurṭa b-baġdaad.* — The land and sea forces are under the command of one commander. *l-quwwaat il-barriyya wil-quwwaat il-bazriyya tazat ʔimrat qaaʔid waazid.* **2.** *šidda.* The storm hasn't reached its full force yet. *l-Ɛaaṣifa ma-wuṣlat šiddatha baƐad.* **3.** *zukum.* She does it from force of habit. *tsawwiiha b-zukm il-Ɛaada.*

in force – *naafiδ, jaari l-mafƐuul.* Is that law still in force? *hal-qaanuun baƐda naafiδ?*

in full force – *b-kaamil Ɛadad-.* The family turned out in full force. *l-Ɛaaʔila ʔijat ib-kaamil Ɛadadha.*

to force – *jubar (u ʔijbaar) n-, ʔakrah (i ʔikraah), riġam (u ʔirġaam), ẓṭarr (a ẓṭiraar), ġuṣab (u ġaṣub).* You can't force me to sign. *ma-tigdar tijburni ʔamẓi.* — You can't force these things; we'll just have to wait. *ma-tigdar itsawwi hal-ʔašyaaʔ ġaṣban, laazim nintiẓir.* — We'll have to force our way in. *laazim nidxul bil-ʔikraah.*

forced – *ẓṭiraari*.* The plane made a forced landing in the desert. *ṭ-ṭiyyaara nizlat nizuul iẓṭiraari.*

forecast – *nubuuʔa* pl. *-aat.* His forecast didn't turn out. *nubuuʔta ma-tzaqqiqat.*

to forecast – *tnabbaʔ (a tanabbuʔ) b-.* They forecast cooler weather. *tnabbʔaw ib-jaww ʔabrad.*

forehead – *guṣṣa* pl. *guṣaṣ, jabha* pl. *-aat.*

foreign - *ʔajnabi*, blaadi*, maal iblaad.* That's a foreign make. *haay šuġuḷ ʔajnabi.*
foreigner - *ʔajnabi* pl. *ʔajaanib.* Before the war many foreigners came here. *gabḷ il-ʒarb ihwaaya ʔajaanib ʔijaw ihnaa.*
forest - *ġaaba* pl. *-aat.*
forever - *lil-ʔabad.* I'm afraid I'll be stuck in this place forever. *ʔaxša raʒ-aḍṭarr ʔabqa b-hal-makaan lil-ʔabad.*
to **forget** - *nisa (a nasi, nisyaan) n-.* She has forgotten everything. *hiyya nisat kullši.*
to **forgive** - *saamaʒ (i musaamaʒa), ʕifa (i ʕafi) ʕan, ġtifar (i ġtifaar) l-.* He'll never forgive you for that. *ʔabadan ma-ysaamʒak ʕala haaḍa.*
fork - **1.** *čaṭal* pl. *-aat.* Could you hand me a knife and fork? *tigdar tinṭiini siččiina w-čaṭal?* **2.** *mafraq* pl. *mafaariq, muftaraq* pl. *-aat.* When we get to the fork, you take the right road, and I'll take the road on the left. *lamma niji lil-mafraq, ʔinta ʔuxuḍ ṭariiq il-yamiin, w-ʔaani ʔaaxuḍ ṭariiq il-yisaar.*
  to fork - *tšaʕʕab (a tašaʕʕub), ftiraq (i ftiraaq).* The road forks beyond the village. *ṭ-ṭariiq yitšaʕʕab min wara l-qarya.*
form - **1.** *šikil* pl. *ʔaškaal.* The sculptor uses many new forms. *n-naʒʒaat yistaʕmil ihwaaya ʔaškaal jidiida.* **2.** *ṣiiġa* pl. *-aat, šikil* pl. *ʔaškaal.* Can you put your question in a different form? *tigdar itṣiiġ suʔaalak ib-ġeer ṣiiġa?* **3.** *qaalab* pl. *qwaalib.* They built a form to pour the concrete into. *sawwaw qaalab ʒatta yṣubbuun ič-čimantu bii.* **4.** *stimaara* pl. *-aat.* You'll have to fill out this form. *laazim timli hal-istimaara.* **5.** *sikli*.* It's only a matter of form, but you'll have to do it. *haaḍa fadd šii šikli, bass laazim itsawwii.*
  to form - **1.** *šakkal (i taškiil) t-, ʔallaf (i taʔliif) t-.* He formed a new cabinet. *šakkal wizaara jidiida.* **2.** *kawwan (i takwiin) t-.* I haven't formed an opinion yet. *baʕad ma-kawwanit raʔi li-hassa.*
formal - *rasmi*.* You needn't be that formal. *ma-aku ʒaaja tṣiir hal-gadd rasmi.*
formalities - *šakliyyaat, rasmiyyaat.* She's very careful to observe the formalities. *tdiir baalha ʒatta ma-tiṭlaʕ ʕan iš-šakliyyaat.*
former - *saabiq.* The former owner has retired. *l-maalik is-saabiq itqaaʕad.*
formerly - *saabiqan.* This was formerly the business section. *saabiqan haaḍi čaanat il-manṭiqa t-tijaariyya.*
fort - *ʒuṣin* pl. *ʒuṣuun.* There's an old fort on the hill. *ʔaku fadd ʒuṣin qadiim ʕat-tall.*
fortieth - *l-ʔarbaʕiin.* That's the fortieth day he's refused to eat meat. *haaḍa l-yoom il-ʔarbaʕiin il-muḍrib bii ʕan ʔakl il-laʒam.*
to **fortify** - *ʒaṣṣan (i taʒṣiin) t-.* The island was fortified. *j-jaziira čaanat muʒaṣṣana.*
fortress - *qalʕa* pl. *qilaaʕ, ʒuṣin* pl. *ʒuṣuun.*
fortunate - **1.** *saʕiid.* That was a fortunate occurrence. *haaḍi čaanat ṣidfa saʕiida.* **2.** *maʒḍuuḍ.* He was fortunate to get a bargain like that. *čaan maʒḍuuḍ lil-ʒuṣuul ʕala šarwa miθil haay.*
fortunately - *l-ʒusn il-ʒaḍḍ.* Fortunately, I got there in time. *l-ʒusn il-ʒaḍḍ, wuṣalit ihnaak ʕal-wakit.*
fortune - **1.** *θarwa* pl. *-aat.* She inherited a large fortune. *wurθat θarwa ṭaʔila.* **2.** *ʒaḍḍ* pl. *ʒḍuuḍ.* I had the good fortune to meet her the other day. *čaan ʒaḍḍ saʕiid ʔan atʕarraf ʕaleeha ḍaak il-yoom.* **3.** *faal.* She told my fortune. *fitʒat-li faal.*
fortune teller - *fattaaʒ* (pl. *-iin*) *faal.*
forty - *ʔarbaʕiin.*
forward - **1.** *ʔila l-ʔamaam.* Forward, march! *ʔila l-ʔamaam, sirr!* **2.** *li-giddaam.* They sent four men forward to investigate. *dazzaw ʔarbaʕ riyaajiil li-giddaam yitʒarruun.* **3.** *hjuum.* They have two good forwards on their soccer team. *ʕidhum ʔiθneen ihjuum mumtaaziin ib-fariiq kurat il-qadam maalhum.* **4.** *mitjaasir* pl. *-iin.* They beat him up because he was so forward with girls. *buṣṭoo li-ʔan čaan kulliš mitjaasir ʕal-banaat.*
  to forward - *dazz (i dazz) n-.* Your mail will be forwarded to your new address. *bariidak raʒ-yindazz ʔila ʕinwaanak ij-jidiid.*
foul - **1.** *faawul* pl. *-aat.* Touching the ball with your hand in soccer is a foul. *ṭaxxat iṭ-ṭooba bil-ʔiid faawul ib-kurat il-qadam.* **2.** *ġaadir, qaḍir.* That was a foul blow. *haay čaanat ḍarba ġaadra.* **3.** *jaayif.* Where does that foul smell come from? *har-riiʒa j-jaayfa mneen tiji?* **4.** *fšaar.* He uses foul language a lot. *yiʒči kalaam ifšaar ihwaaya* or *yfaššir ihwaaya.*
to **found** - *ʔassas (i taʔsiis) t-.* When was the club founded? *swakit in-naadi tʔassas?*
foundation - **1.** *ʔasaas* pl. *-aat.* The flood damaged the foundations of the building. *l-fayaḍaan dammar ʔasaasaat il-binaaya.* -- Your remarks are completely without foundation. *taʕliiqaatak ma-ʔilha ʔasaas.* **2.** *muʔassasa* pl. *-aat.* They're setting up a charitable foundation. *da-yʔassisuun muʔassasa xeeriyya.*
fountain - *šadirwaan* pl. *-aat.* There's a fountain in in the square. *ʔaku šadirwaan bis-saaʒa.*
fountain pen - *paandaan* pl. *-aat, qalam* (pl. *ʔaqlaam*) *ʒibir.* I'll have to fill my fountain pen. *laazim ʔatrus paandaani.*
four - **1.** *ʔarbaʕ.* I bought it for four fils. *štireeta b-ʔarbaʕ ifluus.* -- We took four girls to the movie. *ʔaxaḍna ʔarbaʕ banaat lis-siinama.* **2.** *ʔarbaʕa.* Hold four of these in your hand. *ʔilzam ʔarbaʕa minhum ib-iidak.* -- Multiply this number by four. *ʔuḍrub har-raqum ib-ʔarbaʕa.* **3.** *ʔarbaʕt.* He has to take the medicine four times a day. *laazim yišrab id-duwa ʔarbaʕt awqaat bil-yoom.* -- He stayed with us four days. *buqa ʕidna ʔarbaʕt iyyaam.*
fourteen - *ʔarbaaṭaʕaš.*
fourteenth - *raabiʕ ʕašar, l-ʔarbaaṭaʕaš.*
fourth - **1.** *rubuʕ* pl. *ʔarbaaʕ.* Only one fourth of the students were paying attention. *bass rubuʕ iṭ-ṭullaab čaanaw daayiriin baalhum.* **2.** *raabiʕ.* He died on May fourth. *maat bir-raabiʕ min ʔayyaar.*
fox - *θaʕlab* pl. *θaʕaalib.* A fox is killing our chickens. *fadd θaʕlab da-yuktul dijaajna.*
fraction - **1.** *kasir* pl. *ksuur.* Leave out the fractions and just give me the round numbers. *ʔutruk l-iksuur w-inṭiini bass il-ʔarqaam iṣ-ṣaʒiiʒa.* **2.** *juzuʔ* pl. *ʔajzaaʔ.* He got only a fraction of his father's fortune. *ʒaṣṣal ʕala bass juzuʔ min θarwat ʔabuu.*
fracture - *kasir* pl. *kusuur.* The fracture is healing slowly. *l-kasir da-yilʒam ib-buṭuʔ.*
  to fracture - *kisar (i kasir) n-.* He fell off the bicycle and fractured a bone. *wugaʕ imnil-paaysikil w-kisar waaʒid min iʕḍaama.*
frame - **1.** *ʔiṭaar* pl. *-aat, čarčuuba* pl. *čaraačiib.* I'd like to have a frame for this picture. *ʔariid ʔiṭaar il-haṣ-ṣuura.* **2.** *haykal* pl. *hayaakil.* The frame of the hut is wood. *l-haykal maal il-kuux xišab.* **3.** *bunya* pl. *-aat.* He has a heavy frame. *ʕinda bunya xašna.* **4.** *ʒaala* pl. *-aat.* He's not in a very good frame of mind; better ask him later. *hassa huwwa muu b-xooš ʒaala fikriyya; ʔisʔala baʕdeen.*
  to frame - *čarčab (i čarčaba) t-.* I'll have the picture framed. *raʒ-ačarčib iṣ-ṣuura.*
  **They framed him. *ḍabbaw iṣ-ṣuuč ib-rugubta.*
France - *fraansa.*
frank - *ṣariiʒ.* Be frank with me. *kuun ṣariiʒ wiyyaaya.*
frankly - *b-ṣaraaʒa.* Frankly, I don't know. *b-ṣaraaʒa, ma-aʕruf.*
frantic - *jinuuni*.* He made frantic efforts to free himself. *sawwa muʒaawalaat jinuuniyya ʒatta yxaḷḷis nafsa.*
freckles - *namaš.*
free - **1.** *ʒurr* pl. *ʔaʒraar.* He's a free man again. *huwwa ʒurr min jidiid.* -- You're free to go at any time. *ʔinta ʒurr itruuʒ išwakit-ma triid.* **2.** *faariġ.* Will you be free tomorrow? *raʒ-itkuun faariġ baačir?* **3.** *balaaš, majjaanan.* I got it free. *ʔaxaḍitha balaaš.* **4.** *majjaani*, balaaš.* The admission to the play is free tonight. *d-duxuul lir-ruwaaya l-leela majjaani.* **5.** *ṣaxi* pl. *ʔaṣxiyaaʔ.* He's free with his money. *huwwa ṣaxi b-ifluusa.*
  **He has a free and easy way about him. *yʒiiṭ nafsa b-jaww ma-bii takalluf.*
  to free - **1.** *ʔaṭlaq (u ʔiṭlaaq) siraaʒ-.* They freed the prisoners. *ʔaṭliqaw siraaʒ il-masaajiin.* **2.** *ʒarrar (i taʒriir) t-.* Our army freed the city from the invaders. *jeešna ʒarrar il-madiina mnil-ġuzaat.* **3.** *xallaṣ (i txilliṣ).* They tried for a half hour, but were unable to free the car from the mud. *tʒaawlaw nuṣṣ saaʕa w-ma-gidraw yxalliṣuun is-sayyaara mniṭ-ṭiin.*
freedom - *ʒurriyya.*
freely - **1.** *b-ṣaraaʒa.* He admitted freely that he took it. *ʕtiraf ib-ṣaraaʒa ʔinna ʔaxaḍha.* **2.** *b-ʒurriyya.* You can speak freely. *tigdar tiʒči b-ʒurriitak.* **3.** *b-saxaaʔ.* He spends his

money freely. *yiṣruf ifluusa b-saxaa?.*

to **freeze** - 1. *jimad (i jamid) n-.* The water in the pitcher froze during the night. *l-ṃaay jimad bid-doolka ?aθnaa? il-leel.* -- He froze to death. *jimad imnil-barid w-maat.* 2. *jammad (i tajmiid) t-.* They're building a plant to freeze food. *da-yibnuun maεmal il-tajmiid il-?aṭεima.* -- The government has frozen all foreign accounts. *l-ẓukuuma jammidat kull il-iẓsaabaat il-?ajnabiyya.* 3. *θallaj (i taθliij) t-.* We'll freeze this winter if we don't get a better heater. *raẓ-inθallij haš-šita ?iδa ma-ništiri ṣooba ?aẓsan.* -- My feet are frozen. *rijlayya mθallija.*

freight - 1. *šaẓin.* Including freight and insurance the car will cost a thousand dinars. *wiyya š-šaẓin wit-ta?miin is-sayyaara raẓ-itkallif ?alif diinaar.* 2. *?ujrat šaẓin.* How much is the freight on this trunk? *šgadd ?ujrat iš-šaẓin εala haṣ-ṣanduug?* 3. *ẓimil.* He owns a freight company. *yimlik šarikat ẓimil.*

freight car - *εarabat* (pl. *-aat*) *ẓimil.*

freighter - *baaxirat* (pl. *bawaaxir*) *ẓimil.*

French - 1. *fransi, fransaawi.* He speaks very good French. *yitkallam ifransi kulliš zeen.* 2. *fransi*.* Do you like French wines? *yεijbak iš-šaraab il-ifransi?*

Frenchman - *fransi* pl. *-iyyiin.* Our neighbor is a Frenchman. *jiiraanna fransi.*

frequently - *ġaaliban.* I see him frequently. *?ašuufa ġaaliban.*

fresh - 1. *taaza.* Are these eggs fresh? *hal-beeδ taaza?* 2. *naqi*.* Let's go out for some fresh air. *xalli niṭlaε ništamm hawa naqi.* 3. *εaδib.* The well water turned out to be fresh. *ṭilaε ṃayy il-biir εaδib.* 4. *waqiẓ, wakiẓ.* I can't stand that fresh kid. *ma-aqdar atẓammal hal-walad il-waqiẓ.*

friction - 1. *ẓtikaak.* Oiling the wheel would cut down the friction. *tadhiin ič-čarix yqallil il-iẓtikaak.* 2. *tawattur.* There's friction between the two countries. *?aku tawattur been id-dawulteen.*

Friday - *jimεa* pl. *jimaε.*

friend - *ṣadiiq* pl. *?aṣdiqaa?, ṣaaẓib* pl. *?aṣẓaab.* Are we friends again? *hassa rjaεna ?aṣdiqaa??*

to make friends - *ṭṣaadaq (a taṣaaduq).* He makes friends easily. *haaδa yiṭṣaadaq b-suhuula.*

friendly - *widdi*.* We came to a friendly agreement. *wuṣalna ?ila ttifaaq widdi.* -- The argument was settled in a friendly way. *l-xilaaf inẓall ib-ṭariiqa widdiyya* or *l-xilaaf inẓall widdiyyan.*

friendship - *ṣadaaqa* pl. *-aat, ṣuẓba.* Our friendship lasted forty years. *ṣadaaqatna daamat ?arbaεiin sana.*

fright - *xoof.* You gave me an awful fright. *xawwafitni xooš xoof.*

to **frighten** - *xawwaf (u taxwiif) t-.* You can't frighten me! *ma-tigdar itxawwufni!*

to be frightened - *xaaf (a xoof).* Don't be frightened. *la-txaaf.*

frog - *εagruuga* pl. *-aat, εagaariig* coll. *εagruug.*

from - 1. *min.* He just received a check from his father. *huwwa hastawwa stilam ṣakk min ?abuu.* 2. *εan, min.* I live ten miles from the city. *?askun ib-biεid εašir ?amyaal εan il-madiina.*

from now on - *minnaa w-hiiči, minnaa w-ġaadi.* From now on I'll be on time. *minnaa w-hiiči raẓ-akuun εal-wakit.*

where ... from - *mneen.* Where are you from? *meen ?inta?* or *?inta min ?ay balad?*

front - 1. *waajiha* pl. *-aat.* The front of the house is painted white. *waajihat il-beet maṣbuuġa ?abyaδ.* 2. *jabha* pl. *-aat.* Were you at the front during the war? *činit bij-jabha ?aθnaa? il-ẓarub?* 3. *?awwal.* The table of contents is in the front of the book. *jadwal il-muẓtawiyyat ib-?awwal l-iktaab.* 4. *?amaami*.* We had seats in the front row. *maqaaεidna čaanat bis-sira l-?amaami.*

in front - 1. *giddaam.* Let's meet in front of the post office. *xal-niltigi giddaam daa?irt il-bariid.* 2. *li-giddaam.* He always sits in front. *haaδa daa?iman yugεud li-giddaam.* 3. *?amaam, giddaam.* The officer is marching in front of his men. *δ-δaabuṭ yimši ?amaam jinuuda.*

to **frown** - *εabbas (i taεbiis) t-.* Why is he frowning? *leeš imεabbis?*

fruit - *faakiha* pl. *fawaakih.* Do you have any fresh fruit? *εindak faakiha taaza?*

to bear fruit - *?aθmar (u ?iθmaar).* This tree doesn't bear fruit. *haš-šajara ma-tiθmur.*

to **fry** - 1. *gaḷḷa (i tagliya).* Shall I fry the fish? *triid agaḷḷi s-simač?* 2. *tgaḷḷa (a tagaḷḷi).* The meat is frying now. *l-laẓam da-yitgaḷḷa.*

fuel - 1. *wuquud.* We use coal, wood, and oil as fuels here. *nistaεmil il-faẓam wil-xišab win-nafuṭ ka-wuquud ihnaa.* 2. *baanziin.* Their fuel ran out over the desert. *baanziinhum xilaṣ foog iṣ-ṣaẓraa?.*

to **fulfill** - 1. *ẓaqqaq (i taẓqiiq) t-.* Her wishes were all fulfilled. *raġbaatha kullha tẓaqqiqat.* 2. *qaam (u qiyaam) b-.* We couldn't fulfill the terms of the contract. *ma-gidarna nquum ib-šuruuṭ il-εaqid.*

full - 1. *malyaan, matruus.* Is the kettle full? *l-kitli malyaan?* -- The book is full of mistakes. *l-iktaab matruus ġalaṭ.* 2. *kaamil.* I paid the full amount. *difaεt il-mablaġ kaamil.* -- Are you working full time now? *da-tištuġuḷ dawaam kaamil hassa?* 3. *šabεaan.* I'm full. *?aani šabεaan.*

in full - *b-kaamil-.* I paid the bill in full. *dfaεit il-qaa?ima b-kaamilha.*

fully - 1. *tamaaman.* Are you fully aware of what is going on? *?inta da-tuεruf tamaaman iš-da-yṣiir?* 2. *b-ṣuura kaamla.* He described it fully. *wuṣafha b-ṣuura kaamla.* 3. *maa la-yqill εan.* There were fully 200 people at the reception. *čaan ?aku maa la-yqill εan il-miiteen šaxiṣ bil-ẓafla.*

fume - *ġaaz* pl. *-aat.* The escaping fumes were poisonous. *l-ġaazaat iṭ-ṭaalεa čaanat saamma.*

fun - *winsa.* Fishing is a lot of fun. *ṣeed is-simač kulliš winsa.*

to make fun of - *qašmar (u qašmara) t-, δiẓak (a δiẓik) n- εala.* Are you making fun of me? *da-tqašmurni?*

function - 1. *šuġuḷ* pl. *?ašġaaḷ.* What's his function in the office? *šinu šuġla bid-daa?ira?* 2. *munaasaba* pl. *-aat.* I saw him at one of the functions at the embassy. *šifta b-?iẓda l-munaasabaat bis-safaara.*

to function - *štiġaḷ (u štiġaal).* The radio doesn't function properly. *r-raadyo ma-da-yištuġuḷ zeen.*

fund - 1. *δaxiira* pl. *-aat.* He has an inexhaustible fund of jokes. *εinda δaxiira ma-tixlaṣ min in-nukat.* 2. *εtimaad* pl. *-aat.* The government established a fund to care for the poor. *l-ẓukuuma fitẓat iεtimaad liṣ-ṣarif εal-fuqaraa?.*

funds - *?amwaal.* He misappropriated public funds. *?asaa? istiεmaal il-?amwaal il-εaamma.*

fundamental - *jawhari*, ?asaasi*.* That's a fundamental difference. *haaδa xtilaaf jawhari.*

funeral - *janaaza* pl. *jnaayiz.* I'm going to his funeral. *raẓ-aruuẓ ij-janaazta.*

funnel - 1. *raẓaati* pl. *-iyyaat, miẓgaan* pl. *maẓaagiin.* The funnel is too big for the bottle. *r-raẓaati kulliš čibiir εal-buṭil.*

funny - 1. *muδẓik.* That story is very funny. *hal-quṣṣa kulliš muδẓika.* 2. *hazali*.* He's a very funny actor. *haaδa mumaθθil kulliš hazali.* 3. *ġariib.* Funny, I can't find my pen. *ġariib, ma-da-agdar algi paandaani.*

funny bone - *damaar* (pl. *-aat*) *εikis.* He hit me on the funny bone. *δirabni εala damaar εiksi.*

fur - *faru.* Most fur comes from Canada and Russia. *?akθar il-faru yiji min kanada w-ruusya.*

furious - *θaayir, haayij.* My boss was furious when I arrived late. *ra?iisi čaan θaayir min wuṣalit mit?axxir.*

furnace - *firin* pl. *?afraan.*

to **furnish** - 1. *?aθθaθ (i ta?θiiθ) t-.* I rented a furnished house. *?ajjarit beet im?aθθaθ.* 2. *jahhaz (i tajhiiz) t-.* The management will furnish you with everything you need. *l-?idaara raẓ-itjahhzak ib-kull-ma tiẓtaaj.* 3. *jaab (i jeeb) n-, qaddam (i taqdiim) t-.* Can you furnish proof? *tigdar itjiib daliil?*

furniture - *?aθaaθ.*

further - 1. *baεad, ?akθar, ?aaxar.* Do you need any further information? *tiẓtaaj maεluumaat baεad?* or *tiẓtaaj maεluumaat ?uxra?* 2. *?aaxar.* I'm closing my store until further notice. *raẓ-asidd il-maxzan maali ?ila ?išεaar ?aaxar.* 3. *?abεad.* He threw the rock further than me. *δurab il-iẓjaara ?abεad minni.*

furthermore - *bil-?iδaafa ?ila haaδa.* Furthermore he's not a member. *bil-?iδaafa ?ila haaδa, huwwa muu εuδu.*

fuse - 1. *fyuuz* pl. *-aat.* The fuse blew out. *ṭagg il-ifyuuz.* 2. *fitiila* pl. *fitaayil.* He lit the fuse and ran. *šiεal il-fitiila w-rikaδ.*

fuss - *δajja* pl. *-aat.* Don't make such a fuss over

him. *la-tsawwi hiiči ṣajja zawla.*
to fuss - *liεab (a liεib) n-.* He's always fussing with his tie. *εala ṭuul yilεab ib-booyinbaağa.*
fussy - *nazis.* He's very fussy about his food. *huwwa kulliš nazis bil-ʔakil.*

future - **1.** *mustaqbal.* This job has no future. *haš-šağla ma-biiha mustaqbal.* **2.** *muqbil.* He introduced his future son-in-law to us. *qaddam-ilna nisiiba l-muqbil.*

G

Gabriel - *jubraaʔiil.*
gag - **1.** *kammaama* pl. *-aat.* Take the gag out of his mouth. *ṭalliε il-kammaama min zalga.* **2.** *nukta* pl. *nukaat.* There are a few good gags in the movie. *ʔaku šwayyat xooš nukaat bil-filim.*
to gag - **1.** *kammam (i takmiim, tkimmim) t-.* They gagged him with a handkerchief. *kammimoo b-čiffiyya.* **2.** *thawwaε (a thuwwuε).* I got sick and began to gag. *nafsi gaamat tilεab w-gumt athawwaε.*
gain - *ribiz* pl. *ʔarbaaz.* This table shows our net gain for the year. *haj-jadwal ybayyin ribizna ṣ-ṣaafi lis-sana.*
to gain - **1.** *kisab (i kasib) n-, zaṣṣal (i tazṣiil) t-, ktisab (i ktisaab).* What did he gain by that? *š-zaṣṣal min haay?* -- He gained my confidence. *ktisab θiqati.* **2.** *rubaz (a ribiz) n-, kisab (i) n-, zaṣṣal (i) t-.* I gained ten dollars in the card game. *rbazit εašir doolaaraat ib-liεb il-waraq.* **3.** *zaad (i ziyaada).* I weighed myself and realized that I had gained four pounds. *wzanit nafsi w-šifit ʔanni zidit ʔarbaε paawnaat.* **4.** *tqaddam (a taqaddum), tgarrab (a tagarrub).* Can't you drive any faster? The car behind us is gaining on us. *ma-tigdar itsuug ʔasraε? s-sayyaara l-waraana da-titqaddam minna.* **5.** *θabbat (i taθbiit, tθibbit).* He tried to climb the hill, but he couldn't gain a footing. *zaawal yiṣεad it-tall laakin ma-gidar yθabbit qadama.*
galaxy - *majarra* pl. *-aat.*
gale - *εaaṣifa* pl. *εawaaṣif.* The gale caused great damage. *l-εaaṣifa sabbibat ʔaṣraar baliiğa.*
gall - *jasaara.* He's got an awful lot of gall. *εinda jasaara hwaaya.*
gall bladder - *maraara* pl. *-aat.*
gallery - *galari* pl. *-iyyaat.* Our seats are in the back of the gallery. *karaasiina b-ʔaaxir il-galari.*
gallon - *gaḷin* pl. *-aat.* The American gallon isn't exactly four liters. *l-gaḷin il-ʔamriiki muu ʔarbaε latraat tamaam.*
gallows - *mašnaqa* pl. *mašaaniq, ṣallaaba* pl. *-aat.* They erected a gallows in the center of town. *niṣbaw mašnaqa b-nuṣṣ il-wlaaya.*
galosh - *čazma* pl. *čizam.*
to **galvanize** - *ğalwan (i tğilwin, ğalwana) t-.* This factory galvanizes metals. *hal-maεmal yğalwin il-maεaadin.* -- This pail is galvanized. *haṣ-ṣaṭal imğalwan.*
gamble - *muqaamara* pl. *-aat.* It was a pure gamble, but we had to risk it. *čaanat fadd muqaamara ʔakiida laakin iṣṭarreena njaazif.*
to gamble - **1.** *liεab (a liεib) iqmaar, qaamar (i muqaamara).* They gambled all night. *liεbaw iqmaar ṭuul il-leel.* **2.** *jaazaf (i mujaazafa).* He was gambling with his life. *čaan da-yjaazif ib-zayaata.*
to gamble away - *xiṣar (a xaṣaara) bil-iqmaar.* He gambled his whole salary away. *xiṣar raatba kulla bil-iqmaar.*
gambling - *qmaar.* He spends all his money gambling. *yiṣruf kull ifluusa bil-iqmaar.*
game - **1.** *liεba* pl. *liεab, ʔalεaab.* We bought a game for our son. *štireena fadd liεba l-ʔibinna.* **2.** *liεba* pl. *-aat, daas* pl. *duus.* The children played a game of hopscotch. *j-jahhaal liεbaw liεbat tuukiyya.* **3.** *liεba* pl. *-aat, liεab, geem* pl. *-aat, šooṭ* pl. *ʔašwaaṭ.* The referee called the end of the game. *l-zakam εilan nihaayat il-liεba.* **4.** *ṣeed.* There's a lot of game in this area. *ʔaku ṣeed ihwaaya b-hal-manṭiqa.* **5.** *wujaε.* I've got a game leg. *εindi wujaε rijil.* **6.** *mistiεidd, zaaṣir.* I'm game for anything. *ʔaani mistiεidd il-ʔay šii.*
**I can see through his game. *εaaruf kull malaaεiiba.*
gang - **1.** *εiṣaaba* pl. *-aat.* The head of the gang was a notorious criminal. *raʔiis il-εiṣaaba čaan fadd mujrim maεruuf.* **2.** *jamaaεa* pl. *-aat.* He runs around with a good gang. *da-yimši wiyya xooš jamaaεa.* **3.** *jamaaεa* pl. *-aat, zumra* pl. *zumar.* He runs around with a bad gang. *da-yimši wiyya zumra muu zeena.* **4.** *jooga* pl. *-aat.* We saw a gang of workmen with shovels in the back of the truck. *šifna joogat εummaal wiyyaahum karakaat ib-ʔaaxir il-loori.*
gangrene - *gangariin.*
gap - **1.** *fatza* pl. *-aat.* They're building a road through the mountain gap. *da-yibnuun ṭariiq bil-fatza lli been ij-jibaleen.* **2.** *θağra* pl. *-aat.* Our infantry opened a wide gap in the enemy's lines. *mušaatna fatzaw θağra waasεa b-xuṭuuṭ il-εadu.* **3.** *faraağ.* Your transfer will leave a gap in this office. *naqlak raz-yitruk faraağ ib-had-daaʔira.* **4.** *naqiṣ.* There's a large gap in his education. *ʔaku naqiṣ kabiir ib-θaqaafta.*
garage - *garaaj* pl. *-aat.*
garbage - *zibil, zbaala.*
garden - **1.** *zadiiqa* pl. *zadaayiq.* These flowers are from our garden. *hal-warid imnil-zadiiqa maalatna.* **2.** *janna* pl. *janaaʔin.* Garden of Eden. *jannat εadan.* -- Hanging Gardens of Babylon. *janaaʔin baabil il-muεallaqa.*
gargle - *ğarğara.* Water and salt is a good gargle. *l-mayy wil-miliz xooš ğarğara.*
to gargle - *tğarğar (a tğirğir).* You have to gargle three times a day. *laazim titğarğar iθlaθ marraat bil-yoom.*
garlic - *θuum.*
garment - *hidim, hduum, malaabis.*
to **garnish** - *zarwag (i tzirwig) t-.* The cook garnished the fish with parsley and lemon. *ṭ-ṭabbaax zarwag is-simča b-ikrafus w-nuumi zaamuṣ.*
garter - *ʔaaṣqi* pl. *-iyyaat.*
gas - **1.** *ğaaz* pl. *-aat.* We use gas for cooking. *nistaεmil il-ğaaz liṭ-ṭabux.* -- Cabbage always gives me gas. *l-lahhaana twallid εindi ğaazaat daaʔiman.* -- The dentist uses an anesthetic gas. *ṭabiib il-ʔasnaan yistaεmil ğaaz muxaddir.* **2.** *paanziin.* He had enough gas for ten miles. *čaan εinda paanziin ykaffi l-εašr amyaal.*
to gas - **1.** *sammam (i tasmiim, tsimmim) t- bil-ğaaz, xinag (u xanig) n- bil-ğaaz.* They gassed their prisoners during the war. *sammamaw masaajiinhum bil-ğaaz xilaal il-zarub.* **2.** *xalla (i txilli) t- paanziin b-.* I gassed the car on my way to work. *xalleet paanziin bis-sayyaara b-ṭariiqi liš-šuğuḷ.*
gasket - *gaazgeeta* pl. *-aat* coll. *gaazgeet.*
gasoline - *paanziin.*
gasoline station - *mazaṭṭat* (pl. *-aat*) *paanziin.*
to **gasp** - *lihaθ (a lahiθ).* We were gasping when we reached the top of the hill. *činna nilhaθ min wuṣalna r-raas it-tall.*
gastric - *maεidi*.*
gate - **1.** *baab* (pl. *biibaan*) *xaarijiyya, baab* (pl. *biibaan*) *barraaniyya.* Who opened the gate? *minu fitaz il-baab il-xaarijiyya?* **2.** *daxaḷ.* The manager is counting the gate now. *l-mudiir da-yizsib id-daxaḷ hassa.*
to **gather** - **1.** *jimaε (a jamiε) n-, lamm (i lamm) n-.* The children gathered firewood. *l-ʔaṭfaal jimεaw zaṭab.* **2.** *ltamm (a ltimaam), tjammaε (a tajammuε).* Many people gathered in front of the platform. *naas ihwaaya ltammaw giddaam il-manaṣṣa.* **3.** *stantaj (i stintaaj), fiham (a fahim) n-.* From what you say, I gather that you don't like him. *min illi tguula ʔastantij ʔinta ma-tzibba.* **4.** *stajmaε (i stijmaaε).* The patient gathered strength after the operation. *l-mariiṣ istajmaε quwaa baεad il-εamaliyya.*
gauge - **1.** *geej* pl. *-aat, miqyaas* pl. *maqaayiis.* The gasoline gauge isn't working. *l-geej maal il-paanziin ma-da-yištuğul.* — Bring me a guage so I can measure these wires. *jiib-li fadd miqyaas zatta aqiis hal-waayraat.* **2.** *mitin.* I want a roll of wire in this gauge. *ʔariid laffat waayar ib-hal-mitin.* **3.** *εiyaar* pl. *-aat.* He hunts with a twelve gauge

shotgun. *yṣiid ib-bunduqiyya ɛiyaar iθnaɛaš.*
to gauge - **1.** *qaas (i qiyaas) n-.* This gauges the thickness. *haaδa yqiis is-sumuk.* **2.** *qaddar (i taqdiir) t-.* I would gauge the distance to be two hundred meters. *ʔaqaddir il-masaafa miiteen matir.*
gauze - *gooz.*
gavel - *maṭraqa* pl. *-aat.*
gay - *mibtihij, farzaan.* The children were gay. *j-jahhaal čaanaw mibtihijiin.*
gazelle - *ġazaal* pl. *ġizlaan.*
gear - **1.** *dišli* pl. *-iyyaat.* I broke a tooth off the gear. *ksarit sinn imnid-dišli.* **2.** *geer.* Shift into second gear. *baddil il-geer ɛaθ-θineen.* **3.** *ġaraaḍ.* We put the fishing gear in the trunk of my car. *xalleena ġaraaḍ ṣeed is-simač ib-ṣanduug sayyaarti.* **4.** *ʔaalaat.* Fix the steering gear. *ṣalliz ʔaalaat is-sikkaan.*
gelatin - *jalaatiin.*
to geld - *xiṣa (i xaṣi) n-.* The army gelds all its horses. *j-jeeš yixṣi kull il-xeel maala.*
gem - *jawhara* pl. *jawaahir.* These gems are invaluable. *haj-jawaahir ma-titθamman.*
general - **1.** *ɛaamm.* Have you heard anything about the general elections? *smaɛit ʔay šii ɛan il-intixaabaat il-ɛaamma?* **2.** *ɛumuumi*.* They gave him a general anesthetic. *nṭoo banj ɛumuumi.* **3.** *jiniraal* pl. *-aat* (not applied to Arab officer of that rank). They nominated the general to the presidency of the republic. *raššizaw ij-jiniraal ir-riʔaast ij-jamhuuriyya.* **4.** (= four-star general, Iraqi Army). *ɛamiid* pl. *ɛumadaaʔ* He was promoted general. *raffiɛoo ɛamiid.*
in general - *b-ṣuura ɛaamma, ɛal-ɛumuum.* In general, things are all right. *b-ṣuura ɛaamma, l-ʔazwaal zeena.*
brigadier general - *zaɛiim* pl. *zuɛamaaʔ.*
lieutenant general - *fariiq* pl. *furaqaaʔ.*
major general - *ʔamiir liwaaʔ* pl. *ʔumaraaʔ ʔalwiya.*
general delivery - *šibbaač il-bariid.* Send the letter to me in care of general delivery. *dizz-li l-maktuub ib-waasṭat šibbaač il-bariid.*
generally - *b-ṣuura ɛaamma, ɛal-ɛumuum.* He's generally here before eight. *huwwa ɛal-ɛumuum ihnaa qabḷ iθ-θimaanya.*
generation - *jiil* pl. *ʔajyaal.* His family has been in America for four generations. *ɛaaʔilta ṣaar-ilha ʔarbaɛ ajyaal ib-ʔamriika.*
generous - *kariim* pl. *kuramaaʔ, saxi* pl. *ʔasxiyaaʔ, barmaki* pl. *-iyya.* Don't be so generous! *la-tkuun hal-gadd barmaki!*
genius - **1.** *nubuuġ, ɛabqariyya.* That man has genius. *δaak ir-rijjaal ɛinda ɛabqariyya.* **2.** *naabiġa* pl. *nawaabiġ, ɛabqari* pl. *ɛabaaqira.* He's a genius in mathematics. *huwwa naabiġa bir-riyaaḍiyyaat.*
gentle - **1.** *laṭiif.* A gentle breeze was coming from the sea. *nasiim laṭiif čaan da-yiji mnil-bazar.* **2.** *wadiiɛ, haadiʔ.* This horse is very gentle. *hal-izṣaan kulliš wadiiɛ.*
gentleman - **1.** *sayyid* pl. *saada.* Will you see what this gentleman wants, please? *baḷḷa ma-tšuuf has-sayyid š-yriid?* -- Ladies and gentlemen. *sayyidaati w-saadati.* **2.** *rijjaal* pl. *ryaajiil.* There are two gentlemen outside waiting for you. *ʔaku rijjaaleen da-yintaḍruuk barra.*
gently - **1.** *yawaaš, ɛala keef-.* He knocked gently on the door. *dagg il-baab ɛala keefa.* **2.** *yawaaš, ɛala keef-, b-luṭuf.* You'll have to treat him gently. *laazim itɛaamla b-luṭuf.*
genuine - *ʔaṣli*.* This suitcase is genuine leather. *hal-junṭa jilid ʔaṣli.*
geography - *juġraafiya.*
geometry - *handasa.*
germ - *jarθuum* pl. *jaraaθiim.* Don't eat that! It's full of germs. *la-taakul haay. kullha jaraaθiim.*
German - **1.** *ʔalmaani* pl. *-iyyiin, ʔalmaan.* Are there many Germans here? *ʔaku hwaaya ʔalmaan ihnaa?* **2.** *ʔalmaani.* He speaks German. *yitkallam ʔalmaani.* **3.** *ʔalmaani*.* I bought a German watch. *štireet saaɛa ʔalmaaniyya.*
Germany - *ʔalmaanya.*
gesture - *ʔišaara* pl. *-aat.* His gestures are very expressive. *ʔišaaraata kulliš muɛabbira.*
to get - **1.** *stilam (i stilaam).* When did you get my letter? *šwakit istilamit maktuubi?* **2.** *zaṣṣal (i tziṣṣil, zuṣuul) t-.* We can get apples cheaper here. *nigdar inzaṣṣil it-tiffaaz ib-ʔarxaṣ ihnaa.* -- Try to get him on the telephone. *zaawil itzaṣṣila bit-talifoon.* **3.** *dabbar (u tadbiir, tdubbur) t-, zaṣṣal (i) t-.* Can you get me another copy? *tigdar itdabbur-li nusxa lux?* **4.** *ʔaxaδ (u ʔaxaδ) n-, zaṣṣal (i) t-.* He got the highest grade in the class. *ʔaxaδ ʔaɛla daraja biṣ-ṣaff.* **5.** *xalla (i txilli).* Can you get him to go there? *tigdar itxallii yruuz l-ihnaak?* -- Get him to do it for you. *xallii ysawwi-lk-iyyaaha.* **6.** *jaab (i jeeba) n-.* Go get my hat. *ruuz jiib šafuqti.* **7.** *waṣṣal (i twiṣṣil).* Can you get this message to him? *tigdar itwaṣṣil-la hal-xabar?* **8.** *wuṣal (a wuṣuul), jaa (i majiiʔ).* We got to Baghdad the next day. *wuṣalna l-baġdaad θaani yoom.* **9.** *ṣaar (i).* Do you think he'll get well again? *tiɛtiqid raz-yṣiir zeen marra lux?*
**Do you get the idea? *tšuuf išloon?*
**He got sentenced to a year in jail. *nzikam sana zabis.*
**He got hit in the mouth. *nḍurab ib-zalga.*
**He got hurt in the accident. *tɛawwar bil-zaadiθ.*
**He is getting treated at the hospital. *da-yitɛaalaj bil-mustašfa.*
**His face got real red. *wičča zmarr kulliš.*
**The grass is getting green. *l-zašiiš da-yixḍarr.*
**He got drunk. *sikar.*
**He went to get a drink of water. *raz-yišrab jurɛat mayy.*
**I got four hours sleep. *nimit ʔarbaɛ saaɛaat.*
**His lying really gets me. I hate it. *čiδba yxabbuḷni. ʔamuut minna.*
**I got to bed early, but I couldn't sleep. *ntirazit bil-ifraaš min wakit laakin ma-gdart anaam.*
**We get twenty miles to the gallon in our new car. *nṭalliɛ ɛišriin miil bil-gaḷin ib-sayyaaratna j-jidiida.*
**Get lost! *walli!*
**You beat me three games in a row, but I'll get even tomorrow night. *ġiḷabitni tlaθ liɛbaat wazda wara l-lux, raz-atḷaawak wiyyaak baačir bil-leel.*
**I'll get even with him for the death of my brother. *raz-antiqim minna ɛala mootat axuuya.*
to get about - *daar (u door) b-, ftarr (a farr) b-.* He gets about the house in a wheelchair. *yduur bil-beet ib-kursi ʔabu čruux.* -- A rumor got about that he was going to resign. *fadd ʔišaaɛa daarat bi-ʔanna raz-yistiqiil.*
to get across - **1.** *fahham (i tafhiim) t-.* I wasn't able to get the idea across to him. *ma-gdart afahhima l-fikra.* **2.** *ɛubar (u ɛabur) n-.* I got across the river in a boat. *ɛbarit iš-šaṭṭ ib-balam.*
to get ahead - *tqaddam (a taqaddum).* He'll never get ahead in business with that attitude. *wala raz-yitqaddam bit-tijaara b-hal-waḍiɛ.*
to get a glimpse of - *limaz (a lamiz) n-.* I got a glimpse of a man wearing a red shirt. *limazit rijjaal laabis θoob ʔazmar.*
to get along - **1.** *dabbar (u tadbiir) ʔamur˜.* We get along on very little money. *ndabbur ʔamurna. b-išwayya fluus.* **2.** *twaalam (a tawaalum), tlaaʔam (a talaaʔum).* We get along well with each other. *nitwaalam zeen waazid wiyya l-laax.* **3.** *miša (i maši), raaz (u rawaaz).* I'll have to be getting along now. *laazim ʔamši hassa.* **4.** *tqaddam (a tqaddum).* He's getting along in years. *da-yitqaddam bil-ɛumur.*
**How are you getting along? *šloon ʔazwaalak?* or *šloon da-timši?*
to get around - **1.** *ztaal (a ztiyaal), tmaḷḷaṣ (a tamaḷḷuṣ).* They tried to get around the tax regulations. *zaawilaw yiztaaluun ɛala niḍaam iḍ-ḍaraayib.* **2.** *tjawwal (a tajawwul), jaal (u tajwaal).* As president, naturally he gets around a lot. *b-ṣifta raʔiis, ṭabɛan yitjawwal ihwaaya.* **3.** *ntišar (i ntišaar).* The story got around quickly. *l-izčaaya ntišrat bil-ɛajal.* **4.** *ftarr (a farr), daar (u door).* She can't get around the house very easily. *ma-tigdar itduur bil-beet bis-suhuula.*
to get at - **1.** *zaṣṣal (i tazṣiil) t-, twaṣṣal (a tawaṣṣul).* His family won't let him get at the money that's in his name in the bank. *ʔahla ma-yxalluu yzaṣṣil l-ifluus illi b-isma bil-bang.* -- We didn't get at the real reason. *ma-twaṣṣalna lis-sabab il-zaqiiqi.* **2.** *naaš (u nooš) n-.* I can't get at the bolt from here. *ma-agdar anuuš il-burġi minnaa.*
to get away - **1.** *tmaḷḷaṣ (a tamaḷḷuṣ).* I'm sorry but I couldn't get away. *ʔaasif bass ma-gdarit atmaḷḷaṣ.* **2.** *nhizam (i haziima, nhizaam), hirab (u harab), filat (i falit).* The criminal got away. *l-mujrim inhizam.* **3.** *waxxar (i tawxiir, twixxir) t-.* Get the children away from the stove. *waxxir*

ij-jahhaal imniṭ-ṭabbaax. 4. tirak (u tarik) n-, nhizam (i haziima, nhizaam). I want to get away from town for a few days. ʔard atruk l-wlaaya muddat čam yoom.
**You won't get away with it. haay ma-tfuut-lak.

to get back - 1. rijaɛ (a rujuuɛ). When did you get back? šwakit rijaɛit? -- I have to get these books back before noon. laazim arajjiɛ hal-kutub gabḷ iδ-δuhur. 2. starjaɛ (i stirjaaɛ), rajjaɛ (i tarjiiɛ, trijjiɛ). I want to get my money back. ʔariid astarjiɛ ifluusi.
3. ntiqam (i ntiqaam) min. He got me back for fighting with his brother. ntiqam minni l-iɛraaki wiyya ʔaxuu.

to get behind - 1. saanad (i musaanada). The industrialists are getting behind him for the presidency. rijjaal iṣ-ṣinaaɛa da-ysaanduu lir-riʔaasa. 2. tʔaxxar (a taʔaxxur). We've started to get behind in our work. bdeena nitʔaxxar ib-šuguḷna.

to get by - 1. dabbar (u tadbiir) nafis~. I get by on thirty dinars a month. ʔadabbur nafsi b-itlaθiin diinaar biš-šahar. 2. xallaṣ (i taxliiṣ, txilliṣ) min. How did you get by the guard? šloon xallaṣit imnil-ʒaaris?

to get in - 1. dixal (u duxuul) n-, xašš (u xašš) n-. How did you get in the house? šloon dixalit bil-beet? 2. wuṣal (a wuṣuul), ṭabb (u ṭabb). What time did the train get in? šwakit ṭabb il-qiṭaar? 3. xaššaš (i taxšiiš) t-, fawwat (i tafwiit) t-, daxxal (i tadxiil) t-. Get the clothes in before it rains. xaššiš il-ihduum gabuḷ-ma tumṭur.
**I'd like to get in a game of tennis before it rains. ʔard alɛab fadd liɛbat tanis gabuḷ-ma tumṭur.

to get off - 1. nizal (i nuzuul) min. I'll get off the train at the next station. raʒ-anzil imnil-qiṭaar bil-maʒaṭṭa j-jaaya. 2. δabb (i δabb) n-. He got off a couple of funny jokes. δabb nukutteen muδʒika or δabb-la nukutteen muδʒika. 3. šaal (i šeel) n- ɛan. Get your elbows off the table. šiil iɛkuusak ɛann il-meez. 4. nizaɛ (a naziɛ) n-. Get your clothes off and take a bath. ʔinzaɛ ihduumak w-xuδ ʒammaam. 5. xilaṣ (a xalaaṣ). He got off with a light sentence. xilaṣ ib-ɛuquuba baṣiiṭa.
**The team got off to a bad start. l-fariiq bida bidaaya muu zeena.
**He told the boss where to get off and left. farraġ simma bil-mudiir w-ṭilaɛ.

to get on - 1. ṣiɛad (a ṣuɛuud) n-, rikab (a rukuub) n-. These passengers got on in Kirkuk. har-rukkaab ṣiɛadaw ib-karkuuk. 2. libas (a libis) n-. Help me get my coat on. saaɛidni ʔalbas qappuuṭi. 3. stimarr (i stimraar). Get on with your work. Don't mind me. stimirr ib-šuġḷak. la-tdiir-li baal.

to get out - 1. ṭilaɛ (a ṭuluuɛ) n-. I got out of the office at five. ṭilaɛit imnid-daaʔira bil-xamsa. -- We must not let this news get out. ma-laazim inxalli hal-xabar yiṭlaɛ. 2. ṭallaɛ (i taṭliiɛ) t-. Get this beggar out of the store. ṭalliɛ hal-imjaddi mnid-dukkaan. 3. xilaṣ (a xalaaṣ), xallaṣ (i taxliiṣ, txallaṣ). He got out of it by paying a fine. xilaṣ minha b-dafiɛ ġaraama. 4. waxxar (i tawxiir), twaxxar (a tawaxxur). Get out of my way! waxxir min darbi! 5. ʒaṣṣal (i taʒṣiil) t-. You can't get much out of him. ma-tigdar itʒaṣṣil minna šii. 6. ʒaṣṣal (i taʒṣiil) t-, rubaʒ (a ribiʒ) n-. How much did you get out of this deal? šgadd ʒaṣṣalit ib-haṣ-ṣafqa. 7. nizal (i nizuul). I'll have to get out at the next stop. laazim anzil bil-mawqif ij-jaay.
**How much can I get out of this camera? hal-kaamira šgadd raʒ-atjiib-li?

to get over - 1. txallaṣ (a taxalluṣ) min. I had a cold, but I'm getting over it now. čaanat ɛindi našla laakin da-atxallaṣ minha hassa. 2. ṭallaɛ (i taṭliiɛ) min fikir~. He still hasn't gotten over his wife's death. baɛda ma-ṭallaɛ moot marta min fikra. 3. tnaʒʒa (a tanaʒʒi), twaxxar (a tawaxxur). Get over a little. Let me sit down. tnaʒʒa šwayya, xalli ʔagɛud.

to get rid of - txallaṣ (a taxalluṣ) min. How can I get rid of him? šloon agdar atxallaṣ minna?

to get through - 1. ntiha (i ntihaaʔ), xallaṣ (i txilliṣ). Can you get through in two hours? tigdar itxalliṣ ib-saaɛteen? 2. faat (u foot) min, marr (u marr, muruur) min. You can't get through here. ma-tigdar itfuut minnaa.

to get together - 1. tlaaga (a tlaagi), jtimaɛ (i jtimaaɛ). Let's get together during lunch. xal-nitlaaga wakt il-ġada. 2. ttifaq (i ttifaaq). We weren't able to get together on a good solution. ma-gdarna nittifiq ɛala ʒall zeen.

to get up - 1. gaam (u goom), giɛad (u gaɛda). I get up at six every morning. ʔaani ʔagɛud yoomiyya s-saaɛa sitta ṣ-ṣubuʒ. 2. gaɛɛad (i tgiɛɛid) t-, fazzaz (i tfizziz) t-. Would you get me up in the morning, please? balḷa ma-tgaɛɛidni ṣ-ṣubuʒ rajaaʔan? 3. ṣiɛad (a ṣaɛid) n-. We had a hard time getting up the hill. laaqeena ṣuɛuuba b-ṣaɛdat ij-jibil.

ghost - rooʒ pl. ʔarwaaʒ, šabaʒ pl. ʔašbaaʒ. I don't believe in ghosts. ma-aɛtiqid bil-ʔarwaaʒ. -- He read a story about the Holy Ghost. qira quṣṣa ɛan ir-rooʒ il-qudus. -- He hasn't a ghost of a chance in this matter. ma-ʔila wala šabaʒ ʔamal ib-hal-qaδiyya.

ghoul - ġuul pl. ġiilaan.

giant - ɛimlaaq pl. ɛamaaliqa. Compared to me, he's a giant. bin-nisba ʔili, huwwa ɛimlaaq.

Gibraltar - jabal ṭaariq.

gift - 1. hadiyya pl. hadaaya. Thank you for your nice gift. ʔaškurak ɛala hadiyytak il-laṭiifa. 2. mawhiba pl. mawaahib. He has a gift for drawing. ɛinda mawhiba bir-rasim.

gifted - mawhuub, mulham. He's a gifted boy. huwwa walad mawhuub.

to **giggle** - karkar (i tkirkir). The girls kept on giggling. l-banaat δallaw ykarkiruun.

ginger - skanjabiil.

giraffe - zuraafa pl. -aat.

girder - šeelmaana pl. -aat coll. šeelmaan. They reinforced the roof with girders. qawwaw is-saguf ib-šeelmaan.

girdle - koorsee pl. koorsaat. She went in to buy a girdle. dixlat tištiri koorsee.

girl - bint pl. banaat, bnayya pl. -aat. That girl is nice. hal-bint laṭiifa.

girlfriend - ṣadiiqa pl. -aat. She went to the movie with her girlfriends. raaʒat lis-siinama wiyya ṣadiiqaatha.

to **give** - 1. niṭa (i naṭi) n-. Please give me the letter. ʔarjuuk inṭiini l-maktuub. -- I'll give you five dollars for it. raʒ-anṭiik biiha xamas doolaaraat. 2. wihab (i wahib) n-, niṭa (i) n-. The king gave a car to the foreign minister in recognition of his service. l-malik wihab sayyaara l-waziir il-xaarijiyya ka-ɛtiraaf ib-xadamaata. 3. niṭa (i) n-, tbarraɛ (a tabarruɛ) b-. We gave money to the poor. nṭeena fluus lil-fuqra. 4. ballaġ (i tabliiġ, ʔiblaaġ) t-. Give him my regards. balliġa taʒiyyaati. 5. sabbab (i tasbiib, tsibbib) l-. This noise gives me a headache. haṣ-ṣoot ysabbib-li wujaɛ raas. -- This fellow gives me a lot of trouble. haš-šaxaṣ da-ysabbib-li hwaaya mašaakil. 6. ʔalqa (i ʔilqaaʔ) n-, qaddam (i taqdiim) t-. Who's giving the speech this evening? minu raʒ-yilqi l-xiṭaab hal-masa? 7. tʒalʒal (a taʒalʒul). The window's stuck; it won't give. š-šibbaač imšakkil, ma-yitʒalʒal.

to give away - fiša (i ʔifšaaʔ) n-, baaʒ (u booʒ) n- b-. Don't give away my secret! la-tifši sirri!

to give back - rajjaɛ (i tarjiiɛ) t- l-, radd (i radd) n- l-. Please give me back my pen. rajjiɛ-li qalam il-ʒibir maali min faδlak.

to give in - ʔaδɛan (a ʔiδɛaan). Don't give in to your son every time he asks for something. la-tiδɛan il-ʔibnak kull wakit yuṭlub minnak šii.

to give off - niṭa (i naṭi) n-, biɛaθ (a baɛiθ) n-. This flower gives off a strange odor. hal-warid da-yinṭi riiʒa ġariiba.

to give out - 1. wazzaɛ (i tawziiɛ, twazzaɛ) t-. Who's giving out the candy? minu da-ywazziɛ il-ʒalawiyyaat? 2. xilaṣ (a xalaaṣ). My supply of ink is giving out. l-ʒibir il-mawjuud ɛindi da-yixlaṣ.

to give up - 1. baṭṭal (i tbiṭṭil), tirak (u tarik) n-. I'm going to give up smoking. raʒ-abaṭṭil it-tadxiin. 2. sallam (i tasliim, tsillim). The police gave him twenty-four hours to give up. š-šurṭa nṭoo muhla ʔarbaɛa w-ɛišriin saaɛa ʒatta ysallim. 3. ʔayyas (i tʔiyyis). After ten days searching for him, we gave up. baɛad ɛaširt iyyaam indawwir ɛalee, ʔayyasna.

to give way - nxisaf (i nxisaaf), xisaf (i xasif). While he was walking the ground gave way, and he fell in a big hole. lamma čaan yimši nxisfat bii l-gaaɛ w-wugaɛ ib-nugra čbiira.

given - muɛayyan, muʒaddad. I have to finish it in a

given time. *laazim axallişha b-xilaal wakit muƐayyan.*

gizzard - *ʒooşla* pl. *ʒawaaşil.* Faisal likes to eat chicken gizzards. *fayşal yʒibb yaakul ʒawaaşil dijaaj.*

glad - **1.** *farʒaan* pl. *-iin.* The children were glad to see us. *l-ʔaṭfaal čaanaw farʒaaniin yšuufuuna.* **2.** *min suruur-, ysurr-.* I'll be glad to help you. *min suruuri ʔasaaƐdak.*

gladly - *b-kull suruur, b-mamnuuniyya.* Would you do me a favor? Gladly! *ʔakallfak ib-fadd šii tsawwii? b-kull suruur!*

glance - *naðra* pl. *aat.* At a glance I knew something was wrong. *b-naðra wiʒda Ɛrafit čaan aku fadd šii muu tamaam.*

to glance - *baawaƐ (i mubaawaƐa).* I glanced at my watch. *baawaƐit ib-saaƐti.*

to glance off - *nʒiraf (i nʒiraaf).* The bullet hit a rock and glanced off. *ṭ-ṭalqa ðurbat iş-şaxra w-inʒirfat.*

gland - *ġudda* pl. *ġudad.*

glare - **1.** *lamaƐaan, bariiq.* The glare hurts my eyes. *l-lamaƐaan yʔaðði Ɛyuuni.* **2.** *xazra* pl. *-aat.* He gave me a glare when I entered. *xizarni xazra lamma dxalit.*

to glare - **1.** *şiṭaƐ (a şaṭiƐ), limaƐ (a lamaƐaan).* The sunlight glared off the surface of the water. *ðuwa š-šamis şiṭaƐ min wijh il-mayy.* **2.** *xanzar (i txinzir), xizar (i xazir).* Why are you glaring at me like that? *luweeš da-txanzir Ɛalayya haš-šikil?*

glaring - *lammaaƐ, şaaṭiƐ.* How can you work in that glaring light? *šloon tigdar tištuġul ib-hað-ðuwa ş-şaaṭiƐ?*

glass - **1.** *gziiz, zujaaj.* This pitcher is made of glass. *had-doolka min igziiz.* **2.** *glaaş* pl. *-aat.* Bring me a glass of water. *jiib-li fadd iglaaş mayy.* **3.** *zujaaji*.* Some acids must be kept in glass containers. *baƐað il-ʒawaamið laazim tinʒufuð ib-ʔawƐiya zujaajiyya.*

glasses - *manðara, manaaðir* pl. *manaaðir.* I can't read without glasses. *ma-agdar aqra bila manaaðir.*

gleam - *bariiq, lamaƐaan.* There was a gleam in his eye. *čaan ʔaku bariiq ib-Ɛeena.*

to gleam - *limaƐ (a lamaƐaan), birag (i barig).* The floor was gleaming. *l-gaaƐ čaanat da-tibrig.*

glider - *ṭayyaara* (pl. *-aat*) *širaaƐiyya.*

glisten - *tlaʔlaʔ (a talaʔluʔ), tʔallaq (a taʔalluq), limaƐ (a lamaƐaan), šaƐƐ (i šuƐaaƐ).* The stars were glistening in the sky. *n-nijuum čaanat titlaʔlaʔ bis-sima.*

globe - *kura* (pl. *-aat*) *ʔarðiyya.* The teacher brought a globe to class for our geography lesson. *l-muƐallim jaab kura ʔarðiyya l-dars ij-juġraafiya maalna.*

gloomy - **1.** *mdalhim.* Yesterday was a gloomy day. *l-baarʒa čaanat id-dinya mdalihma.* **2.** *mdalhim, kaʔiib.* He's always gloomy. *huwwa daaʔiman imdalhim* or ***huwwa daaʔiman gaaluḅ wijja.*

glorious - **1.** *raaʔiƐ, badiiƐ, faaxir, laṭiif.* We spent a glorious day at the fair. *gðeena yoom raaʔiƐ bil-maƐrað.* **2.** *majiid.* Yesterday was a glorious day in the history of the country. *l-baarʒa čaan yoom majiid ib-taariix il-balad.*

glory - *majid, Ɛaðama.* He spoke on the glory of our ancestors. *ʒiča Ɛan majd ajdaadna.*

glove - *čaff* pl. *čfuuf.* I bought a pair of gloves yesterday. *štireet zooj ičfuuf il-baarʒa.*

**This suit fits him like a glove. *hal-badla raahma Ɛalee miθl il-miʒbas.*

glove compartment - *čakmača* pl. *-aat.*

glue - *şamuġ, šriis.* I bought a bottle of glue. *štireet šiišat şamuġ.*

to glue - *lizag (i lazig) n-, şammaġ (i tşummuġ) t-.* He glued the two boards together. *lizag il-looʒteen suwa.*

**She stood glued to the spot. *wugfat imbasumra.*

glutton - *šarih* pl. *-iin, nahim* pl. *-iin.* Don't be such a glutton. *la-tkuun hal-gadd šarih.*

**He's a glutton for punishment. *huwwa miθl ič-čalib il-yʒibb daamġa.*

to **gnash** - *gazgaz (i tgizgiz).* He gnashed his teeth. *gazgaz isnuuna.*

to **gnaw** - **1.** *girað (u garið) n- b-.* A mouse was gnawing at the rope. *fadd faara čaanat tigruð bil-ʒabil.* **2.** *garmaṭ (u tgurmuṭ) t- b-.* The dog gnawed the bone. *č-čalib garmaṭ bil-Ɛaðum.*

to **go** - **1.** *raaʒ (u rooʒa) n-.* I go to the movies once a week. *ʔaruuʒ lis-siinama marra bil-isbuuƐ.* **2.** *raaʒ (u rooʒa) n-, miša (i maši) n-.* This train goes to Baghdad. *hal-qiṭaar yruuʒ il-baġdaad.* **3.** *miša (i) n-.* The car goes sixty miles an hour. *s-sayyaara timši sittiin miil bis-saaƐa.* -- Red doesn't go with yellow. *l-aʒmar ma-yimši wiyya l-aşfar.* **4.** *štiġal (u štiġaal), miša (i).* This engine won't go on poor gas. *hal-makiina ma-tištuġul ib-baanziin duuni.* **5.** *miša (i), ʔija (i majiiʔ).* The first line of the poem goes this way. *ʔawwal beet imnil-qaşiida yimši haš-šikil.* **6.** *jara (i jarayaan), miša(i), şaar (i şeera).* Whatever he says goes. *lli yguula yijri.* **7.** *buqa (a baqaaʔ).* They went without food for three days. *buqaw iblayya ʔakil itlatt iyyaam.*

to go ahead - **1.** *tfaððal (a).* Go ahead and eat. *tfaððal ʔukul.* **2.** *stamarr (i stimraar), raaʒ (u) ib-faal~.* I'll just go ahead with what I'm doing. *ʔaani raʒ-astimirr biš-šii lli da-asawwii* or *ʔaani raʒ-aruuʒ ib-faali biš-šii lli da-asawwii.*

to go at - **1.** *jaa (i majiiʔ).* You're not going at it the right way. *ʔinta ma-da-tijiiha mniṭ-ṭariiq iş-şaʒiiʒ.* **2.** *raaʒ (u rooʒa) Ɛala, hijam (i hujuum) Ɛala.* He went at the man with a knife. *hijam Ɛar-rijjaal bis-siččiina.*

to go back - *rijaƐ (a rujuuƐ).* She went back to the house. *rijƐat lil-beet.* -- This style of architecture in Spain goes back to the time of the Arabs in Andalusia. *haṭ-ṭiraaz maal il-binaaʔ b-aşpaanya yirjaƐ il-zamaan il-Ɛarab bil-ʔandalus.*

to go back on - *traajaƐ (a taraajuƐ) Ɛan.* I never go back on my word. *ma-atraajaƐ Ɛan kalimti.*

to go by - **1.** *marr (u muruur) n-, faat (u foota) n-.* Are you going by the grocer's on you're way to work? *raʒ-itmurr Ɛal-baggaal ib-ṭariiqak liš-šuġul?* **2.** *miša (i maši) n- Ɛala, tibaƐ (a tabiƐ) n-.* Don't go by this map. *la-timši Ɛala hal-xariiṭa.* **3.** *staƐmal (i stiƐmaal).* He goes by an assumed name. *yistaƐmil ʔisim mustaƐaar.*

to go down - **1.** *nizal (i nuzuul).* Prices are going down. *l-ʔasƐaar da-tinzil.* **2.** *ġaab (i ġeeba).* The sun is going down. *š-šamis da-tġiib.*

to go in - **1.** *dixal (u duxuul) n-, xašš (u xašš) n-.* They went in at four o'clock. *dixlaw is-saaƐa ʔarbaƐa.* **2.** *štirak (i štiraak), tšaarak (a tašaaruk).* Would you like to go in with me on this transaction? *yƐijbak tištirik wiyyaaya b-haş-şafqa?*

to go in for - *htamm (a htimaam) b-, Ɛind- raġba.* I don't go in for sports. *ma-Ɛindi raġba bir-riyaaða.*

to go into - *dixal (u duxuul) n- b-, xašš (u xašš) n- b-.* He went into politics. *dixal bis-siyaasa.*

to go off - **1.** *θaar (u θoora).* The bomb went off. *l-qumbula θaarat.* **2.** *xitam (i xitaam) n-.* We go off the air at ten in the evening. *nixtim il-ʔiðaaƐa s-saaƐa Ɛašra masaaʔan.*

to go on - **1.** *stimarr (i stimraar).* This can't go on any longer. *haay ma-mumkin tistimirr baƐad ʔakθar.* **2.** *nƐilag (i nƐilaag).* The light went on. *ð-ðuwa nƐilag.*

**Go on! I don't believe that. *yeezi Ɛaad! ma-aşaddig haaða.*

to go out - **1.** *nṭufa (i nṭifaaʔ).* The candle just went out. *hassa nṭufat iš-šamƐa.* **2.** *ṭilaƐ (a ṭalƐa).* He just went out. *hastawwa ṭilaƐ.* **3.** *zaal (u zawaal).* The use of the horse and buggy went out with the advent of the automobile. *stiƐmaal il-iʒşaan wil-Ɛarabaana zaal ib-majiiʔ is-sayyaara.*

to go over - **1.** *raajaƐ (i muraajaƐa) t-.* Let's go over the details once more. *xalli nraajiƐ it-tafaaşiil marra lux.* **2.** *miša (i maši).* It was a good product, but it didn't go over. *čaanat xooš biðaaƐa laakin ma-mišat.* **3.** *Ɛubar (u Ɛabur) n-.* We didn't go over the bridge. *ma-Ɛubarna j-jisir.*

to go through - **1.** *Ɛubar (u Ɛabur, Ɛubuur) n-.* He went through the red light. *Ɛubar ið-ðuwa l-ʔaʒmar.* **2.** *marr (u marr, muruur) b-.* That poor woman has gone through a lot of hardships. *hal-mara l-maskiina marrat ib-maşaayib ihwaaya.*

to go through with - *sawwa (i tsiwwi) t-, naffað (i tanfiið, tniffið) t-.* Did you go through with your plan? *naffaðit xiṭṭak?*

to go under - *ġaaş (u ġooş) n-.* He went under and drowned. *ġaaş w-ġirag.*

to go up - **1.** *şiƐad (a şaƐid) n-.* We watched him going up the mountain. *baawaƐna Ɛalee yişƐad ij-jibal.* **2.** *şiƐad (a), rtifaƐ (i rtifaaƐ).* The price of meat is going up. *siƐr il-laʒam da-yirtifiƐ.*

to go with - **1.** *riham (a rahum) wiyya, miša (i maši) wiyya.* This tie doesn't go with the suit. *har-ribaaṭ ma-yirham wiyya l-qaaṭ.* **2.** *tibaƐ*

(*a tabiE*). The trip and all that went with it cost me a hundred dinars. *s-safra w-maa yitbaEha kallfatni miit diinaar.*
goal - 1. *hadaf* pl. *ʔahdaaf, ġaraḍ* pl. *ʔaġraaḍ, maqṣad* pl. *maqaaṣid.* He has set himself a very high goal. *ẓaṭṭ giddaama fadd hadaf Eaali.* **2.** *gooḷ* pl. *gwaaḷ, hadaf* pl. *ʔahdaaf.* Our team made three goals in the first half. *fariiqna sawwa itlaθ igwaaḷ biš-šooṭ il-ʔawwal.*
goat - 1. *ṣaxal* pl. *ṣxuul, Eanza* pl. *-aat* coll. *Eanz.* He raises goats. *yrabbi ṣxuul.* **2.** *ḍaẓiyya* pl. *ḍaẓaaya.* He's always the goat. *huwwa daaʔiman iḍ-ḍaẓiyya.*
**Don't let him get your goat. *la-txallii yġuθθak.*
goatee - *liẓya* (pl. *liẓa*) *kuusa.* He has a goatee. *Einda liẓya kuusa.*
God - *ʔaḷḷaah, ʔillaah.* God forbid. *la-samaẓ aḷḷaah.* -- In the name of God, the Merciful, the Compassionate. *b-ism illaah ir-raẓmaan ir-raẓiim.* -- God willing. *ʔin šaaʔ aḷḷaah.*
god - *ʔilaah* pl. *ʔaaliha.* They worship false gods. *yEibduun il-ʔaaliha.*
goggles - *manaaḍir, manḍara* pl. *manaaḍir.*
going - 1. *daarij, maaši, jaari.* The going rate on the dinar is two dollars and eighty cents. *s-siEir id-daarij lid-diinaar huwwa doolaareen w-iθmaaniin sant.* **2.** *maaši.* They have a going concern. *Eidhum šarika maašya.*
going to - *raẓ-.* I'm going to bake a cake. *ʔaani raẓ-aṭbux keek.*
goiter - *taḍaxxum il-ġudda d-daraqiyya.*
gold - 1. *ðahab.* Is that real gold? *haaða ðahab ẓaqiiqi?* **2.** *ðahabi**. They awarded him a gold medal. *hidoo-la madaalya ðahabiyya.*
goldsmith - *ṣaayiġ* pl. *ṣiyyaaġ.*
golf - *goolf.*
gonorrhea - *sayalaan, ganooriya.*
good - 1. *faaʔida* pl. *fawaaʔid, maṣlaẓa* pl. *maṣaaliẓ.* I did that for your own good. *sawweet haaða l-maṣlaẓtak.* **2.** *xeer.* He doesn't know the difference between good and evil. *ma-yiErif il-fariq been il-xeer wiš-šarr.* **3.** *zeen, yimši.* This coupon is good for ten days. *hal-koopoon zeen il-muddat Eaširt iyyaam* or *hal-koopoon yimši l-muddat Eaširt iyyaam.* **4.** *zeen, xooš.* He does good work. *ysawwi xooš šuġuḷ* or *ysawwi suġuḷ zeen.* **5.** *xooš, zeen, ṭayyib.* The weather isn't good today. *j-jaww muu ṭayyib il-yoom.* -- He did me a good turn yesterday. *sawwaa-li fadd xooš dagga l-baarẓa.* -- He's from a good family. *huwwa min Eaaʔila ṭayyba.* **6.** *ṣaaliẓ.* He's a good Moslem. *huwwa muslim ṣaaliẓ.* **7.** *bil-qaliil.* There's a good dozen eggs in the refrigerator. *ʔaku bil-qaliil darzan beeḍ biθ-θallaaja.* **8.** *Eaaqil* pl. *Euqqaal, zeen* pl. *-iin.* The children were good all day. *l-ʔaṭfaal čaanaw Euqqaal ṭuul il-yoom.*
**One good turn deserves another. *zeeniyya b-zeeniyya.*
**If you ask him to do something, it's as good as done. *ʔiða tuṭlub minna ysawwi šii, ẓisba ṣaar.*
a good deal - *hwaaya.* He spent a good deal of time in Baghdad. *giḍa wakit ihwaaya b-baġdaad.*
a good many - *xooš Eadad min, Eadad zeen min.* There are a good many foreigners in the hotel. *ʔaku xooš Eadad imnil-ʔajaanib bil-ʔuteel.*
a good while - *mudda ṭwiila.* I haven't seen him for a good while. *ma-šifta min mudda ṭwiila.*
for good - *nihaaʔiyyan, bil-marra.* I've given up smoking for good. *qṭaEit it-tadxiin nihaaʔiyyan.*
good and - *kulliš.* Make the tea good and strong. *sawwi č-čaay kulliš ṭoox.*
Good Friday - *j-jumEa l-Eaḍiima, j-jumEa l-ẓaziina.*
not good enough for - 1. *muu maal.* These shoes aren't good enough for school. *hal-ẓiðaaʔ muu maal madrasa.* **2.** *muu maal, muu gadd.* This girl's not good enough for him. *hal-bint muu gadda.*
to be good - 1. *Eiqal (a).* Both of you be good when the guests arrive. *ʔintu l-iθneen Euqlu min yijuun il-xiṭṭaar.* **2.** *ṣilaẓ (a ṣalaaẓ).* This clay is good for making bricks. *haṭ-ṭiin yiṣlaẓ il-Eamal iṭ-ṭaabuug.*
to do good - *faad (i faaʔida).* The vacation did him good. *l-Euṭla faadata.*
to make good - 1. *sawwa (i tsiwwi) zeen.* I'm sure he'll make good in the city. *ʔaani mitʔakkid raẓ-ysawwi zeen bil-madiina.* **2.** *waffa (i) b-, wufa (i wafi).* He made good his promise. *waffa b-waEda.*
good-bye - *maEa s-salaama, f-iimaan illaah.*
to say good-bye - *waddaE (i tawdiiE).* We said good-bye to him at the airport. *waddaEnaa bil-maṭaar.*
good-for-nothing - *talaf, ma-yiswa šii.* Your brother is a good-for-nothing! *ʔaxuuč ma-yiswa šii!*
good-looking - *jaððaab, ẓilu.* She's a good-looking girl. *hiyya bnayya ẓilwa.*
good-natured - *ẓabbuub, ʔaxlaaqa laṭiifa, xooš ṭabuE.* He's good-natured. *huwwa Einda xooš ṭabuE.*
goodness - *xeer, ṭiib, zeeniyya.* She's full of goodness. *kuulha ṭiib.*
goods - *biḍaaEa* pl. *baḍaayiE.* We import many goods from abroad. *nistawrid baḍaayiE ihwaaya mnil-xaarij.*
goose - *wazza* pl. *-aat* coll. *wazz.* We ate a goose for dinner. *ʔakalna wazza bil-Eaša.*
**The police are going to cook his goose. *š-šurṭa raẓ-itšuuf šuġuḷha wiyyaa.*
gorgeous - *badiiE, zaahi, raayiE.* It was a gorgeous day. *čaan fadd nahaar badiiE.*
gorilla - *ġurilla* pl. *-aat.*
gospel - *ʔinjiil* pl. *ʔanaajiil.* He memorized the four gospels. *ẓufaḍ il-ʔanaajiil il-ʔarbaEa.*
gossip - *ẓači Ean-naas, ẓači wara n-naas.* She likes to hear gossip. *yiEjibha tiṣmaE il-ẓači Ean-naas.*
to gossip - *ẓiča (i ẓači) wara n-naas, qišab (i qašib).* She's always gossiping. *hiyya daaʔiman tiẓči wara n-naas.*
got - *Eind.* He's got a nice house. *Einda xooš beet.*
got to - *laazim.* I've got to leave now. *laazim aruuẓ hassa.*
gourd - *qarEa* pl. *-aat* coll. *qaraE.* The colocynth is a variety of gourd. *l-ẓanḍal nooE imnil-qaraE.*
to **govern - 1.** *ẓikam (u ẓukum) n-.* He governed the country well. *huwwa ẓikam il-balad zeen.* **2.** *ḍubaṭ (u ḍabuṭ) n-.* This invention governs the heat of the room. *hal-ixtiraaE yuḍbuṭ ẓaraarat il-ġurfa.*
government - *ẓukuuma* pl. *-aat.* Who heads the new government? *minu yirʔas il-ẓukuuma j-jidiida?*
governor - 1. *ẓaakim* pl. *ẓukkaam.* I read an article on the governor of New York State. *qireet maqaal Ean ẓaakim wlaayat inyuu yoork.* **2.** *mutṣarrif* pl. *-iin.* The governor of Basra province visited Syria. *mutṣarrif liwaaʔ ib-baṣra zaar suurya.*
gown - 1. *dišdaaša* pl. *dišaadiiš.* The boy put the tail of his gown in his mouth and ran. *l-walad xalla ðyaal dišdaašta b-ẓalga w-rikaḍ.* **2.** *roob* pl. *ʔarwaab.* The students wore black gowns for graduation. *ṭ-ṭullaab libsaw ʔarwaab sooda l-ẓaflat it-taxarruj.*
evening gown - *swaaree* pl. *-iyyaat.*
to **grab - 1.** *lizam (a lazim) n-, ligaf (u laguf) n-.* The police grabbed the thief in the market. *š-šurṭa lizmat il-ẓaraami bis-suug.* **2.** *tnaawaš (a tanaawuš), ligaf (u laguf) n-.* He grabbed a bottle off the shelf. *tnaawaš fadd buṭil imnir-raff.* **3.** *himaš (i hamiš) n-.* Don't grab. You'll get your share. *la-tihmiš raẓ-taaxuð ẓuṣṣṭak.*
grace - 1. *rašaaqa, xiffa.* She walks with grace. *timši b-rašaaqa.* **2.** *widd.* He wants to get into her good graces. *yriid yiksib widdha.*
to say grace - *samma (i tasmiya).* Say grace before you eat! *sammu gabuḷ-ma taakul!*
grade - 1. *daraja* pl. *-aat.* He received the highest grades in the class. *ẓaṣṣal Eala ʔaEla darajaat biṣ-ṣaff.* **2.** *ṣaff* pl. *ṣfuuf.* What grade is your son in? *b-yaa ṣaff ʔibnak?* **3.** *ṣinif.* Do you have a better grade of wool than this? *Eindak ṣinif ṣuuf ʔaẓsan min haaða?* **4.** *nẓidaar* pl. *-aat, Ealwa* pl. *-aat.* The truck couldn't climb the grade. *l-loori ma-gidar yiṣEad il-inẓidaar.*
**He'll never make the grade. *mustaẓiil yigdar ydabburha.*
to grade - 1. *ṣannaf (i tṣinnif, taṣniif) t-.* We grade potatoes according to size. *nṣannif il-puteeta ẓasab il-kubur.* **2.** *Eaddal (i tEiddil, taEdiil) t-.* They're grading the road. *yEaddiluun iṭ-ṭariiq.*
gradual - *tadriiji**. I noticed a gradual improvement. *laaẓaḍit taqaddum tadriiji.*
gradually - *bit-tadriij.* He's gradually getting better. *da-yitẓassan bit-tadriij.*
graduate - 1. *xirriij* pl. *-iin, mitxarrij* pl. *-iin.* Most of the graduates of our university have good positions. *ʔakθar il-xirriijiin min jaamiEatna Eidhum waḍaayif zeena.* **2.** *Eaali.* He is doing graduate study in America. *da-yidrus diraasa Eaalya b-ʔamiirka.*
to graduate - *xarraj (i taxriij, txirrij) t-.* Our university graduates four hundred students per year. *jaamiEatna txarrij ʔarbaE miit ṭaalib bis-sana.*
to be graduated - *tdarraj (a tadarruj).* Taxes are

graduated according to income. *ḍ-ḍaraayib titdarraj ẓasb id-daxal.*
grain – **1.** *ẓabba* pl. *ẓabaabi.* A few grains of salt were on the table. *šwayyat ẓabaabi miliẓ čaanat ɛal-meez.* **2.** *ẓabb* pl. *ẓubuub.* Canada exports meat and grain. *kanada tṣaddir il-luẓuum wil-ẓubuub.* **3.** *ṭabuɛ.* That goes against my grain. *haaδa ḍidd ṭabɛi.* **4.** *δarra.* There isn't a grain of truth in the story. *ma-aku δarra min ẓaqiiqa b-hal-quṣṣa.* **5.** *ɛuruug il-xišab.* Don't plane against the grain. *la-trandij ḍidd iɛruug il-xišab.*
gram – *ġraam* pl. *-aat.* Give me four grams of saffron. *nṭiini ʔarbaɛ iġraamaat zuɛufraan.*
grammar – **1.** *qawaaɛid, naẓu.* I never studied Arabic grammar. *ʔaani ʔabad ma-drasit qawaaɛid il-luġa l-ɛarabiyya.* **2.** *ktaab* (pl. *kutub*) *qawaaɛid.* Do you have a good grammar for beginners? *ɛindak iktaab qawaaɛid zeen lil-mubtadiʔiin?*
grand – **1.** *čibiir.* The dance will take place in the grand ballroom. *ẓaflat ir-riqiṣ raẓ-iṭṣiir bil-qaaɛa č-čibiira.* **2.** *kulli*, ɛaamm.* The grand total comes to three hundred and seventeen. *l-majmuuɛ il-kulli ywaṣṣil iθlaθ miyya w-isbaɛtaɛaš.* **3.** *ɛaḍiim, mumtaaz.* We saw grand scenery on our way to Europe. *šifna manaaḍir ɛaḍiima b-ṭariiqna l-ʔooruppa.* -- That's a grand idea. *haaδi fikra ɛaḍiima.*
granddaughter – *ẓafiida* pl. *-aat.*
grandfather – *jidd* pl. *jduud, ʔajdaad.*
grandmother – *jiddiyya* pl. *-aat, biibi* pl. *-iyyaat.*
grandson – *ẓafiid* pl. *ʔaẓfaad.*
grant – *manẓa* pl. *minaẓ.* He received a grant for further study from the government. *stilam imnil-ẓukuuma manẓa lil-istimraar bid-diraasa.*
to grant – **1.** *minaẓ (a maniẓ) n-.* They granted us the entire amount. *minẓoona l-mablaġ ib-kaamla.* **2.** *ɛtiraf (i ɛtiraaf), sallam (i tsillim, tasliim).* I grant that I was wrong. *ʔaani ʔaɛtirif ib-ʔanni činit ġalṭaan.*
granted – **1.** *mamnuuẓ.* The money which was orginally granted has been spent. *l-ifluus illi čaanat bil-ʔaṣil mamnuuẓa nṣirfat.* **2.** *min il-maqbuul, min il-imsallim.* Granted that your philosophy is correct, but its application is difficult. *min il-maqbuul ʔan falsaftak ṣaẓiiẓa, laakin taṭbiiqha ṣaɛub.*
to take for granted – **1.** *ftiraḍ (i ftiraaḍ), ẓisab (i ẓasib).* I took it for granted that he'd be there. *ftiraḍit raẓ-ykuun ihnaak.* **2.** *stiġall (i stiġlaal).* We were friends until he started taking me for granted. *činna ʔaṣdiqaaʔ ʔila ʔan bida yistiġillni.*
grape – *ɛinba* pl. *-aat* coll. *ɛinab.*
grapefruit – *sindiyya* pl. *-aat* coll. *sindi.*
graph – *rasim bayaani* pl. *rusuum bayaaniyya, xaṭṭ bayaani* pl. *xuṭuuṭ bayaaniyya.*
to **grasp** – **1.** *čallab (i tčillib, tačliib) t- b-, lizam (a lazim) n-, kumaš (u kamuš) n-, ligaf (u laguf) n-.* She grasped the rope with both hands. *čallbat bil-ẓabil b-iideenha θ-θinteen.* **2.** *fiṭan (a faṭin) n- ɛala, fiham (a fahim) n-.* Do you grasp what I mean? *da-tufṭun ɛal-illi da-aguula?*
grass – **1.** *θayyil.* Did you cut the grass? *gaṣṣeet iθ-θayyil?* **2.** *ẓašiiš.* The farmer cut some grass and gave it to the cow. *l-fallaaẓ gaṣṣ ẓašiiš w-inṭaa lil-haayša.* **3.** *ɛišib.* The sheep are grazing on grass in the desert. *l-ġanam da-tirɛa bil-ɛišib bil-barr.*
grasshopper – *jaraada* pl. *-aat* coll. *jaraad.*
grate – *šibča* pl. *-aat.* The easiest way to cook the meat is to put a grate on three stones. *ʔashal ṭariiqa ṭ-ṭabx il-laẓam hiyya ʔann itxalli š-šibča ɛala tlaθ iẓjaaraat.*
to grate – **1.** *ẓakk (u ẓakk) ib-randa.* Grate the carrots when you have time. *ẓukki j-jizar bir-randa lamma ykuun ɛindič wakit.* **2.** *kazbar (u tkuzbur) jilid-.* The scratching of chalk on a blackboard grates on me. *šaxṭat it-tabaasiir ɛas-sabbuura tkazbur jildi.*
grateful – *mimtann, šaakir, mitšakkir.* I'm grateful to you for your help. *ʔaani mimtann ʔilak ɛala musaaɛadtak.*
to **gratify** – *raḍḍa (i tarḍiya, triḍḍi), šabbaɛ (i tašbiiɛ, tšibbiɛ).* He gratified her every wish. *šabbaɛ kull raġba min raġbaatha.*
gratifying – *murḍi.* Your grades this semester are very gratifying. *darajaatak hal-faṣil kulliš murḍiya.*
gratitude – *mtinaan, šukur, ɛtiraaf bij-jamiil.* I don't know how to express my gratitude. *ma-da-aɛruf šloon aɛbur ɛan imtinaani.*
grave – **1.** *gabur* pl. *gbuur.* The coffin was lowered into the grave. *t-taabuut itnazzal bil-gabur.* **2.** *sayyiʔ.* His condition is grave. *ẓaalta sayyiʔa.* **3.** *faḍiiɛ.* That's a grave mistake. *δiič fadd ġalṭa faḍiiɛa.* **4.** *waxiim.* Children's playing with matches brings grave consequences. *liɛb il-ʔaṭfaal biš-šixxaaṭ yjiib ɛawaaqib waxiima.*
gravel – *ẓaṣu.* The path is covered with gravel. *ṭ-ṭariiq imġaṭṭa bil-ẓaṣu.*
gravestone – *marmara* pl. *-aat.*
graveyard – *maqbara* pl. *maqaabir.*
gravity – *jaaδibiyya.*
gravy – *marga, marag.* Do you want only gravy on the rice? *triid marga xaalya foog it-timman?*
gray – **1.** *riṣaaṣi, rumaadi.* Gray and red go together well. *r-rumaadi wil-ʔaẓmar yitwaalmuun zeen.* -- **2.** *riṣaaṣi*, rumaadi*.* He always wears gray suits. *daaʔiman yilbas badlaat rumaadiyya.*
to **graze** – **1.** *riɛa (a raɛi).* The sheep grazed in the fields. *l-ġanam riɛa bil-ẓuquul.* **2.** *gišaṭ (a gašiṭ) n-, xidaš (i xadiš) n-.* The bullet grazed his shoulder. *r-riṣaaṣa gišṭat čitfa.*
grease – **1.** *dihin* pl. *duhuun, šaẓam, dasam.* Don't leave the grease in the pan. *la-titruk id-dihin biṭ-ṭaawa.* **2.** *griiz.* Do you need any grease for your car? *tiẓtaaj ʔay igriiz iṣ-ṣayyaartak?*
to grease – **1.** *dahhan (i tdihhin, tadhiin) t-.* Grease the pan before you put the meat in. *dahhin iṭ-ṭaawa gabuḷ-ma txalli l-laẓam.* **2.** *šaẓẓam (i tašẓiim, tšiẓẓim) t-.* Our best mechanic greased your car. *ʔaẓsan il-miikaaniikiyyiin maalna šaẓẓam sayyaartak.*
greasy – **1.** *mdahhan, dasim.* The dishes are still greasy. *l-immaaɛiin baɛadha mdahhna.* **2.** *dihiin, dasim.* You eat a lot of greasy foods. *taakul ihwaaya ʔakil dihiin.*
great – **1.** *ɛaḍiim* pl. *ɛuḍamaaʔ, kabiir* pl. *kubbaar, kubaraaʔ.* He's one of the greats of contemporary poetry. *huwwa min ɛuḍamaaʔ iš-šiɛir il-muɛaaṣir.* **2.** *ɛaḍiim, kabiir.* She's a great singer. *hiyya muġanniya ɛaḍiima.* -- That's a great idea. *haaδi fikra ɛaḍiima.* **3.** *kabiir, ɛaḍiim, baliiġ, jasiim.* The war did great damage. *l-ẓarb azdaθat ʔaḍraar kabiira.* **4.** *jasiim, kabiir, ɛaḍiim.* He's in great danger. *huwwa b-xaṭar jasiim.* **5.** *baliiġ, kabiir.* His father's death left a great mark on him. *wafaat ʔabuu tirkat ʔaθar baliiġ bii.* **6.** *kabiir, hwaaya.* He was in great pain. *čaan ɛinda ʔalam ihwaaya.* **7.** *hwaaya, kulliš.* They live in a great big house. *ysiknuun ib-beet kulliš ičbiir.*
Great Britain – *briiṭaanya l-ɛuḍma.*
greatly – *b-ṣuura kabiira, b-ṣuura ɛaḍiima.* She exaggerated greatly. *baalġat ib-ṣuura kabiira.*
Greece – *l-yunaan.*
greedy – **1.** *nahim* pl. *-iin, šarih* pl. *-iin.* He's very greedy when we sit down to eat. *huwwa kulliš nahim lamma nugɛud naakul.* **2.** *tammaaɛ, jašiɛ.* He's a greedy merchant. *huwwa taajir tammaaɛ.*
Greek – **1.** *yunaani* pl. *-iyyiin.* His father is a Greek. *ʔabuu yunaani.* **2.** *yunaani.* He speaks Greek. *yiẓči yunaani.* **3.** *yunaani*.* Do you like Greek wines? *yɛijbak šaraab yunaani?*
green – *ʔaxḍar* f. *xuḍra* pl. *xuḍur.* The Iraqi flag is black, white, and green with red and yellow in the middle. *l-ɛalam il-ɛiraaqi ʔaswad w-abyaḍ w-axḍar wiyya ʔaẓmar w-aṣfar bin-nuṣṣ.*
to turn green – *xḍarr (a xḍiraar).* The grass turns green in the spring. *l-ɛišib yixḍarr bir-rabiiɛ.*
**He's still green at this work. *baɛda lzeemi b-haš-šuġuḷ.*
greens – *xuḍra.* You should eat some greens everyday. *laazim taakul išwayya xuḍra kull yoom.*
to **greet** – *sallam (i tasliim, tsillim) ɛala, ẓayya (i taẓiyya).* He greeted him with a wave of the hand. *sallam ɛalee b-iida.* **2.** *staqbal (i stiqbaal).* They greeted him with applause. *staqbiloo bit-taṣfiiġ.*
greeting – *taẓiyya* pl. *-aat, stiqbaal* pl. *-aat, salaam* pl. *-aat.* We never expected such a warm greeting. *ʔabadan ma-twaqqaɛna hiič taẓiyya ẓaarra.*
grenade – *qumbula* (pl. *qanaabil*) *yadawiyya.*
grief – *ẓuzun, ġamm, ẓasra.* She couldn't conceal her grief. *ma-gidrat tixfi ẓuzunha.*
grill – *šibča* pl. *-aat.* I don't like the grill on your new car. *ma-aẓibb šibčat sayyaartak ij-jidiida.* -- Take the meat off the grill as soon as it's done. *šiil il-laẓam imniš-šibča bass-ma yistiwi.*
to grill – **1.** *šuwa (i šawi) n- ɛaš-šibča.* They grilled the meat in the garden. *šuwaw il-laẓam*

Ɛaš-šibča bil-ẓadiiqa. 2. *ṭawwal (i taṭwiil) ib-ʔasʔilat~.* The police grilled the prisoner for hours. *š-šurṭa ṭawwilat ib-ʔasʔilatha l-maẓbuus il-Ɛiddat saaƐaat.*

grim - *mƐabbas.* His face was grim. *čaan wijja mƐabbas.*

grin - *btisaama waafẓa.* There was a grin on his face. *čaan ʔaku btisaama waafẓa Ɛala wujja.*

to grin - *kaššar (i tkiššir).* He grinned at me. *kaššar Ɛalayya.*

grind - 1. *ṭaẓin* pl. *-aat.* I bought a medium grind of coffee. *štireet gaẓwa maṭẓuuna ṭaẓin waṣiṭ.* 2. *šidda* pl. *-aat, šadaaʔid.* It was a long grind, but we made it. *čaanat fadd šidda ṭwiila laakin dabbarnaaha.*

to grind - 1. *ṭiẓan (a ṭaẓin) n-, jiraš (i jariš) n-.* We saw the miller grinding flour. *šifna ṭ-ṭaẓẓaan yiṭẓan iṭ-ṭaẓiin.* 2. *čirax (a čarix) n-.* He ground the meat for hamburger. *čirax il-laẓam lil-kabaab.* -- How much does he charge to grind knives? *šgadd yaaxuδ Ɛala čarx is-sičaačiin?* -- He keeps on grinding out one novel after the other. *δall yičrax ib-har-ruwaayaat waẓda wara l-lux.* 3. *giraṭ (u gariṭ) b-.* He grinds his teeth in his sleep. *yigruṭ b-isnuuna b-nooma.*

grip - 1. *laẓma, qabδa, maska.* He has a strong grip. *Ɛinda fadd qabδa qawiyya.* 2. *yadda* pl. *-aat.* I can't carry it. It doesn't have a grip. *ma-agdar ašiilha. ma-biiha yadda.* 3. *junṭa* pl. *junaṭ.* Where can I check my grip? *ween agdar aʔammin juniṭṭi?* 4. *laẓma.* I can carry the trunk if I can get a grip. *ʔagdar ašiil iṣ-ṣanduug ʔiδa bii laẓma.*

to grip - *liẓam (a laẓim) n-, kumaš (u kamiš) n-.* He gripped her arm tightly. *kumaš ʔiidha b-quwa.*

gripe - *tašakki* pl. *-iyyaat.* Don't tell me your gripes. *la-tgul-li b-tašakkiyyaatak.*

to gripe - *tšakka (a tašakki, tšikki).* He gripes about everything. *yitšakka min kullši.*

gripping - *muʔaθθir.* It was a very gripping film. *čaan filim muʔaθθir kulliš.*

grit - 1. *ẓasu.* Chicken gizzards are full of grit. *ẓawaaṣil id-dijaaj matruusa ẓasu.* 2. *Ɛaziim* pl. *Ɛazaaʔim.* That boy has grit. *hal-walad Ɛinda Ɛaziim.*

to grit - *gaẓgaẓ (i tgiẓgiẓ) b-.* He gritted his teeth and set to work. *gaẓgaẓ b-isnuuna w-bida yištuġul.*

groan - *winiin, taʔawwuh* pl. *-aat.* We heard his groans all night. *smaƐna winiina ṭuul il-leel.*

to groan - *wann (i wniin), tʔawwah (a taʔawwuh).* The sick man was groaning. *l-mariiδ čaan ywinn.*

grocer - *baggaal* pl. *bgaagiil.* Our grocer sells nice apples. *baggaalna ybiiƐ xooš tiffaaẓ.*

groceries - *miswaag.* Would you deliver these groceries to our house? *ma-twaddi hal-miswaag il-beetna?*

grocery store - *dukkaan* (pl. *dkaakiin*) *ibgaala.*

groom - 1. *Ɛirriis* pl. *Ɛirsaan.* That man's the father of the groom. *har-rijjaal ʔabu l-Ɛirriis.* 2. *saayis* pl. *siyyaas.* The groom is walking the horse. *s-saayis da-ymašši l-iẓṣaan.*

to groom - *handam (i handama) t-.* He grooms himself nicely. *yhandim nafsa zeen.* -- Her children are always well-groomed. *ʔaṭfaalha daaʔiman imhandimiin.*

groove - *ẓazz* pl. *ẓzuuz.* We watched the carpenter chisel a groove in the board. *tfarrajna Ɛan-najjaar yiẓfur ẓazz bil-xišba.*

to **grope** - *tlammas (a tlimmis), tẓassas (a tẓissis).* He groped for the switch in the dark. *tlammas is-suwiič biδ-δilma.*

gross - 1. *glooṣ* pl. *-aat.* These are sold in grosses only. *haay tinbaaƐ bil-iglooṣaat bass.* 2. *faδiiƐ.* That was a gross mistake. *δiič čaanat fadd ġalṭa faδiiƐa.* 3. *xaliiƐ.* He told us a gross story. *ẓičaa-nna quṣṣa xaliiƐa.* 4. *majmuuƐ Ɛaamm.* How much was your gross income? *šgadd čaan majmuuƐ id-daxal il-Ɛaamm maalak?*

grouchy - *magluub il-wijih, mġayyim.* He's always grouchy. *huwwa daaʔiman magluub il-wijih.*

ground - 1. *gaaƐ* pl. *giiƐaan, ʔariδ* pl. *ʔaraaδi.* Leave it on the ground. *xalliiha Ɛal-gaaƐ.* -- The ground in this area is not fit for agriculture. *l-gaaƐ ihnaa muu ṣaalẓa liẓ-ẓiraaƐa.* 2. *saaẓa* pl. *-aat.* This palace has beautiful grounds. *hal-qaṣir bii saaẓaat jamiila.* 3. *mukaan* pl. *-aat, ʔamaakin; maẓall* pl. *-aat.* Are there any good fishing grounds near here? *ʔaku ʔamaakin iṣ-ṣeed is-simič qariib minnaa?* 4. *ʔarδi* pl. *-iyyaat.* Connect the ground to the radio. *šidd il-ʔarδi bir-raadyo.* 5. *ʔasaas* pl. *ʔusus.* On what grounds did you jail him? *Ɛala ʔay ʔasaas isjantuu?* 6. *tilif.* Don't put the coffee grounds down the drain. *la-txalli t-tilif maal il-gahwa bil-balluuƐa.* 7. *ʔarδi*.* The dining room is on the ground floor. *qaaƐat iṭ-ṭaƐaam biṭ-ṭaabiq il-ʔarδi.*

to ground - 1. *šakkal (i taškiil, tšikkil) t- ʔarδi.* You have to ground the battery before you use it. *laaẓim itšakkil ʔarδi l-paaṭri gabuḷ-ma tistaƐmila.* 2. *minaƐ (a maniƐ) n- min iṭ-ṭayaraan.* The Aviation Commission grounded four pilots this month. *lajnat iṭ-ṭayaraan minƐat ʔarbaƐ ṭayyaariin imniṭ-ṭayaraan haš-šahar.*

to ground out - *sarrab (i tasriib, tsirrib) t- kahrabaaʔ.* He grounded out the circuit with a screwdriver. *sarrab il-kahrabaaʔ imnil-ittiṣaal ib-darnafiis.*

group - *jamaaƐa* pl. *-aat, jooga* pl. *-aat.* The class was divided into three groups. *ṣ-ṣaff čaan imqassam ʔila θlaθ jamaaƐaat.*

to group - 1. *qassam (i taqsiim) t- ʔila jamaaƐaat.* Group the children according to age. *qassim il-ʔaṭfaal ʔila jamaaƐaat ẓasb il-Ɛumur.* 2. *tjammaƐ (a tajammuƐ), ltamm (a ltimaam).* The students grouped around the teacher to see the experiment. *ṭ-ṭullaab itjammiƐaw ẓawl il-muƐallim ẓatta yšuufuun it-tajruba.*

grove - *bistaan* pl. *basaatiin.* He's working in an orange grove. *yištuġul ib-bistaan purtaqaal.*

to **grow** - 1. *nima (i nami).* Cactus grows in the desert. *ṣ-ṣubbeer yinmi bil-barr.* 2. *nima (i nami), kubar (a kubur).* Your boy has certainly grown a lot. *ʔibnak bila šakk kubar ihwaaya.* 3. *ṣaar (i ṣeer).* His financial condition grew worse. *ẓaalta l-maaliyya ṣaarat ʔatƐas.* 4. *ziraƐ (a zariƐ) n-.* He grows flowers in the garden. *yizraƐ warid bil-ẓadiiqa.*

to grow up - *ruba (a riba).* My friend grew up in Najef. *ṣadiiqi ruḅa bin-najaf.*

growl - *hamhama* pl. *-aat.* The dog's growl scared the children. *hamhamt ič-čalib xawwifat ij-jahhaal.*

to growl - *hamham (i thimhim).* The dog began growling before it barked. *č-čalib bida yhamhim gabuḷ-ma nibaẓ.*

grown-up - 1. *čibiir, kabiir* pl. *kbaar.* The admission price for grown-ups is fifty fils. *ʔujrat id-duxuul lil-ikbaar xamsiin filis.* 2. *kabraan, čibiir.* She has a grown up daughter. *Ɛidha bnayya kabraana.*

growth - *numuww.* He spoke on economic growth. *tkallam Ɛan in-numuww il-iqtiṣaadi.* -- They say smoking stunts the growth. *yguuluun it-tadxiin yʔaxxir in-numuww.* **He has two day's growth. *liẓiita maal yoomeen.*

grudge - *ẓaqid* pl. *ʔaẓqaad, δaġiina* pl. *δaġaaʔin.* Forget your grudges and be friends. *ʔinsu l-ʔaẓqaad w-ṣiiru ʔaṣdiqaaʔ.*

grudgingly - *b-imtiƐaaδ.* He gave in grudgingly. *staslam b-imtiƐaaδ.*

gruesome - *faδiiƐ.* The scene of the automobile accident was a gruesome sight. *manδar ẓaadiθ is-sayyaara čaan manδar faδiiƐ* or ***manδar ẓaadiθ is-sayyaara čaan manδar taqšaƐirr minna l-ʔabdaan.*

gruff - *xašin, ġaliiδ, faδδ.* He has a gruff voice. *Ɛinda ṣoot xašin.*

to **grumble** - *damdam (i tdimdim).* He grumbles every-time we ask him for help. *ydamdim kull-ma nuṭlub minna musaaƐada.*

guarantee - *δamaan* pl. *-aat, ṣoogarta* pl. *-aat, taʔmiin* pl. *-aat.* This watch has a five year guarantee. *has-saaƐa biiha xamas isniin δamaan.* 2. *δamaan* pl. *-aat.* What guarantee do I have that he'll pay me? *šinu δ-δamaan huwwa raẓ-yidfaƐ-li.*

to guarantee - 1. *δuman (u δamaan) n-, kifal (i kafaala) n-.* We guarantee our product for a year. *nuδmun ʔintaajna l-sana wiẓda.* 2. *δuman (u δamaan) n-, ṣoogar (i tṣoogir) t-.* I can't guarantee that he'll be here tomorrow. *ma-agdar aṣoogir raẓ-ykuun ihnaa baačir.*

guard - 1. *ẓaaris* pl. *ẓurraas.* The guard didn't let me enter. *l-ẓaaris ma-xallaani ʔaxušš.* 2. *muraafiq* pl. *-iin.* The king got off the plane with his personal guards. *l-malik nizal imniṭ-ṭayyaara maƐa muraafiqiina l-xaaṣṣiin.* 3. *ẓaami* pl. *-iin.* The army is the country's guard against enemy attack. *j-jeeš ẓaami l-waṭan min hujuum il-ʔaƐdaaʔ.*

to guard - 1. *ẓiras (i ẓiraasa) n-, ẓima (i ẓami) n-.* The army is guarding the town. *j-jeeš da-yiẓris il-balad.* 2. *ẓima (i ẓami) n-.* This toothpaste guards the teeth against decay. *hal-maƐjuun yiẓmi*

l-ʔasnaan imnit-taʔakkul.
to be on one's guard – *ʒtiras (i ʒtiraas).* You have to be on your guard with her. *laazim tiʒtiris minha.*
guardian – *waṣi* pl. *waṣaat.* He was appointed guardian of his brother's son. *čaan mitɛayyin waṣi ɛala ʔibin ʔaxuu.*
guess – *taxmiin* pl. *-aat, taqdiir* pl. *-aat, ʒazir.* That wasn't right, but it's a good guess. *haaða ma-čaan ṣaʒiiʒ, laakin xooš taxmiin.*
to guess – **1.** *ʒizar (i ʒazir) n-, xamman (i taxmiin) t-, qaddar (i taqdiir) t-.* Guess how much money I've got in my pocket. *ʔiʒzir išgadd ɛindi fluus ib-jeebi.* **2.** *ð̣ann (u ð̣ann) n-.* I guess he's sick. *ʔað̣unna huwwa mariið̣.*
guest – *xuṭṭaar* pl. *xṭaaṭiir* coll. *xuṭṭaar, ð̣eef* pl. *ð̣yuuf.* Our guests ate all our food. *xuṭṭaarna ʔaklaw kull ʔakilna.*
guide – **1.** *daliil* pl. *ʔadillaaʔ.* Our guide showed us the things in the museum. *d-daliil maalna farrajna ɛal-ʔašyaaʔ il-mawjuuda bil-matʒaf.* **2.** *daliil* pl. *-aat.* All the theatres are listed in the guide. *kull is-siinamaat imsajjla bid-daliil.*
to guide – **1.** *dalla (i tdilli) t-, ʔaršad (i ʔiršaad).* Mister can you direct us to this address? *s-sayyid, tigdar itdalliina ɛala hal-ɛinwaan?* **2.** *dawwar (i tadwiir) t-, farrar (i tafriir, tfirrir) t-.* She guided us around the ruins. *dawwaratna been il-ʔaaθaar.*
guilt – *ðanib, jurum.* He admitted his guilt. *ɛtiraf ib-ðanba.*
guilty – *muðnib.* The judge found him not guilty. *l-ʒaakim wujada ġeer muð̣nib.*
guitar – *qiiθaara* pl. *-aat.*
gulf – **1.** *xaliij* pl. *xiljaan.* We swam in the Persian Gulf. *sbaʒna bil-xaliij il-faarisi.* **2.** *huwwa ɛamiiqa.* There's a gulf between us. *ʔaku huwwa ɛamiiqa beenaatna.*
gull – *nɛeeja* pl. *-aat* coll. *nɛeej, bɛeeja* pl. *-aat* coll. *bɛeej.* The sea gulls followed our ship. *nɛeej il-mayy tibaɛ markabna.*
gum – **1.** *laθθa* pl. *-aat.* This toothpaste is good for the gums. *hal-maɛjuun xoos lil-laθθa.* **2.** *ɛilič* pl. *ɛluuč.* Do you have some gum? *ɛindak šwayyat ɛilič?* **3.** *ṣamuġ.* We import gum arabic from the Sudan. *nistawrid iṣ-ṣamuġ il-ɛarabi mnis-suudaan.*
to gum – *lizag (i lazig) n-, ṣammaġ (u tṣummuġ) t-.* Did you gum the labels? *lzagt il-biṭaaqaat?*
gun – **1.** *bunduqiyya* pl. *-aat, banaadiq* coll. *banaadiq, tufga* pl. *tufag.* The soldiers were carrying their guns in the parade. *j-jinuud čaanaw šaayliin banaadiqhum bil-istiɛraað̣.* **2.** *ṭalqa* pl. *-aat.* They fired a twenty-one gun salute for the visiting king. *ð̣irbaw waaʒid w-ɛišriin ṭalqa taʒiyya lil-malik iz-zaaʔir.*
**Don't jump the gun! *la-titsarraɛ bil-ʔumuur!*
**They gunned him down. *waggɛoo bil-banaadiq.*
gunpowder – *baaruud.*
gust – *ʒabba* pl. *-aat.* A gust of wind blew the boy's cap off. *ʒabbat hawa waggɛat ɛaraqčiin il-walad.*
gutter – *saagya* pl. *swaagi, majra* pl. *majaari.* My cigarettes fell in the gutter. *jigaarti wugɛat bil-majra.*
**His mind's in the gutter. *yiʒči fasaad.*
guy – *walad* pl. *wilid.* He's a good guy. *huwwa xooš walad.*
gym – **1.** *qaaɛat* (pl. *-aat*) *riyaað̣a.* The party will be in the gym. *l-ʒafla raʒ-itkuun ib-qaaɛat ir-riyaað̣a.* **2.** *riyaað̣a.* We have gym three times a week. *ɛidna riyaað̣a tlaθ marraat bil-isbuuɛ.*
to **gyp** – *ġašš (u ġišš) n-, ġulab (u ġalub) n-.* He gypped me. *ġaššni.*
gypsy – *kaawli* pl. *-iyya, ġajari* pl. *-iyya.* That woman is a gypsy. *hal-mara kaawliyya.*

H

habit – **1.** *ɛaada* pl. *-aat.* That's a bad habit. *haaði ɛaada muu zeena.* **2.** *hduum.* Have you seen my riding habit? *šifit ihduum ir-rukuub maalti?*
to get into the habit of – *tɛawwad (a taɛwiid) ɛala.* I got into the habit of smoking at college. *tɛawwadit ɛat-tadxiin min činit bil-kulliyya.*
haggard – *mamṣuuṣ.* He looks very haggard. *ybayyin ɛalee mamṣuuṣ kulliš.*
hail – *ʒaaluuba* pl. *-aat* coll. *ʒaaluub.* That's hail, not rain. *haaða ʒaaluub, muu muṭar.*
to hail – **1.** *ðabb (i ðabb) ʒaaluub.* It's hailing, not raining. *da-tðibb ʒaaluub, ma-da-tumṭur.* **2.** *ṣaaʒ (i ṣiiʒ) n-.* The doorman hailed a passing cab. *l-bawwaab ṣaaʒ taaksi faayit.* **3.** *raʒʒab (i tarʒiib, truʒʒub) t- b-.* The critics hailed it as the best play of the year. *n-nuqqaad raʒʒibaw biiha b-iɛtibaarha ʔaʒsan tamθiiliyya has-sana.* **4.** *ʒayya (i tʒiyyi) t-.* The crowd hailed him as he entered the city. *j-jumuuɛ ʒayyoo min dixal il-madiina.*
hair – *šaɛra* pl. *-aat* coll. *šaɛar.* What color is her hair? *šinu loon šaɛarha?*
**He's always getting into people's hair. *daaʔiman yitdaaxal b-šuʔuun il-ʔaaxariin.*
haircut – *ziyaan* pl. *-aat, ziyaan* (pl. *-aat*) *raas.* Where'd you get that funny haircut? *ween zayyanit hal-izyaan il-muð̣ʒik?*
to get a haircut – *zayyan (i tziyyin) t- šaɛar˜.* I have to get a haircut. *laazim azayyin šaɛri.*
hair-dresser – *ʒallaaq* (pl. *-iin*) *tajmiil.*
half – *nuṣṣ* pl. *nṣaaṣ.* I'll give him half of my share. *raʒ-anṭii nuṣṣ ʒuṣṣṭi.* — I got it for half price at a sale. *štireetha b-nuṣṣ qiima bit-tanziilaat.* — We'll be there at half past eight. *nkuun ihnaak s-saaɛa θmaanya w-nuṣṣ.*
halfway – **1.** *muu kaamil.* Halfway measures will not suffice. *ʔijraaʔaat muu kaamla muu kaafya.* **2.** *b-nuṣṣ iṭ-ṭariiq.* We ran out of gas halfway to town. *xilaṣ il-baanziin ib-nuṣṣ iṭ-ṭariiq lil-madiina.*
**I'm willing to meet him halfway. *ʔaani mustaɛidd atsaahal wiyyaa.*
hall – **1.** *mamarr* pl. *-aat.* Mr. Ani lives at that end of the hall. *s-sayyid ɛaani yiskun ib-ðiič ij-jiha min il-mamarr.* **2.** *mijaaz* pl. *-aat.* We need a new rug for our hall. *niʒtaaj zuuliyya jidiida lil-imjaaz.* **3.** *qaaɛa* pl. *-aat.* He gave his speech in a large hall. *ʔalqa xiṭaaba b-qaaɛa čbiira.*
halt – *tawaqquf.* There's been a halt in steel production. *ṣaar tawaqquf b-ʔintaaj il-ʒadiid.*
to halt – **1.** *wugaf (a wuguuf).* Halt! Who's there? *ʔoogaf, minu hnaak?* **2.** *waggaf (u twugguf) t-.* He halted the soldiers in front of the barracks. *waggaf ij-jinuud ʔamaam iθ-θakana.*
halting – *mitraddid.* He spoke in a halting voice. *ʒiča b-ṣoot mitraddid.*
ham – *laʒam xanziir.* Would you like some ham for breakfast? *triid išwayya laʒam xanziir lir-riyuug?*
hammer – **1.** *čaakuuč* pl. *čwaakiič.* Please hand me the hammer. *min fað̣lak, naawišni č-čaakuuč.* **2.** *miṭraqa* pl. *miṭaariq.* The students were carrying a flag with a picture of a hammer and sickle on it. *ṭ-ṭullaab čaanaw šaayliin ɛalam bii ṣuurat miṭraqa w-minjal.*
to hammer – **1.** *dagg (u dagg), dagdag (i tdigdig).* Our neighbor has been hammering all day long. *jaarna ṭuul in-nahaar čaan da-ydigguun.* — Hammer this nail in please. *dugg hal-bismaar rajaaʔan.* **2.** *raṣṣax (i tarṣiix).* He hammered the rules into me. *raṣṣax it-taɛliimaat ɛindi.*
hand – **1.** *ʔiid* pl. *ʔiidteen, ʔiideen.* Where can I wash my hands? *ween ʔagdar aġsil ʔiidi?* — My hand was very strong. I had three queens. *ʔiidi čaanat qawiyya. čaan ɛindi tlaθ qizaz.* — He asked for her hand from her father. *ṭulab iidha min ʔabuuha.* — The matter is not in my hands. *l-qað̣iyya muu b-iidi.* — Just keep your hands off that! *waxxir ʔiidak min haay!* — This job has to be done by hand. *haš-šuġuḷ laazim yṣiir bil-ʔiid.* **2.** *yad, ʔiid.* He must have had a hand in that. *laazim čaan ʔila yad biiha.* — **3.** *miil* pl. *ʔamyaal, myaala; ɛagrab* pl. *ɛagaarib.* The minute hand doesn't work. *miil id-daqaaʔiq ma-yištuġul.* **4.** *jiha.* On the other hand, he wants it finished. *w-min jiha lux, yriidha tixlaṣ.* **5.** *yadawi*.* He wanted to blow up the factory with a hand grenade. *raad yinsif il-maɛmal ib-qumbula yadawiyya.*

**I can't lay my hands on it right now. *ma-agdar aζaṣṣilha hassa.*
on hand - *jawwa l-ʔiid, ζaaδ̣ir, mawjuud.* We haven't that size on hand. *ma-εidna hal-ζajim jawwa l-ʔiid.*
to hand - *niṭa (i naṭi) n-, naawaš (u munaawaša) t-.* Please hand me that pencil. *baḷḷa nṭiini hal-qalam.*
to hand in - *sallam (i tsillim) t-.* I'm going to hand in my application tomorrow. *raζ-aruuζ baačir ʔasallim εariiδ̣ti.*
to hand out - *wazzaε (i tawziiε) t-, farrag (i tafriig) t-.* Hand these tickets out! *wazziε hal-biṭaaqaat!*
handbag - *janṭat* (pl. *-aat, junaṭ*) *ʔiid.*
hand brake - *handibreek* pl. *-aat.*
handcuff - *kalabča* pl. *-aat.* Here every policeman carries a pair of handcuffs. *kull šurṭi hnaa yšiil kalabča wiyyaa.*
to handcuff - *kalbač (i tkilbič) t-.* They handcuffed the prisoners. *kalbičaw l-masaajiin.*
hand drill - *mizraf yadawi* pl. *mazaaruf yadawiyya.*
handful - *čaff* pl. *čfuuf.* He took a handful of nuts. *ʔaxaδ fadd čaff čarazaat.*
handkerchief - *čaffiyya* pl. *-aat, čfaafi.*
handle - **1.** *yadda* pl. *-aat.* My suitcase needs a new handle. *yinraad ij-janiṭṭi yadda jidiida.* **2.** *εurwa* pl. *εaraawi.* The handle of this teapot is broken. *hal-quuri εuruuta maksuura.*
**At the slightest occasion he flies off the handle. *yθuur min ʔadna šii.*
to handle - **1.** *εaamal (i muεaamala).* He knows how to handle people. *yuεruf išloon yεaamil in-naas.* **2.** *lizam (a lazim) n-.* Look at it all you want, but don't handle it. *baawiε εaleeha šgadd-ma triid, bass la-tilzamha.* **3.** *tεaaṭa (a taεaaṭi) b-.* We don't handle that commodity. *ma-nitεaaṭa b-has-silεa.* **4.** *δ̣ubaṭ (u δ̣abuṭ) n-.* I can't handle him anymore. *baεad ma-agdar ʔaδ̣ubṭa.* **6.** *dabbar (u tadbiir) t-.* I simply can't handle all the work by myself. *mnil-waaδ̣iζ ʔaani ma-agdar adabbur kull iš-šuğuḷ waζdi.* **7.** *staεmal (i stiεmaal).* Do you know how to handle a revolver? *tuεruf išloon tistaεmil musaddas?*
**Handle that glass with care. *diir baalak εala haj-jaama!*
handmade - *šuğuḷ ʔiid.* That's all handmade. *haaδa kulla šuğuḷ ʔiid.*
handsome - *wasiim.* He's a handsome man. *huwwa rajul wasiim.*
**That's a handsome sum of money. *haaδa xooš mablağ imnil-maal.*
handwriting - *kitaaba, xaṭṭ iid.* His handwriting is illegible. *kitaabta ma-tinqiri.*
handy - **1.** *mufiid.* This potato peeler is very handy. *hal-gaššaara maal il-puteeta mufiida.* **2.** *maahir.* He's a very handy fellow in everything. *huwwa waaζid maahir ib-kullši.* **3.** *jawwa ʔiid.* Have you got a pencil handy? *jawwa ʔiidak qalam?*
to come in handy - *faad (i faaʔida).* A knowledge of typing will come in handy to you some day. *taεallum iṭ-ṭaabiεa yfiidak fadd yoom.*
**The extra money comes in very handy. *l-ifluus il-ʔiδ̣aafiyya ʔilha makaan mufiid min tiji.*
to **hang** - **1.** *šinaq (u šaniq) n-, ṣilab (u ṣalub) n-.* He was hanged yesterday. *l-baarζa nšinaq.* **2.** *εallag (i taεliig) t-.* Can't you hang the picture a little higher? *ma-tigdar itεallig iṣ-ṣuura šwayya ʔaεla?* -- Where can I hang my coat? *ween aεallig sitirti?* **3.** *tεallag (a taεallug).* He hung from the limb and started swinging. *tεallag bil-ğuṣun w-gaam yitmarjaζ.* **4.** *dandal (i tdindil).* Why are you hanging your head? *leeš imdandil raasak?*
**His life hung by a thread. *ζayaata čaanat waagfa εala šaεra.*
to hang around - *raabaṭ (u muraabaṭa).* He's always hanging around the tavern. *εala-ṭuul imraabuṭ bil-mayxaana.*
to hang on - *lizam (a lazim) n-.* I hung on with all my strength. *ʔaani lizamit ib-kull quuti.*
to hang onto - **1.** *lizam (a) n-, čallab (i tčillib) t-.* I hung onto the dog as long as I could. *lizamit ič-čalib ṭuul-ma gidarit.* **2.** *baqqa (i tbiqqi) t-.* I'll hang on to the stock until its price goes up again. *raζ-abaqqi l-ʔashum ʔila ʔan yirtifiε siεirha.* **3.** *xalla (i txilli) t- εind~.* Hang onto this money for me. *xallii-li hal-ifluus εindak.*
to hang out - **1.** *šarr (u šarr) n-, εallag (i taεliig) t-.* Did you hang the wash out? *šarreeti l-ihduum barra?* **2.** *dandal (i tdindil) t-.* The rope is hanging out the window. *l-ζabil imdandal imniš-šibbaač.*
to hang up - *εallag (i taεliig) t-.* Hang up your hat and coat. *εallig šafuqtak w-sitirtak.*
**He got angry and hung up on me. *ziεal εalayya w-sadd it-talafoon ib-wujhi.*
hangar - *garaaj* (pl. *-aat*) *ṭayyaaraat.*
hanger - *tiεlaaga* pl. *-aat.* Put your coat on a hangar. *xalli sitirtak εat-tiεlaaga.*
hangover - *xmaariyya.* Take yourself a shot to get rid of the hangover. *ʔuxuδ-lak fadd peek ζatta tiksir il-ixmaariyya.*
to **happen** - **1.** *ζidaθ (i ζuduuθ), ṣaar (i ṣeer), wuqaε (a wuquuε).* When did that happen? *šwakit ζidθat?* -- What happened to the typewriter? Did someone use it? *š-ṣaayir biṭ-ṭaabiεa? ʔaζζad istaεmalha?* **2.** *ṣaadaf (i taṣaaduf).* I don't happen to agree with you this time. *ṣaadaf ʔan ma-ʔattifiq wiyyaak hal-marra.* -- He doesn't happen to be here. *ṣaadaf ʔan ma-ykuun ihnaa.*
**Everything happens to me. *kull il-bala da-yinzil εala raasi.*
happily - **1.** *b-saεaada.* They are spending their married life happily. *da-yigδ̣uun ζayaathum iz-zawjiyya b-saεaada.* **2.** *b-suruur, b-faraζ.* She does her work happily. *tsawwi šuğuḷha b-suruur.*
happiness - *saεaada, suruur, faraζ.*
happy - *saεiid, farζaan, masruur.* I'm very happy you won. *ʔaani saεiid li-ʔannak irbaζit.*
**Happy New Year! *kull εaam w-intum ib-xeer!*
**Happy birthday! *εiid milaadak saεiid!*
harbor - *miinaaʔ* pl. *mawaani, marfaʔ* pl. *maraafiʔ.*
hard - **1.** *qawi*.* I can't sleep on a hard mattress. *ma-agdar ʔanaam εala fraaš qawi.* -- His death was a hard blow to us. *wafaata čaanat ṣadma qawiyya εaleena.* **2.** *yaabis.* The bread is hard as a rock. *l-xubuz yaabis miθl il-ζjaara.* **3.** *mujidd.* He's a hard worker. *huwwa εaamil mujidd.* **4.** *ṣaεub.* It's hard for me to climb stairs. *ṣaεub εalayya ʔaṣεad id-daraj.* -- Those were hard times. *čaanat ʔawqaat ṣaεba.* -- He's a hard man to get along with. *huwwa rajul ṣaεub titfaaham wiyyaa.* **5.** *b-jidd.* He worked hard all day. *štiğal ib-jidd ṭuul il-yoom.* **6.** *b-quwwa, ζeel.* It was raining hard when he left. *čaanat tumṭur ib-quwwa lamman ṭilaε.* -- He hit him on the head hard. *δ̣uraba εala raasa ζeel.* **7.** *jaamid, qawi*.* This ice cream is extremely hard. It can't be cut even with a knife. *had-doondirma jaamda kulliš, ma-tingaṣṣ ζatta bis-siččiina.*
hard and fast - *θaabit.* In this case you can't make hard and fast rules. *b-hal-ζaala ma-tigdar itζuṭṭ qawaaεid θaabta.*
hard of hearing - *samiε θigiil.* He's hard of hearing. *samεa θigiil.*
to be hard up for - *ζtaaj (a ζtiyaaj).* He's always hard up for money. *huwwa εala-ṭuul yiζtaaj ifluus.*
to try hard - *ζaawal (i muζaawala) t- jahd~, jtihad (i jtihaad).* He tried hard to do it right. *ζaawal kull jahda ζatta ysawwiiha zeen.*
to **harden** - *tṣallab (a taṣallub), jimad (a jamid), sakk (u sakk).* How long will it take the cement to harden? *šgadd yirraad liš-šibintu ζatta yitṣallab?*
hardly - **1.** *b-ṣuεuuba, mniṣ-ṣaεub.* I hardly believe that. *b-ṣuεuuba ʔaṣaddigha.*
You can hardly expect me to believe that. *la-titṣawwar raζ-aṣaddig δaak ib-suhuula.* **2. *bil-kaad.* He had hardly begun to speak when ... *bil-kaad bida yiζči lamman ...*
hardly ever - *mnin-naadir, naadiran.* I hardly ever go out. *mnin-naadir aṭlaε barra.*
harm - *δ̣arar, ʔaδiyya.* You can never undo the harm you've done. *ma-tigdar itziil iδ̣-δ̣arar illi sawweeta.* -- No harm done! *ma-ζidaθ ʔay δ̣arar!*
to harm - *δ̣arr (u δ̣arar) n-, ʔaδδa (i tʔiδδi) t-.* A vacation wouldn't harm you. *l-εuṭla ma-raζ-itδ̣urrak.* -- This dry weather has harmed the crops a lot. *haj-jaww ij-jaaff ʔaδδa z-ziriε ihwaaya.*
harmful - *muδ̣irr, muʔδi.* This drought is harmful for the crops. *hal-maζal muδ̣irr liz-ziriε.*
harmonica - *haarmooniika* pl. *-aat.*
harmony - **1.** *nsijaam.* There was perfect harmony between the two. *čaan aku nsijaam kaamil been iθ-θineen.* -- This song has beautiful harmony. *hal-uğniya biiha nsijaam laṭiif.* **2.** *mitnaasiq, mittifiq, mitlaaʔim.* His plans are in complete harmony with mine. *mašaariiεa kulliš mitnaasqa wiyya maalti.*
harness - *εidda* pl. *εidad.* I just bought a new

harness for my horse. *hastawwni štireet Eidda l-izṣaani.*
to harness - 1. *sarraj (i tsirrij) t-.* Has he harnessed the horses? *sarraj il-xeel?* 2. *staxdam (i stixdaam).* Man is attempting to harness atomic energy. *l-?insaan da-yzaawil yistaxdim iṭ-ṭaaqa δ-δarriyya.*
harp - *qiiθaar, qiiθaara* pl. *-aat.*
to harp - *dagg (u dagg) n-.* Stop harping on the same subject. *bass-Eaad itdugg Eala nafs il-mawδuuE.*
harsh - 1. *qaasi.* Those are harsh terms. *haay šuruuṭ qaasya.* 2. *muxaddiš.* This soap contains no harsh ingredients. *ma-aku Eanaaṣir muxaddiša b-haṣ-ṣaabuun.*
harvest - *mazṣuul.* We had a good harvest. *mazṣuulna čaan zeen.*
to harvest - *ziṣad (i zaṣid) n-.* When you harvest the wheat around here? *šwakit tiziṣduun il-zunṭa b-hal-manṭiqa?*
haste - *Eajala, surEa.*
**Haste makes waste. *l-Eajala mniš-šeeṭaan.*
hastily - *b-Eajala, b-surEa.* They took leave hastily. *ṭilEaw ib-Eajala.*
hasty - *b-surEa, mitsarriE.* You mustn't make hasty decisions. *ma-laazim tittixiδ qaraaraat ib-surEa.*
**I wouldn't be hasty about it, if I were you. *loo b-makaanak ma-astaEjil biiha.*
hat - *šafqa* pl. *-aat, birneeṭa* pl. *-aat.*
to **hatch** - *faggas (i tafgiis).* The hen sits on the eggs until they hatch. *d-dijaaja tguff Eal-beeδ zatta yfaggis.*
hatchet - *balṭa* pl. *-aat.*
hate - *kuruh, buġuδ.* His dislike gradually turned into hate. *bit-tadriij Eadam mazabbta tzawwlat ?ila kuruh.*
to hate - *kirah (a kuruh) n-.* I hate people who are selfish. *?akrah in-naas il-?anaaniyyiin.*
hatred - *karaaha, buġuδ, karaahiyya.*
haul - 1. *ṣeed.* The fishermen had a good haul today. *ṣayyaadiin is-simač ṭallEaw xooš ṣeed hal-yoom.* 2. *zimil* pl. *zumuula.* This haul is too big for the truck. *hal-zimil kulliš čabiir Eal-loori.*
**It's a long haul from here to Bagdad. *masaafa ṭawiila minnaa l-baġdaad.*
to haul - 1. *jarr (u jarr) n-, sizab (a sazib) n-.* The horses were unable to haul the heavy load. *l-xeel ma-gidrat itjurr il-ziml iθ-θigiil.* -- They hauled me out of bed at six this morning. *jarrooni mnil-ifraaš saaEa sitta l-yoom iṣ-ṣubuz.*
**He hauled off as if he meant to hit me. *traajaE w-tzaffaz Eabaalak čaan yriid yiδrubni.*
to haul down - *nazzal (i tanziil) t-.* Has the flag been hauled down yet? *l-Ealam itnazzal loo baEad?*
to **have**: no verbal equivalent, paraphrased with prepositions: 1. *Eind, wiyya.* I have two tickets for the theater. *Eindi biṭaaqteen lit-tamθiiliyya.* -- Do you have a pencil you can lend me? *Eindak qalam tigdar itEiirni?* -- Who had the book last? *minu ?aaxir waazid čaan Einda l-iktaab?* -- He has a heart disease. *Einda maraδ qalb.* -- I have a headache. *wiyyaaya wujaE raas.* -- Do you have the key? *wiyyaak il-miftaaz?* 2. *?il-, b-.* The room has three windows. *l-ġubba ?ilha tlaθ išbaabiič.* -- The argument has no end. *l-mujaadala ma-biiha nihaaya.* -- The streets have no sidewalks. *š-šawaariE ma-biiha ?arṣifa.* 3. *Eind, ?il-.* He has a very uncouth uncle. *?ila Eamm kullis ?adabsizz.* -- She has beautiful eyes. *Eidha Eyuun zilwa.* -- You have a talent for music. *?ilak mawhiba bil-mawsiiqa.* 4. *xalla (i txilli).* Have him wash my car. *xallii yiġsil sayyaarti.*
**Have you had a haircut today? *zayyanit hal-yoom?*
**Has he done his job well? *sawwa šuġla zeen?*
**How long have you been in Baghdad? *šgadd ṣaar-lak ib-baġdaad?*
**How long have you been waiting for me? *šgadd ṣaar-lak tintiδirni?*
**I've been standing here for two hours. *ṣaar-li waaguf ihnaa saaEteen.*
**I'm having my teeth treated. *da-adaawi snaani.*
**We're having a house built. *da-nibni beet.*
**I'll have to have my appendix out. *laazim asawwi Eamaliyyat il-muṣraan il-?aEwar.*
**Good stockings are simply not to be had. *j-juwaariib iz-zeen mustaziil tinligi Eind ?azzad.*
**Please have a seat. *tfaδδal, istariiz!*
**He has it in for you. *huwwa δammha ?ilak.*
**Let's have the knife! *nṭiini s-siččiin!*
**What did she have on? *š-čaanat laabsa?*
**Wouldn't it be better to have it out with him right now? *muu ?azsan loo txallušha wiyyaa hassa?*
I had better, you had better, etc. - *?azsan-li, ?azsal-li, ?azsan-lak,* etc. You'd better do it right away. *?azsal-lak sawwiiha hassa.*
to have to: (present and future) 1. *laazim, Eal-, waajib Eal-.* I have to go get my wife. *laazim ?aruuz ?ajiib zawijti.* -- We'll have to throw a party for these people. *laazim insawwi zafla l-haj-jamaaEa.* 2. *δṭarr (a δṭiraar), njubar (i njibaar).* I had to leave early. *δṭarreet ?aruuz min-wakit.* -- They had to fire him. *δṭarraw yfuṣluu.*
**You have to have new shoes. *laazmak qundara jidiida.*
not to have to - *ma-aku zaaja, muu δaruuri, ma-aku lzuum, ma-laazim.* You don't have to go. *ma-aku zaaja truuz.* -- You won't have to sign again. *ma-aku lzuum timδi marra lux.* -- You didn't have to shout like that. *ma-čaan laazim itṣayyiz hiiči.*
hawk - *ṣagur* pl. *ṣguur.*
hay - *tibin.* The hay isn't dry yet. *t-tibin baEda maa yaabis li-hassa.*
**It's time to hit the hay. *ṣaar wakt in-noom!*
**Let's make hay while the sun shines. *xalli nistiġill il-furṣa gabuḷ-ma tfuut.*
hay fever - *zumma l-qašš.*
haystack - *beedar* (pl. *biyaadir*) *tibin.*
hazard - *xaṭar* pl. *?axṭaar, muxaaṭara* pl. *-aat.* Factory workers are exposed to hazards very much. *Eummaal il-maEaamil muEarraδiin lil-?axṭaar kaθiira.*
hazelnut - *findiqa* pl. *-aat* coll. *findiq, bunduga* pl. *-aat* coll. *bundug.*
hazy - 1. *mġawwaš.* It's rather hazy today. *Eal-?akθar id-dinya mġawwša l-yoom.* 2. *mubham.* Your ideas are hazy. *?afkaarak mubhama.*
he - *huwwa.* He's very glad. *huwwa kulliš masruur.* -- He came yesterday. *(huwwa) jaa l-baarza.*
head - 1. *raas* pl. *ruus.* My head hurts. *raasi yoojaEni.* -- Lettuce is ten fils a head. *raas il-xass ib-Eašr ifluus.* -- I need nails with larger heads. *?aztaaj ibsaamiir raasha ?akbar.* -- I can't make head nor tail of the story. *ma-da-agdar algi l-hal-quṣṣa laa raas wala ?asaas.* -- He sold five head of cattle. *baaE xamis ruus hooš.* -- Begin at the head of the page. *?ibdi min raas iṣ-ṣafza.* -- The mayor rode at the head of the procession. *ra?iis il-baladiyya miša Eala raas il-mawkib.* 2. *Eaqil* pl. *Euquul.* He has a good head for arithmetic. *Einda xooš Eaqil bil-izsaabaat.* 3. *ra?iis* pl. *ru?asaa?.* He's the head of the gang. *huwwa ra?iis il-Eiṣaaba.* 4. *rabb* pl. *?arbaab.* He's the head of the family. *huwwa rabb il-Eaa?ila.* 5. *ṣadir.* We were sitting at the head of the table. *čiina gaaEdiin ib-ṣadr il-meez.*
**That's over my head. *?aani ?aṭraš biz-zaffa.*
**You hit the nail on the head. *?inta lgafitha.*
**My friend is head over heels in love. *ṣadiiqi waagiE bil-ġuraam.*
**That may cost him his head. *haaδi mumkin itkallfa zayaata.*
**Heads or tails? *ṭurra loo kitba?* or *šiir loo xaṭṭ?*
**I can't keep everything in my head. *ma-agdar atδakkar kullši.*
**The man is positively out of his head. *har-rijjaal Eaqla muu b-raasa.*
**I don't want to go over his head. *ma-ariid aruuz l-illi ?aEla minna.*
**Things had to come to a head sooner or later. *l-?ašyaa? laazim fadd yoom tooṣal zaddha.*
**Everyone kept his head. *kull waazid zaafaδ Eala ttizaana.*
to head - 1. *ri?as (a ri?aasa).* He hopes to head the department some day. *yit?ammal yir?as il-qisim fadd yoom.* 2. *wajjah (i tawjiih) t-.* He headed the car at me to murder me. *wajjah is-sayyaara Ealayya zatta ymawwitni.* 3. *tfawwaq (a tafawwuq) Eala.* My boy heads his class at school. *?ibni mitfawwiq Eala ṭullaab ṣaffa bil-madrasa.* 4. *ttijah (i ttijaah), raaz (u).* They're heading for Bagdad. *humma mittajhiin ?ila baġdaad.* -- Where are you headed? *li-ween mittijih?* or *li-ween raayiz?*
**You're heading in the wrong direction. *?inta maaxiδ ittijaah ġalaṭ.*
**His name heads the list of candidates. *?isma b-raas qaa?imat il-muraššaziin.*
headache - 1. *wijaE* (pl. *-aat*) *raas, ṣudaaE.* I've a

bad headache. *Eindi wijaE raas šadiid.* -- This problem is really a headache. *hal-muškila ʒaqiiqatan wijaE raas.*
**The noise gives me a headache. *l-laġwa da-twajjiE raasi.*
headdress - *libaas raas.*
heading - *ttijaah* pl. *-aat.* The plane took a new heading. *ṭ-ṭayyaara ʔaxδat ittijaah ijdiid.*
headlight - *laayt* pl. *-aat.*
headline - *Einwaan* pl. *Eanaawiin.* What are the headlines in today's paper? *šinu l-Eanaawiin maal jariidat il-yoom?*
headlong - *Eala raas.* He plunged headlong into the river. *čayyat biš-šaṭṭ Eala raasa.*
headquarters - **1.** *markaz* (pl. *maraakiz*) *qiyaada, maqarr* (pl. *-aat*) *qiyaada.* This officer was attached to headquarters. *haδ-δaabuṭ čaan mirtibuṭ ib-markaz il-qiyaada.* **2.** *markaz Eaamm* pl. *maraakiz Eaamma, maqarr Eaamm* pl. *maqarraat Eaamma.* For further information, apply to party headquarters. *lil-ʒuṣuul Eala maEluumaat ʔakθar qaddim ṭalab lil-maqarr il-Eaamm lil-ʒizib.*
headwaiter - *raʔiis* (pl. *ruʔasaaʔ*) *booyaat.*
to make **headway** - *tqaddam (a taqaddum).* We made headway slowly in the sand. *tqaddamna b-buṭuʔ bir-ramal.*
head wind - *riiʒ imEaakis* pl. *riyaaʒ imEaaksa.* We had strong head winds all the way. *ṣaadfatna riyaaʒ imEaaksa qawiyya ṭuul iṭ-ṭariiq.*
to **heal** - **1.** *liʒam (a laʒim) n-.* The treatment is healing the wound successfully. *l-muEaalaja da-tilʒam ij-jariʒ kulliš zeen.* **2.** *nliʒam (i nliʒaam).* The wound isn't healing properly. *j-jariʒ ma-da-yinliʒim zeen.*
health - **1.** *ṣiʒʒa.* How's his health? *šloon ṣiʒʒta?* **2.** *ṣiʒʒi*.* He's working on a new health project. *da-yištuġul ib-mašruuE ṣiʒʒi jdiid.*
healthy - *ṣiʒʒi*.* This isn't a healthy climate. *haj-jaww muu ṣiʒʒi.*
**She looks very healthy. *mbayyna Ealeeha ṣ-ṣiʒʒa.*
heap - *kooma* pl. *-aat.* What's this heap of sand for? *luweeš hal-kooma maal ir-ramal?*
to heap - *kawwam (u tkuwwum) t-, kaddas (i takdiis) t-.* The table was heaped with all kinds of food. *ʔalwaan il-ʔakil čaanat imkawwma Eal-meez.*
to **hear** - *simaE (a samiE) n-.* I didn't hear anything. *ma-simaEit ʔay šii.* -- I won't hear of it! *ma-ariid asmaEha.* -- Well then, I'll expect to hear from you. *zeen ʔiδan, ʔatwaqqaE asmaE minnak.*
**You can't hear yourself in this noise. *min hal-laġwa ma-yinsimiE šii.*
hearing - **1.** *muraafaEa* pl. *-aat.* The hearing was set for June sixth. *tEayyan yoom il-muraafaEa sitta ʒuzayraan.* **2.** *samiE.* His hearing is very poor. *samEa kulliš δaEiif.*
to lose one's hearing - *ṭrašš (a ṭrišaaš).* When did he lose his hearing? *šwakit iṭrašš?*
hearse - *Earabaanat* (pl. *Earabaayin*) *jinaaza, sayyaarat* (pl. *-aat*) *jinaaza.*
heart - **1.** *qalb* pl. *quluub, galub* pl. *gluub.* His heart is weak. *qalba δaEiif.* -- It breaks my heart to let him go. *šii yfaṭṭir il-galub ʔan axalli yruuʒ.* -- I didn't have the heart to tell him. *galbi ma-nṭaani ʔaguul-la.* **2.** *ġeeb.* I learned the poem by heart. *ʒfuδṭ il-qaṣiida Eal-ġeeb.* **3.** *ʒaqiiqa* pl. *ʒaqaayiq, ʔasaas* pl. *ʔusus.* I want to get to the heart of this matter. *ʔariid atwaṣṣal ʔila ʒaqiiqat hal-mawδuuE.*
**I haven't got the heart to do it. *galbi ma-yinṭiini ʔasawwiiha.*
**Cross my heart! I didn't do it! *ʔaqsim b-illaah il-Eaδiim, ma-sawweetha.*
**He's a man after my own heart. *huwwa fadd waaʒid ṃayya miθil ṃayyi.*
**Don't lose heart! *la-tifqid šajaaEtak!*
**At heart he's really a good fellow. *jawhara zeen.*
hearts - *kuupa.* Hearts are highest. *l-kuupa ʔaEla šii.*
to take to heart - *ʔaxaδ (u ʔaxiδ) n- ib-jidd.* He's taking it very much to heart. *huwwa maaxiδha kulliš ib-jidd.*
heart attack - *sakta* (pl. *-aat*) *qalbiyya* (fatal), *nawba* (pl. *-aat*) *qalbiyya.*
heartily - **1.** *b-šahiyya, b-raġba.* We ate heartily. *ʔakalna b-šahiyya.* **2.** *min kull galub-.* We laughed heartily. *δʒakna min kull galubna.*
hearty - *dasim.* We had a hearty meal. *ʔakanna ʔakla dasma* or *ʔakanna b-šahiyya.*
**He's hale and hearty in spite of his age. *matruus ṣiʒʒa b-raġum sinna* or *kulla ṣiʒʒa b-raġum sinna.*
heat - **1.** *ʒaraara, ṣuxuuna.* I can't stand the heat. *ma-agdar atʒammal il-ʒaraara.* -- The stove doesn't give enough heat. *ṣ-ṣooba ma-tinṭi ʒaraara kaafya.* **2.** *šooṭ* pl. *ʔašwaaṭ.* My horse won the first heat. *ʒṣaani ġulub biš-šooṭ il-ʔawwal.*
**It happened in the heat of the battle. *ṣaarat min čaanat il-maEraka ʒaamya.*
in heat - *mithayyija.* Our cat's in heat. *bazzuunatna mithayyija.*
to heat - **1.** *daffa (i tdiffi) t-.* The room is well heated. *l-ġurfa mdaffaaya zeen.* **2.** *ʒima (a ʒami).* The living-room radiator doesn't heat up. *ṣoobat ġurfat il-gaEda ma-da-tiʒma.* -- It'll be five minutes before the iron heats up. *l-ʔuuti yinraad-la xamis daqaayiq ʒatta yiʒma.* **3.** *ʒima (i) n-, saxxan (i tsixxin) t-.* I'll have to heat up some water first. *ʔawwal laazim aʒmi šwayya ṃaay.*
heater - *ṣooba* pl. *-aat, madfaʔa* pl. *-aat, madaafiʔ.*
heat-resistant - *muqaawum lil-ʒaraara.* Is that glass heat-resistant? *haz-zujaaj muqaawum lil-ʒaraara?*
heaven - *janna.* When the good man dies he goes to heaven. *r-rajul iṣ-ṣaaliʒ min ymuut yruuʒ lij-janna.*
**She was in seventh heaven. *čaanat fi-ʔawj is-saEaada.*
**For heaven's sake, stop that noise! *daxiil ʔaḷḷa baṭṭil hal-ʒiss!* or *yaa mEawwad, baṭṭil hal-laġwa!*
**Only heaven knows how often I've tried. *bass ʔaḷḷa yidri čam marra ʒaawalit.*
heavy - **1.** *θigiil* pl. *θgaal.* Is that box too heavy for you? *haṣ-ṣanduug kulliš θigiil Ealeek?* -- I can't take heavy food. *ma-agdar aakul šii θgiil.* **2.** *čbiir, kabiir* pl. *kbaar.* He had to pay a heavy fine. *δṭarr yidfaE ġaraama čabiira.* **3.** *qawi*, šadiid.* We can't leave in that heavy rain. *ma-nigdar inruuʒ b-hal-muṭar il-qawi.*
**He's a heavy drinker. *huwwa sikkiir.*
Hebrew - **1.** *Eibri*, Eibraani*.* Do you know the Hebrew alphabet? *tuEruf il-ʒuruuf il-Eibriyya?* **2.** *Eibriyya, Eibri.* Do you speak Hebrew? *titkallam bil-Eibriyya?*
hedge - *siyaaj* (pl. *-aat*) *yaas.*
heel - *čaEab* pl. *čEuub.* I have a blister on my heel of my foot. *Eindi buṭbaaṭa b-čaEab rijli.* -- These shoes need new heels. *hal-qundara tiʒtaaj čaEab jidiid.*
hegira - *hijra.*
height - **1.** *rtifaaE* pl. *-aat.* How do you determine the height of a triangle? *šloon itEayyin irtifaaE il-muθallaθ?* **2.** *ʔooj.* He was then at the height of his power. *b-δaak il-wakit čaan ib-ʔooj quuta.* **3.** *ġaaya* pl. *-aat.* That's the height of stupidity. *haaδi ġaayat il-ġabaaʔ.*
heir - *wariiθ, waariθ* pl. *waraθa.* He's the sole heir. *huwwa l-waariθ il-waʒiid.*
hell - *jahannam, jaʒiim.* He died and went to hell. *maat w-raaʒ ij-jahannam.*
hello - *halaw.* Hello, operator! You've cut me off. *halaw, maʔmuurat il-baddaala, qiṭaEti l-xaṭṭ Eanni.*
helmet - *xuuδa* pl. *xuwaδ.*
help - *musaaEada, muEaawana, maEuuna.* Do you need any help? *tiʒtaaj ʔay musaaEada?*
**It's difficult to get help these days. *ṣaEub tilgi ʔaʒʒad yEaawinak hal-ʔayyaam.*
**Help! *y-ahl ir-raʒam!*
to help - **1.** *saaEad (i musaaEada) t-, Eaawan (i muEaawana) t-, Eaan (i Eoon).* Please help me. *min faḍlak saaEidni.* **2.** *saaEad (i musaaEada) t-.* She helps us out on Sunday. *hiyya tsaaEidna biš-šuġuḷ yoom il-ʔaʒʒad.*
**I can't help it, but that's my opinion. *š-ʔasawwi,* or *la-tluumni, haaδa raʔyi.*
**I couldn't help but see it. *ma-gdarit ʔilla ʔašuufha.*
**Sorry, that can't be helped. *mitʔassif, ma-mumkin titġayyar.*
to help oneself - *tfaδδal (a tafaδδul).* Please help yourself! *tfaδδal!*
helper - *ṣaaniE* pl. *ṣinnaaE.* He has two helpers. *Einda ṣaanEeen.*
helpful - **1.** *xaduum.* She's always very helpful. *hiyya daaʔiman kulliš xaduuma.* **2.** *mufiid.* You've given me a very helpful hint. *nṭeetni fadd ʔišaara kulliš mufiida.*
helping - *taris maaEuun.* I had two helpings. *ʔakalit taris maaEuuneen.*
helpless - *Eaajiz* pl. *-iin, Eajaza.* A baby is helpless. *ṭ-ṭifil Eaajiz Ean kullši.*

hem – *zaašya* pl. *zawaaši*. I want to let out the hem. *ʔariid afukk il-zaašya.*
to hem – *kaff (u kaff) n-*. Mother, hem this skirt for me. *yoom kuffii-li t-tannuura.*
to hem in – *zişar (i zaşir) n-, zaaṭ (u zooṭ) n-*. The house is hemmed between two tall buildings. *l-beet mazşuur been binaayteen Eaalya.*

hen – *dijaaja* pl. *-aat*, coll. *dijaaj*.

her – *-ha*. I saw her last week. *šifitha bil-isbuuE il-maaδi.* -- That was very nice of her. *haaδi čaanat kulliš zilwa minha.* -- This is her house. *haaδa beetha.*

herb – *Eišib* pl. *ʔaEšaab*. In Iraq they still use herbs as remedies. *bil-Eiraaq baEadhum yistaEmiluun il-ʔaEšaab ka-ʔadwiya.*

herd – *qaṭiiE* pl. *quṭEaan*. Who owns this herd? *minu şaazib hal-qaṭiiE?*
to herd – *zišar (i zašir) n-, jimaE (a jamiE) n-*. They herded us all in to a small room. *zišroona kullna b-fadd ġurfa şġayyra.*

here – *hnaa, hnaaya*. We can't stay here. *ma-nigdar nibqa hnaa.* -- Let's cross the street (from) here. *xal-nuEbur iš-šaariE minnaa.* -- The papers here say nothing about the accident. *j-jaraayid ihnaa ma-tiktib ʔay šii Ean il-zaadiθa.*
**Here's the book. *haaδa l-iktaab* or *haak il-iktaab.*
**Here's to you! *l-şizztak* or *l-naxbak!*

hereafter – **1.** *missa ġaadi, baEdeen*. Hereafter I'll be more alert. *missa ġaadi akuun mintibih ʔazyad.* **2.** *l-ʔaaxra*. Some people believe in the hereafter. *baEaδ in-naas yiEtiqduun bil-ʔaaxra.*

hernia – *fatiġ* (pl. *ftuug*) *riiz*.

hero – *baṭal* pl. *ʔabṭaal*.

heroic – *buṭuuli**.

hers – (m.) *maalha*, (f.) *maalatha*. My hat is bigger than hers. *šafuqti ʔakbar min maalatha.*
**A friend of hers told me. *şadiiq min ʔaşdiqaaʔha gaal-li.*

herself – *nafisha, ruuzha*. She fell on the stairs and hurt herself. *wugEat Ead-daraj w-ʔaδδat nafisha* or *wugEat Ead-daraj w-tʔaδδat.* -- She did it by herself. *hiyya sawwatha b-nafisha.*
**She's not herself today. *hiyya muu Eala baEaδha hal-yoom.*

to **hesitate** – *traddad (a taraddud)*. He hesitated a moment before he answered. *traddad fadd lazδa gabul-ma jaawab.* -- Don't hesitate to call if you need me. *la-titraddad itxaaburni ʔiδa tiztaajni.*

hesitation – *taraddud*. He answered without hesitation. *jaawab ibduun taraddud.*

hiccup – *šihheega* pl. *-aat, šahga* pl. *-aat*. I have the hiccups again. *hamm jatni š-šihheega.*

hide – *jilid* pl. *jiluud*. These hides still have to be tanned. *haj-jiluud laazim baEad tindibiġ.*
to hide – **1.** *δamm (u δamm) n-, xifa (i xafi) n-, xaffa (i txiffi) t-*. He hid the money in the drawer. *δamm il-ifluus bil-imjarr.* **2.** *xifa (i xafi) n-*. The trees hide the view. *l-ʔašjaar tixfi l-manδar.* **3.** *xital (i xatil)*. Let's hide in the garage. *xalli nixtil bil-garaaj.*

hideous – **1.** *bašiE*. That's a hideous face you have! *šloon wujih bašiE Eindak!* **2.** *qabiiz*. Where did you buy that hideous hat? *mneen ištireeti haš-šafqa l-qabiiza?*

hieroglyphics – *l-hiirooġliifiyya.*

high – **1.** *mustawa (mnil-irtifaaE)*. Prices have reached a new high. *l-ʔasEaar wuşlat ʔila mustawa jidiid imnil-irtifaaE.* **2.** *Eaali*. I have a high opinion of him. *raʔyi bii kulliš Eaali.* -- The airplane is too high to see. *ṭ-ṭayyaara kulliš Eaalya ma-tinšaaf.* **3.** *ṭaab*. Now shift into high gear. *hassa zuṭṭha Eala ṭaab giir.*
**That building is eight stories high. *hal-ibnaaya rtifaaEha θman ṭabaqaat.*

highlight – *ʔahamm munaasaba* pl. *-aat*. Our party was the highlight of the season. *zaflatna čaanat ʔahamm munaasaba bis-sana.*

highly – **1.** *kulliš*. She seemed highly pleased. *δiharat kulliš mamnuuna.* **2.** *b-kull xeer*. He spoke very highly of him. *jaab δikra b-kull xeer.*

high school – *madrasa* (pl. *madaaris*) *θaanawiyya.*

high tide – *madd*. Let's wait till high tide. *xalli nintiδir lamman yşiir il-madd.*

highway – *ṭariiq* pl. *ṭuruq*. The highway between Baghdad and Najef is completely paved. *ṭ-ṭariiq been baġdaad win-najaf kulla mballaṭ.*

hike – *safra* (pl. *-aat*) *maši; mašya*. Let's go on a hike! *xalli nițlaE safra maši* or *xalli nsawwi mašiya.*
to hike – *miša (i maši)*. We hiked five miles. *mišeena xams amyaal.*

hill – *tall* pl. *tlaal*. What's on the other side of the hill? *š-aku bij-jiha θ-θaanya mnit-tall?*

him – *-a*. I've seen him. *šifta.*

himself – *nafsa, ruuza*. He hurt himself badly. *ʔaδδa nafsa kulliš* or *tʔaδδa kulliš.* -- Did he do it by himself? *huwwa b-nafsa sawwaaha?*
**He's quite beside himself. *ma-yidri b-nafsa.*
**He's himself again. *rijaE il-zaalta ṭ-ṭabiiEiyya.*
**He's not himself today. *haaδa muu Eala baEδa l-yoom.*

to **hinder** – *Eawwag (u taEwiig) t-*. You're hindering me in my work. *ʔinta tEawwugni b-šuġli.*

hinge – *nurmaada* pl. *-aat*. One of the hinges of the door is broken. *wizda min nurmaadaat il-baab maksuura.*
to hinge – *twaqqaf (a tawaqquf)*. Everything hinges on his decisions. *kullši yitwaqqaf Eala qaraara.*

hint – **1.** *ʔišaara* pl. *-aat, talmiiza* pl. *-aat, tanwiiha* pl. *-aat*. Can't you give me a hint? *ma-tigdar tinṭiini fadd ʔišaara?*
**There's just a hint of mint in this drink. *ʔaku riizat niEnaaE bil-mašruub.*
to hint – *ʔaššar (i tʔiššir) t-, lammaz (i tlimmiz, talmiiz) t-, nawwah (i tanwiih) t-*. He hinted that something was up. *ʔaššar bi-ʔan ʔaku fadd šii.*

hip – *wirik* pl. *ʔawraak.*

hire – *ʔujra, kari*. We have boats for hire. *Eidna blaam lil-ʔujra.*
to hire – **1.** *ʔajjar (i tʔijjir, taʔjiir) t-, kira (i kari) n-*. We hired the boat for the whole day. *ʔajjarna l-balam lil-yoom kulla.* **2.** *ʔajjar (i tʔijjir, taʔjiir) t-, šaġġal (i tašġiil) t-, staxdam (i stixdaam)*. We have to hire some people. *laazim inʔajjir baEaδ in-naas.*

his – *-a*, (m.) *maala*, (f.) *maalta*. Have you got his address? *Eindak Einwaana?* -- This car is his. *haaδi s-sayyaara maalta.*
**I met a friend of his. *qaabalit waazid min ʔaşdiqaaʔa.*

hiss – *faziiz, fiziiz, nafxa* pl. *-aat*. I heard the hiss of a snake. *simaEit faziiz zayya.*
to hiss – *nifax (u nafux), fazz (i fiziiz)*. Snakes hiss. *l-zayyaat tinfux.*

historian – *muʔarrix* pl. *-iin.*

historic – *taariixi**.

history – *taariix*. Have you studied European history? *dirasit taariix ʔooruppi?* -- That picture has quite a history. *haş-şuura ʔilha taariix.*

hit – *ʔişaaba* pl. *-aat, δarba* pl. *-aat*. There are two hits in the bull's-eye. *ʔaku ʔişaabteen ib-markaz il-hadif.*
**His song became a hit over night. *ġannuuta nšiharat ib-yoom w-leela.*
to hit – **1.** *δirab (u δarub) n-*. The ball hit the door. *l-kura δurbat il-baab.* -- Who hit you? *minu δirabak?* **2.** *şidam (i şadim) n-*. The news hit me hard. *l-ʔaxbaar şidmatni şadma Eaniifa.* **3.** *şidam (i), δirab (u)*. The car hit him and broke his leg. *s-sayyaara şidmata w-kisrat rijla.* **4.** *ṭaxx (u ṭaxx) n-, δurab (u)*. I hit my knee against the door. *ṭaxxeet rukubti bil-baab.*
to hit it off – *tlaaʔam (a talaaʔum)*. They hit it off pretty well after they met. *tlaaʔmaw kulliš zeen baEad-ma ltiqaw.*
**How did you hit on the right answer? *šloon jaa j-jawaab?*

hitch – *taEqiid*. Everything came off without a hitch. *kullši čaan ibduun taEqiid.* -- That's where the hitch comes in! *hnaa maşdar it-taEqiid!*
**I'm sure there's a hitch somewhere. *ʔaani mitʔakkid aku fadd liEba b-haš-šii.*
to hitch – *rubaṭ (u rabuṭ) n-*. Hitch your horse to the post. *ʔurbuṭ izşaanak bil-Eamuud.* **2.** *šakkal (i tšikkil), čallab (i tčillib)*. Did you hitch the horses to the wagon yet? *šakkalit il-xeel bil-Earabaana loo-baEad?*

hive – *xaliyya* pl. *-aat*. We have six hives of honey bees. *Eidna sitt xaliyyaat maal zanaabiir il-Easal.*

hives – *šira, šaraE*. I've got hives. *Eindi šira.*

to **hoard** – *xizan (i xazin) n-*. They're hoarding sugar. *da-yxiznuun šakar.*

hoarse - *mabʒuuʒ.* He's hoarse today. *ṣoota mabʒuuʒ il-yoom.*
hobby - *huwaaya, walaε.* His latest hobby is collecting stamps. *huwaayta l-ʔaxiira jamε iṭ-ṭawaabiε.*
hog - *xanziir* pl. *xanaaziir.* He raises hogs. *huwwa yrabbi xanaaziir.*
**Don't be such a hog! *la-tkuun šarih!*
to **hold** - **1.** *šaal (i šeel) n-.* She's holding the baby in her arms. *šaayla j-jaahil b-iidha.* **2.** *lizam (a lazim) n-.* That knot will hold. *hal-εugda tilzam.* -- Hold your tongue! *ʔilzam ilsaanak* or *sidd ʒalgak!* -- The room holds twenty people. *l-ġurfa tilzam εišriin šaxiṣ.* **3.** *kumaš (a kamiš) n-, lizam (a).* Hold him! *ʔukumša!* **4.** *sawwa (i tsuwwi) t-, qaam (u qiyaam) n-.* When shall we hold the election? *šwakit nsawwi l-intixaab?* **5.** *εind-.* He holds a high position. *εinda markaz εaali.* **6.** *εiqad (u εaqid) n-, εigad (u εagid) n-.* The meetings are held once a week. *l-ijtimaaεaat tinεiqid marra bil-isbuuε.* **7.** *ṭṭabbaq (a ṭṭubbuq).* This rule doesn't hold in every case. *hal-ʔamur ma-yiṭṭabbaq εala kull ʒaala.* **8.** *jiδab (i jaδib) n-.* That speaker knows how to hold his audience. *hal-xaṭiib yuεruf išloon yijδib il-mustamiεiin.*
to hold back - *minaε (a maniε) n-, lizam (a lazim) n-.* I wanted to go, but he held me back. *ʔaani ridit aruuʒ, bass huwwa minaεni.*
to hold on - *ntiδ̣ar (i ntiδ̣aar).* Can you hold on for a minute? *tigdar tintiδ̣ir fadd daqiiqa?*
to hold on to - **1.** *čallab (i tačliib, tčillib) t-, b-, lizam (a lazim) n-, kumaš (a kamiš) n-.* Hold on to me. *čallib biyya.* **2.** *ʒaafaδ̣ (u muʒaafaδ̣a) t-, εala, ʒtifaδ̣ (u ʒtifaaδ̣) b-.* Can you hold on to that job just a little longer? *tigdar itʒaafuδ̣ εala δiič iš-šaġla l-mudda šwayya ʔaṭwal?*
to hold out - *qaawam (u muqaawama).* We would have held out for months if we had had enough food. *loo čaan εidna ʔakil kaafi čaan qaawamna ʔašhur.*
to hold over - *maddad (i tmiddid) t-.* The movie was held over for another week. *tmaddad εarδ̣ il-filim ʔila sbuuε laax.*
to hold up - **1.** *εaṭṭal (i tεiṭṭil, taεṭiil) t-, ʔaxxar (i tʔixxir, taʔxiir) t-.* You're holding me up. *ʔinta da-tεaṭṭilni.* **2.** *qaawam (u muqaawama) t-.* Will these shoes hold up? *hal-qanaadir itqaawum?* **3.** *silab (i salib) n-.* Two men held me up yesterday. *salbooni θneen il-baarʒa.*
to get hold of - **1.** *liga (i lagi) n-.* Where can I get hold of him? *ween ʔagdar algii?* **2.** *lizam (a lazim).* Stop crying. Get hold of yourself. *baṭṭil il-bači. ʔilzam nafsak.*
holdup - *tasliib* pl. *-aat.* He had nothing to do with the holdup. *ma-ʔila daxal bit-tasliib.*
**What's the holdup? *šinu-lli mεaṭṭilna?*
hole - **1.** *zuruf* pl. *zruuf.* There is a hole in his pants. *ʔaku zuruf ib-panṭaruuna.* **2.** *ʒufra* pl. *ʒufar.* Who dug that hole? *minu ʒifar δiič il-ʒufra?*
**He lives in a dingy hole. *yiskun ib-makaan raziil.*
**I'm five dinars in the hole. *εindi xams idnaaniir εajiz.*
holiday - *εuṭla* pl. *εuṭal.*
Holland - *hoolanda.*
hollow - **1.** *mjawwaf.* These walls seem to be hollow. *hal-iʒyaaṭiin itbayyin imjawwfa.* **2.** *mamṣuuṣ.* Her cheeks are hollow. *xduudha mamṣuuṣa.*
holy - *muqaddas.*
home - **1.** *beet* pl. *byuut.* My home is in Baghdad. *beetna b-baġdaad.* -- We're building a new home. *da-nibni beet ijdiid.* -- Make yourself at home. *l-beet beetak* or *εtubur haaδa beetak.* **2.** *balad* pl. *buldaan; bilaad; waṭan.* Where's your home? (country) *ween baladak?* **3.** *daaxil.* At home and abroad ... *bid-daaxil wil-xaarij ...*
homeless - *bduun maʔwa.* Thousands of people were made homeless by the flood. *ʔaalaaf in-naas ṣaaraw ibduun maʔwa mnil-fayaδ̣aan.*
homemade - *šuġuḷ beet.* This is homemade jelly. *haaδi mrabba šuġuḷ beet.*
to be **homesick** - *ʒann (i ʒaniin).* I'm homesick for my country. *ʔaani da-ʔaʒinn il-waṭani.*
home town - *balda, madiina, wlaaya.* He's from my home town. *huwwa min balidti.*
homework - *waajib beeti* pl. *waajibaat beetiyya; waδ̣iifa* (pl. *waδ̣aayif*) *beetiyya.* Have you done all your homework? *sawweet kull waajibaatak il-beetiyya?*
honest - *mustaqiim, ʔamiin.* Do you think he's honest? *tiftikir huwwa mustaqiim?* -- He has an honest face. *ybayyin εala wujha ʔamiin.*
**An honest man is as good as his word. *r-rajul iš-šariif gool w-fiεil.*
honestly - **1.** *ṣidug, b-šarafi, fil-ʒaqiiqa, ʒaqiiqatan.* I was honestly surprised. *ṣidug ʔaani činit mitεajjib.* **2.** *b-ṣaraaʒa.* Honestly, I don't know what to do with you. *b-ṣaraaʒa ma-adri š-raʒ-asawwi wiyyaak.*
honesty - *stiqaama, ʔamaana.* There's no question about his honesty. *ma-aku šakk b-istiqaamta.* -- Honesty is the best policy. *l-ʔamaana ʔaʒsan ṭariiq.*
to **honk** - *ṭawwaṭ (u ṭṭuwwuṭ), dagg (u dagg) n-.* Honk three times, and I'll come down. *ṭawwuṭ itlaθ marraat w-ʔaani ʔanzil.*
honor - *šaraf.* It's an honor to be elected. *mniš-šaraf waaʒid yuntaxab.* -- On my honor! *b-šarafi!* -- We gave a banquet in his honor. *sawweena daεwa εala šarafa* or *sawweena daεwa takriiman ʔila.*
to honor - **1.** *šarraf (i tširruf) t-, karram (u takriim) t-.* I feel very much honored. *ʔaani ašεur kulliš mukarram.* **2.** *qibal (a qabuul) n-.* We can't honor this check. *ma-nigdar niqbal hač-čakk.*
hood - **1.** *ġiṭa, ġuṭa* (pl. *ġuṭaayaat, ġuṭaawaat*) *raas.* This raincoat has a hood attached to it. *hal-imšammaε imšakkal bii ġiṭa raas.* **2.** *panid.* Lift up the hood and check the car's oil. *šiil il-panid w-ʔufʒas dihin il-sayyaara.*
hoof - *ʒaafir* pl. *ʒawaafir.* There's a nail in our horse's hoof. *ʔaku bismaar ib-ʒaafir iʒṣaanna.*
**We had to hoof it. *δ̣ṭarreena nduggha maši.*
cloven hoof - *δ̣ilif* pl. *ʔaδ̣laaf.*
hook - **1.** *tiεlaaga* pl. *-aat.* Hang your coat on the hook. *εallig sitirtak bit-tiεlaaga.* **2.** *čillaab* pl. *člaaliib, čingaal* pl. *čanaagiil.* We need a new hook for the crane. *nriid čillaab jidiid lis-silink.* **3.** *šuṣṣ* pl. *šṣuuṣ.* What kind of hook are you using to fish? *yaa nooε šuṣṣ da-tistaεmil ib-ṣeed is-simač?*
**He intends to get rich, by hook or by crook. *yriid yṣiir zangiin b-ʔay wasiila.*
to hook - **1.** *ṣaad (i ṣeed) n-.* How many fish did you hook? *čam simča ṣidit?* **2.** *čangaḷ (i tčingiḷ), šakkal (i tšikkil), čallab (i tčillib).* Help me hook this chain. *saaεidni ʔačangiḷ haz-zanjiil.* **3.** *ligaf (u laguf) n-.* She finally hooked him. *ʔaxiiran hiyya lugfata.*
to hook up - *šakkal (i tšikkil) t-.* I haven't hooked up the new radio yet. *li-hassa baεad ma-šakkalt ir-raadyo.*
hop - *ṭafra* pl. *-aat, gamza* pl. *-aat.* It's just a short hop by plane. *biṭ-ṭayyaara kullha ṭafra.*
to hop - *gumaz (u gamuz), ṭufar (u ṭafur).* She hopped with joy. *gumzat imnil-faraʒ.*
to hop around - *gammaz (u tgummuz), ṭaffar (u ṭṭuffur).* He was hopping around on one leg. *čaan da-ygammuz εala fadd rijil.*
hope - *ʔamal* pl. *ʔaamaal.* Don't give up hope. *la-tigṭaε il-ʔamal.*
to hope - *tmanna (a tamanni), tʔammal (a taʔammul).* She had hoped to see you. *čaanat titmanna tšuufak.*
**I hope you didn't catch cold. *nšaaḷḷa ma-axaδit barid.*
hopeful - *εind- ʔamal, mitʔammil.* I am hopeful. *εindi ʔamal.*
hopeless - *mayʔuus min-.* The situation is completely hopeless. *l-ʒaala kulliš mayʔuus minha.*
horizon - *ʔufuq* pl. *ʔaafaaq.*
horizontal - *ʔufuqi*.*
horn - **1.** *girin* pl. *gruun.* That cow's horn is broken. *girin δiič il-haayša maksuur.* **2.** *hoorin* pl. *-aat.* Blow your horn next time! *dugg il-hoorin maalak il-marra j-jaaya!* **3.** *buuq* pl. *ʔabwaaq.* Can you play this horn? *tigdar itdugg hal-buuq?*
hornet - *zambuur* pl. *zanaabiir.*
horrible - *faδ̣iiε.* It was a horrible sight. *čaan manδ̣ar faδ̣iiε.*
horrid - *muzεij, kariih.*
horrors - *faδ̣aaεa* pl. *-aat.* The horrors of war are indescribable. *faδ̣aaεat il-ʒarb ma-tinwuṣuf.*
horse - (m.) *ʒṣaan* pl. *ʒuṣan,* coll. *xeel,* (f.) *faras* pl. *fruusa,* coll. *xeel.*
**A team of wild horses couldn't drag me there. *ma-ʔaruuʒ ihnaak loo tjurrni b-εarabaana.*
**You shouldn't look a gift horse in the mouth. *l-hadiyya muu b-θamanha.*
horse race - *sibaaq il-xeel, reesiz.*
hose - **1.** *buuri* (pl. *bwaari*) *laastiig, ṣoonda* pl.

-*aat*. The hose is still in the garden. *buuri l-laastiig baɛda bil-ẓadiiqa*. **2.** *jwaariib*. We just got a new shipment of women's hose. *hastawwna stilamna šaẓnat ijwaariib nisaaʔiyya jidiida*.
hospital – *mustašfa* pl. -*ayaat*, *quṣṭaxaana* pl. -*aat*, *xastaxaana* pl. -*aat*, *xastaxaayin*.
hospitality – *karam*, *ẓusun ḍiyaafa*.
host – *muḍayyif* pl. -*iin*, *ṣaaẓib* (pl. *ʔaṣẓaab*) *id-daɛwa*. He's a wonderful host. *huwwa kulliš xooš muḍayyif*.
hostess – *muḍayyifa* pl. -*aat*. She's a charming hostess. *hiyya muḍayyifa kulliš laṭiifa*. -- She works as a hostess with Iraqi Airlines. *tištuġul muḍayyifa bil-xuṭuuṭ ij-jawwiyya l-ɛiraaqiyya*.
hot – **1.** *ẓaarr*. Do you have hot water? *ɛindak maay ẓaarr?* -- This mustard sure is hot. *hal-xardal ṣudug ẓaarr*. **2.** *ẓaadd*. He has a hot temper. *ɛinda ṭabuɛ ẓaadd*. **3.** *qawi**. The scent is still hot. *riiẓat iṣ-ṣeed la-tazaal qawiyya*.
**I made it hot for him. *nṭeeta daris ma-yinsaa*.
**I haven't had a hot meal in three days. *ṣaar-li tlaθt iyyaam ma-maakil ṭabux*.
**We were hot on his trail. *činna da-ntibɛa blayya kalal*.
hotel – *ʔuteel* pl. -*aat*, *findiq* pl. *fanaadiq*.
hour – **1.** *saaɛa* pl. -*aat*. I'll be back in an hour. *raẓ-arjaɛ baɛad saaɛa*. -- I'm taking nine hours a week in night school. *ʔaani maaxiḍ tisiɛ saaɛaat bil-isbuuɛ bil-madrasa l-masaaʔiyya*. **2.** *dawaam*. See me after hours. *šuufni wara d-dawaam*. -- My hours are from nine to five. *dawaami mnis-saaɛa tisɛa lis-saaɛa xamsa*.
at all hours – *b-ʔay wakit*, *kull wakit*. I can be reached at all hours. *bil-imkaan l-ittiṣaal biyya b-ʔay wakit*.
hour hand – *miil* pl. *myaal*, *ɛaqrab* pl. *ɛaqaarib*.
house – **1.** *beet* pl. *byuut*, *daar* pl. *duur*. I want to rent a house. *ʔariid aʔajjir beet*. **2.** *majlis* pl. *majaalis*. Both houses will meet in joint session tomorrow. *l-majliseen raẓ-yijtamɛuun ib-jalsa muštaraka baačir*.
**The house was sold out. *kull it-tikitaat inbaaɛat*.
to house – *nazzal* (*i tnizzil*) *t-*, *sakkan* (*i tsikkin*, *taskiin*) *t-*. Where are we going to house the visitors? *ween raẓ-innazzil iz-zuwwaar?*
household – *ʔahl il-beet*. We have something for the whole household. *ɛidna ʔašyaaʔ il-kull ʔahl il-beet*.
housemaid – *xaadma* pl. -*aat*, *ṣaanɛa* pl. -*aat*.
housework – *šuġl il-beet*.
how – *sloon*, *keef*. How shall I do it? *šloon asawwiiha?* -- He'll show you how. *raẓ-yraawiik šloon*. -- How do you do? *šloonak?* or *šloon ʔaẓwaalak?*
**My name's Ahmad - How do you do? *ʔismi ʔaẓmad - tšarrafna*.
**That's a fine how-do-you-do! *yaa fattaaẓ*, *yaa razzaaq!*
how come – *šloon*, *šinu s-sabab*, *luweeš*. How come you're still here? *šloon ʔinta baɛdak ihnaa?*
how many – *čam*, *šgadd*. How many oranges shall I take? *čam purtaqaala ʔaaxuḍ?* or *šgadd purtaqaal ʔaaxuḍ?*
how much – **1.** *šgadd*. How much did he pay? *šgadd difaɛ?* **2.** *beeš*, *šgadd*. How much is this? *haay beeš?*
however – *laakin maɛa ḍaalik*, *bass*. I'd like to do it, however I have no time. *yiɛjibni ʔasawwiiha, laakin maɛa ḍaalik ma-ɛindi wakit*.
howl – *ɛawi*. I thought I heard the howl of a wolf. *ftikarit simaɛit ɛawi ḍiib*.
to howl – **1.** *ɛawwa* (*i tɛuwwi*). The dog has been howling all night. *č-čalib ṣaar-la da-yɛawwi ṭuul il-leel*. **2.** *ṭagg* (*u ṭagg*). The audience howled with laughter. *l-mitfarrjin ṭaggaw imniḍ-ḍiẓik*.
to **huddle** – *ltamm* (*a ltimaam*), *tzaaẓam* (*a tazaaẓum*). They huddled in a corner. *ltammaw ib-fadd izwiyya*. -- The sheep huddled close together. *l-ġanam iltammaw waaẓid yamm il-lax*.
hug – *ẓaḍna* pl. -*aat*. She gave him a big hug. *ẓiḍnata fadd ẓaḍna zeena*.
to hug – **1.** *ẓiḍan* (*i ẓaḍin*). She hugged her mother tightly. *ẓiḍnat ʔummha b-quwwa*. **2.** *laazam* (*i mulaazama*). Our boat hugged the coastline all the way. *markabna laazam is-saaẓil ṭuul iṭ-ṭariiq*.
huge – *ḍaxim* pl. -*iin* or *ḍxaam*. The elephant is a huge animal. *l-fiil ẓayawaan ḍaxim*.
hum – *ṭaniin*. What's that strange hum? *šinu haṭ-ṭaniin il-ġariib?*
to hum – **1.** *hamham* (*i thimhim*). What's that tune you're humming? *yaa laẓin da-thamhim?* **2.** *wann* (*i waniin*), *wanwan* (*i twinwin*). This top won't hum. *hal-muṣraɛ ma-da-ywinn*. **3.** *ṭann* (*i ṭaniin*), *ṭanṭan* (*i ṭṭinṭin*). My ears are humming. *ʔiḍni da-ṭṭinn*.
**Things are always humming at this corner. *haz-zuwiyya daaʔiman biiha ẓaraka*.
human – **1.** *bašari**. Is this a human eye? *haay ɛeen basariyya?* **2.** *bašar*, *bani ʔaadam*. I'm only human. *ʔaani bass bašar*.
humble – *mitwaaḍiɛ*. Abraham Lincoln grew up in humble circumstances. *braahaam linkoolin nišaʔ ib-ḍuruuf mitwaaḍɛa*. -- In the beginning he acted very humble. *ʔawwal marra čaan mutawaaḍiɛ ib-taṣarrufa*.
humidity – *ruṭuuba*.
to **humiliate** – *ḍall* (*i ḍall*) *n-*, *ẓaqqar* (*i taẓqiir*) *t-*. Poverty humiliated me in front of a lot of people. *l-fugur ḍallni giddaam naas ihwaaya*.
humor – **1.** *mazaaj*, *keef*. Are you in a good humor today? *mazaajak zeen hal-yoom?* **2.** *tankiit*, *fakaah*. The humor in this magazine is very biting. *t-tankiit ib-hal-majalla kulliš laaḍiɛ*.
humorous – **1.** *muḍẓik*. He told a very humorous joke. *ẓica nukta kulliš muḍẓika*. **2.** *fakih*, *hazali**. He's a very humorous man. *haaḍa fadd rijjaal kulliš fakih*.
hunch – *šuɛuur daaxili*. I have a hunch that something is wrong there. *ɛindi fadd šuɛuur daaxili ʔaku šii muu tamaam ihnaak*.
hunchback – **1.** *ẓidba* pl. *ẓidab*. One has a hunchback. *waaẓid ɛinda ẓidba*. **2.** (m.) *ʔaẓdab* pl. *ẓadbiin*, (f.) *ẓadba* pl. -*aat*. She's a hunchback. *hiyya ẓadba*.
hunched up – *mẓoodib*, *mẓaddib*. Your back hurts because you're sitting all hunched up. *ḍahrak da-yoojɛak li-ʔan ʔinta mẓoodib ib-gaɛidtak*.
hundred – **1.** *miyya*. About a hundred people were present. *ẓawaali miit waaẓid čaanaw ẓaaḍriin*. **2.** *miyya* pl. -*aat*. Hundreds of people were present. *miyyaat in-naas čaanaw ẓaaḍriin*.
Hungarian – **1.** *majari**. He owns a Hungarian ship. *yimluk baaxira majariyya*. **2.** *majari* pl. -*iyyiin*. The Hungarians left at twelve. *l-majariyyiin raaẓaw is-saaɛa θnaɛaš*. **3.** *majari*. He speaks Hungarian very well. *yiẓči majari kulliš zeen*.
Hungary – *l-majar*.
hunger – *juuɛ*. I nearly died of hunger. *mitit imnij-juuɛ ʔilla šwayya*.
hungry – *juuɛaan* pl. -*iin*, *jwaaɛa*. He has to feed ten hungry stomachs. *laazim yṭaɛɛim ɛašir ibṭuun juuɛaana*. -- We didn't go hungry. *ma-ḍalleena jwaaɛa*.
to **hunt** – *ṣaad* (*i ṣeed*) *n-*, *tṣayyad* (*a taṣayyud*). They're hunting rabbits. *da-yṣiiduun ʔaraanib*. -- We're going hunting tomorrow. *baačir raẓ-nitṣayyad*.
to hunt for – *dawwar* (*u tduwwur*) *t- ɛala*. We were hunting for an apartment. *činna da-ndawwur ɛala šiqqa*. -- Help me hunt for my shoes. *saaɛidni ʔadawwur ɛala qundarti*.
to hunt up – *ligaf* (*u laguf*) *n-*, *liga* (*i lagi*) *n-*. How many did you hunt up? *čam waaẓid ligafit?*
hunter – *ṣayyaad* pl. -*iin*.
hunting license – *ʔijaazat* (pl. -*aat*) *ṣeed*.
hurry – *ɛajala*. There's no hurry. *ma-aku ɛajala*.
in a hurry – *mistaɛjil*. I'm in a big hurry. *ʔaani kulliš mistaɛjil*.
to hurry – **1.** *staɛjal* (*i stiɛjaal*). Don't hurry! *la-tistaɛjil!* -- Hurry up! *ʔisriɛ!* or *staɛjil!* **2.** *ɛajjal* (*i taɛjiil*). Don't hurry me! *la-tɛajjilni!* or *la-txalliini ʔastaɛjil!*
to **hurt** – **1.** *wujaɛ* (*a wujaɛ*), *ʔallam* (*i ʔalam*), *ʔaḍḍa* (*i tʔiḍḍi*). My arm hurts. *ʔiidi toojaɛni*. **2.** *ɛawwar* (*i tɛuwwur*) *t-*, *jiraẓ* (*a jariẓ*) *n-*. Where are you hurt? *ween mitɛawwar?* -- I didn't mean to hurt your feelings. *ma-ridit ajraẓ šuɛuurak*. **3.** *ʔallam* (*i ʔalam*) *t-*, *ʔaḍḍa* (*i ʔaḍa*) *t-*. She's easily hurt. *hiyya titʔallam min ʔaqall šii*. **4.** *ʔaḍḍa* (*i tʔiḍḍi*) *t-*, *ḍarr* (*u ḍarr*) *n-*. This will hurt business. *haay raẓ-itʔaḍḍi s-suug*.
**Will it hurt if I'm late? *raẓ-yṣiir ḍarar ʔiḍa ʔaani ʔatʔaxxar?*
husband – *zooj* pl. *ʔazwaaj*, *rajil* pl. *rjuula*.
to **hush up** – **1.** *ṭamṭam* (*u ṭṭumṭum*) *t-*. The scandal was quickly hushed up. *l-faḍiiẓa bil-ɛajal iṭṭamṭumat*. **2.** *sakkat* (*i tsikkit*) *t-*. Try to hush up the child. *ẓaawli tsakkiti j-jaahil*.
husky – **1.** *jaθiiθ* pl. -*iin*, *jθaaθ*. He's quite husky. *huwwa kulliš jaθiiθ*. **2.** *xašin*. His voice is husky. *ṣooṭa xašin*.
hut – *kuux* pl. *kwaax*, *čardaaġ* pl. *čaraadiiġ*.
hyena – *ḍabuɛ* pl. *ḍbaaɛ*.

I

I - *ʔaani.* I'm cold. *ʔaani bardaan.* -- If I ask him, he'll do it. *ʔiδa ʔaani agul-la, ysawwiiha.*
ice - *θalij.* Put some ice in the glasses. *xalli θalij bil-iglaaṣaat.*
ice box - *ṣanduug* (pl. *sanaadiig*) *θalij, θallaaja* pl. *-aat.*
ice cream - *doondirma.* A dish of ice cream, please. *baḷḷa, fadd maaƐuun doondirma.*
iced - *mθallaj.* Do you serve iced tea here? *Ɛidkum čaay imθallaj ihnaa?*
icy - *baarid miθl iθ-θalij, kulliš baarid.* The water is icy cold. *l-maay baarid miθl iθ-θalij.*
idea - *fikra* pl. That's a good idea! *haay xooš fikra.* -- I haven't the faintest idea what he wants. *ma-Ɛindi ʔay fikra Ɛan iš-šii lli-yriid.*
**What gives you that idea? *š-da-yxalliik itfakkir haš-šikil?*
**Who gave you the bright idea? *haaδa minu lli-nṭaak hal-Ɛaqil?*
**I couldn't get used to the idea. *ma-gdarit atƐawwad nafsi Ɛal-haš-šii.*
**Of all the ideas! *min duun kull il-ʔašyaaʔ!*
**She has big ideas. *hiyya ṭamuuḥa.*
**That's the idea! *hassa tamaam!*
**The idea! *hiiči!*
ideal - **1.** *l-maθal il-ʔaƐla.* Our ideal is freedom and independence for all people. *maθalna l-ʔaƐla l-ḥurriyya wil-istiqlaal il-kull iš-šuƐuub.* **2.** *qudwa* pl. *-aat.* He's my ideal. *huwwa quduuti.* **3.** *miθaali**. This is an ideal place for swimming. *haaδa makaan miθaali lis-sibiḥ.*
idealism - *miθaaliyya.*
idealist - *miθaali* pl. *-iyyiin.*
idealistic - *miθaali**.
identical - *fadd šikil, mitšaabih.* The two copies are identical. *han-nusuxteen fadd šikil tamaaman.* -- The two girls are wearing identical dresses. *l-binteen laabsaat infaaniif fadd šikil tamaaman.*
identification card - *hawiyya* pl. *-aat.*
to **identify** - **1.** *Ɛiraf (u Ɛaruf) n-.* The police identified him by his fingerprints. *š-šurṭa Ɛurfoo min ṭabƐat aṣaabƐa.* **2.** *Ɛarraf (u).* Everyone must stand up and identify himself. *kull waaḥid laazim yoogaf w-yƐarruf nafsa.*
**I don't want to identify myself with them. *ma-ariid yinqirin ʔismi wiyyaahum.*
identity - *hawiyya.* The police don't know the identity of the dead man. *š-šurṭa ma-yƐurfuun hawiyyat il-mayyit.*
**The police still do not know the identity of the thief. *š-šurṭa li-hassa baƐad ma-yƐurfuun minu l-ḥaraami.*
ideology - *maδhab* pl. *maδaahib.* He won't support their political ideology. *ma-yʔayyid maδhabhum is-siyaasi.*
idiot - *hibil, ʔablah* pl. *buluh.*
idle - **1.** *Ɛaaṭil.* He is an idle fellow. *huwwa fadd waaḥid Ɛaaṭil.* **2.** *faariġ.* That's just idle talk. *haaδa ḥači faariġ.* **3.** *baṭṭaal, Ɛaaṭil.* He's been idle for some time. *ṣaar-la mudda baṭṭaal.*
**The factory's been idle for years. *l-maƐmal ma-da-yištuġuḷ ṣaar-la sniin.*
**This machine is idle, we can use it. *hal-makiina maḥḥad da-yšaġġilha, nigdar nistaƐmilha.*
**Her tongue is never idle. *lsaanha la-yčill wala yitƐab.*
**Let the motor idle. *xalli l-makiina tištuġul* or ***la-tṭaffi l-makiina.*
idol - *ṣanam* pl. *ʔaṣnaam.* Worshipping idols is forbidden. *Ɛibaadat il-ʔaṣnaam ḥaraam.*
if - *ʔiδa, loo.* If anyone asks for me, say I'll be right back. *ʔiδa ʔaḥḥad siʔal Ɛalayya, gul-la hassa yirjaƐ.* -- I don't know if he'll come or not. *ma-adri ʔiδa raḥ-yiji loo laa.* -- I'll go even if it rains. *ʔaruuḥ ḥatta loo tumṭur.* -- He talks as if he had been there. *yiḥči Ɛabaalak loo huwwa čaan ihnaak.*
ignorance - **1.** *ġabaawa, ġabaaʔ, jahal.* I've never seen such ignorance. *baƐad ib-Ɛumri ma-šaayif hiiči ġabaawa.* **2.** *jahal.* Ignorance of the law is no excuse. *j-jahal bil-qaanuun muu Ɛuδur.*
ignorant - *ġabi* pl. *ʔaġbiyaaʔ, jaahil* pl. *juhalaaʔ.* She's such an ignorant person. *hiyya fadd mara ġabiyya.*
to **ignore** - *tjaahal (a tajaahul).* I would ignore his remark if I were you. *loo b-makaanak atjaahal iḥčaayta.* -- I ignored him. *tjaahalta* or ***ma-dirit-la baal.*
ill - *mariiδ.* He was very ill. *čaan kulliš mariiδ.*
**He can ill afford to quit his job now. *ma-yḥammal waδƐa ybaṭṭil min šuġḷa hassa.*
**He's ill at ease in such company. *huwwa ma-yirtaaḥ wiyya hiiči jamaaƐa.*
illegal - *ġeer qaanuuni*, muu qaanuuni**. This illegal action will be opposed by all responsible governments. *haaδa l-Ɛamal ġeer il-qaanuuni tƐaarδa kull il-ḥukuumaat il-masʔuula.*
illegitimate - *ġeer šarƐi**. He's an illegitimate child. *huwwa walad ġeer šarƐi.*
illiteracy - *ʔummiyya.* The illiteracy rate is high here. *mustawa l-ʔummiyya Ɛaali hnaa.*
illiterate - *ʔummi* pl. *-iyyiin.* The people of this village are all illiterate. *ʔahil hal-qarya kullhum ʔummiyyiin.*
illness - *maraδ* pl. *ʔamraaδ.*
to **illustrate** - **1.** *waδδaḥ (i tawδiiḥ) b-ṣuwar.* The book is illustrated. *l-iktaab imwaδδaḥ ib-ṣuwar.* **2.** *širaḥ (a šariḥ) n-, waδδaḥ (i).* I can illustrate this best by an example. *ʔagdar ʔašraḥ haaδa ʔaḥsan ib-fadd miθaal.*
illustration - **1.** *ṣuura* pl. *ṣuwar.* The catalogue has many illustrations. *l-katalook bii ṣuwar ihwaaya.* **2.** *šikil* pl. *ʔaškaal.* Look at illustration no. 10, on page 115. *šuuf iš-šikil raqam Ɛašra, ṣafḥa miyya w-ixmuṣṭaƐaš.*
ill will - *karah.* His insults caused a lot of ill will. *ʔihaanaata sabbabat karah in-naas ʔila.*
image - **1.** *ṣuura* pl. *-aat.* The image I have of him is that of an old man. *ṣuurta l-maṭbuuƐa b-fikri maal waaḥid šaayib.* -- She's the image of her mother. *hiyya ṣuura min ʔummha.* **2.** *šikil* pl. *ʔaškaal, škuul.* She examined her image in the mirror. *baawƐat šikilha bil-imraaya.*
imaginable - *mumkin taṣawwur-.* He tried everything imaginable. *ḥaawal kullši mumkin taṣawwura.* -- That's hardly imaginable! *haaδa šii ma-mumkin taṣawwura!* or ***haaδa šii ma-yxušš bil-Ɛaqil!*
imaginary - *xayaali**. Juha is an imaginary character. *juḥḥa fadd šaxṣiyya xayaaliyya.*
**Children sometimes live in an imaginary world. *j-jahhaal dooraat yƐiišuun ib-dunya l-xayaal.*
imagination - *xayaal.* That's pure imagination! *haaδa xayaal ṣirf.* -- She has a fertile imagination. *Ɛidha xayaal xaṣib.*
to **imagine** - **1.** *tṣawwar (a taṣawwur).* I can't imagine what you mean. *ma-ʔaqdar atṣawwar iš-da-tuqṣud.* -- I imagine so. *ʔatṣawwar haš-šikil* or ***ʔaδinn!* **2.** *txayyal (a taxayyul).* You're only imagining things. *ʔinta bass da-titxayyal ʔašyaaʔ ma-mawjuuda.*
to **imitate** - *qallad (i taqliid) t-.* He can imitate my voice. *yigdar yqallid ṣooti.*
imitation - **1.** *taqliid.* The Japanese put out a poor imitation of this lighter. *l-yaabaaniyyiin ṭalƐaw fadd taqliid muu zeen il-hal-qiddaaḥa.* **2.** *ṣṭinaaƐi*, čaδδaabi**. This pocketbook is made of imitation leather. *haj-janṭa maƐmuula min jilid iṣṭinaaƐi.* -- This necklace is made of imitation pearls. *hal-iġḷaada msawwaaya min liilu čaδδaabi.*
immature - *muu naaδij.* His actions are immature for his age. *taṣarrufaata muu naaδja bin-nisba l-Ɛumra.*
immediate - *mubaašir.* Ahmad is my immediate superior. *ʔaḥmad raʔiisi l-mubaašir.*
**There's no school in the immediate neighborhood. *ma-aku madrasa yammna mubaašaratan.*
**This amount will take care of your immediate needs. *hal-mablaġ ykaffi lit-tiḥtaajak hassa.*
immediately - *mubaašaratan, ḥaalan.* Immediately afterwards I heard a scream. *mubaašaratan waraaha smaƐit fadd Ɛeeṭa.* -- I'll go there immediately. *raḥ-aruuḥ ihnaak ḥaalan.*
immense - *δaxum, haaʔil.* They have an immense

living room. *εidhum ṣaaloon ḍaxum.* — They stored immense quantities of meat. *xiznaw kammiyyaat haaʔila mnil-lazam.*

immigrant – *muhaajir* pl. *-iin.* About one thousand immigrants enter the country every year. *ζawaali ʔalif muhaajir yduxluun il-balad kull sana.*

immigration – *hujra.* The Immigration Office is in that building. *daaʔirt il-hujra b-hal-binaaya.*

immoral – **1.** *duuni*, naamarbuuṭi*.* That is an immoral act. *haaδa εamal duuni.* **2.** *munζaṭṭ, duuni*.* This man is immoral. *har-rijjaal munζaṭṭ* or ***har-rijjaal ma-εinda qiyam ʔaxlaaqiyya.*

immortal – *xaalid.* Mutanabbi is an immortal Arabic poet. *l-mutanabbi fadd šaaεir εarabi xaalid.*

immunity – **1.** *manaaεa.* Do you have immunity to smallpox? *εindak manaaεa ḍidd ij-jidri?* **2.** *ζaṣaana.* All ambassadors have diplomatic immunity. *kull is-sufaraaʔ εidhum ζaṣaana diblomaasiyya.*

impartial – *munṣif, εaadil, ζaqqaani*.* I'll try to be impartial. *raζ-aζaawil akuun munṣif.*

impatient – *ma-εind- ṣabur.* He is very impatient. *haaδa kulliš ma-εinda ṣabur.* — Don't be so impatient! *la-tkuun hal-gadd ma-εindak ṣabur!*

imperative – **1.** *fiεl ʔamur.* "*ʔiktib*" is the imperative of "*kitab*"? *ʔiktib hiyya fiεl il-ʔamur maal kitab.* **2.** *ʔijbaari*.* It is imperative for all students to attend the meeting. *l-ζuḍuur bil-ijtimaaε ʔijbaari εala kull it-talaamiiδ.*

imperialism – *stiεmaar.* Imperialism is on the decline. *l-istiεmaar ib-ṭariiqa liz-zawaal.*

impersonal – *ġeer šaxṣi*.* I always keep my relations with the staff impersonal. *daaʔiman axalli εalaaqaati wiyya l-muwaḍḍafiin ġeer šaxṣiyya.*

to **imply** – *ṭḍamman (a).* His statement implied he was in favor of the plan. *kalaama ṭḍamman imwaafaqta εal-xiṭṭa.*

impolite – **1.** *muu mhaδδab.* She is very impolite. *hiyya kulliš muu mhaδδaba.* — Why are you so impolite? *leeš hiiči ʔinta muu mhaδδab?* **2.** *xašin.* That was very impolite of him. *haay čaanat kulliš xašna minna.*

import – *stiiraad.* The government encourages the import of raw materials. *l-ζukuuma tšajjiε istiiraad il-mawaadd il-xaam.*

to import – *stawrad (i stiiraad).* Iraq imports a lot of Australian cheese. *l-εiraaq yistawrid ihwaaya jibin ʔustiraali.*

importance – *ʔahammiyya.* You attach too much importance to the problem. *ʔinta hwaaya txalli ʔahammiyya lil-masʔala.* — That's of no importance. *haaδa ma-ʔila ʔahammiyya.*

important – *muhimm.* I want to see you about an important matter. *ʔariid ašuufak ib-qaḍiyya muhimma.* — He was the most important man in town. *huwwa čaan ahamm rajul bil-madiina.*

imports – *waaridaat, mustawradaat.* Our imports still exceed our exports. *waaridaatna baεadha tziid εala ṣaadiraatna.*

to **impose on** – **1.** *staġall (i stiġlaal).* He's imposing on your good nature. *huwwa yistiġill ṭiibat axlaaqak.* **2.** *furaḍ (u faruḍ).* Don't let them impose their will on you. *la-txalliihum yfurḍuun εaleek miθil-ma yirduun.*

imposing – *raaʔi.* That's certainly an imposing building. *haaδi ζaqiiqa binaaya raaʔya.*

imposition – *zaζma* pl. *-aat, takliif* pl. *-aat.* If it's not an imposition, could you give me a ride? *ʔiδa ma-aku zaζma εaleek mumkin itwaṣṣilni?*

impossible – *mustaζiil.* Why is it impossible? *luweeš haaδa mustaζiil?*

**That man is absolutely impossible! *haš-šaxiṣ ʔabadan ma-yinζimil!*

to **impress** – *ʔaθθar (i taʔθiir) t-.* That doesn't impress me. *haaδi ma-tʔaθθirni.*

impression – **1.** *taʔθiir* pl. *-aat.* He made a good impression on me. *čaan taʔθiira εalayya zeen.* **2.** *naḍra, nṭibaaε.* I got a bad impression of him. *ʔaxaδit εanna naḍra muu zeena.* — He tries to give the impression that he's a good fellow. *yζaawil yinṭi l-inṭibaaε ʔinna xooš rijaal.*

under the impression – *εabaal-.* I was under the impression that he wanted to go. *εabaali raad yruuζ.*

impressionism – *nṭibaaεiyya.*

to **imprison** – *ζibas (i ζabis) n-, sijan (i sajin) n-.* The men were imprisoned for two months. *r-riyaajiil čaanaw maζbuusiin li-muddat šahreen.*

to **improve** – **1.** *ζassan (i taζsiin) t-.* I don't know how we can improve our product. *ma-ʔadri šloon mumkin inζassin intaajna.* **2.** *tζassan (a taζassun).* His condition has improved. *ṣiζζta tζassnat.* — Ahmad is improving in school. *ʔaζmad da-yitζassan bil-madrasa.*

improvement – **1.** *taζassun* pl. *-aat.* I don't see any improvement in her condition. *ma-da-ašuuf ʔay taζassun ib-ζaalatha.* **2.** *taζsiin* pl. *-aat.* We're making some improvements in the house. *da-nsawwi baεḍ it-taζsiinaat bil-beet.*

**That's no improvement over our former method. *ma-jaab ay šii jdiid εan ṭariiqatna s-saabiqa.*

impudence – *ṣalaafa, waqaaζa.* Such impudence! *hiiči ṣalaafa!* or *ʔamma waqaaζa!*

impulse – **1.** *ndifaaε.* You've got to control your impulses. *laazim tiḍbuṭ indifaaεak.* **2.** *daafiε* pl. *dawaafiε, baaεiθ* pl. *bawaaεiθ.* I had an impulse to give the beggar a dinar. *ζasseet ib-fadd daafiε anṭi diinaar lil-faqiir.*

impulsive – *mindafiε.* She is a very impulsive person. *hiyya kulliš mindafεa.*

in – **1.** *b-.* There's no heater in my room. *ma-aku sooba b-ġurufti.* — He's in Najaf now. *hassa huwwa bin-najaf.* — He's the smartest student in the entire class. *huwwa ʔaδka ṭaalib biṣ-ṣaff kulla.* — Say it in English. *guulha bil-ingiliizi.* — That in itself isn't important. *hiyya b-ζadd δaata muu muhimma.* — If I were in your place, I would've gone. *loo činit ib-maζallak, čaan riζit.* — Did it happen in the daytime or at night? *ζidθat bin-nahaar loo bil-leel?* — I can finish it in a week. *ʔagdar axalliṣha b-isbuuε.* — Write in ink. *ʔiktib bil-ζibir.* **2.** *baεad.* I'll be back in three days. *raζ-arjaε baεad itlaθt iyyaam.* — I'll pay you in two weeks. *raζ-adfaε-lak baεad ʔusbuuεeen.* **3.** *mawjuud.* He's not in. *huwwa muu mawjuud.* **4.** *waaṣṭa* pl. *-aat.* He has an in at the Ministry of the Interior. *εinda waaṣṭa b-wizaart id-daaxiliyya.*

**He was the only one at the party in tails. *huwwa čaan il-waζiid bil-ζafla laabis ifraak.*

**Sift the flour before you put the water in. *ʔunxuḷ iṭ-ṭaζiin gabuḷ-ma txalli-la ṃayy.*

**Padded shoulders aren't in any more. *s-sitar ib-čattaafiyyaat muu moodat hal-wakit* or *s-sitar ib-čattaafiyyaat iḍmaζallat.*

**Are you in on it with them, too? *ʔinta hamm mištirik wiyyaahum?*

**He has it in for you. *huwwa δaaṃil-lak-iyyaaha.*

**He knows all the ins and outs. *yuεruf il-ʔaku wil-maaku* or *yuεruf xitlaatha.*

**He's in good with the boss. *εilaaqta zeena bil-mudiir.*

**Now we're in for it! *ʔakalnaaha!*

all in – *taεbaan kulliš, hwaaya taεbaan, mayyit imnit-taεab.* I'm all in. *ʔaani taεbaan kulliš.*

inauguration: The inauguration of the President will be next January. *l-iζtifaal ib-tanṣiib ir-raʔiis raζ-ykuun ib-kaanuun iθ-θaani j-jaay.*

incense – *bxuur.*

incentive – *ζaafiz* pl. *ζawaafiz.* It's hard to work without an incentive. *ṣaεub tištuġul biduun wujuud ζaafiz.*

inch – *ʔinj* pl. *-aat.* Bring me a three-inch nail. *jiib-li bismaar ṭuula tlaθ ʔinjaat.*

**He came within an inch of being run over. *huwwa taqriiban raad inqital.*

**He's every inch a soldier. *huwwa jundi b-maεna l-kalima.*

incident – *ζaadiθ* pl. *ζawaadiθ.* There've been several border incidents lately. *ṣaarat εiddat ζawaadiθ εal-ζuduud bil-mudda l-ʔaxiira.* — They crossed the river without incident. *εubraw in-nahar bala-ma yṣiir ζaadiθ.*

incidentally – **1.** *εaraḍan.* He just said it incidentally. *gaal-ha εaraḍan.* **2.** *bil-munaasaba.* Incidentally, I saw our friend Ali the other day. *bil-munaasaba, šifit ṣaaζibna εali δaak il-yoom.*

incinerator – *miζraqa* pl. *maζaariq.*

incline – *munζadar.* I climbed the incline. *ṣεadt il-munζadar.*

to incline – *maal (i mayil).* The minaret inclines to the right. *l-manaara maayla lil-yimna.*

inclined – **1.** *mayyaal.* I'm inclined to believe him. *ʔaani mayyaal ʔila taṣdiiqa.* **2.** *maayil.* Water naturally flows down an inclined surface. *l-ṃaay εaadatan yinζidir εal-ʔarḍ il-maayla.*

to **include** – **1.** *ζtiwa (i) εala.* The dictionary doesn't include technical expressions. *l-qaamuus* *ma-yiẓtiwi ɛala ṣṭilaaẓaat fanniyya.* 2. *daxxal (i tadxiil) t-.* Include this in my bill. *daxxil haaδi ṣimn iẓsaabi.*

included - 1. *wiyya.* The room is five dinars, service included. *ʔiijaar il-ġurfa xams idnaaniir wiyya l-xidma.* 2. *b-ṣimn.* Were you included in the group that was promoted? *činit ib-ṣimn ij-jamaaɛa l-itraffɛaw?*

including - *b-ṣimn-, wiyya.* He earns thirty dollars, including tips. *huwwa yṭalliɛ itlaaθiin doolaar, ib-ṣiminha l-baxšiiš.*

income - *waarid* pl. *-aat, daxal* pl. *madxuulaat.* How much of an income does he have? *sġadd il-waarid maala?*

incompetent - *muu kafu.* The ambassador is incompetent. *s-safiir muu kafu.*

incomplete - *muu kaamil, naagiṣ.* The details of the report are incomplete. *tafaaṣiil it-taqriir muu kaamla.*

inconceivable - *muu maɛquul, ma-yšiila l-ɛaqil.* It's inconceivable that he'd do anything like that. *muu maɛquul ysawwi hiiči šii.*

inconclusive - *muu muqniɛ, muu qaaṭiɛ.* The evidence so far is inconclusive. *l-ʔadilla li-hassa muu muqniɛa.*

inconvenience - *ʔizɛaaj.* The trip caused us a lot of inconvenience. *s-safra sabbibat-inna hwaaya ʔizɛaaj.*

to inconvenience - *θaqqal (i taθqiil) ɛala, ʔazɛaj (i ʔizɛaaj).* I don't want to inconvenience you. *ma-ariid aθaqqil ɛaleek.*

inconvenient - *muu mulaaʔim.* He visited us at a very inconvenient time. *zaarna b-fadd wakit ʔabad muu mulaaʔim.* -- It will be inconvenient to go to the market today. *l-yoom muu hal-gadd mulaaʔim lir-rooẓa lis-suug.*

incorrect - *muu ṣaẓiiẓ, ġalaṭ.* Some of what he said was incorrect. *baɛaṣ illi gaala muu ṣaẓiiẓ.*

increase - *ziyaada* pl. *-aat, rtifaaɛ* pl. *-aat.* Statistics show a considerable increase in population. *l-ʔiẓṣaaʔaat itbayyin ziyaada kabiira bin-nufuus.*

on the increase - *b-irtifaaɛ.* The birth rate is on the increase. *nisbat il-wilaada b-irtifaaɛ.*

to increase - 1. *zayyad (i tazyiid) t-, kaθθar (i takθiir) t-.* You have to increase your output. *laazim itzayyid il-ʔintaaj.* 2. *zaad (i ziyaada) n-.* The population increased tremendously. *zaadat in-nufuus ib-nisba kabiira.*

incredible: **She told an incredible story. *ẓičat iẓčaaya ma-yšiilha l-ɛaqil.*

indecent - *baδiiʔ.* His language is indecent. *luġata baδiiʔa.*

indeed - 1. *ẓaqiiqatan.* That's very good indeed! *haay ẓaqiiqatan kulliš zeena.* 2. *ṣidug.* Indeed? *ṣidug?*

indefinite - *ma-mɛayyan, ma-maẓduud.* We'll be staying for an indefinite period. *raẓ-nibqa ʔila mudda ma-mɛayyna.*

independence - *stiqlaal.* In these days, all African people want independence. *b-hal-ʔayyaam, kull iš-šuɛuub il-ʔafriiqiyya triid istiqlaal.*

**He insists on complete independence in his work. *yṣirr ɛala ʔan maẓẓad ʔabad yitdaxxal ib-šuġla.*

independent - 1. *mustaqill, mistiqill.* Lebanon is an independent state. *lubnaan balad mustaqill.* 2. *ma-mirtibuṭ.* She's independent of her family. *hiyya ma-mirtabṭa b-ɛaaʔilatha.* 3. *miɛtimid ɛala nafs-.* He's been independent ever since he was sixteen. *čaan miɛtimid ɛala nafsa min ɛumra siṭṭaɛaš sana.*

index - *fihrast* pl. *fahaaris.* Look for the name in the index. *dawwur il-ʔisim bil-fihrast.*

index finger - *sabbaaba* pl. *-aat.*

India - *l-hind.*

Indian - 1. *hindi* pl. *hnuud.* Not all Indians are Hindus. *muu kull il-ihnuud hindoos.* 2. *hindi ʔaẓmar* pl. *hnuud ẓumur.* The original inhabitants of America were the Indians. *sukkaan ʔamriika l-ʔaṣliyyiin humma l-ihnuud il-ẓumur.* 3. *hindi**. The Indian delegation arrived yesterday. *l-wafd il-hindi wuṣal il-baarẓa.*

Indian Ocean - *l-muẓiiṭ il-hindi.*

to **indicate** - *dall (u dall) n- ɛala, bayyan (i tabyiin) t-.* His statement indicates that he's serious about the decision. *ẓčaayta tdull ɛala ʔinnahu jiddi b-hal-qaraar.*

indication - *daliil* pl. *dalaaʔil.* Did she give you any indication that she liked you? *bayynat-lak ʔay daliil ɛala ẓubbha?*

Indies - *jazaaʔir il-hind.*

indifference - *ɛadam ihtimaam.* He showed complete indifference in the matter. *bayyan fadd ɛadam ihtimaam kulli b-hal-mawṣuuɛ.*

indifferent - *laaʔubaali.* Don't be so indifferent. *la-tkuun hal-gadd laaʔubaali.*

**Why are you so indifferent to her? *leeš hal-gadd ma-tdiir-ilha baal?* or *leeš ma-tihtamm biiha?*

indigestion - *suuʔ haṣum.* I have indigestion. *ɛindi suuʔ haṣum.*

indignant - *saaxiṭ.* He was indignant at the unfair treatment. *čaan saaxiṭ ɛal-muɛaamala s-sayyiʔa.*

indiscreet - 1. *ma-mitẓaffuṣ.* Your remark was very indiscreet. *ʔinta ma-činit mitẓaffuṣ ib-δiič l-iẓčaaya.* 2. *ma-mitbaṣṣir.* We feel you were indiscreet in your decision. *ʔiẓna niɛtiqid inta ma-činit mitbaṣṣir ib-qaraarak.*

individual - 1. *šaxiṣ* pl. *ʔašxaaṣ, waaẓid.* He's a peculiar individual. *huwwa fadd šaxiṣ ʔaɛmaala ġariiba.* 2. *farid* pl. *ʔafraad.* The communists don't respect the rights of the individual. *š-šuyuuɛiyyiin ma-yihtammuun ib-ẓuquuq il-farid.* 3. *xaaṣṣ.* We each have our individual taste. *kull waaẓid minnina ʔila δawqa l-xaaṣṣ bii.*

**The individual can do nothing. *ʔiid wiẓda ma-tṣaffug.*

individually - 1. *waaẓid waaẓid.* I wish to speak to the students individually. *ʔard aẓči wiyya kull tilmiiδ waaẓid waaẓid.* 2. *kull waaẓid waẓda.* They came individually to the station. *ʔijaw lil-maẓaṭṭa kull waaẓid waẓda.*

Indonesia - *ʔandooniisya.*

Indonesian - *ʔandooniisi** pl. *-iyyiin.* He's an Indonesian. *huwwa ʔandooniisi.*

indoors - *jawwa, b-daaxil.* You'd better stay indoors today. *ʔaẓsan loo tibqa jawwa l-yoom.* -- If it rains the concert will be held indoors. *l-ẓafla l-moosiiqiyya tṣiir ib-daaxil il-qaaɛa ʔiδa tumṭur id-dinya.*

industrial - *ṣinaaɛi**. They are setting up industrial centers all over the UAR. *humma gaaɛid yibnuun maraakiz ṣinaaɛiyya b-kull ʔanẓaaʔ ij-jamhuuriyya l-ɛarabiyya l-muttaẓida.*

industrialist - *ṣinaaɛi* pl. *-iyyiin.* He's a famous industrialist. *huwwa ṣinaaɛi mašhuur.*

industrialization - *taṣniiɛ.* The industrialization of Egypt is making considerable progress. *t-taṣniiɛ ib-maṣir gaaɛid yitqaddam ib-surɛa.*

industry - *ṣinaaɛa* pl. *-aat.* Many industries were developed after the war. *hwaaya ṣinaaɛaat iṭṭawwrat baɛad il-ẓarb.*

inevitable - *ẓatmi*, laa budd min-, ma-mumkin tafaadi-.* This was an inevitable result. *haay čaanat natiija ẓatmiyya.* -- An argument with him is inevitable now. *t-talaaġ wiyyaa ma-mumkin tafaadii hassa.*

inexpensive - *rxiiṣ, muu ġaali.* I bought an inexpensive watch. *štireet saaɛa rxiiṣa.*

infant - *raṣiiɛ* pl. *riṣaɛ.*

infantile - *maal ijhaal, ṣibaani**. His actions are quite infantile. *taṣarrufaata baɛadha maal ijhaal.*

infantile paralysis - *šalal.* He has infantile paralysis. *huwwa muṣaab biš-šalal.*

infantry - *mušaat.*

to **infect** - *ẓammal (i taẓmiil).* The dirt will infect that wound. *l-waṣaaxa tẓammil ij-jariẓ.*

to be infected - *ẓammal (i), ltihab (i ltihaab).* The wound is infected. *j-jariẓ imẓammil.*

infection - 1. *maraṣ* pl. *ʔamraaṣ, ɛadwa.* Is there any way to keep that infection from spreading to the rest of the people? *hal ʔaku ṭariiqa txalli haaδa l-maraṣ ma-yintišir ʔila baaqi n-naas?* 2. *ltihaab* pl. *-aat.* This medicine will get rid of the infection. *haaδa d-duwa raẓ-yiqṣi ɛal-iltihaab.*

infectious - *muɛdi.* He has a very infectious disease. *maraṣa kulliš muɛdi.*

inferior - 1. *waaṭi.* How can you tell that it's an inferior quality? *šloon tuɛruf haaδa min nooɛ waaṭi?* 2. *ʔaqall nooɛiyya.* This material is inferior to that. *haaδi l-maadda ʔaqall nooɛiyya mnil-lux.*

**He is doing inferior work. *šuġla muu zeen.*

inferiority complex - *murakkab naqis.* She has an inferiority complex. *ɛidha murakkab naqis.*

infidel - *kaafir* pl. *kuffaar.*

infidelity - *xiyaana.* Marital infidelity is a sin. *l-xiyaana z-zawjiyya ẓaraam.*

**He suspects his wife of infidelity. *huwwa yṣunn ʔinna zawijta xaaʔina.*

infinite - *ma-ʔil- nihaaya, ma-ʔil- ẓadd.* She has infinite patience. *ɛidha xuluq ma-ʔila nihaaya.*

to be **inflamed** - *ltihab (i ltihaab).* My eye is inflamed. *εeeni miltahba.*
inflammable - *qaabil lil-iltihaab.* Don't smoke here. The gas is inflammable. *la-tdaxxin ihnaa. l-ṗaanziin qaabil lil-iltihaab.*
inflammation - *ltihaab.* The inflammation is going down. *l-iltihaab da-yqill.*
influence - **1.** *taʔθiir, nufuuð.* He has no influence whatsoever. *ma-εinda ʔay taʔθiir.* **2.** *nufuuð.* The people resist outside influence in the country. *š-šaεab yqaawum in-nufuuð il-ʔajnabi b-balada.*
**He was driving under the influence. *čaan ysuuq w-huwwa sakraan.*
to influence - *ʔaθθar (i taʔθiir) εala.* I'm not trying to influence you. *ma-da-aḥaawil aʔaθθir εaleek.* -- He is trying to influence her in his favor *yḥaawil it-taʔθiir εaleeha l-ṣaalḥa.*
influential: **He's an influential man. *huwwa εinda taʔθiir čibiir. huwwa ṣaaḥib nufuuð waasiε.*
influenza - *ʔifluwanza.*
to **inform** - *xabbar (i taxbiir) t-, gaal (u gool) n-.* Keep me informed of your decisions. *xabburni b-kull qaraar tittaxðuu.*
**He's unusually well informed. *εinda εilim ib-kull il-ʔaxbaar.* or *εinda ṭṭilaaε waasiε.*
informant - *muxbir.* We got the news from a reliable informant. *ḥaṣṣalna εal-ʔaxbaar min muxbir mawθuuq bii.*
information - **1.** *maεluumaat, ʔaxbaar.* I can't give you any information about this case. *ma-agdar anṭiik ʔay maεluumaat titεallaq bil-qaðiyya.* **2.** *stiεlaamaat.* Where's the information desk, please? *min faðlak, ween maktab il-istiεlaamaat?*
infraction - *muxaalafa* pl. *-aat.* We'll charge a fine for any infraction of the rules. *raḥ-naðaε ġaraama εala kull muxaalafa lit-taεlimaat.*
ingenious - *baariε.* Your idea is very ingenious. *εamma fikirtak baariε.*
to **inhabit** - *sikan (u sakan).* The Rualla tribe inhabits the northern portion of the Arabian Peninsula. *qabiilat irwaḷa siknat il-qism iš-šamaali mnij-jaziira l-εarabiyya.* -- This area was not inhabited until two years ago. *hal-manṭiqa ma-čaanat maskuuna ʔilla muddat santeen.*
inhabitant - *saakin* pl. *sukkaan.* All the inhabitants of the island are fishermen. *sukkaan ij-jaziira kullhum ṣayyaadiin simač.* -- In 1960 Baghdad had a million inhabitants. *b-sanat ʔalf w-tisiε miyya w-sittiin sukkaan baġdaad čaanaw milyoon.*
to **inhale** - **1.** *ʔaxað (u) nafas.* The doctor told me to inhale. *ṭ-ṭabiib gal-li ʔuxuð nafas.* **2.** *bilaε (a baliε) id-duxxaan.* She's just learning to smoke, but she doesn't inhale. *hastawwha tεallmat tišrab jigaayir bass ma-tiblaε id-duxxaan.*
to **inherit** - *staaraθ (i stiiraaθ), wuraθ (a wariθ) n-.* I inherited the ring from my mother. *staaraθit il-miḥbas min ʔummi.*
inheritance - *wuriθ, miiraaθ.* My uncle left me a small inheritance. *εammi xaḷḷaf-li fadd išwayya wuriθ.*
inhuman - *waḥši**. The terrorists used inhuman methods against the populace. *l-ʔirhaabiyyiin istaεmal ʔasaaliib waḥšiyya ðidd is-sukkaan.*
initial - *ʔawwali**, *bidaaʔi**. The project is still in its initial stages. *l-mašruuε baεda b-maraaḥla l-ʔawwaliyya.*
initially - *mabdaʔiyyan, ʔawwalan, bil-ʔawwal.* Initially, the government is going to appropriate one million dinars. *mabdaʔiyyan, il-ḥukuuma raḥ-itxaṣṣiṣ milyoon diinaar.*
initiative - *himma.* That engineer doesn't have much initiative. *hal-muhandis ma-εinda hal-gadd himma.*
**Someone has to take the initiative so the others will follow. *fadd aḥḥad laazim yibdi ḥatta l-baaqiin ytibεuu.*
to **inject** - **1.** *biεaθ (a baεiθ) n-.* The change injected new life into the project. *t-taġyiir biεaθ ḥayaat ijdiida bil-mašruuε.* **2.** *ðurab (u ðarub) ʔubrat-.* They injected penicillin in his hip. *ðurboo ʔubrat pansiliin ib-wirka.*
injection - *ʔubra* pl. *ʔubar.* Are you getting injections for diabetes? *da-taaxuð ʔubar maal šakar?*
to **injure** - *jiraḥ (a jariḥ) n-.* How many people were injured in the accident? *šgadd naas injirḥaw bil-ḥaadiθa?*
injury - *jariḥ* pl. *jruuḥ.* His injuries were not serious. *jruuḥa ma-čaanat xaṭra.*
ink - *ḥibir.* I need ink for my fountain pen. *ʔaḥtaaj ḥibir il-qalam il-ṗaandaan maali.*
to ink - *xalla(i) ḥibir εala.* Don't ink the pad too heavily. *la-txalli hwaaya ḥibir εal-iṣṭampa.*
inlaid - *mṭaεεam.* That box has a cover inlaid with ivory. *qabaġ il-quuṭiyya mṭaεεam ib-εaaj.*
inner - *daaxli**, *jawwaani**. The inner door is locked. *l-baab id-daaxli maqfuul.*
innocence - *baraaʔa.* How did he prove his innocence? *šloon θibat baraaʔta?*
innocent - **1.** *barii*ʔ pl. *ʔabriyaaʔ.* He's innocent of this charge. *huwwa bariiʔ min hat-tuhma.* **2.** *baṣiiṭ.* He's as innocent as a new-born babe. *huwwa baṣiiṭ miθl iṭ-ṭifil.* **3.** *b-ḥusun niyya.* It was just an innocent remark. *čaanat mulaaḥaða b-ḥusun niyya.*
innovation - *btikaar* pl. *-aat.* The minister introduced many innovations in his department. *l-waziir qaddam εiddat ibtikaaraat il-taṭbiiqha b-daaʔirta.*
to **inoculate** - *ṭaεεam (i taṭεiim) t-.* I haven't been inoculated against yellow fever yet. *ma-ṭṭaεεamit baεad ðidd il-ḥimma ṣ-ṣafraaʔ.*
inoculation - *taṭεiim* pl. *-aat.*
to **inquire** - *staεlam (i stiεlaam), stafsar (i stifsaar).* I'll inquire about it. *raḥ-astaεlim εanha.*
inquiry - **1.** *taḥqiiq.* An inquiry revealed that ... *t-taḥqiiq bayyan εala ʔinna ...* **2.** *stifsaar* pl. *-aat, stiεlaam* pl. *-aat.* We had a lot of inquiries about this subject. *εidna hwaaya stifsaaraat εan haaða l-mawðuuε.*
insane - *majnuun* pl. *majaaniin, mxaḅḅaḷ* pl. *-iin.* That man is insane. *haaða r-rajul majnuun.*
insane asylum - *mustašfa l-imjaaniin.* When did they release him from the insane asylum? *yamta fakkoo min mustašfa l-imjaaniin?*
inscription - *kitaaba maḥfuura, kitaaba manquuša.* Can you read this inscription? *tigdar tiqra hal-kitaaba l-maḥfuura?*
insect - *ḥašara* pl. *-aat.* Insects are a problem here. *l-ḥašaraat fadd muškila hnaa.*
insecticide - *qaatil ḥašaraat.*
to **insert** - *dimaj (i damij).* Insert this sentence in the beginning of your report. *ʔidmij haj-jumla b-bidaayat taqriirak.*
inside - **1.** *daaxil.* May I see the inside of the house? *ʔagdar ašuuf daaxil il-beet?* **2.** *bid-daaxil.* He left it inside. *tirakha bid-daaxil.* **3.** *b-xilaal, b-ðimin.* Inside of five minutes the theater was empty. *b-xilaal xamis daqaayiq ṣaarat is-siinama faarġa.* **4.** *daaxili**. Could you please give us an inside room? *mumkin min faðlak tinṭiina ġurfa daaxiliyya?*
inside out - **1.** *bil-gufa, bil-magluub.* He has his sweater on inside out. *laabis ibluuza bil-gufa.* **2.** *šibir šibir, tamaaman.* He knows the town inside out. *yuεruf il-madiina šibir šibir.* -- He knows his business inside out. *xaatim maṣlaḥta tamaaman.*
to come (or go) inside - *dixal (u duxuul), xašš (u xašš), ṭabb (u ṭabb).* Why don't you come inside? *leeš ma-tidxul?*
insight - *ʔidraak, fahim.* He showed great insight in handling economic problems. *bayyan ʔidraak waasiε b-muεaalajat il-mašaakil l-iqtiṣaadiyya.*
insignia - *εalaama* pl. *-aat, εalaayim; ʔišaara* pl. *-aat.* The cavalry's insignia is crossed rifles. *εalaamat il-xayyaala bunduqiiteen mitqaaṭεa.*
insignificant - *ṭafiif, taafih, muu muhimm.* The difference is insignificant. *l-ixtilaaf ṭafiif.*
to **insinuate** - *lammaḥ (i talmiiḥ) t-.* He insinuated that the prime minister was taking bribes. *lammaḥ εala ʔan raʔiis il-wuzaraaʔ čaan yaaxuð rašwa.*
insinuation - *tasčiim, talmiiḥ* pl. *-aat.* Those insinuations are out of place. *hat-tasčiim ʔabad muu b-maḥalla.*
to **insist** - **1.** *ṣarr (i ʔiṣraar) n-.* Why do you insist on going? *luweeš iṭṣirr εar-rooḥa?* **2.** *laḥḥ (i ʔilḥaaḥ, laḥḥ).* Don't insist if she doesn't want to go. *la-tliḥḥ ʔiða hiyya ma-triid itruuḥ.*
insistent - *laḥuuḥ.* This beggar is very insistent. *hal-imgaddi kulliš laḥuuḥ.*
insolence - *ṣalaafa.* Children, I don't want any more insolence from you. *wilid, bass εaad ṣalaafa.*
insolent - *ṣalif.* He's an insolent fellow. *huwwa fadd waaḥid kulliš ṣalif.*
insomnia - *ʔaraq.* I have insomnia these days. *da-yṣiir εindi ʔaraq hal-ʔayyaam.*
to **inspect** - *fattaš (i taftiiš) t-.* They inspected the baggage carefully. *fattšaw ij-junaṭ kulliš zeen.*
inspection - *taftiiš* pl. *-aat.* Our baggage is ready

for inspection. *jinatna zaaŝra lit-taftiiš.*
inspector - *mufattiš* pl. *-iin.*
inspiration - *wazi, ʔilzaam.* A good poet can't write without inspiration. *š-šaaƐir iz-zeen ma-yigdar yunŝum bala ma-yijii l-wazi.*
to **inspire** - *ʔawza, wuza (i ʔiizaaʔ) n-.* His calm manner inspires confidence. *huduuʔa yuuzi biθ-θiqa.*
to **install** - *niṣab (u naṣub) n-.* A telephone will be installed tomorrow. *baačir raz-yinnuṣub talafoon.*
installation - **1.** *naṣub.* Telephone installation costs 15 pounds. *naṣub talafoon ykallif ixmuṣṭaƐaš diinaar.* **2.** *munšaʔaat, muʔassasa* pl. *-aat.* He was collecting intelligence on military and industrial installations. *čaan da-yijmaƐ maƐluumaat Ɛan il-munšaʔaat iṣ-ṣinaaƐiyya wil-Ɛaskariyya.*
installment - **1.** *qisim mitsalsil* pl. *ʔaqsaam mitsalsila.* The novel is appearing in installments. *r-ruwaaya da-tiṭlaƐ Ɛala ʔaqsaam mitsalsila.* **2.** *qisiṭ* pl. *ʔaqsaaṭ.* You can pay it in five installments. *tigdar tidfaƐha b-xams aqsaaṭ.*
on installments - *bit-taqsiiṭ, bil-ʔaqsaaṭ.* We bought the furniture on installments. *štireena l-ʔaθaaθ bit-taqsiiṭ.*
to pay in installments - *qassaṭ (i taqsiiṭ).* I'll pay you the amount in installments. *Ɛuud aqassiṭ-lak il-mablaġ.*
instance - **1.** *maθal* pl. *ʔamθaal.* This is another instance of his carelessness. *haaŝa maθal laax Ɛala Ɛadam ihtimaama.* **2.** *zaala* pl. *-aat, marra* pl. *-aat.* In this instance you're wrong. *b-hal-zaala ʔinta ġalṭaan.*
for instance - *maθalan.* There are quite a few possibilities, for instance ... *ʔaku Ɛiddat iztimaalaat, maθalan ...*
instant - *lazŝa* pl. *-aat.* Let me know the instant he arrives. *xburni bil-lazŝa lli yooṣal biiha.* -- He was gone in an instant. *xtifa b-lazŝa wizda.*
instantly - *zaalan, fawran.* He came instantly when I called. *jaa zaalan min ṣizzta.*
instead - *badaal, badalan min, b-makaan, Ɛiwaŝan Ɛan.* What do you want instead of it? *š-itriid badaala?* -- He gave me tangerines instead of oranges. *nṭaani laalingi b-bidaal il-purtaqaal.* -- Why don't you do something instead of complaining all the time? *luweeš ma-tsawwi šii badalan min ʔan titšakka Ɛala ṭuul?* -- Can you go instead of me? *tigdar itruuz Ɛiwaŝan Ɛanni?*
to **instigate** - *zarraŝ (i tazriiŝ).* He instigated the strike. *huwwa lli zarraŝ Ɛal-iŝraab.*
instigator - *muzarriŝ* pl. *-iin.*
instinct - *fiṭra, ġariiza.* Women love children by instinct. *n-niswaan yzibbuun l-aṭfaal bil-fiṭra.*
institute - *maƐhad* pl. *maƐaahid.* I'm studying at the Scientific Institute. *ʔaani adrus bil-maƐhad il-Ɛilmi.*
institution - *maƐhad* pl. *maƐaahid.* It's a state institution. *haaŝa maƐhad zukuumi.*
instruction - *muzaaŝaraat.* Professor Ahmed will give instruction in Arabic. *l-ʔustaaŝ ʔazmad raz-yilqi muzaaŝaraat bil-luġa l-Ɛarabiyya.*
instructions - *taƐliimaat.* The head nurse will give you instructions. *raʔiisat il-mumarriŝaat raz-tintiik it-taƐliimaat.*
instructive - *tawjiihi**. The lecture was very instructive. *l-muzaaŝara čaanat kulliš tawjiihiyya.*
instrument - *ʔaala* pl. *-aat.* Lay out the instruments for the operation. *zaŝŝiri l-ʔaalaat lil-Ɛamaliyya.* -- Do you play a musical instrument? *tigdar itdugg Ɛala ʔaala mawsiiqiyya?*
to **insulate** - *Ɛizal (i Ɛazil) n-.* Wrap the tape around the wire to insulate it. *liff it-teep Ɛal-waayir zatta tƐizla.* -- We'll have to insulate the heating pipes. *laazim niƐzil bwaari l-zaraara.*
insulated - *maƐzuul.* A well insulated wire won't give you a shock. *l-waayir il-maƐzuul zeen ma-yintil.*
insulator - *Ɛaazil* pl. *Ɛawaazil, maadda* (pl. *mawaadd*) *Ɛaazila.*
insult - *ʔihaana* pl. *-aat.* I consider that an insult. *ʔaƐtuburha ʔihaana.*
to insult - *ʔahaan (i ʔihaana) n-.* You've insulted him. *ʔinta ʔahanta.*
insurance - *taʔmiin* pl. *-aat.* You can sign the insurance policy tomorrow. *tigdar itwaqqiƐ Ɛaqd it-taʔmiin baačir.*
to **insure** - *ʔamman (i taʔmiin) t- Ɛala.* I have insured my house for 5,000 dinars. *ʔammanit Ɛala beeti b-mablaġ xamist aalaaf diinaar.*
intellectual - **1.** *muθaqqaf* pl. *-iin, Ɛaaqil* pl. *Ɛuqalaaʔ.* Many intellectuals read this magazine. *hwaaya muθaqqafiin yiqruun haaŝi l-majalla.* **2.** *fikri*, ŝihni*, Ɛaqli**. There's an intellectual bond between them. *ʔaku beenhum irtibaaṭ fikri.* -- She's not interested in intellectual matters. *hiyya ma-Ɛidha raġba bil-ʔumuur il-fikriyya.*
intelligence - **1.** *majhuud fikri, majhuud Ɛaqli.* The exam requires a lot of intelligence. *l-imtizaan yirraad-la hwaaya majhuud fikri.* **2.** *stixbaaraat.* He works in the intelligence service. *huwwa yištuġuḷ ib-daaʔirat l-istixbaaraat.*
intelligent - *ŝaki**. She's very intelligent. *hiyya kulliš ŝakiyya.*
to **intend** - *nuwa (i nawi, niyya).* What do you intend to do? *š-tinwi tsawwi?* or *šinu niyytak?* -- I intend to go to Basra in April. *naawi ʔaruuz lil-baṣra b-niisaan.*
intended - *maqṣuud.* That remark was intended for him. *haay il-mulaazaŝa čaanat maqṣuuda ʔila.* **This merchandise is intended for Spain. *haay il-biŝaaƐa maqṣuud biiha truuz l-ispaanya.* or *hal-biŝaaƐa manwi ʔirsaalha l-ispaanya.*
intense - *qawi*, šadiid.* I couldn't stand the intense heat. *ma-gdarit atzammal il-zaraara l-qawiyya.*
intensity - *šidda, quwwa.* I was amazed at the intensity of her anger. *tƐajjabit min šiddat ġaŝabha.*
intensive - **1.** *qawi*, šadiid.* The government is conducting an intensive campaign to stamp out prostitution. *l-zukuuma da-tsawwi zamla qawiyya zatta tiqŝi Ɛal-biġaaʔ.* **2.** *kaθiif.* They're using intensive cultivation to increase their crops. *gaaƐid yistaƐmiluun iz-ziraaƐa l-kaθiifa zatta yziiduun mazaaṣiilhum.*
intention - *niyya, qaṣid.* Was that really your intention? *ṣidug haaŝi čaanat niitak?*
intentional - *Ɛamdi**. That was an intentional killing. *ŝaak čaan qatil Ɛamdi.*
intentionally - *Ɛamdan.* I did it intentionally. *sawweetha Ɛamdan.*
intently - *b-intibaah.* They were listening intently. *čaanaw da-ysimƐuun b-intibaah.*
to **intercept** - *ltiqaṭ (i ltiqaaṭ).* We intercepted a a message from the enemy's headquarters. *ltiqaṭna risaala min markaz il-ʔaƐdaaʔ.*
intercourse - **1.** *ttiṣaal jinsi, jimaaƐ.* Have you had intercourse with her? *ṣaar Ɛindak ittiṣaal jinsi wiyyaaha?* **2.** *Ɛalaaqaat.* We never had any social intercourse with that family. *ʔabad ma-ṣaar Ɛidna Ɛalaaqaat ijtimaaƐiyya wiyya ŝiič il-Ɛaaʔila.*
to have intercourse - *jaamaƐ (i jimaaƐ).* The doctor forbade him to have intercourse. *d-duktoor minaƐa min ij-jimaaƐ.*
interest - **1.** *htimaam.* He shows a special interest in it. *yibdi htimaam xaaṣṣ biiha.* **2.** *maṣlaza* pl. *maṣaaliz.* This is in your own interest. *haay il-maṣlaztak.* **3.** *huwaaya* pl. *-aat.* He has many interests. *Ɛinda hwaaya huwaayaat.* **4.** *walaƐ.* He has a great interest in stamp collecting. *Ɛinda hwaaya walaƐ ib-jamƐ iṭ-ṭawaabiƐ.* **5.** *faaʔida, faayiz.* How much interest does the bank pay? *šgadd faaʔida yinṭi il-þang?* **6.** *zuṣṣa.* Do you have an interest in the business? *Ɛindak zuṣṣa biš-šuġuḷ?*
to interest - **1.** *jiŝab (i jaŝib).* She doesn't interest me at all. *hiyya ma-tijŝibni ʔabad.* **2.** *raġġab (u tarġiib).* Can't you interest him in that? *ma-tigdar itraġġba biiha?*
interested - **1.** *muulaƐ, Ɛind- raġba.* I'm interested in sports. *ʔaani muulaƐ bil-ʔalƐaab ir-riyaaŝiyya.* **2.** *mihtamm, Ɛind- raġba.* I'm interested in these studies. *ʔaani mihtamm ib-hiiči diraasaat.* -- He's more interested in science than art. *mihtamm bil-Ɛiluum ʔakθar imnil-finuun.* **3.** *Ɛind- waahis.* I'm not interested in going. *ma-Ɛindi waahis aruuz.* **4.** *Ɛind- ġaaya.* He's only interested in her money. *ma-Ɛinda ġaaya ġeer ifluusha.*
interesting - *mumtiƐ.* That's an interesting article. *haaŝi maqaala mumtiƐa.*
**What are the most interesting places to visit in Baghdad? *šinu hiyya ʔalṭaf il-mazallaat illi yumkin waazid yzuurha b-baġdaad.*
to **interfere** - **1.** *Ɛaaq (i ʔiƐaaqa).* He'll leave on Sunday if nothing interferes. *ysaafir il-ʔazzad ʔiŝa ma-yƐiiqa fadd šii.* **2.** *tdaxxal (a tadaxxul).* Don't interfere in other people's affairs! *la-titdaxxal ib-šuġuḷ ġeerak!* -- You're interfering with my work. *ʔinta da-titdaxxal ib-šuġli.*
interference - *wašwaša, tadaxxul.* We can't hear that station because there's so much interference in the

air. *ma-nigdar nismaε hal-maζaṭṭa li-ʔan ʔaku hwaaya wašwaša bij-jaww.*

interior - **1.** *daaxil, jawwa.* The interior of their house is very beautiful. *daaxil beethum kulliš ζilu.* or *beethum min jawwa kulliš ζilu.* **2.** *daaxili*, jawwaani*.* The interior walls are covered with cracks. *l-iζyaaṭiin id-daaxiliyya kullha mfaṭṭra.* **3.** *daaxiliyya.* The Ministry of the Interior is on the river. *wizaarat id-daaxiliyya εaš-šaṭṭ.*

intermission - *fatra* pl. *-aat.* I was in the foyer during the intermission. *ʔaθnaaʔ il-fatra činit biṣ-ṣaaloon.*

internal - **1.** *daaxili*.* The internal affairs of the country are in bad shape. *ʔaζwaal il-balad id-daaxiliyya muu zeena.* **2.** *daaxili*, baaṭini*.* He died of internal injuries. *maat natiijat juruuζ daaxiliyya.*

international - *dawli*.* Do you think the International Bank will underwrite this loan? *tiṭṣawwar ʔinna l-bank id-dawli raζ-yiḍmin hal-qarḍ?*

to **interpret** - **1.** *fassar (i tafsiir) t-.* You can interpret it this way, too. *mumkin itfassirha b-haṭ-ṭariiqa hamm.* **2.** *tarjam (i tarjama).* When the ambassador spoke with the king, he interpreted. *min čaan is-safiir yiζči wiyya l-malik huwwa čaan ytarjim.*

interpreter - *mutarjim* pl. *-iin, turjamaan* pl. *-iyya.* I acted as interpreter. *qumt ib-εamal mutarjim.*

to **interrupt** - **1.** *qaaṭaε (i muqaaṭaεa).* Don't interrupt me all the time. *la-tqaaṭiεni daaʔiman.* **2.** *sabbab (i) taεṭiil.* Am I interrupting? *ʔaani da-asabbib taεṭiil?*

interruption - *muḍaayaqa* pl. *-aat, muqaaṭaεa* pl. *-aat.* I can't concentrate on my work with all these interruptions. *ma-agdar arakkiz εala šuġļi min kuθrat il-muḍaayaqaat.*

intersection - *taqaaṭuε* pl. *-aat.* The accident occurred at the intersection. *l-ζaadiθ ζiṣal εind taqaaṭuε iṭ-ṭuruq.*

interval - **1.** *stiraaζa, tawaqquf.* After a short interval we continued on our trip. *baεad istiraaζa qaṣiira kammalna safratna.* **2.** *masaafa* pl. *-aat.* The trees are set at close intervals. *l-ašjaar mazruuεa εala masaafaat mitqaarba.* **3.** *fatra* pl. *-aat.* The bombs are set to go off at five-minute intervals. *l-qanaabil imwaqqata tinfijir ib-fatraat xamas daqaayiq.*

to **intervene** - *tdaxxal (i tadaxxul), twaṣṣaṭ*

to **intervene** - *tdaxxal (i tadaxxul), twaṣṣaṭ* *(i tawaṣṣuṭ).* It won't do any good to intervene in their quarrel. *ma-aku faayda min tadaxxulak beenaathum.*

intervention - *tadaxxul, tawaṣṣuṭ.* Both sides would welcome U.N. intervention in the dispute. *ṭ-ṭarafeen yraaζibuun tadaxxul hayʔat il-ʔumam il-muttaζida bin-nizaaε.*

interview - *muqaabala* pl. *-aat.* The reporter asked for an interview with the minister. *l-muraasil ṭilab muqaabalat il-waziir.*

to interview - *qaabal (i muqaabala).* The reporter interviewed the minister. *l-muraasil qaabal il-waziir.*

intestines - *ʔamεaaʔ.* The doctor removed a part of his intestines. *d-daktoor šaal wuṣla min ʔamεaaʔa.*

intimate - *ṣamiimi*.* We're intimate friends. *ʔiζna ʔaṣdiqaaʔ ṣamiimiyyiin.* or ***ʔiζna ʔaṣdiqaaʔ kulliš.*

into - **1.** *b-.* Put it into the box. *xalliiha biṣ-ṣanduuq.* -- Get into the car. *ʔidxul bis-sayyaara.* -- We have to take that into account, too. *haay hamm laazim inζuṭṭha bil-iζsaab.* **2.** *l-.* Can you translate this into English? *tigdar ittarjum haay lil-ingliizi?*

**Can these boards be made into something useful? *hal-looζaat yimkim yitsawwa minha šii yfiid?* or *hal-looζaat yimkin titζawwal ʔila šii mufiid?*

**Those kids are always into everything. *haj-jihhaal yšaεbiθuun ib-kullši.*

intolerance - *ʔadam it-tasaamuζ.*

intolerant - *mitεaṣṣub.* That man is very intolerant. *haaδa r-rijjaal mitεaṣṣub kulliš.*

intoxicant - *musakkir* pl. *-aat.* The sale of intoxicants to minors is prohibited. *beeε il-musakkiraat il-ġeer il-baalġiin mamnuuε.*

intoxicated - *xadraan, sakraan.* I'm a little intoxicated tonight. *ʔaani šwayya xadraan il-leela.*

intoxicating - *musakkir.* This wine is very intoxicating. *haš-šaraab kulliš musakkir.*

to **introduce** - **1.** *εarraf (u taεriif) t-, qaddam (i taqdiim) t-.* I'd like to introduce you to my father. *ʔaζibb aεarrfak εala ʔabuuya.* **2.** *ʔadxal (i ʔidxaal), daxxal (i tadxiil) t-.* He introduced a number of changes in his government's policy. *huwwa ʔadxal baεḍ it-taεdiilaat εala siyaast il-ζukuuma.* **3.** *qaddam (i taqdiim) t-.* They introduced new proposals in the legislature. *qaddamaw iqtiraaζaat jidiida lil-barlamaan.*

introduction - *muqaddima* pl. *-aat.* It's mentioned in the introduction. *maδkuura bil-muqaddima.*

intrusion - *taṭafful.* Sorry for the intrusion, sir, but we've just been invaded. *ʔaḍruuna mnit-taṭafful, ʔustaaδ, laakin hassa nhijam εaleena.*

intuition - *badiiha, badaaha.* You'll just have to use your intuition. *ma-εaleek ʔilla ʔan tistaεmil badaahtak.*

to **invade** - *ġiza (i ġazu) n-.* Napoleon tried to invade England. *naapilyoon ζaawal yiġzi ʔingiltara.*

invalid - **1.** *εaajiz* pl. *-iin.* For many years my grandmother has been an invalid. *jiddiiti ṣaar-ilha εiddat sanawaat εaajiz.* **2.** *baaṭil, ġeer šarεi*.* A will without a signature is invalid. *l-waṣiyya baaṭla biduun ʔimḍaaʔ.*

invasion - *ġazwa* pl. *-aat.* The invasion has failed. *l-ġazwa fišlat.*

to **invent** - **1.** *xtiraε (i xtiraaε).* Every day they invent something new. *kull yoom yixtarεuun šii jdiid.* **2.** *xtilaq (i xtilaaq).* Did you invent that story? *ʔinta xtilaqit hal-quṣṣa?*

invention - *xtiraaε* pl. *-aat.*

inventor - *muxtariε* pl. *-iin.*

inventory - *jarid.* Our shop takes inventory each year. *ʔiζna nsawwi jarid kull sana.*

to **invest** - *staθmar (a stiθmaar), šaġġal (i tašġiil).* He invested his money in real estate. *huwwa staθmar ifluusa bil-εiqaar.*

to **investigate** - *ζaqqaq (i taζqiiq) t- b-.* They're investigating the case. *da-yζaqqiquun bil-qaḍiyya.*

investigation - *taζqiiq* pl. *-aat.* An investigation has been ordered by the court. *l-maζkama ʔumrat ib-ijraaʔ taζqiiq.*

investment - *makaan istiθmaar.* What is the best financial investment nowadays? *šinu ʔaζsan makaan l-istiθmaar l-ifluus hal-ʔayyaam?*

investor - *mustaθmir* pl. *-iin.* We need more investors. *yinraad-inna mustaθmiriin baεad.*

invisible - *ġeer manḍuur.* Carbon monoxide is an invisible gas. *ʔawwal ʔooksiid il-kaarboon ġaaz ġeer manḍuur.*

invitation - *daεwa* pl. *-aat, εaziima* pl. *εazaayim.* Many thanks for your kind invitation. *ʔaškurak εala daεuutak.*

to **invite** - *εizam (i εaziima) n-, diεa (u daεwa) n-.* Who did you invite to the party? *ʔilman iεzamit lil-ζafla?* -- He invited me to lunch. *εizamni εal-ġada.*

inviting - **1.** *mušahhi.* The food looks very inviting. *l-ʔakil manḍara mušahhi.* **2.** *muġri.* This low price is very inviting. *has-siεir ir-raxiiṣ kulliš muġri.*

**The sea looks inviting today. *l-baζar yiġri εas-sibiζ hal-yoom.*

to **involve** - **1.** *ʔašrak (i ʔišraak).* He involved me in the crime, and I wasn't even there! *ʔašrakni bij-jariima, w-ʔaani ζatta ma-činit ihnaak!* **2.** *ṭṭallab (a taṭallub).* The trip involved a lot of expense. *s-safra ṭṭallibat ihwaaya maṣaariif.*

**The work involves a certain amount of risk. *š-šaġļa biiha xaṭuura.*

involved - *mεaqqad.* That's a very involved process. *haaδa ʔijraaʔ kulliš imεaqqad.*

to get involved - *ζaṭṭ (u ζaṭṭ) nafs~.* I don't want to get involved in this. *ma-ard aζuṭṭ nafsi b-haay.*

iodine - **1.** *yood.* We studied iodine in class today. *drasna l-yood ib-ṣaffna l-yoom.* **2.** *tantaryook, yood.* Put a little iodine on the wound so it doesn't swell up. *xalli šwayyat tantaryook εaj-jariζ ζatta ma-yooram.*

Iran - *ʔiiraan.*

Iranian - *ʔiiraani** pl. *-iyyiin, εajmi** pl. *εajam, faarisi** pl. *-iyyiin, furs.* She's an Iranian. *hiyya ʔiiraaniyya.*

Iraq - *l-εiraaq.* Baghdad is the capital of Iraq. *baġdaad hiyya εaaṣimat il-εiraaq.*

Iraqi - **1.** *εiraaqi* pl. *-iyyiin.* Are there many Iraqis here? *ʔaku hwaaya εiraaqiyyiin ihnaa?* **2.** *εiraaqi*.* Iraqi industry is advancing. *ṣ-ṣinaaεa l-εiraaqiyya da-titqaddam.*

irksome - *muζεij.* He still has to cope with many irksome problems. *baεad εinda hwaaya mašaakil*

muzεija.
iron - 1. ħadiid. You have to be made of iron to stand all that. laazim itkuun min ħadiid ħatta tigdar titħammal kull haaδa. -- They're putting an iron gate up at the entrance way. da-yħuṭṭuun baab ħadiid il-baab il-ħadiiqa. 2. ʔuuti pl. -iyyaat. Is the iron still hot? l-ʔuuti baεda ħaarr? 3. qawi*. He has an iron will. εinda ʔiraada qawiyya.
cast iron - ʔaahiin. This drainpipe is made of cast iron. hal-buuri min ʔaahiin.
to iron - kuwa (i kawi) n-, ḍirab (u ḍarub) n- ʔuuti. Did you iron my shirt? kweeti θoobi?
to iron out - tsaawa (a tasaawi), ṭṣaffa (a taṣaffi). There are still a few things to be ironed out. baεd aku baεḍ il-ʔašyaaʔ laazim titsaawa.
Iron Curtain - s-sitaar il-ħadiidi.
ironical - min mahzalat il-aqdaar. This turn of events is ironical. min mahzalat il-aqdaar ʔan yṣiir hiiči šii.
ironing board - meez (pl. -aat) maal ʔuuti.
irony - εunuf, ṣaraama. He's prone to using irony. huwwa mayyaal ʔila stiεmaal il-εunuf.
irrational - ġeer mittizin. His statements are irrational. kalaama ġeer mittizin.
irregular - 1. ġeer muntaḍam, ġeer munaḍḍam. The awarding of contracts was irregular. ʔaħkaam il-εuquud čaanat ġeer muntaḍma. 2. ġeer niḍaami*. We were attacked by irregular forces. haajmatna quwwaat ġeer niḍaamiyya.
irregularity - talaaεub pl. -aat. Some irregularities were discovered in his accounts. nliga talaaεub b-iħsaabaata.
irrelevant - ma-ʔila εilaaqa. This question is irrelevant to the case. haaδa suʔaal ma-ʔila εilaaqa bil-qaḍiyya.
irresponsible - ma-εind- masʔuuliyya. That child is irresponsible. haṭ-ṭifil ma-εinda masʔuuliyya.
to **irrigate** - ruwa (i rawi) n-, siga (i sagi) n-. We're going to irrigate this field next year. raħ-nirwi haaδa l-ħaqil s-sana l-qaadima.
irrigation - sagi, rawi. We couldn't raise anything on this land without irrigation. ma-nigdar innammi šii εala hal-gaaε bila sagi.
irritable - minfiεil, εaṣabi. He was very irritable this morning. čaan kulliš minfiεil il-yoom iṣ-ṣubuħ.
to **irritate - 1.** ʔaθaar (i ʔiθaara), ʔazεaj (i ʔizεaaj). His remark irritated me. εibaarta ʔaθaaratni. 2. hayyaj (i tahyiij) t-. This soap doesn't irritate the skin. haay iṣ-ṣaabuuna ma-thayyij ij-jilid.
Islam - l-ʔislaam.
Islamic - ʔislaami*. We're studying Islamic history. ʔiħna nidrus it-taariix il-ʔislaami.
island - jaziira pl. jazaaʔir, juzur. I just came from the island of Cyprus. hassa jeet min jaziirat qubruṣ.
to **isolate** - εizal (i εazil) n-. The sick children were isolated. l-ʔaṭfaal il-marḍa čaanaw maεzuuliin.
isolated - mafṣuul, maεzuul. They live in a house isolated from the village. humma yεiišuun ib-beet mafṣuul εan il-qarya.
Israel - ʔisraaʔiil.
Israeli - ʔisraaʔiili*.
issue - 1. εadad pl. ʔaεdaad. I haven't read the last issue. ma-qreet il-εadad il-ʔaxiir. 2. mawḍuuε pl. mawaaḍiiε. This question will be an important issue in the coming elections. has-suʔaal raħ-ykuun mawḍuuε muhimm bil-intixaabaat ij-jaaya. -- I don't want to make an issue of it. ma-ariid asawwiiha mawḍuuε baħiθ.
to issue - ṣaddar (i taṣdiir) t-. Where did they issue the passports? ween ṣaddraw jawaazaat is-safar?
it - 1. huwwa (or) hiyya (respectively). Which is my book? Oh, that's it. yaahu ktaabi? haδaak huwwa. -- Where is my hat? Here it is! ween šafuqti? hiyyaatha! 2. -a (or) -ha (respectively). I can't do it. ma-ʔagdar asawwiiha. -- I knew it! εirafitha. -- I can't give you the money today. I forgot it. ma-ʔagdar anṭiik l-ifluus il-yoom niseetha.
**Who's ''it''? Ali's ''it''. Run before he tags you! bii-man? b-εali. ʔirkuḍ gabuḷ-ma ygiisak!
**It's cold outside. barra baarda.
**It's raining. gaaεid tumṭur.
**It's lovely today. l-yoom kulliš badiiε.
**It doesn't matter. ma-thimm or ma-yhimm.
**It doesn't make any difference. ma-tifruq.
**He's had it! wuṣal ħadda.
itch - ħakka. I've got an itch. εindi ħakka.
to itch - ħakk (u ħakk) n-. The wound itches. j-jariħ da-yħukkni. -- I itch all over. kull jismi da-yħukkni.
**I'm itching to get started. ʔaani kulliš muštaaq abdi.
item - 1. šii pl. ʔašyaaʔ. We don't carry that item. ma-εidna haš-šii. 2. mawḍuuε pl. mawaaḍiiε. Did you see the item in the paper? šift il-mawḍuuε bij-jariida? 3. faqara pl. -aat. How many items are on that bill? čam faqara b-hal-qaaʔima?
to **itemize** - ṣannaf (i taṣniif) t-. Itemize all your expenses. ṣannif kull maṣaariifak.
itself - 1. nafis-. The child hurt itself. j-jaahil εawwar nafsa. -- The car itself isn't damaged, but the driver was injured. s-sayyaara nafisha ma-tʔaδδat, laakin is-saayiq injiraħ. 2. waħid-. The house itself is worth that. l-beet waħda yiswa hal-gadd.
**That speaks for itself. haay ma-yinraad-ilha ħači.
by itself - min keef-. This door closes by itself. hal-baab yinsadd min keefa.
in itself - b-ħadd δaat-. The plan in itself is good. l-mašruuε ib-ħadd δaata zeen.
ivory - εaaj. The knife handle is ivory. ʔiid is-siččiina min εaaj.

J

to **jab** - naġġ (u naġġ) n-. He jabbed me with the pencil. naġġni bil-qalam.
jack - 1. jagg pl. -aat. I left the jack in the garage. trakt ij-jagg bil-garaaj. 2. walad pl. wulid, bajaġ pl. -aat. I've got three jacks. εindi tlaθ wulid.
**You look as if you had hit the jackpot. ybayyin jaaya d-dinya wiyyaak.
to jack up - 1. šaal (i šeel) b-jagg. You'll have to jack up the car. laazim itšiil is-sayyaara b-jagg. 2. rifaε (a rafuε) n-, zayyad (i tazyiid) t-. They've jacked up the price again. rifεaw is-siεir marra θaanya.
jackal - waawi pl. -iyya.
jackass - zmaaḷ pl. zmaayiḷ, ħmaar pl. ħamiir.
jacket - 1. sitra pl. sitar, čaakeet pl. -aat. You can wear that jacket with flannel slacks. tigdar tilbas has-sitra εala panṭaroon faaneela. 2. gišir pl. gšuur. I boiled the potatoes in their jackets. slagt il-puteeta b-igšuurha. 3. ġlaaf pl. -aat. The jacket of the book is all torn. l-iġlaaf maal l-iktaab kulla mšaggag.
jackknife - čaaquuča pl. -aat, siččiina pl. sčaačiin.
jail - sijin pl. sujuun, ħabis. He was sentenced to six months in jail. nħikam sitt išhur bis-sijin.
to jail - ħibas (i ħabis) n-, sijan (i sijin) n-. He was jailed for theft. nħibas li-ʔan baag.
jalopy - sayyaara (pl. -aat) paḷašqa. He bought an old jalopy. štira-la jadd sayyaara paḷašqa.
jam - 1. mrabba pl. -yaat. I prefer homemade jam. ʔafaḍḍil imrabba maal beet. 2. ḍiiq. I'm in an awful jam. ʔaani b-ḍiiq šadiid.
traffic jam - muškilat izdiħaam. The police untangled the traffic jam. šurṭa l-muruur ħallaw muškilat l-izdiħaam.
to jam - 1. šawwaš (i tašwiiš) εala. Somebody is jamming our broadcast. waaħid da-yšawwiš εala ʔiδaaεatna. 2. ħiṣar (i ħaṣir) n-. He jammed his finger in the door. ħiṣar ʔiṣibεa bil-baab. 3. εiṣa (i). The drawer jammed when I tried to open it. l-imjarr εiṣa lamma ridit ʔafitħa. 4. jayyam (i tajyiim) t-, šakkal (i taškiil) t-. The gears are jammed. l-geer imjayyim. 5. zdiħam (i zdiħaam) n-. The elevator was jammed with people. l-maṣεad čaan muzdaħim bin-naas.
janitor - farraaš pl. -iin, fraariiš; bawwaab pl. -iin.

The janitor cleaned the windows last night. *l-farraaš naḍḍaf l-išbaabiik il-ḅaarʒa ḅil-beel.*
January - *kaanuun iθ-θaani.*
Japan - *yaabaan.*
Japanese - **1.** *yaabaani* pl. *-iyyiin.* He's a Japanese. *huwwa yaabaani.* **2.** *yaabaani**. I bought a beautiful Japanese radio. *stireet raadyo yaabaani ʒilu.*
jar - *šiiša* pl. *šiyaaš, šiyaš.* I want a jar of jam. *ʔariid šiišat imraḅḅa.*
to jar - *hazz (i hazz) n-, xaḍḍ (u xaḍḍ) n-.* Don't jar the table when you sit down. *la-thizz il-meez tigƐud.*
jasmine - *yaasmiin.* The jasmine is a common flower in Iraq. *l-yaasmiin warid šaayiƐ ḅil-Ɛiraaq.*
jaundice - *marḍ iṣ-ṣufaar, ʔabu ṣ-ṣufra, ṣ-ṣafar.*
jaw - *fačč* pl. *fčuuč.* He broke his jaw. *kisar fačča.*
jawbone - *Ɛaḍum (pl. Ɛḍaam) fačč.* Samson killed a whole lot of guys with an ass's jawbone. *šamšuun qital naas ihwaaya b-Ɛaḍum fačč maal iʒmaar.*
jealous - *ġayyaar.* She's jealous because you have a new coat. *hiyya ġayyaara li-ʔan Ɛindič qappuuṭ jidiid.*
to be jealous - *ġaar (a).* He became jealous of me because I've got a car. *ġaar minni li-ʔan Ɛindi sayyaara.*
jealousy - *ġiira.* I'm dying of jealousy since he got the new position. *l-ġiira gaaƐid itmawwitni, min ʔaxaḍ waḍiifta j-jidiida.*
jeep - *sayyaara* (pl. *-aat*) *jiiḅ.*
to **jeer** - *sixar (a suxriyya).* The audience jeered at the singer. *l-mutafarrijiin sixraw imnil-muġanni.*
jelly - *mraḅḅa.* I want rolls and jelly. *ʔariid sammuun w-mraḅḅa.*
to **jeopardize** - *Ɛarraḍ (i taƐriiḍ) t- lil-xaṭar.* The incident jeopardized his future. *l-ʒaadiθ Ɛarraḍ mustaqbala lil-xaṭar.*
jeopardy - *xaṭar.* He put his own life in jeopardy. *Ɛarraḍ ʒayaata lil-xaṭar.*

jerboa - *jarbuuƐ* pl. *jaraabiiƐ.*
Jericho - *ʔariiʒa.*
jerk - *rajja* pl. *-aat.* The train stopped with a jerk. *l-qiṭaar wugaf iḅ-rajja.*
to jerk - *Ɛatt (i Ɛatt) n-, nitaš (i natiš) n-.* She jerked the book out of his hand. *Ɛattat l-iktaab min ʔiida.*
jerry-built - *binaaʔ šallaali.* Those houses are jerry-built. *haay l-ibyuut binaaʔha šallaali.*
Jerusalem - *l-qudus.*
Jesus - *Ɛiisa.*
jet - *naffaaθa.* We took a jet plane from Paris to Beirut. *ʔaxaḍna ṭiyyaara naffaaθa min ḅaariis ʔila beeruut.*
jet-black - *(ʔaswad) miθl il-faʒam, ʔaswad ṭoox.* Her hair is jet-black. *šaƐarha miθl il-faʒam.*
Jew - *yahuudi* pl. *-iyyiin.* She is a Jew. *hiyya yahuudiyya.*
jewel - **1.** *jawhara* pl. *-aat, jawaahir* coll. *jawhar.* The dancer had a jewel in her navel. *r-raaqiṣa ʒaaṭṭa jawhara b-ṣurratha.* **2.** *ʒajra* pl. *-aat, ʔaʒjaar* coll. *ʒajar.* My watch has seventeen jewels. *saaƐati biiha ṣḅaaṭaƐaš ʒajar.*
jewels - *jawaahir, mujawharaat.* She pawned her jewels. *rihnat jawaahirha.*
jeweler - *ṣaayiġ* pl. *ṣiyyaaġ, jawharči* pl. *-iyya.* I'm looking for a jeweler to fix my ring. *da-adawwur-li fadd ṣaayiġ yṣalliʒ il-miʒbas maali.*
jewelry - *mujawharaat.* Did you see her jewelry? *šifit mujawharaatha?*
Jewish - *yhuudi**.
to **jibe** - *nṭubaq (u nṭibaaq).* This doesn't jibe with what I saw. *haay ma-tinṭubuq Ɛala lli šifta ʔaani.*
Jidda - *jidda.*
jiffy - *laʒḍa* pl. *-aat.* It'll only take a jiffy. *ma-taaxuḍ ġeer fadd laʒḍa.*
to **jiggle** - *xaḍḍ (u xaḍḍ) n-, ʒazz (i ʒazz) n-.* Stop jiggling the table. *ḅass Ɛaad itxuḍḍ il-meez.*
to **jilt** - *xidaƐ (a xadiƐ) n-.* His fiancee jilted him. *xaṭiibta xidƐata.*
jitters - *hawas, hwaas.* He's got the jitters. *Ɛinda hawas.*
job - *šaġla* pl. *-aat* coll. *šuġuḷ; Ɛamal.* I'm looking for a job. *da-adawwur Ɛala šuġuḷ.* -- It wasn't an easy job to persuade her. *ʔiqnaaƐha ma-čaan fadd Ɛamal sahil.* -- I've got several jobs to do today. *Ɛindi Ɛiddat šaġlaat asawwiiha l-yoom.* -- It isn't my job to tell him that. *ʔaani muu šuġḷi ʔagul-la haay.*
jockey - *jaaki* pl. *-iyya.*

to **join** - **1.** *nḍamm (a nḍimaam) l-, ntima (i ntimaaʔ) l-, štirak (i štiraak) b-.* When did he join the party? *šwakit inḍamm lil-ʒizib?* **2.** *nḍamm (i), ntima (i), ltiʒaq (i ltiʒaaq).* I'm joining the Army. *raʒ-anḍamm lij-jeeš.* **3.** *šakkal (i taškiil) t-.* Would you like to join us? *triid itšakkil wiyyaana?* **4.** *rakkab (u tarkiib) t-, šakkal (i).* How do you join these two parts? *šloon itrakkub haaḍool il-qismeen?* **5.** *ttiṣal (u ttiṣaal) b-.* Where does this road join the main road? *ween haaḍa ṭ-ṭariiq yittiṣil biṭ-ṭariiq ir-raʔiisi?* **6.** *šaarak (i mušaaraka), štirak (i štiraak).* Everybody joined in the singing. *l-kull šaarkaw bil-ġina.* **7.** *waʒʒad (i tawʒiid) t-.* Let's join forces. *xalli nwaʒʒid juhuudna.*
joint - **1.** *mafṣal* pl. *mafaaṣil.* All my joints ache. *kull mafaaṣli toojaƐni.* **2.** *muštarak.* The land is their joint property. *l-ʔaraaḍi muštaraka beenaathum.*
out of joint - *mafṣuux, maxluuƐ.* My knee's out of joint. *rukubti mafṣuuxa.*
to throw out of joint - *xilaƐ (a xaliƐ) n-, fiṣax (i faṣix).* I threw my shoulder out of joint. *xilaƐit čitfi.*
joke - **1.** *nukta* pl. *nukaat.* I've heard that joke before. *ʔaani smaƐit han-nukta gabuḷ.* -- I played a joke on him. *sawweet bii nukta.* or ***qašmarit Ɛalee.* -- He tried to make a joke of the whole thing. *ʒaawal yiġlub il-mawḍuuƐ ʔila nukta.* **2.** *šaqa.* That's carrying the joke too far. *ṭawwaxitha biš-šaqa.* or *riʒit biš-šaqa zaayid.* -- He can't take a joke. *ma-yitʒammal šaqa.*
to joke - *tšaaqa (a šaqa).* This time I'm not joking. *hal-marra ma-da-atšaaqa.* -- All joking aside, are you really going? *ʔitruk iš-šaqa hassa, ṣudug ʔinta raayiʒ?*

to tell jokes - *nakkat (i tankiit).* He's always telling jokes. *huwwa ynakkit Ɛala ṭuul.*
jolly - *mariʒ* pl. *-iin, bašuuš* pl. *-iin.* He's always jolly. *huwwa daaʔiman mariʒ.*
jolt - *rajja* pl. *-aat.* The car stopped with a sudden jolt. *s-sayyaara wugfat iḅ-rajja mufaajʔa.*
to jolt - **1.** *rajj (i rajj) n-.* The explosion jolted the whole house. *l-infijaar rajj il-ḅeet kulla.* **2.** *hazz (i hazz) n-.* The news jolted us. *l-axbaar hazzatna.*
Jordan - *l-ʔardun, l-ʔurdun.* I'm going to Jordan tomorrow. *ʔaani raayiʒ lil-ʔardun baačir.*
Jordanian - **1.** *ʔarduni* pl. *-iyyiin.* Many Jordanians live in Kuwait. *hwaaya ʔarduniyyiin yƐiišuun bil-kuweet.* **2.** *ʔarduni**. The Jordanian embassy was bombed last night. *s-sifaara l-ʔarduniyya nnisfat il-baarʒa bil-leel.*
to **jostle** - *difaƐ (a dafiƐ) n-.* He jostled me as he went by. *huwwa difaƐni min marr min yammi.*
to **jot down** - *qayyad (i taqyiid) t-.* I jotted her telephone number down. *qayyadit raqam it-talafoon maalha.*
journalist - *ṣuʒufi* pl. *-iyyiin.*
journey - *riʒla* pl. *-aat, safra* pl. *-aat.*
jovial - *mariʒ, bašuuš.* There is a jovial fellow! *huwwa kulliš mariʒ!*
joy - *faraʒ* pl. *ʔafraaʒ.* Her eyes were beaming with joy. *Ɛyuunha čaanat tilmaƐ imnil-faraʒ.*
joyful - *saarr, mufriʒ.* It was a joyful occasion. *čaanat munaasaba saarra.*
Judaism - *d-diyaana l-yahuudiyya.*
judge - **1.** *ʒaakim* pl. *ʒukkaam, qaaḍi* pl. *quḍaat.* When is the judge going to pass sentence? *šwakit il-ʒaakim raʒ-yinṭuq bil-ʒukum.* -- The judge ruled that the divorce was valid. *l-qaaḍi Ɛtubar iṭ-ṭalaaq ṣaʒiiʒ.* **2.** *ʒakam* pl. *-iyya, ʒaakim* pl. *ʒukkaam.* The judges awarded his picture the first prize. *l-ʒakamiyya inṭoo j-jaaʔiʒa l-ʔuula Ɛala ṣuurta.* -- The judge said the ball fell outside. *l-ʒakam gaal iṭ-ṭooba ṭilƐat xaarij.*
**You be the judge of that! *ʔinta qarrir!*
**He's as sober as a judge. *huwwa kulliš ṣaaʒi.*
**She's not a good judge of human nature. *ma-tigdar tuʒkum Ɛala ṭabiiƐat in-naas.*
to judge - **1.** *ʒikam (u ʒukum) n- Ɛala.* Don't judge him too harshly. *la-tuʒkum Ɛalee bil-muuzeen.* **2.** *qaas (i qiyaas), ʒikam (u ʒakim) n- Ɛala.* Never judge others by yourself. *la-tqiis in-naas Ɛala nafsak.* or *la-tuʒkum Ɛan-naas ʒasab iƐtiqaadak bass.*
**To judge by his face he isn't very enthusiastic. *min wujja mbayyin ma-mitʒammis.*
judgment - **1.** *taqdiir.* You can rely on his judgment.

tigdar tiƐtimid Ɛala taqdiira. **2.** *ʐukma* pl. *ˀaʐkaam, qaraar* pl. *-aat.* The president of the court will hand down his judgment today. *raˀiis il-maʐkama raʐ-yiṣdur ʐukma l-yoom.* -- Don't make snap judgments. *la-tuṣdir ˀaʐkaam sariiƐa.* — He showed good judgment. *kaan qaraara ʐakiim.* **3.** *raˀi* pl. *ˀaaraaˀ.* In my judgment you're doing the wrong thing. *b-raˀyi ˀinta gaaƐid itsawwi ġalaṭ.*
judicial - *qaanuuni*.* Judicial procedures are very involved. *l-ˀijraaˀaat il-qaanuuniyya kulliš muƐaqqada.*
judicious - *muwaffaq.* He made a judicious selection. *čaan ixtiyaara muwaffaq.*
jug - *jarra* pl. *-aat.* The women carried water jugs on their heads. *n-niswaan šaalaw jarraat il-mayy Ɛala ruushum.*
juice - *Ɛaṣiir.* I'd like a glass of orange juice, please. *ˀariid iglaaṣ Ɛaṣiir purtaqaal, min faḍlak.*
juicy - *rayyaan, malyaan mayy.* These oranges are very juicy. *hal-purtuqaalaat kulliš rayyaana.*
July - *tammuuz.*
jump - **1.** *qafza* pl. *-aat, ṭafra* pl. *-aat.* His jump broke the national record. *qafizta kisrat ir-raqam il-waṭani.* **2.** *gamza* pl. *-aat.* With one jump he was over the wall. *b-gamza wiʐda Ɛubar il-ʐaayiṭ.*
**You don't want him to get the jump on you, do you? *ma-triida ysibqak, tamaam?*
to jump - **1.** *ṭufar (u ṭafur), gumaz (u gamuz).* How high can you jump? *šgadd Ɛilu tigdar tuṭfur?* -- He jumped off the bus before it stopped. *gumaz imnil-paaṣ gabuḷ-ma yoogaf.* **2.** *giḷab (u gaḷub), Ɛibar (u Ɛabur).* We jumped pages seven to twelve. *gḷabna min ṣafʐa sabƐa ˀila θnaƐaš.* **3.** *fazz (i tafziiz).* He jumped when he heard the noise. *fazz min simaƐ iṣ-ṣooṭ.*
**He jumped at the offer. *qibal il-Ɛariḍ raˀsan.* or *qibal il-Ɛariḍ ib-lahfa.*
**Don't jump to conclusions about things. *la-tuʐkum ib-surƐa Ɛal-ˀašyaaˀ.*
**The train jumped the track. *l-qiṭaar ṭilaƐ imnil-xaṭṭ.*
**He can go jump in the lake! *xalli yḍibb nafsa biš-šaṭṭ!*
to jump around - *gammaz (u tgummuz, tagmiiz).* Stop jumping around. *yikfi Ɛaad itgammuz.*
junction - *taqaaṭuƐ il-xuṭuuṭ.*
June - *ʐuzeeraan.*
jungle - *ġaaba* pl. *-aat.* He was lost in the African jungle. *ḍaaƐ ib-ġaabaat ˀafriiqiya.*
junior: **She's a junior in college. *hiyya ṭaaliba b-ṣaff θaaliθ bil-kulliyya.*
junk - **1.** *qalaaqiil.* We'll have to clean the junk out of the storeroom. *laazim innaḍḍuf il-qalaaqiil imnil-maxzan.* **2.** *ġaraaḍ.* Where did you get that junk? *mneen jibit haay il-ġaraaḍ?*
to junk - *wadda (i twiddi) lis-sikraab.* I'm afraid I'll just have to junk that car. *ˀaani xaayif aḍṭarr awaddi s-sayyaara lis-sikraab.*
jurisdiction - *xtiṣaaṣ.* The matter's outside my jurisdiction. *l-qaḍiyya xaarij ixtiṣaaṣi.*
jurist - *faqiih* pl. *fuqahaaˀ.*
jury - *muʐallifiin.*
just - **1.** *Ɛaadil.* That's a just punishment. *haaḍi Ɛuquuba Ɛaadila.* **2.** *mustaqiim, Ɛaadil.* He is a just man. *huwwa rajul mustaqiim.* **3.** *hassa, hastaww-.* I just arrived. *hassa wuṣalit.* or *hastawwni wuṣalit.* **4.** *biḍ-ḍabuṭ, tamaaman.* That's just the word I meant. *haay hiyya l-kalima illi ˀariidha biḍ-ḍabuṭ.* -- That's just what I wanted. *haaḍa tamaaman miθil-ma ridit.* or ***haaḍa lli ridta!* -- He's just like his father. *huwwa biḍ-ḍabuṭ miθil ˀabuu.* -- He is just as lazy as his brother. *huwwa kaslaan miθl axuu biḍ-ḍabuṭ.* -- It was just the other way around. *hiyya čaanat tamaaman bil-Ɛakis.* -- That takes just as long. *haay taaxuḍ nafs il-wakit biḍ-ḍabuṭ.* -- Just what do you mean? *š-tiƐni biḍ-ḍabuṭ?* **5.** *tamaaman.* The table was just covered with dust. *l-meez čaan imġaṭṭa bit-tiraab tamaaman.* **6.** *mujarrad, bass.* He's just a little boy. *huwwa mujarrad ṭifil.* -- I just said one word, and he got mad. *gilit čilma wiʐda bass w-ziƐal.* -- I just want one glass of water. *ˀariid igḷaas waaʐid mayy bass.* **7.** *duub.* You just made it to class on time. *duub wuṣalit liṣ-ṣaff Ɛal-wakit.* **8.** *Ɛal-ʐaaffa, duub.* You just passed the exam. *ˀinta nijaʐit bil-imtiʐaan Ɛal-ʐaaffa.*
**That's just the way it is! *l-ˀumuur hiiči maašya!*
**There's just nothing you can do about it. *kullši ma-tigdar itsawwi.*
**Just a minute! *fadd daqiiqa!*
**Just what did you mean by that crack? *š-tuqṣud ib-haay il-mulaaʐaḍa?*
**Just for that I won't do it. *l-has-sabab ˀaani ma-asawwiiha.*
just right - *Ɛal-maraam.* The water is just right. *l-maay Ɛal-maraam.* -- My coffee's just right. *gahuuti Ɛal-maraam.*
justice - *nṣaaf, Ɛadaala.* Don't expect justice from him. *la-titwaqqaƐ ˀay inṣaaf minna.*
to do justice - *niṣaf (i naṣif) n-, Ɛidal (i Ɛadil) n-.* You're not doing him justice. *ˀinta ma-da-tinṣif wiyyaa.*
**The picture doesn't do you justice. *ṣ-ṣuura ma-tišbahak tamaaman.* or *ṣ-ṣuura muu ʐilwa miθlak.*
justifiable - *ˀila mubarrir.* I think this expenditure is justifiable. *ˀaƐtiqid hal-maṣruuf ˀila mubarrir.*
justified - *muʐiqq.* I think you were perfectly justified in doing that. *ˀaḍunn innak činit kulliš muʐiqq ib-Ɛamalak.* — You were perfectly justified in asking for more pay. *činit tamaaman muʐiqq ib-ṭalabak ib-ziyaadat raatbak.*
to **justify** - *barrar (i tabriir) t-.* She tried to justify her actions. *ʐaawalat itbarrir ˀaƐmaalha.*

K

Kaaba - *l-kaƐba.*
kangaroo - *kanġar* pl. *kanaaġir.*
keen - **1.** *ʐaadd.* He has a keen mind. *huwwa ʐaadd iḍ-ḍakaaˀ.* -- His sense of smell is keen. *ʐaassat iš-šamm maalta ʐaadda.* -- This knife has a keen edge. *ʐaašyat has-siččiina ʐaadda.* **2.** *mitʐammis* pl. *-iin.* I'm not so keen on that. *ˀaani muu kulliš mitʐammis ilha.* or ***ma-Ɛindi walaƐ bii.*
to **keep** - **1.** *ʐtifaḍ (u ʐtifaaḍ) b-.* May I keep this picture? *ˀagdar aʐtufuḍ ib-haay iṣ-ṣuura?* -- If the team wins three times in a row, they get to keep the cup. *l-firqa ˀiḍa tuġlub itlaθ marraat mitataalya tigdar tiʐtufuḍ bil-kaˀis.* -- He keeps the company's books. *huwwa yiʐtifiḍ ib-sijilaat iš-šarika.* **2.** *biqa (a baqi), ḍall (i ḍall).* The policeman asked us to keep moving. *š-šurṭi ṭilab min Ɛidna ˀan nibqa maašiin.* -- He kept talking all the time. *ḍall yiʐči l-wakit kulla.* -- Keep calm! *ˀibqu haadˀiin.* or *ˀihdaˀu.* -- Can't you keep quiet? *ma-tigdar itḍill saakit?* or *ma-tigdar tiskut?* -- He's keeping me company. *huwwa yibqa wiyyaaya.* — This milk won't keep till tomorrow. *hal-ʐaliib ma-yitʐammal yibqa l-baačir.* **3.** *xalla (i taxliya, txilli).* Sorry to have kept you waiting. *mitˀassif li-ˀan xalleetak tintiḍir.* -- Keep to the right. *xalliik Ɛal-yimna.* or *ˀibqa Ɛal-yimna.* -- Keep me posted. *xalliini Ɛala Ɛilim Ɛala ṭuul.* -- Keep that in mind! *xalliiha b-fikrak!* **4.** *ḍamm (u ḍamm) n-, ʐtifaḍ (i ʐtifaaḍ) b-, ʐufaḍ (u ʐafuḍ).* Please keep this for me. *min faḍlak ḍumm-li-yyaaha.* or *rajaaˀan iʐtifiḍ-li biiha.* **5.** *Ɛaṭṭal (i taƐṭiil) t-.* I won't keep you very long. *ma-raʐ-aƐaṭṭlak ihwaaya.* **6.** *ḍamm(u), kitam (i katim), xabba (i taxbiya, txibbi).* Can you keep a secret? *tigdar iṭḍumm sirr?* -- He kept his real intentions from me for quite a while. *xabba qaṣda l-ʐaqiiqi mudda ṭuwiila Ɛanni.* **7.** *baqqa (i tabqiya) t-, ʐtifaḍ (i ʐtifaaḍ), xalla (i txilli).* Shall I keep your dinner warm? *triidni abaqqi b-ˀaklak ʐaarr?* **8.** *ḍibaṭ (u ḍabuṭ).* Does your watch keep good time? *saaƐtak tiḍbuṭ il-wakit zeen?* -- Keep your temper! *ˀuḍbuṭ aƐṣaabak.* or ***haddi nafsak.* **9.** *wufa (i wafaaˀ, wufa).* I rely on you to keep your word. *ˀaani ˀaƐtimid Ɛaleek ˀan toofi b-waƐdak.* **10.** *rabba (i tarbiya).* We've been keeping chickens for the last three years. *ṣaar-inna nrabbi dijaaj il-muddat itlaθ isniin.* **11.** *daar (i ˀidaara) ˀumuur.* She keeps house for her uncle. *hiyya tdiir ˀumuur beet Ɛammha.*
**Everytime we kick him out, he keeps coming back.

kull-ma nṭurda yirjaɛ.
**His wife just found out he's been keeping a mistress. *marta hassa ɛurfat ɛinda ɛašiiqa.*
to keep away - 1. *btiɛad (i btiɛaad).* Keep away from that radio! *btiɛid ɛan haaδa r-raadyo!* 2. *biɛad (i ʔibɛaad).* Keep the children away from the fire. *ʔibɛid ij-jihhaal ɛan in-naar.*
to keep from - 1. *minaɛ (a maniɛ) n- min.* Nobody can keep you from going there. *mazzad yigdar yimnaɛak min ʔan itruuz ihnaak.* 2. *baṭṭal (i tabṭiil) min, btiɛad (i btiɛaad) ɛan.* He can't keep from drinking. *ma-yigdar ybaṭṭil imniš šurub.*
to keep off - *btiɛad (i btiɛaad) ɛan, waxxar (i tawxiir) min.* Keep off the grass! *btiɛid ɛan il-θayyal!* -- Keep your hands off that car! *waxxir ʔiidak min has-sayyaara!* or *la-txalli ʔiidak ɛala has-sayyaara!*
to keep on - *ḍall (i ḍall), buqa (a baqaaʔ), stamarr (i stimraar) b-.* We kept on walking. *ḍalleena nimši.* -- Keep on trying. *stamirr bil-muzaawala.* -- Keep right on talking. *stamirr bil-kalaam.*
to keep out - 1. *minaɛ (a maniɛ).* Ordinary glass keeps out utraviolet rays. *z-zujaaj il-ɛaadi yimnaɛ il-ʔašiɛɛa maa wara l-banafsajiyya.* -- This isn't a beautiful raincoat, but in any event, it keeps out the rain. *haaδa muu qappuuṭ muṭar laṭiif, laakin ɛala kull zaal, yimnaɛ il-muṭar.* 2. *btiɛad (i btiɛaad) ɛan.* Keep out of my garden! *btiɛid ɛan zadiiqti!* -- It's his affair. You'd better keep out of it! *haaδa šuġla. ʔazsan-lak ibtiɛid ɛanna!* 3. *biɛad (i ʔibɛaad).* I'll try to keep him out of trouble. *raz-azaawil abiɛda ɛan il-mašaakil.* -- Keep him out of my way! *ʔibiɛda ɛan ṭariiqi.*
to keep up - 1. *stimarr (i stimraar) ɛala.* Keep it up and see where it gets you! *stamirr ɛaleeha w-šuuf išloon raz-titʔaδδa!* 2. *zaafaḍ (u muzaafuḍa) ɛala.* How much does it cost you per month to keep up your car? *šgadd ykallifak biš-šahar zatta tzaafuḍ ɛala sayyaartak?* 3. *biqa (a baqaaʔ) ɛala.* Keep up the good work. *ʔibqa ɛala šuġlak iz-zeen.* 4. *lazzag (i talziig) t- b-.* I can't keep up with you when you dictate so fast. *ma-agdar ʔalazzig biik min timli ɛalayya b-surɛa.* -- It's hard for me to keep up with the others in the class. *yiṣɛab ɛalayya alazzig bil-ʔaaxariin biṣ-ṣaff.* -- I can't keep up with my work. *ma-da-agdar alazzig axalliṣ šuġli.*
keepsake - *tiδkaar* pl. *-aat.* She gave him her ring as a keepsake. *nṭata mizbasha ka-tiδkaar.*
kernel - *zabbaaya* pl. *-aat* coll. *zabb; zabba* pl. *-aat* coll. *zabb.*
kerosene - *nafuṭ ʔabyaḍ.*
kettle - *quuri* pl. *quwaari, kitli* pl. *-iyyaat.* The water in the kettle is boiling. *l-maay da-yiġli bil-quuri.*
**That's a pretty kettle of fish! *haaδa mawqif muzɛij!* or *hiyya leeṣa!* or *ṣaayra xabiiṣa!*
key - 1. *miftaaz* pl. *mafaatiiz.* I've lost the key to my room. *ḍayyaɛit miftaaz ġurufti.* -- That was the key to the mystery. *haaδa čaan miftaaz il-laġiz.* 2. *zaruf* pl. *zuruuf.* One of the keys on my typewriter gets stuck. *waazid min zuruuf iṭ-ṭaabiɛa maalti yšakkil.* 3. *muhimm.* He holds a key position in the government. *huwwa ɛinda markaz muhimm bil-zukuuma.* 4. *daliil, ʔiiḍaaz.* The key to the map is in the right-hand corner. *daliil il-xariiṭa biz-zuwiyya l-yimna.*
off key - *našaaz.* Who's singing off key? *minu da-yġanni našaaz?*
keyhole - *beet* (pl. *byuut*) *miftaaz.*
khaki - *xaaki.* This merchant doesn't sell anything but khaki. *hat-taajir ma-ybiiɛ ġeer xaaki.*
Khartoum - *xarṭuum.*
kick - 1. *čillaaq* pl. *člaaliiq, dafra* pl. *-aat.* I felt like giving him a good hard kick. *ɛijabni aḍurḅa čillaaq qawi.* 2. *rafsa* pl. *-aat, zagṭa* pl. *-aat, dafra* pl. *-aat.* The horse's kick broke his leg. *rafsat l-izṣaan kisrat rijla.* 3. *radda* pl. *-aat.* The kick of a rifle can break your collar bone. *raddat il-bunduqiyya yimkin tiksir ɛaḍm it-turquwa maalak.* 4. *walaɛ, waahis.* He gets a big kick out of sports. *ɛinda walaɛ bir-riyaaḍa.*
to kick - 1. *ḍirab (u ḍarib) n-.* Kick the ball! *ʔiḍrub iṭ-ṭooba!* 2. *rifas (u rafus) n-.* I hope this horse doesn't kick. *ʔinšaaḷḷa haaδa l-izṣaan ma-yirfus.* 3. *tšakka (a tašakki).* He kicks about everything. *yitšakka min kullši.*
**I can't kick. *ɛal-aḷḷah!*
to kick out - *ṭirad (u ṭarid) n-.* I nearly kicked him out of the house. *taqriiban ṭiradta mnil-beet.*
kicks - *wansa.* What do you do for kicks around here? *š-itsawwi lil-wansa b-hal-manṭiqa?*
kid - 1. *jadi* pl. *jidyaan.* The goat had two kids. *l-maɛza ɛidha jadyeen.* 2. *walad* pl. *ʔawlaad, wilid; ṭifil* pl. *ʔaṭfaal, jaahil* pl. *jihhaal.* We'll feed the kids first. *nṭaɛɛum il-wilid gabuḷ.* -- Don't act like a kid! *la-titṣarraf miθl il-ʔaṭfaal.* 3. *jilid maɛaz.* I bought some kid gloves. *štireet ičfuuf jilid maɛaz.*
**You have to handle her with kid gloves. *laazim itɛaamilha b-riqqa.*
to kid - *tšaaqa (a tašaaqi), mizaz (a maziz), tmaazaz (a maziz).* I'm only kidding. *ʔaani da-atšaaqa.*
to **kidnap** - *xiṭaf (u xaṭuf) n-.* He kidnapped his sweetheart from her family. *xiṭaf zabiibta min ʔahilha.*
kidney - *kilya* pl. *-aat.* He's having trouble with his kidneys. *kilyaata toojɛa.* 2. *čilwa* pl. *čalaawi.* We have kidneys for supper. *ɛidna čalaawi lil-ɛaša l-yoom.*
kill - *qatil, katil.* The wolves closed in on the sheep for the kill. *δ-δiyaab ṭubgaw ɛal-xaruuf il-qatla.* 2. *fariisa* pl. *-aat, faraayis.* The lion returned to its kill the next day. *l-ʔasad rijaɛ il-fariista bil-yoom iθ-θaani.*
to kill - 1. *kital (u katil) n-, qital (u qatil) n-.* Be careful with that car, or you'll kill somebody. *diir baalak min has-sayyaara, la-truuz tuktul ʔazzad.* -- Her son was killed in action. *ʔibinha nqital bil-maɛraka.* 2. *ṭaffa (i taṭfiya).* Be careful, or you'll kill the engine. *diir baalak, la-truuz iṭṭaffi l-makiina.* 3. *qiḍa (i qaḍi) n- ɛala.* I'll give you something to kill the pain. *ʔanṭiik duwa zatta yiqḍi ɛal-ʔalam.* 4. *kital (i katil), ḍayyaɛ (i tḍiyyiɛ).* We played cards to kill time. *lɛabna waraq zatta niktil wakit.*
**I killed two birds with one stone. *ḍrabit ɛaṣfuureen ib-zajar waazid.*
killer - *qaatil* pl. *-iin, qatala.* The killer escaped. *l-qaatil hirab.*
killing - *qatil, katil.* We're trying to stop this useless killing. *nzaawil inwagguf haaδa l-qatil illi ma-bii natiija.*
kilogram - *keelu* pl. *uwaat.* Give me three kilograms of sugar, please. *nṭiini tlaθ keeluwaat šakar, min faḍlak.*
kilometer - *kiilumatir* pl. *-aat.* Our car does more than a hundred kilometers an hour. *sayyaaratna ṭṭalliɛ ʔakθar min miit kiilumatir bis-saaɛa.*
kind - 1. *nooɛ* pl. *ʔanwaaɛ, jins* pl. *ʔajnaas.* This building is the only one of its kind. *haay il-binaaya hiyya l-waziida min nooɛha.* -- We have only two kinds of coffee. *ɛidna nooɛeen bass imnil-gahwa.* -- What kind of car is that? *šinu nooɛ has-sayyaara?* 2. *laṭiif.* She is a very kind person. *hiyya šaxṣiyya laṭiifa.* -- That was a kind thing to do. *haaδa čaan šii laṭiif ʔan itsawwi.*
**Would you be so kind as to mail this letter for me? *ʔiδa tismaz itdizz haaδa l-maktuub bil-bariid.*
kind of - *b-nawɛ min.* I felt kind of sorry for him. *šiɛarit ib-nooɛ imnil-ʔasaf ittijaaha.*
kindergarten - *rawḍat aṭfaal.*
to **kindle** - *šiɛal (i šaɛil) n-.* Were you able to kindle a fire? *gidarit tišɛil in-naar?*
kindling - *ɛuwad.* We could not find kindling to start a fire. *ma-gdarna nilgi ɛuwad nišɛil biiha naar.*
kindly - 1. *šafuuq.* Her grandmother is a kindly old lady. *jiddiyatha mrayya šafuuqa.* 2. *b-luṭuf.* She received us kindly. *staqbilatna b-luṭuf.* 3. *rajaaʔan, min faḍlak.* Kindly stop when your time is up. *rajaaʔan ʔoogaf min yintihi l-wakit.* -- Kindly mind your own business! *min faḍlak, la-titdaxxal.*
kindness - *faḍil* pl. *ʔafḍaal, luṭuf* pl. *ʔalṭaaf.* I appreciate your kindness. *ʔaqaddir faḍlak.*
king - 1. *malik* pl. *muluuk.* Their king died two weeks ago. *malikhum maat min muddat usbuuɛeen.* 2. *šaayib* pl. *šiyyaab, daaġli* pl. *-iyyaat.* I've got three kings. *ɛindi tlaθ šiyyaab.*
kingdom - *mamlaka* pl. *mamaalik.* The Kingdom of Jordan was created after the First World War. *mamlakat il-ʔardun itʔassasat baɛad il-zarb il-ɛaalamiyya l-ʔuula.*
kinship - *qaraaba, garaaba.* Kinship ties are very important among the Arabs. *ṣilat il-qaraaba muhimma jiddan ɛind il-ɛarab.*

Kirkuk - *karkuuk.*
kiss - *boosa* pl. *-aat, qubla* pl. *-aat.* Give me a kiss. *nṭiini boosa!*
to kiss - *baas (u boos) n-.* He kissed him on both checks. *baasa min ixduuda.*
kitchen - *maṭbax* pl. *maṭaabux.* Do you mind if we eat in the kitchen? *εindak maaniε ʔiða naakul bil-maṭbax?*
kitchenware - *ʔadawaat ṭabax.* This store sells kitchenware. *haaða l-maxzan ybiiε ʔadawaat ṭabax.*
kite - *ṭiyyaara* pl. *-aat.* The boys are out flying kites. *l-wilid da-yṭayyiruun ṭiyyaaraat.*
**Aw, go fly a kite! *ruuḥ dawwur-lak šaġḷa!*
kitten - *farix* (pl. *fruux*) *bazzuuna.* Our cat has some little kittens. *bazzuunatna εidha fruux iṣġaar.*
knack - **1.** *mahaara.* He has a knack for photography. *εinda mahaara ʔaxð it-taṣaawiir.* **2.** *sirr.* Now I've got the knack of it. *hassa εraft is-sirr.*
knapsack - *ḥaqiiba* pl. *ḥaqaaʔib.* The boy scouts carried their food in knapsacks. *l-kaššaafa ḥimlaw ʔakilhum ib-ḥaqaaʔib εala ð̣aharhum.*
to **knead** - *εijan (i εajin) n-.* You have to knead the dough thoroughly. *laazim tiεjin il-εajiin zeen.*
knee - *rukba* pl. *-aat, rikab.* My knee hurts. *rukubti toojaεni.*
kneecap - *ṣaabuunat* (pl. *-aat*) *rijil.*
kneel - **1.** *burak (u baruk).* The camel knelt while they tied the load on. *j-jimal burak lamma kaanaw yšidduun il-ḥimil εalee.* **2.** *θina (i θani) rukbat~.* The soldiers knelt and fired. *j-jinuud θinaw rukbaathum w-ʔaṭḷaqaw in-naar.*
knife - *siččiin* pl. *sačaačiin.* He cut himself with a knife. *jiraḥ nafsa bis-siččiin.*
knight - *faras* pl. *-aat.* I'll take the pawn with the knight. *raḥ-aaxuð ij-jundi bil-faras.*
to **knit** - **1.** *ḥaak (u ḥook, ḥiyaaka) n-.* Did you knit these gloves, Mary? *ḥikti č-čufuuf, maryam?* **2.** *liḥam (a ltiḥaam), ltiḥam (i ltiḥaam).* It took a long time for the bone to knit. *l-εað̣am ʔaxað wakit hwaaya ḥatta liḥam.*
knitting - *ḥyaaka.* Did you notice where she left her knitting? *šifit ween xallat iḥyaakatha?*
knob - **1.** *zirr* pl. *zraar, dugma* pl. *dugam.* The maid broke one of the knobs off the radio. *l-xaadma kisrat waaḥid min izraar ir-raadyo.* **2.** *yadda* pl. *-aat.* The door knob still has to be polished. *yaddat il-baab yinraad-ilha talmiiε.*
knock - *dagg.* Did you hear the knock at the door? *simaεit id-dagg εal-baab?*
**Can you find the knock in the engine? *tigdar itšuuf leeš il-makiina tdugg?*
to knock - **1.** *dagg (u dagg).* Someone's knocking at the door. *waaḥid da-ydugg εal-baab.* -- Please knock before you come in. *min fað̣lak, dugg il-baab gabuḷ-ma tidxul.* -- When I drive uphill the engine knocks. *min aṣεad εat-tall, il-makiina tdugg.* **2.** *ntiqad (i ntiqaad), ḥiča (i ḥači) εala.* He's always knocking American capitalism. *haaða daaʔiman yintiqid ir-raasmaaliyya l-ʔameerkiyya.* **3.** *waggaε (i tawgiiε) t-.* I knocked the knife out of his hand. *waggaεit is-saččiina min ʔiida.*
to knock around - *daar (u dawaraan).* He's knocked around all over the world. *huwwa daayir id-dinya kullha.*
**She's been knocked around a lot. *šaafat ṣuεuubaat ihwaaya b-ḥayaatha.*
to knock down - *waggaε (i tawgiiε) t-.* He knocked him down with his fist. *waggaεa b-ð̣arbat jimεa.* -- Be careful not to knock anything down. *diir baalak la-twaggiε šii.*
to knock off - **1.** *waggaε (i tawgiiε) t-, ṭayyar (i taṭyiir) t-.* He nearly knocked my hat off of my head. *taqriiban waggaε iš-šafqa min raasi.* **2.** *xiṣam (i xaṣum), nazzal (i tanziil).* He knocked off ten dinars from the bill. *xiṣam εašr idnaaniir imnil-qaaʔima.* **3.** *xaḷḷaṣ (i taxliiṣ) t-.* We knocked off work at 6 o'clock. *xaḷḷaṣna š-šuġuḷ saaεa sitta.*
**I'll knock your block off! *ʔað̣urbak ð̣arba tiksir raasak!*
**All right, knock it off! *zeen hassa, baṭṭlu!* or *zeen hassa, bass εaad!*
to knock out - **1.** *daṃṃar (u tadṃiir) t-.* The bomb knocked out the radio station. *l-qumbula daṃṃirat maḥaṭṭat l-ʔiðaaεa.* **2.** *qið̣a (i) εala.* He hit him hard and knocked him out. *ð̣uraba ð̣arba qawiyya w-qið̣a εalee.*
to knock over - **1.** *giḷab (u gaḷub) n-.* Who knocked the pail over? *minu giḷab iṣ-ṣaṭil?* **2.** *waggaε (i tawgiiε) t-.* You almost knocked me over. *taqriiban waggaεitni.*
knocker - *daggaaga* pl. *-aat.* The knocker on our door needs fixing. *daggaagat baabna yinraad-ilha taṣliiḥ.*
knot - **1.** *εugda* pl. *εugad.* Can you untie this knot? *tigdar itfukk haay il-εugda?* -- The board is full of knots. *l-looḥa malyaana εugad.* **2.** *εuqda* pl. *-aat, booṣa* pl. *-aat.* The ship's speed is fifteen knots. *s-safiina surεatha xumuṣṭaεaš εuqda.*
to knot - **1.** *εigad (u εagid) n-.* Shall I knot the string? *triid aεgud il-xeeṭ?* **2.** *šadd (i šadd) n-, εiqad (i εaqid) n-.* You have to knot the two ends together. *laazim itšidd iṭ-ṭarafeen suwa.*
knotted - **1.** *mεaggad.* The string is all knotted. *l-xeeṭ kulla mεaggad.* or ***l-xeeṭ kulla εugad.* **2.** *mšannaṭ.* The calf muscle in my leg is all knotted up. *paačat rijli mšanniṭa.*
knotty - *ṣaεub, εawiiṣ.* That's a knotty problem. *haaði muškila ṣaεba.*
to **know** - *εiraf (u maεrifa) n-.* Do you know his address? *tuεruf εinwaana?* -- Do you know Arabic? *tuεruf εarabi?* -- I don't know how to drive a car. *ma-ʔaεruf asuuq sayyaara.* -- Do you know anything about farming? *tuεruf šii εan iz-ziraaεa?* **2.** *dira (i dari) n-, εiraf (u εarif) n-.* I know he's ill. *ʔadri huwwa mariið̣.*
to let someone know - *xabbar (u ʔixbaar).* I'll let you know tomorrow. *ʔaxabbrak baačir.*
well-known - *mašhuur, maεruuf.* He's a well-known author. *huwwa muʔallif mašhuur.*
know-how - *maεrifa, xibra.* He hasn't the kind of know-how that would qualify him for this job. *ma-εinda l-maεrifa l-kaafiya ḥatta tʔahhila l-haay iš-šaġḷa.*
knowingly - *εan qaṣid.* He wouldn't knowingly cheat us. *ma-yixdaεna εan qaṣid.*
**She looked at him knowingly. *nið̣rat-la nað̣ra biiha maεna.*
knowledge - *maεrifa, εilim.* His knowledge of Arabic is poor. *maεrifta bil-εarabi qaliila.* -- To my knowledge he's not there. *ḥasab εilmi huwwa muu hnaak.*
**He likes to display his knowledge. *yḥibb yraawi nafsa faahim.*
**Answer to the best of your knowledge. *jaawub šgadd-ma tuεruf.*
knowledgeable: **He's quite knowledgeable on Iraqi history. *maεrifta waasεa b-taariix il-εiraaq.*
known - *maεruuf.* That's a known fact. *haay ḥaqiiqa maεruufa.*
knuckle - *mafṣal* pl. *mafaaṣil.* I skinned the knuckles of my right hand. *jilaxit mafṣal ʔiidi l-yimna.*
**He sat in the coffee shop cracking his knuckles. *giεad bil-gahwa yṭagtig b-aṣaabεa.*
**You'd better knuckle down and work. *ʔaḥsan-lak loo tibdi tištuġuḷ.*
kohl - *kuḥul.*
Kurd - *kurdi* pl. *ʔakraad.* Most of the Kurds are Muslims. *muεð̣am il-ʔakraad muslimiin.*
Kuwait - *l-kuweet.*

L

label - *εalaama* pl. *-aat, maarka* pl. *-aat, leebil* pl. *-aat.* There's no label on this bottle. *ma-aku εalaama εala hal-butil.*
to label - *εallam (i tεillim).* Please label those jars for me. *min fað̣lak εallim-li haš-šiyaš.*
labor - **1.** *šuġuḷ* pl. *ʔašġaal, εamal* pl. *ʔaεmaal.* Labor alone will cost three hundred dinars. *š-šuġuḷ waḥda ykallif itlaθ miit diinaar.* -- He was sentenced to five years at hard labor. *nḥikam εalee xamis sanawaat bil-ʔašġaal iš-šaaqa.* **2.** *kadd, majhuud.* This task involves a great deal of labor and perseverance. *haš-šaġḷa tiḥtaaj ʔila kadd w-muθaabara.* -- All our labor has been in vain. *kull majhuudna ð̣aaε.* **3.** *l-εummaal.* Labor will

never agree to that proposal. *l-ɛummaal ʔabadan ma-ywaafquun ɛala hal-iqtiraaz.*
to be in labor - *ṭilgat (a ṭalig).* She was in labor nine hours. *ẓallat tiṭlag tisiɛ saaɛaat.*
laboratory - *muxtabar* pl. *-aat.*
laborer - *ɛaamil* pl. *ɛummaal.*
lace - **1.** *danteel.* I'd like five meters of that lace. *ʔariid xamis amtaar min had-danteel.* **2.** *qiiṭaan* pl. *qyaaṭiin.* I need a pair of shoe laces. *ʔaztaaj zooj qiiṭaan il-qundarti.*
to lace - *rakkab (u) qiyaaṭiin.* Wait till I lace my shoes. *ʔintiẓir ʔila ʔan arakkub il-qiyaaṭiin maal qundarti.*
lack - **1.** *naqiṣ.* There's a lack of experts. *ʔaku naqiṣ bil-xubaraaʔ.* **2.** *ɛadam.* He was acquitted for lack of evidence. *firjaw ɛanna l-ɛadam wujuud ʔadilla.* or *ʔaṭliqaw saraaza l-ɛadam il-ʔadilla.* -- For lack of anything else to do I went to the movies. *rizit lis-siinama l-ɛadam wujuud ʔay šii laax asawwii.*
to lack - *niqaṣ (u niqṣaan), ɛaaz (u ɛooz).* Many conveniences are lacking in this hotel. *hal-findiq tinuqṣa hwaaya wasaaʔil raaza.* -- I didn't lack anything there. *ma-ɛaazni šii hnaak.*
lad - *walad* pl. *wulid, ṣabi* pl. *ṣabyaan.*
ladder - *daraj* pl. *daraaj.*
ladle - *čamča* pl. *-aat.*
lady - **1.** *mrayya* pl. *-aat, mara* pl. *niswaan, zurma* pl. *-aat.* Is that lady his mother? *hal-imrayya ʔumma?* **2.** *sayyida* pl. *-aat.* Ladies and Gentlemen! *sayyidaati w-saadati!* -- Where's the ladies' room? *ween ġurfat is-sayyidaat?*
**We've never had a lady president. *ma-ṣaarat ɛidna raʔiisa ʔabadan.*
to **lag** - *tʔaxxar (a taʔaxxur), txallaf (a taxalluf).* He's always lagging behind the others. *daaʔiman mitʔaxxir ɛan il-baqiyya.*
lake - *buzayra* pl. *-aat.* We went bathing in the lake. *rizna nisbaz bil-buzayra.*
lamb - **1.** *ṭili* pl. *ṭilyaan.* Our ewe gave birth to a lamb yesterday. *naɛjatna jaabat ṭili il-baarza.* **2.** *lazam ġanam.* Beef is cheaper than lamb. *lazm il-hooš ʔarxaṣ min lazm il-ġanam.* **3.** *quuzi.* Bring me a dish of lamb and rice. *jiib-li maaɛuun quuzi ɛala timman.*
lame - **1.** (m.) *ʔaɛraj* pl. *ɛarjiin,* (f.) *ɛarja* pl. *-aat.* He seems to be lame. *ybayyin ʔaɛraj.* -- He has a lame leg. *ɛinda rijil ɛarja.* **2.** *waahi.* That's a lame excuse. *haay zijja waahya.*
lamp - *lampa* pl. *-aat.*
lamp shade - *šamsiyya* pl. *-aat.*
lance - *rumuz* pl. *rmaaz.* His lance broke when he was fighting with it. *nkisar ir-rumuz min čaan yzaarib bii.*
to lance - *fijar (i fajir), ẓurab (u ẓarub) naštar.* The doctor lanced the boil. *ṭ-ṭabiib fijar il-zabbaaya.*
land - **1.** *ʔarẓ, gaaɛ, barr.* We were glad to see land again. *firazna b-šooft il-ʔarẓ marra lux.* **2.** *ʔarẓ, gaaɛ.* The land here is very fertile. *l-ʔarẓ ihnaa kulliš xaṣba.* **3.** *ʔarẓ* pl. *ʔaraaẓi.* I have a lot of land near Baghdad. *ɛindi ʔaraaẓi hwaaya yamm baġdaad.*
to land - **1.** *nazzal (i tanziil) t-.* He had to land his plane in the desert. *ẓṭarr ynazzil ṭiyyaarta bis-sazraaʔ.* **2.** *nizal (i nzuul).* The plane landed without trouble. *ṭ-ṭiyyaara nizlat bila mašaakil.* **3.** *ṭallaɛ (i ṭṭilliɛ) imnil-mayy.* I spent a quarter of an hour before I could land the fish. *ṣrafit rubuɛ saaɛa zatta gdarit aṭalliɛ is-simač imnil-mayy.* **4.** *nẓabb (a).* He landed in jail for fighting. *nẓabb bis-sijin li-ʔan čaan yitɛaarak.* -- **We nearly landed in jail. *rizna lil-zabis ʔilla šwayya.* **5.** *zaṣṣal (i zuṣuul) ɛala.* I landed a job after a week of interviews. *zaṣṣalit ɛala šuġuḷ baɛad muqaabalaat muddat isbuuɛ.*
landing - **1.** *nizuul.* They lowered the plane's wheels preparing for the landing. *nazzlaw čuruux iṭ-ṭayyaara stiɛdaadan lin-nizuul.* **2.** *ʔinzaal* pl. *-aat.* The landing took place at dawn. *l-ʔinzaal jira wakt il-fajir.*
landlord - *ṣaazib* (pl. *ʔaṣzaab*) *muluk.*
landmark: **The monument is a landmark in this area. *n-naṣub fadd ɛalaama mumayyiza b-hal-manṭiqa.*
landowner - *ṣaazib muluk* pl. *ʔaṣzaab ʔamlaak.* The big landowners are usually conservatives. *kibaar aṣzaab il-ʔamlaak ɛaadatan muzaafiẓiin.*
landslide - **1.** *nhiyaar* pl. *-aat.* The road through the mountains was blocked by a landslide. *ṭariiq ij-jibal čaan masduud ib-sabab inhiyaar.* **2.** *ʔaġlabiyya saaziqa.* He won the election by a landslide. *faaz bil-intixaab ib-ʔaġlabiyya saaziqa.*
lane - *darub* pl. *druub.* Follow this lane to the main road. *ʔitbaɛ had-darub ʔila ṭ-ṭariiq ir-raʔiisi.*
language - **1.** *luġa* pl. *-aat.* He knows several languages. *yuɛruf ɛiddat luġaat.* **2.** *lahja.* He used strong language in dealing with them. *staɛmal lahja šadiida b-muɛaamalta wiyyaahum.*
lantern - **1.** *faanuus* pl. *fawaaniis.* Walk in front of me with the lantern so I can see the path. *ʔimši bil-faanuus giddaami zatta ašuuf iṭ-ṭariiq.* **2.** *looks* pl. *-aat.* I need a new mantle for my coleman lantern. *ʔaztaaj fatiila jdiida lil-looks maali.*
lap - **1.** *zuẓin, zijir.* She put the baby in her lap. *zaṭṭat iṭ-ṭifil b-zuẓinha.* **2.** *dawra* pl. *-aat, farra* pl. *-aat.* He was in the lead by five yards in the first lap. *čaan bil-muqaddima xams amtaar bid-dawra l-ʔuula.*
to lap - *ṭubag (u ṭabug) n-.* Lap the boards one over the other so the roof won't leak. *ʔuṭbug il-loozaat wizda ɛal-lux zatta s-saguf ma-yxurr.*
to lap up - *liṭaɛ (a laṭiɛ).* The cats lapped up the milk. *l-bazaaziin liṭɛat il-zaliib.*
lapel - *gaḷba* pl. *-aat, yaaxat sitra* pl. *yaaxaat sitar.*
to **lapse** - *buṭal (a buṭlaan), xılaṣ (a xalıṣ), ntıha (i ntihaaʔ).* If I don't pay this premium my insurance policy will lapse. *ʔiẓa ma-adfaɛ hal-qisiṭ taʔmiini yibṭal.*
lard - *šazam xanziir.*
large - **1.** *čibiir, kabiir, waasiɛ.* This room isn't large enough. *hal-ġurfa muu čbiira kaafi* or ***hal-ġurfa kuburha muu kaafi.* -- The mouth of this jar is large enough for me to put my hand in. *zalig hat-tunga maa waasiɛ ib-zeeθ ʔagdar afawwut iidi bii.* **2.** *čbiir, kabiir.* That's the largest table in the house. *haaẓa ʔakbar meez bil-beet.* -- He's a large importer from the Middle East. *huwwa mustawrid kabiir imniš-šarq il-ʔawsaṭ.*
at large - *zurr.* The thief is still at large. *l-zaraami baɛda zurr.*
largely - *bil-ʔakθar.* Our company is made up largely of volunteers. *firqatna mitkawwina bil-ʔakθar min mutaṭawwiɛiin.*
large-scale - *niṭaaq waasiɛ.* The city is studying a large-scale building program. *l-baladiyya da-tidrus manhaj ʔinšaaʔ ʔabniya ɛala niṭaaq waasiɛ.*
lark - *qumbura* pl. *-aat.*
laryngitis - *ltihaab il-zunjara.*
lash - *qamči* pl. *-iyyaat, jalda* pl. *-aat, zooba* pl. *-aat.* They gave him forty lashes for stealing a loaf of bread. *ẓurboo ʔarbaɛiin qamči li-ʔan baag gurṣat xubuz.*
last - **1.** *ʔaaxir.* She spent her last cent on that dress. *ṣurfat ʔaaxir filis ɛidha ɛala han-nafnuuf.* -- She was the last to leave. *hiyya ʔaaxir wizda tirkat.* **2.** *ʔaxiir, maaẓi.* Last year I was in Europe. *s-sana l-maaẓya činit ib-ʔooruppa.* or ***l-ɛaam činit ib-ʔooruppa.* **3.** *ʔaxiir.* The last thing he said was that he didn't want to come. *ʔaxiir šii gaala čaan ma-yriid yiji.* -- He came in last in the race. *čaan il-ʔaxiir bis-sibaaq.* **4.** *bil-ʔaxiir.* He came last. *jaa bil-ʔaxiir.* or *jaa ʔaaxir waazid.*
at last - *ʔaxiiran.* Here we are at last! *wuṣalna ʔaxiiran!*
last night - *l-baarza bil-leel.* Did you sleep well last night? *nimit zeen il-baarza bil-leel?*
last year - *l-ɛaam.* Last year I spent the summer in Lebanon. *l-ɛaam giẓeet iṣ-ṣeef ib-lubnaan.*
to last - **1.** *daam (u dawaam), ṭawwal (i ṭṭuwwul, taṭwiil).* The war lasted six years. *l-zarb daamat sitt isniin.* -- I'm afraid this good weather won't last long. *xaayif ʔan haj-jaww il-zilu ma-yṭawwil ihwaaya.* **2.** *qaawam (u muqaawama).* This suit didn't last at all. *hal-badla ma-qaawmat ʔabadan.* -- Do you think you can last another mile? *tiɛtiqid tigdar itqaawum miil laax?* **3.** *kaffa (i tkiffi).* I don't think my money will last till the end of the month. *ma-aṭṣawwar ifluusi tkaffi l-ʔaaxir iš-šahar.*
lasting - *daaʔim.* Let's hope for a lasting peace. *xalliina niʔmal ib-salaam daaʔim.*
Latakia - *l-laaẓiqiyya.*
latch - *ṣiqqaaṭa* pl. *-aat, ziḷgaaṭa* pl. *-aat, mizlaaj* pl. *mzaaliij.*
late - **1.** *ʔaxiir.* The late news is broadcast at ten o'clock. *l-ʔaxbaar il-ʔaxiira tinẓaaɛ is-saaɛa ɛašara.* **2.** *marzuum.* Your late father was a friend of mine. *l-marzuum abuuk čaan ṣadiiqi.* **3.** *saabiq.*

The late government encouraged exporting. *l-ǥukuuma s-saabiqa šajjiεat it-taṣdiir.* **4.** *mit?axxir.* You're late again! *?inta mit?axxir marra lux.* -- This installment is four days late. *hal-qusiṭ mit?axxir ?arbaεt iyyaam.*
**He is in his late fifties. *εumra qariib imnis-sittiin.*
late afternoon - *l-εaṣir.* I'll be home late in the afternoon. *raǥ-akuun bil-beet il-εaṣir.*
late morning - *ð-ðaǥa l-εaali.* He comes to work late in the morning. *ð-ðaǥa l-εaali yaǥla yiji liš-šuġul.*

lately - *bil-mudda l-?axiira.* I haven't been feeling so well lately. *ma-da-ašεur zeen bil-mudda l-?axiira.*

later - **1.** *baεdeen.* You'll find out later. *raǥ-tuεruf baεdeen.* **2.** *baεad.* One day later a letter came. *w-baεad yoom jaa maktuub.*

latest - *?aaxir.* What's the latest news? *šinu ?aaxir il-axbaar?* -- That's the latest style. *haay ?aaxir mooda.*

lathe - *čarix* pl. *čruux, mixraṭa* pl. *maxaariṭ.*

lather - *waġfa* pl. *-aat* coll. *waġaf, raġwa* pl. *-aat.* Put a little soap lather on so you can shave well. *xalli šwayya waġaf ṣaabuun ǥatta tiǥliq zeen.*
to lather - *riġa (u raġwa), waġġaf (u twuġġuf).* This soap doesn't lather well. *haṣ-ṣaabuun ma-yirġu zeen.*

Latin - **1.** *laatiini**. The language of the Latin American countries is either Spanish or Portugese. *duwal ?ameerka l-laatiiniyya luġatha ?imma spaaniyya ?aw purtuġaaliyya.* **2.** *l-laatiiniyya.* Latin is a dead language. *l-laatiiniyya luġa mayyta.*

latitude - *xaṭṭ* (pl. *xuṭuuṭ*) *εarið.* It's position is at 40 degrees north latitude. *haay mawqiεha εala xaṭṭ εarið ?arbaεiin šimaalan.*

lattice - *xišab imšabbač.* The balcony is hidden by a lattice. *l-balkoon mastuur ib-xišab mšabbač.*

laugh - *ðiǥka* pl. *-aat.* He has an unusual laugh. *εinda ðiǥka ġeer εaadiyya.*
to laugh - *ðiǥak (a ðaǥik).* Everybody laughed at him. *l-kull ðiǥkaw εalee.* -- We laughed up our sleeves at his pronunciation. *ðiǥakna b-εibbna εala talaffuða.*
**That's no laughing matter. *haaða muu šaqa.*

laughingstock - *maðǥaka, masxara.* His gullibility made him a laughingstock in front of everybody. *taṣdiiga b-kullši sawwaa maðǥaka giddaam in-naas.*

laughter - *ðiǥik.* We heard loud laughter behind us. *smaεna ðiǥik εaali waraana.*

launch - *maaṭoor* pl. *-aat.* We went down the river in his launch. *nǥidarna bin-nahar ib-maaṭoora.*
to launch - **1.** *nizal (i nuzuul) n- lil-ṃaay.* Another ship was launched on Monday. *sifiina lux innizlat lil-ṃaay yoom il-iθneen.* **2.** *?aṭlaq (i ?iṭlaaq).* I hear they launched a new satellite. *simaεit ?aṭliqaw kawkab iṣṭinaaεi jidiid.* **3.** *šann (i šann) n-.* The press launched a fierce attack against the Prime Minister. *ṣ-ṣaǥaafa šannat hujuum εaniif εala ra?iis il-wuzaraa?.* **4.** *ftitaǥ (i ftitaaǥ).* They launched the program for fighting illiteracy by holding a convention in Baghdad. *ftitǥaw mašruuε mukaafaǥat il-?uṃṃiyya b-εaqid mu?tamar ib-baġdaad.*

to **launder** - *ġisal (i ġasil) n-, xisal (i xasil) n-.* My landlady launders my clothes for me. *?umm il-beet tiġsil-li hduumi.*

laundress - *ġassaala* pl. *-aat.* We have a laundress who comes to the house. *εidna ġassaala tijiina lil-beet.*

laundry - **1.** *makwi.* Where's the nearest laundry? *ween ?aqrab makwi?* **2.** *ġasiil.* My laundry just came back. *ġasiili hassa jaa.*

laurel - *ġaar.* This soap has laurel oil in it. *haṣ-ṣaabuun bii zeet il-ġaar.*

lavatory - *mirǥaað* pl. *maraaǥiið, xalwa* pl. *xalawi, ?adabxaana* pl. *-aat, ?adabxaayin; beet* (pl. *byuut*) *ṃayy.*

lavish - *b-?ifraaṭ.* They gave him lavish praise. *midǥoo b-?ifraaṭ.*

law - **1.** *qaanuun* pl. *qawaaniin.* That's against the law. *haay ðidd il-qaanuun.* -- He's studying law. *da-yidrus qaanuun.* -- According to the law of nature, the strong devour the weak. *ǥasab qaanuun iṭ-ṭabiiεa l-qawi yaakul ið-ðaεiif.* -- Those people are very law abiding. *haaðool in-naas yiltazmuun bil-qaanuun.* **2.** *ǥukum* pl. *?aǥkaam.* The government is going to do away with martial law. *l-ǥukuuma raǥ-itšiil il-ǥukm il-εurfi.*
by law - *qaanuunan, b-ǥukm il-qaanuun.* That's prohibited by law! *haaða mamnuuε qaanuunan!*
canon law - *šariiε* pl. *šaraayiε.* Islamic law provides that a woman's inheritance is half that of a man. *š-šariiεa l-?islaamiyya tnuṣṣ εala ?an ǥaqq il-mar?a bil-?iriθ nuṣṣ ǥaqq ir-rajul.*

lawn - *θayyal, θayyil.* The lawn still has to be sprinkled. *θ-θayyal baεda laazim yinrašš.*

law school - *kulliyyat* (pl. *-aat*) *il-ǥuquuq.*

lawsuit - *daεwa* pl. *-aat, daεaawi.* Did Adnan win the lawsuit? *εadnaan rubaǥ id-daεwa?*

lawyer - *muǥaami* pl. *-iin.*

lax - **1.** *mitmaahil, mithaawin.* He's rather lax in his work. *huwwa šwayya mitmaahil ib-šuġla.* **2.** *layyin, mitsaahil, mitmaahil, mithaawin.* She's always been much too lax with her children. *daa?iman layyna wiyya ?aṭfaalha.*

laxative - *mushil* pl. *-aat, musahhil* pl. *-aat.*

laxity - *tahaawan.* He was accused of laxity in his work. *ttihmoo b-tahaawunа b-šuġla.*

to **lay** - **1.** *xalla (i txilli) t-, ǥaṭṭ (u ǥaṭṭ) n-.* Lay the book on the table. *xalli l-iktaab εal-meez.* -- He laid aside 50 dinars for emergencies. *xalla xamsiin diinaar εala ṣafǥa lil-iǥtiyaaṭ.* **2.** *bina (i binaa?).* The workmen were laying tile on the ground floor. *l-εummaal čaanaw yibnuun kaaši εaṭ-ṭaabiq il-?awwal.* or *l-εummaal caanaw yṭabbuguun iṭ-ṭaabiq il-?awwal ib-kaaši.* **3.** *ðabb (i ðabb) n-, xalla (i), ǥaṭṭ (u).* Don't lay the blame on me. *la-tðibb il-loom εalayya.* **4.** *baað (i).* The hen laid four eggs. *d-dijaaja baaðat ?arbaεa beeðaat.* **5.** *bayyað (i tabyiið, tbiyyið) t-.* Our hens are laying well. *dijaajna zeen da-ybayyið.* **6.** *traahan (a taraahun).* I'll lay ten to one that he does it. *?atraahan εašra l-waaǥid huwwa raǥ-ysawwiiha.* **7.** *nayyam (i tniyyim) t-, ṭiraǥ (a ṭariǥ) n-.* Lay the barrel on its side. *nayyim il-barmiil εala ṣafuǥta.*
**He's certainly laying it on thick! *hwaaya da-yθaxxinha!*
to lay claim to - *ddiεa (i ddiεaa?) b-.* A distant relative laid claim to the estate. *fadd waaǥid ?ila qaraaba biεiida ddiεa ǥaqq bil-muluk.*
to lay down - **1.** *jiṭal (i jaṭil) n-.* Lay him down gently. *jiṭla εala keefak.* **2.** *tirak (u tarik) n-, ðabb (i ðabb) n-.* They were ready to lay down their arms. *čaanaw mustaεiddiin yitrukuun islaaǥhum.* **3.** *wuðaε (a waðiε) n-.* Let me lay down the rules for the game. *xalli ?aani ?ooðaε qawaaεid il-liεba.*
to lay for - *xital (i xatil) l-, traṣṣad (a taraṣṣud) l-.* They laid for him at the corner. *xitloo-la biz-zuwiyya.*
to lay off - *stağna (i stignaa?) εan, baṭṭal (i tabṭiil).* We have to lay off some workers. *laazim nistaġni εan baεð il-εummaal.* -- You're going to have to lay off the drinking for awhile! *laazim itbaṭṭil imniš-širib fadd mudda!*
to lay out - **1.** *ṣiraf (u ṣarif).* How much did you lay out for the party? *šgadd ṣirafit lil-ǥafla?* **2.** *ǥaddad (i taǥdiid), xaṭṭaṭ (i taxṭiiṭ).* Lay out the dimensions before you start digging. *ǥaddad il-?abεaad qabil-ma tibdi tiǥfur.* **3.** *εirað (i εarið) n-.* The chairman laid out his plans for the future. *mudiir il-majlis εirað xiṭṭata lil-mustaqbal.*
to lay waste - *dumar (u damur) n-.* The whole region was laid waste by the storm. *l-manṭiqa kullha ndumrat bil-εaaṣifa.*

layer - *ṭabaqa* pl. *-aat.* Everything was covered with a thick layer of sand. *kullši čaan imġaṭṭa b-ṭabaqa θxiina mnir-ramuḷ.*

layman - *šaxuṣ εaadi* pl. *?ašxaaṣ εaadiyyiin.* The layman wouldn't be interested in this book. *š-šaxs il-εaadi ma-yihtamm ib-hal-iktaab.*

lazier - *?aksal.* They say he's lazier than me. *yguuluun huwwa ?aksal minni.*

laziness - *kasal.*

lazy - *kaslaan.* Don't be so lazy! *la-tṣiir hal-gadd kaslaan!*

lead - *riṣaaṣ.* Is this made of lead? *haaði maṣnuuεa min riṣaaṣ?* -- Do you have some lead for my pencil? *εindak riṣaaṣ lil-qalam maali?*

lead - **1.** *dawr ra?iisi* pl. *?adwaar ra?iisiyya.* Who's playing the lead? *minu da-yquum bid-dawr ir-ra?iisi?* **2.** *daliil* pl. *?adilla.* The police had a number of leads on the case. *caan εind iš-šurṭa baεð il-?adilla mutaεallqa bil-qaðiyya.* **3.** *muqaddima.* He was in the lead by five yards in the first lap. *čaan bil-muqaddima ib-xamis yaardaat bil-farra* l-ʔuula. -- When the army entered the town the tanks were in the lead. lamma j-jeeš dixal il-madiina čaanat id-dabbaabaat bil-muqaddima. -- **The first hour he had a five-mile lead on us. bis-saaƐa l-ʔuula čaan ġaalubna xams amyaal.

to lead - 1. qaad (u qiyaada). The lieutenant led his men to the top of the hill. l-mulaazim qaad junuuda ʔila foog it-tall. 2. tfawwaq (a tafawwuq) Ɛala, tqaddam (a taqaddum) Ɛala. Ahmed leads his class in arithmetic. ʔazmad mitfawwuq Ɛala tullaab saffa bil-zisaab. 3. gaad (u good) n-. He led the child across the street. gaad ij-jaahil w-Ɛabbara š-šaariƐ. 4. tqaddam (a taqaddum) Ɛala. Iraq leads the all countries in the production of dates. l-Ɛiraaq yitqaddam Ɛala jamiiƐ id-duwal ib-ʔintaaj it-tamur.

to lead the way - tqaddam (a taqaddum). I'll lead the way and you follow. ʔaani raz-atqaddam w-ʔinta tbaƐni.

to lead to - 1. ʔadda (i). Where will all this lead to? haaδa ween raz-yʔaddi? -- Where does this road lead to? ween yʔaddi hat-tariiq? 2. sabbab (i tasbiib), ʔadda (i) ʔila. Drink led to his downfall. š-šurub sabbab xaraaba. -- The information you gave us led to his arrest. l-maƐluumaat l-inteetna-yyaaha ʔaddat ʔila tawqiifa.

to lead up to - qiṣad (u qaṣid). What do you think he was leading up to? l-ʔay šii tiƐtiqid čaan qaaṣid? -- That's just what I was leading up to. haaδa illi činit aquṣda biδ-δabut.

leader - 1. zaƐiim pl. zuƐamaaʔ. The leaders of all parties were present. zuƐamaaʔ kull il-ʔazzaab čaanaw zaaδriin. 2. raʔiis pl. ruʔasaaʔ. Who is the leader of the group? minu raʔiis ij-jamƐiyya? -- I know the band leader. ʔaƐruf raʔiis il-firqa l-mawsiiqiyya.

leading - baariz, kabiir. He's one of the leading scientists in his field. haaδa waazid min abraz il-Ɛulamaaʔ ib-farƐa. -- This is the leading newspaper in Baghdad. haaδi ʔakbar jariida b-baġdaad.

leaf - 1. warga pl. warag. In the fall the leaves turn brown. bil-xariif il-warag yinġulub loona qahwaaʔi. -- If you add an additional leaf to the spring it'll bear a heavier weight. ʔiδa txalli warga lux Ɛas-sipring yitzammal wazin ʔakθar. 2. ṣaziifa. He promised to turn over a new leaf. wuƐad yiftaz ṣaziifa jidiida b-zayaata.

to leaf through - gallab (u tagliib) t- b-. I'm only leafing through the book. bass da-agallub bil-iktaab.

leaflet - manšuur pl. manaašiir.

league - 1. jaamiƐa pl. -aat. The Arab League has its headquarters in Cairo. j-jaamiƐa l-Ɛarabiyya markazha bil-qaahira. 2. ttizaad pl. -aat. The soccer league's having a dinner today. ttizaad kurat il-qadam imsawwi daƐwat Ɛaša l-yoom.

leak: **There's a leak in the boat. ʔaku mukaan bil-balam ytalliƐ mayy.

to leak - 1. tallaƐ (i ttilliƐ) mayy, nadda (i tniddi). The boat is leaking. l-balam da-ytalliƐ mayy. 2. xarr (u xarr). This pot leaks. haj-jidir yxurr. -- The faucet is leaking. l-zanafiyya da-txurr. 3. tsarrab (a tasarrub). The story leaked out somehow. l-quṣṣa tsarrubat b-ṣuura mniṣ-ṣuwar. -- All the water is leaking out. l-mayy kulla da-yitsarrab li-barra.

lean - 1. šiiriz. Do you want lean meat or some with fat on it? triid lazam šiiriz loo bii šazam? 2. mazal, qazat. It was a lean year for farmers. čaanat sanat mazal lil-fallaaziin. 3. naziif, haziil. He's a lean man. huwwa rajul naziif.

to lean - 1. maal (i meel, mayalaan), dannag (i ddinnig). Don't lean out of the window. la-tmiil imniš-šibbaak. 2. maal (i). He leans toward the right in polities. ymiil nazu l-yamiin bis-siyaasa. 3. maal (i), mayyal (i tamyiil) jism˜. She leaned over the balcony and looked to see who was knocking. maalat imnil-baalkoon zatta tšuuf minu čaan ydugg il-baab. 4. tačča (i ttičči), riča (i rači) n-, sinad (i sanid) n-. Don't lean your chair against the wall. la-tirči kursiyyak Ɛal-zaayit. 5. stinad (i stinaad), ntiča (i). There's nothing to lean against. ma-aku šii tistinid Ɛalee. -- May I lean on your arm? ʔagdar astinid Ɛala δraaƐak? -- She leaned on the railing. ntičat Ɛal-imzajjar. 6. nzina (i nzinaaʔ), maal (i). If you lean forward you can see him. ʔiδa nzineet li-giddaam tigdar itšuufa.

leap - tafra pl. -aat, gamza pl. -aat. He cleared the ditch with one leap. Ɛubar is-saagya b-tafra wizda.

to leap - gumaz (u gamuz). He leaped out of bed at the noise. gumaz min ifraaša min simaƐ iṣ-ṣoot.

leap year - sana kabiisa.

to **learn** - 1. tƐallam (i taƐallum). He hasn't learned a thing. ma-tƐallam šii. 2. Ɛiraf (u maƐrifa). He learned the truth too late. Ɛiraf il-zaqiiqa baƐad fawaat il-wakit.

to learn by heart - zufaδ (u zafuδ) Ɛala galb˜, Ɛal-ġeeb. She learned the poem by heart. zufδat il-qaṣiida Ɛala galubha.

lease - Ɛaqid (pl. Ɛuquud) ʔiijaar. We had to sign a lease for one year. δtarreena nwaqqiƐ Ɛaqid iijaar il-muddat sana.

to lease - 1. staʔjar (i stiʔjaar). Did you lease an apartment yet? stiʔjarit šiqqa loo baƐad? 2. ʔajjar (i taʔjiir) t-. The landlord doesn't want to lease the apartment. ṣaazib il-muluk ma-yriid yʔajjir iš-šuqqa.

least - ʔaqall. That's the least of my worries. haay ʔaqall mašaakli. -- She deserves it least of all. hiyya tistaahilha ʔaqall il-kull. -- That's the least you could do for him. haaδa ʔaqall-ma mumkin itsawwii tijaaha.

at least - Ɛal-ʔaqall. These shoes cost at least two dinars. hal-ʔazδiya kallfat Ɛal-ʔaqall diinaareen. -- At least you might have written to me. Ɛal-aqall čaan kitabit-li.

not in the least - ma- ... ʔabadan, ma- ... ʔabad. It doesn't bother me in the least. ma-thimmni ʔabadan. -- It wouldn't surprise me in the least if ... ma-astaġrub ʔabad ʔiδa ...

leather - jilid pl. jluud. The meat is tough as leather. l-lazam qawi miθl ij-jilid.

leave - ʔijaaza pl. -aat. He's taken a three months' leave. ʔaxaδ ʔijaaza tlaθt išhur.

to leave - 1. tirak (u tarik) n-, raaz (u), Ɛaaf (u Ɛoof) n-, miša (i maši). I have to leave now. laazim ʔatruk hassa. or laazim aƐuufkum hassa. -- I'm leaving for good. raz-atruk nihaaʔiyyan. -- The train leaves at two-thirty. l-qitaar yitruk s-saaƐa θinteen w-nuṣṣ. 2. saafar (i safar), tirak, miša, raaz. My father left yesterday for Europe. ʔabuuya saafar il-ʔooruppa l-baarza. 3. xalla (i txilli) t-, tirak (u). He left his food on the plate. xalla ʔakla bil-maaƐuun. -- Where did you leave your suitcase? ween xalleet jinuttak? -- My brother got all the money, and left me out in the cold. ʔaxuuya ʔaxaδ kull il-ifluus w-xallaani aṣaffug ʔiid ib-ʔiid. -- Leave it to me! xalliiha Ɛalayya. -- When he died he left eight grand-children. min maat tirak iθman ʔazfaad. -- He left word that he would be back soon. xalla xabar ʔanna raz-yirjaƐ baƐd išwayya.

**Are there any tickets left for tonight's performance? buqat ʔay bitaaqaat il-zaflat il-leela?

**Eight from fifteen leaves seven. θmaanya min xumuṣtaƐaš yibqa sabƐa.

**Where does that leave me? ʔaani š-raz-ykuun maṣiiri?

to leave out - fawwat (i tafwiit, tfuwwut) t-, ziδaf (i zaδif) n-. When you copy it, don't leave anything out. min tinqulha, la-tfawwit šii.

Lebanese - 1. lubnaani pl. -iyyiin. Most of the Lebanese know how to speak French. ʔakθar il-lubnaaniyyiin yƐurfuun yizčuun fransi. 2. labnaani*. I visited the Lebanese capital twice last summer. zirit il-Ɛaaṣima l-labnaaniyya marrteen biṣ-ṣeef il-maaδi.

Lebanon - lubnaan.

lecture - muzaaδara pl. -aat. It was an interesting lecture. čaanat muzaaδara latiifa.

to lecture - ʔalqa (i ʔilqaaʔ) muzaaδara, zaaδar (i muzaaδara). He's lecturing on international trade. da-yilqi muzaaδara Ɛan it-tijaara d-dawliyya. -- He lectures on zoology at the university. yzaaδir ib-Ɛilm il-zaywaan bij-jaamiƐa. -- He always lectures us when we're late. daaʔiman yilqi Ɛaleena muzaaδara min inkuun mitʔaxxriin. -- Don't lecture me! la-tilqi b-raasi muzaaδara!

lecturer - muzaaδir pl. -iin.

ledge - zaašya pl. zawaaši. The bird hopped onto the ledge of the window. t-teer gumaz il-zaašyat iš-šibbaač.

ledger: (bookkeeping) daftar (pl. dafaatir) zisaab.

leek - kurraaθ.

left - (m.) yisaar, ʔaysar (f.) yisra. Take the other

bag in your left hand. šiil ij-junṭa l-lux b-iidak il-yisra. -- We had seats at the left of the stage. maqaaεidna čaanat εala yisaar il-masraʒ. -- I sat on the speaker's left. gεadit εala yisaar il-xaṭiib. -- Turn left at the next corner. luuf εal-yisra biš-šaariε ij-jaay.

left-handed - yisraawi pl. -iyyiin. He's left-handed. huwwa yisraawi.

leftist - yisaari pl. -iyyiin. He always was a leftist. daaʔiman čaan yisaari.

leg - **1.** rijil pl. rijleen, rijleenaat. I have a pain in my right leg. εindi ʔalam ib-rijli l-yimna. -- The table leg's broken. rijl il-meez maksuura. -- The left pant leg is torn. rijil panṭaruun il-yisra mamzuuga. **2.** marʒala pl. maraaʒil. We're now on the last leg of our trip. ʔiʒna hassa b-ʔaaxir marʒala min safratna. **3.** fuxuδ pl. fxaaδ. Give me a small leg of lamb. nṭiini fuxuδ ġanam iṣġayyir. -- **They say he's on his last legs. yguuluun ʔamra taqriiban mintihi.
**Stop pulling my leg. bass εaad titšaaqa.

legal - qaanuuni*. That's perfectly legal. haaδa tamaaman qaanuuni. -- He's our legal adviser. huwwa mustašaarna l-qaanuuni.

legality - l-qaanuuniyya.

legation - mufawwaδiyya pl. -aat. Where is the Swiss legation? ween il-mufawwaδiyya is-suwiisriyya?

legend - ʔuṣṭuura pl. ʔaṣaaṭiir. The origin of the legend is unknown. manšaʔ il-ʔuṣṭuura ġeer maεluum.

legible - waaδiʒ. His handwriting is hardly legible. kitaabta muu waaδʒa. or kitaabta ma-tinqiri b-suhuula.

legion - **1.** firqa pl. firaq. The Foreign Legion's mostly mercenaries. l-firqa l-ʔajnabiyya muεδamha yitkawwan min murtazaqa. **2.** faylaq pl. fayaaliq, jeeš pl. jyuuš. The Arab Legion's conducting exercises near the border of occupied Palestine. l-faylaq il-εarabi da-yquum ib-tamaariin εala ʒiduud falasṭiin il-muʒtalla.

legislation - tasriiε.

legislator - mušarriε pl. -iin.

legislature - musarriεiin, sulṭa tašriiεiyya.

legitimate - **1.** šarεi*. He is the legitimate heir. huwwa l-wariiθ iš-šarεi. -- Are all her children legitimate? kull wulidha sarεiyyiin? **2.** ṣaʒiiʒ. Those conclusions are not legitimate. haay il-istintaajaat muu ṣaʒiiʒa.

leisure - faraaġ. This job doesn't leave me much leisure. haš-šaġla ma-titruk-li faraaġ kaafi. -- Do it at your leisure. sawwiiha b-faraaġak.

lemon - nuumiyya (pl. -aat) ʒaamδa coll. nuumi ʒaamuδ. Go buy some lemons. ruuʒ ištiri šwayya nuumi ʒaamuδ.

lemonade - šarbat nuumi ʒaamuδ.

lemon juice - εaṣiir nuumi ʒaamuδ.

lemon tea - čaay ʒaamuδ, ʒaamuδ, čaay nuumi baṣra.

to **lend** - **1.** εaar (i ʔiεaara). Can you lend me this book? tigdar itεiirni hal-iktaab? **2.** daayan (i mudaayan) t-, εaar (i). Would you lend me ten dinars? tigdar itdaayinni εašr idnaaniir?
**Lend me a hand, will you? saaεidni šwayya? or baḷḷa ʔiidak išwayya?

length - **1.** ṭuul pl. ʔaṭwaal. Let's measure the length of the room. xalli nqiiṣ ṭuul il-ġurfa. -- He stretched full length on the bed. tmaddad ib-ṭuula εat-taxit. **2.** fatra pl. -aat, mudda pl. -aat. He can do a lot of work in a short length of time. yigdar ysawwi ʔašyaaʔ ihwaaya b-fatrat wakit qaṣiira. **3.** wuṣla pl. wusal. We need a short length of pipe so the faucet will reach. yirraad-inna wuṣlat buuri ṣġayyra ʒatta l-ʒanafiyya twaṣṣil.
**I went to great lengths to get a passport for you. tεabit ihwaaya ʒatta xallaṣit-lak il-paaspoort.
at length - biṭ-ṭafṣiil. They discussed the plan at length. biʒθaw il-xiṭṭa biṭ-ṭafṣiil.

to **lengthen** - ṭawwal (i taṭwiil) t-. These trousers have to be lengthened. hal-panṭaroon laazim yiṭṭawwal.

lengthwise - biṭ-ṭuul. Cut the material lengthwise. guṣṣ il-iqmaaš biṭ-ṭuul.

lengthy - muṭawwal. He made a lengthy speech. xiṭab xuṭba muṭawwala.

lenient - layyin, mitsaahil. You're too lenient with him. ʔinta kulliš layyin wiyyaa.

lens - εadasa pl. -aat. Your camera has a good lens. l-kaameera maaltak biiha xooš εadasa.

lentil - εadasa pl. -aat coll. εadas. Add some lentils to the soup. δiif išwayya εadas biš-šoorba.

leopard - nimir imnaqqaṭ pl. nmuur imnaqqaṭa, fahad pl. fhuud.

leper - majδuum pl. -iin.

leprosy - marδ ij-juδaam.

lesbian - saʒʒaaqiyya pl. -aat.

less - **1.** ʔaqall. I have less money with me than I thought. εindi fluus ʔaqall min-ma εtiqadit. **2.** naaqiṣ. The price is 10 dinars, less the discount. s-siεir εašr idnaaniir naaqiṣ il-xaṣum. -- Five less three leaves two. xamsa naaqiṣ itlaaθa yibqa θneen.

lesson - **1.** daris pl. duruus. Translate lesson five for tomorrow. tarjum id-dars il-xaamis il-baačir. -- I'll have to do my lessons first. laazim asawwi druusi ʔawwal. -- She gives Spanish lessons. tinṭi druus bil-ispaani. **2.** εibra pl. εibar, daris pl. duruus. Let that be a lesson to you. xalli haaδa ykuun εibra ʔilak. -- I hope you've learned a good lesson from that. ʔinsaaḷḷa ʔaxaδit xooš daris min haay.

let - natt, šabaka. That serve was a let. Take two more serves. haδ-δarba čaanat natt. ʔuxuδ-lak baεad δarubteen.
let alone - b-ġaδδ in-naδar εan. He can't even read Arabic, let alone speak it. ma-yuεruf yiqraʔ εarabi, b-ġaδδ in-naδar εan il-ʒači.
let's - xalli, xal-, yaḷḷa. Let's go home. xalli nruuʒ lil-beet. -- Let's not leave the party until twelve o'clock. xal-ma-nitruk il-ʒafla ʒatta s-saaεa θnaεaš.
to let - **1.** xalla (i txilli) t-, simaʒ (a samiʒ) n- l-. He wouldn't let me do it. ma-xallaani asawwiiha. -- This time I'll let it go. hal-marra raʒ-axalliiha tfuut. or hal-marra raʒ-asmaʒ-lak. -- Don't let anybody in. la-txalli ʔaʒʒad yfuut. -- He wouldn't let me out. ma-xallaani aṭlaε. -- Will the customs officials let us pass? εajaban muwaδδafiin il-gumrug raʒ-yismaʒuu-lna bil-muruur? -- I can't let his statement stand. ma-axalli kalaama yruuʒ ib-faala. -- Please let me have the menu. ʔismaʒ-li b-qaaʔimat il-ʔakil. or **nṭiini qaaʔimat il-ʔakil rajaaʔan. -- Can you let me have five dinars until I get paid? tigdar tismaʒ-li b-xams idnaaniir ʔila ʔan ʔaaxuδ raatbi? **2.** tirak (u tarik), xalla (i txilli). Can't you let me alone for five minutes? ma-tigdar titrukni waʒdi xamis daqaayiq?
**Have you rooms to let? εindak ġuraf lil-ʔiijaar?
**I really let him have it! nṭeeta ʒagga b-ʔiida.
to let down - **1.** nazzal (i tanziil) t-. Please let down the store front. baḷḷa ma-tnazzil il-kabangaat. **2.** xayyab (i txiyyib) His son has let him down badly. ʔibna xayyab ʔamala kulliš. -- He let me down when I needed him. xayyabni min iʒtijit ʔila. or εaafni min iʒtijit ʔila. **3.** tmaahal (a tamaahul) He's beginning to let down in his work. bida yitmaahal ib-šuġḷa.
to let go of - hadd (i hadd) n-, ʒall (i ʒall) n-. Don't let go of the rope. la-thidd il-ʒabil.
to let in on - fiša (i faši). Did you let him in on the secret, too? fišeet-la is-sirr hammeena?
to let off - **1.** nazzal (i tanziil) t-. Please let me off at the next stop. nazzilni bil-maʒaṭṭa j-jaaya, min faδlak. **2.** saamaʒ (i musaamaʒa) t-. I'll let you off easy this time. raʒ-asaamʒak hal-marra.
to let on - bayyan (i tabyiin) εala nafs-, xalla (i taxliya) ybayyin εalee. He didn't let on that he knew anything about it. ma-bayyan εala nafsa ʔinnahu yuεruf šii εanha.
to let out - **1.** farraġ (i tafriiġ) t-. Let the water out of the sink. farriġ il-mayy imnil-maġsala. **2.** εarraδ (i taεriiδ) t-. I told the tailor to let out the waist. gitt-la l-xayyaaṭ yεarriδ il-xaṣir.
to let up - xaff (u xaff). The storm has let up. l-εaaṣifa xaffat.

letdown - xeebat (pl. -aat) ʔamal. The failure of our plan was a big letdown. fašal mašruuεna čaan xeebat ʔamal ičbiira.

letter - maktuub pl. makaatiib, risaala pl. risaaʔil. Are there any letters for me? ʔaku ʔay makaatiib ʔili? -- I want to send an airmail letter. ʔariid abεaθ risaala bil-bariid ij-jawwi. **2.** ʒaruf pl. ʒuruuf. The word has five letters. l-kalima biiha xams iʒruuf. **3.** naṣṣ pl. niṣuuṣ. He sticks to the letter of the law. yitqayyad ib-niṣuuṣ il-qaanuun.

letter carrier - ʔabu l-bariid, saaεi (pl. suεaat) bariid.

lettuce - xass.

letup - *ngiṭaaɛ, fakka.* It's been raining without any letup all day. *ṣaar-ilha tumṭur biduun ingiṭaaɛ il-yoom kulla.*
level - **1.** *mustawa* pl. *-ayaat.* His work isn't up to the usual level. *šuġla muu bil-mustawa l-iɛtiyaadi.* -- The Dead Sea is below sea level. *l-bazr il-mayyit tazit mustawa il-bazar.* -- The bookcase is level with the table. *l-maktaba b-mustawa l-meez.* -- The water level this year is very low. *mustawa l-maay has-sana kulliš waaṭi.* **2.** *ṣanif* pl. *ʔaṣnaaf, daraja* pl. *-aat.* There are five salary levels in our office. *ʔaku xamis ʔaṣnaaf lir-rawaatib ib-daaʔiratna.* **3.** *gubbaan* pl. *-aat.* Have you a level handy to check the tiles? *ʔaku jawwa ʔiidak gubbaan zatta niẓbuṭ il-kaaši?.* **4.** *mustawi, ɛadil.* Is the country level or hilly? *l-manṭiqa mustawiya loo jabaliyya?*
**He did his level best. *sawwa l-yigdar ɛalee.*
**He always keeps a level head. *daaʔiman ẓaabuṭ ʔaɛṣaaba.*
**Is he on the level? *huwwa ṣaadiq?*
to level - **1.** *sawwa (i taswiya) t-, ɛaddal (i taɛdiil) t-.* The ground has to be leveled. *l-gaaɛ yinraad-ilha taswiya.* -- The artillery fire leveled the town to the ground. *ẓarub il-madfaɛiyya sawwa l-madiina wiyya l-gaaɛ.* **2.** *wajjah (i tawjiih).* He leveled a number of insults at the president. *wajjah ɛiddat ištaayim lir-raʔiis.* -- He leveled the gun at me and threatened to fire. *wajjah il-bunduqiyya ɛalayya w-haddadni b-ʔiṭlaaq in-naar.*
to level off - *staɛdal (i stiɛdaal), ɛtidal (i ɛtidaal).* The plane leveled off at 10,000 feet. *ṭ-ṭiyyaara staɛdilat ɛal-irtifaaɛ ɛaširt aalaaf qadam.*
lever - *ɛatala* pl. *-aat.*
to **levy** - *firaẓ (u faruẓ) n-, xalla (i taxliya) t-.* The government will levy a tax on gasoline. *l-zukuuma raz-tifruẓ ẓariiba ɛala l-baanziin.*
lewd - *xalaaɛi*.* She did a lewd dance. *gaamat ib-raqṣa xalaaɛiyya.*
liable - **1.** *masʔuul.* You will be liable for any damages. *raz-itkuun masʔuul ɛan kull ẓarar.* **2.** *muztamal.* You're liable to catch cold if you're not careful. *muztamal taaxuð barid ʔiða ma-tdiir baalak.*
**He's liable to forget! *muztamal yinsa.*
liability - *deen* pl. *dyuun.* His liabilities exceed his assets. *dyuuna ʔakθar min-ma yimluk.*
liaison officer - *ẓaabuṭ* (pl. *ẓubbaaṭ) ittiṣaal.*
liar - *kaððaab* pl. *-iin, čaððaab* pl. *-iin.*
libel - *tašhiir, ṭaɛin.* This report is pure libel. *haaða t-taqriir kulla tašhiir.*
liberal - **1.** *mitzarrir.* He has liberal views. *ɛinda ʔaaraaʔ mitzarrira.* -- He's a liberal. *huwwa mitzarrir.* **2.** *saxi*, kariim.* She's very liberal with her money. *hiyya kulliš saxiyya b-ifluusha.*
to **liberate** - *zarrar (i tazriir) t-, ɛitag (i ɛatig) n-.* He liberated his slaves. *zarrar ɛabiida.*
liberty - *zurriyya.* We are all fighting for liberty. *kullna ndaafiɛ ib-sabiil il-zurriyya.*
**He takes too many liberties for his position. *yitɛadda ziduud waẓiifta.*
at liberty - *zurr.* You're at liberty to say what you wish. *ʔinta zurr, tigdar itguul iš-ma triid.*
librarian - *ʔamiin* (pl. *ʔumanaaʔ) maktaba.*
library - *maktaba* pl. *-aat.*
Libya - *liibya.*
Libyan - **1.** *liibi* pl. *-iyyiin.* There are three Libyans in my office. *ʔaku tlaθ liibiyyiin ib-daaʔirti.* **2.** *liibi*.* Where can I buy a Libyan newspaper? *ween agdar aštiri jariida liibiyya?*
license - *ʔijaaza* pl. *-aat.* You need a license to open a restaurant. *tiztaaj ʔijaaza zatta tiftaz maṭɛam.* -- You cannot drive without a license. *ma-tigdar itsuug bila ʔijaaza.*
to license - *ʔajaaz (i ʔijaaza).* They licensed him to practice medicine in Iraq. *ʔajaazoo l-mumaarasat iṭ-ṭibb bil-ɛiraaq.*
licensed - *mujaaz.* He's a licensed pharmacist. *huwwa ṣaydali mujaaz.*
license plate - *quṭɛa* pl. *quṭaɛ.* My car's license plates are dirty. *quṭaɛ sayyaarti waṣxa.*
lick - *laṭɛa* pl. *-aat.* Let him have a lick of your ice cream. *xalli yaaxuð laṭɛa mnid-doondirma maaltak.*
to lick - **1.** *lizas (a lazis) n-, liṭaɛ (a laṭiɛ) n-.* Just look at the cat licking her kitten. *šuuf il-bazzuuna da-tilzas wulidha.* **2.** *ẓirab (u ẓarub) n-, buṣaṭ (u baṣuṭ) n-.* I'm going to lick you if you don't stop. *tara raz-aẓurbak ʔiða ma-tbaṭṭil.* **3.** *warram (i tawriim) t-, ġiḷab (u ġaḷub) n-.* I can still lick you! *baɛadni ʔagdar awarrmak!* -- All right, I'm licked. *ʔaɛtirif ʔaani nġiḷabit.*
licking - *basṭa* pl. *-aat.* What you need is a good licking. *t-tiztaaja basṭa naašfa.*
licorice - *ɛirg is-suus.*
lid - *ġiṭa* pl. *ʔaġṭiya, ġiṭyaat.* Put the lid back on the pot. *rajjiɛ il-ġiṭa ɛal-jidir.*
lie - *ciðba* pl. *-aat* coll. *čiðib, kiðba* pl. *-aat* coll. *kiðib.* Everything he says is a lie! *kullši yguula čiðib!*
to lie - **1.** *kiðab (i kiðib), čiðab (i čiðib).* There's no doubt that he's lying. *ma-aku šakk huwwa da-yikðib.* **2.** *tmaddad (a tamaddud).* He is lying on the couch. *huwwa mitmaddid ɛal-qanafa.* **3.** Most of the town lies on the right side of the river. *muɛẓam il-madiina waaqiɛ ɛaj-jiha l-yimna mnin-nahar.*
**The book is lying on the table. *l-iktaab ɛal-meez.*
to lie down - *tmaddad (a tamaddud), njiṭal (i njiṭaal).* I want to lie down for a few minutes. *ʔariid ʔatmaddad čam daqiiqa.*
**He's lying down on the job. *ma-ðaabb nafsa ɛaš-šuġuḷ.*
lieutenant - *mulaazim* pl. *-iin.*
lieutenant colonel - *muqaddam* pl. *-iin.*
life - **1.** *zayaat.* It was a matter of life or death. *čaanat masʔalat zayaat ʔaw moot.* -- The night life in this town is dull. *l-zayaat il-leeliyya b-hal-balad jaamda.* -- He lost his life in an accident. *fuqad zayaata b-zaadiθ.* -- Such a life! *l-zayaat hiiči,* or *haay hiyya l-zayaat,* or ***haay hiyya d-dinya.* **2.** *quṣṣat* (pl. *quṣaṣ) zayaat.* He's writing a life of the President. *da-yiktib quṣṣat zayaat ir-raʔiis.* **3.** *zayawiyya.* She's full of life. *kullha zayawiyya.* **4.** *ruuz.* He was the life of the party. *huwwa čaan ruuz il-zafla.* -- I can't for the life of me remember where I put it. *loo taaxuð ruuzi ma-agdar atðakkar ween zaṭṭeetha,* or *waḷḷaahi raz-atxabbaḷ ma-agdar atðakkar ween zaṭṭeetha.* **5.** *ʔazyaaʔ.* We visited an exhibition of marine life. *zirna maɛraẓ il-ʔazyaaʔ il-maaʔiyya.* **6.** *muʔabbad.* He was sentenced to life imprisonment. *nzikam ɛalee bis-sijin il-muʔabbad.*
**This bulb has a life of six hundred hours. *hal-igloob yduum sitt miit saaɛa.*
**There he stood as big as life. *wugaf ihnaak waaẓiz miθil iš-šamis.*
**You can bet your life on that. *ʔakiid!* or *bit-taʔkiid.*
life belt - *zizaam* (pl. *-aat, ʔazzima) najaat.*
lifeboat - *zawraq* (pl. *zawaariq) najaat, qaarib* (pl. *qawaarib) najaat.*
life insurance - *taʔmiin ɛal-zayaat.*
lifetime - *ɛumur.* A thing like that happens only once in a lifetime. *miθil haš-šii yṣiir marra bil-ɛumur bass.*
lift - *maṣɛad* pl. *maṣaaɛid, sansoor* pl. *-aat.* Let's take the lift to the fifth floor. *xan-naaxuð il-maṣɛad liṭ-ṭaabiq il-xaamis.*
**A glass of tea in the afternoon gives me a lift. *stikaan čaay il-ɛaṣir yinɛišni.* or *stikaan čaay il-ɛaṣir ygaɛɛid raasi.*
**Can I give you a lift? *ʔagdar awaṣṣlak?*
to lift - **1.** *šaal (i šeel) n-.* He lifted the baby out of the cradle. *šaal iṭ-ṭifil imnil-kaaruuk.* **2.** *rifaɛ (a rafuɛ).* The good news lifted our spirits. *l-ʔaxbaar iz-zeena rifɛat maɛnawiyyaatna.* **3.** *rifaɛ (a rafuɛ) n-, šaal (i šeel) n-.* After two weeks the ban was lifted. *baɛad isbuuɛeen il-maniɛ inrifaɛ.* **4.** *zaal (u zawaal).* Toward noon the fog lifted. *zaal iẓ-ẓubaab zawaali ẓ-ẓuhur.*
**I won't lift a finger for him no matter what. *waḷḷa ma-asaaɛda loo kullši yṣiir.*
light - **1.** *ẓuwa* pl. *-aayaat, ʔaẓwiya.* The light is too glaring. *ẓ-ẓuwa kulliš ṣaaṭiɛ.* -- The lights of the town came on one by one. *ʔaẓwiyat il-madiina štiɛlat waazid baɛd il-laax.* -- Don't cross until the light changes to green. *la-tuɛbur gabuḷ-ma yitbaddal iẓ-ẓuwa ʔila ʔaxẓar.* **2.** *šixxaaṭa, naar.* Do you have a light? *ɛindak šixxaaṭa?* **3.** *ẓaawi, ẓuwi*.* It's staying light much longer. *d-dinya tibqa ẓaawya mudda ʔaṭwal.* **4.** *ʔabyaẓ, kaašif.* She has a light complexion. *loon wujihha ʔabyaẓ.* **5.** *faatiz, kaašif.* She prefers light colors. *tfaẓẓil il-ʔalwaan il-faatza.* -- I want a light blue hat. *ʔariid šafqa maawiyya faatiz.* **6.** *xafiif.* Why don't you take your light coat? *leeš ma-taaxuð paaltuwwak il-xafiif?* -- There was a light rain today. *ṣaarat maṭra xafiifa l-yoom.* -- I had a light breakfast today. *ryuugi čaan xafiif il-yoom.* --

**He's very light-fingered. ?iida ṭwiila.
**He's at last seen the light. w-?aaxiiran iktišaf il-ζaqiiqa.
to bring to light - ?aδhar (i ?iδhaar). The investigation brought many new facts to light. t-taζqiiq ?aδhar ζaqaa?iq ijdiida.
to come to light - δihar (a δuhuur). A number of problems came to light during our research. baεδ il-mašaakil δihrat ?aθnaa? baζiθna.
to light - šiεal (i šaεil) n-. Wait till I light the fire. ?intiδir ζatta ?ašεil in-naar. -- Light a match. ?išεil šixxaaṭa. 2. warraθ (i tawriiθ) t-, šiεal (i šaεil) n-. I want to light my pipe first. ?ariid awarriθ il-paayip maali ?awwal. -- Is your cigarette still lit? jigaartak baεadha mwarrθa? 3. δawwa (i taδwiya) t-. The hall was brightly lighted. l-qaaεa čaanat imδawwaaya zeen. -- The street is poorly lighted. š-šaariε taδwiita muu zeena.
to light up - limaε (a lamiε). The children's eyes lit up. εyuun il-?aṭfaal limεat.
lightbulb - gloob pl. -aat.
to lighten - 1. birag (i barig), wumaδ (a wamiiδ) It's thundering and lightening. da-tirεid w-tibrig. 2. xaffaf (i taxfiif), kišaf (i kašif). Add a little white paint to lighten the color. xalli šwayya booya beeδa ζatta txaffif il-loon. 3. xaffaf (i), nazzal (i tanziil). If you don't lighten the weight, the tires will blow out. ?iδa ma-txaffif il-wazin tara t-taayiraat itdugg.
lighthouse - fanaar pl. -aat, manaara pl. -aat.
lighting - ?iδaa?a, taδwiya. The lighting is bad here. l-?iδaa?a muu zeena hnaa.
lightning - 1. ṣaaεiqa pl. ṣawaaεiq. Lightning struck the church steeple. ṣ-ṣaaεiqa nizlat εala burj il-kaniisa. 2. barq. There's thunder and lightning. ?aku barq w-raεad.
like - 1. miθil. You're just like my sister. ?inti biδ-δabuṭ miθil ?uxti. -- He ran like mad. rikaδ miθl il-majnuun. -- There's nothing like traveling! ma-aku šii miθil is-safar! 2. miθil-ma. She's just like I pictured her. hiyya biδ-δabuṭ miθil-ma ṭṣawwaritha.
**That's more like it! haaδa ?aqrab ?ila! or hassa ?aζsan!
**That's just like him. haay daggaata. or haay εamaayla.
**Did you ever see the likes of it? šaayif šabiih ?ila? -- What's the weather like today? šloon ij-jaww il-yoom?
**Like father, like son. ?ibn il-wazz εawwaam.
**I don't feel like dancing. ma-εindi raġba lir-riguṣ.
**It looks like rain. tbayyin raζ-tumṭur.
like this, like that - 1. hiiči. It's not like that at all. muu hiiči ?abadan. -- Ordinarily, we do it like this. εaadatan hiiči nsawwiiha. 2. miθil haaδa. I want something like this. ?ariid šii miθil haaδa.
to like - 1. ζabb (i ζubb) n-. I don't like cats. ma-aζibb il-ibzaaziin. or **ma-tiεjibni l-ibzaaziin. -- He never liked to do it. ?abadan ma-ζabb ysawwiiha or **ma-yεijba ysawwiiha. -- Would you like another cup of coffee? tζibb finjaan gahwa laax? or **yεijbak finjaan gahwa laax? 2. šaaf (u). How do you like this town? š-itšuuf hal-madiina?
likelihood - ζtimaal pl. -aat. There is a great likelihood that he'll come. ?aku ζtimaal kabiir huwwa raζ-yiji.
in all likelihood - εala l-?arjaζ. In all likelihood he'll get the job. εala l-?arjaζ huwwa raζ-yaaxuδ iš-šaġla.
likely - muζtamal. That's more likely. haaδa muζtamal ?akθar.
lilac - leelaaqi*. She bought a lilac blouse. štirat ibluuz leelaaqi.
lily - zanbaqa pl. zanaabiq coll. zanbaq.
lily-of-the-valley - sawsana pl. -aat coll. sawsan.
limb - fariε pl. furuuε. He sawed off a limb from the tree. gaṣṣ fariε imniš-šajara.
lime - kilis. The soil doesn't contain enough lime. t-turba ma-biiha kilis kaafi.
limestone - ζajar il-kilis, ζajar jiiri.
limit - ζadd pl. ζuduud. There's a limit to everything. ?aku ζadd il-kullši. **I've reached the limit of my patience. nifaδ ṣabri.
**The speed limit is thirty-five miles an hour. s-surεa l-masmuuζa xamsa w-tlaaθiin miil bis-saaεa.
to limit - ζaddad (i taζdiid) t-, ζiṣar (u ζaṣir) n-. Please limit your talk to three minutes. min faδlak ζaddid kalaamak l-itlaθ daqaayiq.
limited - maζduud. Our time is limited. wakitna maζduud.
limp - 1. raaxi, raxi*. He has a limp handshake. ?iida raaxya min yṣaafuζ. 2. εaraj. He has a slight limp when he walks. bii šwayya εaraj min yimši. **His arm hung limp. ?iida haddilat.
to limp - εiraj (i εarij), gizal (i gazil). He limps noticeably. huwwa da-yiεrij ib-ṣuura mbayyna.
linden - zeezafuun.
line - 1. xaṭṭ pl. xuṭuuṭ. Draw a line between these two points. ?irsim xaṭṭ been han-nuquṭṭeen. -- There's heavy traffic on that line. ?aku zdiζaam εala hal-xaṭṭ. -- There's a new air lines company serving Baghdad. ?aku šarikat xuṭuuṭ jawwiyya jdiida tmurr ib-baġdaad. 2. ṣaff pl. ṣfuuf, xaṭṭ pl. xuṭuuṭ, sira pl. -aawaat. There's a long line of cars ahead of us. ?aku ṣaff iṭwiil imnis-sayyaaraat giddaanma. -- Keep in line! ?ibqa bis-sira! 3. saṭir pl. sṭuur. I still have a few lines to write. baεad-li čam saṭir laazim aktibha. 4. xaṭṭ pl. xuṭuuṭ, tajεiid pl. -aat, tajaaεiid. There are deep lines in his face. ?aku xuṭuuṭ εamiiqa b-wučča. 5. ṣanif pl. ?aṣnaaf, nooε pl. ?anwaaε. He handles three lines of shirts. huwwa ybiiε itlaθ ?aṣnaaf imniθ-θiyaab. 6. ζabil pl. ζbaal The wash is still hung out on the line. l-ihduum baεadha mašruura εal-ζabil.
**Boy, does he have a smooth line! ?amma εinda ṭariiqat balif εajiiba!
**It's along the line of what we discussed. titmaaša wiyya l-mawδuuε illi biζaθnaa.
**Drop me a line. ?iktib-li čam kalima. or εala l-?aqall iktib-li salaam.
**He was killed in the line of duty. nkital min čaan y?addi waajba.
**What line is he in? šinu šuġla?
**That's not in my line. haay muu sagiḷti. or haaδa muu xtiṣaaṣi.
to keep in line - δibaṭ (u δabuṭ) n-. I can't keep the soldiers in line any more. baεad ma-agdar aδbuṭ ij-jinuud.
to line - baṭṭan (i tabṭiin) t-. The jacket is lined with nylon. s-sitra mbaṭṭina b-naayloon.
to line up - ṣṭaff (a ṣṭfaaf). Have the boys line up in the hall. xalli l-wilid yiṣṭaffuun bil-qaaεa. -- People lined up all along the streets to watch the parade. n-naas iṣṭaffaw εala ṭuul iš-šawaariε ζatta yitfarrjuun εal-istiεraaδ.
linen - 1. kittaan. This tablecloth is made of linen. ġiṭa l-meez maṣnuuε min kittaan. 2. čaraačif. The linen is changed every week. č-čaraačif titbaddal kull isbuuε.
liner - baaxira pl. -aat. We took a liner to Europe. ?axaδna baaxira ?ila ?ooruppa.
to linger - biqa (i baqaa?). We'd better not linger around here. ?aζsan ma-nibqa hnaa.
linguist - luġawi pl. -iyyiin.
linguistic - luġawi*.
linguistics - l-luġawiyyaat.
lining - bṭaana pl. -aat. My coat needs a new lining. sitirti tiζtaaj ibṭaana jidiida.
link - ζalaqa pl. -aat. One link of my watch chain is broken. fadd ζalaqa min zanjiil saaεati maksuura.
to link - ribaṭ (u rabuṭ) n-. You have to link the two ends of the chain. laazim tirbuṭ iz-zanjiil imniṭ-ṭarafeen. -- How can you link me with the crime? šloon tirbuṭni bij-jariima?
lint - nifaaya. Lint from the fabrics collects under the furniture. nifaayt il-iqmaaš da-titjammaε jawwa l-?aθaaθ.
lion - ?asad pl. ?usuud, sabiε pl. sbaaε.
lion cub - šibil pl. ?ašbaal.
lioness - labwa pl. -aat.
lip - 1. šiffa pl. -aat, šifaayif, šfaaf. I bit my lip. εaδδeet šiffti. 2. jasaara. I don't want anymore lip from you! ma-ariid minnak jasaara baεad.
lipstick - ζamrat šafaayif.
liquid - saa?il pl. sawaa?il. He's only allowed to drink liquids. bass masmuuζ-la yišrab sawaa?il. -- Do you have liquid soap? εindak ṣaabuun saa?il?
to liquidate - ṣaffa (i taṣfiya) t-. The company had to be liquidated to pay off its debts. š-šarika tṣaffat ζatta tidfaε idyuunha.
**His political opponents had him liquidated. xuṣuuma s-siyaasiyyiin txaḷḷiṣaw minna.
liquor - mašruub pl. -aat. He doesn't touch liquor. ma-yišrab mašruub.
lira - leera pl. -aat.

lisp - *laθġa.* She speaks with a lisp. *hiyya tiζči b-laθġa.*
to lisp - *liθaġ (i laθiġ).* Her youngest son lisps when he talks. *ʔibinha ṣ-ṣiġayyir yilθiġ min yiζči.*
list - *qaaʔima* pl. *qawaaʔim.* His name is not on the list. *ʔisma muu bil-qaaʔima.*
to list - 1. *sajjal (i tasjiil) t-.* This item isn't listed. *haay il-faqara ma-msajjala.* 2. *maal (i meel).* The ship is listing to port. *s-safiina maayla εala jaanibha l-aysar.*
to **listen** - 1. *ʔaṣġa (ʔiṣġaaʔ), stimaε (stimaaε).* They listened intently. *ʔaṣġaw b-ihtimaam.* -- She'll listen to reason. *tiṣġi lil-ζači l-maεquul.* 2. *simaε (a samiε) n-.* Now listen! *ʔismaε!* -- Listen! Somebody's coming. *ʔismaε, waaζid da-yiji.*
to listen in - *tṣannaṭ (a taṣannuṭ)* Somebody must be listening in. *waaζid laazim ykuun da-yitṣannaṭ.*
to listen to - *simaε (a samiε) n-, stimaε (i stimaaε) l-.* I like to listen to classical music. *ʔaζibb asmaε moosiiqa klaasiikiyya.* -- Why didn't you listen to me? *leeš ma-smaεit kalaami?*
listener - *mustamiε* pl. *-iin.*
liter - *litir* pl. *-aat.* Olive oil is sold by the liter, sir. *zeet iz-zeetuun inbaaε bil-litraat ʔustaað.*
literal - *ζarfi*.* This is a literal translation. *haay tarjuma ζarfiyya.*
literally - *ζarfiyyan.* Please translate this literally. *ʔarjuuk, tarjumha ζarfiyyan.* -- They took the order literally. *ṭabbuqaw il-ʔamur ζarfiyyan.*
literature - 1. *ʔadab* pl. *ʔaadaab.* Have you read a great deal of Arabic literature? *qireet ihwaaya mnil-ʔadab il-εarabi.* 2. *muʔallafaat.* The ministry has sent out a lot of literature on the topic. *l-wizaara ʔaṣdirat ihwaaya muʔallafaat bil-mawḍuuε.*
litter - 1. *wuṣax, qaḍaara.* The alley is full of litter. *d-darbuuna malyaana wuṣax.* 2. *naqqaala* pl. *-aat, sadya* pl. *-aat.* They carried him out on a litter. *šaaloo bin-naqqaala.* 3. *dafεa* pl. *-aat.* The cat just had a litter of kittens. *l-bazzuuna hassa jaabat dafεa mnil-ibzaaziin l-iṣġaar.*
to litter - *waṣṣax (i tawṣiix) t-.* Don't litter the road with trash. *la-twaṣṣix iṭ-ṭariiq bil-izbaala.*
little - 1. *ṣġayyir* pl. *ṣġaar.* She has a little girl. *εidha bnayya ṣġayyra.* -- We need a little table in this room. *niζtaaj meez iṣġayyir ib-hal-gubba.* 2. *šwayya.* I have a little money. *εindi šwayya fluus.* -- I can speak a little French. *ʔagdar ʔaζči šwayya fransi.* 3. *qaliil, ðaʔiil.* It's of little importance. *ʔahammiyyatha qaliila.*
**He's little better than a thief. *huwwa tlatt irbaaε ζaraami.*
**That's of little value to me. *ma-ʔila qiima bin-nisba ʔili.*
in a little while - *baεd išwayya.* I'll come back in a little while. *raζ-arjaε baεd išwayya.*
little by little - *tadriijiyyan.* Little by little he calmed down. *hida tadriijiyyan.*
live: **I bought some live fish. *štireet simač baεda yilbuṭ.* **Careful, that's a live wire. *diir baalak, hal-waayir yintil.*
to live - 1. *εaaš (i εeeš).* He lived a happy life. *εaaš ζayaat saεiida.* -- Before the war I lived in France. *gabl il-ζarb εišit b-ifransa.* -- Live and learn! *εiiš w-šuuf!* -- The people on this island live on nothing but fish. *sukkaan haj-jaziira yεiišuun bass εas-simač.* -- I couldn't live on so little. *ma-agdar ʔaεiiš ib-hal-muqdaar.* 2. *sikan (u sukna, sakin), εaaš (i εees).* Does anyone live in this house? *ʔaku ʔaζζad yiskun ib-hal-beet?*
**He has barely enough to live on. *huwwa duub ykaffi εiišta.* or *huwwa bil-kaad ysidd εiišta.*
**He always worked hard and never really lived. *buqa ykidd ṭuul ζayaata laakin ma-thanna b-εiišta.*
**She won't live out the winter. *ma-raζ-iṭṭawwil ir-rabiiε.*
to live up to - *tmassak (a tamassuk) b-.* They didn't live up to the terms of the contract. *ma-tmassikaw b-šuruuṭ il-εaqid.*
**He didn't live up to my expectation. *ma-ṣaar miθil-ma twaqqaεit.*
live coal - *jamra* pl. *-aat* coll. *jamur.* There are still live coals in the brazier. *ʔaku baεad jamur bil-manqala.*
lively 1. *našiṭ.* He's a lively boy. *huwwa walad našiṭ.* 2. *šayyiq.* We had a lively conversation. *ṣaar beenaatna munaaqaša šayyiqa.*
**Step lively! *ζarrik nafsak!*
liver - *kabda* pl. *kabid.* Do you care for liver? *yεijbak il-kabid.*
livestock - *maašiya* pl. *mawaaši.* We can't get feed for our livestock. *ma-nigdar indabbur εalaf lil-maašiya maalatna.*
living - 1. *εiiša, maεiiša.* Living is awfully expensive here. *l-εiiša kulliš ġaalya hnaa.* -- Living conditions are very bad. *ḍuruuf il-maεiiša kulliš muu zeena.* -- He'll have to earn his own living. *laazim ydabbur maεiišta b-nafsa.* 2. *ζayy.* Arabic is a living language. *l-luġa l-εarabiyya luġa ζayya.* 3. *ṭibq il-ʔaṣil.* He's the living image of his father. *huwwa ṣuura ṭibq il-ʔaṣil min ʔabuu.* 4. *ṭayyib, εaayiš.* I don't know whether he's still living. *ma-adri ʔiða čaan baεda ṭayyib.* -- Is your grandmother still living? *jiddiitak baεadha εaayša?*
living room - *ġurfat (pl. ġuraf) gaεda.*
lizard - *breeεṣi* pl. *-iyya, ḍabb, ʔabu breeṣ.*
load - *ζimil* pl. *ʔaζmaal, ζmuulaat.* The load is too heavy for him. *l-ζimil kulliš iθgiil εalee.* -- I ordered a load of sand. *waṣṣeet εala ζimil ramul.* -- It took a load off my mind. *nzaaζ ζiml ičbiir εan čitfi.*
**He has loads of money. *εinda fluus bil-koom.*
to load - 1. *ζammal (i taζmiil) t-.* Load the cases on the truck. *ζammil iṣ-ṣanaadiig bil-loori.* -- The cargo is just being loaded. *l-biḍaaεa hassa da-titζammal.* 2. *ζašša (i taζšiya) t-, εabba (i tεibbi) t-.* He loaded the gun. *ζašša l-bunduqiyya.* 3. *rakkab (u tarkiib) t-.* Do you know how to load film in a camera? *tuεruf išloon itrakkub filim bil-kaamira?* 4. *kawwam (i takwiim) t-.* We're loaded with work. *š-šuġuḷ mkawwam εaleena.*
loaf - *ṣammuunat (pl. -aat) loof.* Please give me three loaves of bread. *baḷḷa nṭiini tlaθ ṣammuunaat xubuz loof.*
to loaf - *tkaasal (a takaasul).* He was loafing on the job. *čaan yitkaasal ib-šuġḷa.*
loafer - 1. *čata* pl. *-awaat.* He's a loafer. *huwwa čata.* 2. *ζiðaaʔ qabaġli.* Have you seen my other loafer? *šifit takk ζiðaaʔi l-qabaġli l-laax?*
loam - *ġaryan.*
loan - *sulfa* pl. *-aat* coll. *sulaf, qariḍ* pl. *quruuḍ.* I'd like to get a loan from the bank. *ʔariid ʔaaxuð sulfa mnil-bank.*
to loan - 1. *daayan (i mudaayana), dayyan (i ddiyyin).* She loaned him 250 fils. *daaynata miiteen w-xamsiin filis.* 2. *εaar (i ʔiεaara).* He loaned me an interesting book. *εaarni ktaab laṭiif.*
loan shark - *muraabi* pl. *-iin.*
lobby - *madxal* pl. *madaaxil.* I'll meet you in the lobby after the movie. *ʔasuufak bil-madxal baεd il-filim.*
local - 1. *maζalli*.* The local papers say nothing about the accident. *ṣ-ṣuζuf il-maζalliyya ma-tiðkur šii εan il-ζaadiθ.* -- He wasn't familiar with local conditions. *ma-čaan εinda maεrifa biḍ-ḍuruuf il-maζalliyya.* 2. *daaxili*.* How much is a local call? *šgadd itkallif il-mukaalama d-daaxiliyya?* 3. *mawḍiεi** A local anesthetic will do. *banj mawḍiεi yikfi.*
to **locate** - 1. *εayyan (i taεyiin) t- mawqiε-.* I couldn't locate him. *ma-gdarit ʔaεayyin mawqiεa.* 2. *ζaddad (i taζdiid) t- maζall-, εayyan (i taεyiin) t- maζall-.* I can't locate the trouble. *ma-agdar aζaddid maζall il-xalal.*
located - *waaqiε.* Where is your new store located? *ween waaqiε maxzanak l-ijdiid?*
location - *mawqiε* pl. *mawaaqiε.* The location of the hotel is ideal. *mawqiε il-findiq mumtaaz.*
lock - *quful* pl. *qfaal.* The lock needs oiling. *l-quful yiζtaaj tadhiin.*
to lock - 1. *qufal (u qaful) n-.* Don't forget to lock the door when you leave. *la-tinsa tuqful il-baab min tiṭlaε.* -- I'm locked out. *nqufal il-baab εalayya.* 2. *šakkal (i taškiil) t-.* The bumpers of the two cars were locked together. *daεεaamiyyaat is-sayyaarteen šakkilat ib-baεaḍha.*
to lock up - *ζibas (i ζabis) n-.* He was locked up. *huwwa čaan maζbuus.*
locker - *ṣanduug* pl. *ṣnaadiig.* I left my racquet in the locker. *tirakit ir-rikit maali biṣ-ṣanduug.*
lockjaw - *guzaaz.*
locksmith - *ʔabu qfaal.* Do you know of a good locksmith near here? *tuεruf ʔabu qfaal zeen qariib minnaa?*
locomotive - *makiinat (ph. makaayin) qiṭaar.*
locust - *jarraada* pl. -aat coll. *jarraad.*
lodge - 1. *kapra* pl. *-aat, kuux* pl. *kwaax.* We have a

hunting lodge in the north. *εidna kaprat ṣeed biš-šimaal.* 2. *maʒfal* pl. *maʒaafil.* Is there a Masonic lodge in Baghdaad? *ʔaku maʒfal maasooni b-baġdaad?.*
to lodge - 1. *ʒišag (i ʒašig) n-.* A piece of wood is lodged in the machine. *ʔaku wuṣlat xišab maʒšuuga bil-makiina.* 2. *qaddam (i taqdiim) t-.* He lodged a complaint with the police. *qaddam šakwa liš-šurṭa.*
log - *jiδiε* (pl. *jδuuε*) *šajara.* The people put a log across the road to stop traffic. *n-naas xallaw jiδiε iš-šajara biš-šaariε ʒatta ywaggfuun is-sayyaaraat.*
**He sat there like a bump on a log. *giεad ihnaak miθl iṣ-ṣanam* or *giεad ihnaak miθl il-ʔaṭraš biz-zaffa.*
**I slept like a log. *nimit miθil l-iʒjaara.* or *nimit miθl il-looʒ.* or *nimit miθil il-mayyit.*
logic - *manṭiq.* Your logic is faulty. *manṭiqak ġeer maεquul.*
logical - *manṭiqi*.*
logically - *manṭiqiyyan*
lone - *waʒiid.* He was the lone surviver. *čaan il-waʒiid ʔilli nijaʒ.*
lonely - *muuʒiš.* This place is quite lonely in winter. *hal-maʒall kulliš muuʒiš biš-šita.*
lonesome - *b-wiʒda.* She feels very lonesome. *tišεur ib-wiʒda.*
to be lonesome for - *šiεar (u šuεuur) ib-wiʒša ʔil-* I'm very lonesome for you. *ʔašεur ib-wiʒša ʔilak.*
long - 1. *ṭuwiil* pl. *ṭwaal.* We had to make a long detour. *δṭarreena nsawwi farra ṭwiila.* -- It's a long way to the top of the mountain. *ṭ-ṭariiq ṭuwiil ʔila qummat ij-jibal.* — He got there a long time after we did. *wuṣal baεad ma-jiʔna b-mudda ṭwiila.* 2. *hwaaya.* Did you stay long at the party? *buqeet ihwaaya bil-ʒafla?*
**The room is twenty feet long. *l-ġurfa ṭuulha εišriin qadam.*
**How long is it? *šgadd ṭuula?*
**The child cried all night long. *ṭ-ṭifil biča ṭuul il-leel.*
**How long will it take? *šjadd yiṭṭawwal?* or *šgadd taaxuδ wakit?*
**So long! *maεa s-salaama.*
**Everything will work out in the long run. *bil-mada l-baεiid il-ʔumuur raʒ-titʒassan.*
long ago - *min zamaan, min mudda ṭwiila.* I knew that long ago. *εirafitha min zamaan.*
as long as 1. *šgadd-ma.* You can keep it as long as you wish. *tigdar itxalliiha εindak išgadd-ma triid.* 2. *madaam, maadaam.* It doesn't bother me as long as the work gets done. *ma-yhimmni madaam iš-šuġuḷ da-yimši.* — As long as you're here, you might as well have dinner with us. *madaam inta hnaa, δall itεašša wiyyaana.*
to long - *štaaq (a štiyaaq), ʒann (i ʒaniin).* I'm longing to see my mother and father again. *mištaaq ašuuf ʔummi w-ʔabuuya marra lux.* --She's longing for a man. *tištaaq ir-rijjaal.* — He's longing for home. *da-yʒinn il-ʔahla.*
long-distance call - *muxaabara* (pl.-*aat*) *xaarijiyya.* Please, I'd like to make a long-distance call. *min faδlič, ʔariid asawwi muxaabara xaarijiyya.*
longer - 1. *ʔaṭwal.* This table is longer than that one. *hal-meez ʔaṭwal min δaaka.* 2. *ʔakθar, mudda ʔaṭwal.* He wanted to stay longer, but I was sleepy. *raad yibqa ʔakθar, bass ʔaani činit naεsaan.* 3. *ʔakθar, ʔazyad.* I can't stand it any longer. *ma-agdar atʒammalha ʔakθar.*
longshoreman - *εaamil* (pl. *εummaal*) *šaʒin.*
look - *naδra* pl. -*aat.* You can see with one look that the town is dirty. *b-naδra wiʒda tigdar tuεruf il-madiina waṣxa.*
**He gave her an angry look. *baawaε εaleeha b-zaεal.*
**Take a good look! *lak, baawiε zeen!*
to look - 1. *tfarraj (a tafarruj).* I enjoy looking at pictures. *ʔaʒibb ʔatfarraj εaṣ-ṣuwar.* 2. *baawaε (i mubaawaεa).* She looked at me when I came into the room. *baawεat εalayya min fitit lil-ġurfa.* — Don't look now but the president just came in. *la-tbaawiε, ir-raʔiis hassa dixal.* — She didn't so much as look at me. *ʒatta mbaawaεa ma-baawaεatni.* 3. *baawaε (i mubaawaεa), šaaf (u šoof).* Look, a falling star! *baawiε! ʔaku najma da-toogaε.* — May I look at Ahmad's file? *ʔagdar ašuuf malaffat aʒmad.* 4. *bayyan (i tabyiin).* You look well. *mbayyin εaleek ṣiʒʒtak zeena.* — It looks like rain. *tbayyin raʒ-tumṭur.*
to look after - *daar (i deera) baal~.* Do you have someone to look after the child? *εindak ʔaʒʒad ydiir baala εaṭ-ṭifil?* -- Looking after this kid is no picnic. *deert il-baal εala haj-jaahil muu šaqa.*
to look down on - *ʒtiqar (i ʒtiqaar).* You mustn't look down on people just because they're poor. *ma-laazim tiʒtiqir in-naas li-ʔanhum fuqaraaʔ.*
**She looks down her nose at everyone. *šaayfa nafisha* or *šaayla xašimha εan-naas.*
to look for - *dawwar (u tadwiir) εala.* We're looking for rooms. *da-ndawwur εala ġuraf.* -- He's always looking for trouble. *huwwa daaʔiman ydawwur εala mašaakil.*
to look forward to - 1. *ntiδar (i ntiδaar).* We're looking forward to our vacation impatiently. *da-nintiδir εuṭlatna yoom yoom.* — We're looking forward to the nineteenth of May when you're going to get married. *da-nintiδir yoom itsaaṭaεaš maayis illi raʒ-titzawwaj bii.* 2. *štaaq (a štiyaaq).* I'm looking forward to seeing you. *ʔaani muštaaq ašuufak.*
to look into - *biʒaθ (a baʒiθ) n-.* We'll have to look into the matter. *laazim nibʒaθ il-mawδuuε.*
to look on - 1. *baawaε (i mubaawaεa), tfarraj (a tafarruj).* I was just looking on. *činit bass da-abaawiε.* 2. *εtibar (u εtibaar).* They looked on her as a stranger. *εtibrooha ġariiba εanhum.*
to look out - 1. *daar (i deera) baal~.* Look out! *diir baalak!* 2. *ʔašraf (i ʔišraaf), ṭall (i ṭall)* The big window looks out on the garden. *š-šibbaak ič-čibiir yišrif εala l-ʒadiiqa.*
to look over - *šaaf (u šoof)* Will you look over these papers? *tismaʒ itšuuf hal-ʔawraaq?*
to look up - 1. *šaal (i šeel) raas~.* He didn't even look up when I called him. *ʒatta raasa ma-šaala min ṣiʒit-la.* 2. *niδar (u naδar) b-iʒtiraam.* She looks up to him. *tunδur-la b-iʒtiraam.* 3. *dawwar (u tadwiir) t- εala.* I have to look up this word in a dictionary. *laazim adawwur εala hal-kalima bil-qaamuus.* 4. *tʒassan (a taʒassun).* Things are beginning to look up. *l-ʔumuur bidat titʒassan.*
**Look me up some time, won't you? *zuurni fadd yoom.*
lookout - 1. *raqiib* pl. *ruqabaaʔ* A lookout was placed on every hill. *ʒaṭṭaw raqiib εala raas kull tall.* 2. *masʔuuliyya, šaġla.* It's your lookout now. *haay masʔuuliitak.*
to be on the lookout for - *xalla (i) εeen~ εala.* Be on the lookout for a black '59 Cadillac license number 354. *xalli εeenak εala sayyaara kaadiilaak sooda, moodeel tisεa w-xamsiin, raqam qiṭεatha tiaθ miyya w-ʔarbaεa w-xamsiin.*
looks - *maδhar* pl. *maδaahir.* To judge by his looks, he's a criminal. *min maδhara, ybayyin εalee mujrim.*
**From the looks of things it may take much longer than we thought. *εala-ma yiδhar, il-masʔala raʒ-taaxuδ ʔakθar min-ma δanneena.*
loom - *nool* pl. *nuwaal.*
loop - *ʒalaqa* pl. -*aat.* Run the rope through this loop. *fawwit il-ʒabil min hal-ʒalaqa.*
to loop - *laff (i laff).* He looped the rope over the post. *laff il-ʒabil εal-εamuud.*
loophole - *majaal* (pl. -*aat*) *lit-tamalluṣ.* Many loopholes have been left in this law. *ʔaku hwaaya majaalaat lil-tamalluṣ ib-hal-qaanuun.*
loose - 1. *raaxi.* The button is loose. *d-dugma raaxya.* 2. *mahduud, maʒluul.* Do you ever let the dog loose? *txalluun ič-čalib mahduud?* 3. *faasid.* She has loose morals. *ʔaxlaaqha faasda.*
**He must have a screw loose! *laazim ykuun mašxuuṭ* or *laazim εinda xeeṭ.*
**She has a loose tongue. *ma-tδumm iʒčaaya.*
to turn loose - *hadd (i hadd) n-.* Don't turn the dog loose! *la-thidd ič-čalib!*
to **loosen** - *raxxa (i tarxiya) t-.* Can you loosen this screw? *tigdar itraxxi hal-burġi?* -- I want to loosen my shoelaces. *ʔariid araxxi qiiṭaan qundarti.*
loot - *ġaniima, booga.* The thieves hid the loot in a tree. *l-ʒaraamiyya δammaw il-ġaniima biš-šajara.*
to loot - *nihab (i nahib) n-, silab (salib) n-.* The enemy looted the town. *l-εadu nihab il-madiina.*
lopsided - *εooja.* The picture's lopsided. *ṣ-ṣuura εooja.*
to **lose - 1.** *δayyaε (i taδyiiε) t-, fiqad (u faqid) n-.* I lost my pencil again. *δayyaεit qalami marra lux.* — I lost track of them after the war. *δayyaεit ʔaθarhum baεad il-ʒarb.* — I've lost all my strength, since I got sick. *δayyaεit kull quuti min itmarraδit.* — Don't lose your way! *la-tδayyiε ṭariiqak!* 2.

xisar (a xasaara) n-, fiqad (u faqid) n-. He lost his entire fortune during the war. *xisar kull θaruuta ʔaθnaaʔ il-ḥarb.* -- I'm afraid he'll lose the game. *xaayif ykuun yixṣar il-liʕba.* 3. *fiqad (u faqid) n-.* After a few steps he lost his balance. *čam xuṭwa w-fiqad tawaazna.* -- He lost his life in the fire. *fuqad ḥayaata bil-ḥariiq.* -- He loses his temper easily. *yifqud ʔaʕṣaaba bil-ʕajil.* -- They lost their son in the war. *fiqdaw ibinhum bil-ḥarb.* 4. *qaṣṣar (i taqṣiir), ʔaxxar (i taʔxiir).* My watch loses three minutes a day. *saaʕti tqaṣṣir itlaθ daqaayiq bil-yoom.* 5. *tilaf (i talif) n-.* My things were lost in the fire. *ġaraaḍi ntilfat bil-ḥariiq* or *ġaraaḍi raaḥat bil-ḥariiq.*

**I lost a part of what he said. *faatni baʕḍ illi gaala.*

**I'm losing my hair. *saʕri da-yoogaʕ.*

to lose face - *ṣaxxam (i taṣxiim) wijih˜, sawwad (i taswiid) wijih˜.* He lost face when he couldn't come through on his promise. *ṣaxxam wičča min ma-gidar yoofi b-waʕda.*

loser - *xasraan* pl. *-iin.* He was the loser. *huwwa čaan il-xasraan.*

**He's a real loser. *ḥaasibta waagfa.*

losing - *xaasir.* They are fighting a losing battle. *daaxiliin maʕraka xaasra.*

loss - 1. *xasaara* pl. *xasaaʔir.* They suffered heavy losses. *tkabbidaw xasaaʔir jasiima.* -- I sold the house at a loss. *biʕt il-beet ib-xasaara.* 2. *faqid, fuqdaan.* She is griefstricken at the loss of her husband. *hiyya ḥaziina ʕala faqid zawujha.*

**He's never at a loss for an excuse. *ma-yiṣʕab ʕalee ʕuδur.* or *ʕuδra b-raas ilsaana.*

**She's never at a loss for an answer. *ma-yiʕṣa ʕaleeha jawaab.*

**I'm at a loss to explain his absence. *ʕiṣa ʕalayya ʔaʕruf ġiyaaba.*

lost - *nafquud, ḍaayiʕ.* I'm going to run an ad about my lost watch. *raḥ-anšur ʔiʕlaan ʕan saaʕati l-mafquuda.*

to be lost - *ḍaaʕ (i ḍiyaaʕ).* My shirt was lost in the laundry. *θoobi ḍaaʕ ʕind il-mukawwi.* -- I hope nothing is lost in the moving. *ʔinšaaḷḷa ma-yḍiiʕ šii bit-taḥwiil.*

**Since his wife's death he's completely lost. *txarbaṭ min maatat zawujta.*

**He was lost in thought. *čaan ḍaarub daalġa.*

**I'm lost when it comes to mathematics. *yḍiiʕ ʕalayya l-iḥsaab min tiji yamm ir-riyaaḍiyyaat.*

lot - 1. *qaṭʕat* (pl. *quṭaʕ*) *ʔarḍ.* How big is your lot? *šgadd kubur quṭʕat il-ʔariḍ maaltak.* 2. *l-maktuub-l.* I don't envy his lot. *ma-aḥisda ʕal-maktuub-la.* 3. *dafʕa* pl. *-aat.* I'll send the books in three separate lots. *raḥ-adizz il-kutub ʕala tlaθ dafʕaat.* 4. *qurʕa.* Let's draw lots. *xalli nsawwi qurʕa.*

**He's a bad lot. *huwwa duuni,* or *huwwa muu xooš walad.*

a lot - *hwaaya, kθiir.* I ate a lot. *ʔakalit ihwaaya.* -- We like him a lot. *nḥibba hwaaya.* -- I still have a lot of work. *baʕad ʕindi hwaaya šuġuḷ.* -- She's a lot better than people think. *hiyya hwaaya ʔaḥsan min-ma n-naas yḍinnuun.*

lots of - *hwaaya, kθiir.* She has lots of money. *ʕidha hwaaya fluus.* -- We had lots of fun at the dance. *hwaaya twannasna bir-rigiṣ-*

loud - 1. *ʕaali.* She has a loud, unpleasant voice. *ʕidha ṣoot ʕaali muzʕij.* 2. *barraaq.* I don't like loud colors. *ma-aḥibb il-ʔalwaan il-barraaqa.*

loud-speaker - *sammaaʕa* pl. *-aat, mukabbir* (pl. *-aat*) *ṣoot.*

lounge - *ġurfat* (pl. *ġuraf*) *l-istiraaḥa.* We had coffee in the lounge. *šrabna gahwa b-ġurfat l-istiraaḥa.*

to lounge around - *tfattal (a tafattul).* I like to lounge around the house on holidays. *ʔaḥibb atfattal bil-beet bil-ʕuṭla.*

louse - *gamḷa* pl. *-aat* coll. *gamul.*

love - *ḥubb.* Love is blind. *l-ḥubb ʔaʕma.* -- He must be in love. *laazim ykunn waagiʕ bil-ḥubb.* or ***laazim da-yḥibb.*

**You can't get it for love or money. *ma-mumkin titḥaṣṣal mahma kaan.*

to love - *ḥabb (i ḥubb) n-.* He loves her very much. *huwwa yḥibbha hwaaya.* -- I love apples. *ʔaḥibb it-tiffaaḥ.* -- I love to dance. *ʔaḥibb arguṣ.*

**Would you like a cup of coffee? - I'd love one! *yʕijbak finjaan gahwa? ʔii, waḷḷa b-makaana!*

lovely - *badiiʕ, laṭiif.* They have a lovely home. *ʕidhum beet badiiʕ.*

loving - *muḥibb.* This is my loving wife. *haay zoojti l-muḥibba.*

low - 1. *naaṣi, waaṭi.* Do you want shoes with high or low heels? *triidiin ḥiδaaʔ čaʕab ʕaali loo naaṣi?.*-- That plane is flying too low. *haṭ-ṭayyaara da-ṭṭiir kulliš naaṣi.* 2. *waaṭi, ḍaʕiif, naazil.* He always gets low marks. *daaʔiman yḥaṣṣil ʕala darajaat waaṭya.* -- His pulse is low. *nabḍa waaṭi.* -- She spoke in a low voice. *tkallmat ib-ṣawṭ waaṭi.* -- You have very low blood pressure. *ḍaġṭak kulliš waaṭi.* 3. *maʕquuč.* I feel very low today. *ʔaani šwayya maʕquuč il-yoom.* 4. *waaḥid.* Put the car in low. *xalli s-sayyaara ʕal-waaḥid.* 5. *ḥaqaara, danaaʔa.* That was low of him. *caanat ḥaqaara minna.*

**He made a low bow. *nḥina hwaaya.*

**The sun is quite low already. *š-šamis taqriiban raḥ-itġiib.*

**I have a low opinion of him. *raʔyi muu zeen bii.*

**Our funds are getting low. *raṣiidna da-yinxufuḍ.*

lower - 1. *ʔanṣa, ʔawṭa.* This chair is lower than that one. *hal-kursi ʔanṣa mnil-laax.* 2. *jawwaani*.* Put it on the lower shelf. *ḥuṭṭha bir-raff ij-jawwaani.*

to lower - 1. *nazzal (i tanziil) t-.* Lower the lifeboats. *nazzil zawaariq in-najaat.* -- He lowered himself in their eyes. *nazzal nafsa b-ʕeenhum.* -- They will lower the price some day. *raḥ-ynizzluun is-siʕir fadd yoom.* 2. *naṣṣa (i tanṣiya) t-, waṭṭa (i tawṭiya) t-.* He lowered his voice when he saw her come in. *naṣṣa ṣooṭa min šaafha tidxul.*

loyal - 1. *muxliṣ* pl. *-iin.* He has always been loyal to the government. *daaʔiman čaan muxliṣ lil-ḥukuuma.* 2. *wafi* pl. *ʔawfiya, muxliṣ* pl. *-iin.* You couldn't have a more loyal friend. *ma-tilgi ṣadiiq ʔawfa minna.* -- I've always been a loyal friend, haven't I? *daaʔiman činit-lak ṣadiiq wafi, muu?*

loyalty - *ʔixlaaṣ.* Nobody questioned his loyalty to the government. *maḥḥad šakk ib-ʔixlaaṣa lil-ḥukuuma.* -- You can depend on his loyalty. *tigdar tiʕtimid ʕala ʔixlaaṣa.*

lubricant - *dihin tašḥiim*

to **lubricate** - *šaḥḥam (i tašḥiim) t-.* Please lubricate the car. *min faḍlak šaḥḥim is-sayyaara.*

lubrication - *tašḥiim*

luck - 1. *ḥaḍḍ.* My luck has changed. *ḥaḍḍi staʕdal.* 2. *tawfiiq, ḥaḍḍ.* I wish you all the luck in the world. *ʔatmannaa-lak kull it-tawfiiq.* -- Now you try your luck! *hassa ʔinta jarrub ḥaḍḍak.*

Good luck! *muwaffaq inšaaḷḷah!* or *ḥaḍḍ saʕiid.*

luckily - *min ḥusn il-ḥaḍḍ.* Luckily, he doesn't bite. *min ḥusn il-ḥaḍḍ ma-yʕaḍḍ.*

lucky 1. *saʕiid.* It was a lucky coincidence. *čaanat ṣidfa saʕiida.* 2. *maḥḍuuḍ.* You can consider yourself lucky. *tigdar tiʕtibur nafsak maḥḍuuḍ* -- You're a lucky fellow. *ʔinta waaḥid maḥḍuuḍ.*

luggage - *junaṭ.* We stowed our luggage on the back seat of the car. *xalleena junaṭna bil-maqʕad il-xalfi bis-sayyaara.*

lukewarm - 1. *daafi, faatir.* Take a lukewarm bath. *ʔuxuδ ḥammaam daafi.* 2. *ma-mihtamm.* He's very lukewarm about your plan. *huwwa ma-mihtamm il-mašruuʕak.*

lull - **We went out during the lull in the storm. *ṭlaʕna min xaffat il-ʕaaṣifa.*

to lull to sleep - *nawwam (i tanwiim) t-.* Her singing lulled the boy sleep. *ġinaaha nawwam iṭ-ṭifil.*

lullaby - *leeluwwa* pl. *-aat.*

lumber - *xišab.* How much lumber will be needed for the book shelves? *šgadd xišab tiḥtaaj l-irfuuf il-kutub.*

luminous - *fisfoori*.* Has your watch got a luminous dial? *saaʕtak biiha myaal fisfooriyya?*

lump - 1. *kutla* pl. *-aat.* What are you going to do with that lump of clay? *š-raḥ-itsawwi b-kutlat iṭ-ṭiin haay?* 2. *waram* pl. *wruum.* He has a big lump on his forehead. *ʔaku waram ib-guṣṣṭa.* 3. *qaalab* pl. *qwaalib, fuṣṣ* pl. *fṣuuṣ.* I take only one lump (of sugar) in my coffee. *ʔaani ʔaaxuδ qaalab waaḥid il-gahuuti.*

lump sugar - *qand.*

lumpy - 1. *mfaṣṣaṣ.* The sugar is lumpy. *š-šakar imfaṣṣaṣ.* 2. *mʕaggad.* This pillow is very lumpy. *hal-imxadda mʕaggida.*

lunar - *qamari*.* The Moslem holidays follow the lunar calendar. *l-ʕuṭal l-islaamiyya titbaʕ it-taqwiim il-qamari.*

lunatic - *mxabbaḷ* pl. *maxaabiiḷ, majnuun* pl. *majaaniin.* He's acting like a lunatic. *da-yitṣarraf miθl il-imxabbaḷ.*

lunch - *ġada* pl. *-aayaat.* It's time for lunch. *ṣaar wakt il-ġada.*
to lunch - *tġadda (a ġada).* Will you lunch with me? *titġadda wiyyaaya?*
lung - *riʔa* pl. *-aat.* His left lung is infected. *riʔata l-yiṣra muṣaaba.*
**The boy yelled at the top of his lungs. *l-walad ɛaaṭ ib-ɛilu ʐissa.*
to **lurk** - *xital (i xatil).* We found him lurking in an alley. *šifnaa xaatil bid-darbuuna.*
lute - *ɛuud* pl. *ɛawaad.* The lute is out of tune. *l-ɛuud ma-manṣuub.*
luxury - **1.** *taraf.* They lived in unbelievable luxury. *ɛaašaw b-taraf faðiiɛ.* **2.** *faxim.* They're building a luxury hotel. *da-yibnuun findiq faxim.*
luxuries - *kamaaliyyaat.* They're raising the tax on luxuries. *da-yʐayyduun iḍ-ḍariiba ɛal-kamaaliyyaat.*
lying - *kiðib, čiðib.* Lying won't get you anywhere. *l-kiðib ma-yfiidak.*
lyre - *qiiθaara* pl. *-aat.*

M

machine - *makiina* pl. *makaayin, ʔaala* pl. *-aat.* The machine is working again. *l-makiina gaamat tištuġuḷ marra lux.*
machine gun - *raššaaša, raššaas* pl. *-aat, maṭrillooz* pl. *-aat.*
machinery - *makaayin, ʔaalaat.*
mad - **1.** *majnuun* pl. *majaaniin, mxabbaḷ* pl. *mxaabiiḷ.* He is a little mad and unpredictable. *haaða šwayya majnuun w-ma-tigdar tuɛruf iš-yiṭlaɛ minna.* -- He drove like mad. *saaq miθl il-imxabbaḷ.* **2.** *mačluub.* He was bitten by a mad dog. *ɛaðða čalib mačluub.* **3.** *ʐaɛlaan, ġaðbaan.* What are you mad about? *ɛala weeš ʐaɛlaan?* or *š-imʐaɛɛlak?* or *ʔeeš biik ʐaɛlaan?*
to drive mad - *jannan (i tjinnin) t-, xabbaḷ (u txubbuḷ) t-.* The heat is driving me mad. *l-ʐarr raʐ-yjanninni.*
to be mad about - *txabbaḷ (a txubbuḷ) ɛala.* She's mad about him. *hiyya mitxabbḷa ɛalee.* -- My boy is mad about ice cream. *ʔibni yitxabbaḷ ɛad-doondirma.*
to be mad at - *ziɛal (a zaɛal) n- ɛala, min.* She's mad at me again. *ziɛlat ɛalayya marra lux,* or *hiyya hamm zaɛlaana ɛalayya.*
madam - *xaatuun* pl. *xwaatiin, sayyida* pl. *-aat.* Is somebody waiting on you, Madam? *xaatuun, ʔaʐʐad faðð šuġḷič?*
madman - *majnuun* pl. *majaaniin, mxabbaḷ* pl. *mxaabiiḷ.*
magazine - *majalla* pl. *-aat.* Where can I buy the magazine? *mneen ʔagdar ʔaštiri l-majalla?*
magnificent - *faaxir, nafiis, mumtaaz.*
to **magnify** - *kabbar (u takubbur) t-.* This lens magnifies six times. *hal-ɛadasa tkabbur sitt marraat.*
magnifying glass - *mukabbira* pl. *-aat.* You can only see it with a magnifying glass. *ma-tigdar itšuufha ʔilla b-mukabbira.*
maid - *xaddaama* pl. *-aat, xaadma* pl. *-aat.* We let our maid go. *baṭṭalna xaddaamatna.*
old maid - *ɛaanis* pl. *ɛawaanis, ɛizba* pl. *-aat.* She acts like an old maid. *titṣarraf ɛabaalak fadd waʐda ɛaanis.* -- **She died an old maid. *maatat ibnayya.*
mail - *bariid* pl. *burud, maktuub* pl. *makaatiib.* The mail is delivered at four o'clock. *l-bariid yitwaʐʐaɛ saaɛa ʔarbaɛa.* -- Is there any mail for me? *ʔaku makaatiib ʔili?*
mails - *bariid, muwaaṣalaat bariidiyya.* The storm held up the mails. *l-ɛaaṣifa ɛaṭṭilat il-muwaaṣalaat il-bariidiyya.*
to mail - *dazz(i)n- bil-bariid.* Did you mail the package? *ʔinta dazzeet ir-ruʐma bil-bariid?* -- Please mail the letter for me. *ʔarjuuk dizz-li l-maktuub bil-bariid.* or *ʔarjuuk ðibb-li l-maktuub bil-bariid.*
mailbox - *ṣanduug (pl. ṣanaadiig) bariid.*
mailman - *muwaʐʐiɛ (pl. -iin) bariid.*
main - **1.** *ʔabbi* pl. *-iyyaat.* The main has burst. *l-ʔabbi ṭagg.* **2.** *ʔasaasi*, raʔiisi*.* That's one of our main problems. *haðiič waʐda min mašaakilna l-ʔasaasiyya.* -- Did you inquire at the main office? *siʔalit bid-daaʔira r-raʔiisiyya?* -- You've forgotten the main thing. *nseet iš-šii l-ʔasaasi.*
in the main - *ɛala l-ɛumuum, bil-ɛumuum, ġaaliban.* The discussion revolved in the main around two questions. *l-munaaqaša daarat ɛala l-ɛumuum ʐawul masʔalteen.* -- I agree with him in the main. *ʔaani ġaaliban ʔattifiq wiyyaa.*
mainly - *ɛala l-ʔakθar.* He comes mainly on Tuesdays. *ɛala l-ʔakθar yiji ʔayyaam l-iθlaaθaa.*
to **maintain** - **1.** *ṣarr (i ʔiṣraar) n- ɛala.* He maintains that he was there. *huwwa yṣirr ɛala ʔinna čaan ihnaak.* **2.** *ʐtifað (u ʐtifaað) b-.* They have moved to Karrada, but they have decided to maintain their house in Fadhil. *ntiqlaw lil-karraada laakin qarriraw yiʐtafð ib-beethum il-ɛatiig bil-faðil.*
maintenance - *ṣiyaana.*
major - **1.** *raʔiis awwal* pl. *ruʔasaaʔ awwaliin.* Has anyone seen the major? *ʔaʐʐad šaaf ir-raʔiis il-ʔawwal?* **2.** *mawðuuɛ raʔiisi* pl. *mawaaðiiɛ raʔiisiyya.* What's your major? *šinu mawðuuɛak ir-raʔiisi?* **3.** *ʔakθar, ʔakbar, ʔaɛðam.* The major part of my income goes for rent. *l-qism il-ʔakbar min daxli yruuʐ lil-ʔiijaar.*
majority - *ʔakθariyya, ʔaġlabiyya.* The majority was against it. *l-ʔakθariyya ɛarrḍat il-mawðuuɛ.* -- The majority of the students were sick. *ʔaġlabiyyat it-talaamiiʐ čaanaw wajɛaaniin.*
make - *maarka* pl. *-aat, nooɛ* pl. *ʔanwaaɛ.* What make is your radio? *r-raadyo maalak yaa maarka?* or ***r-raadyo maalak šuġuḷ man?*
to make - **1.** *sawwa (i tsiwwi) t-, ɛimal (a ɛamal) n-.* He made a big mistake. *sawwa ġalṭa čbiira.* **2.** *ṣinaɛ (a ṣaniɛ) n-, ɛimal (a ɛamal) n-, sawwa (i tsiwwi) t-.* This factory makes bottles. *hal-maɛmal da-yiṣnaɛ ibṭaala.* **3.** *sawwa (i tsiwwi) t-.* They made him president. *sawwoo raʔiis.* -- How much do you make a week? *šgadd itsawwi bil-isbuuɛ?* -- You'll have to make a few changes. *laazim itsawwi šwayya tabdiilaat.* **4.** *xalla (i txilli) t-.* Onions make my eyes water. *l-buṣal yxalli ɛyuuni tidmaɛ.* **5.** *ṣaar (i ṣeera).* He'd really make a good king. *huwwa ʐaqiiqatan yṣiir xooš malik.* **6.** *laʐʐag (i tliʐʐig) b-.* Do you think we'll make the train? *tiɛtiqid raʐ-inlaʐʐig bil-qiṭaar?* **7.** *dabbar (u tadbiir, ddubbur).* How does he make his living? *šloon ydabbur ɛiišta?*
**He made a fool of himself in front of the people. *rtikab ʐamaaqa giddaam in-naas.*
to make a choice - *xtaar (a xtiyaar).* You have to make a choice. *laazim tixtaar.*
to make off with - *baag (u boog) n-.* They made off with our car. *baagaw sayyaaratna.*
to make out - **1.** *farzan (i tfirzin) t-.* Can you make out the date on the postmark? *tigdar itfarzin it-taariix ɛala ṭamgat il-bariid?* **2.** *mila (i mali) n-.* Have you made out the application blank? *mleet il-ɛariiða?* **3.** *sawwa (i tsiwwi).* How did you make out in the exam yesterday? *šloon sawweet bil-imtiʐaan il-baarʐa?*
to make time - *siraɛ (i ʔisraaɛ).* We can make time if we take the other road. *nigdar nisriɛ ʔiða ʔaxaðna ṭ-ṭariiq iθ-θaani.*
to make up - **1.** *sawwa (i tsiwwi) t-.* Make up a list of all the things you need. *sawwi qaaʔima b-kull il-ʔašyaaʔ illi tiʐtaajha.* **2.** *xilaq (i xaliq) n-.* He made up a story about his absence. *xilaq quṣṣa ɛan ġiyaaba.* **3.** *tṣaalaʐ (a taṣaaluʐ).* They've made up again. *tṣaalʐaw marra lux.* **4.** *ɛawwað (u taɛwiið, tɛuwwuð)* You can make up the hours you didn't work yesterday, today. *tigdar itɛawwuð is-saaɛaat illi ma-štaġlitha il-baarʐa, l-yoom.*
makeshift - *rtijaali*.* This is just a makeshift arrangement. *haaða fadd tartiib irtijaali.*
make-up - *ʐwaaga.* Shall I put a little more make-up on? *ʔaʐuṭṭ iʐwaaga šwayya ʔaʐyad?*
**She uses an awful lot of make-up. *titʐawwag akθar imnil-laaʐim.*
makings - *qaabliyya* pl. *-aat.* The boy has the makings of an actor. *l-walad ɛinda qaabliyya yṣiir*

mumaθθil.
male – *δakar* pl. *δkuur, faζal* pl. *fζuul.* Is that dog a male or female? *hač-čalib faζal loo niθya?*
male nurse – *muḍammid* pl. *-iin.*
malicious – *ζaquud, xabiiθ, masmuum.* That was a malicious remark. *haδiič čaanat fadd iζčaaya masmuuma.*
malt – *šiεiir imnaggaε.*
Malta – *maalṭa.*
man – **1.** *rijjaal* pl. *riyaajiil, rajul* pl. *rijaal, zlima* pl. *zilim.* Who's that man? *minu har-rijjaal?* -- He's not the man for it. *haaδa muu zlimatha.* or ***ma-yiṭlaε min ζaggha.* -- What does the man in the street say about it? *š-yguul εanha rajul is-šaariε?* -- Tell the men to unload the furniture from the truck. *gul lir-riyaajiil xalli yfarrġuun il-ʔaθaaθ min il-loori.* **2.** *ʔinsaan.* Man used to live in caves. *l-ʔinsaan čaan yεiiš bil-kuhuuf.*
**One officer and four men volunteered. *ḍaabuṭ waaζid w-ʔarbaε junuud iṭṭawwεaw.*
to **manage** – **1.** *daar (i dawaraan) n-.* Who manages the estate? *minu ydiir il-muqaaṭaεa?* -- He managed the store for six years. *daar il-maxzan sitt isniin.* **2.** *dabbar (u tadbiir, tdubbur) t-.* How did you manage to get the tickets? *šloon dabbarit il biṭaaqaat?* -- Can you manage on your salary? *tigdar itdabbur nafsak ib-raatbak?* or ***tigdar itεiiš εala maεaašak?* -- We have to manage very carefully on our small salary. *laazim indabbur umuurna zeen ζatta nεiiš εala raatibna l-qaliil.* **3.** *ḍubaṭ (u ḍabuṭ) n-.* I can't manage the children. *ma-agdar aḍbuṭ εala j-jihaal.* **4.** *dastar (i dastara) t-, rattab (i tartiib) t-.* Wasn't that cleverly managed? *ma-čaanat δiič imdastara b-mahaara?*
management – *ʔidaara* pl. *-aat.* Complain to the management! *štiki εind il-ʔidaara!*
manager – **1.** *mudiir* pl. *mudaraaʔ.* Where is the manager? *ween il-mudiir?* **2.** *mudabbir.* His wife is a good manager. *marta mudabbira tamaaman.*
mankind – *j-jins il-bašari, l-bašar, l-ʔinsaan.*
manner – *ṭariiqa* pl. *ṭuruq, ʔisluub* pl. *ʔasaaliib.* I liked the manner in which he went about the job. *εijbatni ṭariiqta biš-šuġuḷ.*
manners – *ʔadab, ʔaxlaaq.* She has no manners. *maa εidha ʔadab.*
to **manufacture** – *ṣinaε (a ṣunuε) n-, εimal (a εamal) n-.* What do they manufacture here? *š-yṣinεuun ihnaa?*
manufacturer – *ṣaaζib maṣnaε* pl. *ʔaṣζaab maṣaaniε, muntij* pl. *-iin.*
manure – *samaad* pl. *ʔasmida.*
many – *hwaaya, mitεaddid, εadiid, kiθiir.* I have many reasons. *εindi hwaaya ʔasbaab.* -- Many a person has been fooled by that. *hwaaya naas itqašmuraw bii.*
how many – *šgadd, čam.* How many tickets do you want? *šgadd itriid biṭaaqaat?*
map – *xariiṭa* pl. *xaraayiṭ.* I want a map of Asia. *ʔariid xariiṭa maal ʔaasya.* --Is it possible to get a road map of Iraq? *mumkin taζṣiil xariiṭa l-ṭuruq il-εiraaq?*
to map – *xaṭṭaṭ (i taxṭiiṭ) t-.* The mapping of this area will be finished in a week. *taxṭiiṭ hal-manṭiqa yixlaṣ baεd isbuuε.*
to map out – *εayyan (i taεyiin) t-.* Have you mapped out your route yet? *εayyanit ṭariiq safarak loo baεad?*
maple – *sfandiyaan.*
marble – **1.** *marmar, ruxaam.* The statue is made of marble. *t-timθaal imsawwa min marmar.* **2.** *duεbulla* pl. *-aat, daεaabil* coll. *duεbul.* I used to play marbles, too. *ʔaani hamm činit ʔalεab duεbul.*
March – *ʔaaδaar, maart.* I plan to stay here until March. *niiti ʔabqa hnaa ʔila ʔaaδaar.*
march – **1.** *mašya* pl. *-aat, masiir, masiira.* We still have a long march ahead of us. *baεad giddaamna mašya ṭwiila.* **2.** *maarš* pl. *-aat, moosiiqa masiir.* The band began with a march. *j-jawq bida b-maarš.*
to march – *miša (i miši) n-, ziζaf (a zaζif) n-.* Did you see the soldiers marching? *šift ij-jinuud da-yimšuun?*
mare – *faras* pl. *ʔafraas.*
margin – **1.** *haamiš* pl. *hwaamiš, ζaašya* pl. *ζawaaši.* Leave a wide margin on the left side. *ʔitruk haamiš εariiḍ bij-jiha l-yisra.* **2.** *ζadd* pl. *ζduud.* We're operating on a very small margin of profit. *da-ništuġuḷ εala ζadd ḍaʔiil imnir-ribiζ.* **3.** *ζtiyaaṭi.* I'm allowing a margin for incidental expenses. *ʔaani ζaaṭiṭ iζtiyaaṭi lin-naθriyyaat.* **4.** *fariq* pl. *fruuq.* We won by a narrow margin. *ġilabna b-fariq qaliil.*
mark – **1.** *εalaama* pl. *-aat.* Make a mark next to the names of those present. *ζuṭṭ εalaama yamm ʔasmaaʔ il-ʔašxaaṣ il-ζaaḍriin.* **2.** *daraja* pl. *-aat.* He always gets good marks in mathematics. *huwwa daaʔiman yaaxuδ darajaat zeena bil-ζisaab.* **3.** *ʔaθar* pl. *ʔaaθaar.* He left his mark in the world. *tirak-la ʔaθar bid-dinya.*
You hit the mark that time. *ʔinta ṣibt il-hadaf δiič il-marra.* or ***ζčaaytak čaanat εal-jariζ.*
**I don't feel quite up to the mark today. *ʔaani muu εala baεḍi hal-yoom.*
**Where did you get those black and blue marks? *mneen jattak hal-kadmaat wir-raḍḍaat?*
to mark – **1.** *ʔaššar (i taʔšiir) t-.* I've marked the important parts of the article. *ʔaššarit il-ʔaqsaam il-muhimma mnil-maqaala.* -- I marked the date red on the calendar. *ʔaššarit εal-yoom ib-qalam ʔaζmar bit-taqwiim.* **2.** *εallam (i taεliim) t-.* The road is well marked. *ṭ-ṭariiq zeen imεallam.* **3.** *ζaṭṭ (u) b-baal˜.* Mark my word. *ζuṭṭ iζčaayti b-baalak.* **4.** *ζaṭṭ (u) ʔism˜ εala.* Have you marked your laundry? *ζaṭṭeet ʔismak εala hduumak it-tinġisil?* **5.** *ṣallaζ (i taṣliiζ) t-.* When will you mark our examination papers? *šwakit iṭṣalliζ ʔawraaq l-imtiζaan maalatna?*
to mark down – **1.** *sajjal (i tasjiil) t-, qayyad (i taqyiid) t-.* I've marked down the things I want. *sajjalt il-ʔašyaaʔ il-ʔariidha.* -- Mark down my address. *qayyid εinwaani.* **2.** *raxxaṣ (i trixxiṣ) t-.* They have marked the coats down from 20 to 15 dinars. *raxxṣaw il-maεaaṭif min εišriin ʔila xmuṣṭaεaš diinaar.*
market – *suug* pl. *swaag.* Everything is cheaper at the market. *kullši ʔarxaṣ bis-suug.* -- A new market is being built here. *suug jidiid da-yinbini hnaa.* -- They bought it on the black market. *ištirooha bis-suuq is-sawdaaʔ.*
**There is no market here for cars. *s-sayyaaraat maa εaleeha raġba hnaa.*
to be in the market for – *dawwar (u tadwiir) εala, raad(i) yištiri.* Are you in the market for a good car? *da-triid tištiri sayyaara zeena?* -- She's still in the market (for a husband). *baεadha da-tdawwur εala rijjaal.* or ***baεadha da-tintiḍir xaṭiib.*
to market – *nazzal (i tanziil) t- lil-beeε, εiraḍ (i εariḍ) n- lil-beeε, baaε (i beeε) n-.* The farmers market their produce in town. *l-fallaaζiin ynazzluun mantuujaathum lil-beeε bil-wlaaya.*
to do **marketing** – *tsawwag (a miswaag).* She does her marketing in the morning. *hiyya titsawwag iṣ-ṣubuζ.*
marriage – *zawaaj.* She has a daughter from her first marriage. *εidha bnayya min zawaajha l-ʔawwal.* -- Before her marriage she worked in an office. *gabuḷ zawaajha čaanat tištuġuḷ ib-daaʔira.*
married – *mitzawwij* pl. *-iin.*
to **marry** – **1.** *zawwaj (i tazwiij) t-.* They married their daughter to her first cousin. *zawwjaw binithum l-ibin εammha.* **2.** *tzawwaj (tazawwuj).* Is she going to marry him? *raζ-titzawwaja?* -- Were you married in the courthouse or at home? *ʔinta tzawwajit bil-maζkama loo bil-beet?* **3.** *εiqad (i) zawaaj.* Who married you? *minu εiqad zawaajkum?*
marvelous – *badiiε, εaal, εajiib.*
marsh – *mustanqaε* pl. *-aat, hoor* pl. *ʔahwaar.*
marshal – *maaršaal* pl. *-iyya, mušiir* pl. *-iin.*
masculine – *muδakkar.* ''Window'' is a masculine noun while ''door'' is feminine. *š-šibbaač ʔisim muδakkar wil-baab ʔisim muʔannaθ.*
to **mash** – *hiras (i haris) n-.* I want to mash the potatoes. *ʔariid ahris il-puteeta.*
mass – **1.** *jumhuur* pl. *jamaahiir.* He has the masses with him. *εinda j-jamaahiir wiyyaa.* **2.** *kammiyya* pl. *-aat.* He's collected a mass of material about it. *jimaε kammiyya čibiira εan il-mawḍuuε.*
mass production – *ʔintaaj bij-jumla.* We're not geared to mass production. *ʔiζna ma-mithayyʔiin lil-ʔintaaj bij-jumla.*
master – *sayyid* pl. *saada.* No man can serve two masters. *ma-aku ʔaζζad yigdar yixdim saada θneen.* -- He is master of the situation. *huwwa sayyid il-mawqif.* or ***huwwa msayṭir εal-mawqif.*
to master – *ttiqan (i ttiqaan).* He mastered English in a relatively short time. *ttiqan il-ʔingiliizi b-mudda qaṣiira nisbiyyan.*

masterpiece - **1.** *fariida* pl. *faraa?id.* His poem is one of the masterpieces of Arabic literature. *qaşiidta min faraa?id il-?adab il-Ɛarabi.* **2.** *tuzfa* pl. *tuzaf.* The Iraqi Museum contains a number of masterpieces of Sumerian art. *l-matzaf il-Ɛiraaqi bii Ɛiddat tuzaf min il-fann il-soomari.*

match - **1.** *Ɛuudat šixxaaṭ, šixxaaṭa* pl. *šixxaaṭ.* Give me a box of matches, please. *rajaa?an inṭiini quuṭiyya maal šixxaaṭ.* **2.** *musaabaqa* pl. *-aat.* Who won the match? *minu ġilab il-musaabaqa?* **3.** *nidd.* He's a match for anybody. *huwwa nidd il-kull waazid.* -- I'm no match for him. *?aani muu nidd ?ila.* or ***?aani muu min wazna.* or ***maa Ɛindi qaabliita.*

to be a match - *traaham (a taraahum), twaalam (a tawaalum).* These colors aren't a good match. *hal-?alwaan ma-titraaham.*

to match - **1.** *ṭaabag (u muṭaabaga).* This rug matches the other one in size exactly. *haz-zuuliyya ṭṭaabug il-lux bil-kubur tamaaman.* **2.** *zaazam (i muzaazama).* No one can match our prices. *mazzad yigdar yzaazimna b-?asƐaarna.* **3.** *waašag (i muwaašaga) t-.* You'll never be able to match this color. *ma-raz-tigdar itwaašig hal-loon ?abadan.*

**I'll match you for the coffee. *xall-insawwi ṭurra kitba Ɛal-gahwa.*

material - **1.** *maadda* pl. *mawaadd.* We use only the best materials. *?izna bass nistaƐmil azsan il-mawaadd.* **2.** *maƐluumaat.* He's collecting material for a book. *huwwa da-yijmaƐ maƐluumaat il-fadd iktaab.* **3.** *qmaaš* pl. *?aqmiša.* Can you wash this material? *hal-iqmaaš yinġisil?* **4.** *maaddi** She's only interested in material things. *hiyya bass mihtamma bil-?ašyaa? il-maaddiyya.* **5.** *jawhari** There is no material difference between the two. *ma-aku xtilaaf jawhari been l-iθneen.*

matter - **1.** *qaḍiyya* pl. *qaḍaaya, mawḍuuƐ* pl. *mawaaḍiiƐ.* I'll look into the matter. *?aani raz-anḍur bil-qaḍiyya.* -- This is no laughing matter. *haay muu qaḍiyyat šaqa.* -- What's the matter? *šinu l-qaḍiyya?* **2.** *mas?ala* pl. *masaa?il.* It's a matter of life and death. *haay mas?alat zayaat w-moot.* -- It's not a matter of price. *muu mas?alat siƐir.*

**Something's the matter with his lungs. *ri?ta biiha šii.*

**What's the matter with you? *š-biik?*

**That doesn't matter. *ma-yxaalif* or *ma-yhimm.*

as a matter of course - *b-ṭabiiƐt il-zaal.* We did it as a matter of course. *sawweenaa b-ṭabiiƐt il-zaal.*

as a matter of fact - *bil-zaqiiqa, bil-waaqiƐ.* As a matter of fact I wasn't there. *bil-zaqiiqa ?aani ma-činit ihnaak.*

for that matter - *bin-nisba l-hal-mawḍuuƐ.* For that matter he can stay where he is. *bin-nisba l-hal-mawḍuuƐ yigdar yibqa b-muzalla.*

matter-of-fact - *waaqiƐi*, Ɛamali*.* He's a very matter-of-fact person. *huwwa fadd šaxiş kulliš waaqiƐi.*

no matter how - *šloon-ma.* No matter how we distribute them, there won't be enough for everyone. *šloon-ma nqassimhum, ma-raz-ykuun ?aku kaafi l-kull waazid.*

no matter how much - *šgadd-ma.* No matter how much you rush me, it won't get done any sooner. *šgadd-ma txalliini ?astaƐjil, ma-raz-tixlaş ib-saaƐ.*

no matter what - **1.** *loo š-ma, š-ma, loo kull-ma, ma-yxaalif.* We're going no matter what you say. *loo š-ma tguul ?inta, ?izna raz-inruuz.* **2.** *š-ma.* No matter what I do, it doesn't please him. *š-ma ?asawwi, ma-yƐijba.*

matters - **1.** *?umuur.* You're only making matters worse. *?inta bass da-tƐaqqid il-umuur.* **2.** *?ašyaa?* You take matters too seriously. *?inta taaxuḍ il-?ašyaa? ib-jidd ?akθar imnil-laazim.*

matting - **1.** (light) *zaşiir* pl. *ziṣraan.* We're going to cover the floor with matting for the summer. *raz-nufruš il-gaaƐ ib-ziṣraan Ɛaṣ-ṣeef.* **2.** (heavy) *baariyya* pl. *bwaari.* We need some matting to make a partition here. *yirraad-inna čam baariyya zatta nsawwi zaajiz ihnaa.*

mattress - *doošag* pl. *dwaašig.*

mature - *naaḍij.* The boy is very mature for his age. *l-walad kulliš naaḍij bin-nisba l-Ɛumra.*

maximum - *l-zadd il-?aƐla l-, ?aqṣa.* The maximum salary for this position is eighty dinars a month. *l-zadd il-?aƐla l-raatib hal-waḍiifa θmaaniin diinaar biš-šahar.* -- The maximum penalty for this crime is ten years in prison. *?aqṣa Ɛuquuba l-haj-jariima hiyya Ɛašr isniin zabis.*

**I'm willing to pay twenty dinars, but that's the maximum. *?aani mistiƐidd adfaƐ Ɛišriin diinaar, laakin haaḍa ?azyad šii.*

May - *maayis, ?ayyaar.*

may - **1.** *mumkin.* May I keep this pencil? *mumkin ?aztufuḍ ib-hal-qalam?* or ***tismaz-li ?aztufuḍ ib-hal-qalam.* -- May I have the next game? *mumkin ?alƐab il-liƐba j-jaaya?* -- May I meet with you at five o'clock? *mumkin ?aji ?awaajhak saaƐa xamsa?* -- **May I offer you a cup of coffee? *?agdar aqaddim-lak fadd finjaan gahwa?* **2.** *mumkin, yimkin, yjuuz.* That may be so. *yimkin hiiči.* -- I may be able to come. *?aani yimkin ?agdar aji.* **3.** *rubba-ma, muztamal, yimkin, mumkin.* I may have said it. *rubba-ma ?aani gilitha.*

**Be that as it may... *wa-loo haaḍa hiici...*

maybe - *yimkin, mumkin, muztamal, rubba-ma.* Maybe he's not at home. *yimkin muu bil-beet.*

meadow - *marƐa* pl. *maraaƐi, giṣiil.* I want to rent some meadow land for my horse. *?ariid a?ajjir qiṭƐat giṣiil l-iẓṣaani.*

meager - *qaliil, ḍa?iil, ṭafiif.* The results were meager. *n-nataa?ij čaanat qaliila.*

meal - *?akla* pl. *-aat, wajba* pl. *-aat.* Three meals a day aren't enough for him. *ma-tkaffii tlaθ ?aklaat bil-yoom.* -- I haven't eaten a decent meal in weeks. *ṣaar-li čam isbuuƐ ma-maakil wajba biiha xeer.*

mean - **1.** *xissa* pl. *xisas.* It was mean of him to treat you like that. *čaanat xissa minna yƐaamlak haš-šikil.* **2.** *xasiis, la?iim.* That's a mean trick. *haḍiič fadd ziila xasiisa.* **3.** *waḍiiƐ.* He says very mean things to me. *ygul-li ?ašyaa? kullis waḍiiƐa.* **4.** *muuḍi* pl. *-iyya, wakiiz* pl. *wukkaz.* Those mean boys in the street are teasing me. *hal-wulid il-muuḍiyya bid-darub da-yḍawwjuuni.* **5.** *šaris.* Our neighbors have a mean dog. *jiiraanna Ɛidhum čalib šaris.*

**He plays mean. *ybiiƐ naḍaala.*

to mean - **1.** *Ɛina (i maƐna) n-, qiṣad (u qaṣid) n-, nuwa (i niyya) n-.* What do you mean by that? *š-tiƐni b-haay?* -- You mean to say you saw everything? *yaƐni ?inta šifit kullši?* -- I didn't mean any harm. *?aani ma-qṣadit ?ay ?aḍiyya.* -- What do you mean to do? *š-tinwi tsawwi?* **2.** *hamm (i).* It means a lot to me to see him tonight. *yhimmni kulliš ?ašuufa hal-leela.* **3.** *čaan (ykuun) qaṣid-.* I meant to call, but I forgot. *čaan qaṣdi ?axaabur laakin niseet.*

**His friendship means a lot to me. *ṣadaaqta Ɛaziiza Ɛalayya.*

**That remark was meant for you. *hal-mulaazaḍaat ?inta nƐineet biiha.*

**Is the book meant for me? *l-maqṣuud ib-hal-iktaab ?an ?aaxḍa ?aani?* or *yaƐni haaḍa l-iktaab ?ili?*

meaning - *maƐna* pl. *maƐaani.* This word has several meanings. *hal-kilma ?ilha Ɛiddat maƐaani.* -- What's the meaning of this? *šinu maƐna haay?*

means - **1.** *wasiila* pl. *wasaa?il.* It was just a means to an end. *ma-čaanat ġeer wasiila l-fadd ġaaya.* -- He doesn't have the means to do it. *maa Ɛinda l-wasaa?il zatta ysawwiiha.* **2.** *qaabliyya* pl. *-aat.* He lives beyond his means. *yuṣruf ?akθar min qaabliita.*

**She married a man of means. *tzawwjat rijjaal ?aḷḷa mfaḍḍil Ɛalee.*

by all means - **1.** *min kull la-budd.* By all means take the job. *min kull la-budd, ?iqbal hal-waḍiifa.* **2.** *maƐluum.* Could I have the book now? By all means! *tismaz-li bil-iktaab hassa? maƐluum!*

by means of - *b-waasṭat.* -- You can regulate it by means of a screw. *tigdar itnaḍḍimha b-waasṭat burġi.*

by no means - *?abadan muu, muṭlaqan muu.* He's by no means stupid. *huwwa ?abadan muu ġabi.*

meanwhile - *b-hal-?aθnaa?, xilaal hal-fatra.*

measles - *zaṣba.*

measly - *mšazzaṭ.* He can't get along on his measly salary. *ma-yigdar ydabbur ?amra b-hal-maƐaaš il-imšazzaṭ.*

measure - **1.** *miqyaas* pl. *maqaayiis.* A table of

weights and measures. *jadwal bil-ʔawzaan wil-maqaayiis.* **2.** *qiyaas* pl. *-aat.* What is his waist measure? *šinu qiyaas xiṣra?* **3.** *čeela* pl. *-aat, keela* pl. *-aat.* How much is popcorn by the measure? *beeš čeelt iš-šaamiyya?* **4.** *ʔijraaʔ* pl. *-aat.* We'll have to take strong measures. *laazim nittixið ʔijraaʔaat ʒaazima.* **5.** *wazin* pl. *ʔawzaan.* This word is on the measure ''Faεlaan''. *hal-kalima εala wazin ''faεlaan''.*

to measure - 1. *qaas (i qiyaas) n-.* Measure the height of the window exactly. *qiis irtifaaε iš-šibbaač bið-ð̣abuṭ.* -- We'll have to measure the room before we buy the rug. *laazim inqiis il-ġurfa gabuḷ-ma ništiri s-sijjaada.* **2.** *čaal (i čeel) n-.* He measured out two measures of watermelon seeds and put them in a bag. *čaal čeelteen ʒabb raggi w-ʒaṭṭa b-čiis.*

measurement - *qiyaas* pl. *-aat.* Are these measurements correct? *hal-qiyaasaat ṣaʒiiʒa?* -- Did the tailor take your measurements? *l-xayyaaṭ ʔaxað qiyaasaatak?*

meat - *laʒam* pl. *luʒuum.* Do you have any meat today? *εindak laʒam hal-yoom?*

mechanic - *miikaaniiki* pl. *-iyyiin, fiitarči* pl. *-iyya.*

mechanical - *miikaaniiki**

medal - *wisaam* pl. *ʔawsima, madaalya* pl. *-aat.*

to **meddle -** *tdaxxal (a tadaxxul), tdaaxal (a tadaaxul).* He likes to meddle in other people's business. *huwwa yεijba yitdaxxal ib-šuʔuun in-naas.*

medical - *ṭibbi** I'm under medical treatment. *ʔaani taʒt il-εilaaj iṭ-ṭibbi.* or *ʔaani taʒt it-tadaawi.* -- Look it up in the medical dictionary. *ṭalliεha bil-qaamuus iṭ-ṭibbi.*

medicine - 1. *duwa* pl. *ʔadwiya.* This medicine tastes bitter. *had-duwa ṭaεma murr.* -- Have you taken your medicine yet? *ʔaxaðit id-duwa maalak loo baεad.* **2.** *ṭibb.* My daughter is studying medicine. *binti da-tidrus ṭibb.*

Mediterranean sea - *l-baʒr il-ʔabyað̣ il-mutawaṣṣiṭ, l-baʒr il-mutawaṣṣiṭ.*

medium - 1. *mitwaṣṣiṭ, muεtadil.* He's of medium height. *ṭuula mitwaṣṣiṭ.* **2.** *εan-nuṣṣ.* I like my steak medium-broiled. *ʔariid l-isteek maali mašwi εan-nuṣṣ.*

**It's hard to find a happy medium. *mniṣ-ṣaεub tilgi ʒall waṣaṭ.*

medium-sized - *mitwaṣṣiṭ.* It's a medium-sized task. *hiyya fadd šaġla mitwaṣṣṭa.*

to **meet - 1.** *jtimaε (i jtimaaε).* The committee is going to meet at Ahmad's house. *l-lujna raʒ-tijtimiε ib-beet ʔaʒmad.* **2.** *tlaaqa (i talaaqi), ltiqa (i ltiqaaʔ).* Let's meet at the coffee shop at six o'clock. *xal-nitlaaqa bil-qahwa saaεa sitta.* **3.** *waajah (i muwaajaha) t-, ṣaadaf (i muṣaadafa) t-, laaga (i mulaagaa) t-.* Did you meet him on the street? *waajahta biš-šaariε?.* **4.** *qaabal (i muqaabala) t-, tlagga (a talaggi), staqbal (i stiqbaal).* He met us with a smile. *qaabalna b-ibtisaama.* -- Will you please meet them at the train station? *baḷḷa ma-truuʒ titlaggaahum ib-muʒaṭṭat il-qiṭaar?* **5.** *tεarraf (a taεarruf) b-.* I met him at a party last night. *tεarrafit bii b-ʒafla l-baarʒa bil-leel.* -- I'm interested in meeting some artists. *yiεjibni ʔatεarraf εala baεð̣ il-fannaaniin.* **6.** *twaṣṣal (a).* The two ends of the wire don't meet. *nihaayteen it-teel ma-yitwaṣṣaluun.* **7.** *ttifaq (i ttifaaq).* We hope this pipe will meet with your specifications. *nitʔammal hal-buuriyyaat tittifiq wiyya mawaaṣafatkum.* **8.** *waffa (i tawfiya) b-.* They couldn't meet their obligations. *ma-gidraw ywaffuun b-iltizaamaathum.* **9.** *sadd (i sadd).* I can barely meet my expenses. *bil-kaad ʔagdar asidd maṣaariifi.* **10.** *ʒaqqaq (i taʒqiiq) t-.* My demands are easily met. *taʒqiiq ṭalabaati muu ṣaεub.*

**I'll be glad to meet you halfway. *maa εindi maaniε insawwi taswiya beenaatna.*

**Pleased to meet you. *ʔatšarraf.* or *tšarrafna.*

to meet with - *ʒiṣal (a ʒuṣuul) εala.* I think this will meet with your approval. *ʔaεtiqid haaða š-šii raʒ-yiʒṣal εala riðaaʔak.*

meeting - 1. *jtimaaε* pl. *-aat, jalsa* pl. *-aat.* There were five hundred people at the meeting. *čaan ʔaku xamis miit šaxiṣ bil-ijtimaaε.* -- The committee meeting lasted two hours. *jalsat il-lujna stamarrat saaεteen.* **2.** *muqaabala* pl. *-aat.* I arranged for a meeting of the two. *rattabit fadd muqaabala beenaathum.*

melody - *naġma* pl. *-aat, laʒan* pl. *ʔalʒaan.*

to **melt - 1.** *ðaab (u ðawabaan), maaε (u mawaεaan).* The ice is all melted. *θ-θalij kulla ðaab.* **2.** *mawwaε (i tamwiiε) t-.* Melt the butter. *mawwiε iz-zibid.*

member - *εuð̣u* pl. *ʔaεð̣aaʔ* Are you a member of this club? *ʔinta εuð̣u b-han-naadi?* -- We'll have to amputate the injured member. *laazim nigṭaε il-εuð̣u l-muṣaab.*

membership - *εuð̣wiyya* pl. *-aat.* Our membership is down to less than one hundred. *l-εuð̣wiyya εidna nizlat ʔila ʔaqall min miyya.*

memory - 1. *ðaakira.* My memory is not what it used to be. *ðaakirti muu miθil-ma čaanat.* **2.** *ðikra* pl. *-ayaat.* I have pleasant memories of this town. *εindi ðikrayaat ʒilwa b-hal-madiina.*

menace - *xaṭar* pl. *ʔaxṭaar.* He's a menace to society. *huwwa xaṭar εal-mujtamaε.* -- The menace of atomic war occupies everyone's mind. *xaṭar il-ʒarb ið-ðarriyya šaaġil baal kull in-naas.*

to **mend - 1.** *raaf (u rwaaf) n-, xayyaṭ (i xyaaṭ, txiyyiṭ) t-.* When will you mend my jacket? *yamta raʒ-itruuf sitirti?* **2.** *liʒam (a laʒim) n-.* Have the tinsmith mend the crack in this pan. *xalli t-tanakči yilʒam il-faṭir bij-jidir.* -- The broken bone will take some time to mend. *l-εað̣um il-maksuur yriid-la mudda ʒatta yilʒam.* **3.** *ʒassan (i taʒsiin) t-.* You'll have to mend your ways. *laazim itʒassin ʔaxlaaqak.* or **laazim tiεqal.*

to mention - *ðikar (u ðikir) n-.* He didn't mention the price. *ma-ðikar is-siεir.* or *ma-jaab ṭaari s-siεir.* -- I heard his name mentioned. *smaεit isma nðikar.* -- I would also like to mention... *hamm ʔaʒibb ʔaðkur ʔan...*

**Thank you very much. Don't mention it. *ʔaškurak jiddan. mamnuun.* or *l-εafu.*

**That's not worth mentioning. *ma-tistiʒiqq ið-ðikir.* or *haaða muu šii.*

menu - *qaaʔimat* (pl. *qawaaʔim*) *ʔakil.*

merchandise - *bið̣aaεa* pl. *bað̣aayiε, silεa* pl. *silaε.* The merchandise arrived in good order. *l-bið̣aaεa wuṣlat ib-ʒaala zeena.*

merchant - *taajir* pl. *tijjaar.*

merchant marine - *ʔisṭool tijaari.*

mercury - 1. (quicksilver) *zeebag.* **2.** (mercuric chloride) *sleemaani.* **3.** (planet) *εuṭaarid.*

mercy - *raʒma* pl. *-aat, raʔfa* pl. *-aat.* He pleaded for mercy. *ṭilab ir-raʒma.* -- He has no mercy. *maa εinda raʒma.*

mere - *bass, mujarrad.* The mere thought of it disturbs me. *mujarrad it-tafkiir biiha yizεijni.* -- She's a mere child; too young to get married. *hiyya mujarrad ṭifla, muu b-sinn iz-zawaaj.*

merely - *faqaṭ, laa ġeer.* I was merely joking. *čaan qaṣdi n-nukta, laa ġeer.*

merit - *qiima* pl. *qiyam.* There is little of merit in his book. *ʔaku qiima qaliila l-kitaaba.*

to merit - *staahal (i), staʒaqq (i stiʒqaaq), stawjab (i).* I think he merits a raise. *ʔaεtiqid yistaahil tarfiiε.*

merry - *mariʒ.*

mess - 1. *xarbaṭa* pl. *-aat, hoosa* pl. *-aat.* Did you see the mess the painters left? *šift il-xarbaṭa l-xallooha ṣ-ṣabbaaġiin waraahum.* -- I can't find anything in this mess. *ma-agdar ʔalgi ʔay šii b-hal-hoosa.* **2.** *wurṭa* pl. *wuraṭ.* You certainly got yourself into a nice mess! *laakin ʔinta ṣidug imwaggiε nafsak ib-fadd wurṭa mlabilba.* **3.** *qaaεat* (pl. *-aat*) *ṭaεaam.* I'm invited to dinner at the officer's mess. *ʔaani madεu lil-ʔakil ib-qaaεat ṭaεaam ið̣-ð̣ubbaaṭ.*

**The house is an awful mess. *l-beet waaguf ṭuul.* or *l-beet kulliš imxarbaṭ.*

to mess - 1. *štirak (i štiraak) bil-ʔakil.* You will mess with the officers during your tour of duty here. *raʒ-tištirik wiyya ð̣-ð̣ubbaat bil-ʔakil muddat iltiʒaaqak ihnaa.* **2.** *liεab (a liεib) n-.* Don't mess with the radio! *la-tilεab bir-raadyo!*

to mess up - 1. *waṣṣax (i twiṣṣix) t-.* Don't mess up the floor with your wet feet. *la-twaṣṣix il-gaaε ib-rijlak l-imballila.* **2.** *xarbaṭ (i xarbaṭa) t-.* Who messed up the papers on my desk? *minu xarbaṭ il-ʔawraaq εala meezi?*

message - *xabar* pl. *ʔaxbaar, risaala* pl. *rasaaʔil, maktuub* pl. *makaatiib.* Did anyone leave a message for me? *ʔaʒʒad tirak-li xabar?* -- Could you take a message for him? *ʔagdar aʒuṭṭ-la xabar εindak?* -- Did you give him the message? *ballaġta r-risaala?*

messenger - 1. *muwazziε* (pl. *-iin*) *barq.* The telegraph office employs ten messengers. *daa?irt il-barq tistaxdim ɛašir muwazziɛiin.* 2. *farraaš* pl. *-iin, faraariiš.* The messenger from the Director's office wants to speak to you. *farraaš il-mudiir yriid ykallmak.* 3. *ṭaariš* pl. *ṭawaariiš.* A messenger came from the village to invite us to the wedding. *jaana ṭaariš imnil-qarya zatta yiɛzimna ɛal-ɛiris.*

metal - *maɛdan* pl. *maɛaadin.*

method - *ṭariiqa* pl. *ṭuruq, ?isluub* pl. *?asaaliib.* He's discovered a new method. *ktišaf ṭariiqa jidiida.*

middle - 1. *nuṣṣ* pl. *nṣaaṣ.* I'm leaving the middle of next week. *?aani raayiz ib-nuṣṣ il-?isbuuɛ ij-jaay.* 2. *mitwaṣṣiṭ.* He's a man of middle height. *huwwa fadd rijjaal mitwaṣṣiṭ iṭ-ṭuul.* 3. *waṣaṭ, nuṣṣ.* He was standing in the middle of the room. *čaan waaquf ib-waṣaṭ il-ġurfa.* -- The man fell in the middle of the street. *r-rijjal wugaɛ ib-nuṣṣ iš-šaariɛ.* 4. *waṣṭaani*.* Open the middle window. *fukk iš-šibbaač il-waṣṭaani.* 5. *?aθnaa?.* He got up in the middle of the session and walked out. *gaam ib-?aθnaa? ij-jalsa w-ṭilaɛ barra.*

**I'm in the middle of packing. *?aani maxbuuṣ da-alimm ġaraaði.*

**He's in his middle forties. *ɛumra been il-?arbaɛiin wil-xamsiin.*

middle-aged - *mutwaṣṣiṭ bil-ɛumur.* She's a middle-aged woman. *hiyya fadd wazda mutwaṣṣṭa bil-ɛumur.*

Middle Ages - *l-quruun il-wusṭa.*

Middle East - *š-šarz il-?awsaṭ.*

midnight - *nuṣṣ il-leel.* It was past midnight when we fell asleep. *čaanat baɛad nuṣṣ il-leel lumman iġfeena.*

might - 1. *quwwa.* Might makes right, as they say. *l-zaqq lil-quwwa, miθil-ma yguuluun.* 2. *ɛaðama* pl. *-aat.* The might of the Babylonian kings will never be forgotten. *ɛaðamat il-miluuk il-baabiliyyiin ?abadan ma-tinnisi.*

mighty - 1. *ɛaðiim, haa?il.* He got together a mighty force and stormed the city. *jimaɛ quwwa ɛaðiima w-inqaðð ɛal-madiina.* 2. *qawi*, šadiid.* A mighty wind destroyed their crops. *fadd riiz qawwiyya dammirat zaaṣlaathum.* 3. *kulliš.* He's done mighty little work today. *huwwa ṭallaɛ kulliš šwayya šuġuḷ hal-yoom.*

mild - 1. *muɛtadil.* This is a mild climate. *haaða jaww muɛtadil.* 2. *laṭiif.* The sun is mild today. *š-šamis laṭiifa l-yoom.* 3. *baarid.* Do you have a mild tobacco. *ɛindak titin baarid.* 4. *ðaɛiif, xafiif.* He suffered a mild heart attack last winter. *ṣaarat ɛinda nawba qalbiyya ðaɛiifa š-šita l-faat.*

mile - *miil* pl. *?amyaal.* It's three miles from here. *hiyya b-biɛid itlaθ amyaal minnaa.*

military - *ɛaskari*.* They have military discipline. *ɛidhum ðabuṭ ɛaskari.*

milk - *zaliib.* The milk has turned sour. *l-zaliib zammað.*

**There's no use crying over spilt milk. *l-faat maat.*

to milk - *zilab (i zalib) n-.* Do you know how to milk a cow? *tuɛruf išloon tizlib baqara?* -- They tried to milk him of his money. *zaawlaw yziłbuun kull ifluusa minna.*

mill - 1. *ṭaazuuna* pl. *ṭawaaziin, maɛmal* pl. *maɛaamil.* When are you going to take the grain to the mill? *šwakit raz-taaxuð il-zubuub liṭ-ṭaazuuna?* 2. *maɛmal* pl. *maɛaamil.* We ordered the paper straight from the mill. *ṭlabna l-waraq ra?san imnil-maɛmal.*

miller - *ṭazzaan* pl. *-iin.*

million - *milyoon* pl. *malaayiin.* New York has seven and half million inhabitants. *nyuuyoork biiha sabiɛ malaayiin w-nuṣṣ imnis-sukkaan.* -- I've got a million things to do before dinner. *laazim asawwi milyoon šii gabḷ il-ɛaša.*

mind - 1. *fikir* pl. *?afkaar.* He had a very keen mind. *čaan ɛinda fikir kulliš zaadd.* -- He doesn't know his own mind. *ma-yistiqirr ɛala fikir.* -- I have something else in mind. *ɛindi ġeer šii b-fikri.* 2. *baal.* Keep your mind on your work. *diir baalak ɛala šuġlak.* or *?izšir fikrik ib-šuġlak.* -- What's on your mind? *šaku ɛala baalak?* or ***š-da-tfakkir?* 3. *ðihin* pl. *?aðhaan.* The thought went through my mind that I had seen him before. *l-fikra marrat ib-ðihni ?aani šifta gabuḷ.* 4. *ɛaqliyya* pl. *-aat.* He has a good mind. *ɛaqliita zeena.* 5. *ra?i* pl. *?aaraa?.* To my mind she's the right person for the job. *b-ra?yi ?aani hiyya š-šaxiṣ il-mulaa?im liš-šaġla.*

**You can't be in your right mind. *haaða zači maal waazid ɛaaqil?* or *?inta xarfaan?*

**My mind is not clear on what happened. *ma-?aɛruf biš-šabuṭ iš-ṣaar.*

**I have a good mind to tell him so. *ɛaqli yigṭaɛ agul-la.*

to call to mind - *ðakkar (i taðkiir, tðikkir) t- b-.* That calls to mind a story I know. *haay tðakkir ib-fadd quṣṣa ?aɛrufha.*

to make up one's mind - *staqarr (i stiqraar) ɛala qaraar.* We'll have to make up our minds shortly. *laazim nistaqirr ɛala qaraar baɛad fatra qaṣiira.*

to set one's mind on - *ṣammam (i taṣmiim).* She has her mind set on going shopping today. *hiyya ṣammimat itruuz titsawwag il-yoom.*

to mind - *daar (i dayaraan) baal~.* Don't mind what he says. *la-tdiir baalak l-ill-yguula.* -- Who's going to mind the baby? *minu raz-ydiir baala ɛaj-jaahil?* -- My son doesn't mind me anymore. *?ibni baɛad ma-ydiir-li baal.* -- Mind your own business. *diir baalak ɛala šuġlak.* or ***ma-ɛaleek min šuġuḷ ġeerak.*

**I hope you don't mind me leaving now. *?aani ?at?ammal maa ɛindak maaniɛ ?iða ?aruuz hassa.*

**I don't mind going alone. *maa ɛindi maaniɛ ?aruuz wazdi.*

**I don't mind the hot weather anymore. *tɛallamit ɛaj-jaww il-zaarr.*

mine - 1. *manjam* pl. *manaajim.* Who owns this mine? *minu yimlik hal-manjam?* 2. *luġum* pl. *?alġaam.* Their ship ran into a mine. *baaxirathum iṣṭidmat ib-luġum.*

to mine - 1. *ṭallaɛ (i taṭliiɛ) t-.* How much coal did they mine in May? *šgadd fazam ṭallɛaw imnil-manjam xilaal maayis?* 2. *liġam (u laġum) n-.* The roads are mined. *ṭ-ṭuruq malġuuma.*

miner - *ɛaamil (pl. ɛummaal) manjam.* The miners live near the mine. *ɛummaal il-manjam ysiknuun yamma.*

mine sweeper - *kaasizat* (pl. *-aat*) *?alġaam.*

minimum - *?aqall, zadd ?adna.* What's the minimum? *šinu ?aqall šii.* -- The minimum wage is three dinars a week. *?aqall ?ujra θlaθ dinaaniir bil-?isbuuɛ.*

minister - 1. *qass* pl. *qasasa.* Our church has a new minister. *kaniisatna biiha qass jidiid.* 2. *waziir* pl. *wuzaraa?.* Three ministers have resigned. *tlaθ wuzaraa? istaqaalaw.* -- He was appointed minister to Portugal. *tɛayyan waziir mufawwað bil-purtaġaal.*

minor - 1. *baṣiiṭ, ṭafiif, taafih.* I made only minor changes. *bass sawweet tabdiilaat baṣiiṭa.* -- That's a minor matter. *haaða fadd šii taafih.* 2. *qaaṣir* pl. *-iin, quṣṣaar.* As long as the boy is a minor, his uncle will be his guardian. *madaam il-walad qaaṣir, ɛamma raz-yibqa waṣi ɛalee.*

minority - *?aqalliyya.* We were in the miniority. *činna mnil-?aqalliyya.*

minute - *daqiiq, ṣġayyir.* It was so minute it could hardly be seen. *hal-gadd-ma ṣġayyra bil-kaad tinšaaf.* -- I have checked the most minute detail. *raajaɛit zatta ?adaqq it-tafaaṣiil.*

minute - 1. *daqiiqa* pl. *daqaayiq.* I'll be back in five minutes. *raz-arjaɛ xilaal xamis daqaayiq.* -- I'll drop in for a minute. *raz-amurr fadd daqiiqa.* 2. *lazða* pl. *-aat.* Just a minute, please. *fadd lazða, min faðlak.*

**I'll call you the minute I know. *raz-axaabrak ?awwal-ma yṣiir ɛindi xabar.*

minutes - *mazðar* pl. *mazaaðir.* The secretary will read the minutes of the last meeting. *s-sikirteer raz-yiqra mazðar ij-jalsa s-saabiqa.*

miracle - *muɛjiza* pl. *-aat.*

mirror - *mraaya* pl. *-aat.* Look at yourself in the mirror. *šuuf nafsak bil-imraaya.*

miscarriage - *?ijhaað, ṭariz.* She had a miscarriage. *ṣaar ɛidha ?ijhaað.* or ***hiyya ṭirzat.*

mischief - *?aðiyya* pl. *-aat.* That boy is always up to some mischief. *hal-walad daa?iman wara l-?aðiyya.*

miser - *šaziiz* pl. *-iin, baxiil* pl. *buxalaa?.*

miserable - 1. *taɛiis* pl. *tuɛasaa?, baa?is* pl. *bu?asaa?, miskiin* pl. *masaakiin.* I feel miserable today. *?ašɛur taɛiis hal-yoom.* or ***talfaan hal-yoom.* or ***nafsi maqbuuða.* -- She makes life miserable for him. *da-tsawwi zayaata taɛiisa.* or ***da-tnaqqiṣ ɛiišta.* or ***da-tmarmur zayaata.* 2. *mhalhal.* They live in a miserable shack. *ysiknuun ib-fadd kuux imhalhal.* or ***saakniin ib-beet miθl il-xaraaba.* 3. *kasiif.* What miserable weather! *šloon jaww kasiif!*

misery - *taɛaasa, šaqaa?, bu?s, ðanak.* They lived in utter misery. *ɛaašaw ib-taɛaasa.*

misfortune - *muṣiiba* pl. *maṣaayib, nakba.* It won't be a great misfortune if you don't get it. *yaʕni ma-raz-iṭṣiir fadd muṣiiba ʔiδa ma-tiğdar itzaṣṣla.*
to **misjudge** - *xitaʔ (i xataʔ) n- bil-zukum.* We mustn't misjudge the seriousness of the situation. *ma-laazim nixtiʔ bil-zukum ʕala xuṭuurat il-zaala.*-- You misjudge him. *ʔinta xitaʔit bil-zukum ʕalee.*
to **mislead** - *xidaʕ (a xudaaʕ) n-.* This advertisement misleads the reader. *hal-ʔiʕlaan yixdaʕ il-qaariʔ.*
misleading - *xaddaaʕ.* The description is misleading. *l-wuṣuf xaddaaʕ.*
misprint - *ğalaṭ maṭbaʕi* pl. *ʔağlaaṭ maṭbaʕiyya, ğalṭa* (pl. *-aat*) *maṭbaʕiyya.*
miss - 1. *ʔaanisa* pl. *-aat.* How do you do, Miss Suad? *šloon keefič, ʔaanisa suʕaad?* 2. *xaṭya* pl. *-aat.* You have two hits and three misses. *ʕindak ʔiṣaabteen w-itlaθ xaṭyaat.*
**A miss is as good as a mile. *l-ğalṭa ğalṭa w-law ib-ğadd iš-šaʕra.*
to miss - 1. *xiṭa (i xaṭi) n-.* You missed the target. *xiṭeet il-hadaf.* -- Our house is so easy to find you can't miss it. *beetna yinliği b-suhuula, ma-tiğdar taxṭii.* -- He missed hitting me by a hair. *ḍarubta xiṭatni b-šaʕra.* 2. *tfaawat (a tafaawut) wiyya.* I missed him at the station. *tfaawatit wiyyaa bil-mazaṭṭa.* 3. *stawzaš (i stiwzaaš) l-* I'll miss you terribly. *raz-astawziš-lak kulliš ihwaaya.* or **makaanak raz-ybayyin.*
**Don't miss this picture. *la-tfuutak hal-filim.*
**Do you think I'll miss my train? *tiʕtiqid raz-yfuutni l-qiṭaarʔ.*
**You haven't missed a thing. *ma-faatak fadd šii muhimm.*
**You missed the point of my story. *faatak mağza zčaayti.*
missing - *ḍaayiʕ.* The child has been missing for three days. *ṭ-ṭifil ṣaar-la tlaθt iyyaam ḍaayiʕ.*
mist - *ḍubaab xafiif.*
mistake - 1. *ğalaṭ* pl. *ʔağlaaṭ, ğalṭa* pl. *-aat.* How did you make such a mistake? *šloon ğalaṭit hiiči ğalṭa.* -- Sorry, I took it by mistake. *ʔaasif ʔaxaδitha bil-ğalaṭ.* -- There must be some mistake. *laazim ʔaku fadd šii ğalaṭ.* 2. *ṣuuč.* Sorry, my mistake. *mitʔassif, ṣuuči.* or *ʔaasif, haay ğaliṭṭi.*
to make a mistake - *štibah (i štibaah).* Make no mistake, this is a serious matter. *la-tištibih, il-mawḍuuʕ jiddi.*
to mistake - 1. *fiham (a fahim) ğalaṭ, ʔasaaʔ (i ʔisaaʔa) fihim-.* I mistook his intention. *fihamit niita ğalaṭ.* -- Please don't mistake me. *ʔarjuuk la-tsiiʔ fihmi.* 2. *štibah (i štibaah) b-* Sorry, I mistook you for someone else. *ʔaasif, ištibahit biik ib-šaxiṣ ʔaaxar.*
mistaken - 1. *ğalṭaan, xaaṭiʔ.* That's a mistaken belief. *haaδa ʕtiqaad ğalṭaan.* -- There you're mistaken. *ʔinta ğalṭaan ib-hiiči.* 2. *xaṭaʔ b-* It was a case of mistaken identity. *čaanat qaḍiyyat xaṭaʔ bit-tašriif.*
to **mistreat** - *ʔasaaʔ (i ʔisaaʔa) n- muʕaamala-.* The servant mistreated the children. *l-xaadim ʔasaaʔ muʕaamalat ij-jihhaal.*
mistress - 1. *ṣaaziba* pl. *-aat, sayyida* pl. *-aat.* The dog didn't recognize his mistress. *č-čalib ma-ʕiraf ṣaazibta.* 2. *ʕašiiqa* pl. *-aat, rfiija* pl. *-aat.* She's his mistress. *hiyya rfiijta.*
to **mix** - 1. *xubaṭ (u xabuṭ) n-.* I mixed yellow and red. *xbaṭit ʔaṣfar w-azmar.* -- Mix the paint well before you use it. *ʔuxbuṭ iṣ-ṣubuğ zeen gabuḷ-ma tistaʕmila.* 2. *traaham (a taraahum).* Pickles and milk don't mix. *ṭ-ṭurši wil-zaliib ma-yitraahmuun.* 3. *txaalaṭ (a taxaaluṭ), xtilaṭ (i xtilaaṭ).* We don't mix much with our neighbors. *ʔizna ma-nitxaalaṭ ihwaaya wiyya jwaariinna.* 4. *daxxal (ı tadxiil, tdixxil) nafis~.* She likes to mix in other people's business. *hiyya yiʕjibha tdaxxil nafisha b-šuğuḷ in-naas.*
to mix in - *tdaaxal (a tadaaxul), tdaxxal (a tadaxxul).* Don't mix in, this is none of your business. *la-titdaaxal, haaδa muu šuğlak.* --
to mix up - 1. *xarbaṭ (u xarbaṭa, txurbuṭ) t-.* Don't mix up the cards. *la-txarbuṭ il-biṭaaqaat.* 2. *šawwaš (i tašwiiš)t-, ʔarbak (i ʔirbaak) n-.* Don't mix me up. *la-tšawwišni.* 3. *daxxal (i tadxiil tdixxil) t-.* Don't mix me up in your argument. *la-tdaxxilni b-jadalkum.*
mixed up - 1. *hoosa* pl. *-aat.* Your work is all mixed up. *šuğlak hoosa.* 2. *mitxarbuṭ, mirtibik.* I'm so mixed up I don't know what I'm doing. *ʔaani hal-gadd-ma mitxarbuṭ ma-da-ʔaʕruf iš-da-asawwi.*
mixture - *maziij* pl. *-aat, xaliiṭ* pl. *-aat.*
mix-up - *xarbaṭa* pl. *-aat, xaraabiiṭ.* There was an awful mix-up. *ṣaarat fadd xarbaṭa faḍiiʕa.*
to **moan** - *wann (i wann).* I could hear him moaning in the next room. *ğdarit asimʕa ywinn ib-ğurfat il-lux.*
mob - 1. *ğawğaaʔ.* The mob almost lynched him. *l-ğawğaaʔ taqriiban ʕalliqoo.* 2. *jamaaʕa* pl. *-aat.* There's a mob of people waiting for you. *ʔaku fadd jamaaʕa b-intiḍaarak.*
to mob - 1. *hijam (i hujuum) ʕala.* The girls mobbed him for his autograph. *l-banaat hijmaw ʕalee b-ṭalab tawqiiʕa.* 2. *tkaddas (a takaddus) ʕala.* People mob the stores before the holiday. *l-maxaazin titkaddas ʕaleeha n-naas gabuḷ il-ʕiid.*
model - 1. *namuuδaj* pl. *namaaδij.* He's working on the model of a bridge. *huwwa da-ysawwi namuuδaj il-fadd jisir.* 2. *muudeel* pl. *-aat.* This is the latest model. *haaδi ʔaaxir muudeel.* 3. *ʕaariḍa* pl. *-aat.* She is a clothes model in a fashionable dress shop. *hiyya ʕaariḍat ʔazyaaʔ ib-maxzan ʕaṣri.* 4. *miθaal* pl. *muθul, qidwa* pl. *-aat.* They took him as a model. *ttixδoo ka-qidwa.* 5. *miθaali*, namuuδaji*.* She's a model wife. *hiyya zawja miθaaliyya.*
to model - 1. *ʕiraḍ (u ʕariḍ) n-.* She models women's clothing. *tiʕruḍ ʔazyaaʔ nisaaʔiyya.* 2. *tšakkal (i).* The boy has begun to model himself after his hero. *l-walad bida yitšakkal ib-šikil baṭala.*
moderate - *muʕtadil, mutwaṣṣiṭ.* He has moderate political views. *ʔafkaara s-siyaasiyya muʕtadla.*
modern - *zadiiθ, ʕaṣri*, ʕal-mooda.* She has a modern kitchen. *ʕidha fadd maṭbax ʕaṣri.*
modest - *muztašim, mutwaaḍiʕ.* She's a very modest person. *hiyya fadd wazda kulliš muztašma.* -- The king is modest. *l-maalik mitwaaḍiʕ.*
moist - *raṭib, nadi, naadi, mballal.*
to **moisten** - *ballal (i tabliil, tbillil) t-.* Moisten the stamp. *ballil iṭ-ṭaabiʕ.*
moisture - *rṭuuba, nida.*
mold - 1. *ʕfuuna.* There was a layer of mold on the cheese. *čaan ʔaku ṭabaqa mnil-iʕfuuna ʕaj-jibin.* 2. *qaalab* pl. *qwaalib.* You can use this mold for the pudding. *tiğdar tistaʕmil hal-qaalab lil-puding.*
to mold - 1. *ʕaffan (i taʕfiin) t-.* If you leave the cheese here it will mold. *ʔiδa titruk ij-jibin ihnaa yʕaffin.* 2. *kayyaf (i takyiif) t-, šakkal (i taškiil) t-.* Mold the clay with your hands. *kayyif iṭ-ṭiin ib-iidak.*
moldy - *mʕaffin, mitʕaffin.* The bread is moldy. *l-xubuz imʕaffin.*
mole - 1. *xuld* pl. *zaywaanaat xuld.* We've a mole in our garden. *ʕidna fadd xuld ib-zadiiqatna.* 2. *šaama* pl. *-aat.* He has a large mole on his cheek. *ʕinda šaama čbiira ʕala xadda.*
molecule - *juzayʔa* pl. *-aat.*
moment - *lazḍa* pl. *-aat.* Wait a moment. *ntiḍir lazḍa.*
at a moment's notice - *b-ʔay lazḍa.* Be ready to leave at a moment's notice. *kuun zaaḍir itğaadir b-ʔay lazḍa.*
at the moment - *b-hal-wakit, b-hal-lazḍa.* At the moment I can't give you any further information. *b-hal-wakit ma-agdar anṭiik ʔay maʕluumaat ʔakθar.*
in a moment - *b-xilaal lazḍa, baʕad lazḍa.* I'll give you your change in a moment. *ʔanṭiik baqiyyat ifluusak ib-xilaal lazḍa.*
monastery - *deer* pl. *ʔadyira.*
Monday - *yoom iθ-θineen.*
money - *fluus.* Do you take American money? *tiqbal ifluus ʔamriikiyya?*
**He has money to burn. *ʕinda fluus miθl iz-zibal.*
**You can't get that for love or money. *guwwa mruwwa ma-titzaṣṣal.*
money order - *zawaala* (pl. *-aat*) *maaliyya.*
monk - *raahib* pl. *ruhbaan.*
monkey - *šaadi* pl. *šwaadi, qird* pl. *quruud.*
monopoly - *ztikaar.*
monotonous - **The work here is monotonous but the salary is good. *š-šuğuḷ ihnaa yimši ʕala fadd namaṭ laakin ir-raatib zeen.*
monster - *ğuul* pl. *ʔağwaal, siʕluwwa* pl. *-aat.*
month - *šahar* pl. *ʔašhur.* He came last month. *ʔija b-šahar il-faat.*
monthly - 1. *šahri*.* He writes for a monthly magazine. *huwwa yiktib ib-majalla šahriyya.* -- You can pay the amount in monthly installments. *tigdar tidfaʕ il-mablağ ib-ʔaqsaaṭ šahriyya.* 2. *šahriyyan.* He comes to Baghdad monthly. *yiji l-bağdaad*

šahriyyan.
**You can make a monthly payment of five dinars. *tigdar tidfaε xams idnaaniir biš-šahar.*

monument - *naṣub tiδkaari.* pl. *ʔanṣiba tiδkaariyya.*

mood - **1.** *mizaaj* pl. *ʔamzija.* He's in a good mood today. *mizaaja zeen il-yoom.* **2.** *wahas, xulug.* I'm not in the mood for that. *ʔaani maa εindi wahas l-haay.*

moody - *maqhuur.*

moon - *gumar* pl. *ʔaqmaar.* There's a ring around the moon tonight. *ʔaku ḥalqa daayir madaayir il-gumar hal-leela.*

full moon - *badir* pl. *bduur.* Is there a full moon tonight? *l-gumar badir hal-leela?*

mop - *mimsaḥa* pl. *-aat.* Take a wet mop. *ʔuxuδ fadd mimsaḥa mballila.*

to mop - *misaḥ (a masiḥ) n-.* Did you mop the floor? *misaḥt il-gaaε?* -- He mopped his forehead. *misaḥ guṣṣta.*

to mop up - *qiḍa (i qaḍaaʔ) n- εala.* The government forces mopped up the remnant of the rebels. *l-ḥukuuma qiḍat εala ʔaaxir baqaaya θ-θuwwaar.*

moral - **1.** *maġza, ḥikma* pl. *ḥikam.* And the moral of the story is... *w-maġza l-quṣṣa huwwa...* **2.** *ʔadabi* ʔaxlaaqi*.* Children have a moral obligation to support their parents. *l-ʔabnaaʔ εaleehum masʔuuliyya ʔadabiyya yεiiluun il-waalideen.*

morals - *ʔaxlaaq.* He has no morals at all. *maa εinda ʔaxlaaq ʔabadan.* or ***huwwa ʔaxlaaqsizz.* -- She's a woman of low morals. *hiyya mara ʔaxlaaqha waaṭya.*

morale - *r-ruuḥ il-maεnawiyya, l-maεnawiyya.* The morale of the troops was excellent. *maεnawiyyat ij-jinuud čaanat mumtaaza.*

morality - *nazaaha.* We do not question the morality of his actions. *ma-nšukk ib-nazaahat ʔaεmaala.*

more - *ʔakθar, ʔazyad.* He is asking for more money. *da-yriid ifluus ʔakθar.* or ***da-yriid ifluus baεad.* -- He has more money than he needs. *εinda ʔakθar ifluus min-ma yiḥtaaj.* -- That's more likely. *haδiič muḥtamala ʔakθar.* -- He got more and more involved in the matter. *twarraṭ bil-mawḍuuε ʔakθar fa-ʔakθar.* -- The price will be a little more. *raḥ-yṣiir is-siεr išwayya ʔazyad.*
**What's more? I don't believe him. *wil-ʔakθar min haaδa, ʔaani ma-aṣaddig bii.*

more or less - *šii εala šii, nawεan-ma.* I believe that report is more or less true. *ʔaεtiqid hat-taqriir šii εala šii ṣaḥiiḥ.*

once more - *marra lux.* Try once more. *jarrub marra lux.*

some more - *baεad.* Won't you have some more soup? *ma-triid baεad šoorba?*

the more... the more - *kull-ma... kull-ma.* The more money they get, the more they want. *kull-ma yḥaṣṣluun εala fluus kull-ma yirduun baεad.* -- The more I see him, the more I like him. *kull-ma ʔašuufa, kull-ma ʔaḥibba ʔazyad.*
**The more I give him, the more he wants. *šgadd-ma ʔantii yriid baεad ʔazyad.* or *εeena ma-tišbaε.*

moreover - *w-εalaawatan εala δaalik.*

morning - *ṣubuḥ, ṣabaaḥ* pl. *-aat.* He works from morning till night. *yištuġuḷ imniṣ-ṣubuḥ lil-leel.*

in the morning - *ṣ-ṣubuḥ.* She's only here in the morning. *hiyya hnaa bass iṣ-ṣubuḥ.* -- We stayed up till one in the morning. *siharna lis-saaεa waḥda ṣ-ṣubuḥ.*

this morning - *l-yoom iṣ-ṣubuḥ.* There was a lot to do this morning. *čaan ʔaku hwaaya šuġuḷ il-yoom iṣ-ṣubuḥ.*

mortal - **1.** *zaaʔil* pl. *-iin.* We are mortal and God is immortal. *ʔiḥna zaaʔiliin w-ʔaḷḷa daaʔim.* **2.** *bašari* pl. *-iyyiin* coll. *bašar.* That isn't for ordinary mortals. *haaδa fawq mustawa l-bašar.*

mortality - **1.** *wufiyyaat.* Infant mortality here is still a serious problem. *wufiyyaat il-ʔaṭfaal ihnaa li-hassa muškila čibiira.* **2.** *fanaaʔ.* It is difficult for human beings to accept the idea of their mortality. *l-bašar yiṣεab εaleehum qubuul fikrat fanaaʔhum.*

mortar - **1.** *muuna.* Mortar is made from sand and slaked lime. *l-muuna msawwaaya mnir-ramuḷ wij-juṣṣ.* **2.** *haawan* pl. *hawaawiin.* Pound the coffee beans in a mortar. *dugg il-bunn ib-haawan.*

mortgage - *rahan* pl. *ruhuun.* The interest on the mortgage is due. *l-faayiz εar-rahan istaḥaqq.*

to mortgage - *rihan (i rahan) n-.* He had to mortgage his house. *ḍṭarr yirhin beeta.*

Moslem - *mislim* pl. *-iin.*

mosquito - *bagga* pl. *-aat.* coll. *bagg.* We were all bitten up by the mosquitos. *ʔakalna l-bagg kullatna.*

moss - *ṭuḥlub.*

most - **1.** *ʔakθar-ma, ʔaqṣa-ma.* That's the most I can pay. *haaδa ʔakθar-ma ʔagdar adfaεa.* **2.** *muεḍam, ʔakθar.* Most of the day I'm at the office. *ʔaani bid-daaʔira muεḍam in-nahaar.* -- Most people went home early. *ʔakθar in-naas raaḥaw lil-beet min wakit.* -- He's on the road most of the time. *huwwa msaafir ʔakθar il-ʔawqaat.* -- Who did most of the work? *minu ṭallaε ʔakθar iš-šuġuḷ?* **3.** *kulliš.* The talk was most interesting. *l-ḥadiiθ čaan kulliš mumtiε.*
**We'd better make the most of our time. *ʔaḥsan-inna nḥaawil nistifiid wakitna ʔakθar-ma yimkin.*

at the most - *εal-ʔakθar.* At the most it's worth ten dinars. *εal-ʔakθar yiswa εašir danaaniir.*

mostly - *εala l-ʔaġlab, εala l-ʔakθar.* He's mostly right. *huwwa ṣaḥiiḥ εal-ʔaġlab.* -- The audience consisted mostly of women. *l-ḥaaḍriin čaanaw εala l-ʔakθar niswaan.*

moth - *εiθθa* pl. *-aat* coll. *εiθθ.*

moth ball - *duεbullat* (pl. *-aat*) *naftaaliin.*

moth-eaten - *maεθuuθ.*

mother - *ʔumm* pl. *ʔummahaat, waalda* pl. *-aat.* She takes care of us like a mother. *tdiir baalha εaleena εabaalak ʔummna.*

to mother - *daara (i mdaaraa) t- miθl il-ʔumm.* She mothers him all the time. *tdaarii miθil il-ʔumm εala-ṭuul.*

mother-in-law - **1.** *ḥamaat* pl. *ḥamawaat.* My mother-in law is living with us. *ḥamaati saakna wiyyaana.* **2.** *mart* (pl. *niswaan*) *il-εamm.* The bride and her mother-in-law never get along. *l-εaruusa w-mart il-εamm ma-yitraahmuun.*

mother tongue - *luġa* (pl. *-aat*) *ʔaṣliyya.* What is your mother tongue? *šinu luġatak il-ʔaṣliyya?*

motion - **1.** *ḥaraka* pl. *-aat.* All of her motions are graceful. *kull ḥarakaatha rašiiqa.* **2.** *qtiraaḥ* pl. *-aat.* I'd like to make a motion. *ʔariid aqaddim iqtiraaḥ.*

to motion - *ʔaššar (i taʔšiir), ʔooma (i ʔoomaaʔ, ʔiimaaʔ).* He motioned the taxi to stop. *ʔaššar lit-taaksi ḥatta yoogaf.* -- He motioned me to come. *ʔoomaa-li ʔaji.*

motionless - **1.** *bila ḥaraka.* The patient slept motionless all night. *l-mariiḍ naam bila ḥaraka ṭuul il-leel.* **2.** *jaamid.* I stayed in my place motionless with fear until it was clear there was no snake. *biqeet jaamid ib-makaani mnil-xoof ʔila ʔan itbayyan-li ma-čaan ʔaku ḥayya.* **3.** *raakid.* The surface of the water was motionless. *ṣaṭḥ il-maay čaan raakid.* **4.** *waaquf.* The air is motionless. *l-hawa waaquf.*

motion picture - *filim* pl. *ʔaflaam.*

to **motivate** - *ḥaθθ (i ḥaθθ) n-.* We are trying to find some way to motivate our son to study. *da-ndawwir εala ṭariiqa nḥiθθ biiha ʔibinna εala d-diraasa.*

motivation - *ḥaθθ.* The motivation of the employees in their work is a part of the duties of the Personnel Section. *ḥaθθ il-mustaxdamiin εaš-šuġuḷ min waajibaat šuεbat iḍ-ḍaatiyya.*

motive - *daafiε* pl. *dawaafiε, baaεiθ* pl. *bawaaεiθ.* What is the motive behind the crime? *šinu d-daafiε lij-jariima?* -- My motives are strictly honorable. *bawaaεθi jiddan šariifa.*

motor - *maaṭoor* pl. *-aat, makiina* pl. *makaayin.* I let the motor run. *xalleet l-maaṭoor yištuġuḷ.*

motorcycle - *maatoorsikil* pl. *-aat.*

to **mount** - **1.** *rikab (a rukuub) n-.* He mounted his horse and rode off. *rikab ḥṣaana w-raaḥ.* **2.** *ṣiεad (a ṣuεuud) n-, ṭilaε (a ṭuluuε) n-.* They mounted the steps slowly. *ṣiεdaw id-daraj yawaaš yawaaš.* **3.** *niṣab (u naṣub) n-, rakkab (i tarkiib) t-.* The machine will be mounted on concrete blocks. *l-makiina raḥ-tinnuṣub εala qawaalib konkiriit.* -- I'd like to have this picture mounted and framed. *ʔariid haṣ-ṣuura titrakkab w-titčarčab.* -- Can you mount this stone in a ring for me? *tigdar itrakkub hal-ḥajar ib-maḥbas ʔiliyya?*

mountain - *jibal* pl. *jibaal.* How high is the mountain? *šgadd εulu δaak ij-jibal?* -- We're going to spend a month in the mountains. *raḥ-niġḍi šahar bij-jibaal.*
**Don't make a mountain out of a molehill. *la-tsawwi mnil-ḥabba gubba.*

mountainous - *jabali**

mounted police - *šurṭi xayyaal* pl. *šurṭa xayyaala,*

swaari pl. -iyya. He's a member of the mounted police corps. huwwa b-silk iš-šurṭa l-xayyaala.
to **mourn** - biča (i bači) εala. The widow is still mourning the death of her husband ten years ago. l-ʔarmala baεadha tibči εala zoojha l-maat qabuḷ εašir isniin.
mourning - εaza. The mourning period is seven days. muddat il-εaza sabiεt iyyaam.
in mourning - (m.) mitεazzi pl. -iin, (f.) mitεazzaaya pl. -aat. She's in mourning because of her brother's death. hiyya mitεazzaaya b-sabab moot ʔaxuuha.
mouse - faara pl. -aat coll. faar.
mouth - 1. ḥalig pl. ḥluug. I've got a bad taste in my mouth. ḥalgi ṭaεma muu ṭayyib. -- The story passed from mouth to mouth. l-iḥčaaya ntiqlat min ḥalig il-ḥalig. 2. maṣabb pl. -aat. Qurna is at the mouth of the Shatt al-Arab. l-qurna ṣaayra εala maṣabb šaṭṭ il-εarab. 3. madxal pl. madaaxil, baab pl. biibaan. The dog stopped at the mouth of the cave. č-čalib wugaf ib-baab il-kahif.
**They live from hand to mouth. duub ygidruun ysidduun ramaqhum.
**Don't look a gift horse in the mouth. la-tiεtiriḍ εal-hadiyya š-ma čaan nawuεha. or l-hadiyya muu b-θaminha.
mouth wash - ġasiil ḥalig.
move - 1. ḥaraka pl. -aat. Every move I make hurts. kull ḥaraka ʔasawwiiha tʔaδδiini. 2. door pl. ʔadwaar. It's your move. hassa doorak. or **ʔilak il-liεab. 3. xaṭwa pl. -aat. He can't make a move without asking his wife. ma-yigdar yixṭi xaṭwa blayya ma-yguul il-marta.
to be on the move - 1. riḥal (a raḥiil). The Bedouins are always on the move. l-badu daaʔiman yirḥaluun. 2. tnaqqal (a tanaqqul). He never lives in one town for long; he's always on the move. ma-yiθbit fadd wlaaya, εala ṭuul yitnaqqal.
**My boy can't sit still; he's always on the move. ʔibni ma-yugεud raaḥa; εabaalak maakuuk.
to move - 1. ḥarrak (i taḥriik, tḥirrik) t-. She can't move her foot. ma-tigdar itḥarrik rijilha. -- You'll have to move your car. laazim itḥarrik sayyaartak. 2. tḥarrak (a taḥarruk). I can't move. ma-agdar atḥarrak. -- Don't move, or I'll shoot. la-titḥarrak, tara ʔarmiik. 3. ntiqal (i ntiqaal), tḥawwal (a taḥawwul). Do you know where they are moving to? tuεruf li-ween da-yintaqluun? 4. qtiraḥ (i qtiraaḥ). I move we adjourn the session. ʔaani ʔaqtiriḥ inʔajjil ij-jalsa. 5. ʔaθaar (i ʔiθaara) ḥanaan-. She moved me with her tears. ʔaθaarat ḥanaani b-dimuuεha. 6. liεab (a laεib). It's your play. I just moved. haaδa doorak. ʔaani hassa lεabit. 7. giḷab (u gaḷub) n-. We moved heaven and earth to get it. gḷabna d-dinya ḥatta gdarna nḥaṣṣilha.
**They move in the best circles. mittaṣliin ib-ʔaḥsan jamaaεaat.
**I was moved to tears. bičeet imnit-taʔaθθur.
to move along - miša (i maši), tḥarrak (a taḥarruk). Things are finally moving along now. l-ʔumuur ʔaxiiran bidat timši šwayya.
to move away - 1. ntiqal (i ntiqaal), tḥawwal (a taḥawwul). They moved away a long time ago. ṣaar-ilhum ihwaaya min intiqlaw minnaa. or tḥawwlaw min zimaan. 2. waxxar (i twixxir) t-. Move the table away, please. waxxir il-meez, min faḍlak.
to move on - miša (i maši), tḥarrak(a). Move on! yaḷḷa, imši!
to be moved - tʔaθθar (a taʔθθur). I was deeply moved. tʔaθθarit kulliš. or **nkisar xaaṭri kulliš.
movement - 1. ḥaraka pl. -aat. They watched his movements closely. raaqbaw ḥarakaata b-diqqa. -- He never belonged to any political movement. ma-ntima b-ʔay ḥaraka siyaasiyya. 2. faṣil pl. fṣuul. That theme is from the second movement of the Fifth Symphony. hal-laḥan imnil-faṣl iθ-θaani mnis-simfooniyya l-xaamsa. 3. makiina pl. makaayin. I checked your watch; the movement is dirty. fuḥaṣit saaεtak; il-makiina waṣxa.
movie - filim pl. ʔaflaam. Is there a good movie playing tonight? ʔaku filim zeen da-yištuġul hal-leela?
movies - siinama pl. -aat. We rarely go to the movies. ʔiḥna naadiran inruuḥ lis-siinama.
to **mow** - gaṣṣ (u gaṣṣ) n-. I'm mowing the lawn. da-aguṣṣ iθ-θayyil.
Mr. - sayyid pl. saada. Could I speak to Mr. Mounir? ʔagdar akallim is-sayyid muniir?
Mrs. - sayyida pl. -aat. Address the letter to Mrs. Ali Sheesh. εinwin ir-risaala ʔila s-sayyida εali šiiš.
much - hwaaya, kaθiir. I haven't much time. maa εindi hwaaya wakit. -- I feel much better today. ʔašεur ihwaaya ʔaḥsan hal-yoom.
how much - šgadd. How much will it cost me? šgadd raḥ-itkallifni? or beeš raḥ-iṭṣiir εalayya?
that much - 1. hal-miqdaar. I think that much will be enough for you. ʔaεtiqid hal-miqdaar ykaffiik. 2. hal-gadd. I didn't know you liked it that much. ma-činit ʔadri tḥabba hal-gadd. -- I can tell you that much. ʔagdar agul-lak hal-gadd.
very much - kulliš ihwaaya, jiddan, jaziil. We didn't like it very much. ma-εijbatna kulliš ihwaaya. -- Thank you very much. šukran jaziilan. or ʔaškurak jiddan.
mucus - 1. (nasal) mxaaṭ. 2. (bronchial) balġam.
mucus membrane - ġišaaʔ muxaaṭi pl. ʔaġšiya muxaaṭiyya.
mud - ṭiin, waḥal. The car got stuck in the mud. s-sayyaara εiṣat bit-ṭiin.
muddy - 1. mṭayyan, mwaḥḥal. Your shoes are muddy. qundartak imṭayyna. 2. xaabuṭ. This water is muddy. hal-maay xaabuṭ.
muggy - waxim. It's awfully muggy today. d-dinya kulliš waxma l-yoom.
mule - baġal pl. bġaal.
multiplication table - jadwal (pl. jadaawil) iḍ-ḍarb.
to **multiply** - 1. ḍirab (u ḍarub) n-. Multiply three by four! ʔuḍrub itlaaθa b-arbaεa! 2. tkaaθar (a takaaθur). Rabbits multiply quickly. l-ʔaraanib titkaaθar ib-surεa.
to **mumble** - tamtam (i ttimtim, tamtama). He is always mumbling. huwwa εala ṭuul da-ytamtim.
mumps - nukaaf.
municipal - baladi*.
municipality - baladiyya pl. -aat.
murder - ḥaadiθ (pl. ḥawaadiθ) qatil, katil. The murder was not discovered until a few days later. ḥaadiθ il-qatil ma-nkišaf ʔilla baεad muruur εiddat ʔayyaam.
to murder - 1. kital (u katil) n-. He was accused of having murdered his wife. huwwa ntiham ib-katil marta. 2. laaṣ (u looṣ) n-. She murdered that song. laaṣat hal-ġaniyya.
murderer - qaatil pl. qatala.
muscle - εaḍala pl. -aat. All my muscles hurt. εaḍalaati kullha toojaεni.
museum - matḥaf pl. mataaḥif. I've seen the museum. ʔaani šaayfa lil-matḥaf.
mushroom - fṭirra pl. -aat. coll. fṭirr. Are these mushrooms poisonous? hal-ifṭirr saamm?
music - 1. moosiiqa. Where's the music coming from? mneen da-tiji hal-moosiiqa? 2. nooṭa pl. -aat. I didn't bring my music with me. ma-jibt in-nooṭa maalti wiyyaaya.
musical - moosiiqi*.
musical instrument - ʔaala (pl. -aat) moosiiqiyya. Do you play any musical instrument? ʔinta tdugg fadd ʔaala moosiiqiyya?
musician - moosiiqaar pl. -iyya.
must - 1. lizuum. There is no such thing as must. ma-aku fadd šii ʔisma lizuum. 2. laazim. He must be sick. huwwa laazim mariiḍ. -- You must never forget that. laazim ʔabad ma-tinsaa. or ma-laazim tinsa haaδa ʔabadan. 3. waajib εala. You must pray five times a day. waajib εaleek iṭṣalli xamis marraat bil-yoom.
mustache - šaarib pl. šwaarib.
mustard - xardal.
to **mutilate** - šawwah (i tašwiih) t-. The machine mutilated his hand. l-makiina šawwhat ʔiida. -- The police found the body badly mutilated. š-šurṭa ligaw ij-juθθa mušawwaha kulliš.
mutiny - εiṣyaan pl. -aat.
to **mutter** - tamtam (i ttimtim, tamtama). He muttered something to himself. tamtam ib-fadd šii beena w-been nafsa.
mutton - laḥam ġanam.
mutual - 1. mutabaadal. This treaty provides for mutual aid in case of war. hal-muεaahada tnuṣṣ εala fadd taεaawun mutabaadal ib-ḥaalat il-ḥarb. 2. muštarak. The two prime ministers issued a mutual statement. raʔiiseen il-wuzaraaʔ ṭallεaw bayaan muštarak.
**He's a mutual friend of ours. huwwa ṣadiiq iṭ-ṭarafeen. or huwwa ṣadiiqna θneenna.

muzzle - **1.** *kammaama* pl. *-aat.* Dogs are not allowed on the street without muzzles. *mamnuuɛ tark ič-čilaab biš-šaariɛ bila kammaamaat.* **2.** *fawha* pl. *-aat.* Don't point the muzzle of the gun at anyone. *la-tneešin fawhat il-bunduqiyya ɛala ʔaẓẓad.*

to muzzle - *kammam (i takmiim) t-.* That dog ought to be muzzled. *hač-čalib laazim yitkammam.* -- The press is muzzled. *ʔafwaah iṣ-ṣuḥuf imkammima.*

mysterious - *ġaamiḍ, mubham.*

mystery - **1.** *lagiz* pl. *ʔalġaaz.* How they stole it is still a mystery. *šloon baagoo li-hassa lagiz.* **2.** *ġumuuḍ.* The meeting is surrounded with mystery. *l-ijtimaaɛ muḥaaṭ bil-ġumuuḍ.*

mystery story - *quṣṣa (pl. quṣaṣ) pooliisiyya.* I like to read mystery stories. *yiɛjibni ʔaqra quṣaṣ pooliisiyya.*

N

nag - **1.** *kidiiš* pl. *kidaayiš.* He put all his money on that nag. *xalla kull ifluusa b-hal-kidiiš.* **2.** *niqnaaqiyya* pl. *-aat.* His wife's a real nag. *marta niqnaaqiyya tamaam.*

to nag - *naqnaq (i tniqniq).* Her husband got sick of her nagging. *zawijha ḍaaj imn itniqniqha.*

nail - **1.** *bismaar* pl. *bsaamiir.* Don't hammer the nail in too far. *la-tdugg il-bismaar kulliš zaayid.* **2.** *ʔiḍfir* pl. *ʔaḍaafir.* She painted her nails red. *ṣubġat ʔaḍaafirha b-ʔaḥmar.*

**You hit the nail on the head. *jibitha b-mukaanha.*

to nail - *basmar (i tbismir) t-.* Please nail the board to the wall. *min faḍlak basmir il-xišba bil-ḥaayiṭ.*

**It's difficult to nail him down to anything. *ma-yinṭi lazma.*

naked - **1.** *mṣallax* pl. *mṣaaliix, ɛaryaan* pl. *-iin.* They took a picture of their son naked. *ʔaxḏaw ṣuurat ṭifihum imṣallax.* **2.** *mujarrad.* You can see the satellite with the naked eye. *tigdar itšuuf il-qamar il-iṣṭinaaɛi bil-ɛeen il-mujarrada.*

name - **1.** *ʔisim* pl. *ʔasmaaʔ, ʔasaami.* I've heard of his name before. *ʔaani saamiɛ b-isma gabuḷ.* -- Please give me your full name; your first name, your father's first name and your family name. *ʔarjuuk inṭiini ʔismak il-kaamil, ʔismak, ʔism abuuk, w-laqabak.* **2.** *šuhra* pl. *-aat, ʔisim* pl. *ʔasmaaʔ, ʔasaami; sumɛa* pl. *-aat.* He made a good name for himself in industry. *sawwaa-la xooš isim biṣ-ṣinaaɛa.*

to name - **1.** *samma (i tasmiya, tsimmi) t-.* They named their son Ali Sheesh. *sammaw ʔibinhum ɛali šiiš.* **2.** *ɛadd (i ɛadd) n-, samma (i tasmiya, tsimmi) t-.* Can you name all the planets? *tigdar itɛidd kull il-kawaakib is-sayyaara?* **3.** *ɛayyan (i taɛyiin) t-.* The president named his ministry yesterday. *r-raʔiis ɛayyan wizaarta l-baarḥa.*

namely - *w-huwwa, w-hiyya, yaɛni.* I have only one wish, namely, that we leave soon. *ɛindi raġba wiḥda, w-hiyya nruuḥ qariiban.*

nap - **1.** *ġafwa* pl. *-aat.* I took a short nap after lunch. *ʔaxaḏit ġafwa ṣġayyra baɛad il-ġada.* **2.** *xamla* pl. *-aat.* The nap's all worn off this rug. *l-xamla kullha maḥkuuka min haz-zuuliyya.*

to nap - *ġufa (i ġafu).* The baby napped all afternoon. *ṭ-ṭifil ġufa ṭuul il-ɛaṣir.*

**The inspectors caught us napping. *l-mufattišiin lizmoona ɛala ġafla.*

napkin - *čaffiyya* pl. *čfaafi.*

narcotics - *muxaddiraat.*

narghile - *nargiila* pl. *-aat, ġarša* pl. *-aat.*

narrow - **1.** *ḍayyig.* This is a narrow street. *haaḏa šaariɛ ḍayyig.* -- His opinions on education are very narrow. *ʔaraaʔa bit-taɛliim kullis ḍayyga.* **2.** *ḍayyiq, qaliil.* Our company's margin of profit is very narrow. *majaal ribiḥ šarikatna kulliš ḍayyiq.*

**I had a narrow escape. *njeet ib-qeed šaɛra minha.* or *xḷaṣit b-iɛjuuba.*

narrows - *maḍiiq* pl. *maḍaayiq.* We watched the ship pass through the narrows. *šifna l-baaxira tmurr bil-maḍiiq.*

to narrow - **1.** *ḍaaq (i ḍiiq).* The road narrows a mile from here. *ṭ-ṭariiq yḍiiq masaafat miil imn ihnaa.* **2.** *ḍayyaq (i taḍyiiq, tḍiyyiq) t-.* The government is narrowing the road instead of widening it. *l-ḥukuuma da-tḍayyiq iṭ-ṭariiq badal-ma twassiɛa.*

to narrow down - *ḥiṣar (u ḥaṣir) n-.* We narrowed down the suspicion to three men. *ḥṣarna t-tuhma b-iθlaθ riyaajiil.*

nasty - **1.** *qabiiḥ.* Spitting on the floor is a nasty habit. *t-tafil ɛal-gaaɛ ɛaada qabiiḥa.* **2.** *malɛuun, qabiiḥ.* Don't be so nasty! *la-tṣiir hal-gadd malɛuun!* **3.** *kasiif.* London has nasty weather. *landan biiha jaww kasiif.*

nation - *balad* pl. *bilaad, buldaan; ʔumma* pl. *ʔumam.* The entire nation mourned his death. *l-balad kullha ḥiznaw ɛala moota.*

national - **1.** *waṭani*.* Can you sing the national anthem? *tigdar tiqra n-našiid il-waṭani?* **2.** *muwaaṭin* pl. *-iin.* We hired four Egyptian nationals. *šaġġalna ʔarbaɛ muwaaṭiniin miṣriyyiin.*

nationalism - **1.** *qawmiyya.* He gave a speech on Arab nationalism. *ʔalqa xiṭaab ɛan il-qawmiyya l-ɛarabiyya.* **2.** *waṭaniyya.* He's one of the advocates of Iraqi nationalism. *huwwa waaḥid imnil-munaaṣiriin lil-waṭaniyya l-ɛiraaqiyya.*

nationality - *jinsiyya.*

native - **1.** *ahil* pl. *ʔahaali.* The natives of the island were very nice. *ʔahaali j-jaziira čaanaw kulliš ṭayybiin.* -- He's a native of Najaf. *huwwa min ʔahl in-najaf.* or ***huwwa najafi.* **2.** *ʔaṣli*.* His native language is Arabic. *luġata l-ʔaṣliyya ɛarabiyya.* **3.** *waṭani*.* They attended the festival in their native costumes. *ḥiḍraw il-mahrajaan ib-malaabishum il-waṭaniyya.*

**Potatoes are native to America. *l-puteeta ʔaṣilha min ʔameerka.*

natural - *ṭabiiɛi*.* We visited a natural cave south of the town. *zirna fadd kahaf ṭabiiɛi januub il-balda.* -- The fruit in this picture looks natural. *l-faakiha b-haṣ-ṣuura tbayyin ṭabiiɛiyya.* -- The use of natural rubber is declining. *stiɛmaal il-maṭṭaaṭ iṭ-ṭabiiɛi da-yqill.*

naturally - *ṭabɛan, biṭ-ṭabuɛ.* Naturally she's a little afraid. *ṭabɛan hiyya xaayfa šwayya.*

nature - **1.** *ṭabiiɛa.* My girl friend enjoys the beauty of nature. *ṣadiiqti titmattaɛ ib-jamaal iṭ-ṭabiiɛa.* -- I can't tell you anything about the nature of my work. *ma-agdar agul-lak ʔay šii ɛan ṭabiiɛat šuġḷi.* **2.** *ṭabuɛ, xulug, ṭabiiɛa.* He has a very good nature. *ɛinda xooš ṭabuɛ.* **3.** *fiṭra.* He's an artist by nature. *huwwa fannaan bil-fiṭra.* **4.** *qabiil.* I enjoy doing things of this nature. *ʔartaaḥ min ɛamal ʔašyaaʔ min hal-qabiil.*

nature lover - *ɛaašiq (pl. ɛuššaaq) ṭabiiɛa.*

naughty - *wakiiḥ, wakiḥ.* You've been very naughty today. *činit kulliš wakiiḥ il-yoom.*

nauseated - **I feel nauseated. *ʔašɛur nafsi da-tilɛab.*

naval - *baḥri*.* He studied at the naval academy. *diras bil-kulliyya l-baḥriyya.*

navel - *ṣurra* pl. *ṣurar.*

navy blue - *ʔazrag ṭoox.* I bought a navy blue suit. *štireet qaaṭ ʔazrag ṭoox.*

near - *giriib min, qariib min, b-qurub.* The ball landed near us. *ṭ-ṭooba wugɛat qariib minna.* -- That's a little nearer to the truth. *haaḏa šwayya ʔaqrab liṣ-ṣidug.*

to near - *girab (a gurub) min.* The semester is nearing its end. *l-faṣl id-diraasi yigrab min intihaaʔa.* -- We neared the city about five o'clock. *girabna mnil-madiina ḥawaali s-saaɛa xamsa.*

nearby - *ɛan qurub.* The children stood nearby watching the fire. *l-aṭfaal wugfaw ɛan qurub yitfarrjuun ɛal-ḥariiq.*

Near East - *š-šarq il-ʔadna.*

nearly - *ɛala wašak, bit-taqriib, taqriiban.* She's nearly twenty years old. *ɛumurha ɛala wašak itkuun ɛišriin sana.*

neat - **1.** *ʔaniiq, mhandam.* She always looks very neat. *hiyya daaʔiman tiḍhar kulliš ʔaniiqa.*

2. *naδiif.* He turns out neat work. *da-yṭalliƐ šuğuḷ naδiif.* 3. *mrattab.* His desk is always neat. *meeza daa?iman imrattab.*
necessary - 1. *laazim, luzuum.* He eats more than is necessary. *yaakul ?akθar imnil-luzuum.* 2. *δaruuri*, laazim.* I'll stay if it's absolutely necessary. *raz-abqa ?iδa kulliš δaruuri.*
necessity - 1. *δaruura, zaaja, ztiyaaj, luzuum.* There's no necessity for it. *ma-aku δaruura ?ilha.* -- Necessity is the mother of invention. *l-zaaja ?umm il-ixtiraaƐ.* 2. *ztiyaaj* pl. *-aat, zaaja* pl. *-aat.* My necessities are few. *ztiyaajaati qaliila.*
neck - *rugba* pl. *rugab.* Wrap the scarf around your neck. *liff il-laffaaf Ɛala rugubtak.* -- The bottle has a very narrow neck. *l-buṭil rugubta kulliš δayyga.*
necklace - *glaada* pl. *glaayid.*
neckline - *fatzat ṣadir.*
necktie - *booyinbaağ, bayinbaağ* pl. *-aat, ribaaṭ* pl *?arbiṭa.*

nectarine - *xooxa* (pl. *-aat*) *imrakkuba* coll. *xoox imrakkab.*
need - 1. *zaaja* pl. *-aat, zawaayij; ztiyaaj* pl. *-aat.* There is a need for a better hospital here. *?uku zaaja ?ila mustašfa ?azsan ihnaa.* 2. *δiiq.* You're certainly a friend in need. *?inta zaqiiqatan ṣadiiq Ɛind iδ-δiiq.*
needs - *mutaṭallibaat, zaajaat, ztiyaajaat, zawaayij.* My salary just covers our needs. *raatbi ykaffi mutaṭallibaatna bass.*
if need be - *?iδa qtiδat il-zaaja, Ɛind il-lizuum, Ɛind il-zaaja, ?in lizam il-zaal.* I'll go myself if need be. *?aruuz ib-nafsi ?iδa qtiδat il-zaaja.*
in need of - *b-zaaja ?ila.* He's badly in need of a vacation. *huwwa kulliš ib-zaaja ?ila Ɛuṭla.*
to need - *ztaaj (a ztiyaaj).* I need a new coat. *?aztaaj sitra jdiida.*
**I need to leave at five o'clock. *laazim aruuz is-saaƐa xamsa.*
needle - 1. *?ubra* pl. *?ubar.* Bring me a needle so I can sew on this button. *jiib-li fadd ?ubra zatta ?axayyiṭ had-dugma.* -- The phonograph needle is worn out. *?ubrat il-funnuğraaf saayfa.* 2. *muxyaṭ* pl. *maxaayiṭ.* The upholsterer uses a curved needle in his work. *d-doošamči yistaƐmil muxyaṭ maƐwuuj ib-šuğḷa.*
needy - *muztaaj* pl. *-iin, faqiir* pl. *fuqaraa?.* He donated money to the needy. *tbarraƐ b-ifluus lil-muztaajiin.*
negative - 1. *jaama* pl. *-aat.* Make four prints from this negative. *?iṭbaƐ ?arbaƐ ṣuwar Ɛala haj-jaama.* 2. *saalib.* Hook this wire to the negative terminal of the battery. *?urbuṭ hal-waayir bil-quṭb is-saalib maal il-paaṭri.* 3. *nafi.* Put this sentence in the negative. *zawwil haj-jumla ?ila n-nafi.*
neglect - *?ihmaal.* They fired him due to his neglect. *fuṣloo Ɛala ?ihmaala.*
to neglect - *himal (i ?ihmaal).* Don't neglect to water the plants. *la-tihmil tisgi z-zariƐ.*
to **negotiate** - *tfaawaδ (a tafaawuδ) Ɛala.* They're negotiating a peace treaty. *da-yitfaawδuun Ɛala ttifaaqiyyat is-salaam.*
negotiation - *mufaawaδa* pl. *-aat.* The negotiations lasted a week. *l-mufaawaδaat ṭawwlat isbuuƐ.*
Negress - *Ɛabda* pl. *-aat.*
Negro - *Ɛabid* pl. *Ɛabiid.*
neighbor - *jaar* pl. *jiiraan, jiiraan* pl. *jwaariin.* My neighbor visited me this morning. *jiiraani zaarni haṣ-ṣubuz.*
neighborhood - 1. *jiiraan, jwaariin.* The whole neighborhood was there. *kull ij-jiiraan čaanaw ihnaak.* 2. *ṭaraf* pl. *?aṭraaf, mazalla* pl. *-aat.* We live in a good neighborhood. *niskun ib-mazalla zeena.* -- We talked for an hour in the neighborhood coffee shop. *zičeena saaƐa b-gahwat iṭ-ṭaraf.*
in the neighborhood of - *b-zuduud.* Your bill will run in the neighborhood of five hundred dinars. *l-qaa?ima maaltak raz-itwaṣṣil ib-zuduud il-xamis miit diinaar.*
neighboring - *mujaawir.* The neighboring village was flooded. *l-qariya l-mujaawra čaanat ğargaana.*
neither - *wala.* Neither one of the two was there. *wala waazid imnil-iθneen čaan ihnaak.*
neither ...nor - *laa... wala.* This word is neither Turkish nor Persian. *hač-čilma laa turkiyya wala faarsiyya.*
nephew - 1. (fraternal) *?ibin* (pl. *wulid*) *?ax.* 2. (sororal) *?ibin* (pl. *wulid*) *?uxt.*
nerve - 1. *Ɛaṣab* pl. *?aƐṣaab.* That noise is getting on my nerves. *haṣ-ṣoot da-ydugg ib-?aƐṣaabi.* -- Instead of removing the tooth, he deadened the nerves around it. *badal-ma yišlaƐ is-sinn, kital il-?aƐṣaab illi zaawla.* 2. *jasaara, Ɛeen.* You mean you've got the nerve to ask such a question? *?amma Ɛindak jasaara tis?alni hiič su?aal.*
nervous - *Ɛaṣabi*.* The last few days I've been very nervous. *l-?ayyaam il-?axiira činit kulliš Ɛaṣabi.* -- His mother had a nervous breakdown last year. *?ummha ṣaar Ɛidha nhiyaar Ɛaṣabi s-sana l-faatat.*
nest - *Ɛišš* pl. *Ɛšuuš.*
net - 1. *šibča* pl. *šibač.* He caught a lot of fish in his net. *ṣaad simač ihwaaya b-šibičta.* -- He jumped over the tennis net. *ṭufar foog sibčat it-tanis.* 2. *ṣaafi.* The net weight is a kilo and a half. *l-wazn iṣ-ṣaafi kiilo w-nuṣṣ.*
mosquito net - *kulla* pl. *kulal.*
to net - *rubaz (a ribiz).* We netted four hundred dollars. *rbazna ?arbaƐ miit doolaar.*
The Netherlands - *l-?araaδi l-munxafiδa.*
neutral - 1. *muzaayid* pl. *-iin.* He prefers to remain a neutral. *yfaδδil yuhqa muzaayid.* 2. *booš.* He left the car in neutral. *xalla s-sayyaara Ɛal-booš.* 3. *ziyaadi*, muzaayid.* He fled to a neutral country. *nhizam ?ila balad ziyaadi.* 4. *mutƐaadil.* He changed the acid into a neutral solution. *ğayyar il-zaamuδ ?ila mazluul mutƐaadil.*
neutrality - *ziyaad.* What's your opinion on neutrality? *šinu hiyya fikirtak Ɛan il-ziyaad?* -- The policy of the government is one of positive neutrality? *šinu hiyya fikirtak Ɛan il-ziyaad?* -- *?ijaabi.*
never - 1. *?abadan.* I've never seen Najef. *ma-šaayif in-najaf ?abadan.* 2. *?abadan, qaṭƐan.* Never do that again. *la-tsawwi hiiči šii marra lux ?abadan.*
**Never mind, I'll buy you another. *la-tdiir baal, raz-aštirii-lak waazid laax.*
**Never mind, let it go for now. *Ɛiifha, xalliiha hassa.*
**Never mind, I'll do it myself. *ma-yxaalif, asawwiiha b-nafsi.*
nevertheless - *maƐa δaalik, bir-rağum min δaalik.* Nevertheless, I still can't believe it. *maƐa δaalik, ?aani ma-mumkin aṣaddig biiha.*
new - 1. *jidiid.* Are these shoes new? *hal-qanaadir jidiida?* -- What's new today? *šaku šii jidiid il-yoom?* 2. *taaza, jidiid.* Is there any new news about it? *?aku ?axbaar taaza Ɛanha l-yoom?*
**I feel like a new man. *da-?ašƐur Ɛabaalak maxluuq min jidiid.*
new moon - *hlaal* pl. *?ahilla.* The new moon will be visible either tomorrow or the day after. *l-ihlaal raz-yhill loo baačir loo Ɛugba.*
news - *xabar* pl. *?axbaar, naba?* pl. *?anbaa?.* Did you hear the news on the radio this morning? *smaƐit il-?axbaar bir-raadyo l-yoom iṣ-ṣubuz?* -- We'll have to break the news to him gently. *laazim ingul-la l-xabar ib-luṭuf.* -- That isn't news to me. *haaδa muu xabar jidiid Ɛalayya.*
newspaper - *jariida* pl. *jaraayid.*
newsreel - *?axbaar siinamaa?iyya.* I missed the newsreel last night. *ma-lzagit l-?axbaar is-siinamaa?iyya l-baarza bil-leel.*
new year - *raas is-sana.*
next - 1. *jaay, taali.* We're coming to Baghdad next month. *jaayiin il-bağdaad iš-šahar ij-jaay.* -- Next time do it right! *l-marra j-jaaya sawwiiha zeen!* -- It's your turn next. *l-jaaya noobtak.* 2. *wara, baƐad.* I'm next after you. *?aani waraak.* 3. *baƐdeen.* What shall I do next? *baƐdeen is-raz-asawwi?* 4. *θaani.* The next day he got sick. *l-yoom iθ-θaani tmarraδ.* or ***l-yoom l-baƐda tmarraδ.*
next door to - *b-ṣaff.* The tailor lives next door to us. *l-xayyaaṭ yiskun ib-ṣaffna.* -- We live next door to the school. *niskun ib-ṣaff il-madrasa.*
next to - *yamm, b-ṣaff.* Sit down next to me. *?ugƐud yammi.*
nib - *sillaaya* pl. *-aat, riiša* pl. *riyaš.*
to **nibble** - *garmaṭ (u tgurmuṭ) t-.* Some mouse has been nibbling on this cheese. *fadd faara čaanat itgarmuṭ ib-haj-jibin.*
nice - *laṭiif, zeen, xooš, zilu.* She had on a

nice dress. *čaanat laabsa fistaan laṭiif.* -- Our doctor has a nice way with his patients. *ṭabiibna muεaamalta zeena wiyya l-marδ̣a.* -- He's a nice polite little boy. *huwwa fadd walad laṭiif w-mʔaddab.* -- That wasn't very nice of him to say that. *ma-čaanat ʒilwa minna yguulha.* -- Did you have a nice time? *ǧδ̣eet xooš wakit?* or ***twannasit?* --The room is nice and warm. *hal-ġurfa zeena w-daafya.*

nicely - *tamaam, zeen, xooš.* Our daughter has learned to sew nicely. *bittna tεallimat itxayyiṭ zeen.*
**This will do nicely. *haaδa yʔaddi l-ġaraδ̣.*

nickname - *laqab* pl. *ʔalqaab.*

niece - **1.** (fraternal) *bint* (pl. *banaat*) *ʔax.* **2.** (sororal) *bint* (pl. *banaat*) *ʔuxt.*

night - *leela* pl. *-aat, layaali.* He only stayed with us one night. *buqa wiyyaana fadd leela wiʒda.*
**Good night! *tiṣbaʒ εala xeer!*

night club - *malha* pl. *malaahi.* She sings in the night clubs. *hiyya tġanni bil-malaahi.*

nightgown - **1.** *dišdaaša* (pl. *dišaadiiš*) *noom.* My father prefers a nightgown to pajamas. *ʔabuuya yfaδ̣δ̣il id-dišdaaša εal-bijaama.* **2.** *θoob* (pl. *θyaab*) *noom.* I bought my wife a nylon nightgown. *štireet iz-zawijti θoob noom naayloon.*

nightingale - *bilbil* pl. *balaabil.*

night watchman - *ʒaaris leeli* pl. *ʒurraas leeliyyiin, naaṭuur* pl. *nuwaaṭiir, čarxači* pl. *-iyya, peeṣwaan* pl. *-iyya.*

nine - **1.** *tisεa.* The train leaves at nine o'clock. *l-qiṭaar yiṭlaε saaεa tisεa.* **2.** *tisiεt.* I lived there for nine months. *sikanit ihnaak tisiεt išhur.* **3.** *tisiε.* The atmosphere will be full of radioactivity in another nine years. *j-jaww raʒ-ykuun bii ʔišεaaε δarri baεad tisε isniin.*

nineteen - *tṣaaṭaεaš.*

nineteenth - *l-iṭṣaaṭaεaš.* This is the nineteenth of the month. *haaδa l-yoom il-iṭṣaaṭaεaš imniš-šahar.*

ninetieth - *t-tisεiin.*

ninety - *tisεiin.*

ninth - **1.** *taasiε.* This is the ninth of the month. *haaδa l-yoom it-taasiε imniš-šahar.* **2.** *tusuε* pl. *ʔatsaaε.* Subtract two ninths from five ninths. *ʔiṭraʒ tusεeen min xams atsaaε.*

nip - **1.** *εaδ̣δ̣a* pl. *-aat.* The dog took a good nip of my leg. *č-čalib ʔaxaδ xooš εaδ̣δ̣a min rijli.* **2.** *maṣṣa* pl. *-aat.* He took himself a good nip out of the bottle. *ʔaxaδ-la xooš maṣṣa mnil-buṭil.*

nippy - **1.** *bii garṣat barid.* The air is nippy this morning. *l-hawa bii garṣat barid haṣ-ṣubuʒ.* **2.** *ʒaadd.* This is a nippy cheese. *haj-jibin ṭaεma ʒaadd.*

nitrogen - *niitroojiin.*

no - **1.** *laa.* Answer me, yes or no. *jaawubni, ʔii loo laa.* -- Do you always have to say no? *ma-tguul ġeer laa?* **2.** *muu.* This pen is no good. *hal-qalam muu zeen.*
**This screwdriver is no good for this job. *had-darnafiis ma-yfiid il-haš-šuġuḷ.*
**This bicycle is no good anymore. *hal-paaysikil ma-bii faaʔida baεad.*
**He has no money. *ma-εinda fluus.*
**No smoking! *t-tadxiin mamnuuε!*
**There are no more seats. *ma-aku maqaaεid baεad.*
**No sooner did we arrive than the telephone rang. *wiyya-ma wṣalna dagg it-talifoon.*
**I have no doubt of it whatsoever. *ma-εindi kull šakk biiha ʔabadan.*

noble - *nabiil* pl. *nubalaaʔ.* That was very noble of you. *haaδa čaan εamal nabiil minnak.*

nobleman - *nabiil* pl. *nubalaaʔ, šariif* pl. *ʔašraaf, šurafaaʔ.*

nobody - **1.** (imp.) *laʒʒad, wala waaʒid.* Nobody may leave this room. *laʒʒad yiṭlaε imnil-ġurfa.* **2.** *maʒʒad, wala waaʒid.* Nobody saw us, I'm sure. *maʒʒad šaafna, ʔaani mitʔakkid.* -- Nobody came to the party at all. *wala waaʒid jaa lil-ʒafla ʔabadan.*

nod - *hazzat* (pl. *-aat*) *raas.* He greeted us with a nod. *sallam εaleena b-hazzat raas.*
to nod - **1.** *hazz (i hazz) n-.* She nodded her head yes. *hazzat raasha qaabla.* **2.** *ġaffa (i tġiffi).* He began to nod over his book. *gaam yġaffi εala ktaaba.*
to nod to - **1.** *ʔaššar (i taʔšiir, tʔiššir) l- b-raas˜.* The teacher nodded to me to go on reading. *l-muεallim ʔaššar-li b-raasa ʔastimirr bil-qiraaʔa.* **2.** *sallam (i salaam) εala b-raas˜.* She nodded to me as she passed. *sallimat εalayya b-raasha lamma marrat.*

noise - **1.** *δ̣ajiij, ṣooṭ.* The noise of the traffic keeps me awake at night. *δ̣ajiij il-muruur yxalliini gaaεid ṭuul il-leel.* **2.** *ʒiss* pl. *ʒsuus.* I heard a noise downstairs, and I went down to investigate. *smaεit fadd ʒiss jawwa w-nizilt id-daraj ʔašuuf šaku.* **3.** *laġwa* pl. *-aat, δ̣awδ̣aaʔ.* The noise of the crowd at the auction gave me a headache. *laġwat in-naas bil-mazaad dawwxat raasi.*

to **nominate** - *raššaʒ (i taršiiʒ) t-.* He's going to nominate himself for the member from the third district in Baghdad. *raʒ-yraššiʒ nafsa naaʔib εan il-manṭiqa θ-θaaliθa b-baġdaad.*

noncommissioned officer - *δ̣aabuṭ* (pl. *δ̣ubbaaṭ*) *ṣaff.*

none - *maʒʒad, wala waaʒid.* None of my friends could help me. *maʒʒad min ʔaṣdiqaaʔi gidar ysaaεidni.* -- None of the women know anything about it. *wala waʒda mnin-niswaan tuεruf šii εanna.*
**That's none of your business! *haaδa muu šuġḷak!*

nonsense - *kalaam faariġ, ʒači xaruṭ.* Now you're talking nonsense. *hassa da-tiʒči kalaam faariġ.* or *hassa ʒačyak xaruṭ.*

noodles - *šaεriyya.*

noon - *δ̣uhur.* It wasn't as hot at noon today as it was yesterday noon. *ma-čaanat ʒaarra l-yoom iδ̣-δ̣uhur miθil-ma čaanat il-baarʒa δ̣-δ̣uhur.*

nor - *w-laa.* I haven't seen it nor do I want to see it. *ma-šifta w-laa ʔariid ʔašuufa.*

normal - *εtiyaadi*.* His temperature is normal. *darajat ʒaraarta εtiyaadiyya.*

normally - *εtiyaadiyyan, ʒasab il-εaada.*

north - *šimaal.* The wind is coming from the north. *l-hawa jaay imniš-šimaal.* -- Mosul is north of Baghdad. *l-mooṣil ib-šimaal baġdaad.*

northern - *šimaali*.* You can find snow in the northern part of Iraq. *tigdar tilgi θiluuj bil-qism iš-šimaali mnil-εiraaq.*

Norway - *n-narwiij.*

Norwegian - *narwiiji** pl. *-iyyiin.*

nose - **1.** *xašim* pl. *xšuum.* He can't breathe through his nose because of the operation. *ma-yigdar yitnaffas min xašma b-sabab il-εamaliyya.* **2.** *muqaddama* pl. *-aat.* There was a fire in the nose of the aircraft. *čaan ʔaku ʒariiq ib-muqaddamat iṭ-ṭayyaara.*
**He sticks his nose into everything. *ydaxxil nafsa b-kullši.*

nostril - *manxar* pl. *manaaxir.*

not - **1.** *muu.* He is not a man. *huwwa muu rajjaal.* **2.** *ma-* He did not come. *huwwa ma-ʔija.* **3.** *la-* Do not go. *la-truuʒ.*
not at all - **1.** *muu kulliš.* I'm not at all sure. *ʔaani muu kulliš mitʔakkid.* **2.** *ma...ʔabadan, muu. .. ʔabadan.* They're not at all happy in their new home. *humma muu farʒaaniin ib-beethum ij-jidiid ʔabadan.* **3.** *l-εafu.* Thank you very much. Not at all. *ʔaškurak ihwaaya. l-εafu.*

to **notarize** - *ṣaddaq (i taṣdiiq) t-.* I have a friend that can notarize this document. *εindi ṣadiiq yigdar yṣadiq hal-waraqa.*

notary public - *kaatib εadil* pl. *kuttaab εadil, kuttaab εuduul.*

notch - *θalma* pl. *-aat.* There's a notch on the edge of the table. *ʔaku θalma εala ʒaaffat il-meez.*
to notch - *θilam (i θalim) n-.* He notched the ruler with his knife. *θilam il-maṣṭara b-siččiinta.*

note - **1.** *waraqa* pl. *-aat.* He left a note on the table and went out. *tirak waraqa εal-meez w-ṭilaε.* **2.** *nooṭa* pl. *-aat.* Try to sing this note. *ʒaawil itganni han-nooṭa.* **3.** *mulaaʒaδ̣a* pl. *-aat.* The teacher wrote several notes on the margin of my paper. *l-muεallim kitab εiddat mulaaʒaδ̣aat εala haamiš waraqti.* **4.** *εalaama* pl. *εalaaʔim, ʔaθar* pl. *ʔaaθaar.* There was a note of fear in his voice. *čaan ʔaku ʔaθar xoof ib-ṣoota.* **5.** *kumpiyaala* pl. *-aat.* He gave me a note for the balance. *nṭaani kumpiyaala εala baqiyyat il-ifluus.*
notes - *ruʔuus aqlaam.* I didn't take notes in class today. *ma-ʔaxaδit ruʔuus aqlaam biṣ-ṣaff il-yoom.*
of note - *maεruuf, malʒuuδ̣.* He's written three books of note. *kitab iθlaθ kutub maεruufa.*
to note - **1.** *δikar (u δikir) n-, nawwah (i tanwiih) t-.* He noted our assistance in a letter to the manager. *δikar musaaεadatna b-kitaab*

lil-mudiir. 2. *laazaδ (i mulaazaδa) t-.* Note the beautiful carving. *laaziδ in-naqš ij-jamiil.*
notebook - *daftar* pl. *dafaatir.*
nothing - 1. *ma-aku, laa šii.* Something is better than nothing. *šii ʔazsan min laa šii.* 2. *ma-... šii.* We did nothing all afternoon. *ma-sawweena šii ṭuul il-ƐaṢir.*
for nothing - *b-balaaš, majjaanan.* He gave me this shirt for nothing. *nṭaani haθ-θoob ib-balaaš.*
notice - 1. *ʔiƐlaan* pl. *-aat.* Did you read the notice on the bulletin board? *qreet il-ʔiƐlaan Ɛal-looza?* 2. *ʔišƐaar* pl. *-aat.* They fired him without notice. *ṭallƐoo mniδ-δuġuḷ b:duun ʔišƐaar.* 3. *xabar.* You'll have to give notice a month before you move. *laazim tinṭi xabar gabuḷ šahar min wakit-ma titzawwal.*
**I don't know how it escaped my notice. *ma-adri šloon faatat Ɛalayya.*
to notice - 1. *laazaδ (i mulaazaδa) t-, ntibah (i ntibaah).* Did you notice if he was in his office or not? *laazaδit iδa kaan ib-daaʔirta loo laa?* 2. *laazaδ (i mulaazaδa) t-.* Everybody noticed his tie. *kull waazid laazaδ irbaaṭa.*
to **notify** - *ballaġ (i tabliiġ, tbilliġ) t-, xabbar (u txubbur) t-, ʔaƐlam (i ʔiƐlaam) n-.* Notify me when you arrive. *xabburni lamma tooṢal.*
notion - 1. *meel* pl. *miyuul.* I had a notion to stay home today. *čaan Ɛindi meel ʔabqa bil-beet il-yoom.* 2. *fikra* pl. *fikir.* I haven't any notion what he wants. *ma-Ɛindi ʔay fikra š-yriid.*
notorious - *mašhuur.* He's a notorious criminal. *huwwa mujrim mašhuur.*
noun - *ʔisim* pl. *ʔasmaaʔ.*
nourishing - *muġaδδi.* We ate a nourishing breakfast. *ʔakalna riyuug muġaδδi.*
nourishment - *ġiδaaʔ, quut, taġδiya.* He needs more nourishment. *yriid-la ġiδaaʔ ʔakθar.*
novel - 1. *ruwaaya* pl. *-aat, quṢṢa* pl. *quṢaṢ.* I read a good novel last night. *qreet xooš ruwaaya l-baarza bil-leel.* 2. *jidiid.* That's a novel idea. *haaδi fikra jidiida.*
November - *tišriin iθ-θaani.*
now - *hassa, l-ʔaan.* I have to go now. *laazim ʔaruuz hassa.*
by now - *hassa, l-ʔaan.* He should have been here by now. *laazim ykuun hassa hnaa.*
from now on - *min hassa w-jaay, minnaa w-raayiz, minnaa w-hiič.* From now on I'll keep quiet. *minnaa w-hiič raz-askut.*
just now - *hastaww-, hassa, l-ʔaan.* I talked to him just now. *hastawwni zčeet wiyyaa.*
now and then - *been zeen w-ʔaaxar, been mudda w-mudda, been fatra w-fatra, ʔazyaanan.* I hear from him now and then. *ʔasmaƐ minna been zeen w-ʔaaxar.*
up to now - *l-zadd il-ʔaan, li-hassa.* I haven't been sick up to now. *ma-tmarraδit il-zadd il-ʔaan.*
nowadays - *hal-ʔayyaam.* Nowadays, every house has television. *hal-ʔayyaam kull beet bii talafizyoon.*
nowhere - *ma-... b-ʔay mukaan.* He's nowhere to be seen. *ma-yinšaaf ib-ʔay mukaan.*
nozzle - *raas* pl. *ruus.* The hose needs a new nozzle. *Ṣ-Ṣoonda yriid-ilha raas jidiid.*
nuclear energy - *ṭ-ṭaaqa n-nawawiyya.*
nucleus - *nawaat* pl. *nuwaayaat* coll. *nuwa.*
nude - *mṢallax* pl. *-iin, mṢaaliix; Ɛaryaan* pl. *-iin, Ɛraaya.*
nudge - *naġġa* pl. *-aat.* He gave me a nudge when she walked by. *nṭaani naġġa lamma marrat.*
to nudge - *naġġ (u naġġ) n-.* Don't nudge me! *la-tnuġġni.*
nuisance - *δawaaj, δawajaan.* Neckties are a nuisance. *l-ʔarbiṭa δawajaan.*
numb - 1. *xadraan.* My fingers are numb from the cold. *ʔaṢaabƐi xadraana mnil-barid.* 2. *mitxaddir, xadraan.* I feel completely numb. *ʔašƐur kull jismi mitxaddir.*
to numb - *xaddar (i taxdiir) t-.* The blow numbed my shoulder. *δ-δarba xaddrat čitfi.*
number - 1. *raqam* pl. *ʔarqaam, numra* pl. *numar.* What's your house number? *šgadd raqam beetkum?* — Did you write down the number? *ktabit ir-raqam?* 2. *Ɛadad* pl. *ʔaƐdaad.* A number of cars are still available at reduced prices. *Ɛadad imnis-sayyaaraat baƐda mawjuud ib-ʔasƐaar muxaffaδa.* 3. *Ɛidda.* He's been imprisoned a number of times. *nsijan Ɛiddat marraat.*
**I've got his number. *ʔaƐruf duwaa.*
to number - *raqqam (u truqqum, tarqiim), nammar (u tnummur) t-.* Number the boxes from one to ten. *raqqum il-Ɛilab min waazid ila Ɛašra.*
**His days are numbered. *ʔayyaama maƐduuda.*
numeral - *raqam* pl. *ʔarqaam.*
nun - *raahiba* pl. *-aat.*
nurse - 1. *mumarriδa* pl. *-aat.* The patient needs a nurse. *l-mariiδ yiztaaj mumarriδa.* 2. *murabbiya* pl. *-aat.* The children are out in the park with their nurse. *j-jahhaal barra bil-zadiiqa wiyya murabbiyathum.*
wet nurse - *daaya* pl. *-aat.*
to nurse - 1. *riδaƐ (a raδiƐ) n-.* They brought a woman to nurse the baby. *jaabaw mara tirδaƐ ij-jaahil.* 2. *Ɛtina (i Ɛtinaaʔ) b-.* He's nursing his broken leg. *da-yiƐtini b-rijla l-maksuura.*
nursery - 1. *rawδa* pl. *-aat.* I take my child to the nursery at eight o'clock every day. *ʔaaxuδ ibni lir-rawδa s-saaƐa θmaanya kull yoom.* 2. *maštal* pl. *mašaatil.* I bought these flowers at the nursery. *štireet hal-warid imnil-maštal.*
nut - 1. *čaraza* pl. *-aat* coll. *čaraz; karaza* pl. *-aat* coll. *karaz.* This shop sells all kinds of nuts. *hal-baggaal ybiiƐ jamiiƐ ʔanwaaƐ ič-čarazaat.* 2. *Ṣammuuna* pl. *-aat.* This nut doesn't fit the bolt. *haṢ-Ṣammuuna ma-tirham Ɛal-burġi.* 3. *mxabbaḷ* pl. *-iin, mxaabiiḷ.* He's a real nut. *huwwa mxabbaḷ tamaam.*
nut cracker - *kassaarat* (pl. *-aat*) *jooz.*
nutmeg - *joozbawwa.*
nylon - *naayloon.* He bought nylon socks. *štira jwaariib naayloon.*

O

oak - *balluuṭ.*
oar - *mijdaaf* pl. *majaadiif.* The oars are in the boat. *l-majaadiif bil-balam.*
oasis - *waaza* pl. *-aat.*
oats - *hurṭumaan.* They plant a lot of oats here. *hwaaya yzirƐuun hurṭumaan ihnaa.*
obedience - *ṭaaƐa.*
obedient - *ṭaayiƐ, muṭiiƐ.*
to **obey** - *ṭaaƐ (i ṭaaƐa) n-, xiδaƐ (a xaδiƐ) n-.* He doesn't obey me. *huwwa ma-yṭiiƐni.* — I can't obey that order. *ma-agdar aṭiiƐ hal-ʔamur.*
object - 1. *šii* pl. *ʔašyaaʔ, zaaja* pl. *-aat.* He was struck on the head with a heavy object. *nδirab Ɛala raasa b-šii θigiil.* 2. *qaṢid, maqṢad* pl. *maqaaṢid.* What is the object of that? *šinu l-qaṢid min δaak?*
to **object** - *Ɛtiraδ (i Ɛtiraaδ), maanaƐ (i mumaanaƐa).* I don't know why you object to it. *ma-aƐruf leeš da-tiƐtiriδ Ɛaleeha.* — **I hope you don't object to my smoking. *ʔatʔammal ma-Ɛindak maaniƐ ʔiδa ʔadaxxin.*
objection - *ƐtiraaΔ* pl. *-aat, maaniƐ* pl. *mawaaniƐ.* He didn't raise any objection. *ma-ʔaθaar ʔay iƐtiraaδ.* — Is there any objection? *ʔaku ʔay maaniƐ?*
objectionable - *ma-maqbuul.*
objective - *hadaf* pl. *ʔahdaaf.* We reached our objective. *wuṢalna hadafna.*
obligated - *mamnuun, mumtann.* We're very much obligated to you. *ʔizna mamnuuniin ihwaaya minnak.*
obligation - *waajib* pl. *-aat, ltizaam* pl. *-aat, rtibaaṭ* pl. *-aat.* He can't meet his obligations. *ma-yigdar ywaffi ltizaamaata.*
**We're under no obligation to him. *ʔizna muu marbuuṭiin bii.*
obligatory - *ʔijbaari*.* Military service is obligatory. *l-xidma bij-jeeš ijbaariyya.*
to **oblige** - *jubar (u ʔijbaar).* His illness obliged him to leave school for a year. *maraδṭa jubrata yitruk il-madrasa l-sana wizda.*
to be obliged - *δṭarr (a δṭiraar), njubar (u njibaar).* I was obliged to take shelter in a cave. *δṭarreet altiji bil-kahaf.*
obscene - *baδiiʔ.*
observance - *ztifaal, ztiraam.* The parade is a part of the observance of Army Day. *l-istiƐraaδ qisim imnil-ztifaal ib-yoom ij-jeeš.*
observant - *mulaaziδ.* He is observant and has a good

mind. *huwwa fadd waaẓid mulaaẓiδ w-ɛaaqil.*
observation - 1. *muɛaayana.* He entered the hospital for observation. *dixal il-mustašfa lil-muɛaayana.* 2. *mulaaẓaδa* pl. *-aat.* In his speech he made a number of acute observations on the political situation. *b-xiṭaaba sawwa ɛiddat mulaaẓaδaat ẓaadda ɛan il-ẓaala s-siyaasiyya.*
observatory - *marṣad jawwi* pl. *maraaṣid jawwiyya.*
to **observe** - 1. *laaẓaδ (i mulaaẓaδa).* Did you observe the reaction she had? *laaẓaδit radd il-fiɛil iṣ-ṣaar ɛidha?* 2. *raaɛa (i muraaɛaat).* Which holidays do you observe in Iraq? *yaa ɛuṭal itraaɛuun bil-ɛiraaq?* — All employees here are expected to observe the regulations. *kull il-mustaxdamiin ihnaa mafruuδ biihum yraaɛuun it-taɛliimaat.*
obstacle - *ɛaqaba* pl. *-aat, maaniɛ* pl. *mawaaniɛ.* He had to overcome many obstacles before he was successful. *δṭarr yitġallab ɛala hwaaya ɛaqabaat gabuḷ-ma yitwaffaq.*
obstinate - *ɛaniid* pl. *-iin, ɛanuud* pl. *-iin.* It won't do you any good to be obstinate about it. *ma-yfiidak itṣiir ɛaniid ib-hal-xuṣuuṣ.*
to **obtain** - *ẓaṣṣal (i taẓṣiil) t-.* He obtained all of his education abroad. *ẓaṣṣal kull taɛliima l-ɛaali bil-xaarij.*
obvious - *waaδiẓ, δaahir, mbayyin.* It's obvious that he doesn't want to do it. *mnil-waaδiẓ ʔanna ma-yriid ysawwiiha.* — His annoyance is obvious from his voice. *nziɛaaja mbayyin min ṣoota.*
obviously - *mnil-waaδiẓ, mniδ-δaahir.* She was obviously wrong. *mnil-waaδiẓ čaanat ġalṭaana.*
occasion - *munaasaba* pl. *-aat.* A dress like this can be worn for any occasion. *fistaan miθil haaδa yinlibis ib-kull munaasaba.* — What's the occasion? *šinu l-munaasaba?*
occasionally - *ʔaẓyaanan.* Except for a trip to Basra occasionally, I never leave Baghdad. *ma-ɛada safra lil-baṣra ʔaẓyaanan, ʔabad ma-aṭlaɛ min baġdaad.*
occupation - 1. *šuġuḷ* pl. *ʔašġaal, mihna* pl. *mihan.* What's your occupation? *šinu šuġḷak?* 2. *ẓtilaal.* Where were you during the occupation? *ween činit ib-zaman il-iẓtilaal?*
occupied - *muẓtall.* He is a refugee from occupied Palestine. *haaδa laajiʔ min falaṣṭiin il-muẓtalla.*
to **occupy** - 1. *ẓtall (a ẓtilaal).* The Turks occupied the town first. *l-ʔatraak iẓtallaw il-madiina bil-ʔawwal.* 2. *sikan (u sukna) n-.* The house hasn't been occupied for years. *l-beet ma-nsikan min isniin.* 3. *šiġal (i ʔišġaal) n-.* Studying occupies all my time. *d-diraasa da-tišġil kull waqti.* — The boss is occupied at the moment. *r-raʔiis mašġuul hassa.*
to **occur** - 1. *ṣaar (i), ẓidaθ (i ẓuduuθ), wugaɛ (a waguɛ).* When did the accident occur? *šwakit ṣaar il-ẓaadiθ?* 2. *ʔija (i).* The name occurred twice in the same chapter. *ʔija l-ism marrteen ib-nafs il-faṣil.* 3. *xiṭar (u xuṭuur).* That would never have occurred to me. *δaak wala čaan yixṭur ɛala baali.* 4. *tbaadar (a tabaadur).* Suddenly it occurred to me that I forgot to lock the door. *fujʔatan itbaadar-li ʔanni niseet ʔaqful il-baab.*
ocean - *muẓiiṭ* pl. *-aat.* The U.S.A. lies between two oceans. *l-wilaayaat il-muttaẓida waaqɛa been muẓiiṭeen.*
o'clock - *saaɛa.* The train leaves at seven o'clock. *l-qiṭaar yitruk saaɛa sabɛa.*
October - *tišriin il-ʔawwal.*
oculist - *ṭabiib (pl. ʔaṭibbaaʔ) iɛyuun.*
odd - 1. *šaaδδ* pl. *-iin, ġariib* pl. *-iin.* He's a very odd person. *huwwa fadd waaẓid šaaδδ.* 2. *tak.* Haven't you seen an odd glove anywhere? *ma-šifit tak čaff ib-fadd makaan?* 3. *fardi*.* Pick an odd number. *ʔixṭaar raqam fardi.* 4. *w-ksuur.* It cost me thirty-odd dinars. *kallifatni tlaaθiin diinaar w-ksuur.* 5. *mitfarriġ.* He does all the odd jobs around the house. *huwwa ysawwi kull il-ʔašġaal il-mitfarrġa bil-beet.* 6. *mxaalaf.* We only have a few odd pairs left. *ɛidna bass fadd čam zooj imxaalfa buqat.*
odor - *riiẓa* pl. *riyaẓ, rawaayiẓ.* What is that bad odor I smell? *šinu har-riiẓa j-jaayfa lli qaaɛid aštammha.*
of - 1. *min.* I have a complete edition of his works. *ɛindi nusxa kaamla min muʔallafaata.* — The watch is of gold. *s-saaɛa min δahab.* 2. *maal.* The roof of our house is very high. *ṣ-ṣaṭiẓ maal beetna kulliš ɛaali.*
**Could I have a glass of water, please? *ʔagdar ʔaaxuδ glaaṣ maay rajaaʔan.*
**He's a manager of a big store. *huwwa mudiir maxzan čibiir.*
off - *min.* This thing has been off the market for a year. *haš-šii mixtifi mnis-suug min sana.* or *haš-šii ṣaar-la sana mnis-suug.* -- There's a button off your jacket. *ʔaku dugma waagiɛ min sitirtak.*
**The post office isn't far off. *daaʔirat il-bariid muu kulliš biɛiida.*
**Our maid is off today. *xaadmatna ɛidha ɛuṭla l-yoom.* or *xaadmatna ma-da-tištuġul il-yoom.*
**He's a little off. *huwwa šwayya ɛinda xyuuṭ.* or *šwayya ɛaqla laaɛib.*
**He was off in a flash. *ġaab miθl il-barq.*
**They aren't so badly off. *humma muu kulliš miẓtaajiin.*
**They are very well off. *humma kullis iznaagiin.*
**The ship anchored three miles off shore. *l-baaxira δabbat ʔangar itlaθ ʔamyaal ɛan is-saaẓil.*
**June is still three months off. *baɛad itlaθt išhur il-ẓuzeeraan.* or *ẓuzeeraan baɛad-la tlaθt išhur yaḷḷa yiji.*
**His figures are way off. *ẓsaabaata kullha ġalaṭ.*
**This is an off year for wheat. *haay muu xooš sana lil-ẓunṭa.*
**I'm going to take a week off soon. *raẓ-aaxuδ isbuuɛ ɛuṭla qariiban.*
**This thing has been off the market for a year. *naš-šii mixtifi mnis-suug min sana.* or *haš-šii ṣaar-la sana mnis-suug.*
**There's a button off your jacket. *ʔaku dugma waagiɛ min sitirtak.*
**Hands off! *waxxir iidak min haay!*
**They've broken off relations. *qiṭɛaw ɛalaaqaathum.*
**The branch broke off. *nkisar il-ġuṣin.*
**One leg of the table has come off. *nšilɛat rijil imnil-meez.*
**Ladies are requested to take their hats off. *maṭluub imnim-niswaan yšiiluun šafaqaathum.*
**When does the plane take off? *šwakit iṭṭiir iṭ-ṭayyaara?*
off and on - *ʔaẓyaanan, marraat.* She works off and on. *hiyya tištuġul ʔaẓyaanan.*
to **offend** - *ʔasaaʔ (i ʔisaaʔa) ʔila.* I hope I didn't offend you. *inšaḷḷa ma-ʔasaʔit ʔilak.*
offense - 1. *ʔisaaʔa* pl. *-aat.* I didn't mean any offense. *ma-qṣadit ʔay ʔisaaʔa.* 2. *muxaalafa* pl. *-aat.* Is this your first offense? *haaδi ʔawwal muxaalafa ʔilak?*
to take offense - *staaʔ (a stiyaaʔ), tkaddar (a takaddur).* He took offense at my remark. *staaʔ min mulaaẓaδti.*
offensive - 1. *musiiʔ.* His behavior was offensive to the local people. *taṣarrufa čaan musiiʔ lis-sukkaan il-maẓalliyyiin.* 2. *makruuh, kariih.* It has an offensive odor. *biiha riiẓa kariiha.*
offer - *ɛariδ* pl. *ɛuruuδ.* He made me a good offer. *sawwaa-li xooš ɛariδ.*
to offer - 1. *qaddam (i taqdiim) t-.* May I offer you a cup of coffee? *ʔagdar aqaddim-lak finjaan gahwa?* 2. *ɛiraδ (i ɛariδ) n-.* He offered me a hundred dinars for it. *ɛiraδ ɛalayya miit diinaar biiha.* 3. *tbarraɛ (a tabarruɛ), ɛiraδ (i ɛariδ).* My brother-in-law offered to help me paint the house. *nisiibi tbarraɛ yɛaawinni b-ṣubġ il-beet.* 4. *bayyan (i tabyiin) t-.* Didn't they offer any resistance? *ma-bayynaw ʔay muqaawama?*
offhand - *b-ṣuura murtajala.* I can't tell you offhand. *ma-agdar agul-lak ib-ṣuura murtajala.*
**He treated me in an offhand manner. *ma-qaddarni.* or *ɛaamalni buruud.*
office - 1. *maktab* pl. *makaatib, daaʔira* pl. *dawaaʔir.* You can see me in my office. *tigdar itšuufni b-maktabi.*— The offices close at five o'clock. *d-dawaaʔir tinsadd is-saaɛa xamsa.* 2. *markaz* pl. *maraakiz, manṣib* pl. *manaaṣib.* He has a high office in the government. *ɛinda markaz ɛaali bil-ẓukuuma.*
**The whole office was invited. *kull il-muwaδδafiin čaanaw madɛuwwiin.*
officer - 1. *δaabuṭ* pl. *δubbaaṭ.* He was an officer during the last war. *čaan δaabuṭ bil-ẓarb il-ʔaxiir.* 2. *šurṭi* pl. *šurṭa.* Ask the officer how we get to the station. *ʔisʔal iš-šurṭi šloon noosal lil-maẓaṭṭa.* 3. *ɛuδu (pl. ʔaɛδaaʔ) ʔidaara.* Are you an officer of this club? *ʔinta min ʔaɛδaaʔ ʔidaarat n-naadi?*
official - 1. *maʔmuur* pl. *-iin.* The customs official who examined my bags was very thorough. *maʔmuur il-gumrug illi fuẓaṣ junaṭi čaan kulliš daqiiq.*

2. *muwaδδaf* pl. *-iin.* He's a State Department official. *huwwa muwaδδaf min wizaart il-xaarijiyya.* 3. *rasmi*.* He is here on official business. *huwwa hnaa b-šuġuḷ rasmi.*

officially - *rasmiyyan.* It was announced officially. *nЄilnat rasmiyyan.*

often - 1. *hwaaya, kaθiir.* Do you see him often? *tšuufa hwaaya?* -- He is absent often. *haaδa yġiib kaθiir.* 2. *ġaaliban, ġaaliban-ma.* He often spends his afternoons with us. *ġaaliban-ma yigδi Єaṣriyyaata wiyyaana.*

how often - 1. *čam marra.* How often do you go to the movies in a month? *čam marra truuz lis-siinama biš-šahar?* 2. *yaa-ma.* How often I have wished that I had gone to college. *yaa-ma ʔatmanna loo daaxil kulliyya.*

to **ogle** - *baṣbaṣ (i baṣbaṣa) t- l-.* The boys stand in front of the school and ogle the girls as they come out. *l-wulid yoogfuun giddaam il-madrasa w-ybaṣbiṣuun lil-banaat min yṭilЄuun.*

oil - 1. *nafuṭ, zeet.* Oil is the most important export in Iraq. *n-nafuṭ ʔahamm ṣaadiraat il-Єiraaq.* -- We need some oil for the stove. *niztaaj nafuṭ liṭ-ṭabbaax.* 2. *dihin* pl. *duhuun.* Vegetable oil is often used for cooking. *d-dihn in-nabaati hwaaya mustaЄmal liṭ-ṭabux.* 3. *zeet* pl. *zyuut.* I really prefer olive oil on the salad. *ʔaani bil-zaqiiqa ʔafaδδil zeet iz-zeetuun Єaz-zalaaṭa.*

to oil - *dahhan (i tadhiin) t-.* The sewing machine needs to be oiled. *makiint il-ixyaaṭa yird-ilha titdahhan.*

oilcake- *kisba* pl. *kisab.* Our water buffalo lives on oilcakes. *jaamuusna yЄiiš Єal-kisba.*

oilcan - *yaaġdaan* pl. *-aat.*

oilcloth - *qmaaš imšammaЄ* pl. *ʔaqmiša mšammЄa.*

ointment - *malzam* pl. *malaazim, dihin* pl. *duhuun.*

O.K. - 1. *muwaafaqa, muṣaadaqa, qubuul.* I need his O.K. *ʔaztaaj muwaafaqta.* 2. *zeen.* Everything is O.K. now. *hassa kullši zeen.*

**I'll go along, if it's O.K. with you. *ʔaruuz wiyyaak, ʔiδa ma-Єindak maaniЄ.*

to O.K. - *waafaq (u muwaafaqa), ṣaadaq (i muṣaadaqa).* He has to O.K. it first. *laazim ywaafuq Єaleeha ʔawwal.*

old - 1. *Єatiig, qadiim.* I gave all my old clothes to the poor. *nṭeet kull ihduumi l-Єatiiga lil-fuqaraaʔ.* -- Is this an old model? *haay nooЄha qadiima?* 2. *čibiir* pl. *kbaar.* He's pretty old. *huwwa kulliš čibiir.*

**How old are you? *šgadd Єumrak?*

old man - *šaayib* pl. *šiyyaab.* My uncle is an old man, but he is still very active. *Єammi šaayib laakin la-yzaal kulliš našiiṭ.*

old woman - *Єajuuz, Єajuuza* pl. *Єajaayiz.* She's an old woman now. *hassa hiyya Єajuuz.*

old-fashioned - 1. *rajЄi*, mitЄaṣṣub.* She's very old-fashioned in her ideas. *hiyya kulliš rajЄiyya b-ʔafkaarha.* 2. *min ṭiraaz qadiim.* His clothes are old-fashioned, but of good quality. *malaabsa min ṭiraaz qadiim laakin min nooЄiyya zeena.*

to **omit** - *ziδaf (i zaδif) n-.* Omit that word. *ʔizδif hač-čilma.*

on - 1. *Єala.* He sat on the speaker's left. *giЄad Єala yisaar il-xaṭiib.* -- The drinks are on the house. *š-šurub Єala zsaab il-mazall.* 2. *Єala, foog.* Put it on the table. *xalliiha Єal-meez.* 3. *b-.* On what day? *b-ʔay yoom?* -- Do you sell on credit? *tbiiЄ ib-ʔaqṣaaṭ?* -- I live on Rashid St. *ʔaskun ib-šaariЄ ir-rašiid.* -- Who's on the team? *minu bil-firqa?* -- What's on the radio today? *šaku bir-raadyo l-yoom?* 4. *Єan.* His lecture was on Arab solidarity. *muzaaδarta čaanat Єan it-taδaamun il-Єarabi.*

**Are you open on Friday? *tfattiz ij-jumЄa?*

**Is the gas on? *l-ġaaz mašЄuul?*

and so on - *w-ʔila ʔaaxirihi.* I need paper, ink, and so on. *ʔaztaaj waraq, zibir w-ʔila ʔaaxirihi.*

once - 1. *marra wizda, fadd marra, marra.* I've seen him only once. *šifta marra wizda bass.* -- He feeds the dog once a day. *yṭaЄЄum ič-čalib marra bil-yoom.* 2. *fadd yoom.* This was once the business section. *fadd yoom haaδa čaan il-markaz it-tijaari.*

at once - 1. *suwa, marra wizda, fadd marra.* Everything came at once. *kullši ʔija marra wizda.* 2. *zaalan, b-saaЄ, sariiЄan.* Come at once. *b-saaЄ taЄaal.*

once in a while - *baЄδ il-ʔazyaan, ʔazaanan, dooraat.* Once in a while I like a good glass of cold buttermilk. *baЄδ il-ʔazyaan ʔazibb fadd iglaaṣ liban baarid.*

one - 1. (m.) *waazid* (f.) *wazda.* Count from one to a hundred. *Єidd imnil-waazid lil-miyya.* -- One or two will be enough. *waazid ʔaw iθneen kaafi.* -- It's almost one o'clock. *s-saaЄa zawaali l-wazda.* -- One never knows. *l-waazid iš-midrii.* -- One of us can buy the tickets. *waazid minnina yigdar yištiri l-biṭaaqaat.* 2. *fadd, waazid.* I have one question I want to ask. *Єindi fadd suʔaal ʔariid ʔasʔala.* 3. (m.) *ʔabu* (f.) *ʔumm.* The one with the cover is the best box for our purpose. *ʔabu l-ġiṭa ʔazsan ṣanduug il-ġaraδna.* or ***lli bil-ġiṭa ʔazsan ṣanduug il-ġaraδna.* -- The one with the top down is my car. *ʔumm it-tanta n-naazla s-sayyaara maalti.*

**I prefer the more expensive one. *ʔafaδδil il-ʔaġla.*

**Take that one. *ʔuxuδ haδaak.*

**One of these days, I'll be back. *fadd yoom imnil-ʔayyaam ʔarjaЄ.*

**On the one hand he wants it finished, on the other hand he doesn't give us the material. *min jiha yriidha tixlaṣ w-min jiha ma-da-yinṭiina l-mawaadd.*

one another - *waazid il-laax.* They like one another. *yzibbuun waazid il-laax.*

one at a time - *waazid waazid.* Let them in one at a time. *xaššišhum waazid waazid.*

onion - *buṣla* pl. *-aat* coll. *buṣal.*

only - 1. *bass.* I was going to buy it, only he told me not to. *čaan ištireetha bass huwwa gal-li laa.* -- This is only for you. *haaδi bass ʔilak.* 2. *waziid.* He's our only child. *huwwa ʔibinna l-waziid.*

open - 1. *maftuuz, mafkuuk.* He may have come in through an open window. *yjuuz dixal min šibbaač maftuuz.* -- The dining room is not open yet. *ġurfat il-ʔakil maa maftuuza li-hassa.* 2. *šaaġir.* Is the job still open? *l-waδiifa baЄadha šaaġra?* 3. *maftuug.* The shoulder seam of your jacket is open. *xyaaṭ čitif sitirtak maftuug.* 4. *ṭaliq.* He's in the open air all day long. *huwwa bil-hawa iṭ-ṭaliq ṭuul il-yoom.*

to open - 1. *fitaz (a fatiz) n-, fakk (u fakk) n-.* Open the door please. *ʔiftaz il-baab, min faδlak.* -- They opened an account at the bank. *fitzaw izsaab bil-bang.* 2. *fattaz (i taftiiz).* We open every day at 9 A.M. *nfattiz saaЄa tisЄa ṣ-ṣubuz kull yoom.* 3. *šaqq (u šaqq) n-.* The government is going to open a new highway through the mountains. *l-zukuuma raz-itšuqq ṭariiq jidiid yixtiriq ij-jibaal.* -- The police opened a way through the crowd for us. *š-šurṭa šaqqoo-nna ṭariiq been ij-jamaahiir.* 4. *bida (i bidaaya) n-.* When does hunting season open? *šwakit yibdi mawsim iṣ-ṣeed?* 5. *nfitaz (i nfitaaz).* The door opens easily now. *l-baab hassa da-yinfitiz ib-suhuula.*

**He's always open to reasonable suggestions. *huwwa daaʔiman yiqbal iqtiraazaat maЄquula.*

to open onto - *ṭilaЄ (a ṭaliЄ) Єala.* Our room opens onto a balcony. *ġurfatna tiṭlaЄ Єala baalkoon.*

to open up - *fakk (u fakk) n-, fitaz (a fatiz) n-.* Open up the package. *fukk ir-ruzma.* -- Can you open up the safe? *tigdar itfukk il-qaaṣa?*

opening - 1. *fatza* pl. *-aat.* The opening isn't big enough. *l-fatza muu čibiira kifaaya.* 2. *bidaaya.* We missed the opening of his speech. *ma-lazzagna Єala bidaayat xiṭaaba.* 3. *ftitaaz* pl. *-aat.* Were you at the opening of the exhibition? *činit b-iftitaaz il-maЄraδ?* 4. *šaaġir* pl. *šawaaġir.* We'll call you as soon as we have an opening. *nxaabrak ʔawwal-ma yṣiir Єidna šaaġir.*

opera - *ʔoopra* pl. *-aat.*

opera house - *daar* (pl. *duur*) *ʔoopra.*

to **operate** - 1. *šaġġaḷ (i tašġiiḷ) t-.* How do you operate this machine? *šloon itšaġġiḷ hal-makiina?* 2. *štiġal (u štiġaal).* This machine operates on electricity. *hal-makiina tištuġul bil-kahrabaaʔ.* 3. *sawwa (i taswiya) Єamaliyya.* The doctor says he'll have to operate on her. *d-daktoor gaal laazim ysawwii-lha l-Єamaliyya.*

operation - 1. *Єamaliyya* pl. *-aat.* This is her third operation. *haay θaaliθ Єamaliyya ʔilha.* 2. *zaraka* pl. *-aat.* One machine does the whole process in a single operation. *makiina wazda tquum ib-kull il-Єamaliyya b-zaraka wazda.* 3. *stiЄmaal.* They just put this line into operation. *hassa xallaw hal-xaṭṭ bil-istiЄmaal.*

opinion - *raʔi* pl. *ʔaaraaʔ, fikir* pl. *ʔafkaar.* I have a very high opinion of him. *fikirti Єanna*

kulliš zeena. -- What's your opinion? *šinu raʔyak?* -- We'll have to get the opinion of an expert. *laazim naaxuδ raʔi xabiir.* --
opponent - *muεaariδ* pl. *-iin, munaafis* pl. *-iin, xaṣum* pl. *xṣuum.* He's a dangerous opponent. *huwwa munaafis xaṭir.*
opportunity - *furṣa* pl. *furaṣ.* When will you have an opportunity to see him? *šwakit yṣiir εindak furṣa tšuufa?* -- This is a big opportunity for you. *haay furṣa čbiira ʔilak.*
to **oppose** - **1.** *εaaraδ (i muεaaraδa).* He's the one who opposed your admission to the club. *huwwa lli εaaraδ intimaaʔak lin-naadi.* **2.** *naafas (i munaafasa).* He opposed me in the last election. *naafasni bil-intixaabaat il-ʔaxiira.*
opposite - **1.** *muqaabil, gbaal.* We live opposite the library. *niskun igbaal il-maktaba.* **2.** *muεaakis, muxaalif, εakis.* He came from the opposite direction. *ʔija mnij-jiha l-muεaakisa.* -- This is just the opposite of what I meant. *haaδa tamaaman muxaalif il-ma εneeta.* or *haaδa tamaaman εaks il-εineeta.*
opposition - *muεaaraδa* pl. *-aat.* The proposal met with unexpected opposition. *l-iqtiraaʒ waajah muεaaraδa ğeer mutawaqqaεa.*
to **oppress** - *ṭiğa (i ṭuğyaan) n- εala.* They oppressed the poor and the weak. *ṭiğaw εala l-fuqaraaʔ wiδ-δuεafaaʔ.*
oppressive - *mδaayiq, mustabidd.* The heat's oppressive today. *l-ʒarr il-yoom imδaayiq.*
optician - *naδδaaraati* pl. *-iyya, ṣaaʒib* (pl. *ʔaṣʒaab*) *naδδaaraat.*
optimism - *tafaaʔul.*
optimist - *mitfaaʔil* pl. *-iin.*
optimistic - *mitfaaʔil.* Don't be so optimistic. *la-tkuun hal-gadd mitfaaʔil.*
or - *loo, ʔaw.* He's coming today or tomorrow. *huwwa jaay il-yoom loo baačir.*
oral - *šafahi**, *šafawi**. She passed the oral examination. *nijʒat bil-imtiʒaan iš-šafahi.*
orally - *šafahiyyan, šafawiyyan.*
orange - **1.** *purtaqaala* pl. *-aat,* coll. *purtaqaal.* How much are the oranges? *beeš il-purtaqaal?* **2.** *purtaqaali**. Her dress was orange and white. *nafnuufha čaan purtaqaali w-ʔabyaδ.*
orange juice - *šarbat purtaqaal, εaṣiir purtaqaal.*
orchard - *bistaan* pl. *basaatiin.*
orchestra - *firqa* (pl. *firaq*) *mawsiiqiyya, jooq mawsiiqi* pl. *ʔajwaaq mawsiiqiyya.*
order - **1.** *ʔamur* pl. *ʔawaamir.* I'm just obeying orders. *ʔaani bass da-aṭiiε il-ʔawaamir.* **2.** *ṭalab* pl. *-aat.* Waiter, I'd like to change my order. *booy, ʔariid ʔabaddil iṭ-ṭalab maali.* **3.** *tartiib* pl. *-aat.* Please put these cards in order. *min faδlak xalli hal-biṭaaqaat ʒasab it-tartiib.* **4.** *niδaam* pl. *-aat.* The police restored order quickly. *š-šurṭa staεaadat in-niδaam ib-surεa.*
**I disposed of it in short order. *dabbaritha bil-εajal.*
in order - **1.** *b-maʒall.* Your remark is quite in order. *mulaaʒaδtak ib-maʒallha tamaaman.* **2.** *mrattab, mnaδδam.* I'd like to see your room in order just once. *b-wuddi ʔašuuf ğuraftak imrattaba wa-law marra.* **3.** *kaamil.* His papers are in order. *ʔawraaqa kaamla.* **4.** *ʒasab.* Line up in order of height. *ṣṭaffu ʒasab iṭ-ṭuul.*
in order to - *ʒatta,* I've come from Amara in order to see you. *jaay imnil-iεmaara ʒatta ʔašuufak.*
made to order - **1.** *tufṣaal, tuuṣaa.* All his suits are made to order. *kull quuṭa tufṣaal.* **2.** *tuuṣaa.* Did you buy your furniture ready-made or is it made to order? *štireet ʔaθaaθak ʒaaδra loo tuuṣaa?*
out of order - *xarbaan.* The fan is out of order. *l-paanka xarbaana.*
to order - **1.** *ʔumar (u ʔamur) n- b-.* He ordered their arrest. *ʔumar ib-tawqiifhum.* **2.** *ṭilab (u ṭalib) n-.* Order the taxi for six o'clock. *ʔuṭulba lit-taksi yiji saaεa sitta.* **3.** *waṣṣa (i tawṣiya).* I ordered a new set of tires for the car. *waṣṣeet εala taxum taayaraat jidiid lis-sayyaara.*
to order around - *tʔammar (a taʔammur) εala.* Don't order me around! *la-titʔammar εalayya!*
ordinary - *εtiyaadi**, *εaadi**. He's just an ordinary mechanic. *huwwa miikaaniiki εtiyaadi.*
ore: **He brought in a piece of copper ore for analysis. *jaab qiṭεa min nuʒaas xaam lit-taʒliil.*
organ - *εuδu* pl. *ʔaεδaaʔ.* Our lesson in Health today was on the genital organs. *darasna b-εilm iṣ-ṣiʒʒa l-yoom čaan εann il-ʔaεδaaʔ it-tanaasuliyya.*
organization - **1.** *tanδiim* pl. *-aat, tartiib* pl. *-aat.* The material is good, but the organization is poor. *l-maadda zeena laakin it-tanδiim muu zeen.* **2.** *munaδδama* pl. *-aat.* He is a member of our organization. *huwwa εuδu b-munaδδamatna.*
to **organize** - *naδδam (i tanδiim) t-, rattab (i tartiib) t-.* They have asked me to organize the election campaign for them. *ṭulbaw minni ʔanaδδim-ilhum ʒamlat il-intixaabaat.* -- We'll call you up as soon as we get ourselves organized. *nxaabrak ʔawwal-ma nrattib ʔumuurna.*
**All the employees in our plant are organized. *kull il-εummaal ib-maṣnaεna minδammiin lin-naqaaba.*
Orient - *š-šarq.*
oriental - *šarqi**.
origin - **1.** *ʔaṣil* pl. *ʔuṣuul.* Darwin named his book 'The Origin of the Species'. *daarwin samma ktaaba "ʔaṣl il-ʔanwaaε."* **2.** *ʔasaas* pl. *ʔusus.* I'm trying to get at the origin of the trouble between them. *ʔaʒaawil atwaṣṣal ʔila ʔasaas il-miškila beenhum.* **3.** *taʒarruk.* We will pay your way back to your point of origin. *raʒ-nidfaε-lak nafaqaat ir-rujuuε ʒatta nuqṭat taʒarrukak.* **4.** *manšaʔ* pl. *manaašiʔ.* All importers must submit a certificate of origin for their goods. *kull il-mistawridiin laazim ybirʒuun šahaadaat manšaʔ il-baδaaʔiεhum.* **5.** *maṣdar* pl. *maṣaadir.* What is the origin of this information? *hal-ʔaxbaar maṣdarha mneen?*
original - **1.** *ʔaṣli**. The original plan was altogether different. *l-mašruuε il-ʔaṣli čaan mixtilif tamaaman εan haay.* **2.** *mubtakir, mubtadiʔ.* This architect has original ideas. *hal-muhandis in-naašiʔ εinda ʔafkaar mubtakira.*
originally - *ʔawwalan, ʔaṣlan, bil-ʔaṣil.* Originally he wanted to be a doctor. *bil-ʔawwal raad yṣiir ṭabiib.*
to **originate** - **1.** *ṣidar (u ṣuduur), nišaʔ (a nišuuʔ).* Where did this rumor originate? *hal-išaaεa mneen ṣidrat?* **2.** *tʒarrak (a taʒarrak).* Where does this train originate? *hal-qiṭaar imneen yitʒarrak?*
orphan - *yatiim* pl. *ʔaytaam.*
orphanage - *maytam* pl. *mayaatim, daar* (pl. *duur*) *ʔaytaam, maεhad* (pl. *maεaahid*) *ʔaytaam.*
ostrich - *naεaama* pl. *-aat* coll. *naεaam.*
other - **1.** (m.) *ʔaaxar* (f.) *ʔuxra* pl. *ʔaaxariin, θaani* pl. *-iin.* All the others got a raise but me. *kull il-ʔaaxariin itraffεaw ʔilla ʔaani.* **2.** (m.) *laax* (f.) *lux, θaani.* Take the other car, I'm going to wash this one. *ʔuxδ is-sayyaara l-lux, raʒ-ʔağsilha l-haay.* -- I can't tell one from another. *ma-da-aεruf waaʒid imnil-laax.* **3.** *baaqi* pl. *-iin.* Put six on the shelf and leave the others in the box. *ʒuṭṭ sitta εar-raff w-itruk il-baaqiin bis-ṣanduug.*
**I saw your friend the other day. *δaak il-yoom šifit ṣadiiqak.*
**Send me someone or other, it doesn't matter who. *dizz-li yaahu l-čaan, ma-yhimm.*
**We have to get it done on time somehow or other. *laazim inxallṣa εal-wakit ib-ṭariiqa-ma.*
every other - *been ... w-.* Our poker group meets every other week. *jamaaεt il-pookar maalatna tijtimiε been isbuuε w-isbuuε.*
otherwise - **1.** *ma-εada.* Otherwise, I'm satisfied with him. *ma-εada haay, ʔaani raaδi wiyyaa.* **2.** *laεad.* What would you do otherwise? *laεad šii tsawwi?* **3.** *w-ʔilla.* I have to return the book today, otherwise I'll have to pay a fine. *laazim ʔarajjiε l-iktaab il-yoom w-ʔilla laazim ʔadfaε ğaraama.*
ought - *yinbiği.* I ought to tell him but it's hard to. *yinbiği ʔagul-la laakin yiṣεab εalayya.*
ounce - *ʔoons* pl. *-aat.*
our - *-na;* (m.) *maalna* (f.) *maalatna* (with preceding definite noun). Their house is larger than our house. *beethum ʔakbar min beetna.*
ours - (m.) *maalna* (f.) *maalatna.* This book is ours. *hal-iktaab maalna.*
ourselves - *nafisna, ʔanfusna.* We're just hurting ourselves. *ʔiʒna da-nʔaδδi nafisna bass.*
to **oust** - *ʔaqṣa (i ʔiqṣaaʔ).* Their main purpose is to oust the prime minister from his office. *ğaraδhum ir-raʔiisi yiqṣuun raʔiis il-wuzaraaʔ min waδiifta.*
out - *barra.* They were out when we called them.

čaanaw barra min xaabarnaahum.
**The lights are out. δ-δuwa maṭfi.
**Straw hats are out of fashion. šafqaat il-xuṣṣ raayӡa moodatha.
out of - **1.** min. He did it out of spite. sawwaaha min ӡiqid. **2.** bila, blayya. She's out of work. hiyya blayya šuġuḷ. **3.** xaarij. I'm from out of town. ʔaani min xaarij il-madiina.
**That's out of the question. haaδa maa mumkin.
**We're out of bread. l-xubiz xaḷṣaan.
**I have been out of work for two months. ṣaar-li šahreen baṭṭaal.
**You're out of step. mašyak ma-muntaδam.

outbreak - **1.** nušuub, ndilaaƐ. We left Europe a little before the outbreak of the war. trakna ʔooruppa šwayya gabuḷ nušuub il-ӡarub. **2.** ḍuhuur. There's an outbreak of cholera in that district. ʔaku ḍuhuur maraḍ il-kooleera b-hal-manṭiqa.

outfit - **1.** lawaazim. We bought our son a complete Scout outfit for his birthday. štireena lawaazim kaššaafa kaamla l-ʔibinna l-yoom Ɛiid miilaada. **2.** malaabis. She bought her wedding outfit in Paris. štirat malaabis Ɛirisha b-paariis. **3.** waӡda pl. -aat. Corporal Muhammad was transferred to another outfit. naaʔib il-Ɛariif imӡammad inniqal il ġeer waӡda. **4.** jamaaƐa pl. -aat. I wouldn't work for such an outfit. ma-aštuġul il-hiiči jamaaƐa.
to outfit - jahhaz (i tajhiiz) t-. You'll be able to outfit your expedition in Mosul. b-ʔimkaankum itjahhizuun baƐθatkum imnil-muuṣiḷ.

to **outgrow** - kubar (a kabur) Ɛala. The children have outgrown their clothes. j-jahaal kubraw Ɛala hduumhum.

outlet - **1.** manfaδ pl. manaafiδ, maxraj pl. maxaarij. The lake has two outlets. l-buӡayra biiha manfaδeen. -- Our company is looking for new outlets. šarikatna tdawwur manaafiδ taṣriif jidiida. -- Children have to have an outlet for their energies. j-jahaal laazim ykuun Ɛidhum manfaδ in-našaaṭhum. **2.** nuqṭa pl. nuqaṭ, sookeet pl. -aat. We need another electrical outlet in this room. niӡtaaj nuqṭa kahrabaaʔiyya θaanya b-hal-ġurfa.

outline - **1.** malmaӡ pl. malaamiӡ. We learned to recognize the planes from their outlines. tƐallamna nmayyiz iṭ-ṭayyaaraat min malaamiӡha. **2.** ruus aqlaam. Did you make an outline of what you're going to say yet? sawweet ruus aqlaam l-illi tguula, loo baƐad?

outlook - **1.** tabaašiir. The outlook for the future isn't very bright. tabaašiir il-mustaqbal ma-tbayyin zeena. **2.** naδra pl. -aat. His outlook on life is narrow. naδirta lil-ӡayaat ḍayyqa.

to **outnumber** - faaq (u) bil-Ɛadad. In that class the girls outnumber the boys. b-δaak iṣ-ṣaff il-banaat yfuuquun il-wulid bil-Ɛadad.

out-of-the-way - minƐizil. Our house is on an out-of-the-way street. beetna Ɛala šaariƐ minƐizil.

outpost - markaz (pl. maraakiz) ʔamaami, nuqṭa (pl. nuqaṭ) ʔamaamiyya.

outrage - ʔisaaʔa pl. -aat. This is an outrage to my personal dignity. haaδi ʔisaaʔa l-karaamti š-šaxṣiyya.
to outrage - ʔasaaʔ (i ʔisaaʔa) l-. His behavior outraged the whole community. taṣarrufa ʔasaaʔ lil-mujtamaƐ kulla.

outrageous - muhawwil. Don't buy anything there; he charges outrageous prices. la-tištiri ʔay šii hnaak; haaδa yuṭlub ʔasƐaar muhawwila.

outright - muṭbaq. That's an outright lie. haaδa čiδib muṭbaq.

outside - **1.** barra, xaarij. He's outside. huwwa barra. -- He lives outside the city. yiskun xaarij il-madiina. **2.** barraani*. You left the outside door open. xalleet il-baab il-barraani maftuuӡ.

outsider - xaariji pl. -iyyiin, barraani pl. -iyyiin. We don't permit outsiders to attend our meetings. ma-nismaӡ lil-xaarijiyyiin yiӡδaruun ijtimaaƐaatna.

outskirts - ʔaṭraaf. Many people have orchards on the outskirts of the city. naas ihwaaya Ɛidhum basaatiin ib-ʔaṭraaf il-madiina.

outstanding - **1.** baariz. He's an outstanding scholar. huwwa Ɛaalim baariz. **2.** mubdiƐ. He's an outstanding performer on the lute. haaδa Ɛaazif mubdiƐ Ɛal-Ɛuud. **3.** mawquuf. We still have a number of outstanding bills to collect. Ɛidna baƐad Ɛadad imnil-qawaaʔim il-mawquufa.

oven - **1.** tannuur pl. tanaaniir. Our neighbor's wife has an oven, and she sells the bread she bakes. marit jiiraanna Ɛidha tannuur w-itbiiƐ il-xubuz il-tixubza. **2.** firin pl. fruun. Baking the fish at home is a lot of bother; let's send it to the neighborhood oven. ṭabx is-simač bil-beet dooxa; xall indizza lil-firin maal iṭ-ṭaraf.

over - **1.** foog, fooq. My room is over the kitchen. ġurufti foog il-maṭbax. -- I don't know exactly, but over a hundred at least. ma-aƐruf biḍ-ḍabuṭ, laakin Ɛal-ʔaqall foog il-miyya. **2.** Ɛala. Don't pull the cover over your head. la-tjurr il-ġiṭa Ɛala raasak. **3.** ʔakθar min. That village is over a mile away. δiič il-qarya tibƐid ʔakθar min miil waaӡid.
**The water is over your head there. ma-raӡ-itgayyiš ihnaak.
**Let's go over the details once more. xalli nraajiƐ it-tafṣiilaat marra θaanya.
all over - b-kull makaan. I've looked all over, but I can't find it. dawwarit ib-kull mukaan laakin ma-da-agdar ʔalgaaha.
over again - marra θaanya. Do it over again. sawwiiha marra θaanya. or **Ɛiidha!
over and over again - Ɛiddat marraat. He asked the same question over and over again. siʔal nafs is-suʔaal Ɛiddat marraat.
over there - hnaak. What's that over there? šinu δaak l-ihnaak.
to get over - xallaṣ (i taxliiṣ) t- min. I got over my cold in a week. xallaṣit imnin-našla b-isbuuƐ.

overcoat - qappuuṭ pl. qapaapiiṭ.

to **overcome** - **1.** tġallab (a taġallub) Ɛala. She had many difficulties to overcome. čaan Ɛidha hwaaya ṣuƐuubaat titġallab Ɛaleeha. -- She was overcome with grief. čaan mitġallib Ɛaleeha l-ӡuzun. **2.** qiδa (i qaδaaʔ) Ɛala. The gas almost overcame me. čaan qiδa Ɛalayya l-ġaaz.

to **overdo** - **1.** laӡӡ (i laӡӡ). It doesn't hurt to eat fatty meat, but don't overdo it. ma-yxaalif taakul ʔakil dasim, bass la-tliӡӡ. **2.** kaθθar (i takθiir). I like spices, but our cook overdoes it. tiƐjibni l-ibhaaraat laakin ṭabbaaxna da-ykaθθir minha.

to **overflow** - ṭufaӡ (a ṭafuӡ), faaḍ (i feeḍ). Don't put so much water in the glass; it will overflow. la-txalli ṃayy ihwaaya bil-iglaaṣ w-ʔilla yiṭfaӡ.

overfull - ṭaafiӡ.

to **overlook** - **1.** ġufaḷ (u ġafuḷ) Ɛan. I must have overlooked it. laazim ʔaani ġfalit Ɛanha. **2.** tġaaδa (a taġaaδi) Ɛan. I'll overlook your mistakes this time, but don't do it again. raӡ-atġaada Ɛan ʔaġlaaṭak hal-marra laakin la-tƐiidha marra θaanya. **3.** ʔašraf (i ʔišraaf), ṭall (i ʔiṭlaal), ṣayṭar (i ṣayṭara). My window overlooks the garden. šibbaač ġurufti yišrif Ɛal-ӡadiiqa.

overnight - leela. He got rich overnight. ṣaar zangiin ib-leela.
to stay overnight - baat (a beetuuta). I'm going to stay overnight in Najaf. raӡ-abaat ib-najaf.

oversight - sahu, ġafla. That must have been an oversight. laazim haaδa sahu.

to **oversleep**: **I overslept this morning. ʔaxaδni n-noom il-yoom iṣ-ṣubuӡ.

overthrow - nqilaab pl. -aat. The foreign correspondents predicted the overthrow a month ago. l-muraasiliin il-ʔajaanib itnabbiʔaw bil-inqilaab gabuḷ šahar.
to overthrow - giḷab (u gaḷub) n-. They overthrew the government. gilbaw niδaam il-ӡukum.

overtime - ʔiḍaafi*. I had to work 2 hrs. overtime last night. ḍṭarreet aštuġul saaƐteen ʔiḍaafiyya l-baarӡa bil-leel. -- Beginning next month our office will be on an overtime basis. Ɛtibaaran imniš-šahr il-qaadim daaʔiratna raӡ-itquum ib-ʔaƐmaal ʔiḍaafiyya.

to **owe**: **How much do I owe you? šgadd tiṭlubni? or šgadd ʔaani madyuun ʔilak? or šgadd ʔaani maṭluub-lak? or šgadd ʔilak Ɛalayya? -- **You still owe me 20 dinars. ʔinta la-zilit maṭluub-li Ɛišriin diinaar or ʔinta la-zilit madyuun-li Ɛišriin diinaar. -- **I owe a lot of money. ʔaani mindaan ifluus ihwaaya.

owl - buuma pl. buwam.

own - Ɛuhda, masʔuuliyya. From here on, your on your own. minnaa w-hiiči, ʔinta Ɛala Ɛuhudtak. or minnaa w-faayit, inta w-nafsak. -- As soon as you are familiar with the filing system here, you'll be on your own. ӡaal-ma tlimm ib-niδaam il-faaylaat ihnaa, raӡ-itkuun Ɛala masʔuuliitak. -- He's been on his own ever since he was sixteen. min čaan Ɛumra sittaƐaš sana ṣaar masʔuul Ɛan nafsa.
**I have my own room. Ɛindi ġurfa ʔili waӡdi.

**Are these your own things? *haay ʔašyaaʔ mulkak ʔinta?*
to own – *milak (u muluk) n–.* He owns a house. *huwwa yimluk fadd beet.*

owner – *ṣaaẓib* pl. *ʔaṣẓaab, maalik* pl. *mullaak.* Who is the owner of the store? *minu ṣaaẓib had-dukkaan?*

ownership – *milkiyya* pl. *-aat.* You'll have to pay me in full before I transfer the ownership into your name. *laazim tidfaƐ-li kull il-mablaġ gabuḷ-ma ʔanqul il-milkiyya b-ismak.*
ox – *θoor* pl. *θiiraan.*
oxygen – *ʔooksijiin.*
oyster – *maẓẓaara* pl. *-aat* coll. *maẓẓaar.*

P

pace – **1.** *xaṭwa* pl. *-aat.* Take a pace forward. *tqaddam xaṭwa li-giddaam.* **2.** *surƐa.* This worker sets the pace for the others on the job. *hal-Ɛaamil yẓaddid surƐat iš-šuġuḷ lil-ʔaaxariin.*
to keep pace with – *jaara (i mujaaraat).* I can't keep pace with him at work. *ma-agdar ajaarii biš-šuġuḷ.*
to pace off – *qaas (i qees) n– bil-xaṭwaat.* Pace off a hundred feet. *qiis bil-xaṭwaat miit qadam.*
to pace up and down – *txaṭṭa (a taxaṭṭi), tmašša (a tamašši).* He paced up and down the room. *ḍall yitxaṭṭa bil-ġurfa.*
Pacific Ocean – *l-muẓiiṭ il-haadi.*
pack – **1.** *qaṭiiƐ* pl. *qiṭƐaan.* They went at the food like a pack of hungry wolves. *nizlaw Ɛal-ʔakil miθil qaṭiiƐ imniδ-δiyaab ij-juuƐaana.* **2.** *ẓimil* pl. *ẓmuul.* The donkeys were loaded with heavy packs. *z-zumaayiḷ čaanat imẓammila ẓmuul iθgaal.* **3.** *dasta* pl. *-aat.* Where is that new pack of cards? *ween dastat il-waraq ij-jidiida?*
**That's a pack of lies! *haaδa čiδb ib-čiδib!* or *haaδa kulla šeelmaan!*
to pack – **1.** *lamm (i lamm).* Have you packed your stuff yet? *lammeet ġaraaḍak loo baƐad?* or ***ẓaḍḍart ij-junṭa maaltak?* **2.** *ẓišak (i ẓašik) n–.* They packed more people into that little room. *ẓiškaw baƐad naas ib-δiič il-ġurfa ṣ-ṣiġayyra.* **3.** *diẓas (a daẓis) n–.* The doctor packed cotton in my ear. *ṭ-ṭabiib diẓas guṭin b-iδni.* **4.** *dačč (i dačč) n–.* Don't pack the clothes into the suitcase tightly. *la-tdičč l-ihduum bij-junṭa dačč.*
to pack up – *lamm (i lamm) n–.* He packed up his things and left. *lamm kull ġaraaḍa w-raaẓ.*
package – **1.** *ruzma* pl. *ruzam.* The mailman brought a package for you. *muwazziƐ il-bariid jaab-lak ruzma.* **2.** *paakeet* pl. *-aat.* Do you sell the coffee in the bulk or in packages? *tbiiƐ il-gahwa fraaṭa loo p-paakeetaat?*
packed – **1.** *mqappuṭ, matruus.* The bus was packed this morning. *l-paaṣ čaan imqappuṭ iṣ-ṣubuẓ.* **2.** *malyaan, matruus.* The store was packed with people. *l-maxzan čaan malyaan naas.* **3.** *mƐallab.* This fish is packed in Norway. *has-simač imƐallab bin-narwiij.*
**My things are all packed. *ġaraaḍi ẓaaḍra bij-junṭa.*
**Are these sardines packed in olive oil? *has-saardiin ib-dihin zeet?*
pack-horse – *kidiiš* pl. *kidšaan.*
pack-saddle – *jilaal* pl. *-aat.*
pact – *miiθaaq* pl. *mawaaθiiq.*
pad – **1.** *čibna* pl. *-aat, čiban.* I need a pad to put my typewriter on. *ʔaẓtaaj čibna ʔaẓuṭṭ Ɛaleeha ṭ-ṭaabiƐa maalti.* **2.** *mindar* pl. *manaadir.* Who took my chair pad? *minu ʔaxaδ mindar il-kursi maali?* **3.** *ṣṭampa* pl. *-aat.* I have the stamp, but I can't find the pad. *l-xatam hiyyaata, laakin ma-da-ʔalgi l-iṣṭampa.* **4.** *daftar* pl. *dafaatir.* Bring me one or two pads of note paper. *jiib-li daftar ʔaw daftareen waraq miswadda.* **5.** *kattaafiyya* pl. *-aat.* I had the tailor take the pads out of the shoulders of this jacket. *xalleet il-xayyaaṭ yṭalliƐ il-kattaafiyyaat min ičtaafaat has-sitra.*
to pad – *ẓašša (i tẓišši) t–.* I want the shoulders padded. *ʔariid l-ičtaafaat titẓašša.*
padding – *ẓašwa.*
padlock – *quful* pl. *qfaal, ʔaqfaala.*
page – *ṣafẓa* pl. *-aat, ṣaẓiifa* pl. *ṣaẓaayif.* The book is two hundred pages long. *l-iktaab bii miiteen ṣafẓa.*
pail – *ṣaṭil* pl. *ṣṭuul, ṣaṭla* pl. *-aat.* Get a pail of water! *jiib ṣaṭil maay!*
pain – *ʔalam* pl. *ʔaalaam, wujaƐ* pl. *ʔawjaaƐ.* I feel a sharp pain in my back. *da-aẓiss fadd wujaƐ šadiid ib-ḍahri.*
to take pains – *ʔajhad (i ʔijhaad) nafis~, daqqaq (i tadqiiq) t–.* She takes great pains with her work. *tijhid nafisha kulliš ib-šuġuḷha.*
to pain – *ʔallam (i taʔliim) t–.* It pains me to have to say this but ... *yiʔlimni ʔan laazim aguul haaδa laakin ...*
painful – **1.** *ʔaliim, muʔlim.* That was a painful experience. *haay čaanat fadd tajruba ʔaliima.* **2.** *muzƐija, faḍiiƐa.* Our progress was painfully slow. *taqaddumna čaan baṭiiʔ ʔila daraja muzƐija.*
**It is painful to watch him. *manḍara yiksir il-galub.*
**Was the extraction of the tooth painful? *šalƐ is-sinn ʔaδδaak?* or *šalƐ is-sinn wujaƐak?*
paint – *ṣubuġ* pl. *ʔaṣbaaġ, booya* pl. *-aat.* The paint isn't dry yet. *ṣ-ṣubuġ baƐda ma-yaabis.*
to paint – **1.** *ṣubaġ (u ṣubuġ) n–.* What color are you going to paint the house? *yaa loon raẓ-tuṣbuġ il-beet?* **2.** *risam (i rasim) n–.* She paints in oils. *tirsim biz-zeet.*
paint brush – *firča* pl. *firač.*
painter – **1.** *ṣabbaaġ* pl. *-iin, ṣbaabiiġ.* The painters will finish the kitchen tomorrow. *ṣ-ṣabbaaġiin raẓ-yxallṣuun il-muṭbax baačir.* **2.** *rassaam* pl. *-iin.* He is a famous painter. *haaδa rassaam mašhuur.*
painting – **1.** *lawẓa* pl. *-aat, ṣuura* pl. *ṣuwar.* This is a beautiful painting. *haaδi lawẓa badiiƐa.* **2.** *rasim.* I'm especially interested in Persian painting. *ʔaani mihtamm ib-ṣuura xaaṣṣa b-fann ir-rasim il-ʔiiraani.* **3.** *ṣubuġ.* Painting the house was hard. *ṣubġ il-beet čaan ṣaƐub.*
pair – *zooj* pl. *zwaaj, ʔazwaaj.* I bought myself a pair of gloves. *štireet-li zooj ičfuuf.*
**I bought a new pair of scissors. *štireet imgaṣṣ jidiid.*
pajamas – *beejaama* pl. *-aat.*
pal – *rafiiq* pl. *rufqaan, ṣaaẓib* pl. *ʔaṣẓaab.* You're a real pal. *ʔinta ẓaqiiqatan xooš rafiiq.*
to pal around – *tṣaaẓab (a taṣaaẓub), tƐaašar (a taƐaašur).* They've palled around for years. *tṣaaẓbaw muddat isniin.* or *ṣaar-ilhum mitƐaašriin muddat isniin.*
palace – *qaṣir* pl. *qṣuur.*
palate – *sagif ẓalig* pl. *sguuf iẓluug.*
pale – **1.** *ʔaṣfar, šaaẓib.* Why are you so pale? *š-biik hiiči ʔaṣfar?* **2.** *faatiẓ, ʔaačuġ.* She had on a pale blue dress. *čaanat laabsa nafnuuf ʔazrag faatiẓ.*
to turn pale – *ṣfarr (a), šiẓab (a šuẓuub), mtiqaƐ (i mtiqaaƐ).* When he heard that, he turned pale. *min simaƐha, ṣfarr loona.*
Palestine – *falasṭiin.*
Palestinian – *falasṭiini** pl. *-iyyiin.*
palm – **1.** *čaff* pl. *čfuuf.* My palm is all calloused. *čaffi kulla mbasmir.* **2.** *naxḷa* pl. *-aat* coll. *naxaḷ.* We have four palm trees in our garden. *Ɛidna ʔarbaƐ naxḷaat ib-ẓadiiqatna.* **3.** *šajarat* (pl. *-aat* coll. *šajar) jooz hind.* We don't grow any coconut palms here. *ma-nizraƐ šajar jooz hind ihnaa.*
palm shoot – *fisiila* pl. *fisaayil.*
palpitation – *xafaqaan.*
pamphlet – *kurraasa* pl. *-aat.*
pan – **1.** *jidir* pl. *jduur, jduura.* I need a bigger pan for the rice. *ʔaẓtaaj jidir ʔakbar lit-timman.* **2.** *ṭaawa* pl. *-aat.* Use this pan for the eggs. *staƐmil haṭ-ṭaawa lil-beeḍ.*
to pan out badly – *fišal (a fašal), xaab (i xayba).* My scheme panned out badly. *xuṭṭṭi fišlat.*
to pan out well – *nijaẓ (a najaaẓ).* My scheme panned out well. *xuṭṭṭi nijẓat.*
pane – *jaama* pl. *-aat* coll. *jaam.* The storm blew in several panes. *l-Ɛaaṣifa kisrat Ɛiddat jaamaat.*
panel – **1.** *ẓalaqa* pl. *-aat.* A panel of well-known educators discussed the problem on TV. *ẓalaqa min mašaahiir il-murabbiin biẓθaw il-muškila bit-talafizyoon.* **2.** *hayʔa* pl. *-aat.* A panel of

three experts will study this problem. *hay?a min itlaθ xubaraa? raz-tudrus il-muškila.*
panic - *δuʕur, ruʕub.*
pansy - *ward iṣ-ṣuura.*
to **pant** - *lihaθ (a lahiθ).* He came panting up the stairs. *ṣiʕad id-daraj da-yilhaθ.*
pants - 1. *panṭaruun* pl. *-aat, panaaṭiir.* My pants have to be pressed. *laazim panṭaruuni yinδurub ?uuti.* 2. *širwaal* pl. *šaraawiil.* You can tell he's a Kurd from his baggy pants. *tigdar tiʕurfa kurdi min širwaala.*
paper - 1. *waraqa* pl. *-aat, ?awraaq* coll. *waraq, kaaġada* pl. *-aat, kwaaġid,* coll. *kaaġad.* Do you have a sheet of paper? *ʕindak fadd ṭabqa waraq?* -- Some important papers are missing. *baʕδ il-?awraaq il-muhimma δaayʕa.* 2. *jariida* pl. *jaraayid.* Where is today's paper? *ween jariidt il-yoom?*
paper weight - *θiggaala* pl. *-aat.*
parachute - *parašuut* pl. *-aat, maδalla* pl. *-aat.*
parade - *stiʕraaδ* pl. *-aat.* Did you see the parade yesterday? *šift il-istiʕraaδ il-baarza?*
paradise - *janna, firdaws.*
paragraph - *faqara* pl. *-aat.* This is the beginning of a new paragraph. *haaδi bidaayat faqara jidiida.*
parallel - *muwaazi, muzaaδi.* Draw a parallel to this line. *?irsim muwaazi l-hal-xaṭṭ.* -- The road runs parallel to the river. *ṭ-ṭariiq muzaaδi lin-nahar.*
paralysis - *šalal, faalaj.*
to **paralyze** - *šall (i šalal) n-.* This disease sometimes paralyses the victim's legs. *hal-maraδ ?azyaanan yšill rijleen il-muṣaab.*
paralyzed - 1. *mašluul* pl. *-iin, minšall* pl. *-iin.* He is completely paralyzed. *haaδa mašluul tamaaman.* -- She has been paralyzed ever since she had that stroke. *hiyya minšalla min ṣaabat δiič iṣ-ṣadma.* 2. (m.) *?aʕδab* pl. *-iin,* (f.) *ʕaδba* pl. *-aat.* He has a paralyzed hand. *ʕinda ?iid ʕaδba.* 3. *mgarram* pl. *-iin.* He can't walk because he is paralyzed. *ma-yigdar yimši li-?an imgarram.* 4. *mʕaṭṭal.* Communications were completely paralyzed. *l-muwaaṣalaat čaanat imʕaṭṭla tamaaman.*
paramount - *ʕaδiim, kabiir.* That's of paramount importance. *haaδa ʕaδiim il-?ahammiyya.*
parapet - *suur* pl. *?aswaar.* Stay behind the parapet or you'll get killed. *?ibqa wara s-suur w-?illa tinqitil.*
parasite - *ṭufayli* pl. *-iyyaat.*
parasitical - *mitṭaffil.*
parasol - *šamsiyya* pl. *-aat.*
parcel - *ruzma* pl. *ruzam, laffa* pl. *-aat.* You forgot your parcels. *?inta niseet ruzamak.*
**I'll send it by parcel post. *raz-?adizzha ruzma bil-bariid.*
**Where is the parcel post window? *ween šibbaak ir-ruzam?*
pardon - *marzama* pl. *-aat.* His pardon was refused. *nrufδat marzamta.*
**I beg your pardon, I did'nt mean to step on your foot. *l-ʕafu, ma-qṣadit aduus ʕala rijlak.*
to pardon - 1. *ʕifa (i ʕafu) n- ʕan.* He pardoned me this time. *ʕifa ʕanni hal-marra.* 2. *ġufar (u) n-.* God will pardon my sins. *?aḷḷa raz-yuġfur iδnuubi.*
**Pardon me, I didn't hear what you said. *ʕafwan, ma-smaʕit iš-gilit.*
**Pardon me, when does the movie begin? *?ismaz-li, šwakit yibdi l-filim?*
to **pare** - 1. *gaššar (i tagšiir, tgiššir) t-.* Pare the potatoes and put them in a pan of cold water. *gaššri l-puteeta w-zuṭṭiiha b-jidir maay baarid.* 2. *gaṣṣ (u gaṣṣ) n-.* You should be more careful when you pare your nails. *laazim itdiir baalak ?azyad min itguṣṣ iδaafrak.* 3. *qallal (i taqliil) t-.* You'll have to pare down your estimates, or else they'll turn down the budget. *laazim itqallil taxmiinaatak w-illa yrufδuun il-miizaaniyya.*
parentage - *?aṣil.* She is of good parentage. *haaδi ?aṣilha zeen.*
parenthesis - *qaws* pl. *?aqwaas.* Put the word between parentheses. *zuṭṭ ič-čilma been qawseen.*
parents - *waalideen, ?abaween.* Respect for one's parents is a virtue. *ztiraam il-waalideen faδiila.* -- May God keep your parents! *?aḷḷa yxalli waaldeek.*
**Both my parents are still living. *?ummi w-?abuuya θneenhum baʕadhum ṭayybiin.*
parish - *?abrašiyya* pl. *-aat.*
park - *zadiiqa* pl. *zadaayiq.* There is a beautiful public park in the center of the city. *?aku zadiiqa ʕaamma laṭiifa b-nuṣṣ il-wlaaya.*

to park - *waggaf (u tawgiif), parrak (i tpirrik).* You can park your car here. *tigdar itwagguf sayyaartak ihnaa.*
parking - *wuguuf.* Car parking is prohibited here. *wuguuf is-sayyaaraat mamnuuʕ ihnaa.*
parking place - *mawqif* pl. *mawaaqif.* There's a parking place for cars behind the building. *?aku mawqif lis-sayyaaraat wara l-ibnaaya.*
Parliament - *barlamaan* pl. *-aat, majlis* (pl. *majaalis*) *?umma.*
parlor - *ġurfat* (pl. *ġuruf*) *xuṭṭaar, ġurfat* (pl. *ġuruf*) *istiqbaal.*
to **parole** - **He was paroled. *nfakk w-itxalla tazt il-muraaqaba.*
parrot - *biibimattu* pl. *-uwaat, babaġaa?* pl. *-aat.*
parsley - *krafus, maʕdinoos, jaʕfari.*
part - 1. *juzu?* pl. *?ajzaa?, qism* pl. *?aqsaam.* That part of the work isn't finished yet. *haj-juzu? imniš-šuġuḷ baʕad ma-xilaṣ.* -- This little screw is a very important part of the machine. *hal-burġi l-iṣġayyir fadd juzu? kulliš muhimm imnil-makiina.* -- Can you get spare parts for your bicycle? *tigdar tilgi ?ajzaa? iztiyaaṭiyya lil-paaysikil maalak?* -- The fence is part wood and part stone. *l-zaajiz qisim xišab w-qisim zajar.* 2. *dawr* pl. *?adwaar.* He played the part of a king in the play. *maθθal dawr malik bit-tamθiiliyya.* 3. *manṭiqa* pl. *manaaṭiq, naaziya* pl. *?anzaa?, nawaazi; ṭaraf* pl. *?aṭraaf.* What part of the city are you from? *?inta min yaa manṭiqa mnil-wlaaya.* -- **I haven't traveled much in these parts. *?aani ma-msaafir ihwaaya b-hal-manṭiqa.*
**For my part I have no objection. *min jihti, ma-ʕindi maaniʕ.*
for the most part - *ʕal-?akθar, ʕal-?aġlab.* His company is made up, for the most part, of volunteers. *zaδiirta mitkawwna ʕal-?akθar min miṭṭawwʕiin.* -- For the most part, the weather has been nice this summer. *ʕal-?aġlab iṭ-ṭaqis čaan laṭiif haṣ-ṣeef.*
in part - *nawʕan maa, b-baʕδ, b-qisim min.* I agree with you in part. *?aani ?attifiq wiyyaak nawʕan maa.*
on the part of - *min jaanib, min qibal.* We regret any discrimination against a minority on the part of a government official. *ni?saf il-?ay tafriqa δidd il-?aqalliyya min jaanib ?ay muwaδδaf zukuumi.*
to take part in - *štirak (i štiraak) b-, saaham (i musaahama).* Are you going to take part in the discussion? *raz-tištirik bil-munaaqaša?*
to take the part of - *lizam (a lazim) n- jaanib.* He always takes his brother's part. *daa?iman yilzam jaanib ?axuu.*
to part - 1. *ftiraq (i ftiraaq).* They parted as friends. *ftirqaw ka-?aṣdiqaa?.* 2. *tfaarag (a tafaarug).* Let's part here. *xalli nitfaarag ihnaa.* 3. *waxxar (i twuxxur, tawxiir) t-.* She parted the curtains and looked out. *waxxirat iṭ-pardaat w-baawʕat li-barra.* 4. *furag (u farig) n-.* He parts his hair on the left side. *yufrug šaʕra ʕal-yisra.*
to part with - *txalla (a txalli) ʕan.* I wouldn't part with that book for any price. *ma-?atxalla ʕan δaak il-iktaab ib-?ay θaman.*
partial - 1. *mitzayyiz, muġriδ.* He tries not to be partial. *yzaawil ?an ma-ykuun mitzayyiz.* 2. *juz?i** This is only a partial solution. *haaδa fadd zall juz?i bass.*
to be partial to - 1. *zaaba (i muzaabaa).* He's always been partial to his youngest daughter. *daa?iman yzaabi binta ṣ-ṣiġayyra.* 2. *faδδal (i tafδiil) t-.* He's partial to blondes. *yfaδδil iš-šugur.*
partiality - *muzaabaat.* The other employees resent the partiality in his recommendations for advancements. *baqiit il-mustaxdamiin istankiraw il-muzaabaat ib-tawṣiyaata lit-tarfiiʕ.*
partially - *nawʕan maa, juz?iyyan.* You are partially right. *?inta ṣaziiz nawʕan maa.* -- It's partially finished. *xalṣaana juz?iyyan.*
to **participate** - *štirak (i štiraak), šaarak (i mušaaraka), saaham (i musaahama).* They have invited us to participate in the project. *diʕoona ništirik bil-mašruuʕ.*
participation - *stiraak, mušaaraka, musaahama.*
participle: (active) *?isim faaʕil,* (passive) *?isim mafʕuul.*
particle - *δarra* pl. *-aat, zabba* pl. *-aat.* There isn't a particle of truth in that story. *ma-aku δarra mnil-zaqiiqa b-hal-quṣṣa.* -- The inflammation is from a particle of dirt on the eyeball. *l-iltihaab min δarrat wuṣax ʕala kurat il-ʕeen.*

particular - 1. *tafşiil* pl. *tafaaşiil*. For further particulars write to the publishers. *lil-ʒuşuul Eat-tafaaşiil ʔakθar, ʔiktib lin-našir.* -- My wife will give you all the particulars. *marti tinţiik kull it-tafaaşiil.* 2. *xaaşş*. Our city has its own particular problems. *madiinatna Eidha mašaakilha l-xaaşşa biiha.* 3. *muEayyan*. For no particular reason, he stopped visiting us. *baţţal yzuurna bduun sabab muEayyan.* 4. *muqarrab* pl. *-iin*. He is no particular friend of mine. *haaδa muu fadd şadiiq muqarrab ʔili.* 5. *diqdaaqi* pl. *-iyyiin*. My husband is very particular about his food. *zooji kulliš diqdaaqi b-ʔakla.* 6. *biδ-δaat*. This particular dress costs more. *hal-badla biδ-δaat itkallif ʔakθar.*

in particular - 1. *b-şuura xaaşşa, Eala l-xuşuuş.* I remember one man in particular. *ʔatδakkar fadd rijjaal ib-şuura xaaşşa.* 2. *Eala wajh it-taEyiin.* Are you looking for anything in particular? *da-tdawwur Eala fadd šii Eala wajh it-taEyiin?*

particularly - *b-şuura xaaşşa*. He is particularly interested in science. *huwwa mihtamm ib-şuura xaaşşa bil-Eiluum.*

partition - 1. *ʒaajiz* pl. *ʒawaajiz*. We are going to put in a partition here. *raʒ-inʒuţţ ʒaajiz ihnaa.* 2. *taqsiim*. The partition of Palestine took place as a result of a decision taken by the United Nations. *taqsiim falaşţiin jira Eala ʔaθar qaraar ittixδata l-ʔumam il-muttaʒida.* 3. *nqisaam*. The disagreement caused the partition of the party. *l-xilaaf sabbab inqisaam il-ʒizib.*

partly - *juzʔiyyan, baEδan*. The book is only partly finished as yet. *l-iktaab xalşaan juzʔiyyan bass il-ʒadd il-ʔaan.*

partner - 1. *šariik* pl. *šurakaaʔ*. My business partner is coming back tomorrow. *šariiki biš-šuğuļ raajiE baačir.* 2. *şaaʒib* pl. *ʔaşʒaab*. My partner and I have been winning every game. *ʔaani w-şaaʒbi da-nirbaʒ kull liEba.*

partridge - *qabač*. I bought a pair of partridges. *štireet zooj iţyuur qabač.*

part-time - *nuşş dawaam*. Do you have any part-time work in this office? *ʔaku waδiifa nuşş dawaam ib-hal-maktab?*

party - 1. *ʒizib* pl. *ʔaʒzaab*. What political party do you belong to? *ʔinta l-yaa ʒizib siyaasi mintimi?* 2. *ţaraf* pl. *ʔaţraaf, jaanib* pl. *jawaanib*. Neither of the two parties appeared at the trial. *ţ-ţarafeen ma-ʒiδraw bil-muʒaakama.* -- Both parties agreed to the terms. *j-jaanibeen waafqaw Eaš-šuruuţ.* 3. *ʒafla* pl. *-aat*. She likes to give big parties. *yiEjibha tqiim ʒaflaat faxma.* 4. *Eaziima* pl. *Eazaayim*. Good-night; it was a lovely dinner party. *tişbaʒuun Eala-xeer; Eaziimatkum čaanat mumtaaza.*

**I won't be a party to that. *ʔaani ma-aʒuţţ nafsi b-haay.*

party line - 1. *xaţţ muštarak* pl. *xuţuuţ muštaraka*. Our telephone is on a party line. *talafoonna Eala xaţţ muštarak.* 2. *manhaj ʒizib*. The party leader called upon all members to hold to the party line. *raʔiis il-ʒizib diEa kull il-ʔaEδaaʔ lit-tamassuk ib-manhaj il-ʒizib.*

pass - 1. *mamarr* pl. *-aat*. The pass is covered with snow in winter. *l-mamarr yinţumar biθ-θalij biš-šita.* 2. *biţaaqat* (pl. *-aat*) *muruur*. You'll need a pass to get through the gate. *tiʒtaaj biţaaqat muruur yaļļa tigdar itfuut imnil-madxal.* 3. *maʔδuuniyya* pl. *-aat*. He has a weekend pass. *Einda maʔδuuniyya b-nihaayat hal-isbuuE.*

to pass - 1. *marr (u muruur) b-*. I pass this bank building every day. *ʔamurr ib-binaayat hal-bang kull yoom.* -- The play finally passed the censor. *t-tamθiiliyya ʔaxiiran marrat bir-raqiib.* 2. *marrar (i tamriir) t-, Eabbar (u taEbiir) t-*. They passed the buckets from hand to hand. *marriraw iş-şuţuul min ʔiid il-ʔiid.* 3. *faat (u fawt) n- min*. The train passes here at three o'clock. *l-qiţaar yfuut minnaa s-saaEa tlaaθa.* 4. *ţilaE (a ţuluuE) n-, ğilab (u ğulub) n-*. Pass that car! *ʔiţlaE δiič is-sayyaara!* 5. *qaδδa (i taqδiya) t-*. He passed most of the time reading. *qaδδa ʔakθar il-wakit bil-qaraaʔa.* 6. *muδa (i muδi)*. The days pass quickly when you're busy. *l-ʔayyaam timδi b-surEa min waaʒid ykuun mašğuul.* 7. *nijaʒ (a najaaʒ) b-, Eubar (u Eubuur)*. Did you pass the examination? *nijaʒit bil-imtiʒaan?* 8. *Eubar (u Eabur), marr (u muruur) b-*. You passed through a red light. *Ebarit δuwa ʔaʒmar.* 9. *ntiqal (i ntiqaal)*. The farm passes from father to son. *l-mazraEa tintiqil imnil-ʔab lil-ʔibin.* 10. *maššа (i tamšiya) t-*. The censor refused to pass the film. *r-raqiib rufaδ ymašši l-filim.* 11. *naawaš (u munaawaša)*. Will you please pass me the bread? *ma-tnaawušni l-xubuz min faδlak?* 12. *şaddaq (i taşdiiq) t-*. The House of Representatives passed the bill unanimously. *majlis in-nuwwaab şaddaq il-laaʔiʒa bil-ʔijmaaE.* 13. *şaaʒ (i şeeʒ) paaş*. It's your turn; I passed. *hassa doorak; ʔaani şiʒit paaş.*

to pass around - 1. *dawwar (u tadwiir) t-, farrar (u tafriir) t-*. They passed around cookies. *dawwiraw l-ikleeča Eal-kull.* 2. *ţašš (u ţašš) n-, nišar (u našir) n-*. Pass the word around so that everyone hears. *ţušš l-iʒčaaya ʒatta l-kull ysimEuun.* **We passed around the hat to help him pay his hospital bill. *jimaEnaa-la fluus ʒatta nsaaEda yidfaE maşaariif il-mustašfa.*

to pass away - *twaffa (a), maat (u moot)*. Her mother passed away last week. *ʔummha twaffat isbuuE il-faat.*

to pass by - *marr (u muruur) min yamm, b-*. He passed right by me without seeing me. *marr min yammi tamaaman w-ma-šaafni.*

to pass judgment on - *ʒikam (u ʒukum) n- Eala*. Don't pass judgment on him too quickly. *la-tuʒkum Ealee kulliš bil-Eajal.*

to pass off - 1. *fawwat (u tafwiit) t-, marrar (i tamriir) t-*. He tried to pass off an imitation as the original. *ʒaawal yfawwut šii mzayyif ka-šii ʒaqiiqi.* 2. *Eabbar (u taEbiir)*. He tried to pass himself off as an officer. *ʒaawal yEabbur nafsa ka-δaabuţ.*

to pass on - *waşşal (i tawşiil), ʔafša (i ʔifšaaʔ)*. Don't pass this on to anyone. *la-twaşşil haay l-aʒʒad.*

to pass out - **Several people passed out from the heat. *Eiddat ʔašxaaş ğaabat ruuʒhum imnil-ʒarr.* **They passed out from drinking too much. *fuqdaw waEiihum min kuθrat iš-šurub.*

to pass sentence - *ʔaşdar (u ʔişdaar) ʒukum*. The court will pass sentence today. *l-maʒkama raʒ-tuşdur ʒukum il-yoom.*

to pass through - 1. *marr (u muruur) min, faat (u foot) min*. You can't pass through there. *ma-tigdar itmurr minnaak.* 2. *fawwat (i tafwiit) t-*. Pass the rope through here. *fawwit il-ʒabil minnaa.*

to pass up - 1. *fawwat (i tafwiit), δayyaE (i taδyiiE)*. You ought not to pass up an opportunity like that. *ma-laazim itfawwit hiiči furşa.* 2. *naawaš (u munaa waša) t-*. Pass your papers up to the front row. *naawšu ʔawraaqkum lis-sira l-ʔamaami.*

passable - *maqbuul*. The work is passable. *š-šuğuļ maqbuul.*

passage - 1. *mamarr* pl. *-aat*. We had to go through a dark passage. *δţarreena nisluk mamarr muδlim.* 2. *maqţaE* pl. *maqaaţiE*. He read us several passages from his book. *qiraa-lna Eiddat maqaaţiE minn iktaaba.* 3. *Eabra* pl. *-aat*. The passage across the river by boat takes a half hour. *Eabrat in-nahar bil-balam taaxuδ nuşş saaEa.*

passenger - 1. *raakib* pl. *rukkaab, Eibri* pl. *-iyya*. The bus holds thirty passengers. *l-paaş yilzam itlaaθiin raakib bass.* 2. *musaafir* pl. *-iin*. The passengers must go through customs. *l-musaafiriin laazim ymurruun bil-gumrug.*

passer-by - *Eaabir* (pl. *-iin*) *sabiil, maarr* pl. *-iin*. Some passer-by must have picked it up. *laazim ʔaxaδha fadd Eaabir sabiil.*

passing - 1. *wafaat, moot*. The whole nation mourned his passing. *l-ʔumma kullha ʒiznat Eala wafaata.* 2. *Eaabir, zaaʔil, waqti**. It's just a passing fancy. *haaδa fadd walaE Eaabir.* 3. *najaaʒ*. I got passing grades in all my subjects. *ʒaşşalit darajaat najaaʒ ib-kull idruusi.* 4. *muruur, ţuluuE*. Passing on the right is dangerous. *l-muruur Eal-yamiin xaţar.* 5. *Eubuur*. After passing through the sand, you'll hit a hard surface. *baEd il-Eubuur imnir-ramul, raʒ-itşaadif gaaE qawiyya.*

passion - 1. *walaE, wahas*. He has a passion for music. *Einda walaE bil-mawsiiqa.* 2. *Eaaţifa* pl. *Eawaaţif*. You should try to control your passions better. *laazim itʒaawil itşayţir Eala Eawaaţfak ʔakθar.*

passionate - *Eaaţifi**. She has a very passionate nature. *hiyya Eaaţifiyya.*

passive - 1. *majhuul*. Change this sentence to the passive voice. *ʒawwil haj-jumla ʔila şiiğat il-majhuul.* 2. *salbi**. Passive resistance is a

peaceful but effective weapon. *l-muqaawama s-salbiyya ṭariiqa salmiyya w-laakinha silaaẓ naffaaδ.*
**He is a passive spectator. *haaδa mitfarrij maa-la daxal.*

Passover - *ʕiid il-fuṣẓ.*

past - 1. *maaδi* pl. *mawaaδi.* The police uncovered some suspicious activities in his past. *š-šurṭa ktišfat ʔaʕmaal mašbuuha b-maaδiyya.* -- That's a thing of the past. *haaδa fadd šii bil-maaδi.* or **haaδa ṣaar taariix.* 2. *faayit.* Where were you this past week? *ween činit bil-isbuuʕ il-faayit?* 3. *mitjaawiz.* I am past that stage. *ʔaani mitjaawiz hal-marẓala.*
**It's five minutes past twelve. *s-saaʕa θnaaʕaš w-xamsa.*
**It's way past my bedtime. *faat wakit noomi b-ihwaaya.*
**The worst part of the trip is past. *ʔaswaʔ qisim imnis-safra faat.*
**He walked past me. *faat min yammi.*
in the past - *gabuḷ, bil-maaδi, bis-saabiq.* That has often happened in the past. *haay ẓidθat ihwaaya gabuḷ.*

paste - *ṣamuġ, širiis.* Where did you put the paste jar? *ween ẓaṭṭeet šiišt iṣ-ṣamuġ?*
to paste - *lizag (i lazig) n-, lazzag (i talziig) t-.* Paste these labels on the boxes. *ʔilzig hal-ʕalaamaat ʕaṣ-ṣanaadiig.*

pastime - *tasliya, lahu.* What is your favorite pastime? *šinu hiyya tasliitak il-maẓbuuba?*

pastry - *ẓalawiyyaat.*

pastry shop - *maẓall* (pl. *-aat*) *ẓalawiyyaat.*

pasture - *marʕa* pl. *maraaʕi.* Are the cows still in the pasture? *l-baqaraat baʕadhum bil-marʕa?*

pat - *ṭabṭaba* pl. *-aat.* I got a congratulatory pat on the shoulder. *ẓaṣṣalit ṭabṭubat ʕafaarim ʕala čitfi.*
to pat - *ṭabṭab (u ṭabṭaba) t-.* He patted him encouragingly on the shoulder. *ṭabṭab ʕala čitfa b-tašjiiʕ.* -- He patted the dog. *ṭabṭab-la lič-čalib.*

patch - 1. *rugʕa* pl. *rugaʕ.* I'll have to put a patch on it. *laazim aẓuṭṭ rugʕa.* 2. *qiṭʕa* pl. *qiṭaʕ, wuṣla* pl. *wuṣal.* He raises alfalfa and rents out patches of it to people who have horses. *yizraʕ jatt w-yʔajjir qiṭaʕ minna lin-naas il-ʕidhum xeel.* 3. *lazga* pl. *-aat.* He had a patch over his eye for days. *ẓaṭṭ lazga ʕala ʕeena ʔayyaam.*
to patch - *raggaʕ (i targiiʕ).* Mother had to patch my trousers. *ʔummi δṭarrat itraggiʕ panṭarooni.*
to patch up - *faδδ (u faδδ) n-.* Have they patched up their quarrel yet? *faδδaw il-xilaaf beenaathum loo baʕad?*

patchwork - *talziig, talṭiiš.*

patent - *baraaʔa* pl. *-aat.* I have applied for a patent to protect my rights on my new invention. *qaddamit ṭalab ʕala baraaʔa lil-muẓaafuδa ʕala ẓuquuqi bil-ixtiraaʕ maali.*
to patent - *sajjal (i tasjiil) t-.* You ought to patent your process. *laazim itsajjil ṭariiqtak.*

path - 1. *darub* pl. *druub.* A narrow path leads to the river. *fadd darub δayyiq yʔaddi ʔila n-nahar.* 2. *sabiil* pl. *subul.* He put many obstacles in my path. *ẓaṭṭ ihwaaya ʕaqabaat ib-sabiili.*

patience - *ṣabur.* I lost my patience. *nifaδ ṣabri.*

patient - 1. *mariiδ* pl. *marδa, wajʕaan* pl. *wjaaʕa.* How's the patient today? *šloon il-mariiδ il-yoom?* 2. *ṣabuur, ṭuwiil.* He is a very patient man. *huwwa kulliš ṣabuur.* or *haaδa kulliš ṭuwiil.*

patriarch - *baṭriiq* pl. *baṭaariqa.*

patriot - *waṭani* pl. *-iyyiin.*

patriotism - *waṭaniyya.*

patrol - *dawriyya* pl. *-aat.* We sent a patrol out to reconnoiter. *dazzeena dawriyya lil-istiṭlaaʕ.* -- Ali went out on patrol. *ʕali ṭilaʕ dawriyya.*
to patrol - *ṭaaf (u ṭawafaan).* An armored police car patrols the streets all night. *sayyaarat šurṭa musallaẓa ṭṭuuf iš-šawaariʕ ṭuul il-leel.*

pattern - 1. *naqiš* pl. *nquuš.* This rug has a nice pattern. *haz-zuuliyya naqišha laṭiif.* 2. *faṣaal* pl. *-aat.* Where did you get the pattern for your new dress? *ween ligeeti l-faṣaal il-badaltič ij-jidiida?* 3. *šaakila* pl. *-aat, ṭiraaz* pl. *-aat.* All his thefts are on this pattern. *kull sariqaata ʕala haṭ-ṭiraaz.*

pause - *waqfa* pl. *-aat, sakta* pl. *-aat, tawaqquf* pl. *-aat.* After a short pause the speaker continued. *l-xaṭiib istimarr baʕad waqfa qaṣiira.*
to pause - *twaggaf (a twugguf).* He paused in his work to greet us as we entered. *twaggaf ʕan šuġḷa ẓatta ysallim ʕaleena min daxalna.*

to pave - 1. *ballaṭ (i tabliiṭ).* They are paving this street. *da-yballiṭuun haš-šaariʕ.* 2. *mahhad (i tamhiid) t-.* Their efforts paved the way for independence. *majhuudhum mahhad iṭ-ṭariiq lil-istiqlaal.*

pavement - *tabliiṭ* pl. *-aat, tamhiid* pl. *-aat, ʔarδiyya* pl. *-aat.* The pavement is very narrow here. *t-tabliiṭ ihnaa kulliš δayyig.*

paw - *ʔiid* pl. *-een, -eenaat, rijil* pl. *-een, -eenaat.* The dog has hurt his paw. *č-čalib ʕawwar ʔiida.*

pawn - 1. *liʕba* pl. *-aat, liʕab.* We are tired of being nothing but a pawn in their political schemes. *ʕijazna ʔiẓna bass liʕba b-xuṭaṭhum is-siyaasiyya.* 2. *jundi* pl. *junuud.* You have lost another pawn. *xsarit jundi laax.*
to pawn - *rihan (a rahan) n-.* I had to pawn my watch. *δṭarreet ʔarhan saaʕti.*

pawnshop - *maẓall* (pl. *-aat*) *ruhuunaat.*

pawn ticket - *waṣil* (pl. *wuṣuulaat*) *rahan.*

pay - *raatib* pl. *rawaatib, maʕaaš* pl. *-aat.* How is the pay on your new job? *šloon ir-raatib ib-šuġḷak ij-jidiid?*
to pay - 1. *difaʕ (a dafiʕ) n-.* How much did you pay for your car? *šgadd difaʕit ib-sayyaartak?* -- I would like to pay my bill. *ʔariid adfaʕ qaaʔimti.* 2. *gaam (u qiyaam) b-.* He paid all the expenses. *gaam ib-kull il-maṣaariif.*
**That doesn't pay. *maa min waraaha faayda.* or *š-šaġla ma-tiswa.* or *haay ma-ṭṭaʕʕum xubuz.*
**You couldn't pay me to do that. *loo tinṭiini fluus id-dinya ma-asawwiiha.*
to pay attention - *daar (i deer, dayaraan) baal~, ntibah (i ntibaah).* The pupils didn't pay attention today at all. *t-talaamiiδ ma-daaraw baalhum il-yoom ʔabad.* -- Pay no attention to him. *la-tdiir-la baal.* or **ma-ʕleek minna.*
to pay a visit - *zaar (u ziyaara), raaẓ (u rooẓ) xuṭṭaar ʕala.* I must pay him a visit. *laazim azuura.* -- Let's pay our new neighbors a visit. *xalli nruuẓ xuṭṭaar ʕala jiiraanna j-jiddad.*
to pay back - 1. *waffa (i tawfiya).* I'll pay you back the dinar on Monday. *ʔawaffii-lak id-diinaar yoom iθ-θineen.* 2. *rajjaʕ (i tarjiiʕ) t-.* When are you going to pay me back what you owe me? *šwakit raẓ-itrajjiʕ-li deeni?*
to pay down - *difaʕ (a dafiʕ) ʕarabuun.* They require you to pay one-third down and the rest in monthly installments. *yriiduuk tidfaʕ θulθ il-mablaġ ʕarabuun wil-baaqi b-ʔaqṣaaṭ šahriyya.*
to pay for - *difaʕ (a dafiʕ) n- b-, ʕala.* How much did you pay for the car? *šgadd difaʕit bis-sayyaara?* -- He said he would pay for the rest of us. *qaal raẓ-yidfaʕ ʕaleena kullna.*
**I paid dearly for my mistakes. *ġaliṭṭi kallfatni ġaali.*
to pay for itself - *ṭallaʕ (i taṭliiʕ) t- fluus~.* This machine will pay for itself in five months. *hal-makiina raẓ-iṭṭalliʕ ifluusha b-xamist išhur.*
to pay off - 1. *waffa (i tawfiya), saddad (i tasdiid).* He paid off his debts. *waffa kull idyuuna.* 2. *sadd (i sadd) n- ẓsaab.* He sold the farm and paid off the help. *baaʕ il-mazraʕa w-sadd iẓsaab il-ʕummaal.*
to pay out - 1. *ṣiraf (u ṣaruf) n-.* We paid out more than we took in today. *l-yoom ṣirafna ʔakθar min dixaḷna.* 2. *raxxa (i tarxiya) t-.* Pay out the rope slowly. *raxxi l-ẓabil ʕala keefak.*
to pay up - 1. *waffa (i tawfiya) t-, saddad (i tasdiid) t-.* In a month I'll have it all paid up. *b-xilaal šahar raẓ-awaffiiha kullha.* 2. *ʔadda (i taʔdiya) t-.* I paid up all my debts on payday. *ʔaddeet kull idyuuni yoom il-maʕaaš.*

payment - 1. *dafiʕ.* Prompt payment is requested. *r-rajaaʔ id-dafiʕ ib-surʕa.* 2. *qiṣiṭ* pl. *ʔaqṣaaṭ, dafʕa* pl. *-aat.* I have two more payments on my car. *buqaa-li qiṣṭeen ʕala sayyaarti.* -- I paid up the debt in three payments. *sawweet id-deen itlaθ dafʕaat.*

pea - *bazaalyaaya* pl. *-aat* coll. *bazaalya.*

peace - 1. *salaam, silm.* The whole world wants peace. *kull id-dinya triid is-salaam.* 2. *ʔamin.* The police are doing all they can to maintain peace. *š-šurṭa da-ysawwuun kull-ma yigdaruun lil-muẓaafaδa ʕala l-ʔamin.* 3. *huduuʔ.* If only I could work in peace! *loo bass ʔagdar ʔaštiġuḷ ib-huduuʔ!*
**He doesn't give me any peace. *ma-yxalli baali yirtaaẓ.*
**I'm doing it just to keep the peace. *ʔaani*

da-asawwiiha čifyaan šarr.
**Leave me in peace! *fukk yaaxa minni!* or *juuz ɛanni!* or *ɛuufni!*
to make peace - *ṣaalaʒ (i muṣaalaʒa) t-.* He tried to make peace between them. *ʒaawal yṣaaliʒ beenhum.*
peaceful - 1. *haadiʔ.* Everything is so peaceful around here. *kullši šgadd haadiʔ ihnaa.* 2. *musaalim* pl. *-iin.* He is very peaceful. *haaδa kulliš musaalim.* 3. *silmi*.* There is no peaceful solution to this problem. *ma-aku ʒall silmi l-hal-muškila.*
peach - *xooxa* pl. *-aat* coll. *xoox.* These peaches are very juicy. *hal-xoox kulliš rayyaan.*
peacock - *ṭaawuus* pl. *ṭwaawiis.*
peak - 1. *qumma* pl. *qumam.* We climbed to the peak of the mountains. *tsallaqna l-qummat ij-jibal.* 2. *ʔawj, δarwa.* He was then at the peak of his power. *kaan ib-ʔawj quuta b-δaak il-wakit.*
peanut - *fistiqat* (pl. *-aat*) *ɛabiid* coll. *fistiq ɛabiid.*
pear - *ɛarmuuṭa* pl. *-aat* coll. *ɛarmuuṭ.* How much is a kilo of pears? *beeš il-kiilo l-ɛarmuuṭ?*
pearl - *liiluwwa* pl. *-aat* coll. *liilu.*
peasant - 1. *fallaaʒ* pl. *-iin, flaaliiʒ.* The peasant took some tomatoes to market. *l-fallaaʒ nazzal ṭamaaṭa lis-suuq.* 2. *mɛeedi* pl. *miɛdaan.* You peasant, why don't you learn some manners? *ʔay mɛeedi, leeš ma-titɛallam išwayya ʔuṣuul?*
pebble - *ʒaṣwa* pl. *-aat* coll. *ʒaṣu.* The path is covered with pebbles. *l-mamarr imġaṭṭa bil-ʒaṣu.*
peck - *nagra* pl. *-aat.* Give me another peach, some bird took a peck out of this one. *ʔinṭiini ġeer xooxa, haay fadd ṭeer maaxiδ-la nagra minha.*
to peck - *nigar (u nagir) n-, naggar (i tangiir) t-.* The birds are pecking at the fruit again; chase them away. *l-iṭyuur hamm da-ynaggiruun bil-faakiha; ruuʒ kiššhum.*
peculiar - 1. *ġariib, šaaδδ.* He's a peculiar fellow. *huwwa fadd waaʒid ġariib.* -- The incident was hushed up under peculiar circumstances. *l-ʒaadiθa tlaġmuṭat ib-δ̣uruuf šaaδδa.* 2. *xaaṣṣ.* This style turban is peculiar to the people in the north. *haš-šikil laffa xaaṣṣa b-ʔahl iš-šimaal.*
peculiarity - *xaaṣṣiyya* pl. *-aat, xawaaṣṣ.* They are easy to identify from certain peculiarities in their speech. *mnis-sihuula tiɛrufhum min xawaaṣṣ muɛayyana b-ʒačiihum.*
pedal - 1. *ᵽaaydaar* pl. *-aat.* One of the pedals on this bicycle is longer than the other. *waaʒid imnil-ᵽaaydaaraat ib-hal-ᵽaaysikil ʔaṭwal imnil-laax.* 2. *rijil* pl. *rijleen.* Does your sewing machine have a pedal or do you operate by hand? *makiint il-ixyaaṭa maaltič maal rijil loo maal iid?* 3. *doosa* pl. *-aat.* My foot slipped off the pedal. *rijli zilgat imnid-doosa.*
to pedal - *δ̣irab (u δ̣arub) ᵽaaydaar.* His legs are still too short to pedal a bicycle. *rijlee baɛadha kulliš igṣayyra l-δ̣arb il-ᵽaaydaar.*
to **peddle** - *dawwar (u tduwwur) b-.* The farmer sent his son to peddle tomatoes in this neighborhood. *l-fallaaʒ dazz ibna ydawwur bit-ṭamaaṭa b-hal-imʒalla.*
peddler - *dawwaar* pl. *-iin.*
pedestrian - *maarr* pl. *-iin, maarra; maaši* pl. *mušaat.* Drivers must watch out for pedestrians crossing the street. *s-suwwaaq laazim yintibhuun ɛal-maarriin il-da-yiɛburuun iš-šaariɛ.*
pediatrician - *ṭabiib* (pl. *ʔaṭibbaaʔ*) *ʔaṭfaal.*
pedigree - *ʔaṣil* pl. *ʔaṣaal, nasab* pl. *ʔansaab.* This horse's pedigree goes back for fifty years. *hal-iʒṣaan ʔaṣla yirjaɛ il-xamsiin sana.*
pedigreed - *ʔaṣiil.*
peel - *gišir* pl. *gšuur.* These oranges have a thick peel. *hal-ᵽurtaqaal bii qišir θixiin.*
to peel - *gaššar (i tgiššir) t-.* I have to peel the potatoes. *laazim ʔagaššir il-ᵽuteeta.* -- My skin is peeling. *jildi da-ygaššir.*
to peel off - *tgaššaṭ (a).* The whitewash is peeling off the ceiling. *l-ibyaaδ̣ da-yitgaššaṭ imnis-saguf.*
peep - 1. *waṣwaṣa* pl. *-aat.* The peeps of the baby chicks made their mother run over to them. *waṣwaṣaat ifruux id-dijaaj xallat ʔummhum turkuδ̣ ɛaleehum.* 2. *ṭagga* pl. *-aat.* I don't want to hear another peep out of you. *ma-ariid ʔasmaɛ wala ṭagga baɛad.* 3. *naδ̣ra* pl. *-aat.* Take a peep into the room. *ʔilqi naδ̣ra bil-ġurfa.*
to peep - 1. *waṣwaṣ (u waṣwaṣa).* The baby chicks are peeping because their mother left them. *fruux id-dijaaj da-ywaṣwuṣuun li-ʔan ʔummhum qaamat min ɛaleehum.* 2. *baawaɛ (u mbaawaɛa), daʒʒag (i tadʒiig).* He peeped through the hole in the fence. *baawaɛ min zurf is-siyaaj.*
peeved - *zaɛlaan.* She was peeved about the remark you made. *čaanat zaɛlaana ɛal-iʒčaaya lli ʒičeetha.*
peg - 1. *watad* pl. *ʔawtaad.* He tripped over a tent peg and fell. *ɛiθar ib-watad čaadir w-wugaɛ.* 2. *ɛuuda* pl. *ɛuwad, xišba* pl. *xišab.* There are some pegs on the wall to hang your clothes on. *ʔaku ɛuwad bil-ʒaayiṭ xaaṭir itɛallig ihduumak biiha.*
pelican - *ʔabu jraab* pl. *ṭyuur ʔabu jraab; bajaɛa* pl. *-aat* coll. *bajaɛ.*
pelvis - *ʒawδ̣* pl. *ʔaʒwaaδ̣.*
pen - 1. *sillaaya* pl. *-aat.* This pen scratches. *has-sillaaya da-tšaxxiṭ.* 2. *ᵽaandaan* pl. *-aat, qalam* (pl. *ʔaqlaam*) *ʒibir.* This is an expensive fountain pen. *haaδa ᵽaandaan ġaali.* 3. *zariiba* pl. *zaraayib.* We'll have to build a pen for the sheep. *laazim nibni zariiba lil-ġanam.*
penal code - *qaanuun il-ɛuquubaat.*
penalty - *ɛuquuba* pl. *-aat, jazaaʔ* pl. *-aat.* The penalty is ten years' imprisonment. *l-ɛuquuba ɛašr isniin ʒabis.*
pencil - *qalam* pl. *qlaam.* Give me that pencil, please. *nṭiini δaak il-qalam, min faδ̣lak.*
pending - 1. *rahn.* They have cancelled all permits, pending further investigation. *liġaw kull il-ʔijaazaat, rahn it-taʒqiiqaat il-ʔiδ̣aafiyya.* 2. *muɛallaq.* The matter is still pending. *hal-qaδ̣iyya baɛadha muɛallaqa.* or **hal-qaδ̣iyya baɛad ma-mabtuut biiha.*
pendulum - *raqqaaṣ* pl. *-aat.*
to **penetrate** - 1. *xtiraq (i xtiraaq).* The enemy tanks penetrated our lines. *dabbaabaat il-ɛadu xtirqat xuṭuuṭna.* 2. *tġalġal (a taġalġul).* The Locust Control Expedition penetrated deep into the desert. *firqat mukaafaʒat ij-jaraad itġalġilat biṣ-ṣaʒraaʔ.*
peninsula - *šibih jaziira* pl. *ʔašbaah juzur.*
penitentiary - *sijin* pl. *sijuun.*
penknife - *čaaquuča* pl. *-aat, čawaaqiič; siččiinat* (pl. *sačaačiin*) *jeeb.*
penname - *ʔisim mustaɛaar* pl. *ʔasmaaʔ, ʔasaami mustaɛaara.*
penny - *beeza, filis.* I'm broke, I haven't got a penny. *ʔaani miflis; maa ɛindi beeza.*
pension - *taqaaɛud.* He gets a pension from the government. *yaaxuδ taqaaɛud imnil-ʒukuuma.*
to pension - *ʒaal (i ʔiʒaala) n- ɛat-taqaaɛud.* He was pensioned last year. *nʒaal ɛat-taqaaɛud is-sana l-faatat.*
people - 1. *naas.* What will people say? *s-raʒ-yguuluun in-naas?* 2. *šaɛab* pl. *šuɛuub.* The government always sounds out the opinion of the people in serious matters. *l-ʒukuuma daaʔiman titʒassas raʔy iš-šaɛab ʒawl il-ʔumuur il-xaṭiira.* 3. *qawm* pl. *ʔaqwaam.* The Babylonians were a people who built up a powerful kingdom in ancient times. *l-baabiliyyiin qawm binaw mamlaka qawwiyya bil-ɛuṣuur il-qadiima.* 4. *ɛaalam.* Were there many people at the meeting? *čaan ʔaku ɛaalam ihwaaya bil-ijtimaaɛ?* 5. *ʔahal.* I want you to meet my people. *ʔariidak titɛarraf ɛala ʔahli.* 6. *šaxiṣ* pl. *ʔašxaaṣ.* I only knew a few people at the party. *ɛirafit čam šaxiṣ bass bil-ʒafla.*
pep - *ʒayawiyya, našaaṭ.* Where do you get your pep? *minneen jattak hal-ʒayawiyya?* -- He's full of pep today. *huwwa l-yoom matruus našaaṭ.*
to pep up - *naššaṭ (i tanšiiṭ) t-.* I need something to pep me up. *ʔaʒtaaj fadd šii ynaššiṭni.*
pepper - 1. *filfil.* Pass me the pepper, please. *naawušni l-filfil, min faδ̣lak.* 2. *filfila* pl. *-aat* coll. *filfil.* See if you can find some nice peppers in the market. *šuuf ʔiδa tigdar tilgi čam filfila zeena bis-suug.*
peppermint - *niɛnaaɛ.*
per - 1. *b-.* How much do you sell the oranges for per dozen? *šloon itbiiɛ il-ᵽurtiqaal bid-darzan?* -- He makes sixty dinars per month. *yṭalliɛ sittiin diinaar biš-šahar.* 2. *ɛala, ɛan.* They charge two dinars per person. *yaaxδuun diinaareen ɛala kull nafar.*
**We paid fifty cents per person. *dfaɛna xamsiin filis kull waaʒid.*
per cent - *bil-miyya.* The cost of living has risen ten per cent. *kulfat il-maɛiiša rtifɛat ɛašra bil-miyya.* -- Our bank pays two percent interest. *l-bang maalna yidfaɛ faaʔida θneen bil-miyya.* -- We'll each share fifty percent of the profits. *raʒ-nitqaasam il-maʒsuul kull man bil-miyya xamsiin.*
percentage - *nisba* (pl. *nisab*) *miʔawiyya.*

perennial - **1.** *ζaayil.* These plants are perennial. *han-nabaataat ζaayla.* or ***han-nabaataat itζiil.* **2.** *muzmin.* He is a perennial candidate for the House of Representatives. *haaδa fadd muraššaζ muzmin lin-niyaaba.*

perfect - **1.** *kaamil.* Nothing is perfect. *ma-aku šii kaamil.* **2.** *tamaam.* This is perfect nonsense. *haay laġwa tamaam.* **3.** *maδ̣buuṭ, tamaam.* He speaks perfect French. *yiζči fransi maδ̣buuṭ.* **4.** *muζkam, maδ̣buuṭ, mutqan.* Their plan was perfect. *xiṭṭathum čaanat muζkama.* -- This process is not perfect yet. *haṭ-ṭariiqa baƐadha muu mutqana.*

to perfect - **The method hasn't been perfected yet. *ṭ-ṭariiqa baƐad li-hassa ma-wuṣlat darajat il-kamaal.*

perfection - *kamaal.*

perfectly - **1.** *tamaaman.* He was perfectly satisfied. *čaan raaδ̣i tamaaman.* **2.** *biδ̣-δ̣abuṭ, b-ʔitqaan, Ɛal-maδ̣buuṭ.* He did it perfectly the first time. *ʔawwal marra sawwaaha biδ̣-δ̣abuṭ.* **3.** *kulliš.* I know him perfectly well. *ʔaƐurfa kulliš zeen.*

to **perform** - **1.** *sawwa (i taswiya) t-, qaam (u qiyaam) b-.* Who performed the operation? *minu sawwa l-Ɛamaliyya?* -- The acrobats performed the most difficult feats. *l-pahlawaaniyya qaamaw ib-ʔaxṭar il-ζarakaat.* **2.** *ʔadda (i taʔdiya) t-.* He performed his duty. *ʔadda waajba.* **3.** *maθθal (i tamθiil).* This group of players has been performing this play for two years. *haj-jamaaƐa l-mumaθθiliin ymaθθiluun har-ruwaaya muddat santeen.*

performance - **1.** *Ɛariδ̣.* Did you like the performance of the dancing troupe? *Ɛijabak Ɛariδ̣ hal-firqa r-raaqiṣ?* **2.** *tamθiiliyya* pl. *-aat.* What time does the performance begin? *šwakit tibdi t-tamθiiliyya?*

perfume - *riiζa* pl. *riyaζ.*

to perfume - *Ɛaṭṭar (i taƐṭiir) t-.* She perfumes her handkerchiefs. *tƐaṭṭir ičfaafiiha.*

perhaps - **1.** *rubbama, yimkin.* Perhaps I'll come to the meeting. *rubbama ʔaji lil-ijtimaaƐ.* **2.** *balki, yimkin, yjuuz.* Perhaps he is sick. *balki mariiδ̣.*

period - **1.** *mudda* pl. *mudad.* He worked here for a short period. *štiġal ihnaa mudda qaṣiira.* **2.** *fatra* pl. *-aat.* This is an important period in our history. *haay fatra muhimma b-taariixna.* **3.** *nuqṭa* pl. *nuqaṭ.* You forgot to put a period here. *niseet itζuṭṭ nuqṭa hnaa.* **4.** *daris* pl. *druus.* I have the third period free. *Ɛindi faraaġ bid-dars iθ-θaaliθ.* **5.** *Ɛaada.* Doctor, my period is late this month. *daktoor, Ɛaadti tʔaxxrat haš-šahar.*

period of grace - *muhla.* The period of grace expires on the tenth. *l-muhla tixlaṣ yoom Ɛašra biš-šahar.*

periodical - *dawri**. He suffered periodical setbacks. *Ɛaana naksaat dawriyya.* -- I subscribe to a number of periodical magazines. *ʔaani mištirik ib-Ɛadad imnil-majallaat id-dawriyya.*

perjury - *šahaadat zuur.* She committed perjury. *šihdat šahaadat zuur.*

permanent - **1.** *parmanaant.* I need a permanent. *šaƐri yirraad-la parmanaant.* **2.** *daaʔimi**, *θaabit.* I have no permanent address. *ma-Ɛindi Ɛinwaan θaabit.* -- This is a permanent job. *haaδa šuġuḷ daaʔimi.*

permission - *ruxṣa, ʔiδin.* Did you get his permission? *ʔaxaδit ruxṣa minna?*

to ask permission - *starxaṣ (i stirxaaṣ).* He asked permission of his supervisor to leave an hour early. *starxaṣ min il-mulaaζiδ̣ maala yiṭlaƐ saaƐa gabḷ id-dawaam.*

permit - *ʔijaaza* pl. *-aat.* You need a permit before you can start building. *tiζtaaj ʔijaaza gabuḷ-ma tballiš bil-binaaʔ.*

to permit - **1.** *simaζ (a simaaζ) n- l-, niṭa (i) ruxṣa.* I can't permit that. *ma-asmaζ il-hiiči šii.* **2.** *raxxaṣ (i tarxiiṣ) t-.* My supervisor permitted me to leave early. *l-mulaaζiδ̣ maali raxxaṣni ʔaṭlaƐ Ɛala wakit.*

permitted - *masmuuζ l-, mraxxaṣ.* No one is permitted to enter this building. *maζζad masmuuζ-la yidxul hal-binaaya.* -- Is smoking permitted? *masmuuζ it-tadxiin?*

perpendicular - *Ɛamuudi**.

to **perpetuate** - *xallad (i taxliid) t-.* This deed will perpetuate his name in history. *hal-Ɛamal raζ-yxallid ʔisma bit-taariix.*

to **perplex** - *ζayyar (i taζyiir) t-.* His lack of interest in his studies perplexes me. *qillat ihtimaama b-druusa tζayyirni.*

perplexing - *mζayyir.* This is a very perplexing problem. *haay fadd muškila kulliš imζayyira.*

perplexity - *ζiira.* I was in such a state of perplexity I didn't know what to do. *činit ib-fadd šikil ζiira ma-Ɛrafit š-asawwi.*

per se - *b-ζaδδaat-.* It's not worth much per se, but it has sentimental value. *ma-tiswa šii b-ζaδδaata laakin il-ʔasbaab Ɛaaṭifiyya.*

to **persecute** - *δ̣ṭihad (i δ̣ṭihaad).* He imagines people are persecuting him. *yitṣawwar in-naas da-yiδ̣ṭahduu.*

persecution - *δ̣ṭihaad.* He suffers from a persecution complex. *mibtili b-Ɛuqdat iδ̣ṭihaad.*

to **persevere** - *waaδ̣ab (i muwaaδ̣aba), daawam (i tadwiim).* If you persevere in your efforts, you might get the promotion. *ʔiδa twaaδ̣ub Ɛala juhuudak yimkin itζaṣṣil it-tarfiiƐ.*

Persia - *ʔiiraan, bilaad il-furs.*

Persian - **1.** *faarsi** pl. *furs, Ɛajami** pl. *-iyyiin, ʔiiraani** pl. *-iyyiin.* He's a Persian. *huwwa faarsi.* **2.** *faarsi.* Translate that into Persian. *tarjam haaδi lil-faarsi.*

to **persist** - **1.** *laζζ (i ʔilζaaζ, laζζ) n-, lajj (i lajj) n-.* The boy persisted with his questions until the old man got angry. *l-walad laζζ ib-ʔasʔilta ʔila ʔan ir-rijjaal iš-šaayib ġiδ̣ab.* **2.** *daam (u dawaam), ṭawwal (i taṭwiil).* The effects of the disease persisted a long time. *nataaʔij il-maraδ̣ daamat mudda ṭuwiila.* **3.** *tmaada (a tamaadi).* He persisted in lying. *tmaada bil-kiδib.*

persistent - **1.** *muṣirr.* He is persistent in his efforts to obtain a higher education. *muṣirr Ɛala juhuuda lil-ζuṣuul Ɛala θaqaafa Ɛaalya.* **2.** *mθaabir.* Your son doesn't learn quickly, but he is very persistent. *ʔibnak ma-yitƐallam ib-surƐa, laakin huwwa kulliš imθaabir.*

person - **1.** *šaxiṣ* pl. *ʔašxaaṣ.* He is the same person. *huwwa nafs iš-šaxiṣ.* **2.** *ʔaadmi* pl. *ʔawaadim, ʔinsaan* pl. *naas.* He is a nice person. *haaδa xooš ʔaadmi.* or *huwwa ʔinsaan ṭayyib.* **3.** *nafar* pl. *ʔanfaar.* We have place for two more persons. *Ɛidna makaan in-nafareen baƐad.* **4.** (m.) *waaζid* (f.) *waζda.* She's a nice person. *hiyya fadd waζda laṭiifa.*
**What sort of a person is he? *huwwa šinu min šii?*

in person - *biδ-δaat, šaxṣiyyan, b-nafs-.* Please deliver this to him in person. *ʔarjuuk sallim-la haay biδ-δaat.*

personal - **1.** *šaxṣi**. He asks too many personal questions. *yisʔal ihwaaya ʔasʔila šaxṣiyya.* -- He would like to discuss a personal matter with you. *da-yriid yiζči wiyyaak Ɛala fadd mawδ̣uuƐ šaxṣi.* **2.** *xaaṣṣ, xuṣuuṣi**. These are my personal belongings. *haay ġaraaδ̣i l-xaaṣṣa.*

personality - *šaxṣiyya* pl. *-aat.* She has a loveable personality. *Ɛidha šaxṣiyya maζbuuba.*

personally - *šaxṣiyyan.* I'd like to speak to him personally. *ʔariid aζči wiyyaa šaxṣiyyan.* -- Personally I don't like him. *šaxṣiyyan ʔaani ma-ʔamiil ʔila.*

personnel - **1.** *muwaδ̣δ̣afiin, mustaxdamiin.* We don't have enough personnel. *ma-Ɛidna muwaδ̣δ̣afiin kaafiin.* **2.** *δaatiyya.* He's the director of the personnel section. *haaδa mudiir qism iδ-δaatiyya.*

perspiration - *Ɛarag.*

to **perspire** - *Ɛirag (a Ɛarag).* I perspire a lot at night. *ʔaƐrag ihwaaya bil-leel.*

to **persuade** - *qannaƐ (i taqniiƐ), ʔaqnaƐ (i ʔiqnaaƐ).* He persuaded me to go. *qannaƐni ʔaruuζ.*

persuasion - *taqniiƐ, ʔiqnaaƐ.* We had to use persuasion to get him to agree. *staƐmalna l-ʔiqnaaƐ ζatta nxallii ywaafuq.*

pertinent - *Ɛaaʔid.* I don't think these facts are pertinent to the case. *ma-aδ̣inn hal-waqaaʔiƐ Ɛaaʔida lil-qaδ̣iyya.*

perversion - *nζiraaf.* Sexual perversion can be treated. *l-inζiraaf ij-jinsi yimkin yitƐaalaj.*

pervert - *minζirif* pl. *-iin.* A sexual pervert approached me on the street. *ndagg biyya fadd waaζid minζirif jinsiyyan biš-šaariƐ.*

to pervert - *ʔafsad (i ʔifsaad).* He was accused of perverting the youth. *ntiham ib-ʔifsaad iš-šabaab.*

pessimism - *tašaaʔum.*

pessimist - *mitšaaʔim.*

to be **pessimistic** - *tšaaʔam (a tašaaʔum).* Don't be pessimistic. *la-titšaaʔam.*

pest - **1.** *bala.* The sparrows have become a pest in the orchard. *l-Ɛaṣaafiir ṣaayra bala bil-ζadiiqa.*

2. ḥašara pl. -aat. The government has begun a campaign against insect pests. l-ḥikuuma šaanna ḥamla εal-ḥašaraat.
to **pester** - bazzaε (i tbizziε) t-. He pestered me to death with his questions. bazzaεni b-ʔasʔilta.
pestle - ʔiid (pl. ʔiideen) haawan.
pet - 1. ḥaywaan ʔaliif pl. ḥaywaanaat ʔaliifa. We're not allowed to keep pets in our apartments. maa masmuuḥ inrabbi ḥaywaanaat ʔaliifa b-binaayatna. 2. (m.) walad imdallal pl. wulid imdallaliin; (f.) bitt, bnayya mdallala pl. banaat imdallalaat. She's her mother's pet. hiyya l-ibnayya l-mdallila εid ʔummha.
to pet - massad (i tamsiid) t- l-. Don't pet the dog! la-tmassid-la lič-čalib.
petition - εariiδ̣a pl. εaraayiδ̣, εarδ̣aḥaal pl. -aat, maδ̣baṭa pl. maδ̣aabuṭ. Why don't you get up a petition? leeš ma-tqaddim εariiδ̣a?
to petition - qaddam (i taqdiim) εariiδ̣a. The villagers petitioned the central government for a new school building. ʔahl il-qura qaddimaw εariiδ̣a lil-ḥukuuma il-markaziyya li-ʔajal binaaya jadiida lil-madrasa.
petitioner - mustadεi pl. -iin.
petroleum - nafuṭ.
petty - 1. ṭafiif, zahiid. This is a petty sum. haaδa mablaġ ṭafiif. 2. taafih. I'm tired of these petty objections. yikfi hal-iεtiraaδ̣aat hat-taafha.
petty expenses - naθriyyaat.
pharaoh - firεoon pl. faraaεiin.
pharmacist - ṣaydali pl. ṣayaadila.
pharmacy - ṣaydaliyya pl. -aat.
phase - marḥala pl. maraaḥil, ṭawr pl. ʔaṭwaar. The second phase of the project will begin next month. l-marḥala θ-θaanya mnil-mašruuε raḥ-tibdi š-šahr ij-jaay.
Ph. D. - diktooraa. He has a Ph. D. in economics. εinda diktooraa bil-iqtiṣaad.
phenomenon - δ̣aahira pl. δ̣awaahir. This is a strange phenomenon. haay δ̣aahira ġariiba.
phenomenal - xaariq. He has a phenomenal memory. εinda δaakira xaariqa.
philanthropic - 1. xayri*, birri*. Philanthropic societies provide the schools for orphans with food and clothing. j-jamεiyyaat il-xayriyya tzawwid madaaris il-ʔaytaam bil-ʔakil wil-hiduum. 2. ʔinsaani*. That's not a very philanthropic idea. hal-fikra muu fikra ʔinsaaniyya kulliš.
philanthropist - rajul muḥsin pl. rijaal, riyaajiil muḥsiniin.
philanthropy - ḥubb il-ʔinsaaniyya, εamal (pl. ʔaεmaal) ʔiḥsaan, xeer.
philologist - luġawi pl. -iyyiin.
philology - εilm il-luġaat.
philosopher - faylasuuf pl. falaasifa.
philosophic - falsafi*.
philosophy - falsafa.
phone - talafoon pl. -aat. You're wanted on the phone. da-yriiduuk εat-talafoon.
to phone - talfan (i ttilfin) l-, xaabar (i muxaabara). I'll phone you after lunch. raḥ-atalfin-lak baεd il-ġada.
phonograph - gramafoon pl. -aat, funuġraaf pl. -aat.
phony - 1. mlaffaq. That story is phony. hal-qiṣṣa mlaffaqa. 2. daεi, muddaεi. The guy is a phony. haaδa waaḥid muddaεi.
phosphorus - fusfoor.
photograph - rasim pl. rsuum, ṣuura pl. ṣuwar, taṣwiir pl. taṣaawiir. Where can I have a passport photograph taken? ween ʔagdar ʔaaxuδ rasim maal paaṣpoort.
to photograph - ʔaxaδ (u ʔaxiδ) ṣuura. Have you photographed the statue? ʔaxaδit ṣuurat it-timθaal?
photographer - muṣawwir pl. -iin, rassaam pl. -iin.
phrase - εibaara pl. -aat, qawl pl. ʔaqwaal. This phrase is not a complete sentence. hal-εibaara muu jumla kaamla.
to phrase - 1. εabbar (i taεbiir) εan-. Can you phrase it in a better way? tigdar itεabbur εanha b-ṭariiqa ʔaḥsan? 2. ṣaaġ (u ṣiyaaġa) n-. He phrased his speech so as to appeal to the masses. ṣaaġ xiṭaaba b-ṣuura tʔaθθir bij-jamaahiir.
physical - 1. jismi*, badani*, jismaani*. Avoid every form of physical exertion. tḥaaša ʔay irhaaq jismi. 2. ṭabiiεi*. This contradicts all physical laws. haaδa ynaaqiδ̣ kull il-qawaaniin iṭ-ṭabiiεiyya.
physical education - riyaaδ̣a, r-riyaaδ̣a l-badaniyya.
physical exercise - riyaaδ̣a, tamriin.
physician - daktoor pl. dakaatra, ṭabiib pl. ʔaṭibbaaʔ.
physicist - fiizyaaʔi pl. -iyyiin, fiizyaawi pl. -iyyiin.
physics - fiizya, fiizyaaʔ. He is studying physics. da-yidrus fiizya.
physiology - faslaja.
physique - bunya pl. -aat, qalaafa pl. -aat. He has a nice physique. εinda xooš bunya.
pianist - εaazif (pl. -iin) piyaano.
piano - pyaano pl. pyaanwaat.
pick - 1. qazma pl. -aat. The men were carrying picks and shovels. l-εummaal čaanaw šaayliin qazmaat w-karakaat. 2. riiša pl. riyaš coll. riiš. The pick for my lute broke. r-riiša maal εuudi nkisrat. 3. xiira. This is the pick of the lot. haaδa xiirat il-mawjuud. 4. xiyaar. I have three apples; take your pick. εindi θlaθ tiffaaḥaat; ʔilak il-xiyaar. 5. nuxba pl. nuxab, zubda. These men are the pick of the army. haj-jinuud nuxbat ij-jeeš.
to pick - 1. ḥuwa (i ḥawi) n-. When are you going to pick the fruit? šwakit raḥ-taḥwi il-meewa? 2. xtaar (a xtiyaar) stanga (i stingaaʔ). You certainly picked a nice time for an argument. bila šakk ʔinta xtaareet il-wakit il-munaasib lil-mujaadala. 3. nagnag (i tnignig) b-. Don't pick at your food! la-tnagnig ib-ʔaklak! 4. naġbaš (u naġbaša) b-. Don't pick your teeth! la-tnaġbuš b-isnuunak. 5. nagbar (u tnugbur) b-. Don't pick your nose! la-tnagbur ib-xašmak! 6. fašš (i fašš) n-. Someone must have picked this lock. fadd ʔaḥḥad laazim fašš hal-qufal.
**They picked him to pieces. šarroo εal-ḥabil. or tnaawšoo.
**I have a bone to pick with you. εindi ḥsaab ʔariid ʔaṣaffii wiyyaak.
**Are you trying to pick a quarrel with me? ʔinta da-tdawwur-lak ḥirša wiyyaaya?
to pick on - šadd (i šadd) duub˜ wiyya. He's been picking on me all day. šaadd duuba wiyyaaya n-nahaar kulla.
to pick out - xtaar (a xtiyaar), stanga (i stingaaʔ). He picked out a very nice gift for his wife. xtaar hadiyya kulliš ḥilwa l-zawijta.
to pick up - 1. šaal (i šeel) n-. Please pick up the paper from the floor. baḷḷa ma-tšiil ij-jariida mnil-gaaε. -- The bus stopped here to pick up passengers. l-paaṣ wugaf ihnaa ḥatta yšiil rukkaab. 2. ligaṭ (u lagiṭ) n-. I picked up quite a bit of Italian on my trip. ligaṭit miqdaar la-baʔs bii mnil-ḥači l-ʔiiṭaali b-safurti. 3. lizam (a lazim) n-, kumaš (u kamuš) n-. The police picked up several suspects. š-šurṭa lizmaw baεδ̣ il-muštabih biihum. 4. ktisab (a ktisaab). The train gradually picked up speed. l-qiṭaar iktisab surεa tadriijiyyan.
pickle - ṭuršiyya pl. -aat, coll. ṭurši pl. ṭaraaši. Do you have any pickles? εindak ṭurši?
**He's in a pretty pickle now. huwwa mitwarriṭ hassa. or huwwa waagiε ib-maʔzaq hassa.
to pickle - čibas (i čabis), kammax (u tkummux). Did you pickle the turnips I brought you? čibasti š-šalġam illi jibta ʔilič?
pickled - mxallal. Buy a bowl of pickled beets. štirii-li kaasa šuwandar imxallal.
pick pocket - naššaal pl. -iin, δ̣arraab (pl. -iin) jeeb.
picnic - nuzha pl. -aat.
picture - 1. ṣuura pl. ṣuwar, rasim pl. rusuum. They have some beautiful pictures for sale. εidhum baεδ̣ iṣ-ṣuwar il-badiiεa lil-beeε. -- This is my picture when I was in the army. haaδa rasmi min činit bij-jeeš. 2. filim pl. ʔaflaam. Was the picture good? l-filim čaan zeen? 3. fikra pl. ʔafkaar. I have to get a clear picture of it first. laazim yṣiir εindi fikra waaδ̣ḥa εanna ʔawwal.
to give a picture of - ṣawwar (u taṣwiir). He gave you a false picture of it. ṣawwar-lak-iyyaaha ġalaṭ.
to picture - 1. ṣawwar (u taṣwiir) t-. This novel pictures life a thousand years ago. har-ruwaaya tṣawwur il-ḥayaat gabuḷ ʔalif sana. 2. tṣawwar (a taṣawwur). I pictured it differently. tṣawwaritha ġeer šikil.
pictures - siinama, ʔaflaam. She has been in pictures since she was a child. tiṭlaε bis-siinama min hiyya baεadha ṭifla.
piece - 1. wuṣla pl. wuṣal. May I take a piece of the watermelon. ʔagdar ʔaaxuδ wuṣla mnir-raggi? -- Sew these two pieces together. xayyṭi hal-wuṣilteen suwa. 2. qiṭεa pl. qiṭaε. Get a piece of wire and fasten them together. jiib qiṭεa

min is-silk w-urbuṭhum suwa. **3.** *maqṭuuɛa* pl. *maqaaṭiiɛ.* What is the name of the piece the orchestra is playing? *š-ism hal-maqṭuuɛa l-da-tiɛzifha l-firqa?*

**I gave him a good piece of my mind! *zaffeeta!* or *wabbaxta zeen!*

to fall to pieces - *tfaṣṣax (a tafaṣṣux).* The book is falling to pieces. *l-iktaab itfaṣṣax.* or **l-iktaab ṣaar wuṣla-wuṣla.*

to go to pieces - 1. *nhaar (a nhiyaar).* She went completely to pieces. *nhaarat tamaaman.* **2.** *tfallaš (a tafalluš).* Sooner or later their business is bound to go to pieces. *ˀawwal w-taali tijaarathum laazim titfallaš.*

to tear to pieces - *šaggag (i tšiggig), maḷḷax (i tmiḷḷix).* The dog tore my shoe to pieces. *č-čalib maḷḷax qundarti.*

piece work - *bil-qiṭɛa, bil-wizda.* They work piece work. *yištuġluun bil-qiṭɛa.*

pier - 1. *dinga* pl. *dinag.* The bridge rests on four piers. *j-jisir murakkab ɛala ˀarbaɛ dinag.* **2.** *raṣiif* pl. *ˀarṣifa.* We were standing on the harbor's pier waiting for the boat. *čiina waagfiin ɛala raṣiif il-miinaaˀ da-nintiðir il-markab.*

to **pierce** - *nigab (u nagub) n-, ziraf (u zaruf) n-.* Bullets can not pierce this armored plate. *ˀirṣaaṣ ma-yigdar yingub hal-zadiid il-mudarraɛ.*

pig - *xanziir* pl. *xanaaziir.*

pigeon - *zamaama* pl. *-aat* coll. *zamaam.*

wild pigeon - *ṭwaarni* pl. *-iyya.*

pigeonhole - *xaana* pl. *-aat.* You'll find it in one of the pigeon holes of the desk. *tilgiiha b-wazda min xaanaat il-meez.*

to pigeonhole - *nayyam (i tniyyim).* Apparently they have pigeonholed our request. *yiðhar nayyimaw iṭ-ṭalab maalna.*

pigeon house - *burij* pl. *braaj, bruuj.*

pigheaded - *ɛnaadi* pl. *-iyya, ɛanuud* pl. *-iin.* He is so pigheaded that he won't even listen to my explanation. *haaða hal-gadd iɛnaadi zatta ma-yismaɛ iš-šariz maali.*

pile - 1. *koom, kooma* pl. *kwaam.* Leave space between the piles of sand and gravel. *xalli masaafa been ikwaam ir-ramul wil-zaṣu.* -- This pile of letters needs to be answered. *haay kooma mnil-makaatiib yinraad-ilha jawaab.* **2.** *θarwa* pl. *-aat.* He made his pile during the war. *jimaɛ θaruuta bil-zarub.*

to pile - 1. *kawwam (u takwiim) t-, kaddas (i takdiis) t-.* Pile the bricks next to the wall. *kawwum iṭ-ṭaabuug yamm il-zaayiṭ.* **2.** *dizas (a dazis) n-.* We piled all the suitcases into the trunk of the car. *dizasna kull ij-junaṭ ib-ṣanduug is-sayyaara.* **3.** *ndizas (i ndizaas).* We all piled into one car. *kullna ndizasna b-fadd sayyaara.*

to pile up - *traakam (a taraakum).* My debts are piling up. *dyuuni da-titraakam.*

piles - *buwaasiir.* He was operated on in the hospital for piles. *sawwoo-la ɛamaliyyat buwaasiir bil-mustašfa.*

pilgrim - *zajji* pl. *zijjaaj.*

pilgrimage - *zajj.*

pill - *zabba* pl. *zabaabi* coll. *zubuub.*

pillar - *ɛamuud* pl. *ˀaɛmida, ɛawaamiid; dalag* pl. *-aat; dinga* pl. *dinag.* A large pillar blocked my view of the stage. *fadd ɛamuud ičbiir sadd manðar il masraz min giddaami.*

pillow - *mxadda* pl. *mxaadiid.*

pillowcase - *beet imxadda* pl. *byuut imxaadiid.*

pilot - 1. *rubbaan* pl. *rabaabina, qabṭaan* pl. *qabaaṭina.* The ship is waiting for the pilot. *l-baaxira da-tintiðir ir-rubbaan.* **2.** *ṭayyaar* pl. *-iin.* He is an Air Force pilot. *huwwa ṭayyaar bil-quwwa j-jawwiyya.*

pimple - 1. *zungiṭa* pl. *zanaagiṭ.* Her face is full of pimples. *wujihha mṭallaɛ zanaagiṭ.* **2.** *zabba* pl. *zubuub* coll. *zabb.* When he grew up he got rid of his adolescent pimples. *min kubar xallaṣ min zabb iš-šabaab.*

pin - *danbuus* pl. *danaabiis.* She stuck herself with a pin. *čakkat nafisha b-danbuus.* -- She wore a silver pin. *libsat danbuus fuððα.*

**I was on pins and needles. *činit ɛala ˀazarr imnij-jamur.* or *činit gaaˀid ɛala naar.*

hairpin - *furkeeta* pl. *-aat.*

to pin - 1. *dambas (i tdimbis).* Pin your handkerchief to your coat. *dambis ič-čiffiyya b-sitirtak.* **2.** *ɛiṣa (a ɛaṣi).* The two men were pinned under the car. *r-rijjaaleen ɛiṣaw jawwa s-sayyaara.*

to pin down - *lizam (a lazim).* We couldn't pin him down to anything definite. *ma-gdarna nilzama b-šii ˀakiid.*

to pin on - 1. *šakkal (i tšikkil), ɛallag (i tɛillig).* I'll pin it on for you. *ˀaani ˀašakkil-lak-iyyaaha.* -- She pinned a flower on her dress. *šakkilat warda ɛala badlatha.* **2.** *θabbat (i taθbiit) t-.* The police pinned the crime on him. *š-šurṭa θabbitat ij-jariima ɛalee.*

to pin up - 1. *šakkal (i tšikkil) li-foog, ɛallag (i tɛillig) li-foog.* Let me pin up the hem first. *xalli ˀawwal ˀašakkil il-zaašya li-foog.* **2.** *farkat (i tfurkit) t-.* She pinned up her hair. *farkitat šaɛarha.* or *zaaṭṭa furkeeta ib-šaɛarha.*

pinch - 1. *nitfa* pl. *nitaf, rašša* pl. *-aat.* Add a pinch of salt to the soup. *ðiif fadd nitfa miliz ɛaš-šoorba.* **2.** *garṣa* pl. *-aat.* The boy gave his little sister a good pinch. *l-walad giraṣ ˀuxta ṣ-ṣiġayyra garṣa qawiyya.*

in a pinch - *ɛind ið-ðuruura, b-wakt ið-ðiiq.* In a pinch it will do. *ɛind ið-ðuruura haay itsidd il-zaaja.* -- You can always count on him in a pinch. *b-imkaanak daaˀiman tigdar tiɛtimid ɛalee b-wakt ið-ðiiq.*

to pinch - 1. *giraṣ (u gariṣ) n-, garraṣ (i tagriiṣ) t-.* Don't pinch! *la-tigruṣ!* -- The door pinched my finger. *l-baab girṣat iṣibɛi.* **2.** *ðayyag (i taðyiig) t- ɛala, ˀaðða (i taˀðiya) t-.* Where does the shoe pinch your foot? *minneen il-qundara da-ṭðayyig ɛala rijlak.*

pine - *ṣnoobara* pl. *-aat* coll. *ṣnoobar.* These pine trees are almost fifty years old. *ˀašjaar l-iṣnoobar haay ɛumurha zwaali xamsiin sana.*

pineapple - *ˀananaas.*

pine wood - *xišab čaam.*

pink - 1. *wardi**. She was wearing a pink dress. *čaanat laabsa nafnuuf wardi.* **2.** *qranfila* (pl. *-aat) wardiyya* coll. *qranfil wardi.* We had pinks in this place last year. *čaan ɛidna b-hal-mazall qranfil wardi s-sana l-maaðiya.*

pious - *middayyin* pl. *-iin, taqi* pl. *ˀatqiyaaˀ, ṣaaliz* pl *-iin.* He is a very pious man. *huwwa rajjaal middayyin ihwaaya.*

pipe - 1. *buuri* pl. *bwaari, ˀinbuub* pl. *ˀanaabiib.* The pipe has burst. *l-buuri ṭagg.* -- The oil pipe line runs from Kirkuk to Tripoli. *ˀanaabiib in-nafuṭ timtadd min kirkuuk ˀila ṭaraabluṣ.*

2. *paayp* pl. *-aat.* He smokes a pipe. *ydaxxin paayp.*

to pipe - **We pipe our water from a spring. *naaxuð il-maay bil-buwaari mnil-ɛeen.*

piracy - *qarṣana.*

pirate - *qurṣaan* pl. *qaraaṣina.*

pistachio - *fistiqa* pl. *-aat* coll. *fistiq.*

pistol - *musaddas* pl. *-aat, warwar* pl. *waraawur.*

piston - *pistin* pl. *-aat, pasaatin.*

pit - 1. *manjam* pl. *manaajim.* No one was in the pit when the explosion occurred. *mazzad čaan bil-manjam min ṣaar l-infijaar.* **2.** *nuwaaya* pl. *-aat* coll. *niwa.* The boy swallowed an olive pit. *l-walad bilaɛ nuwaayat zeetuun.*

pitch - 1. *zifit.* What's the difference between pitch and tar? *šinu l-farig been iz-zifit wil-giir?* **2.** *ðarba* pl. *-aat, šamra* pl. *-aat.* That was a good pitch. *haaði čaanat xooš ðarba.* **3.** *zaalik, daamis.* It was pitch dark when we came home. *čaan ðalam daamis lumman jeena lil-beet.*

to pitch - 1. *nuṣab (u naṣub) n-.* Where shall we pitch the tent? *ween ninṣub il-xeema?* **2.** *šumar (u šamur) n-.* Pitch it out of the window. *šmurha mniš-šibbaak.*

to pitch in - *tšallah (a tašalluh), šammar (u tašmiir) ɛann is-saaɛid.* We pitched in and helped him. *tšallahna w-nizalna nɛaawna.*

pitcher - *doolka* pl. *-aat.* Please get me a pitcher of water. *baḷḷa jiib-li doolka maay.*

pitiable - *murθi.* He is in a pitiable condition. *zaalta murθiya.* or **zaalta yinriθii-lha.*

pitiful - *muˀlim, ˀaliim.* That was a pitiful sight. *ðaak čaan fadd manðar muˀlim.*

pity - 1. *šafaqa.* I don't want your pity. *ma-ariid šafaqtak.* **2.** *zasaafa.* It's a pity you can't come. *zasaafa ma-tigdar tiji.* **3.** *zeef.* It's a pity he is only seventeen, otherwise I could have employed him. *yaa zeef ɛumra ṣbaaṭaɛaš, w-ˀilla čaan šaġġalta.*

**She took pity on him. *gaḷubha nkisar ɛalee.*

to pity - *šifaq (i šafaqa) n- ɛala, riθa (i raθaaˀ) n- l-.* She doesn't want anyone to pity her.

ma-triid aẓẓad yišfiq Ɛaleeha. -- I pity them.
ʔarδi l-ẓaalhum.

place – *maẓall* pl. *-aat, makaan* pl. *-aat.* Please put it back in the same place. *ʔarjuuk rajjiƐha b-nafs il-maẓall.* -- If I were in his place I wouldn't have done it. *loo b-makaana, ma-čaan sawweetha.* -- Do you know a good place to eat? *tuƐruf fadd makaan zeen waaẓid yaakul bii?* -- Do you know the place where we stopped reading? *tuƐruf il-maẓall il-wuṣalnaa bil-qiraaya?* -- What is the name of this place? *š-isim hal-maẓall?* -- How many places did you set at the table? *kam maẓall ẓaδδarit Ɛal-meeẓ?*
**Somebody ought to put him in his place. *fadd aẓẓad laazim ywaggfa Ɛind ẓadda.*
**His heart is in the right place. *xooš ʔaadmi.* or *ʔadmi ṭayyib.* or *qaḷba naδiif.*
  in place of – *badaal, Ɛiwaδ.* May I have another book in place of this one? *tismaẓ tinṭiini kitaab laax badaal haaδa?*
  in the first place – *ʔawwalan, gabuḷ kullši.* In the first place, we can't leave until tomorrow. *gabuḷ kullši, ʔizna ma-nigdar niṭlaƐ ʔilla baaƐir.*
  to place – 1. *ẓaṭṭ, (u ẓaṭṭ) n-, wuδaƐ (a waδiƐ) n-, xalla (i txilli) t-.* Place the table next to the window. *ẓuṭṭ il-meeẓ ib-ṣaff iš-šibbaak.* 2. *xalla (i) t-.* Place the guest of honor next to the host. *xalli δeef iš-šaraf yamm ʔabu d-daƐwa.* 3. *Ɛayyan (i taƐyiin) t-.* We have placed all of our graduates. *Ɛayyanna kull il-mitxarrjiin min Ɛidna* or **ligeena l-kull il-mitxarrjiin šuġuḷ.* 4. *wajjah (i tawjiih) t-.* A charge was placed against him. *fadd tuhma twajjihat δidda.* 5. *ʔalqa (i ʔilqaaʔ).* He placed the responsibility for the damage on the proper man. *ʔalqa masʔuuliyyat it-talaf Ɛala l-faaƐil il-ẓaqiiqi.* 6. *tδakkar (a taδakkur).* I've met him before, but I can't place him. *ʔaani mlaagii gabuḷ, bass ma-ʔatδakkar minu huwwa.*

plague – *ṭaaƐuun* pl. *ṭwaaƐiin.*

plain – 1. *sahil* pl. *suhuul.* There is a wide plain between the two mountain ranges. *ʔaku sahil waasiƐ been silsilteen ij-jibaal.* 2. *baṣiiṭ* pl. *-iin, buṣaṭaaʔ.* They are plain people. *humma naas buṣaṭaaʔ.* -- We have a plain home. *Ɛiddna beet baṣiiṭ.* 3. *Ɛtiyaadi*. She is a plain-looking woman, but very intelligent. *haay waẓda malaamiẓha Ɛtiyaadiyya, laakin kulliš δakiyya.* 4. *waaδiẓ. δaahir.* It is quite plain that he is after her money.
**It is as plain as the nose on your face. *waaδẓa miθil Ɛeen is-šamis.*
**The ship now is in plain view. *l-baaxira hassa mbayyna.*
**I told him the plain truth. *git-la l-ẓaqiiqa miθil-ma hiyya.*

plan – 1. *xariiṭa* pl. *xaraayiṭ, muxaṭṭaṭ* pl. *-aat, taṣmiim* pl. *taṣaamiim.* The plan for the new house is ready. *l-xariiṭa maal il-beet ij-jidiid ẓaaδra.* 2. *xiṭṭa* pl. *xuṭaṭ, tadbiir* pl. *tadaabiir.* Have you made any plans yet for the future? *fakkarit ib-ʔay xuṭaṭ lil-mustaqbal loo baƐad?* -- This is an excellent plan. *haaẓa fadd tadbiir mumtaaz.* 3. *mašruuƐ* pl. *mašaariiƐ.* They have great plans for beautifying the city. *Ɛidhum mašaariiƐ Ɛaδiima t-tajmiil il-madiina.* 4. *manhaj* pl. *manaahij.* What are your plans for tomorrow? *šinu manhajak baaƐir?*
  to plan – 1. *rattab (i tartiib) t-, dabbar (u tadbiir) t-.* Our trip was carefully planned. *safratna čaanat kulliš zeena mrattba.* 2. *naδδam (u tanδiim) t-.* He doesn't know how to plan his time. *ma-yuƐruf išloon ynaδδum wakta.* 3. *sawwa (i) xariiṭa.* Who planned your house? *minu sawwa l-xariiṭa maal beetak?* 4. *ṣammam (i taṣmiim) t-.* Who planned your garden for you? *minu ṣammam-lak il-ẓadiiqa maaltak?* 5. *nuwa (i niyya) n-.* Where do you plan to spend the summer? *ween tinwi tigδi ṣ-ṣeef?* 6. *ẓisab (i ẓsaab) n-, ẓsaab~, dabbar (u tadbiir) t- ʔamr~.* On the salary I get, I have to plan very carefully. *bir-raatib illi ʔastilma, ʔaani muṭṭarr ʔaẓsib iẓsaabi b-digga.*
  to plan on – *Ɛtimad (i Ɛtimaad) Ɛala.* You'd better not plan on it. *ʔaẓsan-lak la-tiƐtimid Ɛalee.*

plane – 1. *mustawa* pl. *-ayaat.* The discussion was not on a very high plane. *l-munaaqaša ma-čaanat Ɛala mustawa kulliš Ɛaali.* 2. *randaj* pl. *ranaadij.* I borrowed a plane from the carpenter. *ṭlabit randaj imnin-najjaar.* 3. *ṭiyyaara* pl. *-aat.* What sort of plane is this? *haṭ-ṭiyyaara min ʔay*

nooƐ? 4. *mustawi.* I studied plane geometry for two years. *drasit il-handasa l-mustawiya santeen.*
  to plane – 1. *ṣaffa (i tṣiffi) t-, δirab (u δarib) n- randaj, saawa (i taswiya) t-.* These boards have to be planed. *hal-looẓaat laazim tiṭṣaffa.*
  to plane down – *randaj (i trindij) t-, saawa (i musaawaat) t-.* We'll have to plane the door down. We'll have to plane the door down. *laazim išwayya nrandij il-baab.*

planet – *kawkab sayyaar* pl. *kawaakib sayyaara.*

planned – *marsuum.* We'll carry out the project as planned. *raẓ-innaffiδ il-xuṭṭa miθil-ma marsuuma.*

plant – 1. *nabaat* pl. *-aat, ẓariƐ.* What kind of plants are they? *humma min ʔay nooƐ imnin-nabaataat.* -- I water the plants every day. *ʔasgi z-zariƐ kull yoom.* 2. *maƐmal* pl. *maƐaamil, maṣnaƐ* pl. *maṣaaniƐ.* The manager showed me around the plant. *l-mudiir farrajni Ɛal-maƐmal.*
  to plant – 1. *ziraƐ (a zariƐ) n-.* We planted flowers in our garden. *zraƐna warid ib-ẓadiiqatna.* 2. *šiƐax (i šaƐix) n-, rakkaz (i tarkiiz) t-.* The boy scouts planted the flag in the sand and put up their tents around it. *l-kaššaafa šiƐxaw il-Ɛalam bir-ramuḷ w-nuṣbaw xayaamhum daayir daayra.* 3. *xaššaš (i taxšiiš) t-, daxxal (i tadxiil, ʔidxaal) t-.* The teacher planted bad ideas in the students' minds. *l-muƐallim xaššaš ib-Ɛuquul iṭ-ṭullaab ʔaaraaʔ muu zeena.*
**They planted mines in the road to protect their retreat. *ʔalgimaw iṭ-ṭariiq ẓatta yiẓmuun taraajiƐhum.*

plaster – 1. *bayaaδ, juṣṣ.* The plaster on the wall is all cracked. *l-ibyaaδ Ɛal-ẓaayiṭ kulla mfaṭṭar.* 2. *lazga* pl. *-aat.* The nurse applied a mustard plaster to my back. *l-mumarriδa ẓaṭṭat lazgat xardal Ɛala δahri.* 3. *jiṭṣ.* Her arm is still in a plaster cast. *ʔiidha baƐadha b-qaalab jiṭṣ.* -- This figure is made of plaster of Paris. *hat-timθaal imsawwa min jiṭṣ.*
  to plaster – *bayyaδ (i tibyaaδ) t-.* Have they finished plastering the walls yet? *xalliṣaw tibyaaδ il-iẓyaaṭiin loo baƐad.*

plastic – *plastik.*

plastic surgery – *jiraaẓat it-tajmiil.*

plate – 1. *maaƐuun* pl. *mwaaƐiin.* There's a crack in the plate. *ʔaku faṭir bil-maaƐuun.* 2. *šikil* pl. *ʔaškaal.* The illustration is on Plate Three. *t-tamθiiẓ Ɛala šikil raqam itlaaθa.* 3. *looẓa* pl. *-aat.* It's very difficult to get plates for this camera. *kulliš ṣaƐub tinligi looẓaat il-hal-kaamira.* 4. *ṭaxum* pl. *ṭxuum.* I didn't know she wore a plate. *ma-činit adri tilbas ṭaxum.* 5. *pleeta* pl. *-aat.* The floor of the tank is one single plate. *gaaƐ taanki l-maay ipleeta wiẓda.*
  to plate – *labbas (i talbiis) t-.* They make these knives of steel and then plate them with silver. *ysawwuun has-sičaaƐiin min fuulaaδ w-baƐdeen ylabbisuuha bil-fuδδa.*

platform – 1. *raṣiif* pl. *ʔarṣifa.* Let's meet on the railway platform. *xal-nitlaaga Ɛala raṣiif il-maẓaṭṭa.* 2. *daƐča* pl. *-aat.* Back up the truck to the loading platform. *rajjiƐ it-tirak maalak il-daƐƐat il-ẓimil.* 3. *manaṣṣa* pl. *-aat.* There is a platform for the speaker in the front part of the room. *ʔaku manaṣṣa lil-xaṭiib bij-jiha l-ʔamaamiyya bil-ġurfa.* 4. *masraẓ* pl. *masaariẓ, marsaẓ* pl. *maraasiẓ.* The speakers were all seated on the platform. *l-xuṭabaaʔ kaanaw qaaƐdiin Ɛal-masraẓ.*

platoon – *faṣiil* pl. *faṣaaʔil.*

platter – *balam* pl. *blaam.* The platter won't hold the whole melon. *l-balam ma-yilzam kull ir-raggiyya.*

plausible – *maƐquul.* His explanation is plausible but I don't agree with him. *ʔiiδaaẓaata maƐquula bass ma-attifiẓ wiyyaa.*

play – 1. *liƐib.* The children are completely absorbed in their play. *l-ʔaṭfaal miltihiin bil-liƐib tamaaman.* 2. *tamθiiliyya* pl. *-aat.* I heard an amusing play on the radio in spoken Iraqi. *smaƐit tamθiiliyya muẓẓika bir-raadyo b-zači Ɛiraaqi.* 3. *masraẓiyya* pl. *-aat.* That company is going to perform three plays of Shakespeare this week. *hal-firqa raẓ-itquum ib-tamθiil iθlaθ masraẓiyyaat šakspiir hal-isbuuƐ.* 4. *riwaaya* pl. *-aat.* We don't often get to see plays by professional actors here. *ma-da-yṣaadif inṣuuf riwaayaat min qibal mumaθθiliin muẓtarifiin ihnaa.* 5. *malƐab.* The steering wheel has too much play. *s-sukkaan bii hwaaya malƐab.*
  to play – 1. *liƐab (a laƐib) n-.* The children are playing in the garden. *j-jihaal da-yliƐbuun*

bil-zadiiqa. -- We played for money. *liεabna εala fluus.* **2.** *dagg (i dagg) n-, εizaf (i εazif) n-.* He plays the violin very well. *ydugg kamanja kulliš zeen.* **3.** *qaam (u qiyaam) ib-door, maθθal (i tamθiil) t-.* Who is playing the lead? *minu da-yquum ib-door il-baṭal?* **4.** *štiġal (u šuġul), nεiraδ (i εariδ).* What film is playing tonight? *yaa filim da-yištiġul hal-leela?* **5.** *δabb (i δabb) n-.* He played his highest card. *δabb ʔaεla waraqa b-iida.* **6.** *sawwa (i taswiya).* He played a joke on me. *sawwa biyya nukta.*

to play a role - 1. *maθθal (i tamθiil) t-.* They asked me to play the role of the Juliet in the play *ṭilbaw minni ʔamaθθil juuleet bil-masraziyya.* **2.** *liεab (a laεib) door.* He played an important role in the negotiations. *liεab door muhimm bil-mufaawaδaat.*

to play around - 1. *δayyaε (i taδyiiε) wakit.* You've been playing around long enough. *yikfi baεad itδayyiε waktak.* **2.** *εibaθ (a εabiθ), liεab (a laεib).* Stop playing around with the radio. *bass εaad, la-tiεbaθ bir-raadyo.*

to play fair - *ʔanṣaf (i ʔinṣaaf).* He didn't play fair with me. *ma-ʔanṣaf wiyyaaya.*

to play up - *ʔaδhar (i ʔiδhaar).* He played up her good qualities. *ʔaδhar ṣifaatha z-zeena.*

player - 1. *laεuub* pl. *luwaaεiib.* One of the players got hurt during the game. *waazid imnil-luwaaεiib itʔaδδa ʔaθnaaʔ il-liεib.* **2.** *mumaθθil* pl. *-iin.* There was a party for the players after the play. *caanat zafla lil-mumaθθiliin baεd it-tamθiil.*

playground - *malεab* pl. *malaaεib.*

playing card - *warqa* pl. *-aat.*

plea - 1. *ltimaas* pl. *-aat, rajaaʔ* pl. *-aat.* He ignored my plea. *ma-daar baal l-iltimaasi.* **2.** *tawassul* pl. *-aat.* All my pleas were in vain. *kull tawassulaati raazat εabaθ.*

to **plead - 1.** *twassal (a tawassul), ltimas (i ltimaas), rija (u rajaaʔ).* She pleaded with him to stay. *twassalat bii yibqa.* **2.** *traafaε (a taraafuε).* I have retained the best lawyer in town to plead my case. *lizamit ʔazsam muzaami bil-wlaaya zatta yitraafaε ib-daεuuti.*

**Do you plead guilty? *ʔinta muδnib ʔam laa?*

pleasant - 1. *laṭiif* pl. *-iin, luṭafaaʔ.* She's a pleasant person. *hiyya fadd wazda laṭiifa.* **2.** *mubhij.* We spent a rather pleasant evening there. *gδeena hnaak fadd leela mubhija nawεan-ma.* **3.** *saεiid.* Good-bye! Have a pleasant trip! *maεa s-salaama! ʔatmannaa-lak safra saεiida!* **4.** *saarr.* What a pleasant surprise! *haay šloon mufaajaʔa saarra!*

**It isn't pleasant for me to have to do this. *yuʔsifni ʔan ʔaδṭarr asawwiiha.* or *ma-yhuun εalayya ʔasawwiiha.*

please - *rajaaʔan, balḷa, luṭfan, min faδlak, ʔarjuuk.* Please shut the door. *rajaaʔan sidd il-baab.*

to please - 1. *εijab (i ʔiεjaab) n-.* How does this hat please you? *šloon tiεijbak haš-šafqa?* -- Do as you please. *sawwi lli yεijbak.* or ***b-keefak.* **2.** *ʔarδa (i ʔirδaaʔ).* He's hard to please. *huwwa fadd waazid ṣaεub ʔirδaaʔa.* **3.** *raδδa (i tarδiya, triδδi) t-.* You can't please the whole world. *ma-tigdar itraδδi kull il-εaalam.* **4.** *sarr (i suruur) n-.* Your letter pleased me very much. *maktuubak sarrni hwaaya.*

to be pleased - *kayyaf (i tkiyyif), nsarr (a nsiraar).* He was pleased with it. *kayyaf biiha.*

pleasing - 1. *laṭiif.* He has a pleasing personality. *εinda šaxṣiyya laṭiifa.* **2.** *zilu.* She has a pleasing voice. *εidha ṣoot zilu.*

pleasure - 1. *laδδa* pl. *-aat.* I get a lot of pleasure out of the work. *ʔašεur ib-laδδa biš-šuġuḷ.* or ***ʔaltaδδ biš-šuġuḷ.* **2.** *mitεa* pl. *mitaε.* Watching him swim was a real pleasure. *šoofta yisbaz čaanat mitεa lil-εeen.* **3.** *lahu, hazal.* Business before pleasure. *š-šuġuḷ gabḷ il-lahu.* **4.** *suruur.* We accepted their invitation to dinner with great pleasure. *qibalna εaziimathum εal-εaša b-kull suruur.*

**The pleasure is all mine. *ʔaani l-mamnuun.*

pleat - *kasra* pl. *-aat, θanya* pl. *-aat.* Do you want the dress with or without pleats? *triidiin il-badla biiha kasraat loo laa?*

to pleat - *kassar (i tkissir) t-, θanna (i tθinni) t-.* Are you going to pleat the skirt or leave it straight? *ʔinti raayza tθanniin it-tannuura loo txalliiha εadla.*

plebiscite - *stiftaaʔ* pl. *-aat.*

pledge - *εahad* pl. *εuhuud.* He didn't keep his pledge. *ma-wufa b-εahda.*

to pledge - 1. *ʔaxaδ (u ʔaxiδ) εahad min.* He pledged me to secrecy. *ʔaxaδ εahad minni bil-kutmaan.* **2.** *tεahhad (a taεahhud).* I pledged to vote for him in the election. *tεahhadit ʔanṭii ṣooṭi bil-intixaab.*

plentiful - *waafir, ġaziir, mabδuul.*

plenty - 1. *hwaaya, kθiir.* You have plenty of time. *εindak ihwaaya wakit.* -- You have to get plenty of sleep. *laazim itnaam ikθiir.* **2.** *mitwaffir, hwaaya, kθiir.* There is plenty of rice in the market. *t-timman mitwaffir bis-suug.*

pleurisy - *δaat ij-janb.*

pliable - *layyin.*

pliers - *čillaabteen* pl. *-aat, plaayis* pl. *-aat.*

plight - *waδiε* pl. *ʔawδaaε.* We are aware of their plight and will do everything we can to help them. *ʔizna nidri waδiεhum w-raz-insawwi kull-ma nigdar εalee zatta nεaawinhum.*

plot - 1. *muʔaamara* pl. *-aat, dasiisa* pl. *dasaayis.* The plot was discovered in time. *l-muʔaamara nkišfat bil-waqt il-munaasib.* **2.** *qiṭεa* pl. *qiṭaε, wuṣla* pl. *wuṣal.* We bought a plot of land near the river. *štireena qiṭεat gaaε εan-nahar.* **3.** *silsila (pl. -aat) zawaadiθ.* The story has an interesting plot. *l-quṣṣa silsilat zawaadiθha mumtiεa.*

plot of land (leased) - *εaraṣa* pl. *-aat.*

to plot - *tʔaamar (a taʔaamur).* They plotted against the government. *tʔaamraw δidd il-zukuuma.*

plow - *mizraaθ* pl. *mazaariiθ.* You need a heavier plow. *tiztaaj mizraaθ ʔaθgal.*

to plow - *ziraθ (i zariθ) n-, kirab (u karub, karaab) n-.* I'll need all day to plow this field. *ʔaztaaj ṭuul in-nahaar zatta ʔazriθ hal-zaqil.*

to **pluck -** *nitaf (i natif) n-.* Did you pluck the chicken yet? *ntafitha lid-dijaaja loo baεad?*

plug - 1. *qabaġ* pl. *-aat, saddaad* pl. *-aat.* The sink needs a new plug. *l-muṣlux yirraad-la qabaġ jidiid.* **2.** *plakk* pl. *-aat.* Your car needs a new set of plugs. *sayyaartak yinraad-ilha ṭaxum plakkaat jidiid.*

to plug - *sadd (i sadd) n-.* Plug the hole. *sidd iz-ziruf.* -- The pipe is plugged. *l-buuri masduud.*

to plug in - *šakkal (i taškiil, tšikkil) plakk.* Plug in the fan. *šakkil il-plakk maal il-imhaffa.*

plum - *εinjaaṣa* pl. *-aat* coll. *εinjaaṣ.*

plumber - *ʔabu (pl. ʔahal) buuriyyaat.*

plumb line - *šaahuul* pl. *šwaahiil.*

plump - *matruus, θixiin.* She is a little on the plump side. *haay išwayya matruusa.*

to **plunge - 1.** *ġaṭṭ (u ġaṭṭ), ġiṭaṣ (u ġaṭiṣ).* He plunged into the water. *ġaṭṭ bil-maay.* -- When he heard the boy shouting in the river, he plunged in after him and pulled him out. *min simaε il-walad da-yṣayyiz bin-nahar, ġiṭaṣ εalee w-jarra.* **2.** *čayyat (i tčiyyit).* He plunged into the burning house. *čayyat bil-beet id-da-yiztirig.* **3.** *ġaṭṭaṣ (i tġiṭṭiṣ).* He plunged his hand into the cold water. *ġaṭṭaṣ ʔiida bil-maay il-baarid.*

plural - *jamiε* pl. *jumuuε.* What is the plural of ''beet''? *šinu jamiε "beet"?*

broken plural - *jamiε taksiir.*

sound plural - *jamiε saalim.*

plus - *zaayid, w-.* Four plus three is seven. *ʔarbaεa zaayid itlaaθa ysawwi sabεa.*

plywood - *xišab imεaakas.*

pneumonia - *δaat ir-riʔa.*

pocket - *jeeb* pl. *jyuub.* Put this in your pocket. *zuṭṭ haay ib-jeebak.*

to pocket - *δirab (u δarib) εala, laff (i laff).* His partner pocketed all the profits. *šariika δirab εalee kull il-ʔarbaaz.*

pocketbook - 1. *janṭat (pl. jinaṭ) ʔiid.* The thief stole the pocketbook from the woman and ran away. *l-zaraami baag janṭat il-ʔiid mnil-imrayya w-inhizam.* **2.** *jizdaan* pl. *jizaadiin.* He took out his pocketbook and gave me some change. *ṭallaε jizdaana w-inṭaani xurda.*

pocketknife - *čaaquuča* pl. *čawaaqiič.* May I borrow your pocketknife? *ʔagdar aṭlub ič-čaaquuča maaltak?*

podium - *manaṣṣa* pl. *-aat.* The conductor stepped up onto the podium. *raʔiis il-firqa l-mawsiiqiyya ṣiεad εal-manaṣṣa.*

poem - *qaṣiida* pl. *qaṣaayid.* This book contains all his poems. *hal-iktaab yizwi kull qaṣaayda.*

poet - *šaaεir* pl. *šuεaraaʔ.*

poetry - *šiεir* pl. *ʔašεaar.* My brother writes beautiful poetry. *ʔaxuuya yinδum šiεir badiiε.*

point – **1.** *nabbuula* pl. *-aat.* I broke the point of my pencil. *kisarit nabbuult il-qalam maali.* **2.** *raas* pl. *ruus, ṭaraf* pl. *ʔaṭraaf.* I broke the point of my knife. *kisarit raas is-siččiina maalti.* **3.** *nuqṭa* pl. *nuqaṭ.* Our team scored 23 points. *fariiqna sajjal itlaaθa w-ʕišriin nuqṭa.* -- We have gone over the contract point by point. *dirasna l-ʕaqid nuqṭa nuqṭa.* -- Women are his weak point. *n-nisaaʔ nuqṭat iδ-δuʕuf ʕinda.* **4.** *l-maqṣuud, beet il-qaṣiid, qaṣid.* You missed the point. *faatak il-maqṣuud.* or *faatak beet il-qaṣiid.* **5.** *mawδuuʕ* pl. *mawaaδiiʕ.* That is beside the point. *haaδa xaarij il-mawδuuʕ.* **6.** *ʒadd* pl. *ʒduud.* I can understand it up to a certain point. *ʔagdar aftihimha ʔila ʒadd muʕayyan.* **7.** *naaʒiya* pl. *nawaaʒi, maziyya* pl. *mazaaya.* He has good points, too. *ʕinda nawaaʒi* or *bii mazaaya.* **8.** *muujib.* There is no point in getting there before they open the doors. *ma-aku muujib inkuun ihnaak gabuḷ-ma yiftaʒuun il-baab.* **9.** *markaz* pl. *maraakiz.* The police set up their strong point at the entrance to the city. *š-šurṭa ʒaṭṭaw markaz quwwathum ib-madxal il-madiina.*
**Come to the point and stop beating about the bush. *guul il-ʒaqiiqa w-la-ṭδull tithazzam.*
on the point of – *ʕala wašak.* We were on the point of leaving when company arrived. *činna ʕala wašak da-niṭlaʕ min joona xuṭṭaar.*
point of view – **1.** *wajhat* (pl. *-aat*) *naδar.* Our points of view differ. *wajhaat naδarna tixtilif.* **2.** *jiha* pl. *-aat, naaʒiya* pl. *nawaaʒiyya.* From this point of view he's right. *min haj-jiha huwwa muʒiqq.*
to the point – *biṣ-ṣamiim, muṣiib.* His comments are always to the point. *taʕliiqaata daaʔiman biṣ-ṣamiim.*
to make a point of – *ʒaṭṭ (u ʒaṭṭ) ʕal-baal˜.* Make a point to be on time. *ʒuṭṭ ʕala baalak itkuun ʕal-wakit.*
to point – **1.** *šaar (i ʔišaara) n-, ʔaššar (i taʔšiir) t-.* The arrow points north. *s-sahim yšiir liš-šimaal.* -- Point to the man you mean. *ʔaššir ʕar-rijjaal illi tiʕnii.* -- Point out the place you told me about. *ʔaššir ʕal-makaan illi git-li ʕanna.* **2.** *dall (i tdilli) n-, dalla (i tdilli) t-.* All the signs point towards a cold winter. *kull il-maδaahir itdill ʕala šita baarid.* **3.** *wajjah (i tawjiih) t-.* Don't point the gun at me! *la-twajjih il-bunduqiyya ʕalayya!*
pointed – **1.** *mnabbal, ʒaadd.* Be careful with that pointed stick. *diir baalak min hal-ʕaṣaaya l-imnabbla.* **2.** *ʒaadd.* She's always making pointed remarks. *hiyya daaʔiman itʕalliq taʕliiqaat ʒaadda.*
poise – *razaana, ttizaan.* She never loses her poise. *ʔabadan ma-tifqud razaanta.*
poised – *raziin.* She is very poised for her age. *kulliš raziina bin-nisba l-ʕumurha.*
poison – **1.** *simm, samm* pl. *smuum.* Don't touch it, it's a poison. *la-ṭṭuxxa, haaδa simm.* **2.** *saamm.* They're using poison gases in their war against the royalists. *yistaʕmiluun ġaazaat saamma b-ʒarubhum δidd il-malakiyyiin.*
to poison – **1.** *samm (i samm) n-.* Our dog has been poisoned. *čalibna nsamm.* **2.** *sammam (i tasmiim) t-.* Our dog got poisoned from eating rotten meat. *čalibna tsammam min ʔakal laʒam jaayif.*
poisonous – *saamm, musimm.*
to **poke** – *naġġ (u naġġ) n-.* He'll wake up if you poke him. *yigʕud ʔiδa tnuġġa.*
poker – *ṗookar.* Do you know how to play poker? *tuʕruf tilʕab ṗookar?*
polar – *quṭbi*.* This is a polar bear. *haaδa dibb quṭbi.*
pole – **1.** *mardi* pl. *maraadi.* The water was so shallow they had to use the pole to push the boat. *l-ṃaay čaan kulliš δaʒil iδṭarraw yistaʕmiluun il-mardi l-dafʕ il-balam.* **2.** *ʕamuud* pl. *ʕawaamiid, ʔaʕmida.* The car hit a telephone pole. *s-sayyaara δurbat ʕamuud talafoon.* **3.** *zaana* pl. *-aat.* The pole broke just as he went over the bar. *nkisrat iz-zaana min da-yugmuz foog il-ʕaariδa.* **4.** *quṭub* pl. *ʔaqṭaab.* How cold does it get at the poles? *šgadd iṭṣiir baarda bil-quṭbeen?*
to pole – *maššа (i tmišši) bil-mardi.* In the marshes they pole the boats from one place to another. *bil-ʔahwaar ymaššuun il-mašaaʒiif bil-mardi min mukaan il-mukaan.*
police – *šurṭa.*
to police – *xufar (u xafar) n-.* The streets are well-policed. *š-šawaariʕ zeen maxfuura.*
police blotter – *sijil waqaaʔiʕ iš-šurṭa.*
policeman – *šurṭi* pl. *šurṭa.*
police station – **1.** *markaz* (pl. *maraakiz*) *šurṭa.* Where is the nearest police station? *ween ʔaqrab markaz šurṭa?* **2.** *maxfar* (pl. *maxaafir*) *šurṭa.* There is a police station halfway between the two villages. *ʔaku maxfar iš-šurṭa b-nuṣṣ iṭ-ṭariiq illi been il-qariiteen.*
policy – *siyaasa* pl. *-aat.* I make it a policy to be on time. *min siyaasti ʔan ʔakuun ʕal-wakit.* -- We can't support his policy. *ma-nigdar inʔayyid siyaasta.* **2.** *ʕaqid* pl. *ʕuquud.* Don't let your life-insurance policy lapse. *la-txalli ʕaqd it-taʔmiin maalak itfuut muddta.*
polish – **1.** *ṣubuġ* pl. *ʔaṣbaaġ.* I need some brown polish for my new shoes. *ʔaʒtaaj išwayya ṣubuġ qahwaaʔi l-ʒiδaaʔi j-jidiid.* **2.** *ṣaqil, tahδiib.* He needs a little more polish. *yiʒtaaj išwayya ṣaqil baʕad.*
to polish – **1.** *lammaʕ (i talmiiʕ) t-, ṣiqal (i ṣaqil) n-.* I haven't polished the furniture yet. *baʕad ma-lammaʕit il-ʔaθaaθ.* -- The silver needs polishing. *l-fuδδiyyaat tiʒtaaj talmiiʕ.* **2.** *ṣubaġ (u ṣabuġ) n-.* I didn't have time to polish my shoes. *ma-ṣaar ʕindi wakit ʔaṣbuġ qundarti.*
polite – *mujaamil, muʔaddab.* He's not very polite. *huwwa muu mujaamil kulliš.*
political – *siyaasi*.* Do you belong to any political party? *ʔinta mintimi l-ʔay ʒizib siyaasi?*
politician – *siyaasi* pl. *-iyyiin.*
politics – *siyaasa.* I'm not interested in politics. *s-siyaasa muu šuġḷi.* or *s-siyaasi ma-thimmni.*
pollen – *ṭaliʕ.*
to **pollinate** – *laggaʒ (i talgiiʒ) t-.* Date palms are pollinated by hand. *n-naxal yitlaggaʒ bil-ʔiid.*
polls – *markaz intixaabi* pl. *maraakiz intixaabiyya.*
to **pollute** – *lawwaθ (i talwiiθ) t-, naggas (i tangiis) t-.* First we must find what is polluting the water in the well. *ʔawwalan laazim inšuuf šinu lli da-ylawwiθ il-ṃaay bil-ḅiir.*
polygamy – *taʕaddud iz-zawjaat.*
pomegranate – *rummaana* pl. *-aat* coll. *rummaan.*
pond – *burka* pl. *burak, buʒayra* (pl. *-aat*) *ṣġayyra.*
pool – **1.** *burka* pl. *burak.* The police found him lying in a pool of blood. *š-šurṭa ligata majṭuul ib-burkat damm.* **2.** *ʒooδ* pl. *ʒwaaδ.* The new pool has improved the appearance of our garden. *l-ʒooδ ij-jidiid ʒassan manδar ʒadiiqatna.* **3.** *ṗuul, bilyaard.* Do you play pool? *tilʕab ṗuul?*
swimming pool – *ʒooδ* (pl. *ʔaʒwaaδ*) *sibaaʒa, masbaʒ* pl. *masaabiʒ.* They have a very large swimming pool. *ʕidhum ʒooδ sibaaʒa čbiir.*
poor – **1.** *faqiir* pl. *fuqaraaʔ, fuqra, fuqaara.* He is well-known for his generosity to the poor. *huwwa kulliš maʕruuf ib-karama ʕal-fuqaraaʔ.* -- Many poor people live in this neighborhood. *hwaaya naas fuqra yʕiišuun ib-hal-manṭiqa.* **2.** *miskiin* pl. *masaakiin; xaṭiyya.* The poor fellow is blind. *l-miskiin ʔaʕma.* **3.** *duuni*.* This is poor soil for raising wheat. *haaδi turba duuniyya l-ziraaʕat il-ʒunṭa.* **4.** *δaʕiif* pl. *δiʕaaf.* He's very poor in arithmetic. *huwwa kulliš δaʕiif bil-ʒisaab.* **5.** *rakiik* pl. *rkaak.* That was a poor article in today's paper. *δiič čaanat fadd maqaala rakiika b-jariidat il-yoom.*
poorly – **She was poorly dressed. *libisha mbahdal.* -- **The book is poorly written. *l-kitaab rakiik.* -- **His business was doing so poorly he has decided to sell out. *šuġḷa čaan muu zeen ʔila daraja qarrar yṣaffii.*
to do poorly – *tdahwar (a tduhwur).* He's doing poorly after the operation. *ṣiʒʒta tdahwurat wara l-ʕamaliyya.*
to **pop** – **1.** *ṭagg (u ṭagg).* The balloon popped. *n-nuffaaxa ṭaggat.* **2.** *ṭagṭag (i ṭagṭaga).* Come listen; the corn's popping! *taʕaal ismaʕ; l-ʔiδra da-ṭṭagṭig!*
Pope – *ṗaaṗa, ḅaaba.*
poppy – *xišxaaša* pl. *-aat* coll. *xišxaaš.*
popular – **1.** *šaʕbi*.* They played only popular songs. *qaddimaw ʔaġaani šaʕbiyya bass.* **2.** *maʒbuub.* He's very popular with the masses. *huwwa kulliš maʒbuub imnij-jamaahiir.* **3.** *šaayiʕ, daarij.* That's a popular notion, but it's wrong. *haaδa fadd raʔi šaayiʕ laakin ġalaṭ.*
**It's a very popular restaurant. *haaδa fadd maṭʕam ʕalee hwaaya rijil.*
populated – *ʔaahil, maʔhuul, maskuun.* This area is

not populated. *hal-manṭiqa maa ma?huula.*
population - *sukkaan, nifuus.* The population has doubled in the last twenty years. *ṭḍaaεaf εadad is-sukkaan bil-εišriin sana l-?axiira.*
porcelain - *ṣiini*.* We gave her a tea set of fine porcelain. *nṭiinaaha ṭaxum maal čaay imniṣ-ṣiini l-faaxir.*
porch - *ṭarma* pl. *-aat, ṭaraami.*
porcupine - *gunfuδ* pl. *ganaafuδ.*
pore - *masaama* pl. *-aat, masaam.* The dust got into the pores and caused inflammation. *l-εajaaj xašš bil-masaamaat w-sabbab iltihaab.*
pork - *laẓam xanziir.*
port - *miinaa?* pl. *mawaani.* The ship is at anchor in the port. *l-baaxira δaabba ?angar bil-miinaa?.*
portable - *safari*.* I want to buy a portable typewriter. *?ariid ?aštiri ?aalat ṭaabiεa safariyya.*
porter - *ẓammaal* pl. *-iin, ẓmaamiil.* Can I call you a porter? *?agdar ?aṣiiẓ-lak ẓammaal?*
portion - **1.** *qisim* pl. *?aqsaam, juzi?* pl. *?ajzaa?.* A large portion of the city was destroyed by fire. *qisim čibiir imnil-madiina tdammar bin-naar.* **2.** *wuṣla* pl. *wuṣal, qiṭεa* pl. *qiṭaε.* Just give me a small portion of meat and a vegetable. *bass inṭiini wuṣla ṣġayyra mnil-laẓam w-fadd xuḍra.*
Portugal - *burtuġaal.*
Portugese - *burtuġaali** pl. *-iyyiin.*
pose - *waḍεiyya* pl. *-aat.* Let's try another pose to make sure we have a good picture. *xalli njarrub waḍεiyya lux ẓatta nit?akkad iṣ-ṣuura zeena.*
to pose - *?axaδ (u ?axiδ) waḍεiyya.* They posed for the photographer in front of the fountain. *?axδaw waḍεiyya lil-muṣawwir giddaam il-naafuura.* -- The photographer posed me like this. *l-muṣawwir xallaani ?aaxuδ hiič waḍεiyya.*
to pose a question - *?aθaar (i ?iθaara) su?aal.* I'll pose the questions, and you answer them. *?aani ?aθiir il-?as?ila w-inta jaawubha.*
position - **1.** *waḍiε* pl. *?awḍaaε, waḍεiyya* pl. *-aat.* I'm not in a position to pay right now. *?aani muu b-waḍiε ?agdar adfaε hassa.* **2.** *mawqif* pl. *mawaaqif.* This places me in a very difficult position. *haay itẓuṭṭni b-mawqif ẓarij.* -- What is your position on this subject? *šinu mawqifak ib-hal-mawḍuuε?* **3.** *markaz* pl. *maraakiz, maqaam* pl. *-aat.* A man in your position has to be careful of his appearance. *rajul ib-maqaamak laazim yihtamm ihwaaya b-maḍhara.* -- He was accused of using his position as director for his own personal interests. *ntiham b-istiġlaal markaza ka-mudiir il-muṣlaẓta l-xaaṣṣa.* -- Our army has abandoned the forward positions. *jeešna txalla εan il-maraakiz il-?amaamiyya.* **4.** *waḍiifa* pl. *waḍaayif, manṣab* pl. *manaaṣib.* He has a good position with a wholesale house. *εinda waḍiifa kulliš zeena b-maẓall beeε bij-jumla.*
positive - **1.** *mit?akkid.* I'm positive that he was there. *?aani mit?akkid huwwa čaan ihnaak.* **2.** *?iijaabi*.* The Arab policy is one of positive neutrality in world affairs. *siyaasat il-εarab hiyya l-ẓiyaad il-?iijaabi biš-šu?uun il-εaalamiyya.* **3.** *bil-?iijaab.* I expect a positive answer. *?atwaqqaε jawaab bil-?iijaab.*
positively - **1.** *bit-ta?kiid.* Do you know it positively? *tuεrufa bit-ta?kiid?* **2.** *ẓaqiiqatan.* This is positively awful. *haay ẓaqiiqatan faḍiiεa.* -- The way she talks is positively vulgar. *?amma ẓaqiiqatan tiẓči b-?adabsizz luġiyya.*
to **possess** - *milak (i muluk) n-, mtilak (i mtilaak).* That's all I possess. *haaδa kull-ma ?amlik.*
**What possessed you to do that? *š-jaak w-sawweet haay?*
possession - *ẓiyaaza, mulkiyya.* How long has that been in your possession? *šgadd ṣaar-ilha b-ẓiyaaztak?*
**They lost all their possessions. *fuqdaw kull-ma yimilkuun* or *fuqdaw kull il-čaan εidhum* or *xiṣraw il-?aku wil-maaku.*
to take possession - *stilam (i stilaam), ?axaδ (u ?axiδ) ẓiyaaza.* The new owner hasn't taken possession of the house yet. *l-maalik ij-jidiid baεad ma-stilam il-beet.*
possibility - *ẓtimaal* pl. *-aat.* I see no other possibility. *ma-ašuuf ?aku ?ay iẓtimaal ?aaxar.*
possible - *mumkin.* Call me, if possible. *xaaburni, ?iδa mumkin.* or *xaaburni, ?iδa b-imkaanak.*
possibly - *mumkin, min il-mumkin.* Could you possibly call me? *mumkin itxaaburni?*
post - **1.** *εamuud* pl. *εawaamiid, ?aεmida.* We need new posts for our fence. *niẓtaaj εawaamiid jidiida lil-imẓajjar maalna.* **2.** *mawqiε* pl. *mawaaqiε, mawḍiε* pl. *mawaaḍiε.* A good soldier never deserts his post. *j-jundi z-zeen mustaẓiil yitruk mawḍiεa.* **3.** *mukaan* pl. *-aat, ?amaakin.* This ambassador has served in numerous posts. *has-safiir xidam ib-?amaakin mutaεaddida.*
to post - **1.** *waggaf (u twugguf) t-, ẓaṭṭ (u ẓaṭṭ) n-.* Post two men at each exit. *wagguf rijjaaleen ib-kull maẓall xuruuj.* **2.** *εallag (i taεliig) t-.* Post the sign on the wall. *εallig il-?iεlaan εal-ẓaayiṭ.* -- The order has been posted since yesterday. *l-qaraar ṣaar-la mεallag imnil-baarẓa.*
postage - **1.** *?ujrat (pl. ?ujuur) bariid.* How much is the postage on a registered letter? *šgadd ?ujrat il-bariid εala maktuub musajjal?* -- There is postage due on this letter. *hal-maktuub ?ujurta naaqṣa.* **2.** *ṭawaabiε.* The letter didn't have enough postage. *l-maktuub ma-čaan εalee ṭawaabiε kaafya.*
postal rate - *?ujrat (pl. ?ujuur) bariid; rasim (pl. rusuum) bariid.*
post card - *poost kaard* pl. *-aat, biṭaaqa* pl. *-aat, kaart* pl. *-aat.* Did you get my post card? *stilamt il-biṭaaqa maalti?*
to be **posted** - *ṭṭilaε (i ṭṭilaaε).* He's pretty well posted. *haaδa muṭṭaliε zeen.* -- Keep me posted! *xalliini εala ṭṭilaaε.* or *xalliini εala mustamirr.* or *xalliini εala εilim.*
poster - *?iεlaan (pl. -aat) diεaaya.*
postman - *pooṣṭači* pl. *-iyya; muwazziε (pl. -iin) bariid.*
postmark - *xatim (pl. ?axtaam) bariid; ṭamġa* pl. *-aat.* The postmark is illegible. *xatm il-bariid ma-yinqiri.*
to postmark - *xitam (i xatim) n-, ṭumaġ (u ṭamuġ) n-, ṣaqqaṭ (i taṣqiiṭ) t-.* The letter was postmarked May fifteenth. *l-maktuub maxtuum xumuṣṭaεaš maayis.*
post office - *daa?irat (pl. dawaa?ir) bariid, pooṣṭa* pl. *-aat.* We have five post offices. *εidna xamis dawaa?ir bariid.* -- The post office is open from nine to six. *l-pooṣṭa maftuuẓa mnit-tisεa lis-sitta.*
post-office box - *ṣanduuq (pl. ṣanaadiiq) bariid.*
to **postpone** - *?ajjal (i ta?jiil) t-, ?axxar (i ta?xiir) t-, εawwag (i taεwiig) t-.* I can't postpone the appointment. *ma-aqdar a?ajjil il-mawεid.*
posture - *wagfa* pl. *-aat.* She has poor posture. *wagfatha ma-ẓilwa.*
pot - *jidir* pl. *jduur.* There is a pot of soup on the stove. *?aku jidir šoorba εaṭ-ṭabbaax.*
potato - *puteetaaya* pl. *-aat* coll. *puteeta.*
potential - **1.** *muẓtamal.* We must consider him a potential enemy. *laazim niεtabra εadu muẓtamal.* **2.** *qudrat ?intaaj.* The industrial potential of our country is enormous. *qudrat il-?intaaj iṣ-ṣinaaεiyya d-dawlatna haa?ila.* **3.** *kaamin.* Water has great potential power. *l-maay bii quwwa kaamina haa?la.* **4.** *stiεdaad, qaabliyya.* He has the potential to become a good engineer. *εinda qaabliyya ?an yiṣbaẓ muhandis mumtaaz.*
potentiality - *?imkaaniyya.*
potter - *faxxaar* pl. *-iin, kawwaaz* pl. *-iin.*
pottery - *xazaf.*
poultry - *ṭiyuur daajina.*
pound - *paawan* pl. *-aat.* The metric pound is a bit more than the American pound. *l-paawan il-matri šwayya ?azyad imnil-paawan il-?amriiki.* How much is the English pound in American money? *šgadd yiswa l-paawan il-?ingiliizi bif-filuus il-?amriiki?*
**An ounce of prevention is worth a pound of cure. *dirham wiqaaya xayrun min qinṭaar εilaaj.*
to pound - **1.** *dagg (u dagg) n-.* We pounded on the door for five minutes before they heard us. *daggeena εal-baab muddat xamis daqaayiq gabuḷ-ma samεoona.* -- I wish our upstairs neighbors wouldn't pound kubba at seven in the morning. *?atmanna loo δoola l-gaaεdiin foogaana ma-ydugguun kubba saaεa sabεa ṣ-ṣubuẓ.* **2.** *xufaq (u xafaqaan), dagg (u dagg).* His heart was pounding with anxiety. *galba čaan da-yuxfuq imnil-qalaq.*
to **pour** - **1.** *ṣabb (u ṣabb) n-, daar (i deer).* Please pour me a cup of coffee. *?arjuuk ṣubb-li fadd kuub gahwa.* **2.** *tdaffaq (a tadaffuq).* The water was pouring out of the faucet. *l-maay čaan da-yitdaffaq imnil-buuri.* **3.** *zaxx (u zaxx).* It's pouring out. *da-tzuxx barra.*
**The crowd was just then pouring out of the theater. *j-jamaahiir čaanaw da-yṭilεuun*

imnis-siinama fadd ṭalεa.

to pour off – *čabb (i čabb) n- min.* Pour the water off of the rice. *čibb il-maay imnit-timman.*

to pour out – 1. *čabb (i čabb) n-.* Pour out the water and fill the glass with milk. *čibb il-maay w-itrus il-iglaaṣ bil-ḥaliib.* 2. *šika (i šakwa).* She poured out her troubles to me. *šikat-li hmuumha.*

poverty – *fuqur, εooz.* He is living in great poverty. *da-yεiiš ib-fuqur mudqaε.*

poverty-stricken – *faqiir* pl. *fuqaraaʔ, fuqra fuqaara.*

powder – 1. *poodra.* You've got too much powder on your nose. *ʔaku hwaaya poodra εala xašmič.* 2. *masḥuuq* pl. *masaaḥiiq.* What is that white powder in this bag? *šinu hal-masḥuuq il-ʔabyaḍ ib-hač-čiis?* 3. *baaruud.* There is enough powder here to blow up the whole town. *ʔaku hnaa baaruud kaafi l-nasf il-madiina b-kaamilha.*

to powder – 1. *siḥan (a saḥin) n-.* The pharmacist powdered some tablets and put the powder in capsules. *ṣ-ṣaydali siḥan čam ḥabbaaya w-xalla l-masḥuuq bil-kapsuulaat.* 2. *ḥaṭṭ (u ḥaṭṭ) n- poodra εala.* She powdered her nose. *ḥaṭṭat poodra εala xašimha.*

power – 1. *quwwa* pl. *-aat, ṭaaqa* pl. *-aat.* The machine is operated by electrical power. *l-makiina tištuġuḷ bil-quwwa l-kahrabaʔiyya.* -- The power has been turned off. *l-quwwa ngiṭεat.* -- The purchasing power is improving. *l-quwwa š-širaaʔiyya da-titḥassan.* 2. *stiṭaaεa, ʔimkaan, quwwa, ṭaaqa.* I will do everything in my power. *raḥ-asawwi kull-ma b-istiṭaaεti.* or *******raḥ-asawwi kull-ma yiṭlaε min ʔiidi.* 3. *ṣalaaḥiyya* pl. *-aat.* Parliament has complete power in this matter. *l-barlamaan εinda ṣalaaḥiyya taamma b-hal-mawḍuuε.* 4. *ḥukum.* How long has this party been in power? *hal-ḥizib išgadd ṣaar-la bil-ḥukum?* 5. *ṣayṭara.* He lost all power on his followers. *fuqad kull ṣayṭara εala ʔatbaaεa.* 6. *ṣulṭa, nufuuð.* He wields a lot of power. *εinda nufuuð čibiir.*

to come into power – *ʔija (i majiiʔ) lil-ḥukum.* When did the Republicans come into power? *j-jumhuuriyyiin šwakit ʔijaw lil-ḥukum?*

powerful – *qawi** pl. *-iyyiin, ʔaqwiyaaʔ.* He has a powerful voice. *εinda ṣawṭ qawi.*

powerless – **I'm sorry, but I'm powerless in this matter. *mitʔassif laakin maa b-ʔiidi šii b-hal-qaḍiyya.*

practical – *εamali*.* That isn't very practical. *haay muu kulliš εamaliyya.*

practically – 1. *b-ṣuura εamaliyya, εamaliyyan.* You have to look at things practically. *laazim tinḍur lil-ʔumuur ib-ṣuura εamaliyya.* 2. *taqriiban.* We're practically there. *taqriiban wuṣalna.*

practice – 1. *tamriin.* I need more practice. *ʔaḥtaaj tamriin baεad.* -- Practice makes perfect. *t-tamriin ywaṣṣil lil-ittiqaan.* 2. *εaada* pl. *-aat.* I've made it a practice to get to work on time. *ṣaarat εaada εindi ʔaruuḥ lid-daaʔira εal-wakit.* 3. *taṣarruf* pl. *-aat.* They complained of his dictatorial practices. *štikaw min taṣarrufaata d-diktaatooriyya.*

**Dr. Ali has a wide practice. *d-diktoor εali εinda mураajiεiin ihwaaya.*

in practice – *εamaliyyan, bil-εamal, bit-taṭbiiq.* It is easy in theory, but difficult in practice. *hiyya sahla naḍariyyan laakin ṣaεba εamaliyyan.* -- He put his theory into practice. *wuḍaε naḍariita mawḍaε it-taṭbiiq.*

to practice – 1. *tdarrab (a tadarrub), tmarran (a tamarrun).* He's practicing on the piano. *da-yitdarrab εal-ipyaano.* 2. *maaras (i mumaarasa), zaawad (i muzaawada).* How long has he been practicing medicine? *šgadd ṣaar-la ymaaris iṭ-ṭibb?* 3. *ṭabbaq (i taṭbiiq).* I wish he would practice what he preaches. *yaa reet yṭabbuq illi yguula.*

praise – *madiḥ, θanaaʔ.* The praise went to his head. *l-madiḥ kabbar raasa.*

to praise – 1. *midaḥ (a madiḥ), ʔaθna (i θanaaʔ) εala.* Everybody praises his work. *j-jamiiε yiθnuun εala šuġḷa.* 2. *ḥimad (i ḥamid) n- b-.* I don't want to praise myself, but. . . *ma-ariid ʔaḥmid ib-nafsi, laakin. . .* --

**He praised her to the skies. *ṣaεεadha lis-samawaat.*

prank – *nukta* pl. *nukat, ḥiila* pl. *ḥiyal.* That's a silly prank. *haay mukta saxiifa.* -- They played a prank on me. *sawwaw biyya nukta.*

to **pray** – 1. *ṣalla (i ṣalaat).* Moslems are expected to pray five times a day. *mafruuḍ bil-muslimiin yṣalluun xams awqaat bil-yoom.* 2. *diεa (i duεaaʔ) n-.* I'll pray for you. *raḥ-ʔadεii-lak.*

prayer – *ṣalaa, ṣalaat* pl. *ṣalawaat; daεwa* pl. *-aat, duεaaʔ* pl. *ʔadεiya.*

to **preach** – 1. *wuεað (a waεið) n-.* I heard him preach at the mosque in the month of Ramadhan. *simaεta yooεað bij-jaamiε ib-šahar ramaḍaan.* 2. *baššar (i tabšiir) t- b-.* The prophet first preached the Islamic religion to the people of Mecca. *r-rasuul baššar bid-diyaana l-ʔislaamiyya l-ʔahil makka bil-ʔawwal.*

preacher – *waaεið* pl. *wuεεaað, xaṭiib* pl. *xuṭabaaʔ.*

precaution – *ḥtiyaaṭ* pl. *-aat.* You should take better precautions against fire. *laazim tittixið iḥtiyaaṭaat ʔaḥsan ḍidd in-naar.*

to **precede** – *sibaq (i sabiq) n-.* A strange silence preceded the storm. *huduuʔ ġariib sibaq il-εaaṣifa.*

to give **precedence** – *badda (i tbiddi) t-, qaddam (i taqdiim) t-.* I gave him precedence over myself. *baddeeta εala nafsi.*

precedent – *saabiqa* pl. *sawaabiq.* This will constitute a dangerous precedent. *haaða yšakkil saabiqa xaṭra.*

precepts – *furuuḍ, taεaaliim.* He follows the precepts of Islam implicitly. *yittibiε furuuḍ il-ʔislaam ib-ḥaðaafiirha.*

precious – 1. *θamiin, nafiis.* He gave me a very precious gift. *nṭaani hadiyya kulliš θamiina.* 2. *ġaali, εaziiz.* Your friendship is precious to me. *ṣadaaqtak ġaalya εindi.* 3. *kariim.* Emeralds are precious stones. *z-zumurrad ḥajar kariim.*

precipitation – 1. *ṣuquuṭ il-muṭar.* What's the average annual precipitation in this area? *šgadd muεaddal ṣuquuṭ l-muṭar is-sanawi b-hal-manṭiqa?* 2. *raasib.* What's this white precipitation in this bottle? *šinu har-raasib il-ʔabyaḍ ib-hal-buṭul?* 3. *tarassub.* When precipitation is over take it off the fire. *baεad-ma yikmil it-tarassub šiila min in-naar.*

precise – 1. *daqiiq.* He is very precise in his work. *huwwa kulliš daqiiq ib-šuġḷa.* 2. *biḍ-ḍabuṭ.* Those were his precise words. *haay čaanat kalimaata biḍ-ḍabuṭ.*

precisely – 1. *b-ṣuura daqiiqa.* Translate this precisely. *tarjum haaða b-ṣuura daqiiqa.* 2. *biḍ-ḍabuṭ.* That is precisely what I had in mind. *haaða biḍ-ḍabuṭ nafs iš-šii l-čaan εala baali.*

precision – 1. *diqqa, ḍabuṭ.* The measurements must be taken with precision. *l-qiyaasaat laazim tinnixið ib-diqqa.* 2. *daqiiq.* This company specializes in the manufacturing of precision instruments. *haš-šarika mitxaṣṣiṣa b-ṣunε il-ʔaalaat id-daqiiqa.*

predecessor – *salaf* pl. *ʔaslaaf.*

predestination – *qaḍaaʔ w-qadar.*

to **predict** – *tnabbaʔ (a tanabbuʔ) b-, tkahhan (a takahhun) b-.* He predicted this. *tnabbaʔ ib-haaða.*

prediction – *nubuuʔa* pl. *-aat.*

predominant – *ġaalib.* Red is the predominant color for cars this year. *l-ʔaḥmar huwwa l-loon il-ġaalib ib-sayyaaraat has-sana.*

preface – *muqaddima* pl. *-aat.*

to **prefer** – *faḍḍal (i tafḍiil) t-.* I prefer the brand I've been using. *ʔafaḍḍil in-nawε illi da-astaεmila.* -- I prefer brunettes to blondes. *ʔafaḍḍil is-sumur εaš-šuqur.*

preference – *ʔafḍaliyya* pl. *-aat, ʔaqdamiyya* pl. *-aat.* I don't give preference to anyone. *ma-anṭi ʔafḍaliyya l-ʔaḥḥad.*

**I have no preference. *ma-aku fariq.* or *kulla siwa.* or *ma-tufruq εindi.*

pregnancy – *ḥabal* pl. *-aat, ḥbaala* pl. *-aat.* How many pregnancies have you had? *čam iḥbaala ṣaarat εindič?* or ***čam baṭin jibti?*

pregnant – *ḥibla, ḥaamil.*

to become pregnant – *ḥibal (a ḥabil).* She became pregnant a year after we were married. *ḥiblat baεad sana min itzawwajna.*

prejudice – 1. *taḥayyuz* pl. *-aat, taḥazzub* pl. *-aat.* So far as I can see he hasn't any prejudices at all. *ḥasib-ma ʔašuuf maa εinda ʔay taḥayyuzaat ʔabadan.* 2. *taεaṣṣub.* Prejudice and ignorance are hard to combat. *t-taεaṣṣub wij-jahil ṣaεub itḥaarubhum.*

prejudiced – 1. *mitḥayyiz* pl. *-iin, mitḥazzib* pl. *-iin.* The judge is obviously prejudiced in the case. *l-qaaḍi mnil-waaḍiḥ mitḥayyiz bid-daεwa.* 2. *mitεaṣṣib* pl. *-iin.* He is prejudiced against the new ways. *huwwa mitƐaṣṣib ð̣idd it-taqaaliid il-ḥadiiθa.*

preliminary - *tamhiidi*, btidaaʔi*.* This is just a preliminary investigation. *haaða bass taḥqiiq tamhiidi.*

premature - *gabuḷ ʔawaan-.* I am afraid that step was premature. *ʔaxša hal-xaṭwa čaanat gabuḷ ʔawaanha.*

premier - **1.** *raʔiis (pl. ruʔasaaʔ) wuzaraaʔ.* The Premier is scheduled to speak to Parliament tomorrow. *l-muqarrar yuxṭub raʔiis il-wuzaraaʔ bil-barlamaan baačir.* **2.** *ḥafla (pl. -aat) ftitaaḥiyya.* We attended the premier of the film in a body. *ḥið̣arna l-ḥafla l-iftitaaḥiyya lil-filim ib-limmatna.*

premium - *qiṣiṭ* pl. *ʔaqṣaaṭ.* I have to pay the premium on the insurance policy. *laazim ʔadfaƐ il-qiṣiṭ maal Ɛaqd it-taʔmiin.*

preparation - **1.** *taḥð̣iir* pl. *-aat, stiƐdaad* pl. *-aat.* The preparations for the trip took us a week. *l-istiƐdaadaat lis-safra ṭawwilat Ɛidna sbuuƐ.* -- The plans are still in a state of preparation. *l-xiṭaṭ baƐadha b-door it-taḥð̣iir.* **2.** *tahayyuʔ, taʔahhub, taḥð̣iir, stiƐdaad.* War preparation consumes a large part of the budget. *t-tahayyuʔ lil-ḥarub yistahlik qisim kabiir imnil-miizaaniyya.*

to **prepare** - **1.** *ḥað̣ð̣ar (i taḥð̣iir) t-, staƐadd (i stiƐdaad).* Did you prepare for tomorrow's exam? *staƐaddeet lil-imtiḥaan maal baačir.* **2.** *hayyaʔ (i tahiyyiʔ).* Have the nurse prepare the patient for the operation. *xalli l-mumarrið̣a thayyiʔ il-mariið̣ lil-Ɛamaliyya.* -- You had better prepare him for the shock first. *gabuḷ kullši ʔaḥsan-lak ithayyiʔa liṣ-ṣadma.* -- Prepare for the worst. *hayyiʔ nafsak il-ʔaswaʔ il-iḥtimaalaat.*

prepared - **1.** *ḥaað̣ir* pl. *-iin, mistiƐidd* pl. *-iin.* We are prepared to do whatever you suggest. *ʔiḥna ḥaað̣riin insawwi lli tiqtarḥa.* **2.** *jaahiz, ḥaað̣ir.* The papers are all prepared except for the signature. *l-ʔawraaq kullha jaahza maa Ɛada t-tawqiiƐ.*

preposition - *ḥaruf* (pl. *ḥuruuf) jarr.*

to **prescribe** - *wuṣaf (i waṣuf) n-.* The doctor prescribed these pills for me. *ṭ-ṭabiib wuṣaf-li hal-ḥubuub.*

prescription - *waṣfa* pl. *-aat, raačeeta* pl. *-aat.*

presence - **1.** *ḥuð̣uur.* The document has to be signed in your presence. *l-waθiiqa laazim titwaqqaƐ ib-ḥuð̣uurak.* **2.** *wujuud.* They resented the presence of the foreign army strongly. *Ɛaarð̣aw wujuud ij-jeeš il-ʔajnabi b-šidda.*

presence of mind - *surƐat xaaṭir-.* I admire your presence of mind. *tiƐjibni surƐat xaaṭrak.*

present - **1.** *hadiyya* pl. *hadaaya.* Did you give him a present for his birthday? *nṭeeta hadiyya b-munaasabat Ɛiid miilaada.* **2.** *ḥaað̣ir.* We live in the present, not in the past. *ʔiḥna nƐiiš bil-ḥaað̣ir muu bil-maað̣i.* **3.** *mawjuud* pl. *-iin, ḥaað̣ir* pl. *-iin.* All of his friends were present. *kull ʔaṣdiqaaʔa čaanaw mawjuudiin.* **4.** *ḥaali*.* In my present position I can't do anything else. *b-wað̣Ɛi l-ḥaali ma-agdar asawwi ʔay šii ʔaaxar.*

at present - *ḥaaliyyan, bil-waqt il-ḥaali.* They aren't working at present. *ma-yištaġluun ḥaaliyyan.*

for the present - *l-hassa, l-ʔaan, muwaqqatan.* That will be enough for the present. *haay tikfi l-hassa.* -- We are out of pencils for the present. *l-iqlaam xalṣaana muwaqqatan.*

to present - **1.** *qaddam (i taqdiim) t-.* The ambassador is going to present his credentials tomorrow. *s-safiir raḥ-yqaddim ʔawraaq iƐtimaada baačir.* **2.** *ṭallaƐ (i taṭliiƐ), xilaq (u xaliq).* Each case presents new difficulties. *kull qað̣iyya Ɛala ḥida tṭalliƐ mašaakil jidiida.* **3.** *Ɛirað̣ (u Ɛarið̣) n-.* Why don't you present the facts as they are? *leeš ma-tiƐruð̣ il-ḥaqaayiq miθil-ma hiyya.*

to present with - *hida (i ʔihdaaʔ) n-.* The company presented him with a gold watch. *š-šarika hidata saaƐa ðahab.*

to **preserve** - **1.** *ḥaafað̣ (i muḥaafað̣a), ṣaan (u ṣiyaana) n-.* I did this in order to preserve my dignity. *sawweet haaða ḥatta ʔaḥaafuð̣ Ɛala karaamti.* **2.** *ʔabqa (i ʔibqaaʔ).* We are trying to preserve what is left. *da-nḥaawil il-ʔibqaaʔ Ɛal-baqiyya l-baaqya.* **3.** *ḥufað̣ (u ḥafuð̣) n-.* The refrigerator will preserve the meat until we can use it. *θ-θallaaja tuḥfuð̣ il-laḥam ʔila ʔan nigdar nistaƐmila.*

preserved - **1.** *maḥfuuð̣.* The specimens are preserved in formaldehyde solution in the laboratory. *n-namaaðij maḥfuuð̣a b-maḥluul il-formaldahaayd bil-muxtabar.* **2.** *mḥaafuð̣ Ɛala.* The house is well-preserved. *l-beet imḥaafuð̣ Ɛalee zeen.*

preserves - *mrabba* pl. *-ayaat.*

to **preside** - *traʔʔas (a taraʔʔus).* Ali presided over the meeting. *Ɛali traʔʔas ij-jalsa.*

president - **1.** *raʔiis* pl. *ruʔasaaʔ.* He has been appointed president of the board of directors. *tƐayyan raʔiis il-majlis il-ʔidaara.* -- The President of the republic announced the formation of a new cabinet. *raʔiis ij-jamhuriyya ʔaƐlan taškiil wuzaara jidiida.* **2.** *muḥaafið̣* pl. *-iin.* He was president of the Central Bank. *čaan muḥaafið̣ il-bang il-markazi.*

press - **1.** *ṣaḥaafa.* Will the press be admitted to the conference? *raḥ-yusmaḥ liṣ-ṣaḥaafa tiḥð̣ar il-muʔtamar?* **2.** *maṭbaƐa* pl. *maṭaabuƐ.* The manuscript is ready to go to press. *l-mibyað̣ð̣a jaahza truuḥ lil-maṭbaƐa.* **3.** *makbas* pl. *makaabis.* Can you operate a date press? *tigdar itšaġġul makbas tumuur?* **4.** *miƐṣaara* pl. *-aat.* I operate this fruit-juicing press. *ʔaani ʔašaġġil hal-miƐṣaara maal fawaakih.*

**The film had a good press. *l-filim inmidaḥ bij-jaraayid.*

in the press - *taḥt iṭ-ṭabuƐ.* The book is still in the press. *l-iktaab baƐda taḥt iṭ-ṭabuƐ.*

to press - **1.** *ð̣urab (u ð̣arub) n- ʔuuti.* They pressed my suit nicely. *ð̣urab il-qaaṭ maali xooš ʔuuti.* **2.** *daas (u doos) n-.* Press the button. *duus iz-zirr.* **3.** *Ɛaṣṣar (i taƐṣiir) t-.* They pressed the grapes and fermented them. *Ɛaṣṣiraw il-Ɛinab w-xammiroo.* **4.** *kibas (i kabis) n-, čibas (i čabis) n-.* This is where the cured dates are pressed and packaged. *haaða l-makaan illi ykibsuun bii t-tamur w-yḥuṭṭuu bil-paakeetaat.* **5.** *ð̣ayyaq (i tað̣yiiq) Ɛala.* His creditors are pressing him. *d-dayyaana da-yð̣ayyquun Ɛalee.* **6.** *laḥḥ (i ʔilḥaaḥ) b-.* I wouldn't press the matter any further, if I were you. *loo b-makaanak ma-aliḥḥ bil-mawð̣uuƐ baƐad.* **7.** *ð̣iġaṭ (u ð̣aġiṭ) Ɛala.* The party is pressing the President to appoint him to the Commission. *l-ḥizib da-yuð̣ġuṭ Ɛala r-raʔiis ḥatta yƐayyina bil-hayʔa.*

to press together - *daas (u doos) n-, raṣṣ (u raṣṣ) n-.* Press the peppers together tightly so you can get them all in the pot. *duus il-filfil ib-quwwa ḥatta tigdar itdaxxil kullhum bij-jarra.*

presser - *ʔuutači* pl. *-iyya.* I worked as a presser for five years. *štiġalit ʔuutači l-muddat xams isniin.*

pressing - *mustaƐjal.* I have a pressing engagement. *Ɛindi mawƐid mustaƐjal.*

pressure - *ð̣aġiṭ.* We work under constant pressure. *ništuġuḷ taḥat ð̣aġiṭ mustamirr.*

to put pressure on - *ð̣iġaṭ (u ð̣aġiṭ) n- Ɛala, laḥḥ (i ʔilḥaaḥ).* We'll have to put pressure on him. *laazim inliḥḥ Ɛalee.*

prestige - *maqaam, hayba, makaana.* He has great prestige. *Ɛinda maqaam Ɛaali.*

to **presume** - *tṣawwar (a taṣawwur), ð̣ann (u ð̣ann).* I presume he is at home. *ʔatṣawwar huwwa bil-beet.*

to **pretend** - **1.** *ddiƐa (i ddiƐaaʔ), ziƐam (i zaƐim).* He pretended that he was a doctor. *ddiƐa ʔanna ṭabiib.* **2.** *tð̣aahar (a tað̣aahur).* He's just pretending! *haaða da-yitð̣aahar!*

**He pretended not to know a thing about it. *sawwa nafsa ma-yuƐruf ʔay šii Ɛanha.*

pretense - **1.** *ddiƐaaʔ* pl. *-aat.* His pretense fooled no one. *ddiƐaaʔa ma-xidaƐ ʔaḥḥad.* **2.** *ḥiila* pl. *ḥiyal, tað̣aahur* pl. *-aat.* His illness is only a pretense. *marað̣a ma-huwwa ʔilla ḥiila.*

pretext - *Ɛuður* pl. *ʔaƐðaar, ḥijja* pl. *ḥijaj.* He's just looking for a pretext. *huwwa da-ydawwur-la fadd Ɛuður.*

pretty - **1.** *ḥilu.* She's a very pretty girl. *hiyya fadd ibnayya kulliš ḥilwa.* **2.** *xooš.* That's a pretty mess! *ʔamma haay xooš xarbaṭa.* **3.** *laa baʔis b-.* It tastes pretty good. *ṭaƐamha laa baʔis bii.*

**He's sitting pretty. *haaða mayya biṣ-ṣadir.*

pretty much - *taqriiban.* He eats pretty much everything. *yaakul kullši taqriiban.* -- It's pretty much the same. *hiyya nafs iš-šii taqriiban.*

to **prevail** - **1.** *jira (i jari), miša (i maši).* This custom still prevails. *hal-Ɛaada baƐadha maašya.* **2.** *saad (u siyaada).* This opinion prevails at the moment. *har-raʔi ysuud bil-waqt il-ḥaað̣ir.*

to prevail over - *tġallab (a taġallub) Ɛala.* The opinion of the majority prevailed over the desires of the minority. *raʔi l-ʔakθariyya tġallab Ɛala* raǵbaat il-ʔaqalliyya.

to prevail upon - *qannaɛ (i taqniiɛ) t-.* Can't we prevail upon you to come along? *ma-raz-nigdar inqanniɛak tiji wiyyaana?*

to **prevent** - *minaɛ (a maniɛ) n-.* The police prevented the crowd from entering. *š-šurṭa minɛaw in-naas imnid-dixuul.*

preventive - *wiqaaʔi*.* My son has decided to specialize in preventive medicine. *ʔibni qarrar yitxaṣṣaṣ biṭ-ṭibb il-wiqaaʔi.*

previous - *saabiq, maaδi.* I met him on a previous visit. *tɛarrafit bii b-ziyaara saabqa.* -- He has no previous experience in that field. *ma-ɛinda xibra saabiqa b-hal-miidaan.*

previously - *saabiqan, min gabuḷ.*

prey - *ǵaniima* pl. *ǵanaayim.* He is an easy prey for dishonest schemers. *haaδa ǵaniima baarda b-iid il-zayyaaliin.*

price - **1.** *siɛir* pl. *ʔasɛaar.* The prices are very high here. *l-ʔasɛaar kulliš mirtafɛa hnaa.* **2.** *θaman* pl. *ʔaθmaan.* I wouldn't do that for any price. *ma-asawwi haaδa mahma kaan iθ-θaman.* **I want it regardless of price. *ʔariida mahma kallaf.*

to price - **1.** *saɛɛar (i tasɛiir) t-, saam (u soom) n-.* This merchant prices his goods too high for me. *hat-taajir ysaɛɛir baδaayɛa kulliš ǵaali ɛalayya.* **2.** *ɛaamal (i muɛaamala) ɛala.* I priced this radio in several stores. *ɛaamalit ɛala har-raadyo b-ɛiddat mazallaat.*

to **prick** - *čakk (u čakk) n-, niǵaz (u naǵiz) n-.* I pricked my finger with a pin. *čakkeet ʔiṣibɛi b-danbuus.*

to prick up - *šantar (i šantara).* The horse pricked up his ears. *l-izṣaan šantar ʔiiδaana.*

prickly heat - *zaṣaf.*

pride - **1.** *ɛizza.* Don't you have any pride in yourself? *maa ɛindak ʔay ɛizzat nafis?* -- It is a matter of national pride. *haay masʔalat ɛizza qawmiyya.* **2.** *faxar.* He is the pride of his school. *haaδa faxar madrasta.* **3.** *ʔanafa, kibriyaaʔ.* His pride is unbearable. *kibriyaaʔa ma-tinzimil.*

to take pride - *ftixar (i ftixaar), ɛtazz (a ɛtizaaz).* He takes great pride in his work. *huwwa hwaaya yiɛtazz ib-šuǵḷa.*

to pride oneself on - *tbaaha (a tabaahi) b-.* She prides herself on her good cooking. *titbaaha b-ṭabixha z-zeen.*

priest - *qass, qissiis* pl. *-iin, qasaawusa, qissaan; xuuri* pl. *-iyya, xawaarna.*

priesthood - *kahanuut.* He is going to enter the priesthood. *raz-yidxul il-kahanuut.*

primarily - *bil-ʔaṣil, bid-daraja l-ʔuula, ʔawwalan ʔaṣliyyan.* I am primarily a clerk, but I work as a driver. *ʔaani bil-ʔaṣil kaatib w-laakin ʔaštuǵuḷ ka-saayiq.* -- This is primarily a matter for the court. *haay bid-daraja l-ʔuula šuǵḷat il-mazkama.*

primary - **1.** *raʔiisi*, ʔasaasi*.* His primary objective is profit. *hadafa r-raʔiisi huwwa r-ribiz.* **2.** *ʔawwali*.* The primary elections will be held next month. *l-intixaabaat il-ʔawwaliyya raz-itṣiir iš-šahr ij-jaay.* **3.** *btidaaʔi*.* He hasn't even completed primary school. *huwwa ma-kammal zatta l-madrasa l-ibtidaaʔiyya.*

prime - **1.** *mumtaaz, faaxir, xooš.* This butcher sells only prime meat. *hal-gaṣṣaab ybiiɛ lazam mumtaaz bass.* **2.** *ɛizz, zahra.* He died in the prime of life. *maat ib-zahrat il-ɛumur.*

prime minister - *raʔiis* (pl. *ruʔasaaʔ*) *wuzaraaʔ.*

primitive - *bidaaʔi*.* Primitive societies lived on hunting. *l-mujtamaɛaat il-bidaaʔiyya ɛaašat ɛaṣ-ṣeed.* -- The gufa is a primitive type of water transportation. *l-guffa nawɛ bidaaʔi min il-muwaaṣalaat il-maaʔiyya.*

primus stove - *preemis* pl. *-aat.*

prince - *ʔamiir* pl. *ʔumaraaʔ.*

princess - *ʔamiira* pl. *-aat.*

principal - **1.** *mudiir* pl. *mudaraaʔ.* The principal called the teachers into his office. *l-mudiir jimaɛ il-muɛallimiin ib-ǵurufta.* **2.** *mablaǵ ʔaṣli* pl. *mabaaliǵ ʔaṣliyya.* Have you paid anything on the principal? *dfaɛit šii mnil-mablaǵ il-ʔaṣli.* **3.** *ʔasaasi*, raʔiisi*.* The principal cause of the delay is lack of money. *s-sabab ir-raʔiisi lit-taʔxiir huwwa ɛadam wujuud il-ifluus.*

principality - *ʔimaara* pl. *-aat.* We have a branch office in the principality of Bahrein. *ɛidna daaʔira farɛiyya b-ʔimaarat il-bazreen.*

principle - **1.** *qaaɛida* pl. *qawaaɛid.* I make it a principle to save some money every month. *sawweetha qaaɛida ʔawaffur fadd mablaǵ kull šahar.* **2.** *mabdaʔ* pl. *mabaadiʔ.* He is a man of principles. *haaδa waazid ṣaazib mabdaʔ.*

a matter of principle - *ka-mabdaʔ, ka-qaaɛida.* I don't do such things as a matter of principle. *ka-mabdaʔ, ma-asawwi hiiči ʔašyaaʔ.*

print - **1.** *ṭabuɛ.* The print in this book is too small. *ṭ-ṭabuɛ ib-hal-iktaab kulliš naaɛim.* **2.** *baṣma* pl. *-aat, ṭabɛa* pl. *-aat.* The prints left by his fingers were found on the doorknob. *baṣmaat ʔaṣaabɛa nligat ɛala yaddat il-baab.* **3.** *ʔaθar* pl. *ʔaaθaar.* It was easy to follow his footprints in the sand. *čaan imnis-suhuula taɛaqqub ʔaaθaar ʔaqdaama ɛar-ramul.* **4.** *nusxa* pl. *nusax.* How many prints shall I make of each picture? *kam nusxa ʔaṭalliɛ min kull ṣuura.* **5.** *rasim maṭbuuɛ* pl. *rusuum maṭbuuɛa.* The museum has a fine collection of prints. *l-matzaf bii xooš majmuuɛa mnir-rusuum il-maṭbuuɛa.* **6.** *mnaqqaš.* You always look good in a print. *ʔinti daaʔiman titlaɛiin zilwa b-nafnuuf imnaqqaš.*

to print - *ṭubaɛ (a ṭabuɛ) n-.* We can print them for you for twenty fils per page. *nigdar niṭbaɛ-lak-iyyaahum ib-ɛišriin filis iṣ-ṣaziifa.* -- The letter was printed in yesterday's paper. *l-maktuub inṭubaɛ ib-jariidat il-baarza.* **Print your name. *ʔiktib ismak ib-zuruuf minfaṣla.*

printed matter - *maṭbuuɛaat.* What are the postage rates for printed matter? *šgadd il-ʔujra il-bariidiyya ɛal-maṭbuuɛaat.*

printer - *ṭabbaaɛ* pl. *-iin.*

print shop - *maṭbaɛa* pl. *maṭaabiɛ.*

prior - **1.** *gabuḷ.* Prior to the war the cost of living was much lower. *gabḷ il-zarub takaaliif il-maɛiiša čaanat ihwaaya ʔaqall.* **2.** *saabiq.* Have you had any prior experience in this type of work? *ɛindak xibra saabqa b-han-nooɛ šuǵuḷ.*

priority - **1.** *ʔasbaqiyya, ʔafδaliyya.* This job has priority over the others. *haš-šaǵla ʔilha ʔasbaqiyya ɛal-baaqi.* **2.** *tawjiib.* It is our policy to give priority to regular customers. *tawjiib il-miɛaamiil il-ɛittag min siyaasatna.*

prism - *manšuur* pl. *manaašiir.*

prison - **1.** *sijin* pl. *sujuun.* The prison is heavily guarded. *s-sijin ɛalee ziraasa qawiyya.* **2.** *zabis.* The court sentenced him to five years in prison. *l-mazkama zukmat ɛalee bil-zabis xams isniin.*

prisoner - *sajiin* pl. *sujanaaʔ, masjuun* pl. *masaajiin, mazbuus* pl. *mazaabiis.* A prisoner has just escaped. *fadd sajiin hastawwa nhizam.*

prisoner of war - *ʔasiir* pl. *ʔusaraaʔ, ʔasra.*

to take prisoner - *ʔassar (i taʔsiir) t-.* We took the wounded soldier prisoner. *ʔassarna j-jundi l-majruuz.*

private - **1.** *jundi* pl. *junuud.* I was a private in the second world war. *činit jundi bil-zarub il-ɛaalamiyya θ-θaanya.* **2.** *xaaṣṣ.* This is my private property. *haaδa mulki l-xaaṣṣ.* **3.** *xuṣuuṣi*, xaaṣṣ.* Do you have a single room with a private bath? *ɛindak ǵurfa biiha zammaam xuṣuuṣi?*

in private - *ɛala nfiraad.* I'd like to talk to you in private. *ʔard azči wiyyaak ɛala nfiraad.*

privates - *ɛawra* pl. *-aat.* Do not expose your privates under any circumstances. *la-tikšif ɛawurtak ib-ʔay zaal min l-azwaal.*

privation - *zirmaan.*

privilege - **1.** *mtiyaaz* pl. *-aat.* He was deprived of all privileges. *nziram min kull il-imtiyaazaat.* **2.** *zaqq* pl. *zuquuq.* If you want to leave, it's your privilege. *ʔiδa triid itruuz, haaδa zaqqak.* **It would be a privilege to do this for you. *ʔakuun mamnuun ʔaquum-lak ib-hal-xidma.* or *ysurrni ʔasawwii-lak haaδa.*

prize - *jaaʔiza* pl. *jawaaʔiz.* Who won the first prize? *minu ribaz ij-jaaʔiza l-ʔuula?*

probability - *ztimaal* pl. *-aat.* That is well within the bounds of probability. *haaδa jiddan δimin niṭaaq il-iztimaal.*

probable - *muztamal.* It might be possible, but it is not very probable. *haay mumkina bass muu kulliš muztamala.*

probably - *mnil-muztamal.* You'll probably meet him on the train. *mnil-muztamal raz-itlaagii bil-qiṭaar.*

most probably - *ʔaǵlab iδ-δann.* Most probably he is the one that should be blamed for it. *ʔaǵlab iδ-δann huwwa lli laazim yinlaam ɛaleeha.*

probation - *tajruba.* He is still on probation. *baᶜda taɀt it-tajruba.*
problem - 1. *muškila* pl. *mašaakil.* We all have our problems. *kullatna ᶜidna mašaakilna.* -- That's your problem. *haaδi muškila txuṣṣak ʔinta.* 2. *masʔala* pl. *masaaʔil.* I couldn't solve the second problem. *ma-gdart aɀill il-masʔala θ-θaanya.*
problematical - *muškil.*
procedure - 1. *ʔuṣuul.* What is the usual procedure? *šinu l-ʔuṣuul il-muttabaᶜaʔ* 2. *ʔijraaʔ* pl. *-aat.* The procedures for terminating the services of an employee are in this directive. *l-ʔijraaʔaat il-ʔinhaaʔ xadamaat muwaδδaf mawjuuda b-han-niδaam.*
to **proceed** - 1. *stamarr (i stimraar), miša (i maši).* They have decided to proceed according to the original plan. *ṣammimaw ᶜala ʔan yistimirruun ɀasb il-xiṭṭa l-marsuuma.* -- Then he proceeded to talk about the differences in the two dialects. *baᶜad δaalik istamarr yiɀči ᶜan il-xilaaf bil-lahijteen.* 2. *daawam (i dawaam).* We stopped the car to look at the view and then proceeded on our way. *waggafna s-sayyaara l-mušaahadat il-manδar w-baᶜdeen daawamna b-seerna.* 3. *kammal (i takmiil) t-.* Let's proceed with the class. *xalli nkammil id-daris.*
proceeding - *ʔijraaʔ* pl. *-aat.* I watched the proceedings with great interest. *laaɀaδit seer il-ʔijraaʔaat ib-šooq ᶜaδiim.*
proceeds - *waaridaat, ʔiiraad.* The proceeds will go to charity. *l-waaridaat itruuɀ lil-xayraat.*
process - 1. *ṭariiqa* pl. *ṭuruq.* Our engineers have developed a new process. *muhandisiinna ṭallᶜaw ṭariiqa jidiida.* 2. *ᶜamaliyya* pl. *-aat, muᶜaamala* pl. *-aat.* That will be a long drawn-out process. *haay raɀ-itkuun ᶜamaliyya ṭuwiila.*
to process - *ṣaffa (i taṣfiya) t-.* This refinery can process enough oil to cover our internal gasoline needs. *hal-maṣfa yistaṭiiᶜ yṣaffi kammiyyat nafuṭ itsidd ɀaajatna d-daaxiliyya mnil-banziin.*
**The consulate is going to process your visa. *l-qunṣuliyya raɀ-tijri muᶜaamalat il-viiza maaltak.*
procession - 1. *mawkib* pl. *mawaakib.* The procession of the President and his official guest will pass through this street. *mawkib ir-raʔiis w-ḍeefa r-rasmi raɀ-ymurr min haš-šaariᶜ.* 2. *zaffa* pl. *-aat.* The wedding procession will leave from the restaurant at seven o'clock. *z-zaffa raɀ-tiṭlaᶜ imnil-maṭᶜam saaᶜa sabᶜa.* 3. *janaaza* pl. *-aat.* All of his old friends walked in his funeral procession. *kull ʔaṣdiqaaʔa l-ᶜittaq mišaw ib-janaazta.*
to **proclaim** - *ʔaᶜlan (i ʔiᶜlaan).* They proclaimed the 14th of July a holiday. *ʔaᶜlinaw yoom ʔarbaṭaᶜaš tammuuz ᶜuṭla.*
proclamation - *ʔiᶜlaan* pl. *-aat, balaaġ* pl. *-aat.*
to **procure** - *ɀaṣṣal (i taɀṣiil) t-.* They hired me to procure fresh vegetables and meat for them from local sources. *staxdimooni ɀatta ʔaɀaṣṣil-ilhum xuδrawaat w-laɀam taaza mnil-maṣaadir il-maɀalliyya.*
produce - *maɀṣuul* pl. *-aat, maɀaaṣiil.* The farmers sell their produce on market day. *l-fallaɀiin ybiiᶜuun maɀṣuulaathum ib-yoom il-gaᶜda.*
to produce - 1. *ʔantaj (i ʔintaaj).* We don't produce enough grain to cover our needs. *ma-nintij ɀubuub kaafya tsidd ɀaajatna.* 2. *ṭallaᶜ (i taṭliiᶜ) t-.* How many cars do they produce a month? *čam sayyaara yṭallᶜuun biš-šahar.* 3. *ʔabraz (i ʔibraaz).* Can you produce any written proof? *tigdar tibriz fadd daliil xaṭṭi?*
product - *mantuuj* pl. *-aat.* This company is getting ready to put a new product on the market. *haš-šarika da-tistiᶜidd il-tanziil mantuuj jidiid lis-suug.*
production - *ʔintaaj* pl. *-aat.*
productive - *muntij, muθmir.* He's a very productive writer. *huwwa fadd kaatib kulliš muntij.*
profession - 1. *mihna* pl. *mihan, ɀirfa* pl. *ɀiraf.* My son is preparing himself for the legal profession. *ʔibni da-yhayyiʔ nafsa l-mihnat il-muɀaamaat.* 2. *silk.* He is in the teaching profession. *huwwa b-silk it-taᶜliim.*
professional - 1. *muɀtarif* pl. *-iin, mumtahin* pl. *-iin.* He's a professional gambler. *huwwa fadd qumarči muɀtarif.* 2. *ṣaaɀib mihna* pl. *ʔaṣɀaab mihan.* All of our friends are professional people. *kull ʔaṣdiqaaʔna min ʔaṣɀaab il-mihan.*
professor - *ʔustaaδ* pl. *ʔasaatiδa, proofisoor* pl. *-iyya.*
proficiency - When I applied for the job, they gave me a proficiency test in typing. *lamma qaddamit ᶜal-waδiifa, ʔinṭooni mtiɀaan kafaaʔa biṭ-ṭibaaᶜa.*
proficient - *baariᶜ.* How long did it take you to become proficient in English? *šgadd ʔaxaδak ʔila ʔan ṣirit baariᶜ bil-ingiliizi?*
to become proficient - *biraᶜ (a baraaᶜa).* You can't expect to become proficient in typing and shorthand in a month. *la-tintiδir tibraᶜ biṭ-ṭibaaᶜa wil-ixtizaal xilaal šahar.*
profit - 1. *ribiɀ* pl. *ʔarbaaɀ.* I sold it at a profit. *biᶜitha b-ribiɀ.* 2. *faaʔida* pl. *fawaaʔid, maksab* pl. *makaasib.* I don't expect to get any profit out of that. *ma-atwaqqaᶜ ʔay faaʔida min waraaha.*
to make a profit - *ribaɀ (a ribiɀ).* He makes a profit of at least 10% on every item. *yirbaɀ ᶜala l-ʔaqall ᶜašra bil-miyya ᶜala kull silᶜa.*
to profit - *ntifaᶜ (i ntifaaᶜ) stafaad (i stifaada).* Did you profit much from the lecture? *stafaadeet ihwaaya mnil-muɀaaδara?*
**One profits from his mistakes. *l-waaɀid yitᶜallam min ʔaġlaaṭa.*
profitable - *murbiɀ, mufiid, naafiᶜ.* Is it a profitable business? *haš-šaġla murbiɀa?*
profound - *ᶜamiiq.* He had a profound influence on me. *čaan ʔila taʔθiir ᶜamiiq ᶜalayya.*
profusion - *kuθra.* There is a profusion of roses blooming in the garden. *ʔaku kuθra b-ward ij-juuri mfattaɀ bil-ɀadiiqa.*
program - 1. *manhaj* pl. *manaahij.* The program sells for a dirham. *l-manhaj da-yinbaaᶜ ib-dirham.* -- What's on our program tonight? *šinu manhajna hal-leela?* 2. *barnaamij* pl. *baraamij.* How did you like the program? *šloon ᶜijabak il-barnaamij?*
progress - *taqaddum.* The students are making good progress. *t-talaamiiδ da-yṣiir ᶜidhum taqaddum maɀsuus.* -- Are you making any progress with your book? *da-yṣiir ᶜindak ʔay taqaddum b-iktaabak?*
to progress - 1. *tɀassan (a taɀassun).* You've progressed a lot in the six weeks I've been away. *ʔinta hwaaya tɀassanit xilaal il-ʔasaabiiᶜ is-sitta lli ġibit biiha.* 2. *tqaddam (a taqaddum), traqqa (a triqqi).* Our country has progressed fast during the past few years. *baladna tqaddam sariiᶜ xilaal is-sanawaat il-ʔaxiira.* 3. *tqaddam (a taqaddum).* We progressed slowly toward the enemy. *tqaddamna b-buṭuʔ ᶜala l-ʔaᶜdaaʔ.*
progressive - *mitjaddid* pl. *-iin, mitqaddim* pl. *-iin, mitdarrij* pl. *-iin.* He's a progressive teacher. *huwwa muᶜallim mitjaddid.*
progressively - *bit-tadriij.* The war grew progressively worse. *l-ɀarub saaʔat bit-tadriij.*
to **prohibit** - 1. *minaᶜ (a maniᶜ) n-.* The law prohibits smoking here. *l-qaanuun yimnaᶜ it-tadxiin ihnaa.* 2. *ɀarram (u taɀriim) t-.* The Moslem religion prohibits alcoholic drinks. *l-ʔislaamiyya ɀarramat šurb il-xamur.*
project - *mašruuᶜ* pl. *mašaariiᶜ.* We're working on a project together. *da-ništuġuḷ suwa b-fadd mašruuᶜ.*
to project - 1. *ᶜiraδ (u ᶜaruδ) n-.* The film was projected on the wall. *l-filim inᶜiraδ ᶜal-ɀaayiṭ.* 2. *ṭilaᶜ (a ṭuluuᶜ), biraz (u bariz, buruuz).* The rear end of our new car projects one foot out of our garage. *muʔaxxar sayyaaratna j-jidiida yiṭlaᶜ qadam waaɀid imnil-garaaj.*
projector - *prujaktar* pl. *-aat.*
to **prolong** - *ṭawwal (i taṭwiil) t-.* You are only prolonging the agony. *ʔinta bass da-ṭṭawwil il-ᶜaδaab.*
prominent - *baariz, muᶜtabar.* He's a prominent artist. *huwwa fannaan baariz.* -- He has a prominent chin. *ᶜinda fadd ɀinič baariz.*
promise - 1. *waᶜad* pl. *wuᶜuud.* You didn't keep your promise. *ma-wuffeet ib-waᶜdak.* 2. *ʔamal, tabaašiir.* There is some promise of change. *ʔaku ʔamal bit-taġyiir.*
to promise - *wuᶜad (a waᶜad), niṭa (i naṭi) n- kalaam.* We promised him a present. *wuᶜadnaa b-hadiyya.* -- Promise me that you won't do it again. *ʔooᶜidni ʔan ma-tsawwiiha marra lux.*
promising - *mbaššir bil-xeer.* The horse lost the race after a promising start. *l-iɀṣaan xiṣar is-sibaaq baᶜad bidaaya mbaššra bil-xeer.*
promissory note - *kumpyaala* pl. *-aat.*
to **promote** - 1. *raffaᶜ (u tarfiiᶜ) t-.* He was promoted to captain. *traffaᶜ ʔila raʔiis.* 2. *šajjaᶜ (i tšijjiᶜ) t-.* Most countries promote their foreign trade. *ʔakθar id-duwal itšajjiᶜ tijaaratha l-xaarijiyya.*
promotion - *tarfiiᶜ.* My promotion is overdue. *tarfiiᶜi tʔaxxar.*

prompt - **1.** *sariiƐ, Ɛaajil.* I expect a prompt reply. *ʔatwaqqaƐ jawaab sariiƐ.* **2.** *bil-wakit.* He's prompt in paying his debts. *yidfaƐ deena bil-wakit.*
to prompt - *zaffaz (i tziffiz) t-.* What prompted you to say that? *šinu lli zaffazak itguul haay?*
promptly - **1.** *biδ-δabuṭ.* We start promptly at five. *nibdi saaƐa xamsa biδ-δabuṭ.* **2.** *zaalan, Ɛal-fawr.* The police arrived promptly. *š-šurṭa wuṣlat zaalan.*
pronoun - *δamiir* pl. *δamaaʔir.*
to **pronounce** - **1.** *lufaδ (u lafuδ) n-.* Am I pronouncing the word correctly? *da-alfuδ il-kalima ṣaziiz?* **2.** *nitaq (u nutuq) n- b-.* The judge will pronounce sentence tomorrow. *l-zaakim raz-yinṭuq bil-zukum bil-Ɛuquuba baačir.*
pronounciation - *lafuδ* pl. *ʔalfaaδ.* That's not correct pronunciation. *hal-lafuδ muu ṣaziiz.*
proof - **1.** *burhaan* pl. *baraahiin, daliil* pl. *ʔadilla.* What proof do you have of that? *šinu burhaanak Ɛala haay?* **2.** *ʔiθbaat.* There's definite proof that he killed her. *ʔaku ʔiθbaat ʔakiid ʔannahu huwwa lli qitalha.* **3.** *miswadda* pl. *-aat.* I've just finished reading proof on my new article. *hastawwni xallaṣit iqraayat il-miswadda l-maqaalti j-jidiida.*
propaganda - *diƐaaya.*
to **propagate** - **1.** *kaθθar (i takθiir).* There are many ways of propagating this plant. *ʔaku ṭuruq mutaƐaddida t-takθiir hal-ʔašjaar.* **2.** *nišar (u našir) n-.* The first four caliphs propagated the Islamic religion. *l-xulafaaʔ ir-raašidiin nišraw il-ʔislaam.*
propeller - *parawaana* pl. *-aat.*
proper - **1.** *ṣaziiz, laayiq.* That isn't the proper way to handle people. *haaδi muu ṭ-ṭariiqa ṣ-ṣaziiza l-muƐaamalat in-naas.* **2.** *munaasib, mulaaʔim.* This isn't the proper time to ask questions. *haaδa muu l-wakt il-mulaaʔim il-suʔaal ʔasʔila.* **3.** *ʔaṣli*.* In 1937 the Japanese invaded China proper. *sana ʔalf w-tisiƐ miyya w-sabƐa w-tlaaθiin l-yaabaaniyyiin ġizaw ʔarδ iṣ-ṣiin il-ʔaṣliyya.* **4.** *muxtaṣṣ.* You have to talk to the proper person. *laazim tizči wiyya š-šaxṣ il-muxtaṣṣ.*
properly - **1.** *ka-ma yajib, zasb il-ʔuṣuul.* I'll show you how to do it properly. *raz-araawiik išloon itsawwiiha ka-ma yajib.* **2.** *b-liyaaqa.* Can't you behave properly? *ma-tigdar titṣarraf ib-liyaaqa?*
property - **1.** *muluk* pl. *ʔamlaak.* All the furniture is my property. *kull il-ʔaθaaθ mulki.* -- He has a mortgage on his property. *msawwi rahan Ɛala mulka.* **2.** *xaaṣṣiyya* pl. *xawaaṣṣ, xaṣaaʔiṣ.* One of the properties of copper is its reddish color. *wazda min xawaaṣṣ iṣ-ṣifir loona l-ʔazmar.*
prophecy - *nubuuʔa* pl. *-aat.*
to **prophesy** - *tnabbaʔ (a tanabbuʔ).* He prophesied that the world would come to an end this coming year. *tnabbaʔ il-Ɛaalam raz-yintihi s-sana j-jaaya.*
prophet - *nabi* pl. *ʔanbiyaaʔ.*
proportion - **1.** *tanaasub.* That picture is all out of proportion. *t-tanaasub ib-haṣ-ṣuura kulla ġalaṭ.* **2.** *nisba.* Everybody is paid in proportion to what he does. *kull waazid yaaxuδ bin-nisba š-šuġla.* **3.** *fiʔa* pl. *-aat, qisim* pl. *ʔaqsaam.* A small proportion of the people approved. *fiʔa qaliila mnin-naas waafqaw.*
**His expenses are entirely out of proportion to his income. *maṣruufaata ma-titnaasab wiyya waaridaata ʔabadan.*
proportional - **1.** *nisbi*.* These figures show the proportional distribution of population. *hal-ʔarqaam itbayyin it-tawziiƐ in-nisbi lis-sukkaan.* **2.** *mitnaasib.* Your wages will be proportional to your education. *ʔujuurak raz-itkuun mitnaasba wiyya diraastak.*
proportioned - *mitnaasiq, mitnaasib.* Her figure is well-proportioned. *jisimha zilu mitnaasiq.*
proposal - **1.** *Ɛariδ* pl. *Ɛuruuδ.* He made me an interesting proposal. *qaddam-li Ɛariδ muġri.* **2.** *qtiraaz* pl. *-aat.* Your proposal met with the approval of all members. *qtiraazak naal muwaafaqat kull il-ʔaƐδaaʔ.* **3.** *xuṭba* pl. *-aat.* Our daughter had two proposals at the same time. *binitna jattha xuṭubteen ib-nafs il-wakit.*
to **propose** - *qtiraz (i qtiraaz).* I propose we go to the movies. *ʔaqtiriz inruuz lis-siinama.*
to propose to - *xiṭab (u xuṭba) n-, ṭilab (u ṭalab) n- ʔiid.* He proposed to her. *xiṭabha* or *ṭilab ʔiidha.*
proposition - **1.** *Ɛariδ, Ɛiraδ* pl. *Ɛuruuδ.* He made me an excellent proposition. *Ɛiraδ Ɛalayya Ɛariδ mumtaaz.* **2.** *šaġla* pl. *-aat.* It is a paying proposition. *haay šaġla murbiza.* **3.** *qtiraaz* pl. *-aat.* Your proposition is very sound. *qtiraazak kulliš maƐquul.*
proprietor - *maalik* pl. *millaak, ṣaazib* pl. *ʔaṣzaab.*
pros and cons - *mazaasin w-masaawiʔ.*
prose - *naθir.*
rhymed prose - *sajiƐ.*
to **prosecute** - *qaam, ʔaqaam (i ʔiqaama) n- daƐwa Ɛala.* Do you think the government will prosecute him? *tiftikir il-zukuuma raz-itqiim daƐwa Ɛalee?*
prosecutor - *mištiki* pl. *-iin, muddaƐi* pl. *-iin.*
prospect - **1.** *ʔamal* pl. *ʔaamaal.* What are his prospects of getting a job? *šgadd Ɛinda ʔamal bil-zuṣuul Ɛal-waδiifa?* **2.** *fikra* pl. *fikir.* I don't like the prospect of having to work with him. *fikrat iš-šuġuḷ wiyyaa ma-tiƐjibni.*
**This boy has good prospects. *hal-walad Ɛinda mustaqbal zeen.*
prospective - *muntaδar, mutawaqqaƐ, maʔmuul.* He is my prospective son-in-law. *huwwa nisiibi l-muntaδar.*
prostitute - *gazba* pl. *gzaab, muumis* pl. *-aat, Ɛaahra* pl. *-aat.*
prostitution - *daƐaara, baġaaʔ.*
to **protect** - **1.** *zima (i zami) n-.* I wear these glasses to protect my eyes. *ʔaani ʔalbas hal-manaaδir ʔazmi Ɛyuuni.* **2.** *zaafaδ (u muzaafaδa) t- Ɛala.* I will protect your interests. *ʔaani raz-azaafuδ Ɛala maṣlaztak.* **3.** *daafaƐ (i difaaƐ) Ɛan.* Everyone must protect his own property. *kull waazid laazim ydaafiƐ Ɛan mulka.* **4.** *wuqa (i wuqaaya) n-.* This medicine protects the eyes from disease. *had-duwa yooqi l-Ɛeen imnil-ʔamraaδ.*
protection - *zimaaya.* There is no protection against that. *ma-aku zimaaya δidd haay.*
protectorate - *mazmiyya* pl. *-aat.*
to **protest** - **1.** *ztajj (a ztijaaj).* I protest! *ʔaani ʔaztajj!* **2.** *ʔaṣarr (i ʔiṣraar) n- Ɛala.* He protested his innocence throughout the trial. *ʔaṣarr Ɛala baraaʔta ṭuul il-muzaakama.*
Protestant - *prootistaani** pl. *-iyyiin.*
Protestantism - *prootistaaniyya.*
protocol - *prootookool.*
proton - *prootoon* pl. *-aat.*
proud - **1.** *faxuur.* I am proud of you. *ʔaani faxuur biik* or ***ʔaani ʔaftixir biik.* **2.** *ʔaanuuf.* She is too proud, to ask for someone's help. *haay ʔaʔnaf min ʔan tistanjid ib-ʔazzad.*
to **prove** - *ʔaθbat (i ʔiθbaat), barhan (i tburhin) t-.* I can prove I didn't do it. *ʔagdar aθbit ib-ʔanni ma-sawweetha.*
to prove to be - *ṭilaƐ (a ṭuluuƐ).* The rumor proved to be lies. *hal-zači ṭilƐat čiδib.*
proverb - *maθal* pl. *ʔamθaal, qawl maʔθuur* pl. *ʔaqwaal maʔθuura.*
to **provide** - **1.** *jahhaz (i tajhiiz, tjihhiz) t-, zawwad (i tazwiid) t-.* The university is going to provide the laboratory with modern equipment. *j-jaamiƐa raz-itjahhiz il-muxtabar ib-lawaazim zadiiθa.* **2.** *hayyaʔ (i thiyyiʔ) t-.* We will provide the place for the meeting. *raz-inhayyiʔ il-mukaan lil-ijtimaaƐ.* **3.** *waffar (u tawfiir) t-.* We provided all means of comfort. *waffarna kull ʔasbaab ir-raaza.*
to provide for - **1.** *Ɛaal (i ʔiƐaala).* He has to provide for the whole family. *laazim yƐiil il-Ɛaaʔila kullha.* **2.** *zisab (i ʔizsaab) n- ʔizsaab.* The law provides for such special cases. *l-qaanuun yizsib izsaab miθil hal-qaδaaya l-xaaṣṣa.* **3.** *ztaaṭ (a ztiyaaṭ).* We will provide for a long winter. *raz-niztaaṭ ʔila šita ṭawiil.*
provided, providing - *b-šarṭ, Ɛala šarṭ.* I'll go, provided you come with me. *ʔaruuz ib-šarṭ tiji wiyyaaya.*
province - *liwaaʔ* pl. *ʔalwiya.* Iraq is divided into fourteen provinces. *l-Ɛiraaq minqisim ʔila ʔarbaataƐaš liwaaʔ.*
provision - *naṣṣ* pl. *nuṣuuṣ.* There is no provision made for this in the law. *ma-aku naṣṣ Ɛala haaδa bil-qaanuun.*
provisions - *tajhiizaat, maʔuuna.* Our provisions are running low. *tajhiizaatna da-tqill.*
to **provoke** - **1.** *ʔaθaar (i ʔiθaara) n-.* His remark provoked a roar of laughter. *mulaazaδta ʔaθaarat Ɛaaṣifa mniδ-δizik.* **2.** *stafazz (i stifzaaz).* Don't provoke him. *la-tistafizza.* -- His behavior is provoking. *taṣarrufa yistafizz il-waazid.*

**He's provoked about it. *huwwa migtaa§ Ɛanha.*

prune - *Ɛinjaaṣa* (pl. *-aat*) *myabbisa* coll. *Ɛinjaaṣ imyabbas.*

to prune - *qallam (i taqliim) t-.* The rosebushes need to be pruned. *Ɛruug il-warad yinraad-ilha titqallam.*

psychiatrist - *ṭabiib nafsaani* pl. *ʔaṭibbaaʔ nafsaaniyyiin.*

psychology - *Ɛilm in-nafs.*

public - 1. *Ɛumuum, naas.* Is this park open to the public? *hal-ẓadiiqa maftuuẓa lil-Ɛumuum?* 2. *Ɛaamm.* Public opinion is against him. *r-raʔi l-Ɛaamm §idda.* -- Public health requires these measures. *ṣ-ṣiẓẓa l-Ɛaamma tiṭṭallab hal-ʔijraaʔaat.* 3. *Ɛumuumi*.* Is there a public telephone here? *ʔaku talafoon Ɛumuumi hnaa?* 4. *Ɛalani*, Ɛumuumi*.* I bought this rug at a public auction. *štireeṭ has-sijjaada b-mazaad Ɛalani.*

**He embezzled public funds. *xtilas ʔamwaal id-dawla.*

**Such books will always find a public. *hiiči kutub itšuuf-ilha qurraaʔ daaʔiman.*

in public - *giddaam in-naas.* You shouldn't behave like this in public. *ma-laazim titṣarraf hiiči giddaam in-naas.*

publication - 1. *našir.* What is the date of publication? *šwakit taariix in-našir?* 2. *našra* pl. *-aat.* This is a useful publication. *haay našra mufiida.*

publicity - *diƐaaya.* That's what I call clever publicity. *haaδa lli ʔasammii diƐaaya maahra.*

to **publish** - *nišar (u našir) n-.* He hopes to publish his new book very soon. *yitʔammal yinšur iktaaba j-jidiid qariiban.*

publisher - *naašir* pl. *-iin.*

publishing house - *daar našir.*

puddle - *nugra* pl. *nugar, burka* pl. *burak.* Careful, don't step into the puddle! *diir baalak, la-tixṭi bin-nugra!*

puff - *nafas.* I got sick after only one puff. *nafsi liƐbat baƐad nafas waaẓid.*

pull - 1. *jarra* pl. *-aat.* One more pull and we'll have it open. *jarra lux baƐad raẓ-tinfakk.* 2. *waaṣṭa* pl. *-aat, xaaṭraana, §ahar.* You need a lot of pull to get a job here. *tiẓtaaj ihwaaya waaṣṭaat yaḷḷa tigdar itẓaṣṣil šuğuḷ ihnaa.*

to pull - 1. *jarr (u jarr) n-.* Don't pull so hard! *la-tjurr hal-gadd ẓeel.* 2. *šilaƐ (a šaliƐ) n-.* This tooth must be pulled. *has-sinn laazim yinšiliƐ.*

**Don't pull any funny stuff! *la-tbiiƐ šaṭaara b-raasi!*

**Don't try to pull the wool over my eyes! *la-tẓaawil itƐabbur Ɛalayya qiriš qalb!* or *la-tẓaawil itlaflifni!*

**He pulled a fast one on me. *doolabni.* or *§irabni kalak.*

**I pulled a big boner. *sawweet min nafsi ma§ẓaka.*

**Pull over to the side! *ʔoogaf Ɛala ṣafẓa!* or *ʔuṭbug!*

to pull apart - 1. *faakak (i tfaakuk) t-.* It took three men to pull them apart. *tlaθ riyaajiil yaḷḷa gidraw yfaakikuuhum.* 2. *faṣṣax (i tafṣiix) t-.* I had to pull the radio apart in order to find what was wrong. *§ṭarreet ʔafaṣṣix ir-raadyo ẓatta ʔalgi l-Ɛeeb.*

to pull down - 1. *nazzal (i tanziil) t-.* Shall I pull down the shades? *ʔanazzil il-ṗardaat?* 2. *hidam (i hadim) n-.* They're going to pull down all the old houses. *raẓ-yhidmuun kull il-ibyuut il-Ɛatiiga.*

to pull in - *ṭabb (u ṭabb), wuṣal (a wuṣuul).* When did your train pull in? *qiṭaarak išwakit ṭabb?*

to pull oneself together - *šadd (i šadd) n- ẓeel~.* Pull yourself together! *šidd ẓeelak!*

to pull out - 1. *šilaƐ (a šaliƐ) n-.* The children pulled out all the weeds. *l-ʔaṭfaal šilƐaw kull il-ẓašiiš.* 2. *ṭilaƐ (a ṭuluuƐ).* The train will pull out any minute. *l-qiṭaar raẓ-yiṭlaƐ ib-ʔay laẓ§a.*

to pull through - *dabbar (u tadbiir) t-, Ɛubar (u Ɛabar).* We were afraid she might not pull through it. *činna xaayfiin ma-raẓ-itdabburha.*

to pull up - 1. *ṭubag (u ṭabug).* The car pulled up in front of the house. *s-sayyaara ṭubgat giddaam il-beet.* 2. *jarr (u jarr) n-.* Pull up a chair! *jurr-lak fadd kursi!*

pulley - *bakra* pl. *-aat.*

pulse - *nabu§.* The nurse took my pulse. *l-mumarri§a ʔax§at nab§i.*

pump - 1. *ma§axxa* pl. *-aat.* We have a pump in our country house. *Ɛidna ma§axxa b-beetna r-riifi.* 2. *ṗamṗ* pl. *-aat.* I need a new pump for the bicycle. *ʔaẓtaaj ṗamṗ jidiid lil-ṗaaysikil.*

to pump - 1. *§axx (u §axx) n-.* Shall I pump some water? *ʔa§uxx išwayya ṃaay?* 2. *stadraj (i stidraaj).* Don't let him pump you. *la-txallii yistadrijak.*

to pump up - 1. *§axx (u §axx) n-.* Our water is pumped up from the spring. *l-ṃaay maalna yin§axx imnil-Ɛeen.* 2. *nufax (u nafux) n-.* Will you please pump up the front tires? *baḷḷa ma-tinfux it-taayaraat il-giddaamiyya?*

pumping station - *maẓaṭṭat* (pl. *-aat*) *§axx.*

pumpkin - *šijrat* (pl. *-aat* coll. *šijar*) *ʔaskala.*

punch - 1. *§arbat* (pl. *-aat*) *jimiƐ, lakma* pl. *-aat, books* pl. *-aat.* The punched knocked him down. *§arbat ij-jimiƐ waggƐata.* 2. *quwwa.* His speech lacked punch. *ẓadiiθa čaan yinquṣṣa l-quwwa.* 3. *šarbat* pl. *šaraabit.* Would you like some more punch? *tẓibb tišrab baƐad šarbat?*

to punch - 1. *ziraf (u zaruf) n-, gira§ (u garu§) n-.* The conductor punched our tickets. *mufattiš il-ṗaaṣ ziraf tiktaatna.* 2. *§irab (u §arub) n-.* Shut up, or I will punch you in the nose. *ʔinčabb, tara ʔa§urbak bil-xašma.*

puncture - *zuruf* pl. *zuruuf, nugub* pl. *nguub, ṗančar* pl. *-aat.* Is there a puncture in the tire? *ʔaku zuruf bit-taayar?*

to puncture - *ziraf (u zaruf) n-, nigab (u nagub) n-.* He has a punctured eardrum. *ṭablat ʔiδna mazruufa.*

to **punish** - 1. *Ɛaaqab (i muƐaaqaba) t- Ɛala.* Violations will be severely punished. *l-muxaalafaat yitƐaaqab Ɛaleeha b-šidda.* 2. *niṭa (i naṭi) n- qaṣaaṣ.* I think he's been punished enough. *ʔaƐtiqid inniṭa qaṣaaṣ kaafi.*

punishment - *Ɛuquuba* pl. *-aat, qaṣaaṣ* pl. *-aat.* The punishment was too severe. *l-Ɛuquuba čaanat kulliš qaasya.*

**Our car has taken a lot of punishment. *sayyaaratna štiƐal diinha.*

punitive - *taʔdiibi*.* We have to send a punitive expedition to the strike area. *laazim indizz ẓamla taʔdiibiyya l-manṭiqt il-ʔi§ṭiraab.*

pupil - 1. *tilmiiδ* pl. *talaamiiδ, ṭaalib* pl. *ṭullaab.* She has twenty pupils in her class. *Ɛidha Ɛišriin tilmiiδ ib-ṣaffha.* 2. *buʔbuʔ* pl. *baʔaabiʔ.* The pupil of the left eye is dilated. *l-buʔbuʔ maal il-Ɛeen il-yisra twassaƐ.*

puppy - *juru* pl. *juriwaat, juraawa; buuji* pl. *bwaaj.*

purchase - *šarwa* pl. *-aat.* This boat was a wonderful purchase. *hal-balam čaan xooš šarwa.*

to purchase - *štira (i štiraaʔ).* We're going to purchase a new home this fall. *raẓ-ništri beet jidiid hal-xariif.*

pure - 1. *xaaliṣ.* The necktie is pure silk. *r-ribaaṭ ẓariir xaaliṣ.* 2. *naqi*.* Do you have pure alcohol? *Ɛindak kuhuul naqiyya?* 3. *ṣirf, baẓt.* That's pure nonsense. *haaδi lağwa ṣirfa.*

purely - *baẓt, ṣirf.* This is a purely political matter. *haaδa maw§uuƐ siyaasi baẓt.*

purge - *taṭhiir* pl. *-aat.* This government needs a purge of all corruption. *hal-ẓukuuma tiẓtaaj ʔila taṭhiir il-fasaad.*

to purge - *ṭahhar (i taṭhiir) t-.* The government is planning to purge its police department. *l-ẓukuuma naawiya ṭṭahhir silk iš-šurṭa.*

to **purify** - *ṣaffa (i taṣfiya) t-.* This water needs to be purified. *hal-ṃaay laazim yitṣaffa.*

purple - *šaraabi*.*

purpose - *ğara§* pl. *ʔağraa§, muraad, mabğa, qaṣid, ğaaya* pl. *-aat.* What's the purpose of all this? *šinu l-ğara§ min kull haaδa?* -- He left without achieving his purpose. *tirak bala-ma ynaal ğara§a.* -- What purpose did he have in doing that? *šinu čaan ğara§a min iswayyaat haay?* -- You can use this tool for many purposes. *tigdar tistaƐmil hal-ʔaala l-Ɛiddat ğaayaat.*

on purpose - *Ɛan qaṣid, Ɛamdan, qaṣdan, qaṣṭani.* I left my coat home on purpose. *ʔaani trakit qaṗṗuuṭi bil-beet Ɛan qaṣid.*

purse - 1. *junṭa* pl. *-aat, junaṭ.* This purse doesn't go well with my new dress. *haj-junṭa ma-tirham zeen wiyya badilti j-jidiida.* 2. *jaaʔiza* pl. *jawaaʔiz.* The purse was divided among the winners. *j-jaaʔiza tqassmat been ir-raabẓiin.*

to **pursue** - 1. *taabaƐ (i mutaabaƐa) t-.* I don't want to pursue the subject any further. *ma-ariid ataabiƐ hal-mawðuuƐ baƐad ʔazyad.* 2. *Ɛaqqab (i tƐiqqib) t-, tƐaqqab (a tƐiqqib).* The police are pursuing the smugglers. *š-šurṭa da-tƐaqqib il-muharribiin.* 3. *tibaƐ (i tabiƐ) n-.* We all pursue the policies of our party. *kullna nitbaƐ siyaasat ʒizibna.*

pursuit plane - *ṭiyyaara* (pl. *-aat*) *muṭaarida.*

pus - *qeeʒ, jaraaʒa.*

push - *dafƐa* pl. *-aat.* He gave me such a push that I nearly fell over. *nṭaani fadd šikil dafƐa xallatni ʔoogaƐ taqriiban.*

to **push** - 1. *difaƐ (a dafiƐ) n-.* Push the table over by the window. *ʔidfaƐ il-meez il-yamm is-sibbaač.* -- He was pushed way back. *ndifaƐ lil-ʔaxiir.* 2. *difaƐ (a dafiƐ) n-, daffaƐ (i tadfiiƐ) t-.* Don't push! *la-tidfaƐ!* 3. *čifat (i čafit).* The people pushed into the elevator. *n-naas čiftaw lil-maṣƐad.* 4. *daas (u doos) n-.* Did you push the button? *dist iz-zirr?* 5. *ðabb (i ðabb) n-.* He tried to push the blame on me. *ʒaawal yðibb il-loom Ɛalayya.* 6. *xalla (i txilli) t-.* What pushed you to do it? *š-xallaak itsawwiiha?*

**I tried to push my way through the crowd. *ʒaawalit ʔašuqq ṭariiqi been ij-jamaahiir.*

to **push off** - *ṭilaƐ (a ṭuluuƐ, ṭiluuƐ).* Right after we pushed off, the boat capsized. *baƐad-ma ṭilaƐna b-išwayya ngilab il-balam.*

pus - *qeeʒ, jaraaʒa.*

to **put** - 1. *ʒaṭṭ (u ʒaṭṭ) n-, xalla (i txilli) t-.* Put the table over there. *ʒuṭṭ il-meez ihnaak.* -- Put an ad in the paper. *ʒuṭṭ iƐlaan bij-jariida* or *ʔunšur.* 2. *wuðaƐ (a waðiƐ) n-.* That puts me in an embarrassing position. *haaða yooðaƐni b-waðiƐ ʒarij.* -- I'll have to put an end to this situation. *raʒ-ʔooðaƐ ʒadd il-hal-ʒaala.*

**I wouldn't put any faith in that story. *hal-iʒčaaya ma-Ɛaleeha Ɛtimaad.*

**Why don't you put it straight to him? *leeš ma-tgul-la-yaaha b-ṣaraaʒa?*

**Put it this way; we don't like each other. *b-kalima ʔuxra; ʔiʒna waaʒid ma-yʒibb il-laax.*

to **put across** - 1. *fahham (i tafhiim).* I don't know how to put it across to him that... *ma-da-ʔadri šloon afahhma ʔinna...* 2. *ʔanha (i ʔinhaaʔ), xaḷḷaṣ (i taxliiṣ).* Did you put the deal across? *ʔanheet iṣ-ṣafqa?*

to **put aside** - 1. *xalla (i txilli) t- Ɛala ṣafʒa.* She's been putting aside a little money each month. *da-txalli šwayya fluus Ɛala ṣafʒa kull šahar.* 2. *ðabb (i ðabb) n- Ɛala ṣafʒa.* Put that newspaper aside and let us finish this. *ðibb ij-jariida Ɛala ṣafʒa w-xalli nxaḷḷuṣ haay.*

to **put away** - *ðamm (u ðamm) n-.* Put your jewelry away in a safe place. *ðumm mujawharaatak ib-makaan ʔamiin.* -- Put your summer clothes away. *ðumm ihduumak iṣ-ṣeefiyya.*

to **put back** - *rajjaƐ (i tarjiiƐ) t-, radd (i radd) n-.* Put the book back where you got it. *rajjiƐ il-iktaab imneen-ma ʔaxaðta.*

to **put to bed** - *nayyam (i tanyiim), nawwam (u tanwiim).* I have to put the kids to bed. *laazim ʔanayyim il-ʔaṭfaal.*

to **put down** - 1. *nazzal (i tnizzil, tanziil) t-, ʒaṭṭ (u ʒaṭṭ) n-.* Put the box down here. *nazzil iṣ-ṣanduug ihnaa.* 2. *kitab (i kitaaba) n-.* Put down your name and address. *ʔiktib ʔismak w-Ɛinwaanak.* 3. *qimaƐ (a qamiƐ) n-, ʔaxmad (i ʔixmaad) n-.* The army put down the revolution. *j-jeeš qimaƐ iθ-θawra.*

to **put in** - 1. *ṣiraf (u ṣaruf) n-.* They put in a lot of time on that job. *ṣirfaw ihwaaya wakit Ɛala haš-šuguḷ.* 2. *rakkab (u tarkiib) t-.* Did they put in a new windowpane? *rakkbaw jaama jidiida liš-šibbaač?*

to **put in a word for** - *ʒiča (i ʒači) l-, tšaffaƐ (a tšiffiƐ).* I want you to put in a word for me with the director. *ʔariidak tiʒčii-li wiyya l-mudiir.*

to **put in order** - *rattab (i trittib, tartiib) t-, naððam (u tniððim, tanðiim) t-.* He's putting his affairs in order. *da-yrattib ʔumuura.*

to **put into words** - *Ɛabbar (u taƐbiir) t- Ɛan.* This is something hard to put into words. *haaða fadd šii ṣaƐub it-taƐbiir Ɛanna.*

to **put off** - 1. *nayyam (i tanyiim).* I can't put the matter off any longer. *ma-agdar anayyim il-qaðiyya baƐad.* 2. *Ɛaṭṭal (i taƐṭiil, tƐiṭṭil) t-, Ɛawwag (i taƐwiig) t-.* Let's put off the decision until tomorrow. *xalli nƐaṭṭil il-qaraar li-baačir.* 3. *ʔajjal (i tʔijjil, taʔjiil) t-.* I can't put off the appointment. *ma-agdar aʔajjil il-mawƐid.* 4. *maaṭal (i mumaaṭala) t-.* Can't you put him off for a while? *ma-tigdar itmaaṭla mudda?*

to **put on** - 1. *libas (a libis) n-.* Put your hat on! *ʔilbas šafiqtak!* -- Which dress shall I put on? *ʔay badla ʔalbas?* 2. *šiƐal (i šaƐil) n-, Ɛilag (i Ɛalig) n-, fitaʒ (a fatiʒ) n-, fakk (u fakk) n-.* Put on the light, please. *baḷḷa ʔišƐil ið-ðuwa.*

**I've put on three pounds. *zaad wazni tlaθ paawnaat.*

**Don't you think her accent is put on? *ma-tiftikir lahjatha mitṣannƐa?*

to **put oneself out** - *tkallaf (a takalluf), ġaθθ (u ġaθθ) n- nafs~.* Don't put yourself out on my account. *la-titkallaf Ɛala muudi.*

to **put out** - 1. *ṭaffa (i ṭṭiffi, taṭfiya) t-.* The fire was put out quickly. *l-ʒariig iṭṭaffa bil-Ɛajal.* -- Put out the light before you leave. *ṭaffi ð-ðuwa gabuḷ-ma truuʒ.* 2. *ṭallaƐ (i ṭṭilliƐ, taṭliiƐ) t-.* Put him out if he makes too much noise. *ṭallƐa barra ʔiða ysawwi laġwa hwaaya.* 3. *nišar (u našir) n-.* Who's putting out your book? *minu da-yinšur iktaabak?*

to **put over on** - *Ɛabbar (u taƐbiir) t- Ɛala.* You can't put anything over on him. *ma-tigdar itƐabbur Ɛalee šii.*

to **put through** - *naffað (i tanfiið) t-.* He put his own plan through. *naffað mašruuƐa l-xaaṣṣ.*

to **put to death** - *Ɛidam (i ʔiƐdaam) n-.* The criminal was put to death this morning. *l-mujrim inƐidam hal-yoom iṣ-ṣubuʒ.*

to **put together** - 1. *ʒaṭṭ (u ʒaṭṭ) n- suwa.* Don't put the dog and the cat together, they will fight. *ma-tʒuṭṭ il-čalib wil-bazzuun suwa tara yitƐaarkuun.* 2. *rakkab (u tarkiib) t-.* We must put the pieces together. *laazim inrakkub il-wuṣal suwa.*

to **put up** - 1. *niṣab (u naṣub) n-.* New telephone poles are being put up. *Ɛawaamiid talafoon jidiida yinnuṣbuun.* 2. *Ɛirað (u Ɛarið) n-, nazzal (i tanziil) t-.* The farm will be put up for sale this week. *l-mazraƐa raʒ-tinƐirið lil-beeƐ hal-isbuuƐ.* 3. *Ɛammar (u taƐmiir) t-, bina (i binaaʔ, bani) n-.* This building was put up in six months. *hal-binaaya tƐammrat ib-sitt išhur.* 4. *ʒaṭṭ (u ʒaṭṭ) n-.* We put up a fence around the house. *ʒaṭṭeena siyaaj daayir-ma daayir il-beet.* 5. *xalla (i txilli) t-, ʒaṭṭ (u ʒaṭṭ) n-.* Each of them put up a thousand dollars. *kull waaʒid minhum xalla ʔalif duulaar.* 6. *ʔabda (i ʔibdaaʔ) n-.* They didn't put up a fight. *ma-ʔabdaw muqaawama.*

**Who'll put up the bail for him? *minu raʒ-yitkallafa?*

**Can you put us up for the night? *tigdar itbayyitna?*

to **put up to** - *dalla (i tdilli) t-.* His friends put him up to it. *ʔaṣdiqaaʔa dalloo Ɛaleeha.*

to **put up with** - *tʒammal (a tʒimmil).* I don't know why you put up with it. *ma da-ʔadri lweeš titʒammalha.*

puzzle - 1. *ʒazzuura* pl. *-aat, ʒazaaziir.* Can you solve the puzzle? *tigdar itʒill hal-ʒazzuura?* 2. *laġiz* pl. *ʔalġaaz.* That is a puzzle to me. *haaði laġiz bin-nisba ʔili.*

to **puzzle** - *ʒayyar (i tʒiyyir) t-.* His letter had us puzzled. *maktuuba ʒayyarna.*

to **puzzle out** - *ʒizar (i ʒazir) n-, ʒall (i ʒall) n-.* I can't puzzle it out. *ma-agdar ʔaʒzirha.*

pyramid - *haram* pl. *ʔahraam.*

Q

quack - *dajjaal* pl. *-iin, mušaᶜwiδ* pl. *-iin.* The Ministry of Health has been able to track down a great many quacks and prevent them from practicing medicine. *wizaart iṣ-ṣiẓẓa twaffqat bil-ᶜuθuur ᶜala d-dajjaaliin ihwaaya w-maniᶜhum min mumaarasat iṭ-ṭibb.*
quadrangle - *šikil rubaaᶜi* pl. *ˀaškaal rubaaᶜiyya.*
quake - *zilzaal* pl. *zalaazil, hazza* (pl. *-aat*) *ˀarδiyya.*
qualification - **1.** *muˀahhila* pl. *-aat.* Do you think she has the necessary qualifications for the job? *tiᶜtiqid ᶜidha l-muˀahhilaat il-laazima lil-waδiifa.* **2.** *taẓaffuδ.* I agree to it with some qualification. *ˀawaafiq ᶜalee maᶜa baᶜδ it-taẓaffuδ.*
qualified - *ˀahil, ṣaaliẓ, laayiq.* He is well-qualified for the position. *haaδa ˀahil jiddan lil-waδiifa.* -- He is not qualified to marry into such a rich and famous family. *haaδa muu ˀahil yitzawwaj min ᶜaaˀila mašhuura ġaniyya miθil haay.*
to **qualify** - **1.** *ẓaddad (i taẓdiid) t- maᶜna.* I want to qualify my previous statement. *ˀariid ˀaẓaddid maᶜna kalaami s-saabiq.* **2.** *ˀahhal (i taˀhiil) t-.* That does not qualify you for this kind of job. *haaδa ma-yˀahhlak il-han-nooᶜ šuġuḷ.* **3.** *ṣilaẓ (a ṣalaaẓ), laag (i liyaaq).* You don't qualify for the job. *ma-tiṣlaẓ lil-waδiifa.*
quality - **1.** *xiṣla* pl. *xiṣal, ṣifa* pl. *-aat.* He has many good qualities. *ᶜinda hwaaya xiṣal zeena.* **2.** *miiza* pl. *-aat.* This machine has special qualities. *hal-makiina biiha miizaat xaaṣṣa.* **3.** *nawᶜiyya* pl. *-aat.* It is a matter of quality, not quantity. *l-masˀala masˀalat nawᶜiyya muu kammiyya.*
quandary - *ẓiira.*
quantity - *kammiyya* pl. *-aat, miqdaar* pl. *maqaadiir.* We have a sufficient quantity on hand for the present. *ᶜidna kammiyya kaafya mawjuuda bil-wakt il-ẓaaδir.* -- **This item is available in quantity. *hal-maadda mitwaffra b-kammiyyaat čibiira.*
quarantine - *ẓajir ṣiẓẓi, ᶜazil.* You will have to spend three days in quarantine. *laazim tibqa tlaθt iyyaam bil-ẓajir iṣ-ṣiẓẓi.*
to quarantine - *ẓijar (u ẓajir) n-.* They quarantined all the passengers on the plane. *ẓijraw kull rukkaab iṭ-ṭiyyaara.*
quarrel - **1.** *ᶜarka* pl. *-aat.* The policeman broke up the quarrel in the street. *š-šurṭi faδδ il-ᶜarka biš-šaariᶜ.* **2.** *xiṣaam* pl. *-aat.* The quarrel between the two politicians has become serious. *l-xiṣaam been is-siyaasiyyeen ṣaar jiddi.* **3.** *nizaaᶜ* pl. *-aat.* The farmers took their quarrel over water rights to the Bureau of Irrigation. *l-fallaaẓiin waṣṣlaw nizaaᶜhum ᶜala ẓuquuq is-saqi l-daaˀirt ir-rayy.*
to quarrel - **1.** *tᶜaarak (a ᶜarka).* This man quarrels with everyone. *haaδa yitᶜaarak wiyya l-kull.* **2.** *txaaṣam (a taxaaṣum), tjaadal (a tajaadul).* The committee members quarreled over financial matters. *ˀaᶜδaaˀ il-lujna txaaṣmaw ẓawl iš-šuˀuun il-maaliyya.* **3.** *tnaazaᶜ (a tanaazuᶜ).* The sons of the deceased quarreled over his estate the day after he died. *wild il-marẓuum itnaazᶜaw ᶜala tarakta ˀawwal yoom baᶜad wafaata.*
quarrelsome - **1.** *jadali*.* He is so quarrelsome nobody likes him. *haaδa fadd waaẓid jadali maẓẓad yẓibba.* **2.** *qarač.* She is the most quarrelsome women in the whole neighborhood. *haay ˀakθar wiẓda qarač bil-maẓalla.* **3.** *wakiiẓ, wakiẓ.* He is a quarrelsome boy, always picking fights with the other children. *haaδa walad wakiẓ kull wakit ydawwir ᶜarkaat wiyya l-wulid il-baaqiyyiin.*
quarry - *maqlaᶜ* pl. *maqaaliᶜ, maẓjar* pl. *maẓaajir.* All the stone is from a local quarry. *kull iṣ-ṣaxar min maqlaᶜ maẓalli.*
quarter - **1.** *rubuᶜ* pl. *ˀarbaaᶜ, čaarak* pl. *čwaariik.* It's a quarter to seven. *saaᶜa sabᶜa ˀilla rubuᶜ.* **2.** *rubuᶜ* pl. *ˀarbaaᶜ.* Three quarters of the harvest was damaged. *tlatt irbaaᶜ il-maẓṣuul tilaf.* **3.** *ẓayy* pl. *ˀaẓyaaˀ.* These are the old quarters of the city. *haay il-ˀaẓyaaˀ il-qadiima mnil-madiina.* **4.** *maskan* pl. *masaakin.* The officers' quarters are at the far end of the camp. *masaakin iδ-δubbaaṭ ib-nihaayat il-muᶜaskar.* **5.** *waṣaṭ* pl. *ˀawṣaaṭ.* It is maintained in some quarters that the plan will not work. *yguuluun ib-baᶜδ il-ˀawṣaaṭ ˀann il-xiṭṭa ma-raẓ-tinjaẓ.*
to quarter - *sakkan (ı taskiin) t-.* They quartered the troops in the schoolhouse during the emergency. *sakknaw ij-jinuud ib-binaayt il-madrasa ˀaθnaaˀ ẓaalt iṭ-ṭawaariˀ.*
quarterly - **1.** *majalla* (pl. *-aat*) *faṣliyya.* This article appeared in the quarterly published by the society. *hal-maqaal innišar bil-majalla l-faṣliyya lli tuṣdurha j-jamᶜiyya.* **2.** *kull itlaθt išhur, ˀarbaᶜ marraat bis-sana.* We pay the interest on the loan quarterly. *nidfaᶜ il-faayiz ᶜala d-deen kull itlaθt išhur.*
quarter-master - *δaabuṭ* (pl. *δubbaaṭ*) *ˀiᶜaaša.*
quarters - *maskan* pl. *masaakin.* Did you find decent quarters? *ligeet-lak fadd maskan muẓtaram?*
at close quarters - *mitlaaẓim, maxbuuṣ.* They fought at close quarters. *tᶜaarkaw mitlaaẓmiin.*
quartz - *kwaarits.*
quaver - *raᶜša* pl. *-aat, rajfa* pl. *-aat.* There was a quaver in her voice as she asked the question. *čaan ˀaku raᶜša b-ẓissha min siˀlat is-suˀaal.*
to quaver - *riᶜaš (i raᶜiš), rijaf (i rajif).* The old man is feeble, and his voice quavers when he talks. *š-šaayib δaᶜiif w-ẓissa yirᶜiš min yiẓči.*
quay - *raṣiif* pl. *ˀarṣifa.*
queasy - **I feel queasy from all the rich food. *nafsi da-tilᶜab min kull il-ˀakil id-dasim.*
queen - **1.** *malika* pl. *-aat.* Her majesty, the Queen, has come! *ṣaaẓibat ij-jalaala, l-malika, jatti!* **2.** *waziir* pl. *wuzaraaˀ.* I am going to take your queen with the knight. *raẓ-aaxuδ waziirak bil-iẓṣaan.* **3.** *bnayya* pl. *banaat, qizza* pl. *-aat.* I have two jacks and three queens in my hand. *ᶜindi waladeen w-itlaθ banaat b-iidi.*
queer - **1.** *nimuuna, ᶜantiika.* He is a queer bird. *haaδa fadd waaẓid nimuuna.* **2.** *šaaδδ.* What a queer idea! *šloon fikra šaaδδa!*
to **quell** - *qimaᶜ (a qamiᶜ) n-, ˀaxmad (i ˀixmaad) n-.* Troops were quickly dispatched to quell the uprising. *j-jiyuuš indazzat ib-surᶜa ẓatta tiqmaᶜ iθ-θawra.*
to **quench** - *ruwa (i rawi) n-.* This won't quench my thirst. *haaδa ma-yirwi ᶜaṭaši.*
querulous - *naẓis.* She has become a querulous old lady. *ṣaayra fadd ᶜajuuz naẓsa.*
query - *stifhaam* pl. *-aat, stiᶜlaam* pl. *-aat.* This pamphlet should answer any queries there might be. *hal-kurraasa laazim itjaawab ᶜala kull il-istifhaamaat.*
quest - *baẓθ.* The quest for happiness continues all our life. *l-baẓθ ᶜan is-saᶜaada yistamirr ṭuul ᶜumurna.*
question - **1.** *suˀaal* pl. *ˀasˀila.* Have you any further questions. *ᶜindak ˀasˀila lux?* **2.** *qaδiyya* pl. *qaδaaya.* It was a question of saving a human life. *čaanat qaδiyyat ˀinqaaδ ẓayaat bašariyya.* **3.** *masˀala* pl. *masaaˀil.* It's still an open question. *baᶜadha masˀala biiha ˀaxiδ w-radd.*
**That's completely out of the question. *haaδa mustaẓiil.* or *haay la-tsoolifha.* or *haay ṭalliᶜha min l-iẓsaab.*
beyond question - *ma-bii suˀaal, foog iš-šubhaat, ma-maškuuk bii.* His honesty is beyond question. *nazaahta ma-biiha suˀaal.*
in question - *maqṣuud, maᶜni.* The gentleman in question was not there. *r-rijjaal il-maqṣuud ma-čaan ihnaak.*
to ask a question - *siˀal (a suˀaal) n-.* They asked a lot of questions. *siˀlaw ihwaaya ˀasˀila.*
to question - **1.** *stajwab (i stijwaab).* The police questioned him all night long. *š-šurṭa stajwiboo ṭuul il-leel.* **2.** *šakk (u šakk) n- b-.* I question his sincerity. *ˀašukk ib-ˀixlaaṣa.*
question mark - *ᶜalaamat* (pl. *-aat*) *istifhaam, ᶜalaamat* (pl. *-aat*) *suˀaal.*
questionnaire - *qaaˀimat* (pl. *-aat*) *ˀasˀila.*
queue - *sira* pl. *-aawaat.* The queue in front of the ticket window was so long I didn't want to wait. *s-sira qiddaam šibbaak il-biṭaaqaat čaan hal-gadd ṭuwiil ma-ridt antiδir.*
to queue up - *lizam (a) n- sira.* People usually queue up for the buses at rush hours. *n-naas ᶜaadatan yilzamuun sira ᶜal-paaṣ wakt il-izdiẓaam.*
quick - **1.** *sariiᶜ, ᶜaajil.* That was a quick decision. *haaδa čaan qaraar sariiᶜ.* -- All his movements are quick. *kull ẓarakaata sariiᶜa.* **2.** *laẓam ẓayy.* I

cut my fingernail to the quick. *gaṣṣeet iẟifri lil-laẓam il-ẓayy.*
**His remark touched the quick. *ẓičaayta wuṣlat il-laẓam il-ẓayy.* or *ẓičaayta daggat bil-Ɛaẟum.*
to be quick - *staƐjal (i stiƐjaal).* Be quick about it. *staƐjil biiha.*
to **quicken** - *Ɛajjal (i tƐijjil) t- b-, sarraƐ (i tasriiƐ) t-.* He quickened his steps. *Ɛajjal ib-xaṭwaata.*
quickly - *b-surƐa, bil-Ɛajal.* He does things quickly. *ysawwi kullši b-surƐa.*
quicksilver - *zeebag, sleemaani.*
quick-tempered - *ẓaadd iṭ-ṭabuƐ.* She is very quick-tempered. *hiyya kulliš ẓaaddat iṭ-ṭabuƐ.* or **raasha ẓaarr.*
quiet - **1.** *haadi?.* I live in a quiet neighborhood. *?askun ib-ṭaraf haadi?.* **2.** *ṣanṭa, haadi?.* It is very quiet here. *kulliš ṣanṭa hnaa.* **3.** *saakit, ṣanṭa.* Why are you so quiet? *leeš saakit?* or *š-biik hal-gadd ṣanṭa?* **4.** *sukuut, ṣanṭa.* Quiet, please! *sukuut, rajaa?an!* or *ṣanṭa, rajaa?an!*
to keep quiet - *buqa (a baqaa?) saakit, sikat (u sukuut).* Why didn't you keep quiet? *lweeš ma-buqeet saakit?*
to quiet - **1.** *hadda (i tahdiya, thiddi) t-, sakkat (i taskiit) t-.* Samira, go see if you can quiet the baby. *samiira, ruuẓi šuufi ?iẟa tgidriin ithaddiin j-jaahil.* **2.** *hida? (a huduu?).* Let's wait until the excitement quiets down a bit. *xal-nintiẟir ?ila ?an yihda? il-ẓamaas.* -- She quieted down after a while. *hid?at baƐad fadd fatra.*
quilt - *lẓaaf* pl. *liẓfaan.*
quince - *sfarjala* pl. *-aat* coll. *sfarjal, ẓeewaaya* pl. *-aat, ẓeewaat* coll. *ẓeewa.*
quinine - *kiniin, kiina, qanaqiina.*
to **quit** - **1.** *baṭṭal (i tbuṭṭul) t- min.* He quit his job yesterday. *baṭṭal min šuġla l-baarẓa.* -- Quit it! *baṭṭil!* or **bass Ɛaad!* or **juuz* -- Let's call it quits! *xalli nbaṭṭil!* **2.** *jaaz (u jooz) n-.* I told him a thousand times to quit and he didn't. *gilit-la ?alif marra yjuuz laakin ma-jaaz.*
**It's time to quit. *ṣaar wakt it-tabṭiila.* or *ṣaar wakt il-ẓalla.* or *paaydoos.*
quite - **1.** *hwaaya, kulliš.* That's quite possible. *haay kulliš jaa?iz.* -- It turned quite cold during the night. *burdat kulliš ihwaaya bil-leel.* **2.** *ṣudug* That was quite an experience. *haay ṣudug čaanat tajruba.* **3.** *tamaaman, b-ẟabuṭ, kulliš.* Are you quite sure that you can't go? *?inta mit?akkid tamaaman ma-tigdar itruuẓ?*
quiz - *xtibaar* pl. *-aat.* The teacher gives us a short quiz everyday. *l-muƐallim yinṭiina xtibaar qaṣiir kull yoom.*
quorum - *niṣaab.* We couldn't vote on the bill because we didn't have a quorum. *ma-gidarna nṣawwiṭ Ɛal-laa?iẓa li-?an ma-ẓiṣal in-niṣaab.*
quota - *koota, ẓiṣṣa, taxṣiiṣaat.* There is some talk of increasing the quota for foreign cars next year. *?aku ẓači ẓawl ziyaadat il-koota lis-sayyaaraat il-?ajnabiyya sant ij-jaaya.*
quotation - **1.** *stišhaad* pl. *-aat.* His speech was full of quotations. *ẓadiiθa čaan malyaan bil-istišhaadaat.* **2.** *siƐir* pl. *?asƐaar.* This newspaper publishes the stock market quotations. *haj-jariida tinšur ?asƐaar il-boorṣa.*
quotation mark - *Ɛalaamat* (pl. *-aat*) *ẓaṣir.*
to **quote** - **1.** *stašhad (i stišhaad) b-.* That's quoted on page ten. *haay mustašhad biiha b-ṣafẓa Ɛašra.* **2.** *Ɛiraẟ (i Ɛariẟ) n-, niṭa (i) n-.* What price did he quote you? *šinu s-siƐir il-Ɛiraẟ-ilk-iyyaa?*
**Don't quote me. *la-tinqulha Ɛann ilsaani.*
quotient - *ẓaaṣil il-qisma.* If you divide fifteen by five the quotient is three. *?aẟa tqassim ixmuṣṭaƐas Ɛala xamsa ẓaaṣil il-qisma tlaaθa.*

R

rabbit - *?arnab* pl. *?araanib.*
race - **1.** *sibaaq* pl. *-aat, reesiz.* When does the race start? *šwakit yibdi s-sibaaq?* **2.** *jinis* pl. *?ajnaas.* The yellow race is found in eastern Asia. *j-jins il-?aṣfar mawjuud ib-šarq ?aasya.*
to race - *tsaabaq (a musaabaqa), tġaalab (a taġaalub, muġaalaba).* Let's race. *xal-nitsaabaq.*
**Don't race the engine. *la-tijhid il-makiina.*
**The car raced through the streets. *s-sayyaara čaanat ṭayra biš-šawaariƐ.*
rack - **1.** *raff* pl. *rfuuf.* Put the books back on the rack. *rajjiƐ il-kutub Ɛar-raft.* -- Put your baggage up on the rack. *ẓuṭṭ junaṭak Ɛar-raff.* **2.** *tiƐlaaqa* pl. *-aat.* I hung my coat on the rack. *Ɛallaqit sitirti Ɛat-tiƐlaaqa.* **3.** *mišjab* pl. *mašaajib.* The soldiers put the guns on the rack. *j-junuud ẓaṭṭaw il-banaadiq bil-mišjab.*
**Don't rack your brains over it. *la-tdawwux raasak biiha.*
racket - **1.** *hoosa* pl. *-aat.* The children are making an awful racket. *l-?aṭfaal da-ysawwuun ġeer hoosa.* **2.** *liƐba* pl. *liƐab.* This whole business is nothing but a racket. *haš-šaġla liƐba mnil-?asaas.* **3.** *rakit* pl. *-aat, maẟrab* pl. *maẟaarib.* Her racket is much too heavy for you. *r-rakit maalha kulliš θigiil Ɛaleeč.*
radiator - *raadeeta* pl. *-aat.* Something is wrong with the radiator of my car. *?aku šii bir-raadeeta maal sayyaarti.*
radical - **1.** *miṭṭarrif* pl. *-iin.* I consider him a radical. *?aani ?aƐtabra miṭṭarrif.* -- He has very radical views. *Ɛinda wajhaat naẟar kulliš miṭṭarrfa.* **2.** *?asaasi*.* He wants to make some radical changes. *yriid ysawwi baƐẟ it-taġyiiraat il-?asaasiyya.*
radio - *raadyo* pl. *-uwwaat.* Was it announced over the radio? *nẟaaƐat bir-raadyo?*
to radio - *ẟaaƐ (i ?idaaƐa) n-.* They radioed from the plane that they were in trouble. *ẟaaƐaw imniṭ-ṭayyaara bi-?an Ɛidhum muškila.*
radio station - *maẓaṭṭat* (pl. *-aat*) *?iẟaaƐa.*
radish - *fijlaaya* pl. *-aat* coll. *fijil.* Shall I slice up the radishes? *?agaṣgiṣ il-fijil?*
raft - *čalač* pl. *člaač, kalak* pl. *klaak.*
rag - *xirga* pl. *xirag, wuṣla* pl. *wuṣal.* Do you have a rag to dust the table? *Ɛindič fadd wuṣla l-masẓ il-meez?*
to **rage** - **1.** *haaj (i hiyaaj, hayajaan), ẓtadd (a ẓidda), θaar (u θawra).* He raged like a bull. *haaj miθl iθ-θoor.* **2.** *gabb (u gabb).* The storm raged all night long. *l-Ɛaaṣifa ẟallat gaabba ṭuul il-leel.*
ragged - *mxalgan.* They were wearing ragged clothes. *čaanaw laabsiin ihduum imxalgina.*
rail - *sičča* pl. *sičač, sikka* pl. *sikak.* A loose rail caused the accident. *faad qisim raaxi mnis-sičča sabbab il-ẓaadiθ.*
railing - *mẓajjar* pl. *-aat.* Hold on to the railing. *?ilzam l-imẓajjar.*
railroad - *qiṭaar* pl. *-aat, sikkat* (pl. *sikak*) *ẓadiid.* I prefer to go by railroad. *?afaẟẟil aruuẓ bil-qiṭaar.* -- Our house is near the railroad. *beetna yamm is-sikka.*
railroad station - *maẓaṭṭat* (pl. *-aat*) *qiṭaar.*
rain - *muṭar* pl. *?amṭaar.* We stayed home because of the rain. *bqeena bil-beet ib-sabab il-muṭar.*
to rain - *muṭar (u muṭar).* It rained hard all morning. *muṭrat ib-quwwa ṭuul iṣ-ṣubuẓ.*
rainbow - *qooz qazaẓ, gooz gadaẓ.*
raincoat - *mšammaƐ* pl. *-aat.*
rainy - *mumṭir.*
raise - *ziyaada* pl. *-aat, tarfiiƐ* pl. *-aat.* They gave me a raise. *nṭooni ziyaada.*
to raise - **1.** *šaal (i šeel) n-.* Use the jack to raise the car. *staƐmil ij-jagg il-šeel is-sayyaara.* -- They didn't even raise their heads from their work as we passed. *wala šaalaw ruushum min šuġulhum min marreena.* **2.** *rufaƐ (a rafuƐ) n-.* All those in favor, raise your hands. *kull il-mu?ayyidiin, ?irfaƐu ?iideekum.* -- They raised the siege and withdrew. *rifƐaw il-ẓiṣaar w-insiẓbaw.* **3.** *rtifaƐ (i rtifaaƐ)* The bread won't raise without yeast. *l-Ɛajiin ma-yirtifiƐ bala xumra.* **4.** *Ɛalla (i taƐliya) t-.* Raise the picture a little; it's not all on the screen. *Ɛalli ṣ-ṣuura šwayya, muu kullha Ɛal-parda.* -- Raise the volume a little on the radio. *Ɛalli ẓiss ir-raadyo šwayya.* **5.** *ṣaƐƐad (i taṣƐiid) t-.* He showed us how they raise and lower the irrigation gates. *raawaana šloon yṣaƐƐiduun w-ynazziluun ?abwaab is-saqi.* **6.** *zayyad (i tazyiid, ziyaada) t-.*

The rent will be raised on October first. *l-ʔajaar raẓ-yitzayyad ib-ʔawwal tišriin ʔawwal.* — The company has promised to raise our salaries all across the board. *š-šarika wuƐdat itzayyid rawaatibna jamiiƐan.* **7.** *raqqa (i tarqiya) t-.* They raised him from clerk to supervisor. *raqqoo min kaatib ʔila mulaaẓiδ.* **8.** *ziraƐ (a zariƐ) n-.* They raise a lot of wheat here. *yzirƐuun ihwaaya ẓunṭa hnaa.* **9.** *rabba (i tarbiya) t-.* She has raised nine children. *rabbat tisiƐ ʔaṭfaal.* — Most farmers here raise sheep. *ʔakθar iz-zurraaƐ ihnaa yrabbuun ġanam.* **10.** *dabbar (u tadbiir) t-.* I couldn't raise the money. *ma-gdarit adabbur l-ifluus.* **11.** *jimaƐ (a jamiƐ) n-.* Our club is raising money to aid the flood victims. *naadiina da-yijmaƐ ifluus il-ʔiġaaθat mankuubi l-fayaδaan.*
**The kids are raising the roof again. *j-jihaal da-yguḷbuun id-dinya marra lux.*
to raise a question - *ʔaθaar (i ʔiθaara) mawδuuƐ.* Who raised the question? *minu ʔaθaar il-mawδuuƐ?*

range - **1.** *ṭabbaax* pl. *-aat.* We just bought a new range. *hastawwna štireena ṭabbaax jidiid.* **2.** *marƐa* pl. *maraaƐi.* In the spring the sheep go out on the range. *bir-rabiiƐ il-ġanam yruuẓuun lil-marƐa.* **3.** *saaẓa* pl. *-aat, maydaan* pl. *mayaadiin.* The new recruits spent their first day on the firing range today. *l-mujannadiin ij-jiddad giδaw yoomhum il-ʔawwal ib-saaẓt ir-rami hal-yoom.* **4.** *mada* pl. *-aayaat, marma* pl. *maraami, niṭaaq* pl. *ʔanṭiqa.* The tanks were out of range of our guns. *d-dabbaabaat čaanat xaarij niṭaaq madaafiƐna.*
to range - **1.** *traawaẓ (a taraawuẓ).* The prices range from one to five dinars. *l-ʔasƐaar titraawaẓ min diinaar ʔila xamis danaaniir.* **3.** *tjawwal (a tajawwul).* The bedouin range the western desert with their flocks. *l-badu yitjawwaluun biṣ-ṣaẓraaʔ il-ġarbiyya wiyya qiṭƐaanhum.*

rank - **1.** *rutba* pl. *rutab.* What's the officer's rank? *šinu rutbat haδ-δaabuṭ?* **2.** *kaθθ.* His face was covered by a rank growth of beard. *wuččа čaan imġaṭṭa b-liẓya kaθθa.*

rapid - *sariiƐ.*

rare - **1.** *naadir.* That's a rare flower. *haaδi warda naadra.* **2.** *Ɛan-nuṣṣ.* I'd like my steak broiled rare. *ʔariid il-laẓam maali mašwi Ɛan-nuṣṣ.*

rarely - *naadiran, mnin-naadir.* That rarely happens. *haaδa naadiran yiẓduθ.*

rascal - *šiiṭaan, šayṭaan* pl. *šayaaṭiin.*

rash - **1.** *ẓaṣaf.* There is a rash on his face. *ʔaku ẓaṣaf ib-wuččа.* **2.** *mooja* pl. *ʔamwaaj.* Last month there was a rash of robberies. *š-šahr il-faat čaan ʔaku moojat boog.* **3.** *mitsarriƐ, bala tarawwi, bala ʔimƐaan.* Don't make any rash promises. *la-tinṭi wuƐuud bala tarawwi.*

rat - *jreedi* pl. *-iyya.*

rate - **1.** *siƐir* pl. *ʔasƐaar, ʔujra* pl. *ʔujur, ʔujuur.* What are the rates for single rooms? *šgadd siƐr il-ġurfa ʔumm sariir waaẓid?* — What are the new rates for airmail? *šinu l-ʔujuur ij-jidiida lil-bariid ij-jawwi?* — The rate of interest is four per cent. *siƐr il-faaʔida ʔarbaƐa bil-miyya.* **2.** *muƐaddal.* At this rate we'll never get done. *Ɛala hal-muƐaddal wala raẓ-inxalliṣ.*
at any rate - *Ɛala kull ẓaal.* At any rate, I'd like to see you. *Ɛala kull ẓaal, ʔaani da-ariid ašuufak.*
first-rate - *daraja ʔuula, ṣinif ʔawwal, mumtaaz.* It's definitely a first-rate hotel. *haaδa bila šakk ʔuteel daraja ʔuula.*

rather - **1.** *šwayya, nawƐan-ma.* The play was rather long. *r-ruwaaya čaanat nawƐan-ma ṭwiila.*
**I would rather wait. *ʔaani ʔafaδδil antiδir.*
**I'd rather die than give in. *ʔaani ʔafaδδil il-moot Ɛat-tasliim.*

ration - *quṣƐa* pl. *quṣaƐ, taƐyiin* pl. *-aat.* Our rations consisted of bread and soup. *quṣƐatna čaanat xubuz w-šoorba.*
to ration - *wazzaƐ (i tawziiƐ) bil-biṭaaqaat, ẓaddad (i taẓdiid) t- tawziiƐ.* Sugar was rationed. *š-šakar itwazzaƐ bil-biṭaaqaat.* — They rationed the meats. *ẓaddidaw tawziiƐ il-laẓam.*

rattle - *xirxaaša* pl. *xaraaxiiš.* They bought the baby a rattle. *štiraw xirxaaša liṭ-ṭifil.*
to rattle - **1.** *ṭarbag (i ṭarbaga), xašxaš (i xašxaša, txišxiš) t-.* Do you have to rattle the dishes that way? *ʔaku muujib iṭṭarbig hiiči bil-immaaƐiin?* — There is a kind of snake that rattles. *ʔaku nooƐ imnil-ẓayyaat itxašxiš.* **2.** *šawwaš (i tašwiiš) t-, xarbaṭ (u xarbaṭa) t-.* Don't rattle me. *la-tšawwišni.*
to rattle on - *θarθar (i θarθara), liġa (i laġwa).* She can rattle on like that for hours. *tigdar itθarθir haš-šikil il-muddat saaƐaat.*

to rave - *hiδa (i hiδyaan).* He raved like a madman. *hiδa miθl il-majnuun.*

raw - **1.** *niyy.* The meat is almost raw. *l-laẓam niyy taqriiban.* **2.** *miltihib.* My throat is raw. *zarduumi miltihib.*
**He got a raw deal. *ṣaaba ġubun.*

ray - **1.** *šuƐaaƐ* pl. *ʔašiƐƐa.* Ordinary panes of glass keep out ultraviolet rays. *j-jaam il-Ɛaadi yimnaƐ il-ʔašiƐƐa fooq il-banafsajiyya.* **2.** *baṣiiṣ.* There's still a ray of hope. *li-hassa ʔaku fadd baṣiiṣ imnil-ʔamal.*

rayon - *rayoon.*

razor - *muus* pl. *mwaas.* I have to strop my razor. *laazim ʔaẓidd il-muus maali.*
safety razor - *makiinat* (pl. *makaayin*) *ziyaan.* I can't find my safety razor. *ma-da-agdar algi makiinat iz-ziyaan maalti.*

razor blade - *muus* pl. *mwaas, mwaasa.* Please buy me a dozen razor blades. *ʔarjuuk ištirii-li darzan imwaasa.*

to **reach** - **1.** *madd (i madd) ʔiid˜.* The little fellow reaches for everything he sees. *haz-zaƐṭuuṭ ymidd ʔiida Ɛala kullši yšuufa.* — He reached into his pocket. *madd ʔiida b-jeeba.* **2.** *mtadd (a mtidaad).* The garden reaches all the way to the river. *l-ẓadiiqa timtadd liš-šaṭṭ.* **3.** *wuṣal (a wuṣuul) ʔila.* The rumor even reached us. *l-ʔišaaƐa wuṣlat ẓatta ʔilna.* — The radio reaches millions of people. *r-raadyo yooṣal ʔila malaayiin imnin-naas.* — We reached the city at daybreak. *wuṣalna l-wlaaya wučč iṣ-ṣubuẓ.* **4.** *ttiṣal (i ttiṣaal) b-.* There was no way of reaching him. *ma-čaan ʔaku fadd ṭariiqa nittiṣil bii.* **5.** *naaš (u nooš) n-.* Can you reach that shelf? *tigdar itnuuš δaak ir-raff?* **6.** *naawaš (u mnaawaša).* Reach me the hammer. *naawušni č-čaakuuč.*

reaction - **1.** *radd fiƐil.* What was his reaction? *š-čaan radd il-fiƐil Ɛinda?* **2.** *tafaaƐul.* You can speed up the reaction if you beat the mixture. *tigdar itsarriƐ it-tafaaƐul ʔiδa tsaxxin il-maziij.*

reactionary - *rajƐi**.

to **read** - **1.** *qira (a qraaya) n-.* You should read this book. *laazim tiqra hal-iktaab.* — The text reads differently. *l-matin yiqra ġeer šikil.* — Please read it to me. *ʔarjuuk iqraa-li-yyaaha.* **2.** *ʔaššar (i taʔšiir) t- Ɛala.* The thermometer reads 35 degrees. *l-miẓraar yʔaššir xala xamsa w-itlaaθiin daraja.*

reader - **1.** *qaariʔ* pl. *qurraaʔ.* This newspaper has more than a million readers. *haj-jariida ʔilha ʔazyad min milyoon qaariʔ.* **2.** *ktaab* (pl. *kutub*) *muṭaalaƐa.* Do you have my English reader? *Ɛindak iktaab il-muṭaalaƐa l-ʔingiliizi maali?*

readily - *bila taraddud, b-surƐa, bil-Ɛajal.* He admitted it readily. *Ɛtiraf biiha bila taraddud.* — She consented readily. *qiblat ib-surƐa.*

reading - *qiraaʔa.* He got excellent in reading. *ʔaxaδ jayyid jiddan bil-qiraaʔa.*

ready - **1.** *ẓaaδir.* When will dinner be ready? *šwakit ykuun il-Ɛaša ẓaaδir?* **2.** *mistiƐidd, ẓaaδir.* I'm ready for anything. *ʔaani mistiƐidd il-kullši.* **3.** *jaahiz.* The house is ready for occupancy. *l-beet jaahiz lis-sikna.* **4.** *jawwa l-ʔiid.* I don't have any ready cash just now. *ma-aku fluus jawwa ʔiidi hassa.*
to get ready - **1.** *staƐadd (i stiƐdaad), tẓaδδar (a taẓaδδur).* Get ready, go! *ʔistaƐiddu, ʔibdaʔ!* — My brother is getting ready to go out. *ʔaxuuya da-yitẓaδδar liṭ-ṭalƐa.* **2.** *ẓaδδar (i taẓδiir) t-.* My wife is getting the food ready. *marti da-tẓaδδir il-ʔakil.*

ready-made - *jaahiz, ẓaaδir.* Do you buy your clothes ready-made? *tištiri hduumak jaahza?*

real - **1.** *ẓaqiiqi**. That's not his real name. *haaδa muu ʔisma l-ẓaqiiqi.* **2.** *ʔaṣli**. Is this real silk? *haaδa ẓariir ʔaṣli?* **3.** *min ṣidug.* That's what I call a real friend. *haaδa l-asammii ṣadiiq min ṣidug.* **4.** *waaqiƐ.* That never happens in real life. *haaδa ʔabad ma-yiẓduθ bil-waaqiƐ.*

real estate - *ʔamlaak.*

reality - *ẓaqiiqa, waaqiƐ.*

to **realize** - **1.** *ẓaqqaq (i taẓqiiq) t-.* He never realized his ambition to become a doctor. *ʔabadan ma-ẓaqqaq ṭumuuẓa bi-ʔan yṣiir ṭabiib.* **2.** *ṭallaƐ (i taṭliiƐ) t-.* He realized quite a profit on that deal. *ṭallaƐ xooš ribiẓ ib-δiič iš-šaġla.* **3.** *tṣawwar (a taṣawwur).* I simply can't realize he's dead. *ma-da-agdar aṭṣawwar ʔanna mayyit.* — I didn't realize it was so late. *ma-tṣawwarit hal-gadd il-wakit mitʔaxxir.* **4.** *ʔadrak (u ʔidraak).* Does he realize how sick he is? *da-yidruk išgadd mariiδ huwwa?*

5. *qaddar (i taqdiir) t-*. He doesn't realize how much work is involved. *ma-da-yqaddir išgadd biiha šuğuḷ.* -- I never realized the danger. *ma-qaddart il-xaṭar ʔabadan.*

really - 1. *ẓaqiiqatan, ṣ-ṣudug.* Do you really mean it? *ʔinta ẓaqiiqatan tiƐniiha.* -- I really wanted to stay at home. *ṣ-ṣudug ʔaani ridit ʔabqa bil-beet.* 2. *bil-ẓaqiiqa.* He is really younger than he looks. *huwwa bil-ẓaqiiqa ʔaṣğar min-ma ybayyin Ɛalee.*
**I really don't know. *waḷḷa ma-adri.*

rear - 1. *ḍahar* pl. *ḍuhuur.* The rear of the house is being painted. *ḍahr il-beet da-yinṣubuğ.* 2. *maqƐad* pl. *maqaaƐid.* She fell on her rear. *wugƐat Ɛala maqƐadha.* 3. *xalfi**. The rear row is empty. *s-sira l-xalfi faariğ.* 4. *warraani**. The rear windows haven't been cleaned yet. *š-šibaabiič il-warraaniyya baƐad ma-tnaḍḍfat.*
in the rear - *bil-xalf, li-wara.* The emergency exit is in the rear. *baab iṭ-ṭawaari bil-xalf.*

to **rearrange** - *ʔaƐaad (i ʔiƐaada) tartiib, tanḍiim.* You ought to rearrange the furniture. *laazim itƐiid tartiib il-ʔaθaaθ.*

reason - 1. *daaƐi* pl. *dawaaƐi.* She really has no reason for acting like that. *ẓaqiiqatan ma-aku daaƐi hiyya titṣarraf haš-šikil.* 2. *baaƐiθ* pl. *bawaaƐiθ.* I see no reason for complaint. *ma-ašuuf baaƐiθ liš-šakwa.* 3. *sabab* pl. *ʔasbaab, Ɛilla* pl. *Ɛilal.* Is that the reason you didn't go? *haaḍa sabab Ɛadam rooẓtak?* 4, *Ɛaqil, ṣawaab.* Please use your reason. *rajaaʔan ẓakkum Ɛaqlak.* -- If this keeps up, I'll lose my reason. *ʔiḍa haay raẓ-tistimirr ʔaani raẓ-afqud ṣawaabi.*
to reason - *tẓaajaj (a taẓaajuj), tfaaham (a tafaahum).* You can't reason with him. *ma-tigdar titẓaajaj wiyyaa.*

reasonable - 1. *maƐquul.* She's a very reasonable person. *hiyya fadd waẓda kulliš maƐquula.* 2. *mnaasib.* They sell their books at reasonable prices. *ybiiƐuun kutubhum ib-ʔasƐaar imnaasba.*

reasonably - *b-Ɛaqil.* He acted reasonably. *ṭṣarraf ib-Ɛaqil.*

to **rebel** - *Ɛiṣa (a Ɛiṣyaan).* The troops rebelled against their commander. *j-junuud Ɛiṣaw Ɛala qaaʔidhum.*
**My stomach simply rebelled. *nafsi ma-qiblat.*

to **recall** - 1. *tḍakkar (a taḍakkur).* Do you recall whether he was there or not? *titḍakkar ʔiḍa huwwa čaan ihnaak loo laa?* 2. *stadƐa (i stidƐaaʔ).* I read in the paper that your government has recalled its ambassador. *qireet bij-jariida ẓukuumatkum istadƐat safiirha.*

receipt - 1. *waṣil* pl. *wuṣuulaat.* Please give me a receipt. *rajaaʔan inṭiini waṣil.* 2. *daxaḷ.* The receipts were low today. *d-daxaḷ čaan qaliil hal-yoom.* 3. *wuṣuul.* Please acknowledge receipt of this letter. *rajaaʔan ʔaƐlimuuna b-wuṣuul hal-maktuub.*
to receipt - **Please receipt this bill. *ʔarjuuk ʔaššir hal-qaaʔima Ɛtiraafan bil-wuṣuul.*

to **receive** - 1. *stilam (i stilaam).* Did you receive my telegram? *stilamit barqiiti?* 2. *qubaḍ (u qabuḍ) n-.* You'll receive your salary in case on the first of the month. *raẓ-tiqbuḍ raatbak ib-ʔawwal iš-šahar.* 3. *staqbal (i stiqbaal).* They received us cordially. *staqbiloona b-tarẓiib.*

receiver - 1. *simmaaƐa* pl. *-aat.* You didn't put the receiver back on the hook. *ma-rajjaƐt is-simmaaƐa b-makaanha.* 2. *mustalim* pl. *-iin.* Write the receiver's name legibly. *ʔiktib ism il-mustalim ib-wuḍuuẓ.*

recent - 1. *ẓadiiθ.* . Television is a comparatively recent invention. *t-talafizyoon fadd ixtiraaƐ ẓadiiθ nisbiyya.* 2. *jidiid.* Don't you have any recent issues? *ma-Ɛindak ʔay ʔaƐdaad jidiida?.* 3. *ʔaxiir.* Did you hear of the recent revolution in the north? *simaƐit Ɛan iθ-θawra l-ʔaxiira biš-šimaal?*

recently - *ʔaxiiran, ẓadiiθan.* I heard it recently. *smaƐitha ʔaxiiran.*

reception -!1. *stiqbaal.* He gave us a warm reception. *staqbalna stiqbaal ẓaarr.* 2. *ltiqaaṭ.* Reception is poor today on the radio. *l-iltiqaaṭ muu zeen hal-yoom bir-raadyo.* 3. *ẓaflat* (pl. *-aat*) *istiqbaal.* Have you been invited to the reception? *nƐizamit il-ẓaflat l-istiqbaal?*

recess - 1. *furṣa* pl. *furaṣ, fatra* pl. *-aat.* We have a short recess at ten in the morning. *naaxuḍ furṣa gṣayyra saaƐa Ɛašra ṣ-ṣubuẓ.* 2. *liiwaan* pl. *lawaawiin.* The recesses of the mosque are cool. *lawaawiin il-masjid baarda.*

recipe - *waṣfa* pl. *-aat.* Do you have a simple recipe for a cake? *Ɛindič fadd waṣfa baṣiiṭa maal keek?*

reckless - *ʔahwaj.* He's reckless driver. *huwwa fadd saayiq ʔahwaj.*

recognition - *taqdiir, Ɛtiraaf.* He didn't get the recognition he deserved. *ma-ẓaṣṣal Ɛala t-taqdiir illi yistiẓiqqa.*

to **recognize** - 1. *Ɛiraf (u maƐrifa) n-.* At first I didn't recognize you. *bil-ʔawwal ma-Ɛraftak.* 3. *Ɛtiraf (i Ɛtiraaf).* The United States does not recognize that country. *l-wilaayaat il-muttaẓida ma-tiƐtirif ib-had-dawla.*

to **recommend** - *waṣṣa (i tawṣiya) b-.* I recommended her highly to him. *waṣṣeeta kulliš biiha.* or *nṭeeta biiha tawṣiya qawwiyya.*

recommendation - *tawṣiya* pl. *-aat.* I did it on your recommendation. *sawweetha ẓasab tawṣiitak.*

record - 1. *qayd* pl. *qiyuud.* I can't find any record of that bill. *ma-da-agdar algi ʔay qayd ib-hal-qaaʔima.* 2. *sijill* pl. *-aat.* He has a criminal record. *Ɛinda sijill sawaabiq.* 3. *taariix.* That was the worst earthquake on record. *haaḍa čaan ʔaswaʔ zilzaal bit-taariix.* or *haaḍa čaan ʔawsaʔ zilzaal imsajjal.* 4. *ṣṭiwaana* pl. *-aat, qawaana* pl. *-aat.* They have a good selection of classical records. *Ɛidhum xooš majmuuƐa mnil-iṣṭiwaanaat il-iklaasiikiyya.* 5. *raqam qiyaasi* pl. *ʔarqaam qiyaasiyya.* He broke all records in free style swimming. *kisar kull il-ʔarqaam il-qiyaasiyya bis-sibaaẓa l-ẓurra.* -- We had a record crop this year. *ṣaar Ɛidna maẓṣuul qiyaasi has-sana.*
to record - 1. *sajjal (i tasjiil) t-.* Have you recorded everything he said? *sajjalit kullši gaala?* -- Can I use your tape recorder to record something? *ʔagdar astaƐmil il-musajjil maalak ẓatta ʔasajjil šii?* 2. *qayyad (i taqyiid) t-.* Record all payments in this book. *qayyid kull il-madfuuƐaat ib-has-sijill.*

to **recover** - 1. *tšaafa (a tašaafi), tƐaafa (a taƐaafi).* He recovered from his illness quickly. *bil-Ɛajal itšaafa min maraḍa.* 2. *starjaƐ (i stirjaaƐ).* Did you finally recover your watch? *taaliiha starjaƐit saaƐtak?* 3. *staradd (i stirdaad), staƐaad (i stiƐaada).* He recovered his balance immediately. *staradd muwaazanta bil-Ɛajal.*

recovery - *šafaaʔ.* He's on the road to recovery. *huwwa b-ṭariiqa liš-šafaaʔ.*

red - 1. (m.) *ʔaẓmar* (f.) *ẓamra,* pl. *ẓumur.* I want to buy a red hat. *ʔard aštiri šafqa ẓamra.* 2. *ʔaẓmar.* Red is not becoming to her. *l-ʔaẓmar ma-yluug-ilha.*
**I'd rather be dead than Red. *ʔafaḍḍil il-moot Ɛaš-šuyuuƐiyya.*
**I saw red when I heard that. *faar dammi min ismaƐitha.*

Red Crescent - *l-hilaal il-ʔaẓmar.*

Red Cross - *ṣ-ṣaliib il-ʔaẓmar.*

to **reduce** - 1. *xaffaḍ (u taxfiiḍ) t-, nazzal (i tanziil) t-.* We reduced the prices ten per cent. *xaffaḍna l-ʔasƐaar Ɛašra bil-miyya.* 2. *qallal (i taqliil) t-, naggaṣ (i tangiiṣ) t-.* We have to reduce our expenses. *laazim inqallil maṣaariifna.* 3. *ḍaƐƐaf (i taḍƐiif), nazzal (i tanziil).* He can reduce his weight whenever he wants to. *yigdar ynazzil wazna šwakit-ma yriid.*

to **refer** - 1. *ẓawwal (i taẓwiil) t-, ẓaal (i ʔiẓaala) n-.* They referred me to the manager. *ẓawwlooni Ɛal-mudiir.* 2. *šaar (i ʔišaara) n-.* She referred to it in her book. *šaarat ʔilha b-iktaabha.*

reference - 1. *marjiƐ* pl. *maraajiƐ.* You may give my name as a reference. *tigdar tinṭi ʔismi ka-marjiƐ.* 2. *ktaab* (pl. *kutub*) *tawṣiya.* May I see your references? *ʔagdar ašuuf kutub it-tawṣiya maaltak?*

to **reflect** - *Ɛikas (i Ɛakis) n-.* The mirror reflects the light. *l-imraaya tiƐkis iḍ-ḍuwa.* 2. *fakkar (i tafkiir).* I need time to reflect on it. *ʔariid wakt afakkir biiha.*

reflection - 1. *xayaal.* You can see your reflection in the water. *tigdar itšuuf xayaalak bil-maay.* 2. *taƐriiḍ.* That's no reflection on you. *haaḍa muu taƐriiḍ biik.*

reform - *ʔiṣlaaẓ* pl. *-aat.* He introduced many reforms. *ʔadxal ʔiṣlaaẓaat ihwaaya.*
to reform - 1. *ʔaṣlaẓ (i ʔiṣlaaẓ).* He's always trying to reform the world. *daaʔiman yriid yiṣliẓ id-dinya.* 2. *nṣilaẓ (i).* I'm sure he'll reform. *ʔaani mitʔakkid raẓ-yinṣiliẓ.*

refreshing - *munƐiš.* On the banks of the Tigris the breeze is always refreshing. *Ɛala ḍifaaf dijla l-hawa daaʔiman munƐiš.*

refreshments - *muraṭṭibaat.* Refreshments were served during the intermission. *twazzƐat il-muraṭṭibaat ʔaθnaaʔ il-fatra.*

refrigerator - *θillaaja* pl. *-aat.*

refugee - *laajiʔ* pl. *-iin.*

refund – *ʔirjaaε* pl. *-aat, tarjiiε* pl. *-aat.* No refunds without a receipt. *ʔirjaaε il-mabaaliġ ma-ykuun ʔilla b-waṣil.*
  to refund – *rajjaε (i tarjiiε) t-, ʔaεaad (i ʔiεaada) n-.* I'll refund your expenses. *εuud arajjiε-lak maṣaariifak.*
refusal – *rafuδ̣.* I didn't expect a refusal from him. *ma-twaqqaεit minna r-rafuδ̣.*
refuse – *ʔawsaax.* You'll find a refuse box outside. *tilqi ṣanduug ʔawsaax barra.*
  to refuse – *rufaδ̣ (u rafuδ̣) n-.* He doesn't refuse me anything. *ma-yirfuδ̣-li ʔay ṭalab.*
regard – **1.** *xuṣuuṣ, šaʔn.* In that regard, I agree with you. *b-hal-xuṣuuṣ attifiq wiyyaak.* **2.** *εtibaar.* He has no regard at all for others. *maa εinda ʔayy iεtibaar lil-ʔaaxariin.* **3.** *ʒtiraam* pl. *-aat.* Give my regards to your wife. *qaddim iʒtiraamaati l-zawujtak.*
  to regard – **1.** *εtibar (u εtibaar).* We regard him as an authority on law. *niεtabura ʒujja bil-qaanuun.* **2.** *qaddar (i taqdiir).* I regard him highly. *ʔaani ʔaqaddra hwaaya.*
region – *manṭiqa* pl. *manaaṭiq, ʔiqliim* pl. *ʔaqaaliim.*
register – *sijill* pl. *-aat, qayd* pl. *qyuud.* Did you sign the register? *waqqaεit is-sijill?*
  to register – *sajjal (i tasjiil) t-.* He's not registered at this hotel. *huwwa ma-mitsajjil ib-hal-ʔuteel.* -- I couldn't vote because I forgot to register. *ma-gdarit aṣawwut li-ʔan niseet ʔasajjil.* -- Where can I register this letter? *ween ʔagdar ʔasajjil hal-maktuub.*
registered – *musajjal.* I got a registered letter today. *stilamit maktuub musajjal hal-yoom.* --
regret – **1.** *ʔasaf.* I had to decline the invitation with regret. *δ̣ṭarreet ʔaεtiδir εan id-daεwa maεa l-ʔasaf.* **2.** *εtiδaar.* Mr. and Mrs. Doe send their regrets. *s-sayyid wis-sayyida flaan yqaddimuun iεtiδaarhum.*
  **I'd rather wait than have regrets later. *ʔaani ʔafaδ̣δ̣il antiδ̣ir εala ʔan ʔakuun mitnaddim baεdeen.*
  to regret – **1.** *tʔassaf (a taʔassuf), ʔisaf (a ʔasaf).* I've always regretted not having traveled much. *tʔassafit daaʔiman bi-ʔanni ma-saafarit ihwaaya.* **2.** *nidam (a nadam).* He regretted having said it. *nidam εala goolatha.*
regrettable – *muʔsif.* This is a regrettable mistake. *haaδi ġalṭa muʔsifa.*
regular – **1.** *εtiyaadi*, εaadi*.* The regular price is 5 dinars. *s-siεr il-iεtiyaadi xams idnaaniir.* **2.** *muntaδ̣am.* His pulse is regular. *nabδ̣a muntaδ̣am.* **3.** *mnaδ̣δ̣am.* He lives a very regular life. *yεiiš ʒayaat imnaδ̣δ̣ma kulliš.*
regularly – *b-intiδ̣aam.* He pays regularly. *huwwa yidfaε b-intiδ̣aam.*
to **regulate** – **1.** *naδ̣δ̣am (i tanδ̣iim) t-.* I can't regulate the temperature. *ma-da-agdar ʔanaδ̣δ̣im il-ʒaraara.* **2.** *δ̣ubaṭ (u δ̣abuṭ) n-.* Can you regulate the carburetor? *tigdar tuδ̣buṭ il-kaabreeta?*
regulation – *niδ̣aam* pl. *ʔanδ̣ima.* That's against police regulations. *haaδi muxaalifa l-ʔanδ̣imat iš-šurṭa.*
rein – *rašma* pl. *-aat.*
to **reject** – *rufaδ̣ (u rafuδ̣) n-.* My application was rejected. *εariiδ̣ti nrufδ̣at.*
related – *mitεalliq.* I want all the information related to this matter. *ʔariid kull il-maεluumaat il-mitεalliqa b-hal-ʔamur.*
  **We're related on my mother's side. *εidna qaraaba min jihat ʔummi.*
  **That's a related matter. *haaδa mawδ̣uuε ʔila εalaaqa.*
relation – **1.** *εalaaqa* pl. *-aat.* The relations between the two countries are strained. *l-εalaaqaat been il-baladeen itwattrat.* **2.** *ṣila* pl. *-aat, εalaaqa* pl. *-aat.* Why don't you talk to him, you have better relations with him. *leeš maa ʔinta tiʒči wiyyaa, ṣiltak bii ʔaʒsan.* **3.** *qariib* pl. *qaraayib.* Are they all your relation? *haδoola kullhum qaraaybak?*
relationship – *εalaaqa.* What's the relationship between those two? *šinu l-εalaaqa been hal-iθneen?*
relative – **1.** *qariib* pl. *ʔaqribaaʔ, garaayib.* He is a relative of mine. *haaδa qariibi.* or *haaδa garaaybi.* **2.** *nisbi*.* He said: Everything in life is relative. *gaal: kullši nisbi bil-ʒayaat.*
to **relax** – **1.** *raxxa (i tarxiya) t-.* Relax your muscles. *raxxi εaδ̣alaatak.* **2.** *rtaaʒ (a raaʒa).* I can't relax until it's finished. *ma-agdar artaaʒ ʔila ʔan tixlaṣ.* **3.** *hidaʔ (a huduuʔ).* Relax! Nobody's going to hurt you. *ʔihdaʔ, maʒʒad raʒ-yʔaδδiik.*
release – *ʔifraaj (*pl. *-aat) εan-, ʔiṭlaaq siraaʒ.* The lawyer has applied for her release. *l-muʒaami qaddam ṭalab lil-ʔifraaj εanha.*
  to release – **1.** *ʔafraj (i ʔifraaj) n- εan, ʔaṭlaq (i ʔiṭlaaq) n- siraaʒ.* The police released him right away. *š-šurṭa ʔafrajaw εanna ʒaalan.* **2.** *fakk (u fakk) n-.* Release the safety catch. *fukk miftaaʒ il-ʔamaan.*
reliable – **1.** *εalee εtimaad.* He is a reliable person. *huwwa fadd šaxiṣ εalee εtimaad.* -- **This is a reliable firm. *haaδi fadd šarika tiεtimid εaleeha.* **2.** *mawθuuq b-.* I got it from a reliable source. *ʒaṣṣalitha min maṣdar mawθuuq bii.*
relief – **1.** *faraj.* There is no hope of immediate relief from the heat. *ma-aku ʔamal faraj qariib imnil-ʒarr.* **2.** *ʔiεaana.* They want to organize a relief committee. *yriiduun yšakkluun lujna lil-ʔiεaana.*
  to give relief – *rayyaʒ (i taryiiʒ) t-.* Did the medicine give you any relief? *d-duwa rayyaʒak išwayya?*
to **relieve** – **1.** *xaffaf (u taxfiif) t-.* This will relieve your headache. *haay raʒ-itxaffuf wujaε raasak.* **2.** *raaʒ (i ʔiraaʒa).* Why don't you tell me the story and relieve me of my anxiety. *leeš ma-tiʒčii-li l-qiṣṣa w-itriiʒni min qalaqi.* **3.** *xallaṣ (i taxliis) t-.* We're trying to find a servant to relieve my wife of the cleaning. *da-nʒaawil nilqi xiddaama ʒatta nxalliṣ marti mnit-tanδ̣iif.*
  **We relieve one another. *ʔiʒna nʒill waaʒid maʒall il-laax.*
religion – *diin* pl. *ʔadyaan.*
religious – **1.** *mitdayyin* pl. *-iin, taqi* pl. *-iyyiin.* He's very religious. *huwwa kulliš mitdayyin.* **2.** *diini.** He belongs to a religious order. *huwwa min ʔatbaaε ṭariiqa diiniyya.*
to **rely on** – *εtimad (i εtimaad) εala.* You can't rely on him. *ma-tigdar tiεtimid εalee.*
to **remain** – *δ̣all (a), buqa (a baqaaʔ).* He remained silent. *δ̣all saakit.* -- There remains nothing else for us to do but wait. *ma-yibqaa-nna šii nsawwii ġeer nintiδ̣ir.*
  **That remains to be seen. *haaδi raʒ-itbayyin baεdeen.*
remaining – *baaqi.* What did you do with the remaining cards? *š-sawweet bil-biṭaaqaat il-baaqya?*
remains – **1.** *ʔaaθaar.* I'm anxious to see the historical remains. *ʔaani muštaaq ʔašuuf il-ʔaaθaar it-taariixiyya.* **2.** *mayyit* pl. *moota.* The remains were taken to Najaf for burial. *l-mayyit inʔixaδ lin-najaf lid-dafin.*
remark – *mulaaʒaδ̣a* pl. *-aat.* That remark wasn't called for. *hal-mulaaʒaδ̣a maa ʔilha daaεi.*
remarkable – *fawq il-εaada, xaariq.* What's so remarkable about it. *šinu l-fawq il-εaada biiha?*
remedy – *εilaaj* pl. *-aat, duwa* pl. *ʔadwiya.* That's a good remedy for colds. *haaδa xooš εilaaj lin-našla.*
  to remedy – *εaalaj (i muεaalaja) t-, daawa (i mudaawaat) t-.* I don't know how that can be remedied. *ma-ʔadri haay išloon titεaalaj.*
to **remember** – *tδakkar (a taδakkur), tfaṭṭan (a tafaṭṭun).* It was in May, as far as I remember. *čaanat ib-maayis, ʒasab-ma ʔatδakkar.*
  **I simply can't remember his name. *ʔisma ʔabad ma-da-yiji εala baali.*
  **He always remembers us at Christmas. *daaʔiman nuxtur εala baala b-εiid il-miilaad.*
  **Remember to turn out the light. *la-tinsa ṭṭaffi δ̣-δ̣uwa.*
  **Remember me to your father. *sallim-li εala ʔabuuk.*
to **remind** – **1.** *δakkar (i taδkiir).* He reminded me of my promise. *δakkarni bil-waεad maali.* -- He reminds me of his father. *yδakkirni b-ʔabuu.* **2.** *jaab (i) b-baal, δakkar (i taδkiir).* Remind me about it later. *jiibha b-baali baεdeen.*
reminder – *taʔkiid* pl. *-aat.* I'll send him a reminder, if he doesn't pay by tomorrow. *ʔadizz-la taʔkiid ʔiδa ma-yidfaε baačir.*
remnant – *baqiyya* pl. *baqaaya, faδ̣la* pl. *-aat.* How much do you want for those three remnants? *hal-itlaθ baqaaya maal l-iqmaaš beeš itbiiεhum?*
remote – *kulliš biεiid.* There's a remote possibility that it will succeed. *ʔaku ʒtimaal kulliš biεiid raʒ-yinjaʒ.*
to **remove** – **1.** *nizaε (a naziε) n-, šaal (i šiyal) n-.* Please remove your hat. *ʔarjuuk ʔinzaε šafugtak.* **2.** *zaal (i ʔizaala), šaal (i).* This should remove all doubt. *haay laazim itziil kull šakk.*

3. *rawwaz (i tarwiiz) t-, zaal (i), šaal (i).* That cleaner will remove all stains. *hal-maadda l-munaȿȿifa trawwiz kull il-lakkaat.* 4. *Ɛizal (i Ɛazil) n-.* He was removed from office. *nƐizal imnil-waȿiifa.* 5. *niqal (u naqil) n-.* The phone was removed from here. *t-talafoon inniqal minnaa.*

to **renew** - *jaddad (i tajdiid) t-.* I went to the police to renew my license. *rizit liš-šurṭa ʔajaddid ʔijaazti.*

rent - *ʔiijaar* pl. *-aat.* How much rent do you pay for your house? *šgadd tidfaƐ ʔiijaar ib-beetak?*

to rent - 1. *ʔajjar (i taʔjiir) t-, staʔjar (i stiijaar).* I rented a room for three months. *ʔajjarit ġurfa l-itlaθt išhur.* -- They rented a garage. *staʔjiraw garaaj.* 2. *ʔajjar (i taʔjiir).* He rented me the room for one month. *ʔajjarni l-ġurfa šahar waazid.*

repair - 1. *taşliiz* pl. *-aat.* The car needs only minor repairs. *s-sayyaara tiztaaj taşliizaat başiiṭa bass.* 2. *taƐmiir* pl. *-aat, tarmiim* pl. *-aat, taşliiz* pl. *-aat.* This house needs a lot of repairs. *hal-beet yirraad-la hwaaya taƐmiir.*

to repair - 1. *şallaz (i taşliiz) t-.* He repaired the radio for me. *şallaz-li r-raadyo.* 2. *rammam (i tarmiim) t-, Ɛammar (u taƐmiir) t-, şallaz (i).* When are you going to repair this house? *šwakit raz-itrammim hal-beet?*

to **repeat** - *Ɛaad (i ʔiƐaada) n-, karrar (i takriir) t-.* Repeat what I just said. *Ɛiid illi gilta hassa.* -- They repeat everything they hear. *ykarriruun kullši l-ysimƐuu.*

to **replace** - 1. *zall (i zall) mazall, ʔaxaδ (u ʔaxiδ) mukaan.* We haven't been able to get anyone to replace her. *ma-da-nigdar nilgi ʔazzad yzill mazallha.* 2. *baddal (i tabdiil) t-.* They replaced some tubes and made other repairs in the t.v. set. *baddilaw baƐaȿ laampaat w-sawwaw taşliizaat ʔuxra b-jihaaz it-talafizyoon.* 3. *stabdal (i stibdaal).* The prime minister is going to replace two members of his cabinet. *raʔiis il-wuzaraaʔ raz-yistabdil Ɛuȿween min ʔaƐȿaaʔ wizaarta.*

reply - *jawaab* pl. *ʔajwuba, radd* pl. *ruduud.* I never received a reply to my letter. *ʔabad ma-stilamit jawaab il-maktuubi.*

to reply - *jaawab (u ʔijaaba), radd (i radd).* He replied to my letter immediately. *jaawab Ɛala maktuubi zaalan.*

report - *taqriir* pl. *taqaariir.* I've already read the report. *ʔaani qreeta lit-taqriir.*

to report - 1. *ruwa (i rawi) n-.* The newspapers reported the accident in detail. *j-jaraayid ruwat il-zaadiθ bit-tafşiil.* 2. *ballaġ (i tabliiġ) t-Ɛan.* Somebody must have reported him to the police. *fadd ʔazzad laazim ballaġ iš-šurṭa Ɛanna.*

to report to - *raajaƐ (i muraajaƐa).* Tomorrow report to the director for your work. *bukra raajiƐ il-mudiir Ɛan šuġlak.*

**To whom do I report? *minu l-marjaƐ maali?*

report card - *waθiiqat (pl. waθaayig) darajaat.* She always comes home with good report cards in her hand. *daaʔiman tiji lil-beet w-b-ʔiidha waθaayiq darajaat mumtaaza.*

reporter - *şuzufi* pl. *-iyyiin.*

to **represent** - *maθθal (i tamθiil) t-.* Who is representing the defendant? *minu da-ymaθθil il-muddaƐa Ɛalee?* -- What does this symbol represent? *har-ramiz š-ymaθθil?*

representative - 1. *mumaθθil* pl. *-iin.* He is the European representative of a big concern. *haaδa l-mumaθθil l-ʔooruppi l-šarika čibiira.* 2. *naaʔib* pl. *nuwwaab.* Who's the representative from your district? *minu n-naaʔib min manṭiqtak.*

reproach - *taƐniif, muʔaaxaδa.* I didn't mean that as a reproach. *ma-qşadit il-muʔaaxaδa.*

to reproach - *waaxaδ (u muwaaxaδa) t-, zijar (u zajir) n-.* My mother is always reproaching me for my extravagance. *ʔummi daaʔiman twaaxiδni Ɛala ʔisraafi.*

reputation - 1. *sumƐa, šuhra, şiit.* He has a good reputation. *Ɛinda sumƐa ṭayyba.* 2. *maƐruuf Ɛan.* He has a reputation for being a good worker. *maƐruuf Ɛanna b-ʔanna šaaġuul.*

request - *ṭalab* pl. *-aat, rajaaʔ* pl. *-aat.* They granted the request. *waafqaw Ɛaṭ-ṭalab.* -- I am writing you at the request of a friend. *ʔaani da-ʔaktib-lak binaaʔan Ɛala rajaaʔ şadiiq.*

to request - *trajja (a tarajji) min.* I must request you to leave this place. *ʔaani muȿṭarr ʔatrajja minnak titruk hal-mazall.*

to **require** - 1. *stalzam (i stilzaam).* A thing like that requires careful study. *fadd šii miθil haaδa yistalzim diraasa daqiiqa.* 2. *ztaaj (a ztiyaaj), nraad (a) l-, ṭṭallab (a taṭallub).* That requires no proof. *haaδa ma-yiztaaj ʔay ʔiθbaat.* -- How much time will that require? *haay šgadd yinraad-ilha wakit?* -- How much money does that require? *šgadd ifluus haay tiṭṭallab?* 3. *ṭilab (u ṭalab) n-.* Do you require a deposit? *tiṭlubuun taʔmiinaat?* 4. *stadƐa (i stidƐaaʔ), qtiȿa (i qtiȿaaʔ).* The situation requires firm measures. *l-zaala tistadƐi ʔijraaʔaat şaarima.*

requirement - 1. *mutaṭallab* pl. *-aat.* The requirements for graduation are numerous. *mutaṭallabaat it-taxarruj kaθiira.* 2. *ztiyaaj* pl. *-aat, zaaja* pl. *-aat.* He asked us to estimate what our manpower requirements in the crafts will be. *ṭilab min Ɛidna nqaddir išgadd raz-itkuun zaajatna mnil-Ɛummaal il-maahriin.* 3. *šarṭ maṭluub* pl. *šuruuṭ maṭluuba.* Does he meet our requirements? *titwaffar bii š-šuruuṭ il-maṭluuba?*

to **resemble** - *šibah (a šibih), ṭilaƐ (a ṭuluuƐ) Ɛala.* Don't you think he resembles his mother? *ma-tiƐtiqid yišbah ʔumma?* or *ma-tiƐtiqid ṭaaliƐ Ɛala ʔumma?*

reservation - 1. *zajiz* pl. *zujuuz.* I want to cancel my reservation. *ʔariid ʔalġi l-zajiz maali.* 2. *tazaffuȿ* pl. *-aat.* He said it with some reservation. *qaalha maƐa baƐȿ it-tazaffuȿ.*

reserve - 1. *ztiyaaṭi.* I'm afraid we'll have to dig into our reserves. *ʔaƐtiqid raz-niȿṭarr nistaƐmil il-iztiyaaṭi maalna.* -- One-fifth of the world's oil reserves are in Kuwait. *xumis iztiyaaṭi l-Ɛaalam mnin-nafuṭ bil-kuwayt.* 2. *ztiyaaṭ.* He is a reserve officer. *haaδa ȿaabuṭ iztiyaaṭ.*

to reserve - 1. *zijaz (i zajiz) n-.* Can you reserve a place for me? *tigdar tizjiz-li mazall?* 2. *zufaȿ (u zufuȿ) n-.* He reserved the right of using the car for himself. *zufaȿ zaqq istiƐmaal is-sayyaara l-nafsa.*

reserved - 1. *haadiʔ* pl. *-iin.* I found him very reserved. *šifta kulliš haadiʔ.* 2. *mazjuuz.* All seats are reserved. *kull il-mazallaat mazjuuza.*

to **resign** - *staqaal (i stiqaala).* He resigned as chairman of the committee. *staqaal min riʔaasat il-lujna.*

resignation - 1. *stiqaala* pl. *-aat.* He handed in his resignation today. *qaddam istiqaalta l-yoom.* 2. *stislaam, ʔiδƐaan.* He received the news with resignation. *tqabbal il-ʔaxbaar b-istislaam.* 3. *tasliim.* We have nothing left but resignation to the will of God. *ma-Ɛidna ġeer it-tasliim l-ʔiraadat ʔaḷḷa.*

resigned to - *raaȿi b-.* She's resigned to her fate of remaining an old maid for the rest of her life. *raaȿya b-qismatha tibqa bnayya ṭuul Ɛumurha.*

to **resist** - *qaawam (u muqaawama) t-.* He tried to resist, but the police arrested him. *zaawal yqaawum laakin iš-šurṭa ʔalqat il-qabuȿ Ɛalee.* -- I couldn't resist the temptation. *ma-gdarṭ aqaawum il-ʔiġraaʔ.*

resistance - *muqaawama.* He didn't put up any resistance. *ma-bayyan ʔay muqaawama.*

to **resole** - *zaṭṭ (u zaṭṭ) n- naƐal.* I'm having my shoes resoled. *da-azuṭṭ naƐal il-qundarti.*

resolution - *qaraar* pl. *-aat.* The resolution was adopted unanimously. *l-qaraar itşaddaq bil-ʔijmaaƐ.*

resort - *maljaʔ* pl. *malaajiʔ.* As a last resort I can turn to him. *ka-ʔaaxir maljaʔ agdar arjaƐ ʔila.*

health resort - *maşazz* pl. *-aat.* She's not going to a health resort this year. *ma-raz-itruuz lil-maşazz has-sana.*

summer resort - *maşiif* pl. *maşaayif.* Do you know a nice summer resort? *tuƐruf fadd maşiif laṭiif?*

to resort - *ltijaʔ (i ltijaaʔ).* I don't want to resort to force. *ma-ʔariid altijiʔ lil-quwwa.*

resource - 1. *wasiila* pl. *wasaaʔil.* I have exhausted all resources. *stanfaδit kull il-wasaaʔil.* 2. *mawrid* pl. *mawaarid.* Oil is one of our important resources. *n-nafuṭ ʔazad mawaaridna l-muhimma.*

respect - 1. *ztiraam.* He has won the respect of everyone. *ktisab iztiraam ij-jamiiƐ.* 2. *jiha* pl. *-aat, naazya* pl. *nawaazi.* We were satisfied in every respect. *činna raaȿiin min kull ij-jihaat.*

to respect - *ztiram (u ztiraam).* I respect your opinion. *ʔaani ʔazturum raʔyak.* -- You must respect your elders. *laazim tizturum il-ʔakbar minnak.*

respectable - *muztaram* pl. *-iin, muƐtabar* pl. *-iin.* Respectable people don't go in a place like that. *n-naas il-muztaramiin ma-yṭubbuun hiiči makaan.*

respected - *muḥtaram* pl. *-iin, muεtabar* pl. *-iin.* He is a respected business man in this city. *huwwa fadd rajul ʔaεmaal muḥtaram ib-hal-wlaaya.*
responsibility - *masʔuuliyya* pl. *-aat.* I'll take the responsibility. *ʔaani raḥ-atḥammal il-masʔuuliyya.*
responsible - *masʔuul* pl. *-iin.* They held him responsible for the damage. *εtibroo masʔuul εann iδ̣-δ̣arar.*
rest - **1.** *baaqi, baqiyya.* Eat some now and save the rest. *ʔukul qisim hassa w-δ̣umm il-baaqi.* -- You raise the money, and I'll do the rest. *ʔinta dabbur l-ifluus w-ʔaani εalayya l-baaqi.* -- Where are the rest of the boys? *ween baqiyyat il-wulid?* **2.** *raaḥa.* I went to the mountains for a rest. *riḥit lij-jibaal il-ṭalab ir-raaḥa.* **3.** *stiraaḥa* pl. *-aat.* Let's take a short rest. *xal-naaxuδ fadd istiraaḥa gṣayyra.*
at rest - *raakid, waaguf.* Wait until the pointer is at rest. *ʔintiδ̣ir ʔila ʔan ykuun il-muʔaššir raakid.*
**This will put your mind at rest. *haay raḥ-itrayyiḥ fikrak.*
to take a rest - *staraaḥ (i stiraaḥa), rtaaḥ (a raaḥa).* Let's take a little rest. *xal-nirtaaḥ išwayya.*
to rest - **1.** *rtaaḥ (a raaḥa), staraaḥ (a stiraaḥa).* Rest awhile. *ʔirtaaḥ išwayya.* **2.** *rayyaḥ (a taryiiḥ), ʔaraaḥ (i ʔiraaḥa).* Try to rest your eyes. *ḥaawil itrayyiḥ εeenak.* **3.** *wugaε (a wuguuε).* The whole responsibility rests on him. *kull il-masʔuuliyya toogaε εalee.* **4.** *tačča (i tatčiya, ttičči) t-.* The ladder was resting against the wall. *d-daraj čaan mittačča εal-ḥaayiṭ.*
**The decision rests with you. *l-qaraar b-iidak.*
to rest assured - *ṭmaʔann (i ṭmiʔnaan).* Rest assured that I'll do what you want. *ṭmaʔinn raḥ-ʔasawwi lli triida.*
restaurant - *maṭεam* pl. *maṭaaεum, looqanṭa* pl. *-aat.* Is there a good restaurant around here? *ʔaku maṭεam zeen ib-hal-manṭiqa?*
restless - *qaliq* pl. *-iin.* I'm very restless today. *ʔaani kulliš qaliq il-yoom.*
to **restore** - **1.** *staεaad (i stiεaada).* The police restored order. *š-šurṭa staεaadaw in-niδ̣aam.* **2.** *rajjaε (i tarjiiε) t-.* All the stolen goods were restored. *kull il-masruuqaat trajjεat.* **3.** *jaddad (i tajdiid) t-.* The government is going to restore this old mosque. *l-ḥukuuma raḥ-itjaddid haj-jaamiε il-εatiig.*
to **restrain** - **1.** *ṣayṭar (i ṣayṭara) εala.* She couldn't restrain her curiosity. *ma-gidrat itṣayṭir εala fuδ̣uulha.* **2.** *δ̣ubaṭ (u δ̣abuṭ) n-.* Can't you restrain your children? *ma-tigdar tuδ̣buṭ ijhaalak?*
rest room - *mirḥaaδ̣* pl. *maraaḥiiδ̣, ʔadabxaana* pl. *ʔadabxaayin, xalwa* pl. *xalaawi, beet* (pl. *byuut*) *maay.*
result - *natiija* pl. *nataaʔij.* The results were very satisfactory. *n-nataaʔij kaanat kulliš murδ̣iya.*
retail - *bil-mufrad.* He sells wholesale and retail. *ybiiε bij-jumla w-bil-mufrad.*
to retail - *baaε (i beeε) n- bil-mufrad.* This coat retails at about thirty dinars. *hal-qappuuṭ yinbaaε bil-mufrad ib-ḥawaali tlaaθiin diinaar.*
to **retire** - **1.** *nsiḥab (i nsiḥaab).* He has retired from public life. *nsiḥab imnil-ḥayaat il-εaamma.* **2.** *tqaaεad (a taqaaεud).* He'll be able to retire next year. *ykuun b-imkaana yitqaaεad is-sana j-jaaya.*
retreat - *taraajuε* pl. *-aat, taqahqur* pl. *-aat, nsiḥaab* pl. *-aat.* The retreat was orderly. *t-taraajuε čaan muntaδ̣am.*
to retreat - *traajaε (a taraajuε), tqahqar (a taqahqur), nsiḥab (i nsiḥaab).* They were forced to retreat after two day's fighting. *δ̣ṭarraw yitraajεuun baεad qitaal yoomeen.*
return - **1.** *waarid* pl. *-aat.* How much of a return did you get on your investment? *šgadd waarid ʔijak min tašgiil ifluusak?* **2.** *rajεa* pl. *-aat, εawda* pl. *-aat.* I found many things changed on my return. *b-rajiεti šift ihwaaya ʔašyaaʔ mitbaddla.* **3.** *murajjaε.* I didn't use my return ticket. *ma-staεmalit biṭaaqati l-murajjaε.*
to return - **1.** *rijaε (a rujuuε).* When did you return? *šwakit rijaεit?* -- I've returned to my original idea. *rjaεit ʔila raʔyi l-εatiig.* **2.** *rajjaε (i tarjiiε) t-.* She didn't return my visit. *ma-rajjεat-li z-ziyaara.* **3.** *εaad (i ʔiεaada), rajjaε (i tarjiiε).* Don't forget to return the book. *la-tinsa tεiid l-iktaab.*
returns - *nataaʔij.* Have the election returns come in yet? *nataaʔij il-intixaabaat wuṣlat loo baεad?*
**Many happy returns! *ʔaḷḷa yεiida εaleek bis-suruur.*
revenge - *θaar, ntiqaam.*
to revenge - *θiʔar (a θaar), ntiqam (i ntiqaam).* He revenged the death of his father. *θiʔar qatil ʔabuu.* or **ʔaxaδ θaar ʔabuu.*
reverse - **1.** *gufa, θaani.* Don't forget to fill in the reverse side of the card. *la-tinsa titrus gufa l-kaart.* or *la-tinsa titrus il-wujj iθ-θaani mnil-kaart.* **2.** *bagg.* Put the transmission in reverse. *xalli l-giir εal-bagg.*
to reverse - **1.** *rijaε (a rujuuε) li-wara.* Tell him to reverse. *gul-la yirjaε li-wara.* **2.** *εikas (i εakis) n-.* In order to put it together, reverse the procedure. *ḥatta trakkibha, ʔiεkis il-εamaliyya.*
review - *muraajaεa* pl. *-aat.* He publishes book reviews in this magazine. *yinšur muraajaεaat bil-kutub ib-hal-majalla.*
to review - *niqad (u naqid) n-.* Who's going to review the play? *minu raḥ-yinqud it-tamθiiliyya?*
review lesson - *daris* (pl. *druus*) *muraajaεa.*
to **revolt** - *θaar (u θawra).* Why did they revolt? *leeš θaaraw?*
revolution - **1.** *θawra* pl. *-aat.* He was the hero of the revolution and was later killed. *čaan baṭal iθ-θawra w-baεdeen inkital.* **2.** *farra* pl. *-aat.* How many revolutions does this motor make per minute? *čam farra tiftarr hal-makiina bid-daqiiqa?*
to **revolve** - **1.** *daar (u dawaraan).* The moon revolves around the earth. *l-gumar yduur ḥawl il-ʔarδ̣.* **2.** *ftarr (a ftiraar).* The wheel revolves on its axle. *č-čarix yiftarr ḥawil maḥwara.*
reward - *jaaʔiza* pl. *jawaaʔiz, mukaafaʔa* pl. *-aat.* He was promised a substantial reward. *nwiεad ib-jaaʔiza θamiina.*
to reward - *jaaza (i mujaazaat) t-, kaafaʔ (i mukaafaʔa) t-.* He was well rewarded for his diligence. *zeen itkaafaʔ εala jtihaada.*
rhyme - *qaafiya* pl. *qawaafi.* This word doesn't fit the rhyme. *hač-čilma ma-tiji εal-qaafiya.*
rhymed prose - *sajiε.*
rib - **1.** *δ̣ilaε* pl. *δ̣luuε.* He's so thin you can see his ribs. *huwwa δ̣iεiif ʔila daraja tšuuf iδ̣luuεa.* -- Two ribs of my boat were broken. *nkisrat δ̣ilεeen min iδ̣luuε il-balam maali.* **2.** *siim* pl. *syaam.* The wind broke one of the ribs of my umbrella. *l-hawa kisar siim min isyaam šamsiiti.*
ribbon - **1.** *qirdeela* pl. *-aat.* She was wearing a blue ribbon in her hair. *čaanat laabsa qirdeela zarga b-šaεarha.* **2.** *šariiṭ* pl. *šaraayiṭ.* I need a new ribbon for my typewriter. *ʔaḥtaaj šariiṭ jidiid il-ʔaalat iṭ-ṭaabiεa maalti.*
rice - **1.** *timman.* I'd like a pound of rice. *ʔariid paawan timman.* **2.** *šilib, timman.* This man is one of the biggest rice merchants in Iraq. *haaδa min ʔakbar tujjaar iš-šilib bil-εiraaq.*
rich - **1.** *zangiin* pl. *zanaagiin, ġani* pl. *ʔaġniyaaʔ.* He is a rich man. *haaδa waaḥid zangiin.* **2.** *θari* pl. *ʔaθriyaaʔ.* He comes from a rich family. *huwwa min εaaʔila θariyya.* **3.** *dasim.* The food is too rich. *l-ʔakil kulliš dasim.* **4.** *xaṣib.* It's rich soil. *hiyya ṭurba xaṣba.*
rickets - *kusaaḥ.*
riddle - *laġiz* pl. *ʔalġaaz, ḥazzuura* pl. *-aat.*
ride - **1.** *rukba* pl. *rukab.* It's only a short ride by bus. *hiyya muu ʔazyad min rukbat paaṣ qaṣiira.* **2.** *farra* pl. *-aat.* Let's take a ride in the car. *xalli nsawwii-nna fadd farra bis-sayyaara.* or *xal-niṭlaε bis-sayyaara.*
**He gave me a ride all the way. *waṣṣalni b-sayyaarta kull iṭ-ṭariiq.*
to ride - **1.** *rikab (a rukuub) n-.* Do you know how to ride a motorcycle? *tuεruf tirkub maaṭoorsikil?* -- We rode in a beautiful car. *rikabna b-sayyaara ḥilwa.* **2.** *miša (i maši).* This car rides smoothly. *has-sayyaara timši miθl id-dihin.*
**Stop riding me! *bass εaad itliḥḥ!* or *ma-tfukk yaaxa εaad!*
ridiculous - *saxiif, saxaafa.* Don't be ridiculous! *la-tṣiir saxiif!* -- That's ridiculous. *haay saxaafa.* or *haaδa šii saxiif.*
rid of - *xalṣaan min.* I'm glad I'm rid of it. *ʔaani farḥaan xalṣaan minna.*
to get rid of - *xilaṣ (a xalaaṣ) min, txallaṣ (a taxalluṣ) min.* I got rid of her at last. *ʔaxiiran*

ixlaşit minha.
rifle - *bunduqiyya* pl. *banaadiq, tufga* pl. *tufag.*
right - **1.** *ʒaqq* pl. *ʒuquuq.* I insist on my rights. *ʔaani ʔaşirr Ɛala ʒuquuqi.* -- You have no right to say that. *ma-ʔilak ʒaqq itguul haay.* -- He's right. *l-ʒaqq wiyyaa.* **2.** (m.) *yamiin* (f.) *yimna.* I've lost the glove for my right hand. *ðayyaƐit ič-čaff maal ʔiidi l-yimna.* **3.** *qaaʔim.* A right angle has ninety degrees. *z-zaawiya l-qaaʔima biiha tisƐiin daraja.* **4.** *munaasib.* He came just at the right time. *ʔija bil-wakt il-munaasib tamaaman.* **5.** *şaʒiiʒ.* Are we going the right way? *ʔiʒna da-nimši Ɛaṭ-ṭariiq iş-şaʒiiʒ?* **6.** *raʔsan, fadd raas, Ɛadil.* I'm coming right home from the office. *raʒ-ʔaji mniš-šuġuḷ lil-beet raʔsan.* **7.** *tamaaman.* The house is right next to the church. *l-beet yamm il-kaniisa tamaaman.* **8.** *zeen.* We'll leave tomorrow if the weather is right. *niṭlaƐ baačir ʔiða j-jaww zeen.*
**You can't be in your right mind. *ʔinta laazim muu b-kaamil Ɛaqlak.*
**It serves him right! *yistaahil!* or *yistaʒiqq!*
**Go right ahead. *fuut ib-faalak.* or *twakkal Ɛal-aḷḷa!*
**He's right here next to me. *hiyyaata hnaa b-şaffi.*
right away - *ʒaalan, raʔsan, fawran.* Let's go right away or we'll be late. *xalli nruuʒ ʒaalan w-ʔilla nitʔaxxar.* -- Tell him to come to see me right away. *gul-la yiji ywaajihni fawran.*
right now - *hassa.* I'm busy right now. *ʔaani mašġuul hassa.*
right off - *fawran.* I can't answer that right off. *ma-agdar ajaawub Ɛala haay fawran.*
rightful - *šarƐi*.* He is the rightful owner of the house. *huwwa l-maalik iš-šarƐi lil-beet.*
right-hand - (m.) *yamiin* (f.) *yimna.* The school is on the right-hand side of the street. *l-madrasa Ɛaj-jiha l-yimna mniš-šaariƐ.*
**He's the boss's right-hand man. *huwwa l-ʔiid il-yimna lir-raʔiis.*
rim - *ʔaṭaar* pl. *-aat.* The rim of my glasses is broken. *ʔaṭaar manaaðri maksuur.*

ring - **1.** *miʒbas* pl. *maʒaabis, xaatam* pl. *xawaatim.* She wears a ring on her right hand. *tilbas miʒbas b-iidha l-yimna.* **2.** *ʒalqa* pl. *-aat.* Tie the rope to the iron ring. *šidd il-ʒabil ib-ʒalaqt il-ʒadiid.* **3.** *dagga, ranna.* That bell has a peculiar ring. *haj-jaras ʔila ranna ġariiba.* **4.** *ring* pl. *-aat.* I had the mechanic put in a new set of rings. *xalleet il-fiitarči yʒuṭṭ-li ṭaxum ringaat jidiida.*
to give a ring - *dagg (u) talafoon.* Give me a ring tomorrow. *dugg-li talafoon baačir.*
to ring - **1.** *rann (i rann).* The noise is still ringing in my ears. *l-laġwa baƐadha da-trinn ib-ʔiðni.* **2.** *dagg (u dagg).* The phone rang. *dagg it-talafoon.* -- Did you ring the bell? *daggeet ij-jaras?*
**Somehow it doesn't ring true. *ʔašu ma-tbayyin şudug.*
rinse - *xaðða* pl. *-aat.* Two rinses will be enough. *xaððteen itkaffi.*
to rinse - **1.** *xaðð (u xaðð) n-.* I rinse my wash twice. *ʔaani ʔaxuðð il-ġasiil maali marrteen.* -- Rinse the glasses under the faucet. *xuðð il-iglaaşaat jawwa il-buuri.* **2.** *maðmað (u maðmaða) t-.* Rinse out your mouth with water and a little salt. *maðmuð ʒalgak ib-maay w-šwayya miliʒ.*
riot - **1.** *hayaaj, Ɛarbada, šaġab.* Two people were killed in the riot. *šaxşeen inkitlaw ʔaθnaaʔ il-hayaaj.* -- The riot was caused by several drunkards. *l-Ɛarbada sababha čam sakraan.*
**He's a riot. *haaða fadd imşannifči.*
to riot - *šaaġab (i mušaaġaba).* They ignored the presence of the police and kept on rioting all night. *ʔahmilaw wujuud iš-šurṭa w-ðallaw yšaaġbuun ṭuul il-leel.*
rip - **1.** *šagg* pl. *šguug, mazig* pl. *mzuug.* Do you know you have a rip in your jacket? *tidri ʔaku mazig ib-sitirtak?* **2.** *fatig* pl. *ftuug.* There is a rip in the seam of your shirt under the arm. *ʔaku fatig ib-θoobak jawwa ʔubṭak.*
to rip - **1.** *mizag (i mazig) n-, šagg (u šagg) n-.* I ripped my pants climbing the fence. *šaggeet panṭurooni ʔaθnaaʔ-ma činit ʔatšalbah Ɛas-siyaaj.* **2.** *fitag (i fatig) n-.* I have to rip out the seams. *laazim ʔaftig l-ikwaaka.*
ripe - **1.** *laaʒig, naaðij.* The apples aren't ripe yet. *t-tiffaaʒ baƐda maa laaʒig.* **2.** *mithayyiʔ.* The situation is ripe for trouble. *l-waðiƐ mithayyiʔ lil-mašaakil.*
**He lived to a ripe old age. *Ɛammar ihwaaya.*
to **rise** - **1.** *ṭilaƐ (i ṭuluuƐ), ʔašraq (i šuruuq).* The sun rises early. *š-šamis tiṭlaƐ min wakit.* **2.** *şiƐad (a şuƐuud).* Over there the road rises again. *hnaak iṭ-ṭariiq yişƐad marra lux.* **3.** *rtifaƐ (i rtifaaƐ), şiƐad (i şuƐuud).* The river is rising rapidly. *n-nahar da-yirtifiƐ bil-Ɛajal.* -- Prices are still rising. *l-ʔasƐaar baƐadha da-tirtifiƐ.* **4.** *gaam (u qiyaam).* All rose from their seats. *kullhum gaamaw min makaanaathum.* **5.** *nnufax (u nnifaax).* The cake is rising. *l-keeka da-tinnufux.*
**He rose from the ranks. *haaða maslaki.*
risk - *muxaaṭara* pl. *-aat, mujaazafa* pl. *-aat.* I can't take such a risk. *ma-agdar asawwi hiiči mujaazafa.*
to risk - *xaaṭar (i muxaaṭara) b-, jaazaf (i mujaazafa) b-.* He risked his life to save her. *xaaṭar ib-ʒayaata ʒatta yungiðha.* -- He's risked his entire fortune. *jaazaf ib-kull θaruuta.*
**He risked his life. *ʒaṭṭ ʒayaata Ɛala čaffa.*
rival - *munaafis* pl. *-iin, muzaaʒim* pl. *-iin.* They were rivals for many years. *čaanaw munaafsiin il-baƐaðhum il-muddat isniin ihwaaya.* -- He works for a rival company. *yištuġul ib-fadd šarika muzaaʒima.*
river - *nahar* pl. *ʔanhaar, ʔanhur; šaṭṭ* pl. *šṭuuṭ.* What's the name of this river? *han-nahar š-isma?*
road - *ṭariiq* pl. *ṭuruq, darub* pl. *druub.* Where does this road go to? *haṭ-ṭariiq li-ween ywaşşil?* -- He's on the road to recovery. *huwwa b-ṭariiq liš-šafaaʔ.*
to go on the road - **1.** *ṭilaƐ (a) yiftarr.* Our salesman is going on the road next week. *d-dawwaar maalna raʒ-yiṭlaƐ yiftarr ʔisbuuƐ ij-jaay.* **2.** *sawwa (i) jawla, qaam (u) b-jawla.* Next month our team is going on the road for two weeks. *š-šahr ij-jaay fariiqna raʒ-ysawwi jawla l-muddat ʔisbuuƐeen.*
roar - **1.** *hadiir.* We can hear the roar of the waterfall from here. *nigdar nismaƐ hadiir iš-šallaal minnaa.* **2.** *zaʔiir.* It sounded like the roar of a lion. *čaan Ɛabaalak zaʔiir maal ʔasad.*
to roar - **1.** *ziʔar (a zaʔiir).* When he's angry he roars like a lion. *Ɛinda-ma yiġðab yizʔar miθl il-ʔasad.* **2.** *qahqah (i qahqaha).* They roared with laughter. *qahqihaw imniš-šaʒik.*
to **roast** - *šuwa (i šawi) n-.* You didn't roast the meat long enough. *ma-šuweet il-laʒam mudda kaafya.* There's leg of lamb roasted in the oven for dinner. *ʔaku rijil quuzi mašwi lil-Ɛaša.*
to **rob** - **1.** *baag (u boog) n-.* I've been robbed. *nbaageet.* **2.** *sallab (i tasliib) t-, nihab (a nahib) n-.* They'll rob you of your last cent. *raʒ-ysallibuun ʔaaxir filis Ɛindak.*

robbery - **1.** *booga* pl. *-aat, sariqa* pl. *-aat.* When was the robbery committed? *šwakit şaarat il-booga?* **2.** *tasliib, nahab, boog.* That's highway robbery! *haaða tasliib!*
robe - **1.** *roob* pl. *-aat.* Please get me my robe and my slippers. *ʔarjuuk jiib-li r-roob win-naƐal maali.* **2.** *zbuun* pl. *-aat, Ɛabaaya* pl. *Ɛibi.* The chiefs who come from their tribes wear inner and outer robes. *š-šiyuux illi yjuun min Ɛašaayiirhum ylibsuun zbuunaat w-Ɛibi.*
rock - **1.** *şaxra* pl. *şaxar.* They had to blast the rock. *ðṭarraw ynisfuun iş-şaxra.* **2.** *ʒjaara* pl. *ʒjaar.* He was throwing rocks. *čaan da-yšammur iʒjaar.*
to rock - **1.** *htazz (a htizaaz).* The floor rocked under our feet. *l-gaaƐ ihtazzat jawwa rijleena.* -- The boat's rocking. *l-balam da-yihtazz.* **2.** *hazz (i hazz) n-.* She rocked the cradle until the baby fell asleep. *hazzat il-kaaruuk ʔila ʔan naam ij-jaahil.* **3.** *xaðð (u xaðð) n-.* She showed us how to rock the churn to make butter. *šawwfatna šloon inxuðð iš-šičwa ʒatta nsawwi zibid.*
rocky - *şaxri*.* This soil is too rocky for farming. *hal-ʔarð şaxriyya, ma-tişlaʒ liz-ziraaƐa.*
rod - *šiiš* pl. *šyaaš.* The parts are connected by an iron rod. *l-wuşal mittaşla waʒda bil-lux ib-šiiš.*
lightning rod - *maaniƐat* (pl.*-aat*) *şawaaƐiq.* Most large buildings have lightning rods. *ʔakθar il-Ɛimaaraat biiha maaniƐaat şawaaƐiq.*
role - *door* pl. *ʔadwaar.* He played an important role. *liƐab door muhimm.*

roll - 1. *laffa* pl. *-aat.* He used up a whole roll of wrapping paper. *staεmal laffa kaamla min waraq it-tağliif.* **2.** *ṣammuuna* pl. *-aat,* coll. *ṣammuun.* Shall I get bread or rolls? *š-aaxuδ xubuz loo ṣammuun?*

roll of film - *filim* pl. *ʔaflaam.* I'd like two rolls of 120 film. *ʔariid filmeen ʒajam miyya w-εišriin.*

to roll - 1. *daεbal (i tdiεbil) t-, daʒraj (i daʒraja, tdiʒrij) t-.* Don't roll the barrel. *la-tdaεbil il-barmiil.* **2.** *tdaεbal (a tadaεbul), tdaʒraj (a tadaʒruj).* The ball rolled under the table. *ṭ-ṭooba tdaεbilat jawwa l-meez.* **3.** *tmaayal (a tamaayul).* The ship was rolling heavily. *l-baaxira čaanat da-titmaayal ib-šidda.* **4.** *dačč (a) n- b-roola.* The tennis court must be rolled. *saaʒt it-tanis laazim tindačč bir-roola.* or *saaʒt it-tanis yird-ilha doos bir-roola.* **5.** *laff (i laff) n-.* I roll my own cigarettes. *ʔaani ʔaliff jigaayri.*

to roll around - 1. *tmarğal (a tmurğul).* The buffalo rolled around in the mud. *j-jaamuusa tmarğilat biṭ-ṭiin.* **2.** *tdaεbal (a tdiεbil).* The marbles rolled around in the box. *d-duεbul itdaεbal biṣ-ṣanduug.*

to roll out - 1. *furaš (u furiš) n-.* The servant rolled out the mattress on the bedstead. *l-xaadim furaš id-doošag εas-sariir.* **2.** *fakk (u fakk) n-.* Roll the dough out thin. *fukki l-εajiin xafiif.*

to roll over - 1. *giḷab (u gaḷub) n-.* The nurse rolled the patient over. *l-mumarriδa guḷbat il-mariiδ.* --The horse rolled over on the grass. *l-iʒṣaan ngiḷab εala ṣafʒat il-lux εal-ʒašiiš.* **2.** *tgaḷḷab (a tguḷḷub).* I rolled over in bed. *tgaḷḷabit bil-ifraaš.*

to roll up - *laff (i laff) n-.* We rolled up the rug. *laffeena z-zuuliyya.*

rollcall - *tiεdaad.* Did the sergeant take a roll call? *l-εariif sawwa tiεdaad.*

Roman - *roomaani*.* Use Roman numerals. *ʔistaεmil ʔarqaam roomaaniyya.*

Rome - *rooma.*

roof - 1. *ṣaṭiʒ* pl. *ṣṭuuʒ.* In Iraq people sleep on the roof in the summer. *bil-εiraaq in-naas ynaamuun biṣ-ṣaṭiʒ biṣ-ṣeef.* **2.** *saguf* pl. *sguuf.* I burned the roof of my mouth. *ʒragit saguf ʒalgi.*

room - 1. *ġurfa* pl. *ġuraf, gubba* pl. *gubab.* Where can I get a furnished room? *ween ʔalgi ġurfa mʔaθθiθa?* **2.** *mukaan* pl. *-aat.* Is there any room left for my baggage? *buqa mukaan ij-junaṭi?* **3.** *manaam, sakan.* What do they charge for room and board? *šgadd yaaxδuun εala l-ʔakil wil-manaam?*

roomy - *waasiε, raʒib.* We have a roomy apartment. *εidna fadd šaqqa waasεa.*

rooster - *diič* pl. *dyuuča.*

root - *εirig* pl. *εruug, jaδir* pl. *jδuur.* The roots of this tree are very deep. *εruug haš-šajar kulliš ġamiija.* -- The root of the tooth is decayed. *εirg is-sinn xaayis.*

to take root - 1. *ṭallaε (i taṭliiε) εuruug.* How can you tell whether the cutting has taken root? *šloon tuεruf ʔiδa l-qalam ṭallaε εuruug?* **2.** *diraj (u duruuj).* The custom never really took root. *l-εaada bil-ʒaqiiqa ʔabad ma-dirjat.*

to root out - *staʔṣal (i stiʔṣaal).* We must root out crime. *laazim nistaʔṣil il-ʔijraam.*

**He stood there as if rooted to the spot. *wugaf ihnaak εabaalak mitbasmur ib-mukaana.*

rope - *ʒabil* pl. *ʒbaal.* He was leading the calf by a rope. *čaan gaayid il-εijil ib-ʒabil.*

**Give him enough rope and he'll hang himself. *raxxii-la l-ʒabil išwayya w-šuuf išloon yidmur nafsa.*

**I'm at the end of my rope. *ʔaani stanfaδit kull-ma b-ṭaaqti.*

**He knows all the ropes. *yuεruf kull il-idruub.*

to rope off - *giṭaε (a gaṭiε) b-ʒabil.* They roped off the street for the parade. *giṭεaw iš-šaariε ib-ʒabil lil-istiεraaδ.*

rose - *wardat (pl. -aat) juuri,* coll. *warid juuri.* He brings me roses everyday. *yjiib-li warid juuri yoomiyya.*

rosebush - *hiraš (pl. hruuš) warid juuri.*

to rot - *xaas (i xayasaan).* The fruit is rotting on the trees. *l-fawaakih da-txiis εal-ʔašjaar.*

rotten - 1. *xaayis.* The peaches are rotten. *l-xoox xaayis.* **2.** *qaδir.* They played a rotten trick on us. *liεbaw εaleena fadd liεba qaδra.*

rough - 1. *xašin.* Why are your hands so rough? *leeš ʔiidak hiiči xašna?* -- He has a rough voice. *εinda ʒiss xašin.* -- The bench is made of rough planks. *l-maṣṭaba msawwaaya min looʒ xašin.* -- She isn't used to such rough work. *ma-mitεallma εala hiiči šuğuḷ xašin.* **2.** *waεir.* This road is very rough. *haṭ-ṭariiq kulliš waεir.* **3.** *taqriibi*.* This will give you a rough idea. *haaδa yinṭiik fikra taqriibiyya.*

roughly - 1. *b-qaswa.* You've got to treat him roughly. *laazim itεaamla b-qaswa* or *laazim tiqsi wiyyaa.* **2.** *taqriiban.* Can you tell me roughly how much it will be? *tigdar itgul-li taqriiban išgadd raʒ-itkuun?*

roughneck - *qaasi* pl. *qusaat.*

round - 1. *jawla* pl. *-aat.* He was knocked out in the first round. *nδirab nookaawt ib-ʔawwal jawla.* **2.** *doora* pl. *-aat.* Let's have another round of coffee. *xal-nišrab doora θaanya gahwa.* -- The watchman made his last round and went to bed. *n-naaṭuur daar doorta l-ʔaxiira w-raaʒ ynaam.* **3.** *mdawwar, daaʔiri*.* I bought a round copper tray. *štireet ṣiiniyya ṣifir imdawwura.*

to round off - 1. *qarrab (u taqriib) t-.* Round off your answer to the nearest ten. *qarrub jawaabak l-ʒadd il-εašaraat.* **2.** *kawwar (u takwiir) t-.* I'm not interested in details, round off the result and give me it. *maa εalayya b-tafaaṣiil; kawwur-li n-natiija w-inṭiini-yyaaha.* **3.** *εaddal (i taεdiil) t-.* Round off the edges a little. *εaddil il-ʒawaaši šwayya.*

to round out - *kammal (i ʔikmaal) t-.* I need this to round out my collection. *ʔaani ʔaʒtaaj haay ʒatta ʔakammil majmuuεti.*

round trip - *roozа w-jayya, rawaaʒ w-majiiʔ.* How much is the round trip? *šgadd itkallif ir-rooʒa wij-jayya?*

round-trip ticket - *biṭaaqa (pl. -aat) murajjaε.* He bought a round-trip ticket. *štira biṭaaqa murajjaε.*

rout - *haziima* pl.*-aat, hazaaʔim.* The demonstration ended with the complete rout of the students. *l-muδaahara ntihat ib-haziima kaamla min qibal iṭ-ṭullaab.*

route - *ṭariiq* pl. *ṭuruq.* Which route did you take? *ʔay ṭariiq ʔaxaδit.*

row - *hoosa* pl. *-aat, lağwa* pl. *-aat, lağaawi.* My neighbors made a terrible row last night. *jiiraani sawwa hoosa faδiiεa il-baarʒa bil-leel.* -- I had a row with him. *ṣaar εindi lağwa wiyyaa.*

row - *sira* pl. *-aayaat, -aawaat.* We had seats in the first row. *čaan εidna maqaaεid bis-sira l-ʔawwal.*

in a row - *marra wara l-lux, marra εala marra.* He won three times in a row. *ribaʒ itlaθ marraat marra εala marra.*

to row - *jidaf (i jadif) n-.* We rowed across the lake. *jidafna l-ṣafʒat il-lux imnil-buʒayra.*

rowboat - *balam* pl. *blaam.*

royal - *maliki*.*

rub - *farka* pl. *-aat.* One rub with this material will remove the spot. *farka wiʒda b-hal-maadda trawwiʒ il-lakka.*

to rub - 1. *jallağ (i tajliiğ) t-.* My shoes rub at the heel. *qundarti da-tjalliğ rijli mnič-čaεab.* **2.** *misaʒ (a masiʒ) n-.* Keep rubbing it until it shines. *δall imsaʒ biiha ʔila ʔan itguum tilmaε.* **3.** *furak (u farik) n-.* He rubbed his hands together to get warm. *furak ʔiid ib-ʔiid ʒatta yiʒma.* -- Rub his back with alcohol. *ʔufruk δahra kuʒuul.*

to rub against - *ʒakk (u ʒakk) n- b-, tnassaʒ (a tmissiʒ) b-.* The cat rubbed against my leg. *l-bazzuuna ʒakkat nafisha b-rijli.*

to rub down - *dallak (i tadliik).* The public baths employ men to rub down their customers. *l-ʒammaamaat iš-šaεbiyya tšağğul čam rijjaal ydallikuun il-maεaamiil.*

to rub in - *furak (u farik) n- b-.* Rub the salve in well. *ʔufruk zaayid ib-dihin.*

**I know I'm wrong, but you don't have to rub it in. *ʔadri ʔaani ġalṭaan bass ma-aku ʒaaja tεiid w-tiṣqul.*

to rub out - *misaʒ (a masiʒ) n-.* You forgot to rub out the price. *niseet timsaʒ is-siεir.*

rubber - 1. *maṭṭaaṭ, laastiik.* These tires are made of synthetic rubber. *hat-taayaraat maṣnuuεa min maṭṭaaṭ iṣṭinaaεi.* **2.** *kaaluuš.* I lost one of my rubbers yesterday. *δayyaεit farda min kaaluuši l-baarʒa.*

rubbish - 1. *zibil.* Don't mix the rubbish in with the garbage. *la-tuxbuṭ iz-zibil wiyya baqaaya* *l-ʔakil.* **2.** *xaruṭ.* Don't talk such rubbish! *la-tiʒči hiiči xaruṭ!*

rude - *jilif* pl. *ʔajlaaf.* Don't be so rude! *la-tṣiir hal-gadd jilif.*

rudeness - *jalaafa.* His rudeness is inexcusable. *jalaafta ma-yinṣufuʒ Ɛanha.*

rug - *sijjaada* pl. *-aat, zuuliyya* pl. *zwaali.*

ruin - *xaraab, damaar, halaak.* You'll be the ruin of me. *raʒ-itkuun sabab damaari.*

to ruin - **1.** *tilaf (i ʔitlaaf), dumar (u damur).* The rain will ruin the crop. *l-muṭar raʒ-yitlif il-maʒṣuul.* **2.** *xarrab (u taxriib) t-, dammar (u tadmiir) t-.* The volcano ruined the city. *l-burkaan xarrab il-wlaaya.* **3.** *hilak (i halaak).* The war ruined them. *l-ʒarub hilkathum.* **4.** *dumar (u damur) n-, dammar (u tadmiir) t-.* His new suit is completely ruined. *badilta j-jidiida ndumrat tamaaman.*

ruins - **1.** *xaraayib.* The city is in ruins. *l-madiina ṣaayra xaraayib.* **2.** *ʔaṭlaal, ʔaaθaar.* They discovered the ruins of an old temple. *ktišfaw ʔaṭlaal maƐbad qadiim.*

rule - **1.** *ʒukum.* In old times Spain was under Arab rule. *b-zamaan il-qadiim ʔispaanya čaanat taʒat ʒukum il-Ɛarab.* **2.** *niδaam* pl. *ʔanδima.* That's against the rules. *haaδa muxaalif lil-ʔanδima.* **3.** *ʔuṣuul.* I'm sticking to the rules. *ʔaani mitqayyid bil-ʔuṣuul.* **4.** *qaaƐida* pl. *qawaaƐid.* This rule doesn't apply here. *hal-qaaƐida ma-tinṭubuq ihnaa.*

as a rule - *Ɛtiyaadiyyan.* As a rule, I don't smoke. *Ɛtiyaadiyyan ʔaani ma-adaxxin.*

to rule - *ʒikam (u ʒukum) n-.* They wanted to rule the entire world. *raadaw yʒukmuun id-dinya kullha.*

to rule out - *nifa (i nafi) n-.* This doesn't rule out the other possibility. *haaδa ma-yinfi l-iʒtimaal il-laax.*

ruler - **1.** *ʒaakim* pl. *ʒukkaam.* He was an absolute ruler. *čaan ʒaakim muṭlaq.* **2.** *maṣṭara* pl. *maṣaaṭir.* The ruler is too short. *l-maṣṭara kulliš iqṣayyra.*

to **rumble** - **1.** *ṭargaƐ (i ṭargaƐa).* We heard trucks rumbling over the bridge. *smaƐna looriyaat da-ṭṭargiƐ Ɛaj-jisir.* **2.** *qarqar (i qarqara).* My stomach is rumbling. *baṭni da-tqarqir.*

rumor - *ʔišaaƐa* pl. *-aat.* The rumor spread like wildfire. *l-ʔišaaƐa ntišrat miθl il-barq.*

run - **1.** *darub* pl. *druub.* The city bus makes ten runs to Kufa every day. *paaṣ il-ʔamaana yruuʒ Ɛašra druub lil-kuufa kull yoom.* **2.** *salit.* You've got a run in your stocking. *jwaariibič bii salit.* or ***jwaariibič insilat minna xeeṭ.*

in the long run - *bil-mudda, Ɛala muruur iz-zaman, wiyya l-wakit.* In the long run you'll get tired of that. *bil-mudda raʒ-tiƐjaz minha.*

to run - **1.** *rikaδ (u rikiδ).* Don't run so fast. *la-tirkuδ hiiči sariiƐ.* **2.** *miša (i maši).* My car runs smoothly. *sayyaarti timši miθl id-dihin.* **3.** *štiġal (u šuġul).* Why do you keep the motor running? *leeš da-txalli l-makiina tištuġul?* -- How many weeks has this movie been running? *hal-filim čam isbuuƐ ṣaar-la da-yištuġul?* or *hal-filim išgadd ṣaar-la maƐruuδ?* **4.** *šaġġal (i tašġiil) t-.* Can you run a washing machine? *tigdar itšaġġil makiina maal ġasl ihduum?* **5.** *kišaf (i kašif).* The color runs. *l-loon yikšif.* **6.** *faat (u foot).* How often does this bus run? *kull išgadd hal-paaṣ yfuut?* **7.** *jira (i jarayaan).* The irrigation ditch has water running through it. *s-saagya da-yijri biiha maay.* -- Does that run in the family? *haaδa yijri b-damm il-Ɛaaʔila?* **8.** *daar (i ʔidaara) n-.* He's been running the business for three years. *ṣaar-la tlaθ isniin da-ydiir iš-šuġuḷ.* **9.** *marr (u marr).* The road runs right in front of my house. *š-šaariƐ ymurr giddaam beeti.* **10.** *wuṣal (a wuṣuul), bilaġ (i buluuġ).* The casualties ran into thousands. *l-ʔiṣaabaat wuṣlat ʔila ʔaalaaf.* **11.** *fawwat (i tafwiit) t-.* Run the rope through this loop. *fawwit il-ʒabil min hal-ʒalqa.* **12.** *txallal (a taxallul).* The theme runs through the novel from beginning to end. *l-fikra titxallal il-quṣṣa mnil-bidaaya lin-nihaaya.*

to run across - *ṣaadaf (i muṣaadafa) t-.* Maybe I'll run across him someday. *yimkin ʔaṣaadfa fadd yoom.*

to run aground - *gayyaš (i tagyiiš).* My boat ran aground. *balami gayyaš.*

to run around - **1.** *xawwar (u taxwiir), daar (u dawaraan), ftarr (a farr).* Where have you been running around? *ween činit da-txawwur?* **2.** *miša (i maši), ṣaaʒab (i muṣaaʒaba).* He's running around with a bad crowd. *mṣaaʒib-la muu xooš jamaaƐa.*

to run away - **1.** *hirab (u huruub, harab), farr (u firaar).* His wife has run away. *marta hurbat.* -- The thief ran away before the police arrived. *l-ʒaraami farr gabuḷ-ma tiji š-šurṭa.* **2.** *nhizam (i haziima), Ɛallag (i taƐliig).* When he saw us, he ran away. *min šaafna nhizam.* or ***min šaafna šammaƐ il-xeeṭ.*

to run down - **1.** *tqaṣṣa (a taqaṣṣi).* We ran down all the clues. *tqaṣṣeena kull il-ʔadilla.* **2.** *siʒag (a saʒig) n-.* He was run down by a truck. *nsiʒag ib-sayyaarat loori.* **3.** *ʒiča (i ʒači) Ɛala.* She's always running her friends down behind their backs. *haay daaʔiman tiʒči Ɛala ʔaṣdiqaaʔha waraahum.* **4.** *xilaṣ (a xalaaṣ) naṣub-.* The clock has run down. *s-saaƐa xilaṣ naṣubha.*

to run dry - *nišaf (a našif), yibas (a yibis).* The well ran dry last summer. *l-biir nišaf is-sana l-faatat.*

to run errands - *ṭṣaxxar (a taṣaxxur).* I don't have time to run errands for you. *maa Ɛindi wakit aṭṣaxxar-lak.*

to run for - *raššaʒ (i taršiiʒ) t- l-.* Who's running for the lower house from this district? *minu mraššiʒ lin-niyaaba min hal-manṭiqa?*

to run into - **1.** *diƐam (a daƐim) b-.* He ran the car into a tree. *diƐam is-sayyaara b-šajara.* **2.** *ṣaadaf (i muṣaadafa).* We ran into them in Paris last summer. *ṣaadafnaahum ib-paariis iṣ-ṣeef il-maaδi.*

**He's running into debt. *da-ywaggiƐ nafsa b-deen.*

to run low - *šaʒʒ (i šaʒʒ).* My money is running low. *fluusi da-tšiʒʒ.*

to run off - **1.** *Ɛallag (i taƐliig), hirab (a huruub), nhizam (i nhizaam).* He ran off with the club's funds. *ʔaxaδ ifluus in-naadi w-Ɛallag.* **2.** *ṭufaʒ (a ṭafuʒ).* The water ran off the fields. *l-maay ṭufaʒ imnil-ʒuquul.*

to run out - **1.** *xilaṣ (a xalaaṣ), nifaδ (a nafaaδ).* Our supply of sugar has run out. *xilaṣ mawjuudna mniš-šakar.* -- All their supplies ran out. *nifδat kull maʔuunathum.* **2.** *hajjaj (i tahjiij) t- min.* They ran him out of town. *hajjijoo mnil-balad.*

to run over - **1.** *ṭufaʒ (a ṭafuʒ).* Watch out that the bathtub doesn't run over. *diir baalak la-txalli il-baanyo yiṭfaʒ.* **2.** *siʒag (i saʒig) n-.* Watch out you don't run over the children. *diir baalak la-tisʒag ij-jihhaal.* **3.** *raajaƐ (i muraajaƐa).* Run over your part before the rehearsal. *raajiƐ doorak gabḷ it-tadriib.*

to run the risk - *tʒammal (a taʒammul) xaṭar, xaaṭar (i muxaaṭara), jaazaf (i mujaazafa).* He ran the risk of losing all his money. *tʒammal xaṭar xaṣaarat kull ifluusa.*

rundown - **1.** *puxta, xaraaba.* The house is rundown. *l-beet ṣaayir puxta.* or *l-beet ġaadi xaraaba.* **2.** *minhaar, minʒatt, talfaan.* His health is rundown; he needs a tonic. *ṣiʒʒta minʒatta, yriid-la muqawwiyyaat.* **3.** *minhadd, barbaad.* She looks terribly rundown. *ybayyin Ɛaleeha minhadda tamaaman.* or *ybayyin Ɛaleeha ṣaayra barbaada.* **4.** *mulaxxaṣ* pl. *-aat.* They gave us a rundown on the news. *nṭoona mulaxxaṣ il-ʔaxbaar.*

rung - *darja* pl. *-aat.* The top rung of the ladder is broken. *d-darja l-foogaaniyya maal id-daraj maksuura.*

runner - *raakuuδ* pl. *ruwaakiiδ.* He's a famous runner. *haaδa fadd raakuuδ mašhuur.*

rupture - *fatiq* pl. *ftuuq.* He has a rupture. *Ɛinda fatiq.*

ruse - *ʒiila* pl. *ʒiyal, xudƐa* pl. *xudaƐ.* We had to resort to a ruse. *δ̣ṭarreena niltiji ʔila xudƐa.*

rush - **1.** *bardiyya* pl. *-aat* coll. *bardi.* This mat is made of rushes. *hal-ʒaṣiir min bardi.* **2.** *Ɛajala.* What's the rush for? *Ɛala weeš hal-Ɛajala?* **3.** *zdiʒaam.* Let's wait till the rush is over. *xal-nintiδir ʔila ʔan yixlaṣ il-izdiʒaam.*

to rush - **1.** *xubaṣ (u xabṣa) n-.* Don't rush me, I'm going to do it. *la-tuxbuṣni ʔaani raʒ-asawwiiha.* **2.** *staƐjal (i stiƐjaal).* Don't rush, we have lots of time. *la-tistaƐjil, Ɛidna hwaaya wakit.* -- She rushed through her work and was done by noon. *staƐjilat ib-šuġuḷha w-xallṣat iδ-δuhur.* **3.** *maššа (i tamšiya) t- bil-Ɛajal.* They rushed the bill through. *maššaw il-laaʔiʒa* *bil-εajal.* **4.** *wadda (i tawdiya) bil-εajal.* They rushed him to the hospital. *waddoo lil-mustašfa bil-εajal.* **5.** *hijam (i hujuum).* The blood rushed to his head. *d-damm hijam ʔila raasa.*

Russia – *ruusya.*

Russian – **1.** *ruusi** pl. *ruus.* Those technicians are Russians. *hal-fanniyyiin ruus.* **2.** *ruusi.* They have a class in Russian I want to join. *εidhum daris bir-ruusi ʔariid ʔaštirik bii.*

rust – *zinjaar, ṣadaʔ.* Before you paint the fence, scrape off the rust. *ḥukk iz-zinjaar gabuḷ-ma tiṣbuġ is-siyaaj.*

to rust – *zanjar (i zinjaar) t-, ṣadda (i ṣuduuʔ).* Oil the machine or it will rust. *dahhin il-makiina wa-ʔilla tzanjir.*

to **rustle** – *xašxaš (i xašxaša).* I thought I heard something rustle. *ʔaðinn ismaεit šii yxašxiš.*

rusty – *mzanjir, mṣaddi.* He scratched his hand on a rusty nail. *jilaġ ʔiida b-bismaar imzanjir.* — The knife is rusty. *s-siččiina mṣaddya.*

**I'm afraid my French is a little rusty. *ʔaxša l-ifransi maali yinraad-la ṣaqil.*

rut – *nugra* pl. *nugar.* Keep out of the ruts made by the cars ahead of us. *twaxxar imnil-nugra s-sawwatha s-sayyaaraat il-gabuḷna.*

in rut – *ḥaamya, mithayyja.* Don't let the dog out; she's in rut. *la-txalli č-čalba tiṭlaε; tara ḥaamya.*

S

sack – *čiis* pl. *čyaas.* I want a sack of rice. *ʔariid čiis timman.*

sacred – *muqaddas.* The mosque is a sacred place. *j-jaamiε makaan muqaddas.*

**Nothing is sacred to him. *ma-yuεruf il-ḥaraam.*

sacrifice – **1.** *taðḥiya* pl. *-aat.* They made many sacrifices for their children. *hwaaya qaddimaw taðḥiyaat il-wilidhum.* **2.** *xaṣaara.* I sold my car at a big sacrifice. *biεit sayyaarti b-xaṣaara čbiira.*

to sacrifice – *ðaḥḥa (i taðḥiya) t-.* She sacrificed her life to him. *ðaḥḥat ḥayaatha min ʔajla.*

sad – *ḥaziin.* Why is he so sad? *leeš huwwa hal-gadd ḥaziin?*

saddle – *sarij* pl. *sruuj.* Can you ride without a saddle? *tigdar tirkab bila sarij?*

to saddle – *sarrij (i tasriij) t-.* Do you know how to saddle a horse? *tuεruf išloon itsarrij l-iḥṣaan?*

**He saddled me with all his troubles. *ðabb kull maṣaayba b-raasi.* or *ðabb kull ihmuuma εalayya.*

safe – **1.** *qaaṣa* pl. *-aat, xzaana* pl. *-aat, xazaayin.* We keep our safe in the office. *ʔiḥna nḥuṭṭ qaaṣatna bid-daaʔira.* **2.** *b-ʔamaan.* You are safe now. *ʔinta hassa b-ʔamaan.* **3.** *ʔamiin, maʔmuun.* This neighborhood isn't quite safe. *hal-manṭiqa muu hal-gadd ʔamiina.* **4.** *saliim.* That's a safe guess. *haaða taxmiin saliim.*

**Is the bridge safe for cars? *j-jisir yitḥammal sayyaaraat?*

**To be on the safe side, let's ask him again. *ḥatta nkuun mitʔakkidiin, xalli nsiʔla marra lux.*

safe and sound. *ṣaaġ saliim.* He's back safe and sound. *rijaε ṣaaġ saliim.*

safely – *b-salaama.* They arrived safely. *wuṣlaw ib-salaama.*

safety – *salaama.* This is for your personal safety. *haaði l-salaamtak iš-šaxṣiyya.*

**First the children were brought to safety. *ʔaxðaw il-aṭfaal bil-ʔawwal ʔila makaan amiin.*

safety razor – *makiinat* (pl. *makaayin*) *ḥilaaqa, zyaan.*

to **sag** – **1.** *hubaṭ (u habuṭ), rtixa (i rtixaaʔ).* The bookshelf sags in the middle. *raff il-kutub haabuṭ imnin-nuṣṣ.* **2.** *xisaf (u xasuf).* The mattress sags in the middle. *l-ifraaš xaasif imnin-nuṣṣ.*

Sahara Desert – *ṣ-ṣaḥraaʔ il-kubra.*

sail – *šraaε* pl. *-aat.* The wind tore the sail. *l-hawa šagg l-išraaε.*

to sail – *tirak (u tarik), ṭilaε (a ṭluuε).* The boat sails at five. *s-safiina titruk saaεa xamsa.*

**We go sailing every week. *kull isbuuε niṭlaε bil-balam ʔabu širaaε.*

**Do you know how to sail a boat? *tuεruf išloon itquud balam širaaεi?*

sailboat – *balam širaaεi* pl. *blaam širaaεiyya.*

sailor – *baḥḥaar* pl. *baḥḥaara.* How many sailors are on the boat? *čam baḥḥaar ʔaku εas-safiina?*

sake – *xaaṭir, muud, ʔajil.* I did it for your sake. *sawweetha εala muudak.* — He gave his life for his country's sake. *ðaḥḥa b-nafsa min ʔajil bilaada.* — At least do it for your son's sake! *εal-aqall sawwiiha l-xaaṭir ibnak.*

**For the sake of argument, let's say he did go. *xalli niftirið ʔinna raaḥ.*

salad – *zalaaṭa.*

salary – *raatib* pl. *rawaatib, maεaaš* pl. *-aat.* How can you manage on that salary? *šloon itdabbur ʔamrak ib-har-raatib?*

sale – **1.** *beeε.* The sale of alcoholic drinks to minors is prohibited. *beeε il-mašruubaat liṣ-ṣiġaar mamnuuε.* — Our neighbor's house is for sale. *beet jiiraanna lil-beeε.* — Sales of cotton goods have doubled this year. *beeε il-mantuujaat il-quṭniyya tðaaεaf has-sana.* **2.** *tanziiluul.* I bought this coat at a sale. *štireet hal-qappuuṭ min maḥall εinda tanziilaat.*

salesclerk – *bayyaaε* pl. *-a, -iin.* He's a salesclerk in a department store. *huwwa bayyaaε ib-maḥall tijaari.*

salesman – *bayyaaε* pl. *-a, -iin.* One of our salesmen will call on you tomorrow. *waaḥid min bayyaaεiinna raḥ-yzuurak baačir.*

salt – **1.** *miliḥ.* Pass me the salt, please. *naawušni l-miliḥ rajaaʔan.* **2.** *mmallaḥ.* Do you have salt cheese? *εindak jibin immallaḥ?*

to salt – *mallaḥ (i tamliiḥ) t-.* Did you salt the soup? *mallaḥti š-šoorba?*

to salt away – *xazzan (i taxziin) t-, ṣammad (u taṣmiid) t-.* He salted away a tidy sum of money. *haada xazzan xooš kammiyya mnil-ifluus.*

salt flat – *ṣabxa* pl. *-aat.*

salt shaker – *mamlaḥa* pl. *mamaaliḥ.*

salt works – *mamlaḥa* pl. *mamaaliḥ.* We visited the salt works near Basra. *ziirna l-mamlaḥa qurb il-baṣra.*

salty – *maaliḥ.* The fish is awfully salty. *s-simač kulliš maaliḥ.*

same – **1.** *nafis.* I can be back on the same day. *ʔagdar arjaε ib-nafs il-yoom.* — We're the same age. *ʔiḥna b-nafs il-εumur.* or ***ʔiḥna εumurna suwa.* — Thanks, the same to you! *šukran, ʔatmannaa-lak nafs iš-šii.* or ***ʔinta hammeen.* **2.** *suwa.* That's all the same to me. *kullha suwa εindi.* or **haay kullha fadd šii bin-nisba ʔili.*

all the same – *maεa ðaalik.* All the same, I want to see it. *maεa ðaalik, ʔariid ašuufha.*

sample – *namuuðaj* pl. *namaaðij, namuuna* pl. *namaayin.* Do you have a sample of the material with you? *εindak namuuðaj imnil-iqmaaš jaayba wiyyaak?*

sand – *ramuḷ.*

sandal – *naεal, naεaal* pl. *niεil.*

sandwich – *sandwiiča* pl. *-aat.* Take a few sandwiches along. *ʔuynð wiyyaak čam sandwiiča.*

to sandwich in – *ḥiṣar (i ḥaṣir) n-.* He was sandwiched in between two stout women. *nḥiṣar been niswaan iθneen ismaan.*

sanitary – *ṣiḥḥi**. Your kitchen is not sanitary enough. *maṭbaxak muu ṣiḥḥi kaafi.*

sarcastic – *mithakkim* pl. *-iin.*

sardine – *sardiina* pl. *-aat* coll. *sardiin.*

satisfaction – *rtiyaaḥ, ʔirðaaʔ.* It gives me great satisfaction to hear that. *ʔašεur b-irtiyaaḥ čibiir min asmaεha.*

**Was everything settled to your satisfaction? *ntihat il-masʔala miθil-ma triid?* or *kullši čaan ṣaayir εala keefak?*

satisfactory – *murði.* His condition is satisfactory. *ḥaalta murðiya.*

to be satisfactory – *wufa (i wafooʔ) bil-maraam.* This room is quite satisfactory. *hal-ġurfa toofi bil-maraam tamaaman.*

to **satisfy** – **1.** *ʔarða (i ʔirðaaʔ) n-, raððа (i tarðiya) t-.* Your answer doesn't satisfy me. *jawaabak ma-yirðiini.* — I'm not satisfied with my new apartment. *ʔaani ma-raaði εala šuqqti j-jidiida.* — You can't satisfy everybody. *ma-tigdar itraðði kull waaḥid.* **2.** *qinaε (a qanaaεa) n-.* We'll have to be satisfied with less. *laazim niqnaε ib-ʔaqall.*

Saturday - *s-sabit, yoom is-sabit.*
sauce - **1.** *marga* pl. *-aat* coll. *marag.* How do you make the sauce for this dish? *šloon itsawwi l-marga maal hal-ʔakla?* **2.** *ṣooṣ* pl. *-aat, ṣaaṣ* pl. *-aat.* Put some sauce on your kabob. *xalli šwayya ṣooṣ ɛala l-kabaab.*
saucepan - *jidir* pl. *jduur, jduura; gidir* pl. *gduur, gduura.*
saucer - *maaɛuun* pl. *mwaaɛiin, ṣaẓan* pl. *ṣẓuun.*
Saudi - *suɛuudi* pl. *-iyyiin.* I met a Saudi yesterday. *laageet fadd suɛuudi l-baarẓa.*
Saudi Arabia - *l-mamlaka l-ɛarabiyya s-suɛuudiyya.*
savage - **1.** *waẓši* pl. *-iyyiin, wuẓuuš; hamaji* pl. *-iyyiin, hamaj.* You're behaving like a savage. *ʔinta tiṭṣarraf miθl il-wuẓuuš.* **2.** *qaasi.* He started a savage attack on the government. *bida hijuum qaasi ɛal-ẓukuuma.*
to **save** - **1.** *ʔanqaδ (u ʔinqaaδ) n-.* He saved her life. *ʔanqaδ ẓayaatha.* **2.** *ḍamm (u ḍamm) n-, ẓtifaḍ (u ẓtifaaḍ) b-.* Could you save this for me until tomorrow? *tigdar iṭḍumm-li haay ʔila baačir?* — Why do you save these old papers? *lweeš tiẓtifuḍ ib-hal-ʔawraaq il-ɛatiiga?* **3.** *ẓijaz (i ẓajiz) n-.* Is this seat being saved for anyone? *hal-makaan maẓjuuz il-ʔaẓẓad?* **4.** *jimaɛ (a jamiɛ) n-, jammaɛ (i tajmiiɛ) t-.* He saves stamps. *yijmaɛ ṭawaabiɛ.* **5.** *waffar (i tawfiir) t-, ddixar (a ddixaar).* Have you saved any money? *waffarit ʔay ifluus?* **6.** *xallaṣ (i taxliiṣ) t- min, jannab (i tajniib) t- min.* You could have saved yourself the trouble. *čaan xallaṣit nafsak min-had-dooxa.*
**Save your breath. He's not listening. *la-ttaɛɛib nafsak, huwwa ma-daayir-lak baal.*
savings - *muddaxaraat.* He's used up all his savings. *ṣiraf kull muddaxaraata.*
saw - *minšaar* pl. *manaašiir.* Could I borrow a saw from you? *ʔagdar aṭlub minšaar minnak?*
to saw - *gaṣṣ (u gaṣṣ) n-, širaẓ (a šariẓ) n-.* He's been sawing wood all morning. *ṣaar-la mniṣ-ṣubuẓ yguṣṣ xišab.*
to **say** - **1.** *gaal (u gool) n-.* What did you say? *š-gilit?* — The paper says rain. *j-jariida tguul raẓ-tumṭur.* — What does the sign say? *š-itguul haay il-ʔišaara?* — I'll meet you, say, in an hour. *ʔašuufak, xalli nguul baɛad saaɛa.* — They say he speaks several languages. *yguuluun huwwa yitkallam ɛiddat luġaat.* **2.** *kitab (i kitaaba) n-, δikar (u δikra) n-, gaal (u gool) n-.* The papers didn't say a thing about it. *j-jaraayid ma-kitbat ʔay šii ɛanha.*
**There's much to be said for his suggestion. *qtiraaẓa yistiẓiqq il-ihtimaam.*
to say good-by - *waddaɛ (i tawdiiɛ) t-.* I said good-by to him yesterday. *waddaɛta l-baarẓa.*
to say nothing of - *min ɛada.* It takes a lot of time, to say nothing of the expense. *taaxuδ ihwaaya wakit haay min ɛada l-maṣaariif.*
saying - *qawl* pl. *ʔaqwaal, maθal* pl. *ʔamθaal.* That's a very common saying. *haaδa qawl kulliš šaayiɛ.*
**That goes without saying. *haaδa ma-bii munaaqaša.*
scaffold - *skalla* pl. *-aat, ʔaskala* pl. *-aat.* He fell from the scaffold. *wugaɛ min ɛal-iskalla.*
scale - *miqyaas* pl. *maqaayiis.* I bought myself a new scale. *štireet-li fadd miqyaas jidiid.* — The scale is one to one thousand. *miqyaas ir-rasim waaẓid ɛala ʔalif.* **2.** *sullam* pl. *salaalim.* She practices musical scales all day. *titdarrab ɛala s-sullam il-mawsiiqi ṭuul in-nahaar.* **3.** *gišir* pl. *gšuur, filis* pl. *fluus.* The fish has big scales. *s-simča ɛidha gšuur ikbaar.* **4.** *miizaan* pl. *mawaaziin, miyaaziin.* Put the meat on the scales. *xalli l-laẓam bil-miizaan.*
to scale - **1.** *ṣiɛad (a ṣaɛuud) n-ɛala, tsallaq (a tasalluq).* Ten of us scaled the wall. *ɛašra minna ṣiɛdaw ɛal-ẓaayiṭ.* **2.** *gaššar (i tagšiir) t-.* The fish hasn't been scaled yet. *s-simča ma-tgašširat baɛad.*
scandal - *faḍiiẓa* pl. *faḍaayiẓ.*
scar - *ʔaθar (pl. ʔaaθaar) jiriẓ, ʔuxut.* He has a scar on his right cheek. *ɛinda ʔaθar jiriẓ ɛala xadda l-ʔayman.*
scarce - *naadir.* Gold coins have become scarce. *l-ɛumla δ-δahabiyya ṣaayra naadra jiddan.*
**Eggs are scarce at this time of year. *l-beeḍ yqill ib-hal-wakit imnis-sana.*
scarcely - *bil-kaad.* I scarcely know him. *ʔaani bil-kaad ʔaɛurfa.*
scare - *fazaɛ, fazza.* You gave me an awful scare. *fazzaɛitni fazaɛ faḍiiɛ.* or ***xawwafitni hwaaya.*
to scare - **1.** *xawwaf (i taxwiif) t-.* The dog scared me to death. *č-čalib xawwafni hwaaya.* **2.** *xaaf (a xoof) n-.* I scare easily. *ʔaani ʔaxaaf bil-ɛajal.*
**We were scared stiff. *jimadna mnil-xoof.*
**Where did he scare up the money? *mneen jaab l-ifluus?* or *mneen dabbar l-ifluus?*
scarf - *laδδaaf* pl. *-aat.*
scarlet - *qirmizi*.*
to **scatter** - *tfarraq (a tafarruq), ṭaššar (i taṭšiir) t-.* The crowd scattered when the police arrived. *j-jamhuur itfarraq min wuṣlat iš-šurṭa.* — The books were scattered all over the floor. *l-kutub čaanat imṭaššara b-kull ṣafẓa ɛal-gaaɛ.*
scene - **1.** *mašhad* pl. *mašaahid, manḍar* pl. *manaaḍir.* That's in the third scene of the second act. *haaδa bil-mašhad iθ-θaaliθ imnil-faṣl iθ-θaani.* **2.** *furja* pl. *-aat.* Don't make a scene. *la-tsawwiina furja.*
behind the scenes - *jawwa l-ɛabaa, wara s-sitaar.* Nobody knows what's going on behind the scenes. *maẓẓad yidri š-da-yṣiir jawwa l-ɛabaa.*
scenery - **1.** *mašaahid, manaaḍir.* Who designed the scenery? *minu ṣammam il-mašaahid?* **2.** *manaaḍir.* We didn't have time to look at the scenery. *ma-ṣaar ɛidna wakit inšuuf il-manaaḍir.*
scent - **1.** *riiẓa* pl. *-aat.* The dogs have got the scent. *č-čilaab šammaw ir-riiẓa.* **2.** *ẓassat iš-šamm.* Our dog has a keen scent. *čalibna ɛinda ẓassat iš-šamm ẓaadda.*
to scent - **1.** *štamm (a štimaam) riiẓat-.* The dogs have scented the fox. *č-čilaab ištammaw riiẓat iθ-θaɛlab.* **2.** *ɛaṭṭar (i taɛṭiir) t-.* She scented the clothes. *ɛaṭṭirat il-ihduum.*
schedule - *jadwal* pl. *jadaawil.* We'll have to work out a schedule if we want to finish on time. *laazim insawwi jadwal ʔiδa ridna axalliṣ ɛal-wakit.*
on schedule - *ɛal-wakit.* The train arrived on schedule. *l-qiṭaar wuṣal ɛal-wakit.*
to schedule - *ẓaddad (i taẓdiid) t- wakit, ɛayyan (i taɛyiin) wakit.* The meeting's scheduled for tomorrow. *l-ijtimaaɛ itẓaddad wakta baačir.*
scheme - **1.** *xuṭṭa* pl. *xuṭaṭ, mašruuɛ* pl. *mašaariiɛ, manhaj* pl. *manaahij.* Has he thought up a new scheme? *haaδa fakkar ib-xuṭṭa jidiida?* **2.** *tartiib* pl. *-aat.* We've changed the color scheme. *ġayyarna tartiib il-alwaan.*
to scheme - *dabbar (u tadbiir) t-, muʔaamara.* They're always scheming. *humma ɛala ṭuul ydabbruun muʔaamaraat.*
scholar - *ɛaalim* pl. *ɛulamaaʔ, ṭaalib (pl. ṭullaab) ɛilim.* He's a great scholar. *huwwa ɛaalim čibiir.*
school - *madrasa* pl. *madaaris.* Do you go to school? *ʔinta truuẓ lil-madrasa?*
science - *ɛilim* pl. *ɛiluum.* He's more interested in science than art. *ɛinda raġba bil-ɛilim ʔakθar imnil-fann.*
scientific - *ɛilmi*.*
scientist - *ɛaalim* pl. *ɛulamaaʔ.*
scissors - *mugaṣ* pl. *mugaṣṣaat, mgaaṣa, mgaṣṣ* pl. *-aat, mgaaṣiiṣ.* The scissors are dull. *l-mugaṣ ʔaɛma.*
to **scold** - *zaff (i zaff) n-, razzal (i tarziil) t-.* My mother scolded me. *ʔummi zaffatni.*
to **scorch** - *ẓirag (i ẓarig) n-.* I nearly scorched my dress. *ẓragit badilti ʔilla šwayya.*
**The sun is scorching hot. *š-šamis da-tilfaẓ.*
scorcher - **It's a scorcher today. *hal-yoom ẓaarr.*
score - **1.** *majmuuɛ.* What's the score? *šgadd il-majmuuɛ?* or ***šgadd ṣaarat in-nuqaaṭ?* **2.** *θaar.* I have a score to settle with him. *ɛindi θaar wiyyaa laazim ʔanhii.*
**Scores of people died in the epidemic. *ɛadad čibiir maat imnil-wabaaʔ*
to score - *sajjal (i tasjiil) t-.* We scored five points in the second half. *sajjalna xamis nuqaaṭ bin-nuṣṣ iθ-θaani.*
scorpion - *ɛagrab* pl. *ɛagaarub.*
scoundrel - *saafil* pl. *safala, minẓaṭṭ* pl. *-iin.*
to **scour** - *jilaf (ijalif) n-.* She scoured the kettle. *jilfat il-quuri.*
scouring pad - *ṣummaaṭa* pl. *-aat, jillaafa* pl. *-aat.*
scrambled eggs - *beeḍ maṭruug.*
scrap - **1.** *wuṣla* pl. *wuṣal.* That's only a scrap of paper. *haaδi mjarrad wuṣlat waraq.* **2.** *ɛarka* pl. *-aat.* They had an awful scrap last night. *čaanat beenaathum ɛarka θixiina l-baarẓa bil-leel.*
to **scrape** - **1.** *gišaṭ (i gašiṭ) n-.* He scraped his hand on the rock. *gišaṭ ʔiida biṣ-ṣaxra.*
to scrape off - *ẓakk (u ẓakk) n-.* Scrape the

paint off before you paint. *ẓukk iṣ-subuġ gabuḷ-ma tiṣbuġ.*

to scrape together - *lamm (i lamm) n-, jimaʕ (a jamiʕ) n-.* I couldn't scrape the money together. *ma-gdarit alimm il-ifluus.*

scrap metal - *sikraab.* He deals in scrap metal. *yištuġuḷ bis-sikraab.*

scratch - **1.** *xadiš* pl. *xuduuš, txirmuš* pl. *-aat.* What's that scratch on your cheek? *šinu hal-xadiš ib-xaddak?* **2.** *šuxuṭ* pl. *šxuuṭ.* How'd that scratch get on the table? *mneen jaa haš-šuxuṭ ʕal-meez?*

**We escaped without a scratch. *nhizamna min duun ʔay ʔaδδa.*

**After the fire he had to start from scratch. *baʕd il-ẓariiq iḍṭarr yibdi mnil-ʔawwal.*

to scratch - **1.** *xaddaš (i taxdiiš) t-, xidaš (i xadiš) n-.* Be careful not to scratch the furniture. *diir baalak la-txaddiš il-ʔaθaaθ.* **2.** *šixaṭ (u šaxuṭ) n-.* This pen scratches. *hal-qalam yišxuṭ.*

to scratch out - *šiṭab (u šaṭub) n-, šixaṭ (u šaxuṭ) n-.* Scratch out the last sentence. *ʔišṭub ij-jumla l-ʔaxiira.*

scream - *ṣarxa* pl. *-aat, ṣeeẓa* pl. *-aat, ṣyaaẓ.* I thought what I heard was a scream. *ḍanneet illi smaʕitha ṣarxa.*

**He's a scream! *huwwa kulliš muḍẓik.*

to scream - *ṣirax (u ṣraax).* The child screamed with fright. *ṭ-ṭifil ṣirax imnil-xoof.*

screen - **1.** *sitaar* pl. *sataaʔir, ẓaajiz* pl. *ẓawaajiz.* Change behind the screen. *baddil wara s-sitaar.* **2.** *šaaša* pl. *-aat.* He looks older on the screen. *ybayyin ʔakbar min ʕumra ʕaš-šaaša.* **3.** *teel.* We need a new screen on that window. *niẓtaaj teel jidiid ʕala haaδa š-šibbaak.*

screw - *burġi* pl. *baraaġi.* These screws need tightening. *hal-baraaġi tiẓtaaj taqwiya.*

to screw - *buram (u barum) n-.* He screwed the nut on the bolt. *buram ij-jooza ʕal-burġi.*

**Screw the cap on tight. *šidd il-qabaġ zeen.*

**Things are all screwed up at work. *kull il-masaaʔil imxarbuṭa biš-šuġuḷ.*

**If I can screw up enough courage, I'll ask for a raise. *ʔiδa ʔagdar ašidd ẓeeli, raẓ-aṭlub ziyaadat raatib.*

screw driver - *darnafiis* pl. *-aat, mfall* pl. *-aat.*

to **scrub** - *furak (u farik) n-.* We've got to scrub the floor. *laazim nifruk il-gaaʕ.*

sculptor - *naẓẓaat* pl. *-iin, maθθaal* pl. *-iin.*

scythe - *minjal* pl. *manaajil.*

sea - *baẓar* pl. *biẓaar.* How far are we from the sea? *šgadd nibʕid imnil-baẓar?* -- The Nile empties into the Mediterranean Sea. *n-niil yṣubb bil-baẓr il-ʔabyaḍ il-mutawaṣṣiṭ.*

seal - **1.** *faqma* pl. *-aat.* We watched them feed the seals. *tfarrajna ʕaleehum yṭaʕʕmuun il-faqmaat.* **2.** *ṭamġa* pl. *-aat, xatim* pl. *ʔaxtaam.* The papers bore the official seal. *l-ʔawraaq ẓaamla ṭ-ṭamġa r-rasmiyya.* **3.** *xatim* pl. *ʔaxtaam.* Somebody must have broken the seal. *waaẓid laazim kaasir il-xatim.*

to seal - *sadd (i sadd) n-, lizag (i lazig) n-.* Have you sealed the letter yet? *saddeet il-maktuub loo baʕad?*

seam - *xyaaṭ* pl. *-aat.* Rip open the seam. *ʔiftig l-ixyaaṭ.*

search - *baẓiθ* pl. *buẓuuθ, taftiiš* pl. *-aat.* The police made a thorough search. *š-šurṭa qaamat ib-baẓiθ šaamil.*

to search - **1.** *fattaš (i taftiiš) t-.* We'll have to search you. *laazim infattišak.* **2.** *dawwar (i tadwiir) t-.* I've searched the whole house. *dawwarit il-beet kulla.* **3.** *biẓaθ (a baẓiθ) n-, dawwar (i), fattaš (i).* We searched for him everywhere. *biẓaθna ʕalee b-kull makaan.*

seasick - **I was terribly seasick on my last trip. *ṣaabni dawaar baẓar kulliš qawi bis-safra l-faatat.*

seasickness - *dawaar baẓar.*

season - **1.** *faṣil* pl. *fuṣuul.* Which season do you like best, winter or summer? *yaa faṣil itẓibb ʔakθar, š-šita loo ṣ-ṣeef?* **2.** *mawsim* pl. *mawaasim.* This is the best season for swimming. *haaδa ʔaẓsan mawsim lis-sibiẓ.*

to season - *ẓaṭṭ (u) bahaaraat ʕala.* What did you season the meat with? *š-ẓaṭṭeet ʕal-laẓam?*

seasoned - *mjarrub.* They were seasoned troops. *čaanaw ijnuud imjarrubiin.*

seat - *maqʕad* pl. *maqaaʕid.* This seat needs fixing. *hal-maqʕad yiẓtaaj taṣliiẓ.* -- The pants are tight in the seat. *l-panṭuroon ḍayyig imnil-maqʕad.*

to have a seat - *giʕad (u guʕuud) n-.* Please have a seat. *tfaḍḍal, ʔugʕud.*

to seat - **1.** *gaʕʕad (i tagʕiid) t-.* Seat the children in the front row. *gaʕʕid il-ʔaṭfaal biṣ-ṣaff il-ʔamaami.* **2.** *lizam (i lazim) n-, kaffa (i takfiya) t-.* The theater seats five hundred people. *s-siinama tilzam xamis miit saxiṣ.*

second - **1.** *θaanya* pl. *θawaani.* He ran a hundred yards in ten seconds. *rikaḍ miit yarda b-ʕašir θawaani.* **2.** *laẓḍa* pl. *-aat.* Wait a second. *ʔintiḍir laẓḍa.* **3.** *θaani.* Will you please give me the second book from the left? *baḷḷa ma-tinṭiini l-iktaab iθ-θaani lli min ʕal-yisra?* -- Give me a second class ticket to Basra, please. *rajaaʔan inṭiini taδkara daraja θaanya lil-baṣra.*

in the second place - *θaanyan.* In the first place I have no time, and in the second place I don't want to go anyway. *ʔawwalan ma-ʕindi wakit, w-θaanyan ʔaani ma-ariid aruuẓ ʕala kull ẓaal.*

to second - *θanna (i taθniya) t-, ʕala.* I second the motion. *ʔaθanni ʕal-iqtiraaẓ.*

second-hand - **1.** *mustaʕmal.* He bought the book second-hand. *štira l-iktaab mustaʕmal.* **2.** *min maṣdar θaanawi.* I only know that story secondhand. *ʔaʕruf hal-quṣṣa min maṣdar θaanawi bass.*

secondly - *θaanyan.* Secondly, I don't want to go anyway. *θaanyan ma-ariid aruuẓ ʕala kull ẓaal.*

second-rate - *daraja θaanya.* It's definitely a second-rate hotel. *bit-taʔkiid haaδa findiq daraja θaanya.*

secret - **1.** *sirr* pl. *ʔasraar.* Let me in on the secret. *xabburni ʕan is-sirr.* **2.** *sirri*.* They have a secret plan. *ʕidhum xuṭṭa sirriyya.*

secretary - *sikirteer* pl. *-iyya.* She's my secretary. *hiyya s-sikirteera maalti.* -- I talked to the second secretary at the embassy. *ẓčeet wiyya s-sikirteer iθ-θaani bis-safaara.*

secretly - *bis-sirr, sirran, bil-xifya.* They met secretly. *jtimʕaw bis-sirr.*

sect - *maδhab* pl. *maδaahib, ṭaaʔifa* pl. *-aat, ṭawaaʔif.*

section - **1.** *juzuʔ* pl. *ʔajzaaʔ.* You'll find it in section three of chapter one. *tšuufa bij-juzʔ iθ-θaaliθ imnil-faṣl il-ʔawwal.* **2.** *qisim* pl. *ʔaqsaam, manṭiqa* pl. *manaaṭiq.* I was brought up in this section of Baghdad. *ʔaani rbeet ib-hal-qism min baġdaad.*

secure - **1.** *mḍoogar, maḍmuun.* It's a secure investment. *hiyya šaġla mḍoogra.* **2.** *bil-amaan.* Nobody feels secure these days. *maẓẓad yišʕur bil-amaan hal-ʔayyaam.* **3.** *mašduud.* Is the load secure? *l-ẓimil mašduud zeen?*

to secure - *ḍiman (i ḍamaan) n-.* His future is secured. *mustaqbala maḍmuun.*

security - **1.** *ṭamaʔniina.* We feel a sense of security if we lock our door at night. *nišʕur ib-ṭamaʔniina ʔiδa qfalna baabna bil-leel.* **2.** *ḍamaan.* What security can you give me? *ʔay ḍamaan tigdar tinṭiini?* **3.** *rahin* pl. *ruhuun.* I had to leave my watch as security. *ḍṭarreet aẓuṭṭ saaʕati ka-rahin.* **4.** *ʔamin.* The meeting of the security council lasted an hour. *jtimaaʕ majlis il-ʔamin ṭawwal saaʕa.*

securities - *ʔashum w-sanadaat.* He's invested most of his money in securities. *šaġġaḷ muʕḍam amwaala bil-ʔashum wis-sanadaat.*

to **see** - **1.** *šaaf (u šoof) n-.* May I see your passport? *ʔagdar ašuuf jawaaz safarak?* **2.** *tṣawwar (a taṣawwur), šaaf (u šoof) n-.* I don't see it that way. *ma-aṭṣawwarha hiiči.* **3.** *ltiga (i ltigaaʔ).* I'd like to see more of you. *ʔaẓibb altigi wiyyaač ʔakθar.*

**Anybody can see through him. *ʔay waaẓid yigdar yuʕruf šaku b-gaḷba.*

**I'll see you through this year. *raẓ-abqa asaaʕdak ʔila nihaayat haay is-sana.*

**Please see to it that this letter is mailed today. *rajaaʔan itʔakkad bi-ʔan hal-maktuub yruuẓ bil-bariid il-yoom.*

**See to it that you are on time. *tʔakkad min ʔan tiji ʕal-wakit.*

to see one home - *waṣṣal (i tawṣiil) t- lil-beet.* May I see you home? *tismaẓii-li awaṣṣlič lil-beet?*

seed - *bazra* pl. *-aat* coll. *bazir, ẓabba* pl. *-aat, ẓubuub* coll. *ẓabb.* Did you buy any seeds? *štireet bazir?* -- Some types of oranges have no seeds. *baʕaḍ ʔanwaaʕ il-purtaqaal ma-biiha ẓabb.*

to seed - *biδar (i baδir) n-, ṭašš (u ṭašš) n- bazir.* When did you seed this field? *šwakit biδarit hal-ẓaqil?*

to **seem** - **1.** *bayyan (i tabyiin) t-.* I seem to be in-

terrupting. *ybayyin ʔanni da-aqaaṭiε.*
2. *bida (u badu).* It seems to me he wanted to go last week. *yibduu-li čaan yriid yruuz̧ δaak il-isbuuε.* or *εala ma-aεtiqid raad yruuz̧ δaak il-isbuuε.*

to **seize** - 1. *kumaš (u kamuš) n-, lizam (a lazim) n-.* He seized the rope with both hands. *kumaš il-z̧abil b-iidteena.* 2. *milak (i malik) n-, lizam (a) n-.* Fear seized him. *milaka l-xoof.* 3. *sayṭar (i sayṭara) t- εala, lizam (a) n-.* The police seized his papers. *š-šurṭa sayṭarat εala ʔawraaqa.* 4. *ġtinam (i ġtinaam), ntihaz (i ntihaaz).* If I don't seize this opportunity, it may be too late. *muz̧tamal yruuz̧ εalayya kullši ʔiδa ma-aġtinim hal-furṣa.*

seldom - *naadiran, naadiran-ma.* I seldom see him in the coffee shop. *naadiran-ma ʔašuufa bil-gahwa.*

to **select** - *ntixab (i ntixaab), xtaar (a xtiyaar).* Have you selected anything yet? *ntixabit šii loo baεad?*

selection - *majmuuεat il-ʔaškaal.* We have a big selection of shirts. *εidna majmuuεat il-ʔaškaal imniθ-θiyaab.*

selfish - *ʔanaani*.* How can anyone be so selfish? *šloon waaz̧id yigdar ykuun hal-gadd ʔanaani?*

to **sell** - 1. *baaε (i beeε) n-.* Did you sell your old car? *biεit sayyaartak il-qadiima?* — Sorry the tickets are all sold out. *maεa l-ʔasaf, it-taδaakir inbaaεat kullha.* 2. *nbaaε (a).* How are the glasses selling? *šloon da-tinbaaε l-iglaaṣaat?*
**He sold us out to the enemy. *xaanna wiyya l-ʔaεdaaʔ.* or *huwwa wiša biina lil-ʔaεdaaʔ.*

Semite - *saami* pl. *-iyyiin.* The Semites established the first civilization in Iraq. *s-saamiyyiin ʔanšaʔuu ʔawwal z̧aδaara bil-εiraaq.*

Semitic - *saami*.* Arabic is a Semitic language. *l-luġa l-εarabiyya hiyya luġa saamiyya.*

to **send** - *dazz (i dazz) n-, ʔarsal (i ʔirsaal) n-, biεaθ (a baεiθ) n-.* Send it by mail. *dizzha bil-bariid.*
to send for - *stadεa (i stidεaaʔ).* Have you sent for the doctor? *stadεeet ṭabiib?*
to send in - *daxxal (i tadxiil) t-.* Send him in. *daxxla.* or ***xallii yidxul.*
to send out for - *dazz (i dazz) n- εala.* Shall I send out for ice cream? *triid adizz εala doondirma?*

senior - *ʔaqdam, ʔasbaq.* He's the senior man in the office. *huwwa ʔaqdam waaz̧id bil-maktab.*

sensation - 1. *δajja, z̧amaas.* His speech created a sensation. *z̧adiiθa ʔaθaar δajja čibiira.* 2. *šuεuur.* It's a very pleasant sensation. *huwwa fadd šuεuur laṭiif.*

sense - 1. *z̧aassa* pl. *-aat.* My dog has a keen sense of smell. *čalbi εinda z̧aassat šamm qawiyya.*
2. *ʔidraak, εaqil.* I hope he has sense enough to take a taxi. *ʔaamal ʔan ykuun εinda ʔidraak kaafi z̧atta yaaxuδ taksi.* 3. *šuεuur.* It gives us a sense of security. *tinṭiina šuεuur bil-iṭmiʔnaan.*
**There's no sense in doing that. *ma-ʔilha maεna tsawwiiha.*
in a sense - *min naaz̧iya, min jiha.* That's true, in a sense. *min naaz̧iya haaδa ṣaz̧iiz̧.*
to sense - *z̧ass (i z̧iss) n-, ʔadrak (i ʔidraak) n-.* I sensed right away that something was wrong. *z̧asseet raʔsan ʔaku fadd šii ġalaṭ.*

senseless - *ma-biiha εaqil.* It would be senseless to go out in this rain. *ma-biiha εaqil ʔiδa tiṭlaε barra b-hal-muṭar.*

sensible - *εaaqil, mudrik.* Be sensible! *kuun εaaqil!*

sensitive - *z̧assaas.* I'm sensitive to cold. *ʔaani z̧assaas lil-barid.*

sentence - 1. *jumla* pl. *jumal.* I didn't understand the last sentence. *ma-ftihamt ij-jumla l-ʔaxiira.*
2. *z̧ukum* pl. *ʔaz̧kaam.* The judge has just pronounced sentence. *l-z̧aakim hassa ʔaṣdar il-z̧ukum.*
to sentence - *z̧ikam (u z̧ukum) n-.* He was sentenced to five years. *nz̧ikam xams isniin.*

sentry - *z̧aaris* pl. *z̧urraas.* The sentry didn't let me pass. *l-z̧aaris ma-xallaani ʔafuut.*

separate - *minfiṣil.* Could we have separate rooms? *nigdar naaxuδ ġuraf minfaṣla?*
to separate - 1. *farraq (i tafriiq) t-.* I could hardly separate those two. *b-ṣuεuuba gdarit atfarriq haθ-θineen.*
2. *qassam (i taqsiim) t-.* Separate the group into five sections. *qassim ij-jamaaεa ʔila xamis aqsaam.*

separately - *εala z̧ida.* Can you buy each volume separately? *tigdar tištiri kull juzuʔ εala z̧ida?*

September - *ʔayluul.*

sergeant - *εariif* pl. *εurafaaʔ*

series - *silsila* pl. *-aat.* He's written a series of articles about it. *kitab silsilat maqaalaat εanha.*

serious - 1. *jiddi* pl. *-iyyiin.* Why are you so serious? *leeš ʔinta hal-gadd jiddi?* 2. *muhimm.* It isn't serious. *muu šii muhimm.* 3. *xaṭar, xaṭiir.* That's a serious mistake. *haaδa ġalṭa xaṭra.*
**Are you serious? *da-tiz̧či jidd?*

seriously - *jiddiyyaat, εan jidd.* Don't take it so seriously. *la-taaxuδha jiddiyyaat.* — I'm seriously considering getting married. *ʔaani jiddiyyaat da-afakkir biz-zawaaj.*

sermon - *xuṭba* pl. *-aat.* The Imam gave a good sermon Friday. *l-ʔimaam xuṭab xuṭba zeena yoom ij-jumεa.*

servant - *xaadim* pl. *xadam, xiddaam.* I'm not your servant. *ʔaani muu xaadim maalak.*

serve - *sirv, seef.* Whose serve is it? *b-iid man is-sirv?*
to serve - 1. *qaddam (i taqdiim) t-.* Shall I serve the drinks now? *ʔaqaddim il-mašruubaat hassa?*
2. *xidam (i xadim).* He served in the Navy. *xidam bil-baz̧riyya.*
**This will serve as a substitute. *haay raz̧-itquum maqaamha.*
**Dinner is served! *l-εaša z̧aaδir.* or *l-εaša jaahiz.* **That serves you right! *tistaahilha!*

service - 1. *xidma.* The service is bad in this restaurant. *l-xidma muu zeena b-hal-maṭεam.* — This is a civil service regulation. *haaδa qaanuun il-xidma l-madaniyya.* 2. *jeeš, jayš.* How long have you been in the service? *šgadd ṣaar-lak bij-jayš?*

service station - *maz̧aṭṭat (pl. -aat) paanziin, paanziinxaana* pl. *-aat.* Let's stop at the next service station. *xal-noogaf ib-muz̧aṭṭat il-paanziin ij-jaaya.*

set - *ṭaxum* pl. *ṭxuum, majmuuεa* pl. *-aat.* We have a whole set of these ash trays. *εidna ṭaxum kaamil min haṭ-ṭablaat ij-jigaayir.*
all set - *z̧aaδir.* Everything all set? *kullši z̧aaδir?*
to set - 1. *z̧aṭṭ (u z̧aṭṭ), xalla (i).* Set it on the desk. *z̧uṭṭha εal-meez.* 2. *niṣab (u naṣub) n-.* I set my watch by the station clock. *niṣabit saaεati εala saaεat il-muz̧aṭṭa.* 3. *εayyan (i taεyiin) t-, z̧addad (i taz̧diid) t-.* Why don't you set the time? *leeš ma-tεayyin il-wakit?* 4. *karrak (i takriik) t-.* Is the hen setting on the eggs? *d-dijaaja mkarrika εal-beeδ?* 5. *jabbar (u tajbiir) t-.* The doctor will have to set your arm. *ṭ-ṭabiib laazim yjabbur ʔiidak.* 6. *rakkab (i tarkiib) t-.* He set the stone in a ring for me. *rakkab-li l-z̧ajar εal-miz̧bas.* 7. *ġurab (u ġarub) n-.* The sun has already set. *š-šamis ġurbat.* 8. *ṣaffaf (i taṣfiif) t-.* I want my hair washed and set. *ʔariid šaεri yinġisil w-yiṭṣaffaf.* 9. *bida (i bidaaya).* He set to work immediately. *bida bil-εamal z̧aalan.*
10. *z̧aδδar (i taz̧δiir) t-.* Quick, set the table! *z̧aδδiri l-meez bil-εajil.*
**You've got to set a good example. *laazim tijεal min nafsak maθal il-ġeerak.*
to set ahead - *qaddam (i taqdiim) t-.* I set my watch five minutes ahead. *qaddamit saaεti xams diqaayiq.*
to set at - *z̧addad (i taz̧diid) t-.* He set the price at fifty dinars. *z̧addad is-siεir ib-xamsiin diinaar.*
to set down - *nazzal (i tanziil) t-.* Set the box down gently. *nazzil iṣ-ṣanduug εala keefak.*
to set free - *ʔaṭlaw (i ʔiṭlaaq) siraaz̧.* The prisoners were set free. *l-masjuuniin ʔaṭliqaw saraaz̧hum.*
to set off - *fajjar (i tafjiir) t-.* They didn't have time to set off the explosives. *ma-čaan εidhum wakit yfajjruun il-mutafajjiraat.*
to set on - *šayyaš (i tašyiiš) t-, εala.* He set the dogs on me. *šayyaš ič-čilaab εalayya.*
to set out - *twajjah (a tawajjuh), saafar (i safar).* He set out for home on Monday. *twajjah il-beeta yoom iθ-θineen.*
to set straight - *εaddal (i taεdiil) t-.* Can you set me straight on this? *tigdar itεaddilni b-haay?*
to set up - 1. *niṣab (u naṣub) n-.* The new machines have just been set up. *l-makaayin ij-jidiida hassa nnuṣbat.* 2. *ʔassas (i taʔsiis) t-.* Are you going to set up housekeeping? *raz̧-itʔassis beet?* — His father set him up in business. *ʔabuu ʔassas-la šuġul.*

to **settle** - 1. *ṣaffa (i taṣfiya) t-.* He settled his bill with his creditors. *ṣaffa z̧saaba maεa d-dayyaana.*

2. *ʒall (i ʒall) n–*. You must settle the misunderstanding between yourselves. *laazim itʒilluun il-xilaaf beenaatkum.* 3. *stawṭan (i stiiṭaan).* The Americans settled their country gradually. *l-amriikaan istawṭinaw baladhum bit-tadriij.* 4. *sakkan (i taskiin) t–*. The government is going to settle farmers on the newly developed land. *l-ʒukuuma raʒ-itsakkin il-fallaaʒiin bil-ʔaraaḍi l-mustaθmara ʒadiiθan.* 5. *staqarr (i stiqraar).* The Bedouin don't want to settle anywhere. *l-badu ma-yriiduun yistiqirruun ib-ʔay mukaan.* 6. *ṭaax (u ṭoox).* The wall has settled a little. *l-ḥaayiṭ ṭaax išwayya.* 7. *trassab (a tarassub).* Wait until the coffee grounds have settled. *ntiḍir ʔila ʔan yitrassab it-tilif maal il-gahwa.* 8. *niha (i nahi) n–*. That settles the matter. *haaδa yinhi l-masʔala.*
settled people – *ʒaḍar.* There is a great difference in the lives of nomad and settled peoples. *ʔaku fariq čibiir ib-ʒayaat il-badu wil-ʒaḍar.*
settlement – 1. *ttifaaq* pl. *-aat.* They couldn't reach a settlement. *ma-gidraw yooṣluun ʔila ttifaaq.* 2. *maʔwa* pl. *maʔaawi, mustaqarr* pl. *-aat.* We uncovered the remains of an ancient settlement. *ktišafna ʔaaθaar maʔwa qadiim.*
seven – 1. *sabiε.* He's seven years old. *εumra sabiε siniin.* 2. *sabiεt.* I was there seven days. *buqeet ihnaak sabiεt iyyaam.* 3. *sabεa* pl. *-aat.* These numbers are all sevens. *har-raqum kullha sabεaat.*
seventeen – *ṣbaaṭaεaš.*
seventeenth – *l-iṣbaaṭaεaš.*
seventh – *saabiε.*
seventieth – *s-sabεiin.*
seventy – *sabεiin.*
several – *εidda.* I'd like to stay here for several days. *ʔard abqa hnaa εiddat ʔayyaam.*
severe – 1. *qaasi.* It was a very severe winter. *čaan iš-šita qaasi.* 2. *šadiid, ʒaadd.* She complains of severe pains. *hiyya tiški min ʔaâlaam šadiida.*
to **sew** – *xayyaṭ (i taxyiiṭ) t–*. She sews her own clothes. *txayyiṭ ihduumha b-nafisha.* — Please sew the buttons on for me. *rajaaʔan xayyiṭ-li d-dijam.*
sewer – *burbux* pl. *baraabix.* The sewer is clogged. *l-burbux masduud.*
sex – 1. *jinis.* In your application, state your age and sex. *b-ṭalabak ʔiδkur il-εumur wij-jinis.* 2. *jinsi*.* She's got a lot of sex appeal. *εidha hwaaya jaaδibiyya jinsiyya.*
sexual – *jinsi*.* He has sexual relations with her. *εinda εilaaqa jinsiyya wiyyaaha.*
sexy – *muhayyij.* She's a very sexy girl. *hiyya fadd bint kulliš muhayyija.*
shabby – 1. *mšaggig.* His suit looks shabby. *badilta tbayyin imšaggiga.* 2. *xasiis, danii ʔ.* That was very shabby of him. *haay čannat kulliš xasiis minna.*
shade – 1. *ḍill, fayy.* Let's stay in the shade. *xal-nibqa biḍ-ḍill.* 2. *parda* pl. *-aat.* Pull down the shades. *nazzil il-pardaat.* 3. *loon* pl. *ʔalwaan.* This red is too dark a shade. *haaδa l-loon il-ʔaʒmar išwayya ṭoox.*
shadow – *xayaal* pl. *-aat.* The trees cast long shadows. *l-ʔašjaar itsawwi xayaalaat iṭwiila.*
**There is not a shadow of doubt about it. *ma-biiha šakk ʔabadan.*
to shadow – *raaqab (i muraaqaba) t–*. They assigned a detective to shadow him. *εayynaw šurṭi sirri ʒatta yraaqba.*
shady – That's a shady business. *haay šaġla mašbuuha.*
**It's shady over here. *biiha fayy ihnaa.*
shaft – *šaft* pl. *-aat.* The shaft on this machine is bent. *šaft hal-makiina maεwuuj.*
to **shake** – 1. *hazz (i hazz) n–*. He shook his head. *hazz raasa.* 2. *xaḍḍ (u xaḍḍ) n–*. Shake it well before using it. *xuḍḍha zeen gabuḷ-ma tistaεmilha.* 3. *rajj (u rajj) n–*. The earthquake shook everything in the city. *z-zalzila rajjat kullši bil-madiina.*
**Come on, shake a leg! *yaḷḷa, staεjil!*
to shake hands – *ṭṣaafaʒ (a taṣaafuʒ).* They shook hands. *ṭṣaafʒaw.*
shaky – 1. *mirtiεiš.* I'm still shaky. *ʔaani baεadni mirtiεiš.* 2. *mgaḷgaḷ.* The table's shaky. *l-meez imgaḷgaḷ.*
shall – *raʒ-, εuud.* We shall see who's right. *raʒ-inšuuf minu maḍbuuṭ.*
**I'll never go there. *ʔabad ma-aruuʒ ihnaak.*
**Shall I wait? *triid antiḍir?*
shallow – 1. *ḍaʒil.* The lake is very shallow in this area. *l-buʒayra kulliš ḍaʒla b-hal-manṭiqa.* — He's a very shallow person. *huwwa fadd waaʒid kulliš ḍaʒil.* 2. *muu ġamiij.* Put it in a shallow bowl. *ʒuṭṭha b-minčaasa muu ġamiija.*
shame – 1. *xajal.* Haven't you any shame? *ma-εindak ʔay xajal?* or ***ma-tistiʒi ʔabad?* 2. *εeeb.* Shame on you! *εeeb εaleek.*
**What a shame you can't come! *maεa l-ʔasaf ma-tigdar tiji.*
shape – 1. *šikil* pl. *ʔaškaal.* What shape is the table? *šloon šikla lil-meez.* 2. *ʒaala* pl. *-aat.* What shape is the car in? *šloon ʒaalat is-sayyaara?* 3. *waḍεiyya* pl. *-aat, ʒaala* pl. *-aat.* I'm in bad shape. *waḍεiiti muu zeena.*
in shape – *ʒaaḍir.* Is everything in shape? *kullši ʒaaḍir?*
out of shape – *muεaqqač, maεquuč.* The hat's all out of shape. *š-šafqa kullha mεaqqača.*
to shape up – *tʒassan (i taʒassun).* Things are gradually shaping up. *l-ʔašyaaʔ tadriijiyyan da-titʒassan.*
share – 1. *ʒuṣṣa* pl. *ʒuṣaṣ, sahim* pl. *ʔashum.* Everybody has to pay his share. *kull waaʒid laazim yidfaε ʒuṣṣta.* 2. *sahim* pl. *ʔashum.* How many shares did you buy? *čam sahim ištireet?*
to share – *tšaarak (i tašaaruk) b–*. Let's share the cake. *xalli nitšaarak bil-keeka.*
to share with – *šaarak (i mušaaraka) b–*. Will you share my lunch with me? *tigdar itšaarakni bil-ġada?*
shareholder – *musaahim* pl. *-iin.*
shark – *koosaj* pl. *kwaasij.*
loan shark – *muraabi* pl. *-iin.*
sharp – 1. *ʒaadd.* Do you have a sharp knife? *εindak siččiina ʒaadda?* 2. *laaδiε, saliiṭ.* She has a sharp tongue. *εidha lsaan laaδiε.* 3. *biḍ-ḍabuṭ, tamaaman.* We have to be there at five o'clock sharp. *laazim inkuum ihnaak saaεa xamsa biḍ-ḍabuṭ.*
**Keep a sharp eye on him. *raaqba zeen.*
to **sharpen** – 1. *ʒadd (i ʒadd) n–*. This knife needs sharpening. *has-siččiina tiʒtaaj ʒadd.* 2. *qaṭṭ (u qaṭṭ) n–, bira (i bari) n–*. Sharpen the pencil for me, please. *quṭṭ-li l-qalam min faḍlak.*
shave – *ʒilaaqa* pl. *-aat, ziyaan* pl. *-aat.* I want a shave and a haircut. *ʔariid ʒilaaqat wujji w-ziyaan šaεari.*
to shave – *zayyan (i zyaan) t–, ʒilaq (i ʒalooqa) n–*. Who shaved you? *minu zayyanak?* or *minu ʒilaq wiččak?*
she – *hiyya, haaδi, haay.* She is a capable woman. *hiyya mrayya muqtadra.*
**She was in town last night. *čaanat bil-balad il-baarʒa bil-leel.*
shed – *εambaar* pl. *εanaabiir, maxzan* pl. *maxaazin.* Put the tools back in the shed. *rajjiε il-ʔadawaat lil-εambaar.*
to shed – 1. *ʔalqa (i ʔilqaaʔ) n–*. That sheds some light on the matter. *haaδa yilqi ḍaww εal-mawḍuuε.* 2. *nizaε (a naziε), δabb (i δabb) n–*. As soon as I got into my room I shed all my clothes. *ʔawwal-ma wuṣalit il-ġurufti nizaεit kull ihduumi.* 3. *δiraf (i δarif) n–*. She shed bitter tears. *δirfat dumuuε ʒaarra.* 4. *δabb (i δabb).* My dog's shedding his hair. *čalbi da-yδibb šaεra.* 5. *minaε (a maniε).* This overcoat doesn't shed water at all. *hal-qappuuṭ ma-yimnaε il-muṭar bil-marra.*
sheep – *xaruuf* pl. *xurfaan, ġanma* pl. *ʔaġnaam* coll. *ġanam.*
sheer – 1. *ṣirf.* That's sheer nonsense. *haaδi saxaafa ṣirf.* 2. *šaffaaf.* I'd like some sheer material like voile. *ʔariid iqmaaš šaffaaf miθl il-waayil.*
sheet – 1. *čarčaf* pl. *čaraačif.* Shall I change the sheets? *triid aġayyir ič-čaraačif?* 2. *quṭεa* pl. *-aat.* Please give me a sheet of paper. *rajaaʔan inṭiini fadd quṭεat waraq.* 3. *ṭabqa* pl. *-aat, looʒa* pl. *-aat.* We bought a sheet of plywood. *štireena ṭabqat xišab muεaakis.*
**She turned as white as a sheet. *wujihha ṣaar ʔaṣfar miθl il-kurkum.*
sheik – *šeex* pl. *šyuux.*
shelf – *raff* pl. *rfuuf.* The shelves are empty. *r-rufuuf xaalya.*
shell – 1. *gišir* pl. *gšuur.* The hazelnut shell is hard. *gišr il-findig qawi.* 2. *qumbula* pl. *qanaabil.* A shell exploded near our house. *fadd qumbula nfijrat yamm beetna.* 3. *ṣidfa* pl. *-aat.* coll. *ṣidaf.* What'll I do with the shells of the snails? *š-asawwi b-ṣidaf il-ʒalazuun haay?*
to shell – 1. *gaššar (i tagšiir) t–*. Do you want to shell the nuts? *triid itgaššir ij-jooz?* 2. *fallas (i tafliis) t–, gaššar (i tagšiir) t–.*

The peas have to be shelled. *l-bazaalya laazim titfallas.* **3.** *§irab (u §arib) n- bil-qanaabil.* The army shelled the town. *j-jayš §irbaw il-madiina bil-qanaabil.*

shelter - *malja?* pl. *malaaji?, ma?wa* pl. *-aat.* We found shelter in a hut during the storm. *ttixaδna l-kuux malja? ?aθnaa? il-Eaaşifa.*

to shelter - *?aawa (yi?wi ?iiwaa?).* They sheltered and fed us. *?aawoona w-ţaEEmoona.*

shepherd - *raaEi* pl. *raEyaan.*

shield - *diriE* pl. *duruuE.* He has a collection of shields and swords. *Einda majmuuEa min id-duruuE wis-siyuuf.*

to shield - **1.** *zima (i zimaaya) n-, zifa§ (a zafi§) n-.* You ought to shield your eyes against the sun. *laazim tizmi Eeenak imniš-šamis.* **2.** *tsattar (a tasattur) Eala, zima (i zimaaya) n-.* He must be shielding someone. *laazim da-yitsattar Eala fadd ?azzad.*

shift - *dafEa* pl. *-aat, wajba* pl. *-aat.* Our workers work in two shifts. *Eummaalna yištağluun Eala dafiEteen.*

to shift - **1.** *baddal (i tabdiil) t- geer.* You ought to shift into second. *laazim itbaddil geer Eaθ-θineen.* **2.** *ğayyar (i tağyiir) t-, baddal (i tabdiil) t-.* We have to shift the meeting to Tuesday. *laazim inğayyir il-ijtimaaE ?ila θ-θilaaθaa.* **3.** *tğayyar (a tağayyur).* The direction of the wind has shifted. *l-hawa tğayyar ittijaaha.*

**I've always had to shift for myself. *?aani činit mi§ţarr daa?iman ?adabbur ?umuuri b-nafsi.*

shin - *saaq.* I got kicked in the shinbone. *?akalit §arba Eala Ea§mat saaqi.*

shine - *lamEa.* See if you can take the shine out of these pants. *šuuf ?iδa tigdar itwaxxir il-lamEa min hal-panţaroon.*

to shine - **1.** *šaEE (i šaEE) n-, limaE (a lamiE) n-.* Her eyes were shining with joy. *Eyuunha čaanat da-tšiEE imnil-faraz.* **2.** *baddaE (i tabdiiE) t-.* He's good in all his subjects, but mathematics is where he shines. *haaδa zeen ib-kull idruusa bass ybaddiE Eala l-?axaşş bir-riyaa§iyyaat.* **3.** *subağ (u sabuğ) n-.* I have to shine my shoes. *laazim ?aşbuğ qundarti.*

**The sun isn't shining today. *š-šamis ma-ţaalEa l-yoom.*

ship - *baaxira* pl. *bawaaxir.* When does the ship leave? *šwakit itğaadir il-baaxira?*

to ship - *šizan (a šazin) n-, dazz (i dazz) n-.* Has the case been shipped yet? *ş-şanduug inšizan loo baEad?*

shipment - *šazna* pl. *-aat, ?irsaaliyya* pl. *-aat.* We've just received a new shipment of shoes. *hassa stilamna šazna jdiida mnil-?azδiya.*

shipwreck - *zuţaam safiina.*

shirt - *θoob* pl. *θyaab, qamiiş* pl. *qumşaan.* Are my shirts back from the laundry? *θyaabi rijEat imnil-makwi?*

**He'd give you the shirt off his back. *?iida muu ?ila.* or *huwwa kulliš barmaki.*

**Keep your shirt on, I'll be right there. *la-taxbusni, ?aani jaay.*

shish kebab - *tikka.*

to **shiver** - *rijaδ (i rajiδ) n-, riEaš (i raEiš) n-.* The child shivered with cold. *ţ-ţifil rijaf imnil-barid.*

shock - **1.** *şadma* pl. *-aat.* His death was a great shock to us all. *mootta čaanat şadma Eaniifa Ealeena kullna.* — He's still suffering from shock. *baEad yqaasi mniş-şadma.* **2.** *natil.* You can get a bad shock from this machine. *mumkin taakul natil qawi min hal-makiina.* **3.** *koom* pl. *?ikwaam.* They stacked up the wheat in shocks. *kaddisaw l-zunţa Eala šikil ikwaan.*

to get a shock - *nnital (i).* I got a shock from the lamp. *nnitalit inni§-§aww.*

to shock - *şiEaq (a şaEiq) n-, şidam (i şadim) n-.* I was shocked by the death of his father. *nşiEaqit ib-xabar moot ?abuu.*

shockproof - *§idd il-kasar.* This watch isn't shockproof. *has-saaEa muu §idd il-kasar.*

shoe - **1.** *qundara* pl. *qanaadir, ziδaa?* pl. *?azδiya.* I'd like a pair of shoes. *?ariid zooj qanaadir.* **2.** *naEal* pl. *nEaalaat.* The horse lost one shoe. *l-izşaan waggaE naEal min inEaalaata.*

to shoe - *naEEal (i tanEiil).* The horse needs shoeing. *l-izşaan yirraad-la tanEiil.*

shoehorn - *karata* pl. *-aat.*

shoelace - *qiiţaan* pl. *qyaaţiin.* I want a pair of shoelaces. *?ariid zooj iqyaaţiin.*

shoemaker - *qundarči* pl. *-iyya.* Is there a shoemaker nearby? *?aku qundarči qariib minnaa?*

shoe polish - *şubuğ qanaadir.*

shoeshine - *şubuğ qundara.* I need a shoeshine. *?aztaaj şubuğ qundara.*

to **shoot** - **1.** *rima (i rami), ?aţlaq (i ?iţlaaq).* He shot the gun four times. *rima l-bunduqiyya ?arbaE marraat.* **2.** *§urab (u §arub) b-rişaaş.* He shot him in the back and killed him. *§uraba rişaaş ib-§ahra w-mawwata.* **3.** *xiţaf (u xaţuf) n-.* The car shot past us. *s-sayyaara xuţfat min yammna.* **4.** *maddad (i tamdiid), tallaE (i taţliiE).* The seed, when it starts growing, shoots out roots. *l-zabba min tinbit itmaddid ijduur.* **5.** *?axaδ (u ?axiδ) n-.* I shot eight pictures today. *?axaδit θaman şuwar il-yoom.*

**You ought to be shot for that. *yinraad-lak taEliig Ealeeha.*

to shoot down - *waggaE (i tawgiiE) t-.* They shot down one of our planes. *waggaEaw wizda min ţiyyaaraatna.*

shop - *dukkaan* pl. *dakaakiin, mazall* pl. *-aat. maxzan* pl. *maxaazin.* There are many shops on this street. *?aku hwaaya dakaakiin ib-haš-šaariE.*

to shop - *tsawwag (a tsuwwug).* We shop at the market. *?izna nitsawwag imnis-suug.*

**I want to shop around before I buy the present. *?ariid aduur išwayya w-aaxuδ fikra gabuļ-ma ?aštiri l-hadiyya.*

shopping - *miswaag.* I still have a lot of shopping to do. *baEad Eindi hwaaya miswaag.*

shore - *saazil* pl. *sawaazil.* How far is it to the shore? *šjadd yibEid is-saazil?*

short - **1.** *šooţ* pl. *-aat.* There was a short in your radio. *saar šooţ ib-waayaraat ir-raadyo maalak.* **2.** *gşayyir.* He's rather short. *huwwa gşayyir.* — She wears short dresses. *tilbas malaabis igşayyra.* — Cut my hair short. *guşş šaEri gşayyir.* **3.** *naaqiş.* His books are short today. *zsaaba naaqiş hal-yoom.*

in short - *muxtaşar il-kilaam, xaşm il-zači.* In short, I can't come. *muxtaşar il-kilaam, ma-agdar ?aji.*

to cut short - *ğaşşar (i tagşiir) t-.* They had to cut their trip short. *§ţarraw ygaşşruun safrathum.*

to run short - *nugaş (u naguş).* Our ammunition is running short. *δaxiiratna da-tinguş.*

shortage - **1.** *naqiş, qilla.* The shortage of materials is reducing our production. *naqş il-mawaadd il-?awwaliyya da-yxaffuş intaajna.* **2.** *Eajiz, naqiş.* The auditors discovered a shortage in his accounts. *l-mudaqqiqiin iktišfaw Eajiz b-izsaabaata.*

shortcoming - *Eeeb* pl. *Eiyuub.* The house has many shortcomings. *l-beet bii Eiddat Eiyuub.*

short cut - *ţariiq muxtaşar* pl. *ţuruq muxtaşara.* He knows a short cut to the beach. *yuEruf ţariiq muxtaşar liš-šaaţi.*

to **shorten** - *gaşşar (tgişşir) t-.* Shorten the pants for me, please. *gaşşir-li l-panţaroon rajaa?an.*

shorter - *?aqşar, ?agşar.* These pants are shorter than mine. *haay il-panţaroonaat ?aqşar min maalti.*

shortly - *baEd išwayya.* He'll be here shortly. *raz-ykuun ihnaa baEd išwayya.*

shorts - **1.** *lbaas* pl. *-aat, libsaan.* He ordered six pairs of shorts. *waşşa Eala sitt libsaan.* **2.** *panţaroon igşayyir* pl. *-aat igşayyra.* The girls all wore shorts and sweaters. *kull il-banaat libsaw panţaroonaat igşayyra w-bluuzaat şuuf.*

short wave - *mawja qaşiira.* You can get short wave too, on this radio. *tigdar itzaşşil Eala mawja qaşiira hamm ib-har-raadyo.*

shot - **1.** *ţalqa* pl. *-aat.* Did you hear a shot? *smaEit ţalqa?* **2.** *niišaanči* pl. *-iyya, neešinči,* pl. *-iyya.* He's a good shot. *huwwa xoδs niišaanči.* **3.** *laqţa* pl. *-aat, şuura* pl. *şuwar.* We got good shots of the prime minister. *?axaδna xooš laqţaat il-ra?iis il-wuzaraa?* **4.** *?ubra* pl. *?ubar.* Are you getting shots? *da-taaxuδ ?ubar?* **5.** *mitwattir.* His nerves are all shot. *?aEşaaba mitwattra.* **6.** *mistahlak.* That machine's all shot. *haay il-makiina mistahlika.*

**He thinks he's a big shot. *yitşawwar nafsa fadd šaxşiyya.*

to take a shot - *?aţlaq (i ?iţlaaq) rişaaş.* Somebody took a shot at him. *fadd waazid ?aţlaq Ealee rişaaş.*

shoulder - *čitif* pl. *čtaaf, čtaafaat.* His shoulders are broad. *čtaafa Eariiδa.*

**I gave it to him straight from the shoulder. *kallamta b-şaraaza.*

**We'll have to put our shoulders to the wheel.

laazim nibδil ʔaqṣa juhudna.

to give the cold shoulder - *tjaahal (i tajaahul), ɛaamal (i muɛaamala) ib-buruud.* Why'd you give him the cold shoulder? *leeš itjaahalta?*

to shoulder - 1. *xalla (i txilli) t- ɛala čitif-.* He shouldered the sack of wheat and walked home. *xalla čiis il-ẓunṭa ɛala čitfa w-miša lil-beet.* 2. *ʔaxaδ (u) ɛala ɛaatiq-, tẓammal (a taẓammul).* He shouldered the responsibility. *ʔaxaδ il-masʔuuliyya ɛala ɛaatqa.* — Why should I shoulder the blame for it? *leeš ʔaani laazim atẓammal il-loom?* 3. *tnakkab (a tanakkub).* The soldiers shouldered their rifles and marched off. *j-jinuud itnakkbaw banaaduqhum w-mišaw.*

to **shout** - *ṣayyaẓ (i tṣiyyiẓ) t-, ṣaaẓ (i ṣyaaẓ) n-.* You don't have to shout! *ma-aku ẓaaja tṣayyiẓ!*

**The speaker was shouted down by the crowd. *ṣyaaẓ ij-jamaahiir xalla l-xaṭiib yiskut.*

shouting - *ṣyaaẓ.* Your shouting is getting on my nerves. *ṣyaaẓkum da-ysawwiini ɛaṣabi.*

shove - *dafɛa* pl. *-aat.* He gave me a shove that knocked me over. *difaɛni dafɛa waggaɛatni.*

to shove - 1. *daffaɛ (i tadfiiɛ) t-, daɛɛač (i tadɛiič) t-.* Don't shove! *la-tdaffiɛ!* 2. *difaɛ (a dafiɛ) n-.* They shoved him in front of a bus. *difɛoo giddaam il-baaṣ.*

to shove around - *jaawaz (a tajaawuz) ɛala.* People keep shoving him around. *n-naas yjaawzuun ɛalee.*

shovel - *karak* pl. *-aat, mijraf* pl. *-aat.* You'll need a pickax and shovel. *raẓ-tiẓtaaj qazma w-karak.*

to shovel - *kuraf (u karuf).* Shovel this sand into the truck. *ʔukruf ir-ramul w-δibba bil-loori.*

show - 1. *ɛariḍ* pl. *ɛuruuḍ.* Other than that, how did you like the show? *ma-ɛada haaδa, šloon ɛijabak il-ɛariḍ?* 2. *door* pl. *ʔadwaar, ɛariḍ* pl. *ɛuruuḍ.* When does the first show start? *s-saaɛa beeš yibdi d-door il-ʔawwal?*

to show - 1. *raawa (i muraawaʔa) t-, bayyan (i tabyiin) t-.* Show me how you do it. *raawiini šloon itsawwiiha.* 2. *bayyan (i tabyiin) t-.* Only his head showed above water. *bass raasa bayyan min foog il-maay.* 3. *dalla (i tdilli).* Could you show me the way? *tigdar itdilliini ṭ-ṭariiq?* 4. *ɛiraḍ (i ɛariḍ) n-.* What are they showing at the theater this evening? *š-raẓ-yɛirḍuun bis-siinama hal-leela?* 5. *ʔaḍhar (i ʔiḍhaar) n-.* The investigation didn't show a thing. *t-taẓqiiqaat ma-ʔaḍharat šii.* 6. *ḍihar (i ʔiḍhaar).* I'm going to show you for what you are. *raẓ-aḍihrak ɛala ẓaqiiqtak.*

**This picture shows a new automobile. *haṣ-ṣuura marsuuma sayyaara jdiida.*

to show around - *farraj (i tafriij) t- ɛala.* She's showing her guests around the town. *da-tfarrij iḍyuufha ɛal-madiina.*

to show off - *tbaaha (i tabaahi), raawa (i muraawaʔa) nafs~.* He's just showing off. *huwwa bass da-yitbaaha.* — He likes to show his children off. *yɛijba yitbaaha b-awlaada.*

to show up - 1. *jaa (i majiiʔ), bayyan (i tabyiin) t-.* Nobody showed up. *maẓẓad jaa.* 2. *ḍihar (a ḍuhuur).* Yellow shows up well against a black background. *l-ʔaṣfar yiḍhar zeen ɛala gaaɛiyya sooda.*

showcase - *jaamxaana* pl. *-aat.* Let me see that ring in the showcase. *raawiini l-miẓbas illi bij-jaamxaana.*

shower - 1. *zaxxa* pl. *-aat.* We were caught in a heavy shower. *lizmatna zaxxa qawiyya.* 2. *duuš* pl. *-aat.* Does your new apartment have a shower? *š-šiqqa j-jidiida maaltak biiha duuš?*

to shower - *ġarrag (i tġirrig) t-.* Their friends showered them with presents. *ʔaṣdiqaaʔhum ġarrgoohum bil-hadaaya.*

show-off - *mbahaayči* pl. *-iyya.* He's a big show-off. *huwwa mbahaayči.*

shrewd - *miqtidir, ẓaadiq.* He's a shrewd businessman. *huwwa fadd rajul ʔaɛmaal miqtidir.*

shrill - *rafiiɛ.* She has a shrill voice. *ɛidha ẓiss rafiiɛ.*

shrimp - 1. *rubyaan.* We're having shrimp for dinner. *raẓ-ykuun ɛidna rubyaan bil-ɛaša.* 2. *qizim* pl. *ʔaqzaam.* He's a little shrimp. *huwwa qizim.* or **haaδa nuṣṣ neeča.*

to **shrink** - 1. *xašš (u xašš) n-.* Does this material shrink when washed? *hal-iqmaaš yxušš bil-ġasil?* 2. *nkumaš (i nkimaaš).* The meat shrank when we cooked it. *l-laẓam inkumaš min ṭubaxnaa.* 3. *tjabjab (a tajabjub).* He shrinks from responsibility. *haaδa yitjabjab imnil-masʔuuliyya.*

shrub - *šujayra* pl. *-aat.*

to **shrug** - *hazz (i hazz) n-.* He shrugged his shoulders. *hazz ičtaafa.*

to **shuffle** - 1. *xarbaṭ (u txurbuṭ) t-, xilaṭ (i xaliṭ) n-.* Have the cards been shuffled? *l-waraq itxarbaṭ?* 2. *šaẓẓaṭ (i tašẓiiṭ) b-.* Stop shuffling your feet; you're ruining your shoes! *bass ɛaad itšaẓẓiṭ ib-rijlak, muu ɛidamit qundartak!*

to **shut** - 1. *sadd (i sadd) n-.* Please shut the door! *sidd il-baab rajaaʔan!* 2. *ẓibas (i ẓabis) n-.* Who shut the dog in the garage? *minu ẓibas ič-čalib bil-garaaj?*

to shut down - *ɛazzal (i tɛizzil).* Why'd the factory shut down? *leeš il-maɛmal ɛazzal.*

to shut off - 1. *giṭaɛ (a gaṭiɛ) n-, gaṣṣ (u gaṣṣ) n-.* The workers shut off our water for two days. *l-ɛummaal giṭɛaw il-maay ɛanna li-muddat yoomeen.* 2. *sadd (i sadd) n-.* Shut off the water. *sidd il-maay!*

to shut up - *sikat (u sukuut) n-.* Shut up! *ʔiskut!* or **nčabb!*

shutter - 1. *ʔabajoor* pl. *-aat.* Open the shutters, please. *fukk il-ʔabajooraat, min faḍlak.* 2. *ẓaajiz* pl. *ẓawaajiz, ẓaajib* pl. *ẓujjaab.* The lens shutter in my camera is stuck. *ẓaajiz il-ɛadasa maal kaamarti mšakkal.* 3. *kabang* pl. *-aat.* The storekeeper shut the door and rolled down the shutter. *ṣaaẓib il-maẓall sadd il-baab w-nazzal il-kabang.*

shy - *xajuul* pl. *-iin.* Don't be so shy! *la-tkuun hal-gadd xajuul.* or **la-tistiẓi.*

to shy - *jifal (i jafil).* The horse shied at the car. *l-iẓṣaan jifal imnis-sayyaara.*

to shy away from - *tjannab (a tajannub).* He shies away from hard work. *yitjannab iš-šuġuḷ iš-šaaq.*

sick - *mariiḍ* pl. *marḍa.* He's sick in bed. *huwwa mariiḍ bil-ifraaš.* — The sick are given the best of care. *l-marḍa ydaaruuhum zeen.*

**I get sick when I fly. *nafsi tilɛab min aṭiir.*

**I'm getting sick and tired of this job. *malleet min iš-šaġḷa.* or *bizɛat nafsi mniš-šaġḷa.*

to be taken sick - *tmarraḍ (a tamarruḍ).* He was suddenly taken sick. *ɛala ġafla tmarraḍ.*

sickle - *minjal* pl. *manaajil.*

sickness - *maraḍ* pl. *ʔamraaḍ.*

side - 1. *jiha* pl. *-aat, ṣoob* pl. *ʔaṣwaab, jaanib* pl. *jawaanib.* On this side of the street there are only a few houses. *min haj-jiha mniš-šaariɛ ʔaku šwayya ẓwaaš bass.* — I saw him on the other side of the city. *šifta biš-ṣoob iθ-θaani mnil-madiina.* 2. *jaanib* pl. *jawaanib.* He is on our side. *huwwa min jaanibna.* 3. *jaanibi*.* Please use the side door. *rajaaʔan istaɛmil il-baab ij-jaanibiyya.* 4. *xaaṣra* pl. *xawaaṣir.* She's a thorn in his side. *waagfa siččiina b-xaaṣirta.*

**To be on the safe side, I asked him again. *siʔalta marrt il-lux ẓatta atʔakkad.*

side by side - *suwa.* They walked along silently side by side. *mišaw bil-hiduuʔ suwa.*

to take sides - *nẓaaz (a nẓiyaaz) ʔila jiha, ʔayyad (i taʔyiid) t- jiha.* It's difficult to take sides on this question. *ṣaɛub waaẓid yinẓaaz ʔila jiha b-hal-qaḍiyya.*

to side with - *nẓaaz (a nẓiyaaz) l-, ʔayyad (i taʔyiid) t- l-.* You always side with him! *ʔinta daaʔiman tinẓaaz-la.*

sidewalk - *raṣiif* pl. *ʔarṣifa.*

siege - *ẓiṣaar* pl. *-aat.*

sieve - *munxuḷ* pl. *manaaxuḷ.*

to **sift** - *nixaḷ (u naxiḷ) n-.* The flour has to be sifted first. *ṭ-ṭaẓiin laazim yinnuxuḷ bil-ʔawwal.*

to **sigh** - *tẓaṣṣar (a taẓaṣṣur), tnahhad (a tanahhud).* What are you sighing about? *leeš da-titẓaṣṣar?*

sight - 1. *naḍar, baṣar.* He lost his sight in the accident. *fuqad naḍara bil-ẓaadiθ.* 2. *manḍar* pl. *manaaḍir.* That's a beautiful sight! *haaδa manḍar jamiil waḷḷa!*

**I recognized you at first sight. *ʔawwal ma-šiftak ɛiraftak.*

**Don't lose sight of him. *la-txallii yġiib ɛan naḍarak.*

**They had orders to shoot him on sight. *čaan ɛidhum ʔawaamir yiṭliquun in-naar ʔawwal-ma yšuufuu.*

sights - *maɛaalim.* Have you seen the sights of the town? *šifit maɛaalim il-madiina?*

by sight - *bil-wujih.* I know him only by sight. *ʔaɛurfa bass bil-wujih.*

in sight - *mbayyin, ḍaahir.* The end is not yet in sight. *n-nihaaya baɛadha ma-mbayyna.*

to catch sight of - *limaẓ (a lamiẓ).* As soon as he caught sight of you, he vanished. *ʔawwal-ma limaẓak, ixtifa.*

sign - 1. *quṭɛa* pl. *quṭaɛ, ʔišaara* pl. *-aat, ɛalaama* pl. *-aat, yaafṭa* pl. *-aat.* What does that sign say? *š-maktuub ɛal-quṭɛa?* 2. *baadira* pl. *-aat.* Is that a good sign? *haay baadira ṭayyba?* 3. *ʔišaara* pl. *-aat.* He gave us a sign to follow him. *nṭaana ʔišaara ntibɛa.* 4. *daliil* pl. *dalaaʔil.* All signs point to an early winter. *kull id-dalaaʔil itšiir ɛala ʔinna š-šita raʒ-yiji mubakkir.*
 to sign - *waqqaɛ (i tawqiiɛ) t-, muδ̣a (i ʔimδ̣aaʔ, maδ̣i) n-.* He forgot to sign the letter. *nisa ywaqqiɛ ir-risaala.* -- Don't forget to sign in. *la-tinsa timδ̣i min tiji.*
 to sign up - *sajjal (i tasjiil).* I signed up for three courses. *sajjalit ib-iθlaθ mawaaδ̣iiɛ.*
 to sign over - *sallam (i tsillim).* He signed over the business to his son. *sallam šuġla l-ʔibna.*
signal - *ʔišaara* pl. *-aat.* We agreed on a signal. *ttifaqna ɛala ʔišaara.* -- We're getting a strong signal from him. *da-nitlaqqa ʔišaara qawiyya minna.*
 to signal - *ʔaššar (i taʔšiir) t-.* Will you signal the waiter, please? *ma-tʔaššir lil-booy, balla?*
signalman - *maʔmuur* (pl. *-iin*) *seer.* The signalman stopped the train in time. *maʔmuur is-seer waggaf il-qiṭaar bil-wakt il-munaasib.*
signature - *tawqiiɛ* pl. *tawaaqiiɛ.* The letter has no signature. *l-maktuub ma-ɛalee tawqiiɛ.*
signet ring - *muhur* pl. *mhaar.* He signs documents with his signet ring. *yumhur il-waθaayiq bil-muhur maala.*
silence - 1. *sukuun, sukuut.* There was complete silence in the room. *čaan ʔaku sukuun šaamil bil-ġurfa.* 2. *hiduuʔ.* They listened in silence. *ntibhaw ib-hiduuʔ.*
 to silence - *sakkat (i taskiit) t-.* I couldn't silence him. *ma-gdart asakkta.*
silent - 1. *saakit.* Why are you so silent? *leeš ʔinta hal-gadd saakit?* 2. *ṣaamit.* She used to play in silent pictures. *čaanat itmaθθil bil-ʔaflaam iṣ-ṣaamita.*
silk - *ʒariir.* How much is this silk? *beeš hal-ʒariir?*
silly - 1. *ʔaʒmaq.* That's a silly thing to do. *haaδa ɛamal ʔaʒmaq.* 2. *saxiif, fuṭiir.* That was a silly thing to say. *kalaamak ṣaxiif.* -- Don't be so silly! *la-ṭṣiir hal-gadd saxiif.* 3. *ʔablah.* He's not so silly as he looks. *huwwa muu hal-gadd ʔablah miθil-ma da-ybayyin ɛalee.*
silver - 1. *fuδ̣δ̣a.* I gave her a lighter made of silver. *nṭeetha qiddaaʒa min fuδ̣δ̣a.* 2. *fuδ̣δ̣i*.* She's wearing a silver ring. *laabsa miʒbas fuδ̣δ̣i.*
similar - *mušaabih, šabiih, mumaaθil.* I know of a similar case. *ʔaɛruf qaδ̣iyya mušaabiha.*
simple - 1. *basiiṭ, sahil.* That's quite a simple matter. *haaδa fadd mawδ̣uuɛ kulliš basiiṭ.* 2. *saaδij* pl. *suδδaj, basiiṭ* pl. *busaṭaaʔ.* I may sound simple to you, but I don't understand it. *mumkin titṣawwarni saaδij, laakin ma-da-aftihimha.*
simplicity - 1. *tabsiiṭ.* For the sake of simplicity let's say that... *min ʔajil tabsiiṭ il-mawδ̣uuɛ xalli nguul...* 2. *basaaṭa.* All his designs are characterized by simplicity. *kull taṣaamiima tiġlib ɛaleeha l-basaaṭa.*
simply - 1. *qaṭɛan.* That's simply impossible! *haaδi mustaʒiila qaṭɛan!* 2. *b-basaaṭa.* He explained it to the children simply. *širaʒha lil-ʔaṭfaal ib-basaaṭa.*
sin - *δanib* pl. *δinuub, maɛṣiya* pl. *maɛaaṣi.* He's committed a lot of sins. *rtikab ɛiddat δinuub.*
 to sin - *ʔaδnab (i ʔiδnaab).* He sins more than he does good. *yiδnib ʔakθar min-ma ysawwi xeer.*
Sinai Peninsula - *šubuh jaziirat siina.*
since - 1. *min.* He hasn't been here since Monday. *ma-caan ihnaa min yoom il-iθneen.* 2. *min wakit-ma, min.* I haven't seen anyone since I got back. *ma-šifit ʔaʒʒad min wakit-ma rijaɛit.* 3. *li-ʔan.* Since I didn't have the money I couldn't go. *ʔaani ma-gdarit aruuʒ li-ʔan ma-čaan ɛindi fluus.*
 ever since - *min δaak il-wakit.* I haven't spoken with him ever since. *ma-ʒčeet wiyyaa min δaak il-wakit.*
sincere - *muxliṣ.* He's a sincere person. *huwwa fadd waaʒid muxliṣ.*
sincerely - *min kull ɛaqil-, min ṣudug, min kull galub-.* You sincerely believe it? *min kull ɛaqlak tiɛtiqid biiha?*
to **sing** - *ġanna (i ġina) t-.* I don't sing very well. *ma-ʔaġanni zeen.*
to **singe** - 1. *ʒirag (i ʒarig) n-.* I singed my eyebrows when I got too close to the fire. *ʒragit ʒawaajbi min itqarrabit lin-naar.* 2. *lahhab (i tlihhib).* After you pluck the chicken's feathers, singe it. *baɛad-ma tintif riiš id-dijaaja, lahhibha.*
singer - *mġanni* pl. *-iin.* He's a well-known singer. *huwwa mġanni maɛruuf.*
single - 1. *ʔaɛzab* pl. *ɛuzzaab.* Are you married or single? *ʔinta mitzawwij loo ʔaɛzab?* 2. *waaʒid.* He made just a single mistake. *sawwa fadd ġalṭa waʒda bass.*
 **He didn't make a single mistake. *ma-sawwa wala ġalṭa.*
 to single out - *xtaar (a xtiyaar), ntixab (i ntixaab).* Why did they single you out? *leeš bass ʔilak xtaarook?*
singular - *mufrad.* ''Boy'' is the singular of ''boys.'' *walad mufrad ʔawlaad.*
sink - *maġsala, maġsal* pl. *maġaasil.* The dishes are still in the sink. *l-imwaaɛiin baɛadha bil-maġsala.*
 to sink - 1. *ġirag (a ġarag) n-.* The ship sank in 10 minutes. *s-safiina ġirgat ib-ɛašir daqaayiq.* 2. *ġarrag (i tġirrig) t-.* They sank three enemy ships. *ġarrigaw itlaθ bawaaxir lil-ɛadu.* 3. *ṭumaṣ (u ṭamuṣ).* The car sank into the mud. *s-sayyaara ṭumṣat biṭ-ṭiin.* 4. *hibaṭ (u hubuuṭ) n-.* The house has sunk ten inches. *l-beet hibaṭ ɛašir injaat.* 5. *tdahwar (a tadahwur).* His health is sinking rapidly. *ṣiʒʒta gaaɛid titdahwar ib-surɛa.*
sip - *šafṭa* pl. *-aat, maṣṣa* pl. *-aat.* I only had a sip of my coffee. *ʔaxaδit šafṭa wiʒda mnil-gahwa.*
 to sip - *rišaf (u rašif) n-, šifaṭ (u šafuṭ) n-.* He sipped the hot coffee. *rišaf il-gahwa il-ʒaarra.*
sir - 1. *sayyid* pl. *saada.* Sir, the colonel is here. *sayyidi, l-ɛaqiid ihnaa.* 2. *ʔustaaδ* pl. *ʔasaatiδa.* Yes sir, I'll call him now. *naɛam ʔustaaδ, raʒ-axaabra hassa.* 3. *ɛamm* pl. *ʔaɛmaam.* No sir, I didn't break the vase. *laa ɛammi, ma-ksart il-mazhariyya.* or *laa ɛammu, ma-ksart il-mazhariyya.*
sister - *ʔuxut* pl. *xawaat.* Do you have any sisters? *ɛindak xawaat?*
sister-in-law - *ʔuxut* (pl. *xawaat*) *mara-, mart ʔaxu-* pl. *mrayyaat ʔuxwa-.* She's my sister-in-law. *hiyya ʔuxut marti.*
to **sit** - *giɛad (u gaɛid), jilas (i jiluus).* We sat in the front row. *gɛadna biṣ-ṣaff il-ʔamaami.*
 to sit in on - *ʒiδ̣ar (a ʒuδ̣uur).* I sat in on all the conferences. *ʒiδ̣arit kull il-muʔtamaraat.*
 to sit up - *sihar (a suhuur).* We sat up all night waiting for him. *siharna ṭuul il-leel nintaδ̣ra.*
sitting - 1. *gaɛda* pl. *-aat.* He finished the food in one sitting. *xallaṣ il-ʔakil ib-gaɛda wiʒda.* 2. *guɛuud, gaɛid.* Sitting at home alone makes her nervous. *guɛuudha waʒʒadha bil-beet ysawwiiha ɛaṣabiyya.*
situation - *mawqif* pl. *mawaaqif.* She saved the situation. *hiyya ʔanqiδat il-mawqif.*
six - 1. *sitta.* Will six be enough? *sitta tkaffi?* 2. *sitt.* They were here six days ago. *čaanaw ihnaa gabuḷ sitt iyyaam.*
 **It's six of one and half a dozen of another. *xooja ɛali, mulla ɛali.*
sixteen - *ṣiṭṭaɛaš.*
sixteenth - *ṣ-ṣiṭṭaɛaš.*
sixth - *saadis.*
sixtieth - *s-sittiin.*
sixty - *sittiin.*
size - 1. *qiyaas* pl. *-aat.* What size shoe do you wear? *ʔay qiyaas qandara tilbas?* 2. *ʒajim* pl. *ʔaʒjaam, ʒujuum.* What size refrigerator are you going to buy? *ʔay ʒajim θallaaja raʒ-tištiri?*
 to size up - *qaddar (i tqiddir) t-.* How do you size up the situation? *šloon itqaddir il-waδ̣iɛ?*
skate - *skeet* pl. *-aat.* A wheel came off my skate. *č-čarix wugaɛ imnil-iskeet maali.*
 to skate - *tzallaj (a tazalluj).* We Baghdadis don't skate. *ʔiʒna l-baġdaadiyyiin ma-nitzallaj.*
skeleton - *haykal* pl. *hayaakil.*
skeptical - *šakkaak.* Don't be so skeptical! *la-tkuun hal-gadd šakkaak.*
sketch - *muxaṭṭaṭ* pl. *-aat.*
to **ski** - *tzaʒlag (a tazaʒlug).* I never learned how to ski on snow. *ʔabad ma-tɛallamit išloon atzaʒlag ɛaθ-θalij.*
to **skid** - *tzaʒlag (a tazaʒlug).* The car started to skid. *s-sayyaara gaamat titzaʒlag.*
skill - *mahaara, baraaɛa.* That requires a lot of skill. *δiič tiṭṭallab ihwaaya mahaara.*
skilled - *maahir* pl. *-iin.* He is a skilled cabinet-maker. *huwwa najjaar moobilyaat maahir.*
skillfully - *b-mahaara, b-baraaɛa.* You got yourself out of that problem very skillfully. *xaḷḷaṣit nafsak imnil-muškila b-mahaara.*
to **skim** - *šaal (i šiyaala) n- il-gišwa.* I skimmed the

milk. *šilt il-gišwa mnil-ẓaliib.*
to skim through - *tṣaffaẓ (a taṣaffuẓ).* I just skimmed through the book. *tṣaffaẓit il-iktaab bass.*
skin - **1.** *jilid* pl. *jluud.* She had very sensitive skin. *ᵋidha jilid kulliš ẓassaas.* **2.** *farwa* pl. *-aat.* How many skins will you need for the coat? *čam farwa tiẓtaaj lis-sitra?* **3.** *gišir* pl. *gšuur.* These apples have a thick skin. *hat-tiffaaẓ gišra θixiin.* **4.** *jildi**. He's got a skin disease. *ᵋinda maraḍ jildi.*
I got a passing grade by the skin of my teeth. *ẓaṣṣalit ᵋala darajt in-najaaẓ ᵋal-ẓaaffa.*
to skin - **1.** *ṣilax (a ṣalix).* After you slaughter the calf, skin it. *baᵋad-ma tiδbaẓ il-ᵋijil ʔiṣlaxa.* **2.** *jilax (a jalix), jilaġ (a jaliġ).* When he fell he skinned his knee. *min wugaᵋ jilax rukubta.*
to **skip** - **1.** *ṭufar (u ṭafur) n-.* Skip a few lines. *ʔuṭfur čam ṣaṭir.* — Can you skip rope? *tuᵋruf tuṭfur ᵋal-ẓabil?* **2.** *ᵋubar (u ᵋabur, ᵋubuur) n-,* I skipped second grade. *ᵋubarit iṣ-ṣaff iθ-θaani.* **3.** *giḷab (u gaḷub) n-.* Skip a few pages. *ʔugḷub ᵋiddat ṣafẓaat.* **4.** *tirak (u tarik).* Skip the hard words. *ʔitruk il-kalimaat iṣ-ṣaᵋba.* **5.** *nhizam (i nhizaam) min.* He skipped town. *nhizam imnil-madiina.*
skirt - *tannuura* pl. *-aat, tnaaniir.* Her skirt is too long. *tannuuratha ṭwiila.*
skull - *jumjuma* pl. *jamaajim.* He fractured his skull. *nkisrat jumjumta.*
skullcap - *ᵋaraqčiin* pl. *-aat.* They wear skullcaps under their headcloths. *yilbasuun ᵋaraqčiin jawwa l-yeešmaaġ.*
sky - *sima* pl. *samawaat.* How does the sky look today? *šloon is-sima l-yoom?*
**The news came out of a clear blue sky. *l-ʔaxbaar nizlat miθl iṣ-ṣaaᵋiqa.*
**He praised her to the skies. *midaẓha hwaaya.*
slack - **1.** *waaguf, kasaad.* Business is slack. *š-šuġuḷ waaguf.* **2.** *baṭiiʔ.* His work has become very slack. *šuġḷa ṣaayir kulliš baṭiiʔ.* **3.** *raxi**. Your tentropes are too slack. *ẓbaal xeemtak raxiyya.*
slacks - *panṭaroon* pl. *-aat.*
to **slap** - *liṭam (u laṭum) n-.* She slapped him when he tried to kiss her. *liṭmata min ẓaawal ybuusha.*
slaughter - *majzara* pl. *majaazir, maδbaẓa* pl. *maδaabiẓ.* The slaughter was terrific. *l-majzara čaanat faḍiiᵋa.*
to slaughter - *δibaẓ (a δabiẓ) n-.* We usually slaughter sheep on holidays. *ᵋaadatan niδbaẓ xaruuf ib-ʔayyaam il-ᵋiid.*
slave - *ᵋabid* pl. *ᵋabiid.* He treats them like slaves. *yᵋaamilhum ᵋabaalak ᵋabiid.*
**I've really slaved today. *štiġaḷit miθl iẓmaar il-yoom.*
sleep - *noom.* Sleep is important. *n-noom muhimm.*
to get sleep - *naam (a noom).* I didn't get enough sleep last night. *ma-nimit kaafi l-baarẓa bil-leel.*
to sleep - *naam (a noom).* Did you sleep well? *nimit zeen?*
**Sleep on it before you decide. *δakkir biiha hal-leela gabuḷ-ma tqarrir.*
sleepy - *naᵋsaan, mnaᵋᵋis.* I'm still sleepy. *baᵋadni naᵋsaan.*
to make sleepy - *naᵋᵋas (i tanᵋiis) t-.* The heat's making me sleepy. *l-ẓaraara tnaᵋᵋisni.*
sleeve - *ridin, rdaan* pl. *ridaanaat.* The sleeves are too short. *r-ridaanaat kulliš igṣaar.*
**He laughed up his sleeve. *ḍiẓak ib-ᵋibba.*
slender - *rašiig.* She's gotten very slender. *ṣaayra kulliš rašiiga.*
slice - **1.** *quṭᵋa* pl. *quṭaᵋ, wuṣla* pl. *wuṣal.* How many slices of bread shall I cut? *čam quṭᵋat xubuz ʔaguṣṣ?* **2.** *šiif* pl. *šyaaf.* Have another slice of watermelon. *ʔuxuδ šiif laax raggi.*
to slice - **1.** *šarraẓ (i tširriẓ) t-.* Do you want to slice the roast? *triid itšarriẓ il-laẓam?* **2.** *šayyaf (i tašyiif).* Slice up the cucumbers. *šayyifi l-ixyaara.*
slide - **1.** *slaayda* pl. *-aat.* He gave a lecture with slides. *niṭa muẓaaḍara b-islaaydaat.* **2.** *ziẓlaaga* pl. *-aat.* The city put a new slide in the playground. *l-baladiyya ẓaṭṭat ziẓlaaga jdiida bil-malᵋab.*
to slide - *zaẓlag (i tziẓlig).* Pick the desk up; don't slide it on the floor. *šiil il-meez, la-tzaẓilga (ᵋal-gaaᵋ).*
slight - **1.** *baṣiiṭ, ṭafiif, qaliil.* There's a slight difference. *ʔaku xtilaaf baṣiiṭ.* **2.** *xafiif.* He has a slight cold. *ᵋinda našla xafiifa.* **3.** *naẓiif.* She's very slight. *hiyya kulliš naẓiifa.*
slightest - *ʔaqall.* I haven't the slightest doubt. *ma-ᵋindi ʔaqall šakka.*
slim - **1.** *naẓiif, ḍaᵋiif.* She's gotten very slim. *ṣaarat kulliš naẓiifa.* **2.** *ḍiᵋiif.* His chances are very slim. *ʔamala kulliš ḍiᵋiif.*
sling - **1.** *miᵋčaal* pl. *maᵋaačiil, miᵋčaan* pl. *maᵋaačiin.* David killed Goliath with a sling. *daawuud qital jaaluut bil-miᵋčaal.* **2.** *ᵋillaaga* pl. *-aat.* They put his broken arm in a sling. *ᵋalligoo ʔiida b-ᵋillaaga.*
slingshot - *muṣyaada* pl. *-aat.* I'm looking for some rubber to make a slingshot. *da-adawwir ᵋala wuṣlat laastiig ẓatta asawwi muṣyaada.*
slip - **1.** *beet* pl. *byuut.* Our pillows need new slips. *mxaadiidna yinraad-ilha byuut jidiida.* **2.** *ʔatag* pl. *-aat.* Your slip is showing. *ʔatagič da-ybayyin.* **3.** *zalla* pl. *-aat, zalga* pl. *-aat.* It was just a slip of the tongue. *čaanat bass zallat ilsaan.* **4.** *wuṣla* pl. *wuṣal.* He wrote it on a slip of paper. *kitabha ᵋala wuṣlat waraq.*
to give someone the slip - *mulaṣ (a maluṣ) min, filat (i falit) min.* He's given us the slip again. *mulaṣ min ᵋidna marra lux.*
to slip - **1.** *zilaq (a zalaq), tzaẓlag (a tziẓlig).* I slipped on the ice. *zlagit ᵋaθ-θalij.* **2.** *ṭilaᵋ (a ṭuluuᵋ) min.* It slipped my mind completely. *ṭilaᵋ min baali tamaaman.*
**He slipped the policeman some money. *ᵋabbar ifluus liš-šurṭi.*
**Wait until I slip into a coat. *ʔintiḍir ʔila ʔan ʔalbas sitra.*
to slip away - *šilaᵋ (a šaliᵋ), nass (i nass).* Let's slip away, before he sees us. *xalli nišlaᵋ gabuḷ-ma yšuufna.*
to slip by - *faat (u foot).* I let the chance slip by me. *xalleet il-furṣa tfuutni.*
to slip out - **1.** *filat (i falit) min.* I really didn't want to tell him, but it just slipped out. *bil-ẓaqiiqa ma-ridt agul-la, bass filtat min ilsaani.* — The bird slipped out of my hand. *l-ᵋaṣfuur filat min ʔiidi.* **2.** *zubag (u zabug), filat (i falit).* The fish slipped out of my hand. *zubgat is-simča min ʔiidi.*
to slip up - **1.** *xarbaṭ (u txurbuṭ).* I slipped up badly on the next question. *xarbaṭit ihwaaya bis-suʔaal iθ-θaani.* **2.** *twahdan (a twihdin).* I don't know how I could have slipped up on that job. *ma-ʔadri šloon itwahdanit ib-haš-šaġḷa.*
slipper - **1.** *naᵋaal* pl. *-aat, niᵋil.* I can't find my slippers. *ma-da-ʔagdar algi naᵋaali.* **2.** *baabuuj* pl. *bwaabiij.* My wife lost her slippers. *zoojti ḍayyᵋat baabuujha.*
slippery - **1.** *zalag.* The streets are very slippery. *š-šawaariᵋ kulliš zalag.* **2.** *mitqallib* pl. *-iin.* He's a slippery character. *huwwa waaẓid mitqallib.*
slit - *fatẓa* pl. *-aat, šagg* pl. *šguug.* Make the slit a bit longer. *sawwi l-fatẓa šwayya ʔaṭwal.*
to slit - *gaṣṣ (u gaṣṣ).* The criminals slit his throat. *l-mujrimiin gaṣṣaw joozta.*
slogan - **1.** *šiᵋaar* pl. *-aat.* The students wrote slogans on the walls. *ṭ-ṭullaab kitbaw šiᵋaaraat ᵋal-ẓiiṭaan.* **2.** *hitaaf* pl. *-aat.* I didn't hear their slogans. *ma-smaᵋit hitaafaathum.*
slope - *munẓadar* pl. *-aat, nẓidaar* pl. *-aat, dihidwaana* pl. *-aat.* Is the slope very steep? *l-munẓadar qawi?*
to slope - *nẓidar (i nẓidaar).* The floor slopes. *l-gaaᵋ minẓadra.*
sloppy - **1.** *mbahdal, mbahδal.* Don't be so sloppy! *la-tkuun hal-gadd imbahdal.* **2.** *mxarbaṭ.* They always do sloppy work. *daaʔiman ysawwuun šuġuḷ imxarbaṭ.*
slot - *fatẓa* pl. *-aat.* Put ten fils in the slot when you want to call from a public phone. *ẓuṭṭ ᵋašr ifluus bil-fatẓa min itriid itxaabur min talafoon ᵋumuumi.*
slow - **1.** *baṭiiʔ.* He's very slow in his work. *huwwa kulliš baṭiiʔ ib-šuġḷa.* **2.** *muʔaxxira, mqaṣṣira.* Your watch is slow. *saaᵋtak imʔaxxira.* **3.** *haadi, xafiif.* Cook the soup over a slow fire. *ʔuṭbux iš-šoorba ᵋala naar haadiya.*
to slow down - **1.** *xaffaf (u taxfiif) t-, tmahhal (a tamahhul).* Slow down when you come to an intersection. *xaffuf min ṭooṣal lit-taqaaṭuᵋ.* — Slow down; I can't keep up with you. *xaffuf mašyak; ma-agdar alaẓẓig biik.* **2.** *tmaahal (a tamaahul).* He's slowing down in his work. *da-yitmaahal ib-šuġḷa.*
slowly - *yawaaš, b-buṭuʔ.* Drive slowly. *suuq yawaaš.*

or **suuq *Eala keefak.*
sly - *makkaar, maakir.*
small - 1. *ṣġayyir* pl. *ṣġaar.* The room is rather small. *l-ġurfa šwayya ṣġayyra.* 2. *basiiṭ, qaliil.* The difference is very small. *l-ixtilaaf kulliš basiiṭ.* 3. *waḍiiE.* That was an awfully small thing to do. *haaδa Eamal waḍiiE.*
smaller - *ʔaṣġar.* I haven't anything smaller. *ma-Eindi šii ʔaṣġar.*
smallpox - *jidri.* We have all been vaccinated against smallpox. *kullatna ṭṭaEEamna ḍidd ij-jidri.*
smart - 1. *laṭiif, ʔaniiq.* That's a smart dress. *haaδi badla laṭiifa.* 2. *δaki* pl. *ʔaδkiyaaʔ* He's a smart boy. *haaδa walad δaki.*
 to smart - *zirag (i zarig).* The wound smarts. *j-jiriz yizrig.*
to **smash** - *kassar (i tkissir) t-, zaṭṭam (a tzuṭṭum) t-.* The boys smashed the window. *l-wilid kassiraw iš-šibbaač.*
smell - 1. *riiza* pl. *-aat.* What's that smell? *šinu har-riiza?* 2. *šamm.* His sense of smell is keen. *zaassat iš-šamm maalta zaadda.*
 to smell - 1. *štamm (a štimaam).* Do you smell gasoline? *tištamm riizt il-baanziin?* 2. *niṭa (i) riiza.* It smells like cooked lamb. *tinṭi riizat lazam il-ġanam il-mašwi.*
smile - *btisaama* pl. *-aat.* She has a charming smile. *Eidha fadd ibtisaama jaδδaaba.*
 **She was all smiles. *wujihha čaan ḍazuuk.*
 to smile - *btisam (i btisaam).* Did I see you smile? *šiftak tibtisim?*
smoke - *duxxaan.* Where's that smoke coming from? *mneen da-yiji had-duxxaan?*
 to smoke - *daxxan (i tadxiin, tdixxin) t-.* Do you smoke? *ʔinta tdaxxin?* -- The stove is smoking again. *ṭ-ṭabbaax da-ydaxxin marra lux.*
smoking - *tadxiin.* Smoking is forbidden here. *t-tadxiin mamnuuE ihnaa!*
smooth - 1. *naaEim, ʔamlas.* Her skin is very smooth. *jilidha kulliš naaEiim.* 2. *haadiʔ* The sea was very smooth. *l-bazar čaan kulliš haadiʔ*
 **I can't get a smooth shave with this blade. *hal-muus ma-ynaEEim zeen.*
 to smooth down - *nawwam (u tanwiim) t-, ṣaffaf (u taṣfiif) t-.* Smooth down your hair. *nawwum šaErak.*
 to smooth out - *Eaddal (i taEdiil) t-, rattab (i tartiib) t-.* Smooth out the tablecloth. *Eaddil ġaṭa l-meez.*
smoothly - *b-huduuʔ, b-salaam.* Everything went smoothly. *kullši miša b-huduuʔ.*
to **smother** - 1. *xinag (u xanig) n-.* He smothered the child with the pillow. *xinag iṭ-ṭifil bil-imxadda.* 2. *xtinag (i xtinaag).* We nearly smothered. *xtinagna ʔilla šwayya.*
to **smuggle** - *harrab (i tahriib) t-.* They smuggled in arms. *harribaw islaaz lid-daaxil.*
snail - *zalazuuna* pl. *-aat* coll. *zalazuun; zalanṭaza* pl. *-aat* coll. *zalanṭaz.*
snake - *zayya* pl. *-aat, zayaaya.*
snap - 1. *ṭabbaaga* pl. *-aat.* I have to sew snaps on my dress. *laazim axayyiṭ ṭabbaagaat Eala nafnuufi.* 2. *zaraka, ruuz.* Put some snap in your marching. *xallu šwayya zaraka b-mašiikum.* 3. *sariiE.* Don't make snap judgments. *la-tinṭi ʔazkaam sariiEa.*
 **The exam was a snap. *l-intizaan čaan basiiṭ.* or *l-imtizaan čaan zalaaṭa.*
 to snap - 1. *ṭagg (u ṭagg).* If the cucumber's fresh and crisp, just bend it and it snaps. *l-ixyaara, ʔiδa hašša, bass tiδniiha ṭṭugg.* 2. *dagg (u dagg).* He snaps two fingers when he sings. *min yġanni ydugg iṣbiEteen.* 3. *niṭar (u naṭir) n-.* I don't know why he snapped at me that way. *ma-adri leeš niṭar biyya hiiči.*
 **Snap out of it! *trukha!* or *ʔinsaaha!*
 **The dog snapped at me. *č-čalib zaawal yEaḍḍni.*
 to snap up - *fall (i fall).* Snap it up! The train leaves in half an hour. *fillha! l-qiṭaar raz-yitzarrak baEad nuṣṣ saaEa.*
snappy - *ʔaniiq* pl. *-iin.* He's a snappy dresser. *huwwa ʔaniiq bil-libis.*
 **Come on, make it snappy. *yaḷḷa, bil-Eajal!*
snapshot - *ṣuura* pl. *ṣuwar.* Where did you take these snapshots? *ween ʔaxaδit haṣ-ṣuwar?*
to **sneak** - *dixal (u duxuul) bil-baskuut.* He must have sneaked into the house. *laazim dixal il-beet bil-baskuut.*
sneaky - *saxtači* pl. *-iyya.* He's pretty sneaky. *huwwa saxtači.*
sneeze - *Eaṭsa* pl. *-aat.* That sure was a loud sneeze. *zaqiiqatan čaanat Eaṭsa qawiyya.*
 to sneeze - 1. *Eiṭaṣ (i Eaṭiṣ).* I sneezed from the dust. *Eiṭaṣit imnil-Eajaaj.* 2. *Eaṭṭaṣ (i tEiṭṭiṣ) t-.* He's been sneezing all morning. *ṣaar-la da-yEaṭṭiṣ imniṣ-ṣubuz.*
to **sniff** - *štamm (a šamm) šamšam (i tšimšim).* He sniffed the food. *štamm riizt il-ʔakil.*
to **snore** - *šixar (u šaxiir).* He snored all night long. *čaan yišxur il-leel kulla.*
snow - *θalij.* How deep is the snow? *šgadd ġumj iθ-θalij?*
 to snow - *θilaj (i θalij).* It snowed all night. *buqat tiθlij il-leel kulla.*
 **We're snowed under with work. *ġiragna biš-šuġuḷ.*
so - 1. *hiiči, ṣudug, ṣaziiz, tamaam.* Isn't that so? *muu hiiči?* 2. *laEad, ʔiδan, yaEni.* So you think it's a good idea. *laEad tiEtiqid haay xooš fikra.* -- So you don't want to go. *yaEni ma-triid itruuz.* -- So what? *šinu, yaEni?* 3. *hamm, hammeen, hammeena.* If I can do it, so can you. *ʔiδa ʔaani ʔagdar asawwiiha, ʔinta hamm tigdar.* 4. *hal-gadd.* Why are you so lazy? *ʔinta leeš hal-gadd kaslaan?* 5. *ʔila daraja.* I'm so tired, I can't work. *ʔaani taEbaan ʔila daraja ma-agdar aštuġuḷ.* 6. *kulliš.* You look so tired! *mbayyin Ealeek kulliš taEbaan.*
 **So long! *fiimaanillaa!* or *maEa s-salaama!*
 **I need five dinars or so. *ʔaztaaj zawaali xams idnaaniir.*
 so as to - *zatta.* I did some of the work so as to make things easier for you. *sawweet qisim imniš-šuġuḷ zatta axaffif Ealeek.*
 so far - *li-hassa, l-zadd il-ʔaan, l-zadd hassa.* I haven't had any news so far. *li-hassa ma-Eindi ʔay ʔaxbaar.* -- How are things? So far, so good. *šloon il-ʔazwaal? li-hassa, kullši zeen.*
 so far as - *zasab-ma.* So far as I know, he's still in Australia. *zasab-ma ʔaEruf huwwa baEda b-ʔusturaalya.*
 so much - 1. *hal-gadd.* Not so much rice please. *muu hal-gadd timman, min faḍlak.* 2. *jiddan, hwaaya.* Thanks ever so much. *ʔaškurak kulliš ihwaaya.*
 so on - *ʔila ʔaaxirihi.* He went to the market and bought potatoes, tomatoes, and so on. *raaz lis-suug w-ištira puteeta, ṭamaaṭa, w-ʔila ʔaaxirihi.*
 so so - *nuṣṣ w-nuṣṣ, yaEni.* How are you? So so. *šloonak? nuṣṣ w-nuṣṣ.*
 so that - *zatta.* I'm telling you so that you'll know. *ʔaani da-agul-lak zatta tuEruf.*
to **soak** - 1. *nigaE (a nagiE) n-.* Leave the beans to soak. *xalli l-baagilla bil-maay zatta tingaE.* 2. *naggaE (i tangiiE, tniggiE) t-.* We soaked the laundry overnight. *naggaEna l-ihduum ṭuul il-leel.* 3. *šarrab (u tšurrub, tašriib) t-.* Soak the bread in the gravy. *šarrib il-xubuz bil-marga.*
 to soak up - *mtaṣṣ (a mtiṣaaṣ), maṣṣ (u maṣṣ).* The sponge will soak the water. *l-isfanja timtaṣṣ il-maay.*
soaked - *mnaggaE* pl. *-iin, mballal* pl. *-iin.* We came home soaked. *wuṣalna lil-beet imnaggaEiin.*
 to get soaked - *tnaggaE (a tanaggaE), tballal (a taballul).* I got soaked because I didn't have an umbrella. *tnaggaEit li-ʔan ma-čaanat Eindi šamsiyya.*
soap - *ṣaabuuna* pl. *-aat* coll. *ṣaabuun.* I want a cake of soap. *ʔariid qaalab ṣaabuun.*
 to soap - *ṣooban (i tṣoobin).* Dad is soaping his face. *ʔabuuya da-yṣoobin wujja.*
 **Soap your face well before shaving. *xalli ṣ-ṣaabuun zeen gabḷ il-zilaaqa.*
sob - *šahgat* (pl. *-aat*) *bači.* We heard sobs in the next room. *smaEna šahgaat bači bil-ġurfa l-muqaabila.*
 to sob - *šihag (a šahig) mnil-bači.* The child sobbed bitterly. *ṭ-ṭifil šihag imnil-bači zeel.*
sober - *ṣaazi* pl. *-iin.* You never find him real sober. *ʔabad ma-tilgii ṣaazi tamaaman.*
 to sober up - *ṣiza (a ṣazi).* He sobered up quickly. *ṣiza bil-Eajal.*
soccer - *kurat il-qadam.* Soccer is a very popular sport in Iraq. *kurat il-qadam fadd liEba kulliš mazbuuba bil-Eiraaq.*
social - *jtimaaEi*.* Social conditions have changed tremendously. *l-ʔazwaal il-ijtimaaEiyya tġayyirat kulliš ihwaaya.*
socialism - *l-ištiraakiyya.*
socialist - *štiraaki* pl. *-iyyiin.*
socialistic - *štiraaki*.*
society - 1. *mujtamaE.* He doesn't feel at ease in society. *ma-yaaxuδ zurriita min huwwa b-mujtamaE.* 2. *jamEiyya* pl. *-aat.* The society was founded ten

years ago. *j-jamƐiyya t?assisat gabuḷ Ɛašr isniin.*
sociological - *jtimaaƐi**. I subscribed to a sociological journal. *štirakit ib-majalla jtimaaƐiyya.*
sociologist - *Ɛaalim jtimaaƐi* pl. *Ɛulamaa? ijtimaaƐiyyiin.*
sociology - *Ɛilm il-ijtimaaƐ.*
sock - **1.** *lakma* pl. *-aat, books* pl. *-aat.* I'd give him a sock on the jaw if I were you. *loo b-makaanak, ?anṭii lakma Ɛala fačča.* **2.** *takk, fardat ijwaariib* pl. *jwaariib.* I want three pairs of socks. *?ariid itlaθ izwaaj ijwaariib.*
soda - *ṣooda, sooda.* Bring me a bottle of soda water. *jiib-li buṭil ṣooda.*
soft - **1.** *raxu.* The ground's too soft to drive on. *l-gaaƐ raxwa; ma-tigdar itsuuq Ɛaleeha.* **2.** *layyin.* The bread is soft. *l-xubuz layyin.* — He's too soft with the prisoners. *huwwa kulliš layyin wiyya l-masaajiin.* **3.** *ḍaƐiif.* He's soft from lack of exercise. *huwwa ḍaƐiif ib-sabab Ɛadam liƐib riyaaḍa.* **4.** *raqiiq, Ɛaδib, naaƐim.* Her voice is soft. *ṣootha raqiiq.* **5.** *xafiif.* A soft light would be better. *tkuun ?azsan loo ḍ-ḍuwa xafiif.* **6.** *sahil.* He's got a soft job. *šagiḷta sahla.*
soft drinks - *muraṭṭabaat.* Only soft drinks are served here. *hnaa Ɛidna bass muraṭṭabaat.*
soil - *turba.* The soil here is very fertile. *t-turba hnaa kulliš xaṣba.*
to soil - *waṣṣax (i tawṣiix, twuṣṣux) t-.* You soiled your suit. *?inta waṣṣaxit qaaṭak.*
soiled - *mwaṣṣax, waṣix.* Everything is soiled. *kullši mwaṣṣax.*
soldier - *jundi* pl. *jnuud.*
sole - **1.** *čaff rijil* pl. *čfuuf rijleenaat.* I have a cut on my sole. *Ɛindi jiriz b-čaff rijli.* **2.** *naƐal.* The soles of the brown shoes are worn. *naƐal il-qundara j-joozi gaayim.* **3.** *waziid* pl. *-iin.* He was the sole survivor. *huwwa čaan il-waziid illi nija.*
to sole - *zaṭṭ (u zaṭṭ) naƐal.* I have to have my shoes half-soled. *laazim azuṭṭ nuṣṣ naƐal il-qundarti.*
solely - *wazid-.* I'm solely responsible. *?aani wazdi l-mas?uul.*
solid - **1.** *ṣatib, jaamid.* Is the ice solid? *θ-θalij ṣaar ṣalib?* **2.** *kaamil.* We waited a solid hour for him. *ntiḍarnaa l-muddat saaƐa kaamla.* **3.** *qawi*, tukma.* This chair doesn't seem very solid to me. *ma-ašuuf hal-iskamli kulliš qawi.* **4.** *xaaḷiṣ.* This ring is made of solid gold. *hal-mizbas maƐmuul min δahab xaaḷiṣ.* **5.** *jaamid* pl. *jawaamid.* All liquids turn into solids by cooling. *jamiiƐ is-sawaa?il titzawwal ?ila jawaamid bil-buruuda.*
solution - **1.** *mazluul* pl. *mazaaliil.* You need a stronger solution. *tiztaaj mazluul ?aqwa.* **2.** *zall* pl. *zuluul.* We'll find some solution for it. *raz-inšuuf-ilha zall.*
to **solve** - *zall (i zall) n-.* I can't solve the riddle. *ma-?aqdar azill il-laġiz.*
some - **1.** *šwayya.* He lent me some money. *daayanni šwayya fluus.* **2.** *baƐaḍ.* Some people can't stand noise. *baƐḍ in-naas ma-ygidruun yitzammaluun iḍ-ḍajja.* **3.** *qisim.* Some of us are going by train and some by car. *qisim min Ɛidna raz-yruuzuun bil-qiṭaar w-qisim bis-sayyaara.* **4.** *zawaali.* We stayed some two or three hours. *buqeena zawaali saaƐateen ?aw itlaaθa.* **5.** *fadd.* You'll regret that some day. *fadd yoom raz-tindam Ɛaleeha.*
somebody - *fadd šaxiṣ, waazid.* Somebody asked for you. *fadd šaxiṣ si?al Ɛannak.*
somehow - **1.** *b-šikil imnil-?aškaal.* We'll do it somehow. *Ɛuud insawwiiha b-šikil imnil-?aškaal.* **2.** *b-ṣuura mniṣ-ṣuwar.* The letter got lost somehow. *l-maktuub ḍaaƐ ib-ṣuura mniṣ-ṣuwar.*
someone - *fadd ?azzad, fadd waazid.* Is there someone here who can play the lute? *?aku fadd ?azzad ihnaa yuƐruf ydugg Ɛuud?*
something - *šii, fadd šii.* Is something the matter? *?aku šii?* — That's something to think about. *haaδa fadd šii yiswa t-tafkiir.* — Something or other reminded me of home. *fadd šii δakkarni b-?ahli.*
sometime - *fadd yoom, fadd wakit.* Why don't you visit us sometime? *leeš ma-tzuurna fadd yoom.*
sometimes - *?azyaanan, baƐḍ il-?azyaan, dooraat, marraat, noobaat.* Sometimes it gets very hot here. *?azyaanan iṭṣiir kulliš zaarra hnaa.*
somewhat - *šwayya, nooƐan-ma.* I feel somewhat tired. *da-?ašƐur išwayya taƐbaan.*
somewhere - *b-fadd makaan, b-fadd mazall.* I saw it somewhere, but I don't remember where. *šifitha b-fadd makaan bass ma-atδakkar ween.*
son - *walad* pl. *wulid, ?ibin* pl. *wulid.* Has he any sons? *?aku Ɛinda wulid?* — Is this your son? *haaδa ?ibnak?*
song - *ġunnuwwa* pl. *-aat, ?uġniya* pl. *?aġaani, ġanniyya* pl. *-aat.* Do you know the song? *tuƐruf il-ġunnuwwa?*
**He always gives me the same song and dance. *daa?iman yƐiid Ɛalayya nafs il-fatlaṗiič.*
**We bought the chair for a song. *štireena l-iskamli b-?axu l-balaas.*
son-in-law - *zooj binit* pl. *?azwaaj banaat, rajil bint* pl. *rjuula banaat.* My son-in-law is no good. *zooj binti ma-yiswa filis.*
soon - *qariiban, baƐd išwayya.* He's coming back soon. *raz-yirjaƐ qariiban.*
**It's too soon to tell what's the matter with him. *baƐad li-hassa ma-nigdar niƐruf šaku bii.*
**I'd just as soon not go. *?afaḍḍil ma-aruuz.* or *?azsan-li ma-aruuz.*
as soon as - *?awwal-ma.* Let me know as soon as you get here. *gul-li ?awwal-ma tooṣal l-ihnaa.*
sooner - *?asraƐ.* The sooner you come, the better. *šgadd-ma tiji ?asraƐ, baƐaḍ ?azsan.*
**No sooner said than done. *?axalliṣ-lak-iyyaaha b-lazḍatha.*
sooner or later - *Ɛaajilan ?aw ?aajilan, ?awwal w-taali.* Sooner or later we'll have to make up our minds. *Ɛaajilan ?aw ?aajilan laazim inqarrir.*
to **soothe** - *sakkan (i taskiin) t-, hadda? (i tahdii?) t-.* This salve will soothe the pain. *had-dihin raz-ysakkin il-wajaƐ.*
sore - **1.** *jariz* pl. *jruuz.* The sore is pretty well healed up. *j-jariz taqriiban lizam.* **2.** *zabb* pl. *zabaabi.* His leg was covered with sores. *rijla čaanat imġaṭṭaaya bil-zabaabi.* **3.** *zassaas.* That's a sore point with him. *haay mas?ala zassaasa bin-nisba ?ila.* **4.** *zaƐlaan* pl. *-iin.* Are you sore at me? *?inta zaƐlaan Ɛalayya?*
**I have a sore toe. *Ɛindi ?iṣbiƐ ib-rijli da-yoojaƐni.*
**Where's the sore spot? *ween manṭiqt il-wajaƐ?*
to get sore - *ziƐal (a zaƐal) n-.* You needn't get sore so quickly. *ma-aku zaaja tizƐal bil-Ɛajal.*
sorrow - *qahar, zizin* pl. *?azzaan.* She can't get over her sorrow. *ma-da-tigdar tinsa qaharha.*
sorry - **1.** *mit?assif* pl. *-iin, ?aasif* pl. *-iin.* I'm really sorry. *?aani zaqiiqatan mit?assif.* — I'm sorry to say it can't be done. *?aasif ?an ?aguul ma-mumkin iṭṣiir.* **2.** *l-Ɛafu, ?aasif, mit?assif.* Sorry! Did I hurt you? *l-Ɛafu, ?aδδeetak?*
**I'm sorry for her. *?ašƐur ib-?asif ittijaahha.*
sort - *nooƐ* pl. *?anwaaƐ, šikil* pl. *?aškaal, ṣinif* pl. *?aṣnaaf.* I can't get along with that sort of person. *ma-agdar attifiq wiyya šaxiṣ min han-nooƐ.*
**What sort of person is he? *huwwa šinu min šii?*
sort of - **1.** *nooƐan-ma, fadd nooƐ.* She's sort of nice. *hiyya laṭiifa nooƐan-ma.* **2.** *taqriiban.* I sort of knew it was going to happen. *taqriiban Ɛirafit haaδa čaan raz-yṣiir.*
to sort - *ṣannaf (i taṣniif) t-, Ɛizal (i Ɛazil) n-.* Have the stockings been sorted? *j-jwaariib iṭṣannifat?*
soul - **1.** *ruuz* pl. *rwaaz.* If someone dies, his soul will go to heaven. *?iδa l-waazid ymuut, truuz ruuza lis-sima.* **2.** *?azzad, ?insaan, nafis.* There wasn't a soul to be seen. *ma-čaan ?azzad mawjuud.*
**He's with us heart and soul. *huwwa wiyyaana tamaaman.*
sound - **1.** *ṣawṭ* pl. *?aṣwaaṭ.* Light travels faster than sound. *ḍ-ḍuwa yintiqil ?asraƐ imniṣ-ṣooṭ.* **2.** *ziss* pl. *zsuus, ṣooṭ* pl. *?aṣwaaṭ.* What was that sound? *š-čaan δaak il-ziss?* **3.** *naġma, ranna.* I recognized her by the sound of her voice. *Ɛirafitha min naġmat zissha.* **4.** *saliim, matiin, qawi*.* He has a sound constitution. *Ɛinda bunya saliima.*
**That's a sound bit of advice. *haay xooš naṣiiza.*
**He's sound asleep. *huwwa ġaat bin-noom.*
safe and sound - *saaġ saliim.* He's back, safe and sound. *rijaƐ saaġ saliim.*
to sound - *bayyan (i tabyiin) t-.* The report sounds good. *t-taqriir ybayyin zeen.*
to sound out - *jass (i jass) nabaḍ-.* I'll have to sound him out first. *laazim ?awwal ajiss nabḍa.*
soup - *šoorba* pl. *-aat.* Bring us the soup. *jiib-ilna š-šoorba.*
sour - *zaamuḍ, mzammuḍ.* The milk has turned sour. *l-zaliib ṣaar zaamuḍ.*
**Don't make such a sour face. *la-tṣiir hiiči*

mεabbis.

source – **1.** *maṣdar* pl. *maṣaadir.* I have it from a reliable source. *ẓaṣṣalit εaleeha min fadd maṣdar mawθuuq bii.* **2.** *ʔasaas* pl. *-aat, ʔusus.* Have you found the source of the trouble? *εirafit ʔasaas il-muškila?* **3.** *manbaε* pl. *manaabiε.* The source of the river is north of here. *manbaε in-nahar imniš-šimaal.*

south – *jinuub.* The wind is coming from the south. *r-riyaaẓ jaaya mnij-jinuub.* — The arrow points south. *s-sahim yʔaššir εaj-jinuub.*

southern – *jinuubi*.* This plant is found only in southern regions. *han-nabaat yinligi bil-manaaṭiq ij-jinuubiyya bass.*

souvenir – *tiδkaar* pl. *-aat.* I want to buy some souvenirs here. *ʔard aštirii-li čam tiδkaar minnaa.*

sovereign – *δaat siyaada.* Iraq is a soverign state. *l-εiraaq dawla δaat siyaada.*

Soviet – *soofyaati*.* They're in the Soviet sphere of influence. *humma b-manṭiqat in-nufuuδ is-soofyaati.*

Soviet Russia – *ruusya s-soofyaatiyya.*

sow – *xanziira* pl. *-aat.*

to **sow** – *biδar (i baδir) n-.* He's sowing the field with wheat. *da-yibδir ẓunṭa bil-ẓaqil.*

space – **1.** *faδaaʔ.* They've just fired another rocket into space. *hassa ʔaṭliqaw ṣaaruux laax lil-faδaaʔ.* **2.** *makaan.* The desk takes up too much space. *l-meez yaaxuδ makaan kulliš ičbiir.* **3.** *majaal* pl. *-aat.* There's a large space between the houses. *ʔaku majaal waasiε been il-beeteen.* **4.** *faδwa* pl. *-aat, saaẓa* pl. *-aat.* There's an open space behind the house. *ʔaku faδwa wara l-beet.* **5.** *xilaal, mudda, fatra.* He did the work in the space of two weeks. *sawwa š-šuğuḷ ib-xilaal ʔusbuuεeen.*

**He was staring out into space. *čaan ṣaafun.* or *čaan δaarub daalğa.*

to space – *baaεad (i mubaaεada) t-.* The posts are spaced a foot apart. *l-εawaamiid mitbaaεida εan-baεaδha masaafa qadam.*

spade – *misẓaa* pl. *masaaẓi.* Grab a spade and dig. *ʔuxuδ-lak misẓaa w-ʔuẓfur.*

**Why don't you call a spade a spade? *leeš ma-tizči l-ẓaqiiqa?*

spare – **1.** *faraağ.* What do you do in your spare time? *š-itsawwi b-wakit faraağak?* **2.** *ẓtiyaaṭi*.* Can you find spare parts for your radio? *tigdar itẓaṣṣil εala ʔadawaat iẓtiyaaṭiyya r-raadyuwwak?* **3.** *zaayid.* Is there any spare room in that car? *ʔaku makaan zaayid b-has-sayyaara?* **4.** *ʔiδaafi*, yadag, speer.* We never travel without a spare tire. *ʔabadan ma-nsaafir bila taayir speer.*

to spare – **1.** *waffar (u tawfiir) t- εan.* You can spare yourself the trouble. *tigdar itwaffur εan nafsak il-ʔizεaaj.* **2.** *xalla (i) min.* Spare me the details. *xalliini mnit-tafaaṣiil.* **3.** *staǧna (i stignaaʔ) εan.* Can you spare the pencil? *tigdar tistağni εan il-qalam?* **4.** *simaẓ (a samiẓ) b-.* Can you spare me a minute of your time? *tismaẓ-li b-daqiiqa min waqtak?* **5.** *ʔabqa (i ibqaaʔ) εala.* The commander spared the captives' lives by putting them in a prison outside the city. *l-qaaʔid ʔabqa εala ẓayaat il-ʔasraaʔ ib-waδiεhum ib-sijin xaarij il-madiina.*

**He spared no expense. *ma-buxal ib-šii.*

sparingly – *b-iqtiṣaad, b-tadbiir.* Use it sparingly. *staεmilha b-iqtiṣaad.*

spark – *šaraara* pl. *-aat.* The fire was started by a spark. *l-ẓariiq bidat ib-fadd šaraara.*

to **sparkle** – *tlaʔlaʔ (a tliʔliʔ).* The moonlight is sparkling on the water. *δuwa il-gumar gaaεid yitlaʔliʔ εal-maay.*

spark plug – *plakk* pl. *-aat.* I need new spark plugs for my car. *ʔaẓtaaj plakkaat jidiida l-sayyaarti.*

sparrow – *εaṣfuur* pl. *εaṣaafiir.*

to **speak** – *ẓiča (i ẓači) n-, tkallam, (a takallum).* Am I speaking clearly enough? *da-ʔaẓči b-wuδuuẓʔ* — May I speak to you? *ʔagdar aẓči wiyyaak?* **It's nothing to speak of. *muu fadd šii yiswa δikir.* or *ma-biiha šii muhimm.*

to speak to – *kallam (i tkillim).* He spoke to me for half an hour. *kallamni l-muddat nuṣṣ saaεa.*

to speak up for – *daafaε (a difaaε) εan.* Nobody spoke up for him. *maẓẓad daafaε εanna.*

speaker – *muẓaddiθ* pl. *-iin, mutkallim* pl. *-iin.* He's an excellent speaker. *huwwa muẓaddiθ mumtaaz.*

speaking – *kalaam, ẓači.* I prefer speaking to writing. *ʔafaδδil il-kalaam εal-kitaaba.*

**We're not on speaking terms. *ʔiẓna ma-nitẓaača.*

spear – *rumuẓ* pl. *rimaaẓ.*

special – *xaaṣṣ, xuṣuuṣi*.* I'm saving it for a special occasion. *ʔaani δaamunha l-munaasaba xaaṣṣa.*

specialty – *xtiṣaaṣ* pl. *-aat.* Children's diseases are his specialty. *ʔamraaδ il-ʔaṭfaal ixtiṣaaṣa.*

specific – *muεayyan.* He proposed specific means to remedy the situation. *qaddam iqtiraaẓaat muεayyana l-muεaalajat il-waδiε.*

specifications – *muwaaṣafaat.* We can build it to your specifications. *nigdar nibniiha ẓasab muwaaṣafaatkum.*

spectator – *mitfarrij* pl. *-iin.*

speech – **1.** *nuṭaq.* He lost his speech after the accident. *fuqad nuṭqa baεd il-ẓaadiθ.* **2.** *xuṭba* pl. *xuṭab.* That was a very good speech. *haay čaanat kulliš xooš xuṭba.*

speed – *surεa.* Let's put on a little speed. *xalli nʔayyid is-surεa šwayya.*

to speed – *εadda (i taεdiya) t- s-surεa, faat (u foota) n- s-surεa, ʔasraε (i ʔisraaε).* You're speeding now. *ʔinta mitεaddi s-surεa hassa.*

to speed up – *εajjal (i taεjiil) t-, staεjal (i stiεjaal).* Can you speed things up a little? *tigdar itεajjil išwayya?*

speed limit – *surεa maẓduuda.* The speed limit is thirty-five miles an hour. *s-surεa l-maẓduuda xamsa w-itlaaθiin miil bis-saaεa.*

spell – **1.** *siẓir.* She's completely under his spell. *maʔxuuδa b-siẓra tamaaman.* or ***hiyya masẓuura bii.* **2.** *nooba* pl. *-aat.* Does she often get spells like that? *hiyya daaʔiman tijiiha hiiči n-noobaat?*

to spell – **1.** *thajja (a thijji).* Please spell your name. *ʔarjuuk ithajja ʔismak.* **2.** *naab (u niyaaba) n- εan.* Let me spell you awhile. *xalliini anuub εannak išwayya.*

to **spend** – **1.** *ṣiraf (u ṣaruf) n-.* We spent a lot of money. *ṣrafna hwaaya fluus.* **2.** *giδa (i gaδi) n-.* I'd like to spend my vacation here. *yiεjibni ʔagδi ʔijaazti hnaa.*

sperm – *mani.*

sphere – **1.** *kura* pl. *-aat.* How do you find the capacity of a sphere? *šloon itẓaṣṣil εala siεat il-kura?* **2.** *manṭiqa* pl. *manaaṭiq.* They're in the Russian sphere of influence. *humma b-manṭiqt in-nufuuδ ir-ruusiyya.*

spice – *bhaar* pl. *-aat.* Do you use spices much in your cooking? *tistaεmiliin ihwaaya bhaaraat biṭ-ṭabux?*

to spice – *xalla (i) bhaaraat.* She spiced the food too much. *xallat ihwaaya bhaaraat bil-ʔakil.*

**The meat is highly spiced. *l-laẓam bii hwaaya bhaaraat.*

spider – *εankabuut* pl. *-aat, εanaakib.*

to **spill** – *čabb (i čabb) n-.* Who spilled the milk? *minu čabb il-ẓaliib?*

spin – *farra* pl. *-aat.* We took a spin in his car. *ʔaxaδna farra b-sayyaarta.*

to spin – **1.** *farr (u farr) n-.* He spun the top. *farr il-muṣraε.* **2.** *ftarr (a farr).* My head is spinning. *raasi da-yiftarr.* or ***raasi daayix.* **3.** *ğizal (i ğazil) n-, fital (i fatil) n-.* The thread isn't spun evenly. *l-xeeṭ ma-mağzuul bit-tasaawi.*

to spin around – *ltaaf (a ltifaaf), ndaar (a).* He spun around and fired. *ltaaf w-ʔaṭlaq riṣaaṣa.*

spinach – *sbeenaağ.*

spine – **1.** *šawka* pl. *-aat.* I've got a spine from the cactus in my hand. *ʔaku šawkat ṣubbeer b-iidi.* **2.** *εamuud faqari, εawaamiid faqariyya.* He broke his spine in the accident. *kisar il-εamuud il-faqari maala bil-ẓaadiθ.*

spiral – *malwi*, lawlabi* ẓalazuuni*.* The minaret has a spiral staircase. *l-manaara biiha daraj malwiyya.*

spirit – **1.** *ruuẓ* pl. *ʔarwaaẓ, jinni* pl. *jinn.* The natives believe in evil spirits. *s-sukkaan yiεtiqduun bil-ʔarwaaẓ iš-širriira.* **2.** *rooẓ* pl. *ʔarwaaẓ.* I assume his spirit went to heaven when he died. *ʔaftiriδ rooẓa raaẓat lij-janna min maat.* **3.** *himma.* That's the proper spirit! *haay il-himma ṣ-ṣaẓiiẓa!*

in good spirits – *mirtaaẓ.* I hope you're in good spirits. *ʔinšaaḷḷa tkuun mirtaaẓ.*

in low spirits – *mahmuum.* He seemed to be in low spirits. *ybayyin εalee mahmuum.*

spiritual – *ruuẓi*.* There's a spiritual bond between them. *ʔaku fadd raabiṭa ruuẓiyya beenaathum.*

spit – **1.** *ṣiix* pl. *ṣiyaax, šiiš* pl. *šiyaaš.* They're roasting a sheep on a spit. *gaaεid yẓammiṣuun il-xaruuf ib-ṣiix.* **2.** *tafla* pl. *-aat, tfaal.* His spit is yellow because he uses snuff. *t-tafla maalta ṣafra li-ʔan yistaεmil barnuuṭi.*

to spit – *tifal (i tfaal), biṣaq (u biṣaaq).* He spat on the ground. *tifal εal-gaaε.*

spite - *nikaaya.* He did it just for spite. *sawwaaha bass lin-nikaaya.*
  in spite of - *b-rağum min, b-rağum εan.* I went in spite of the rain. *riħit ib-rağum min il-muṭar.*
  to spite - *ġaaδ (i ʔigaaδa) n-.* Are you doing that just to spite me? *ʔinta da-tsawwiha ħatta tġiiδni bass?*

to **splash** - **1.** *ṭaffar (i taṭfiir) t-.* The car splashed water on me. *s-sayyaara ṭaffirat εalayya ṃaay.* **2.** *ṭṭaffar (a taṭaffur).* The water splashes in all directions. *l-ṃaay da-yiṭṭaffar il-kull jiha.* **3.** *ṭabbaš (u taṭbiiš, ṭṭubbuš) t-.* The boy splashed through the shallow water. *l-walad ṭabbaš bil-geeš.*

splendid - *raaʔiε, faaxir, mumtaaz.* That was a splendid idea! *δiič čaanat fadd fikra raaʔiεa.*

splint - *jabiira* pl. *jabaayir.* His arm has to be put in splints. *ʔiida laazim tinħaṭṭ bij-jabaayir.*

splinter - *sillaaya* pl. *-aat, liiṭa* pl. *-aat.* I've got a splinter under my nail. *ʔaku sillaaya jawwa ʔiδifri.*

split - **1.** *nšiqaaq* pl. *-aat, xilaaf* pl. *-aat.* There was a split in the party. *čaan ʔaku nšiqaaq bil-ħizib.* **2.** *faṭir* pl. *fṭuur, šagg* pl. *šguug.* There's a split in that board. *ʔaku faṭir ib-hal-looħa.*
  to split - **1.** *filaq (u faliq) n-, šagg (u šagg) n-, filaε (a faliε) n-.* The lightning split the tree from top to bottom. *ṣ-ṣaaεiqa filqat iš-šajara min foog li-jawwa.* **2.** *nšagq (i nšiqaaq).* The party has split into three groups. *l-ħizib inšaqq ʔila tlaθ ʔaqsaam.* **3.** *tgaasam (a tagaasum).* They split the profits with the workers. *tgaasmaw il-ʔarbaaħ wiyya l-εummaal.* **4.** *qassam (i taqsiim) t-.* The directors split the profits between the workers and investors. *l-mudaraaʔ qassmaw il-ʔarbaaħ been il-εummaal wil-mustaθmiriin.* **5.** *fitag (u fatig) n-.* Your pants have split in the seat. *panṭaroonak infitag bil-maqεad.*
  **I nearly split my sides laughing. *ridt amuut imniδ-δiħik.* or *ṭaggat baṭni mniδ-δiħik.*
  to split hairs - *daqdaq (i tdiqdiq).* Don't split hairs, please. *baṭṭla la-tdaqdiq.*

to **spoil** - **1.** *xaas (i xees), jaaf (i jeef).* The apples are beginning to spoil. *t-tiffaaħ da-yibdi yxiis.* **2.** *jaaf (i jeef).* The meat will spoil in this heat. *l-laħam raħ-yjiif ib-hal-ħaraara.* **3.** *fisad (i fasid), xirab (a xarbaan).* The eggs have spoiled. *l-beeδ fisad.* **4.** *dallal (i tadliil) t-.* You're spoiling him. *ʔinti da-tdallilii.*

spoke - *siim* pl. *siyaama.* I broke two spokes in the front wheel. *ksarit siimeen bič-čarx il-giddaami.*

sponge - **1.** *sfanja* pl. *-aat* coll. *sfanj.* Where'd you buy that sponge? *mneen ištireet haay il-isfanja?* **2.** *ṭufeeli* pl. *-iyya, -iyyiin.* He's an awful sponge. *huwwa ṭufeeli.*
  to sponge off - **1.** *misaħ (a masiħ) bil-isfanja.* She sponged off the water. *misħat il-ṃaay bil-isfanja.* **2.** *ṭṭaffal (a taṭafful) εala.* He's always sponging off his friends. *daaʔiman yiṭṭaffal εala ʔaṣdiqaaʔ.*

spoon - *xaašuuga* pl. *xwaašiig.* A spoon fell off the table. *fadd xaašuuga wugεat imnil-meez.*

sport - *liεba* (pl. *-aat*) *riyaaδiyya.* Soccer is a good sport. *kurat il-qadam xooš liεba riyaaδiyya.*

sports - *riyaaδa.* Do you go in for sports? *tħibb ir-riyaaδa?*

spot - **1.** *buqεa* pl. *buqaε, latxa* pl. *-aat, lakka* pl. *-aat.* You have a spot on your tie. *ʔaku buqεa εala ribaaṭak.* **2.** *mukaan* pl. *-aat, ʔamaakin.* I stood in the same spot for a whole hour. *buqeet ib-nafs il-mukaan il-muddat saaεa kaamila.* — A cup of coffee would just hit the spot. *fadd finjaan gahwa hassa ykuun ib-mukaana tamaam.* **3.** *nuqṭa* pl. *nuqaaṭ.* You've touched a sore spot. *ʔinta ṭarraqit ʔila nuqṭa ħassaasa.* **4.** *manṭiqa* pl. *manaaṭiq, mukaan* pl. *-aat, nuqṭa* pl. *nuqaaṭ.* Where is the sore spot? *ween manṭiqat il-ʔalam?*
  on the spot - **1.** *b-laħδatha.* They fired him on the spot. *ṭirdoo b-laħδatha.* **2.** *b-nafs il-makaan.* I was right on the spot when the accident happened. *min ṣaar il-ħaadiθ, činit ib-nafs il-makaan.* **3.** *b-waδiε ħarij.* You put me on the spot. *ʔinta xalleetni b-waδiε ħarij.* or **ħrajit mawqifi.*
  to spot - **1.** *limaħ (a lamiħ) n-.* I spotted him in the crowd. *limaħta bil-xabṣa.* **2.** *mayyaz (i tamyiiz) t-.* I could spot him anywhere. *ʔagdar ʔamayyza ween-ma čaan.*

sprain - *faṣix* pl. *fṣuux.* You've got a bad sprain there. *εindak faṣix qawi.*
  to sprain - *fuṣax (u faṣix) n-.* She sprained her ankle. *fuṣxat marfaq rijilha.*

to **spray** - *rašš (i rašš) n-.* We have to spray the peach trees. *laazim inrišš ʔašjaar il-xoox.*

spread - **1.** *ntišaar, tawassuε.* They tried to check the spread of the disease. *ħaawlaw ywaggfuun intišaar il-maraδ.* **2.** *čarčaf* pl. *čaraačif.* They put new spreads on the beds. *ħaṭṭaw čaraačif ijdiida εač-čarpaayaat.*
  to spread - **1.** *nišar (u našir) n-.* The gardener is spreading manure on the lawn. *l-bustanči da-yinšur l-ismaad εaθ-θayyal.* **2.** *mtadd (a mtidaad), ntišar (a ntišaar).* The fire's spreading rapidly. *n-naar da-timtadd ib-surεa.* — The news spread quickly. *l-ʔaxbaar intišrat bil-εajal.* **3.** *wazzaε (i tawziiε) t-.* The payments were spread over several years. *d-dafεaat itwazzεat εala εiddat isniin.*
  to spread out - **1.** *furaš (u fariš) n-, madd (i madd) n-.* Spread the map out. *ʔufruš il-xariiṭa.* **2.** *mtadd (a mtidaad).* We saw the whole valley spread out below us. *šifna l-waadi kulla mimtadd jawwaana.*

spring - **1.** *rabiiε.* We arrived in spring. *wuṣalna bir-rabiiε.* **2.** *εeen* pl. *εyuun; nabiε, yambuuε* pl. *yanaabiiε.* There's a spring behind our house. *ʔaku εeen wara beetna.* **3.** *zumbalag* pl. *-aat.* The spring in my watch is broken. *z-zumbalag maal saaεti maksuur.* **4.** *sipring* pl. *-aat.* We broke a spring on the car on our trip. *ksarna sipring is-sayyaara b-safratna.*
  to spring - **1.** *gumaz (u gamuz) n-.* He sprang from his seat. *gumaz min kursiyya.* **2.** *ṭilaε (a ṭuluuε).* All the rumors spring from the same source. *kull il-ʔišaaεaat tiṭlaε min nafs il-maṣdar.* **3.** *nibaε (a nabiε).* The plant sprang up overnight. *z-zariε nibaε εala ġafla.*

to **sprinkle** - *rašš (i rašš) n-, ṭašš (a ṭašš) n-.* Have the streets been sprinkled yet? *š-šawaariε inraššat loo baεad?*

spy - *jaasuus* pl. *jawaasiis.* We're going to send a team of spies to Saudi Arabia. *raħ-indizz jamaaεat jawaasiis lil-mamlaka l-εarabiyya s-saεuudiyya.*
  to spy - *tjassas (a tajassus).* They caught him spying on a military installation. *lizmoo da-yitjassas ib-muʔassasa εaskariyya.*

squad - *ħaδiira* pl. *ħaδaayir.* An eight man squad was guarding the intersection. *ħaδiira min iθman irjaal čaanaw yħirsuun it-taqaaṭuε.*

square - **1.** *saaħa* pl. *-aat.* Our windows look out on a large square. *šbaabiična tišrif εala saaħa čbiira.* **2.** *murabbaε* pl. *-aat.* That's not a square, that's a rectangle. *haaδa muu murabbaε, haaδa mustaṭiil.* **3.** *εadil.* He's a pretty square fellow. *huwwa fadd waaħid εadil.*
  **I haven't eaten a square meal in days. *ṣaar ihwaaya ma-maakil ʔakla dasma.*
  **Our back yard is twenty feet square. *s-saaħa l-warraaniyya maalatna εala šikil murabbaε ṭuula w-δilεa εišriin qadam.*
  **This squares our account. *haaδa ysaddid iħsaabna.*

squash - *šijra* pl. *-aat* coll. *šijar.* Buy some squash while you're at the market. *štiri šwayya šijar min itkuun bis-suuq.*
  to squash - **1.** *jiεaṣ (i jaεiṣ) n-, εiqač (i εaqič) n-.* I squashed my hat when I sat down. *jiεaṣit šafuqti min giεadit.* **2.** *ħiṣar (i ħaṣir) n-.* I squashed my finger in the door. *ħṣarit ʔiṣibεi bil-baab.*

to **squeal** - **1.** *ṣirax (u sraax), εaaṭ (i εyaaṭ).* The child squealed with joy. *j-jaahil ṣirax imnil-faraħ.* **2.** *wiša (i wišaaya) n-.* Somebody must have squealed on us to the police. *waaħid laazim ykuun wiša biina liš-šurṭa.*

to **squeeze** - **1.** *εiṣar (i εaṣir) n-.* Don't squeeze my hand so hard. *la-tiεṣir ʔiidi hal-gadd ħeel.* — I'll squeeze the oranges. *raħ-aεṣir il-purtaqaal.* **2.** *diħas (a daħis) n-.* I can't squeeze another thing into my suitcase. *ma-ʔagdar adħas ʔay šii laax ib-jinuṭṭi.*

squirrel - *sinjaab* pl. *sanaajiib.*

to **squirt** - *rašš (i rašš) n-.* The elephant squirted water on the spectators. *l-fiil rašš il-ṃaay εal-mutafarrijiin.*

to **stab** - *tiεan (a ṭaεin) n-.* He was stabbed in the brawl. *ntiεan bil-εarka.* — He's just waiting for a chance to stab me in the back. *da-yintihiz furṣa ħatta yiṭεanni mnil-xalf.*

stable - **1.** *ṣṭabil* pl. *-aat.* Where are the stables?

ween l-iṣṭablaat? 2. *mustaqirr.* They haven't had a stable government for years. *ma-ṣaar Ɛidhum ẓukuuma mustaqirra min mudda ṭwiila.* 3. *θaabit.* A stable currency is absolutely necessary. *wujuud Ɛumla θaabita ẓaruuri jiddan.*

stack - *kudis* pl. *ʔakdaas, koom* pl. *ʔakwaam.* I had to go thru a whole stack of newspapers to find it. *čaan laazim adawwur akdaas imnij-jaraayid ẓatta algaaha.*

to stack - *kaddas (i takdiis) t-, kawwam (u takwiim) t-.* Stack the books in the corner. *kaddis il-kutub biz-zuwiyya.*

staff - *muwaẓẓafiin.* He dismissed part of his staff. *ṭirad qisim min muwaẓẓafii.*

general staff - *qiyaadat il-ʔarkaan.* That officer has been attached to the general staff. *haaδa δ-ẓaabuṭ iltaẓaq ib-qiyaadat il-ʔarkaan.*

stage - 1. *masraẓ* pl. *masaariẓ.* That hall has a nice stage. *haay il-qaaƐa biiha masraẓ ẓilu.* 2. *marẓala* pl. *maraaẓil.* It depends on what stage it's in. *tiƐtimid Ɛala l-marẓala lli hiyya biiha.*

to stage - *qaam (u qiyaam) n- b-.* They staged the robbery in broad daylight. *qaamaw bis-sariqa b-waẓaẓ in-nahaar.*

to **stagger** - *ṭṭootaẓ (a taṭooṭuẓ), trannaẓ (a tarannuẓ).* I saw him stagger out of a bar. *šifta ṭaaliƐ imnil-baar yiṭṭootaẓ.* — The blow staggered him. *δ-ẓarba xallata yiṭṭootaẓ.*

staggering - *muδhil, xayaali*, faẓiiƐ.* The prices are staggering. *l-ʔasƐaar ṣaayra muδhila.* — Expenditures have reached staggering proportions. *l-maṣruufaat wuslat ʔila ẓadd faẓiiƐ.* or ***l-maṣruufaat itjaawzat il-maƐquul.*

stagnant - *xaayis, jaayif.* The water is stagnant. *l-maay xaayis.*

stain - *buqƐa* pl. *buqaƐ, laṭxa* pl. *-aat.* I can't get the stains out of my shirt. *ma-agdar ašiil il-buqaƐ min θoobi.*

to stain - *lawwax (w talwiix) t-.* You've stained your shirt. *lawwaxit θoobak.*

stairs - *daraj* pl. *-aat.* Take the stairs to your right. *ʔuxuδ id-daraj illi Ɛala yamiinak.*

stake - 1. *Ɛamuud* pl. *ʔaƐmida.* You get the stakes for the fence. *ʔinta jiib il-ʔaƐmida maal is-siyaaj.* 2. *θbaat* pl. *-aat, watad* pl. *ʔawtaad.* He drove in a stake to tie up the cow to. *dagg iθbaat ẓatta yšidd il-haayša bii.*

**There's too much at stake. *biiha hwaaya muxaaṭara.*

**His life is at stake. *ẓayaata muhaddada bil-xaṭar.* or *da-yraahin Ɛala ẓayaata.*

**My money's at stake. *jaazafit ib-ʔamwaali.*

stakes - *rihaan, rahin.* They doubled the stakes. *ẓaaƐfaw ir-rihaan.*

to **stall** - 1. *ṭufa (i ṭafi) n-.* The motor's stalled again. *l-muẓarrik inṭufa marra lux.* 2. *maaṭal (i mumaaṭala).* Quit stalling! *la-tmaaṭil, Ɛaad!* or *yeezi mumaaṭala.*

to **stammer** - *tlaƐθam (a tliƐθim), watwat (i twitwit).* He stammers when he talks. *huwwa yitlaƐθam ib-kalaama.*

stamp - 1. *ṭaabiƐ* pl. *ṭawaabiƐ.* Give me five ten-fils stamps, please. *nṭiini xamis ṭawaabiƐ ʔumm Ɛašr ifluus rajaaʔan.* 2. *ṭamġa* pl. *-aat, xatim* pl. *ʔaxtaam.* Where's the ''Air Mail'' stamp? *ween ṭamġat il-bariid ij-jawwi?*

to stamp - 1. *ṭumaġ (u ṭamuġ) n-.* I stamped all the papers. *ṭumaġit kull il-ʔawraaq.* 2. *dagg (u dagg).* She stamped her foot. *daggat rijilha.*

to stamp out - 1. *ʔaxmad (i xamid, xumuud) n- b-rijil-.* He stamped out the fire. *ʔaxmad in-naar ib-rijla.* 2. *qiẓa (i qaẓi) n- Ɛala.* All opposition was ruthlessly stamped out. *kull il-muƐaaraẓa nqiẓat Ɛaleeha.*

stand - *mawqif* pl. *mawaaqif.* He's changed his stand on this matter several times. *ġayyar mawqifa bin-nisba l-mawẓuuƐ Ɛiddat marraat.*

**The witness will take the stand! *š-šaahid yaaxuδ makaana.*

to stand - 1. *wugaf (a wuguuf).* He's standing in the rain. *huwwa waaguf bil-muṭar.* 2. *simad (i ṣumuud), θibat (i θubuut, θabaat).* The soldiers stood their ground. *j-jinuud simdaw ib-maraakizhum.* 3. *buqa (a baqaaʔ) θaabit.* He stood his ground. *buqa θaabit Ɛala mawqifa.* 4. *qaawam (u muqaawama).* The city's defenders stood for three days. *l-mudaafiƐiin Ɛan il-madiina qaawumaw itlaθt iyyaam.* 5. *waggaf (u tawgiif) t-.* Stand the ladder in the corner. *wagguf id-daraj biz-zuwiyya.* 6. *tẓammal (a taẓammul).* I can't stand it any longer there. *ma-agdar atẓammal ʔakθar ihnaak.* 7. *waajah (i muwaajaha), jaabah (i mujaabaha).* You'll have to stand trial if they catch you. *laazim itwaajih muẓaakama ʔiδa lizmook.*

**You don't stand a chance of getting accepted. *ma-aku ʔamal tinqibil.*

**What I said the other day still stands. *ʔilli gilta l-baarẓa baƐda maaši.* or *ʔilli gilta l-baarẓa baƐda ma-tġayyar.*

**You can have it as it stands for 50 dinars. *tigdar taaxuδha miθil-ma hiyya b-xamsiin diinaar.*

to stand by - 1. *ṭubag (u ṭabug).* He always stands by his friends. *daaʔiman yiṭbug wiyya ʔaṣẓaaba.* 2. *biqa (a biqaaʔ) Ɛala.* I'm standing by my decision. *ʔaani baaqi Ɛala qaraari.*

**Stand by, I may need you later. *kuun ẓaaẓir, yimkin ʔaẓtaajak baƐdeen.*

**He stood by, doing nothing. *wugaf miθl il-looẓ.*

to stand for - 1. *ʔayyad (i taʔyiid) t-.* He stands for greater cooperation with neighboring states. *yʔayyid ziyaadat it-taƐaawun maƐa l-ʔaqṭaar il-mujaawira.* 2. *maθθal (i tamθiil).* The olive branch stands for peace. *ġuṣn iz-zaytuun ymaθθil is-salaam.* 3. *qibal (a qubuul) n-.* I won't stand for that sort of treatment. *ma-ʔaqbal hiiči muƐaamala.*

**He stands for equality. *huwwa min duƐaat il-musaawaat.*

to stand on - *Ɛtimad (i) Ɛala.* I'll stand on my record. *ʔaƐtimid Ɛala l-maaẓi maali.*

to stand out - *biraz (i buruuz), ẓihar (u ẓuhuur).* She stands out in a crowd. *hiyya ẓaahra been il-majmuuƐa.* — He stands out in physics. *huwwa kulliš baariz bil-fiizya.*

to stand up - 1. *wugaf (a wuguuf).* Don't bother standing up. *la-tzaẓẓim nafsak w-toogaf.* 2. *qaawam (u muqaawama), ṣumax (u ṣamux), kadd (u kadd).* The car has stood up well. *s-sayyaara ṣumxat zeen.*

**She stood me up at the last minute. *Ɛtidrat ib-ʔaaxir laẓẓa.*

to stand up for - *saaƐad (i musaaƐada) daafaƐ (i difaaƐ).* If we don't stand up for him, no one else will. *ʔiδa ma-saaƐadnaa, maẓẓad raẓ-ysaaƐda.*

standard - 1. *miqyaas* pl. *maqaayiis.* You can't judge him by ordinary standards. *ma-tigdar tuẓkum Ɛalee bil-maqaayiis il-Ɛaadiyya.* 2. *miƐyaar* pl. *maƐaayiir, miqyaas* pl. *maqaayiis.* Their standards are high. *maƐaayiirhum Ɛaalya.* 3. *mustawa* pl. *-ayaat.* Their standard of living is lower than ours. *mustawa maƐiišathum aqall min Ɛidna.* 4. *Ɛtiyaadi*.* We carry all the standard sizes. *Ɛidna kull il-ʔaẓjaam il-iƐtiyaadiyya.*

stand-by - *ẓaalat inδaar.* I'm on stand-by this week. *ʔaani b-ẓaalat inδaar hal-isbuuƐ.*

standing - 1. *maqaam, markaz.* He has a high standing in the community. *maqaama Ɛaali bil-mujtamaƐ.* 2. *saakin, raakid.* It's standing water. *haaδa l-maay saakin.* 3. *wuguuf.* There's standing room only. *ʔaku maẓall lil-wuquuf bass.*

**They're friends of long-standing. *humma ʔaṣdiqaaʔ ṣaar-ilhum zamaan.*

star - 1. *najma* pl. *-aat, njuum.* The sky's full of stars. *s-simaaʔ malyaana njuum.* 2. *baṭal* pl. *ʔabṭaal.* Who was the star in that picture? *minu čaanat il-baṭala b-δaak il-filim?*

**He's my star pupil. *haaδa ʔaẓsan ṭaalib Ɛindi.*

starch - *niša.* Put some starch in the shirts. *xalli šwayya niša liθ-θiyaab.*

to starch - *našša (i tanšiya).* Did you starch the shirts? *naššeet iθ-θiyaab?*

to **stare** - *baẓlaq (i baẓlaqa).* He just stared into space. *baẓlaq bis-sima.*

start - *bidaaya.* It was all wrong from the start. *čaan muxtiʔ imnil-bidaaya.*

**You gave me quite a start. *fazzazitni.* or *jaffalitni.*

to start - 1. *bida (i bidaaya) n-.* The movie has just started. *l-filim hassa bida.* — How did the fire start? *šloon bida l-ẓariiq?* 2. *bida (i bidaaya) n- b-.* Who started this rumor? *minu bida b-hal-ʔišaaƐa?* 3. *šaġġal (i tašġiil) t-, ẓarrak (i taẓriik).* Start the motor. *šaġġil il-muẓarrik.* 4. *šiƐal (i šaƐil) n-.* Let's start a fire and get warm. *xalli nišƐil naar w-nitdaffa.* 5. *tẓarrak (i taẓarruk).* The train started slowly. *l-qiṭaar itẓarrak ib-buṭuʔ.*

starting - *btidaaʔan.* Starting today the bus will stop here. *btidaaʔan imnil-yoom il-baaṣ raẓ-yoogaf ihnaa.*

to **startle** - *jaffal (i tajfiil) t-, fazzaz (i tafziiz) t-.* The noise startled me. *ṣ-ṣawṭ jaffalni.*

to be startled - **1.** *jifal (i jafil).* I was startled by the shot. *jifalit imniṭ-ṭalqa.*

to **starve** - **1.** *jaaƐ (u juuƐ).* Thousands of people starved. *ʔaalaaf imnin-naas jaaƐaw.* **2.** *jawwaƐ (i tajwiiƐ) t-.* We can't attack them, we'll have to starve them out first. *ma-nigdar inhaajimhum hassa, xalli njawwiƐhum ʔawwal.*

**They almost starved to death. *taqriiban maataw imnij-juuƐ.*

state - **1.** *wilaaya* pl. *-aat.* What's the largest state in the U.S.? *šinu hiyya ʔakbar wilaaya bil-wilaayaat il-muttaʒida.* **2.** *dawla* pl. *-aat, duwal, ʒukuuma* pl. *-aat.* The railroads are owned by the state. *s-sikak il-ʒadiidiyya timlikha d-dawla.* **3.** *ʒaala* pl. *-aat, waδ̣Ɛiyya* pl. *-aat, ʒaal* pl. *ʔaʒwaal, waδ̣iƐ* pl. *ʔawδ̣aaƐ.* His affairs are in a bad state. *ʔumuura b-ʒaala mxarbuṭa.* — Don't speak to her when she's in this state. *la-tkallimha w-hiyya b-hal-waδ̣Ɛiyya.* **4.** *ʒukuumi*.* It's a state hospital. *haaδa mustašfa ʒukuumi.* **5.** *xaarijiyya.* He works for the state department. *yištuğul ib-wizaart il-xaarijiyya.*

to state - **1.** *gaal (u gool) n-.* You just stated that you were not there. *hassa gilit ma-činit ihnaak.* **2.** *waδ̣δ̣aʒ (i tawδ̣iiʒ) t-, bayyan (i tabyiin) t-.* The terms are stated in the contract. *š-šuruuṭ imwaδ̣δ̣aʒa bil-Ɛaqid.* — I thought he stated his case well. *ʔaƐtiqid bayyan qaδ̣iita zeena.*

statement - **1.** *bayaan* pl. *-aat.* The prime minister issued his policy statement to parliament. *raʔiis il-wuzaraaʔ qaddam bayaan siyaasta lil-majlis.* **2.** *kašif* (pl. *kšuuf*) *ʒisaab.* My bank sends me a statement each month. *l-bang ydizz-li kašf il-ʒisaab kull šahar.*

static - *wašwaša, xašxaša.* There's so much static I can't get the station. *hwaaya ʔaku wašwaša bir-raadyo; ma-da-agdar aṭalliƐ il-maʒaṭṭa.*

station - *maʒaṭṭa* pl. *-aat.* Get off at the next station. *ʔinzil bil-maʒaṭṭa j-jaaya.* — We're going to visit a radio station. *raʒ-inzuur maʒaṭṭat il-ʔiδaaƐa.*

to station - *xalla (i txilli) t-.* The police stationed a man at the door. *š-šurṭa xallat ʒaaris Ɛal-baab.*

**Where are you stationed? *ween markazak?*

stationery - *qirṭaasiyya.* I need some stationery. *ʔaʒtaaj išwayya qirṭaasiyya.*

statue - *timθaal* pl. *tamaaθiil.*

stay - *baqaaʔ* pl. *-aat.* Our stay in the mountains during the summer was very pleasant. *baqaaʔna bij-jibal biṣ-ṣeef čaan kulliš laṭiif.*

to stay - *buqa (a baqaaʔ).* How long will you stay? *šgadd raʒ-tubqa?* — Are you staying with friends? *baaqi wiyya ʔaṣdiqaaʔak?* — You've stayed away a long time. *buqeet biƐiid mudda ṭuwiila.*

to stay up - *sihar (a sahar).* Our children stay up until nine o'clock. *wilidna yisharuun lis-saaƐa tisƐa.*

steady - **1.** *θaabit.* This needs a steady hand. *haay tiʒtaaj-ilha ʔiid θaabta.* — We kept a good steady pace. *ʒaafaδ̣na Ɛala surƐa θaabta.* **2.** *mustamirr.* He's made steady progress. *ʒaṣṣal Ɛala taqaddum mustamirr.* **3.** *daaʔimi*, mustamirr.* He's one of our steady customers. *huwwa min maƐaamiilna d-daaʔimiyyiin*

to **steal** - *baag (u boog) n-, siraq (u sariq) n-.* He stole all my money. *baag kull ifluusi.*

to steal away - *nass (i nass).* We had to steal away. *δ̣ṭarreena nniss.*

steam - **1.** *buxaar.* There's steam coming from the teapot. *ʔaku buxaar da-yiṭlaƐ imnil-quuri.* **2.** *buxaari*.* He showed us a model of a steam engine. *raawaana nimuuδaj makiina buxaariyya.*

**You'll have to get up some steam if you want to get done on time. *yinraad-lak himma ʔiδa činit itriid itxalliṣ bil-wakit.*

to steam - *baxxar (i tabxiir) t-.* The rice is still steaming. *t-timman baƐda ybaxxir.*

steamer - *baaxira* pl. *bawaaxir.* The steamer sails at 10 o'clock. *l-baaxira titruk is-saaƐa Ɛašra.*

steel - *fuulaaδ.* The bridge is built entirely of steel. *j-jisir mibni kulla min fuulaaδ.*

steep - **1.** *minʒidir ib-šidda, kulliš minʒidir.* Be careful, the stairs are steep. *diir baalak, id-daraj minʒadra b-šidda.* **2.** *Ɛaali.* The price is too steep. *s-siƐir kulliš Ɛaali.*

to steep - *xidar (a xadir) n-.* Let the tea steep a little longer. *xalli č-čaay yixdar ʔakθar.*

to **steer** - **1.** *wajjah (i tawjiih) t-.* Steer the launch in to shore. *wajjih il-maaṭoor Ɛaj-juruf.* — Steer the car to the right of that policeman. *wajjih is-sayyaara b-jihat il-yamiin min haš-šurṭi.* **2.** *deewar (u tdeewur).* Okay, you steer and I'll push. *zeen, ʔinta tdeewur w-ʔaani ʔadfaƐ.* **3.** *dazz (i dazz) n-.* He's steered a lot of customers my way. *dazz-li maƐaamiil ihwaaya.*

**Better steer clear of him. *tčaffa šarra.*

to steer away - *waxxar (i twixxir) t-, baƐƐad (i tabƐiid) t-.* Steer away from those kids. *waxxir is-sayyaara min haj-jihaal.*

steering wheel - *sikkaan* pl. *-aat.*

stem - *saag* pl. *siigaan.* Don't cut the stems too short. *la-tguṣṣ is-siigaan igṣaar.*

step - **1.** *daraja* pl. *-aat.* The steps are carpeted. *d-darajaat mafruuša bis-sijjaad.* **2.** *xuṭwa* pl. *-aat, xuṭaw.* He took one step forward. *tqaddam xuṭwa li-giddaam.* — We built up our business step by step. *bineena šuğulna xuṭwa xuṭwa.* **3.** *ʔijraaʔ* pl. *-aat.* The government is taking steps to wipe out crime. *l-ʒukuuma gaaƐid tittixiδ l-ʔijraaʔaat lil-qaδ̣aaʔ Ɛala jaraaʔim.*

**Watch your step. *laaʒiδ̣ min timši.*

to step - **1.** *wugaf (a wuguuf).* Perhaps if you step on a chair you can reach it. *yimkin itnuuška ʔiδa wugafit Ɛala kursi.* **2.** *daas (u doos).* I stepped into the mud. *disit Ɛaṭ-ṭiin.*

**Step lively! *xuff rijlak!*

to step aside - *tnaʒʒa (a tanaʒʒi), waxxar (i twixxir) t-.* I stepped aside to let him by. *tnaʒʒeet w-xalleeta ymurr.*

to step in - **1.** *dixal (u duxuul).* I saw him step into the store. *šifta yidxul bil-maxzan.* **2.** *tdaxxal (a tadaxxul).* The president himself may have to step in. *r-raʔiis nafsa muʒtamal yitdaxxal.*

to step off - *nizal (i nizuul).* He just stepped off the train. *hassa nizal imnil-qiṭaar.*

to step out - *ṭilaƐ (a ṭuluuƐ).* He just stepped out for a minute. *ṭilaƐ daqiiqa w-yirjaƐ.*

to step up - **1.** *zayyad (i tazyiid) t-.* We'll have to step up the pace. *laazim inzayyid is-surƐa.* **2.** *šaddad (i tašdiid) t-.* The government stepped up its campaign against VD. *l-ʒukuuma šaddidat ʒamlatha δ̣idd il-ʔamraaδ̣ iz-zuhriyya.* **3.** *jaa (yiji majiiʔ) yamm.* A strange man stepped up to me on the street. *šaxiṣ ğariib jaa yammi Ɛaš-šaariƐ.*

sterile - **1.** *muƐaqqam.* Get me a sterile dressing. *jiib-li gooz muƐaqqam.* **2.** *Ɛaqiim, Ɛaaqir.* I think my wife is sterile. *ʔaδ̣inn zawijti Ɛaqiima.*

to **sterilize** - *Ɛaqqam (i taƐqiim) t-.* Sterilize the needle before you use it. *Ɛaqqim il-ʔubra gabuḷ-ma tistaƐmilha.*

sterling - *ʔaṣli*.* That's sterling silver. *haay fuδ̣δ̣a ʔaṣliyya.*

stern - **1.** *muʔaxxira* pl. *-aat.* Sit in the stern of the boat and I'll row. *ʔugƐud ib-muʔaxxirat il-balam w-ʔaani ʔajlif.* **2.** *jaaf, mƐabbis.* He's a stern man. *huwwa jaaf.*

stew - *marga* pl. *-aat* coll. *marag.* We had okra stew and rice. *ʔakalna margat baamya w-timman.*

**He's in a stew again. *huwwa mithayyij marra lux.*

to stew - *ṭubax (u ṭabux) n-.* Shall I stew the chicken or roast it? *triidni ʔaṭbux id-dijaaj ʔaw aʒammuṣa?*

stick - *Ɛuuda* pl. *Ɛuwad, Ɛaṣa* pl. *Ɛiṣi.* He hit me with a stick. *δ̣irabni bil-Ɛuuda.*

to stick - **1.** *naǧǧaz (u tanǧiiz) n-, čakčak (i tčikčik) t-.* Something is sticking me. *fadd šii da-ynaǧǧizni.* **2.** *čakk (u čakk) n-.* I stuck my finger. *čakkeet ʔuṣbaƐi.* **3.** *lizag (a lazig) n-.* This stamp doesn't stick. *haaδa ṭ-ṭaabiƐ ma-yilzag.* **4.** *čallab (i tačliib, tčillib).* The door always sticks in damp weather. *l-baab daaʔiman yčallib bir-riṭuuba.* **5.** *biqa (a baqaaʔ) n-.* Nothing sticks in his mind. *ma-yibqa šii b-damaaǧa.* **6.** *xalla (i txilli) t-.* Just stick it in your pocket. *bass xalliiha b-jeebak.* **7.** *daxxal (i tadxiil) t-, ʒaṭṭ (u ʒaṭṭ).* He sticks his nose into everything. *ydaxxil nafsa b-kullši.* or ***ʒummuṣ bij-jidir yinbuṣ.*

to stick out - *tʒammal (a taʒammul).* Try and stick it out a little longer. *ʒaawil titʒammalha šwayya ʔakθar.*

to stick to - **1.** *tmassak (a tamassuk) b-.* I'm sticking to my opinion. *ʔaani mitmassik ib-raʔyi.* or *ʔaani muṣirr Ɛala raʔyi.* **2.** *lizag (a lazig) n- Ɛala.* That won't stick to a smooth surface. *haaδa ma-yilzag Ɛala saṭiʒ ʔamlas.*

to stick up - *daafaε (i difaaε) n-.* He stuck up for me. *daafaε εanni.*

sticky - **1.** *mdabbug.* My fingers are all sticky with honey. *ʔaṣaabεi mdabbga mnil-εasal.* **2.** *raṭib.* It's awfully sticky today. *kulliš raṭba l-yoom.*
**He's got sticky fingers. *ʔiida ṭwiila.*

stiff - **1.** *yaabis.* His collars are always stiff. *yaaxta εala ṭuul yaabsa.* **2.** *qawi*.* The steering is awful stiff! *l-isteerin kulliš qawi.* **3.** *mitšannij.* My legs are stiff. *rijlayya mitšannija.* **4.** *naašif.* Don't be so stiff! *la-tkuun kulliš naašif!* **5.** *ṣaεub.* Was it a stiff examination? *čaan l-imtiζaan ṣaεub?* **6.** *čibiir.* He paid a stiff fine. *difaε ġaraama čbiira.*
to be stiff - *tṣallab (a taṣallub).* Relax and don't be stiff when you're swimming. *raxxi nafsak; la-titṣallab min tisbaζ.*

still - **1.** *haadiʔ, saakin.* The night was still. *l-leel čaan haadiʔ.* **2.** *waaguf.* The wheels of industry were still. *εajalaat iṣ-ṣinaaεa čaanat waagfa.* **3.** *baεad-, la-zaal (a).* I'm still of the same opinion. *ʔaani baεadni b-nafs ir-raʔi.* -- This box is big, but that box is still bigger. *has-sanduug kabiir, laakin δaak iṣ-ṣanduug baεda ʔakbar.* -- It's still raining. *la-tzaal timṭur.* -- I'm still eating. *la-azaal ʔaakul.* -- They were still playing. *čaanaw la-yzaaluun yilεabuun.*
to hold still - *wugaf (a wuguuf).* Hold still a minute! *ʔoogaf daqiiqa!* or *la-titζarrak!*
to keep still - *sikat (u sukuut).* Why don't you keep still? *leeš ma-tiskut?*

to stimulate - **1.** *nabbah (i tanbiih) t-.* Coffee stimulates the nerves. *l-gahwa tnabbih il-ʔaεṣaab.* -- We stimulated the muscle with an electric current. *nabbahna l-εaδala bit-tayyaar il-kahrabaaʔi.* **2.** *šajjaε (i tašjiiε) t-.* We must stimulate foreign trade. *laazim inšajjiε it-tijaara l-xaarijiyya.*
**Running fast stimulates the breathing. *r-rikiδ is-sariiε yzayyid surεat it-tanaffus.*

stingy - *baxiil* pl. *buxalaaʔ.* Don't be stingy! *la-tṣiir baxiil!*

stir - **1.** *harja* pl. *-aat.* There was a stir in the crowd when he got up to speak. *ṣaarat harja bin-naas min gaam da-yiζči.* **2.** *ζarika* pl. *-aat, xarxaša* pl. *-aat.* I heard a stir in the bush. *simaεit ζarika bid-daġal.*
to stir - **1.** *xaaṭ (u xooṭ).* She forgot to stir the soup. *nisat itxuuṭ iš-šoorba.* **2.** *ζarrak (i taζriik) t-, hazz (i hazz) n-.* The wind stirred the branches. *l-hawya ζarrkat il-ġuṣuun.* **3.** *tζarrak (a taζarruk).* He's stirring. *da-yitζarrak.*

stirring - *muθiir, muhayyij.* He made a stirring speech. *xiṭab xiṭaab muθiir.*

stitch - *nabδa* pl. *-aat.* The injury needed four stitches. *j-jariζ inraad-la ʔarbaε nabδaat.* --
**When is the doctor going to take out the stitches? *yamta ṭ-ṭabiib raζ-yjurr il-xeeṭ?*
**I haven't done a stitch of work today. *ma-štiġalit wala ζabbaaya l-yoom.* or *ma-sawweet wala nitfat šuġul hal-yoom.*
**Don't take big stitches. *la-txayyiṭ xašin.*
to stitch - *xayyaṭ (i taxyiiṭ) t-.* Did you stitch the hem yet? *xayyaṭit il-ζaašya loo baεad?*

stock - **1.** *majmuuεa* pl. *-aat.* He has a large stock of shirts. *εinda majmuuεa čbiira mnil-qumṣaan.* **2.** *saham* pl. *ʔashum.* I advise you not to buy these stocks. *ʔanṣaζak la-tištiri hal-ʔashum.* **3.** *ʔaxmaṣ* pl. *ʔaxaamiṣ.* The stock of a rifle is usually made of wood. *ʔaxmaṣ il-bunduqiyya εaadatan maεmuul min il-xišab.*
**I don't put much stock in what he says. *ma-axalli wazin il-ζačya.* or *ma-aεtimid εala ζačya.*
in stock - *maxzuun.* What colors do you have in stock? *ʔay ʔalwaan maxzuuna εindak?*
out of stock - *xalṣaan.* Sorry, that color is out of stock. *mitʔassif δaak in-nooε xalṣaan.*
to take stock - **1.** *jirad (u jarid) n-.* Next week we're going to take stock. *l-isbuuε ij-jaay raζ-nijrud.* **2.** *raajaε (i muraajaεa).* Let's take stock of what we've done. *xalli nraajiε illi sawweenaa.*
to stock - *xizan (i xazin) n-.* We don't stock that brand. *ma-nixzin hal-maarka* or ****ma-εidna hal-maarka.**

stocked - **1.** *mjahhaz.* Our store is stocked with everything. *maxzanna mjahhaz ib-kullši.* **2.** *maxzuun.* Sorry that color isn't stocked by us. *mitʔassif hal-loon muu maxzuun εidna.*

stock exchange - *boorṣa* pl. *-aat.*

stockholder - *musaahim* pl. *-iin.* I'm a stockholder in that company. *ʔaani musaahim ib-δiič iš-šarika.*

stocking - *juuraab* pl. *juwaariib.* I'd like three pairs of stockings. *ʔaζibb itlaθ izwaaj juwaariib.*

stomach - **1.** *miεda* pl. *-aat.* He has an upset stomach. *miεidta mxarbaṭa.* **2.** *baṭin* pl. *bṭuun.* Don't lie on your stomach. *la-tinbuṭiζ εala baṭnak.*
**I'm sick to my stomach. *nafsi da-tilεab.*
to stomach - *tζammal (a taζammul).* I can't stomach that fellow. *ma-agdar atζammal haš-šaxiṣ.*

stone - **1.** *ζjaara* pl. *-aat.* He killed two birds with one stone. *qital εaṣfuureen b-iζjaara.* **2.** *nuwaaya* pl. *-aat,* coll. *nuwa.* Swallowing peach stones is dangerous. *baliε nuwa l-xoox xaṭar.* **3.** *min iζjaar, ζajari*.* We sat on a stone bench. *giεadna εala maqεad min iζjaar.* -- We noticed a stone statue. *laaζaδna timθaal ζajari.*
**He left no stone unturned. *ma-xalla zwiyya ma-dawwarha.*

stool - **1.** *taxta* pl. *-aat.* When he milks the cow, he sits on a stool. *min yiζlib il-haayša yigεud εala taxta.* **2.** *xuruuj.* We have to make three tests, for the blood, the urine, and the stool. *laazim insawwi θlaθ taζliilaat lid-damm, lil-bool w-lil-xuruuj.*

stoop - *ζanya* pl. *-aat.* He has a slight stoop. *εinda ζanya šwayya.*
to stoop - *nζina (i nζinaaʔ), naṣṣa (i tnaṣṣi).* He stooped to pick up the newspaper. *naṣṣa ζatta yitnaawaš ij-jariida.*
to stoop to - *tnaazal (a tanaazul), nizal (i nuzuul).* I don't think she'd stoop to such a thing. *ma-aδinnha titnaazal il-hiiči šii.*

stop - **1.** *mawqif* pl. *mawaaqif.* You have to get off at the next stop. *laazim tinzil bil-mawqif ij-jaay.* **2.** *waqfa* pl. *-aat.* We have a ten-minute stop in Basra. *εidna waqfat εašir daqaayiq bil-baṣra.* **3.** *ζadd.* We'll have to put a stop to that practice. *laazim nooδaε ζadd il-hal-εaada.* or ****laazim inbaṭṭil hal-εaada.**
to stop - **1.** *wugaf (a wuguuf) n-.* The bus stops on the other side of the street. *l-ṗaaṣ yoogaf ib-ṣafζat il-lux imniš-šaariε.* -- My watch stopped. *saaεti wugfat.* -- I stopped for a drink of water on the way. *wugafit bit-ṭariiq ζatta ʔašrab maay.* **2.** *waggaf (u tawgiif) t-.* Stop the car at the next street. *wagguf is-sayyaara biš-šaariε ij-jaay.* **3.** *baṭṭal (i tabṭiil) t-.* Please stop that noise. *ʔarjuuk baṭṭil hal-ζiss.* -- Stop it! *baṭṭil!* or ****bass εaad!**
to stop over - *wugaf (a wuguuf) b-, biqa (a baqaaʔ) b-.* Why don't you stop over at my house on the way? *leeš ma-toogaf ib-beeti εala ṭariiqak?*
to stop overnight - *baat (a beetuuta).* We'll stop in Hilla overnight. *raζ-inbaat bil-ζilla.*
to stop short - *sakkat (i taskiit) t-.* I stopped him short before he could say much. *sakkatta b-surεa gabul-ma gidar yiζči hwaaya.*
to stop up - *sadd (i sadd) n-.* You're going to stop up the drain. *raζ-itsidd il-balluuεa.*

stopper - *saddaad* pl. *-aat.* Put the stopper in the kettle. *xalli s-saddaad bil-buṭil.*

store - **1.** *maxzan* pl. *maxaazin, maζall* pl. *-aat, dukkaan* pl. *dukaakiin.* I know a store where you can buy a good suit. *ʔaεruf fadd maxzan tigdar tištiri minna badla zeena.* **2.** *δaxiira* pl. *δaxaayir, muuna* pl. *muwan.* We have a sufficient store of food in the basement. *εidna δaxiira kaafya mnil-ʔakil bis-sirdaab.* -- The army has a large store of rifles in the city. *j-jeeš εinda δaxiira čabiira min it-tufag bil-madiina.*
**Who knows what the future has in store for us? *minu yuεruf iš-δaamm-inna l-mustaqbal?*
to store - *xizan (i xazin) n-, δamm (u δamm) n-, ζiraz (i ζariz).* Where shall I store the potatoes? *ween ʔaxzin il-puteeta?*
**I stored up a lot of energy during my vacation. *tnaššaṭit ihwaaya b-εuṭulti.*

storm - *εaaṣifa* pl. *εawaaṣif.* There was a big storm last night. *jatt εaaṣifa čibiira l-baarζa bil-leel.*
to storm - *ṣaarat (i) εaaṣifa.* It's going to storm tonight. *raζ-itṣiir εaaṣifa hal-leela.*

stormy - *εaaṣif.*

story - **1.** *saaluufa* pl. *-aat, suwaaliif, quṣṣa* pl. *quṣaṣ, ζčaaya* pl. *-aat.* Do you want me to tell you a story? *triidni ʔaζčii-lak saaluufa?* -- It's always the same old story. *daaʔiman nafs il-iζčaaya* or *daaʔiman nafs il-quṣṣa l-εatiiga.* **2.** *ṭaabig* pl. *ṭawaabig.* The building has five stories. *l-binaaya biiha xamis ṭawaabiq.*

stout - *simiin* pl. *smaan.* He's a stout man. *huwwa*

rijjaal simiin.
to get stout - *siman (a simin).* He's gotten very stout lately. *siman ihwaaya b-ḥal-ʔayyaam.*
stove - **1.** *ṭabbaax* pl. *-aat, ʔoojaaġ* pl. *-aat.* Put the meat on the stove. *xalli l-laȥam εat-ṭabbaax.* **2.** *ṣooba* pl. *-aat.* I need a stove in my bedroom. *ʔaȥtaaj ṣooba b-ġurfat noomi.*
straight - **1.** *εadil.* Draw a straight line. *ʔirsim xaṭṭ εadil.* -- He gave me a straight answer. *jaawabni jawaab εadil.* -- She's always straight with me. *hiyya daaʔiman εadla wiyyaaya.* -- Is my hat on straight? *šafuqti εadla?* -- She stands very straight. *toogaf kulliš εadil.* -- He worked for fifteen hours straight. *štiġaḷ xumuṣṭaεaš saaεa εadil.* **2.** *εadil, raʔsan.* Go straight home. *ruuȥ εadil lil-beet.* **3.** *saada.* I take my arrack straight. *ʔaaxuδ il-εarag maali saada.* **4.** *tamaam, tamaaman.* Try to get the story straight. *ȥaawil tifham il-quṣṣa tamaam.* -- You didn't get me straight. *ma-fhamitni tamaam.* -- Our house is straight across from the church. *beetna tamaaman gubaal il-kaniisa.*
**He can't think straight. *fikra mšawwaš.*
**Now let's get this straight! I'm the boss here! *fukk εeenak! ʔaani r-raʔiis ihnaa!*
straight ahead - *gubaḷ.* Walk straight ahead. *ʔimši gubaḷ.*
to **straighten** - *εaddal (i taεdiil) t-.* Can you straighten the rod? *tigdar itεaddil iš-šiiš?* -- Straighten the tablecloth. *εaddil čarčaf il-meez.*
to straighten out - **1.** *εaddal (i taεdiil) t-.* Have you straightened out your financial affairs? *εaddalit ʔumuurak il-maaliyya?* **2.** *ṣaalaȥ (i muṣaalaȥa).* Have you straightened out everything between them? *ṣaalaȥit beenhum* or *ṣaalaȥithum?* **3.** *εidal (a εadil), tεaddal (a taεaddul).* Tomorrow everything will straighten out. *bukra kullši yiεdal.*
to straighten up - *εaddal (i taεdiil) t-, rattab (i tartiib) t-.* Will you please straighten up the room? *ʔarjuuk εaddil il-ġurfa.*
strain - **1.** *mataaεib.* He can't stand the strain of modern living. *ma-yigdar yitȥammal mataaεib il-ȥayaat il-ȥadiiθa.* **2.** *šilεaan gaḷub.* Reading this small print is a strain. *qraayat hal-kitaaba n-naaεima šilεaan gaḷub.* **3.** *tawattur.* What caused the strain in relations between the two countries? *š-sabbab tawattur il-εalaaqaat been id-dawilteen?*
**I don't think the rope will stand the strain. *ma-aδ̣inn il-ȥabil raȥ-yitȥammal.*
to strain - **1.** *šilaε (a šaliε, šilεaan) n- gaḷub-, taεεab (i tatεiib) t-.* That last effort strained me. *hal-majhuud il-ʔaxiir šilaε gaḷbi.* -- Reading this small print strained my eyes. *qraayat hal-kitaaba n-naaεima taεεab εeeni.* -- Don't strain yourself. *la-tišlaε gaḷbak* or *la-ttaεεib nafsak.* **2.** *wattar (i tawtiir) t-.* The blockade strained relations between the two countries. *l-ȥiṣaar wattar il-εalaaqaat been id-dawilteen.* **3.** *ṣaffa (i taṣfiya) t-.* She strained the rice. *ṣaffat it-timman.*
strained - **1.** *mitwattir.* Relations between the two countries are strained. *l-εalaaqaat been id-dawilteen mitwattra.* **2.** *mṣaffa.* I prefer strained honey. *ʔafaδ̣δ̣il εasal mṣaffa.*
strainer - *maṣfi* pl. *maṣaafi.*
strait - *maδ̣iiq* pl. *maδ̣aayiq.*
Straits of Gibraltar - *maδ̣iiq jibal ṭaariq.*
strange - *ġariib, εajiib.* All this is strange to me. *kull haaδa ġariib εalayya.* -- What a strange question! *šloon suʔaal ġariib!*
stranger - *ġariib* pl. *ġurabaaʔ.* The stranger gave me a book. *l-ġariib inṭaani ktaab.*
strap - *seer* pl. *-aat, syuur.* The man beat his horse with a leather strap. *r-rijjaal δ̣irab iȥṣaana b-seer jilid.*
straw - **1.** *tibin.* We feed our horse straw. *ninṭi l-iȥṣaan maalna tibin.* **2.** *muṣṣaaṣa* pl. *-aat, guṣba* pl. *-aat* coll. *guṣab.* Please bring me a drinking straw. *ʔarjuuk jiib-li muṣṣaaṣa.*
**That's the last straw! *wuṣlat ȥaddha!*
strawberry - *čilka* pl. *-aat.* coll. *čilak; šilleeka* pl. *-aat.* coll. *šilleek.*
stray - **1.** *taayih.* He was hit by a stray bullet. *nδ̣irab ib-riṣaaṣa taayha.* -- Have you found the stray lamb? *ligeet it-ṭili t-taayih?* **2.** *saayib.* Stray dogs are becoming a problem. *l-ičlaab is-saayba da-tṣiir muškila.*
to stray - *taah (i teeh).* The lamb strayed from the flock. *ṭ-ṭili taah min il-qaṭiiε.*

stream - **1.** *šaṭṭ* pl. *šṭuuṭ, nahar* pl. *ʔanhaar, ʔanhur.* Where can we ford the stream? *ween nigdar niεbur iš-šaṭṭ ixyaaδa?* **2.** *saagya* pl. *suwaagi, saajya* pl. *swaaji.* A little stream flows through our farm. *fadd saagya ṣġayyra tijri b-mazraεatna.* **3.** *seel* pl. *syuul.* A stream of refugees left the city. *seel min il-laajiʔiin tirak il-wlaaya.* **4.** *majra* pl. *majaari.* You interrupted my stream of thought. *giṭaεit majra ʔafkaari.*
to stream - **1.** *jira (i jarayaan).* Tears streamed down her cheeks. *d-dumuuε jirat εala xduudha.*
street - *šaariε* pl. *šawaariε, jaadda* pl. *-aat, darub* pl. *druub.* I met him on the street. *laageeta biš-šaariε.*
streetcar - *traam* pl. *-aat, traamwaay* pl. *-aat.*
street light - *δ̣uwa* (pl. *-aayaat, ʔaδ̣wiya*) *šaariε.* The street lights go on at dark. *δ̣uwaayaat iš-šawaariε tištiεil lamma tṣiir δ̣alma.*
strength - *quwwa.* I don't have the strength to do my work. *ma-εindi quwwa ȥatta ʔasawwi šuġḷi.* -- I've lost all my strength. *fiqadit kull quuti.* -- The strength of the enemy surprised us. *quwwat il-εadu ʔadhišatna.*
**He doesn't know his own strength. *ma-yiεruf nafsa šgadd qawi.*
on the strength of - *binaaʔan εala.* We hired him on the strength of your recommendation. *šaġġaḷnaa binaaʔan εala tawṣiitak.*
strenuous - *mutεib, mujhid.* That's a strenuous job. *haaδi fadd šaġḷa mutεiba.* or ***haaδi fadd šaġḷa tišlaε il-gaḷub.*
stress - *tašdiid* pl. *-aat.* The stress is on the second syllable of the word. *t-tašdiid εala l-maqṭaε iθ-θaani mnil-kalima.*
to stress - **1.** *ʔakkad (i taʔkiid) t- εala, šaddad (i tašdiid) t- εala.* She stressed the importance of honesty. *ʔakkidat εala ʔahammiyyat il-ʔamaana.* **2.** *šaddad (i).* We stress the second syllable of the word. *nšaddid εala l-maqṭaε iθ-θaani mnil-kalima.*
stretch - *masaafa* pl. *-aat, qisim* pl. *ʔaqsaam.* We had to run the last stretch. *njibarna nirkuδ̣ il-masaafa l-ʔaxiira.*
at a stretch - *εala fadd jarra, bala wagfa.* He works about ten hours at a stretch. *yištiġuḷ ȥawaali εašir saaεaat εala fadd jarra.*
to stretch - **1.** *kabbar (u takbiir) t-.* Can you stretch my shoes a little bit. *tigdar itkabbur qundarti šwayya.* **2.** *tkabbar (a takabbur).* The gloves will stretch. *l-ičfuuf titkabbar.* **3.** *maṭṭa (i tamṭiya) t-.* You stretched the elastic too much. *maṭṭeet il-laastiik ihwaaya.* **4.** *tmaṭṭa (a tamaṭṭi) tmaġġaṭ (a tamaġġuṭ).* The lion yawned and stretched. *s-sabiε itθaawab w-itmaṭṭa.*
**The wheat fields stretch out for miles. *ȥuquul il-ȥunṭa mimtadda l-εiddat ʔamyaal.*
to stretch out - *madd (i madd) n-.* He stretched out his hand. *madd ʔiida.*
stretcher - *naqqaala* pl. *-aat, maȥaffa* pl. *-aat, sadya* pl. *-aat.* They took him to the hospital on a stretcher. *šaaloo lil-mustašfa bin-naqqaala.*
strict - *mitšaddid.* His father is very strict. *ʔabuu kulliš mitšaddid.*
strike - *ʔiδ̣raab* pl. *-aat.* How long did the strike last? *l-ʔiδ̣raab išgadd ṭawwal?*
to go on strike - *sawwa (i taswiya) ʔiδ̣raab, ʔaδ̣rab (i ʔiδ̣raab).* We're going on strike tomorrow. *raȥ-insawwi iδ̣raab baačir.*
to strike - **1.** *δ̣irab (u δ̣arub) n-.* Who struck you? *minu δ̣irabak?* **2.** *ṭaxx (u ṭaxx) b-.* The ship struck a rock. *s-sifiina ṭaxxat ib-ṣaxra.* **3.** *wugaε (a wuguuε) εala, δ̣irab (u δ̣arub) n-.* Lightning struck the tree. *ṣ-ṣaaεiqa wugεat εala š-šajara.* **4.** *dagg (u dagg).* The clock just struck ten. *s-saaεa hassa daggat εašra.* **5.** *šiεal (i, šaεil) n-.* Strike a match. *ʔišεil šixxaaṭa.* **6.** *liga (i lagi).* The government struck oil in the north. *l-ȥukuuma ligat nafuṭ biš-šimaal.* **7.** *εiqad (i εaqid) n-.* Did you strike a bargain? *εiqadit ṣafqa?* **8.** *lifat (i lafit) n-.* That was the first thing that struck my eye. *haaδa čaan awwal šii lifat naδ̣ari.*
**It strikes me he's acting very strangely. *ybayyin εalee da-yitṣarraf ib-ṣuura ġeer ṭabiiεiyya.*
**Does that strike a familiar note? *haaδa yjiib šii b-baalak?* or *haaδa yδakkrak ib-šii?*
to strike off - *šiṭab (u šaṭub) n-.* Strike his name off the list. *ʔišṭub isma mnil-qaaʔima.*
to strike out - **1.** *šiṭab (u šaṭub) n-, ȥiδaf (i ȥaδif) n-.* Strike out the first paragraph. *ʔišṭub il-faqara l-ʔuula.* **2.** *tȥarrak (a ȥaraka).* The

patrol struck out into the desert. *d-dawriyya tzarrikat biṣ-ṣazraaʔ.*

to strike up a friendship – *ṭṣaadaq (a taṣaaduq).* The two of them struck up a friendship very quickly. *θneenhum ṭṣaadqaw ib-surεa.*

striker – *muδrib* pl. *-iin.* The strikers have agreed to negotiate. *l-muδribiin waafqaw yitfaawδuun.*

striking – **1.** *zaahi.* She likes to wear striking colors. *tzibb tilbas ʔalwaan zaahya.* **2.** *εajiib.* There's a striking resemblance between the two. *ʔaku šabah εajiib beenaathum.*

string – **1.** *xeeṭ* pl. *xyuuṭ.* This string is too short. *hal-xeeṭ kulliš igṣayyir.* **2.** *watar* pl. *ʔawtaar.* I have to buy a new string for my violin. *laazim ʔaštiri watar jidiid lil-kamanja maalti.*

**He's still attached to his mother's apron strings. *baεda tazat ṣaytarat ʔumma.* or *baεda laazig ib-ʔumma.*

to string – **1.** *liδam (u laδum) n-.* Where can I have my pearls strung? *ween ʔagdar ʔalδum il-liilu maali?* **2.** *waṣṣal (i tawṣiil) t-.* How are you going to string the wire to the garage? *šloon raz-itwaṣṣil il-waayir lil-garaaj?*

string bean – *faaṣuulaaya* pl. *-aat* coll. *faaṣuuliyya, faaṣuulya.*

to **strip** – **1.** *ṣallax (i taṣliix) t-.* They strip the cars of everything valuable before they scrap them. *yṣallixuun is-sayyaaraat min kullši l-yiswa gabuḷ-ma ysakribuuha.* **2.** *šilaε (a šaliε) n-.* The captain stripped the medals from his chest. *r-raʔiis šilaε il-madaalyaat min ṣadra.* **3.** *jarrad (i tajriid) t-.* They stripped the king of all his privileges. *jarridaw il-malik min kull imtiyaazaata.*

to strip off – *nizaε (a naziε).* She stripped off her clothes. *nizεat ihduumha.* or ***ṭṣallxat.*

stripe – **1.** *qalam,* pl. *qlaam.* The tie has red and white stripes. *l-booyinbaaġ bii qlaam zumur w-biiδ.* **2.** *xeeṭ* pl. *xyuuṭ.* If you get drunk again, we'll take your stripes away. *ʔiδa skarit marrt il-lux, naaxuδ ixyuuṭak minnak.*

striped – *mqallam.* She's wearing a striped dress. *laabsa nafnuuf imqallam.*

stroke – **1.** *nfijaar* (pl. *-aat) bid-damaaġ.* He died of a stroke. *maat min ʔaθar infijaar bid-damaaġ.* **2.** *δarba* pl. *-aat.* With a few strokes of the oars, he was in midstream. *b-čam δarbat mijdaaf, wuṣal il-nuṣṣ iš-šaṭṭ.* **3.** *jarra* pl. *-aat.* With a stroke of the pen, he was sentenced to hang. *b-jarrat qalam, inzikam εalee bil-ʔiεdaam.*

**It was a real stroke of luck to get this apartment. *tazṣiil haš-šaqqa čaan zaδδ εadil.*

**At one stroke everything was changed. *kullši tbaddal fadd nooba.*

**He arrived at the stroke of four. *wuṣal is-saaεa ʔarbaεa biδ-δabuṭ.*

to stroke – *massad (i tamsiid) t- l-.* Our cat loves to be stroked. *bazzuunatna tzibb yitmassad-ilha.*

stroll – *mašya* pl. *-aat.* A short stroll won't tire you much. *mašya ṣġayyra ma-ttaεεbak ihwaaya.*

**I'd like to take a stroll around the square. *ʔariid ʔatmašša zawl is-saaza.*

to stroll – *tmašša (a tmašši).* Let's stroll through the town. *xalli nitmašša bil-madiina.*

strong – **1.** *qawi*.* He has strong hands. *εinda ʔiideen qawiyya.* **2.** *šadiid, qawi*.* There's a strong wind blowing today. *ʔaku hawa šadiid da-yhibb il-yoom.*

struggle – **1.** *mašaqqa* pl. *-aat.* I only beat him after a hard struggle. *ma-ġiḷabta ʔilla b-mašaqqa.* **2.** *mukaafaza.* The struggle against illiteracy in Iraq has made progress. *mukaafazat il-ʔummiyya bil-εiraaq itqaddimat.* **3.** *kifaaz* pl. *-aat, mukaafaza* pl. *-aat.* They got their freedom through a long struggle. *zaṣṣlaw εal-istiqlaalhum ib-kifaaz ṭuwiil.* **4.** *tbaaṭaz (a tabaaṭuz).* I've been struggling with this problem for some time. *ṣaar-li mudda da-ʔatbaaṭaz wiyya hal-muškila.* **5.** *jaahad (i jihaad).* The government is struggling to improve economic conditions. *l-zukuuma da-tjaahid zatta tzassin il-ʔazwaal il-iqtiṣaadiyya.*

to struggle against – *kaafaz (i mukaafaza) t-.* We had to struggle against the current. *δṭarreena nkaafiz it-tayyaar.*

**We had a hard struggle to get the piano up to the second floor. *mitna gabuḷ-ma nṣaεεid il-piyaano lit-ṭaabiq iθ-θaani.*

stubborn – *εnaadi, εnuudi* pl. *-iyyiin.* He's terribly stubborn. *huwwa kulliš iεnaadi.*

to get **stuck** – **1.** *nziṣar (i nziṣaar).* I got stuck in the chair. *nziṣarit bil-kursi.* **2.** *ṭumas (u ṭamus). nziṣar (i nziṣaar).* My car got stuck in the mud. *sayyaarti ṭumsat bit-ṭiin.* **3.** *twarraṭ (a tawarruṭ), txoozaq (a taxoozuq).* I got stuck with this car. *twarraṭit ib-has-sayyaara.*

**I got stuck on this passage. *εiṣat εalayya haay ij-jumla.*

stuck-up – *mitkabbur.* She is stuck-up *hiyya mitkabbra.* or ***šaayla xašimha.*

student – *tilmiiδ* pl. *talaamiiδ, ṭaalib* pl. *ṭullaab.* How many students are there at the medical school? *čam tilmiiδ ʔaku b-kulliyyat iṭ-ṭibb?*

studio – *stoodyo* pl. *-waat.* I've got to see a man at the Iraqi Broadcasting Studios. *laazim ʔašuuf fadd rijjaal b-istoodyowaat il-ʔiδaaεa l-εiraaqiyya.*

study – **1.** *diraasa* pl. *-aat.* Has he finished his studies? *xallaṣ diraasta?* **2.** *baziθ* pl. *buzuuθ, ʔabzaaθ.* He has published several studies in that field. *nišar εiddat abzaaθ ib-hal-mawδuuε.*

to study – **1.** *diras (u diraasa) n-.* We studied the map before we started our trip. *dirasna l-xariiṭa gabuḷ-ma nibdi safratna.* — He's studying Chinese. *da-yidrus ṣiini.* **2.** *bizaθ (a baziθ) n-, diras (u daris) n-.* The government is studying the problem. *l-zukuuma da-tibzaθ il-muškila.*

stuff – *ġaraaδ, ʔašyaaʔ.* Throw that old stuff away! *δibb hal-ġaraaδ il-εatiiga!*

**Now we'll see what sort of stuff he's made of. *hassa nšuuf šinu maεdana.*

to stuff – **1.** *zannaṭ (i tazniiṭ).* He stuffs animals for the museum. *yzanniṭ zaywaanaat lil-matzaf.* **2.** *zašša (i tazšiya) t-, εabba (i taεbiya) t-.* Stuff cotton in your ears. *zašši guṭun b-iδnak.* — Can you stuff all these things in one suitcase? *tigdar itεabbi kull hal-ġaraaδ ib-fadd janṭa?* **3.** *tiras (i/u taris) n-, dačč (i dačč) n-.* We stuffed our bellies with food. *daččeena bṭuunna bil-ʔakil.*

stuffed – **1.** *masduud.* My nose is all stuffed up. *xašmi masduud.* **2.** *mazši, nzašša.* We had stuffed turkey for lunch. *tġaddeena diič hindi mazši.*

to **stumble** – *εiθar (a εaθir).* I stumbled over a stone. *εiθarit b-izjaara.*

stupid – **1.** *ġabi, baliid.* He isn't at all stupid. *huwwa muu ġabi ʔabadan.* **2.** *saxiif.* That's a stupid idea. *haay fikra saxiifa.*

sty – *zadigdiga,* pl. *-aat.* I'm getting a sty on my left eye. *da-tiṭlaε-li zadigdiga b-εeeni l-yisra.*

style – **1.** *ʔisluub* pl. *ʔasaaliib.* His style of writing is very poor. *ʔisluuba bil-kitaaba kulliš δaεiif.* **2.** *mooda* pl. *-aat.* It's the latest style. *haay ʔaaxir mooda.* — She's always in style. *hiyya εal-mooda daaʔiman.*

subject – **1.** *mawδuuε* pl. *mawaaδiiε, qaδiyya* pl. *qaδaaya.* I don't know anything about that subject. *ma-aεruf šii εan haaδa l-mawδuuε.* **2.** *raεiyya* pl. *raεaaya.* He is a British subject. *huwwa min raεaaya ʔingiltara.* **3.** *mubtadaʔ.* The subject of this sentence is the word "Ali". *l-mubtadaʔ ib-haj-jumla huwwa l-kalima "εali".* **4.** *muεarraδ.* This schedule is subject to change. *haaδa j-jadwal muεarraδ lit-taġyiir.*

**I'm always subject to colds. *ʔaani ʔannišil ib-surεa.*

to subject – *ʔaxδaε (i xuδuuε).* The Mongols subjected all of Asia to their rule. *l-maġuul ʔaxδiεaw kull ʔaasya l-zukumhum.*

to **submit** – **1.** *qaddam (i taqdiim) t-.* I'll submit my report on Monday. *raz-ʔaqaddim taqriiri yoom iθ-θineen.* **2.** *riδax (u riδuux).* The criminal submitted to search. *l-mujrim riδax lit-taftiiš.* **3.** *xiδaε (a xuδuuε).* The boss forces everyone to submit to his ideas. *r-raʔiis yijbur il-kull yixδaεuun il-ʔaaraaʔa.* **4.** *staslam (i stislam).* His mother had to submit to an operation. *ʔumma δṭarrat tistaslim il-εamaliyya.*

to **subscribe** – **1.** *štirak (i štiraak).* I subscribed to both papers. *štirakit bij-jariidteen.* **2.** *šaarak (i mušaaraka) t-.* I don't subscribe to your opinion. *ma-ʔašaarkak ib-raʔyak.*

substantial – **1.** *čbiir, δaxum.* He lost a substantial sum of money. *xiṣar kammiyya čbiira mnil-ifluus.* or *xiṣar mablaġ δaxum.* **2.** *jawhari*.* I don't see any substantial difference. *ma-ašuuf ʔay faraq jawhari.* **3.** *tukma.* Don't use that ladder; it's not substantial. *la-tistaεmil had-daraj; haaδa muu tukma.*

substantially – *jawhariyyan.* The two are substantially alike. *l-iθneen jawhariyyan yitšaabhuun.*

substitute – **1.** *badal, εuwaδ.* Vegetable oil is occasionally used as a substitue for animal fat. *d-dihin in-nabaati ʔazyaanan yustaεmal ka-badal lid-dihin il-zaywaani.* **2.** *bdaal.* If you can't be here tomorrow, send a substitute. *ʔiδa ma-tigdar*

itkuun ihnaa baačir, dizz waaḥid ibdaalak.
to substitute for - 1. *εawwaḍ (i taεwiiḍ) t-b-makaan-.* I'll substitute red for green. *raḥ-ʔaεawwuḍ ʔaḥmar ib-makaan il-ʔaxḍar.* **2.** *ʔaxaδ (u) makaan-.* Can you substitute for me today? *tigdar taaxuδ makaani l-yoom?*
to **subtract** - *ṭiraḥ (a ṭariḥ) n-.* He subtracted six from ten. *ṭiraḥ sitta min εašra.*
subtraction - *ṭariḥ.*
suburb - *ḍaaḥiya* pl. *ḍawaaḥi.* Their house is in the suburbs of the city. *beethum ib-ḍawaaḥi il-madiina.*
to **succeed** - *jaa (i majiiʔ) wara.* Who succeeded him in office? *minu jaa waraa bil-waḍiifa.* **2.** *nijaḥ (a najaaḥ).* He succeeds in everything he undertakes. *yinjaḥ ib-kull-ma yaaxuδ εala εaatqa.*
success - *najaaḥ* pl. *-aat.* Congratulations on your success! *tahaaniina εala najaaḥak!* -- The play wasn't much of a success. *t-tamθiiliyya ma-ḥaṣṣlat εala najaaḥ ihwaaya.*
successful - *naajiḥ* pl. *-iin.* He's a successful businessman. *huwwa rajul ʔaεmaal naajiḥ.*
successor - *xalaf* (hereditary). The sheik's oldest son becomes his successor. *ʔakbar awlaad iš-šeex yṣiir xalafa.*
such - 1. *hiiči, miθil haaδa.* Such statements are hard to prove. *hiiči εibaaraat yiṣεab barhanatha.* -- I've never heard such nonsense before. *ma-smaεit miθil hal-laġwa gabuḷ.* -- I heard some such thing. *simaεit hiiči šii.* or *simaεit šii min haaδa l-qabiil.* **2.** *hal-gadd.* Don't be in such a hurry. *la-tistaεjil hal-gadd.* -- It was such a long movie that we didn't get out till midnight. *hal-gadd-ma čaan filim ṭuwiil, ma-tlaεna ʔilla l-nuṣṣ il-leel.*
as such - *b-ḥadd δaat-.* The work as such isn't difficult. *š-šuġuḷ ib-ḥadd δaata muu ṣaεub.*
such as - *miθil.* We sell things such as hats and shirts. *nbiiε ʔašyaaʔ miθil šafqaat w-iθyaab.*
to **suck** - *maṣṣ (u maṣṣ) n-.* Our baby sucks his thumb. *ṭifilna ymuṣṣ ibhaama.*
suction - *maṣṣ, mtiṣaaṣ.*
Sudan - *s-suudaan.*
Sudanese - *suudaani** pl. *-iyyiin.*
sudden - *fujaaʔi**. There's been a sudden change in the weather. *ṣaar tabaddul fujaaʔi bij-jaww.*
all of a sudden - 1. *fujʔatan, εala ġafla, baġtatan.* All of a sudden I remembered that I had to mail a letter. *fujʔatan itδakkarit laazim ʔaδibb bil-bariid.*
to **sue - 1.** *štika (i šikaaya).* We sued him for damages. *štikeena εalee b-ṭalab it-taεwiiḍ.* **2.** *ṭilab (u ṭalab).* They'll sue for peace. *raḥ-yṭulbuun iṣ-ṣuluḥ.*
Suez - *s-suwees.*
to **suffer - 1.** *tεaδδab (a εaδδaab), qaasa (i muqaasaat).* Did she suffer very much? *tεaδδbat ihwaaya?* **2.** *tkabbad (a takabbud).* They suffered heavy losses. *tkabbdaw xasaayir faadḥa.*
sufficient - *kaafi.*
to **suffocate** - *xtinag (i xtinaaq).* I nearly suffocated. *taqriiban ixtinagit.*
sugar - *šakar.* Please pass me the sugar. *ʔarjuuk, εabbur-li š-šakar.*
to **suggest - 1.** *qtiraḥ (i qtiraaḥ).* I suggest that we go to the movies. *ʔaqtiriḥ inruuḥ lis-siinama.* **2.** *lammaḥ (i talmiiḥ).* Are you suggesting that I'm wrong? *da-tlammiḥ bi-ʔanni ġalṭaan.* **3.** *δakkar (i taδkiir) b-, jaab (i jeeb) b-baal-.* Does this suggest anything to you? *haaδa yδakkrak ib-šii?* or *haaδa yjiib šii b-baalak?*
suggestion - *qtiraaḥ* pl. *-aat.* Your suggestion is very reasonable. *qtiraaḥak kulliš maεquul.*
suicide - *ntiḥaar* pl. *-aat.* Suicide cases are rare here. *ḥawaadiθ il-intiḥaar naadra hnaa.*
to commit suicide - *ntiḥar (i ntiḥaar).* He committed suicide because he owed a lot of money. *ntiḥar li-ʔan čaan maṭluub ifluus ihwaaya.*
suit - 1. *qaaṭ* pl. *quuṭ, badla* pl. *-aat.* He needs a new suit. *yiḥtaaj qaaṭ jidiid.* **2.** *daεwa* pl. *daεaawi.* If you don't pay today, we shall bring suit. *ʔiδa ma-tidfaε il-ifluus il-yoom, nqiim daεwa εaleek.* **3.** *nooε* pl. *ʔanwaaε, qisim* pl. *ʔaqsaam.* The four suits in cards are: hearts, diamonds, spades and clubs. *ʔanwaaε il-waraq il-ʔarbaεa hiyya kuupa w-dinar w-maača w-sinak.*
**If he takes one, I'll follow suit. *ʔiδa yaaxuδ waaḥid, ʔaani ʔasawwi miθla.*
to suit - 1. *raḍḍa (i tarḍiya).* It's hard to suit everybody. *ṣaεub itraḍḍi kull in-naas.* **2.** *naasab (i munaasaba) t-, waalam (i muwaalama) t-.* These books are suited to the age of the children. *hal-kutub itnaasib εumr il-ʔaṭfaal.* **3.** *waafaq (i muwaafaqa), naasab (i), waalam (i).* Does this suit your taste? *haaδa ywaafiq δawqak?* -- Which day would suit you best? *yaa yoom ywaafqak ʔaḥsan?* **4.** *laag (u loog, liyaaga) l-.* Red doesn't suit you. *l-ʔaḥmar ma-yluug-lak.*
to be suited - 1. *laag (u).* Is she suited for this kind of work? *hiyya laayga l-hal-waḍiifa?* **2.** *ṣilaḥ (a ṣalaaḥiyya).* This land isn't suited for growing wheat. *hal-ʔarḍ ma-tiṣlaḥ il-ziraaεat il-ḥunṭa.* **3.** *laaʔam (i mulaaʔama).* This climate isn't suited for people with TB. *hal-manaax ma-ylaaʔim il-masluuliin.*
**Suit yourself. *keefak.*
suitable - *mnaasib, ṣaaliḥ, mlaaʔim.* We can't find a suitable apartment. *ma-nigdar nilgi beet imnaasib.*
suitcase - *junṭa* pl. *junaṭ.* I have three suitcases and one trunk. *εindi tlaθ junaṭ w-ṣanduug waaḥid.*
sullen - *εabuus, mεabbis.*
sultan - *sulṭaan* pl. *salaaṭiin.*
sultanate - *salṭana* pl. *-aat.*
sultry - *šarji**. It's awfully sultry today. *l-yoom il-hawa kulliš šarji.*
sum - 1. *majmuuε* pl. *-aat.* Just tell me the full sum. *bass gul-li l-majmuuε.* **2.** *mablaġ* pl. *mabaaliġ.* I still owe him a small sum. *baεadni madyuun-la mablaġ iṣġayyir.*
to sum up - *laxxaṣ (i talxiiṣ) t-.* Let me sum up briefly. *xalli ʔalaxxiṣ b-ixtiṣaar.*
Sumeria - *soomar.*
Sumerian - *soomari** pl. *-iyyiin.* The Sumerians lived in lower Iraq. *s-soomariyyiin siknaw jinuub il-εiraaq.*
summary - *xulaaṣa* pl. *-aat, mulaxxaṣ* pl. *-aat.* Read the book and give me a summary. *ʔiqra l-iktaab w-inṭiini l-mulaxxaṣ.*
summer - 1. *ṣeef* pl. *ṣyaaf.* I spent three summers in the mountains. *biqeet itlaθ iṣyaaf bij-jibaal.* -- Does it get hot here in summer? *tṣiir ḥaarra hnaa bis-ṣeef?* **2.** *ṣeefi*, ṣayfi**. I need a new summer suit. *yirraad-li badla ṣeefiyya jdiida.*
summer resort - *maṣiif* pl. *maṣaayif.*
to **summon** - *ṣaaḥ (i ṣeeḥ) n-.* The boss summoned me to his office. *r-raʔiis ṣaaḥni l-ġurufta.*
to summon up - *stajmaε (stijmaaε).* He couldn't summon up the courage to enter the cold water. *ma-gidar yistajmiε šajaaεta ḥatta yxušš bil-maay il-baarid.*
sun - *šamis* pl. *šmuus.* The sun has just gone down. *š-šamis tawwha ġurbat.*
to sun - *šammas (i tšimmis), tšammas (a tšimmis).* We saw a snake sunning himself on a rock. *šifna fadd ḥayya da-tšammis nafisha εala ṣaxra.*
sunbeam - *šuεaaε (pl. ʔašiεεat) šamis.*
Sunday - *yoom (pl. ʔayyaam) il-ʔaḥḥad.*
sundown - *miġrib.* He usually comes home around sundown. *εaadatan yiji lil-beet wakt il-miġrib.*
sunlight - *ḍuwa šamis.*
Sunna - *sunna.* The Sunna consists of the deeds and sayings of the Prophet. *s-sunna hiyya ʔafεaal w-ʔaḥaadiiθ in-nabi.*
Sunni, Sunnite - *sinni** pl. *-iyyiin, sinna.*
sunny - 1. *mišmis.* The front rooms are sunny. *l-ġuraf il-ʔamaamiyya mišmisa.* **2.** *ṣaaḥi.* We'll have a sunny day tomorrow. *baačir id-dinya raḥ-tṣiir ṣaaḥya.*
sunrise - *šuruuq.*
sunset - *l-ġuruub.*
sunshine - *ʔašiεεat šamis, ḍuwa šamis.* The sunshine is strong today. *ʔašiεεat iš-šamis qawiyya l-yoom.*
sunstroke - *ḍarbat (pl. -aat) šamis.* He died of sunstroke. *maat min ḍarbat šamis.*
superior - 1. *raʔiis* pl. *ruʔasaaʔ.* Is he your superior on the job? *huwwa raʔiisak biš-šuġuḷ?* **2.** *mumtaaz.* This is of superior quality. *haaδa min nooε mumtaaz.*
superiority - *tafawwuq.* Their superiority in numbers is weakened by their lack of experience. *tafawwuqhum bil-εadad qallat ʔahammiita l-εadam xibrathum.*
superiority complex - *murakkab iš-šuεuur bil-εaḍama.* He has a superiority complex. *εinda murakkab iš-šuεuur bil-εaḍama.*
superstition - *xuraafa* pl. *-aat.*
superstitious: **He's terribly superstitious. *hwaaya yiεtiqid bil-xuraafaat.*
supervision - *ʔišraaf.* They are under constant supervision. *humma taḥat ʔišraaf mustamirr.*
supper - *εaša* pl. *-aayaat.* I've been invited for supper. *ʔaani maεzuum εala εaša.*

to have supper - *tεašša (a taεašši).* Would you like to have supper with us tonight? *tzibb titεašša wiyyaana hal-leela?*

supplement - **1.** *mulzaq* pl. *malaaziq.* The supplement to the phone book is small this year. *mulzaq daliil it-talafoon has-sana ṣġayyir.* **2.** *ʔiδaafa* pl. *-aat.* The doctor recommended using vitamins as a supplement to the diet. *ṭ-ṭabiib wuṣaf istiεmaal il-fiitaamiinaat ka-ʔiδaafa ʔila l-ġiδaaʔ.*

supply - **1.** *kammiyya* pl. *-aat.* We still have a big supply of bicycles. *baεad εidna kammiyya čibiira mnil-baaysiklaat.* **2.** *δaxiira* pl. *δaxaayir, maxzuun* pl. *-aat.* Our potato supply is almost gone. *δaxiiratna min il-puteeta taqriiban xilṣat.* **3.** *tajhiiz* pl. *-aat.* The hospital needs more medical supplies. *l-mustašfa yiztaaj tajhiizaat ṭibbiyya ʔakθar.*

to supply - **1.** *jahhaz (i tajhiiz) t-.* Our bakery supplies all the big hotels. *maxbazna yjahhiz kull il-ʔuteelaat ič-čibiira.* **2.** *zawwad (i tazwiid) t-.* He always supplies us with cigarettes. *huwwa daaʔiman yzawwidna bij-jigaayir.* **3.** *mawwan (i tamwiin) t-.* We have a contract to supply the police with ammunition. *εidna qunṭaraat inmawwin iš-šurṭa bil-εitaad.*

support - **1.** *taʔyiid.* You can count on my support. *tigdar tiεtimid εala taʔyiidi.* **2.** *dinga* pl. *dinag.* We've got to put supports under the bridge. *laazim inxalli dinag jawwa j-jisir.*

in support of - *taʔyiidan l-.* Can you offer any evidence in support of your statement. *tigdar itqaddim ʔay burhaan taʔyiidan il-εibaartak.*

to support - **1.** *ʔayyad (i taʔyiid) t-, sinad (i sanid) n-.* All the parties are supporting him. *kull il-ʔazzaab da-tʔayyida.* -- I'll support your election campaign. *raz-asnid zamiltak il-intixaabiyya.* **2.** *εaal (i ʔiεaala) n-, εayyaš (i taεyiiš) t-.* He has to support his parents. *laazim yεiil ʔumma w-ʔabuu.* **3.** *diεam (a daεim) n-.* Have you got evidence to support your claim? *εindak daliil yidεam iddiεaaʔak?*

to support oneself - *qaam (u qiyaam) ib-nafs^.* I have supported myself ever since I was fifteen. *qumit ib-nafsi min čaan εumri xmuṣṭaεaš sana.*

to **suppose** - *furaδ (u faraδ), ftiraδ (i ftiraaδ).* Let's suppose that I'm right. *xalli nifruδ ʔaani ṣaziiz.* **2.** *δann (i δann).* I suppose so. *ʔaδinn hiiči.*

supposed to - **1.** *mafruuδ bii.* He's supposed to be rich. *l-mafruuδ bii huwwa ġani.* **2.** *laazim.* I was supposed to go out tonight, but I'm too tired. *čaan laazim ʔaṭlaε hal-leela, laakin ʔaani kulliš taεbaan.*

supposing - *εala fariδ, faraδan.* Supposing he doesn't come tonight, what'll we do? *εala fariδ ma-yiji hal-leela, š-insawwi?*

sure - **1.** *ʔakiid, muʔakkad.* That's a sure thing. *haaδa šii ʔakiid.* **2.** *ṭabεan, maεluum, ʔakiid, muʔakkad.* Sure, I'd be glad to. *ṭabεan, εala εeeni.* **3.** *waḷḷa.* I'd sure like to see him again. *waḷḷa ʔariid asuufa marrt il-lux.* **4.** *mitʔakkid.* Are you sure of that? *ʔinta mitʔakkid min δaak?*

for sure - *bit-taʔkiid.* Be there by five o'clock for sure. *kuun ihnaak saaεa xamsa bit-taʔkiid.*

sure enough - *fiεlan.* You thought it would rain, and sure enough it did. *ʔinta gilit raz-tumṭur, w-fiεlan muṭrat.*

to be sure - *tʔakkad (a taʔakkud).* Be sure to come tomorrow. *tʔakkad tiji baačir.*

**He's sure to be back up nine o'clock. *bit-taʔkiid raz-yirjaε saaεa tisεa.*

to make sure - *tʔakkad (a taʔakkud), tzaqqaq (a tazaqquq).* Make sure that you take everything with you. *tʔakkad taaxuδ kullši wiyyaak.* -- I just wanted to make sure that nothing was wrong. *bass ridit ʔatzaqqaq ma-aku šii.*

surely - *bit-taʔkiid, ʔakiid.* Will you be there? Surely. *raz-itkuun ihnaak? bit-taʔkiid.* -- He can surely do that. *bit-taʔkiid yigdar ysawwi haaδa.*

**I surely thought it would be finished. *činit mitʔakkid raz-tixḷaṣ.*

surface - *saṭiz* pl. *suṭuuz, wujih* pl. *wujuuh.*

surgeon - *jarraaz* pl. *-iin.*

surgery - *jiraaza.*

surplus - **1.** *ziyaada* pl. *-aat.* There is a surplus in the wheat crop this year that they don't know what to do with. *ʔaku ziyaada b-mazṣuul il-zunṭa has-sana ma-yidruun s-ysawwuu biiha.* **2.** *zaayid.* The Labor Office has forbidden the company to discharge its surplus employees. *mudiiriyyat šuʔuun il-εummaal minεat il-istiġnaaʔ εann il-εummaal iz-zaaydiin.*

surprise - **1.** *mufaajaʔa* pl. *-aat.* I've got a surprise for you. *εindi mufaajaʔa ʔilak.* **2.** *dahša* pl. *-aat.* You'll get the surprise of your life. *raz-tindihiš dahša ma-ṣaar miθilha.* or *raz-tindihiš ʔakbar dahša b-zayaatak.*

to catch by surprise - *faajaʔ (i mufaajaʔa) t-, baaġat (i mubaaġata) t-.* The rain caught me by surprise. *l-muṭar faajaʔni.* or *l-muṭar baaġatni.*

to take by surprise - *ʔaxaδ (u) εala ġafla, baaġat (i mubaaġata) t-.* You took me by surprise. *ʔaxaδitni εala ġafla.* or *baaġatitni tamaaman.*

to surprise - *ʔadhaš (i dahša) n-, εajjab (i εajab) t-.* I wanted to surprise you. *ridit ʔadihšak.* or *ridit ʔaεajjbak.* -- Nothing surprises me any more. *ma-aku šii yεajjibni baεad.* -- I'm surprised at you. *ʔaani mitεajjib εaleek.* -- I'm not surprised at anything you do. *š-ma tsawwi ma-yidhišni.*

to **surrender** - **1.** *sallam (i tasliim) t-.* He surrendered to the police. *sallam liš-šurṭa.* **2.** *staslam (i stislaam).* The enemy surrendered. *l-εadu staslam.*

to **surround** - **1.** *zaaṭ (i ʔizaaṭa) n-.* A high fence surrounds the house. *siyaaj εaali yziiṭ il-beet.* **2.** *ṭawwaq (u taṭwiiq) t-, zaaṣar (i ziṣaar, muzaaṣata) t-.* We're surrounded. *ʔizna mṭawwaqiin.*

suspect - *mašbuuh* pl. *-iin.* He's a suspect in that case. *huwwa mašbuuh ib-δiič il-qaδiyya.*

to suspect - *šakk (u šakk) b-, rtaab (a rtiyaab) b-, štibah (i štibaah) b-.* Do you suspect anything? *tšukk ib-šii?* or *tirtaab ib-šii?*

to **suspend** - **1.** *waqqaf (i tawqiif) t-.* The bank has suspended payment due to the robbery. *l-bang waqqaf id-dafiε b-sabab il-booga.* **2.** *fuṣal (u faṣil) n-, ṭirad (u ṭarid) n-.* He was suspended for a year. *nfuṣal il-muddat sana.* -- He was suspended from school for a week. *nṭirad imnil-madrasa l-muddat isbuuε.* **3.** *sizab (a sazib) n-, waqqaf (i).* The department of health suspended the restaurant's license for a month. *wizaart iṣ-ṣizza sizbat ʔijaazat il-maṭεam il-muddat šahar.* **4.** *sadd (i sadd) n-, εaṭṭal (i taεṭiil).* The government suspended the newspaper. *l-zukuuma saddat ij-jariida.* **5.** *εallag (i taεliig) t-.* The worksmen suspended the chandelier from the ceiling by a heavy chain. *l-εummaal εalligaw iθ-θirayya mnis-saguf ib-silsila qawiyya.*

suspense - *ziira.* I can't stand the suspense any longer. *ma-ʔatzammal il-ziira baεad.*

suspicion - *šakk* pl. *škuuk.* What aroused your suspicion? *šinu ʔaθaar šakkak?* or **š-xallaak tirtaab?*

suspicious - **1.** *muriib* pl. *iin.* That place looks suspicious. *hal-mazall ybayyin muriib.* **2.** *šakkaak* pl. *-iin.* My husband is very suspicious. *rajli kulliš šakkaak.*

**I immediately got suspicious. *zaalan šakkeet.* or *zaalan irtaabeet.*

swallow - **1.** *jurεa* pl. *-aat, juraε.* I only took one swallow. *širabit bass jurεa wazda.* **2.** *bint* (pl. *banaat) sinduhind.* The swallows come in the spring and build their nests. *banaat sinduhind yjuun bir-rabiiε w-yibnuun iεšuušhum.*

to swallow - *bilaε (a baliε) n-.* My throat hurts me so much I can't swallow anything. *balεuumi hal-gadd yoojaεni ma-agdar ablaε šii.*

**He swallowed the bait hook, line and sinker. *l-ziila εubrat εalee.*

swamp - *hoor* pl. *ʔahwaar, mustanqaε* pl. *-aat.* How far does the swamp go? *l-hoor išgadd yimtadd?*

to swamp - **1.** *ġirag (a ġarig).* I was swamped with work last week. *ġiragit biš-šuġuḷ l-isbuuε il-faat.* **2.** *tiras (i taris) n-.* A large wave swamped our boat. *fadd mooja čibiira tirsat balamna maay.*

swarm - *jamaaεa* pl. *-aat.* They saw a swarm of bees. *šaafaw jamaaεat nazal.*

to swarm - *εajj (i εajj).* The swamp is swarming with mosquitoes. *l-mustanqaε yεijj bil-baqq.*

to **sway** - **1.** *htazz (a htizaaz).* The trees swayed in the wind. *l-ʔašjaar ihtazzat bil-hawa.* **2.** *ʔaθθar (i taʔθiir) t- εala.* No one can sway him once his mind is made up. *mazzad yigdar yʔaθθir εalee baεad-ma ysawwi fikra.*

to **swear** - **1.** *zilaf (i zalif) n-, ʔaqsam (i qasam) n-.* She swears she's telling the truth. *tizlif da-tguul iṣ-ṣudug.* -- Do you swear to that? *tizlif εala haaδa?* or *tiqsim εala haaδa?* **2.** *šattam (i taštiim) t-, sabb (i sabb) n-.* He swears constantly. *yšattim εala ṭuul.* or *ysibb εala ṭuul.*

to swear in - *zallaf (i tazliif).* They swore the

witness in on the Koran, and later began asking him questions. *zallifaw iš-šaahid bil-qur?aan w-baεdeen gaamaw yis?aluu ?as?ila.*
sweat - *εarag.* He wiped the sweat from his brow. *misaz il-εarag min guṣṣṭa.*
to sweat - *εirag (a εarag).* This kind of work makes you sweat. *han-nooε imniš-šuġuḷ yxalliik tiεrag.*
sweaty - *εargaan.* I'm sweaty all over. *?aani εargaan min foog li-jawwa.*
to **sweep** - **1.** *kinas (u kanis) n-.* Did you sweep the bedroom? *kinasti ġurfat in-noom?* **2.** *sizal (a sazil) n- b-.* Her dress sweeps the ground. *nafnuufha da-yiszal bil-gaaε.*
to sweep away - *ktisaz (i ktisaaz).* The flood waters swept away the town. *ṃaay il-fayaḍaan iktisaz l-wlaaya.*
sweet - **1.** *zilu.* The dates are very sweet. *t-tamur zilu kulliš.* **2.** *zabbuub.* She is a sweet girl. *hiyya bint zabbuuba.*
sweetheart - *zabiib* pl. *?azibbaa?.* She's his sweetheart. *hiyya zabiibta.*
sweets - *zalawiyyaat.* I don't care much for sweets. *ma-azibb il-zalawiyyaat.*
swell - *xooš.* She's a swell person. *hiyya xooš ?aadmiyya.*
to swell - *wuram (a waram).* My finger is all swollen. *?iṣibεi kulla waarum.*
swelling - *waram.* Has the swelling gone down? *l-waram nizal?*
to **swim** - *sibaz (a sibiz, sibaaza).* Do you know how to swim? *tuεruf tisbaz?*
swimming - *sibaaza.* Swimming is the only sport I enjoy. *s-sibaaza hiyya r-riyaaḍa l-waziida lli ?atwannas biiha.*
swimming pool - *masbaz* pl. *masaabiz.*
swing - *marjiiza, marjuuza* pl. *maraajiiz.* We have a swing in our garden. *εidna marjuuza b-zadiiqatna.*
in full swing - *b-?awj.* The party is in full swing. *l-zafla b-?awijha.*
to swing - **1.** *marjaz (i tmirjiz, marjaza) t-.* You swing me, and then I'll swing you. *?inta marjizni w-baεdeen ?aani ?amarjizak.* **2.** *tmarjaz (a tamarjuz).* You'll fall off if you swing so hard. *toogaε ?iḍa titmarjaz hal-gadd zeel.* **3.** *hazz (i hazz) n-.* She swings her arms when she walks. *thizz iideeha lamma timši.*
to swing around - *furr (u farr) n-, deewar (u tdeewur).* Swing the car around. *furr is-sayyaara.*
switch - **1.** *swiič* pl. *-aat.* The light switch is next to the door. *swiič iḍ-ḍuwa yamm il-baab.* **2.** *mugaṣṣ* pl. *-aat.* The last car jumped the track at the switch. *?aaxir faargoon ṭilaε imnis-sikka yamm il-mugaṣṣ.*
to switch - **1.** *zawwal (i tazwiil) t-.* The train was switched to another track. *l-qiṭaar itzawwal ?ila ġeer sikka.* **2.** *daar (i deer) n-.* Switch the radio to short wave. *diir ir-raadyo εal-mooja l-qaṣiira.* **3.** *baadal (i mubaadala) t-.* Let's switch places. *xalli nitbaadal ib-mukaanaatna.*
**I don't know how we switched coats. *ma-aεruf išloon ?axaḍna qaṗṗuuṭ waazid il-laax bil-ġalaṭ.*
to switch off - *ṭaffa (i taṭfiya) t-.* Switch off the light. *ṭaffi ḍ-ḍuwa.*
to switch on - *šiεal (i šaεil) n-.* Switch on the light. *?išεil iḍ-ḍuwa.*
sword - *seef* pl. *syuuf.*
syllable - *maqṭaε* pl. *maqaaṭiε.* The accent is on the first syllable. *t-ta?kiid εala l-maqṭaε il-?awwal.*
symbol - *ramiz* pl. *rumuuz.*
symbolic - *ramzi*.* That sign has the same symbolic meaning all over the world. *hal-?išaara biiha nafs il-maεna r-ramzi b-kull il-εaalam.*
to **symbolize** - *rimaz (i ramiz).* The statue over there symbolizes our struggle against imperialism. *hat-timθaal yirmiz ?ila mukaafazatna lil-istiεmaar.*
to **sympathize with** - **1.** *šaarak (i mušaaraka) b-šuεuur.* I sympathize with you. *?ašaarkak ib-šuεuurak.* **2.** *εiṭaf (u εaṭuf) εala.* I sympathize with the flood victims. *?aεṭuf εala l-mutaḍarririin bil-fayaḍaan.*
sympathy - *εaṭuf.* I have no sympathy for her. *ma-εindi ?ay εaṭuf εaleeha.* or ***galbi ma-yinkisir εaleeha.*
Syria - *suurya.*
Syrian - **1.** *suuri* pl. *-iyyiin, šaami* pl. *-iyyiin.* There were a number of Syrians on the boat. *čaan ?aku εiddat suuriyyiin bil-markab.* **2.** *suuri*, šaami*.* He speaks the Syrian dialect very well. *yizči l-lahja s-suuriyya kulliš zeen.*
system - **1.** *niḍaam* pl. *?anḍima.* They're hoping to change their system of government. *da-yit?ammaluun ybaddiluun niḍaam zukuumathum.* **2.** *jihaaz* pl. *?ajhiza.* We're studying the respiratory system. *da-nidrus jihaaz it-tanaffus.* **3.** *?isluub* pl. *?asaaliib.* I have a better system. *εindi ?isluub ?azsan.* **4.** *jisim* pl. *?ajsaam.* My system can't take it. *jismi ma-yitzammala.*
systematic - *mnaḍḍam.* He's very systematic. *huwwa kulliš imnaḍḍam.*
systematically - *b-ṣuura mnaḍḍama.* You'll have to work more systematically. *laazim tištuġuḷ ib-ṣuura mnaḍḍama ?akθar.*

T

tab - **1.** *εalaama* pl. *-aat.* The tab on this file is worn out. *l-εalaama maal hal-faayil imšaggiga.* **2.** *zsaab* pl. *-aat.* How much is the tab? *šgadd il-izsaab?*
to keep tabs on - *raaqab (i muraaqaba).* The police are keeping tabs on him. *š-šurṭa da-yraaqbuu.*
table - **1.** *meez* pl. *myuuza.* Put the table in the middle of the room. *zuṭṭ il-meez ib-nuṣṣ il-gubba.* **2.** *jadwal* pl. *jadaawil.* The figures are given in the table on page 20. *l-?arqaam mawjuuda bij-jadwal ib-ṣafza εišriin.*
**The tables are turned. *nεiksat il-?aaya.*
to table - *?ajjal (i) in-naḍar b-.* Why has the committee tabled the motion? *lweeš il-lujna ?ajjilat in-naḍar bil-iqtiraa?*
tablecloth - *čarčaf (*pl. *čaraačif) meez, mšammaε* pl. *-aat* (oilcloth).
table of contents - *fihras* pl. *fahaaris, jadwal (*pl. *jadaawil) muztawiyaat.*
tablespoon - *xaašuuga (*pl. *xwaašiig) maal ?akil, qaašuuga (*pl. *qwaašiig) maal ?akil.*
tablet - **1.** *daftar (*pl. *dafaatir) miswadda.* I've used a whole tablet of paper on this case. *xallaṣit daftar miswadda kaamil εala hal-qaḍiyya.* **2.** *zabbaaya* pl. *-aat, zubuub* coll. *zabb.* The doctor told me to take two tablets before each meal. *ṭ-ṭabiib gal-li ?ablaε zabbaayteen gabḷ il-?akil.*
table tennis - *ṗing ṗoong.*
taboo - *mzarram.* It's taboo for girls to go out alone at night. *mzarram εal-banaat yṭilεuun bil-leel wazzadhum.*
tack - **1.** *danbuus* pl. *danaabiis.* Tacks don't hold well on this bulletin board. *d-danaabiis ma-tilzam zeen εala hal-looza maal il-?iεlaanaat.* **2.** *bismaar* pl. *basaamiir.* This tack came out of the sofa. *nšilaε ḥal-bismaar imnil-qanafa.*
to tack - *danbas (itdinbis).* The tailor tacked the sleeve on the coat during the last fitting. *l-xayyaaṭ danbas ir-ridaan bis-sitra b-?aaxir iṗraawa.* -- Tack this notice on the bulletin board. *danbis hal-iεlaan ib-loozat il-iεlaanaat.*
tackle - *ġaraaḍ.* I brought my fishing tackle along. *jibit ġaraaḍ ṣeed is-simač wiyyaaya.*
to tackle - *εaalaj (i muεaalaja).* You've tackled the problem the wrong way. *εaalajit il-muškila b-ṭariiqa muu ṣaziiza.* or *εaalajt il-muškila ġalaṭ.*
**The policeman tackled the thief outside the house. *š-šurṭi kumaš il-zaraami w-waggaεa barra l-beet.*
tact - *labaaqa.* This situation calls for a certain amount of tact. *hal-zaala tiṭṭallab išwayya labaaqa.*
tactic - *taktiik* pl. *-aat, ?isluub* pl. *?asaaliib.* He's still using the same old tactics to get his own way. *baεda da-yistaεmil nafs it-taktiikaat zatta yzaṣṣil illi yriida.* -- The commander changed his tactics to deal with guerrilla warfare. *l-qaa?id baddal ?asaaliiba l-zarbiyya zatta tlaa?im zarb il-εiṣaabaat.*
tag - *biṭaaqa* pl. *-aat.* Put a tag on the package.

ħuṭṭ biṭaaqa εar-ruħma.
to tag after - *liħag (a laħig).* His son has been tagging after him all day. *ʔibna liħaga ṭuul in-nahaar.*
**Can I tag along? *ʔagdar aruuħ wiyyaak?*

tail - 1. *ðeel* pl. *ðyuul.* My dog has a short tail. *čalbi εinda ðeel igṣayyir.* 2. *ðyaal* pl. *-aat.* Put your shirt tail inside your pants. *xaššis iðyaal θoobak bil-panṭiruun.*
**I can't make head or tail of what he says. *ħčaayta ma-biiha laa raas w-laa čaεab.*
**Heads or tails? *ṭurra loo kitba?* or *šiir loo xaṭṭ?*
at the tail end - *b-ʔaaxir, b-čaεab.* We arrived at the tail end of the first act. *wuṣalna b-ʔaaxir il-faṣl il-ʔawwal.* -- We were at the tail end of the line. *činna b-čaεab xaṭṭ il-intiðaar.*
to tail - *tibaε (a tabiε) n-, liħag (a laħig) n-.* There's a car tailing us! *ʔaku sayyaara da-titbaεna!*

tail light - *baaklaayt* pl. *-aat, ðuwa warraani* pl. *ðuwaayaat warraaniyya.* I'm having the tail light on my car fixed. *da-aṣalliħ il-baaklaayt maal sayyaarti.*

tailor - *xayyaaṭ* pl. *-iin, xyaayiiṭ.* Where is there a good tailor? *ween ʔaku xayyaaṭ zeen?*
to tailor - *xayyaṭ (i xiyaaṭa) t-.* He tailored the suit the way I wanted it. *xayyaṭ il-badla miθil-ma riditha.*

tailoring - *xyaaṭa, xyaaṭ.* Tailoring is a trade which brings in good money. *l-ixyaaṭa mihna tjiib xooš ifluus.* -- The tailoring costs much more than the material. *l-ixyaaṭa tkallif ihwaaya ʔakθar imnil-iqmaaš.*

tailor-made - *tifṣaal.* All his clothes are tailor-made. *kull ihduuma tifṣaal.*

tails - *fraak.* We have to wear tails to the party this evening. *laazim nilbas ifraak bil-ħafla hal-leela.*

taint - 1. *ṣnaan.* The milk has an onion taint to it. *l-ħaliib bii ṣnaan buṣal.* 2. *laṭxa* pl. *-aat, waṣma* pl. *-aat.* This will be a taint on my reputation. *haaði raħ-iṭṣiir laṭxa b-sumuεti.*
**Cover the butter or the onions will taint it. *ġaṭṭi z-zibid ħatta la-yaaxuð ṭaεam buṣal.*

take - *daxal.* The take ran to fifty thousand dollars. *d-daxal waṣṣal ʔila xamsiin ʔalf doolaar.*
to take - 1. *ʔaxað (u ʔaxið) n-.* Who took my ties? *minu ʔaxað booyinbaaġaati?* -- Who took first prize? *minu ʔaxað ij-jaaʔiza l-ʔuula?* -- You can take it back; I won't need it any more. *tigdar taaxuðha; baεad ma-aħtaajha.* -- Who took his place? *minu ʔaxað makaana?* -- I'm taking Ahmad to the movies with me. *ʔaani maaxið ʔaħmad lis-siinama wiyyaaya.* -- We took many pictures. *ʔaxaðna hwaaya ṣuwar.* -- Take the measurements of this table. *ʔuxuð qiyaasaat hal-meez.* -- We always take a nap after lunch. *ʔiħna daaʔiman naaxuð ġafwa baεd il-ġada.* -- Did the doctor take your temperature this morning? *ṭ-ṭabiib ʔaxað ħaraartak hal-yoom iṣ-ṣubuħ?* -- Let's take a quick dip. *xalli naaxuð-inna fadd ġaṭṭa.* -- We've taken all the necessary precautions. *ʔaxaðna kull il-iħtiyaaṭaat il-laazma.* -- Take my advice. *ʔuxuð naṣiiħti.* or *ʔiqbil naṣiiħti.* -- Don't take it so seriously! *la-taaxuðha hal-gadd jidd.* -- That takes too much time. *haay taaxuð ihwaaya wakit.* or **haay *tiħtaaj ihwaaya wakit.* -- He takes too many liberties. *yaaxuð ħurriita ʔakθar imnil-laazim.* -- We'll take the room with twin beds. *raħ-naaxuð il-ġurfa ʔumm ifraašeen.* -- My rook will take your pawn. *qaliεti raħ-taaxuð ij-jundi maalak.* or **raħ-*ʔagtul ij-jundi maalak bil-qalεa.* -- Did you take these figures from the latest report? *ʔaxaðit hal-arqaam imnit-taqriir il-ʔaxiir?* 2. *nraad (a).* It won't take much gas to get there. *ma-yinraad ihwaaya baanziin ħatta nooṣul l-ihnaak.* -- That doesn't take much brains. *haay ma-yinraad-ilha hwaaya muxx.* 3. *liħam (a laħim).* She took the child by the hand and led him across the street. *liħmat ʔiid ij-jaahil w-εabbrata iš-šaariε.* 4. *wadda (i).* What else do you want to take along with you? *baεad š-itriid itwaddi wiyyaak?* 5. *šaal (i šeel).* My last smallpox vaccination didn't take. *ʔaaxir marra ðirabit jidri ma-šaal.* 6. *sawwa (i taswiya).* The government is going to take a census next year. *l-ħukuuma raħ-itsawwi ʔiħṣaaʔ infuus is-sana j-jaaya.* 7. *liqa (i ʔilqaaʔ).* Why don't you take a look at the house and tell me what you think? *leeš ma-tilqi naðra εal-beet w-itgul-li raʔyak?* 8. *tħammal (a taħammul).* I'll take the responsibility. *ʔaani raħ-atħammal il-masʔuuliyya.* -- Why should I take the blame for his mistake? *leeš laazim atħammal il-loom εan ʔaġlaaṭa?* 9. *rikab (u rikib) b-, raaħ (u rooħ) b-.* Why don't you take the bus? *leeš ma-tirkab bil-paaṣ?* 10. *bilaε (a baliε) n-.* Take one pill before each meal. *ʔiblaε ħabbaaya gabuḷ kull wajbat ʔakil.* 11. *ṭawwal (i taṭwiil).* How long will the trip from here to the market take? *r-rooħa minnaa lis-suug išgadd iṭṭawwil?* 12. *fiham (a fahim), ʔawwal (i taʔwiil).* He took my remark the wrong way. *fiham qaṣdi bil-ġaḷaṭ.* or *ʔawwal iħčaayti bil-ġaḷaṭ.*
**Take it easy! You've got all day. *la-tistaεjil; εindak il-yoom kulla.*
**Take it easy! Don't let that upset you. *la-tdiir baal; la-txalli haaða yziεjak.*
**He took me at my word. *sawwa ħčaayti maal.*
**How did he take to your suggestion? *εijaba qtiraaħak?* or *gitaε εaqla b-iqtiraaħak?* or *š-čaan raʔya b-iqtiraaħak?*
**I take it you're in trouble again. *ybayyin ʔinta mwarriṭ nafsak marra lux.*
**I took him down a peg or two. *xalleeta yuεruf qadra šinu.* or *kisarit xašma šwayya.*
**She took the stand as witness for the defense. *wugfat ka-šaahda lid-difaaε.*
**Take a look! Isn't that a beautiful horse? *baawiε! hal-iħṣaan muu ħilu?*
**They took the town by storm. *hijmaw fadd hajma w-iħtallaw il-wlaaya.*
**How much will you take for your car? *šgadd itriid ib-sayyaartak?*
to take after - 1. *ṭilaε (a ṭuluuε) εala.* He takes after his father. *ṭaaliε εala ʔabuu.* 2. *rikað (u rikið) wara, εala.* She took after the dog with a stick. *šaalat il-εuuda w-rikðat wara č-čalib.*
to take away - 1. *ʔaxað (u ʔaxið) n-, wadda (i).* The police took him away. *š-šurṭa ʔaxðoo.* or *š-šurṭa waddoo.* -- She took my books away with her. *waddat kutbi wiyyaaha.* 2. *waxxar (i tawxiir) t-.* Please take the dog away from the table. *baḷḷa waxxir ič-čalib imnil-meez.* 3. *ṭiraħ (a ṭariħ) min.* Take three away from five. *ʔiṭraħ itlaaθa min xamsa.* 4. *šaal (i šeel).* Please take those dirty cups away. *baḷḷa ma-tšiil hal-kuubaat il-waṣxa.* 5. *ħaṭṭ (u ħaṭṭ).* His eccentric behavior takes away from his prestige among the students. *tṣarrufa š-šaaðð yħuṭṭ min qadra been it-talaamiið.*
to take back - 1. *siħab (a saħib).* I take back what I said. *ʔasħab kalaami.* 2. *rajjaε (i tarjiiε) t-.* You can take it back to the tailor. *tigdar itrajjiεha lil-xayyaaṭ.* -- We already hired someone else, so we can't take him back now. *εayyanna waaħid ġeera w-baεad ma-nigdar inrajjεa.*
**This music takes me back to my days in Paris. *hal-mawsiiqa tðakkirni b-ʔayyaam paariis.*
to take down - 1. *nazzal (i tanziil) t-.* Take the picture down from the wall. *nazzil iṣ-ṣuura min εal-ħaayiṭ.* 2. *sajjal (i tasjiil) t-.* Take down my address. *sajjil εinwaani.* 3. *ðubaṭ (u ðabuṭ) n-.* Who's taking down the minutes? *minu da-yiðbuṭ ij-jalsa?*
to take for - *tṣawwar (a taṣawwur).* Sorry, I took you for someone else. *l-εafu, tṣawwartak ġeer waaħid.* or **l-εafu, εabaali ġeer waaħid.* -- What do you take me for? A liar? *š-da-tṣawwarni? čaððaab?* or **š-εabaalak? ʔaani čaððaab?*
to take in - 1. *sawwa (i taswiya)* We take in about 30 dinars a day. *da-nsawwi ħawaali θlaaθiin diinaar bil-yoom.* 2. *gaṣṣaf (i tagṣiif).* Will you take this dress in at the waist? *baḷḷa ma-tgaṣṣfiin han-nafnuuf min yamm il-xiṣir?* 3. *tkallaf (a takalluf) b-.* Our uncle took us in after our parents died. *εammna tkallaf biina baεad-ma maataw ʔabuuna w-ʔummna.* 4. *tqašmar (a qašmara).* Have you been taken in again? *tqašmarit marra lux?* 5. *raaqab (i muraaqaba), laaħað (i mulaaħaða).* He sat there, taking it all in. *giεad ihnaak yraaqib kullši.* 6. *ʔaxað (u ʔaxið) n-.* The police took him in for questioning. *š-šurṭa ʔaxðoo lil-markaz lit-taħqiiq.*
to take off - 1. *ʔaxað (u) ʔijaaza.* I'm taking off for the rest of the day. *raħ-ʔaaxuð ʔijaaza baqiit in-nahaar.* 2. *ṭaar (i ṭayaraan)* When does the plane take off? *šwakit iṭṭiir iṭ-ṭiyyaara?* 3. *nizaε (a naziε).* I'm going to take off my coat. *raħ-anzaε il-qappuuṭ maali.* 4. *nazzal (i tanziil), naggaṣ (i tangiiṣ).* He took a few dollars off the

price for me. *nazzal-li čam doolaar imnis-siɛir.*
to take on - 1. *lizam (a lazim) n-.* I took on a new job yesterday. *lizamit šaġla jdiida l-baarʒa.* 2. *šaġġal (i tašġiil) t-, ɛayyan (i taɛyiin) t-.* I hear the factory is taking on some new men. *smaɛit il-maɛmal raʒ-yšaġġil ɛummaal jiddad.* 3. *ʔaxaδ (u ʔaxiδ).* The situation has taken on a new aspect since then. *min δaak il-wakit il-hassa l-ʒaala ʔaxδat maδhar jidiid.* 4. *δaaf (i ʔiδaafa) n-.* We'll take on two more coaches at the next station. *raʒ-inδiif fargooneen lux bil-maʒatta j-jaaya.*
**I'll take him on any day! *ʔaani ʔanaazla ʔay yoom.* or *ʔaani mistaɛidd-la šwakit-ma yriid.*
to take out - 1. *tallaɛ (i tatliiɛ) t-.* Did you take the meat out of the refrigerator? *tallaɛt il-laʒm imniθ-θallaaja?* -- Why do you take it out on me? *leeš da-ttalliɛha b-raasi?* or *leeš da-ttalliɛ ʒeefak biyya.* 2. *wadda (i) b-.* When did he take his children out last? *šwakit čaanat ʔaaxir marra wadda jhaala b-fadd mukaan?*
to take over - *stilam (i stilaam).* He took over my job. *stilam šuġli.* -- Who has taken over the management of the factory? *minu stilam ʔidaarat il-maɛmal?*
to take up - 1. *ʔaxaδ (u ʔaxiδ).* That takes up a lot of space. *haay taaxuδ ihwaaya makaan.* 2. *saɛɛad (i tasɛiid).* Please take this book up with you when you go. *balla ma-tsaɛɛid hal-iktaab wiyyaak min itruuʒ foog?* 3. *ɛaašar (i muɛaašara).* I wouldn't take up with those people if I were you. *ʔaani loo b-makaanak ma-ʔaɛaašir δoola.* or *ʔaani loo b-makaanak ma-ʔamši wiyya δoola n-naas.* or *ʔaani loo b-makaanak ma-ʔatɛaašir wiyya δoola n-naas.* 4. *bida (i badi).* Can you take up where he left off? *tigdar tibdi mneen-ma battal?* 5. *tδaakar (i taδaakur) ɛan.* You'll have to take that matter up with someone else. *laazim titδaakar wiyya ġeeri ɛan hal-mawδuuɛ.*
taken - 1. *maʔxuuδ.* All seats on the bus were taken. *kull il-maqaaɛid bil-paas maʔxuuδa.* or ***l-paas imqapput.* 2. *maʒjuuz.* All seats are taken for tonight's performance. *kull il-maqaaɛid il-ʒaflat hal-leela maʒjuuza.* 3. *muġram.* She's really taken with that dress. *hiyya ʒaqiiqatan muġrama b-δaak in-nafnuuf.*
taking - *ʔaxiδ.* Taking pictures is forbidden here. *ʔaxiδ is-suwar mamnuuɛ ihnaa.*
**She has very taking ways. *tasarrufaatha tisʒar l-waaʒid.*
tale - 1. *saalfa* pl. *swaalif, saaluufa* pl. *-aat, swaaliif.* Children love to listen to fairy tales. *j-jihaal yʒibbuun yismaɛuun swaalif.* 2. *qussa* pl. *qusas.* She made up that tale to get even with them. *xtirɛat hal-qussa ʒatta taaxuδ ʒeefha minhum.*
talebearer - *fattaan* pl. *-iin, -a; waaši* pl. *-iin, wušaat.*
talent - 1. *mawhiba* pl. *mawaahib.* He has a talent for mathematics. *ɛinda mawhiba bir-riyaaδiyyaat.* -- She discovered her artistic talent late in life. *ktišfat mawhibatha l-fanniyya b-ʔawaaxir ɛumurha.* 2. *qaabliyya* pl. *-aat.* He has a talent for getting into trouble. *ɛinda qaabliyya l-xalq il-mašaakil il-nafsa.* or ***ywaggiɛ nafsa b-mašaakil.*
**I never saw so much talent on one program. *b-ɛumri ma-šaayif hal-gadd naas mawhuubiin ib-fadd manhaj.*
talk - 1. *ʒadiiθ* pl. *ʔaʒaadiiθ.* His talk was much too long. *ʒadiiθa čaan ʔatwal imnil-laazim.* -- Her marriage is the talk of the town. *zawaajha saar ʒadiiθ il-majaalis.* 2. *ʒači.* Oh, that's just talk! *haaδa bass ʒači.* -- What kind of talk is that? *haaδa šloon ʒači?* or *šinu hal-ʒači?*
to have a talk with - *ʒiča (i ʒači) wiyya, ʒaača (i).* I had a long talk with him. *ʒačeet wiyyaa ʒači tuwiil.* or *ʒaačeeta fadd mudda twiila.*
**I'd like to have a talk with you. *ʔard aʒči wiyyaak išwayya.* or *ʔard atʒaača wiyyaak išwayya.*
to talk - *ʒiča (i ʒači).* Don't you think he talks too much? *ma-tiɛtiqid huwwa yiʒči hwaaya?* -- How can he talk with food stuffed in his mouth? *šloon yigdar yiʒči w-ʒalga matruus ʔakil?*
to talk into - *qannaɛ (i taqniiɛ), sawwa (i) l-wahas.* Do you suppose we can talk them into coming with us? *tiɛtiqid nigdar inqanniɛhum yjuun wiyyaana?* or *tiɛtiqid nigdar insawwii-lhum wahas yjuun wiyyaana?*
to talk nonsense - *liġa (i laġwa, laaġi).* Don't talk nonsense! *la-tilġi* or *la-tiʒči ʒači faariġ.*
to talk over - *biʒaθ (a baʒiθ, daanaš (i mudaanaša), tδaakar (a muδaakara).* Talk the matter over with him. *ʔibʒaθ il-mawδuuɛ wiyyaa.* or *tδaakar wiyyaa bil-mawδuuɛ.* -- Let's talk it over. *xal-nitdaanaš biiha.*
talkative - *θarθaar* pl. *-iin, laġwi* pl. *-iyya.* I don't like real talkative people. *ma-aʒibb iθ-θarθaariin.*
**Our son knows how to speak, but he's just not talkative. *ʔibinna yuɛruf yiʒči, bass ma-yiʒči hwaaya.*
tall - 1. *tuwiil* pl. *twaal.* She's tall and thin. *hiyya twiila w-δiɛiifa.* 2. *ɛaali.* There aren't many tall buildings in that city. *ma-aku hwaaya bnaayaat ɛaalya b-δiič l-wlaaya.*
**He's one meter, and sixty centimeters tall. *tuula matir w-sittiin santimatir.*
**How tall are you? *šgadd tuulak?*
tallow - *šaʒam.*
to **tally - *ɛadd (i ɛadd) n-.*** They have a machine to tally the votes. *ɛidhum makiina l-ɛadd il-ʔaswaat.*
tamarind - *tamur hind.* Tamarind makes a refreshing drink. *šarbat tamur hind kulliš munɛiš.*
tamarisk - *ʔaθil.*
tambourine - *daff* pl. *dfuuf.*
tame - 1. *ʔaliif.* The birds there are so tame they eat out of your hand. *t-tuyuur ihnaak hal-gadd ʔaliifa taakul min ʔiid il-waaʒid.* 2. *haadiʔ.* All in all, it was a pretty tame evening. *b-suura ɛaamma čaanat fadd leela haadʔa.*
to become tame - *ʔilaf (i ʔulfa).* Birds become tame if you feed them every day. *t-tuyuur yiʔlifuun ʔiδa ttaɛɛumhum yoomiyya.*
to tame - *rawwaδ (i tarwiiδ) t-.* He tames wild animals. *yrawwiδ ʒaywaanaat waʒšiyya.* -- Lions are easily tamed. *s-sibaaɛ titrawwaδ ib-suhuula.*
to tame down - *ɛiqal (a ɛaqil), hidaʔ (a huduuʔ).* He's tamed down a lot since he left school. *ɛiqal ihwaaya baɛad-ma tirak il-madrasa.*
to **tamp - *dačč (i dačč) n-.*** Tamp the earth down well before you lay the tile. *dičč il-gaaɛ zeen gabul-ma tʒutt il-kaaši.*
tamper - *madagga* pl. *-aat.* Do you have a tamper I can borrow? *ɛindak madagga ʔagdar ʔatdaayanha?*
to tamper - *liɛab (a liɛib).* We caught him tampering with the mail. *lizamnaa yilɛab bil-makaatiib.* -- Don't tamper with the radio. *la-tilɛab bir-raadyo.*
tan - 1. *samaar.* Where did you get that nice tan? *mneen jaak has-samaar?* 2. *gahwaaʔi ʔaačuġ, joozi ʔaačuġ.* I lost my tan gloves. *δayyaɛit ičfuufi l-gahwaaʔiyya ʔaačuġ.*
to tan - 1. *dibaġ (u dbaaġa, dabuġ), dabbaġ (u tdubbuġ).* What do you use when you tan hides? *š-tistaɛmiluun min itdibġuun ij-jiluud?* 2. *smarr (a smiraar).* She tans easily. *tismarr ib-suhuula.*
**I'll tan your hide if you don't behave! *tara ʔahri jildak ʔiδa ma-raʒ-itsiir ʔaadmi.* or *tara ʔadabbuġ jildak ʔiδa ma-raʒ-itsiir ʔaadmi.*
tangerine - *laalangiyya* pl. *-aat* coll. *laalingi.*
Tangier - *tanja.*
tangle - 1. *šarbaka* pl. *-aat.* This tangle in the strings can't be undone. *haš-šarbaka bil-ixyuut ma-tinfakk.* 2. *warta* pl. *-aat.* You've certainly got yourself in a tangle this time. *sudug waggaɛit nafsak ib-warta hal-marra.*
to tangle - 1. *ɛaggad (i taɛgiid) t-, sarbak (i šarbaka) t-.* The cat tangled the string. *l-bazzuuna ɛaggidat il-xeet.* 2. *warrat (i tawriit) t-.* Don't tangle with him! *la-twarrit nafsak wiyyaa!*
tangled - 1. *mɛaggad.* The yarn is tangled. *s-suuf imɛaggad.* 2. *makfuuš.* His hair is tangled. *šaɛra makfuuš.*
tank - 1. *taanki* pl. *-iyyaat.* He took a few fish out of the tank. *ʔaxaδ čam simča mnit-taanki.* -- Fill up the tank with gas. *ʔimli it-taanki baanziin.* 2. *dabbaaba* pl. *-aat.* A column of tanks led the attack. *ratil imnid-dabbaabaat itsaddrat il-hijuum.* 3. *ɛanbaar* pl. *ɛanaabiir, taanki* pl. *-iyyaat.* Every house in Baghdaad has a water tank on the roof. *b-kull beet ib-baġdaad ʔaku ɛanbaar maay bis-satiʒ.* 4. *jidir* pl. *jduur, jduura.* The hot-water tank is rusty. *jidir il-ʒammaam maalna mzanjar.*
tanning - *dibaaġa.* Mosul has a tanning factory. *l-moosil biiha maɛmal dibaaġa.*
**His father gave him a good tanning. *ʔabuu bisata basta zeena.*

tap - **1.** *dagga* pl. *-aat.* I heard two taps on the window. *smaƐit daggteen Ɛaš-šibbaač.* **2.** *mzambila* pl. *-aat, ẓanafiyya* pl. *-aat.* The tap on the barrel is dripping. *l-imzambila maal il-barmiil da-tnaggiṭ.* **3.** *naƐalča* pl. *-aat.* Please put taps on these shoes. *baḷḷa dugg il-hal-qundara naƐalčaat.*
**He always has some story on tap. *Ɛinda daaʔiman iẓčaayaat ẓaaḍra.*
to tap - **1.** *nigar (u nagir), dagg (u dagg).* He tapped on the window. *nigar Ɛaš-šabbaač.* **2.** *ẓaṭṭ (u ẓaṭṭ) n- raqaaba Ɛala.* The police tapped his telephone. *š-šurṭa ẓaṭṭaw raqaaba Ɛala talafoona.* **3.** *dagg (u dagg).* She tapped me on the shoulder. *daggat Ɛala čitfi.*
**They tapped the water main for the new house. *jarraw maay imnil-ʔabbi lil-beet ij-jidiid.*
tape - *šariiṭ* pl. *ʔašriṭa, šaraayiṭ.* He has several tapes of Iraqi music. *Ɛinda čam šariiṭ imnil-mawsiiqa l-Ɛiraaqiyya.* -- I'd like five yards of the white tape. *ʔariid xamis yardaat imniš-šariiṭ il-ʔabyaḍ.*
**Getting through this red tape will take a long time. *jtiyaaz har-rasmiyyaat yaaxuḍ wakit ihwaaya.*
to tape - **1.** *lizag (i lazig).* Please tape an address label on that package. *baḷḷa ʔilzig biṭaaqat Ɛinwaan Ɛala ḍiič ir-ruzma.* **2.** *sajjal (i tasjiil) t-.* Last night we taped the President's speech. *l-baarẓa bil-leel sajjalna ẓadiiθ ir-raʔiis.*
tape measure - *šariiṭ (pl. šaraayiṭ) qiyaas.*
tape recorder - *musajjil* pl. *-aat.*
tapeworm - *duuda (pl. diidaan) waẓiida.*
tar - *giir, jiir.*
target - **1.** *niišaan* pl. *-aat, hadaf* pl. *ʔahdaaf.* Did you set up the target? *niṣabt il-hadaf?* **2.** *ġaraḍ* pl. *ʔaġraaḍ, hadaf* pl. *ʔahdaaf.* Our target for this month is to sell 1,000 suits. *ġaraḍna haš-šahar inbiiƐ ʔalif badla.*
tariff - *gumruq, rasim* pl. *rsuum, taƐriifa* pl. *-aat.* The tariff on silk is high. *l-gumruq Ɛal-ẓariir Ɛaali.*
tarnish - **1.** *sawaad.* Clean the tarnish from those spoons. *naḍḍuf is-sawaad min hal-iqwaašiig.* **2.** *zinjaar.* Clean the tarnish off the brass tray. *naḍḍuf iz-zinjaar min iṣ-ṣiiniyya l-iprinj.*
to tarnish - **1.** *swadd (a sawaad).* The silverware will tarnish if you don't keep it in its box. *l-fuḍḍiyyaat tiswadd ʔiḍa ma-tḍummha ib-ṣanduugha.* **2.** *zanjar (i zinjaar).* That brass doorknob will tarnish quickly. *hal-yaddt il-baab il-iprinj itzanjir bil-Ɛajal.*
tarpaulin - *čaadir* pl. *čwaadir.* Cover the load with a tarpaulin. *ġaṭṭi l-ẓimil ib-čaadir.*
tart - *ẓaamuḍ.* The apples have a tart taste. *t-tiffaaẓ bii ṭaƐam ẓaamuḍ.*
task - *šaġla* pl. *-aat.* He is equal to his task. *yitlaƐ min ẓagg haš-šaġla.*
to take to task - *zaff (i zaff) n-.* We'll have to take him to task for his laziness. *laazim inziffa Ɛala kasala.*
taste - **1.** *ṭaƐam.* This meat has a peculiar taste. *hal-laẓam bii fadd ṭaƐam ġariib.* -- I have a bad taste in my mouth. *ʔaku fadd ṭaƐam ma-ṭayyib ib-ẓalgi.* **2.** *ḍawq* pl. *ʔaḍwaaq.* I'd have given you credit for better taste. *tṣawwarit ḍawqak ʔaẓsan min haaḍa.*
**Let me have a taste of it. *xalli ʔaḍuuga.*
to have a taste for - *staḍwaq (i stiḍwaaq).* He has a taste for classical music. *yistaḍwiq il-moosiiqa l-iklaasiikiyya.*
to taste - *ḍaag (u ḍoog), ḍaaq (u ḍooq).* Just taste this coffee! *bass ḍuug hal-gahwa!*
The soup taste good. *š-šoorba ṭaƐamha ṭayyib.* --It tastes of vinegar. *ṭaƐamha yinṭi Ɛala xaḷḷ.* or *bii ṭaƐam xaḷḷ.*
tasteless - **1.** *ma-bii ṭaƐam.* The food is tasteless. *l-ʔakil ma-bii ṭaƐam.* **2.** *ma-bii ḍawq.* Her clothes are tasteless. *libisha ma-bii ḍawq.*
tasty - *laḍiiḍ, ṭayyib.* This food is very tasty. *hal-ʔakil kulliš laḍiiḍ.*
tavern - *mayxaana* pl. *-aat.*
tax - *ḍariiba* pl. *ḍaraayib.* Have you paid your taxes yet? *difaƐt iḍ-ḍaraayib maaltak loo baƐad?*
to tax - *furaḍ (u fariḍ) n- ḍariiba.* Everybody was taxed two dinars. *nfurḍat ḍariiba diinaareen Ɛala kull waaẓid.* -- It is not governmental policy to tax essential commodities. *muu min siyaast il-ẓukuuma tufruḍ ḍariiba Ɛas-silaƐ iḍ-ḍaruuriyya.*
tax collector - *jaabi (pl. jubaat) ḍariiba.*
taxi - *taksi, taaksi* pl. *-iyyaat.* I took a taxi from the station. *ʔaxaḍit taaksi mnil-maẓaṭṭa.*
taxi driver - *saayiq (pl. suwwaaq) taaksi.*
taxpayer - *daafiƐ (pl. -iin) ḍariiba.*
tea - *čaay.* In Iraq they serve tea in small glasses. *bil-Ɛiraaq yqaddmuun ič-čaay b-istikaanaat.*
to **teach** - **1.** *Ɛallam (i taƐliim) t-, darras (i tadriis) t-.* Will you teach me German! *tƐallimni ʔalmaani?* -- He teaches in a boys' school. *huwwa ydarris ib-madrasa maal wilid.* **2.** *Ɛallam (i).* I'll teach him not to disturb me! *raẓ-aƐallma baƐad ma-yizƐijni.*
teacher - *muƐallim* pl. *-iin, mudarris* pl. *-iin.* He always wanted to be a teacher. *daaʔiman raad yṣiir muƐallim.*
teaching - *tadriis, taƐliim.* Teaching Arabic isn't too hard. *tadriis il-Ɛarabi muu kulliš ṣaƐub.*
teachings - *taƐaaliim.* Muslims follow the teachings of the Koran. *l-muslimiin yitbaƐuun taƐaaliim il-qurʔaan.*
tea cup - *kuub (pl. kwaab) čaay.*
tea glass - *stikaan* pl. *-aat.*
tea house - *čaayxaana* pl. *-aat.*
teak - *ṣaaj.* Our dining room table is teak. *meez ʔakilna min ṣaaj.*
tea kettle - *kitli* pl. *-iyyaat.*
team - **1.** *firqa* pl. *firaq.* Our team has won every football game it entered this year. *firqatna ġulbat kull sibaaq kurat qadam dixlat bii has-sana.* **2.** *zooj* pl. *zwaaj, majmuuƐa* pl. *-aat.* That carriage sports a beautiful team of horses. *ḍiič il-Ɛarabaana biiha xooš zooj xeel badiiƐa.*
to team up - *tjammaƐ (a tajammuƐ).* They teamed up against me. *tjammƐaw Ɛalayya.* -- We teamed up in groups of six to play volley ball. *tjammaƐna kull sitta suwa ẓatta nilƐab kurat iṭ-ṭaaʔira.*
team mate - *Ɛuḍu (pl. ʔaƐḍaaʔ) firqa.* He's one of my team mates. *huwwa waaẓid min ʔaƐḍaaʔ firaqti.*
teamwork - *takaatuf, taḍaamun.* Good teamwork allowed us to finish the job ahead of time. *t-takaatuf xallaana nxaḷḷiṣ iš-šuġuḷ gabḷ il-mawƐid.*
tea pot - *quuri* pl. *-iyyaat, quwaari.*
tear - *šagg* pl. *šguug.* Can this tear be mended? *haš-šagg mumkin yitxayyaṭ.*
to tear - **1.** *šagg (u šagg) n-.* Don't tear the paper! *la-tšigg il-warqa!* **2.** *nšagg (a).* Careful, the canvas is tearing! *diir baalak, ič-čaadir da-yinšagg.* **3.** *nitaš (i natiš) n-.* She tore the letter out of his hand. *nitšat il-maktuub min ʔiida.* **4.** *gass (u gaṣṣ) n-, giṭaƐ (a gaṭiƐ) n-.* Tear the coupon out of the magazine. *guṣṣ il-koopoon imnil-majalla.* -- The button tore off. *d-dugma ngiṭƐat.* **5.** *šilaƐ (a).* Who tore this page out of the book? *minu šilaƐ haṣ-ṣafẓa mnil-iktaab?*
to tear down - *fallaš (i tafliiš, tfalliš) t-.* He tore his house down. *fallaš beeta.*
to tear open - *fakk (u fakk), fitaẓ (a fatiẓ).* Who tore the package open? *minu fakk ir-ruẓma?*
to tear up - **1.** *šaggag (i tašgiig).* I hope you tore that letter up. *ʔatʔammal ʔinta šaggagit ḍaak il-maktuub.* **2.** *fakk (u fakk), ẓaffar (u tẓuffur).* The workmen tore up the street in front of the house. *l-Ɛummaal fakkaw iš-šaariƐ igbaaḷ il-beet.*
tear - *damƐa* pl. *-aat,* coll. *dmuuƐ.* Tears ran down her cheeks. *d-dimuuƐ inẓidrat Ɛala xduudha.*
**Tears won't help you. *l-biča ma-yfiidič.*
to tear - *dammaƐ (i tadmiiƐ).* My eyes are tearing. *Ɛyuuni da-tdammiƐ.*
tear gas - *ġaaz musiil lid-dumuuƐ.*
to **tease** - *daahar (i duhur, mudaahara).* Everyone teases him. *l-kull ydaahruu.* -- Don't tease the dog. *la-tdaahir ič-čalib.*
tea shop - *čaayxaana* pl. *-aat.*
teasing - *mdaahara.* I don't like this kind of teasing. *ma-yiƐjibni hiiči mdaahara.*
tea spoon - *xaašuugat (pl. xwaašiig) čaay.*
technical - *fanni*.* The broadcast was called off for technical reasons. *twaqqfat il-ʔiḍaaƐa l-ʔasbaab fanniyya.* -- There are several technical institutes in Iraq. *ʔaku Ɛiddat maƐaahid fanniyya bil-Ɛiraaq.*
technicality - *sabab fanni* pl. *ʔasbaab fanniyya.* We lost the game due to a technicality. *xṣarna s-sibaaq il-sabab fanni.*
technician - *fanni* pl. *-iyyiin.*
technique - *ṭariiqa* pl. *ṭuruq, ʔusluub* pl. *ʔasaaliib.* We'll have to improve our teaching techniques. *laazim inẓassin ṭariiqatna bit-tadriis.*
tedious - *mumill, muḍawwij.*
teen-ager - *muraahiq* pl. *-iin.*
to **telecast** - *Ɛiraḍ (i Ɛariḍ) bit-talafizyoon.*
telegram - *barqiyya* pl. *-aat.* I want to send a telegram. *ʔariid adizz barqiyya.*

telegraph - *barq.* Where's the telegraph office? *ween daaʔirt il-barq?*
to telegraph - *ʔabraq (i ʔibraaq) l-.* Did he telegraph you? *ʔabraq-lak?*
telegraph operator - *maʔmuur (pl. -iin) barq.*
telephone - *talafoon* pl. *-aat.* May I use your telephone, please? *tismaʐ-li ʔastaεmil talafoonak min faḍlak?*
to telephone - *xaabar (u muxaabara).* Did anybody telephone? *ʔaʐʐad xaabar?*
telephone booth - *maqṣuurat (pl. -aat) talafoon.*
telephone call - *muxaabara* pl. *-aat.* I have to pay for every telephone call. *laazim adfaε εala kull muxaabara.*
telephone directory - *daliil (pl. ʔadillat) talafoon.* His name is in the telephone directory. *ʔisma b-daliil it-talafoon.*
telephoning - *muxaabara.* Telephoning won't take much time. *l-muxaabara ma-taaxuδ ihwaaya wakit.*
telescope - *taliskoop* pl. *-aat.*
teletype - *talitaayp.*
to **televise** - *εiraḍ (i εariḍ) bit-talafizyoon.*
television - *talafizyoon.*
to **tell** - **1.** *gaal (u gawl) l-.* Tell him your name. *gul-la š-ismak.* -- Tell me, what are you doing tonight? *gul-li š-raʐ-itsawwi hal-leela.* **2.** *ʐiča (i ʐači), gaal (u).* I wish I could tell you the whole story. *yaa reet ʔagdar ʔaʐčii-lak il-quṣṣa kullha.* **3.** *εiraf (u).* You can tell by his voice that he has a cold. *tigdar tuεruf min ʐissa ʔinna manšuul.* **4.** *ʐizar (i ʐazir).* Nobody could have told that in advance. *maʐʐad čaan yigdar yiʐzir haay li-giddaam.* **5.** *farraq (i tafriiq).* I can't tell one from the other. *ma-ʔagdar afarriq waaʐid imnil-laax.* **6.** *sabbaʐ (i tasbiiʐ).* That old man is always telling his beads. *š-šeex daaʔiman ysabbiʐ ib-masbaʐta.*
**Can your little boy tell time yet? *ʔibnak yigdar yiqra s-saaεa loo baεad?*
**To tell the truth, I don't know. *bil-ʐaqiiqa, ʔaani ma-ʔadri.* or ***walla, ma-ʔaεruf.*
**You can tell by looking at him that he's been working hard. *ybayyin εalee čaan da-yištuġul ib-himma.*
to tell a lie - **1.** *kiδab (i kiδib), čiδab (i čiδib).* I told her a lie to get out of going to the party. *kiδabit εaleeha ʐatta la-aruuʐ lil-ʐafla.* **2.** *čaδδab (i).* He's always telling lies. *εala ṭuul yčaδδib.*
to tell apart - *farraq (i tafriiq) been, mayyaz (i tamyiiz) been.* I can't tell these two materials apart. *ma-agdar afarriq been hal-iqmaašeen.*
teller - *ṣarraaf* pl. *-iin, ṣaraariif.* He has worked ten years as teller in that bank. *štiġal ṣarraaf εašr isniin ib-δaak il-bang.*
temper - **1.** *ṭabuε* pl. *ʔaṭbaaε.* He has an even temper. *ṭabεa haadi.* **2.** *ṣalaaba.* This steel has more temper than iron. *hal-fuulaaδ bii ṣalaaba ʔazyad imnil-ʐadiid.*
to lose one's temper - *ʐtadd (a ʐtidaad).* He loses his temper easily. *yiʐtadd bil-εajal.*
to temper - *siga (i sagi).* In Damascus they have tempered steel for hundreds of years. *biš-šaam yisguun il-fuulaaδ ṣaar-ilhum miyyaat isniin.*
temperamental - *εaṣabi*.* She's very temperamental. *hiyya kulliš εaṣabiyya.* or ***xulugha ḍayyig.*
temperance - *εtidaal.* He lives by temperance. *yεiiš b-iεtidaal.*
temperate - *muεtadil.* He is very temperate in his habits. *huwwa kulliš muεtadil ib-εaadaata.* -- Europe is situated in the temperate zone. *ʔooruppa waaqεa bil-manṭiqa l-muεtadila.*
temperature - **1.** *ṣxuuna, darajat ʐaraara.* Her temperature went down today. *ṣxuunatha nizlat il-yoom.* **2.** *darajat ʐaraara.* What was the highest temperature yesterday? *šgadd čaanat ʔaεla darajat ʐaraara l-baarʐa?*
temple - **1.** *maεbad* pl. *maεaabid.* This church is built on the ruins of a Roman temple. *hal-kaniisa nbinat εala xaraayib maεbad roomaani.* **2.** *tooraat.* I love to spend Friday night in the temple. *ʔaʐibb agḍi masaaʔ ij-jumεa bit-tooraat.* **3.** *ṣaabir* pl. *ṣwaabir.* The bullet struck him in the temple. *r-riṣaaṣa ḍurbata b-ṣaabra.*
temporary - *muwaqqat, waqti.** This is only a temporary solution. *hal-ʐall muwaqqat bass.*
to **tempt** - *ġira (i ʔiġraaʔ).* That doesn't tempt me. *haaδa ma-yiġriini.* or ***haaδa ma-ysawwii-li waahis.*
**I was tempted to tell him the truth. *ṣaar-li waahis ʔagul-la l-ʐaqiiqa.*
temptation - *ʔiġraaʔ* pl. *-aat.*
tempting - *muġri.* He made me a very tempting offer. *εiraḍ εalayya εariḍ muġri.*
ten - **1.** *εašra.* It's ten o'clock. *s-saaεa bil-εasra.* **2.** *εaširt.* We're going on a vacation in ten days. *raayʐiin ib-ʔijaaza baεad εaširt iyyaam.* **3.** *εašir.* He has ten men working for him. *εinda εašir rayaajiil yištaġluu-la.*
tenacious - *muṣirr, εanuud.*
tenaciously - *b-ʔiṣraar.* He holds to his opinion tenaciously. *mitmassik ib-raʔya b-ʔiṣraar.*
tenant - *mistaʔjir* pl. *-iin.* He has been our tenant for ten years. *huwwa mistaʔjir εidna ṣaar-la εašr isniin.*
to **tend** - **1.** *maal (i mayalaan).* He tends to be partial in his judgments. *ymiil lit-taʐayyuz ib-qaraaraata.* **2.** *daar (i) baal~.* Tend to your own business! *diir baalak εala šuġlak.* -- Who's going to tend to the furnace? *minu raʐ-ydiir baala εal-firin?*
tendency - **1.** *mayl* pl. *myuul.* He has a tendency to exaggerate. *εinda mayl lil-mubaalaġa.* **2.** *mayl* pl. *myuul, ttijaah* pl. *-aat.* He has leftist tendencies. *εinda myuul yasaariyya.*
tender - **1.** *fargoon (pl. -aat) wuquud.* Only the locomotive and the tender were derailed. *bass il-makiina w-faargoon il-wuquud ṭilεaw imnis-sičča.* **2.** *ṭari*.* The meat is so tender you can cut it with a fork. *l-laʐam hal-gadd ṭari l-waaʐid yguṣṣa bič-čaṭal.* **3.** *ʐassaas.* The bruise is still tender. *r-raḍḍ baεda ʐassaas.*
tendon - *watar* pl. *ʔawtaar.*
tenement - *beet (pl. byuut) nizil.*
tennis - *tanis.*
tennis court - *saaʐat (pl. -aat) tanis.*
tennis racquet - *rakit* pl. *-aat.*
tennis shoes - *qundara (pl. qanaadir) laastiig, qundarat (pl. qanaadir) riyaaḍa.*
tense - **1.** *mitwattir.* The situation was tense. *l-ʐaala čaanat mitwattra.* -- **He's very tense these days. *ʔaεṣaaba kulliš mitwattra hal-ʔayyaam.* **2.** *ṣiiġa* pl. *ṣiyaġ.* That verb is in the past tense. *hal-fiεil ib-ṣiiġat il-maaḍi.*
tension - *tawattur.* The world is in a state of tension these days. *l-εaalam ib-ʐaalat tawattur hal-ʔayyaam.*
**Those are high tension power lines. *hal-waayaraat biiha quwwa kahrabaaʔiyya εaalya.*
tent - *xeema* pl. *-aat, xiyam; čaadir* pl. *čwaadir.* The tent is made of canvas. *l-xeema maεmuula mnil-junfaaṣ.*
tenth - **1.** *εaašir.* This is the tenth year I've been working at the same job. *haay is-sana l-εaašra ʔaani ʔaštuġul nafs iš-šuġul.* **2.** *εušur* pl. *ʔaεšaar.* It's not even one tenth finished. *ʔaṣlan εušurha ma-xilaṣ.*
**We get paid on the tenth of the month. *niqbuḍ rawaatibna yoom εašra biš-šahar.*
term - **1.** *šarṭ* pl. *šuruuṭ.* He gave us very good terms. *nṭaana šuruuṭ mumtaaza.* **2.** *faṣil* pl. *fuṣuul.* When does the fall school term begin? *šwakit yibdi faṣl id-diraasa lil-xariif?* **3.** *mudda* pl. *mudad.* He spent a four-year term in the presidency. *giḍa muddat ʔarbaε isniin bir-riʔaasa.* **4.** *ṣṭilaaʐ* pl. *-aat.* Do you know the technical term for it? *tuεruf l-iṣṭilaaʐ il-fanni maalha?* **5.** *εibaara* pl. *-aat.* I told him in no uncertain terms what I think of him. *git-la raʔyi bii b-εibaaraat ṣariiʐa.* **6.** *εilaaqa* pl. *-aat.* We're on bad terms. *εilaaqaatna muu zeena.*
**We have been trying to come to terms for months now. *ṣaar-inna ʔašhur da-nriid nitfaaham.* or *ṣaar-inna ʔašhur da-nriid noosal ʔila ttifaaq.*
terminal - **1.** *maʐaṭṭa* pl. *-aat.* We have to pick up the trunks at the freight terminal. *laazim naaxuδ junaṭna min maʐaṭṭat iš-šaʐin.* **2.** *raas* pl. *ruus.* The terminals of the battery are corroded. *ruus il-paatri mzanjira.* **3.** *nihaaʔi*.* You receive a month's terminal pay when you resign. *taaxuδ raatib šahar nihaaʔi εinda-ma tistaqiil.*
to **terminate** - **1.** *ʔanha (i ʔinhaaʔ), fuṣax (u faṣix).* The company terminated his services. *š-šarika ʔanhat xadamaata.* -- The landlord terminated our lease. *ṣaaʐib il-muluk fuṣax εaqd il-ʔiijaar maalna.* **2.** *xilaṣ (a), ntiha (i ntihaaʔ)* My lease terminates in June. *εaqd il-ʔiijaar maali yixlaṣ ib-ʐuzeeraan.*
terminology - *ṣṭilaaʐaat.* Their terminology is not

clear. *ṣtilaaẓaathum muu waaẓẓa.

termites – *ʔarḍa*. Our house has termites. *beetna bii ʔarḍa.*

terrace – *ṭarma* pl. -*aat*. Let's all go sit on the terrace. *xall-inruuẓ kullna nig𝜀ud biṭ-ṭarma.*

terrain – *ʔaraaḍi*. Around Baghdad the terrain is level. *yamm baḡdaad il-ʔaraaḍi minbaṣṭa.*

terrible – 1. *faḍii𝜀*. There was a terrible accident this morning. *čaan ʔaku ṣṭidaam faḍii𝜀 il-yoom iṣ-ṣubuẓ.* 2. *mxarbaṭ*. The weather is terrible. *j-jaww kullis imxarbaṭ.* or **j-jaww kulliš muu zeen.**

terribly – *kulliš*. I'm terribly sorry. *ʔaani kulliš mit ʔassif.*

terrific – 1. *𝜀aḍiim*. His poetry is terrific. *qaṣiidta 𝜀aḍiima.* 2. *haaʔil, šadiid*. Did you hear that terrific explosion today? *sima𝜀t il-infijaar il-haaʔil il-yoom?* -- He's under terrific pressure. *huwwa taẓat ḍaḡiṭ šadiid.*

to terrify – *ri𝜀ab (i ʔir𝜀aab)*. He brought me news that terrified me. *jaab-li xabar ri𝜀abni bii.*

   to be terrified – *rti𝜀ab (i)*. I was terrified. *rti𝜀abit* or **mitit imnil-xoof.**

terrifying – *muxiif, mur𝜀ib.*

territory – *ʔaraaḍi*. We will defend our territory. *raẓ-indaafi𝜀 𝜀an ʔaraaḍiina.*

terror – *xoof, ru𝜀ub*. We were speechless with terror. *činna jaamdiin imnil-xoof.*

terrorism – *ʔirhaab*. The dictator ruled through terrorism. *d-diktaatoor ẓikam bil-ʔirhaab.*

terrorist – *ʔirhaabi* pl. -*iyyiin.*

to terrorize – *ʔarhab (i ʔirhaab)*. The bandits terrorized the countryside. *quṭṭaa𝜀 iṭ-ṭuruq ʔarhibaw in-naas bil-ʔaryaaf.*

test – 1. *mtiẓaan* pl. -*aat*. You have to take a test before you get a driver's license. *laazim taaxuδ imtiẓaan gabuḷ-ma tẓaṣṣil 𝜀ala ʔijaazat siyaaqa.* -- Did you pass all your tests? *nijaẓit ib-kull imtiẓaanaatak?* 2. *faẓiṣ* pl. *fuẓuuṣ*. I had an eye test today. *čaan 𝜀indi faẓṣ i𝜀yuun il-yoom.* 3. *xtibaar* pl. -*aat*. He made several tests during his experiment. *sawwa 𝜀iddat ixtibaaraat ʔaθnaaʔ tajrubta.*

   to test – 1. *mtiẓan (i mtiẓaan)*. I'll test half the class today. *raẓ-amtiẓin nuṣṣ iṣ-ṣaff il-yoom.* -- I was tested in arithmetic today. *mtiẓanit bil-ẓisaab hal-yoom.* 2. *fuẓas (a faẓiṣ)*. Test the brakes. *ʔifẓaṣ l-ibreek.* -- Test this urine for sugar. *ʔifẓaṣ il-bool w-šuuf ʔiδa bii šakar.*

testicle – *xuṣwa* pl. *xaṣaawi.*

to testify – 1. *bayyan (i bayaan)*. Have you anything further to testify? *𝜀indak ba𝜀ad šii tbayyna.* 2. *šihad (a šahaada)*. Can you testify to his honesty? *tigdar tišhad ib-ʔamaanta?*

testimony – *šahaada* pl. -*aat*. Can you add anything further to your testimony? *ʔaku ba𝜀ad šii tḍiifa l-šahaadtak.*

testing – 1. *mtiẓaan*. The system of testing in this school is excellent. *ṭariiqat il-imtiẓaan ib-hal-madrasa mumtaaza.* 2. *tajaarub*. We're about ready to resume atomic testing. *ʔiẓna 𝜀ala wašak in𝜀iid it-tajaarub iδ-δarriyya.*

test tube – *ʔinbuubat* (pl. *ʔanaabiib) ixtibaar.*

tetanus – *l-igzaaz, l-kuzaaz, l-gazzaaz, l-kazzaaz.*

text – *naṣṣ* pl. *nuṣuuṣ*. The text of the speech is on page two. *naṣṣ il-xiṭaab mawjuud ib-ṣafẓa θneen.*

textbook – *ktaab madrasi* pl. *kutub madrasiyya, ktaab muqarrar* pl. *kutub muqarrara.*

textile – 1. *nasiij*. There is a new textile plant in Mosul. *ʔaku ma𝜀mal nasiij jidiid bil-muuṣil.* 2. *qmaaš* pl. *ʔaqmiša, nasiij* pl. *ʔansija*. Egypt is famous for its cotton textiles. *miṣir mašhuura b-ʔaqmišatha l-quṭniyya.*

texture – *malmas* pl. *malaamis*. Silk has a smooth texture. *l-ẓariir malmasa naa𝜀im.*

than – 1. *min*. He's older than his brother. *huwwa ʔakbar min ʔaxuu.* -- I appreciate him more than ever. *ʔaqaddra ʔazyad min gabuḷ.* 2. *badal-ma, bidaal-ma*. I'd rather stay home than go to that dull play. *ʔafaḍḍil abqa bil-beet badal-ma ʔaruuẓ ib-har-ruwaaya l-itḍawwij.*

to thank – *šikar (u šukur)*. I haven't even thanked him yet. *ba𝜀ad li-hassa ma-škarta.*

   Thank goodness! *l-ẓamdu l-illaa.*

thankful – *mamnuun, šaakir*. We are very thankful to you. *ʔiẓna hwaaya mamnuuniin.*

thanks – 1. *šukur*. I don't expect any thanks or praise. *ma-ʔantiḍir ʔay šukur aw θanaaʔ.* 2. *faḍil*. It's no thanks to him that I'm here. *l-faḍil muu*

ʔila b-jayti.

   Thanks a lot. *šukran jaziilan.*

that – 1. (m.) *δaak, haaδaak* (f.) *δii*č, *haaδii*č. What's that? *δaak šinu?* or *šinu haaδaak?* -- That girl is my sister. *δii*č *il-bint ʔuxti.* or *δii*č *l-ibnayya ʔuxti.* -- What does that mean? *šinu ma𝜀na δaak?* or *δii*č *iš-ti𝜀ni?* 2. *lli, l-*. Do you know the story that he told us? *tu𝜀ruf l-iẓčaaya l-ẓičaa-lna-yyaaha?* -- Who's the man that just came in? *minu r-rijjaal illi ʔija hassa?* 3. *ʔann*. They told me that you were ill. *gaaloo-li ʔannak činit waj𝜀aan.* 4. *hal-*. I don't want that much milk. *ma-ariid hal-gadd ẓaliib.*

   at that – 1. *walaw hii*č*i*. Even at that I wouldn't pay more. *walaw hii*č*i ʔaani ma-adfa𝜀 ʔazeed.* 2. *ma𝜀a haaδa*. At that it costs only two dinars. *ma𝜀a haaδa, ykallif diinaareen bass.* 3. *𝜀ala hal-ẓaṭṭa, 𝜀ala haš-šikil*. We'll leave it at that. *xalli nxalliiha 𝜀ala hal-ẓaṭṭa.*

   that is – *ya𝜀ni*. I'll come tomorrow, that is, if it doesn't rain. *ʔaji baačir, ya𝜀ni, ʔiδa ma-muṭrat.*

thaw – *δawabaan θalij, moo𝜀 θalij*. This year the thaw set in rather early. *δawabaan iθ-θalij bida min wakit has-sana.*

   to thaw – *δaab (u) iθ-θalij, maa𝜀 (u) iθ-θalij*. It's thawing. *θ-θalij da-yδuub.* -- Has the refrigerator thawed out yet? *maa𝜀 iθ-θalij il-biθ-θallaaja?*

the – *l-*. The house is big. *l-beet ičbiir.* -- Please pass me the butter. *baḷḷa naawišni z-zibid.*

   The sooner we're paid the better. *kull-ma yinṭuuna fluusna min wakit, ʔaẓsan.*

theater – 1. *qaa𝜀at* (pl. -*aat) tamθiil*. Our theater has a modern stage. *qaa𝜀at it-tamθiil maalatna biiha masraz 𝜀aṣri.* 2. *sinama* pl. -*aat*. Most movie theaters in Baghdad are in Bab el Sharji. *ʔakθar is-siinamaat ib-baḡdaad ib-baab iš-šarji.*

theft – *booga* pl. -*aat, sariqa* pl. -*aat*. The theft was discovered the next morning. *ktišfaw il-booga θaani yoom iṣ-ṣubuẓ.*

their – *-hum*. Do you know their address? *tu𝜀ruf 𝜀inwaanhum?*

theirs – 1. *maalhum*. This book is theirs. *hal-iktaab maalhum.* 2. *maalathum*. We'll go in our car, and they'll take theirs. *nruuẓ ib-sayyaaratna, w-humma yruuẓuun ib-maalathum.*

   Our house isn't as big as theirs. *beetna muu b-gadd beethum.*

   Are you a friend of theirs? *ʔinta ṣadiiqhum?*

them – 1. *-hum*. I don't want to have anything to do with them. *ma-ariid adaxxil nafsi wiyyaahum.* 2. *-ha*. The papers are on the floor; will you please pick them up? *l-ʔawraaq bil-gaa𝜀; ma-tšiilha baḷḷa?*

theme – 1. *mawḍuu𝜀* pl. *mawaaḍii𝜀*. Why did you pick that theme? *lwee*š *intixabit hal-mawḍuu𝜀?* 2. *ʔinšaaʔ* pl. -*aat*. Have you finished your theme for tomorrow? *kitabit il-ʔinšaaʔ maalak maal baačir?*

themselves – *nafishum*. They did it themselves. *humma sawwooha b-nafishum.*

   The pair divided the money between themselves. *θneenhum itqaasmaw l-ifluus beenhum.*

then – 1. *ba𝜀deen, t-taali*. What did he do then? *w-ba𝜀deen iš-sawwa?* 2. *la𝜀ad*. Then everything is O.K. *la𝜀ad kullši zeen.* -- Well, then, let's go. *zeen, la𝜀ad xalli nruuẓ.* 3. *𝜀uud, δaak il-wakit*. Call Tuesday. We'll know by then. *xaabur iθ-θilaaθa, 𝜀uud yṣiir 𝜀iδna ma𝜀luum.* 4. *δaak il-wakit*. He did it right then, rather than waiting. *sawwaaha b-δaak il-wakit, badal-ma yintiḍir.*

   We go to the movies now and then. *nruuẓ lis-siinama been mudda w-mudda.*

   then and there – *ra ʔsan*. Why didn't you take it then and there? *lee*š *ma-ʔaxaδitha ra ʔsan?*

theoretical – *naḍari**. That's a theoretical solution. *haaδa ẓall naḍari.*

theoretically – *naḍariyyan*. Theoretically the experiment should turn out all right. *naḍariyyan it-tajruba laazim tinjaẓ.*

theory – *naḍariyya* pl. -*aat.*

there – *hnaak*. Have you been there? *b-𝜀umrak raayiẓ ihnaak?*

   I'm afraid he's not quite all there. *ybayyin mašxuuṭ.*

   There you are! I was looking all over for you. *hiyyaatak, činit da-adawwir 𝜀aleek ib-kull makaan.*

   there is, are – *ʔaku*. There are a few good hotels in town. *ʔaku 𝜀am ʔuteel zeen bil-wlaaya.* -- Are

there such people? *ʔaku hiiči naas?* -- There aren't enough chairs. *ma-aku skamliyyaat kaafya.*
thereabouts - *ðiič il-ʔaṭraaf.* Are there any banks thereabouts? *ʔaku bang ib-ðiič il-ʔaṭraaf?*
therefore - *li-ðaalik, li-haaða.* Therefore I assume it is so. *li-ðaalik ʔaɛtiqid hiyya haš-šikil.*
thermometer - *tarmoomatir* pl. *-aat.*
these - **1.** *ðoola, haaðoola.* I like these better. *ðoola yɛijbuuni ʔazeed.* -- These are good workmen. *haaðoola xooš ɛummaal.* **2.** *hal-.* These boys are good students. *hal-wulid xooš talaamiið.* -- These cigarettes are Turkish. *haj-jigaayir turkiyya.* -- Everything is very expensive these days. *kullši ġaali hal-ʔayyaam.*
**I'll attend to it one of these days. *raz-asawwiiha yoom imnil-ʔayyaam.*
thesis - **1.** *naðariyya* pl. *-aat, farðiyya* pl. *-aat.* His thesis proved to be right. *naðariita nθibtat ṣizzatha.* **2.** *ʔuṭruuza* pl. *-aat.* He wrote an excellent master's thesis. *kitab ʔuṭruuza mumtaaza l-šihaadat il-maajisteer.*
they - *humma.* They're my friends. *humma ʔaṣdiqaaʔi.* **They're leaving tomorrow. *msaafriin baačir.* **They work for me. *yištiġluu-li.*
thick - *θixiin.* The soup is too thick. *š-šoorba kulliš θixiina.* -- This board isn't that thick. *hal-looza maa hal-gadd θixiina.* -- He's too thick to understand that. *haaða damaaġa θxiin; ma-yifham hiiči ʔašyaaʔ.*
**The crowd was very thick at the scene of the accident. *čaan qaḷaðaaḷig ib-mazall il-zaadiθ.*
**I'll go through thick and thin for him. *ʔatzammal il-murr wil-zaamuð ɛala muuda.*
**Wherever there's a fight, he's in the thick of it. *ween-ma ʔaku ɛarka, tilgii b-nuṣṣha.*
to **thicken** - **1.** *θixan (a θuxuuna).* The sauce will thicken if you leave it on the fire to boil. *l-marga raz-tiθxan ʔiða txalliiha ɛan-naar itfawwur.* **2.** *θaxxin (i taθxiin) t-.* Thicken the sauce with tomato paste. *θaxxin il-marga b-maɛjuun ṭamaaṭa.*
thicket - *daġaḷ* (coll.).
thickness - *θuxun.* What is the thickness of that cardboard? *šgadd θuxun hal-imqawwaaya?*
thickset - *mraṣraṣ.* He's quite thickset. *haaða kulliš mraṣraṣ.*
thick-skinned - *safiiz.* She's thick-skinned, so she didn't mind the insult. *haaði safiiza, w-ma-daarat baal lil-ʔihaana.*
thief - *zaraami* pl. *-iyya.* Stop, thief! *ʔilzamuu l-zaraami!*
thievery - *boog.*
thigh - *fuxuð* pl. *fxaað.*
thimble - *kuštubaan* pl. *-aat.*
thin - **1.** *xafiif.* The paper is too thin. *hal-warqa kulliš xafiifa.* -- That soup is rather thin. *š-šoorba xafiifa šwayya.* **2.** *ðɛiif* pl. *ðaɛfaan.* She's gotten thin. *ṣaayra ðɛiifa.* or *ðuɛfat.* -- Her face has gotten very thin. *wujihha ṣaayir kulliš ðiɛiif.* **3.** *rifiiɛ.* That stick's too thin. *hal-ɛuuda kulliš rifiiɛa.* **4.** *waahi.* That's a pretty thin excuse. *haaða fadd ɛuður kulliš waahi.*
**I'll go through thick and thin for him. *ʔatzammal il-murr wil-zaamuð ɛala muuda.*
to get thin - *ðiɛaf (a ðuɛuf).* You've gotten thin. *ðiɛafit.*
to thin - **1.** *xaff (u xaff).* His hair is thinning. *šaɛra da-yxuff.* **2.** *xaffaf (u taxfiif).* Thin this paint. *xaffuf haṣ-ṣubuġ.*
to thin out - *xaff (u xaff).* Let's wait until this crowd thins out. *xal-nintiðir ʔila ʔan yxuff il-izdizaam.*
thing - *šii* pl. *ʔašyaaʔ, zaaja* pl. *-aat.* Some funny things have been going on here. *šwayya ʔašyaaʔ ġariiba da-tṣiir ihnaa.* -- I don't know the first thing about it. *ma-aɛruf ʔay šii ɛanha.* -- We've heard a lot of nice things about you. *smaɛna hwaaya ʔašyaaʔ zeena ɛannak.* -- It all adds up to the same thing. *ʔawwal w-taali kullha fadd šii.* -- That's an entirely different thing. *haaða fadd šii yixtilif tamaaman.*
**I didn't have a thing to do with it. *ma-čaan ʔili ʔay ɛalaaqa b-haaða.*
the real thing - *min ṣudug.* This time it's the real thing. *han-nooba min ṣudug.*
the thing (to do, etc.) - *ʔazsan šii.* The thing to do is to go home. *ʔazsan šii waazid yruuz lil-beet.*
things - **1.** *hduum.* Put on your things and let's go for a walk. *ʔilbas ihduumak w-xalli nitlaɛ nitmašša.* **2.** *l-ʔumuur, l-ʔazwaal.* Things have got to improve. *l-ʔumuur laazim titzassan.* **3.** *ġaraað.* Have you packed your things yet? *lammeet ġaraaðak loo baɛad?*
of all things - *ɛajiib.* Well of all things, what are you doing here? *ɛajiib, ʔinta š-da-tsawwi hnaa?*
to see things - *txayyal (a taxayyul).* You're just seeing things. *ʔinta bass da-titxayyal.*
to **think** - **1.** *ftikar (i ftikaar), fakkar (i tafkiir).* Don't you think it's too warm? *ma-tiftikir id-dinya kulliš zaarra?* **2.** *ɛtiqad (i ɛtiqaad).* I think he stated it plainly. *ʔaɛtiqid huwwa bayyanha b-wuðuuz.* -- He thinks his son is clever. *yiɛtiqid ʔibna kulliš šaaṭir.* **3.** *ðann (i ðann).* I thought you were from the country. *ðanneet ʔinta min sukkaan il-ʔaryaaf.* -- I don't think I'll go. *ma-aðinn raz-aruuz.* **4.** *šaaf (u šoof).* I don't think it's in your interest to do this. *ma-ašuuf min maṣlaztak itsawwi haay.*
**He's never really learned how to think. *ʔabad ma-tɛallam yistaɛmil fikra.*
**That's what you think, but you're wrong! *haaða raʔyak, laakin ʔinta ġalṭaan!*
**Now he thinks differently. *hassa tbaddal fikra.*
**He thinks nothing of driving all night. *ma-yhimma loo saaq il-leel kulla.*
to think about - *fakkar (i tafkiir) b-.* I've been thinking about it all afternoon. *ṣaar-li n-nahaar kulla da-afakkir biiha.* -- They're thinking about getting married. *da-yfakkruun biz-zawaaj.*
to think out - *tbaṣṣar (a tabaṣṣur) b-.* He doesn't think things out very far. *ma-yitbaṣṣar ihwaaya bil-ʔumuur.*
to think over - *fakkar (i tafkiir) b-, daanaš (i mudaanaša) fikr~.* He's still thinking it over. *baɛda da-ydaaniš fikra.* or *baɛda da-yfakkir biiha.*
thinker - *mufakkir* pl. *-iin.* Plato was a great thinker. *ʔaflaaṭuun čaan mufakkir ɛaðiim.*
thinking - *tafkiir.* Thinking about it won't help. *t-tafkiir biiha ma-bii faaʔida.*
**That's wishful thinking. *haaði tamanniyaat.*
thinly - **Put the paint on thinly. *la-tkaθθir iṣ-ṣubuġ.* **The valley is thinly forested. *hal-waadi bii šwayya ašjaar.* **This area is thinly settled. *hal-manṭiqa ma-mizdazma bis-sukkaan.*
thinner - **1.** *ʔaðɛaf.* He's thinner than his brother. *huwwa ʔaðɛaf min ʔaxuu.* **2.** *ʔaxfaf.* Can you make it a little thinner? *ma-tsawwii šwayya ʔaxfaf?* **3.** *ʔarfaɛ, ʔaðɛaf.* It'll have to be thinner to fit. *laazim itkuun ʔarfaɛ zatta tirham.*
to get thinner - *ðaɛɛaf (u taðɛiif) nafs~.* She wants to get thinner. *triid itðaɛɛuf nafisha.*
thinness - *ðuɛuf.* Her thinness worries me. *ðuɛufha da-yiqliqni.*
third - **1.** *θuluθ, θiliθ.* A third of that will be enough. *θuluθ haay ykaffi.* **2.** *θaaliθ.* We couldn't stay for the third act. *ma-gdarna nibqa lil-faṣl iθ-θaaliθ.*
third-class - **1.** *daraja θaalθa.* Give me one third-class ticket to Basra. *nṭiini tikit daraja θaalθa lil-baṣra.* **2.** *θaaliθ baab, θaaliθ daraja.* This wool is third class. *haṣ-ṣuuf θaaliθ baab.*
thirdly - *θaaliθan.* First of all it's expensive, secondly it's impractical, and thirdly it's difficult to get. *ʔawwalan ġaalya, θaaniyan muu ɛamaliyya, w-θaaliθan ṣaɛub tazṣiilha.*
thirst - **1.** *ɛaṭaš.* I can't quench my thirst. *ma-da-ʔagdar ʔarwi ɛaṭaši.*
**He still has his thirst for adventure. *baɛda yzibb il-muġaamaraat.*
thirsty - *ɛaṭšaan* pl. *ɛaṭaaša, -iin.* I'm very thirsty. *ʔaani kulliš ɛaṭšaan.* -- We all are very thirsty. *kullna činna ɛṭaaša.*
thirteen - *tlaṭṭaɛaš.*
thirteenth - *l-itlaṭṭaɛaš.* He came on the thirteenth. *jaa yoom l-itlaṭṭaɛaš.* -- I stopped reading after the thirteenth page. *baṭṭalt il-iqraaya baɛd iṣ-ṣaziifa l-itlaṭṭaɛaš.* -- Who was thirteenth in the class? *minu ṭilaɛ itlaṭṭaɛaš biṣ-ṣaff?*
thirtieth - *l-itlaaθiin.*
thirty - **1.** *tlaaθiin.* This month has thirty days. *haš-šahar bii tlaaθiin yoom.* **2.** *nuṣṣ.* It's three-thirty. *is-saaɛa tlaaθa n-nuṣṣ.*
this - (m.) *haaða, hal-.* (f.) *haaði, haay,*

hal-. Do you know this man? *tuεruf har-rijjaal?* -- Is this the same tie I saw? *haaδa nafs ir-ribaaṭ iš-šifta?* -- This is on me. *haay εala ζsaabi* or *haaδa εalayya.* -- What's this? *šinu haay?* or *haay šinu?* -- This is just what I wanted to avoid. *haay ič-činit da-ariid ʔatfaadaaha.*
**I'm going to see him this afternoon. *raζ-ašuufa l-yoom il-εaṣir.*
**They talked about this and that. *ζičaw εal-ʔaku wil-maaku.*

thorn - *šooka* pl. *-aat* coll. *šook.* The tree is full of thorns. *š-šajara matruusa šook.*

thorny - **1.** *bii šook.* Watch out, that plant is thorny. *diir baa lak, haz-zariε bii šook!* **2.** *šaaʔik, muζrij.* That is a very thorny question. *haaδa fadd mawδ̣uuε šaaʔik.*

thorough - **1.** *mutqan.* He's very thorough in everything he does. *huwwa kulliš mutqan ib-kullši l-ysawwii.* **2.** *šaamil, kaamil.* He submitted a thorough report. *qaddam taqriir šaamil.*
**He gave him a thorough beating. *biṣaṭa basṭa zeena.*

thoroughbred - *ʔaṣiil.* Those horses are thoroughbreds. *hal-xeel ʔaṣiila.*

thoroughfare - *šaariε* pl. *šawaariε.* Rashid St. is the main thoroughfare in Baghdad. *šaariε ir-rašiid huwwa š-šaariε ir-raʔiisi b-baġdaad.*

thoroughly - **1.** *b-diqqa.* Read it thoroughly. *ʔiqraa b-diqqa.* **2.** *tamaaman.* I'm thoroughly convinced he's wrong. *ʔaani muqtiniε tamaaman ʔanna ġalṭaan.*

those - *δoolaak, δoola.* Who are those people you were talking to? *minu humma δoolaak ič-činit da-tiζči wiyyaahum?*

though - **1.** *maεa ʔann, w-law.* Though he knew it, he didn't tell me anything about it. *maεa ʔanna yuεrufha, ma-gal-li εanha.* -- I bought several shirts, though I didn't need them. *štireet čam θoob w-law ma-aζtaajhum.* **2.** *laakin, bass.* All right, I'll do it! Not now, though. *zeen, εuud asawwiiha! bass muu hassa.* **3.** *maεa haaδa, εal-kull ζaal.* You've ordered it, though, haven't you? *ʔinta waṣṣeet εalee, maεa haaδa, muu?*
as though - *εabaalak.* It looks as though it may rain. *šikilha εabaalak raζ-tumṭur.*

thought - **1.** *tafkiir.* The very thought of it makes me sick. *mujarrad it-tafkiir bii ylaεεb in-nafis.* **2.** *fikra* pl. *-aat, fikar.* The thought occurred to me. *l-fikra xiṭrat-li* or *l-fikra jatti εala baali.* **3.** *muraaεaat.* Can't you show a little thought for others? *ma-tbayyin išwayya muraaεaat lil-ʔaaxariin?*
to be lost in thought - *ṣufan (u ṣafna).* He was lost in thought. *čaan ṣaafun.*
to give thought - *fakkar (u tafkiir) b-.* I'll have to give this matter some thought. *laazim ʔafakkir ib-hal-mawδ̣uuε.*
**Don't give it another thought! *la-tdawwix raasak biiha.* or *la-yibqa baalak yammha.*

thoughtful - *ṣaafun.* Why do you look so thoughtful? *š-biik ṣaafun?*
**It's very thoughtful of you to bring me flowers. *haaδa fadd šuεuur kullis laṭiif minnak itjiib-li warid.*

thoughtless - *ṭaayiš.* That was a thoughtless act. *haaδa fadd taṣarruf ṭaayiš.*
**She's so thoughtless. *ma-traaεi šuεuur il-ʔaaxiriin.*

thousand - *ʔalf* pl. *ʔaalaaf.*

thousandth - **1.** *l-ʔalf.* This is our thousandth shipment. *haaδi rsaaliyyatna l-ʔalf.* **2.** *waaζid imnil-ʔalf.* I own a thousandth of the company. *ʔamluk waaζid imnil-ʔalf min haš-šarika.*

thrashing - *basṭa* pl. *-aat.* Did he ever get a thrashing! *ṣ-ṣudug ʔakal basṭa!*

thread - **1.** *xeeṭ* pl. *xyuuṭ.* Have you a needle and thread? *εindič ʔubra w-xeeṭ?* **2.** *sinn* pl. *snuun.* The thread on this screw is worn out. *sinn hal-burġi saayif.*
to thread - **1.** *liδam (u laδum).* I'll thread the needle for you. *ʔaani ʔalδum-lič il-ʔubra.* **2.** *ṭallaε (i) sinn.* Would you thread this pipe for me? *baḷḷa ma-ṭṭalliε-li sinn il-hal-buuri?*

threat - *tahdiid* pl. *-aat.* Your threats don't scare me. *tahdiidaatak ma-yxawwufni.*

to **threaten** - *haddad (i tahdiid).* He threatened to leave if they didn't increase his salary. *haddad ybaṭṭil ʔiδa ma-yzayyduun maεaaša.* -- The epidemic threatened the whole city. *l-maraδ haddad il-wlaaya kullha.*

three - **1.** *tlaaθa.* Three and three equals six. *tlaaθa w-itlaaθa tsaawi sitta.* **2.** *tlaθt.* I've been here three days. *činit ihnaa tlaθt iyyaam.* **3.** *tlaθ.* He brought three books. *jaab itlaθ kutub.*

to **thresh** - *diras (i draas) n-, daas (u).* In northern Iraq, they still thresh grain by oxen. *b-šimaal il-εiraaq, baεadhum ydirsuun il-ζubuub biθ-θiiraan.*

threshing machine - *makiinat* (pl. *makaayin*) *diraas.*

threshold - *εitba* pl. *εitab.*

thrift - *qtiṣaad.* Scotsmen are known for their thrift. *l-iskutlandiyyiin mašhuuriin bil-iqtiṣaad.*

thrifty - *muqtiṣid.* She's a thrifty housewife. *hiyya fadd ʔumm beet muqtaṣda.*

to **thrill** - **1.** *ṭurab (i ṭarab).* The music thrilled him. *ṭurbata l-mawsiiqa.* **2.** *ʔaθaar (i ʔiθaara) mašaaεir.* Seeing the site of Sumer for the first time thrilled me. *šoofat mawqiε soomar il-ʔawwal marra ʔaθaar mašaaεri.*
to be thrilled - *ṭaar (i) εaqil-.* Jamil was thrilled with his present. *jamiil εaqla ṭaar bil-hadiyya.*

thrilling - *raayiε.* This is a thrilling view! *haaδi fadd manδar raayiε!*

to **thrive** - **1.** *ntiεaš (i ntiεaaš).* The economy is thriving. *l-waδε il-iqtiṣaadi da-yintiεiš.* **2.** *nima (u nimu).* Cattle thrive here. *l-baqar yinmu b-hal-manṭiqa.* **3.** *traεraε (a taraεruε).* The children are thriving. *j-jihaal da-yitraεraεuun.*

throat - *zarduum* pl. *zraadiim, balεuum* pl. *blaaεiim.* The doctor painted my throat with iodine. *ṭ-ṭabiib dihan zarduumi b-yood.*
**He'd cut your throat for two cents. *yguṣṣ rugubtak εala filseen.*
**He jumped down my throat. *miharni.* or *zaffni.*
**She wanted to say something, but the words stuck in her throat. *raadat itguul fadd šii bass εiṣat ič-čilma b-ζaligha.*

to **throb** - *nubaδ (u nabuδ).* The blood is throbbing in my veins. *d-damm da-yinbuδ ib-damaaraati.*

throne - *εarš* pl. *εuruuš.*

through - **1.** *been.* The president's party drove through cheering crowds. *r-raʔiis w-ζašiita marraw ib-sayyaaraathum been ij-jamaahiir il-haatfa.* **2.** *min.* You have to go through the hall to get to the kitchen. *laazim itfuut imnil-hool ζatta truuζ lil-maṭbax.* **3.** *εan ṭariiq.* You'll have to go through the sergeant to see the captain. *laazim itruuζ εan ṭariiq il-εariif ζatta tšuuf ir-raʔiis.* **4.** *b-sabab, b-natiijat.* The work was held up two weeks through his negligence. *wugaf iš-šuġuḷ muddat isbuuεeen b-sabab ihmaala.*
**We went through the woods. *xtiragna l-ġaaba.* or *gṭaεna l-ġaaba fadd ṣafζa lil-lux.*
**The carpenter bored a hole through the wood. *n-najjaar ziraf zuruf bil-xišba.*
**The deal fell through. *ṣ-ṣafqa ma-nijζat.*
**There's no through train from Kirkuk to Basra. *ma-aku qiṭaar yruuζ fadd raas min karkuuk lil-baṣra.*
**Is this a through street? *haaδa šaariε yxarrij?*
through and through - **1.** *mnil-ʔasaas, mnil-εirig.* He's bad through and through. *haaδa muu xooš ʔaadmi mnil-ʔasaas.* **2.** *min foog li-jawwa.* We were soaked through and through. *tnaggaεna min foog li-jawwa.*
to be through - *xaḷḷaṣ (i).* I'll be through work at five o'clock. *ʔaxaḷḷiṣ imniš-šuġuḷ is-saaεa xamsa.*
**I am through with it. *maa-li laazim bii baεad.*
**If you ever do that again, we're through. *tara ʔiδa tsawwi haay marra lux, wala ʔašuuf wiččak baεad.*

throughout - **1.** *ṭuul.* You can get these vegetables throughout the year. *tigdar tilgi hal-xuδra ṭuul is-sana.* **2.** *b-kull ʔanζaaʔ.* This hotel is famous throughout the world. *hal-ʔuteel maεruuf ib-kull ʔanζaaʔ il-εaalam.*

throw - *šamra* pl. *-aat, δabba* pl. *-aat.* That was some throw! *haay šloon šamra ζilwa!*
to throw - **1.** *šumar (u šamur), δabb (i δabb).* Let's see how far you can throw the ball. *xalli nšuuf iš-biεid tigdar tišmur iṭ-ṭooba.* -- He throws himself into it heart and soul. *δaabib nafsa εaleeha min kull galba.* **2.** *waggaε (i), šumar (u).* The horse threw him. *l-ζiṣaan waggaεa.* **3.** *buṭaζ (a baṭiζ).* He threw his opponent in a few seconds. *buṭaζ xaṣma b-čam θaaniya.* **4.** *wajjah (i).* Throw that light this way, please. *baḷḷa wajjih iδ-δ̣uwa*

l-haṣ-ṣafḥa.

to throw away – *δabb (i δabb).* Throw the papers away. *δibb hal-ʔawraaq.* -- He's just throwing his money away. *da-yδibb ifluusa biš-šaṭṭ.*

to throw back – *δabb (i δabb) n–.* Throw the fish back in the river. *δibb is-simča biš-šaṭṭ.*

to throw down – *šammar (u), šumar (u šamur).* Don't throw your things down so carelessly. *la-tšammur ġaraaδak haš-šikil bala htimaam.*

to throw in – *čammal (i tčimmil).* The baker threw in a few extra loaves of bread. *l-xabbaaz čammal čam ṣammuuna.*

**Ahmad threw in the towel. *ʔaḥmad sallam.* or *ʔaḥmad istaslam.*

to throw off – **1.** *nizaɛ (naziɛ).* He threw off his coat and joined the fight. *nizaɛ sitirta w-ištirak bil-ɛarka.* **2.** *txallaṣ (a) min.* How did you manage to throw off your cold? *šloon igdarit titxallaṣ imnin-našla?*

to throw out – **1.** *δabb (i δabb) n–.* I threw my old shoes out. *δabbeet qanaadri l-ɛatiiga.* **2.** *ṭirad (u ṭarid) n–, čallaq (i tčliiq) t–.* She almost threw me out. *yaɛni ʔilla šwayya čaan ṭirdatni.* or *baɛad išwayya tčalliqni.*

**The judge threw the case out of court for lack of evidence. *l-ḥaakim radd id-daɛwa l-ɛadam wujuud ʔadilla.*

to throw up – **1.** *ṭagg (u) b-wijj.* That's the second time you've thrown that up to me. *haay il-marra θ-θaanya ṭṭuggha b-wijji.* **2.** *zaaɛ (u zooɛ), zawwaɛ (i tazwiiɛ).* I throw up whenever I see blood. *kull-ma ašuuf damm ʔazuuɛ.* **3.** *baṭṭal (i) min.* He threw up a good job to run for the election. *baṭṭal min saġla zeena ḥatta yraššiḥ nafsa lil-intixaab.*

thud – *ṭabba* pl. *-aat.* I heard a thud in the next room. *simaɛit ṭabba b-ġuruft il-lux.*

thumb – *ʔibhaam* pl. *-aat.* I burned my thumb. *ḥragit ibhaami.*

**I'm all thumbs today. *š-ma ʔasawwi b-ʔiidi l-yoom ma-yiṭlaɛ tamaam.* or *ʔaani mxarbuṭ il-yoom.*

**He's too much under his wife's thumb. *yimši b-ḥukum marta ʔakθar imnil-laazim.* or *marta raakbata.*

**He sticks out like a sore thumb. *δaakuwa mbayyin.* or *δaakuwa ma-yinδamm.*

to thumb through – *warraq (i).* I thumbed through the telephone book. *warraqit ib-daliil it-talafoon.*

thumb tack – *danbuus* pl. *dnaabiis.* We put up the notice with thumb tacks. *ɛallaqna l-iɛlaan ib-danaabiis.*

thunder – *garguuɛa* pl. *garaagiiɛ, raɛad.* Did you hear the thunder last night? *smaɛt il-garaagiiɛ il-baarḥa bil-leel?*

**A thunder of applause greeted the speaker. *staqbilaw il-xaṭiib ib-fadd ɛaaṣifa mnit-taṣfiiq.*

to thunder – *gargaɛ (i gargaɛa), riɛad (i raɛad).* It's beginning to thunder. *bidat itgargiɛ.* or *bidat id-dinya tirɛid.*

**You shouldn't have let him thunder at you like that. *ma-čaan laazim itxallii yirɛid w-yizbid ɛaleek haš-šikil.*

thunderstorm – *ɛaaṣifa* pl. *ɛawaaṣif.* We missed the thunderstorm. *l-ɛaaṣifa ma-jatti ɛaleena.*

Thursday – *yoom il-xamiis.* That can wait till Thursday. *xalliiha ʔila yoom il-xamiis* or *xalliiha lil-xamiis.*

to thwart – *xayyab (u).* His action thwarted our plans. *tṣarrufa xayyab xiṭaṭna.*

thyme – *zaɛtar, saɛtar.*

tick – **1.** *garaada* pl. *-aat* coll. *garaad.* The dog is covered with ticks. *č-čalib malyaan garaad.* **2.** *doošag* pl. *dwaašig.* We had to sleep on straw ticks. *δṭarreena nnaam ɛala dwaašig maal ḥalfa.* **3.** *dagga* pl. *-aat.* The room is so quiet you can hear the tick of the clock. *l-gubba hiiči ṣanṭa tigdar tismaɛ daggaat is-saaɛa.*

to tick – *dagg (u dagga).* I can hear the watch tick. *da-ʔagdar asmaɛ is-saaɛa tdugg.*

ticket – **1.** *biṭaaqa* pl. *-aat, biṭaayiq; tikit* pl. *-aat.* Can you get us three tickets for the play? *tigdar itdabburna tlaθ biṭaaqaat lir-ruwaaya?* -- You can buy a ticket on the train. *tigdar tištiri tikit bil-qiṭaar.* **2.** *qaaʔimat muraššaḥin.* The National Party has a good ticket. *l-ḥizb il-waṭani ɛinda qaaʔimat muraššaḥiin zeena.*

ticking – **1.** *xaam iš-šaam.* How much is this ticking a yard? *hal-xaam iš-šaam beeš iδ-δiraaɛ?* **2.** *ṭagṭaga.* I just heard a strange ticking in the machine. *hassa smaɛit ṭagṭaga ġariiba bil-makiina.*

tickle – *šaxṭa* pl. *-aat.* I've a tickle in my throat. *ɛindi fadd šaxṭa b-zarduumi.*

to tickle – *daġdaġ (i daġdaġa) t–.* He doesn't laugh even if you tickle him. *ma-yiδḥak ḥatta loo daġdaġta.*

ticklish – *ḥassaas.* That's a ticklish question. *haaδa fadd mawδuuɛ ḥassaas.*

**Are you ticklish? *tġaar ib-suhuula?* or *d-daġdaġa tʔaθθir biik?*

tide: **The tide is coming in. *l-baḥar raḥ-yirtifiɛ.*

high tide – *madd.* It was high tide when the ship came up the river. *s-sifiina dixlat in-nahar wakt il-madd.*

low tide – *jazir.* You can walk out to the island at low tide. *wakt il-jazir tigdar timši lil-jazra.*

to tide over – *ṭallaɛ (i taṭliiɛ), dabbar (u) ʔamur.* Two dinars will tide me over until Monday. *diinaareen iṭṭalliɛni l-yoom iθ-θineen.*

tidy – **1.** *mhandam, mnaδδam, mrattab.* He is a very tidy person. *huwwa fadd waaḥid kulliš imhandam.* **2.** *mrattab, mnaδδam.* Her room is always tidy. *ġurfatha daaʔiman imrattba zeen.* **3.** *čbiir.* He's inherited a tidy fortune. *wiraθ θarwa čbiira.*

tie – **1.** *ṣila* pl. *-aat, raabiṭa* pl. *rawaabiṭ.* The two countries are bound by economic and military ties. *d-dawulteen murtabṭiin ib-ṣilaat iqtiṣaadiyya w-ɛaskariyya.* **2.** *raabiṭa* pl. *rawaabiṭ.* Family ties are stronger in the Middle East than in the West. *r-rawaabiṭ il-ɛaaʔiliyya biš-šarq il-ʔawsaṭ ʔaqwa mnil-ġarb.* **3.** *booyinbaaġ* pl. *-aat, ribaaṭ* pl. *ʔarbiṭa.* He wears expensive ties. *yilbas booyinbaaġaat ġaalya.* **4.** *loog* pl. *-aat.* The ties on this line need replacing. *l-loogaat maal has-sičča yinraad-ilha taġyiir.* **5.** *taɛaadul.* The game ended in a tie. *s-sibaaq intiha b-taɛaadul.*

to tie – **1.** *šadd (i šadd).* I have to tie my shoelaces. *xalli ašidd qiiṭaan qundarti.* **2.** *tɛaadal (a taɛaadul).* They tied us in the last minute's play. *tɛaadlaw wiyyaana b-ʔaaxir laḥδa mnil-liɛib.* **3.** *ɛigad (u ɛagid).* Tie that knot securely. *ʔuɛgud hal-ɛugda zeen.*

**My hands are tied. *ʔaani mčattaf.*

to tie down – *ribaṭ (u rabuṭ).* I don't want to tie myself down. *ʔaani ma-ard arbuṭ nafsi.*

to tie in – *riham (a rahum).* This ties in nicely with what we know. *haaδa yirham zeen wiyya l-nuɛurfa.*

to tie on – *šadd (i šadd) b–, rubaṭ (u rabaṭ) b–.* Tie on another piece of string. *šidd biiha wuṣla lux xeeṭ.*

to tie up – **1.** *rubaṭ (u rabaṭ), šadd (i šadd).* Please tie up these papers for me. *ʔarjuuk urbuṭ-li hal-ʔawraaq ib-xeeṭ.* -- Did you tie up the boat? *rbaṭṭa lil-balam?* **2.** *šaġġal (i tašġiil).* He's tied up all his money in real estate. *šaġġal kull ifluusa b-muɛaamalaat il-ʔamlaak.* **3.** *ɛaṭṭal (i taɛṭiil).* The accident tied up traffic. *l-ḥaadiθ ɛaṭṭal il-muruur.*

tied up – **1.** *mirtibiṭ.* Are you tied up this evening? *ʔinta mirtibiṭ ib-šii hal-leela?* **2.** *mašġuul.* I was tied up all afternoon. *činit mašġuul tamaaman ṭuul wara δ-δuhur.* **3.** *mšaġġal.* I'm sorry, my money's tied up right now. *mitʔassif ifluusi mšaġġila hassa.*

**Rashid St. is generally tied up at noontime. *šaariɛ ir-rašiid ɛaadataan ma-yinfaat bii mnil-xabṣa δ-δuhriyya.*

tiger – *namur* pl. *nmuur, nmuura.* We're going to hunt tigers. *raḥ-inṣiid inmuur.*

tight – **1.** *ḥeel.* Shut your eyes tight. *sidd iɛyuunak ḥeel.* -- Hold tight to the horse's neck. *čallib ib-rugbat l-iḥṣaan ḥeel.* **2.** *δabb, maδbuub.* I tied my shoelaces too tight. *šaddeet qiiṭaan qundarti δabb.* -- Is the jar sealed tight? *qabaġ iš-šiiša maδbuub zeen?* or *qabaġ iš-šiiša masduud δabb?* **3.** *δayyig.* This jacket is too tight for me. *has-sitra kulliš δayyga ɛalayya.* **4.** *sakraan.* Boy was I tight last night! *ʔamma ʔaani ṣudug činit sakraan il-baarḥa bil-leel!* **5.** *baxiil.* He's very tight with his money. *huwwa kullis baxiil b-ifluusa.* **6.** *šaaḥḥ.* Money is very tight now. *l-ifluus šaaḥḥa hassa.*

**I've been in many a tight spot before. *ʔaani yaa-ma waagiɛ ib-warṭa gabuḷ.* or *ʔaani maarr ib-ʔayyaam ɛaṣiiba gabuḷ.*

to sit tight – *ṣubar (u ṣabur).* You just sit tight; and we'll be with you in half an hour.

ʔiṣbur ib-makaanak; ʔiẓna raẓ-inkuun yammak baɛad nuṣṣ saaɛa.
to **tighten** - *ŝabb (u ŝabb).* Tighten the rope. *ŝubb il-ẓabil.*
tightlipped - *skuuti* pl. *-iyya, katuum* pl. *-iin.* Nuri is quite tightlipped. *nuuri kulliš iskuuti.*
tightly - *ŝabb, b-ẓeel.* He tied the package tightly. *šadd ir-ruzma ŝabb.*
Tigris River - *nahar dijla.*
tile - *kaašiyya* pl. *-aat* coll. *kaaši.* A tile fell off the bathroom wall. *kaašiyya wugɛat min ẓaayiṭ il-ẓammaam.*
to tile - *ṭabbag (i taṭbiig) t- b-kaaši.* We have to tile the kitchen floor. *laazim inṭabbug gaaɛ il-muṭbax bil-kaaši.*
till - **1.** *daxal.* Is there any money in the till? *ʔaku fluus bid-daxal?* **2.** *ʔila ʔan, ẓatta.* Wait till I come back. *ntiŝir ʔila ʔan ʔarjaɛ.* **3.** *ʔila, ẓatta.* I won't be able to see you till next week. *ma-raẓ-agdar ašuufak ʔila l-isbuuɛ ij-jaay.*
tilt - *meela* pl. *-aat.* The telephone pole has taken on a bad tilt. *ɛamuud it-talafoon maal meela qawiyya.*
at a tilt - *maayil, mnakkas.* The Iraqi cap is worn at a tilt. *s-sidaara l-ɛiraaqiyya tinlibis maayla.*
to tilt - **1.** *mayyal (i tmiyyil), nakkas (i tankiis).* If you tilt the bottle, you may be able to get it out of the refrigerator. *loo tmayyil il-buṭil muẓtamal tigdar iṭṭalɛa mniθ-θillaaja.* — Tilt your hat forward a bit. *nakkis šafuqtak išwayya.* — Tilt the flag forward during the parade. *nakkis il-ɛalam ʔaθnaaʔ il-istiɛraaŝ.* **2.** *ẓina (i ẓani), mayyal (i).* I can't tilt my head to either side. *ma-ʔagdar ʔaẓni raasi li-ṣafẓa.*
timber - **1.** *ʔašjaar maal xišab.* Iraq has little timber. *l-ɛiraaq ma-bii hwaaya ʔašjaar maal xišab.* **2.** *dalag* pl. *-aat, jiŝaɛ* pl. *jiŝuuɛ.* The timbers on our roof are rotting. *d-dalagaat ib-sagufna xaaysa.*
time - **1.** *wakit* pl. *ʔawkaat.* It's time to leave. *ṣaar wakt ir-rooẓa.* — What time are we to go? *š-wakit raẓ-inruuẓ.* — These are hard times. *haay ʔawkaat ɛaṣiiba.* or ***haaŝi muu xooš ʔayyaam.* **2.** *marra* pl. *-aat, nooba* pl. *-aat.* This is my first time here. *haay ʔawwal marra ʔaji hnaa.* — Four times five equals twenty. *ʔarbaɛ marraat xamsa, ɛišriin.* or *ʔarbaɛa b-xamsa ysaawi ɛišriin.* — Two times two equals four. *marrteen iθneen ysaawi ʔarbaɛa.* **3.** *l-ʔayyaam, z-zaman.* Time will tell. *l-ʔayyaam tikšifha.* **4.** *mudda.* The time is up tomorrow. *l-mudda tixlaṣ baačir.* — I worked a long time. *štiġaḷit mudda ṭwiila.* — He comes to see us from time to time. *yiji yšuufna been mudda w-mudda.* or *yiji yšuufna been ẓiin w-ʔaaxar.* **5.** *tawqiit.* The news in Arabic is broadcast from London at 6 P.M. Greenwich time or 9 P.M. Baghdad local time. *l-ʔaxbaar bil-ɛarabi tinŝaaɛ min landan bil-leel saaɛa sitta ẓasab tawqiit grinič ʔaw saaɛa tisɛa ẓasab tawqiit baġdaad il-maẓalli.* **6.** *tawqiiɛ.* The drum beats the time in music. *d-dumbuk yiŝbuṭ it-tawqiiɛ bil-mawsiiqa.* **7.** *zaman, ʔawaan.* That research is ahead of the times. *hal-buẓuuθ ġaaḷba z-zaman.* That design was too far ahead of its time. *hat-taṣmiim saabiq ʔawaana.* **8.** *muwaqqat.* The revolutionaries set a time bomb in the plane. *θ-θuwwaar ẓaṭṭaw qumbula mwaqqita biṭ-ṭiyyaara.*
**Would you know what time of day it is? *tuɛruf is-saaɛa b-eeš?*
**They gave him a bad time. *ŝawwjoo* or *ʔaŝŝoo hwaaya.*
a long time ago - *min zamaan, gabuḷ mudda ṭwiila.* I met her a long time ago. *tɛarrafit biiha min zamaan.* — She left a long time ago. *raaẓat min zamaan.* or ***ṣaar-ilha hwaaya min raaẓat.*
all the time - *ɛala ṭuul, daaʔiman.* We had good weather all the time. *čaan ij-jaww mumtaaz ɛala ṭuul.* — He's here all the time. *huwwa daaʔiman ihnaa.*
at times - *ʔaẓyaanan, dooraat.* At times I work fourteen hours at a stretch. *ʔaẓyaanan ʔaštuġuḷ ʔarbaaṭaɛaš saaɛa ɛala fadd jarra.* — I see him at times. *ʔašuufa dooraat.*
for the time being - *b-hal-ʔaθnaaʔ, muwaqqatan.* Stay here for the time being. *ʔibqa hnaa b-hal-ʔaθnaaʔ.*
in good time - *b-wakitha.* You'll know it in good time. *ɛuud tuɛrufha b-wakitha.*
in time - **1.** *b-natiija, ʔaxiiran, bil-wakt il-munaasib.* I'm sure we'll come to an agreement in time. *ʔaani mitʔakkid raẓ-nooṣal il-fadd ittifaaq bin-natiija.* **2.** *bil-wakt il-munaasib.* The doctor arrived in time to save her. *d-diktoor wuṣal bil-wakt il-munaasib ẓatta yinquŝha.*
on time - **1.** *ɛal-wakit.* Please be on time. *baḷḷa kuun ɛal-wakit.* **2.** *bil-ʔaqṣaaṭ.* He bought the car on time. *štira s-sayyaara bil-ʔaqṣaaṭ.*
time after time - *marra ɛala marra, yaama w-yaama, marraat.* I've asked him time after time not to do it. *yaama w-yaama ridit minna ma-ysawwiiha.*
to have a good time - *twannas (a winsa).* Did you have a good time? *twannasit?*
to time - **1.** *ɛayyan (i taɛyiin) wakit.* We timed the conference to start after the holiday. *ɛayyanna wakt il-muʔtamar ẓatta yibdi wara l-ɛuṭla.* **2.** *lizam (a) wakit, ŝubaṭ (u) wakit.* Who timed the race? *minu lizam wakt is-sibaaq?*
time keeper - *muwaqqit* pl. *-iin.*
timely - *b-wakit-.* That's a timely article. *haaŝa fadd maqaal ib-wakta.*
timer - *muwaqqit* pl. *-aat.* Set the timer for 5 minutes. *ʔinṣub il-muwaqqit ʔila xamis daqaayiq.*
timesaver: **Canned foods are great timesavers. *l-muɛallabaat itxalli l-waaẓid yiqtiṣid bil-wakit.*
timetable - *jadwal (pl. jadaawil) ʔawqaat.*
timid - *mitwahwih, xajuul.* Don't be so timid! *la-tṣiir hal-gadd mitwahwih.*
timing - *tawqiit.* The hold-up relied on precise timing. *s-sariqa ɛtimdat ɛala tawqiit daqiiq.*
**The timing of his speech was excellent. *xiṭaaḅa jaa bil-wakt il-munaasib.*
tin - **1.** *tanak.* The price of tin went up last week. *ʔasɛaar it-tanak ṣiɛdat bil-isbuuɛ il-faat.* **2.** *quuṭiyya* pl. *qwaati.* Give me a tin of tobacco. *nṭiini quuṭiyyat titin.*
tinder - *ɛilga.* Bring a little tinder so I can start the fire. *jiib-li šwayyat ɛilga ẓatta ašɛil in-naar.*
to **tingle** - *nammal (i).* My foot's tingling. *rijli mnammla.*
to **tinkle** - *ṭagṭag (i ṭagṭaga).* The ice cubes tinkle in the glass. *θ-θalij da-yṭagṭig bil-igḷaaṣ.*
tinsmith - *tanakči* pl. *-iyya.*
tint - *loon* pl. *ʔalwaan.* Use a lighter tint for the wall. *staɛmil loon ʔaftaẓ il-haaŝa l-ẓaayiṭ.*
to tint - **1.** *ṣubaġ (u).* I want my hair tinted blond. *ʔariid ʔaṣbuġ šaɛri ʔašgar.* **2.** *lawwan (i talwiin).* We've tinted one of the photographs. *lawwanna waaẓid imnir-rusuum.*
tiny - *ṣġayyir.* Where'd you get such a tiny radio? *ween ligeet hiiči raadyo ṣġayyir?*
tip - **1.** *raas* pl. *ruus.* They landed on the northern tip of the island. *nizlaw ib-raas ij-jaziira š-šimaali.* — My shoes are worn at the tips. *qundarti saafat imnir-raas.* **2.** *ṭarf* pl. *ʔaṭraaf.* The word is on the tip of my tongue. *č-čilma ɛala ṭarf ilsaani.* **3.** *zaḅaana* pl. *-aat.* Do you have cigarettes with tips? *ɛindak jigaayir ʔumm iz-zaḅaana?* **4.** *naṣiiẓa* pl. *naṣaayiẓ.* Let me give you a tip. *xalli nṭiik fadd naṣiiẓa.* **5.** *ʔixbaariyya* pl. *-aat.* The police found him through a tip. *š-šurṭa ligoo ɛan ṭariiq ixbaariyya.* **6.** *baxšiiš* pl. *-aat.* How much of a tip shall I give the waiter? *šgadd anṭi baxšiiš lil-booy?*
to tip - *niṭa (i) baxšiiš.* Did you tip the porter? *nṭeeta baxšiiš lil-ẓammaal?*
to tip off - *niṭa (i) maɛluumaat, ʔixbaariyya.* Who tipped you off? *minu nṭaak il-maɛluumaat?*
to tip over - **1.** *guḷab (u gaḷub) n-.* The maid tipped the chair over. *l-xaadma guḷbat l-iskamli.* **2.** *ngiḷab (u ngiḷaab).* The boat tipped over. *l-balam ingiḷab.*
tiptoe - *ʔaṭraaf ʔaṣaabiɛ.* The children came in on tiptoe. *j-jihaal xaššaw ɛala ʔaṭraaf il-ʔaṣaabiɛ.*
tiptop - *mumtaaz.* My car's in tiptop condition. *sayyaarti b-ẓaala mumtaaza.*
tire - *taayar* pl. *-aat.* Did you put air in the tires? *nfaxt it-taayaraat?*
to tire - **1.** *taɛɛab (i tatɛiib).* The long journey tired us thoroughly. *s-safra ṭ-ṭwiila taɛɛbatna kulliš.* **2.** *tiɛab (a taɛab, taɛbaan).* I tire very easily in this hot weather. *ʔaani ʔatɛab bil-ɛajal ib-haj-jaww il-ẓaarr.* **3.** *mall (i malal), ŝaaj (u ŝooj, ŝawajaan).* I'm tired of her

nagging. *malleet min nagnagatha.*
tired - *taƐbaan.* He looks tired. *ybayyin taƐbaan.*
tiresome - **1.** *mumill.* What a tiresome person he is! *haaδa ṣudug fadd šaxiṣ mumill.* **2.** *mutƐib.* This is very tiresome work. *haš-šuğuḷ kulliš mutƐib.*
tissue - **1.** *nasiij* pl. *ʔansija.* Was there much tissue injured? *čaan aku hwaaya ʔansija mitʔaδδaaya?* **2.** *čaffiyya (pl. čfaafi) waraq.* Buy me a box of tissues. *štirii-li quuṭiyya čfaafi waraq.*

tissue paper - *waraq xafiif.* Wrap it in tissue paper. *liffha b-waraq xafiif.*
title - **1.** *ʔisim* pl. *ʔasmaaʔ.* Do you know the title of the book? *tuƐruf ʔism il-iktaab?* **2.** *laqab* pl. *ʔalqaab.* What's his title? *šinu laqaba?* **3.** *Ɛinwaan* pl. *Ɛanaawiin.* What's the title of your position? *šinu Ɛinwaan waḍiiftak?* -- The title page is missing from this book. *ṣafḥat il-Ɛinwaan ḍaayƐa min hal-iktaab.* **4.** *mulkiyya* pl. *-aat.* Whose name is the title of the car in? *b-ism man mulkiit is-sayyaara?*
to - **1.** *l-, ʔila.* I have to go to the library. *laazim aruuḥ lil-maktaba.* -- He went through his fortune to the last cent. *ṣiraf kull θaruuta l-ʔaaxir filis.* **2.** *b-.* I told him that to his face. *gilt-ilh-iyyaa b-wučča.* -- What do you say to this? *š-itguul ib-haay.* **3.** *wiyya.* Did you talk to him? *ḥčeet wiyyaa?* **4.** *Ɛala.* Apply this ointment to the inflamed area. *ḥuṭṭ hal-marham Ɛal-manṭiqa l-miltahba.*
**I'm trying to help you. *ʔaani bass da-ariid aƐaawnak.*
**I must go to bed. *laazim anaam.*
**It doesn't mean much to him. *ma-yhimma.*
**It's ten minutes to four. *s-saaƐa ʔarbaƐa ʔilla Ɛašra.*
toad - *Ɛugrugga* pl. *-aat, Ɛagaariig* coll. *Ɛugrugg, Ɛagruug.*
toadstool - *raas (pl. ruus) fṭirr* coll. *fṭirr.*
toast - *naxab* pl. *ʔanxaab.* Let's drink a toast to the newlyweds. *xal-nišrab naxab il-Ɛuruus wil-Ɛirriis.*
to toast - **1.** *ḥammaṣ (i taḥmiiṣ).* Shall I toast the bread? *triidni ʔaḥammiṣ il-xubuz?* **2.** *širab (a) naxab.* Let's toast the host. *xal-nišrab naxab id-daaƐi.*

tobacco - *titin.*
tobacco dealer - *titinči* pl. *-iyya.*
tobacco shop - *maxzan (pl. maxaazin) jigaayir.*
today - *hal-yoom, l-yoom.* What's on the menu today? *šaku Ɛidkum ʔakil hal-yoom?* -- I haven't read today's paper yet. *baƐadni ma-qreet jariidt il-yoom.*
toe - *ʔiṣbiƐ (pl. ʔaṣaabiƐ, ʔaṣaabiiƐ) rijil.* My toes are frozen. *ʔaṣaabiiƐ rijli mθallja.*
**I didn't mean to stop on anybody's toes. *ma-qṣadit il-ʔisaaʔa l-ʔaḥḥad.* or *ma-qṣadit ʔatƐarraḍ l-aḥḥad.*
**I have to be on my toes all the time. *laazim ʔafukk iƐyuuni Ɛala ṭuul.* or *laazim ʔakuun mityaqqiḍ Ɛala ṭuul.*
together - *suwa.* We work together. *ništuğuḷ suwa.* -- I saw my friend and his wife walking together. *šifit ṣadiiqi w-marta yitmaššuun suwa.*
to get together - *jtimaƐ (i jtimaaƐ).* Can we get together some evening? *nigdar nijtimiƐ fadd leela?*
to stick together - *tƐaaḍad (a taƐaaḍud).* Let's stick together in this matter. *xalli nitƐaaḍad ib-hal-masʔala.*
toilet - *mirḥaaḍ* pl. *maraaḥiiḍ, xalaaʔ* pl. *-aat.* Where's the toilet? *ween il-mirḥaaḍ?*
toilet paper - *waraq maraaḥiiḍ, waraq xalaaʔ.* Muslims use water instead of toilet paper. *l-misilmiin yistaƐmiluun maay ibdaal waraq il-maraaḥiiḍ.*
token - **1.** *daliil* pl. *dalaaʔil, Ɛalaama* pl. *-aat, tiδkaar* pl. *-aat.* He gave it to me as a token of his friendship. *nṭaani-iyyaaha ka-daliil Ɛala ṣadaaqta.* **2.** *ʔismi*.* We may be able to satisfy them with a token payment. *yimkin nigdar nirḍiihum ib-fadd mablağ ʔismi.*
tolerance - **1.** *taḥammul.* This steel has high tolerance for heat. *hal-fulaaδ Ɛinda taḥammul qawi lil-ḥaraara.* **2.** *tasaamuḥ.* Tolerance is difficult in religion and politics. *t-tasaamuḥ bid-diin w-bis-siyaasa ṣaƐub.*
tolerant - *mitsaamiḥ.* Our boss is very tolerant. *mudiirna kulliš mitsaamiḥ.*
to **tolerate** - *tsaamaḥ (a) b-.* I won't tolerate inefficiency. *ma-raḥ-ʔatsaamaḥ ib-ḥaalat Ɛadam il-kafaaʔa.*

toll - **1.** *Ɛibriyya* pl. *-aat.* You have to pay a toll on this bridge. *laazim tidfaƐ Ɛibriyya Ɛala haj-jisir.* **2.** *Ɛadad.* The plane crash took a heavy toll of life. *raaḥ Ɛadad ičbiir imniḍ-ḍaḥaaya b-ḥaadiθ iṭ-ṭiyyaara.*
toll bridge: **This is a toll bridge. *haaδa j-jisir yaaxδuun Ɛalee Ɛibriyya.*
tomato - *ṭamaaṭaaya* pl. *-aat* coll. *ṭamaaṭa.* Make the salad with tomatoes and cucumbers. *sawwi z-zalaaṭa min ṭamaaṭa w-ixyaar.*
tomato juice - *Ɛaṣiir ṭamaaṭa.*
tomato sauce - *maƐjuun ṭamaaṭa.*
tomb - **1.** *qabur* pl. *qubuur.* He placed a wreath on the tomb of the unknown soldier. *ḥaṭṭ ʔikliil Ɛala qabr ij-jundi il-majhuul.* **2.** *ḍariiḥ* pl. *ḍaraayiḥ.* They went to visit Husayn's tomb in Karbala. *raaḥaw yzuuruun ḍariiḥ il-ḥusayn ib-karbala.*
tomcat - *hirr* pl. *hruura.*
tomorrow - *baačir.* I'll be back tomorrow. *raḥ-ʔarjaƐ baačir.* -- It'll be in tomorrow's paper. *tiṭlaƐ ib-jariidat baačir.* -- I won't see him till tomorrow morning. *ma-raḥ-ašuufa gabuḷ baačir iṣ-ṣubuḥ.*
ton - *ṭann* pl. *ṭnuun.* We order a ton of coal. *waṣṣeena Ɛala ṭann faḥam.* -- That's a ten-ton truck. *hal-loori ʔabu Ɛašr iṭnuun.*
tone - **1.** *lahja* pl. *-aat, ṣooṭ* pl. *ʔaṣwaaṭ.* You shouldn't speak to her in such a rough tone. *ma-laazim tiḥči wiyyaaha b-hiiči lahja ḥaadda.* **2.** *ṣooṭ* pl. *ʔaṣwaaṭ.* This violin has a beautiful tone. *hal-kamanja ṣootha kulliš ḥilu.* **3.** *loon* pl. *ʔalwaan.* His car is two-tone. *sayyaarta looneen.*
to tone down - *hidaʔ (a huduuʔ), Ɛiqal (a Ɛaqil).* He's toned down a lot since he came here. *hidaʔ ihwaaya min ʔija l-ihnaa.*
tongs - **1.** *maaša* pl. *-aat.* Use tongs to stir the coals. *ḥarrik ij-jamur bil-maaša.* **2.** *milgaṭ* pl. *malaagiṭ.* He picked up a lump of sugar with the tongs. *šaal fuṣṣ šakar bil-milgaṭ.*
tongue - *lisaan* pl. *-aat, lisin, ʔalsina.* Let me see your tongue. *xal-ʔašuuf ilsaanak.* -- She has a sharp tongue. *Ɛidha lsaan ḥaadd.* or *lsaanha miθl is-siččiin.* -- The tongue on my shoe is torn off. *ngiṭaƐ ilsaan qundarti.*
tonic - **1.** *muqawwi* pl. *-iyaat.* What you need is a good tonic. *yinraad-lak fadd muqawwi zeen.* **2.** *toonik.* Do you like gin and tonic? *yƐijbak jin w-toonik?* **3.** *dihin.* The barber put some tonic on my hair. *l-imzayyin ḥaṭṭ dihin ib-šaƐri.*
tonight - *hal-leela, l-leela.* What shall we do tonight? *š-insawwi hal-leela?* -- Have you seen tonight's paper? *šift ij-jariida maalat hal-leela?*
tonnage - *ṭann ḥumuula.* What's the tonnage of that vessel? *čam ṭann ḥumuulat δiič il-baaxira?*
tonsil - *looza* pl. *-aat.* My tonsils are swollen. *loozteeni miltahba.*
tonsilitis - *ltihaab il-loozteen.*
too - *hamm, hammeen.* May I come, too? *ʔagdar ʔaani hamm ʔaji?*
**This is too hot. *haay kulliš ḥaarra.*
**Don't stay away too long. *la-ṭṭawwal barra hwaaya.*
**This board is too long. *hal-looḥa ʔaṭwal imnil-laazim.*
**The play was none too good. *r-ruwaaya ma-čaanat kulliš zeena.*
tool - **1.** *ʔadaat* pl. *ʔadawaat, ʔaala* pl. *-aat.* Be careful with those new tools. *diir baalak Ɛala hal-ʔadawaat ij-jidiida.* **2.** *ʔaala* pl. *-aat.* The mayor is only a tool in the hands of his party. *raʔiis il-baladiyya muu ʔazyad min ʔaala b-iid il-ḥizib maala.*
tooled leather - *jilid mašğuul, jilid manquuš.*
to **toot** - *ṭawwaṭ (u tṭuwwuṭ), dagg (u).* Toot your horn at this corner. *ṭawwuṭ ib-haaδa l-mafrag.*
tooth - *sinn* pl. *snuun.* This tooth hurts. *has-sinn ywajjiƐ.* -- The saw has a broken tooth. *l-minšaar bii sinn maksuur.*
**She has a sweet tooth. *tḥibb il-ḥalaa hwaaya.*
**We fought against it tooth and nail. *qaawamnaaha b-kull šidda.*
toothache - *wajaƐ sinn.* I have a toothache. *Ɛindi wajaƐ sinn.*
toothbrush - *firčat (pl. firač) isnuun.*
tooth paste - *maƐjuun isnuun.*
top - **1.** *raas* pl. *ruus.* The storm broke off the top of our palm tree. *l-Ɛaaṣifa kisrat raas in-naxla maalatna.* -- You'll find that passage at the top of page 32. *tšuuf hal-faqara b-raas ṣafḥa θneen w-iθlaaθiin.* **2.** *qumma* pl. *qumam.* How far is it to

the top of the mountain? *šgadd il-masaafa l-qummat haj-jibal?* **3.** *εilu, ʔaεla.* She shouted at the top of her voice. *ṣaaḥat ib-εilu ḥissha* or ***ṣaaḥat ib-kull ḥissha.* **4.** *foogaani**. There's still one room vacant on the top floor. *li-hassa ʔaku ġurfa faarġa bil-qaaṭ il-foogaani.* — Your handkerchiefs are in the top drawer. *čfaafiyyak bil-imjarr il-foogaani.* **5.** *tanta* pl. *-aat.* It's such nice weather, let's put the top down. *j-jaww kulliš laṭiif, xalli nnaḥḥil it-tanta.* **6.** *muṣraε* pl. *maṣaariε.* Do you know how to spin a top? *tuεruf tilεab muṣraε?* **7.** *foog.* The book is lying on top. *l-iktaab maḥṭuuṭ li-foog.* — We searched the house from top to bottom. *fattašna l-beet min foog li-jawwa.* **8.** *ʔaqṣa.* We drove at top speed all the way down here. *siqna b-ʔaqṣa surεa ṭuul iṭ-ṭariiq l-ihnaa.*

**I don't know why he blew his top. *ma-ʔadri leeš haaj.*

**I slept like a top last night. *nimit miθl il-iḥjaara l-baarḥa bil-leel.*

to top off – *ʔanha (i), xallaṣ (i).* Let's top off the evening with a glass of wine. *xalli ninhi l-leela b-fadd iglaaṣ šaraab.*

**To top it all off, he stole my wallet. *w-ičmaala, baag ij-jiḥdaan maali.* or *foogaaha, baag jiḥdaani.*

topic – *mawδuuε* pl. *mawaaδiiε.* This is quite a timely topic. *haaδa fadd mawδuuε ib-wakta.*

topsoil – *ḥimiij.* The rains are washing away the topsoil. *l-ʔamṭaar da-tijruf iḥ-ḥimiij.*

topsy-turvy – *raas εala εaqib.* Everything was topsy-turvy. *kullši čaan magluub raas εala εaqib.*

torch – *mašεal* pl. *mašaaεil.*

torment – *εaδaab.* I can't stand the torment anymore. *ma-atḥammal il-εaδaab baεad.*

to torment – **1.** *ʔaδδa (i).* Stop tormenting that cat! *bass εaad itʔaδδi hal-bazzuuna.* **2.** *marmar (u tmurmur) l-, εaδδab (i taεδiib).* She tormented her father all day. *hiyya marmurat il-abuuha ṭuul in-nahaar.* or *εaδδibat ʔabuuha ṭuul in-nahaar.*

torn – *mašguug.* Which pocket is torn? *yaa jeeb mašguug?*

tornado – *fittaala* pl. *-aat.*

torpedo – *toorbiid* pl. *-aat.*

torrent – *seel* pl. *siyuul.* The heavy rain caused several small torrents. *l-muṭar il-qawi sabbab εiddat siyuul iṣġayyra.*

**The rain came down in torrents. *l-muṭar gaam yinzil miθl il-girab.*

torrid zone – *l-manṭiqa l-istiwaaʔiyya.* Most of Africa lies within the torrid zone. *muεδam ʔafriiqya waaqεa bil-manṭiqa l-istiwaaʔiyya.*

tortoise – *sulḥafaat* pl. *salaaḥif, ragga* pl. *-aat* coll. *ragg.*

torture – **1.** *εaδaab, marmara.* Life with her is just torture. *l-ḥayaat wiyyaaha εaδaab bass.* **2.** *taεδiib.* Confessions obtained by torture are illegal. *l-iεtiraafaat il-titḥaṣṣal bit-taεδiib muu qaanuuniyya.*

to torture – *εaδδab (i taεδiib).* The police tortured him to get a confession. *š-širṭa εaδδiboo ḥatta yaaxδuun minna εtiraaf.*

to **toss** – **1.** *šimar (u šamur).* Toss me the ball over here. *šmur-li ṭ-ṭooba li-hnaa.* **2.** *tgaḷḷab (u tguḷḷub).* Last night I tossed and turned all night long. *l-baarḥa bil-leel δalleet atgaḷḷab b-ifraaši.*

tot – *ṣġayyruun* pl. *-iin.* She's just a tiny tot. *baεadha ṣġayyruuna.*

total – *majmuuε* pl. *majaamiiε, yakuun* pl. *-aat.* Subtract ten from the total. *ʔiṭraḥ εašra mnil-majmuuε.* — My total earnings for this month were two hundred dollars. *majmuuε il-ḥaṣṣalta haš-šahar miiteen doolaar.*

to total – **1.** *waṣṣal (i).* His income totals two thousand dollars a year. *daxla ywaṣṣil ʔalfeen doolaar bis-sana.* **2.** *ḥisab (i ḥsaab), jimaε (a jamiε).* Let's total up our expenses for the month. *xalli niḥsib maṣruufaatna maal iš-šahar.*

to **totter** – *tmaayal (a tamaayul).* The old man got up and tottered toward the door. *š-šaayib gaam w-itmaayal lil-baab.*

tottering – *mitdaaεi.* The bridge is tottering. *j-jisir mitdaaεi.*

touch – **1.** *ṭaxxa* pl. *-aat.* She jumps at the slightest touch. *tugmaz min ʔaqall ṭaxxa.* or ***tugmaz bass waaḥid ygiisha.* **2.** *malmas.* Silk is soft to the touch. *l-ḥariir naaεim il-malmas.* **3.** *nugṭa* pl. *nugaaṭ.* The soup still needs a touch of salt. *š-šoorba baεadha tiḥtaaj fadd nugṭat miliḥ.* **4.** *ʔaθar* pl. *ʔaaθaar.* The patient has a touch of fever. *l-mariiδ εinda ʔaθar iṣxuuna.*

**The game was touch and go towards the end. *natiijat is-sibaaq čaanat imεalliga.*

to get in touch with – *ttiṣal (i ttiṣaal) b-.* I have to get in touch with him right away. *laazim attiṣil bii ḥaalan.*

to touch – *gaas (i), ṭaxx (u ṭaxx).* Please don't touch that! *baḷḷa la-tgiisha l-haay.* — He won't touch liquor. *ma-ygiis il-mašruub.*

**I touched him for two dinars. *šilaεit minna diinaareen.* or *tdaayanit minna diinaareen.*

to touch off – *ʔadda (i taʔdiya) ʔila.* His remarks touched off a violent argument. *mulaaḥaδaata ʔaddat ʔila fadd jadal εaniif.*

to touch on – **1.** *šaar (i) ʔila, ṭṭarraq (a) ʔila.* The speaker touched on many points during his talk. *l-muḥaaδir šaar ʔila εiddat nuqaaṭ ib-ḥadiiθa.* **2.** *wuṣal (a wuṣuul) ʔila.* His remarks touch on blasphemy. *ḥačya yooṣal ʔila darajt il-kufur.*

to touch up – *sawwa (i) rituuš l-.* They haven't touched up the picture yet. *baεad li-hassa ma-sawwoo-lha rituuš liṣ-ṣuura.*

touched – *mašxuuṭ.* Don't mind him! He's a little touched. *la-tdiir-la baal, haaδa mašxuuṭ.*

to be touched – *tʔaθθar (i taʔaθθur)* She was deeply touched by the story. *tʔaθθrat kulliš imnil-ḥčaaya.*

**I was deeply touched by his kindness. *luṭfa ʔaxjalni.*

touchy – **1.** *mitnarfiz.* She's very touchy. *hiyya kulliš mitnarfiza.* **2.** *ḥassaas.* That's a very touchy subject. *haaδa fadd mawδuuε kulliš ḥassaas.*

tough – **1.** *qawi.* The meat is awfully tough. *l-laḥam kulliš qawi.* **2.** *ṣaεub.* That's a tough assignment. *haay fadd šaġla ṣaεba.* **3.** *larr.* He's a real tough character. *huwwa fadd waaḥid ʔabu jaasim larr.* **4.** *suuʔ.* He's had tough luck. *jaabah suuʔ ḥaδδ.*

**That's a tough nut to crack. *haay fadd muškila ma-tinḥall.*

to **toughen** – *εallam (i) εal-xušuuna.* A year in the army will toughen him. *fadd sana bij-jeeš tεallma εal-xušuuna.*

tour – *jawla* pl. *-aat.* He made a tour through Europe and Asia. *sawwa jawla b-ʔawruppa wib-ʔaasya.*

to tour – *jaal (u jawla).* The troupe is now touring South America. *l-firqa hassa da-tjuul ʔamriika j-jinuubiyya.*

tourist – *saayiḥ* pl. *suwwaaḥ, siyyaaḥ.* Many tourists come here during the summer. *hwaaya suwwaaḥ yijuun ihnaa ʔaθnaaʔ iṣ-ṣeef.*

tourist class – *darajat is-siyaaḥa, daraja θaanya.*

to **tow** – *jarr (u jarr).* Can you tow my boat over to that side? *baḷḷa tigdar itjurr il-balam maali l-δaak iṣ-ṣoob?*

toward(s) – **1.** *b-ittijaah, εala ttijaah.* He drove off toward Karrada. *saaq b-ittijaah il-karraada.* **2.** *qariib, wujj.* I'll be there towards evening. *ʔakuun ihnaak qariib il-miġrib.* **3.** *wiyya, naḥu.* He was very nice toward me. *čaan kulliš laṭiif wiyyaaya.*

towel – *paškiir* pl. *pašaakiir, xaawli* pl. *-iyyaat, manšafa* pl. *manaašif.*

tower – *burij* pl. *braaj.* Lightning struck the tower last night. *ṣ-ṣaaεiqa nizlat εal-burij il-baarḥa bil-leel.*

town – **1.** *wlaaya* pl. *-aat, madiina* pl. *mudun, balda* pl. *-aat.* What's the name of this town? *hal-wlaaya š-isimha?* **2.** *baladi**. He's a member of the town council. *huwwa εaδu majlis baladi.*

tow rope – *ḥabil* (pl. *ḥbaal) maal jarr.*

tow truck – *saaḥiba* pl. *-aat.* Send me a tow truck. *dizz-li s-saaḥiba.*

toxic – *saamm.* These fumes are toxic. *hal-ġaazaat saamma.*

toy – *malaaεiib, laεεaaba* pl. *-aat* coll. *laεεaab.* I'll bring him some toys. *raḥ-ajiib-la malaaεiib.*

to toy – *ṣufan (u).* I was toying with this idea. *činit da-ʔaṣfun ib-hal-fikra.*

trace – *ʔaθar* pl. *ʔaaθaar.* The police found traces of poison in the food. *š-šurṭa ligaw ʔaθar simm bil-ʔakil.* — He disappeared without leaving a trace. *xtifa bala ma-yitruk ʔaθar.*

to trace – **1.** *ttabbaε (a tatabbuε), qtifa (i qtifaaʔ).* They traced him by his footsteps. *ttabbiεoo b-ʔaaθaar ʔaqdaama.* or *qtifaw ʔaaθaar ʔaqdaama.* **2.** *nisab (i nisba).* We traced the story to him. *nisabna l-iʒčaaya ʔila.* **3.** *stansax (i stinsaax).* Did you trace the floor plan? *stansaxit muxaṭṭaṭ il-binaaya?*

tracer – *taʔkiid.* We'll send a tracer after that letter. *raʒ-indizz taʔkiid ɛala δaak il-kitaab.*

trachoma – *traaxooma.*

tracing paper – *waraq istinsaax.*

track – *ʔaθar* pl. *ʔaaθaar.* There were many animal tracks around the spring. *čaan ʔaku ʔaaθaar ʒayawaanaat ihwaaya ʒawl il-ɛeen.* **2.** *darub* pl. *druub.* There is an old track in the desert which leads to the well. *ʔaku darub ɛatiig biṣ-ṣaʒraaʔ yʔaddi lil-biir.* **3.** *xaṭṭ* pl. *xuṭuuṭ, sičča* pl. *sičač.* The train will arrive on Track Two. *l-qiṭaar yooṣal ɛal-xaṭṭ iθ-θaani.* — The tracks between Hilla and Kufa are being repaired. *s-sičča been il-ʒilla wil-kuufa da-tiṭṣallaʒ.* **4.** *zanjiil* pl. *znaajiil.* The left track on the tractor is broken. *z-zanjiil il-ṣafʒat il-yisra maal l-itraaktar magṭuuɛ.* **5.** *ttijaah* pl. *-aat.* You're on the right track. *ʔinta mittijih bil-ittijaah iṣ-ṣaʒiiʒ* or *******ʔinta maaši zeen.*

**I'm afraid you're entirely off the track. *ʔaɛtiqid ʔinta maaši ġalaṭ.*

to keep track of – **1.** *δ̣ubaṭ (u δ̣abuṭ).* Keep close track of your expenses. *ʔiδ̣buṭ maṣruufaatak.* **2.** *raaqab (i mu.aaqaba).* The police kept track of him. *š-šurṭa raaqbata.*

to track – *ttabbaɛ (a tatabbuɛ) ʔaθar.* We tracked the fox to his lair. *ttabbiɛna ʔaθar iθ-θaɛlab lil-ġaar maala.*

to track up – *waṣṣax (i).* You're tracking up the kitchen with your feet. *ʔinta da-twaṣṣix gaaɛ il-muṭbax ib-rijlak.*

tract – **1.** *qiṭɛa* pl. *qiṭaɛ, muqaaṭaɛa* pl. *-aat.* Several oil companies are prospecting in this tract. *ɛiddat šarikaat nafuṭ da-tnaqqib ib-hal-muqaaṭaɛa.* **2.** *kurraasa* pl. *-aat.* The chamber of commerce published a tract on the oil question. *ġurfat it-tijaara nišrat kurraasa ɛan muškilat in-nafuṭ.* **3.** *jihaaz* pl. *ʔajhiza.* Her digestive tract is weak. *jihaaz il-haδ̣um maalha δ̣aɛiif.*

traction – *saʒib.* Rear-engined cars have better traction than others. *s-sayyaaraat illi makiinatha li-wara saʒibha aʒsan min ġeerha.*

tractor – *traaktar* pl. *-aat.*

trade – **1.** *tijaara.* Our trade with the Far East has fallen off. *tijaaratna wiyya š-šarq il-ʔaqṣa qallat.* **2.** *ṣanɛa* pl. *ṣanaayiɛ, mihna* pl. *mihan.* The boy has to learn a trade. *l-walad laazim yitɛallam fadd ṣanɛa.* — I'm a butcher by trade *mihinti gaṣṣaab.* **3.** *šuġuḷ, maɛmiil.* He's taking away my trade. *kassad ɛalayya šuġḷi.* **4.** *tijaari*.* They published new trade regulations. *ʔaṣdiraw ʔanδ̣ima tijaariyya jdiida.*

to trade – **1.** *baddal (i tabdiil).* I've traded my typewriter for a bicycle. *baddalit ʔaalt iṭ-ṭaabiɛa maalti b-paaysikil.* **2.** *taajar (i tijaara).* Iraq trades mostly with England. *l-ɛiraaq ytaajir ɛal-ʔakθar wiyya ʔingiltara.*

trader – *taajir* pl. *tujjaar.*

tradesman – *dukkaanči* pl. *-iyya.*

trade wind – *riiʒ tijaari* pl. *riyaaʒ tijaariyya.*

tradition – *taqliid* pl. *taqaaliid.* This is a tradition we have been following for centuries. *haaδa fadd taqliid ʔiʒna taabɛii min ɛuṣuur.*

traditional – *taqliidi*.*

traffic – **1.** *muruur.* Traffic is heavy on Rashid Street. *l-muruur qawiyya b-šaariɛ ir-rašiid.* **2.** *tijaara.* The United Nations is trying to control the traffic in narcotics. *hayʔat il-ʔumam itriid tuδ̣buṭ tijaarat il-muxaddiraat.*

**This street is closed to traffic. *haaδa š-šaariɛ masduud.*

traffic jam – *zdiʒaam* (pl. *-aat) sayyaaraat.*

traffic light – *ʔaδ̣wiyat* (pl. *-aat) muruur.*

tragedy – **1.** *faajiɛa* pl. *fawaajiɛ.* What a tragedy the accident was! *šloon faajiɛa čaan il-ʒaadiθ!* **2.** *ruwaaya* (pl. *-aat) muʒzina.* The Baghdad Theatre Group is presenting a tragedy this week. *l-firqa t-tamθiiliyya l-baġdaadiyya raʒ-itqaddim ruwaaya muʒzina hal-isbuuɛ.*

tragic – *muʔlim, mufjiɛ.* That accident was tragic. *δaak il-ʒaadiθ čaan muʔlim.*

trail – **1.** *ṭariiq* pl. *ṭuruq.* The trail leads into the woods. *ṭ-ṭariiq yʔaddi l-daaxil il-ġaaba.* **2.** *ʔaθar* pl. *ʔaaθaar.* A trail of blood caught their eye. *ʔaθar imnid-damm lifat naδ̣arhum.*

**The police are on his trail. *š-šurṭa mɛaqqbata* or *š-šurṭa waraa.*

to trail – *liʒag (a).* Somebody trailed me all the way home. *fadd waaʒid liʒagni ṭuul iṭ-ṭariiq lil-beet.*

train – **1.** *qiṭaar* pl. *-aat.* When does the train leave? *šwakit yitʒarrak il-qiṭaar?* **2.** *dyaal* pl. *-aat.* The bride wore a dress with a long train. *l-ɛaruus libsat badla biiha dyaal ṭuwiil.*

to train – **1.** *darrab (u tadriib).* He trains the new employees. *huwwa ydarrub il-muwaδ̣δ̣afiin il-jiddad.* **2.** *tmarran (a tamriin).* He's been training for the fight for weeks. *ṣaar-la ʔasaabiiɛ da-yitmarran lil-mulaakama.*

trainer – **1.** *mudarrib* pl. *-iin.* He's a boxing trainer. *haaδa mudarrib mulaakama.* **2.** *ṭiyyaara* (pl. *-aat) maal tadriib.* That's a trainer for new pilots. *haay ṭiyyaara maal tadriib liṭ-ṭayyaariin ij-jiddad.*

training – **1.** *tamriin, tadriib.* He's still in training. *baɛda taʒt il-tamriin.* **2.** *tadriib.* The Post Office Department maintains a training school for its employees. *mudiiriyyat il-bariid ɛidha madrasat tadriib il-mustaxdamiiha.*

trait – *ṣifa* pl. *-aat, xiṣla* pl. *xiṣal.* She has many fine traits. *ɛidha hwaaya ṣifaat zeena.*

traitor – *xuuʔin* pl. *-iin, xwaana, xawana.*

tramp – *mhatlaf* pl. *-iin, mitšarrid* pl. *-iin.* He looks like a tramp. *huwwa ɛabaalak fadd waaʒid imhatlaf.*

to **trample** – *dawwas (i tadwiis) t-.* The horses trampled the children. *l-xeel dawwisat il-ʔaṭfaal.*

transaction – *muɛaamala* pl. *-aat.* We completed the transaction in the lawyer's office. *kammalna l-muɛaamala b-maktab il-muʒaami.*

to **transcribe** – *stansax (i stinsaax).* Can you transcribe this into Roman script? *tigdar tistansix haaδa ʔila ʒruuf laatiiniyya?*

transcript – *waθiiqa* pl. *waθaayiq.* The registrar requires a transcript of my studies in Baghdad. *musajjil ij-jaamiɛa ṭilab waθiiqa b-diraasti b-baġdaad.*

transfer – *naqil.* I have asked for a transfer to Baghdad. *ṭlabit naqil il-baġdaad.*

to transfer – **1.** *baddal (i tabdiil).* Where do we transfer buses? *ween inbaddil il-paaṣ?* **2.** *niqal (u naqil) n-, ʒawwal (i taʒwiil).* The commander transferred half his forces to the front. *l-qaaʔid niqal nuṣṣ quwwaata lij-jabha.* — He transferred the property to her name. *ʒawwal milkiyyat il-muluk ʔilha.* — He'd like to be transferred. *yriid yinniqil.*

to **transform** – *ʒawwal (i taʒwiil).* This station transforms oil fuel into electric energy. *hal-muʒaṭṭa tʒawwil iṭ-ṭaaqa l-ʒaraariyya maal in-nafuṭ ila quwwa kahrabaaʔiyya.*

transformer – *muʒawwil* pl. *-aat.* The transformer in my radio is burnt out. *l-muʒawwil bir-raadyo maall ʒtirag.*

transfusion – *naqil.* The patient needs a blood transfusion. *l-mariiδ̣ yinraad-la naqil damm.*

transient – *maarr* pl. *-iin, ɛaabir* pl. *-iin.* The airport has sleeping and dining facilities for transients. *l-maṭaar imjahhaz ib-maʒall noom w-ʔakil lir-rukkaab il-maarriin.*

transit – *traansiit.* These goods are in transit. *hal-biδ̣aaɛa traansiit.*

transition – *ntiqaal* pl. *-aat.* Our country is in a period of transition. *bilaadna b-fatrat intiqaal.*

to **translate** – *tarjam (u tarjuma).* How do you translate this? *šloon ittarjum haay?*

translation – *tarjuma* pl. *taraajum.*

translator – *mutarjim* pl. *-iin.*

transmission – *geer* pl. *-aat, transmišin* pl. *-aat.* Something seems to be wrong with the transmission of my car. *l-geer maal sayyaarti bii šii.*

transmitter – *mursila* pl. *-aat.* The Baghdad Radio transmitters are at Abu-Ghrayb. *mursilaat maʒaṭṭat ʔiδaaɛat baġdaad b-abu ġreeb.*

transparent – **1.** *šaffaaf.* The water is quite transparent here. *l-maay šaffaaf ihnaa.* **2.** *makšuuf.* His methods are transparent. *ʔasaaliiba makšuufa.*

to **transplant** – *niqal (u naqil).* I'm going to transplant the seedlings today. *raʒ-ʔanqul il-ištuul il-yoom.*

transport – **1.** *tasfiir.* Our primary concern was the transport of troops. *hammna l-ʔawwal čaan tasfiir ij-jiyuuš.* **2.** *markab* (pl. *maraakib) naqil.* Two transports were sunk by submarines. *l-ġawwaaṣaat ġirgaw markabeen naqil.* **3.** *ṭayyaarat* (pl. *-aat) naqil.* He's piloting a transport. *da-yquud ṭayyaarat naqil.*

to transport – *niqal (u naqil)*. The Navy will transport these troops. *l-baẓriyya raẓ-tunqul haj-jiyuuš*.

transportation – *waaṣṭat naqil*. I'll need some transportation. *yinraad-li waaṣṭat naqil*.

trap – 1. *fuxx* pl. *fxaax*, *šarak* pl. *ʔašraak*. The police set a trap for him. *š-surṭa niṣboo-la fuxx*. 2. *miṣyaada* pl. *-aat*. We caught three rats in the trap. *ṣidna tlaθ ijreediyya bil-miṣyaada*.

to trap – *ẓiṣar (i ẓaṣir)* The boys trapped the cat in a corner. *l-wulid ẓiṣraw il-bazẓuuna biẓ-ẓuwiyya*.

trash – *zibil* pl. *ẓbaalaat*. Burn the trash! *ʔiẓrig iẓ-zibil*. -- We don't buy such trash. *ʔiẓna ma-ništiri hiiči ẓbaalaat*.

travel – *safar* pl. *-aat*. Travel in winter is difficult. *s-safar ṣaɛub biš-šita*. -- Let him tell you about his travels. *xal-yiẓčii-lak ɛala safraata*.

to travel – 1. *saafar (i safar)*. I traveled a lot when I was in the Army. *saafart ihwaaya min činit bij-jeeš*. 2. *ftarr (a farr)*, *daar (u dawaraan)*. He has traveled all over Europe. *ftarr kull ʔawruppa*. 3. *saaẓ (i siyaaẓa)*. She has been traveling for a month. *ṣaar-ilha šahar da-tsiiẓ*.

**He must have been traveling sixty miles an hour. *laazim čaan da-ysuuẓ sittiin miil bis-saaɛa*.

traveller – *musaafir* pl. *-iin*.

travelling salesman – *bayyaaɛ*, *baayiɛ mitjawwil* pl. *bayyaaɛa mitjawwiliin*.

tray – *ṣiiniyya* pl. *ṣawaani*. Put the cups on the tray. *ẓuṭṭ il-kuubaat biṣ-ṣiiniyya*.

treason – *xiyaana*.

treasure – *kanẓ* pl. *knuuẓ*.

treasurer – *ʔamiin* (pl. *ʔumanaaʔ*) *ṣanduug*.

treasury – 1. *xaẓiina* pl. *xaẓaayin*. The country's treasury is almost empty. *xaẓiint id-dawla taqriiban faarġa*. 2. *maaliyya*. He works in the Treasury Department. *yištuġul ib-wizaart il-maaliyya*.

treat – *laθθa* pl. *-aat*. It's a treat to read his books. *qraayat kutba laθθa*. **This time the treat's on me. *hal-marra ɛalayya*. or *hal-marra ɛala ẓsaabi*.

to treat – 1. *ɛaamal (i muɛaamala)*. He treats me like a child. *yɛaamilni ɛabaalak ṭifil*. 2. *ɛaalaj (i muɛaalaja)*. Dr. Ahmad is treating me. *d-daktoor aẓmad da-yɛaalijni*. 3. *difaɛ (a dafiɛ) ɛala*. He treated everybody. *difaɛ ɛal-kull*.

to treat lightly – *stixaff (i stixfaaf)*, *stahwan (i stihaana)*. You shouldn't treat that so lightly. *ma-laazim tistixiff ib-haaδa*.

treatment – *tadaawi*, *muɛaalaja*. I'm going to the doctor's tomorrow for treatment. *ʔaani raayiẓ liṭ-ṭabiib baačir lit-tadaawi*. 2. *muɛaamala* pl. *-aat*. I don't like that kind of treatment. *ma-tiɛjibni hiiči muɛaamala*.

treaty – *muɛaahada* pl. *-aat*. The treaty has to be ratified by the Senate. *l-muɛaahada laazim tiṭṣaddaq min majlis il-ʔaɛyaan*.

tree – *šajara* pl. *-aat*, *ʔašjaar* coll. *šajar*. We have a tree in front of our house. *ɛidna šajara giddaam il-beet*.

trellis – *qamariyya* pl. *-aat*.

to tremble – *rijaf (i rajif)*. He trembled with fear. *rijaf imnil-xoof*.

tremendous – 1. *haaʔil*, *ɛaδiim*. That's a tremendous undertaking. *haaδa mašruuɛ haaʔil*. --There's a tremendous difference between them. *ʔaku xtilaaf ɛaδiim beenaathum*. 2. *ɛaδiim*. They've just got out a tremendous new record. *ṭallɛaw iṣṭiwaana jdiida ɛaδiima*.

tremendously – *kulliš ihwaaya*. Social conditions have changed tremendously. *l-ʔaẓwaal il-ijtimaaɛiyya tġayyrat kulliš ihwaaya*.

tremor – 1. *hazza* pl. *-aat*. Several weak earth tremors took place yesterday. *ɛiddat hazzaat ʔarδiyya xafiifa ṣaarat il-baarẓa*. 2. *raɛša* pl. *-aat*, *rtiɛaaš* pl. *-aat*. He has a tremor in his hand. *ɛinda raɛša b-ʔiida*.

trench – *xandaq* pl. *xanaadiq*. Civilians were forced to dig trenches. *l-madaniyyiin njubraw yuẓufruun xanaadiq*.

trend – *ttijaah* pl. *-aat*. The trend in Iraq is to wear Western suits. *l-ittijaah bil-ɛiraaq hassa naẓu libs il-malaabis il-ġarbiyya*.

to trespass – *tɛadda (a)*. You were trespassing on my property. *ʔinta činit da-titɛadda min gaaɛi*.

trestle – *skalla* pl. *-aat*. The workmen set up a trestle. *l-ɛummaal nuṣbaw iskalla*.

trial – 1. *muẓaakama* pl. *-aat*. The case was never

brought to trial. *d-daɛwa ʔabadan ma-nɛirδat lil-muẓaakama*. -- He's on trial for murder. *huwwa hassa taẓt il-muẓaakama ɛan qaδiyyat qatil*. 2. *tajruba* pl. *tajaarub*. He's been through a lot of trial and tribulation. *marr b-ihwaaya tajaarub w-šadaaʔid*. -- Children learn through trial and error. *l-ʔaṭfaal yitɛallmuun bit-tajruba*. -- I took the radio on trial. *qbalit ir-raadyo ɛala šarṭ it-tajruba*.

to give a trial – *jarrab (u)*. Why don't you give the car a trial? *leeš ma-tjarrub is-sayyaara fadd mudda?* -- We'll give you a week's trial. *raẓ-injarrbak fadd isbuuɛ*.

triangle – *muθallaθ* pl. *-aat*. A triangle has three sides. *l-muθallaθ bii tlaθ aδaaɛ*.

triangular – *muθallaθ iš-šikil*. The race was run on a triangular course. *s-sibaaq jira ɛala saaẓa muθallaθat iš-šikil*.

tribal – *ɛašaaʔiri**. The group is studying tribal customs. *j-jamaaɛa da-tidrus il-ɛaadaat il-ɛašaaʔiriyya*.

tribe – *ɛašiira* pl. *ɛašaayir*, *qabiila* pl. *qabaaʔil*. He's the head of a tribe from the South. *huwwa šeex ɛašiira bij-jinuub*.

tribesman – *ʔibin ɛašaayir*.

tribunal – *hayʔat* (pl. *-aat*) *taẓkiim*. We'll take the dispute to an international tribunal. *raẓ-naaxuδ han-nizaaɛ il-hayʔat taẓkiim dawliyya*.

tributary – *raafid* pl. *rawaafid*. The Diyala river is a tributary of the Tigris. *nahr idyaala min rawaafid nahar dijla*.

tribute – 1. *xaawa* pl. *-aat*, *jizya* pl. *-aat*. The Assyrians exacted tribute from many nations. *l-ʔaašuuriyyiin furδaw xaawa min ihwaaya duwal*. 2. *madiẓ*. He paid you a fine tribute. *midaẓak madiẓ zeen*. or **ʔaθna ɛaleek*.

trick – 1. *ẓiila* pl. *ẓiyal*. I'm on to his tricks. *ʔaani ʔaɛruf ẓiyala*. -- Do you know any card tricks? *tuɛruf ẓiila maal waraq?* 2. *šaṭaara* pl. *-aat*. Don't try your tricks on me! *la-tẓaawil itbiiɛ šaṭaartak ib-raasi*. 3. *nukta* pl. *nukat*. He played a trick on us. *sawwa biina nukta*. 4. *maawi*. Watch out, there's a trick to that! *diir baalak haay biiha waawi!* 5. *darub* pl. *druub*. He knows all the tricks. *yindall kull il-idruub*. 6. *fann* pl. *fnuun*. There's a trick to fixing this dish. *ṭabix haj-ʔakla yinraad-la fann*. 7. *ẓigri**. Have you seen Ali's trick box? *šift iẓ-ṣanduug is-ẓiẓri maal ɛali?* **I've got a trick knee. *rukubti maɛyuuba*. **There's no trick to it. *haay ma-yinraad-ilha šii*. or *haay šaġla. or haay baṣiiṭa*.

to trick – *qašmar (u qašmara)*. He tricked me again. *qašmarni marrt il-lux*. -- They tricked us into signing. *qašmaroona w-xalloona nimδi*.

to trickle – *xarr (u xarr)*. The water trickled out of the faucet. *l-maay xarr imnil-buuri*.

trickster – *ġaššaaš* pl. *-iin*, *ẓayyaal* pl. *-iin*. He has a reputation for being a trickster. *haaδa mašhuur ib-kawma ġaššaaš*.

tricky – *daqiiq*. That's a tricky question. *haaδa fadd mawδuuɛ daqiiq*.

trifle – 1. *šaqa*, *liɛib*. That's no trifle. *haay muu šaqa*. 2. *šii ṭafiif* pl. *ʔašyaaʔ ṭafiifa*, *šii taafih* pl. *ʔašyaaʔ taafha*. Don't bother about trifles. *la-tihtamm bil-ʔašyaaʔ iṭ-ṭafiifa*. 3. *šwayya*, *ʔismin*, *šaɛra*. The trousers are a trifle too long. *l-panṭaruun išwayya ṭwiil*. -- The food was good but just a trifle salty. *l-ʔakil čaan zeen bass ʔismin maaliẓ*. **He was only trifling with her. *čaan da-yilɛab ib-raasha*. **He's no man to trifle with. *haaδa fadd waaẓid yinẓisib-la ẓsaab*.

trifling – *ṭafiif*, *taafih*. That's such a trifling matter! *haaδa šii kulliš ṭafiif*.

trigger – *zinaad* pl. *-aat*. The trigger on this pistol has a light pull. *l-iznaad maal hal-musaddas sahil yindaas*.

trigonometry – *ɛilm il-muθallaθaat*, *ẓsaab il-muθallaθaat*.

trim – 1. *ẓaašya* pl. *ẓwaaši*. Most cars now have chrome trim. *ʔakθar is-sayyaaraat biiha ẓwaaši min neekal*. 2. *taɛdiil* pl. *-aat*. My hair isn't long, but it needs a trim. *šaɛri muu ṭuwiil, laakin yiẓtaaj taɛdiil*. 3. *mrattab*. She always looks very trim. *hiyya daaʔiman kulliš imrattba*. 4. *naẓiif*. She has a trim figure. *ɛidha qiwaam naẓiif*.

to trim – 1. *ɛaddal (i)*. Just trim my hair a little. *bass ɛaddil šaɛri šwayya*. 2. *garṭaf (u* *garṭafa).* I'm trimming my mustache. *da-agarṭuf iswaarbi.* **3.** *ʒawwag (u ʒwaaga) t-.* She trimmed her hat with feathers. *ʒawwgat šafqatha bir-riiš.*

trimming - 1. *naqiš.* The trimming on her dress is red. *n-naqiš εala badlatha ʔaʒmar.* **2.** *ʒbaaša* pl. *-aat.* We had turkey and all the trimmings. *ʔakalna diič hindi w-iʒbaašaata.*
 **He gave me a trimming. *buṣaṭni basṭa zeena.*
 **We really got a trimming in our last game. *ṣudug tdammarna b-liεbatna l-ʔaxiira.*

trip - 1. *safra* pl. *-aat.* How was your trip? *šloon čaanat safirtak?* -- Have a pleasant trip. *ʔatmannaa-lak safra zeena.* **2.** *rooʒa* pl. *-aat, rajεa* pl. *-aat.* The trip there was quicker than the trip back. *r-rooʒa čaanat ʔashal imnir-rajεa.*
 to trip - 1. *εiθar (a εaθir).* Be careful not to trip on the stairs. *diir baalak la-tiεθar bid-daraj.* **2.** *δ̣irab (u) band.* He tripped me. *δ̣irabni band.*
 to trip up - 1. *ligaf (u laguf), ṣaad (i ṣeed).* My professor tripped me up on that question. *l-ʔustaaδ ligafna b-has-suʔaal.* **2.** *ġilaṭ (a ġalaṭ).* I must have tripped up somewhere. *laazim iġlaṭit ib-fadd makaan.*

tripe - 1. *karša.* I can't eat tripe. *ma-agdar aakul il-karša.* **2.** *laġwa, ʒači faaṣix.* That's just tripe! *haaδi laġwa!*

to **triple** - *δ̣aaεaf (u) itlaθ marraat.* He tripled his earnings. *δ̣aaεaf ʔarbaaʒa tlaθ marraat.*

triplet - **She had triplets. *jaabat itlaaθa.*

tripod - *seepaaya* pl. *-aat.*

trite - *baayix.* That joke's too trite. *han-nukta ṣaarat baayxa.*

triumph - *ntiṣaar* pl. *-aat.*

triumphant - *muntaṣir.*

trivial - *taafih, ṭafiif.* That's a trivial matter. *haay fadd šii taafih.*

trolley - *traam* pl. *-aat.* In Cairo they still have trolleys. *baεad ʔaku traamaat bil-qaahira.*

troop - 1. *firqa* pl. *firaq.* My nephew is in a boy scout troop. *ʔibn axuuya b-firqat il-kaššaafa.* **2.** *jundi* pl. *junuud.* Get the troops out of the sun! *xalli j-junuud la-yoogfuun biš-šamis!*
 to troop in - *xašš (u xašš).* The students all trooped in when the bell rang. *t-talaamiiδ xaššaw kullhum min dagg ij-jaraṣ.*

trophy - *kaʔs* pl. *kuʔuus.* Our school took the trophy this year. *madrasatna ʔaxδat il-kaʔs has-sana.*

Tropic of Cancer - *madaar is-saraṭaan.*

Tropic of Capricorn. *madaar ij-jadi.*

tropical - *stiwaaʔi*.* Central Africa has a tropical climate. *ʔafriiqya l-wuṣṭa jawwha stiwaaʔi.*

tropics - *l-manṭiqa l-istiwaaʔiyya.* Much of Africa lies within the tropics. *ʔakθar ʔafriiqya waaqεa bil-manṭiqa l-istiwaaʔiyya.*

trot - *xabab.* That horse has a nice trot. *hal-iʒṣaan xababa ʒilu.*
 to trot - *xabb (u xabb).* The horse trotted around the field. *l-iʒṣaan xabb ʒawl is-saaʒa.*

trouble - 1. *muškila* pl. *-aat.* What's your trouble? *šinu muškiltak?* or ***šbiik?* **2.** *ʔizεaaj* pl. *-aat.* This trouble is quite unnecessary. *haaδa fadd ʔizεaaj ʔabad ma-ʔila muujib.* **3.** *δ̣tiraab* pl. *-aat; qalaaqil.* There's been trouble up at Mosul. *ʔaku δ̣tiraabaat bil-muuṣil.* **4.** *zaʒma* pl. *-aat.* Don't put yourself to any trouble. *la-tjurr zaʒma.* or ***la-titkallaf.* **5.** *warṭa* pl. *-aat.* He's in trouble again. *hamm wugaε ib-warṭa.* or ***hammeena twarraṭ.*
 **What's the trouble? *š-ṣaar?* or *šaku?*
 to trouble - 1. *ʔazεaj (i ʔizεaaj), dawwax (u tdawwux) raas.* I'm sorry, but I'll have to trouble you again. *mitʔassif bass ʔaani miδ̣ṭarr ʔaziεjak marra lux.* **2.** *šawwaš (i tašwiiš) t-.* The news troubled me very much. *l-ʔaxbaar šawwšatni kulliš.* **3.** *qilaq (i qalaq).* What's troubling you? Is it some bad news? *šinu l-qaalqak, ʔaku ʔaxbaar muu zeena?* or *šbiik mitšawwiš, ʔaku ʔaxbaar muu zeena?* **4.** *ʔaδδa (i ʔaδiyya).* My arm has been troubling me ever since my accident. *ʔiidi da-tʔaδδiini min ṣaar il-ʒaadiθ li-hassa.*
 **What's troubling you? Is it your eyes again? *šbiik, hamm iεyuunak?* or *šbiik mazεuuj, hamm iεyuunak?*
 **May I trouble you for a match? *tismaʒ-li b-šixxaaṭa?*

troubled - 1. *εasiir, εaṣiib.* We are living in troubled times. *da-nεiiš ib-ʔayyaam εasiira.* or *da-nεiiš ib-fadd zaman εaṣiib.* **2.** *qaliq.* I've been very troubled about his health lately. *ṣirit kulliš qaliq εala ṣiʒʒta bil-mudda l-ʔaxiira.*

troublesome - 1. *mdawwix.* My tooth has been troublesome. *sinni mdawwixni.* **2.** *muzεij, qallaaq.* That pupil is troublesome today. *hat-tilmiiδ muzεij il-yoom.*

trough - 1. *ʒooδ̣ (pl. ʔaʒwaaδ̣) saqi.* The watering trough leaks. *ʒooδ̣ is-saqi da-yxurr.* **2.** *miεlaf* pl. *maεaalif.* Throw some more food in the trough. *ʒuṭṭ baεad εalaf bil-miεlaf.*

trousers - *panṭaruun* pl. *-aat.*

trousseau - *jhaaz* pl. *-aat.*

trowel - *maalaj* pl. *mwaalij, ʒaffaara* pl. *-aat.*

truce - *hudna* pl. *-aat.* The two countries agreed to a truce. *d-dawilteen ittifqaw εala hudna.*

truck - *loori* pl. *-iyyaat.* Where can I park my truck? *ween ʔagdar awagguf il-loori maali?*
 to truck - *niqal (u) bil-loori, wadda (i) bil-loori.* He trucks his produce to the warehouse. *da-yinqul l-imxaδ̣δ̣ar maala lil-εalwa bil-loori.*

trucker - *saayiq loori* pl. *suwwaaq looriyyaat.* The truckers went on strike today. *suwwaaq il-looriyyaat sawwaw ʔiδ̣raab il-yoom.*

truck farm - *mazraεat* (pl. *-aat*) *xuδ̣ar.*

truck farmer - *zarraaε xuδ̣ar.*

truck farming - *zariε xuδ̣ar.*

true - 1. *ṣudug, ṣaʒiiʒ.* Is that story true? *hal iʒčaaya ṣuδug?* -- He is a true scholar. *huwwa ṭaalib εilim min ṣudug.* **2.** *muxlaṣ, ṣudug.* He's a true friend. *huwwa ṣadiiq muxlaṣ.* -- He stayed true to his principles. *buqa muxliṣ il-mabaadʔa.* **3.** *ṭibq il-ʔaṣil.* I swear this is a true copy. *ʔašhad bi-ʔan haay nusxa ṭibq il-ʔaṣil.*

truffle - *čimaaya* pl. *-aat.* coll. *čima.*

truly - *ʒaqiiqatan, bil-ʒaqiiqa.* I am truly sorry. *ʔaani mitʔassif ʒaqiiqatan.*

trumpet - *buuq* pl. *ʔabwaaq, buuri* pl. *bwaari.*

trunk - 1. *jiδiε* pl. *jδuuε.* The trunk of the tree is completely hollow. *jiδε iš-šajara kulla faariġ.* -- The human body consists of head, trunk, and limbs. *jisim il-ʔinsaan yitkawwan min raas w-jiδiε w-ʔaṭraaf.* **2.** *ṣanduug* pl. *ṣanaadiig.* Are the trunks packed yet? *ṣ-ṣanaadiig kullha matruusa loo baεad?* **3.** *čiswa* pl. *-aat, čisaw, panṭuroon* (pl. *-aat*) *riyaaδ̣a.* These trunks are too tight. *hač-čiswa kulliš δ̣ayyga.* **4.** *raʔiisi*.* The Karbala branch joins the trunk line at Hindiyya. *l-xaṭṭ il-farεi maal karbala yittiṣil bil-xaṭṭ ir-raʔiisi b-saddat il-hindiyya.*

truss - 1. *ʒzaam* pl. *ʒizim.* He has to wear a truss. *laazim yilbas iʒzaam.* **2.** *rabbaaṭ* pl. *-aat.* The new bridge is built with steel trusses. *j-jisir ij-jidiid mabni εala rabbaaṭaat min fuulaaδ.*

trust - 1. *θiqa.* I'm putting my trust in you. *ʔaani ʒaaṭṭ θiqti biik.* **2.** *wiṣaaya* pl. *-aat.* That orphan's money is in a trust. *fluus hal-yatiim maʒṭuuṭa taʒt il-wiṣaaya.* **3.** *ʔtimaan.* I'm investing my money in a trust company. *da-ašaġġil ifluusi b-šarikat iʔtimaan.*
 to trust - 1. *wiθaq (a θiqa) b-, ʔamman (i taʔmiin) b-.* I don't trust him. *ʔaani ma-ʔaθiq bii.* -- Can you trust me until payday? *tigdar itʔammin biyya l-yoom il-maεaaš?* **2.** *tʔammal.* I trust you slept well. *ʔatʔammal nimit zeen.*
 to trust to - *εtimad (i) εala.* You shouldn't trust too much to your memory. *ma-laazim hal-gadd tiεtimid εala δakirtak.*

trustee - *waṣi* pl. *ʔawṣiyaaʔ.* The judge appointed Ahmad as trustee for his nephew's estate. *l-qaaδ̣i εayyan ʔaʒmad waṣi εala ʔamlaak ibin ʔaxuu.*

trusteeship - *wiṣaaya.* This country was under trusteeship a long time. *had-dawla čaanat taʒt il-wiṣaaya mudda ṭuwiila.*

trustful - **He's too trustful. *yʔammin bin-naas ihwaaya.*

trustworthy - *ʔamiin* pl. *ʔumanaaʔ* That man isn't very trustworthy. *haada r-rijaal muu kulliš ʔamiin.*

truth - *ṣudug, ʒaqiiqa, ṣaʒiiʒ, ṣiʒʒa.* That's the truth. *haaδa iṣ-ṣudug.* -- I told him the plain truth. *gitt-la l-ʒaqiiqa miθil-ma hiyya.*

truthful - *ṣaadiq.* Ali is very truthful. *εali kulliš ṣaadiq.*

truthfulness - 1. *ṣidiq.* His truthfulness is beyond question. *ṣidqa ma-bii šakk.* **2.** *ṣiʒʒa.* I'm not challenging the truthfulness of that statement. *ma-da-ʔanaaqiš ṣiʒʒat it-taṣriiʒ.*

try - *muʒaawala* pl. *-aat.* They reached the mountaintop on the first try. *wuṣlaw il-qummat ij-jibal ib-ʔawwal muʒaawala.*
 to try - 1. *jarrab (u tajruba) t-.* I'd like to try it. *yiεjibni ʔajarrubha.* -- Have you tried this medicine yet? *jarrabit had-duwa loo baεad?* **2.** *ʒaawal (i muʒaawala).* Try to reach him in his

office. *zaawil tittiṣil bii b-daaʔirta.* 3. *δaag (u δoog) n-.* Try some of the peppers. I think you'll like them prepared this way. *δuug išwayya mnil-filfil, ʔaδinn yƐijbak maṭbuux hiiči.* 4. *zaakam (u muzaakama).* Who's going to try the accused? *minu raz-yzaakim il-muttaham?* 5. *šaaf (u šoof), naδar (u).* Which judge is trying the case? *yaa zaakim da-yšuuf id-daƐwa?*

to try on – *gaddar (i).* I'd like to try that suit on again. *ʔariid agaddir hal-qaaṭ marra lux.* or *ʔariid ʔašuuf marra lux išloon il-qaaṭ yugƐud Ɛalayya.*

to try out – *jarrab (u tajruba) t-.* I'm going to try out a new car. *raz-ʔajarrub fadd sayyaara jidiida.*

trying – *Ɛaṣiib.* Those were trying times. *haay ʔawqaat Ɛaṣiiba.*

tub – 1. *ṭašit* pl. *ṭšuut.* The wash is still in the tub. *l-ihduum baƐadha biṭ-ṭašit.* 2. *baanyo* pl. *-owaat.* Did you wash out the bath tub after you took a bath? *ġisalt il-baanyo baƐad-ma ʔaxaδit zammaam?*

tube – 1. *ʔinbuuba* pl. *-aat, buuri* pl. *-iyyaat.* They had to feed him through a tube. *δṭarraw yinṭuu ʔakal b-inbuuba.* 2. *čuub* pl. *-aat, čuup* pl. *-aat.* I need a new tube for my bicycle. *ʔaztaaj čuub jidiid lil-paaysikil maali.* 3. *tyuub* pl. *-aat, dabba* pl. *-aat.* I want a large tube of tooth paste. *ʔariid fadd ityuub čibiir maƐjuun maal isnuun.* 4. *lampa* pl. *-aat.* My radio needs a new tube. *r-raadyo maali yinraad-la lampa jidiida.*

tubercular – *masluul.*

tuberculosis – *sill.*

tubing – *buuri* pl. *bwaari.* I need two hundred meters of tubing. *ʔaztaaj miiteen matir buuri.*

tubular – *Ɛala šikil ʔinbuub, Ɛala šikil buuri.*

tuck – *kasra* pl. *-aat, ṭawya* pl. *-aat.* The dress needs some tucks at the waist. *n-nafnuuf yinraad-la čam kasra mnil-xiṣir.*

to tuck in – 1. *laflaf (i tliflif).* Mother used to tuck us in at night. *ʔummi čaanat tlaflifna bil-lizfaan bil-leel.* 2. *xaššaš (i taxšiiš) t-.* Your shirt tail is out; tuck it in your pants. *θoobak ṭaaliƐ; xaššiša bil-panṭuroon.*

to tuck up – *šaal (i šeel) n-.* She tucked up her skirts and ran. *šaalat iδyaalha w-rikδat.*

Tuesday – *yoom iθ-θilaaθaa, yoom it-tilaaθaa.* I'll be back on Tuesday. *ʔarjaƐ yoom it-tilaaθaa.*

tuft – 1. *kafša* pl. *-aat.* The squirrel has only one tuft of hair on its tail. *s-sinjaab Ɛinda bass kafšat šaƐar wazda b-δeela.* 2. *kooma* pl. *kuwam.* There's a rabbit behind that tuft of grass. *ʔaku ʔarnab wara koomt il-zašiiš δiič.* 3. *kaƐkuula* pl. *-aat, kaƐaakiil.* This type of pigeon has a tuft on its head. *han-nooƐ zamaam Ɛinda kaƐkuula.*

tug – *maatoor* pl. *-aat.* Two tugs are towing the barge. *maatooreen da-yjarruun id-duuba.*

to tug – *sazsal (i tsizsil), jarjar (i tjirjir).* Stop tugging at me! *bass Ɛaad itsazsil biyya!*

tug of war – *jarr il-zabil.* Who won the tug of war? *minu gilab ib-jarr il-zabil?*

tuition – *ʔujuur id-diraasa.* Have you paid your tuition yet? *dfaƐit ʔujuur id-diraasa loo bazad?*

tumble – *wagƐa* pl. *-aat, čuqlumba* pl. *-aat.* She took quite a tumble yesterday. *tčaqlibat fadd čuqlumba zeena l-baarza.*

to tumble down – *tčaqlab (a tčiqlib), tdaƐbal (a tdiƐbil).* He tumbled down the stairs. *tčaqlab imnid-daraj.*

tumbler – *glaaṣ* pl. *-aat, bardaaġ* pl. *baraadiiġ.* He brought me some water in a tumbler. *jaab-li šwayya maay ib-bardaaġ.*

tumor – *waram* pl. *wuruum.*

tune – *naġma* pl. *-aat, lazin* pl. *ʔalzaan.* Do you know that tune? *tuƐruf hal-lazin?*

**He keeps harping on the same tune. *yδill ydugg Ɛala nafs il-watar.*

in tune – *manṣuub.* Is your violin in tune? *l-kamanja maaltak manṣuuba?*

**Their government is in tune with the times. *niδam il-zukum maalhum yitlaaʔam wiyya z-zamaan.*

out of tune – 1. *našaaz.* She always sings out of tune. *daaʔiman itġanni našaaz.* 2. *ma-manṣuub.* The lute is out of tune. *l-Ɛuud ma-manṣuub.*

to tune in – *ṭallaƐ (i).* You haven't tuned the station in properly. *ʔinta ma-ṭallaƐt il-muzaṭṭa zeen.* or ***r-raadyo muu Ɛal-mazaṭṭa.*

to tune up – 1. *niṣab (u naṣub) ʔaalaat˜.* The orchestra is tuning up. *l-firqa da-tinṣub ʔaalaatha.* 2. *δubaṭ (u δabuṭ) n-, qassam (i taqsiim) t-.* Did you tune up the motor? *δubaṭṭ il-makiina?*

tuning – *naṣub.* The piano needs tuning. *l-ipyaano yinraad-la naṣub.*

Tunis – *tuunis.*

Tunisia – *tuunis.*

Tunisian – *tuunisi** pl. *-iyyiin.*

tunnel – *nafaq* pl. *ʔanfaaq.*

turban – *Ɛmaama* pl. *-aat, Ɛmaayim; laffa* pl. *-aat, čarraawiyya* pl. *-aat.*

turbine – *tarbiin* pl. *-aat.*

turbulence – *δṭiraab.* There's some turbulence ahead so we'll change course. *raz-inbaddil ittijaahna li-ʔan ʔaku δṭiraab bij-jaww giddaamna.*

turbulent – *miδṭirib.* It is a very turbulent situation. *l-zaala čaanat miδṭarba kulliš.*

Turcoman – *turkumaani* pl. *turkumaan.* Most Turcomans in Iraq live around Kirkuk. *ʔakθar it-turkumaan bil-Ɛiraaq ib-manṭiqat karkuuk.*

turf – *Ɛišib.*

Turk – *turki* pl. *ʔatraak.*

Turkey – *turkiya.*

turkey – *diič hindi* pl. *dyuuča hindiyya, Ɛališiiš* pl. *-aat.*

Turkish – *turki** pl. *ʔatraak.* Is he a Turkish citizen? *huwwa jinsiita turki.* -- How do you say it in Turkish? *šloon itguulha bit-turki?* -- I stopped by the Turkish bath to see Ali. *marreet bil-zammaam it-turki zatta ašuuf Ɛali.*

Turkish delight – *zalquum, luqum.*

Turkish towel – *xaawli* pl. *-iyyaat, paškiir* pl. *pašaakiir.*

turn – 1. *farra* pl. *-aat.* He gave the wheel a half turn. *farr ič-čarix nuṣṣ farra.* -- Give the valve three turns to the right. *furr is-ṣammaam itlaθ farraat lil-yamiin.* 2. *loofa* pl. *-aat.* Take the first turn to the right. *duur ib-ʔawwal loofa Ɛal-yamiin.* 3. *nooba* pl. *-aat, door* pl. *ʔadwaar.* It's my turn now. *hassa noobti.* -- You will be called up in turn. *raz-tinṣaaz bid-door.*

**We encountered difficulties at every turn. *ƐtirSatna ṣuƐuubaat min kull naaziya.*

**The meat is cooked to a turn. *l-lazam maṭbuux Ɛal-ʔuṣuul.*

**Last night he took a turn for the worse. *l-baarza bil-leel ṣizzta tdahwurat.*

**The political situation has taken a turn for the better. *l-zaala s-siyaasiyya ṣaar biiha tazassun.*

good turn – *maƐruuf, zeeniyya* pl. *-aat.* Ali did me a good turn. *Ɛali sawwaa-li zeeniyya.*

to take turns – *tnaawab (a tanaawub).* We'll take turns driving. *raz-nitnaawab bis-siyaaqa.*

to turn – 1. *daar (i deer), farr (u farr).* I can't turn the key. *ma-da-ʔagdar ʔadiir il-miftaaz.* — She turned her back on me. *daarat-li δaharha.* — Turn your chair to the light. *furr il-kursi maalak Ɛaδ-δuwa.* 2. *čirax (u čarix, čiraaxa) n-.* He turned these chess pieces on a lathe. *čirax qutaƐ haš-šitranj bit-toorna.* 3. *gallab (u tagliib) t-.* She turned the pages slowly. *gallubat iṣ-ṣazaayif Ɛala keefha.* -- The police turned the room upside down. *š-šurṭa galliibaw il-ġurfa min foog li-jawwa.* or *š-šurṭa nabbišaw il-ġurfa.* 4. *laƐƐab (i talƐiib).* The sight turned my stomach. *l-manδar laƐƐab nafsi.* 5. *wajjah (i tawjiih) t-, daar (i deer).* Turn the hose on the fire! *wajjih il-buuri Ɛan-naar.* 6. *ṣaar (i).* He's just turned fifty today. *ṣaar Ɛumra xamsiin sana l-yoom.* — They turned traitor. *ṣaaraw xawana.* 7. *gilab (u galub) n-, baddal (i tabdiil) t-.* I want to turn these stocks into cash. *ʔariid ʔaglub has-sandaat ʔila naqid.* 8. *ftarr (a farr).* The wheels turned slowly. *l-ičruux iftarrat yawaaš.* 9. *ltifat (i ltifaat).* She turned to look at him. *ltiftat zatta tbaawiƐ Ɛalee.* 10. *ngilab (u).* The tide of battle will turn. *majra l-maƐraka raz-yingulub.* or *l-ʔaaya raz-tingulub.* 11. *liwa (i lawi) n-.* It's the second time today that I turned my ankle. *haay θaani marra hal-yoom ʔalwi rijli.* 12. *twajjah (i tawajjuh).* I don't know who to turn to. *ma-adri ʔil-man ʔatwajjah.* 13. *tzawwal (a tazawwul).* The water turned to steam. *l-maay itzawwal ʔila buxaar.*

**She turned red. *zmarrat.*

**The milk turned sour. *l-zaliib izmaδδ.*

**They turned pale when they heard the news. *ṣfarraw min simƐaw il-xabar.*

to turn around – 1. *ndaar (a).* Turn around and let me see the back of your jacket. *ndaar w-xalli ʔašuuf δahar sitirtak.* 2. *deewar (u deewara) t-.* Turn around, the street is closed. *deewur, iš-šaariƐ masduud.*

to turn back - *rijaƐ (a rujuuƐ).* Let's turn back. *xal-nirjaƐ.*

to turn down - 1. *rufaδ (u rafuδ) n-, radd (i radd) n-.* The management turned down my application. *l-ʔidaara rufδat ṭalabi.* 2. *ṭawwa (i), Ɛiwaj (i).* Please don't turn down the corners of my book. *la-tiƐwij ẓawaaši l-waraq b-iktaabi.* 3. *naṣṣa (i tanṣiya), nazzal (i tanziil).* Will you turn down the radio, please? *naṣṣi r-raadyo, min faδlak.* 4. *faat (u foot) n- b-, deewar (u deewara) t- b-.* Turn down this road. *fuut ib-haṭ-ṭariiq.*

to turn in - 1. *xašš (u xuss) min, faat (u foot) min.* Driver, turn in here! *saayiq, xušš minnaa!* 2. *naam (a noom).* We ought to turn in early tonight. *laazim innaam Ɛala wakit hal-leela.* 3. *wiša (i wišaaya) b-.* We turned him in to the police. *wišeena bii biš-šurṭa.* 4. *qaddam (i taqdiim).* He turned in his resignation. *qaddam istiqaalta.* 5. *sallam (i tasliim).* You must turn your gun in to the police. *laazim itsallim bunduqiitak liš-šurṭa.*

to turn into - *ṣaar (i), ngilab (i ngilaab).* The wine turned into vinegar. *š-šaraab ingilab ʔila xall.* — He has turned into a poet. *ngilab šaaƐir.* or *ṣaar šaaƐir.*

to turn loose - *fakk (u fakk), hadd (i hadd).* He turned his dog loose. *fakk čalba.*

to turn off - 1. *sadd (i sadd) n-, qiṭaƐ (a qaṭiƐ) n-.* Did you turn off the gas? *saddeet il-ġaaz?* 2. *ṭaffa (i taṭfiya).* Turn off the radio. *ṭaffi r-raadyo.*

to turn on - 1. *šiƐal (i šaƐil) n-.* Why don't you turn on the light? *leeš ma-tišƐil iδ-δuwa?* 2. *fakk (u fakk) n-, šiƐal (i šaƐil) n-.* Who turned on the radio? *minu fakk ir-raadyo?*

to turn out - 1. *ṭirad (u ṭarid) n-.* They turned me out of my room in the hotel. *ṭirdooni min ġurufti bil-ʔuteel.* 2. *gilab (u galub) n-.* Turn the right side of the material out. *ʔuglub l-iqmaaš Ɛala wučča.* 3. *ṭallaƐ (i taṭliiƐ) t-, ʔantaj (i ʔintaaj).* The factory turns out 500 pairs of shoes a day. *l-maƐmal yṭalliƐ xamis miit zooj qanaadir bil-yoom.* 4. *ṭilaƐ (a ṭuluuƐ) n-.* How did the elections turn out? *šloon ṭilƐat natiijt il-intixaabaat?* — The snapshots didn't turn out right. *ṣ-ṣuwar ma-ṭilƐat zeen.* 5. *ẓiδar (a ẓuδuur).* A large crowd turned out for the meeting. *jamaaƐa čibiira mnin-naas ẓiδrat il-ijtimaaƐ.*

to turn over - 1. *gilab (u galub) n-.* I nearly turned over the table. *baƐad išwayya ʔaglub il-meez.* 2. *ngilab (u ngilaab).* Our boat turned over. *balamna ngilab.* 3. *sallam (i tasliim) t-.* Every-one has to turn over his weapons to the police. *l-kull laazim ysallmuun ʔasliẓathum liš-šurṭa.* — He turned his business over to his son. *sallam šuġla l-ʔibna.* 4. *gallab (u tagliib).* Turn it over in your mind before you give me your answer. *gallubha b-Ɛaqlak zeen gabul-ma tinṭiini jawaab.*

to turn up - 1. *δihar (a δuhuur), ṭilaƐ (a ṭuluuƐ).* I guess the file will probably turn up when we're not looking for it. *ʔaƐtiqid hal-faayil Ɛala l-ʔakθar raẓ-yiδhar min ma-da-ndawwir Ɛalee.* 2. *nubaṣ (u nabuṣ), δihar (a δuhuur).* The missing man suddenly turned up here in Baghdad. *r-rijjaal iδ-δaayiƐ fujʔatan nubaṣ ihnaa b-baġdaad.*

turning - 1. *taẓawwul.* That was the turning point. *haay čaanat nuqṭat it-taẓawwul.* 2. *taraajuƐ, nukuuṣ.* There'll be no turning back now. *ma-aku majaal lit-taraajuƐ.*

turnip - *šalġama* pl. *-aat* coll. *šalġam.*

turnkey - *sajjaan* pl. *-iin.*

turnover - 1. *taġyiir* pl. *-aat.* There's a big turn-over of employees in this office. *ʔaku hwaaya taġyiir bil-muwaδδafiin ib-had-daaʔira.* 2. *beeƐ w-šira.* My uncle's store has a big turnover. *ʔaku hwaaya beeƐ w-šira b-dukkaan Ɛammi.* 3. *kleecaaya* pl. *-aat* coll. *kleeča.* They served date turnovers with tea. *qaddmaw kleeča maal tamur wiyya čaay.*

turpentine - *tarpantiin.*

turquoise - *feeruuz, šaδir.* My sister has a turquoise stone in her ring. *ʔuxti Ɛidha faṣṣ feeruuz bil-miẓbas maalha.*

turret - *burij* pl. *ʔabraaj.* The old castle has turrets on the walls. *l-qalƐa l-Ɛatiiqa biiha ʔabraaj bil-iẓyaaṭiin.* — The tank returned with its turret damaged. *d-dabbaaba rijƐat ib-burij imẓaṭṭam.*

turtle - *ragga* pl. *-aat* coll. *ragg, sulẓafaat* pl. *salaaẓif, rafuš* pl. *rfuuš.*

turtledove - *fuxtaaya* pl. *-aat, faxaati.*

turtleneck sweater - *bluuz (pl. -aat) ʔabu rugba.* He's wearing a turtleneck sweater. *yilbas bluuz ʔabu rugba.*

tusk - *naab* pl. *ʔanyaab.*

tutor - *muƐallim xuṣuuṣi* pl. *muƐallimiin xuṣuuṣiyyiin.* You need a tutor in mathematics. *yinraad-lak muƐallim xuṣuuṣi bir-riyaaδiyyaat.*

tuxedo - *qaaṭ (pl. quuṭ) smookin.*

twang - *xanna.* He talks with a twang. *Ɛinda xanna b-ẓačya.*

tweezers - *mingaaš* pl. *-aat, minaagiiš.*

twelfth - *l-iθnaƐaš.*

twelve - *θnaƐaš.*

twentieth - *l-Ɛišriin.*

twenty - *Ɛišriin.*

twice - 1. *marrteen, noobteen.* I was invited there twice. *ʔaani marrteen maƐzuum ihnaak.* 2. *δiƐf.* That way will take twice as long. *haṭ-ṭariiq yaaxuδ δiƐf il-mudda.* — I paid twice as much. *dfaƐit δiƐf hal-miqdaar.*

twig - *ġuṣun iṣġayyir* pl. *ʔaġṣaan iṣġayyra.*

twin - *toom* pl. *twaam.* Those two boys are twins. *hal-waladeen toom.* — She's his twin sister. *hiyya ʔuxta t-toom.*

twine - *suutli.* I need some more twine to tie this package. *ʔariid išwayya laax suutli ẓatta ʔašidd ir-ruzma.*

to twine - *tsallaq (a tasalluq).* The grapevine twines around the trellis. *Ɛarag il-Ɛinab yitsallaq Ɛala šiič il-qamariyya.*

twinge - *naġza* pl. *-aat.* I just felt a twinge in my side. *ẓasseet fadd naġza b-xaaṣirti.*

to **twinkle** - *tlaʔlaʔ (a talaʔluʔ).* The stars were twinkling. *n-nijuum čaanat da-titlaʔlaʔ*

to **twirl** - 1. *farr (u farr).* He twirled his umbrella. *farr šamsiita.* 2. *ftarr (a).* The pencil twirled on the end of the string. *l-qalam l-imƐallag bil-xeeṭ gaam yiftarr.* 3. *fital (i fatil), biram (u barum).* The officer twirled his moustache. *δ-δaabuṭ fital išwaarba.*

twist - 1. *barma* pl. *-aat.* He gave the donkey's tail a good twist. *buram δeel iz-zumaal barma qawiyya.* 2. *wuṣla* pl. *-aat.* Add a twist of lemon peel. *ẓuṭṭ fadd wuṣlat gišir nuumi ẓaamuδ.*

to twist - 1. *luwa (i lawi) n-.* He twisted my arm until it hurt. *luwa ʔiidayya ʔila ʔan gaamat toojaƐni.* — I nearly twisted my ankle. *luweet rijli ʔilla šwayya.* — Twist the two ends of the wire together. *ʔilwi nihaayteen il-waayar suwa.* 2. *farr (u farr) n-.* Twist the screw two more turns to the right. *furr il-burġi marrteen lux lil-yimna.* 3. *tlawwa (a talawwi).* The road twists through the mountains. *ṭ-ṭariiq yitlawwa been ij-jibaal.*

**She twisted him around her little finger. *labista b-iṣbaƐha miθl il-miẓbas.*

twister - *fitteela* pl. *-aat.* The twister blew off the garage roof. *l-fitteela ṭayyrat sagf il-garaaj.*

to **twitch** - *raff (u raff).* My eye is twitching. *Ɛeeni da-truff.*

to **twitter** - *waṣwaṣ (i waṣwaṣa).* The sparrows are twittering. *l-Ɛaṣaafiir da-twaṣwiṣ.*

two - 1. *θneen, θinteen.* There's no one here but the two of us. *ma-aku ʔaẓẓad ihnaa ġeer ʔiẓna θ-θineen.* — It is two o'clock. *s-saaƐa θinteen.* — The two of you come here! *θneekum taƐaalu hnaa!* — They came in by twos. *dixlaw iθneen iθneen.* 2. *-een.* He owns two houses and two cars. *yimluk beeteen w-sayyaarteen.* — A two-passenger car is not big enough for our family. *sayyaara maal nafareen maa kaafya l-Ɛaaʔilatna.*

two-faced - *ʔabu wijheen.* He's two-faced and sneaky; don't trust him. *haaδa ʔabu wijheen w-ẓayyaal; la-taθiq bii.*

two hundred - *miiteen.*

type - 1. *nooƐ* pl. *ʔanwaaƐ, šikil* pl. *ʔaškaal.* What type of shoe did you have in mind? *ʔay nooƐ qundara Ɛaqlak qaaṭiƐ bii.* 2. *faṣiila* pl. *faṣaaʔil.* Do you remember your blood type? *titδakkar min ʔay faṣiila dammak?* 3. *ẓarf* pl. *ẓruuf.* Which kind of type do you want? *ʔay nooƐ imnil-iẓruuf itriid?* 4. *ṣinif* pl. *ʔaṣnaaf.* He's not my type. *haaδa muu min ṣinfi.*

to type - 1. *ṭubaƐ (a ṭabuƐ) n-.* Can you type? *tigdar titbaƐ?* 2. *ṣannaf (i taṣniif) t-.* Nurse, have you typed that blood yet? *yaa mumarriδa, ṣannafti had-damm loo baƐad?*

typesetter - *munaδδid* pl. *-iin.*

typewriter - *ṭaabiƐa* pl. *-aat.* Bring the typewriter here. *jiib iṭ-ṭaabiƐa hnaa.*

typewriting - *ṭabuƐ, ṭibaaƐa.* Do they teach type-writing at this school? *yƐallimuun ṭabuƐ*

ib-hal-madrasa?
typhoid - *tiifo.*
typhus - *tiifoos.*
typical - **1.** *ʔaṣli**. This is a typical example of an old Iraqi house. *haaδa namuuδaj ʔaṣli lil-beet il-ɛiraaqi l-qadiim.* **2.** *ṣamiim* pl. *-iin.* He's a typical Iraqi. *huwwa ɛiraaqi ṣamiim.*
**That's typical of him. *haaδi daggaata.*
typist - *kaatib* (pl. *kuttaab*) *ṭaabiɛa.* He's a good typist. *haaδa xooš kaatib ṭaabiɛa.*
tyranny - *δulum, stibdaad.*
tyrant - *δaalim* pl. *δullaam, mustabidd* pl. *-iin.* He's a tyrant in the office, but he's active in community welfare. *haaδa δaalim bid-daaʔira, laakin ysawwi xeer ihwaaya lil-mujtamaɛ.*

U

udder - *dees* pl. *dyuus, δariɛ* pl. *δruuɛ, θadi* pl. *θidaaya.*
uglier - *ʔabšaɛ, ʔaqbaz.* She's uglier than her sister. *hiyya ʔabšaɛ min ʔuxutha.*
ugly - **1.** *qabiiz, bašiɛ.* She's so ugly! *hiyya kulliš qabiiza.* **2.** *muġriδ, qabiiz.* They're spreading ugly rumors about him. *da-yšayyɛuun ʔišaaɛaat muġriδa ɛanna.*
ulcer - *qurza* pl. *-aat, quraz.*
ulterior - *xafi.* I think there is an ulterior motive behind his action. *ʔaɛtiqid ʔaku ġaraδ xafi b-ɛamala.*
ultimate - *nihaaʔi*, ʔaxiir, ʔaaxar.* Is this your ultimate goal? *haay ġaaytak in-nihaaʔiyya?* or *haaδi ʔaaxar ġaaya triidha?*
ultimatum - *ʔinδaar nihaaʔi* pl. *ʔinδaaraat nihaaʔiyya.* We issued an ultimatum to the enemy. *dazzeena ʔinδaar nihaaʔi lil-ɛadu.*
ultra - **1.** *miṭṭarrif.* He is ultra-Conservative. *huwwa muzaafiδ miṭṭarrif.* **2.** *fooq.* We studied ultra-violet rays in physics. *dirasna l-ʔašiɛɛa fooq il-banafsajiyya bil-fiizyaa?*
umbilical cord - *zabil* (pl. *zbaal*) *ṣurra.*
umbrella - *šamsiyya* pl. *-aat, šamaasi.*
umpire - *zakam* pl. *muzakkimiin, muzakkim* pl. *-iin.*
un- - **1.** *ma-, muu, ġeer.* This is an unusual situation. *haaδi zaala ma-ɛtiyaadiyya.* -- Last night we had unexpected company. *l-baarza bil-leel joona xuṭṭaar ma-mutwaqqaɛiin.* --That's very unlikely. *haay kulliš ma-muztamala.* -- I am uncomfortable here! *ʔaani muu mirtaaz ihnaa.* -- His trip is still uncertain. *safirta baɛadha muu ʔakiida.* -- I'm still uncertain as to whether I'll go. *ʔaani li-hassa ġeer mitʔakkid ʔiδa raz-aruuz.* -- The climate here is unhealthy. *j-jaww ihnaa ġeer ṣizzi.* **2.** *ma-.* It's quite unlike anything I've seen before. *haaδa ma-yišbah ʔay šii ʔaani šaayfa gabuḷ.* -- This is undesirable. *hiiči šii ma-yinraad.* -- This is unfit to eat. *haaδa ma-yiṣlaz lil-ʔakil.* **3.** *biduun, bila.* This radio has an unconditional guarantee. *har-raadyo bii taɛahhud biduun šarṭ.* -- That's undoubtedly the reason he quit. *haaδa bila šakk sabab ṭaliɛta.* -- The fort was left unmanned. *l-qalɛa ntirkat biduun junuud.* -- He did it unconsciously. *sawwaaha bila šuɛuur.* **4.** *xilaaf.* That's quite unlike him. *haay tamaaman xilaaf ɛaadta.* **5.** *ma-ʔil-.* That remark is uncalled for. *hal-izčaaya ma-ʔilha muujib.* -- Your fears are unfounded. *xoofak ma-ʔila muujib.* -- The statement is unfounded. *hal-izčaaya ma-ʔilha ʔasaas.* -- It was an unparalleled success. *čaan fadd najaaz ma-ʔila maθiil.*
**She's been so unfortunate. *ɛala ṭuul hiyya ma-čaanat mazδuuδa.*
**He was unfaithful to his wife. *čaan da-yxuun zawujta.* or *ma-čaan muxliṣ iz-zawujta.*
**He is unusually bright. *δakaaʔa ʔakθar imnil-iɛtiyaadi.*
to un- - *fakk* (*u fakk*). I can't unlatch the door. *ma-agdar ʔafukk il-lisaan maal il-baab.* -- He unbuttoned his shirt. *fakk id-dugma maal θooba.* or *fakk θooba.* -- They uncoupled the engine at Hindiyya. *fakkaw makiint il-qiṭaar bil-hindiyya.* -- He unbuckled his belt. *fakk izzaama.*
unabridged - *kaamil.* This is the unabridged edition of his book. *haaδi n-nusxa l-kaamila min iktaaba.*
unanimous - *ʔijmaaɛi**. It needs unanimous approval. *tiztaaj ʔila muwaafaqa ʔijmaaɛiyya.*
unanimously - *bil-ʔijmaaɛ.* They elected him unanimously. *ntixaboo bil-ʔijmaaɛ.*
unarmed - *ʔaɛzal.* The robber was unarmed. *l-zaraami čaan ʔaɛzal.*
unbeliever - *kaafir* pl. *kuffaar.*
uncertainty - *ziira.* Don't leave us in such uncertainty. *la-txalliina b-hiiči ziira.*
uncivil - *xašin, jaaff.* He was very uncivil to us. *čaan kulliš xašin wiyyaana.*
uncle - *ɛamm* pl. *ɛmuum* (paternal), *xaaḷ* pl. *xwaaḷ* (maternal).
unclean - *nagis.* I can't pray now; I'm unclean. *hassa ma-agdar aṣalli li-ʔanni nagis.*
uncomfortable - *mitδaayiq.* I felt uncomfortable when my father was there. *zasseet mitδaayiq min ʔabuuya čaan ihnaak.*
uncompromising - *mitɛannit* pl. *-iin, mɛaanid* pl. *-iin.* The union leaders are very uncompromising. *zuɛamaaʔ in-naqaaba kulliš mitɛannitiin.*
unconscious - *ġaayba ruuz~.* He's still unconscious. *baɛda ġaayba ruuza.*
uncouth - *xašin.*
to **uncover** - **1**. *kaššaf* (*i takšiif, tkiššif*). Don't uncover that pot. *la-tkaššif ij-jidir.* **2.** *ktišaf* (*i ktišaaf*). I uncovered something new in that case. *ktišafit fadd šii jdiid bid-daɛwa.*
uncovered - *makšuuf, mkaššaf.* Their heads are uncovered. *ruushum makšuufa.*
under - **1.** *jawwa, tazat.* The slippers are under the bed. *n-naɛal jawwa č-čarpaaya.* -- Can you swim under water? *tigdar tisbaz jawwa l-maay?* **2.** *tazat.* Are you under medical treatment? *ʔinta tazt it-tadaawi hassa?* -- The police put him under surveillance. *š-šurṭa zaṭṭoo tazt il-muraaqaba.* **3.** *b-.* Under the new system, there will be elections soon. *bin-niδaam ij-jidiid raz-itṣiir intixaabaat qariiban.* -- Under these circumstances that could never happen. *b-hiiči δuruuf δiič ʔabad ma-tṣiir.* **4.** *ʔaqall min, tazat, jawwa.* This meat weighs under a kilo. *hal-lazam wazna ʔaqall min keelu.* -- They cannot vote since they are under legal age. *ma-ygidruun yṣawwtuun li-ʔan jawwa s-sinn il-qaanuuni.* **5.** *jawwaani**. Their underclothing is wool. *hduumhum ij-jawwaaniyya min ṣuuf.* **6.** *naaʔib* pl. *nuwwaab.* He's the under-secretary of defense. *huwwa naaʔib waziir id-difaaɛ.*
**I'm under contract with the government. *ʔaani maaδi ɛaqid wiyya l-zukuuma.*
**Don't forget you are under oath. *la-tinsa ʔinta zaalif yamiin.*
**Is the fire under control? *n-naar mṣayṭar ɛaleeha?*
underarm - *ʔubuṭ* pl. *ʔubaaṭ* This salve will prevent underarm perspiration. *had-dihin yimnaɛ il-ɛarag imnil-ʔubuṭ.*
underdog - *miskiin* pl. *masaakiin.* He always helps the underdog. *huwwa daaʔiman yɛaawun il-masaakiin.*
underground - **1.** *jawwa l-gaaɛ.* The city has underground telephone lines. *ʔaslaak it-talafoon maal hal-wlaaya jawwa l-gaaɛ.* **2.** *muqaawama sirriyya.* He served with the underground during the war. *xidam wiyya l-muqaawama s-sirriyya ʔaθnaaʔ il-zarb.*
underhand - *min jawwa.* Throw the ball underhand. *ʔušmur iṭ-ṭooba min jawwa.*
underlying - *ʔasaasi**. Do you understand the underlying causes? *tuɛruf il-ʔasbaab il-ʔasaasiyya?*
to **undermine** - *zufar* (*u zafur*) *n- jawwa.* The river undermined the wall and brought it down. *n-nahar zufar jawwa l-zaayiṭ w-waggaɛa.* -- He undermined my position and got me fired. *huwwa l-zufar jawwaaya w-xallaani ʔanṭirid.*
underneath - *jawwa.* I found the ball underneath the bed. *ligeet iṭ-ṭooba jawwa č-čarpaaya.*
undernourishment - *suuʔ taġδiya.*
underpants - *lbaas* pl. *-aat, libsaan.*
underprivileged - *mazruum* pl. *-iin.* He built a hospital for underprivileged children. *bina mustašfa*

lil-ʔaṭfaal il-maḥruumiin.
to **underrate** – *staxaff (i stixfaaf) b-, qallal (i taqliil) min.* We underrated his strength. *staxaffeena b-quuta.*
to **undersell** – *kisar (i).* That store undersold us. *δaak il-maḥall kisarna.*
undershirt – *faaniila* pl. *-aat.*
to **understand** – *ftiham (i ftihaam), fiham (a fahim).* He doesn't understand Russian. *ma-yiftihim ruusi.* -- I understand from his letter that he likes his work. *ʔafham min maktuuba š-šaġḷa εijbata.*
understanding – **1.** *ʔidraak.* He has keen understanding. *εinda xooš ʔidraak.* **2.** *tafaahum.* There's a close understanding between them. *ʔaku beenaathum tafaahum zeen.* **3.** *mudrik.* He's a very understanding man. *huwwa fadd waaḥid mudrik.*
**They've reached an understanding on the Berlin question. *tfaahmaw εala qaδ̣iyyat barliin.*
understood – *mafhuum.* Of course that's understood! *ṭabεan haay mafhuum!*
to **undertake** – **1.** *qaam (u qiyaam) b-.* I hope you're not planning to undertake that trip alone. *ʔatʔammal ʔinta ma-raḥ-itquum ib-has-safra waḥdak.* **2.** *tkaffal (a takafful).* He undertook to pay for his nephew's education. *tkaffal ib-maṣaariif taθqiif ʔibn axuu.*
undertaking – **1.** *taḥammul.* His undertaking that responsibility was a big favor. *taḥammula hal-masʔuuliyya čaan fadd luṭuf kabiir.* **2.** *mašruuε* pl. *mašaariiε.* The government is encouraging industrial undertakings. *l-ḥukuuma da-tšajjiε il-mašaariiε iṣ-ṣinaaεiyya.*
undertaker – *mġassil* pl. *-iin.*
underwear – *hduum jawwaaniyya.*
underworld – *muḥiiṭ ʔijraam.* He grew up in the underworld. *nišaʔ ib-muḥiiṭ il-ʔijraam.*
to **underwrite** – *δ̣iman (i δ̣amaan).* Will the International Bank underwrite this loan? *l-bang id-dawli raḥ-yiδ̣min hal-qarδ̣?*
to **undo** – **1.** *ḥall (i ḥall), fall (i fall), fakk (u fakk).* Help me undo this knot. *εaawinni nḥill hal-εugda.* **2.** *εaddal (i taεdiil).* We'll need a week to undo this mess. *yinraad-ilna sbuuε ḥatta nεaddil hal-xarbaṭa.*
**Now it's happened; it can't be undone. *hassa baεad ṣaarat w-ma-aku majaal lit-taraajuε.*
undoing – *xaraab.* Drink was the cause of his undoing. *š-šurub čaan sabab xaraaba.*
to **undress** – **1.** *nazzaε (i tnizziε, tanziiε).* I'll undress the children. *ʔaani raḥ-anazziεhum lij-jahaal.* **2.** *nizaε (a naziε) hiduum.* The phone rang just as I was undressing. *dagg it-talifoon ʔawwal-ma bdeet anzaε ihduumi.*
undulent fever – *ḥummat maalṭa.*
unduly – *ʔakθar imnil-laazim.* You are unduly severe. *ʔinta qaasi ʔakθar imnil-laazim.*
undying – *ʔila l-ʔabad.* You have my undying gratitude. *raḥ-abqa mamnuun ʔilak ʔila l-ʔabad.*
uneasily – *b-qalaq.* He sat waiting there uneasily. *giεad da-yintiδ̣ir ib-qalaq.*
uneasy – **1.** *mitqayyid.* I feel uneasy in his company. *ʔaḥiss mitqayyid min ʔakuun wiyyaa* or ***ma-ʔaaxuδ ḥurriiti hal-gadd min ʔakuun wiyyaa.* **2.** *ma-mistiqirr.* This is an uneasy situation. *hal-waδ̣iε ma-mistiqirr.* **3.** *mitšawwiš.* He left his wife very uneasy. *xalla marta mitšawwša kulliš.*
unemployed – *εaaṭil* pl. *-iin, baṭṭaal* pl. *-a.* He's unemployed now. *huwwa hassa εaaṭil.*
unemployment – *εaṭaala, baṭaala.* Unemployment this year is less than before. *l-εaṭaala has-sana ʔaqall min gabuḷ.*
UNESCO – *yuuniskoo.*
unexpectedly – *εala ġafḷa.* The accident occurred unexpectedly. *l-ḥaadiθ ṣaar εala ġafla.*
unfinished – *εan-nuṣṣ, ma-xalṣaan, naagiṣ.* The contractor left the work unfinished. *l-qunṭarči tirak iš-šuġuḷ εan-nuṣṣ.*
unfortunate – *muʔsif.* That's an unfortunate mistake! *haaδi ġalṭa muʔsifa.*
unfortunately – *l-suuʔ il-ḥaδ̣δ̣.* Unfortunately, negotiations aren't advancing very well. *l-suuʔ il-ḥaδ̣δ̣, il-mufaawaδ̣aat ma-da-titqaddam hal-gadd zeen.*
ungrateful – *naakir (pl. -iin) ij-jamiil.* He's an ungrateful boy. *hal-walad naakir ij-jamiil.*
unharmed – *salaamaat.* He escaped unharmed. *ṭilaε salaamaat.*
to **unhitch** – *ḥall (i ḥall), fakk (u fakk).* They unhitched the horses from the carriage. *ḥallaw il-xeel imnil-εarabaana.*
to **unhook** – *fakk (u fakk).* Unhook the garden gate, please. *baḷḷa ma-tfukk baab il-ḥadiiqa.*
unification – *tawḥiid.* The foreign ministers are considering unification of the country. *wuzaraaʔ il-xaarijiyya da-ydursuun tawḥiid il-balad.*
uniform – **1.** *badla (pl. -aat) rasmiyya.* They gave us new uniforms. *nṭoona badlaat rasmiyya jdiida.* **2.** *εala namaṭ waaḥid.* Their products aren't of very uniform quality. *muntajaathum muu εala namaṭ waaḥid.*
uniformity – *tanaasuq.* We need more uniformity in our administrative practices. *niḥtaaj ʔila tanaasuq ʔakθar bil-ʔidaara,*
to **unify** – *waḥḥad (i tawḥiid).* Bismarck unified Germany. *bismaark waḥḥad ʔalmaanya.*
unilateral – *min jaanib waaḥid.* We will not accept any unilateral decision. *ma-niqbal qaraar min jaanib waaḥid.*
union – **1.** *ttiḥaad* pl. *-aat.* Racial segregation is still in vogue in the Union of South Africa, unfortunately. *t-tamyiiz il-εunṣuri baεda mawjuud b-ittiḥaad januubi ʔafriiqya l-suuʔ il-ḥaδ̣δ̣.* **2.** *naqaaba* pl. *-aat.* Are you a member of the union? *ʔinta εuδ̣u bin-naqaaba?*
unique – *wahiid.* It was a unique experience. *čaanat tajruba waḥiida min nooεha.*
unison – *ṣoot waaḥid.* Repeat this statement in unison. *εiidu haj-jumla b-ṣoot waaḥid.*
unit – **1.** *qisim* pl. *ʔaqsaam.* This book is divided into twelve units. *l-iktaab imqassam ʔila θnaεaš qisim.* **2.** *wiḥda* pl. *-aat.* He's been assigned to another unit. *nniqal il-ġeer wiḥda.*
to **unite** – **1.** *ttiḥad (i ttiḥaad).* Egypt and Syria united to form the UAR. *miṣir w-suurya ttiḥdaw w-sawwaw ij-jamhuuriyya l-εarabiyya l-muttaḥida.* **2.** *waḥḥad (i tawḥiid).* Saladin united the Muslims against the Crusaders. *ṣalaaḥ id-diin waḥḥad il-muslimiin δ̣idd iṣ-ṣaliibiyyiin.*
United Arab Republic – *j-jamhuuriyya l-εarabiyya l-muttaḥida.*
United Nations – *l-ʔumam il-muttaḥida.*
United States – *l-wilaayaat il-muttaḥida.*
unity – **1.** *ttiḥaad.* The Arabs need unity. *l-εarab yinraad-ilhum ittiḥaad.* **2.** *wiḥda.* Arab unity is the goal of many parties. *l-wiḥda l-εarabiyya ġaayat ihwaaya ʔaḥzaab.*
universal – **1.** *εaamm.* There is universal agreement on that. *ʔaku ttifaaq εaamm εal-haay.* **2.** *εaalami.** Gandhi had a universal message. *ġaandi risaalta čaanat εaalamiyya.*
universe – *εaalam, koon, dinya.*
university – **1.** *jaamiεa* pl. *-aat.* How many students are there at this university? *šgadd ʔaku ṭullaab ib-haj-jaamiεa?* **2.** *jaamiεi*.* University life is loads of fun. *l-ḥayaat ij-jaamiεiyya kulliš laṭiifa.*
unknown – *majhuul.* We visited the grave of the unknown soldier. *zirna qabr ij-jundi l-majhuul.*
unless – **1.** *ʔilla ʔiδa.* We're coming, unless it rains. *ʔiḥna jaayiin ʔaḷḷaahumma ʔilla ʔiδa tumṭur id-dinya.* **2.** *ʔiδa ma-.* Unless you tell me why, I won't do it. *ʔiδa ma-tgul-li leeš, tara ʔaani ma-asawwiiha.*
to **unload** – *farraġ (i tafriiġ) t-.* They haven't unloaded the ship's cargo yet. *baεad ma-farrġaw ḥumuulat il-markab.* -- Unload your gun before you go in the car. *farrig it-tufga maaltak gabuḷ-ma txušš bis-sayyaara.*
unlucky – **1.** *mašʔuum.* It was an unlucky coincidence. *čaanat fadd ṣidfa mašʔuuma.* **2.** *ma-maḥδ̣uuδ̣.* I don't know why I'm so unlucky. *ma-adri leeš ʔaani hal-gadd ma-maḥδ̣uuδ̣.*
to **unmask** – *bayyan (i tabyiin), kišaf (i kašif).* They unmasked the traitor. *bayynaw il-xaaʔin.*
unoccupied – *faariġ.* That house is unoccupied. *δaak il-beet faariġ.*
unpleasant – *muzεij.* I got some unpleasant news today. *jatni šwayya ʔaxbaar muzεija l-yoom.*
unrest – *qalaaqil.* We heard there's unrest in Najaf. *smaεna ʔaku qalaaqil bin-najaf.*
unruly – *wakiiḥ, wakiḥ.* He's an unruly child. *huwwa walad wakiiḥ.*
unstable – *qaliq.* This chemical compound is unstable. *hal-murakkab il-kiimyaawi qaliq.*
to **untangle** – **1.** *ḥall (i ḥall), fakk (u fakk).* Can you please untangle this string? *baḷḷa ma-tḥill hal-ixyuuṭ l-imčabbina.* **2.** *faδ̣δ̣ (u faδ̣δ̣).* The police untangled the traffic jam. *šurṭat il-muruur*

faδδaw izdizaam is-sayyaaraat.

untidy - *mxarbaṭ.* His wife is very untidy. *marta kulliš mxarbaṭa.*

to **untie** - *fakk (u fakk).* Can you untie this knot for me? *tigdar itfukk-li hal-ɛuqda?* -- Wait till I untie the package. *ntiδir ˀila ˀan ˀafukk ir-ruzma.*

until - **1.** *l-, zatta.* Wait until tomorrow. *ntiδir il-baačir.* **2.** *ˀila ˀan, zatta.* Wait until he comes. *ntiδir ˀila ˀan yiji.*

to **unveil** - *zaaz (i) sitaar ɛan.* The president will unveil the monument next week. *raˀiis ij-jamhuriyya raz-yziiz is-sitaar ɛan in-naṣub it-tiδkaari l-isbuuɛ ij-jaay.*

up - **1.** *foog.* I'm up here. *ˀaani foog ihnaa.* -- Would you please put it up there? *baḷḷa ma-tzuṭṭa foog ihnaak?* -- You can find a nice room for a dinar and up. *tigdar tilgi ġurfa zeena hnaa min diinaar w-foog.* **2.** *gaaɛid.* Is he up already? *huwwa min hassa gaaɛid imnin-noom?* **3.** *ɛaks.* Shall we head up the river? *ma-xal-nittijih ɛaks il-maay?* **4.** *matruuk, ɛala.* The decision is up to you. *l-qaraar matruuk ˀilak* or *l-qaraar ɛaleek.*
**Your time is up. *xilaṣ waktak.*
**He was walking up and down the room. *čaan da-yruuz w-yiji bil-gubba.*
**We all have our ups and downs. *haay id-dinya, yoom ˀilak w-yoom ɛaleek* or *haay id-dinya, yoom tiṣɛad yoom tinzil.*
up to - **1.** *l-zadd.* Because of the storm, trains were up to two hours late. *b-sabab il-ɛaaṣifa il-qiṭaaraat čaanat mitˀaxxra l-zadd saaɛteen.* **2.** *gadd.* He isn't up to the job. *huwwa muu gadd haš-šaġla.*
**What's he up to this time? *han-nooba šaku ɛinda?*
up to now - *li-hassa.* Up to now he hasn't answered. *baɛad li-hassa ma-jaawab.*

uphill - **This road goes uphill for a mile and then descends. *haṭ-ṭariiq yiṣɛad fadd miil w-baɛdeen yinzil.*

upkeep - *ṣiyaana.* My car requires a lot of expenses for upkeep. *sayyaarti yinraad-ilha hwaaya maṣaariif liṣ-ṣiyaana.*

upper - *foogaani*.* The fire started on the upper floor. *n-naar bidat imnil-qaat il-foogaani.*
**Write the page number in the upper right-hand corner. *zuṭṭ ˀarqaam iṣ-ṣafzaat li-foog bij-jiha l-yimna.*

to **uproot** - *šilaɛ (a šaliɛ), qilaɛ (a qaliɛ).* The storm uprooted several trees. *l-ɛaaṣifa šilɛat čam šajara.*

upset - **1.** *maqluuq, mitšawwiš.* He was all upset. *čaan kulliš maqluuq.* **2.** *mitxarbuṭ.* I have an upset stomach. *miɛidti mitxarbuṭa.*
to upset - **1.** *giḷab (u gaḷub), waggaɛ (i twuggiɛ).* Be careful or you'll upset the pitcher. *diir baalak, tara raz-tugḷub id-doolka.* -- You're upsetting the boat! *ˀinta raz-tugḷub il-balam!* **2.** *xarbaṭ (u).* Nothing ever upsets him. *ma-aku fadd šii yxarbuṭa.*

upside down - *bil-magḷuub.* That picture is upside down. *haṣ-ṣuura maztuuta bil-magḷuub.*
to turn upside down - *giḷab (u gaḷub).* They turned the whole house upside down. *guḷbaw il-beet kulla.*

upstairs - **1.** *foogaani*.* The upstairs apartment is vacant. *š-šiqqa l-foogaaniyya faarġa.* **2.** *foog.* He's upstairs. *huwwa foog.* **3.** *foog, li-foog.* Bring our bags upstairs. *ṣaɛɛid jinaṭna li-foog.*

up-to-date - **1.** *ɛala ˀaaxir ṭarz, ɛala ˀaaxir ṭiraaz, zadiiθ.* She has an up-to-date kitchen. *ɛidha maṭbax ɛala ˀaaxir ṭarz.* **2.** *l-zadd il-yoom.* My books are posted up to date. *dafaatri t-tijaariyya mnaδδma l-zadd il-yoom.*

urge - *daafiɛ* pl. *dawaafiɛ.* I felt the urge to tell him what I thought of him. *zasseet ib-fadd daafiɛ agul-la raˀyi bii.*
to urge - **1.** *zaθθ (i).* If you urge her a bit, she'll do it. *hiyya tsawwiiha loo šwayya tziθθha.* **2.** *šajjaɛ (i tašjiiɛ).* She urged us to stay longer. *šajjɛatna nibqa mudda ˀaṭwal.* **3.** *zarraδ (i tazriiδ).* His mother urged him to commit the crime. *ˀumma zarriδata ysawwi haj-jariima.*

urgent - *mustaɛjal.* I have an urgent request. *ɛindi fadd ṭalab mustaɛjal.*

use - **1.** *stiɛmaal* pl. *-aat.* How long has this method been in use? *šgadd ṣaar-ilha haṭ-ṭariiqa bil-istiɛmaal.* **2.** *faaˀida.* Will that be of any use to you? *haay biiha faaˀida ˀilak?* or ***haay itfiidak?* — What's the use of arguing? *šinu l-faaˀida mnil-mujaadala?* **3.** *zaaja.* I have no use for that. *ma-ˀili zaaja b-haay.* or ***ma-aztaaj haay.*
**It's no use, we've got to do it. *ma-aku čaara, ˀizna laazim insawwiiha.*
to make use of - *staġall (i stiġlaal).* He made good use of the opportunity. *staġall il-furṣa zeen.*
to use - *staɛmal (i stiɛmaal).* I can't use that. *ma-agdar astaɛmil haay.* — What toothpaste do you use? *yaa maɛjuun isnuun tistaɛmil?* -- We'll use this room as a classroom. *raz-nistaɛmil hal-ġurfa ka-ṣaff.*
to use up - *stahlak (i stihlaak), stanfaδ (i stinfaaδ), xallaṣ (i taxliiṣ), ṣiraf (u ṣaruf).* We've used up all our supplies. *stanfaδna kull il-mawjuud il-ɛidna.* -- His car uses up a lot of gasoline. *sayyaarta tistahlik ihwaaya ḅaanziin.*

used - **1.** *čaan.* I used to live here. *činit askun ihnaa.* -- He used to eat in restaurants before he got married. *čaan da-yaakul bil-maṭaaɛim gabuḷ-ma tzawwaj.* **2.** *mitɛawwid.* I'm not used to hard work. *ˀaani ma-mitɛawwid ɛala š-šuġuḷ iṣ-ṣaɛub.*
to get used to - *taɛawwad (a) ɛala.* She's gotten used to getting up at seven o'clock. *hiyya tɛawwdat ɛal-gaɛda s-saaɛa sabɛa.*

useful - *mufiid, naafiɛ.* A maid is useful around the house. *l-xaddaama mufiida bil-beet.* -- I've found this book very useful. *šifit hal-iktaab kulliš naafiɛ.*

useless - *ma-aku faaˀida, ma-bii faaˀida.* It's useless to try to convince him. *ma-aku faaˀida tzaawil itqannɛa.* --This map is useless to me. *hal-xariiṭa ma-biiha faaˀida ˀili.*

usher - *tašriifaati* pl. *-iyya, daliil* pl. *-iin, ˀadillaaˀ.* The usher will show you your seats. *t-tašriifaati raz-yraawiikum maqaaɛidkum.*
to usher - *dalla (i tdilli) t-.* We were ushered to our seats. *tdalleena ɛala maqaaɛidna.*

usual - *ɛtiyaadi*.* Our usual hours are from 8 to 3. *dawaamna l-iɛtiyaadi mniθ-θamaanya ˀila θ-θalaaθa.* -- We'll meet at the usual place. *raz-niltiqi bil-mukaan il-iɛtiyaadi.*
as usual - *kal-ɛaada, ɛal-ɛaada.* It's raining, as usual. *da-tumṭur kal-ɛaada.* -- Everything went along as usual. *kullši miša ɛal-ɛaada.*

usually - *ɛaadatan.* I usually visit them twice a week. *ɛaadatan ˀazuurhum marrteen bil-isbuuɛ.*

utensil - *ˀadaat* pl. *ˀadawaat.* We bought some new cooking utensils. *štireena ˀadawaat ṭabux ijdiida.*

utmost - **1.** *kulliš.* The matter is of the utmost importance. *l-qaḍiyya kulliš muhimma.* **2.** *ˀaqṣa.* He expended the utmost energy. *biδal ˀaqṣa juhda.*

utter - *kulliš.* Things are in a state of utter confusion in the office. *l-ˀumuur kulliš imxarbuṭa bid-daaˀira.*
to utter - *gaal (u gool).* I couldn't utter a single word. *ma-gdart aguul wala čilma.*

V

vacant - **1.** *faariġ, xaali.* The house has been vacant for a week. *l-beet ṣaar-la sbuuɛ faariġ.* -- Next to our house there is still a vacant lot. *yamm beetna ˀaku saaza faarġa.* **2.** *šaaġir* pl. *šawaaġir.* We have no position vacant at the moment. *ma-ɛidna waḍiifa šaaġra hassa.*

to **vacate** - *farraġ (i tafriiġ), ṭilaɛ (a ṭuluuɛ) min.* When are you going to vacate the house? *šwakit raz-itfarriġ il-beet?*

vacation - *ɛuṭla* pl. *ɛuṭal.* The children are looking forward to their vacation. *j-jahaal da-yintaδruun ɛuṭlathum ib-faariġ iṣ-ṣabur.*
on vacation - *mujaaz, bil-ˀijaaza.* Ali is on vacation. *ɛali mujaaz.*

vague – *mubham, muu waaδiʒ.* He gave me a vague answer. *jaawabni jawaab mubham.*
vaguely – *muu b-wuδuuʒ.* I remember him vaguely. *ma-atδakkara b-wuδuuʒ.*
vain – *maġruur, šaayif nafs~.* She's terribly vain. *hiyya kulliš maġruura.*
in vain – *ƐabaΘan.* The doctor tried in vain to save the boy's life. *d-daktoor ƐabaΘan ʒaawal yinquδ ʒayaat il-walad.*
valid – **1.** *ṣaʒiiʒ.* I don't think your argument is valid. *ma-aƐtiqid jadalak ṣaʒiiʒ.* **2.** *ṣaaliʒ, naafiδ, il-mafƐuul.* Is my license still valid? *ʔijaazti baƐadha ṣaalʒa?*
**Your passport isn't valid any more. *ṗaaṣṗortak xilṣat il-mudda maalta.*
valley – *waadi* pl. *widyaan.*
valuable – *Θamiin, nafiis.* That's a valuable ring. *haaδa miʒbas Θamiin.*
valuables – *ʔašyaaʔ Θamiina.* You'd better lock your valuables in the safe. *ʔaʒsan loo tʒuṭṭ ʔašyaaʔak iΘ-Θamiina bil-qaaṣa.*
value – **1.** *qiima* pl. *qiyam.* This coin has no value. *hal-qiṭƐat in-nuquud ma-ʔilha qiima.* — Even though it's rare, it's of no value to me. *walaw hiyya naadra, bass mu-ʔilha qiima bin-nisba ʔili.* **2.** *wazin.* I don't attach any value to his opinions. *ma-anṭi ʔay wazin il-ʔaaraaʔa.*
to value – **1.** *Ɛtazz (a Ɛtizaaz) b-, qaddar (i taqdiir).* I value his friendship very highly. *hwaaya ʔaƐtazz ib-ṣadaaqta.* **2.** *Θamman (i taΘmiin), saam (u soom).* What do you value your house at? *beeš itΘammin beetak?* or **š-tiftikir beetak yiswa?*
valve – *ṣammaam* pl. *-aat.* The worker opened a valve to let oil into the pipeline. *l-Ɛaamil fakk iṣ-ṣammaam ʒatta n-nafuṭ yijri bil-buuri.* **2.** *walf* pl. *-aat.* Your valves need adjusting. *l-walfaat yinraad-ilha δabuṭ.*
to **vanish** – *xtifa (i xtifaaʔ).* My pencil has vanished. *qalami xtifa.*
vapor – *buxaar* pl. *ʔabxira.* On sunny days a lot of vapor goes into the atmosphere. *bil-ʔayyaam il-mušmiša hwaaya buxaar yiṣƐad lij-jaww.*
variable – *muu Θaabit.* The weather is variable these days. *j-jaww muu Θaabit hal-ʔayyaam.*
variety – **1.** *taškiila* pl. *-aat.* We have a wide variety of shirts. *Ɛidna taškiila čbiira mniΘ-Θiyaab.* **2.** *nooƐ* pl. *ʔanwaaƐ.* How many varieties of apples grow in your orchard? *čam nooƐ imnit-tiffaaʒ Ɛindak ib-bistaanak?* **3.** *tanawwuƐ.* There's not much variety in my life. *ma-aku tanawwuƐ ib-ʒayaati.*
various – *mixtalif.* I have various reasons. *Ɛindi ʔasbaab mixtalfa.*
varnish – *waarniiš.* How long does it take the varnish to dry? *šgadd yṭawwil il-waarniiš ʒatta yeebas?*
to varnish – *δirab (u δarub) waarniiš.* We just varnished the doors. *tawwna δirabna l-buub waarniiš.*
to **vary** – *xtilaf (i xtilaaf).* The length varies in each case. *ṭ-ṭuul yixtilif ib-kull ʒaala.*
vase – *mazhariyya* pl. *-aat.*
veal – *laʒam Ɛijil.*
vegetable – *mxaδδar* pl. *-aat, mxaaδiir.*
vehicle – *Ɛajala* pl. *-aat.*
veil – *ṗuuši* pl. *ṗwaaši, ṗuušiyya* pl. *-aat.* Many Iraqi women still wear veils. *hwaaya niswaan Ɛiraaqiyyaat baƐadhum yilibsuun ṗuušiyya.*
vein – *damaar* pl. *-aat, wariid* pl. *ʔawrida.* The medicine has to be injected into the vein. *d-duwa laazim yinδurub bid-damaar.*
velvet – *qadiifa.*
venereal disease – *maraδ zuhri* pl. *ʔamraaδ zuhriyya.* Gonorrhea is a venereal disease. *s-sayalaan maraδ zuhri.*
Venice – *l-bunduqiyya.*
venom – *samm* pl. *sumuum.*
vent – *majra (*pl. *majaari) hawa, manfaδ (*pl. *manaafiδ) hawa, baadgiir* pl. *-aat.* Open the vent! *fukk majra l-hawa.*
to give vent – *naffas (i tanfiis).* She gave vent to her anger. *naffisat Ɛan gaḷubha.*
ventilation – *tahwiya* pl. *-aat.* This room need ventilation. *hal-ġurfa yinraad-ilha tahwiya.*
venture – *mujaazafa* pl. *-aat, muxaaṭara* pl. *-aat.* It was a dangerous venture. *čaanat mujaazafa xaṭra.* — I'm going into a new business venture. *raʒ-asawwi fadd mujaazafa tijaariyya.*
to venture – **1.** *xaaṭar (i muxaaṭara), jaazaf (i mujaazafa).* I wouldn't venture to go out in this weather. *ma-ard axaaṭir aṭlaƐ ib-hiici jaww.* **2.** *jaazaf (i mujaazafa).* Nothing ventured, nothing gained. *ma-tjaazif, kullši ma-tʒaṣṣil.*
verb – *fiƐil* pl. *ʔafƐaal.*
verbal – *šafahi*, šafawi*.* We have a verbal agreement. *beenaatna Ɛaqid šafahi.*
verdict – *ʒukum* pl. *ʔaʒkaam, qaraar* pl. *-aat.* The court issued the verdict. *l-maʒkama ṣaddrat il-ʒukum.*
verge – **1.** *ʒaaffa.* She's on the verge of a breakdown. *hiyya Ɛala ʒaaffat l-inhiyaar il-Ɛaṣabi.* **2.** *wašak.* I was on the verge of telling him. *činit Ɛala wašak agul-la.*
verse – **1.** *šiƐir.* The play is written in verse. *r-ruwaaya Ɛala šikil šiƐir.* **2.** *beet* pl. *ʔabyaat.* Let's read the first verse of the poem. *xalli niqra ʔawwal beet imnil-qaṣiida.* **3.** *qisim* pl. *ʔaqsaam.* Let's sing only the first verse. *xalli nġanni ʔawwal qisim bass.*
version – *ruwaaya* pl. *-aat.* I heard another version. *simaƐit ruwaaya lux.*
versus – *δidd.* This is the case of the cotton company versus the ministry of agriculture. *haaδa daƐwat šarikat il-guṭin δidd wizaarat iz-ziraaƐa.*
vertical – *Ɛamuudi*.* The Nabi Shiit minaret in Mosul isn't vertical. *manaarat in-nabi šiit il-bil-mooṣil muu Ɛamuudiyya.*
very – **1.** *kulliš.* The bank is not very far from here. *l-bang muu kulliš biƐiid minnaa.* — We're very satisfied with the new cook. *ʔiʒna kulliš mirtaaʒiin min iṭ-ṭabbaax ij-jidiid.* **2.** *biδ-δabuṭ, nafs, biδ-δaat.* That's the very thing I want. *haaδa iš-šii illi ariida biδ-δabuṭ.* **3.** *nafs, biδ-δaat.* She left that very day. *raaʒat ib-nafs il-yoom.*
**He came the very next day. *ma-ṭawwal iΘ-Θaani yoom w-ʔija.*
vessel – *sifiina* pl. *sufun, markab* pl. *maraakub.* Several large vessels were docked in the harbor. *Ɛiddat sufun ikbaar waččat bil-miinaaʔ.*
vest – *yalag* pl. *-aat, ʒaxma* pl. *-aat, ʒixam.* He usually wears a vest. *Ɛaadatan yilbas yalag.*
vestige – *ʔaΘar* pl. *ʔaaΘaar.*
veteran – **1.** *muʒaarib* pl. *-iin.* He's an old veteran. *haaδa muʒaarib qadiim.* **2.** *mdarrab* pl. *-iin, muʒannak* pl. *-iin.* He's a veteran politician. *huwwa siyaasi mdarrab.*
**He's a veteran of the North African campaign of World War II. *ʒaarab ib-šimaal ʔafriiqya bil-ʒarb iΘ-Θaanya.*
veterinarian – *bayṭari* pl. *-iyya, beeṭaar* pl. *-iyya.* The veterinarian can tell you what's wrong with your horse. *l-bayṭari yigdar ygul-lak iš-bii l-iʒṣaan maalak.*
viaduct – *jisir* pl. *jsuura.*
to **vibrate** – *htazz (a htizaaz), rijaf (i rajif).* Pluck the string and watch it vibrate. *ʔuδrub il-watar w-šuufa šloon yihtazz.* — The steering wheel vibrates at high speed. *l-isteerin yirjif min itsuuq ib-surƐa.*
vice – **1.** *raδiila* pl. *raδaayil.* Gambling is a vice. *liƐb il-iqmaar raδiila.* **2.** *naaʔib* pl. *nuwwaab.* He's the vice-president. *huwwa naaʔib ir-raʔiis.*
vicinity – **1.** *manṭiqa.* Is there a tailor in this vicinity? *ʔaku xayyaaṭ ib-hal-manṭiqa?* or **ʔaku xayyaaṭ qariib minnaa.* **2.** *ʒawaali.* The weather is bad in the vicinity of Washington. *j-jaww muu zeen ʒawaali waašinṭan.*
vicious – *šaris, xabiiΘ.* The dog is vicious. *č-čalib šaris.*
**She has a vicious tongue. *lsaanha waṣix* or *lsaanha yguṣṣ.*
victim – *δaʒiyya* pl. *δaʒaaya.* He was the victim of an auto accident. *raaʒ δaʒiyyat ʒaadiΘ taṣaadum.*
victor – *mintiṣir* pl. *-iin.* We were the victors in that struggle. *ʔiʒna činna l-mintiṣriin ib-δaak il-kifaaʒ.*
victorious – *mintiṣir.* The victorious army entered the city. *j-jayš il-mintiṣir dixal l-wlaaya.*
victory – *ntiṣaar* pl. *-aat, naṣir* pl. *ʔanṣaar.* That was a great victory. *čaan fadd intiṣaar ƐaΘiim.*
view – **1.** *manδar* pl. *manaaδir.* You have a nice view from here. *Ɛindak xooš manδar minnaa.* **2.** *raʔi* pl. *ʔaaraaʔ.* Our views differ. *ʔaaraaʔna tixtilif.* **3.** *naδar.* In view of these developments, we'll have to change our plans. *bin-naδar ʔila hat-taṭawwuraat, laazim inġayyir xuṭaṭna.* — Here's my point of view. *haay wujhat naδari.*

in view - *mbayyin.* Is the ship in view? *s-sifiina mbayyna?*
to come into view - *bayyan (i).* The ship finally came into view. *s-sifiina taaliiha bayynat.*
vile - **1.** *qaδir* pl. *-iin, saafil* pl. *safala.* He's really a vile person. *huwwa fadd waaħid kulliš qaδir.* **2.** *muzεij.* What vile weather we're having! *ġeer jaww muzεij haaδa!*
village - *qarya* pl. *qura.* He lives in the village. *da-yiskun bil-qarya.*
vinegar - *xaḷḷ.*
to **violate** - *xaalaf (i muxaalafa).* That's not the first time he's violated the law. *haay muu ʔawwal marra yxaalif biiha l-qaanuun.*
violation - *muxaalafa* pl. *-aat.* He has three violations on his record. *εinda tlaθ muxaalafaat.*
violent - **1.** *εaniif* pl. *-iin.* He's a violent person. *huwwa fadd waaħid kulliš εaniif.* **2.** *ħaadd.* We had a violent argument. *ṣaarat beenaatna munaaqaša ħaadda.* **3.** *faδ̣iiε.* He died a violent death. *mootta čaanat faδ̣iiεa.*
violet - **1.** *wardat* (pl. *-aat,* coll. *warid) banafša.* We have violets in our garden. *εidna warid banafša b-ħadiiqatna.* **2.** *banafsaji*.* Her dress is violet. *badlatha banafsajiyya.*
violin - *kamanja* pl. *-aat.*
virgin - **1.** *baakir, baakra* pl. *bawaakir, bnayya* pl. *-aat.* She's a virgin. *hiyya baakir.* **2.** *εaδraaʔ* pl. *εaδaara.* He told the story of the Virgin Mary. *ħiča quṣṣat maryam il-εaδraaʔ.*
virtue - **1.** *ħasana* pl. *-aat.* His virtues are undeniable. *ħasanaata ma-tunkar.* **2.** *faḍil.* He has risen to this position by virtue of his education. *wuṣal il-hal-manṣab ib-faḍil θaqaafta.*
visa - *viiza* pl. *-aat, taʔšiira* pl. *-aat.*
vise - *mangana* pl. *-aat.*
visibility - *mada r-ruʔya.* The visibility is limited today. *mada r-ruʔya maħduuda hal-yoom.*
visible - *mbayyin, waaδ̣iħ.* The ship isn't visible yet. *l-baaxira baεad li-hassa ma-mbayyna.*
vision - *naδ̣ar.* His vision is getting poor. *naδ̣ara da-yiδ̣εaf.* -- He's a man of great vision. *huwwa fadd waaħid εinda naδ̣ar baεiid.*
visit - *ziyaara* pl. *-aat.* That was an unexpected visit. *δiič čaanat fadd ziyaara ma-mutawaqqaεa.*
to pay a visit - *zaar (u ziyaara) n-.* He paid me a visit last week. *zaarni bil-isbuuε il-faat.*
to visit - *zaar (u ziyaara).* He wanted to visit you. *raad yzuurak.* -- Have you visited our museum yet? *zirt il-matħaf maalna loo baεad?*
visitor - *xiṭṭaar, zaaʔir* pl. *zuwwaar.* We're having visitors tonight. *εidna xiṭṭaar hal-leela.* -- No visitors are allowed in this ward. *z-zuwwaar mamnuuε yduxluun ib-har-radha.*
vital - **1.** *ħayawi*.* It's of vital importance to me. *haaδa fadd šii ħayawi bin-nisba ʔila.* **2.** *muhimm.* He's well posted on the vital issues of the day. *huwwa miṭṭiliε εala kull il-ʔašyaaʔ il-muhimma l-iṭṣiir.*
vitality - *ħayawiyya.* He has a lot of vitality. *εinda ħayawiyya mumtaaza.*
vitamin - *fiitaamiin* pl. *-aat.*
vivid - **1.** *xaṣib.* He has a vivid imagination. *εinda xayaal xaṣib.* **2.** *barraaq, zaahi.* He uses vivid colors in his paintings. *yistaεmil ʔalwaan barraaqa bir-risuum maalta.* **3.** *waaδ̣iħ.* He gave us a vivid description of his experience. *nṭaana waṣuf waaδ̣iħ εan tajaaruḅa.*

vocal cords - *ħbaal ṣawtiyya.*
voice - *ṣoot* pl. *ʔaṣwaat, ħiss* pl. *ħsuus.* His voice carries well. *ħissa yinsimiε zeen.*
to voice - *jaahar (i mujaahara).* Don't be afraid to voice your opinions. *la-txaaf itjaahir ib-muεaaraδ̣tak.*
void - *malġi, baaṭil.* This check is void. *haṣ-ṣakk mafεuula baaṭil.* -- The contract is null and void. *l-εaqid mafεuula baaṭil.*
to void - *baṭṭal (i tabṭiil).* I'll void the check. *raħ-abaṭṭil ič-čakk.*
volcano - *burkaan* pl. *baraakiin.*
volley-ball - *kurat iṭ-ṭaaʔira.*
volt - *voolt* pl. *-aat.*
volume - **1.** *jizuʔ* pl. *ʔajzaaʔ, mujallad* pl. *-aat.* The book was published in two volumes. *l-iktaab innišar ib-juzʔeen.* **2.** *ħajim* pl. *ħjuum.* What's the volume of this tank? *šinu ħajim hal-εumbaar?* **3.** *jumla.* The factory's producing clothing in volume. *l-maεmal da-yintij ihduum bij-jumla.*
voluntarily - *b-ixtiyaar-, min keef-.* He did it voluntarily. *sawwaaha b-ixtiyaara.*
voluntary - *xtiyaari*.* Education is voluntary after 16. *d-diraasa xtiyaariyya baεad sinn iṣ-ṣiṭṭaεaš.*
volunteer - *miṭṭawwiε* pl. *-iin.* Can you get some volunteers to do it? *tigdar tilgi fadd čam miṭṭawwiε ysawwuuha?*
to volunteer - **1.** *εiraδ̣ (u εariδ̣), tbarraε (a tabarruε) b-.* He volunteered his services. *εiraδ̣ xadamaata.* **2.** *ṭṭawwaε (a taṭawwuε).* Who'll volunteer for this job? *minu yiṭṭawwaε il-haš-šaġḷa?*
to **vomit** - *zaaε (u zooε), zawwaε (i tazwiiε), δabb (i δabb) min raas~, giḷab (u gaḷub).* He got drunk and vomited. *sikar w-zawwaε.*
vote - **1.** *ṣawt* pl. *ʔaṣwaat.* They elected him by a majority of 2000 votes. *ntixboo b-akθariyyat ʔalfeen ṣawt.* **2.** *taṣwiit.* Minors have no vote. *l-iṣġaar ma-εidhum ħaqq it-taṣwiit.* -- The motion was put to a vote. *ħaṭṭaw l-iqtiraaħ bit-taṣwiit.*
to vote - **1.** *ntixab (i ntixaab), ṣawwat (i taṣwiit).* I couldn't vote in the last elections. *ma-gdart antixib bil-intixaabaat il-faatat.* -- Who'd you vote for? *ʔilman intixabit?* **2.** *ṣawwat (i taṣwiit).* Shall we vote on it? *nṣawwit biiha?* **3.** *qarrar (i taqriir).* The board voted five hundred dinars for relief. *l-majlis qarrar taxṣiiṣ xamis miit diinaar lil-ʔiεaanaat.*
to vote down - *rufaδ̣ (u) bit-taṣwiit.* They voted down the proposal. *rufδ̣aw l-iqtiraaħ bit-taṣwiit.*
voter - *naaxib* pl. *-iin, muntaxib* pl. *-iin.* We have 200 voters in this section. *εidna miiteen naaxib ib-hal-muħalla.*
to **vouch** - *šihad (a šahaada).* I vouch for him. *ʔaani ašhad-la.*
to **vow** - **1.** *tεahhad (a taεahhud).* He vowed not to do it again. *tεahhad ma-ysawwiiha baεad.* **2.** *ħilaf (i ħalif).* He vowed to avenge his brother's death. *ħilaf yaaxuδ θaar ʔaxuu l-maat.*
voyage - *safra* pl. *-aat.*
vulgar - **1.** *baδiiʔ.* He uses vulgar language. *yistaεmil ħači baδiiʔ.* **2.** *faδ̣δ̣, xašin.* He's a vulgar person. *haaδa fadd waaħid faδ̣δ̣.*
vulnerable - *εurḍa.* Our position is vulnerable to attack. *mawqifna εurḍa lil-hijuum.*
vulture - *ħdayya* pl. *-aat.* Vultures eat only carrion. *l-iħdayyaat yaakluun fṭaayis bass.*
vulva - *farij* pl. *fruuj.*

W

to **wad** - *kaεbar (u kaεbara).* He wadded up the paper and threw it away. *kaεbar il-waraq w-δabba.*
to **waddle** - *tdaεbal (a tdiεbil).* The duck waddled over to the water. *l-baṭṭa tdaεbilat lil-ṃayy.*
to **wade** - **1.** *xaaδ̣ (u xooδ̣) n-.* The soldiers waded ashore. *j-jinuud xaaδ̣aw lis-saahil.* -- We waded across the stream. *giṭaεna š-šaṭṭ xooδ̣.* **2.** *δabb (i δabb) nafs~.* I waded into my work. *δabbeet nafsi εaš-šuġuḷ.*
waders - *ʔaħδiyat xooδ̣.* He bought a pair of waders to go fishing. *štira ʔaħδiyat xooδ̣ ħatta yṣiid simač.*
to **wag** - *hazz (i hazz) n- b-.* The dog wagged its tail. *č-čalib hazz ib-δeela.*

wage - *ʔujra* pl. *ʔujuur.* They're not paying a decent wage. *ma-ydifεuun ʔujra zeena.*
to wage - *θaar (i ʔiθaara).* They can't wage a long war. *ma-ygidruun yθiiruun ħarb iṭwiila.*
wage rates - *mustawa ʔujuur.* Wage rates are rising. *mustawa l-ʔujuur da-yirtifiε.*
wagon - *εarabaana* pl. *-aat.* Hitch the horses to the new wagon. *šidd il-xeel bil-εarabaana j-jidiida.*
waist - *xiṣir* pl. *xṣuur, xaaṣra* pl. *xawaaṣir.* I took the pants in at the waist. *gaṣṣafit il-panṭaruun min yamm il-xiṣir.*
wait - *ntiδ̣aar* pl. *-aat.* The hour's wait was aggravating. *saaεat l-intiδ̣aar čaanat muzεija.*

to lie in wait - *traṣṣad (a taraṣṣud).* They were lying in wait for us. *čaanaw mitraṣṣdiinna.*
to wait - **1.** *ntiδar (i ntiδaar), ṣṭubar (u ṣṭubaar, ṣabur).* Wait a moment. *ntiδir išwayya.* -- Have you been waiting long? *ṣaar-lak ihwaaya mintiδir?* -- I can hardly wait to see him. *ma-da-agdar aṣṭubur ɛala šoofta.* **2.** *tʔajjal (a taʔajjul).* Can that business wait till tomorrow? *hal-masʔala mumkin titʔajjal il-baačir?* **3.** *ɛaṭṭal (i taɛṭiil) t-.* We'll wait dinner for him. *ɛuud inɛaṭṭil il-ɛaša ɛala muuda.* **4.** *ṣubar (u ṣabur).* I can't wait till that day comes. *ma-da-agdar aṣbur ʔila ʔan yiji δaak il-yoom.*
to wait for - *ntiδar (i ntiδaar).* I'll wait for you until five o'clock. *ʔantiδrak il-saaɛa xamsa.* -- Wait for his answer. *ntiδir jawaaba.*
to wait on - *šaaf (u) šuġuḷ.* Will you please wait on me now? *baḷḷa ma-tšuuf šuġḷi ɛaad?*
waiter - *booy* pl. *-aat.* He's a waiter in a restaurant. *huwwa booy maal maṭɛam.*
waiting room - *ġurfat* (pl. *ġuraf*) *intiδaar.* Is there a waiting room at the airport? *ʔaku ġurfat intiδaar bil-maṭaar?*
to **wake** - *gaɛɛad (i tgiɛɛid).* Please wake me at seven o'clock. *baḷḷa gaɛɛidni saaɛa sabɛa.*
to wake up - **1.** *fazzaz (i) mnin-noom, gaɛɛad (i) mnin-noom.* The noise woke me up in the middle of the night. *ṣ-ṣoot fazzazni mnin-noom ib-nuṣṣ il-leel.* **2.** *giɛad (u).* I didn't wake up until eight this morning. *ma-gɛadt imnin-noom ʔilla saaɛa θmaanya ṣ-ṣubuḥ.*
**It's high time you wake up to the fact that.... *laazim itfukk ɛeenak muu θixnat....*
walk - *mašya.* Did you have a nice walk? *ʔaxaδit-lak xooš mašya?* -- You can recognize him by his walk. *tigdar itɛurfa min mašiita.*
to go for a walk - *tmašša (a tamašši).* Let's go for a walk. *xalli nitmašša.*
to walk - **1.** *miša (i miši).* Shall we walk or take the bus? *raḥ-nimši loo naaxuδ paaṣ?* -- Can the baby walk yet? *j-jaahil yigdar yimši loo baɛad?* **2.** *mašša (i).* Did you walk the dog? *maššeet ič-čalib?*
to walk down - *nizal (i).* We were walking down the stairs. *činna da-ninzil id-daraj.*
to walk out on - *ṭilaɛ (a), baṭṭal (i).* Our girl walked out on us. *l-xaddaama ṭilɛat.*
to walk up - *ṣiɛad (a ṣuɛuud).* He can't walk up the stairs. *ma-yigdar yiṣɛad id-daraj.*
wall - *ḥaayiṭ* pl. *ḥiiṭaan, ḥyaaṭiin.* Hang the picture on this wall. *ɛallig iṣ-ṣuura ɛala hal-ḥaayiṭ.* -- Only the walls are still standing. *bass l-iḥyaaṭiin baɛadha baaqya.*
to wall up - *bina (i bnaaya).* They're walling up the doorways and windows in that building. *da-ybnuun iš-šabaabiič wil-ibwaab maal hal-ibnaaya.*
wallet - *jazdaan* pl. *-aat, jazaadiin.* I lost my wallet. *δayyaɛit jazdaani.*
walnut - **1.** *jooza* pl. *-aat* coll. *jooz.* Let's buy some walnuts. *xal-ništiri jooz.* **2.** *xišab jooz.* This table is made of walnut. *hal-meez imsawwa min xišab jooz.*
walnut tree - *jooza, šajrat* (pl. *-aat, ʔašjaar* coll. *šajar*) *jooz.* We have a walnut tree in our garden. *ɛidna jooza b-ḥadiiqatna.*
want - *maṭlab* pl. *maṭaaliib.* My wants are very modest. *maṭaaliibi basiiṭa.*
**I'll take it for want of something better. *raḥ-aqbalha li-ʔan ma-aku šii ʔaḥsan.*
to want - *raad (i ʔiraada) n-.* He knows what he wants. *yuɛruf š-yriid.* -- I want two sandwiches. *ʔariid sandwiičteen.* -- How much do you want for your furniture? *šgadd itriid anṭiik ib-hal-ʔaθaaθ?* -- I want to go swimming. *ʔariid asbaḥ.*
want ad - *ʔiɛlaan* pl. *-aat.*
wanted - *maṭluub.* He is wanted by the police. *huwwa maṭluub imniš-šurṭa.*
war - *ḥarb* pl. *ḥuruub.* Where were you during the last war? *ween činit ʔaθnaaʔ il-ḥarb il-ʔaxiira?*
holy war - *jihaad.*
ward - *qaawuuš* pl. *qwaawiiš, radha* pl. *-aat.* They had to put him in the ward because all the rooms were taken. *δṭarraw yḥuṭṭuu bil-qaawuuš li-ʔan kull il-ġuraf mašġuuḷa.*
warden - *mudiir* (pl. *mudaraaʔ*) *sijin.*
wardrobe - **1.** *qanṭoor* pl. *-aat.* What are your clothes doing in my wardrobe? *ɛajab ḥaaṭiṭ ihduumak bil-qanṭoor maali?* **2.** *ṭaxum ihduum.* She bought herself a complete wardrobe. *štirat ṭaxum kaamil ihduum.*
warehouse - *maxzan* pl. *maxaazin.*
warm - **1.** *daafi.* It's warm today. *j-jaww daafi l-yoom.* **2.** *dafyaan.* Are you warm enough? *ʔinta dafyaan zeen?*
to warm - **1.** *daffa (i).* Come in and warm yourself by the fire. *taɛaal jawwa w-daffi nafsak yamm in-naar.* **2.** *ḥima (i ḥami) n-.* Please warm up the soup for me. *baḷḷa ḥmii-li š-šoorba.*
to warm up - *maal (i).* I can't warm up to him. *ma-agdar amiil ʔila.*
warmth - *ḥamaawa.* The warmth of the fire reached me over here. *jatni ḥamaawat in-naar l-ihnaa.*
to **warn** - **1.** *ḥaδδar (i taḥδiir).* They warned me about him. *ḥaδδrooni minna.* **2.** *niδar, ʔanδar (i ʔinδaar).* The government warned that demonstrators would be jailed. *l-ḥukuuma ʔanδirat ib-ḥabs illi ysawwuun muδaaharaat.*
warning - *taḥδiir* pl. *-aat.* The government broadcast a warning about the flood. *l-ḥukuuma ʔaδaaɛat taḥδiir ɛan il-fayδaan.*
to **warp** - **1.** *ɛakkaf (u).* This wood will warp. *han-nooɛ imnil-xišab yɛakkuf.* **2.** *tɛawwaj (a).* The records will be warped in the heat. *l-iṣṭiwaanaat titɛawwaj bil-ḥaraara.*
wash - *hduum maġsuula.* The maid hung the wash on the line. *l-xaddaama šarrat l-ihduum il-maġsuula ɛal-ḥabil.*
to wash - **1.** *ġisal (i ġasil) n-.* Wash these shirts, please. *baḷḷa, ġisli hal-ihduum.* -- This floor hasn't been washed yet. *l-gaaɛ baɛadha ma-nġislat.* **2.** *ġassal (i), ġisal (i).* Did you wash your face? *ġassalit wujjak?*
to wash away - *jiraf (u jaruf) n-.* Last year the flood washed away the bridge. *s-sant il-faatat il-fayaδaan jiraf ij-jisir.*
to wash up - *ġassal (i), ġisal (i).* I'd like to wash up before supper. *ʔariid aġassil gabuḷ il-ʔakil.*
**He's washed up. *ntiha ʔamra.*
**Our plans for a trip are all washed up. *mašruuɛna maal is-safra fišal.*
waste - **1.** *tabdiid.* That's plain waste. *haaδa tabdiid waaδiḥ.* **2.** *maδyaɛa.* It's a waste of time and energy. *haay maδyaɛa lil-wakit wij-jahid.*
**Haste makes waste. *l-ɛajala mniš-šayṭaan.*
to go to waste - **1.** *baar (u boor).* A good cook doesn't let anything go to waste. *ṭ-ṭabbaaxa z-zeena ma-txalli šii ybuur.* **2.** *raaḥ (u) ɛabaθ, δaaɛ (i δiyaaɛ).* His talents are going to waste. *qaabliyyaata raayḥa ɛabaθ.*
to lay waste - *dumar (u damur) n-.* The storm has laid waste the entire area. *l-ɛaaṣifa dumrat il-manṭiqa kullha.*
to waste - *δayyaɛ (i taδyiiɛ).* He wastes a lot of time talking. *yδayyiɛ ihwaaya wakit bil-ḥači.*
wastebasket - *sallat* (pl. *slaal*) *muhmalaat.*
watch - *saaɛa* pl. *-aat.* By my watch it's five. *bil-xamsa ḥasab saaɛati.*
to watch - **1.** *tfarraj (i) ɛala.* I've been watching this program for about an hour. *ṣaar-li ḥawaali saaɛa da-atfarraj ɛala hal-manhaj.* **2.** *baawaɛ (i mubaawaɛa), šaaf (u).* Watch how I do it. *baawiɛ išloon da-asawwiiha.* **3.** *daar (i) baal˜.* Who's going to watch the children? *minu raḥ-ydiir baala ɛaj-jihaal?* **4.** *raaqab (u muraaqaba).* That fellow needs close watching. *haaδa waaḥid laazim yraaqba zeen.* **5.** *fakk (u) ɛeen˜, daar (i) baal˜.* Watch yourself with him. *fukk ɛeenak zeen wiyyaa.*
to watch out - *daar (i) baal˜.* Watch out when you cross the street. *diir baalak min tuɛbur iš-šaariɛ.*
to watch out for - *traqqab (a).* I'll be watching out for you to arrive at the station. *raḥ-atraqqab wuṣuulak lil-maḥaṭṭa.*
watchmaker - *saaɛači* pl. *-iyya.*
watchman - *ḥaaris* pl. *ḥurraas.*
water - *ṃaay, ṃayy.* Please give me a glass of water. *baḷḷa ṇṭiini glaaṣ ṃaay.*
to water - **1.** *siga (i sagi) n-.* I water the garden every day. *ʔaani ʔasgi l-ḥadiiqa yoomiyya.* -- Have the horses been watered yet? *sgeet il-xeel loo baɛad?* **2.** *dammaɛ (i tadmiiɛ).* My eyes are watering. *ɛyuuni da-tdammiɛ.* **3.** *saal (i seel).* The cake makes my mouth water. *l-keeka xallat luɛaabi ysiil.*
waterfall - *šallaal* pl. *-aat.*
watermelon - *raggiyya* pl. *-aat* coll. *raggi.*
waterproof - **1.** *δidd il-muṭar.* Is this coat waterproof? *hal-miɛṭaf δidd il-muṭar?* **2.** *δidd il-ṃayy.* Is this watch waterproof? *has-saaɛa δidd il-ṃayy?*
wave - **1.** *mooja* pl. *ʔamwaaj* coll. *mooj.* The waves are very high today. *l-mooj kulliš ɛaali l-yoom.*

2. *mawja* pl. *-aat*. A wave of enthusiasm swept the country. *fadd mawja mnil-ḥamaas ištaaḥat il-balad.*
to wave - 1. *rafraf (i rafrafa) t-*. The flags were waving in the breeze. *l-iɛlaam čaanat da-trafrif bil-hawa.* 2. *ʔaššar (i taʔšiir).* I waved to him with my hand. *ʔaššarit-la b-iidi.*

wax - *šamiɛ.*

way - 1. *ṭariiq* pl. *ṭuruq*. Is this the way to Baghdad? *haaδa ṭ-ṭariiq il-baġdaad?* — Are you going my way? *raayiḥ ɛala ṭariiqi?* 2. *ṭariiqa* pl. *ṭuruq*. That's just his way of dealing with employees. *haaδi ɛaadatan ṭariiqat muɛaamalta lil-muwaδ̣δ̣afiin.* — There are different ways of doing things. *ʔaku ɛiddat ṭuruq.* 3. *šikil*. You shouldn't treat people this way. *ma-laazim itɛaamil in-naas ib-haš-šikil.* — That's the way he wants it. *yriidha haš-šikil.* 4. *darub*. Do you know your way around here? *tuɛruf darbak ib-hal-manṭiqa?* or ***tindall hal-manṭiqa?* 5. *maṣaariif*. He paid my way. *huwwa difaɛ l-maṣaariif maalti.* — I paid my own way at college. *dfaɛit maṣaariif daraasti min jeebi l-xaaṣṣ.* 6. *ʔamir*. He'll make his way wherever he is. *yigdar ydabbur ʔamra ween-ma tδibba.*
**Everything is going along (in) the same old way. *kullši baɛda miθil-ma čaan.*
**Everything turned out the way they wanted. *kullši ṣaar miθil-ma raadaw.*
**Have it your own way! *miθil-ma triid.* or *keefak.*
**I'm afraid he's in a bad way. *ʔaxaaf ḥaalta muu zeen.*
**I don't see my way clear to do it now. *ma-ašuuf imnil-munaasaba ʔasawwiiha hassa.*
**Christmas is still a long way off. *baɛad ihwaaya l-krismas.*
a long way - *biɛiid*. The school is a long way from our house. *l-madrasa biɛiida ɛan beetna.*
by the way - *bil-munaasaba*. By the way, are you coming with us tonight? *bil-munaasaba ʔinta jaay wiyyaana hal-leela?*
by way of - 1. *ɛala ṭariiq*. We went by way of Damascus. *riḥna ɛala ṭariiq iš-šaam.* 2. *ɛala sabiil*. He said it by way of a joke. *gaalha ɛala sabiil in-nukta.*
in a way - *min jiha, nooɛan-ma*. In a way he's right. *min jiha huwwa ṣaḥiiḥ.*
in no way - *ʔabadan*. This is in no way better than what you had before. *haay ʔabadan muu ʔaḥsan min illi čaanat ɛindak gabuḷ.*
in the way of - *min*. What have you got in the way of radios? *šaku ɛidkum imnir-raadyowaat?*
in what way - *šloon*. In what way is that better? *šloon haay aḥsan?*
out of the way - *muu ɛar-rijil*. This place is somewhat out of the way. *hal-maḥall išwayya muu ɛar-rijil.*
right of way - *ṭariiq*. You shouldn't have gone through, I had the right of way. *ma-čaan laazim itfuut, ṭ-ṭariiq čaan ʔili.*
to get under way - *tqaddam (a), btida (i)*. The project is slowly getting under way. *l-mašruuɛ da-yitqaddam išwayya šwayya.*
to give way - *ngiṭaɛ (i)*. The rope's giving way. *l-ḥabil da-yingiṭiɛ.*
to go out of one's way - 1. *tkallaf (a)*. I don't want you to go out of your way for my sake. *ma-ariidak titkallaf ɛala muudi.* 2. *biδal (i baδil) juhuud~*. We went out of our way to make him comfortable. *bδalna juhuudna ḥatta nxallii yirtaaḥ.*

way out - *maxraj* pl. *maxaarij*. I don't see any way out of this mess. *ma-da-ašuuf ʔay maxraj min hal-wurṭa.*

we - *ʔiḥna*. We're not the ones responsible. *ʔiḥna muu l-masʔuuliin.*
**We have a house in Najef. *ɛidna beet bin-najaf.*
**We haven't seen him. *ma-šifnaa.*

weak - 1. *xafiif*. Would you like your tea weak or strong? *triid čaayak xafiif loo ṭoox?* 2. *δ̣aɛiif*. He's still weak from his illness. *baɛda δ̣aɛiif imnil-maraδ̣.* — The bridge is weak. *j-jisir δ̣aɛiif.*

to **weaken - 1.** *δ̣aɛɛaf (u)*. The flood weakened the bridge. *l-fayaδ̣aan δ̣aɛɛaf ij-jisir.* 2. *ʔaδ̣ɛaf (u ʔiδ̣ɛaaf)*. Aspirin weakens you. *l-ʔaspariin yδ̣iɛfak.*

weakness - *nuqṭat (pl. nuqaaṭ) δ̣uɛuf*. That's his biggest weakness. *haaδi ʔahamm nuqṭat δ̣uɛuf ɛinda.*

wealth - *θarwa*. They wasted the wealth of the nation. *δ̣ayyɛaw θarwat il-balad.*

wealthy - *zangiin* pl. *znaagiin, ġani* pl. *ʔaġniyaaʔ*. She married a wealthy merchant. *tzawwjat fadd taajir zangiin.*

weapon - *slaaḥ* pl. *ʔasliḥa*. All weapons have to be turned over to the police. *kull il-ʔasliḥa laazim titsallam liš-šurṭa.*

wear - 1. *hduum*. I'm sorry, we carry only men's wear. *mitʔassif, ɛidna hduum iryaajiil bass.* 2. *libis*. There's still a lot of wear left in this suit. *hal-qaaṭ baɛad bii libis ihwaaya.*
**The cuffs are showing signs of wear. *r-ridaanaat mbayyna saayfa.*
to wear - 1. *libas (a libis) n-*. He never wears a hat. *ʔabad ma-yilbas šafqa.* -- What did she wear? *š-libsat?* 2. *ṭawwal (i)*. This coat didn't wear well. *hal-miɛṭaf ma-ṭawwal ihwaaya.*
**She wears her hair short. *hiyya tguṣṣ šaɛarha gṣayyir.*
to wear down - *gaam (u)*. These heels are all worn down. *hal-ičɛuuba maal iqnaadir kullha gaamat.*
**We finally wore him down. *taaliiha nazzalnaa ɛan baġiḷta.*
to wear off - 1. *burad (a)*. Wait till the excitement wears off. *ntiδ̣ir ʔila ʔan tibrad il-hoosa.* 2. *raaḥ (u)*. The paint has worn off my car in several spots. *ṣ-ṣubuġ maal sayyaarti raaḥ min čam makaan.*
to wear out - 1. *stahlak (a stihlaak)*. The tires are all worn out. *t-taayaraat kullha stahilkat.* — Our furniture is worn out. *ʔaθaaθna stahlak.* 2. *šaggag (i) t-*. He wore out his shoes quickly. *šaggag qundarta bil-ɛajil.* 3. *hilak (i halaak)*. Just don't wear yourself out! *la-tihlik nafsak.*

weather - *jaww, ṭaqis, manaax*. How is the weather today? *šloon ij-jaww il-yoom?*
**I'm a little under the weather today. *ma-da-aḥiss hal-gadd zeen hal-yoom.*
to weather - *dabbar (i tadbiir) ʔamr~*. How did you weather the flood? *šloon dabbarit ʔamrak bil-fayaδ̣aan.*

to **weave -** *ḥaak (u ḥook, ḥyaaka) n-*. The children wove this rug at school. *l-ʔaṭfaal ḥaakaw hal-ibṣaaṭ bil-madrasa.*

weaver - *ḥaayič, ḥaayik* pl. *ḥiyyaač*. He's a weaver. *huwwa ḥaayič.*

wedding - *ɛiris* pl. *ʔaɛraas*. I was at the wedding but not at the reception. *činit bil-ɛiris bass muu bil-ḥafla.*

Wednesday - *l-ʔarbaɛaa.*

weeds - *ḥašiiš*. The whole garden is full of weeds. *l-ḥadiiqa matruusa ḥašiiš.*
to weed - *šilaɛ (a šaliɛ) ḥašiiš*. I've got to weed the garden. *laazim ʔašlaɛ il-ḥašiiš imnil-ḥadiiqa.*

week - *sbuuɛ* pl. *ʔasaabiiɛ*. I'll be back in three weeks. *raḥ-arjaɛ ib-xilaal itlaθ asaabiiɛ.*
by the week - *sbuuɛiyya*. They pay by the week. *ydifɛuun isbuuɛiyya.*

weekend - *ɛuṭlat isbuuɛ* pl. *ɛuṭal ʔasaabiiɛ*. We decided to spend the weekend at the lake. *qarrarna nigδ̣i ɛuṭlat il-isbuuɛ bil-buḥayra.*

weekly - 1. *sbuuɛi**. He publishes a weekly newspaper. *yṭalliɛ jariida sbuuɛiyya.* 2. *marra bil-isbuuɛ, sbuuɛiyyan*. This magazine appears weekly. *hal-majalla titlaɛ marra bil-isbuuɛ.*

to **weep -** *biča (i)*. She wept bitter tears. *bičat ib-ḥurga.*

to **weigh -** *wuzan (i wazin) n-*. Please weigh this package for me. *baḷḷa ʔoozin-li har-ruzma.* — He always weighs his words carefully. *daaʔiman yoozin iḥčaayaata zeen.*
**This piece of meat weighs four pounds. *hal-wuṣlat il-laḥam wazinha ʔarbaɛ keeluwwaat.*
**The responsibility weighs heavily on me. *hal-masʔuuliyya kulliš zaḥma.*

weight - 1. *ɛyaar* pl. *-aat*. The weights are under the scale. *l-iɛyaaraat jawwa l-miizaan.* 2. *wazin, θugul*. Did you put down the weight of the package? *sajjalit wazn ir-ruzma?* — Don't attach too much weight to what he says. *la-tinṭi hwaaya wazin il-ḥačya.* 3. *ḥsaab, wazin*. His opinion carries great weight. *raʔya yinḥisib-la ḥsaab.* or *raʔya ʔila wazin.*

weird - *ġariib*. That's a weird story. *haay iḥčaaya ġariiba.*

welcome - 1. *stiqbaal* pl. *-aat*. They gave us a warm welcome. *staqbiloona stiqbaal ḥaarr.* or ***raḥḥibaw biina zeen.* 2. *ɛal-maraam*. This is a welcome change in government policy. *hat-taġyiir ib-siyaasat il-ḥukuuma čaan ɛal-maraam.*
**You're always welcome here. *šwakit ma-tiji ʔahlan wa-sahlan.* or *haaδa miθil beetkum.*
**You're welcome. *ʔahlan wa-sahlan.* or *mamnuun.*
to welcome - *staqbal (i), raḥḥab (i) b-*. They

welcomed us warmly. *staqbiloona bit-tirzaab.* or *razzibaw biina.*
to **weld** - *lizam (i lazim).* He's welding the bumper on my car. *da-yilzim id-daƐƐaamiyya maal sayyaarti.*
welfare - *raxaaʔ.* The welfare of the country depends on this project. *raxaaʔ il-bilaad yiƐtimid Ɛala haaδa l-mašruuƐ.*
well - 1. *biir* pl. *byaar.* They're digging a well back of the house. *da-yzaffruun biir wara l-beet.* 2. *zeen.* Do you know him well? *tƐurfa zeen?* — I'm not feeling well today. *ʔaani ma-da-aziss hal-gadd zeen il-yoom.* — The new business is doing very well. *š-šuġuḷ zeen da-yimši.* — Please let me do it. Very well. *baḷḷa xalliini asawwiiha. zeen.* 3. *hwaaya.* There were well over 1000 people. *čaanaw ihwaaya ʔazyad min ʔalif waazid.* 4. *haa.* Well, where did you come from? *haa, mneen jeet?*
**Leave well enough alone. *ʔazsan-lak itxalliiha miθil-ma hiyya.*
as well as - *miθil-ma, miθil.* He talks Arabic as well as I do. *yizči Ɛarabi miθil-ma ʔazči ʔaani.* or *yizči Ɛarabi miθli.*
**He knows Arabic as well as several other languages. *yuƐruf Ɛarabi w-yuƐruf luġaat ʔuxra.*
**He couldn't very well refuse to come. *ma-čaan aku majaal yirfuδ id-daƐwa.*
**He could very well change his mind. *ʔaku ztimaal kabiir ybaddil fikra.*
to get well - *ṭaab (i), ṣaar (i) zeen.* First I must get well again. *xalli ʔaṭiib ʔawwal.* — I hope you get well soon! *nšaalla tṣiir zeen Ɛan qariib.*
well-behaved - *Ɛaaqil, mʔaddab.* She's a well-behaved child. *haay fadd ṭifla kullis Ɛaaqla.*
well-done - *maṭbuux zeen, mištiwi zeen.* The meat is well-done. *l-lazam maṭbuux zeen.*
well-to-do - *zangiin.* His family is well-to-do. *Ɛaaʔilta zangiina.*
west - 1. *ġarb.* The wind is from the west. *l-hawa mnil-ġarb.* — The sign points west. *s-sahim yʔaššir Ɛal-ġarb.* 2. *ġarbi*.* There's a west wind today. *ʔaku hawa ġarbi l-yoom.*
western - *ġarbi*.* The Syrian Desert extends into the western part of Iraq. *baadiyat iš-šaam timtadd lil-qism il-ġarbi mnil-Ɛiraaq.*
westward - *lil-ġarb.* They headed westward. *ttijhaw lil-ġarb.*
wet - 1. *mballal, mitnaggiƐ, mnaggaƐ.* My socks are wet. *jwaariibi mballila.* — I'm wet through and through. *ʔaani mitnaggiƐ min foog li-jawwa.* 2. *raṭib.* We had a wet summer. *marr Ɛaleena ṣeef raṭib.* 3. *jdiid.* The paint is still wet. *ṣ-ṣubuġ baƐda jdiid.* or **ṣ-ṣubuġ baƐda ma-yaabis.*
to get wet - *tnaggaƐ (a tniggiƐ), tballal (a).* I got wet yesterday in the rain. *tnaggaƐit imnil-muṭar il-baarza.*
to wet - *baal (u bool).* The baby wet his pants. *ṭ-ṭifil baal b-ilbaasa.*
whale - *zuuta* pl. *-aat, zuwat* coll. *zuut.*
what - 1. *š-.* What would you like to eat? *š-yƐijbak taakul?* 2. *šinu.* What things are missing? *šinu l-ʔašyaaʔ in-naagṣa?* — What's the color of the gloves? *šinu loon ič-čufuuf?* 3. *šloon, šgadd.* What beautiful flowers you have in your garden! *šloon zilu hal-warid il-Ɛindak bil-zadiiqa.* — What nonsense! *šloon laġwa* 4. *beeš.* What time is it? *s-saaƐa beeš?* 5. *yaa.* Do you know what train we're supposed to take? *tuƐruf yaa qiṭaar laazim naaxuδ?* 6. *lli.* That's just what I wanted to avoid. *haaδa š-šii lli ridt atzaašaa.*
**He certainly knows what's what. *muʔakkad huwwa yuƐruf š-aku š-ma-aku.*
**He didn't get there in time, but what of it? *ma-wuṣal l-ihnaak Ɛal-wakit, bass š-yhimm?*
**What about me? *w-ʔaani?*
what...for - *luweeš, leeš, ʔilweeš.* What did you do that for? *luweeš sawweetha haay?*
what's more - 1. *bil-ʔiδaafa.* (And) what's more, he is very efficient. *w-bil-ʔiδaafa l-haaδa, huwwa qadiir.* 2. *hamm.* I'm leaving, and what's more, I'm taking the furniture. *raz-aruuz w-aaxuδ il-ʔaθaaθ hamm.*
whatever - 1. *š-ma.* Whatever he does is all right with me. *š-ma ysawwi ma-yxaalif.* — Do whatever you want. *sawwi š-ma triid.* — She's lost whatever respect she had for him. *δayyƐat iš-ma čaan Ɛidha mnil-iztiraam ʔila.* 2. *š-.* Whatever made you do that? *š-xallaak itsawwi haay?* 3. *ʔabadan.* I have no money whatever. *ma-Ɛindi fluus ʔabadan.*
whatsoever - *ʔabadan.* I have no money whatsoever. *ma-Ɛindi fluus ʔabadan.*
wheat - *zunṭa.* They raise a lot of wheat in Iraq. *yzirƐuun ihwaaya zunṭa bil-Ɛiraaq.*
wheel - *čarix* pl. *čruux.* This wheel on that wagon is broken. *č-čarix maal hal-Ɛarabaana maksuur.*
to wheel - *difaƐ (a dafiƐ) n-.* Wheel the baby carriage into the garage. *ʔidfaƐ Ɛarabaant ij-jaahil lil-garaaj.*
to wheel around - *ftarr (a).* He wheeled around suddenly and fired. *Ɛala ġafla ftarr w-šawwat.*
when - 1. *šwakit, ʔeemta.* When can I see you again? *šwakit ašuufak murra lux?* 2. *min, lamma, lamman.* When he calls up tell him I'm not here. *min yxaabur gul-la ʔaani ma-hnaa.* — When the work is done you can go. *tigdar itruuz min yixlaṣ iš-šuġuḷ.* — I wasn't home when he called. *ma-činit bil-beet lamma xaabar.*
**There are times when I enjoy being alone. *tiji awqaat yiƐjibni ʔakuun il-wazdi.*
whenever - 1. *swakit-ma.* Come to see us whenever you have time. *zuurna šwakit-ma yṣiir Ɛindak wakit.* 2. *kull-ma.* Whenever we have a picnic it rains. *kull-ma nsawwi safra, tguum tumṭur.*
**Whenever did you find time to write? *šloon dabbarit wakit zatta tiktib?*
where - 1. *ween.* Where is the nearest hotel? *ween aqrab ʔuteel?* — Where does the difference lie? *ween l-ixtilaaf?* 2. *illi.* We found him just where we expected him to be. *lgeenaa bil-makaan illi twaqqaƐna nilgii bii.* — They will send them where they're needed most. *Ɛuud ydizzuuhum il-makaan illi yiztaajuuhum bii hwaaya.*
where...from - *mneen.* Where does your friend come from? *ṣadiiqak mneen?*
wherever - *ween-ma.* Wherever you are, don't forget to write me. *la-tinsa tiktib-li ween-ma tkuun.* — Wherever you go in this country you'll find good roads. *ween-ma truuz ib-hal-balad, kull iṭ-ṭuruq zeena.*
whether - *ʔiδa, loo.* I'd like to know whether he's coming. *ʔard aƐruf ʔiδa raz-yiji loo laa.*
whey - *rooba.*
which - 1. *yaa, ʔay.* Which bag did you pick out? *yaa janṭa ʔaxaδti?* 2. *yaahu.* Which is yours? *yaahu maalak?* 3. *lli.* Please return the book which you borrowed. *baḷḷa rajjiƐ l-iktaab illi ṭlabta.*
whichever - *ʔay.* Take whichever one you want. *ʔuxuδ ʔay waazid itriida.*
while - 1. *šwayya, fadd mudda, fadd fatra.* You'll have to wait a while. *laazim tintiδir išwayya.* 2. *min, lamma, b-ʔaθnaaʔ-ma.* He came while we were out. *ʔija min činna ṭaalƐiin.* 3. *bayna-ma.* Some people live in luxury, while others are dying of starvation. *baƐaδ in-naas yƐiišuun ib-baδax bayna-ma ġeerhum mayytiin imnij-juuƐ.* 4. *ma-daam.* I want to go in while it's still light. *ʔariid aruuz ma-daam baƐadha δaawya.*
to while away - *giδa (i giδyaan).* I while away my time reading. *da-agδi wakti ʔaqra.*
whip - *qamči* pl. *qamaači, qirbaač* pl. *qaraabiič.* The driver snapped the whip. *l-Ɛarabanči ṭagg il-qamči maala.*
to whip - *δirab (u) bil-qamči.* He whipped the horse mercilessly. *δirab il-xeel maalta bil-qamči bala razam.*
whisky - *wiiski.*
whisper - *hamis.* I heard a whisper in the next room. *smaƐit hamis bil-ġurfa l-yammna.*
in a whisper - *mšaawra.* They spoke in a whisper so that no one would hear them. *zičaw imšaawra zatta lazzad yismaƐhum.*
to whisper - *himas (i), šaawar (i mušaawara).* She whispered the word in my ear. *himsat ič-čilma b-ʔiδni* or *šaawratni bič-čilma.*
whistle - 1. *ṣaafira* pl. *-aat.* The policeman lost his whistle. *š-šurṭi δayyaƐ iṣ-ṣaafira maalta.* 2. *maaṣuula* pl. *-aat.* The boy broke his whistle. *l-walad kisar il-maaṣuula maalta.* 3. *ṣoofra* pl. *-aat.* The signal was one long and two short whistles. *l-ʔišaara čaanat ṣoofra ṭwiila w-ṣoofirteen igṣaar.*
to whistle - *ṣoofar (i ṣoofra).* He whistled as he walked along. *čaan da-yimši w-yṣoofir.* — He whistled to the cab. *ṣoofar-la lit-taksi.*
white - 1. *ʔabyaδ.* She wore a white dress at the party. *libsat nafnuuf abyaδ bil-zafla.* 2. *bayaaδ.* I put the whites of four eggs in the cake. *zaṭṭeet bayaaδ arbaƐ beeδaat bil-keeka.*
whitewash - *byaaδ.* The whitewash is peeling off the walls. *l-ibyaaδ maal il-zaayiṭ da-yoogaƐ.*

to whitewash - *bayyaṣ (i tabyiiṣ) t-.* How long will it take you to whitewash the garage? *šgadd mudda yinraad-lak ɀatta tbayyiṣ il-garaaj?*
who - **1.** *minu.* Who used this book last? *minu ʔaaxir waaɀid istaƐmal hal-iktaab?* **2.** *lli.* Did you notice the man who just passed by? *laaɀaṣṭ ir-rijjaal il-marr minnaa hassa?* **3.** *man.* Who did you give it to? *ʔil-man inṭeetha?*
who...for - *Ɛala man.* Who are you looking for? *Ɛala man da-tdawwur?*
whoever - *minu-ma.* Whoever wants it may have it. *minu-ma yriidha xal-yaaxuδha.*
whole - *kaamil, kull.* I intend to stay a whole week. *b-niiti ʔabqa sbuuƐ kaamil.* -- He ate the whole thing himself. *ʔakal kullši waɀda.*
on the whole - *b-ṣuura Ɛaamma, šii Ɛala šii.* On the whole, I agree with you. *b-ṣuura Ɛaamma ʔaani attifiq wiyyaak.*
wholesale - *bij-jumla.* They sell only wholesale. *ma-ybiiƐuun ġeer bij-jumla.* -- The president gave out wholesale pardons. *raʔiis ij-jamhuuriyya ṭallaƐ Ɛafu bij-jumla.*
wholesale price - *siƐir ij-jumla.* What's the wholesale price? *šinu siƐr ij-jumla?*
whooping cough - *suƐaal diiki.* My kids all have whooping cough. *wuldi kullhum Ɛidhum suƐaal diiki.*
whore - *gaɀba* pl. *-aat, gɀaab.*
whose - **1.** *maal man.* Whose watch is this? *maal man has-saaƐa?* **2.** *lli.* There's the lady whose bag you found yesterday. *haaδi l-imrayya lli lgeet janṭatha l-baarɀa.*
why - *luweeš, leeš, ʔilweeš.* Why is the train so crowded this morning? *luweeš il-qiṭaar hal-gadd xabṣa l-yoom?*
**Why, what do you mean? *haa! š-tuqṣud?*
**Why there he is! *haa, hiyyaata.*
that's why - *li-haaδa, l-has-sabab.* That's why I didn't call you. *li-haaδa ma-xaabartak.*
wick - *ftiila* pl. *ftaayil.*
wide - **1.** *Ɛariiṣ.* The garage doorway isn't wide enough. *l-baab maal il-garaaj muu hal-gadd Ɛariiṣa.* — The window is very wide. *š-šibbaač Ɛariiṣ ihwaaya.* **2.** *čbiir, waasiƐ.* We have a wide selection of shoes. *Ɛidna majmuuƐa čbiira mnil-ʔaɀδiya.* **3.** *waasiƐ.* Our firm has wide commercial connections. *šarikatna Ɛidha Ɛalaaqaat tijaariyya waasƐa.*
**The window is two feet wide. *š-šibbaač Ɛurṣa fuuteen.*
wide-awake - *ṣaaɀi.* I'm wide awake. *ʔaani ṣaaɀi tamaaman.*
**He's a wide-awake fellow. *Ɛeena mafkuuka zeen.*
wide-eyed - **He looked at me wide-eyed. *fakk iƐyuuna mitƐajjib.*
to **widen** - *Ɛarraṣ (i taƐriiṣ) t-.* They're going to widen our street. *raɀ-yƐarrṣuun šaariƐna.*
wide open - *Ɛala gfaaha.* He left the door wide open. *xalla l-baab mafkuuka Ɛala gfaaha.*
widespread - **1.** *mintišir.* How widespread is this opinion? *šgadd mintašra hal-fikra?* **2.** *šaayiƐ.* This custom is widespread here. *hal-Ɛaada šaayƐa hnaa.* **3.** *waasiƐ, šaamil.* The hailstorm caused widespread damage. *l-ɀaaluub sabbab ṣarar waasiƐ.*
widow - *ʔarmaḷa* pl. *ʔaraamiḷ.*
widower - **That man is a widower. *har-rijjaal marta mayyta.*
width - *Ɛuruṣ.* What's the width of this window? *šgadd Ɛuruṣ haš-šibbaač?* — The room is nine feet in width. *l-ġurfa Ɛuruṣha tisiƐ fuutaat.* — We need double-width material for the drapes. *niɀtaaj iqmaaš ʔabu Ɛurṣeen lil-pardaat.*
wife - *zawja* pl. *-aat.* She's the wife of the prime minister. *haay zawjat raʔiis il-wuzaraaʔ.*
wild - **1.** *waɀši*.* There are no wild animals in this area. *ma-aku ɀaywaanaat waɀšiyya b-hal-manṭiqa.* **2.** *wakiiɀ, wakiɀ.* The children are too wild. *l-wulid kulliš wukkaɀ.* **3.** *mitɀammis.* I'm not wild about it. *ʔaani muu kulliš mitɀammis Ɛaleeha.*
**He lead a wild life when he was young. *čaan ṭaayiš min čaan iṣġayyir.*
**My boy is wild about ice cream. *ʔibni ymuut Ɛad-doondirma.*
to go wild - **1.** *tɀammas.* The crowd went wild when they heard the news. *n-naas itɀammsaw min simƐaw il-axbaar.* **2.** *haaj (i).* The crowd went wild and attacked the embassy. *n-naas haajaw w-hijmaw is-safaara.*
to run wild - *nhadd (a).* The dog has run wild since his master died. *č-čalib inhadd min maat ṣaaɀba.*
wilderness - *čool* pl. *čwaal.* They wandered in the wilderness. *taahaw bič-čuwaal.*
wilds - **Their house is way out in the wilds. *beethum ib-ʔaaxir id-dinya.*
will - **1.** *ʔiraada.* He has a strong will. *Ɛinda ʔiraada qawiyya.* **2.** *waṣiyya* pl. *waṣaaya.* He died without making a will. *maat bala-ma yiktib waṣiyya.*
at will - *b-keef-.* They come and go at will. *yruuɀuun w-yijuun ib-keefhum.*
to will - *waṣṣa (i tawṣiya).* He willed all his property to the hospital. *waṣṣa kull ʔamlaaka lil-mustašfa.*
will - **1.** *Ɛuud.* I'll meet you at three o'clock. *Ɛuud ašuufak saaƐa tlaaθa.* -- We'll see what can be done. *Ɛuud inšuuf iš-nigdar insawwi.* **2.** *raɀ-.* They'll be surprised to see you here. *raɀ-yitƐajjbuun min yšuufuuk ihnaa.* — I thought that would happen. *ṭṣawwarit hiiči šii raɀ-yṣiir.* -- I won't be able to do that. *ma-raɀ-agdar asawwi haay.* — He won't get anywhere that way. *ma-raɀ-yooṣal in-natiija b-haṭ-ṭariiqa.*
**Won't you come in for a minute? *baḷḷa ma-txušš išwayya?*
**Will you please reserve a room for me. *baḷḷa-ma tiɀjiz-li ġurfa?*
**This hall will hold a thousand people. *hal-qaaƐa tilzam ʔalif waaɀid.*
**What would you like to drink? *š-yƐijbak tišrab?*
**We would rather live outside of town. *ʔiɀna nfaṣṣil niskun xaarij l-wlaaya.*
**Would you rather go to the theater? *tfaṣṣil itruuɀ lis-siinama?*
**He would never take the job. *ʔabad ma-yiqbal haš-šuġuḷ.*
**He'll go for days without smoking. *ʔaɀyaanan yibqa Ɛiddat ʔayyaam bala ma-ydaxxin.*
willing - **I'm willing to try anything. *ma-Ɛindi maaniƐ š-ma-ykuun.* or *ʔaqbal asawwi kullši.*
will power - *quwwat ʔiraada.* He has amazing will power. *Ɛinda quwwat ʔiraada Ɛajiiba.*
to **wilt** - *δibal (a δabil).* The flowers have wilted. *l-warid δibal.*
to **win** - **1.** *ġilab (u ġuḷub).* I'm going to win this time. *raɀ-aġlub hal-marra.* — Which team do you think will win? *yaa firqa titṣawwar raɀ-tuġlub?* **2.** *ribaɀ (a rabiɀ).* I won five hundred fils. *rbaɀit xamis miit filis.*
to win over - *stimaal (i).* Can you win him over to our side? *tigdar tistimiila j-jaanibna?* or *tigdar itqannƐa yṣiir wiyyaana?*
winch - *bakra* pl. *-aat.*
wind - *hawa.* There was a violent wind last night. *čaan ʔaku hawa kulliš Ɛaali l-baarɀa bil-leel.*
**There's something in the wind. *ybayyin aku šii bij-jaww.*
**I took the wind out of his sails. *faššeet ijraaba.*
to get wind of - *ɀass (i), Ɛiraf (u) b-.* I got wind of the story yesterday. *ɀasseet bil-quṣṣa l-baarɀa.*
to **wind** - **1.** *tƐarraj (a taƐarruj).* The road winds through the mountains. *ṭ-ṭariiq yitƐarraj been ij-jibaal.* **2.** *laff (i laff) n-.* Wind it around my finger. *liffha daayir-ma daayir ib-ṣibƐi.* **3.** *kawwak (u takwiik) t-.* I forgot to wind my watch. *nseet akawwuk saaƐti.*
to wind up - **1.** *laff (i laff) n-.* Will you help me wind up this yarn? *ma-tƐaawunni ʔaliff haṣ-ṣuuf?* **2.** *rattab (i tartiib).* They gave him two weeks' time in which to wind up his affairs. *nṭoo sbuuƐeen ɀatta yrattib ʔumuura.*
to get **winded** - *nihat (a).* I get winded easily when I run. *ʔanhat bil-Ɛajil min arkuṣ.*
winding sheet - *čifan* pl. *čfaana.*
windmill - *ṭaaɀuunat* (pl. *ṭwaaɀiin) hawa, makiina* (pl. *makaayin) hawaaʔiyya.*
window - **1.** *šibbaač* pl. *šbaabiič.* Please open the windows. *baḷḷa fukk iš-šibaabiič.* **2.** *jaamxaana* pl. *-aat.* Put these on display in the window. *ʔiƐriṣ hal-ʔašyaaʔ bij-jaamxaana.*
windowpane - *jaama* pl. *-aat.* The stone broke the windowpane. *l-iɀjaara kisrat ij-jaama.*
windpipe - *qaṣaba* (pl. *-aat) hawaaʔiyya.*
windshield - *jaama* (pl. *-aat) giddaamiyya.*
windy - **It's windy today. *ʔaku hawa hwaaya l-yoom.*
wine - *šaraab.* Do you have aged wine? *Ɛindak šaraab muƐattaq?*
wing - **1.** *jnaaɀ* pl. *-aat.* The pigeon broke its wing. *ṭ-ṭeer inkisar ijnaaɀa.* — The office is in the left wing of the building. *d-daaʔira bij-jinaaɀ il-Ɛal-yisra mnil-binaaya.* **2.** *ɀimaaya.* She took him under her wing. *šimlata b-ɀimaayata.*

**I watched the play from the wings. *tfarrajit Ear-ruwaaya min ṣafzat il-masraz wara l-parda.*

wink - 1. *ġamza* pl. *-aat.* She gave me a knowing wink. *ġumzat-li ġamzat waazid yidri.* 2. *lazδa.* I didn't sleep a wink. *ma-ġumδat Eeeni wala lazδa.*

**He was gone in a wink. *ġaab miθil lamz il-baṣar.*

to wink - *ġumaz (u ġamuz).* Did she wink at you? *ġumzat-lak?*

winter - *šita* pl. *-aayaat.* We don't travel in winter. *ma-nsaafir biš-šita.*

to **wipe** - *naššaf (i tanšiif) t-.* I'll wash the dishes if you wipe them. *?aġsil l-imwaaEiin ?iδa ?inta tnaššifhum.*

to wipe off - *misaz (a masiz) n-.* First let me wipe off the dust. *xalli ?amsaz it-tiraab ?awwal.*

to wipe out - *qiδa (i qaδaa?) n- Eala.* The earthquake wiped out the whole town. *z-zilzaal qiδa Eal-wlaaya kullha.*

wire - 1. *silk* pl. *?aslaak, siim* pl. *syuuma, waayir* pl. *-aat.* The wire isn't strong enough. *s-silk muu hal-gadd qawi.* 2. *barqiyya* pl. *-aat.* Send him a wire. *dizz-la barqiyya.*

by wire - *barqiyyan.* I'll let you know by wire. *Euud axabbrak barqiyyan.*

to wire - *dazz (i dazz) barqiyya l-.* He wired me to meet him at the station. *dazz-li barqiyya aluugii bil-muzaṭṭa.*

wisdom - *Eaqil.* That needs courage and wisdom. *haay yinraad-ilha šajaaEa w-Eaqil.*

wise - *Eaaqil.* He's a very wise man. *huwwa fadd waazid kulliš Eaaqil.*

**When are you going to get wise to yourself? *šwakit raz-yiji Eaqlak ib-raasak?*

**Don't be such a wise guy. *?iθgal išwayya.*

to put one wise - *fahham (i tafhiim) t-.* Don't you think we ought to put him wise? *ma-tiEtiqid ?azsan infahhma š-aku š-ma-aku?*

wish - 1. *raġba* pl. *-aat.* My wishes are easily satisfied. *raġbaati sahil tazqiiqha.* 2. *tamanniya* pl. *-aat.* Best wishes for the New Year! *?aṭyab it-tamanniyaat ib-munaasabat raas is-sana.*

to wish - *tmanna (a tamanni).* We wished him luck on his trip. *tmanneenaa-la safra mwaffqa.* -- I wish I could stay here longer. *?atmanna loo ?agdar abqa mudda aṭwal.* -- I wouldn't wish it on my worse enemy. *ma-atmannaaha l-Eaduwwi.*

**I wish I'd done that. *yaareet sawweetha.*

to wish for - *tmanna (a tamanni).* What do you wish for most? *š-titmanna hassa ?azyad šii?*

witch - *sazzaara* pl. *-aat, saazira* pl. *-aat.*

with - 1. *wiyya, maEa.* I'll have lunch with him today. *raz-atġadda wiyyaa l-yoom.* -- Do you want something to drink with your meal? *yEijbak tišrab šii wiyya l-?akil?* -- He took the book with him. *?axaδ l-iktaab wiyyaa.* 2. *maEa, b-.* With pleasure! *maEa l-mamnuuniyya.* 3. *b-.* With all the money he's spent he should have a better house than that. *b-hal-ifluus l-iṣrafha čaan laazim ykuun Einda beet ?azsan min haaδa.* -- The house was crawling with ants. *l-beet čaan yruuš bin-namil.* 4. *bin-nisba ?il-.* With him it's all a matter of money. *bin-nisba ?ila hiyya mawδuuE ifluus bass.* 5. *raġum.* With all the work he's done he still isn't finished. *raġum kull iš-šuġuḷ is-sawwaa huwwa li-hassa baEad ma-mxalliṣ.* 6. *Eind.* He's staying with us. *huwwa naazil Eidna.* 7. *min.* She was beaming with happiness. *wujihha čaan da-yiδzak imnil-faraz.*

to **withdraw** - 1. *sizab (a sazib) n-.* I withdraw the motion. *?aszab il-iqtiraaz.* 2. *nsizab (i nsizaab).* Because of health reasons I will withdraw from the elections. *?aani raz-ansizib imnil-intixaabaat il-?asbaab ṣizziyya.*

to **wither** - *δibal (a).* Her face is withered. *wujihha δablaan.*

within - 1. *xilaal.* I expect an answer within three days. *?atwaqqaE jawaab xilaal itlaθt iyyaam.* 2. *δimin.* Speeding is forbidden within the city limits. *s-surEa mamnuuEa δimin zuduud l-wlaaya.* -- This is within my authority. *haay δimin ṣulṭaati.* 3. *ib-xilaal.* The letters came within a short period. *l-makaatiib wuṣlat ib-xilaal fatra qaṣiira.*

**We're within 3 miles of the city. *?izna b-biEid itlaθ amyaal imnil-wlaaya.*

without - *blayya, bala, biduun, min ġeer.* Can I get in without a ticket? *?agdar axušš iblayya tikit?* -- He left without permission. *ṭilaE biduun ?ijaaza.* -- She left the room without saying a word. *tirkat il-ġurfa blayya-ma tguul wala čilma.*

witness - *šaahid* pl. *šhuud.* The witnesses haven't been examined yet. *š-šuhuud baEad ma-nsi?law li-hassa.*

to witness - 1. *šihad (a) Eala.* We witnessed his signature. *šhadna Eala tawqiiEa.* 2. *šaaf (u šoof).* Did you witness the accident? *šift il-zaadiθ min ṣaar?* 3. *tfarraj (a tafarruj) Eala.* A huge crowd witnessed the game. *hwaaya naas itfarrjaw Eas-sibaaq.*

witty - *mnakkit laaδiE.* He's very witty. *huwwa mnakkit laaδiE.*

wolf - *δiib* pl. *δiyaab.* The wolves have been killing our sheep. *δ-δiyaab da-yaakluun xurfaanna.*

**He's a wolf in sheep's clothing. *bil-wujih imrayya w-bil-gufa sillaaya.* or *jawwa Eanaamta ?aku miit ibliis.*

woman - *mara* pl. *niswaan, mrayya* pl. *-aat.* That woman is selling yoghurt. *δiič il-mara da-tbiiE liban.*

womb - *razam* pl. *?arzaam.*

wonder - *muEjiza* pl. *-aat.* The medicine works wonders. *had-duwa ysawwi muEjizaat.* -- It's a wonder that you got here at all. *wuṣuulak ihnaa b-zadd δaata čaan muEjiza.*

**No wonder it's cold with the window open. *ṭabEan itṣiir barda ?iδa iš-šibbaač mafkuuk.*

to wonder - *stağrab (u stiġraab).* I shouldn't wonder if it were true. *ma-astaġrub ?iδa čaanat ṣudug.*

**I was wondering where you were. *ridt aEruf Eajaban inta ween.*

**I wonder what he'll do now. *Eajaban iš-raz-ysawwi hassa.*

wonderful - *mumtaaz.* That's a wonderful book. *haaδa ktaab mumtaaz.*

wood - 1. *xišab.* What kind of wood is this? *šinu nooE hal-xišab?* 2. *zaṭab.* Those people are collecting wood for the fire. *δoola da-ylimmuun zaṭab lin-naar.*

wooden - *min xišab.* The pan has a wooden handle. *ṭ-ṭaawa biiha yadda min xišab.* -- The room is divided by a wooden partition. *l-ġurfa maqsuuma b-zaajiz min xišab.*

woods - *ġaaba* pl. *-aat.* Is there a path through the woods? *?aku ṭariiq imnil-ġaaba?*

**We're not out of the woods yet. *baEadha zaalatna ma-mistaqirra.*

wool - *ṣuuf.* The blanket is made of pure wool. *hal-baṭṭaaniyya ṣuuf xaaliṣ.*

woolen - *min ṣuuf.* I bought a woolen sweater. *štireet ibluuz min ṣuuf.*

woolens - *ṣuufiyyaat.* Did you put moth balls in your woolens? *zaṭṭeet naftaaliin wiyya ṣ-ṣuufiyyaat maaltak?*

word - 1. *čilma, kalima* pl. *-aat.* We have to learn fifty new words between now and tomorrow. *laazim nizfaδ xamsiin čilma minnaa l-baačir.* -- How do you spell that word? *šloon tithajja hač-čilma?* -- I don't want to hear another word about this. *ma-ariid asmaE wala čilma baEad Ean hal-mawδuuE.* -- I remember the tune, but I forget the words. *?atδakkar l-lazan bass naasi l-kalimaat.* 2. *waEad.* He gave his word that he would finish the job in time. *niṭa waEad yxalliṣ iš-šuġuḷ ib-wakta.* 3. *xabar.* Try to send them word we need reinforcements. *zaawil itdizz-ilhum xabar Ean zaajatna lil-musaaEada.*

**You can take his word for it. *Etimid Eala zčaayta.*

**He doesn't let you get a word in edgewise. *ma-yxalli ?azzad yizči.*

**In a word, no. *muxtaṣar mufiid, laa.*

to word - *rattab (i tartiib) kalimaat.* How do you want to word the telegram? *šloon itriid itrattib kalimaat il-barqiyya?*

wording - **The wording of this sentence is bad. *Eibaaraat haj-jumla ma-mrattba.*

work - 1. *šuġuḷ* pl. *?ašġaaḷ.* The Department of Public Works is being reorganized. *?aEaadaw tanδiim mudiiriyyat il-?ašġaaḷ il-Eaamma.* -- The work is boring. *š-šuġuḷ yδawwij.* -- He's been out of work since the factory closed. *huwwa gaaEid bila šuġuḷ min saddaw il-maEmal.* 2. *mu?allafa* pl. *-aat.* All of that author's works are very popular. *kull mu?allafaat hal-kaatib naajza.* 3. *Eamal* pl. *?aEmaal.* All that painter's works are very popular. *kull ?aEmaal haaδa r-rassaam naajza.* 4. *qiṭEa* pl. *qiṭaE.* That work of art is in the Egyptian museum. *hal-qiṭEa l-fanniyya bil-matzaf il-miṣri.*

**It took a lot of work to convince him we were right. *tEabna yaḷḷa qannaEnaa.*

to work - 1. *štiġaḷ (u štiġaal).* I work from eight to five. *?aštuġuḷ imniθ-θimaanya lil-xamsa.* -- The elevator doesn't work. *l-maṣEad ma-yištuġuḷ.*

2. *šaǧǧal*. He works his employees very hard. *yšaǧǧil̩ Ɛummaala kulliš ihwaaya.* — Do you know how to work an adding machine? *tuƐruf išloon itšaǧǧil̩ makiinat iʒsaabaat?* 3. *nijaʒ (a najaaʒ).* This trick doesn't always work. *hal-liƐba muu daa?iman tinjaʒ.* 4. *fakk (u).* I had to work my way through the crowd. *δṭarreet afukk-li ṭariiq been in-naas bil-itdiffiƐ.*

to work loose – *rixa (a).* Several screws have worked loose on the machine. *čam burǧi rixat bil-makiina.*

to work on – 1. *qannaƐ (i).* We're working on him to give us the day off. *da-nqannƐa ʒatta yinṭiina yoom Ɛuṭla.* 2. *štiǧal̩ (u) b-.* The mechanic is just working on your car now. *l-miikaaniiki da-yištuǧul̩ ib-sayyaartak hassa.*

to work out – 1. *rattab (i tartiib) t-, hayya? (i tahyii?) t-.* The plan is well worked out. *l-mašruuƐ mitrattib zeen.* 2. *nijaʒ (a najaaʒ).* How do you think this idea would work out? *šgadd tiṭṣawwar hal-fikra raʒ-tinjaʒ?* 3. *miša (i miši).* How did things work out? *šloon mišat il-?umuur?*

worker – *Ɛaamil* pl. *Ɛummaal.* He's the best worker in my factory. *haaδa ?aʒsan Ɛaamil bil-maƐmal maali.*

**He's a hard worker. *haaδa kulliš šaaǧuul̩.*

working hours – *dawaam.* May I call you during working hours? *?agdar axaabrak ?aθnaa? id-dawaam?*

workman – *Ɛaamil* pl. *Ɛummaal.*

works – *makiina* pl. *makaayin.* The works of that clock need repairing. *l-makiina maal has-saaƐa yinraad-ilha taṣliiʒ.*

water works – *?isaalat maa?.* The water works are outside the city. *?isaalat il-maa? barra l-wlaaya.*

world – 1. *dinya.* He's traveled all over the world. *daar id-dinya kullha.* — I wouldn't hurt him for anything in the world. *ma-?aδδii loo yinṭuuni mulk id-dinya.* 2. *Ɛaalam.* The Red Cross is a world-wide organization. *mu?assasat iṣ-ṣaliib il-?aʒmar mintašra b-kull il-Ɛaalam.*

**Where in the world have you been? *b-yaa zwiyya činit δaamum nafsak?*

**It will do him a world of good to go somewhere else. *hwaaya l-maṣlaʒta loo yruuʒ il-ǧeer makaan.*

**My father thinks the world of you. *?abuuya yqaddrak kulliš ihwaaya.*

worm – *duuda* pl. *-aat* coll. *duud.* Do you use worms for bait? *?inta tistaƐmil duud liṭ-ṭuƐum?*

wormy – *mdawwid.* These dates are wormy. *hat-tamur kulla mdawwid.*

worn – *mistahlik, gaayim.* My coat is pretty worn. *sitirti mistahlika.*

worn-out – *taƐbaan kullis.* He looks worn-out. *ybayyin Ɛalee taƐbaan kulliš.*

worry – *dooxat raas, qalaq.* Her son gave her a great deal of worry. *?ibinha sabbab-ilha hwaaya dooxat raas.*

to worry – 1. *šawwaš (u), qilaq (i qalaq) n-.* His silence worries me. *sukuuta da-yšawwušni.* 2. *tšawwaš (a).* I'm worried about him. *fikri mitšawwiš Ɛalee.*

**I won't let that worry me. *ma-adawwux raasi b-haay.*

**The future doesn't worry him. *ma-yxaaf imnil-mustaqbal.*

**I don't have time to worry about that. *ṣ-ṣidug ma-Ɛindi wakt il-haay.*

worse – 1. *?amarr, ?angas.* He's feeling worse this morning. *hal-yoom ṣiʒʒta baƐad amarr.* — The weather is worse now than it was in the morning. *j-jaww hassa ?angas imniṣ-ṣubuʒ.* 2. *?aswa?.* His business is going from bad to worse. *šuǧl̩a da-yiṭṭawwar min sayyi? ?ila ?aswa?.* 3. *?atƐas.* He's even worse off now. *ʒaalta hassa baƐad ?atƐas.*

**He's none the worse for it. *ma-ṣaaba ?ay δarar min waraaha.*

**Her condition is getting worse and worse. *ʒaalatha da-titdahwar.*

worship – *Ɛibaada.* The worship of idols was prevalent before Islam. *Ɛibaadat il-?aṣnaam čaanat mawjuuda gabl̩ il-?islaam.*

to worship – *Ɛibad (i Ɛbaada) n-.* He worships his wife. *yiƐbidha l-marta.*

worst – 1. *?aswa?.* But wait, I haven't told you the worst. *yawaaš, baƐad ma-git-lak ?aswa? šii.* 2. *?angas.* I got the worst piece. *jatni ?angas wuṣla.* 3. *?atƐas.* That's the worst accident I've seen in my life. *δaak ?atƐas ʒaadiθ taṣaadum šaayfa b-Ɛumri.*

**I get the worst of it when I argue with him. *kull-ma atnaaqaš wiyyaa, ?aani ?aakulha.*

**We're over the worst of it. *šarrha faat.*

at worst – *b-?atƐas il-ʒaalaat.* At worst, the storm won't last longer than a week. *b-?atƐas il-ʒaalaat, il-Ɛaaṣifa ma-ṭṭawwil ?azyad min isbuuƐ.*

worth – 1. *qiima* pl. *qiyam.* He didn't appreciate her true worth. *ma-qaddar qiimatha l-ʒaqiiqiyya.* 2. *ʒagg.* Give me 10 fils worth of peanuts. *?inṭiini ʒagg Ɛašr ifluus fistiq Ɛabiid.*

**Give me fifty fils worth of almonds. *nṭiini b-xamsiin filis looz.*

**Did you get your money's worth in the night club last night? *Ɛaad ṭallaƐt ifluusak il-ʒaṭṭeetha bil-malha l-baarʒa bil-leel?*

to be worth – 1. *siwa (a).* It's worth the trouble. *tiswa dooxt ir-raas.* — That horse is worth five hundred dinars. *hal-iʒṣaan yiswa xamis miit diinaar.* 2. *stiʒaqq (i stiʒqaaq).* His idea is worth trying. *fikirta tistiʒiqq it-tajruba.*

**Pay him what he's worth. *?inṭii Ɛala gadd taƐaba.*

**He's worth about two million dinars. *yimlik-la fadd milyooneen diinaar.*

**I'll make it worth your while. *?araδδiik.* or *ma-titnaddam.*

worthless – *ma-il- qiima.* That money is worthless now. *hal-ifluus baƐad ma-ilha qiima.*

**The painting is practically worthless. *haṣ-ṣuura ma-tiswa šii.*

worthy – *nabiil.* They did it for a worthy cause. *sawwooha l-ǧaaya nabiila.*

wound – *jariʒ* pl. *jruuʒ.* It will be a couple of months before the wound in his leg is healed. *yinraad-la šahreen ʒatta j-jariʒ illi b-rijla yṭiib.*

to wound – *jiraʒ (a jariʒ) n-, jarraʒ (i tajriiʒ).* Several men were wounded in the action. *čam waaʒid injirʒaw ib-δaak il-hijuum.* — The explosion wounded three soldiers. *l-infijaar jiraʒ itlaθ jinuud.*

to **wrap** – *laff (i laff) n-, ǧallaf (i).* Shall I wrap it up for you? *triid aliff-ilk-iyyaaha?*

**He's all wrapped up in his work. *δaabib nafsa Ɛaš-šuǧul̩.* or *minhimik biš-šuǧul̩.* or *ṭaamuṣ biš-šuǧul̩.*

wrapping paper – *waraq taǧliif.*

wreath – *?ikliil* pl. *?akaaliil.*

wreck – 1. *?anqaaδ.* The bodies are still buried in the wreck. *j-jiθaθ baƐadha madfuuna bil-?anqaaδ.* 2. *ʒaadiθ* pl. *ʒawaadiθ.* Was anybody killed in the wreck? *?aʒʒad maat bil-ʒaadiθ?*

**He's a complete wreck. *?aƐṣaaba minhaara.*

to wreck – 1. *ʒaṭṭam (u taʒṭiim).* The collision wrecked the car. *t-taṣaadum ʒaṭṭamha lis-sayyaara.* 2. *dammar (u tadmiir).* The explosion wrecked the whole plant. *l-infijaar dammar il-maƐmal.* 3. *dumar (u damur) n-.* The strike wrecked his business. *l-?iδraab dumar šuǧl̩a.*

wrench – *ṣpaana* pl. *-aat, ṣpaayin.*

to **wrestle** – 1. *tṣaaraƐ (a taṣaaruƐ).* He likes to wrestle better than box. *yƐijba yitṣaaraƐ ?azyad min-ma yitlaakam.* 2. *Ɛaalaj (i muƐaalaja) t-.* I've been wrestling with this problem for hours. *ṣaar-li tlaθ saaƐaat da-aƐaalij hal-qaδiyya.*

wretched – *δaayij.* I still feel wretched. *baƐadni δaayij.*

to **wring** – 1. *Ɛiṣar (u Ɛaṣir).* Wring out the clothes. *?iƐṣur il-ihduum.* 2. *luwa (i lawi).* She wrung the chicken's neck. *luwat rugbat id-dijaaja.*

wringer – *Ɛaṣṣaara* pl. *-aat.* The wringer on my washing machine is broken. *Ɛaṣṣaart il-ǧassaala maalti maksuura.*

wrinkle – *tajƐiid* pl. *tajaaƐiid.* Her face is full of wrinkles. *wujihha matruus tajaaƐiid.*

to wrinkle – 1. *Ɛaknaš (i tƐikniš) t-.* He wrinkled his forehead. *Ɛaknaš wujja.* 2. *tƐaqqač (a taƐaqqič).* This silk wrinkles easily. *hal-ʒariir yitƐaqqač bil-Ɛajil.*

wrist – *rusuǧ* pl. *?arsaaǧ.* You've got a sprained wrist. *?aku Ɛindak rusuǧ mafṣuux.*

wrist watch – *saaƐat (pl. -aat) iid.*

to **write** – *kitab (i kitba, kitaaba) n-.* Write your name on the first line. *?iktib ismak Ɛala ?awwal saṭir.*

to write down – *sajjal (i tasjiil).* Write down that telephone number before you forget it. *sajjil har-raqam maal it-talafoon gabul̩-ma tinsaa.*

to write off – *ʒisab (i ʒsaab) n-.* You'd better write that off as a bad debt. *?aʒsan-lak iʒsib had-deen mayyit.*

writer – *kaatib* pl. *kuttaab.* My son wants to become a story writer. *?ibni yriid iyṣiir kaatib quṣaṣi.*

writing – *kitba, kitaaba* pl. *-aat.* I can't read his

writing. *ma-agdar aqra kitibta.*
**I don't get around to writing. *ma da-yṣiir Ɛindi wakit ʔaktib.*
in writing - *maktuub.* I'd like to have that in writing. *ʔariid haay maktuuba.*
writings - *kitaabaat.* I don't understand his writings. *ma-agdar aftihim kitaabaata.*
wrong - **1.** *ġalaṭ.* He admitted that he was in the wrong. *Ɛtiraf ib-ġalaṭa.* — I must have added the figures up wrong again. *laazim hamm ijmaƐit l-ʔarqaam ġalaṭ.* — You're heading in the wrong direction. *ttijaahak muu ṣaziiz.* or *ttijaahak ġalaṭ.* **2.** *ġalṭaan.* I'm afraid you're wrong. *ʔaƐtiqid inta ġalṭaan.* -- I'll admit that I was completely wrong about him. *ʔaƐtirif ʔaani činit ġalṭaan ib-raʔyi bii.* **3.** *muu tamaam.* Something is wrong with the telephone. *ʔaku šii muu tamaam ib-hat-talafoon.*
**He got out on the wrong side of the bed. *hal-yoom wujja magluub.*
**Is anything wrong with you? *yoojƐak šii?*
**What's wrong with you? *š-biik?*
to do wrong - *ġilaṭ (a ġalaṭ).* He thinks he can do no wrong. *yiƐtiqid huwwa ʔabad ma-yiġlaṭ.*
to wrong - *ḍilam (u ḍulum) n-, ġidar (i ġadir) n-.* He thinks he's been wronged. *yiƐtiqid inna huwwa maḍluum.*
wrongfully - *ḍulman w-Ɛidwaanan, bil-taƐaddi.* He was wrongfully accused of incompetence. *ttihmoo b-Ɛadam il-qaabliyya ḍulman w-Ɛidwaanan.*

X

X-ray - **1.** *ʔašiƐƐat* (pl. *-aat*) *ʔeeks.* Who discovered the X-ray? *minu ktišaf ʔašiƐƐat ʔeeks?* **2.** *ʔašiƐƐa* pl. *-aat.* May I see the X-ray? *ʔagdar ašuuf il-ʔašiƐƐa?*
to X-ray - *ʔaxað (u ʔaxið) ʔašiƐƐa l-.* The dentist X-rayed my teeth. *ṭabiib il-ʔasnaan ʔaxað ʔašiƐƐa l-isnuuni.*

Y

yard - **1.** *yaarda* pl. *-aat.* I'd like to have five yards of this material. *ʔariid xamis yaardaat min hal-iqmaaš.* **2.** *saaza* pl. *-aat.* The house has a yard for the children to play in. *l-beet bii saaza yliƐbuun biiha j-jihaal.* **3.** *skalla* pl. *-aat.* You may be able to get that at the lumber yard. *balki tigdar tilgiiha bil-iskalla maal xišab.*
yarn - *ġazil.* I'll take six balls of that green yarn. *ʔariid xamis laffaat min ðaak il-ġazil il-ʔaxḍar.*
to **yawn** - *tθaawab (a taθaawub).* He began to yawn from drowsiness. *bida yitθaawub imnin-naƐas.*
year - *sana* pl. *-awaat, sniin.* He's thirty years old. *Ɛumra tlaaθiin sana.* -- I haven't seen him for years. *ṣaar-li sniin ma-šaayfa.*
**Year in, year out, the same routine. *sana txušš, sana tiṭlaƐ, ma-aku taġyiir.*
yearly - *sanawi**. How much is the yearly rent? *šgadd il-ʔajaar is-sanawi?*
**My uncle pays us a yearly visit. *Ɛammi yzuurna marra bis-sana.*
yeast - *xumra* pl. *-aat, xamiira* pl. *-aat.*
yell - *Ɛeeṭa* pl. *-aat.* He let out a yell and died. *Ɛaaṭ fadd Ɛeeṭa w-maat.*
to yell - *Ɛayyaṭ (i taƐyiiṭ).* Don't yell; you'll wake the neighbors. *la-tƐayyiṭ, raz-itgaƐƐid ij-juwaariin.*
yellow - *ʔaṣfar.* She's wearing a yellow dress. *laabsa nafnuuf aṣfar.*
**He's yellow. *haaða jabaan.*
yes - *ʔii, naƐam, bali.* Yes, I'll be glad to go. *ʔii, aruuz maƐa l-mamnuuniyya.*
yes man - *ʔabu bali.* He's a yes man. *haaða ʔabu bali.*
yesterday - *l-baarza.* I saw him yesterday. *šifta l-baarza.*
yet - **1.** *baƐad* (with negative). Haven't you read the book yet? *ma-qreet l-iktaab baƐad?* -- He hasn't come yet. *ma-jaa baƐad.* **2.** *loo baƐad.* Did you see the new play yet? *šift it-tamθiiliyya j-jidiida loo baƐad?* -- Have you selected anything yet? *stangeet šii loo baƐad?* **3.** *laakin, bass.* He didn't want to go, yet he had to. *ma-raad yruuz laakin iḍṭarr.* **4.** *maƐa haaða.* And yet you can't help liking him. *maƐa haaða ma-tigdar ʔilla tzibba.*
to **yield** - **1.** *ṭallaƐ (i taṭliiƐ) t-, jaab (i jeeb).* His business doesn't yield much profit. *maṣlazta ma-ṭṭilliƐ ihwaaya ribiz.* **2.** *nitaj (i ʔintaaj) n-.* This farm yields a pretty good income. *hal-mazraƐa tintij xooš waarid.* **3.** *xiḍaƐ (a xuḍuuƐ), ʔaðƐan (i ʔiðƐaan), riḍax (a ruḍuux).* We'll never yield to force. *ʔabadan ma-nixḍaƐ lil-quwwa.*
yoghurt - *laban.*
yolk - *ṣafaar.*
you - **1.** (m.) *ʔinta* (f.) *ʔinti* (pl.) *ʔintum.* Are you the new clerk? *ʔinta l-kaatib ij-jidiid?* **2.** (m.) *-ak,* (f.) *-ič,* (pl.) *-kum.* I haven't seen you in a long time. *ma-šiftak min zamaan.*
young - *jaahil.* Who's that young man? *minu ðaak ir-rijjaal ij-jaahil?* -- She's very young for her age. *tbayyin jaahla bin-nisba l-Ɛumurha.*
**The night is still young. *l-leel baƐda b-ʔawwala.*
young people - *šabaab.* The young people had a lot of fun. *š-šabaab itwannsaw ihwaaya.*
yours - *maal-.* This hat is yours, sir. *haš-šafqa maalak, yaa ʔustaað.* This doll is yours. *hal-laƐƐaaba maaltič.* -- My bag is bigger than yours. *jinuṭṭi ʔakbar min maaltak.*
**Is he a friend of yours, Mr. Smith? *haaða min ʔaṣdiqaaʔak, yaa mistir smiθ?*
yourself - *nafs-.* Did you hurt yourself? *ʔaððeet nafsak?*
youth - *šabaab.* He had to work hard in his youth. *ḍṭarr yištuġul ihwaaya b-šabaaba.*
yo-yo - *yooyo* pl. *-owaat.*

Z

zebra - *zibra* pl. *-aat.*
zero - *ṣifir* pl. *ṣfaara.* Add another zero. *zuṭṭ ṣifir laax.* -- The temperature is zero. *darajat il-zaraara ṣifir.*
zinc - *qaṣdiir, tuutya.*
Zion - *ṣahyuun.*
Zionism - *ṣ-ṣahyuuniyya.*
Zionist - *ṣahyuuni** pl. *-iyyiin, ṣahaayna.*
zipper - *zanjiil* pl. *zanaajiil.* I broke the zipper on my sweater. *ksarit iz-zanjiil maal ibluuzi.*
zither - *qaanuun* pl. *qawaaniin.*
zone - *manṭiqa* pl. *-aat, manaaṭiq.* Iraq is located in the temperate zone. *l-Ɛiraaq waaqiƐ bil-manṭiqa l-muƐtadila.*
zoo - *zadiiqat* (pl. *zadaayiq*) *zaywaanaat.*
zoology - *Ɛilim il-zaywaanaat.*

NOTES

NOTES

NOTES

NOTES

NOTES